REFERENCE BOOK GUIDES

China: A Handbook

PURPOSE — This reference book presents both a comprehensive survey of Chinese affairs and specific information on subjects concerning mainland China.

ORGANIZATION — Arranged in 3 parts: 1 contains general information on China; 2, DOCUMENTS, includes texts of major government documents; 3, DATA, contains specific facts and statistics.

The TABLE OF CONTENTS (pg. 7-9) gives the author's name, chapter title and pg. no. There is also a LIST OF TABLES, CHARTS, AND FIGURES, as well as a LIST OF MAPS. The INDEX is at the back (pg. 899-915).

PROCEDURE — To find specific information, turn to the INDEX and alphabetically locate your subjects and their pg. nos. Turn there. To find more general information, turn to the TABLE OF CONTENTS.

FOR EXAMPLE — You are interested in finding information on the Han dynasty. Refer to the INDEX and you'll find:

Index

Halpern, A. M., 'Communist China and
    Peaceful Coexistence', 296

Subjects ➡ Han dynasty, 634, 635

Han language, 706-7

Han people, and national minorities, 116–
    17, 680–81, 685, 778   **Pg. nos.**

Hangchow Bay, geology of, 34

Hankow (Wuhan): in civil wars, 133, 138,

- - - - - - - -

Or you may want information on the population of China.

Here is a part of the TABLE OF CONTENTS: **Page number**

Chapter   **Author**

China: A Handbook. Yuan-li Wu, ed. N.Y.: Praeger, 1973.

CHINA

HANDBOOKS TO THE MODERN WORLD

CHINA

A Handbook

Edited by

Yuan-li Wu

PRAEGER PUBLISHERS

New York · Washington

BOOKS THAT MATTER

Published in the United States of America in 1973
by Praeger Publishers, Inc.
111 Fourth Avenue, New York, N.Y. 10003

Library of Congress Catalog Card Number: 72–101683

Printed in Great Britain

The editor wishes to acknowledge
his appreciation of having had the opportunity
to work with the many contributors to this volume.
In particular, he wishes to thank Grace H. Wu
for her contribution to Parts Two and Three of the volume.

CONTENTS

7

PART TWO: DOCUMENTS

PART THREE: DATA

9

LIST OF TABLES, CHARTS, AND FIGURES IN PART ONE

LIST OF MAPS

Part I

1

INTRODUCTION

YUAN-LI WU

THIS is a reference book on mainland China intended for the general readership. It seeks to present both a comprehensive survey of Chinese affairs and specific information on subjects that are likely to interest the occasional reader. This volume appears at a time when Communist China stands at the crossroads. After twenty years of rule on the Chinese mainland and many internal and external political changes culminating in the Cultural Revolution of 1966–69, the government in Peking is about to embark upon the post-Mao-Chou era. Certain sharp discontinuities in past trends may begin to surface. Yet the directions, if new, really cannot be fully discerned until several years from now. There always is the danger of taking transitory phenomena for enduring traits. Yet, whatever may happen, the continuum of history requires that the student of contemporary affairs begin with a reliable base line. The purpose of this volume is to provide such a base line through the collection of survey articles in the main body of the volume. Most of these articles have had a cut-off date in 1969–70. However, some allowance has been made for the more recent developments in 1971 and China's changing relations with the United States and the Soviet Union. A small number of extracts of documents and data compilations are provided in Parts II and III for ready consultation by the occasional reader.

China has undergone radical upheavals in many respects and on a vast scale during the past twenty years. In the midst of all the change, however, certain factors are almost totally, if not absolutely, constant. Still other factors can change but slowly in any short span of time. The physical geography of the country, the land forms, the climate, the distribution of inland waters, and the soils and vegetation of the geographical regions fall into this category. They are largely determined by nature and are unlikely to change perceptibly in the short run. Within the physical environment, the agricultural resources provided by nature are also relatively constant; so are the ways in which these land resources are utilized. Because of the vastness of the country, changes in land utilization, irrigation, terracing, rural transportation, and even agricultural technology do not normally lend themselves to rapid revolution. The same may be said of the natural, nonagricultural resources, including the size and distribution of the mineral reserves, water power, and so forth. The first three chapters of Part I, written respectively by Hsieh, Buck, and Wang, are devoted to an examination of these constant and slow-changing factors.

While the physical and natural environment is largely given, what man does with it is by no means predetermined. Not only can the environment be modified in the long run, but even the short-term results of man's efforts can be remarkably varied at times. This is true particularly when the stock of knowledge is augmented through importation and vigorous dissemination and when institutions that serve to channel and organize man's efforts are subjected to revolutionary change· These truisms are

19

graphically illustrated when we consider the manner in which estimates of China's natural resources that can be readily exploited have changed during the last two decades and when we examine, both in Buck's chapter and in a later chapter by K. C. Yeh, the changes in the Chinese land tenure system and farm organization under the present regime.

What man does with his environment is a function of his numbers, his aspirations, his skill, the manner in which his efforts are organized, and the impediments, domestic and foreign, that he must overcome, including obstacles that he puts in his own way. In a sense, the rest of Part I is an attempt to describe these aspects of Chinese history in the last two decades.

To begin with, the Aird chapter treats the question of numbers. As the reader will note, it is not easy to get a simple answer to the apparently innocent question: How many Chinese are there? From the methodological point of view, the student of Chinese affairs is well advised to go through this chapter for a full initiation into the problem posed by uncertainty of data. (A no less significant introduction can be found in Buck's discussion on cultivated and arable land.) What is not immediately apparent to the reader, however, is another very significant point; namely, that this very uncertainty of data may have plagued the Chinese government and economic planners even more acutely in their policy-making and daily operations than it has the student of Chinese affairs who examines China from abroad.

The reader who has patiently read through the chapters on geography, land and natural resources, and the demographic facts and speculations will find himself in a position to address a set of questions that deal with the manner in which the Chinese have made use of their environment and how well or poorly they have done. At this point, we come up against an important distinction between a totalitarian society and a pluralistic one, which influences our approach to and planning of the book. If we were dealing with a pluralistic society, we should now begin with a discussion of Chinese history, of social institutions and mores, of the value system or systems that are used in judging success or failure and that drive men onward, and of the cultural, religious, and ethical factors that define or circumscribe man's behavior. On the other hand, in dealing with a totalitarian regime, of which contemporary China is by all counts a reasonable facsimile, we must begin with an understanding of the nature of the central decision-making body in which most power has been concentrated, that is, the Chinese Communist Party. For it is the Communist Party that prescribes the nation's long-term goals as well as its short-term objectives, that organizes the national effort to achieve these goals, and that determines both the strategic and tactical approaches to given situations.

The Communist Party of China is a party with a militant and doctrinaire ideology. However, it does not operate in a historical vacuum, and the development of its doctrines cannot be divorced entirely from modern Chinese history. For it is also a party that sought actively to seize political power, and for long periods the attempt was made by military means. Thus it could not ignore the real world it had to reckon with. The doctrinal development of the Chinese Communist Party must therefore be viewed in the light of its protracted political and military struggle—both internally with the Chinese Nationalists and externally in dealing with foreign powers. In addition, one must not lose sight of the fact that throughout the entire history of the Chinese Communist Party, the Russians have been very deeply involved, both as a mentor and doctrinal source and as an ally that, from time to time, played a double game. Thus the Party's internal development and struggle on the domestic front have been intertwined with its external policy as well as the external relations of Republican China, of which it was, before 1949, only an illegal and for most of the time insurgent part.

The long article by Lindsay describes the development of Communist doctrines in the light of changing situations and the varied roles of the Party played from 1920 to

1949. Those three decades were punctuated by a number of about-faces by the Party, including a period of alliance with the Kuomintang (KMT); the return to illegitimacy with the Nanchang uprising; the civil war, ending with the historic march to northwest Central China; the formation of the united front after the Sian incident; the long interplay during the Yenan period, which involved the Communists, the KMT, and the United States; and the civil war after 1945 that culminated with the Communist seizure of power in 1949.

The Leninist origin of the Chinese Communist Party as a group of radical political agitators and the twists and turns dictated by the changing fortunes of guerrilla warfare and occasionally desperate political situations must be read in the light of contemporary history. Furthermore, the period when the Chinese Communist Party was an opposition party—before its seizure of national power—needs to be contrasted with developments after 1949. Even after 1949, however, one cannot lose sight of the need for the Communists to change their tune as their hold on state power weakened or gained strength. At the beginning, when political power was not yet consolidated, doctrine to some degree had to give way to the need for consolidation; besides, the building of a totalitarian society could not be accomplished in one day. However, when the people's confidence in the Party had been built up, it became possible to experiment with 'free criticism.' The political risks of too much freedom led once more to yielding to the demands for consolidation, both within the country and within the Party. Thus, the different elements of Communist doctrine that gained ascendancy from time to time often varied with the fortunes of the Party like a swinging pendulum. Still, throughout the five decades since the inception of the Chinese Communist Party, its political objectives and the totalitarian and centralist character of its organization have remained relatively constant.

The fact that the Chinese Communist Party is a political organization whose aim was to seize power, and, once power had been secured, to rule a nation-state requires that we understand (1) the nature and growth of the Party as an organization and (2) the structure of the state organs and government agencies employed in the exercise of political power. For the decisions made by the Party must be carried out both through the Party organs and through the governmental machinery, the latter being in turn subject to supervision by the Party at various levels. Furthermore, the Party derives additional strength from a large number of mass organizations, which act as a front and an outer circle of support for the central core of cadres. How this entire apparatus has grown in size and complexity and how the Party constitution has evolved to its present form are described in some detail in the Kallgren article. The following chapter by Houn focuses on the state organs, including the basic functions and principles of the state constitution and the National People's Congress; the State Council and the machinery of central government; the apparatus of local government; and the structure and role of the judiciary. Virtually all the analyses—as well as others in chapters yet to follow—raise the question of whether, after the Cultural Revolution and the Ninth Party Congress, and especially after the purge of Lin Piao, which signaled the beginning of a new effort to consolidate and rebuild political power, the Chinese Communist Party can be successful in reconstituting the Party machinery and Party unity that were both deliberately and inadvertently torn down. The student of Chinese history will recall the many misfortunes the Chinese nation has weathered and survived over several thousand years. Yet to be aware of this is not to assume that the Chinese Communist Party as a political institution and an organizational form will necessarily survive every cataclysm it encounters and sometimes creates for itself. The post-Mao and/or Chou period will constitute one such occasion of radical change, and it may be some time before one can expect any real stability.

When there is uncertainty about abstract political form and when unity and the balance of power within the Party are in doubt, one can turn for additional light to more tangible, albeit not necessarily more tractable, elements, such as the Party elite.

The assumption is that from the background, previous experience, and past associations of the individuals, as well as their present groupings, one may be able to detect where power resides and what might therefore be the trends of future policy. Such an analysis of the top central and regional elite is found in the chapter by Weiss, which also gives the general reader a glimpse of some of the personalities. Of course, an attempt to deduce from the personal histories of the individuals and the known presence or lack of cohesiveness among them the course of events that must necessarily be shaped by many other elements as well is the pursuit of an elusive quarry. Nevertheless, such an analysis serves to remind us that man's action can never be divorced from the actor himself and that the vagaries of human nature could indeed play a crucial part at some critical juncture of history. In this regard, not the least intriguing issue that faces the student of contemporary China is the role the military has come to play as a result of the struggles and purges within the Chinese Communist Party. A knowledge of the background of some of the military leaders and how they have risen to positions of real power may well constitute the basis of understanding of the future trend of development in the post-Mao period, of which only a bare beginning is being witnessed.

As noted earlier, the successive shifts of general policy and approach to China's problems are partly a result of conflicts between preoccupation with ideological doctrines and the practical need to hang onto power when opposition threatens to become overwhelming. It is only natural for men in power to wish to continue to exercise it. It is also natural for an authoritarian regime to do everything possible, including the ruthless use of physical and psychological coercion, to suppress opposition in order to perpetuate its rule. While Communist doctrine postulates the withering away of the state as the coercive means of maintaining authority in a society of opposing class interests, Communist Parties that rule nation-states, like other prototypes of authoritarianism, have never hesitated to use coercion to bolster their own power. Thus, in order to understand how a Communist Party carries out its decisions through the state apparatus and peripheral organizations one must look beyond the visible structure of government and the legitimate lines of command for the transmission of orders and information feedback. The realities of the 'dictatorship of the proletariat' cannot be easily conveyed in purely analytical terms.

The backbone of Mao's dictatorship of the proletariat is the People's Liberation Army (PLA). The PLA was not only instrumental in winning the Chinese civil war, it also played a vital role in external ventures in Korea—albeit under the name of 'volunteers'—and India and in border skirmishes with the Soviet Union. The PLA poses a continuous threat to Taiwan and, as a potential source of support for North Korea's Kim Il Sung, to the Republic of Korea. It was to certain elements of the PLA that Mao had to appeal for support when the Cultural Revolution threatened to get out of hand. The PLA apparently oversees China's nuclear weapons program. Thus, the PLA is the final repository of power and the ultimate guardian of the Chinese Communist Party. The very life of the Communist Party of China and China's present tenuous claim to great-power status in a military sense depend upon the unity and cohesiveness of the PLA and its political leanings. The future course China will follow after Mao will be set largely by the PLA. For these reasons it is pertinent to examine the relationship between the Party and the army along with such characteristics of the PLA as its capability, organization, doctrine, and strategy, all largely based upon its past experience in guerrilla warfare, enriched by the lessons it has learned through modernization and participation in the Korean War and from its Soviet mentors. Ellis Joffe surveys these topics.

To recapitulate, while Lindsay examines the history and doctrine of the Chinese Communist Party, Kallgren and Houn describe the formal—and informal—structures of government and Party that are used to carry out the orders of the Party-state leadership. This analysis then is modified and supplemented by the personalities of the leadership, including some of the military elite, as investigated by Weiss. Finally, the chapter by Joffe deals with the physical means of coercive power to which final appeal is inevitably made. Having dealt with these aspects of structure, organization, and means for the implementation of Party decisions, we shall be in a position to examine the actual performance of China under the Chinese Communists.

In this connection, the analysis below may be regarded as composed of two parts. The first discusses China's record in dealing with foreign countries and groups; the second deals with domestic economic, social, and cultural developments. Because the area of foreign policy is very broad in scope, the discussion is subdivided into (1) an historical analysis of the significant changes and episodes in Chinese foreign policy since 1949 and (2) more detailed accounts of Chinese relations with a few countries that are more likely to exert a stronger influence on China than others. Included among the latter are the United States, the Soviet Union, and Japan. A separate chapter is reserved for discussion of countries of the 'third world,' which China aspires to lead. These detailed accounts of China's external relations are further supplemented by two articles of special interest. The first deals with Chinese concepts and practice of international law, a subject that could become vitally important if the breakdown of China's self-imposed isolation after the end of the Cultural Revolution continues after Mao. The second discusses the overseas Chinese, a group whose sympathy and support have traditionally been sought by all revolutionary parties or factions that have ruled or aspired to rule the Chinese mainland.

In his discussion of Chinese foreign policy, Hinton distinguishes the following periods: alliance with Stalin, peaceful coexistence, the emergence of a 'harder line,' the campaign against Khrushchevian revisionism, and the post-Khrushchev era. The reader will find in this analysis a continuous thread of conflict between pragmatic considerations and doctrinaire positions. One of the most important considerations the Communist Chinese leaders have had to entertain has been the need for external material support of a military nature, which in the early years of the regime could be expected from no other source but the Soviet Union. The degree of independence that China can assert has proved to be a function of its own perception of its strength. Both open pronouncements and implied policy have been influenced to a large degree by the course of development of China's nuclear weapons program. Chinese disappointments with the Soviet Union in the 1958 Taiwan Strait crisis, during the 1962 war with India, and in the apparent lack of consistent and wholehearted Soviet support for Chinese nuclear weapons development, as well as China's serious concern about hostile Soviet intentions in 1969, all played an important role in the shaping of Chinese policy at critical moments. Hinton's chapter provides the reader with the necessary background for his own speculation as to where China will go next.

In the discussion of China's relations with the major powers, the reader's attention is drawn first to the China policy of the United States at the time of the fall of the Chinese mainland to the Communists, a most controversial issue of U.S. domestic policy in the 1950's. Myers then traces the further development of America's China policy, including especially the impact of the Korean conflict. U.S.–China relations must, however, be examined also from the point of view of China, for, even as there is a China policy issue for Washington, so is there a U.S. problem for China. How the Chinese perceive developments in the United States and the rationale of American policy toward China is obviously not without effect on the determination of Chinese policy toward the United States. In this connection, there are certain parameters that must be taken into account in the assessment of the prospects of the U.S.–China relations. Among these are the 'two Chinas' issues; the existence of mutual defense arrangements between the U.S. and the Republic of China; the doctrinaire hostility of Chinese Communism toward the United States as a capitalist society; the role the United States has played in blocking the expansion of Chinese influence in Asia; the part the United States could play, and might be induced to play, in the eyes of

Peking, in maneuvers between China and the Soviet Union with respect to each other; and China's desire to cultivate new trade partners, among which the United States may or may not be included, as alternatives to the Communist countries. These are all elements that enter into the future development of U.S.–China relations.

In particular, inherent in the U.S.-Soviet-China triangle are possibilities of radical realignments of future international relations. The development of Chinese relations with the Soviet Union is marked by ideological affinity and the practical considerations of Soviet aid, which have been absent in the development of U.S.–China relations. However, the most interesting issue, discussed at length by Michael, is the historical evolution that took place between 1950 and 1963. That period saw the Sino-Soviet alliance deteriorate to the point of an open break and witnessed the evolution of an ideological conflict into serious differences in state relations. Until the border skirmishes of 1969, few would have considered seriously the possibility of open Soviet–Chinese military hostilities. Yet the differences are real and well documented, and one may very well raise the question whether the fundamental, political problems between the two countries, as well as between the two large Communist Parties, both vying for leadership in the international movement, can ever be accommodated short of the subservience of one to the other. Since it is hard to envisage the subordination of Soviet interests to those of China, one can only conclude that the realistic alternatives are (1) subordination of China to the Soviet Union, at least to the extent of following parallel policies with respect to certain principal issues of concern to both, and (2) the continuation of the present conflict. An important question is whether such a continuation of conflict can be contained at a safe level indefinitely and what role China's development of an independent nuclear capability might play in the future.

Other than the United States and the Soviet Union, the country of the greatest importance to China is probably Japan. In the opinion of some observers, it was the invasion of China by Japan that contributed decisively to the Chinese inflation and the overtaking of China by chaos. The Sino-Soviet Treaty of 1950 was concluded in light of the possible rearmament of Japan. Yet between 1950 and 1969 the relative positions of China and Japan have greatly altered. Far from being the common enemy of both China and the Soviet Union, Japan has now become a major supplier of industrial equipment to China and a potentially large investor in the economic development of Soviet Siberia. At the same time, while the Sino-Soviet Treaty has in effect fallen into abeyance, Japan's growing military capability and the signs of possible accelerated rearmament after the reversion of Okinawa and in the light of the new China policy of the United States pose some rather serious long-term problems for China. Furthermore, while Japan has kept its nuclear options open, China has already proceeded well down the road toward an independent nuclear weapons capability. In addition, Japan's effort to tread the narrow line that separates politics from economics has been a constant obstacle in the development of friendly relations. Yet the developing economic relations between the two countries, albeit fluctuating at times, continue to constitute an ameliorating factor in the over-all relations between them. This very complex set of factors has influenced Sino-Japanese relations in the twenty-year period since 1949 and is inextricably entwined with Japan's domestic politics and with China's changing foreign policy. A detailed account of these subjects is provided in Humphreys's article.

There are many other countries whose relations with China are worth investigating. From China's standpoint, as King Chen shows, these countries can be roughly divided into two 'intermediate zones,' which lie between the Communist countries and the United States and the principal capitalist nations. Chinese relations with the 'third world,' which corresponds approximately to the 'first intermediate zone,' follow certain recognizable patterns. Official relations, economic and military assistance, cultural exchanges, and various forms of 'people's diplomacy' are carried out to further strengthen ties with China, which may result in the establishment of revolutionary bases for the support of 'wars of national liberation.' In this regard, both the Chinese state and the Chinese Communist Party play their respective roles. Not infrequently, international forums involving Afro-Asian groups are utilized for the benefit of the Chinese Communist Party in its unceasing effort to wrest leadership of the international revolutionary movement away from the Soviet Union. In the 'second intermediate zone,' Chinese relations with such countries as the United Kingdom, France, West Germany, Canada, and Australia follow the more traditional approach of diplomacy and trade. These countries are regarded by China as avowedly capitalist. However, the 'contradictions' in their relations with the United States are exploitable. The principal task for Chinese diplomacy, therefore, is to widen the potential gulf between them and the United States.

One of the puzzling issues facing those who have had to deal with officials from Peking is the Chinese concept of international law. Not only is it important that we understand the Chinese view of the nature and role of international law, the principle of sovereignty, and the concept of peaceful coexistence, but for some readers it may be necessary also to acquire a rudimentary knowledge of Chinese theory and practice with respect to some specific issues. Among the items listed by Chiu are: territorial waters, air and outer space, 'unequal treaties,' succession to treaties concluded by former Chinese governments, the treatment of foreigners and their property, diplomatic and consular immunity and privileges, and so forth.

The overseas Chinese, discussed briefly by Chiu, are the subject of a much lengthier account by C. H. Wu, who describes the overseas Chinese community, including its geographic distribution, social structure, and places of origin, and the different attitudes of host countries, especially in Southeast Asia. He then analyzes Peking's varying policies toward the overseas Chinese and the dependent families of those overseas Chinese who have returned to China. In particular, the impact of the overseas Chinese on remittances to China and on China's international payments is examined in some detail. This is followed by an account of the organizational aspects of both the Communist Party and the government in their dealings with the overseas Chinese.

After chapters on Chinese foreign policy, which offer the reader an opportunity to evaluate Communist China's performance in the external arena, we turn to the domestic scene and, in the first place, to economics. John Aird describes China's fundamental demographic problem, together with the theories and policies that have been advanced to deal with it. The main issue, apparently, has been a continuing struggle between the Malthusians and those who deny on doctrinaire grounds the existence of a population problem. As one examines repeated shifts of China's population policy, one may indeed come to despair of the emergence of a stable and rational attitude as long as Maoism prevails. Unfortunately for China, even if Maoism does not prevail, the very size of the Chinese population may present monumental problems that cannot be readily solved.

Since a most convenient measure of economic performance in the aggregate is the national income, both the different available estimates of China's national product and income and their time trends are presented in K. C. Yeh's chapter, which draws largely on his previous joint work with Ta-chung Liu. Yeh's paper is followed by three others dealing, respectively, with the agricultural sector; economic development and industrialization; and money, banking, and finance. These are followed by a chapter on the development of China's external economic relations. The three chapters on the domestic economy are worthy of special attention for what they reveal about the manner in which economic development and planning can be carried out in a primarily agricultural economy that has only a small industrial base. The many policy issues that must be resolved in choosing an appropriate strategy of development include the choice of priorities, the provision of incentives, the determination of the rate of accumulation, the ever present need to guard against inflation, the distribution of output, and a host of other technical and economic problems. How China has succeeded in some of these respects and during some periods, but has failed in other respects and other periods, is clearly set forth by Yeh with respect to agriculture, by Lau with respect to the nonagricultural sectors, and by Ecklund in the area of money and banking. As for external trade, the account by Hung includes estimates of both China's foreign trade and its external credit relationships. If any major discontinuity is to occur in Chinese affairs after Mao, knowledge about the 'base line' described in these four papers will be indispensable for projection and understanding.

The next article provides a link between the economic infrastructure and what the Marxists would describe as the social and cultural superstructure of the Chinese society. No economy can progress far without a technological base. Nor can one develop an independent, sophisticated military capability without appropriate developments in science and technology. At the same time, how any nation develops its scientific and technological manpower and to what ends and in what manner this manpower is used will largely determine the directions the nation's culture will follow. The Berberet article provides both a historical account of Chinese science and technology and a survey of the development of science and technology under the present regime. It covers the organization of scientific and technological policy and offers an evaluation of the progress to date along with the prospects of the future advancement of Chinese science and technology.

The evaluation of the Chinese performance in promoting both national and Party goals must not be confined to political and economic terms. How these developments have affected the Chinese as individual human beings and as members of both large and small groups is examined next. A chapter on health and medicine by Worth looks at the inherent health problems and the policies and measures that have been adopted to tackle them. This is followed by a review of changes in Chinese society and social institutions by William Liu; a survey of education by Theodore Chen, including educational philosophy and the school system and its accomplishments; and a detailed account of developments in the Chinese language and observations on Chinese literature, including in particular the content and progress of language reform, the emergence of simplified characters, phonetic spelling, and developments in the languages of racial minorities. Contemporary developments in Chinese literature are covered in the second part of the article by the late S. H. Chen, which provides a bird's-eye view of what has happened to poetry, fiction, and good writing in general, of which traditional China was never in short supply. A most fascinating account along the same lines by Richard Yang deals with opera, modern drama, motion pictures, music, painting, and the graphic arts.

Upon completing the first twenty-nine chapters of Part I, the reader will have succeeded in obtaining a comprehensive view of contemporary Chinese affairs. However, the articles are intended to *survey* the many facets of China today, and they contain a cut-off date; they do not encompass all there is to know about mainland China up to the minute. For those students who want to pursue studies on China, the final chapter by Ma serves as a guide for further reading. It contains an account of the bibliographical tools available in this country and elsewhere, including U.S. Government publications, foreign publications, Communist Chinese sources, and the publications on China of some of the principal research institutions.

It is fitting that our *tour d'horizon* ends with the observations by Chen and Yang on literature and art. Apparently, twenty years of Communist rule have not been able to stifle totally the expressions of the human spirit (the same may be said of the Soviet Union). This brings us to the question whether traditional China and its values, which succeeded in Sinicizing many alien ideas and invaders in the past, will once more weather through Communism and Maoist ideas. There are those who believe so. But others are less sanguine: they detect in Maoism and the Communist totalitarian ideology elements that are not without their Chinese foundations in the distant past.

Nor can one ignore the revolutionary changes that have taken place in the methods of psychological conditioning and indoctrination and in the cruder means of coercion and repression. Hitlerism was not defeated from within, nor have we any indisputable evidence that any significant peaceful change within the Soviet Union will take place in the foreseeable future. There is little ground, therefore, to believe that the Chinese case will be an exception. The uncertain element lies with generational change, for no one can foretell what the next generation will bring, in spite of the conformity of education and the indoctrination of the Party line.

Even more uncertain is whether the present changing Sino-Soviet-American relationship might not produce some major changes. In particular, how irreconcilable are the differences between Peking and Moscow? How much risk is either side prepared to take? And if there should be war, one may legitimately raise the question whether China itself can survive as a national entity, not to mention its traditional values and its accomplishments up to the present. It is clear that these questions cannot—and will not—be answered in this volume. The reader must be left with his own judgments and musings.

These points should be added: First, a few documents (Part II) have been selected for reference. Unfortunately, space does not permit the inclusion of a greater number. Second, the data section (Part III) contains information on various political and economic subjects, as well as matters of general interest. The details can be seen in the table of contents. Finally, for the benefit of those readers who are not familiar with the transliteration of Chinese names, it should be mentioned that the Wade-Giles system of transliteration has been used throughout, with the exception of some proper names (mostly place names) for which traditional spelling has been preserved because of usage of long standing.

Menlo Park, California
June, 1972

2

PHYSICAL GEOGRAPHY

CHIAO-MIN HSIEH

THE GEOLOGICAL STRUCTURE

THE present land forms of China cannot be understood without knowledge of the country's geological structure and its underlying rocks.

Beneath all young deposits in China—that is, below the sands of great plains, loess valley bottoms, and other consolidated conglomerates, sandstones, shales, and limestones—lies an ancient complex of hard crystalline rocks which form the foundation of China's continent. During the geological periods, this ancient land mass was never wholly submerged by the sea. Although the oldest rocks are distributed extensively in China, they have come to the surface in only a few localities.

The three old masses standing out on the surface of China are structurally so rigid that they are called massifs and shields. The best preserved of these permanent massifs is *Tibetia*, which is in the western part of China. Extending from the southeast in the provinces of Fukien and Chekiang, as well as in Shantung and Liaoning, is the remnant of the old land of *Cathaysia*, which contains the granites and porphyries. The third remnant of old rock is found in Inner Mongolia and is called *Gobia*. This Paleozoic massif is partly buried by Tertiary sand and clays and by basalt flows.

A great thickness of deposits has been laid down between these three old crystalline hard rocks. During geological time, from the beginning of the Paleozoic period up to the Jurassic, shallow seas occasionally invaded the land, leaving limestones, sandstones, and shales. During the Carboniferous and Jurassic periods, coal beds were deposited over widespread areas.

Inherited from the three old land masses, the structural patterns in China have three distinctive strike sets. The first is the northeast-southwest, or the Cathaysia, trend, which is reflected in the mountain ranges of the Liaotung and Shantung peninsulas; the ranges in Fukien province; the Great Khingan range between Mongolia and Manchuria; and T'aihang Mountains bounded by the loess plateau and the North China plain, the Yangtze Gorge, and the eastern edge of the Yünnan-Kweichow plateau.

The second strike set extends from west to east. It is represented by the Yin mountain range, which divides North China from Mongolia, and is developed in the land mass of Gobia. Another important west-east trend is the mountain range of Chinling, a continuation of the K'unlun, which separates the Yangtze from the Yellow (Huang) River and forms the backbone of China. Another east-west strike is the Nanling in South China, which is also the divide between the Yangtze and the Hsi (West) rivers.

The third structural trend runs from north to south and is well developed in the land mass of Tibetia. It is reflected in the Holan and Liupan mountains, and in the Hengtuan mountain ranges on the eastern edge of the Tibetan Plateau.

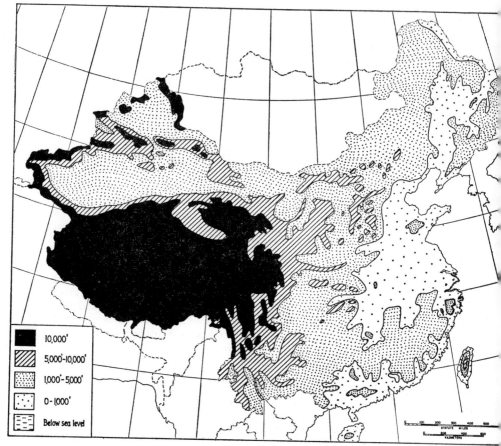

■	10,000'
▨	5,000'-10,000'
░	1,000'-5,000'
⋮	0-1,000'
▤	Below sea level

Map 1   Relief

LAND FORMS

The land forms of China are varied and complex, ranging from the 8,880-meter peak of Mount Chomolunga (Everest) to the depth of the Turfan depression at 283 meters below sea level. They include extensive plateaus, desert sand dunes, alpine glaciers, alluvial plains, precipitous canyons, and irregular coasts. Unique landscapes are formed by loess hills and limestone karst.

China's checkerboard structure is the result of three characteristics: (1) The land declines from the west to the east; (2) most of the major mountain ranges run from the west to the east; and (3) there is a wide variety of land forms.

Incline from west to east. Starting in the extreme west from the Tibetan Plateau, 'the roof of the world,' the west-east inclination is like a three-section staircase divided by two notable steps. The highest step consists of the K'unlun and Ch'ilien mountains, which are the northern boundary of Tibet, and the Taliang Mountains, which are the eastern edge of the Tibetan Plateau. The altitude of this step roughly coincides with the 3,000-meter (10,000-foot) contour line. The second step, which is 2,000 meters lower, follows the Great Khingan Mountains, the T'aihang Range, the Wu Mountains—which are the Yangtze gorges—and the eastern border of the Yünnan-Kweichow upland; its altitude roughly coincides with the 1,000-meter (3,000-foot) contour line.

30

Between these two steps are a number of plateaus and basins, such as the Tarim basin, Inner Mongolia, the loess plateaus in Northwestern and North China, and the limestone plateau in the south. The Szechwan basin, with its large tract lying below 1,000 meters, is a notable exception in the high tablelands.

East of the second step is a depression belt where the elevation is less than 500 meters. This belt extends over the Manchuria plain, the North China plain, and the mid-Yangtze lake region.

Still farther east are the elevated land masses of the Eastern Manchuria upland, the Shantung Peninsula, and the southeastern coastal hills. The land mass ends at the Yellow Sea, the East China Sea, and the South China Sea.

West-east orientation of major mountain ranges. At intervals across the above-mentioned elevated and depressed stretches, the major mountains or watersheds run in general from west to east. In the west, they are the T'ien range, which divides Sinkiang in half, the K'unlun, which separates Sinkiang from Tibet, and the Himalayas, which form the mighty boundary between China and India.

The eastern regions are also cut by three mountain ranges. In the far north, the Yin range separates Inner Mongolia from the North China plain. To the south, the Chinling Range lies between the North China plain and central China, and still farther south, the Nanling Mountains divide Central China from South China.

This combination of longitudinal descending steps and latitudinal folded belts of mountains superimposed upon each other gives China's land surface a checkerboard pattern.

Varied land forms. With respect to slope and relief, the land of China may be classified as plain, basin, hill, plateau, and mountain. About 14 per cent of the land is plain; 16 per cent, basin; 34 per cent, plateau; 9 per cent, hill; and 30 per cent, mountains. The distribution of elevation is as follows:

Elevation	Per cent
Over 5,000 meters (16,404 feet)	16
2,000–5,000 meters (6,561–16,404 feet)	17
1,000–2,000 meters (3,280–6,561 feet)	35
500–1,000 meters (1,640–3,280 feet)	18
Under 500 meters (1,640 feet)	14
	100

Plains. Coastal plains formed by river deposits and interior plains cover more than a million square kilometers, or 10 per cent of China's territory; they provide its principal farmlands. The notable coastal plains, each with an area of 300,000 square kilometers, are the North China plain in the lower reaches of the Yellow River, the Manchuria plain, and the middle and lower Yangtze deltas. The Canton delta is also a small plain. Rich soils, extensive irrigation, and centuries of intensive farming have made these areas not only the granary of China but also one of the world's greatest centers of agricultural production. The most important interior plains, which are smaller, are the Chengtu plain, with an area of 6,000 square kilometers, the Wei plains, and the Ninghsia plains, all of which have been widely irrigated to form agricultural centers supporting large populations.

Basins. About one-sixth of the total land area of China consists of basins, of which the four largest are the Szechwan, the Tarim, the Dzungarian, and the Tsaidam. Fringed by lofty mountains, these basins are a part of the basic structure of the land, rather than the result of erosion or cataclysm. Aside from Szechwan, where special climatic conditions provide ample rainfall, the inland location of these basins causes a dry climate, which has made the areas surrounding the basins into steppe and desert regions. Local peasants use melted snow from the permanently white-capped surrounding mountains to irrigate their fields, which appear as fertile and picturesque oases. The Szechwan basin (elevation under 500 meters) is called the 'heavenly country' by the Chinese, because the rich soils and humid climate permit the cultivation of a wide variety of crops. Four major rivers cross the basin, giving the province its name, Szechwan, meaning 'four rivers.'

Hilly regions. The hilly regions constitute about 9 per cent of China's total land area. Age-old erosion is responsible for the low elevation, mostly under 500 meters, of these hills. Their gentle slopes, interspersed with fluvial plains and small basins, make them ideal for terracing and the cultivation of a wide variety of crops and trees. A few mountains of over 1,000 meters, such as T'ai Mountain in Shantung, Huang Mountain in Anhwei, Lu Mountain in Kiangsi, and T'ienmu in Chekiang, are nationally known tourist and pilgrimage centers because of their traditional religious significance, as evidenced by heavy concentrations of temples.

Plateaus. Located in West and Central China, the plateaus occupy one-third of the country's total land area and include the four principal areas of Tibet, Inner Mongolia, the loess plateau of Shansi and Shensi, and the limestone plateau of Yünnan and Kwangsi. Each has its own appearance and special features. Tibet, with an average elevation of over 4,000 meters, is the world's most extensive tableland. Here are found endless snow-covered peaks, rich salt lakes, steppe tundras, and relatively flat valleys. The Inner Mongolia plateau, bounded on the south by the Great Wall, on the east by the Great Khingan Mountains, and on the west by the Ch'ilien Mountains, is broad and flat, and rather uniform in its surface.

Averaging 1,000 meters in elevation, the loess (*huang-t'u*) plateau is covered with a thick layer of fertile loess, which forms a broad undulating surface. The sparseness of vegetation leaves the fine loess open to erosion by wind and water. The limestone plateau in Yünnan and Kwangsi stands at an elevation of 1,000–2,000 meters. Water erosion has led to well-developed karst topography, including isolated peaks, many pinnacles, gaping sinkholes and caverns, and lapiers, as well as small, fertile intramontaine plains, known locally as *pa-tze.*

Mountains. The mountains of China both reflect the geological structure of the land and provide the skeleton around which it is formed. The mountains are ranged in three principal directions. Those produced by the Yen Shan revolution of the Cretaceous Period run from the northeast to the southwest; those built during the earlier Caledonian and Hercynian revolution of the Paleozoic era strike east-west; and others, formed during the Cenozoic period, have a north-south orientation.

The Cathaysian Mountains, running northeast-southwest, include the Ch'angpai in eastern Manchuria and the Wui (Wuyi) in Fukien.

The east-west oriented mountains, which resemble the fingers of a giant hand stretching across China, include the T'ienshan, the Altyn, the K'unlun, the Nanling, and the Himalayas. At longitude 96° E., the east-west direction of the Himalayas suddenly turns to the south, forming the Hengtuan (horizontal cut) mountains, which are north-south oriented ranges. The erosive action of the Nu, the Lants'ang, and the Gold Sand rivers has cut gorges into these mountains.

SPECIAL LAND FORMS

Loess. Loess covers more than 200,000 square kilometers of North China and is an important natural feature in Kansu, Honan, Shansi, and Shensi provinces. It is a loose, fine yellow silt composed of quartz and aluminum oxide and varying in size from 1/16 to 1/32 cm. in diameter. It has no layers but is well developed in vertical joints and usually forms gorge-like gullies, whose banks rise several decameters above the floor, making transportation difficult.*

* A kilometer is about .62 miles; a centimeter measures .39 inches; a decameter is approximately 32.81 feet.

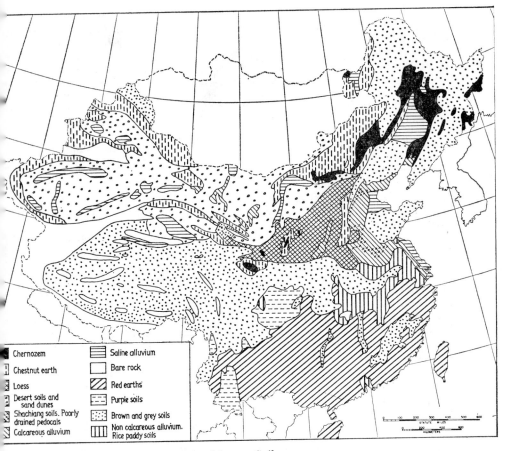

Map 2 Soils

The accumulation of loess began in the middle of the Pliocene Period, when North China was mostly grassland. Apparently, strong winds deposited silt from the Gobi desert on the grasslands, and thus loess was formed. The loess is more than 100 feet deep in places, burying the original bedrock land form and forming an undulating tableland. Even today, North China's 'wind of sand' or dust storms in the spring indicate that loess accumulation is still in progress.

The wind-laid silt of loess is deposited in a thick, loose mantle and is easily dissolved by underground water, which produces depressions, earthquakes, and landslides. Terracing on the loess surface and destruction of plant cover have made soil erosion a serious problem in the area. The silt content of the rivers and the rate of erosion in the region are a function of the extent of the loess area. To compare the Yungting and Tach'ing rivers as an example, the drainage area of the former consists of 21 per cent loess, while that of the latter has only 9 per cent; the silt content of the Yungting River is twenty-five times that of the Tach'ing.

An unusual and noted use of loess is for the construction of cave dwellings, which are cool in summer and warm in winter. These constructions form very comfortable homes, from which the farmer must climb to the 'roof' in order to cultivate his farm.

Karst. Kwangsi, Kweichow, and Yünnan are classic examples of karst topography. High temperatures and heavy rainfall have for centuries caused erosion of the massive limestone that dominates this region, and the long solution of the limestone has resulted in the spectacular landscapes for which the area is known. In some places, isolated hills rise almost vertically from the ground as the only remnants of the original mass of limestone, while in others deep sinkholes and canyons cut the original surface. Still other areas have been eroded into a profusion of steep hills.

Caves and underground drainage channels penetrate the subterranean regions; creeks that begin on the surface suddenly disappear to become underground streams. Kweilin, the capital of Kwangsi, has the reputation of having the most beautiful scenery in China. As a matter of fact, karst scenery is often the dominant characteristic of Chinese landscape painting.

Glaciation. Modern research has produced evidence of Ice Age glaciation in many parts of China, including the mountains of northwestern Hupei, the Lu Mountains and surrounding plains, the Huang and parts of Tapieh Mountains, the Yangtze valley, and the mountains on the western border of the Red Basin of Szechwan. Other areas with traces of glacial action include the Great Khingan, Ch'ilien (Nan), and T'ien areas, as well as Kweichow, Yünnan, and northern Kwangsi, and even the Western Hills of Peking.

The corrie type of polyglaciation (leaving round depressions in hillsides) apparently predominated in both northern and southern China, with periods of warm (genial and subtropical) climate interspersed with the glacial periods.

Although research has uncovered much new information in recent years, important questions remain. For example, what is the origin of the boulder and clay deposits found only partly preserved on terraces that have been leveled down to plains, often covered with new deposits of loess or other soils? Where can the line of demarcation be drawn between glacial and interglacial periods, and during what geological ages did these periods occur? Did arctic and tropical flora and fauna, whose fossils are found together, live at the same time or successively in the same region? Is there any relation between glacial and fluvio-glacial deposits and the different formations of loess? What is the division of physiographic stages according to alternating glacial and interglacial climates? What effect has postglacial erosion had on the prior erosion of land surfaces during the glacial and interglacial periods?

Coastlines. China's 12,500-mile coastline, extending from the mouth of the Yalu River on the Chinese-Korean border in the north to the mouth of the Peilun River on the Chinese-Vietnamese border in the south, is one-half as long as the Equator. The coast is of two types: sandy and rocky. Generally speaking, Hangchow Bay, just south of Shanghai, divides China's coast into two parts; north of the bay the coast is sandy, with the exception of the rocky shores of the Shantung and Liaotung peninsulas; south of the bay, it is rocky. The sandy coast is associated with the plains; it has shallow water offshore, many spits and sandbars, and great possibilities for the development of the salt and chemical industries. The rocky coast is irregular, with many islands and some drowned rivers. Most of it has excellent harbors and fishing grounds.

The northern part of Kiangsu Province and the land along the Po Hai Gulf coast, both of which are sandy, are famous salt-producing areas; they are also rich in marine products. The Shantung and Liaotung peninsulas, with their rocky coasts and their many harbors and islands, provide favorable facilities for fishing.

The rocky coast south of Hangchow Bay is interrupted occasionally by patches of sandy shoreline at the mouths of some rivers. The rocky coasts have many indentations that are suitable for the construction of ports and for a highly developed fishing industry.

The coast of China includes both submergent and emergent types. It is believed that emergence characterized the formation of the coast north of Hangchow Bay and submergence the formation of the coast south of it.

However, the coast of China has not been stable, especially the southeastern coast, where the irregular rocky coastline, the many drowned rivers, the many islands and bays, the lack of large deltas, and the spits and bars all definitely point to submergence. Conversely, the wave-cut terraces, marine shell deposits, and shallow water offshore are evidences of emergence. As a whole, the coast of southeastern China is of a compound type, which was first submergent in the early Tertiary Period and was raised in the Quaternary.

CLIMATE

In a country so large and so varied in land forms, the climate is necessarily diversified. Distinction can be made among equatorial, tropical, subtropical, warm temperate, temperate, and frigid zones, while humidity areas can be classified in three categories—humid, arid, and semiarid. The varied climate has produced a wide variety of flora and fauna.

Control factors. Three factors control China's climate: monsoons, mountain barriers, and cyclones. The monsoons result from the distribution of land and water. China is on the western edge of the great Eurasian continent, facing the Pacific Ocean to the east. This location subjects it to the unique wind system of eastern Asia.

In the winter, the heat of the earth radiates quickly, and the interior land mass becomes extremely cold, causing the air pressure to rise drastically. On the other

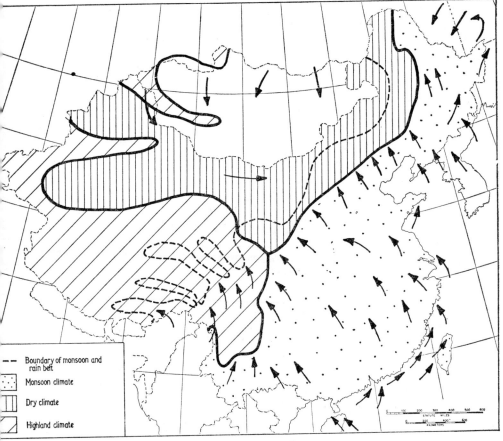

Map 3   Climate

35

hand, the Pacific Ocean retains some heat, and the temperature of the land near the sea accordingly becomes higher, which produces low pressure.

In the summer, the land becomes warmer than the ocean, and thus low pressure develops on the land, while high pressure shifts to the ocean. As the winds always blow from the region of high pressure to that of low, this change in pressure centers causes the wind to change its direction every half-year. In winter, it blows from the land to the ocean, and in summer, from the ocean to the land. During the winter monsoon, the wind directions in North China are usually north and northwest, while in Central China they are north and northeast. The summer monsoon is dominated by south, east, and southeast winds in the north, and by southeast winds in the south.

The winter wind consists chiefly of a fresh polar continental air mass (PC) and land-transformed or sea-transformed polar continental air (LNPC or SNPC). Generated by the Mongolian anticyclone in winter, these air masses are cold and stable and influence a great part of China. The summer monsoon consists of three air masses with different origins: the tropical maritime (TM), the equatorial maritime (EM), and the polar maritime (PM). They are warm and unstable air masses. Of the three, the last is not tropical in origin and is least important. Because the winds that blow from the continent are dry and cold, and those that blow from the ocean are moist and warm, rainfall reaches its maximum in summer and its minimum in winter.

The west-east disposition of the mountain ranges affects the climate by presenting barriers to the rain-bearing winds from the south in summer, and to the cold winds from the north in winter. Three pairs of cities, Sian and Wanhsien, Chengchow and Hankow, and Nanking and Hsüchou, are examples of the influence of the mountain barriers on rainfall. Both cities of each pair are located on the same longitude, but each pair is separated by the Ch'inling range. Wanhsien, Hankow, and Nanking, all south of the range, have an annual rainfall of more than 750 millimeters; Sian, Chengchow, and Hsüchou, all north of the range, have only half as much annual rainfall—375 millimeters or about 15 inches.

At China's latitude, extratropical cyclones are usually the sole cause of weather changes, especially in the spring. About 70 per cent of these cyclones originate in China, 27 per cent in Siberia, and 2 per cent in India. The highest incidence of cyclones occurs in April and the lowest in August, with the spring season accounting for 35.3 per cent of a year's storms. Winter accounts for 26.2 per cent, autumn for 20.2 per cent, and summer for only 18.3 per cent. Typhoons are an important factor in the climate, especially during August and September on the southeastern coast.

Temperature and rainfall. Temperature and the amount of rainfall indicate the climate of a region. In China, the temperature in the north and that in the south are not much different in summer, but they differ markedly in winter. During the winter, the isotherms are close together, extending from west to east, parallel with the latitude; in the summer, they are far apart, having a longitudinal orientation and in general lying parallel to the coast. During January, the coldest month of the year, as one travels from Canton in the south to Harbin in the north, the temperature decreases by 3 degrees Fahrenheit for every 1 degree of latitude. When the traveler leaves Canton, he needs only light garments, and when he reaches Hankow he needs a light coat, but as he goes farther north and reaches Peking he needs a heavy overcoat. Finally, when he arrives at Harbin, he will be well advised to put on a fur coat and a fur cap. He experiences different climatic conditions, from pleasant sunshine to Arctic rigors—the difference in temperature is some 80 degrees. On the other hand, during July, the warmest month of the year, the difference in temperature between Canton and Harbin is less than 18 degrees Fahrenheit.

Rainfall in different parts of China shows even more variation than the temperature. Atmospheric moisture in China comes mostly from the Pacific, so that the rainfall decreases as a traveler goes from the southeast to the northwest. It is 2,000 mm.

annually along the southeastern coast, 750 mm. in the Chinling range, and less than 375 mm. along the Yellow River.* The land northwest of Sinkiang Province is so dry that it depends for its water supply on the melting of snow on the top of the T'ien Mountains, the most important mountain range in the area.

In addition to orographic rain produced in mountainous areas, rainfall originates in thunderstorms, cyclones and typhoons. Table 2–1 shows the percentage distribution of the latter three types of rainfall in various cities. China can be divided roughly into three humidity zones—humid, arid, and semiarid—according to annual rainfall. The humid zone includes areas south of the Chinling range and the Huai River, where the annual rainfall averages 750 mm. and sometimes reaches 1,500 mm. in the southeastern coastal hilly regions. These areas are well known for their rice, tea, and subtropical fruits and plants. The arid zone includes the areas north of the Yin and K'unlun mountains, such as Sinkiang, Inner Mongolia, and other parts of the northwest, where the annual rainfall is less than 250 mm. Here the air is dry, and with the exception of the irrigated oases, most of the land is steppe and desert. Shortage of rain here is due, first, to the long distance from the sea, and second, to mountains and plateaus, which prevent the moist wind from blowing in from the southeastern coastal areas. The land lying between the two zones is a semiarid zone with an average annual rainfall of 500 mm.

Table 2–1—Types of Rainfall in Various Cities

	Canton	Nanking	K'unming	Chengtu	Peking	Huhehot	K'uch'e
Thunderstorm	17	13	12	16	15	28	28
Typhoon	21	4	0	0	3	0	0
Cyclone	62	83	88	84	82	72	72

Chang Chi-yün, ed., *Chung-Kuo ti Tzu-jan Huan-ching,* (*The Physical Environment of China*) (Taipei, Taiwan: 1955), p. 103.

China's rainfall not only is unevenly distributed throughout the country but also varies widely from season to season and year to year. Disparity is greatest in the lower Yellow River region and the Northwest. For example, Peking's average annual rainfall over a period of sixty-seven years (1870–1937) was 630 mm., but the extremes for a single year ranged from 1,084 mm. to 168 mm. The Hsi River area has the most consistent rainfall.

More than 80 per cent of the annual rainfall occurs between May and October, during the summer monsoon. In the semiarid and arid regions, the heaviest rainfall is concentrated in July and August. The coincidence of the time of the heaviest precipitation with the highest temperature is beneficial to agriculture, especially rice cultivation.

The lengths of the seasons also vary. Some places have a long winter and practically no summer, while others are warm all year and have no real winter. Using monthly average temperature as a guide for dividing the four seasons, we can regard summer as the period when temperatures are above 72 degrees Fahrenheit (22 degrees Centigrade), and winter as that when temperatures are below 50 degrees. Spring and autumn are the periods when temperatures are between these extremes. According to this classification, in the areas south of the Nanling range there is no winter; but summer lasts for five to eight months. In contrast, most of the Tibetan plateau and northern Heilungkiang have long winters and no summer. The rest of the country enjoys four seasons, although winter is longer than summer in the north, the reverse being true in the south.

China has four important climatic boundaries that are closely related to cultivation. The first is the 21-degree Fahrenheit (— 6-degree Centigrade) (January) isotherm,

* A millimeter is roughly .04 inches.

which roughly coincides with the Great Wall and is the southern boundary of the area growing spring and winter wheat. The second is the isohyet of 750 mm., which parallels the Chinling range and the Huai River and coincides with the 50-degree (10-degree) isotherm. This line is the northern limit of rice cultivation. The third is the isohyet of 1,250 mm., which is the southern limit of wheat cultivation. The fourth boundary is the 43-degree (6-degree) (January) isotherm, which separates the double-rice crop-area from that growing a single rice crop; the boundary between them coincides with the 32-degree (0-degree) isotherm south of the Nanling range.

Climatically, moving southward, China can therefore be divided into several belts, which are closely related to the types of crops grown. The details are as follows:

Name of Belt	Location	Crops	Growing Season
Seipei	North of the Great Wall	Spring wheat	140 days
Hopei	North of the Yellow River	Wheat and millet	222 days
Huaipei	North of the Huai River	Wheat and cotton	250 days
Huainan	South of the Huai River	Rice and bamboo	285 days
Kiangnan	South of the Yangtze River	Silk and tea	300 days
Lingnan	South of the Nanling range	Two crops of rice, olives, lichee nuts, sugar cane, oranges and other fruit	All year
Hainan	Hainan Island	Palm trees and tropical fruits	All year

HYDROGRAPHY

Drainage patterns. China's river systems carry 2,784 cubic kilometers of water a year, which is about 9 per cent of the world's fresh water and is surpassed in quantity only by the waters of the Soviet Union and Brazil. The river systems are essential to agricultural and industrial development and are among China's most valuable natural resources. A number of ambitious programs are aimed at harnessing the rivers to provide irrigation, electricity, and transportation on a large scale. Simultaneous efforts to curb soil erosion are designed to control flooding and to make previously barren areas fertile. More than 95,000 kilometers of the streams are considered navigable, and the water energy has the potential for generating 540 million kilowatts of electric power.*

China's general surface configuration—high elevations in the west and low lands in the east—has the result that most rivers flow from west to east and empty into the Pacific Ocean. However, the central plateau regions are surrounded by mountains and thus provide a second or interior drainage watershed. Nearly 36 per cent of China's rivers flow into the great basins of this area, and the waters are absorbed into the arid bottoms. A majority of such streams originate from the western slopes of the mountains bordering the plateau regions. The drainage pattern can be seen in Table 2-2.

East of the 'continental divide,' a vertical line that runs from the lower Great Khingan range in Inner Mongolia to the border with India via northwestern Ninghsia, the Kansu corridor, the western border of Tsinghai, and the western third of Tibet, the rivers flow out to the sea, while west of the 'divide' they flow inward to the interior plains and basins. Interior streams are generally short, shallow, and poorly

* In comparison, the United States has 44.5 million kilowatts of developed hydroelectric power and 124 million kilowatts of undeveloped potential. See National Conference Board, *Economic Almanac 1967–68*, 18th ed. (New York: Macmillan, n.d.), p. 95.

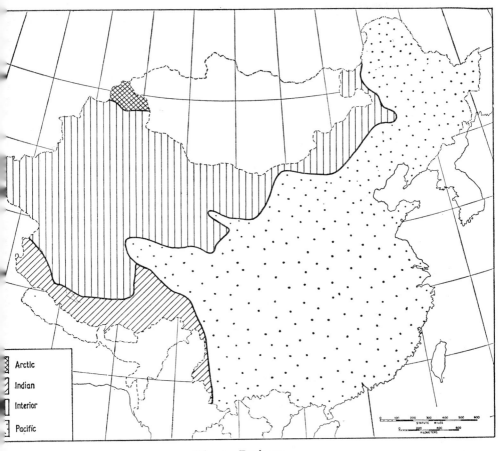

Map 4   Drainage

defined, often carrying water only during the rainy season and ending when all the water is finally absorbed into the sand. The Tarim River is, however, a notable exception to this rule.

Table 2–2—River Drainage Pattern

Destination of River System	Area (sq. km.)		Per Cent	
Total flow out	*6,144,630*		*64.0*	
Pacific Ocean		5,440,540		56.7
Indian Ocean		663,750		6.9
Arctic Ocean		40,340		0.4
Interior	3,452,370		36	
Total	9,597,000		100	

Distribution of China's rivers and their characteristics. Three areas of China provide the sources of most major Asian rivers. The Central Asian plateau is the origin of such long rivers as the Yangtze, the Yellow, the Heilungkiang (Amur), the Lants'ang (upper Mekong), the Yalutsangpu (upper Brahmaputra), the Ganges, and the Indus. The second important river-source area includes the Great Khingan range on the eastern border of Inner Mongolia, the T'aihang range, the eastern edge of the Shansi

39

plateau, and the Yünnan-Kweichow plateau. Major rivers originating there include the Sungari, Liao, Huai, Hai, Luan, Pearl, Red, and Hsi. The third area is spread over most of the east coast of China, including the Ch'angpai Mountains in Manchuria, the Shantung hills, the southeastern coastal hills, and Wuling. These regions are the origins of the many short coastal rivers, including such streams as the Tumen and the Yalu, on the Chinese-Korean border. In the southeastern coastal area the streams are associated with rivermouth cities. Thus, the Ch'ient'ang River is associated with Hangchow, the Wu with Wenchou, the Lung with Amoy, and the Han with Swatow.

China's rivers are distributed in eight geographic areas, each with its distinctive characteristics.

1. In the *Northeast* (Manchuria and the Maritime Provinces), where the major rivers are the Heilungkiang, Sungari, Tumen, Yalu, and Liao, the highest water level occurs in August, which is the rainy season. Melting snow and ice also produce a high flow in the spring, but floods result from damming by ice floes rather than from the high volume of water. The rivers of this area are frozen from late October or early November to March. Since water comes only from underground sources during this period, the lowest water levels occur in January and February.

2. *North China* includes the Liao, Huai, Hai, and Yellow Rivers, all of which have their highest water levels in August. In the north, melting snow brings a high water point in the spring, but elsewhere, as the volume of snow is limited, floods as a rule are caused only by sudden showers. The lowest water level occurs in May and June, when high temperature and dry weather cause a high evaporation rate, except for the Yellow River, which is fed by the melting snows of Tsinghai and has its low point in December and January. Dry climate and sandy soil make erosion particularly severe in this area.

3. In *South China*, the plentiful rainfall of the tropics and semitropics creates large rivers, such as the Huai, the Ch'ient'ang, Ou, Wei, Pearl, and Yangtze rivers. There is no freezing, and water is high from April to September, with the highest levels and floods occurring during the July–August typhoon season.

4. In the *Southwest*, the main rivers are the upper Yangtze, upper and middle Yü, upper Hsi, Red, Lants'ang, Min, and Nu rivers. Since this region is little affected by snow and ice, the high water level occurs during the July–August rainy season, and the lowest levels coincide with the dry weather of February. The depth of the river beds in the mountainous areas means that these rivers seldom overflow.

5. The *Tsinghai–Tibet* area is the source of many rivers. Its streams include the upper Indus, the upper Yalutsangpu, the upper Nu (Salween), the Lants'ang, and the headwaters of the Yangtze and Yellow rivers. Melting snow and ice cause a high spring water level, but the gradualness of the melting process causes the high season to be poorly defined. Rains from July to September make those months the season of highest water levels. The waters are frozen from October to March.

6. The streams of *Inner Mongolia* are poorly defined and dispersed over wide plains, where many areas have no real streams because of sand, high winds, gully diversion, low rainfall, and a high evaporation rate. The main water source is rainfall, so that many of the streams carry water only when it rains. Underground sources feed a few tiny streams, which are the most dependable in this arid region.

7. In the *Northwest*, melting snow and glaciers from the T'ien, K'unlun, and Ch'ilien mountains provide the chief water source for the desert and semidesert areas. Although snow begins to melt in March, absorption and a high evaporation rate keep the water level quite low, except for the period from June to August. The flow is steady during this season when there is rain, but dispersal in the steppe and desert lands leaves little water at the lower reaches of these streams, which are dry from October to late May.

8. The *Altai area* includes the Oerhch'issu and Wulunku (Urungu) rivers, which are fed by plentiful snow and rainfall. Spring floods are caused by the coincidence of spring rains with the melting of snow, while the midseason high-water levels occur in July. From August to October, the water level is average. Freezing from November to March causes low water levels from November to April.

SOILS AND VEGETATION

Soils. The study of soils in China has had a long history. As early as the fourth century B.C., ancient records of soil distribution were given in the *Yü Kung*, an ancient book on the mountains and rivers of China. Since 1930, soil surveys and laboratory studies have been carried on by Chinese as well as foreign scholars. The natural process of soil formation takes place through time, while the geographical distribution of soils is expressed in space.

The geographical distribution of lowland soils results in the formation of different soil zones at different latitudes, according to their distance from the sea, the effect of high mountains, and the changes in climate and vegetation. Generally speaking, forest soils, which are usually regarded as of the oceanic type, develop in the relatively humid monsoon climate of the region near the sea, while dry steppe and desert soils, which are always regarded as belonging to the continental soil type, are formed under semiarid and arid climate conditions of the inland regions. Intermediate between the forest soils and the steppe and desert soils is a transitional zone of forest-steppe soil.

In China, the oceanic type of forest soils includes podzolic soils of brown earth, yellow and red earth, red earth, and laterites. The continental type in Inner Mongolia and Northwest China includes chernozems, chestnut earth, brown earth, and desert soils. From east to west, the soils change in Northeast China and Inner Mongolia from podzolic soils to gray-forest soils, leached chernozems (black earth), chernozems, dark chestnut soils, light chestnut soils, brown soils, and desert soil. In North and Northwest China, soils range from brown earth to gray earth and desert soils. In Central China, it is yellow soils in the north and yellow and red earths in the south; to the west it is yellow earth and mountain soils. In South China, no sharp regional difference appears.

Vegetation. Of the 4 million square miles of China, approximately one-half consists of woodland and the other half of grassland and desert. The woodland is concentrated in the eastern section; the grassland and desert, in the western lands.

One feature of the vegetation of China rarely found in other parts of the world is that the woodland extends in an unbroken expanse of continuous forest communities from the tropical rain forest to the boreal coniferous forest. The woodland is divided into six major forest types, which form broad bands on the land surface in a more or less latitudinal sequence. From north to south, there are the boreal coniferous forest, the mixed northern hardwood forest, the temperate deciduous broad-leaf forest, the mixed forest, the evergreen broad-leaf forest, and the rain forest.

The grassland-desert is essentially in the region of internal drainage in the heartland of the Eurasian land mass. The vegetation forms concentric rings of desert scrub, alkaline-saline plant communities, steppe, and—farther away from the center—vast expanses of short and tall grass. The concentric rings encircle a salt lake (*nor*), a dried-up lake basin, or an immense desert, such as the Hanhai and the Takla Makan. Along the periphery of the concentric zones is the woodland-grassland transitional belt.

Superimposed upon the general pattern of latitudinal bands of forest types and concentric rings of grassland-desert is the altitudinal differentiation of vegetation types. In the mountains, the vegetation ranges from the rain forest on the lower slopes through the evergreen broad-leaf forest, the deciduous broad-leaf forest, and

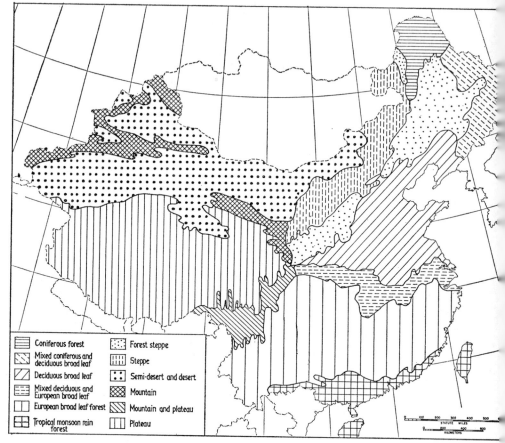

Coniferous forest | Forest steppe
Mixed coniferous and deciduous broad leaf | Steppe
Deciduous broad leaf | Semi-desert and desert
Mixed deciduous and European broad leaf | Mountain
European broad leaf forest | Mountain and plateau
Tropical monsoon rain forest | Plateau

Map 5   Vegetation

the boreal coniferous forest of spruce and fir, to the alpine scrub and meadow and the area of perpetual snow.

No genuine understanding of the vegetation in China and its ramifications is possible without recognition of the fact that the nation is founded on two great natural plant formations—the woodland in the East and the grassland-desert complex in the inland West. Table 2–3 sets forth concisely the contrasting geographical traits of East and West.

Table 2–3—Geographical Traits of West and East

The West	The East
1. Grassland and desert; trees confined to high elevations and areas near water supply	1. Essentially woodland, except under unfavorable local habitat conditions
2. Except for arable grassland, primary land use is grazing	2. Land cleared primarily for crop cultivation.
3. Nomadic	3. Permanent settlement
4. Sparsely populated except in limited irrigation area	4. Densely populated except in the underdeveloped frontiers and in the montane-boreal regions

42

| 5. High plateaus, basins without external drainage, high mountain ranges; essentially an internal drainage area | 5. Alluvial plains, broad river valleys, basins with external drainage, hills, dissected plateaus, and mountains |
| 6. Mountain ranges 6,000–7,000 meters; highest peak: 8,882 meters | 6. Mountain ranges to 3,000 meters; highest peak rarely exceeds 4,000 meters. |

Adapted from Wang Chi-wu, *The Forest of China: With a Survey of Grassland and Desert Vegetation* (Cambridge, Mass.: Harvard University Press, 1961).

SELECTED BIBLIOGRAPHY

CHANG, JEN-HU. 'The Climate of China According to the New Thornthwaite Classification,' *Annals of the Association of American Geographers*, 45 (Washington, D.C.: Association of American Geographers, 1955): 393–403.

Collected Scientific Papers, 1919–1949. Vol. 1: 'Meteorology.' Peking: n. p, 1954.

CRESSEY, GEORGE B. *Land of the 500 Million: A Geography of China.* New York: McGraw-Hill Book Company, 1955. Comprehensive bibliography attached at the end of the book.

GHERZI, E. *The Meteorology of China.* 2 vols. Macao: n. p., 1951.

HOU, CHEN, and WANG. 'The Vegetation of China with Special Reference to the Main Soil Types,' *Report for the 6th International Congress of Soil Science.* Peking: Institute of Botany, Academia Sinica, 1956.

HSIEH, CHIAO-MIN. *The Coast of Southeast China: Submergent or Emergent?* Taipei, Taiwan: Chinese Institute of Geography (paper for U.S. Office of Naval Research), 1962.

HUANG, T. K. *On the Major Tectonic Forms of China,* Vol. 20 of Memoir Series A. Chungking: Geological Survey of China, 1945.

HSIEH, CHIAO-MIN, and JEAN KAN. *Typhoons on the Southeastern Coast of China and Taiwan.* Taipei, Taiwan: The Chinese Institute of Geography, 1962.

KOVDA, V. A. 'Soil and Natural Environment of China' (translated from Russian). Washington, D.C.: JPRS 5967, 1960.

LEE, J. S. *The Geology of China.* London: Murby, 1939.

MA, YUNG-CHIH. 'General Principles of Geographical Distribution of Chinese Soils,' *Report for the 6th International Congress of Soil Science.* Peking: Institute of Soil Science, Academia Sinica, 1956.

MIKUNOV, V. F. 'New Works on Tectonics of China,' *International Geology Review*, Vol. 7, No. 1. Washington, D.C.: American Geological Institute, 1965.

RICHARDSON, S. D. *Forestry in Communist China.* Baltimore: The Johns Hopkins Press, 1966.

THORP, JAMES. *Geography of the Soils of China.* Nanking: The National Geological Survey of China, 1936.

WANG, CHI-WU. *The Forest of China: With a Survey of Grassland and Desert Vegetation.* Cambridge: Harvard University Press, 1961.

3

LAND AND AGRICULTURAL RESOURCES

JOHN LOSSING BUCK

INTRODUCTION

THE Chinese Communists inherited their richest agricultural asset—the farmer—but have changed his status from that of entrepreneur to laborer on collective farms with land, implements, and labor animals owned by the state. The farmers were placed under the management of cadres appointed primarily for their ideological purity. There is only one landlord for all of China, who learned from bitter experience during the Great Leap failure that ill-advised directions from Peking on farm operations decreased rather than increased production. Another lesson was the necessity of allowing farmers to have individual plots for their own use to raise vegetables, fruits, hogs, and chickens.

A considerable portion of this chapter will portray the situation before the Communist regime as a setting for an appraisal of developments under that regime.

THE LAND AND ITS AMELIORATION

Like all large countries, China has a great land area, with soils and climate both favorable and unfavorable for adequate agricultural production.

The agricultural land for twenty-two provinces of the pre-Communist, pre-1945 period[1] has been classified into two major regions and eight agricultural areas: The Wheat region of North China has three subdivisions, the Spring Wheat Area, the Winter Wheat Millet Area, and the Winter Wheat Kaoliang Area; the Rice Region of Central and South China has five subdivisions, the Yangtze Rice-Wheat Area, the Rice-Tea Area, the Szechwan Rice Area, the Double-Cropping Rice Area, and the Southwest Rice Area. Boundaries are deliniated on the basis of type of land, soils, elevation, climate, and type of utilization for crop production, without regard to provincial boundaries.[2]

Revision of a few provincial boundaries by the Communist government[3] from time

---

[1] Chahar, Suiyüan, Ninghsia, Tsinghai, Kansu, Shensi, Shansi, Hopei, Shantung, Kiangsu, Anwhei, Honan, Hupei, Szechwan, Yünnan, Kweichow, Hunan, Kiangsi, Chekiang, Fukien, Kwangtung, and Kwangsi.

[2] John Lossing Buck, *Land Utilization in China*; idem, *Land Utilization in China—Statistics*; and idem, *Land Utilization in China—Atlas* (Shanghai: The Commercial Press, 1937).

[3] Information on changes in boundaries was kindly supplied by Grace H. Wu, Research Associate Assistant, Hoover Institution, Stanford, Calif.

to time do not alter the boundaries of the two agricultural regions or the eight agricultural areas. New provincial boundaries are as follows: In November, 1952, Chahar was incorporated into Shansi and Hopei.[4] In June, 1954, Suiyüan was incorporated into Inner Mongolia.[5] Ninghsia was incorporated into Kansu in June, 1954,[6] but in October, 1958, it was separated from Kansu and made an autonomous region.[7] Jehol was abolished and parts of it incorporated into Hopei, Liaoning, and Inner Mongolia in July, 1955.[8] Sikang was incorporated into Szechwan in the same month.[9]

Soils

There are two major soil groups within the twenty-two provinces. They were described by James Thorp, of the National Geological Survey in Peking, as the calcium soils in the Wheat Region north of the Huai River and the Ch'inling Mountains and the leached, or acid, soils in the Rice Region to the south.[10] Each of these two has many subgroups varying in agricultural productivity. For instance, in Hopei Province, south of Tientsin, there are considerable amounts of alkaline or saline soils, which extend to the coast, where meager crops or no crops at all are produced.

In parts of the North China Plain there are Shachiang soils, which have lime concretions in the subsoil and are very poor. In Suhsien, northern Anhwei, these soils are traditionally classified as 'iron' land. This is the lowest grade of four local classifications of land, 'gold, silver, copper, and iron,' which are taxed accordingly. In the same general area, there are depressions called 'lake land,' which flood in summer but usually dry out in time for a winter wheat crop. For a summer crop on this 'lake land,' rice and sesame seeds are planted together. If there is flooding, a rice crop will be harvested; if not, a crop of sesame will be obtained.

Thorp has estimated that some nine-tenths of the soil of China has been transported by water or wind. There is no evidence of glacial soils, important to agriculture, in China.[11] Most of the large areas of alluvial soils have no stones. Consequently, plowshares and moldboards of thin gray cast iron have been used for centuries.

Over the centuries, immense areas of the land surface have been modified for cultivation by the use of (1) terracing to avert soil erosion and conserve water, (2) irrigation, and (3) dikes to prevent flooding from streams and rivers, as well as a sea wall along the coast of Kiangsu and Chekiang, about 300 miles in length, to protect crop land. This modification of land represents a prodigious amount of labor. To accomplish so much construction was a formidable task; much of the terracing on hill and mountain slopes would be impossible for modern earth-moving equipment.

Terracing

Terracing of land is prevalent in both North and South China, a practice that has saved millions of acres from destruction by erosion. Sample studies of 240 localities in 156 *hsien* of 21 provinces reveal 24 per cent of the cultivated area as terraced.[12] In some localities, like the loess areas in Kansu, the terraces still slope rather steeply,

---

[4] *Jen-min Shou-ts'e, 1953 (People's Handbook)*, Peking, annual, p. 128.
[5] *Ibid., 1955*, p. 230.
[6] *Ibid.*, and *1959*, 1: 222.
[7] *Ibid., 1959*, 1: 241.
[8] *Ibid., 1956*, p. 241.
[9] *Ibid.*
[10] Buck, *Land Utilization in China*, Chapter V, pp. 130–61.
[11] *Ibid.*, p. 130.
[12] Buck, *Land Utilization in China—Statistics* (Shanghai: The Commercial Press, 1937), Table 20, pp 53–54.

with consequent erosion. Substantial areas in Kansu have been lost to cultivation through such erosion. However, in eastern Shansi, near P'ingtingchou, on rather steep slopes, terraces with retaining stone walls are prevalent, and land is leveled with an inward slant. The top of the stone wall facing is protected with a stone spillway for any heavy runoff. Some of these retaining walls are ten to fifteen feet in height.

Even more dramatic is the terracing of rugged loess highlands in the valley of the Ching River, Shensi Province, where very narrow terraces follow the land contours around sharply eroded steep hillsides as very narrow ribbons.[13]

Irrigation

In 1929–33, the estimated proportion of cultivated land reported as irrigated for 240 localities in 186 *hsien* of 21 provinces was 47 per cent.[14] Data from 16,456 farms in 164 localities in 151 *hsien* of 22 provinces reveal that 45.8 per cent of the crop area[15] (cultivated area) was irrigated. However, the weighted average for the eight agricultural areas indicates that 40.5 per cent of the crop area was irrigated. The area irrigated in 112 localities between the periods 1904–9 and 1929–33 increased from 36.4 to 38.5 per cent.[16] The increase was most pronounced in the Winter Wheat Kaoliang area of the North China Plain, from 4.3 to 14.4 per cent, chiefly by well irrigation. This trend in the plain has continued under the Communist regime, although a substantial number of new wells delivered water too alkaline or too saline. The extent to which well irrigation can be developed in this area is still questionable.

Some of the data issued by the Communist government and intended as an indication of trends in irrigation are especially misleading. For instance, Communist data from three sources[17] report 16 million, 20.2 million, and 26 million hectares irrigated in 1949, all of which are underestimates. For succeeding years, gradual statistical increases occur until 1956, when there was a sharp increase, followed by a further increase for 1957. The 1957 figures given were 34.7 million and 38.3 million hectares, from two different sources. These may be compared with 40.5 million hectares in 1929–33 for the twenty-two provinces. In 1958, a Communist figure of 66.7 million hectares was recorded through an oversight in the method of calculation. The corrected amount is 37.6 million hectares. The Russian water expert M. M. Krylov estimated the irrigated area of mainland China at 39.8 million hectares in 1957.[18]

Examples of successful irrigation projects developed in past centuries, which are still functioning, are the canalized area of the Yangtze Delta and the diversion of water to the Chengtu Plain in Szechwan Province.

The Yangtze Delta canals. I have been unable to find any record of the period of construction of the tremendous network of Yangtze Delta canals. Construction of these canals probably occurred before work commenced on the first segment of the Grand Canal from the Yangtze River at Chenchiang to Ch'ingchiangpu.[19] Here grain was transported via the Huai, Yellow, and Lo rivers to Ch'angan (Sian), the capital

---

[13] *Ibid.*, p. 214, Table 12; and *idem, Land Utilization in China—Atlas*, p. 141, photo No. 3.
[14] Buck, *Land Utilization in China—Statistics*, p. 53, Table 20.
[15] *Ibid.*, p. 214, Table 12.
[16] *Ibid.*, p. 52, Table 19; and *idem, Land Utilization in China*, p. 188, Table 17.
[17] State Statistical Bureau, *Economic Statistical Abstract*, February, 1960, p. 120, cited in John Lossing Buck, Owen L. Dawson, and Yuan-li Wu, *Food and Agriculture in Communist China* (New York: Praeger Publishers, 1966), p. 156.
[18] See M. M. Krylov, 'Brief Review of the Underground Water of Communist China,' in Buck, Dawson, and Wu, *Food and Agriculture*, p. 155.
[19] L. Richard, *Comprehensive Geography of the Chinese Empire*, translated into English (Tusewei Press, 1908), p. 428.

of Shensi, where there was a very large population and a short supply of grain.[20] The canals are used for irrigation by pumping water from them to the rice fields and for transportation of goods and passengers to and from markets and, to a smaller degree, from the farmsteads to the rice fields. George P. Cressey estimated the length of these canals at 150,000 miles and, for the whole Yangtze Plain from Shanghai to Ich'ang, at least 250,000 miles.[21]

F. H. King counted 190 canals,[22] which he crossed by rail from Chiahsing (Kashing) to Hangchou, a distance of 62 miles. While traveling by rail the 162 miles between Shanghai and Nanking, he counted 593 canals in the canalized area from Shanghai to Lungt'an (near Ch'angchou).

Rainfall in this canalized area is plentiful for crops other than rice. However, rice provides more food per unit of land and justifies the extra labor and cost of pumping water from the canals.

The irrigated Chengtu Plain. Li Ping, Governor of Szechwan during the Ch'in dynasty in the third century B.C., conceived and executed a large project for the irrigation of the Chengtu Plain, which had been subject to frequent famines from drought. He had a diversion channel constructed from a branch of the Ming River at Kuanhsien, Szechwan, through the nose of a mountain. Two additional main branch channels were constructed to lead the water onto the plain to other smaller channels and then to the many smaller branch channels throughout the plain, irrigating more than 1 million acres. The original construction was completed by Li Ping's son, Li Er-wang, more than 2,100 years ago.

For centuries, farmers from the villages in the plain in late winter and early spring have customarily participated in the annual cleaning of the diversion channel of flood debris deposited each year. The bamboo 'sausages' (about 20 feet long, made of woven bamboo, and filled with large stones) for protecting the lower sides of the channel are also repaired or replaced annually. To carry out this work, each year each farming village is assigned a quota of men, bamboo, and equipment, such as carrying baskets and shovels. The system described above has been properly maintained down through the centuries, and excellent crops of wheat, rice and other crops are produced.

Li Ping's dictum, carved in stone at a large memorial temple overlooking the Ming River and the diversion channel, was: 'Dig the channels deep; keep the dikes low.' Knowing the weakness of man, Li Ping had a large piece of iron buried in the diversion channel at the depth to which debris should be removed each year. In 1942, I saw the top of this iron marker, measuring about 2 by 2 feet at the exposed surface.

In the hilly and mountainous regions of Szechwan and South China, runoff water is channeled into the millions of terraced and bunded rice fields that constitute a high proportion of the cultivated land. In fact, traditionally irrigation water was obtained largely through the simple recognition that water runs downhill. Local persons specializing in designing terraces and irrigation channels utilized this fact.

Ponds

A feature in rolling and hilly lands in Szechwan and other parts of the Rice Region is the construction of ponds at the margin between cultivated land and uncultivated slopes. Very shallow channels lead water runoff into these ponds. Only one good crop

---

[20] C. P. FitzGerald, *China: A Short Cultural History*, 3rd ed. (New York: Praeger Publishers, 1961), pp. 320–23.

[21] George B. Cressey, *Land of the 500 Million: A Geography of China* (New York: McGraw Hill Book Co., 1955), p. 192.

[22] F. H. King, *Farmers of Forty Centuries* (Madison, Wis.: Mrs. F. H. King, publisher and editor, 1911), pp. 98–102, with two sketch maps of the major canals and the sea wall; reprint, New York: Harcourt, Brace, 1926.

in four years can be expected, but farmers hope for enough rain in the other years. It has proved to be a hazardous practice, because in dry years water is insufficient. In Huayang *hsien*, east of the Ch'engtu Plain, farmers term the practice 'gambling with Heaven.' A considerable number of farmers have given up growing rice in favor of other crops requiring less water, such as corn and soybeans interplanted.

Diking for Water Control

The Yangtze flood plain from Nanking to Ich'ang is a spiderweb consisting of large dikes along the river and a maze of others of varying sizes throughout the plain. In 1931, two weeks of rain dropped 24 inches of water throughout the watershed of the Yangtze and Huai rivers. Dikes broke and the entire plain was flooded to an average maximum height of 9 feet above the level of farmers' fields. Some 25 million farmers were affected, and many suffered severe losses. Fortunately, a great many farming villages and hamlets are built on raised mounds of earth. Many farmers had oval-shaped tubs normally used to collect water-grown crops from ponds and lagoons, which also served as a means of escape from flood water to high ground.

According to official claims, a similar flood in 1954 reached a higher level at Hankow than did the 1931 flood. The Communist government raised the dikes at and near Hankow to a higher level. However, as the National Flood Relief Commission had previously pointed out,[23] raising the dikes too high would build up the bottom of the river bed with silt and lead to the same danger as that posed by the silting of the Yellow River (see below).

Water Control in Communist China

The Chinese had effective local organizations for irrigation and flood control measures, such as building and maintaining channels and dikes. However, local physical conflicts often occurred in areas where they were ineffective or where no such organizations existed. With the advent of the Communist government, changes of personnel caused dissatisfaction among farmers and a reported deterioration in maintenance.

Under the Communist government, emphasis was at first placed on large dams and reservoirs. The most ambitious multiple-purpose project was the huge Sanmen Gorge Dam in southwestern Honan, where the Yellow River bends sharply from Shensi to Honan. It was designed by the Russians for flood control for the North China Plain and for hydroelectric power. Its construction was halted with the withdrawal of Russian assistance in mid-1960. Chinese engineers have criticized the project since its first proposal on the grounds that the high percentage of silt in the Yellow River would probably cause rapid silting of the reservoir.

The first large conservation project was the drainage of the Huai River waters from the Hungtzu Lake to the Grand Canal, thence to the Yangtze River and through a new channel to the sea, a project begun by the Nationalist government. In addition to the drainage aspect, the Chinese Communists built a number of reservoirs along the upper reaches of the Huai River and also dug large channels north of the river to irrigate adjoining farm lands. Whether or not this was successful in increasing crop production is subject to question because of the nature of the soil and the low level of the river water in the spring, when the important crop of wheat is in the growth stage.

In 1964, a Japanese economist told me that the Communist government had diverted water from the Yellow River in a part of the North China Plain into reser-

---

[23] *Report of the National Flood Relief Commission* (Shanghai: National Flood Relief Commission, 1933); see also, *The 1931 Flood in China: An Economic Survey* (Nanking: The University of Nanking, Bulletin No. 1 [New Series], April, 1932), with excellent map of the flooded area and places where data were obtained in the economic survey.

voirs from which irrigation channels were constructed to farmers' fields, primarily for growing rice. Presumably, the reservoirs would silt up rapidly from the high percentage of silt in the river. Moreover, the soils are porous and are not rice soils, since they lack a heavy subsoil.

There were some other large projects for irrigation, but there are no adequate data on their effectiveness in increasing crop production. However, there are reports of new irrigated areas that are becoming waterlogged and of the development of alkaline and saline salts, which have decreased rather than increased production. A number of water-conservation projects were undertaken in the 1950's, but the Soviet expert M. H. Korniev claims that there were many costly failures.[24]

A 1969 report indicates that greater attention has been paid recently to improved water control on existing irrigated and diked farm land by millions of people in several provinces of the Rice Region.[25]

Table 3-1—Ownership of Farm Land and Tenancy, Twenty-two Provinces, China, 1919–68

	Per Cent of Farm Operators		
Sources	Owners	Part-owners	Tenants
Ministry of Agriculture and Forestry, Peking, 1919 (1)	59	18	23
Land Utilization in China, 1929–33 (2)			
(a) Farm survey	54	40	6
(b) Farm survey	54	29	17
(c) Agricultural survey	44	23	33
National Agricultural Research Bureau (for a year between 1931 and 1937) (3)	46	24	30
Communist government (1957–68) (mainland China) (4)			100

Sources: (1) Compiled from *Statistical Report of Ministry of Agriculture and Forestry* (Peking, 1919) by C. M. Chiao in his monograph, *Farm Tenancy in the Hsien of Quinsan and Nantung, Kiangsu Province and Suhsien in Anhwei Province* (Nanking: University of Nanking, Bulletin 30 [Chinese Series]), the initial study of tenancy in China by a trained agricultural economist. (2) (a) The farm survey of 16,786 farms in twenty-two provinces where farmers who owned their farmsteads but rented all crop land were classified in the part-owner group in Buck, *Land Utilization in China*, p. 196, Table 22, and idem, *Land Utilization in China—Statistics*, pp. 57–59, Table 22. (b) farmers owning their farmsteads but renting their crop land were classified as tenants, *ibid*. (c) Estimates for 236 localities, 146 *hsien*, 20 provinces, 1929–33, *ibid*. (3) The National Agricultural Research Bureau, *Crop Reports Estimates* in 1931–37, quoted by T. H. Shen, *Agricultural Resources of China* (Ithaca, N.Y.: Cornell University Press, 1951), p. 96; these data are estimates of crop reports published by the National Agricultural Research Bureau, Nanking, for a year in 1931–37 period. (4) All farmers assumed reduced to the status of laborers except for small private plots for producing vegetables, hogs, chickens, and eggs for own use, or for sale. This includes all mainland China, not only twenty-two provinces.

---

[24] See Buck, Dawson, and Wu, *Food and Agriculture*, p. 159.
[25] Colin McCullough, 'Spring Planting Started in China', *The New York Times*, March 23, 1969.

LAND OWNERSHIP AND UTILIZATION

Ownership of cultivated land. Because virtually all land under the Communist system is owned by the state, discussion of private land ownership must deal with the pre-1949 period. Broad categories of ownership of farm land in China for 1929–33 for 111 *hsien* in 20 provinces, obtained from official *hsien* records, indicated the following percentage distribution of ownership: private land, 93.3 per cent (fee simple); government land, 1.0 per cent (mostly hill and mountain land); school land, 0.7 per cent; temple land, 1.8 per cent; soldiers' land, 2.3 per cent; official ancestral land, 0.4 per cent; charity land, 0.1 per cent; other, 0.4 per cent.[26]

Farm ownership and tenancy. Data on the percentage of farmers who were owners, part-owners, and tenants on private land vary from 44 to 59 per cent for owners, 24 to 29 per cent for part-owners and 17 to 31 per cent for tenants (including tenants who own their own farmsteads but rent their crop land). The fact that part-owner farmers owned more land than they rented to increase the size of the farm indicates that they belong to the owner class rather than the tenant class. Owners averaged 4.22 acres per farm; part-owners rented 1.80 acres and owned 2.45 acres, a total of 4.25 acres; tenant farmers rented an average of 3.56 acres[27] (see Table 3–1).

From about 1920 to 1949, propaganda and misinformation about the farm tenancy situation were widespread. The more serious cases of unfairness to tenants occurred wherever there was a concentration of absentee landlords collecting rent through agents, such as in the lower Yangtze Delta area, the West River delta area near Canton and, to some extent, Szechwan Province.

Three economic studies of tenancy for 203 farms in Szechwan Province in 1940–41, for 285 farms in a four-province survey of Central China in 1934–35, and for 510 farms in a *Chinese Farm Economy* survey reveal that the landlords received 28.4 per cent of farm receipts as compared with their being responsible for 27.6 per cent of all farm expenses. The average interest rate received by landlords on investment and expenses for 3,777 tenant farms in nine widely scattered areas was 10.1 per cent, or one-tenth of 1 per cent greater than the prevalent bank rate of 10 per cent on fixed deposits.[28]

A proposal for a land tenure law was presented to the National Government by a number of Chinese economists in the early 1930's, but it was not accepted. Revisions were made, and finally, in Chungking in the early 1940's, a law was passed giving the provinces power to initiate land reform in the form of Tenant Land-Purchase Projects. A very successful project developed at Peipei (Szechwan) and Lungyen (Fukien) was started in December, 1943, and completed in December, 1947; 32,242 families became owner-farmers under the program. The revised land law of 1946 by the National Government provided that rents should not exceed 8 per cent of the land value.

Fragmentation of land. Traditionally, the farmer's land consisted of scattered plots rather than one contiguous area of land and averaged 5.4 plots per farm. One reason for this was to share good and inferior land with neighbors; for instance, in rice areas with both lowland and upland, it was considered unfair for a farmer to have all his

---

[26] Buck, *Land Utilization in China,* p. 193, Table 19; and *idem, Land Utilization in China—Statistics,* pp. 35–36, Table 7.

[27] *Ibid.,* p. 197, Table 23; and *ibid.,* p. 60, Table 23 (in hectares).

[28] John Lossing Buck, 'Farm Tenancy in China', in *Economic Facts,* No. 5. 33 and 34 (Chengtu: Department of Agricultural Economics, College of Agriculture and Forestry, University of Nanking, June and July, 1944); issued as book under title *Farm Tenancy in China,* by same publisher. A summary of data from many research studies by the same institution. A list of twenty-seven studies on various aspects of tenancy is given in *Economic Facts,* No. 34, some of which are not now available.

land in either type. As an additional advantage, different kinds of crops may be grown according to the diverse soil and water conditions of the different plots. This assists in reducing peaks of labor. However, there is loss of time in travel back and forth. Collective and commune farming under the present regime may have partially eliminated this problem, but laborers still have to travel the same distance from the village to the farther fields.[29]

The cultivated land. Statistics on the amount of cultivated land for mainland China vary by from 81 million to 115 million hectares during 1928–67.[30] The low figure of 65.8 million hectares for the twenty-two provinces used by the National Agricultural Research Bureau for computing production in 1931–37 was based on the *Statistical Monthly* data that do not include large amounts of unregistered land, popularly called 'black land.' Land surveys in several *hsien* in the 1930's revealed great discrepancies in official land data. As explained below in the notes to the table on Land and Agricultural Resources in the Data Section, estimates of the amount of unregistered land were obtained from local persons by the Land Utilization in China project field investigators. The average of these estimates indicates that it would be appropriate to increase the official cultivated land estimate of 65.8 million hectares by a factor of 1.337. The average of the highest estimates gives a factor of 1.425. Thus, the cultivated land for the twenty-two provinces becomes 88 million hectares or, alternatively, 93.8 million hectares. Likewise, if these factors are also applied to official data for Manchuria, Sinkiang, and Jehol,[31] an increase from 14.7 million hectares to 19.7 million or 20.9 million hectares would be obtained. For mainland China as a whole, it is possible that 115 million hectares represents the cultivated area in 1929–33. This is the same amount as estimated by Lieu and Chen in 1928.[32] Whether or not the 115 million hectares is too high will be tested in a later section on quantity of food grains in relation to population. T. H. Shen regards Yang's estimate of 134 million hectares for mainland China and Taiwan as too high.[33] A perusal of Yang's computations verifies this contention.[34]

The exact amount of cultivated land will never be known unless it is measured and unless information is obtained on annual gains or losses.

In 1955–57 the Communist regime encouraged farmers to produce crops on previously uncultivated land, which caused erosion and meager crops on mountain and

---

[29] Graves interspersed in cropland took up 1.1 per cent of the crop area and interfered with farm operations. See Buck, *Land Utilization in China*, p. 177, Table 9. In the early days of the Communist government some, if not most, of these scattered graves were removed or destroyed.

[30] See the table on Land and Agricultural Resources in the Data Section, Part III of this volume.

[31] A Japanese economist who was with the South Manchurian Railroad for thirty years suggested to me in 1964 that more than 40 per cent of the cultivated land in Manchuria did not appear in the official statistics.

[32] D. K. Lieu and Chung-min Chen, 'Statistics of Farm Land in China,' *Chinese Economic Journal*, 2, No. 3 (Chinese Government Bureau of Economic Information, March, 1928): 181–213.

[33] T. H. Shen, *Agricultural Resources of China* (Ithaca, N.Y.: Cornell University Press, 1951), p. 6.

[34] Shu-chia Yang, 'Fundamental Problems of Chinese Agriculture,' *National Reconstruction*, Vol. 5 (New York: Chinese Institute in America, July, 1944). Yang used the highest *Land Utilization in China* estimate for cultivated land of 232 million acres (362,082 square miles) or 93.8 million hectares. He then made an error by adding 53 million acres for land in the twenty-two provinces excluded from the eight agricultural areas. The exclusion in *Land Utilization in China* was made for contiguous nonagricultural land outside of an agricultural area boundary but within the provincial boundary, primarily because of the topography and elevation of the land excluded. Other areas included by Yang are 42 million acres for the

hill slopes. Consequently, a new mandate was issued to increase yields on a smaller percentage of cultivated land. Communist data on cultivated land in *Ten Great Years*, for the 1949–58 period, reveal a decrease from 112 million hectares in 1956 to 107.8 million in 1958.

Amount of crop hectares in all crops. Crop hectares are the number of crops planted and harvested on the same hectare of cultivated land during one year. The extent of multiple cropping measured in this manner is employed as a multiple cropping index. For instance, 50 hectares of cultivated land with 25 hectares in one crop a year, 15 hectares with two crops a year and 10 hectares with three crops a year yield $\dfrac{85 \text{ hectares in crop hectares}}{\text{on 50 hectares cultivated land}} \times 100 =$ an index of multiple cropping of 170. The index in the Rice Region is 163.2; in the Wheat Region, where the growing season is shorter, it is 131. In the Spring Wheat Area, it is only 107. There is very little, if any, multiple cropping in Manchuria, Jehol (which is today part of Hopei, Liaoning, and Inner Mongolia), and Sinkiang because the growing season is shorter than in the Wheat Region.

Given the data from Buck, Dawson, and Wu, *Food and Agriculture in Communist China*, for the percentage of cultivated land in the Wheat and Rice regions of twenty-two provinces and for the index of multiple cropping, the following computations for crop hectares are possible.[35] The new cultivated land totals are 93.8 million hectares for the twenty-two provinces and 20.9 million hectares for Manchuria, Jehol and Sinkiang.[36]

Wheat Region	50.9% × 93.8m/ha =	47.7m/ha
Rice Region	49.1% × 93.8m/ha =	46.1m/ha
Total		93.8m/ha

Index of multiple cropping:

Wheat Region	131.0 × 47.7m/ha =	62.5m/crop hectares
Rice Region	163.2 × 46.1m/ha =	75.2m/crop hectares
Manchuria, Jehol, and Sinkiang		
(No multiple cropping)	× 20.9m/crop hectares	
Mainland China total	158.6m/crop hectares	

The index of multiple cropping for mainland China as a whole is 139.7 (158.6m/ha ÷ 115m/ha cultivated land).

Arable uncultivated land. Various estimates of arable uncultivated land are presented in the table on Land and Agricultural Resources in the Data Section of this volume, with full explanations in the notes. For mainland China, they vary from 18 to 28 million hectares between 1914 and 1963. *Land Utilization in China* sample studies in 1929–33 for the eight agricultural areas of the twenty-two provinces indicate 24 million arable hectares, of which cultivation would be feasible for no more than 15 million hectares, and then only if the institutional problems of its utilization could be remedied first. For example, the local population may be unwilling to permit graves or pasture land to be used for crops.

'northeastern four provinces,' 2 million acres for Sinkiang and, also, 2 million acres for Taiwan, which is not a part of mainland China. By deleting the 53 million acres of the twenty-two provinces and the 2 million acres for Taiwan, an area of 111.7 million hectares is obtained. This is between the amounts of 108 million hectares (line 4 B) and 115 million hectares (line C) in the table on Land and Agricultural Resources in the Data Section.

[35] P. 52, columns 6 and 7.

[36] Buck, *Land Utilization in China*, p. 165, Table 3.

More than one-half of the uncultivated land was reported in the following productive uses for 155 *hsien* of 20 provinces: trees and bushes, 28.1 per cent; forest, 22.8 per cent; grass (principally harvested dry in the autumn for fuel), 23.8 per cent; pasture, 11.9 per cent; reeds, 5.2 per cent; other uses, 8.2 per cent.[37]

These productive uses of uncultivated land indicate that such land has economic usefulness. The problem is whether or not cultivation would offer greater rewards. For instance, land that is at present used for dry grass harvested in the autumn, if planted to crops, could supply fuel from their stalks. In parts of the North China Plain, stubble with roots is gathered after harvest for fuel. If coal or electricity should become available at reasonable rates for heating and cooking, some of the arable uncultivated land now used to produce fuel might then be cultivated.

Most of the grass areas in South China, including parts of the Yangtze Valley, are rolling country and have clay soils; large amounts of fertilizer and heavy equipment would be required to prepare the soils for cultivation. Possibly they should be developed as improved pasture lands.

In the 1950's the Communist government obtained provincial estimates of wastelands (arid, saline, marshy, and red-soil hills in twenty-four provinces) amounting to 54.7 million hectares. This was followed by on-the-ground surveys, which netted only 35.4 million hectares in twenty provinces. For ten of these provinces, a classification was made of wastelands requiring little or no reconditioning, slight reconditioning, and much reconditioning, as well as those not ready for utilization. The first three categories amounted to 14.4 million hectares for ten provinces, of which 10.4 million hectares are in Sinkiang and Heilungkiang. Adding O. L. Dawson's estimate for the other ten provinces of 3.7 million hectares, a total of 18.1 million hectares of reclaimable wastelands is indicated for mainland China as a whole.[38]

The PLA and Agriculture

The role of Lin Piao's army in Chinese society.[39] In addition to its military functions, the PLA governs and is in charge of economic development in much of Sinkiang and Tibet and manages the important land reclamation and water conservation projects in China. It also plays an important role as a major producer of contemporary art, literature, and films.

In the mid-1950's, the PLA directed land reclamation and settlement in Sinkiang for farming in large farm units. Later, it initiated and carried out economic development in Tibet. More recently, it has been participating in pastoral and agricultural development in Inner Mongolia.[40] In the past, good pastoral lands there were broken up for cultivation, only to meet with crop failure because of a dry climate and insufficient water for cultivation.

The Chinese Communists have encouraged the settlement of Chinese in Inner Mongolia. There is danger for the future, because the ratio between Chinese and Mongols, 3:1 in 1947, is now about 15:1. The emphasis on agriculture in an area with inadequate water for farming may lead to further destruction of land resources if the Communists attempt to convert good pasture land to farm land, especially if the immigrating Chinese are farmers.

---

[37] Buck, *Land Utilization in China—Statistics*, p. 33, Table 6, and pp. 44–46, Table 14.

[38] Owen L. Dawson, *Communist China's Agricultural Development and Future Potential* (Washington, D.C.: Office of External Research, Department of State, 1968), pp. 67–70.

[39] Chalmers, Johnson, 'Lin Piao's Army and Its Role in Chinese Society,' Part I, *Current Scene*, 4, No. 13, (July 1, 1966): 1–10; and Part II, *Current Scene*, 4, No. 14, (July 15, 1966): 1–11.

[40] William Heaton, 'Inner Mongolia: Aftermath of the Revolution,' *Current Scene*, 9, No. 4, (April 7, 1971): 11, 13.

The PLA has developed viable, well-organized projects and has created discipline among participants in these projects. It is undoubtedly the most important organization holding the fabric of China together. The PLA is a political as well as a military organization and establishes a political presence in both production projects and in governmental administrative organizations.

The important role of the military in agriculture is suggested by the appointment of Li Shu-jung, formerly the 'Responsible Person of PLA Lanchow Units,' as Vice-Minister of Agriculture.[41]

FOOD GRAIN PRODUCTION

Food grain production and yields. Statistics and estimates on the production of food grains from 1929–32 through 1967 vary from 132 million metric tons to 215 million metric tons (see Table 3–2). The two early estimates for 1929–32 and 1931–37 of 136 and 132 million metric tons are underestimates, mainly because of unregistered cultivated land. The 1929–33 *Land Utilization in China* amount of 183 million metric tons is based on a land correction factor of 1.337 for the twenty-two provinces applied to the National Agriculture Research Bureau (NARB) production estimate of 116 million metric tons for the twenty-two provinces. No correction is made in line 3A of the table for official land data for Manchuria, Jehol, and Sinkiang. Applying the correction factor of 1.337 to these three areas, in line 3B, the total production is 189 million metric tons. If the highest land correction factor of 1.425 is used, the production for the twenty-two provinces and for Manchuria, Jehol, and Sinkiang indicates a possible 201 million metric tons for 1929–33.

Food grain production statistics for 1948–58 of the Communist period, which show low estimates of land and production for 1949–52 and a greatly exaggerated figure of 250 million metric tons for 1958, averaged 163 million metric tons, whereas for 1953–57 the average was 172 million metric tons. For 1967, the estimates vary from 172 million metric tons to 215 million metric tons. The highest estimates are 214 million metric tons by Dawson and 215 million metric tons by the United Nations Food and Agricultural Organization.

The estimated yields per crop hectare vary from 1,430 kg. to 1,665 kg. There are five estimates in the 1,400 kg. bracket, one in the 1,500 kg. bracket and five in the 1,600 kg. bracket. Yields were computed from production estimates divided by crop hectares and are determined by relative differences in total crop hectares and total production.

Table 3–2—Production of Food Grains Related to Population, Production per Capita, Crop Hectares, and Yields per Crop Hectare, 1929–67

Sources	Crop Hectares (millions)	Yield per Hectare (kilograms)	Production (million metric tons)	Population (millions)	Production per Capita (kilograms)
I. Pre-Communist Period					
1. *Statistical Monthly*					
(1929–32)[a]	83	1,639	136	385	353
2. NARB (1931–37)[b]	89	1,483	132	436	303
3. *Land Utilization in China*					
(1929–33) (A)	111	1,649	183	606[c]	302
(B)	117	1,615	189	606	310
(C)	124	1,621	201	606	330

[41] Ellis Joffe, 'The Chinese Army in the Cultural Revolution: The Politics of Intervention,' *Current Scene* 8, No. 18 (December 7, 1970): 22–23, 28.

Sources	Crop Hectares (millions)	Yield per Hectare (kilograms)	Production (million metric tons)	Population (millions)	Production per Capita (kilograms)
4. *Land Utilization in China* (food consumption survey) (1929–33)[d]	—	—	205	606	338
5. NARB (food survey) (1937)[e]	—	—	203	606	335
II. Communist Period					
6. *Ten Great Years*					
(1949–58)	114	1,430	163	597	273
(1953–57)	119	1,448	172	604 or 636	286 or 270
7. *Current Scene* (1967)	120	1,558	187	765 or 805	244 or 232
8. U.N. Food and Agriculture Organization (1967)	—	—	215	780 or 805	276 or 267
9. O. L. Dawson (1967)	128	1,665	214	754 or 805	286 or 265
10. *Monthly Research on China* (1967)	118	1,453	172	765 or 805	225 or 214
11. Union Research Institute (Hong Kong) (1967)	123	1,439	177	765 or 805	231 or 220

[a] Crop hectares, production, and population appear to be underestimates. The *Chinese Postal Guide* for 1928 gives a population of 485 million.

[b] Crop hectares, production, and population also appear to be underestimates. The production for Manchuria, Jehol, and Sinkiang has been included in addition to the bureau's production for twenty-two provinces. The population figure of 436 million comprises 400 million used by the Food and Agriculture Organization in calculating calories from average 1931–37 production for twenty-two provinces and also 36 million population for Manchuria. Shen, *Agricultural Resources of China*, Appendix, Tables 4 and 5.

[c] The population of 606 million is higher than the 592 million previously computed by Buck, Dawson, and Wu, *Food and Agriculture*, pp. 37–40 and Appendix, p. 62, Table 8. A minor reason is the omission of Sikang for absence of firm data and the inclusion of Jehol with Manchuria and Sinkiang. Compilation of data from C. C. Chang, *An Estimate of China's Farms and Crops* (Nanking: University of Nanking, December, 1932), indicates for Manchuria, Jehol, and Sinkiang a food-grain production of 16.3 million metric tons, which is 1.4 million metric tons greater than the 14.9 million metric tons computed in Appendix Table 3, p. 55, chiefly because Jehol is included instead of Sikang. The same data, which also appear in the *Statistical Monthly*, are in a less summarized form. The population data from the above references amount to 32.1 million for Manchuria, Jehol, and Sinkiang, a gross underestimate. At 40.1 million, Buck, Dawson and Wu, *Food and Agriculture*, p. 38, divided into 16.3 million metric tons indicates 406 kgs. per capita production, which is too high. There is no reason to believe that the production of 16.3 million metric tons is too great. Therefore, the 40.1 million population is increased by the average factor of 1.337 used to correct the amount of cultivated land. This gives a population of 53.6 million for the three areas and a production of 304 kg. per capita, which appears more reasonable than the 406 kg. Therefore, the 551.9 million for the twenty-two provinces plus 53.6 million indicates a total population of 606 million. This 606 million is used for lines A, B, and C and in sources 4 and 5.

[d] This food consumption survey of 2,727 farm families, 17,351 persons in 131 *hsien* of

twenty-one provinces, 1929–33, was conducted at the same time as the *Land Utilization in China* study. Data were obtained chiefly in the same localities as for the farm survey but from different families, mainly, but with some exceptions (Buck, *Land Utilization in China*, Chapter 15). Detailed data for each locality appear in Buck, *Land Utilization in China—Statistics*, Chapter 3, pp. 84–121. The computation is as follows: Daily intake of calories from all foods per adult is unit 3,295. At 92.4 per cent from food grains, the intake would be 3,045 calories. At 1.3 persons per adult male unit, the intake is 2,342 calories per person. Dividing by 3,528 calories per kilogram, the intake would be 663.8 grams per day; multiplying by 365 days equals 242.3 kg. per year for processed food grain; dividing by 0.806 for processing factor equals 300 kg. per farm capita unprocessed. For a farm population of 484.8 million times 300 kg. equals 145.4 million metric tons of unprocessed food grains. The nonfarm population consumption of food grains may be computed as 16.8 per cent of the total food grains available for food. Therefore, 145.4 million metric tons divided by 83.2 per cent for farm population gives 174.9 million metric tons available for a total population of 606 million. However, 85.5 per cent of the total production is not used for food. Therefore, 174.9 divided by 85.5 per cent equals 204.56 million metric tons, or 205 million metric tons in a rounded number, for total production. This divided by a total population of 606 million equals 338 kg. of food grain production per capita. (See Buck, Dawson, and Wu, *Food and Agriculture*, pp. 68–69 for above factors used for computations.)

e The National Agricultural Research Bureau conducted a rural food grain consumption survey in 1937 by obtaining data through the bureau's crop reporters. The survey states that the data obtained were for 'the usual amount of consumptio nper person, old and young, not for any one year.' Although 1936 was an unusually good crop year, it seems improbable that it would have influenced farmers to give a higher amount than the usual amount of consumption. The weighted average per person is 286.1 kg., with potatoes reduced one-fourth to equal food grains (Buck, Dawson, and Wu, *Food and Agriculture*, p. 63). The weighted average of 286.1 kg. per capita is considered more accurate than the average of 296.4 kg. by localities. The computations for production per farm capita are as follows:

286.1 kg × 0.806 for processing = 230.6 kg.
230.6 kg. ÷ 365 days = 631.8 grams per day
631.8 grams × 3,528 calories per kg. = 2,229 calories per farm capita per day from food grains.

These data may be compared with the Land Utilization Food Survey, which showed 273.2 kg. of food grains per farm capita, netting 2,129 calories per day. This might indicate some improvement in the food situation of 1935–37 over that during 1929–33. It is well known that the Chinese economy was better in 1935–37 than in the early 1930's. The crop reports of the National Agricultural Research Bureau do not indicate increased production for 1935–37 except for the year 1937. It is surmised that underreporting developed during the later period of 1931–37. O. L. Dawson, former U.S. Agricultural Attaché in China, has suggested it might be as much as 10 per cent.

The 286.1 kg. unprocessed ÷ 0.855 of food grains for other than food uses indicates 335 kg. production per farm capita.

f The population for 1949–58 of 597 million is a ten-year average based on the 1953 census (Buck, Dawson, and Wu, *Food and Agriculture*, p. 40). For 1953–57, the population of 604 million is based on the 1953 census series average for 1953–57 per Aird. The alternative 636 million is based on a 5 per cent underestimate in the 1953 census, Table 1, Model I, p. 42, per John S. Aird, *Estimates and Projections of the Population of Mainland China, 1953–1968*, Bureau of Census, U.S. Department of Commerce, No. 17, Washington, D.C., U.S. Government Printing Office. Quotations from Aird's tables have been rounded in millions. All the remaining items on population for 1967 are also based on Aird's projections (Table 2, Model A). The 765 million is based on the 1953 census. The 805 million is based on an undercount of 5 per cent in the 1953 census. Other possible undercounts of 10 and 15 per cent have not been used in this table. Exceptions are for the Food and Agricultural Organization (FAO) of the United Nations, which used 780 million and for Dawson's own figure for 1967 of 754 millions. Dawson estimates production from the rounded amounts of 128 million crop hectares at 214 million metric tons.

Sources: See the table on Land and Agricultural Resources, Data Section, for notes on sources and for crop hectares, yields, and production.

The chief reason for the significant variation in the average yield per crop hectare for all food grains between the National Agricultural Research Bureau estimate of 1,483 and that of 1,649 kg.[42] in *Land Utilization in China* is the larger yield of rice in the latter. The latter average rice yield was computed and weighted by crop hectares in each type of rice and by seasons grown. This average is 2,930 kg., compared with 2,534 for the National Agricultural Research Bureau. Further evidence is provided by the NARB in the 1937 food survey, which tried to establish the usual amount of consumption. The survey revealed a larger consumption of rice than the NARB estimated production of rice. It is possible that, beginning about 1962, the Communist government perfected its method of computation of rice yields and that the increases over previous years were at least a partial correction in the method of estimating yields.

Dawson's yield of 1,664 kg. per crop hectare for all food grains is the highest of all estimates. His crop hectares in food grains estimated at 128 million is also the highest.

Apparently, the area planted to potatoes and their production increased significantly under the Communist regime, without, however, any significant increase in yield. This was possible because potatoes fitted into the rotation of crops and in the utilization of odd pieces of land. A part of the increase may have been in Irish potatoes, which can be planted to advantage in cool areas or during winter seasons in the warmer regions.

Population and production of food grains. An important test of the claims of the Communist government in agricultural production is the amount of food grains produced per capita (Table 3–2). The numerous reports of advances, such as reclamation of land, mechanization of agriculture, improved seeds, use of insecticides and fungicides, manufacture and use of chemical fertilizers, increase in multiple cropping, an increased amount of green manuring, and irrigation and drainage projects all point to a probable increase in production. However, there is a debit phase of land going out of cultivation through salinity and alkaline accumulation even on newly developed lands; erosion; blowing sand; flooding with debris; and the use of cultivated land for such development projects as railways, roads, industries, and other construction. Furthermore, an unrelenting factor affecting production per capita is the continued increase in population. These considerations pose a difficulty in maintaining production per capita.

Production of food grains per capita is not, of course, the sole criterion of progress. Developments that diminish the drudgery of farm operations should not be overlooked. The rapid progress of mechanized irrigation through the use of electricity is an example that compounds the benefits from timely application of water to growing crops. Finally, it should be borne in mind that the accuracy of computations of production per capita depends upon the degree of reliability of land, production, and population data.

The various estimates of food grain production and of population are tested in Table 3–2 by computing production per capita. The results range from 214 to 338 kg. per capita. The amounts of 353 and 303 kg. per capita computed from the *Statistical Monthly* and the NARB data used by the Food and Agriculture Organization for compiling a food balance sheet[43] are inaccurate, because both production and population are underestimates.

The last two estimates in the table appear to be too low, because if only 214 or 231 kg. per capita had been available, there would have been extreme hunger, which has

---

[42] The yield of 1,649 kg. is lower than the average *Land Utilization in China* yield of 1,671 kg. per crop hectare for the twenty-two provinces (Buck, Dawson, and Wu, *Food and Agriculture*, p. 24), because yields in Manchuria, Jehol, and Sinkiang are lower than in the twenty-two provinces.

[43] Shen, *Agricultural Resources of China*, pp. 378–83.

not been reported. Moreover, 1967 has been reported as a very good crop year. Even the *Current Scene* estimate of 187 million metric tons for 1967, indicates per capita availability of only 232 to 244 kg. Production data from the *Land Utilization in China* farm survey, based on the highest projection of 201 million metric tons, indicates 330 kg. per capita. This is slightly less than the 338 kg. per capita production obtained from data in the *Land Utilization in China* food consumption survey of the same period. It indicates that the projection of 201 million metric tons (line C) may be near the actual production in 1929–33.

The conclusion from the comparative data in Table 3–2 indicates no net progress during the Communist period in production per capita. Most certainly there appears to be a lower per capita production than in 1929–33 and 1937. Such a conclusion, of course, depends upon the degree of accuracy of various estimates. Unfortunately, Communist Chinese data on food production and consumption are insufficient as a cross-check of the five estimates for 1967.

There is no evidence of net progress in 1967 over 1953–57 (270 or 285 kg.). The highest estimates for 1967 are 267 or 276 kg., as computed from the U.N. Food and Agriculture Organization estimate for total production of 215 million metric tons and the 284 kg. per O. L. Dawson's estimate of a total production of 213 million metric tons. Even these two estimates are below those of 330 kg. and 338 kg. obtained from the *Land Utilization* farm and food surveys; they are also below the estimate of 333 kg. of production per capita compiled from the 1937 NARB food survey.

Agricultural Resources Other than Land

Manufacture of farm tools, equipment, and small machines. Although some 7 per cent of the cultivated area of China in 1967 was estimated to have power mechanization,[44] the bulk of farm work is still done by human and animal labor with traditional hand and animal draft equipment. However, the Honan broadcasting unit reported on August 8 and September 23, 1968, that the output of hand-operated tractors in Kiangsi in 1968 had risen sixfold over 1967.

The construction of farm tools, farm equipment, and small machines is now assigned to areas as small as a county or even townships. The chief mechanized equipment to be made is the rice seedlings transplanter. It still requires adjustments in construction to make it a practical but simple machine that can be pulled by a water buffalo. Emphasis is also placed on the small-scale smelting of iron ore wherever it can be mined locally. Iron is an important component of farm tools.

The emphasis on small tools and equipment is a departure from earlier attempts to manufacture large machinery unsuitable for Chinese farm conditions. It also marks a change from the philosophy of Liu Shao-ch'i, who advocated construction of farm machines and equipment in a few large centers.[45]

Tillage implements. Of all the implements, the most numerous are the many different types and shapes of hand hoes. For the cultivation of rice under irrigation, a V-shaped wooden frame with small iron teeth is attached to a bamboo pole some ten feet or more in length. The frame is pulled back and forth between the rows of rice to control weeds.

The plow is of many types. Almost invariably, it has a point, or share, and a moldboard, both of gray cast iron. The beam is usually of wood in South China and of iron in the North China Plain.

Harvesting and threshing equipment. The chief harvesting implement is the sickle,

---

[44] As estimated by Dawson, *Agricultural Development and Future Potential*, p. 158.

[45] Chu-yuan Cheng, 'The Effects of the Cultural Revolution on China's Machine-Building Industry,' *Current Scene*, 8, No. 1 (January 1, 1970): 4–11.

which takes on different shapes. One type in the rice-tea area has a serrated blade. In North China, the sickle has a handle with appropriate curves. A light and ingenious grain cradle is used in northern Anhwei, where the wheat crop is light and extensive in acreage.

Threshing in North China is carried out chiefly by animals pulling a stone roller over cut grain laid on a packed earthen threshing floor. In the Rice Region, rice is threshed by two different methods. One is with a large wooden box with runners, pulled or carried to the rice fields. Small bundles of cut rice are knocked against the inside of the box to loosen the grain. The other method uses a strongly built wooden rack about two and one-half feet high. The head end of a small bundle of rice is knocked against the rack to loosen the grains of rice, which fall to the threshing floor.

Farm transportation. The wheelbarrow is used in all parts of China where the land is comparatively level. The four-wheeled farm cart in the North China Plain is the chief means of transporting crops from the field to the farmstead and to the market town.

A three-wheeled cart is used in northeastern Kiangsu. Boats in the canalized areas, such as the Yangtze delta area, are another means of transport. The donkey is used widely as a pack animal.

Irrigation equipment. In the rice region, the so-called dragon pump is used to raise water from canals and streams. It varies in size and length according to the amount of water to be pumped and the height to which the water must be raised. Depending upon the size and length of the pump, the weight of two, four, six, or eight persons may be needed to turn the cylinder to scoop up the water from the lower end, which is immersed in the water. In the canalized area of Kiangsu, there are many dragon pumps with turnstiles operated by water buffaloes. Windmills are also found in northeast Kiangsu to supply power for operating the dragon pump. The dragon pump is very efficient for low lifts of water, but it operates only at various acute angles, depending on the height of land above the source of water.

By the 1920's, diesel engines began to be used instead of manpower for the dragon pump. Thry were manufactured in China with only one imported item, the carburetor. Production of diesel engines for many types of uses progressed rapidly through the 1930's.

By the early 1930's, electric motor pumps began to be used in Wuchin *hsien* (Kiangsu), with electricity supplied by the power plant in the city of Wuhsi.

Quantity and value of farm equipment. Two economic surveys of farm equipment conducted in the 1930's[46] revealed that in East Central China, in the Rice Region, the average number of pieces of farm equipment owned per farm was 28.9 for 1,384 farms in eleven localities. In North China, there was an average of 17.1 items of important types of equipment per farm on 420 farms, excluding equipment used only by a few farmers and items connected with storage of grain and processing for farm use. The value of this equipment in percentage of land value was 3.3 per cent in East Central China and 2.6 per cent in North China.

In East Central China, there were 39,997 items of implements and equipment owned by 1,384 farmers. For a total of 1,426 farms, there were twenty-eight items per farm. The size of the farm averaged 16.6 mow, or 1.1 hectares of cultivated land. The twenty-eight items, divided by 1.1 hectares, equals 25.45 items per hectare. If this

---

[46] T. Odgen King, *Farm Implements in East Central China*, Bulletin No. 53 (Nanking: College of Agriculture and Forestry, University of Nanking, 1938), also a Ph.D. thesis, Cornell University, Ithaca, New York. See also H. S. Pan, *Economic Feasibility of Mechanization of Chinese Agriculture*, a master's thesis, Department of Agriculture and Economics, Washington State University, Pullman, Washington, 1949. The original manuscript *Farm Implements in North China* is in the possession of J. L. Buck. Both studies provide extensive information about traditional farm equipment, its manufacture, and repair.

number should apply to the whole Rice Region of 46.1 million hectares mentioned earlier, the total number of implements would be 1,163 million.

In the North China study, the 420 farms covered had 7,307 important implements, or 17.4 items per farm. The crop land per farm was 35.7 mow or 2.38 hectares. The 17.4 items per farm divided by 2.38 hectares give 7.31 implements per hectare of cultivated land. If applied to the Wheat Region of 47.7 million hectares, the number of important implements would be 348.7 million. If also applied to the 20.9 million hectares for Manchuria, Jehol, and Sinkiang, there would be 79.7 million more implements, for a total of 428 million. As previously mentioned, the data for North China do not include minor equipment or equipment that may not be used on most farms. The total implements and equipment for all of China in the 1930's would be more than 1,591 million pieces.

Cooperation in the use of implements was generally practiced in both East Central China and North China in the pre-Communist period. Many farmers, especially those with small acreage, borrowed implements from other farmers, and a considerable number of implements were jointly owned by two or more farmers.

A serious deterioration of the farm equipment situation occurred in connection with the operation of the large producers' cooperatives in 1955–57 and that of the communes in 1958. Under collective management, the equipment was less well cared for than it had been in the past. The Communist government placed a major emphasis on mechanization with little, if any, concern for traditional tools and equipment. New manufacturing centers were established in *hsien* cities far from the farmer. The local blacksmiths were brought to these centers, depriving the countryside of repair facilities. Equally unfortunate was the attitude of the engineers at these centers, who considered it beneath their dignity to make or repair simple tools. Consequently, a serious shortage of useful equipment affected production adversely. It was some time after the failures of the large communes during the Greap Leap that the Chinese Communists, out of necessity, gave attention to the production of traditional equipment.

A recent report indicates that Peking now realizes the need to place manufacturing centers nearer to the farmer, who needs the local service of blacksmiths and carpenters. Chi-ming Hou cites evidence that, in 1965, 1 billion small and medium agricultural tools and machines were produced in rural areas from one million metric tons of steel.[47] This represents an average of one kilogram of steel per piece and raises a question as to the actual number of small tools. Hou suggests that this large amount, similar to other claims, is probably an exaggeration.

On the other hand, the iron parts of implements that need replacement from time to time might be economically produced at centers far from the farmer, providing economical transportation to farm markets were maintained. In the 1920's, I visited a native foundry in a suburb of Nanking where gray cast-iron plow shares and plow moldboards were being produced in twenty different types to suit local areas in five provinces served by this foundry. Traditionally, producers of farm implements, whether near or far, utilize the community fairs in winter or early spring for the sale of their products. Various kinds of implements are lined up in rows for inspection and sale at these fairs, which are very impressive affairs.

Mechanization.[48] During the Communist period, great emphasis has been placed on mechanization, although considerable controversy has raged over the speed at which it should take place. There were heated arguments between Mao Tse-tung and Liu

---

[47] Chi-ming Hou, *Sources of Agricultural Growth in Communist China*, Reprint No. 20 (Ithaca, N.Y.: Committee on the Economy of China, Social Science Research Council, 1968), pp. 721–37.
[48] For a comprehensive appraisal of mechanization in Communist China, see Dawson, *Agricultural Development and Future Potential.*

Shao-ch'i as to whether the manufacture of farm machines should be concentrated in large factories or in scattered smaller plants.[49]

At first, probably under the influence of Russian advisers, Communist China produced only tractors and accompanying machinery of large types. These were useful only on state farms in parts of Manchuria and Sinkiang. More recently, attention has been given to the manufacture of smaller tractors, such as the seven-horse-power tractor, for use on small areas. This type of tractor, with complementary equipment for farm operations and transportation, could be quite practical if reasonable in price and cost of operation.

The most successful mechanization aiding the largest number of farmers has been power pumps for irrigation. The greatest stride was in electric motors and pumps and transmission lines from city power plants into the countryside, not only for pumping, but for small industrial enterprises. According to Dawson's calculations from Communist Chinese data, the ratio of mechanical power pumps of three types—the 'camel boiler,' the 'coal-gas engine,' and the 'diesel engine'—to the electrical pumps was 2 to 1 in 1964, although electrical pumping was increasing more rapidly.[50] Dawson estimates that 36.8 per cent of the irrigated area in 1967 was provided with electrical pumping facilities.[51] This includes irrigated area with electrical facilities before the advent of the Communist government.

I have seen no reports of manufacture of small mechanical threshers for rice, wheat and other crops. In the 1920's, the University of Nanking used a small imported thresher on the university farm. An economic study of costs indicated mechanical threshing of grains would be feasible. The chief objection to the American type of thresher was that it crushed the straw, which was used for thatching, making sandals, and other purposes, all of which required a stiff straw. Threshing in the Chinese way is expensive. It is difficult to separate the dirt and small stones from the earthen threshing floors of North China from the grain itself. It was necessary for flour mills in Shanghai to install special cleaning machinery before they could use the wheat. In fact, the millers in the 1930's found it cheaper and easier to buy clean graded wheat from abroad.

Japan's experience in mechanization should be a helpful guide to China. In the summer of 1927, I visited some agricultural economists at Fukuoka. During a field trip, observation was made of an electric pump newly installed by a farmer. The farmer pointed to it and remarked: 'Now I have nothing to do, but I have to pay for it.' However, pumping with electricity developed rapidly, followed by mechanical threshers and small tractors. Farmers sold their horses, which were used partly for transportation, and gradually converted to a cart pulled by the tractor. The buffaloes were also sold and replaced by the milk cow. The fodder and grain that previously fed the buffalo were then used for the cow. In fact, Japanese farmers gradually imported feed to increase the number of cows and even to add some beef animals.

Labor animals. The kinds of labor animals in the twenty-two provinces are water buffaloes, oxen (including yellow cows used as draft animals only), mules, horses, donkeys, and a few camels.[52]

Water buffaloes are used only in the Rice Region. Oxen are important in all parts of China. Mules are found mainly in North China. Horses were owned by only 5.1 per cent of the farmers in North China and 2.3 per cent in South China. Donkeys are

---

[49] *Current Scene*, Vol 6, No. 22 (Hong Kong, December 20, 1968).

[50] Dawson, *Agricultural Development and Future Potential*, p. 160, quoting NCNA, September 20, 1964.

[51] *Ibid.*, p. 162.

[52] Buck, *Land Utilization in China—Atlas*, p. 126, Table 2, listed for 167 localities. The canals were in Tingpien and Yülin of Shensi Province for 1 per cent of the farms.

prevalent in the Wheat Region of North China on 39 per cent of the farms, compared with only 2.9 per cent of farms in the Rice Region.

In South China, usually only one animal, the water buffalo or the ox, is used per plow. In North China, a team of two to five animals is used. For farm work and pulling a cart, a team may consist of many combinations of animals, such as an ox, a donkey, and a mule.

The number of labor animal units per crop hectare for the twenty-two provinces[53] was 0.71. For the Wheat Region, the average was 0.55 units per crop hectare; for the Rice Region, it was 0.83 units.

The total of labor animal units in 1929–33 was 106 million (Table 3–3).[54] The units for the Southwest Rice Area were two crop hectares. The next highest was 0.89 unit for the Double Cropping Rice Area and the third highest was 0.73 labor animal unit for the Spring Wheat Area. The enumerators explained the high number of two units in the Southwest Rice Area as caused by the availability of grazing land. To a certain extent this may also be true for the other two areas. All three areas have more pasture land available than the other five areas.

The larger number of labor animal units (0.83) in the Rice Region than in the Wheat Region (0.58) may be attributed to the need for more animal power to plow and harrow in the wet clay soils of rice fields, which are usually under water. Such plowing is done mainly by the buffalo, which is rated as one and one-third animal units and is slow-moving. Moreover, there is a higher ratio of multiple cropping in the Rice Region than in the Wheat Region. On the other hand, in the Wheat Region of North China, the soils are more friable, the implements are larger and cover more ground in each operation than in the Rice Region, and the draft animals move at a faster pace than do water buffaloes.

The low estimates for 1961 and 1963 (Table 3–3) reflect a true decline in the numbers of labor animals. As a result of the communization of labor animals, beginning with the establishment of agricultural producers' cooperatives in 1957, some farmers slaughtered their animals. Farmers tend to have a strong feeling for their own animals. In the collective farms and the communes, on the other hand, the animals did not receive proper care or feed. Young animals were not trained for work. Animal care was delegated to the lowest-paid person, who was least in ability among the communized farmers.

---

[53] *Ibid.*, p. 299, Table 11, listed for 167 localities. An ox, horse, or mule is considered as one unit; a donkey as one-half a unit; and a water buffalo as one and one-third unit.

[54] The calculations are as follows:

Region	Number of Crop Hectares[a] (millions)	Labor Animal Units per Crop Hectare	Labor Animal Units (millions)
Wheat	62.5	0.55	34.4
Rice	75.2	0.83	62.4
Manchuria, Jehol, and Sinkiang	20.9	0.45[b]	9.4
			106.2 or 106 million units

a See paragraph headed *Amount of crop hectares in all crops*, under subheading 'Land Ownership and Civilization,' above.

b Assuming 0.45 for the adjacent Winter Wheat Kaoliang area would not be an over estimate.

Table 3-3—Number of Labor Animal Units, 1937-67

Sources	Period	22 Provinces (millions)	Manchuria Jehol, and Sinkiang (millions)	Total (rounded in millions)
National Agricultural Research Bureau (1)	1937 and 1935	49.8	2.4	52
Land Utilization in China (2)	1929-33 (2A)	96.9	9.4	106
	1929-33 (2B)	89.9	9.4	99
Communist period (3)	1957	—	—	84
	1961	—	—	51
	1963	—	—	54
O. L. Dawson (4)	1967	—	—	68

Sources: (1) Shen, *Agricultural Resources of China*, pp. 288-90. Dr. Shen states: 'Rough estimates of the number of livestock have been obtained by the National Agricultural Research Bureau. . . . Owing to difficulties of obtaining any estimates, these figures have limited usefulness.' For the purpose of this table, the labor animals have been converted to labor animal units. (2A) Buck, *Land Utilization in China—Statistics*, p. 299, Table 11. (2B) If the two labor animal units for the Southwest Rice Area are replaced by the 0.89 units per crop hectare for the Double Cropping Rice Area, the number for the twenty-two Provinces would be 89.9 million and the total 99 million. (3) Dawson, *Agricultural Development and Future Potential*, p. 183. (4) *Ibid.*, pp. 187, 189. This estimate is based on calculated labor animal requirement for a cultivated area of 110 million hectares, not on a count of animals.

The shortage of labor animals made it necessary for the farmers to pull the plows and harrows themselves. This may have been one of the reasons why city people were sent to the country at that time. The decrease in labor animals also reduced the amount of organic fertilizer available for crops.

There has been slow recovery in the labor animal situation in the 1960's, but no Communist Chinese statistics are available from which to derive the actual number.

FERTILIZER AND TECHNICAL IMPROVEMENTS

Traditional fertilizers. Over the centuries, the Chinese farmer has maintained the fertility of the land by the use of night soil, animal dung, pond and canal mud, oil cakes (refuse after pressing out the oil from oil seed crops, such as soybeans and sesame), and some green manure crops, particularly in the Yangtze delta and on the Chengtu Plain, mainly *Astragulus Sinensis.*

In 1965, it was claimed that the area in green manure crops in the Yangtze River valley had been increased 50 per cent by reducing the area in winter grain crops.[55] For 1929-33 in the Yangtze Rice-Wheat Area, 4.1 per cent of the crop area was growing *Astragulus Sinensis* as a green manure crop. An increase of 50 per cent amounts to 6.2 per cent of the planted area in the crop.

Chemical fertilizers. The use of chemical fertilizers in China dates back to the 1920's, when a British firm introduced ammonium sulphate in the lower Yangtze valley. During 1928-33, the importation of chemical fertilizers, chiefly ammonium sulphate, amounted to 100,000 to 150,000 metric tons a year.

Beginning in 1935, N. L. Chang and H. L. Richardson, in cooperation with the NARB in Nanking, conducted 170 field tests in fourteen provinces on the effectiveness

[55] *ERS Foreign 162*, Foreign Analysis Division, Economic Research Service, U.S. Department of Agriculture, July, 1966.

of chemical fertilizers for wheat, cotton, rice, rapeseed, and corn. The average percentage of localities with plant nutrient deficiencies for the five crops was 73 per cent for nitrogen, 40 per cent for phosphorus, and 14 per cent for potash. The tests indicated that production could be increased 25 per cent in areas where the lack of water was a limiting factor.

The amounts of chemical fertilizer required, based on the above tests, were computed by H. T. Yeh of the NARB at 6,401,000 metric tons of ammonium sulphate, 3,812,000 metric tons of calcium phosphate, and 301,000 metric tons of potassium sulphate. Dr. Shen concludes from these data that for all crops an annual output of 15 million metric tons would be required for China proper.[56]

The manufacture of chemical fertilizers (ammonium sulphate) began in 1937 with the completion of a modern factory at Yungli on the Yangtze, downriver from Nanking. Unfortunately, the Japanese in their attack on China bombed the factory late in 1937. After the Sino-Japanese War, the factory was repaired and production resumed before the takeover by the Communists. Dr. T. H. Shen reports a production of 45,000 tons of ammonium sulphate in 1948.

The Communist government, having the benefit of this previous experience of the requirement for chemical fertilizers, has consistently given high priority to domestic production and to importation of chemical fertilizers (Table 3-4). Countries exporting chemical fertilizers to China include Japan, West Germany, East Germany, England and Jordan. Both domestic production and imports have increased at about the same rate to 6 million metric tons of production in China in 1969 and 6 million metric tons of imports.

The chemical fertilizer industry. In Kiangsu, the capacity for production of nitrogenous fertilizer was officially reported to have trebled in small plants between 1966 and early 1969. Large modern plants were built in Shensi and Hopei. The Shensi plant was the first large modern plant using a new carbonization process, and the Hopei plant was one of the major projects in the Third Five Year Plan. Because most of the equipment was domestically produced, the construction of these new plants signifies a continuous growth of chemical fertilizer equipment during the Cultural Revolution. Chu-yuan Cheng states in an article:

Throughout the Cultural Revolution there was no abatement in capital investment in the chemical fertilizer industry, although production was interrupted during 1967. In Kiangsu Province, over twenty small and medium-sized plants were built after the beginning of the Cultural Revolution, compared with only twelve plants erected before 1966. In Shantung Province, the number of chemical plants built in 1966 was said to equal the number constructed between 1958–1965. During 1967–68 another eighteen plants were added. Shantung's nitrogenous fertilizer output 1966–1968 was seven times that in the previous eight years. In Kiangsu Province the capacity for production of nitrogenous fertilizer trebled. Large modern plants were built in Shensi of which one was the first using a new carbonization process.[57]

Representative centers manufacturing chemical fertilizer[58] are as on page 67.

---

[56] Shen, *Agricultural Resources of China*, p. 38; N. F. Chang and H. L. Richardson, 'The Use of Fertilizers in China,' *Nature*, Vol. 69, No. 3780, April 11, 1942; and 'Scope and Work of the National Agricultural Research Bureau,' miscellaneous publication No. 15, May, 1938.

[57] Chu-yuan Cheng, 'The Effects of the Cultural Revolution on China's Machine-building Industry,' *Current Scene*, 8, No. 1 (January 1, 1970).

[58] 'The Geography of Mainland China: A Concise Sketch,' *Current Scene*, Vol. 7, No. 17 (September 1, 1969).

Table 3–4—Chemical Fertilizer Production and Imports,
Chiefly Nitrogenous and Phosphates, 1952–69

| Year | Production (million metric tons) | Imports | | Total (million metric tons) |
		(Million $ U.S.)	(Million metric tons)	
1952 (1)	0.18	—	—	—
1954 (2)	—	—	0.08	—
1956 (3)	0.66	—	0.84	1.50
1957 (1)	0.63	—	—	—
1958 (4)	1.24	—	1.46	2.70
1959 (3)	2.12	—	—	—
1960	2.48 (3)	70 (5)	2.30 (5)	—
1960 (1)	1.68	—	—	—
1961 (3)	1.40	—	0.88	2.28
1961 (1)	1.43	—	—	—
1962 (3)	2.12	—	1.11	3.10
1963 (3)	2.80	—	1.70	4.50
1964 (3)	3.50	—	1.20	4.70
1965	4.50 (6)	—	2.00 (est.)	6.50
1965 (5)	—	140	4.66	—
1966	5.00 (6)	150 (7)	5.00 (7)	10.00
1966 (8)	4.25	—	4.25	8.50
1967[a]	—	200	6.66	—
1968 (9)	6.00	—	7.00	13.00
1968 (7)	—	200	6.66[b]	—
1969 (7)	6.00	180	6.00[c]	12.00
1972 (3)	estimated requirement of 15 million metric tons			

Note: There may be some variation in nutrient value.
[a] The Cultural Revolution disrupted imports of fertilizer at Chinese ports.
[b] Includes 2.46 million metric tons (ammonium sulphate equivalent) from Japan.
[c] Includes 2.85 million metric tons from Japan.

Sources: (1) Chu-yuan Cheng, *Communist China's Economy, 1949–1962* (South Orange, N.J.: Seton Hall University Press, 1963), pp. 134–37. (2) E. Stuart Kirby, *Contemporary China* (Hong Kong: Hong Kong University Press, 1956), p. 108; includes 12,441 tons of ammonium sulphate and 38,006 tons of phosphate fertilizers, imported from Japan. (3) Owen L. Dawson, 'China's Two-Pronged Agricultural Dilemma,' *Current Scene*, 3, No. 20 (June 1, 1965): 5–6, 10, 13. (4) The Editor, 'China's Economy in 1969: Policy, Agriculture, Industry, Foreign Trade,' *Current Scene*, 8, No. 11 (June 1, 1970): 16; in terms of ammonium sulphate equivalent in 1969 at cost of about $190 million; Japan was principal supplier, but some was imported from West Germany; quantity was about the same level in 1968. (5) Sidney Klein, 'The Cultural Revolution and China's Foreign Trade,' *Current Scene*, 5, No. 19 (November 17, 1967): 3; 'only chemical fertilizer imports in 1965 showed a distinct increase over all other 1969 import data attaining U.S. $140 million, or twice the level of $70 million for imports of fertilizer in 1969. The reason was the regime's acknowledgment of importance of chemical fertilizer to agriculture.' (6) The Editor, 'And Now There Are Four,' *Current Scene*, 4, No. 20 (November 10, 1966): 4; output in terms of ammonium sulphate and normal superphosphate may approach 5 million metric tons in 1966, compared with 4.5 million tons in 1965. (7) The Editor, 'China's Foreign Trade in 1969: The National People's Congress, the Communist Youth League,' *Current Scene*, 8, No. 16 (October 7, 1970): 4, 6; figures on imports from Japan from China Affairs Division, Asian Affairs Bureau, Ministry of Foreign Affairs, Tokyo, and *Current Scene*, 8, No. 9 (May 1, 1970): 3. (8) 'The Geography of Mainland China: A Concise Sketch,' *Current Scene*, 7, No. 17 (September 1, 1969): 18. (9) U.S., Department of Agriculture, Economic Research Service, *The Agricultural Situation in Communist Areas* (Washington, D.C., April 7, 1969), p. 27.

Province	Place	Product
Hupei	Chunghsiang	Phosphate
Kiangsu	Hsinhailien	Phosphate
Kwantung	Canton	Fertilizer
Kweichow	K'aiyang	Phosphate
Szechwan	Luchow[59]	Fertilizer
Tsinghai	Ch'aerhpan Basin	Potassium salts

There are numerous other smaller units of production. For instance, Shantung Province is reported to have scores of units producing fertilizers on a small scale.

One may raise the question of how much of the imported fertilizer and even the manufactured fertilizer actually reached the farmer and was applied properly to the fields.

Although during the Cultural Revolution, 'there was no abatement in capital investment in the chemical industry,' there were serious delays, caused by the Red Guards, in unloading imported fertilizer at Chinese ports.[60]

The quality of fertilizers produced by small plants of much less than 100,000-ton capacity is subject to doubt. The merit of small fertilizer plants as against large plants of 100,000 metric tons capacity or more, varies undoubtedly according to their proximity to transportation facilities and areas of consumption and according to managerial and personnel skills in plants of varied sizes. The quality of the large number of phosphate rock deposits is also an important factor.

Crop improvement. Over the centuries, the Chinese have adapted varieties of crops to the different soils and climates throughout China. However, scientific development of improved seeds was unknown. Crop improvement was begun by the University of Nanking, expanded with the cooperation of plant breeders from Cornell University, and further developed under the National Agricultural Research Bureau established in 1932.

By 1937, considerable distribution of improved seeds had taken place. The program included especially wheat and cotton and was making progress in rice and soybeans. In 1942 as a result of the assistance of Dr. Dykstra of the U.S. Department of Agriculture, the NARB began multiplying seed tubers in areas free of potato virus. The white potato was one crop that could be fitted easily into the rotation of crops. (Part of the reported increase in potato area during 1949–58 may have been in white potatoes.) All Chinese plant breeders had received training and experience in up-to-date plant breeding at the University of Nanking and the National Agricultural Research Bureau during 1925–34, with the assistance of personnel from the Plant Breeding Department, Cornell University, and other United States institutions.

The Communist government inherited these seeds and personnel, except for a few plant breeders who went to Taiwan. The evidence at hand indicates that it was not able to reap full rewards from this legacy because of mismanagement. The adoption, chiefly in North China, of Lysenko's theory of breeding based on environmental factors may have adversely influenced plant breeding for a short time. During the large collective and commune stage, stores of improved seeds were spoiled because of improper storage and care. Potato production has increased because of a larger area in potatoes, although yields per hectare are no greater.

The Communist claims of crop improvement are impressive, but figures on farm yields from the improved varieties are not available.[61]

---

[59] Important complex for the manufacture of urea on a large scale.

[60] Cheng, 'Effects of Cultural Revolution.'

[61] For some detailed information on crop improvement, see *Agricultural Development and Future Potential*, pp. 103–10.

CONCLUSION

In spite of all the Communists' efforts, many of them efficacious if properly implemented, estimates of food grain production per capita for 1967, a good crop year, do not show an increase over 1953–57. The commune type of organization for production was unpopular with the farmers, and by 1960 the government had changed the primary production unit from the county commune to the production teams of some twenty farm families. The production brigade, each composed of about twenty teams, became the unit for accounting and supply of seed, equipment, and fertilizers and for payment of taxes in an amount equivalent to that formerly paid by the tenants to the landlords. This system of organization requires expert management and is difficult to administer adequately, because it depends on efficient performances in other parts of the whole organization, such as production of new equipment, repair of existing equipment, improved seed production and supplies, chemical fertilizer supply, and uninterrupted transportation and manufacture. In fact, only two estimates of 214 and 215 million metric tons for 1967 exceed the three surveys in 1929–37 of 201, 203, and 205 million metric tons (Table 3–2) for food grain production.

During the Cultural Revolution of 1966–68, internal rivalry and fighting between struggling groups for power caused some interruption of transport and industrial output. The recent and continued transfer of millions of young people from the cities to the countryside may be caused in part by a shortage of food in the cities, although the stated purpose is re-education through experience in the countryside.

SELECTED BIBLIOGRAPHY

BUCK, JOHN LOSSING. *Chinese Farm Economy.* Shanghai: The Commercial Press, 1930; Chicago: The University of Chicago Press, 1930. A farm-management and socioeconomic analysis of field data from 2,866 farms and farm families in seventeen localities of seven provinces, including chapters on population, food consumption, and standard of living.

———. *Land Utilization in China.* Shanghai: The Commercial Press, 1937; Chicago: The University of Chicago Press, 1937; 3d ed., New York: Paragon Book Gallery, 1968. An Agricultural-economics study of data collected by a trained staff from 16,786 farms in 168 localities of twenty-two provinces. The data were analyzed and summarized for each of the eight agricultural areas and for the Wheat Region of North China and the Rice Region of Central and South China. The analysis shows relationships among various factors pertinent to the agricultural economy. Chapters on population and standards of living.

———. *Land Utilization in China—Atlas.* Shanghai: The Commercial Press, 1937; Chicago: The University of Chicago Press, 1937. Includes all analyzed data capable of being presented geographically; maps of topography, soils, and climate; and five pages of aerial photographs of the layout of farm land on various types of topography.

———. *Land Utilization in China—Statistics.* Shanghai: The Commercial Press, 1937; Chicago: University of Chicago Press, 1937. Data are tabulated by averages for 100 farms in each of 168 localities for each *hsien*, each province, each of the eight agricultural areas, for Wheat and Rice regions, and for all of China (twenty-two provinces).

BUCK, JOHN LOSSING; OWEN L. DAWSON; and YUAN-LI WU. *Food and Agriculture in Communist China.* New York: Praeger Publishers, 1966. Wu and Buck analyze Communist data on production and consumption. Dr. Wu presents an excellent description of the economics of agriculture in the pre-Communist period, describes the situation under Communism, tests the Communist data on production and consumption, and suggests a possible future trend. Buck makes an upward correction of the cultivated land area used by the NARB (1931–37), giving a more accurate food grain output for that period, and deflates the Communist 1949–58 figures depicting rapid increases. DAWSON describes the fertilizer situation in relation to food supplies, explains the need for additional chemical fertilizers, assesses the irrigated area and Communist attempts to increase irrigation, and evaluates water supplies.

DAWSON, OWEN L. *Communist China's Agricultural Development and Future Potential*. New York: Praeger Publishers, 1968. An excellent presentation and interpretation of a large amount of data on Communist claims of progress and the author's estimates for 1967. It is a valuable source for all research on agriculture in Communist China. The first edition was issued by the Office of External Research, Department of State, Washington, D.C., in 1968.

HOMMEL, RUDOLF P. *China at Work*. New York: The John Day Company, 1937.

KING, F. H. *Farmers of Forty Centuries*. Madison, Wis.: Mrs. F. H. King, 1911; 2d ed., New York: Harcourt Brace, 1926. An interesting account of the author's perceptive observations on a visit to the Far East, including China. Of special interest is his sketch map of the Yangtze canalized area and his praise of the skills of Chinese farmers. Copiously illustrated with photographs.

LIU, TA-CHUNG, and KUNG-CHIA YEH. *The Economy of the Chinese Mainland*. Princeton, N.J.: Princeton University Press, 1965. A scholarly work, portions of which attempt to give a reasonable interpretation of agricultural land and production data before and after the advent of the Communist government. The reader or student will find information for both periods that is not readily available elsewhere.

SCOTT, JAMES CAMERON. *Health and Agriculture in China*. London: Faber & Faber, 1951. A persuasive exposition, based on the author's 1933–41 research in China, on the ill health of farmers caused by bacteria carried in human feces and urine used as fertilizers. Suggestions based on experiments are given on treatment of feces and urine for their safe use as fertilizer.

SHEN, T. H. *Agricultural Resources of China*. Ithaca, N.Y.: Cornell University Press, 1951. An excellent source book on the agriculture of China in its various aspects, many of which are not described elsewhere. Caution is necessary in regard to the production and food tables for 1931–37, because the base cultivated area upon which production was computed was too small, a result of the first attempt under the National Government to obtain data on cultivated area and production.

TREGEAR, THOMAS R. *A Geography of China*. Chicago: Aldine Publishing Company, 1965. Subject matter is arranged under physical, historical, economic, and regional geography and is well illustrated. Description of the physical characteristics of Sinkiang in relation to agricultural development is of particular significance.

4

NATURAL RESOURCES AND THEIR UTILIZATION

K. P. WANG

RESERVES AND PRODUCTION

A COUNTRY must have access to raw materials and industrial-commercial capacity in order to become influential in the world economy. China has most of the natural resources and is increasing its technical know-how. Its human resources are without parallel. The expanding population, however, is exerting great pressure on the land and the limited food supply. Chinese agriculture can be developed to exceed basic needs, but only with tremendous capital investments for fertilizers and equipment. In the present circumstances, agriculture has not been able to provide funds for industrial development on as large a scale as Peking may have hoped.

China is relatively richly endowed with mineral wealth, and is already a significant world producer of many mineral products (see Tables 4-1 and 4-2). The country's over-all resource position has been further enhanced under the Chinese Communists as a result of intensive programs of geological investigation and mineral development carried out by such government agencies as the ministries of Geology, Coal, Petroleum, and Metallurgical Industry. In fact, highly significant new deposits of coal, petroleum, iron, copper, lead and zinc, molybdenum, asbestos, pyrites, and fertilizer raw materials have been found in widespread areas, not to speak of many minerals and metals of which China has long been a major producer, such as tin, tungsten, antimony, mercury, bismuth, fluorspar, magnesite, and talc. Yet such are China's geographical and geologic idiosyncrasies that surpluses and deficiencies exist simultaneously, in both mineral potential and mineral production.

Given favorable development conditions, the country could become an industrial giant. The process may be slow, particularly in terms of diversification of products and production of consumer goods, because of traditional difficulties and the nature of a centralized economy. Most likely, China will not be able to attain first-rank status as a world economic power in the decade ahead.

Mainland China made steady progress in mineral production between 1960 and 1966, which was a banner year. Then came 1967 and the effects of the Cultural Revolution, with politics crippling economics and industrial production. As a consequence, mineral output value (based upon approximate world prices)—mine output plus added value derived from smelting and processing—may have declined 30 per cent from the $4–4.5 billion estimated for 1966.*

The year 1967 began with a militant call to destroy anti-Maoists and ended in a

---

* Unless otherwise indicated, production estimates in this chapter are the author's.

Table 4–1—World Significance of Selected Chinese Minerals, 1965*

Commodity	Approximate Rank in World Output	Share of Estimated World Output (per cent)	Adequacy in Production	Reserves or Resources
Metals:				
Aluminum	9	2	Virtually adequate	Considerable
Antimony	1	24	Large surplus	World's largest
Bismuth	5	7	Large surplus	First rank
Chromite	Insignificant	Very small	Greatly deficient	Unimportant
Copper	10	2	Deficient	Moderate
Gold	Not among first 20	Small	Can use more	Moderate
Iron ore	4	6	Adequate	First rank
Iron, pig	5	6	Adequate	Not applicable
Iron, steel ingot	7	3	Adequate	Not applicable
Lead	9	4	Slight surplus	Moderate
Manganese ore	6	6	Surplus	Considerable
Mercury	4	9	Large surplus	First rank
Molybdenum	5	3	Sizable surplus	First rank
Nickel	Insignificant	Very small	Greatly deficient	Unimportant
Tin	2	13	Large surplus	First rank
Tungsten concentrate	1	30	Large surplus	World's largest
Zinc	11	3	Slight surplus	Moderate
Nonmetals:				
Asbestos	5	4	Moderate surplus	Considerable
Barite	8	3	Slight surplus	Considerable
Cement	8	3	Slight surplus	Extensive raw materials
Fluorspar	5	8	Sizable surplus	Considerable
Graphite	5	7	Adequate	Moderate
Gypsum	13	1	Adequate	Considerable
Magnesite	3	11	Surplus	First rank
Phosphate rock	7	1	Seriously deficient	Considerable
Pyrite	5	6	Can use more	Considerable
Salt	2	13	Slight surplus	First rank
Sulphur	8	2	Surplus	Moderate
Talc	5	4	Surplus	Moderate
Mineral fuels:				
Anthracite	2	12	Adequate	First rank
Bituminous coal	3	15	Adequate	First rank
Coke	5	5	Adequate	First rank
Petroleum, crude	17	0.6	Nearly self-sufficient	Moderate
Petroleum, refined	Not among first 20	0.5	Deficient	Not applicable

* Chinese production estimated by author generally as an order of magnitude rather than as a definite quantity. Consequently, the determinations of world rank and of share of world output can be regarded only as approximations. Moreover these determinations may also be inexact because of incomplete or erroneous reporting of the output of other countries.

Source: Annual issues of U.S. Department of the Interior, *Bureau of Mines Mineral Yearbook*. First appeared in 1965 as *Mineral Yearbook Review of the Mineral Industry of Mainland China*.

Table 4–2—Production of Minerals and Metals in Mainland China*
(Metric tons, unless otherwise specified)

Commodity	1952	1957	1966	1967	1968	1969	1970	1971
Metals:								
Aluminum:								
Bauxite†	0	90,000	400,000	350,000	380,000	450,000	500,000	
Alumina	0	45,000	200,000	175,000	190,000	230,000	250,000	
Metal, refined	0	20,000	100,000	80,000	90,000	120,000	130,000	
Antimony, mine	8,000	15,000	15,000	12,000	12,000	12,000	12,000	
Bismuth, mine	NA	NA	300	250	250	250	250	
Copper, mine	NA	NA	90,000	80,000	90,000	100,000	100,000	
Copper, refined metal	10,000	50,000	100,000	90,000	100,000	100,000	100,000	
Gold (troy ounces)	NA	NA	60,000	50,000	50,000	50,000	50,000	
Iron and Steel:								
Iron ore‡ (thousand tons)	4,290	15,000	40,000	28,000	38,000	40,000	44,000	
Pig iron (thousand tons)	1,928	5,940	20,000	14,000	19,000	20,000	22,000	27,000
Steel ingot (thousand tons)	1,350	5,350	16,000	11,000	15,000	16,000	17,000	21,000
Rolled steel (thousand tons)	1,100	4,260	13,000	9,000	12,000	13,000	14,000	
Lead, mine	NA	NA	100,000	90,000	100,000	100,000	100,000	
Lead, refined metal	7,000	45,000	100,000	90,000	100,000	100,000	100,000	
Magnesium	NA	NA	1,000	1,000	1,000	1,000	1,000	
Manganese ore (thousand tons)	191	700	1,000	700	900	1,000	1,000	
Mercury (76-pound flasks)	NA	NA	26,000	20,000	20,000	20,000	20,000	
Molybdenum, mine	NA	NA	1,500	1,500	1,500	1,500	1,500	
Silver (troy ounces)	NA	NA	800,000	600,000	700,000	800,000	800,000	
Tin, refined	10,000	24,000	22,000	20,000	20,000	20,000	20,000	
Tungsten concentrate (about 68 per cent WO_3 grade)	20,000	15,000	15,000	15,000	15,000	15,000	15,000	
Zinc, mine	NA	NA	100,000	90,000	100,000	100,000	100,000	
Zinc, refined metal	9,000	37,000	90,000	80,000	90,000	90,000	100,000	
Nonmetals:								
Asbestos	NA	NA	140,000	150,000	150,000	160,000	170,000	
Barite	NA	NA	110,000	100,000	120,000	140,000	150,000	
Cement (thousand tons)	2,860	6,860	11,000	80,000	9,000	10,000	10,000	12,000
Fluorspar	NA	NA	250,000	250,000	250,000	250,000	270,000	
Graphite	NA	NA	40,000	30,000	30,000	30,000	30,000	
Gypsum	NA	NA	600,000	500,000	500,000	550,000	550,000	
Magnesite (thousand tons)	NA	NA	1,000	800	900	1,000	1,000	
Phosphate rock (thousand tons)	NA	NA	1,000	1,000	1,000	1,100	1,200	
Pyrite (thousand tons)	NA	NA	1,500	1,500	1,500	1,800	2,000	
Salt (thousand tons)	4,950	8,280	13,000	13,000	15,000	15,000	16,000	
Sulphur	NA	NA	250,000	250,000	250,000	250,000	250,000	
Talc	NA	NA	150,000	150,000	150,000	150,000	150,000	
Mineral Fuels:								
Coal (thousand tons)	66,600	128,000	325,000	225,000	300,000	330,000	360,000	390,000
Coke (thousand tons)	NA	NA	17,000	13,000	15,000	17,000	18,000	
Petroleum, crude (thousand tons)	440	1,440	13,000	11,000	15,000	20,000	24,000	29,000
Petroleum, refined (thousand tons)	NA	NA	12,500	10,000	14,000	19,000	23,000	

* Estimated by author. Estimate for 1971 in crude oil includes 4 million tons of shale oil.

† Excludes bauxite for refractories.

‡ Equivalent 50 per cent Fe ore.

partially successful campaign to restore law and order. Numerous and widespread clashes between industrial workers and technocrats, peasants, soldiers, and Red Guard students took place. The railroad system was disrupted, and there was much unauthorized borrowing of trucks for demonstrations and other activities. By necessity, the Third Five-Year Plan, scheduled to begin in 1966, was indefinitely postponed.

As a result of the intervention of the Chinese People's Liberation Army (PLA), 1968 was a year of somewhat more orderly production in the mining industry, while the trend was generally up in 1969. The year 1970 promised to be a good year, surpassing the previous record in 1966. Considerable new facilities were brought into production during 1969. At the same time, decentralization and the opening up of new, not-too-large mines and other production units became the order of the day. The rationale is not entirely economic. The decline in China's traditional mineral exports, as well as large imports for stockpiling purposes, like decentralization, reflected the war scare in 1969. The decentralization policy, however, was continued in 1970.

IRON AND STEEL

The Cultural Revolution interrupted the recovery of the iron and steel industry from its post–Great Leap low, with 1967 the worst year. As a result of work disruptions at mines and plants, plus serious transport bottlenecks, China's steel production declined at least 30 per cent in 1967. In contrast, 1966 had been an outstanding year, with all major steel centers fulfilling targets before the full force of the Cultural Revolution reached the industrial sector. Some improvement took place in 1968, followed by a good year in 1969; 1970 may turn out to have been another good year.

China's iron ore base has proved much stronger than previously thought. A claim in the late 1950's placed potential reserves at a staggering 100 billion metric tons.* Discounting exaggerations, the workable reserve appears to be at least 5 billion tons. Ore quality and type vary greatly, but this poses no special technological difficulties. Iron ore, like coal, is widely distributed in China.

To complement internal achievements and to fill the technical void created by the Sino-Soviet rift, the Chinese Communists in 1965–66 had embarked upon a program of purchasing foreign steel plants. The biggest deal to be negotiated was with a European consortium headed by the West German firm DEMAG AG to build a $150-million, 3-million-ton annual capacity steel-rolling mill. Negotiations were called off at the end of 1967 and reportedly were broken in early 1968. The Austrians, who were building LD (Linz Donawitz) oxygen converters at the Taiyüan steel works, had to leave without completing construction, but these have apparently been installed. A deal to buy a West German steel tubing plant from Mannesman AG was reportedly signed, but details on construction are lacking. The Hitachi Shipbuilding Company of Japan was negotiating in 1966 to sell a large sintering and pelleting plant to the Chinese Communists; the outcome, too, is unclear. During 1969, however, some 1.2 million tons of finished steel products—consisting mostly of items China cannot readily produce—were imported from Japan as a part of stockpiling for war.

Anshan. Anshan, a large integrated steel center by world standards with ten blast furnaces ranging in size from 585 to 1,513 cubic meters (or about 2,600 metric tons per day)[1] and twenty-five open hearths, had been capable of producing roughly 6

---

* Tonnage figures in this chapter are in metric tons.
[1] See *American Metal Market* (New York: American Metal Market Company, March 4, 1968), pp. 1, 23; also, 'The Mineral Industry of Mainland China,' *Bureau of Mines Minerals Yearbook* (Washington, D.C.: U.S. Department of the Interior), 1969–70.

million metric tons of steel ingots annually. It managed to escape the worst hazards of the Cultural Revolution until mid-August, 1967, when armed struggle and damage to several blast furnaces were reported. Although order was quickly restored, normal operations had been seriously disrupted. It is probable that steel ingot production dropped to 4–5 million tons in 1967. By 1969, however, production may have risen to 6.5 million tons, making it a record year. A number of technological improvements and new products have also been introduced, especially large structural shapes. Anshan has also successfully introduced the practice of injecting slurry coal (sometimes also tar and coal gas) and heavy oil under high temperature and pressure conditions at its No. 9 blast furnace to bring coke consumption down to below 400 kilograms per ton of pig.

Wuhan. Prior to 1969, the Wuhan steel works, with 1,386- and 1,436-cubic-meter blast furnaces, five open-hearth furnaces (four 500-tonners and one 250-tonner), three byproduct coke plants, and various rolling mills, had been rated at about 1.5 million tons of ingot capacity a year. A new open hearth (probably of 500-ton capacity) and a third large blast furnace were brought into operation during 1969, raising the estimated annual ingot capacity to 2.2 million metric tons. While 1966 was apparently a good year, production suffered from fighting during 1967 and 1968. The 1969 crude steel output was estimated at 1.7 million tons.

The Shihchingshan-T'angshan-Tientsin-Peking complex. The Shihchingshan-T'angshan-Tientsin-Peking complex has an annual capacity of more than 1.5 million tons of steel and a planned capacity probably twice as large. Shihchingshan, with three blast furnaces (413, 512, and 963 cubic meters), three coke units, and top-blown oxygen converters, has been the key in this complex. Other facilities include rolling mills and a new blooming mill completed in 1969. Because of its location near the capital, production suffered less at these plants than elsewhere during the Cultural Revolution and was on an upward trend in 1969. Injection of anthracite dust along with other fuels into blast furnaces, a practice thought hazardous by Westerners and Japanese, has been successfully done at Shihchingshan.

Paot'ou. The Paot'ou steel works is oriented around a 1,513-cubic-meter blast furnace, possibly two 600-ton open-hearth furnaces, a sintering plant, and related byproduct coke units and rolling mills, including one large rolling mill completed in 1969. Operational difficulties were finally smoothed out in 1966, when outputs for most items were said to be 50–100 per cent greater than in 1965. Present annual steel capacity is estimated at 800,000 tons a year. Output from the new large rolling mill includes rails, girders and alloy steel I-beams.

Taiyüan. The Taiyüan steelworks was still under construction when the Cultural Revolution began. Five blast furnaces (963 and 291 cubic meters, and three very small ones), various steel furnaces and one rolling mill, including open hearths, electric furnaces, and converters, had already been installed; a second rolling mill began normal production late in 1969. The steel works were 'seized' in early 1967 by anti-Maoists but taken back fairly quickly. Despite some interruptions during the year, output in 1969 probably reached 1 million tons of ingot.

Chungking. Chungking, with three blast furnaces (the largest being 620 cubic meters), at least two open hearths, and all the necessary related equipment to make steel products, is another center capable of producing 800,000 to 1 million tons of steel annually. A somewhat outmoded plant, Chungking did well in 1969, although it had its share of troubles during the Cultural Revolution.

Shanghai and Maanshan. Shanghai has at least eight small steel works. Of these the No. 1 steel works is the most important, including among its facilities two blast furnaces, two open hearths, a number of Bessemer & Thomas converters, and possibly three 'home-made' oxygen top-blower converters. The two blast furnaces, with a combined annual capacity of perhaps 500,000 tons of pig iron, are supplemented by pig iron imported from Maanshan. The Maanshan steel works in nearby Anhwei,

K. P. WANG

with thirteen small blast furnaces ranging from 34 to 255 cubic meters in size, recently built a few modern open-hearth furnaces and a heavy rolling mill. Shanghai and Maanshan together probably can produce 2 million to 3 million tons of steel annually. Steel ingot production in 1969 was estimated at 1.5 million metric tons in Shanghai and 700,000–800,000 tons at Maanshan.

Copper, Lead, Zinc, and Aluminum

Copper. China suffers from a chronic shortage of copper, which has prompted the country to turn more to aluminum for electrical use and to make special efforts to explore for copper. Several sizable porphyry copper deposits reportedly have been found in North China, including ones at Paiyinchang in Kansu and Chungt'iao Mountain in Shansi. Yünnan and T'ungkuan Mountain (south of Nanking) probably also have important copper deposits. Various overtures have been made to purchase Japanese copper smelters in order to exploit sizable reserves already prospected. By the end of 1970, however, no contract had been signed. In the long run, the Chinese should be able to produce considerably beyond the 90,000- to 100,000-ton levels attained in recent years.

Lead and Zinc. A contract was signed with the British firm Imperial Smelting Process, Ltd., in 1966 to use the ISP process in building a lead-zinc plant at Shaokuan in northern Kwangtung. A 30 per cent zinc–16 per cent lead concentrate, presumably from nearby areas, will be smelted to produce 35,000 to 40,000 metric tons of zinc and 18,000 to 20,000 tons of lead annually, roughly 40 and 20 per cent, respectively, of national outputs for recent years. The Chinese have made exchange visits of technicians with the Japanese firm Sumitomo, which has a similar plant. However, by the end of 1969, a bid from Sumitomo to build the plant had not been carried out. Historically, Shuik'ou Mountain in Hunan has been the best known lead-zinc center. Zinc is needed primarily for galvanized sheets, die-castings, and brass; lead for batteries and pipe.

Aluminum. Until 1969 the Fushun reduction plant in Manchuria, rated at perhaps 80,000 to 100,000 tons of metal yearly, had been the key to Chinese aluminum. In recent years, the Chinese sought both European and Japanese help in expanding aluminum facilities. The existence of several new plants in Kirin (west of Changchun), Honan (near Chengchow), and at the Sanmen Gorge on the Yellow River was reported in 1969.[2] Demand for aluminum has greatly increased because of the expansion of facilities for electricity transmission and generation and the shortage of copper.

Tin, Tungsten, Antimony, and Mercury

The international sales of China's important export metals have declined sharply in recent years. Normally, China produces roughly 10 to 15 per cent of the world's tin, 25 to 35 per cent of the world's tungsten, 20 to 25 per cent of the world's antimony, and 8 to 12 per cent of the world's mercury. Exports to the free world have not been built up enough to replace shipments formerly going to the Soviet bloc. In tin, the Soviet Union took 17,700 metric tons in 1960 and only nominal quantities in the late 1960's (e.g., 100 tons in 1967). Accountable free world imports of tin from China averaged 5,000 to 7,000 tons annually in 1962–65, 3,000 tons in 1967–68, and less in 1969. Normal domestic consumption is in the neighborhood of 5,000 to 7,000 tons. Production declined during the Cultural Revolution, but the combined output of the centers at Kochiu (in Yünnan) and Fuch'uan-Hohsien-Chungshan (in Kwangsi) was estimated at 20,000 tons in 1969. This suggests considerable domestic stockpiling.

Chinese tungsten has fared a little better under high-price conditions. In 1960, the

[2] New China News Agency (NCNA), Aug. 24, 1969.

76

Soviet Union imported 18,900 metric tons of concentrates, or the equivalent of 80,000 tons of metal, and, after the Sino-Soviet rift, only 3,000 tons in 1966 and somewhat larger amounts in 1967–69. In contrast, the free world imported about 2,000 tons in 1964, a record 9,000 tons in 1966, 7,000 tons in 1967, and perhaps 5,000 tons a year in 1968–69. Domestic consumption approximates 5,000 tons of tungsten concentrates, about one-third or less of annual production. Kiangsi Province is still the main source of Chinese tungsten.

Antimony production has been in the doldrums, with little change in 1967–69, although domestic consumption and stockpiling have increased. Hsik'uangshan in Hunan Province is the main production center, but Kwangsi has gained in relative significance. China may be the world's leading antimony producer, but output value remains small.

Mercury output probably declined sharply in 1967, although the country was still prominent among world producers. Southwest China, particularly T'ungjen in Kweichow Province, produced the bulk. A great change has taken place in sales, with the Soviet Union importing 35,000 flasks of Chinese mercury in 1962 and only 1,000 flasks annually in 1966–67.

URANIUM AND OTHER METALS

Uranium. Between October, 1964, and October, 1970, China carried out eleven nuclear explosions at Lop Nor in Sinkiang Province. Of these, seven contained thermonuclear or fusion devices. Mainland China is believed to have two plutonium reactor plants. However, U_{235}, rather than the more conventional plutonium, has been consistently used. The processed U_{235} comes from a gaseous diffusion plant that has been in production since 1963 near Lanchou in Kansu Province.[3] Power for the Lanchou plant is furnished by a large hydroelectric facility nearby. By going all out in this very costly nuclear-hydroelectric project based upon U_{235}, the Chinese have probably shortened their nuclear schedule considerably and assured much lower future costs.

Three new uranium mines were reported to have started production in recent years, with a combined initial daily output of 2,500 tons of ore: the Maishan and Chushan in Ch'üannan, Kiangsi Province, and the Hsiachuang in Wengyüan, Kwangtung Province. The Czechs gave technical and financial assistance to the Chinese in building necessary beneficiation and processing facilities at Chuchou in Hunan Province, for which China did not pay cash but gave the Czechs some of the processed uranium.

Manganese, Molybdenum, Chromite, Nickel, Bismuth, Titanium, and other metals. Chinese manganese ore output ranked about fifth in the world, even though production dropped sharply in 1967 from the usual million-ton annual output, primarily because of reduced steel smelting. Hsiangt'an in Hunan Province, Mukuei and Laip'ing in Kwangsi, Ch'inhsien and Fangch'eng in Kwangtung, Tsuni in Kweichow, and Wafangtzu in Manchuria are the main producers. A small surplus is exported. As of 1970, the Chinese apparently had not yet fully developed a large molybdenum deposit in Shansi, nor several other significant discoveries; however, hundreds of tons of concentrates have been exported yearly for some time from existing mines. Chromite is still in short supply, and Albania shipped 83,500 metric tons to China in 1964 —indicative of more recent levels of sales. Failure to get some of the nickel contracted from Le Nickel of France under a four-year contract has prompted China to make inquiries in West Germany and the Netherlands.

---

[3] For particulars, see *Defense Program and Budget,* Fiscal Year 1971 (Washington,.: D.C U.S. Government Printing Office, 1970).

Mainland China has long been an important bismuth producer by world standards. The bulk of the bismuth, found in association with tungsten and other nonferrous metals, was exported. In 1966, the Chinese were exploring the possibility of purchasing a titanium plant from the Japanese. They have also shown interest in titania pigment for some time. Various kinds of rare earth metals and alloys for use in the optical, metallurgical, and nuclear energy industries were produced at Chinchou, Liaoning Province, and elsewhere. In 1966–67, the China National Metals and Minerals Import and Export Corporation reportedly offered gallium and selenium of 99.99 per cent purity for export.

CEMENT AND ASBESTOS

Cement. Cement production in 1969 regained the level of 10 million tons a year that had been reached in 1966. During 1967, when a substantial drop took place, the whole cement industry was badly disrupted by the Cultural Revolution, from raw materials to production, distribution, and consumption. An important indication of development within China was that imports by Hong Kong—the main purchaser of surplus Chinese cement—declined from 910,000 metric tons in 1966 to 475,000 tons during the first eleven months of 1967.

More than half of the approximately fifty large and medium cement plants (100,000-ton to 1-million-ton annual capacity) were mentioned by name in the Chinese press during 1963–66, and it was claimed that more than a dozen modern plants (200,000 to 700,000 tons) and some 100 small plants (mostly less than 100,000 tons) had been built during that period. Some of the larger newly built plants are Tat'ung in Shansi Province, K'unming in Yünnan, Yaohsien in Shensi, Yungteng in Kansu, Chungking in Szechwan, Canton in Kwangtung, Liuchou in Kwangsi, Kueiyang in Kweichow, Mutanchiang in Kirin, and Nanp'ing in Fukien. The largest and newest cement plant is at Hantan, Hopei Province, with an annual output of about 1 million tons. At least two other plants are of similar size.

Asbestos. Production of asbestos—mainly of good grade and the long-fiber, chrysotile type—has continued to increase in China and may hit the 200,000-ton level in a few years' time. In 1967, the country produced perhaps 4 per cent of the world's asbestos and ranked fourth or fifth. The bulk of output came from Shihmien (which literally means asbestos) in Szechwan Province, where a dozen new projects were completed not long ago and where a new large, high-grade ore body was reportedly discovered. Chinese and Canadian asbestos experts have exchanged visits in recent years, and the Chinese were interested in buying Canadian beneficiation equipment for Shihmien. Most of the asbestos is domestically consumed, but some has been exported.

FERTILIZERS AND SALT

Chemical fertilizers. In 1969, the Chinese chemical fertilizer industry, badly disrupted during the Cultural Revolution, produced 8 to 10 million tons of processed fertilizers, all nitrogenous, except for 2 million tons of phosphates. In recent years, considerable emphasis has been placed on producing nonsulphur fertilizers, such as synthetic ammonia, urea, ammonium carbonate, potassium fertilizers, and ground phosphate rock. For example, a 45,000-ton synthetic ammonia plant was completed in Tsinan, Shantung Province. Ammonium carbonate plants were built in Hunan and Hopei provinces as well as the Ninghsia Hui Autonomous Region, among others. A large mixed potassium fertilizer plant was constructed in Canton, but its capacity is unknown. The Chuchou plant in Hunan Province reportedly placed a 200,000-ton 'calcium phosphate' (presumably ground phosphate rock) unit in production. The small plants built in recent years are believed to number several hundred and account for a third of the national capacity.

Imports of fertilizers in 1968–69 were between 5.5 and 6.5 million tons a year. China had contracted for roughly 5.9 million tons of nitrogenous fertilizer from Western Europe and Japan for delivery in 1967. Of that total, Nitrex AG, a Swiss firm heading a European consortium of nitrogenous fertilizer producers and exporters, contracted to deliver 3.5 million tons at about $38 per ton cif; the Japanese Ammonium Sulphate Export Association signed for delivery of 2.4 million tons at about $40 cif. Additional small imports came from the United Kingdom and Italy. The closing of the Suez Canal and the harbor confusion in coastal China resulted in an estimated actual total delivery of about 5 million tons, of which 2.6 million tons came from Europe. In addition, China imported about 750,000 metric tons of phosphate rock from Morocco in 1967. A fertilizer plant bought from Humphreys and Glasgow, Ltd., of the United Kingdom for Luchou near Chungking was reportedly completed. Fertilizer plants have also been purchased from Italy (Montecatini) and Japan, among others.

The supply position of fertilizer raw materials in 1967–68 did not show much change from 1966. Pyrite production of perhaps 1.5 million tons a year prior to 1969 came mainly from Hsiangshan in Anhwei Province and Yingte in Kwangtung. This and byproduct sulphur from nonferrous ores were used in sulphuric acid manufacture. Pyrite production in 1969 was estimated at 1.8 million tons. Additional pyrite was produced in Szechwan and Shansi provinces, but the output is not included in the above estimate, because this pyrite was converted to about 250,000 tons of elemental sulphur, a part of which was ultimately exported. Phosphate rock production totals approximately 1 million tons a year, coming mainly from Chinghsiang in Hupei Province, K'aiyang in Kweichow, and, to a lesser extent, Liuyang in Hunan and Nant'ung in Kiangsu. Mainland China imported not only phosphate rock but also some apatite from Lackay, North Vietnam.

Salt. China retained its position as the world's second largest producer of salt, after the United States. As of late 1970, no significant change in output level had been recorded for several years. Operating conditions were good for the four main producing provinces—Kiangsu, Shantung, Hopei, and Liaoning—which furnished nearly three-fourths of the country's total output. Although most salt was consumed for food purposes, industrial demand was rising. A surplus of salt traditionally has been exported, mainly to Japan; in 1967, China's total salt exports were considerably in excess of 1 million tons and constituted roughly one-tenth of production. The Chinese salt industry produced many byproducts, such as potassium chloride, bromine, boric acid, iodine, and barium chloride.

FLUORSPAR, MAGNESITE, AND OTHER NONMETALS

Fluorspar. Chinese fluorspar production in 1967 was perhaps 7 or 8 per cent of the world total. Output from Chekiang and North China remained steady, but Kwangsi Province has become a significant new source. The bulk of the fluorspar is exported. For 1966, importing countries gave the following figures, in metric tons: Japan, 97,330 (129,291 in 1967); U.S.S.R., 49,700; West Germany, 22,618; Poland, 18,509; the Netherlands, 9,968; Sweden, 5,549; and Belgium, 2,217. One firm, the Kamisho Company of Tokyo, contracted for all of Japan's fluorspar imports from China. Within China, fluorspar is consumed in the manufacture of steel, aluminium, and ceramics, and in atomic energy.

Magnesite. Southern Manchurian magnesite found in a belt extending from Tashihch'iao northeast to Lienshankuan continued to be of great world significance. Output in 1967 probably was down from the million-ton level in recent years, because of the reduced requirements of the steel industry. The Anshan steel works has pioneered in the use of magnesia-alumina refractory bricks for iron and steel smelting in China. Large amounts of magnesite and calcined magnesia have been traditionally available for export.

Barite, steatite, talc, borax, and synthetic diamonds. Barite production was down slightly, but still 2 or 3 per cent of the world total. This industry has good potential, and output can be expanded considerably above the 100,000-ton annual level to meet domestic oil-drilling needs and export demand. Japan imported 8,902 metric tons of barite in 1965; 37,680 tons in 1966; and 26,695 tons in 1967. Poland has imported 5,000 to 8,000 tons annually in recent years. Chinese steatite and talc from Taling (Tashih-ch'iao) in Liaoning Province are world-famous. Somewhere between one-third and one-half of the 1967 output was exported, with Japan, the main purchaser, taking 22,742 tons of steatite and 17,268 tons of talc. A surplus of borax continued, although no information was available on the extensive boron-bearing lake deposits in the Iksaydam area of Tsaidam, Tsinghai Province. It was reported in mid-1967 that a metallurgical plant in Tsingtao had successfully produced synthetic diamonds, presumably on an experimental basis.

COAL

Coal production in 1966 was estimated at a high of 325 million tons. The year 1967 was marked by many open clashes and rival rallies pitting the miners and technocrats against Red Guards. By mid-1967, PLA units either had been or still were stationed at most major Chinese coal-mining centers. Aside from internal production difficulties, the coal industry also faced a crippling transportation bottleneck in its effort to deliver coal to consumers and obtain equipment and supplies for operations. Inability to move coal caused shortages in many regions, which prompted Peking to organize a nationwide campaign to conserve coal.

National coal output in 1967 was down about 100 million metric tons as compared with 1966, or roughly 30 per cent. (Even so, the country still ranked third among world producers.) Steady improvements were registered, however, during 1968, and output in 1969 was estimated at 330 million tons, surpassing the 1966 high.

China has always been noted for extensive and well-distributed reserves of easily mined, high-quality coal, particularly in the North and Northeast. The maximum Communist Chinese claim for coal reserves of 9.6 trillion metric tons (100 billion tons 'verified') no doubt is greatly exaggerated according to Western standards of classification. However, China's coal reserves rank among the foremost in the world, along with those of the United States and the Soviet Union. Large coal reserves have also been uncovered in Central, South, Southwest, and Northwest China, which in the past had been considered inadequate in coal for large-scale industrial development. Most of the coal is bituminous, and seven out of about thirty large coal fields have substantial amounts of coking coal. Reserves of anthracite, although only a small part of the total coal, are also relatively large by world standards.

Fuhsin, Kailan, Huainan, Hokang, Chihsi, and Tat'ung—which normally produce a combined 100 million metric tons annually—suffered the least dislocation in the Cultural Revolution because of their proximity to authority in Peking. Even so Fuhsin, Kailan, Huainan, and Chihsi went through a brief cycle of clashes and PLA occupation. A report that Fushin output had declined 30 per cent in 1967 clearly suggests a considerable drop in production for the leading mines. The several dozen medium-size coal mines of 1 million to 9 million tons yearly capacity also suffered serious work disruption. As an extreme example, the new model P'ingtingshan Coal Mine in Honan Province went through six months of 'civil war' before the PLA stepped in. The Chiaotao Anthracite Mine nearby endured a strike in early 1967. Nevertheless, a few large and many medium mines, such as Fuhsin, Kailan, Chihsi, Shuangyashan, Pench'i, Tzupo, Tsaochuang, and Chinghsing, reported good production performance during 1967 despite political disturbances. The small mines in remote areas were the hardest hit by prolonged work stoppage and transportation tie-ups. By 1969, most of the large combines had recovered and reported good performance.

Capital construction nearly came to a standstill in 1967, with few reports of mine construction activity. Some new coal mines or shafts have since opened: an opencast mine near Chengchow, Honan Province; a modern shaft coal mine in Tat'ung, Tsinghai; a new colliery at Hsinwen, Shantung; and a new opencast mine in Fushun, Manchuria.

PETROLEUM

Crude oil production in 1969 reached 20 million tons, including 2.5 million to 3 million tons of shale oil. Before that, 1967 was a year of confusion for petroleum, although the decline in output was not as great as in other major industries. In contrast, 1966 had been a record year in output and one in which the Chinese Communists could claim self-sufficiency in supply. Political upheavals did not spare petroleum, but supreme efforts were made to restore order and normal operations. It was even claimed that the country's oil production in the first nine months of 1967 topped the corresponding period in 1966. This statement clearly can be discounted when the results from individual fields, such as Tach'ing, Shengli, Karamai, and Yümen, are examined.

Tach'ing, northwest of Harbin in Manchuria, which was discovered in 1959, remained very much in the news. In January, 1967, Premier Chou En-lai publicly denounced the 10,000 Red Guard workers who had left their jobs to attend rallies in Peking. After some work stoppage, the PLA was sent in to take control. Trouble erupted again in August when thousands of anti-Maoists engaged Maoists in open conflict. Again, the PLA moved in swiftly. With a large refinery complex and successful drilling and water-injection practices, Tach'ing had expanded its output to perhaps 5 million tons in 1966. The Institute of Petroleum Industry was transferred to Tach'ing to assist in technology. With the cessation of troubles, crude production in 1968 rose to 8 million to 9 million tons, and another increase of 37 per cent was reported in 1969.

In late May, 1967, armed clashes were reported in Sinkiang between the local military forces and Mao supporters. As a result, operations at the Karamai oil complex (oilfields and refinery at Karamai and another refinery at Tushantze) were suspended and regular oil deliveries to Lanchow were interrupted. PLA units loyal to Peking quickly quelled the armed clashes and restored oil production in Sinkiang. The uneasy truce was maintained for the rest of 1967, so that Sinkiang's oil production in 1967–68 may have kept pace with 1966. The Karamai complex reportedly registered a 160 per cent output increase over a three-year period up until 1966, when many new projects were substantially completed. Annual production of perhaps 2 million tons was achieved in 1966 by drilling new oil wells, rejuvenating abandoned wells, and improving the spacing of wells. Crude production at the complex in 1969 totaled at least 2.5 million tons.

In August, 1967, a Japanese newspaper reported that Lanchow was paralyzed by armed struggle and that oil refining was suspended for a month. The nearby Yümen oilfields, which probably produced more than 2 million tons of crude in 1966, also had 'bloody clashes.' Production in 1969, however, easily topped 2.5 million tons and may be as high as 3 million tons. Yümen has a refinery but normally ships surplus crude to Lanchow.

The general confusion in Shanghai and Szechwan during 1967 must have affected their oil-refining and gas-extraction operations, respectively. Shanghai not only has a large refinery with thermal cracking and platforming units of Chinese design but also has become an important center for producing oil-refining and drilling equipment. Szechwan has China's foremost known natural gas fields, which, however, are relatively small by world standards. The famous Fushin coal mine in Manchuria stopped the production of Coproduct shale oil at least temporarily, possibly because of the

81

competition of surplus natural crude oil from Tach'ing and Shengli, which Fuhsin might be refining. The Mouming shale oil project in Kwangtung Province is believed to be in operation, probably producing 2.5 million tons of crude oil a year.

China has started to look into offshore exploration and drilling for oil. Since South China is short of oil, offshore work may have commenced along the coast of Kwangtung and Hainan provinces. In 1967, equipment for such operations was purchased from West Europe and Rumania. Rumania in particular has been assisting China both in furnishing exploration, production, and refining equipment and in providing technical aid, offshore and onshore.

HYDROELECTRIC POWER

China's resources of water power are extensive. One estimate places the total potential at 535 million kilowatts, with two-fifths in the Yangtze basin, one-fifth in the Tibetan rivers (mainly the Brahmaputra), one-sixth in the other rivers of the Southwest, and 2 to 6 per cent each in the Yellow River Basin, the Hsi River Basin, the rivers of the Northeast (including the Yalu River bordering North Korea), the rivers of the Northwest, and the coastal rivers of the Southeast. Thus, the principal water power resources are concentrated in the Southwest (including the Yangtze basin and Tibetan rivers) and, secondarily, the central provinces, particularly the upstream Yangtze, where markets are limited and population not large.

The Yangtze basin covers 740,000 square miles, with the total length of the main river and its tributaries estimated at 40,000 miles. The annual runoff reportedly exceeds 30 billion cubic feet, and the annual mean discharge tops 1 million cubic feet per second. From the source to Ipin, where the river enters the Szechwan basin, the Yangtze drops 15,700 feet in 840 miles. From Ipin and Ich'ang, where it comes out on the lowlands, the Yangtze drops 710 feet in 630 miles; and from Ich'ang to the mouth, it drops only 130 feet in 1,120 miles.*

The Yellow River is China's second river in size. Its drainage basin covers 300,000 square miles, but the mean annual runoff is only one-twentieth that of the Yangtze. The downstream Yellow River is famous for its yellow silt, hence the name.

Any rational development of China's hydroelectric sources would also have to consider their use for navigation and irrigation. The total length of inland waterways suitable for navigation is better than 55,000 miles (compared with about 22,000 miles for the entire railroad system), one-third of which is navigable by steam and diesel vessels. More than one-third of the cultivated area (estimated at 112 million hectares in 1964) is under irrigation.

Power development has not been commensurate with resources. In 1965, the total net generation of electric power in China was estimated at only 37 billion kilowatt hours, roughly equal to the production in Alabama, Australia, or India in that year. Thermal power has been the mainstay, with hydroelectric power contributing only 8 billion kilowatts, or 21.6 per cent of the total, in 1965. Although installed hydroelectric capacity for that year was only about 3 million kilowatts (compared with 10.5 million kilowatts of thermal capacity), this compares with 200,000 kilowatts in 1952 and 1 million kilowatts in 1957.

Many hydroelectric projects were started by the Communists during the Leap Forward of 1958–60, but most were subsequently abandoned. The better-known and larger hydroelectric installations now in existence include the Hsinnanchiang plant in Chekiang Province, the Sanmenchia project on the upper Yellow River, the Tafengman and Suping plants in Manchuria, and the Tsaoyang (Chaoyang) station in the Hining area of Tsinghai Province. So far it has not been feasible to build a large

---

* A square kilometer is the equivalent of .3861 square miles; a kilometer is .62 miles; a meter is about 39.37 inches.

hydroelectric station to tame the upstream waters of the mighty Yangtze, and it may not be for years to come.[4]

SUMMARY OUTLOOK

In the 1970's, China is expected to maintain its position as one of the three leading world producers of coal, together with the United States and the Soviet Union. In some years, coal output may reach 500 million metric tons. Coal will continue to be the country's principal energy source and should support a sizable thermoelectric power industry. The oil industry may well blossom into a medium-size one, possibly on a par with that of Indonesia. Still in short supply, oil will be significant militarily, indispensable to passenger and short-haul traffic, and secondary to coal for power and energy. Hydroelectric power development will be accelerated, and installed capacity may expand several times over. Atomic energy will also begin to come into its own.

Some time in the 1970's, yearly steel output is expected to reach 20 to 40 million metric tons, somewhat less than half that of Japan and ranking about sixth or seventh in the world. The industry will be capable of making many kinds of steel products but will still be considerably weaker in rolling and fabrication than the more industrialized countries. As for steel-making minerals, tungsten, molybdenum, and manganese will continue to loom large by world standards, and there will be large surpluses for export.

China's major nonferrous metals and light metals industries are expected to expand to beyond 200,000 metric tons annually each for copper, lead, zinc, and aluminum— medium rank by world standards. A few large porphyry copper deposits might be developed, along with smelters, and new aluminum-reduction plants will be built. Meanwhile, there will be a serious shortage of nonferrous metals during the mid-1970's. Export metals like tin, antimony, mercury, and bismuth will continue to be significant in world markets. The country will be able to make most of the high-purity metals it needs.

The cement industry probably will top the 20-million-ton annual output level at some time in the 1970's. Raw materials are no problem, and cement plants will be built according to markets and financial capability. Fertilizer production will rise markedly. Based mainly upon very extensive magnesite resources, refractories will be produced according to demand. There will still be large surpluses of fluorspar and talc. China will always be one of the world's largest salt producers. In line with the rise in industrial demand, the outputs of asbestos and barite are expected to increase greatly.

China's mineral industry will be built up to a new plateau at 50 to 100 per cent greater than the maximum in recent years. This will be accompanied by more diversity and sophistication. Achievements will be notable by developing-country standards, but the lag behind the industrialized countries will not necessarily be reduced. While China's economic influence is expected to rise, there is no evidence that it will break into the inner circle of the world's great industrial powers during the next decade.

SELECTED BIBLIOGRAPHY

'China,' *Far Eastern Economic Review 1970 Yearbook* (Hong Kong: Far Eastern Economic Review, 1970), pp. 97–116. Very good evaluation of the economy as a whole for year in question. Contains good mineral industry and related sections.

The Chinese Coal Industry, July, 1961–March, 1962; Part I, pp. 1–159; Part II, pp. 1–18; Part III, pp. 1–42; Part IV, pp. 1–49; Part V, pp. 1–39; and Part VI, pp. 1–39. Warrington,

---

[4] For additional details on hydroelectric power, see John Ashton, 'Development of Electric Energy Resources in Communist China,' *An Economic Profile of Mainland China*, for the Joint Economic Committee, Congress of the United States (Washington, D.C.: U.S. Government Printing Office, February, 1967), pp. 297–316.

United Kingdom: Joseph Crosfield & Sons, Ltd. Best comprehensive report of Chinese coal industry, in English. Much detail on technical aspects of individual mines.

Chugoku Tairiku no Sekiyu Shigen (Petroleum Resources in Mainland China). Tokyo: Ajia Keizai Kenkyujo, November, 1961. Fairly up-to-date review of principal oilfields and their capabilities.

'Coal and Steel,' *London Mining Journal* (London: Mining Journal Ltd., April 12, 1968), p. 283. Briefly describes some current developments in coal and steel.

Japan Metal Bulletin. Osaka: Sangyo Press, 1965–71. Occasional reports on mainland China, particularly trade in minerals, metals, and equipment with Japan.

London Mining Journal. Annual Review. London: Mining Journal Ltd., 1965–71. Not too detailed but timely annual reviews of the Mineral Industry of Mainland China.

'Mainland China,' *World Mining*, 4, No. 3 (San Francisco: Marshall W. Freeman Publications, March, 1968): 29–33. Based upon recently uncovered report written in early 1960's entitled 'Conspectus of Chinese Industries and Trade' (in Chinese). Article in English mentions many specific deposits, mines, and plants and describes general status of mineral exploration and development.

'Mineral Industry of Mainland China,' *Minerals Yearbook, 1963–65 and 1967–70.* Vol. IV. Washington, D.C.: U.S. Government Printing Office. Reviews on a yearly basis mineral economy of China, with data on developments, production, trade, and individual mineral industries.

'Red China's Steel Plant Growing,' in *American Metal Market* (New York: American Metal Market Company, March 4, 1968), pp. 8, 23. Japanese visitors' report of summer, 1967. China's total steel output clearly exaggerated, but data on leading steel works seem good.

Tekkō Handobukku—Chūkyō (Iron and Steel Handbook—Communist China). Tokyo: Tekko Kaigai Shijo Chosa Iinkai, November 1966. Detailed analysis of steel industry and raw materials, including mines and plants. Also has good information on major coal mines, oilfields, and trade in general.

WANG, K. P. 'The Mineral Resource Base of Communist China,' *An Economic Profile of Mainland China.* Washington, D.C.: U.S. Government Printing Office, February, 1967, pp. 167–95. Comprehensive, up-to-date review of subject, with general analysis of factors affecting development, management and policy problems, and summary outlook. Does not cover Cultural Revolution.

———. 'A Review of Mining and Metallurgy,' *Sciences in Communist China*, Publication No. 68. Washington, D.C.: American Association for the Advancement of Science, 1961, pp. 687–738. Review of Chinese mineral technology up until 1960.

———. 'Rich Mineral Resources Spur Communist China's Bid for Industrial Power,' *Mineral Trade Notes*, Special Supplement No. 59. Washington, D.C.: U.S. Government Printing Office, March, 1960, pp. 1–35. Review of mineral situation in the late 1950's, based upon Chinese technical publications released in those years (no such publications have been available in the 1960's).

WU, Y. L. *Economic Development and Use of Energy Resources in Communist China.* New York: Frederick A. Praeger, Inc., 1963. A good comparative evaluation of various energy sources.

5

OFFICIAL POPULATION DATA*

JOHN S. AIRD

POPULATION is a basic dimension of human society. In any country, the size of the population is a gross measure of the human assets and liabilities, an indicator of the scale of actual or potential human activity within its borders. If the characteristics and distribution of the population are also known, the measure of the human resources and human burdens can be taken more accurately. If these indicators can be followed over time and correlated with measures of other important social, political, and economic factors, much more can be learned about fundamental human relationships. Such knowledge may make it possible to plan the evolution of society toward fulfillment of specific national goals.

No accurate measure has ever been taken of the demographic dimensions of mainland China. The traditional official population records of pre-Communist times were kept primarily for such purposes as taxation, labor levies, and military conscription, which made them unreliable as sources of population data. Some of the special demographic investigations conducted by social scientists in the decades immediately preceding the Communist victory are entitled to more serious consideration, but most of them are limited in scope and coverage. During the First Five-Year Plan period, 1953–57, the Chinese Communists made what must be regarded as the first serious attempt in China's history to build a system of demographic accounting, but the cornerstone of that effort, the census of June 30, 1953, was not wholly successful, and the population registers founded on the census records seem to have crumbled away since and to have no immediate prospect of reconstruction.

The Chinese Communist attitude toward statistics in general and population statistics in particular has always been ambivalent. In the abstract, the Party leaders have subscribed to the Leninist dictum that statistics are essential to socialism. Socialist society was to be a planned society, and planning presupposed statistical measurements to identify society's problems and to gauge the effectiveness of the policies devised for their solution. Especially during the Great Leap Forward period (1958–60), statistics were said to be 'the Party's eyes and ears,' which meant they were to serve the Party as a form of domestic intelligence.[1] But in actual practice statistical

---

* The opinions expressed in this chapter are those of the writer and do not necessarily coincide with the official views of the United States Government.

[1] 'Wei Cheng-chih Tou-cheng Fu-wu, wei Sheng-ch'an Tou-cheng Fu-wu, tsai Ke-chi Tang-wei Ling-tao hsia, Kuan-ch'e Chih-hsing Ch'ün-chung lu-hsien, K'u-chan San-ke yüeh Shih-hsien Ch'üan-kuo T'ung-chi Kung-tso Ta-yao-chin (Fight Hard for Three Months to Achieve a Great Leap Forward in Statistical Work in the Whole Country Under the Leadership of the Party Committee and Thoroughly Carry Out the Mass Line to Serve the Political Struggle and the Production Struggle),' *T'ung-chi Yen-chiu (Statistical Research,)*

data were more often used to prove the success of Party policies than to test their validity. Mao and his colleagues on the Party Central Committee believed that Marxism was 'scientific,' which meant 'true,' and that, having mastered this truth, they were capable of deriving from it policies that were 'correct' for any given stage of China's national development. Their commitment to statistics was based in part on the expectation that statistics would confirm their own insights. When statistics and politics seemed to disagree, as was increasingly the case toward the close of the First Five-Year Plan period, there was no question on which side the need for adjustment lay.

In a truly planned society, statistical objectivity could not have been sacrificed to political convenience without serious functional consequences. But, in China, planning never went much beyond defining long-range goals and setting short-range production targets. As long as planning was either nonquantitative or uncoordinated, it did not need and could not effectively utilize the elaborate products of a modern statistical system. Population data were often used by local civil authorities to determine food and cloth allocations, but they were not of much use in planning such public services as education, housing, and medical care, which were never available in sufficient quantity to pose delicate problems of coordination. Nevertheless, the leadership of the People's Republic of China (P.R.C.) invested considerable effort over the years in various kinds of population investigation. Their investigations testify amply to the seriousness of their interest in population data.

PRINCIPAL SOURCES OF POPULATION DATA

Analysis of the methods used in investigations of the Chinese population undertaken between 1949 and 1964 is hampered, as are many other analyses of the mainland China scene, by lack of reliable information. What can be asserted about these investigations consists mainly of inferences based on extrapolations and generalizations from fragments of evidence that are frequently ambiguous and sometimes contradictory. The evidence includes central directives, supplementary instructions, progress reports, results of special inquiries, complaints, commentaries, and communications of various kinds published in newspapers and journals. Though the items on some investigations constitute a fairly thick file, and though some items are remarkably candid and revealing, they do not give a clear picture of the quantity and quality of statistical work done in the basic units where the actual data-collecting took place. There are instances of conscientious work showing individual initiative and ingenuity and instances of perfunctory work, gross negligence, and fraud, but it is seldom possible to determine with any assurance which was the exception and which was the rule. At no point in the history of Chinese Communist population investigations was the administrative system able to secure absolute conformity to central directives. Nor would conformity have solved all the problems, for the central directives left many important procedural matters to the discretion of local authorities who were not competent to find acceptable solutions. All of the investigations were attended by varying but significant degrees of confusion. None went according to plan.

Urban police registers. Soon after they entered Peking, the Chinese Communists began to devise new procedures for the registration of the urban population. In the fall of 1949, the Republic of China registration regulations were annulled. The old registration forms were declared void, the new household books were placed on sale in Peking. Residents were required to purchase the books, which were then filled out by

---

No. 7, Peking, July 23, 1958, p. 1; and Lai Ping-jang, 'Statistical Work Is the Party's Eyes and Ears,' *Kan-su Jih-pao (Kansu Daily)*, Lanchow, December 22, 1959, translated in *Survey of China Mainland Press*, No. 2231, U.S. Consulate General, Hong Kong; April 5, 1960, pp. 26–27.

police registration cadres on a door-to-door basis.[2] By the spring of 1950, the new system had been instituted in Shanghai,[3] and by the end of the year it was being installed in Canton and Chungking and probably in most other large cities.[4] Standard regulations for urban registration throughout the country were promulgated by the Government Administrative Council in July, 1951. The municipal public security bureaus were instructed to modify their own regulations accordingly.[5] In the fall of 1951, the Kwangtung Provincial Government ordered cities and towns throughout the province to establish registration systems.[6] Similar orders may have been issued in other provinces.

The urban registers were not very successful, either for statistical or for administrative purposes. The initial investigations caught many people who had been able to avoid being listed in previous population records, but there were apparently many others who continued to evade the registers. They had their reasons. The population registers were established primarily for purposes of population control and political surveillance. The household registration books were used as the basis for identity cards, residence certificates, and migration permits, for controlling access to education and employment, and for food and cloth rationing. If the entire system had been under strict management, the population might have been compelled in time to comply with registration regulations in order to claim essential goods and services. But strict management was apparently an administrative impossibility, as is evident from the presence of unauthorized migrants in cities and reports of inflated ration claims and sale of ration coupons, and the problem of noncompliance with registration regulations increased when it became known that the registers were being used to probe political backgrounds, to investigate property holdings, and to compile dossiers of complaints and allegations by local Party cadres, street committees, and 'activists' against particular households and individuals. Even those heads of household inclined to observe the regulations found that the registration cadres in the public security dispatch stations were so incompetent, negligent, arrogant, and officious as to dis-

---

[2] 'Pei-ching-shih Jen-min Cheng-fu Pu-kao (Public Notice of the Peking Municipal People's Government),' *Jen-min Jih-pao (People's Daily)*, Peking, November 17, 1949; 'Yung-hu Hsin-te Hu-k'ou Chih-tu (Support the New Household Registration System,' *Jen-min Jih-pao*, December 4, 1949 (editorial); 'Ching-shih hsin Hu-k'ou Kuei-t'se Shunli T'ui-hsing Shih-min Tzu-tung Ch'üeh-shih Sheng-pao Lou-pao Hsü-pao te Fen-fen Sheng-ch'ing Keng-cheng (New Household Regulations Carried out Smoothly in Peking Municipality; People of the Municipality Report the Truth Voluntarily; Numerous Requests for Correction of Under-reporting and False Reporting),' *Jen-min Jih-pao*, December 4, 1949; 'Ching-chien hsin Hu-k'ou Kung-tso Wan-ch'eng (Establishing of New Household Registration Work Completed in Peking),' *Jen-min Jih-pao*, February 4, 1950; K'o Fu, 'Chien-li ch'i Jen-min te Hu-k'ou Chih-tu (Establish a People's Household Registration System),' *Jen-min Jih-pao*, February 4, 1950.

[3] 'Major Events in Shanghai, 1949–1951,' *Shanghai News*, Shanghai, May 28, 1951, in *Current Background*, No. 78, U.S. Consulate General, Hong Kong, June 4, 1951, p. 2.

[4] 'Kuang-chou Chü-pan Ch'üan-shih Hu-k'ou Teng-chi (Canton Carries Out Household Registration Throughout the Municipality),' *Ta-kung pao (Ta-kung Daily)*, Hong Kong, December 14, 1950; 'Canton Completes Census Taking,' *Nan-fang Jih-pao (Southern Daily)*, Canton, January 16, 1951; translated in *Survey of China Mainland Press*, No. 49, January 16, 1951, p. 14; 'Ch'ung-ch'ing-shih Jen-min Cheng-fu Pu-kao (Public Notice of the Chungking Municipal People's Government),' *Hsin-hua Jih-pao (New China Daily)*, Chungking, July 9, 1953.

[5] 'Ministry of Public Security Promulgates Regulations Governing Urban Population,' NCNA, July 16, 1951; translated in *Survey of China Mainland Press*, No. 137, July 18, 1951, pp. 7–9.

[6] 'Ch'üan-sheng Hsien Shih Hsiang-ts'un Hsü-chen Jen-k'ou I-tung hsü ching Ho-chun (Population Movements in *Hsien* Cities and Rural Market Towns Throughout the Province Must Be Approved),' *Hsing-tao Jih-pao (Hsing-tao Daily)*, Hong Kong, November 2, 1951.

courage the reporting of household changes. From 1952 onward, the registers were also used in repeated and rather unsuccessful efforts to prevent unwanted migrants from moving from the rural areas to the cities. The manifold anxieties and frustrations caused by these policies led the population to resort once again, as in the past, to evasions, falsification of documents, the sale and lending of household books and residence permits, and general obfuscation.

Since the currency of registration records depended upon the voluntary reporting of household changes by the very people the records were used to control, there was not much real possibility of keeping them up to date. The public security police soon found them so inaccurate as to be of little use for surveillance.[7] Supplementary field checks had to be ordered in all the major cities every few years to incorporate unreported changes. The 1953 census directives included a provision that extra census forms be made out in urban areas where the registration 'is not yet well implemented' to be sent to the public security dispatch stations, presumably to correct defective registration records.[8] But in the years that followed, the accumulation of defects continued, particularly during the expulsion of unwanted urban residents in 1955, the Greap Leap Forward population displacements of 1958–59, and the panic migrations of the food crisis years, 1960–61.

The 'land reform' population investigations. While the urban registers were being established in the early 1950's, the local 'land reform' committees were conducting rural population investigations as part of a general survey of the land, property holdings, and 'class status' of peasant households in preparation for the confiscation and redistribution of land, grain stocks, livestock, housing, farm implements, and other property. These investigations were to be conducted in accordance with the general provisions of the Land Reform Law of 1950, which in turn were based on experience with 'land reform' in the territories under Communist control prior to 1949. However, the 1950 Law did not give detailed instructions as to how stock-taking in rural areas was to be carried out.[9] Proper execution of the provisions of the Law would have required a very thorough and highly sophisticated statistical operation. The thoroughness of what was actually attempted is apparent in the press accounts of the setting up of organizations, planning, 'keypoint' experimentation, cadre training, propaganda, checking, and supervision, all of which were already standard features of mass programs in the P.R.C. But a high level of sophistication in the design and management of statistical operations was simply not possible—the necessary expertise was lacking at both local and national levels.

Because of persistent administrative problems, the 'land reform' effort seems to have been marked by confusion from the beginning. Though officials of the Party's Rural

---

[7] For example, see the complaints about surveillance problems caused by faulty population records in 'Ti-shih Chan-k'ai Hu-k'ou P'u-ch'a Teng-chi Kung-tso (Urumchi Municipality Starts Household Investigation and Registration Work),' *Hsin-chiang Jih-pao (Sinkiang Daily)*, Urumchi, January 10, 1953; 'Wu-lu-mu-ch'i-shih Tung-fang Chih-an Kung-tso P'u-p'ien Chan-k'ai (Winter Public Security Work Carried Out Throughout Urumchi Municipality),' *Hsin-chiang Jih-pao*, December 22, 1954; 'T'an T'an Hu-k'ou Wen-t'i (Let's Talk about the Problem of Household Registration),' *Hsin-wan Jih-pao (Hsin-wan Daily)*, Shanghai, June 5, 1955; and 'Kuang-chou-shih Chieh-ho Cheng-tun Liang-shih T'ung-hsiao K'ai-chan Ho-tui Hu-k'ou Kung-tso (Canton Municipality Carries Out Household Registration Work in Conjunction with the Reorganization of State Food Grain Sales),' *Nan-fang Jih-pao*, July 14, 1955.

[8] 'Measures for National Census and Registration of Population,' NCNA, Peking, April 6, 1953; translated in *Current Background*, No. 241, May 5, 1953, p. 35.

[9] *The Agrarian Reform Law of the People's Republic of China*, 2nd ed., Peking: Foreign Languages Press, 1951, pp. 1–16. In supplementary decisions given in the same volume, a great deal of attention is paid to the question of how to determine 'class status.' There are no suggestions on carrying out statistical investigations.

Work Department and the Central Committee sometimes described the progress of 'land reform' in glowing terms in their summary reports, the specific communications of local, provincial, and regional 'land reform' committees with the central authorities cited situation after situation in which excessive zeal, gross negligence, incompetence, or corruption had led to violations of instructions that jeopardized the aims of 'land reform.' There were repeated purges of lower-level cadres and a major purge of cadres at intermediate levels, whose malefactions, reported in the press with detailed statistical breakdown by various subcategories, are enough to cast doubt on other statistics produced during the campaign.

There is also direct evidence that the statistical work was done badly and that not all of its shortcomings were the fault of the cadres alone. In many places, the work seems to have been done in public meetings in which the peasants, led by the 'land reform' cadres and prodded from behind by 'activist' elements with whom the cadres had been able to 'strike roots,' reported on their own land and property holdings as well as those of the wealthy peasants and landlords. The reports were then posted and subjected to general criticism until everyone was 'satisfied' that the data were correct. Each peasant was thus in a position to check his neighbor's report to make sure that there was no cheating,[10] but such a system could not guarantee accurate land records. In some areas, the investigation of landholdings consisted simply in revising 'preliberation' land records, since it was found in practice that this yielded more accurate results than could be obtained by conducting a completely new survey with inexperienced personnel.[11] Whether similar use was made of old population records is not indicated in available sources, but in a rural community, of course, the details of population are more subject to change than the amount of arable land.

Ministry of Public Health vital registration experiments. While the urban registers and the rural population records were being set up, the Ministry of Public Health was trying out a system of vital registration in an increasing number of experimental reporting units in various parts of the country. Unlike the other two efforts, this one seems to have been intended primarily to provide statistical data, though it is possible that the Ministry also hoped its investigations would establish its claim to administrative dominion over an eventual nationwide system of vital statistics reporting. The first reporting areas were apparently selected during or soon after 1950. By the beginning of 1952, there were 33 reporting units in the system, representing a population of 7.5 million. By the beginning of 1953, there were 77 units, distributed among 28 provinces and provincial level municipalities; of the 77 units, 58 were urban, including 9 within Peking itself.[12]

---

[10] For example, see Jao Shu-shih, 'Hua-tung T'u-ti Kai-ke Tien-hsing Shih-yen Ching-yen Tsung-Chia (Summation of Experiences in Model Land Reform Experiments in East China),' *Ta-kung pao*, December 21, 1950; Hou K'ang and Chang Ch'ing-yün, 'Wo-men shih Ju-ho Fen-p'ei Tou-cheng Ko-shih te (How We Distributed the Fruits of Struggle),' *Hsin-chiang Jih-pao*, December 15, 1951; Ch'en Hua, 'T'u-lu-fan Erh-ch'ü I-hsiang San-hsing-cheng-ts'un Fen-p'ei Ko-shih Kung-tso te Chü-t'i Tso-fa (Concrete Measures for Carrying Out Distribution Work in the Third Administrative Village of the First *Hsiang*, Second District, of T'u-lu-fan),' *Hsin-chiang Jih-pao*, January 15, 1952; 'Sui-yüan-sheng Nung-min Hsieh-hui Kuan-yü Mu-ch'ien T'u-ti Kai-ke Yün-tung te Chih-shih (Directive of the Peasants' Association of Suiyüan Province Concerning the Land Reform Movement at Present),' *Sui-yüan Jih-pao (Suiyüan Daily)*, Huhehot, January 23, 1952; and 'Chung-shan Kuan-t'ang-hsiang Fen-p'ei T'u-ti Pan-fa (The Method of Land Distribution in Kuan-t'ang *Hsiang* in Chung-shan),' *Nan-fang Jih-pao*, April 11, 1952.

[11] I Chih, 'Tsen-yang Chin-hsing hsinch'ü T'u-ti Tiao-ch'a Kung-tso (How to Carry Out Land Investigation Work in the New Areas),' *Jen-min Jih-pao*, November 17, 1950.

[12] State Statistical Bureau, 'Chung-hua Jen-min Kung-ho-kuo Kuo-chia T'ung-chi-chü Kuan-yü T'ing-pan Sheng-ming T'ung-chi Shih-pan Kung-tso te I-chien (Opinion of the State Statistical Bureau of the People's Republic of China Concerning the Termination of

At that time, the Ministry of Public Health planned to 'improve' its vital registration work.[13] It drafted tentative regulations to govern the reporting of births and deaths in urban areas and sent them to the Government Administrative Council for approval. In August, 1953, it produced a similar set of regulations for rural vital registration, which were sent to the State Statistical Bureau. But the bureau's response was not favorable. It advised the ministry to 'examine' its vital registration work. As a result of the 'examination,' by October, 1953, the number of urban units was cut back from fifty-eight to fifty-five, and the number of rural units from nineteen to fourteen. The bureau also contended there was duplication between the ministry's vital records and the records kept in the public security dispatch stations,[14] and that reporting to both agencies caused considerable public inconvenience. Investigation of causes of death by the public health authorities sometimes delayed issuance of death certificates needed for burial permits, with consequences that could be distressing, especially during warm weather. After more than a year of study, the bureau ordered the ministry to stop its work on vital registration in November, 1954. The reason given for the decision was not only the duplication of records but also the ruling that compilation of vital statistics under health auspices was implicitly 'bourgeois' and Malthusian, in that it treated vital events as biological phenomena rather than as indicators of the development of production and the improvement of living conditions. The discontinuation of experimental vital registration was thus said to be a blow to 'reactionaries' in China.[15]

The 1953 census. The decision to take a national census was apparently reached some time in 1952. By that time the Chinese Communists had succeeded in establishing political control over most of the mainland and had restored agriculture and industry to something like prewar normalcy. They were ready to install the political and economic institutions by means of which they hoped to transform Chinese society. In the political sphere, they drafted a national constitution to be submitted for approval to a National People's Congress consisting of delegates chosen by local people's congresses, to be convened during 1953, following general elections. In preparation for the general elections, voters were to be registered in conjunction with the country's first national census. The census was to provide data needed for economic planning during the forthcoming First Five-Year Plan period and to answer once and for all the hitherto unanswerable questions regarding the true magnitude of China's population.

Planning for the census seems to have gotten under way during the latter half of 1952. But by April, 1953, when the census directives were issued, it was already apparent that the complex arrangements and procedures would require far more time than had originally been allotted. Local units were to set up their own committees, conduct 'keypoint' experimental investigations, review the results, modify the

---

Vital Statistics Experimental Work),' November, 1954, in State Statistical Bureau, *T'ung-chi Kung-tso Chung-yao Wen-chien Hui-pien (A Compilation of Important Documents on Statistical Work)*, Vol. 1 (Peking: T'ung-chi Ch'u-pan-she, 1955): 592. At that time the three municipalities of Peking, Tientsin, and Shanghai were directly under the central government, hence administratively equal to provinces. In 1958, Tientsin was placed under Hopei Province.

[13] State Statistical Bureau, 'I-chiu-wu-san-nien Ch'üan-kuo T'ung-chi Kung-tso Kang-yao (Tasks for Statistical Work Throughout the Country in 1953),' February 23, 1953; in State Statistical Bureau, *T'ung-chi Kung-tso Chung-yao Wen-chien Hui-pien*, 1: 39.

[14] State Statistical Bureau, *T'ung-chi Kung-tso Chung-yao Wen-chien Hui-pien*, 1: 593–94.

[15] Ku Wei-lin, 'Wo tui T'ing-pan Sheng-ming T'ung-chi Shih-pan Kung-tso te Jen-shih (My Understanding of the Suspension of Vital Statistics Experimental Work),' *T'ung-chi Kung-tso T'ung-hsin (Statistical Work Bulletin)*, No. 1 (Peking: Chi hua T'ung-chi Tsa-chih-she. January 23, 1955), pp. 36–37.

directives and procedures in line with these experiences, train large numbers of census cadres, carry out the full-scale census work, conduct post-enumeration 'rechecks,' tally the results, and forward them to the next higher level. The critical census date had been set for midnight on June 30, 1953, but it was obvious that most of the census field work would have to take place after that date. When complaints were received that preliminary census work was interfering with spring planting and other agricultural tasks of the highest priority, it was decided early in the summer of 1953 to postpone the major census effort until after the fall harvest.

The original timetable had called for completion of field work by September 30 and submission of results to the central census office by November 15, but not even the municipalities were able to hold to that schedule. Peking reportedly had started its basic-level election work by the latter part of October,[16] but it was still in the initial stages at the beginning of December.[17] Shanghai held its census near the end of November.[18] Canton was still struggling to get its census work under way in the latter part of January, 1954.[19] Counting the rural population was further delayed by winter plowing and spring planting in some areas. More than 70 per cent of the enumerating throughout the country took place after the end of December, 1953,[20] and it was not completed in the last of the provinces until May, 1954.[21]

The protracted period of field work further complicated an already difficult task. The greater the lapse of time between the critical date and the date of actual enumeration, the greater the problems of making the census records conform to the demographic situation as it had been on June 30. By the spring of 1954, some of the people who had been living in a particular locality the previous June had died or moved away. The correct particulars as of June 30, 1953, were supposed to be supplied by surviving relatives or neighbors, a somewhat impractical idea. Persons who had moved into the locality after the census date were not to be listed on the census forms, though they were supposed to be included in the voter registration. This seems to have caused further confusion, because some cadres thought voter lists were to be based only on census records. Persons born after the census date and persons who had permanent residence in some other place were not to be included in the count. It was assumed that persons absent from their permanent places of residence would be reported by someone in their home community, but there were no provisions for listing them on transient forms to be sent to the home community as a check. The city of Fuhsin developed such a system, but it seems to have applied only to permanent Fuhsin residents having temporary residence in another part of the same city at the

---

[16] 'Chi-ts'eng Hsüan-chü Tien-hsing Shih-pan Chieh-shu Ch'üan-kuo P'u-hsüan Wen-pu Chan-k'ai (Experimental Election at the Basic Level is Completed: General Election Throughout the Country Unfolds with Firm Step),' Wen-hui Pao (Wenhui Daily), Hong Kong, October 25, 1953.

[17] 'Election Campaign in Peking's Municipal Districts,' NCNA, December 13, 1953; translated in Survey of China Mainland Press, No. 710, December 17, 1953, pp. 24–25.

[18] 'Population Census and Registration of Voters Started in Shanghai,' NCNA, November 28, 1953; translated in Survey of China Mainland Press, No. 699, December 2, 1953, p. 26.

[19] 'Pen-shih Pei-ch'ü Ching-kuo P'u-hsüan Hsüan-ch'uan hou Ch'üan-mien Chan-k'ai Jen-k'ou Tiao-ch'a Hsüan-min Teng-chi Kung-tao (Population Investigation and Registration of Voters Carried Out Throughout the North District of Our City After Election Propaganda),' Kuang-chou Jih-pao (Canton Daily), Canton, January 23, 1954.

[20] 'Chung-yang Hsüan-chü Wei-yüan-hui Pan-kung-shih teng Fa-ch'u Lien-ho T'ung-chih Yao-ch'iu Ke-t'i Tso-hao Jen-k'ou Tiao-ch'a Teng-chi Kung-tso (The Office of Central Election Committee and Other [Offices] Issue Joint Directive Requesting All Areas to Do Population Investigation and Registration Work Well),' NCNA, March 10, 1954; most complete version available in Takung-Pao, Tientsin, March 11, 1954.

[21] 'Basic-Level Elections Completed in Kwangtung,' Wen-hui Pao (Hong Kong), June 4, 1954; translated in Survey of China Mainland Press, No. 822, June 4, 1954, p. 31.

time of census-taking,[22] and there is no evidence that such a method was ever adopted on a national scale or that it was imitated in any other municipality. Probably quite a few migrants in transit and temporary residents absent for some time from their supposedly permanent places of abode were omitted from the count. Since the preponderance of migrants went from rural to urban areas, and since most urban areas were reached by the census registrars long before the counting began in rural areas, a high proportion of the persons who moved during the period from May, 1953, to May, 1954, would have been migrants from areas not yet enumerated to areas in which census work had been concluded. No adequate measures were devised to close this loophole.

Perhaps the most serious deficiency of the census as originally planned was the failure to make any arrangements for a map survey of residences and households to make sure that those families living in out-of-the-way places were not inadvertently omitted. Evidently the census planners had little conception of the magnitude of that problem. If they were aware of the attention paid to it in countries with more census experience, they must have supposed that their own administrative system gave them sufficient control over their people to make special provisions unnecessary.

In general, the Chinese census planners seem to have thought that completeness and accuracy in census work were matters not so much of methods as of motivation. The original census proclamation issued by the Government Administrative Council over Chou En-lai's signature called upon all census personnel to do a good job and 'maintain the principle' of completeness, accuracy, no double-counting, and no omissions.[23] The inadequacy of this approach might have been discovered in good time if the census methodology had been thoroughly pretested in experimental areas before the original census directives were issued. But instead, census planning seems to have been done in committee without benefit of field experience. Polite attention was paid to Soviet advisers, but there is little to indicate whether or not their advice was followed. Chinese scholars with knowledge of foreign census techniques were not consulted. Though the census directives called for experimentation at local levels, there was no provision for altering the over-all census methods on the basis of local experience. The few supplementary directives sent out from the central census office during the year of field work consisted mainly of supplementary explanations of the original directives and optional suggestions for minor changes in procedures. Whatever was wrong with the census plan as initially conceived remained unchanged to the end.

When the final results were released, the census was hailed by census official Pai Chien-hua as the most accurate count ever taken of China's population. A postenumeration check covering nearly 53 million people, 9 per cent of the reported total population of 583 million, was said to have revealed that the rate of omissions was only 0.255 per cent and of double-counting only 0.139 per cent, for a net undercount of 0.116 per cent.[24]

Taken at face value, the claim meant that China's census was the most accurate ever taken in a major country. The claim was not believable. But whether or not Pai and his professional colleagues believed it, other—presumably influential—persons in the Chinese hierarchy must have thought it reasonable, or they would not have risked the prestige of the regime by publicizing it. Their credulity only tended to increase the

[22] 'Measures for Census Report and Registration of Non-Residential Persons Enforced in Fushun,' NCNA, July 6, 1953; translated in Survey of China Mainland Press, No. 605, July 8, 1953, p. 25.

[23] 'Directive on National Census and Registration,' NCNA, April 6, 1953; translated in Current Background, No. 241, May 5, 1953, p. 30.

[24] Pai Chien-hua, '600 Million People—a Great Strength for Socialist Construction of China,' Jen-min Jih-pao, November 1, 1954; translated in Survey of China Mainland Press, No. 926, November 11–12, 1954, p. 33.

skepticism of foreign statisticians, some of whom doubted whether a field enumeration had taken place. There were also some skeptics within the P.R.C., whose doubts became public during the Hundred Flowers period from late 1956 through the spring of 1957.[25] Stung by criticism of the census, spokesmen for the regime became violently defensive and denied all the charges,[26] but, so far as is known, the detailed results of the census were never made generally available. If they contained internal evidence that might have contradicted the accuracy claim, the evidence was kept from the critics.[27]

However, there is enough evidence in the news items describing the checking done in various localities during the 'experimental' period to show that the level of accuracy was far below what the check indicated and that in most cases the methods used to check accuracy constituted no check at all. Article 14 of the original census directive says that, 'to avoid omissions, duplications, and mistakes,' the local census offices 'may, during or on completion of the registration, make selective checks or rechecks to discover mistakes and to correct them immediately.'[28] From this it would appear that making accuracy checks was optional and that timing and methods were left to the discretion of local census committees.

In some areas the checking seems to have been fairly conscientious, but for the most part it was superficial. In three villages in Kirin Province, census records were compared with old household records, residence group chiefs were interviewed, and some household interviews were conducted. What the interviews consisted of was not revealed, but it was reported that comparison with census records showed that the old records had omitted 9.5 per cent of the households and 27.7 per cent of the population.[29] Whether or not the household books listed persons the census omitted was not indicated, but it is obvious that a highly defective record system would not constitute much of a check on the census, particularly if both tended to omit the same kinds of

---

[25] Tai Shih-kuang, *1953 Population Census of China* (Calcutta: Indian Statistical Institute, December 20, 1956), pp. 8–12, 15–18; Ch'en Ta, *New China's Population Census of 1953 and Its Relations to National Reconstruction and Demographic Research* (Stockholm: International Statistical Institute, August 8–15, 1957), pp. 7–9; 'Wei-le Pang-chu Kuo-chia T'ung-chi-chü Cheng-feng Hsüeh Mu-ch'iao Chü-chang Yao-ch'ing Ching Chin Pu-fen Ching-chi-hsüeh T'ung-chi-hsüeh Chiao-shou Chü-hsing Tso-t'an-hui (Director of the State Statistical Bureau Hsüeh Mu-ch'iao Invites University Professors of Economics and Statistics in Peking and Tientsin to Symposium to Help in Rectification of the State Statistical Bureau),' *T'ung-chi Kung-tso (Statistical Work)*, No. 12 (Peking: Chi-hua T'ung chi Tsa-chih-she, June 29, 1957), pp. 1–2.

[26] Pi Shih-lin, 'Wo-kuo 1953-nien te Jen-k'ou Tiao-ch'a shih K'o-hsüeh-te (Our Country's 1953 Population Census Is Scientific),' *T'ung-chi Kung-tso*, No. 24, December 29, 1957, pp. 15–18; and Li Ch'in-k'o, 'Wo-kuo 1953-nien Jen-k'ou P'u-ch'a te Wei-ta Ch'eng-chiu Pu-yung Mo-sha (The Great Achievements of Our Country's 1953 Population Census Are Not to Be Obscured),' *T'ung-chi Yen-chiu (Statistical Research)*, No. 3 (Peking: T'ung-chi Ch'u-pan-she, March 23, 1958), pp. 3–4.

[27] The State Statistical Bureau apparently prepared a report giving 1953 census data on age, sex, and ethnic status for the whole country and population totals by province and *hsien*. The book, entitled *Chung-hua Jen-min Kung-ho-kuo 1953-nien Jen-k'ou Tiao-ch'a Tzu-liao (Results of the 1953 Population Census of the People's Republic of China)*, was advertised for sale in several statistical journals in China in 1958. The advertisement in *T'ung-chi Yen-chiu* listed the contents of the volume and indicated the price, which would imply that it had reached the final stages of preparation and perhaps had been printed. However, no copy of this volume has ever turned up outside of China, and no citation to it has been found in any Chinese article or monograph.

[28] *Current Background*, No. 241, p. 35.

[29] Office of the Kirin Provincial Election Committee, 'Chu-lin-sheng Yü-shu-hsien Yung-fu teng ts'un Chin-hsing Jen-k'ou Tiao-ch'a ho Hsüan-min Teng-chi te Tso-fa (Methods of Carrying Out Population Investigation and Voters Registration in Yung-fu and Other Villages in Yü-shu *Hsien*, Kirin Province),' *Jen-min Jih-pao*, June 28, 1953.

households and the same kinds of individuals within households. Some units used the household records in preparing preliminary household data sheets from which the census forms were filled out. Other units compared the census forms with the voter registration forms, which had been filled out at the same time, and in some areas, the check consisted merely in calling mass meetings at which the people were asked to tell of any errors in census work they might know about. Apparently there were a number of areas in which whatever was done as a 'check' revealed no errors whatsoever. The few instances of omissions and double-counting reported by the census offices that conducted a real check, however inadequate, were then divided by the total population in all areas that claimed they had made accuracy checks, including a large number that reported 100 per cent accuracy.[30] The resulting accuracy figures give no indication of the actual frequency of errors in the census data.

Nationwide population of registration system. The leaders of the P.R.C. were sufficiently confident of the results of their census to try to base a nationwide system of population registers on the census records. The idea seems not to have occurred to the officials of the Ministry of Internal Affairs and the State Statistical Bureau in time to incorporate it in the original census plans. It was broached publicly for the first time at the Second National Civil Administration Conference in Peking in the fall of 1953, but only a few of the provinces had begun to draw up plans for universal registration by the spring of 1954, and the actual work of setting up the system did not begin until the fall of 1954. By April, 1955, the work was said to be under way in all provinces but Shansi. Progress was expected to be 'gradual' because of the many difficulties anticipated,[31] and when the directive on universal registration was issued in July, 1955, the work was evidently still incomplete.[32]

Some of the difficulties were implicit in the circumstances. By the time the effort at permanent registration reached the basic-level units, the census work was already from one to two years past, and a new investigation was necessary to convert the census records to a current demographic profile. But there were no central funds and no central supervision forthcoming to support and guide the effort. Local authorities were expected to resurvey the population in conjunction with various 'central tasks,' such as planned purchase and distribution of food grains and other supplies, but they were also warned not to let registration work interfere with these tasks. The central authorities had had enough experience with the perennially faltering urban police registers to know that setting up rural registers would not be easy, but it proved more difficult than anticipated. One *hsiang* (village) in Kiangsu Province, for example, had made five population surveys for different purposes within the year following the census and had come up with different figures each time.[33] Besides the technical difficulties faced by the local authorities, there seems to have been some conflict in Peking between the Ministry of Internal Affairs and the Ministry of Public Security over which would control what aspect of population record-keeping. The Ministry of Internal Affairs, which had been in charge of census work, seemed to be gaining con-

---

[30] Further discussion of the 1953 census accuracy checks may be found in John S. Aird, 'Population Growth,' Chapter 4 in *Economic Trends in Communist China*, edited by Alexander Eckstein, Walter Galenson, and Ta-chung Liu (Chicago: Aldine Publishing Company, 1968), pp. 239–42.

[31] 'Registration of Persons Gradually Instituted in Various Parts of China,' *Kuang-ming Jih-pao (Kuang-ming Daily)*, Peking, April 2, 1955; translated in *Survey of China Mainland Press*, No. 1040, May 4, 1955, p. 13.

[32] 'State Council's Directive Concerning Establishment of Permanent System for Registration of Persons,' NCNA, Peking, July 2, 1955; translated in *Survey of China Mainland Press*, No. 1082, July 5–6, 1955, pp. 10–13.

[33] 'For Speedy Institution of a Regular System of Registration of Persons' (editorial), *Kuang-ming Jih-pao*, April 2, 1955; translated in *Survey of China Mainland Press*, No. 1040, May 4, 1955, pp. 14–15.

trol of registration in some towns in 1955,[34] but in January, 1956, the Ministry of Public Security was made responsible for all registration work, rural as well as urban.[35] The change meant a further shift in emphasis toward political priorities in population record-keeping.

In very short order, the predictable consequences of the transfer began to be apparent. Toward the end of 1955, the mainland press initiated what was apparently an officially sponsored campaign of 'spontaneous' letters from readers criticizing the mismanagement of population registration by the police. In 1956 the campaign was intensified. The police were charged with bureaucratic officiousness and incompetence. They had made mistakes in putting down names, ages, addresses, and sexes of persons applying for registration or for moving permits. When rushed, they left many blanks unfilled. They lost household books and moving permits. Moreover, they did not seem to care. The press items give the impression that many police cadres regarded population record-keeping as a great bother and expressed their frustration by harassing those who tried to comply with registration regulations.[36] Registration had no more than been established when it began to fulfill a pessimistic prognostication made earlier by one of the provincial internal affairs departments: 'Eventually it will become an operation that no one is responsible for and will gradually dissolve by itself.'[37]

Under such circumstances, the accuracy of population data obtained from the registration records must have left a good deal to be desired. Statistical evidence relating to accuracy is fragmentary and inferential. A technical article by a statistician in the Harbin Bureau of Public Health says that, when the local security police took over vital registration from the public health cadres in 1955, 'the work of checking on abandoned infants ceased,' whereupon the registration of infant deaths apparently declined.[38]

Taking all evidence together, it is reasonable to conclude that registration of births, deaths, migrants, and resident population was never complete and that it became less so with the passing of time. Where the system stood at the end of 1957 is not entirely clear, though some of the innovations in the new set of registration regulations issued on January 9, 1958, suggest that many new loopholes had been discovered since the

---

[34] Ibid., p. 15.

[35] 'Kuo-wu-yüan Kuan-yü Nung-ts'un Hu-k'ou Teng-chi T'ung-chi Kung-tso ho Kuo-chi Kung-tso I-Kuei Kung-an Pu-men Chieh-pan te T'ung-chih (1956-nien i-yüeh shih-san-jih) (Notification of the State Council on the Transfer of Rural Household Registration and Statistical Work and Activities Relating to Nationality Matters to Public Security Organs [January 13, 1956]),' Chung-hua Jen-min Kung-ho-kuo Fa-kuei Hui-pien (Collection of Laws and Regulations of the People's Republic of China), 3 (Peking: Fa-lü Ch'u-pan-she, 1956): 173-75.

[36] For example, see 'Wei-shen-mo pa Wo-te Hu-chi ch'ien tao Ho-nan-sheng ch'ü? (Why Send My Household Registration to Honan Province?),' Nan-fang Jih-pao, January 16, 1956; 'Yen-chung-te Kuan-liao Chu-i Tso-feng (A Serious Bureaucratic Style),' Nan-fang Jih-pao, January 23, 1956; 'Chei Pu-shih Shen-mo hsiao Shih-ch'ing (This Is No Small Matter),' Hsin Hu-nan Pao (New Hunan Daily), Changsha, April 23, 1956; 'Pu chih-tao Na-t'ien ts'ai yu hsia-lo (No Telling When It Will Be Found),' Chien-she Pao (Construction Daily), Kweilin, May 17, 1956; and 'Chih Ch'a I-ke Tzu (A Difference of One Character),' Chi-lin Jih-pao (Kirin Daily), November 23, 1956.

[37] Shansi Province, Civil Administration Department, 'Kung-ku yü Chien-ch'üan Ching-ch'ang Hu-k'ou Teng-chi Chih-tu te Chi-tien I-chien (Several Opinions Concerning the Strengthening and Perfecting of the Regular Household Registration System),' Kuang-ming Jih-pao, August 9, 1955.

[38] Yang Chien-pai, 'Ha-erh-pin Tung-fu-chia ch'ü Chü-min Shou-ming-piao, 1953-1955-nien (A Life-Table for the Population of Tung-fu-chia District, Harbin, 1953-1955),' I-hsüeh-shih yü Pao-chien Tsu-chih (Medical and Health Organization), 2, No. 1 (Peking: Jen-min Wei-sheng Ch'u-pan-she, March 25, 1958): 10. Yang was talking about data from a residential area of a relatively prosperous industrial center.

first set of regulations for general registration had been issued in July, 1955.[39] The deterioration must have been much accelerated under the impact of the Great Leap Forward' of 1958–60, which neglected statistics, planning, record-keeping, and many other mundane considerations in favor of ardent political activism. The food crisis that came next, in 1960–61, and the beginnings of economic recovery in 1962 and 1963 necessarily had a sobering effect, but the efforts of administrative personnel were probably fully absorbed in the essential business of food distribution, economic management, and political control and could not have been spared for work on population records.

At some time in the spring of 1964, a decision was reached in Peking to take another sounding of the population throughout the country. The result was an investigation and correction of registration records, which has been rather widely referred to in the West as China's '1964 census.'[40] It seems to have been less of a 'census' in the Western sense of the term than the 1953 census, and some demographers outside China question whether the 1953 effort should be so designated.[41] What matters more is whether or not the method of investigation succeeded in producing reasonably accurate and useful figures. This question cannot be answered with much assurance, because less is known about the 1964 count than about any of its predecessors since 1949. It was never mentioned in the mainland press. The original directives were never published, nor have any results been released. A rumor current in the P.R.C. in the fall of 1964 implied that, like the 1953 census, the new investigation returned a population total above what the Chinese Communist leaders had expected and that once again, as in 1954, they were concerned lest the figure arouse Malthusian fears among a people so recently on the brink of famine. This time, according to the rumor, they decided to suppress the new population figures. A similar account was recently given by a refugee from the mainland who claims to have taken part in the investigation. He says that a total figure of 'more than 713 million' was circulated in official channels in June, 1966, ostensibly the result of the 1964 investigation, but that some of the cadres involved in the investigation suspected that this was not the originally reported total. They noted that the 1964 figures for 'many hsien and districts' indicated population increases of 30 to 40 per cent over the 1953 census figures, and on this basis they speculated that the national total should have reached 800 million by mid-1964. They also surmised that the regime had substituted a lower figure to conceal the fact that its efforts to reduce population growth rates through birth control and delayed marriage had been a failure.[42] The story is not altogether implausible.

---

[39] 'Regulations of the People's Republic of China Governing Household Registration,' NCNA, January 9, 1958; translated in *Survey of China Mainland Press*, No. 1695, January 21, 1958, pp. 1–5. See also Lo Jui-ch'ing, 'Explanations on Regulations for Household Registration,' NCNA, January 9, 1958; translated in *Survey of China Mainland Press*, No. 1695, January 21, 1958, pp. 5–10, and 'Let Household Registration Work Render Greater Service to the People' (editorial), *Jen-min Jih-pao*, January 10, 1958; translated in *Survey of China Mainland Press*, No. 1695, January 21, 1958, pp. 10–12.

[40] Reports by visitors to the mainland in the spring of 1964 told of a press interview with Ch'en Yi in which he indicated that a nationwide population investigation was planned and of posters in Canton dated June 17, which announced a national population count as of June 30. See for example Derek Davies, 'A New Census,' *Far Eastern Economic Review*, 45, No. 2 (July 9, 1964): 41–42; and 'China Believed to Have Held Census,' *The Times* (London), July 10, 1964, p. 12.

[41] The distinction turns mainly on whether the investigation in question consists of a more or less simultaneous canvass of residences in which the data are taken down in interviews without reference to previous records. Neither the 1953 nor the 1964 investigation can qualify by the strict definition, but the 1964 investigation seems to have been more a check of previous records and less an independent field count than the 1953 investigation.

[42] Hsüeh Feng, 'Chung-kung te 1964-nien Jen-k'ou P'u-ch'a (Communist China's Popula-

In any case, there is no doubt that a population count of some kind took place during the middle of 1964. One foreign account states that the information collected included name, sex, date of birth, place of birth, educational level, marital status, 'family background,' 'class status,' commune and production team in which employed, occupation, height, weight, 'distinctive features,' professional skill, and 'aspirations.'[43] This is a rather long list, far beyond what was ever contemplated for the 1953 census or included in the urban registers, insofar as available evidence shows. So ambitious an effort would imply that those who planned it were too inexperienced in statistical work to know what expectations would be reasonable.

There is no indication of who was in charge of the planning. The field work was reportedly conducted by local committees led by government statistical personnel, local Party leaders, and local public security chiefs. Forms designed by the central authorities were printed by the local committees and distributed to heads of household, who were required to fill them out with the help of household investigation teams, which went from door to door. The completed forms were then brought to registration places, where they were checked against the household books. Presumably discrepancies were queried and the correct information entered in the household books. Some type of 'recheck' operation was also reported. Then the local figures were assembled and transmitted to higher levels, as in previous investigations.[44]

The mainland refugee cited above says that participants in the 1964 investigation generally agreed that the accuracy of the figures 'exceeded 99.8 per cent,' whatever that may mean. However, he also believes that the principal source of inaccuracy was in the counting of 'black persons' and 'black households'—evaders of the population registers—whose numbers he says had greatly increased during the mass transfers of urban residents to rural areas in the early 1960's.[45] Without more substantial statistical and methodological information, the effectiveness of the 1964 investigation cannot be evaluated.

OFFICIAL POPULATION DATA

The inferences about defects in the official population data from the P.R.C. that can be drawn on the basis of a review of methods of investigation and record-keeping are limited by the amount of information in the published sources. Other problems, which the officials and statisticians either did not suspect or did not discuss in the press, may constitute major causes of error. However, some further insights into the deficiencies of the official data can be gained by statistical analysis of the figures themselves. The tests of plausibility and internal consistency that can be applied to the data depend upon how much detail on components, distribution, characteristics, and change is available. The Chinese Communists have released very little of all the data they have gathered, perhaps because they were to some degree aware that their figures would not bear careful scrutiny, but those that have appeared contain enough discrepancies and anomalies to suggest that many more must have been visible in the complete statistical tabulations.

---

tion Census of 1964),' *Tsu-kuo (China Monthly)*, No 56 (Hong Kong, November 1, 1968), pp. 18–19. If the national total as actually reported exceeded the 1953 census figure by 30 to 40 per cent, it would have been somewhere between 757 and 816 million. The fact that no public announcement was made about the 1964 investigation in the press or on radio even in the preparatory stages suggests that the regime had never intended to make the results generally available.

[43] H. T. Wang, 'An Analysis of Mainland China's 1964 Census,' *Free China and Asia*, 11 (Taipei, September, 1964): 7. Hsüeh Feng (*op. cit.*, p. 18) lists many of the same items and adds nationality, religion, relationship to head of household, and 'political profile.'

[44] Hsüeh Feng, *op. cit.*, pp. 17–18.

[45] *Ibid.*, p. 18.

Table 5–1—Official Figures on the Size and Rate of Increase of the Total,
Urban, and Rural Population of Mainland China, 1949–57
(absolute figures in thousands as of year's end)

	Total Population		Urban Population		Rural Population	
Year	Number	Per Cent Increase	Number	Per Cent Increase	Number	Per Cent Increase
1949	541,670	—	57,650	—	484,020	—
1950	551,960	1.90	61,690	7.00	490,270	1.29
1951	563,000	2.00	66,320	7.50	496,680	1.31
1952	574,820	2.10	71,630	8.00	503,190	1.31
1953	587,960	2.29	77,670	8.43	510,290	1.41
1954	601,720	2.34	81,550	4.99	520,170	1.94
1955	614,650	2.14	82,850	1.59	531,800	2.24
1956	627,800	2.14	89,150	7.60	583,650	1.29
1957	646,530	2.98*	—	—	—	—

* Calculated; no growth rate given in the source.
Sources:
1949–56: *T'ung-chi Kung-tso* Data Section, 'Data on China's Population from 1949 to 1956,' *T'ung-chi Kung-tso (Statistical Work)*, No. 11 (Peking: Chi-hua T'ung-chi Tsa-chih-she, June 14, 1957); translated in *Extracts from China Mainland Magazines*, No. 91, U.S. Consulate General, Hong Kong, July 22, 1957, pp. 22–25.
1957: State Statistical Bureau, *Ten Great Years: Statistics of the Economic and Cultural Achievements of the People's Republic of China* (Peking: Foreign Languages Press, 1960), p. 11 (total shown includes Taiwan).

Total population figures. Among figures purporting to represent the total population of the Chinese mainland, it is important to distinguish census or registration data and official estimates based on them from the figures that are commonly quoted in the mainland press and radio without any clear indication of date or coverage. Aside from the State Statistical Bureau's series for 1949–56 and its figure for the end of 1957 published several years later (see Table 5–1), most mainland total population figures are rounded to the nearest 10 million, 25 million, 50 million, or 100 million. The figure of 475 million in use prior to the census was the first of a rather large collection of rhetorical figures that have found currency in the P.R.C. for short periods since 1949. In the early years of the regime, that figure coexisted with a less popular total of 500 million, representing the mainland population with an additional allowance of 25 million for overseas Chinese throughout the world. Both these figures were retired by the 1953 census announcement. For the next five years, the principal rhetorical figure was 600 million. This figure was also intended to stand for the world total of Chinese people, but by the latter part of the First Five-Year Plan period it had been exceeded by the bureau's figures for the mainland population alone and was often cited as a mainland figure.

After the publication of the 1957 year-end total of 646,530,000, a round figure of 650 million began to appear in public speeches by Chinese officials, gradually but never completely displacing the 600 million figure. Both vanished after the release in August, 1966, of the communiqué of the eleventh plenary session of the Eighth Central Committee of the Chinese Communist Party, which concluded with a reference to the '700 million Chinese people.'[46] Since then, this has been the most frequently

[46] 'Communiqué of the Eleventh Plenary Session of the Eighth Chinese Communist Party Central Committee' (adopted August 12, 1966), NCNA (in English), August 13, 1966. The

quoted round figure. Late in the 1960's, however, a figure of 750 million appeared several times,[47] and, in November, 1971, Vice-Premier Li Hsien-nien disclosed that government departments in Peking were using divergent estimates that ranged from below 750 million to 833 million.[48]

Population totals of 630 million, 640 million, 660 million, 670 million, 680 million, 690 million, and 'almost 700' million, evidently intended as round figures to the nearest 10 million, may be found in a number of press items and speeches, some of them by prominent officials.[49] These figures represent an attempt to keep closer track of the growth of the mainland population than the figures rounded to the nearest 50 million or 100 million. However, like the other rhetorical figures, they are almost never cited in a way that clearly identifies the date of reference or the population included. It is never safe to assume that the date of reference is the same as the date of the speech, or that the figure refers to the previous midyear or year end, whichever was closer. Nor is it safe to assume that the figure refers only to the mainland

---

figure seems to have made its first public appearance in the *Jen-min Jih-pao* in June, 1966 ('Wo-men shih Chiu-shih-chieh te P'i-p'an-che [We Are the Critics of the Old World],' *Jen-min Jih-pao*, June 8, 1966). A little later in the same month, the paper published what was ostensibly a letter from Lin Piao dated March 11, 1966, in which the figure was also cited ('Lin Piao T'ung-chih Kung-yeh Chiao-t'ung Chan-hsien Huo-hsüeh Huo-yung Mao Chu-hsi Chu-tso hsieh te I-feng Hsin-chung Chih-chu Mao Chu-hsi T'ien-ts'ai ti pa Ma-k'o-ssu Lieh-ning Chu-i T'i-kao tao Ch'an-hsin te Chieh-tuan Mao Tse-tung Ssu-hsiang Kuan-shu tao Kung Nung chung Ch'ü-neng Chuan-hua wei Chü-ta Wu-chih Li-liang [Comrade Lin Piao's Letter to the Industrial and Communications Front on Their Active Study and Active Application of Chairman Mao's Writings Points Out That Chairman Mao Creatively Elevated Marxism-Leninism to a New Height and That When the Thought of Mao Tse-tung Is Poured into Industry and Agriculture It Will Turn into an Enormous Material Force],' *Jen-min Jih-pao*, June 19, 1966).

[47] E.g., a statement in a broadcast from Radio Lanchow on February 11, 1968. See British Broadcasting Corporation, *Summary of World Broadcasts*, February 16, 1968.

[48] Mamduh Rida, 'Days in China—An Interview with the Number 3 Man in China,' *Al Jumhuriya* (Cairo), November 18, 1971, p. 9.

[49] For example, Wang Kuang-wei predicted the population would reach 640 million during 1957 in 'How To Organize Agricultural Labor Power,' *Chi-hua Ching-chi (Planned Economy)*, No. 8 (Peking: Chi-hua Tung-chi Tsa-chih-she, August 9, 1957); translated in *Extracts from China Mainland Magazines*, No. 100, September 23, 1957, p. 11. Yang Ying-chien cited a total of 660 million in 'Lun Tsung-ho P'ing-heng (Let's Discuss Synthesis and Balance),' *Ching-chi Yen-chiu (Economic Research)*, No 11 (Peking: Ching-chi Yen-chiu Tsa-chih-she, November 17, 1962), p. 2. Ch'en Yi used figures of 680 million in 1959 (Reuters dispatch of February 4, 1959, carried in *The New York Times*, February 5, 1959); 670 million in 1960 (report on an interview with Ch'en Yi in Peking on November 21, 1960, carried in the *Economist*, Tokyo, January 10, 1961); 'almost 700 million' in March, 1961 ('Ch'en Yi Su-pan-te-li-yüeh Chi-hsü Hui-t'an [Ch'en Yi and Subandrio Continue Talks],' *Jen-min Jih-pao*, April 1, 1961); and 650 million in October, 1962 (text of Vice-Premier Ch'en Yi's Televised Interview with Japanese Correspondent, NCNA [in English], October 1, 1962, in *Survey of China Mainland Press*, No. 2833, October 5, 1962, p. 29).

During an interview with Edgar Snow in Peking in November, 1964, Mao reportedly said that 'some people' thought China's population had reached 680 million or 690 million but that he himself did not believe it could be that large. Some Western observers speculated that Mao might have reference to the suppressed results of the 1964 investigation. But, as we have seen, other reports suggested that the 1964 figure should have been at least as high as 713 million, if not much higher. There is an inclination in some quarters to assume that any figure attributed directly to Mao—or Chou or Liu—must be regarded as 'official.' However, Mao has never shown much adeptness in handling figures, particularly population figures, and it is much more likely that he was recalling some of the numbers current in official circles in Peking during 1958 and 1959. See Edgar Snow, 'Interview with Mao,' *New Republic*, February 27, 1965, p. 20.

population, even if only the mainland population would be appropriate to the context.[50]

Several other population totals cited in mainland sources during the First Five-Year Plan period were too specific to be regarded as rhetorical figures. They were apparently compilations or estimates produced outside the State Statistical Bureau, but most of them were not used beyond the publication of the bureau's population data series in June, 1957.[51] Given the confusion and delay in establishing the rural population registers during 1954–56, there was probably ample reason why the bureau was unable to put out a series of population figures before June, 1957, and why, even then, the figures for 1956 were described as partly estimated and subject to revision later.[52] There is also reason to doubt whether the 1954 and 1955 totals consisted entirely of reported figures from the population registers, since very few of those records had been established by the end of 1954, and some were still to be set up after the end of 1955.

The census total as of June 30, 1953, was evidently the base figure from which the bureau's estimates for year end 1952 and year end 1953 were derived, but the method used is not clear. The official natural increase rate for 1953 released at the time of the census results was 20 per thousand population per year. Applied to the census figure, this would give an increment for the year of about 11,650,000, but the increment shown in the bureau's series was 13,140,000, equivalent to a natural increase rate of 22.6 per thousand, or an increase from the start of the year of 2.29 per cent, as shown in the bureau's own tables.[53] The discrepancy is not explained.

---

[50] For example, a newspaper article by the Minister of Food in 1959 cites mainland food production figures with population figures that include an allowance for Taiwan. See Sha Ch'ien-li, 'Liang-shih Chan-hsien te Hui-huang Ch'eng-chiu (Dazzling Success of the Food Grain Front),' *Jen-min Jih-pao*, October 25, 1959.

From time to time, Western scholars have attempted to assign a date of reference to one of the current rhetorical figures in order to extrapolate a hypothetical official population series for the years since 1957. Such efforts involve unwarranted assumptions and are not methodologically sound.

[51] One of these was a set of provincial population totals compiled by the geographer Hu Huan-yung, which add to a mainland total of 604,666,212, presumably as of the end of 1954. Hu says merely that the figures 'are taken from the 1954 universal registration.' Hu Huan-yung, 'Chung-kuo Ke Sheng Ch'ü Mien-chi Jen-k'ou Chih-shih T'u (A Graph of the Area and Population of China by Provinces and Regions),' *Ti-li Chih-shih (Geographical Knowledge)*, No. 9 (Peking: Ti-chih Ch'u-pan-she, 1957), p. 391. The corresponding figure from the State Statistical Bureau release is 601,720,000.

Two other figures, clearly labeled 'estimates,' were cited in articles by Minister of Food Chang Nai-ch'i. One of these was a figure of 603,230,000 for 1955. 'The Food Situation in China,' NCNA, June 26, 1956; translated in *Current Background*, No. 407, August 17, 1956, p. 25. The other was a figure of 616,500,000 for 1956. 'The Present Grain Situation as Seen from Several Groups of Figures,' *Liang-shih (Grain)*, No. 1 (Peking: Liang-shih-pu, January 25, 1957); translated in *Extracts from China Mainland Magazines*, No. 78, April 15, 1957, p. 30. The bureau's annual average population figures for 1955 and 1956 are 608,180,000 and 621,230,000, respectively, or roughly 5 million higher in each case.

Another source gives agricultural population figures for 1952 and 1956 that differ from those issued by the bureau by a few million. [Li Shu-teh, 'Peasants' Burden in 1956: Conditions and Problems,' *Ts'ai-cheng (Finance)*, No. 8 (Peking: Ts'ai-cheng Ch'u-pan-she, August, 1957); translated in *Extracts from China Mainland Magazines*, No. 100, September 23, 1957, p. 18.] Here again, it appears that estimates had been used in lieu of official figures that had not yet appeared when the article was written. After the June, 1957, figures were out, conflicting figures virtually disappeared.

[52] See *Extracts from China Mainland Magazines*, No. 91 (July 22, 1957), p. 22.

[53] *Ibid.*, p. 23. Even more puzzling is the fact that the increment is divided unevenly on either side of the census total, with the larger portion assigned to the first half of 1953 and the smaller portion to the latter half of the year. The effect is to imply a natural increase rate of

The figures for year end 1949, 1950, and 1951 were reportedly based on 'the trend of natural increase of our population in the past,'[54] but from the figures in Table 5-1 it is obvious at a glance that the bureau's statisticians simply assumed increase rates of 1.9, 2.0, and 2.1 per cent per year for 1950, 1951, and 1952, respectively, and extrapolated in reverse from the 1952 year end total. These increase rates are arbitrary and not very plausible, since they imply too much progress in mortality reduction before 1950 and not enough afterward.[55]

The figure for year end 1957—646,530,000—was released in a volume of statistics celebrating the first ten years of the P.R.C. The figure would imply an increase of 2.98 per cent over the year end 1956 total in the June, 1957, series, a rate of increase well beyond that officially claimed for 1957 and not really a continuation of the June, 1957, series. There may have been an upward revision of the 1956 year end figure some time after June, 1957, but, if so, the average annual increase rate for the two-year period 1956-57 would be 2.56 per cent, which is still too high to accord with the corresponding natural increase figures (see below).

No precisely dated figures for the total population of the mainland have been released since the year end 1957 total. The Great Leap Forward of 1958-60 disrupted most statistical operations and resulted in virtually a complete blackout of statistical data of all kinds. There is no evidence that the State Statistical Bureau, which never had primary responsibility for demographic data collection, is still compiling the local population reports from the police registration offices. Since 1957, a few round figures representing the population of particular provinces and municipalities have been cited in local press and radio news items. These were particularly numerous during 1958 and 1959. Many of the figures that appeared at that time were merely rounded versions of figures for 1953 and 1957, but others exceeded the 1957 total by a margin sufficient to show that they were supposed to represent subsequent population growth. There was no indication how these figures were arrived at. Some may have been merely extrapolations, but others may have been derived from the annual registration reports, if such reports were still being compiled at the provincial and municipal levels in spite of Great Leap Forward disruptions.

After 1959, provincial and municipal totals almost disappeared from the mainland press and radio, but very recently a new crop of local population figures has begun to appear, most of them in contexts that are distinctly rhetorical, such as, during the Cultural Revolution, declarations that 'the X million people of Province pledge their loyalty to Chairman Mao.' The appearance of these figures has led some China-watchers to suppose that the central authorities in Peking may once again be compiling a total population figure from the local reports and that the figure of 700 million for the mainland is the product of some such compilation. The fact that so low a population figure does not agree with the magnitude and trend of growth implied by the First Five-Year Plan figures, even with some allowance for higher mortality during the food crisis of 1960-61, led to the further supposition that Peking has either abandoned the First Five-Year Plan population figures or is allowing for a much more serious loss of population during 1960-61 than many Western observers had previously been willing to assume.[56] However, a more careful

26.9 per thousand for the first half of the year and only 18.3 per thousand for the second half. This does not make sense, yet the 1953 census total has never been officially replaced and is still cited occasionally in official publications.

[54] *Ibid.*, p. 22.

[55] Curiously enough, in calculating the average annual population total for 1949, the bureau seems to have reverted to the 1951 increase rate of 2.0 per cent, instead of continuing 'the trend of natural increase of our population' used for 1950, 1951, and 1952. Hence, the increase rate assumed for 1949 is higher than that assumed for 1950. This also makes no sense.

[56] American Consulate General, Hong Kong, Airgram A-523, April 9, 1968, pp. 1-5.

examination of the new figures does not sustain these inferences. The evidence will be discussed in the following section.

Provincial figures. The only available official data giving the distribution of the population within mainland China are three sets of provincial totals: the census figures as of June 30, 1953, a compilation as of year end 1954 published by a Chinese geographer, and the State Statistical Bureau's compilations as of year end 1957. A map showing population density zones was prepared in 1955 for use in secondary schools by a Shanghai map publishing house, based on *hsien* (county) data from the 1953 census (see Map 9), but the *hsien* figures are not available. No provincial figures were ever released for 1955 or 1956, so far as is known, though the provinces must have been required to report figures for those years, and the bureau must have attempted to compile them. Even individual province totals for those years are extremely rare. This is a matter of some significance; it strongly suggests that both central and local authorities were under some constraint to withhold the figures, perhaps because they contained embarrassing anomalies.

Further evidence in support of such a conclusion may be found in comparisons of the three sets of province figures in Table 5–2. Although the figures were supposedly adjusted to 1957 boundaries, there are improbabilities in the figures for certain provinces that cannot be explained in demographic terms. It has already been noted that

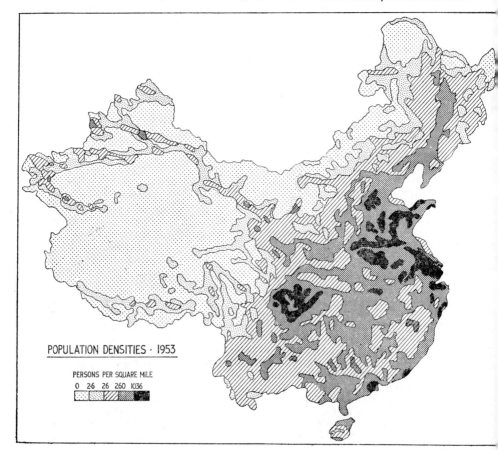

POPULATION DENSITIES · 1953

PERSONS PER SQUARE MILE
0   26   26   260   1036

Map 9   Population Densities in Mainland China: 1953

102

the 1954 provincial figures, which were supposedly taken from registration data as of year end 1954, add to a total higher than that for the same date released by the bureau in June, 1957.[57] The implied annual average increase rates for individual provinces between mid-1953 and year end 1954 also seem too high in some cases. The lowest increase rates are those indicated for Anhwei and Hopei (with Peking and Tientsin included), both about 1.7 per cent.[58] The next lowest rate is for the combined populations of Kansu and Ninghsia, about 2.0 per cent.[59] There is nothing particularly implausible in the high increase rates shown for the three Manchurian provinces or for Ch'inghai and Sinkiang, all of which were presumably receiving substantial net in-migration at this time,[60] but the rates for Kansu and Ninghsia, which are also frontier areas, are curiously low in comparison, and the rate for the Inner Mongolia Autonomous Region (IMAR), about 12.8 per cent, is out of all reason.[61] Most of the rates for the remaining provinces are in the range from 2.0 to 2.4 per cent, except for Fukien and Honan, both about 2.7 per cent; Kiangsu, around 2.9 per cent; and Shensi, which is an unbelievable 3.3 per cent. The percentage increase rate for the mainland as a whole implied by Hu's figures is 2.5 per cent, compared with 2.3 per cent for the same period according to the bureau's June, 1957, series.

The provincial increase rates between year end 1954 and year end 1957 seem to bear no consistent relationship with those implied for the previous year and a half. About half the rates were higher for the 1954–57 period than for the 1953–54 period, and the other half were lower. The changes seem not to conform to an intelligible pattern when related to region, degree of urbanization, or ethnic composition of the provincial population. So far as the total population is concerned, Hu's 1954 total implies an average annual increase of less than 2.3 per cent for the three-year period, whereas the State Statistical Bureau's figure implies an increase of more than 2.4 per cent. Hu's figures and the official vital rates (see below, under heading *Vital rates*) would suggest a slowing of the rate of population growth after 1954, whereas the bureau's total population figures imply a rising rate of increase. Demographically, a rising increase rate would seem more plausible, but it is possible that the annual reports from the province-level units did not conform to demographic plausibility and that the bureau was confronted with a dilemma it could not resolve.

---

[57] See footnote 51, above. Hu Huan-yung's article appeared in September, 1957. In it, he claims to have adjusted the 1954 figures to conform to 1957 boundaries. Yet his figures for Kwangtung and Kwangsi do not fit with the 1953 census figures adjusted to 1957 boundaries given in *Chung-hua Jen-min Kung-ho-kuo Ti-t'u-chi (Atlas of the People's Republic of China)* (Peking: Ti-t'u Ch'u-pan-she, 1957).

[58] Tibet is not included in these comparisons. Hu Huan-yung gives separate figures for Tibet and the Chamdo area, which add to a downward rounded form of the 1953 census total for Tibet-Chamdo. The bureau's 1957 figure is also the 1953 figure, further rounded to the nearest 10,000.

[59] Ninghsia, which was a separate province while the census was under way, had been abolished by the time the census results were announced. It had been re-established as the Ninghsia Hui Autonomous Region before Hu's article appeared.

[60] The implied rate for Liaoning, the most urbanized of China's provinces, was 3.1 per cent; the rate for Kirin was 2.8 per cent. For Heilungkiang on the northern frontier, the rate was 4.8 per cent. For Ch'inghai and Sinkiang the implied rates were 3.6 and 3.7 per cent, respectively.

[61] If we allow a natural increase equivalent to 2.5 per cent a year average for the period, the average rate of net in-migration per year would amount to more than 750,000. There is nothing in the available information on resettlement at that time that would suggest that any such large-scale movement was taking place or that the IMAR could have provided the minimum accommodations needed to receive such an influx. The most likely explanation is a change in the base population figure between 1953 and 1954, but there is no evidence to support this surmise.

Table 5-2—Population of Mainland China, by Province, 1953, 1954, and 1957
(thousands)

Region and Province	Midyear 1953	Year end 1954	Year end 1957
Mainland China	582,603	604,667	646,530
Northeast			
Heilungkiang	11,897	12,761	14,860
Kirin	11,290	11,767	12,550
Liaoning	20,566	21,518	24,090
Inner Mongolia	7,338	8,800	9,200
North			
Hopei	43,348	44,434	48,730
Shansi	14,314	14,786	15,960
Northwest			
Kansu	} 12,928	{ 11,594	12,800
Ninghsia		{ 1,728	1,810
Shensi	15,881	16,664	18,130
Sinkiang	4,874	5,145	5,640
Ch'inghai	1,676	1,768	2,050
East			
Anhwei	30,663	31,426	33,560
Chekiang	22,866	23,590	25,280
Fukien	13,143	13,683	14,650
Kaingsu	47,137	49,229	52,130
Shantung	48,877	50,517	54,030
Central-South			
Honan	44,215	46,026	48,670
Hupei	?7,790	28,654	30,790
Hunan	33,227	34,296	36,220
Kaingsi	16,773	17,297	18,610
Kwangsi	17,591	20,180	19,390
Kwangtung	36,740	35,900	37,960
Southwest			
Kweichow	15,037	15,570	16,890
Szechwan	65,685	68,043	72,160
Yünnan	17,473	18,018	19,100
Tibet and Chamdo Area	1,274	1,273	1,270

Source:

1953: Census data in 1957 boundaries, from *Chung-hua Jen-min Kung-ho-kuo Ti-t'u-chi* (*Atlas of the People's Republic of China*) (Peking: Ti-t'u Ch'u-pan-she, 1957).

1954: Registration data in 1957 boundaries, from Hu Huan-yung, 'Chung-kuo Ke Sheng Ch'ü Mien-chi Jen-k'ou Chih-shih-t'u (A Graph of the Area and Population of China by Provinces and Regions),' *Ti-li Chih-shih* (*Geographical Knowledge*), No. 9 (Peking: Ti-chih Ch'u-pan-she, 1957), pp. 390–91.

1957: Registration data, from State Statistical Bureau, *Ten Great Years: Statistics of the Economic and Cultural Achievements of the People's Republic of China* (Peking: Foreign Languages Press, 1960), p. 11.

The 1964 investigation might have been expected to produce a new round of local population figures like those that had emerged from the urban police registers and 'land reform' population counts of the early 1950's, but for some reason the 1964 effort had no such sequel. Few provincial population figures were cited in the press during the next several years. Then, in 1967 and 1968, while the Cultural Revolution was going through its agonizing contortions, province figures once again began to appear. Some of the 'new' figures were not entirely new. Of the twenty-four 'new' province totals cited in one compilation, ten were either cited in 1959 or earlier or are smaller than figures cited during those years, and three others were equaled or exceeded by figures cited in or projected for 1962.[62] Of the figures for the remaining eleven units, four are so little above the figures current in 1957, 1958, and 1959 as to raise doubts about how 'new' they really are.[63] The figures for the other seven units do represent new orders of magnitude, and since these became available 'new' figures have appeared for six more units, all larger than previously cited figures. Of these thirteen figures, however, several are too low to be plausible as midyear 1964, figures and at least four others seem too low to be plausible as 1967 year end figures.[64]

---

[62] American Consulate General, Hong Kong, op. cit., April 9, 1968, pp. 1–5. The dispatch lists 'new' figures for eight municipalities (Peking, Tientsin, Shanghai, Canton, Wuhan, Chengchow, Paot'ou, and Nanking) and twenty-four mainland provinces (no 'new' figures were available for Fukien or Shensi when the dispatch was prepared). The mainland sources containing the 'new' figures were press and radio dispatches dating from the period from March, 1967, through March, 1968, except for three figures that date from 1960, 1963, and 1964. However, the date of the mainland source must not be taken as the reference date of the figure it cites. The 'new' figure for Anhwei appears to be a downward rounding of the 1953 census figure. The figures for Szechwan and Ch'inghai are apparently downward roundings of their 1957 year end registration figures. The figures for Kansu, Ninghsia, Liaoning, Yünnan, and Kweichow were already current in the mainland press in 1958. The figures for Honan and Hupei were previously cited in 1959. The figure for Sinkiang was previously cited in 1962.

Of the 'new' figures for the eight municipalities, those for Peking, Shanghai, and Paot'ou were previously reported in 1959. The figure for Tientsin is about 25 per cent above the 1957 year end figure, but only about one-third the magnitude of the figure for the population under Tientsin's municipal authority in the latter part of 1958, when that authority extended over adjacent rural areas. The 'new' figures for the other four municipalities are higher than previously available figures, and significantly so in two instances.

[63] Assuming that the 'new' figures date from as early as mid-1964 (the Consulate General compilation assumes that they refer to year end 1965) the average annual increase rates for Hopei and Kangsu are only about 0.6 per cent, and the rates for Kwangtung and Shantung are about 0.8 per cent. If the figures are assumed to refer to some later year, the implied average annual increase rates are lower still.

[64] The first seven units are Chekiang, Heilungkiang, Kirin, and Shansi provinces and the Kwangsi Chuang, Inner Mongolia, and Tibet Autonomous Regions. The six other units are Anhwei, Fukien, Yünnan, Liaoning, and Shensi provinces and the Sinkiang Uigur Autonomous Region. A number of the units on this list are Manchurian provinces or minority regions on the frontiers, both of which have in the past shown rapid increase rates, presumably as a result of large net in-migration rates. This makes it difficult to judge what rates of increase would be reasonable for them during the years since 1957. Presumably Chinese statisticians would also find it difficult to decide what rates of increase to use in making current estimates for these units, and accurate population records probably do not exist.

For the other units, some of the increase rates do not make sense whether the recent figures are assumed to refer to mid-1964 or year end 1967. The figure for Anhwei would imply an annual increase rate of less than 0.7 per cent between year end 1957 and mid-1964. For the units for which migration should not be a major factor, most of the other figures are too high to be plausible as midyear 1964 figures. But the figures for Fukien, Shansi, Liaoning, and Shensi seem too low to be as recent as 1967 figures. Only the Chekiang, Kwangsi, and Yünnan figures make sense as 1967 totals. Those for Kirin, Heilungkiang, IMAR, and Sinkiang are

The appearance of at least thirteen really 'new' figures suggests that in a number of provinces attempts were made in the late 1960's to produce current population figures. For the present, it is not possible to say whether these figures are being obtained in some fashion from population records and reports or whether they are merely crude estimates. Under the circumstances, to derive 'new' mainland population totals by summing old and 'new' province figures or by computing hypothetical average increase rates from arbitrary combinations of these figures without solving the critical problems of reference dates is methodologically unsound.[65] The resulting totals cannot be reliable, and inferences based on them are without foundation.[66]

Rural and urban population figures. The State Statistical Bureau's June, 1957, release also included figures on the rural and urban population for the years 1949–56. The figures for the earlier years of the period were obviously estimated by first calculating a year end 1952 total, assuming rates of increase for the urban component for the years 1950–52, deriving urban figures as of year end for 1949, 1950, and 1951, and then subtracting these figures from the previously estimated total population figures to get the rural population figures as residuals. The urban increase rate for 1953, 8.43 per cent, seems to have been based on reported data, but the rates for 1952 and earlier were obviously obtained by rounding off the 1953 rate to an even 8.0 per cent for 1952 and subtracting 0.5 per cent per year progressively for each of the two prior years.[67]

How the rural and urban figures as of year end 1952 were obtained is not clear. An explanatory note in the source suggests that a part of the 1952 figures consisted of reported data from Peking, Tientsin, Shanghai, Fukien, and Kiangsu, and the rest was computed from midyear figures. This explanation is not adequate. Precensus provincial population figures compiled from local reports by various Chinese atlases and by the *People's Handbook* (*Jen-min shou-ts'e*) during 1952 and 1953 were generally below the corresponding 1953 census totals by a margin greater than the increase rates shown in the State Statistical Bureau's series would imply. Some of the precensus urban population totals are very much smaller than the census figures for the same municipalities. Hence, it is unlikely that the precensus figures could have been used

---

higher, of course, but there is no way of determining whether they are too high, not high enough, or about right.

[65] The latter approach was used in an article in which the 'new' figures for thirteen provinces were taken as 1967 year end figures and implied average annual increase rates were computed for each province with the 1953 census figures as a base. Hypothetical 'weighted' and 'unweighted' average increase rates were then obtained from the thirteen provinces and applied to the mainland population total for 1953 to obtain alternate estimates of the mainland population as of year end 1967. Since many of the figures assumed to be provincial totals as of year end 1967 are not actually 'new' figures, the resulting increase rates are extremely low, yet this fact did not lead the analyst to question the assumptions gratuitously made about the reference date of the figures. See Lois Dougan Tretiak, 'Population Picture,' *Far Eastern Economic Review*, 59, No. 14 (April 4, 1968): 14.

[66] For further discussion of the new provincial figures, see Robert Michael Field, 'Chinese Provincial Population Data,' *The China Quarterly*, No. 44, October–December, 1970, pp. 195–202.

[67] A methodological note in the source states that the urban figures for 1949, 1950, and 1951 are 'based on the rate of population increase in cities and towns in the Northeast and Northwest,' but, though this may apply to the general magnitude, it obviously does not explain the year-to-year rates. See *T'ung-chi Kung-tso* Data Section, *op. cit.*, in *Extracts from China Mainland Magazines*, No. 91, U.S. Consulate General, Hong Kong, July 22, 1957, p. 22. Again, as in the case of the total population estimates, the annual average figure for the urban population in 1949 was calculated by assuming the same increase rate for 1949 as for 1951, ignoring the assumed trend of the urban increase rates for 1950–52. Hence, again, the rate assumed for 1949 is higher than the rate assumed for 1950. This is a further indication of the crudeness of the methodology underlying the bureau's population estimates.

without adjustment to produce 1952 totals that would fit plausibly into a series with the census figures.

The urban and rural totals for 1953 were apparently derived in some fashion from the 1953 census, as the source says, but again, as in the case of the total population figures for 1953, there is a discrepancy between the census figures for the urban and rural population and the annual average figures for 1953 shown in the bureau's series. The census reported an urban population of 77,257,282 and a rural population of 505,346,135 as of midyear 1953.[68] The June, 1957, series gives annual average figures for 1953 of 74,650,000 and 506,740,000, respectively. Thus, the bureau's annual average rural population figure is 1.4 million above the census figure, and its urban figure is 2.6 million below the census figure. A note in the source says that the urban population totals include persons living in market towns in suburban areas but exclude suburban village residents. This may have been intended as an explanation of the discrepancy between the bureau's midyear 1953 urban total and that originally reported in the census communiqué, but it would imply that the census figure had since been revised.

The 1954 and 1955 urban and rural totals were presumably based, at least in part, on registration data. It is possible that the 1954 rural figure was also obtained as a residual by subtracting a reported urban figure from an estimated total population figure, since the rural registers were probably not in a condition to report a rural population total as of year end 1954 or for some time thereafter. But the figures for 1955 at least have the appearance of reported totals, because the urban increase rate is unusually low for that year, and the rural increase rate unusually high. As the source notes, there was an all-out drive that year to rid the cities of recent rural-to-urban migrants by sending them back to their native villages.[69] The low over-all population increase shown for 1955 is also plausible as an indication that many of the expellees removed from the urban registers failed to check in at their native villages but returned without reregistering to the urban areas, causing an increase in general underregistration. The 1956 figures should have been based entirely on data from the registration system, which was about as well established by the end of that year as it was ever going to be, but the source indicates in a footnote to the urban figures that the 7.6 per cent increase rate for that year was an estimate based on reports from only fourteen provinces and the three centrally controlled municipalities, which showed an urban growth rate of 7.66 per cent.[70] Presumably this means that reporting was still so incomplete or so slow that the 1956 year end reports from some municipalities and provinces were not available as of late spring, 1957, when the June, 1957, series was compiled.

The inference to be drawn from all this is that the State Statistical Bureau was obliged to undertake quite a bit of manipulation of the reported data before it could produce a series for urban, rural, and total population for the P.R.C. for the years 1949–56. Without knowing how much manipulation was required or whether the underlying judgments were sound, no confidence can be placed in either the magnitude or the trend of these figures.[71]

---

[68] 'Communiqué on Results of Census and Registration of China's Population,' NCNA, November 1, 1954; translated in *Current Background*, No. 301 (November 1, 1954), p. 2.

[69] *T'ung-chi Kung-tso* Data Section, *op. cit.*, in *Extracts from China Mainland Magazines*, No. 91, U.S. Consulate General, Hong Kong, July 22, 1957, p. 24.

[70] *Ibid.*, p. 23. The reason for rounding downward is not given.

[71] The bureau itself made no great claim for the accuracy of the annual population figures, despite what other officials had said about the accuracy of census data. In January, 1956, an editorial in a statistical journal admitted that population statistics were among those which 'still were incomplete' and that they needed to be 'greatly' strengthened. See 'Shih-ying Kuo-chia Chien-she ti Hsü-yao, Pi-hsü pa T'ung-chi Kung-tso Tso-yao Yu To Yu K'uai, Yu

Even less confidence may be attached to the few figures on the urban population obtainable from scattered sources for the years since 1956. The bureau did not include a new urban population total among its population figures as of year end 1957, but another mainland source indicated an increase in the 'town' population during the First Five-Year Plan period of 38.9 per cent.[72] Applied to the year end 1952 urban figure, this would imply an urban population of 99,490,000 by the end of 1957. There are no official figures to indicate what happened in succeeding years, but it appears that there was a great upsurge in rural-to-urban migration during 1958 and 1959 and that a considerable growth in the urban population took place. According to one Chinese source in the fall of 1959, 'the urban population ... has been increasing very rapidly, particularly since the overall economic big leap forward last year.' The source adds that in '22 big and medium cities' the population had increased by 24.56 per cent between March, 1958, and March, 1959.[73] An increase rate this large applied to the figure previously indicated as the urban population at year end 1957 would imply an urban population in the vicinity of 125 million by the spring of 1959, but it is not possible to say whether the rate for these twenty-two cities would have been above or below the national average. A net increment of 25 million in a little over a year to the already crowded cities of China would have greatly overloaded accommodations and facilities and caused difficulties in the supplying of food and other essential services.

During the crisis of 1960–61, many urban factories were shut down, either for lack of raw materials from agriculture or because of the withdrawal of Soviet technicians and managers, yet the influx of rural population apparently continued, perhaps under the pressure of rural food shortages or in response to the availability of foreign grain to city residents. In the spring of 1961, one source noted that the population of cities and mining areas had increased by 20 million during the three Great Leap Forward years 1958–60.[74] In January, 1964, Po I-po reportedly told Anna Louise Strong in an interview that too much manpower had been drawn into the cities from the rural areas, that the natural calamities had shown that the urban population was too large for the countryside to support, and that until agriculture was mechanized, the urban population must be reduced from 130 million to 110 million.[75]

How this reduction was to be accomplished was not indicated. The regime had not been successful in controlling urban growth in previous years, and its administrative

Hao, Yu Sheng (To Meet the Needs of National Construction, More, Faster, Better, and More Economical Statistical Work Must Be Done),' T'ung-chi Kung-tso T'ung-hsin (Statistical Work Bulletin), No. 2, January 29, 1956, p. 3.

[72] Hsüeh Cheng-hsiu, 'Tentative Treatise on the Relationship Between Increase of Urban Population in Socialist Cities and Development of Industrial and Agricultural Production,' Kuang-ming Jih-pao, October 7, 1963; translated in Survey of Mainland China Press, No. 3093, November 4, 1963, p. 2. There is nothing to show that this percentage figure was based on State Statistical Bureau compilations, but its specificity to three significant digits and the reference to the First Five-Year Plan period imply derivation from official data.

[73] Chou Po-p'ing, 'Supply of Food Grains in China This Year,' China News Service, Canton, October 3, 1959; translated in Survey of China Mainland Press, No. 2126, October 29, 1959, p. 16. The list of twenty-two cities includes only two of fourteen cities with more than 1,000,000 population as of year-end 1957, according to State Statistical Bureau data (see Table 5-3). The 'million-cities' included are Wuhan and Sian. Of the other twenty cities, thirteen had less than 500,000 population in 1957.

[74] Liu Jih-hsin, 'On the Relationship Between Agriculture and Heavy Industry,' Ta-kung Pao (Peking), February 2, 1961; translated in Survey of China Mainland Press, No. 2466, March 29, 1961, p. 4.

[75] Anna Louise Strong, 'Interview with Po I-po on Economic Readjustment,' Ta-kung Pao, January 15, 1964; translated in Survey of China Mainland Press, No. 3152, February 3, 1964, p. 7.

apparatus was probably weaker during the 1960's, following the collapse of the Great Leap and the food crisis, than during the First Five-Year Plan period. Moreover, there had been almost continuous efforts to transfer segments of the urban population to rural areas since 1955. However, by 1960, a mass movement was reportedly under way to resettle young people permanently in the rural areas. According to 'incomplete statistical data' for eighteen provincial level units, 'more than 6 million urban and rural young men and women' had joined the agricultural front line.[76] In 1961, there were reports by foreign correspondents in Peking that 20 million persons had already been dispatched from urban areas and that 30 million more were to follow in 1962.[77] In April, 1962, the reduction of the urban population was one of the points in a ten-point program of economic 'readjustment' announced by Chou En-lai to the Second National People's Congress.[78] In December, 1963, it was reported that 'more than 40 million educated youths' had gone to the countryside and 'dedicated themselves to agriculture' since 1949,[79] and other large-scale transfers were described in press items during 1964, 1965, and the first half of 1966.

These numbers cannot be taken as a measure of the true volume of net migration or even as a reasonable basis for estimates. They do not give any indication of the amount of backflow, which must have been substantial, nor do they indicate clearly what proportion of the numbers reported were rural youth returning to agriculture after their schooling. If as many as 20 million, 30 million, or 40 million urban residents were supposed officially to have been resettled in rural areas by the beginning of 1964, an official estimate of 130 million urban residents remaining—The Po I-po figure—is hard to imagine.

However the resettlement programs may have fared before the summer of 1966, they seem to have received a sharp setback in the next two years, during the Cultural Revolution. Civil control organs, including the public security police responsible for checking unauthorized migration, were paralyzed by that disturbance. Mao's call to his youthful supporters to come to Peking to 'exchange experiences' with other revolutionaries seems to have instituted a period of virtually unrestricted travel, during which many young people recently transferred to rural areas may have been able to escape back to the cities once more. For a time, apparently, it was widely believed that the policy of transferring urban youth to rural areas was devised by Liu Shao-ch'i and had therefore been repudiated by the Maoists, but early in 1968 the policy was declared to be a vital part of Mao's 'proletarian revolutionary line,' and the drive was resumed.[80] If the urban registers are still being maintained, they are probably not now capable of furnishing a demographic profile of the present urban population.

---

[76] 'Over Six Million Young Men and Women Step Onto the First Line of Agriculture in the Country,' *Chung-kuo Ch'ing-nien-pao (China Youth Daily)*, Peking, October 23, 1960; translated in *Survey of China Mainland Press*, No. 2407, December 30, 1960, p. 10. Neither the time period covered by these 'data' nor the size of the urban component was indicated.

[77] Selections from several dispatches by Vasil Magdeski of the Yugoslav news agency, Tanjug, quoted in 'The Chinese Puzzle,' *East Europe*, 2, No. 10 (October, 1962): 25–26.

[78] 'Press Communiqué of the Third Session of the Second National People's Congress of China,' NCNA in English, April 16, 1962; in *Current Background*, No. 681, April 18, 1962, p. 2.

[79] '40 Million Youths Have Gone to Build the Countryside,' *China News Service*, December 9, 1963, cited in *Wen-hui Pao*, December 10, 1963; translated in *Survey of China Mainland Press*, No. 3120, December 16, 1963, pp. 14–15. Later news items quote this figure as though it referred only to urban youths transferred during the drive of the early 1960's. The origin and actual meaning of the figure cannot be determined. See '40 Million Educated Youths Are Eagerly Building the Countryside,' *China News Service*, August 27, 1964, cited in *Ta-kung Pao*, August 28, 1964; translated in *Survey of China Mainland Press*, No. 3293, September 4, 1964, pp. 1–2.

[80] 'Reply to Reader's Questions on Youths Who Have Returned from Frontier Regions to Shanghai,' *Wen-hui Pao*, February 25, 1968, translated in *Survey of China Mainland Press*, No.

Figures for individual cities. Official population figures for particular cities suffer from all of the deficiencies and ambiguities found in other population data from the P.R.C. plus a few special problems of their own. Scattered city population figures are available for the years prior to 1953, but the urban population registers for those years were admittedly quite defective.[81] The official communiqué of November 1, 1954, giving the final census results, included population figures only for the three municipalities under central authority at that time—Peking, Shanghai, and Tientsin.[82] Some census totals were given in census progress reports and in other news dispatches during and after the census-taking, but most of the 1953 census city figures that have since become available appeared not in Chinese but in Soviet sources.[83] The State Statistical Bureau provided a list of cities with a population of more than 500,000 in 1957 in its *Ten Great Years*, which are shown, together with the 1953 figures, in Table 5–3. These figures may give a rough indication of the size and rate of growth of the population in major Chinese cities during the First Five-Year Plan period, but they cannot safely be used to make precise inter-city comparisons, and they certainly cannot be used for extrapolation of future urban growth.

Besides the perennial problems of lapsing urban registers, the accuracy and comparability of the figures for individual cities were prejudiced by unresolved problems of definition. A curious omission in the instructions for the 1953 census is the failure to explain what constitutes a city for demographic purposes. The 1953 census directives state that the home address was to be written in the upper left corner of the household form for city households and in the upper right corner for rural village households,[84] but there were no instructions on how to distinguish urban from rural populations in the vicinity of cities, nor was there any word on how to distinguish a large village from a small town. These problems were apparently not recognized until 1955, when the State Council passed resolutions on the establishment of municipalities and towns and on the criteria for distinguishing urban and rural areas.[85] The new criteria did not

---

4146, March 26, 1968, pp. 15–16; 'Perseveringly Adhere to the Main Orientation of Integrating with Workers and Peasants' (editorial), *Wen-hui Pao*, May 4, 1968, translated in *Survey of China Mainland Press*, No. 4185, May 24, 1968, pp. 10–11. The new drive intensified during the summer and fall of 1968. Analysts in Hong Kong recently estimated the volume of compulsory movement at some 20 million within a two-month period beginning at the end of 1968 and extending into February, 1969. See Stanley Karnow, '20 Million Red Chinese Shunted to Countryside,' *The Washington Post*, February 21, 1969. The policy was still being vigorously enforced in November, 1970.

[81] See, for example, 'Population Census Statistical Work Concluded in Fushun,' NCNA, December 17, 1953, translated in *Survey of China Mainland Press*, No. 716, December 29, 1953, p. 18; and 'Census and Registration Work Completed in Areas with 60 per cent of Population in China,' NCNA, March 10, 1954, translated in *Survey of China Mainland Press*, No. 766, March 13–15, 1954, p. 27.

[82] 'Communiqué of Results of Census and Registration of China's Population,' NCNA, Peking, November 1, 1954; translated in *Current Background*, No. 301, November 1, 1954, pp. 1–2.

[83] Principally A. G. Shiger, *Administrativno-territorial'noye deleniye zarubezhnykh stran (Administrative-Territorial Division of Foreign Countries)*, 2d ed. (Moscow: Izdatel'stvo geograficheskoy literatury, 1957), pp. 142–44, and various volumes of the *Bol'shaya Sovetskaya entsiklopediya (Great Soviet Encyclopedia)*, 2d ed. (Moscow). For a list of 1953 census city population figures from these and other sources, see Morris B. Ullman, *Cities of Mainland China: 1953 and 1958*, U.S. Bureau of the Census, International Population Reports, Series P–95, No. 59, Table 1, pp. 18–29.

[84] 'Directions on Filling Out Census and Registration Forms,' NCNA, April 6, 1953; translated in *Current Background*, No. 241, May 5, 1953, p. 36.

[85] The first was passed at the eleventh meeting of the State Council on June 9, 1955, and the second at the twentieth meeting on November 7, 1955. See *Chung-kuo Jen-min Kung-ho-kuo Fa-kuei Hui-pien (Compilation of Laws and Regulations of the Chinese People's Republic)*, 2 (Peking:

correspond exactly to the *de facto* definitions of the 1953 census, but it was said that the differences were minor and that the new definitions were consistent with 'tradition' and would not 'create any problems.'[86] Whether or not the new criteria ever became operational for statistical purposes is not known.

After 1957, the problem of definitions became infinitely more complex when the

Table 5-3—The Population of Major Cities in the P.R.C., 1953 and 1957
(thousands)

Cities	Mid-1953	Year end 1957	Cities	Mid-1953	Year end 1957
Central Municipalities			Kiangsu		
Peking	2,768	4,010	Nanking	1,092	1,419
Shanghai	6,204	6,900	Hsüchou	373	676
Hopei			Suchou	474	633
Tientsin	2,694	3,200	Wuhsi	582	613
Tangshan	693	800	Chekiang		
Shihchiachuang	373	598	Hangchow	697	784
Shansi			Fukien		
Taiyüan	721	1,020	Foochow	553	616
Liaoning			Honan		
Shenyang	2,300	2,411	Chengchow	595	766
Port Arthur–Dairen	892	1,508	Hupei		
Fushun	679	985	Wuhan	1,427	2,146
Anshan	549	805	Hunan		
Kirin			Changsha	651	703
Changchun	855	975	Kiangsi		
Kirin	435	568	Nanchang	398	508
Heilungkiang			Kwangtung		
Harbin	1,163	1,552	Canton	1,599	1,840
Tsitsihar	345	668	Szechwan		
Shensi			Chungking	1,772	2,121
Sian	787	1,310	Chengtu	857	1,107
Kansu			Kweichow		
Lanchow	397	699	Kweiyang	271	504
Shantung			Yünnan		
Tsinan	680	862	K'unming	699	880
Tsingtao	917	1,121			
Tzupo	184	806			

Sources:

1953: Morris B. Ullman, *Cities of Mainland China* (note 81, above), pp. 35–36.

1957: State Statistical Bureau, *Ten Great Years: Statistics of the Economic and Cultural Achievements of the People's Republic of China* (Peking: Foreign Languages Press, 1960), p. 12.

Fa-lü Ch'u-pan-she, July–December 1955): 409–10; and 'Kuo-wu-yüan Kuan-yü Ch'eng-hsiang Hua-fen Piao-chun te Kuei-ting (State Council Regulations on the Demarcation of Urban and Rural Areas),' *T'ung-chi Kung-tso T'ung-hsin*, No. 12, December 17, 1955, p. 4.

[86] State Statistical Bureau, 'Kuan-yü Ch'eng Hsiang Hua-fen Piao-chun Jo-kan Chu-yao Wen-t'ite Shuo-ming (Explanation of Some Important Questions Concerning the Criteria for the Demarcation of Rural and Urban Areas),' *T'ung-chi Kung-tso T'ung-hsin*, No. 12, December 17, 1955, pp. 5–6.

larger metropolitan centers began to annex contiguous rural units.[87] Much of the newly annexed territory was not urban at all. For example, the area of Peking increased from 4,540 to 8,770 square kilometers in March, 1958, and to 17,000 square kilometers in October, 1958.[88]

The population figures cited in mainland sources may refer to (1) the population in the 'city districts,' (2) the population of the city and its 'suburbs,' (3) the population of the total area under municipal control, (4) the urban population in the city and its 'suburbs,' or (5) the urban population under municipal control.[89] Sometimes the user of the figure does not seem to know what population his figure refers to, and often it is obvious that he has no idea of the reference date of the figure. The confusion introduced in 1958 continues to the present, with the result that it is not possible now to compile an updated list of city figures even for the major municipalities. All recently quoted figures must be regarded with suspicion; the chances are they are older than they seem.[90]

Birth, death, and natural increase rates. The anomalies of the increase rates implied by the official total and province population figures are further complicated when examined in connection with the official data on vital rates. There are only a few vital rates for provinces. Those for sixteen rural areas given in the previously cited paper by Ch'en Ta[91] were presumably based on data from the experimental vital registration work of 1951–54, but none of the sixteen reporting units is larger than a single *hsien*, and several are as small as a single *hsiang* (village). The rates reported strongly suggest that rural vital registration was incomplete and unreliable even under the relatively favorable circumstances of the experimental registration areas in the early 1950's. Without due allowance for underregistration, they may not be taken as even a rough approximation of the levels of birth, death, and natural increase rates in rural China at that time.

Another group of vital rates are those for seven cities for the years 1952–56 and for

---

[87] A decision to allow centrally controlled municipalities and other 'comparatively large cities' to 'assume leadership' over contiguous counties was 'approved' by the Second National People's Congress Standing Committee in September, 1959, but the policy had already been in effect for more than a year. The reasons given for permitting the annexations were: (1) to accord with the rapid progress of socialist construction, (2) to encourage mutual assistance between industry and agriculture, and (3) to facilitate allocation of manpower. 'NPC Decision Granting Large Municipalities Jurisdiction Over *Hsien* and Autonomous *Hsien*,' NCNA, September 17, 1959; translated in *Survey of China Mainland Press*, No. 2101, September 21, 1959, p. 5.

[88] See Appendix D in Ullman, *Cities of Mainland China* (note 83, above), pp. 42–44. A square kilometer is roughly .3861 square miles.

[89] Within cities and municipalities, a part of the resident population was classified as rural for occupational reasons, and some mainland population figures for urban units exclude these while others include them. The differences are sometimes mistaken for inconsistencies in the official totals, and they can be rather large, especially in figures referring to the area under municipal control.

[90] No demographically respectable extrapolations of the urban population of mainland China or of the population in particular cities or groups of cities can be made for the years since 1957 using the currently available information. Attempts to make use of the few figures for the urban population or the population of specific cities that have appeared since 1957 are of questionable value as long as the definition of what constitutes the 'urban' population is uncertain and as long as the figures for the cities are ambiguous as to date and coverage. General trends cannot be assumed if the effects of The Great Leap Forward, the food crisis years, the relocations of urban populations, and the Cultural Revolution on urban growth cannot be determined. To make projections without solving these problems is to produce numbers that may be seriously misleading.

[91] Ch'en Ta, *Population Census of 1953* (note 25, above), p. 25.

two additional cities for 1956 only,[92] but some of the data show signs of incomplete registration of births and deaths in the earlier years of their span, of either increasing completeness or inflation during 1954, and of a further decline in completeness of registration during 1956. There is some evidence to suggest that the data were obtained only from selected residential areas within each municipality. It is not possible to derive from these figures more than a rough estimate of the actual level of birth, death, and natural increase rates for urban areas during the 1950's.[93]

The most important of all the officially released vital rates for China is the series of national vital rates for 1952–57 (see Table 5–4). This series was never published in complete form by an official agency but was issued piecemeal through various channels. Some of the figures were given to foreign visitors to Peking during 1958. Prior to that time, only the 1953 figures were available. They had appeared in an article by Pai Chien-hua at the time of the census communiqué in November, 1954, in which he said that the data came from a collection of rural and urban reporting units containing a total population of 30,180,000.[94] The composition of the 'sample' is curious. It reportedly included twenty-nine 'large and medium' cities, rural units in thirty-five *hsien*, and the 'whole province of Ninghsia,' but this would give it too large an urban component to represent a country that was 85 per cent rural, and the fact that the number of *hsien* represented is given but not the number of provinces suggests that they may not have been widely distributed.[95] The 'sample' was apparently based on convenience rather than on representativeness.

Table 5—4—Official Vital Rates for the P.R.C., 1952–57
(rates per 1,000 population)

Year	Birth Rate	Death Rate	Natural Increase
1952	37.0	18.0	19.0
1953	37.0	17.0	20.0
1954	37.0	13.0	24.0
1955	35.0	12.4	22.6
1956	32.0	11.4	20.6
1957	34.0	11.0	23.0

Source: S. Chandrasekhar, *China's Population: Census and Vital Statistics* (Hong Kong: Hong Kong University Press, 1959), p. 50. (A crude birth rate of 38.0 per thousand given for 1954 in the source is apparently an error.)

[92] Roland Pressat, 'La Population de la Chine et son Economie,' *Population*, 13, No. 4 (October–December, 1958): 572–73.

[93] For discussion of the urban and rural vital rates, see John S. Aird, *The Size, Composition, and Growth of the Population of Mainland China*, U.S. Bureau of the Census, International Population Statistics Reports, Series P-90, No. 15 (Washington, D.C.: U.S. Government Printing Office, 1961), pp. 39–40, 47–49.

[94] Pai Chien-hua, '600 Million People' (note 25, above), p. 33. The investigation that produced these figures is referred to in the translated source as a 'census check,' which has led many people to suppose that the data were collected as part of the 1953 census work. This appears to be an error. Presumably the population totals for some of the reporting areas were census data, but the totals of births and deaths could not have been, since the census instructions included no provisions for collecting such information and the census forms allowed no place for recording it. Some of the vital data probably came from the Ministry of Public Health vital registration experiments, which were discontinued at just about this time, and the rest from the urban registers.

[95] Pai Chien-hua, *loc. cit.* The inclusion of Ninghsia, the Hui minority area far to the north that had just been incorporated into Kansu Province, is rather curious by itself. Vital registration could not have been very advanced in that region by 1954.

Vital rates and absolute totals of births, deaths, and natural increase were obtained from the State Statistical Bureau by a French demographer in August, 1958.[96]

A series of vital rates reportedly given by an unspecified official agency to another foreign visitor in December, 1958 includes vital rates for 1952, 1955, and 1956, as well as those previously released.[97] However, in view of the peculiarities noted in the absolute figures for 1954 and 1957, it is doubtful that any of the rates in this series can be taken as the products of a national reporting system. Instead, it must be assumed that, at best, they are based on registration in a limited and unrepresentative sample of areas, and, at worst, they may have been improvised by methods that would not entitle them to serious consideration.

Data on age and sex. Aside from a few fragmentary figures for small units, the only published age data for the population of China since 1949 were those collected during the 1953 census. Age data were evidently obtained in many of the population investigations in both rural and urban areas prior to the census, but even the local authorities seldom released any of the results, and these data apparently were never compiled and published. Detailed data by age and sex should have been available from the population registers during at least some of the years between the census of 1953 and the disruption of statistical work in 1958, but again, no data have appeared in print to suggest that compilations had been made in Peking.

The 1953 census data were never published in absolute figures for small age groups. Percentage figures to the nearest 0.1 per cent for the population of both sexes were given in ten-year age groups for ages 5 through seventy-four years in Ch'en Ta's paper of August, 1957, and in ten-year age groups for ages twenty through fifty-nine in a journal article of May, 1959, by T'ien Feng-t'iao, an instructor in a school operated by the Ministry of Public Health. Sex ratios for irregular age groups were given by Tai Shih-kuang in his paper of December, 1956. All these figures were presumably obtained from official sources and seem to be essentially in agreement. They are presented in Table 5–5.

The most complete age-sex data from the census were disclosed by T'ien in the form of a population pyramid representing the percentage distribution of the census population in five-year age groups by sex through eighty years of age. Though the pyramid was crudely drawn, readings can be taken from it that, when controlled to the other percentage figures in ten-year age groups for both sexes, seem to give a fairly close approximation of the original census age-sex data. Results of one such reading are given in Table 5–6.

---

[96] Roland Pressat, 'La Population de la Chine et son Economie' (note 92, above), p. 570. The figures for 1953 are incorrectly dated 1952 in Pressat's article. Pressat's absolute totals are as follows:

	Births	Deaths	Natural Increase
1953	21,510,000	9,880,000	11,630,000
1954	21,560,000	7,790,000	13,770,000
1957	21,660,000	6,890,000	14,770,000

The crude rates for 1957 seem to have been derived from absolute totals of births, deaths, and natural increase and some figure for the annual average population. But the birth and natural increase rates for 1954 cannot be obtained by dividing the absolute totals for births and net increase by the official annual average population figure for that year. Moreover, when the absolute totals of births, deaths, and natural increase for 1954 are compared with the corresponding figures for 1957, with allowance for the fact that the original figures seem to have been in units of 10,000, the increment or decrement from 1954 to 1957 is a round figure in each case (births, plus 10 units; deaths, minus 90 units; and natural increase, plus 100 units). This anomaly suggests the possibility that the absolutes were assumed figures.

[97] Chandrasekhar, *China's Population: Census and Vital Statistics, loc. cit.* (see note to Table 5–4).

Table 5-5—1953 Census Age and Sex Data from Ch'en Ta, T'ien Feng-t'iao,
and Tai Shih-kuang
(age distributions in percentages; sex ratios are numbers of males
per 100 females)

Ch'en Ta's Age Data		T'ien Feng-t'iao Age Data		Tai Shih-kuang's Sex Ratios	
All ages	100.0	All ages	99.99	All ages	107.7
0 to 4 years	15.6	0 to 6 years	20.44	Under 1 year	104.9
5 to 14 years	20.3	7 to 19 years	24.58	1 and 2 years	106.2
15 to 24 years	17.3	20 to 29 years	16.00	3 to 6 years	110.0
25 to 34 years	14.6	30 to 39 years	13.29	7 to 13 years	115.8
35 to 44 years	12.0	40 to 49 years	10.57	14 to 17 years	113.7
45 to 54 years	9.3	50 to 59 years	7.85	18 to 35 years	111.5
55 to 64 years	6.5	60 years and		36 to 55 years	106.8
65 to 74 years	3.4	over	7.26	56 years and	
75 years and				over	86.7
over	1.0				

Sources: Ch'en's data: Ch'en Ta, *New China's Population Census of 1953, and Its Relations to National Reconstruction and Demographic Research*, Table 4, p. 23.

T'ien's data: T'ien Feng-t'iao, 'Wo-kuo Chi-hua Sheng-yü ho Jen-k'ou Tseng-chih Wen-t'i (The Problem of Planned Birth and Population Increase in China),' *Jen-min Pao-chien (People's Health)*, 1, No. 5 (May 1, 1959): 462.

Tai's data: Tai Shih-kuang, *1953 Population Census of China* (note 25, above), p. 21.

Table 5-6—1953 Census Age and Sex Data from T'ien's Population Pyramid
(age distributions are percentage figures; sex ratios are
numbers of males per 100 females)

Ages	Both Sexes	Male	Female	Sex Ratio
All ages	100.00	51.82	48.18	107.6
0 to 4 years	15.59	8.02	7.57	105.9
5 to 9 years	10.94	5.79	5.16	112.2
10 to 14 years	9.39	5.06	4.33	117.1
15 to 19 years	9.11	4.80	4.30	111.6
20 to 24 years	8.24	4.29	3.95	108.4
25 to 29 years	7.75	4.13	3.63	113.7
30 to 34 years	6.89	3.67	3.22	114.0
35 to 39 years	6.40	3.33	3.07	108.6
40 to 44 years	5.56	2.87	2.69	106.4
45 to 49 years	5.01	2.56	2.45	104.6
50 to 54 years	4.24	2.16	2.08	103.9
55 to 59 years	3.61	1.82	1.78	102.2
60 to 64 years	2.90	1.41	1.49	95.2
65 to 69 years	2.04	0.95	1.08	88.1
70 to 74 years	1.37	0.57	0.80	72.0
75 to 79 years	0.64	0.26	0.38	68.3
80 years and over	0.32	0.12	0.21	57.5

Source: Derived from age-sex pyramid given in T'ien, 'Wo-kuo Chi-hua Sheng-yü ho Jen-k'ou Tseng-chih Wen-ti,' p. 463. Percentage figures were originally calculated to three decimal places and have been independently rounded. Sex ratios were calculated on the unrounded figures.

Figures by sex for the population 'directly surveyed' during the 1953 census were also given in the November, 1954, release. These figures apparently were not obtained as a tally from the original returns but were derived by multiplying the figure of 574,205,940 persons 'directly surveyed' by percentage figures for the male and female proportions, which seem to have been available only to four significant digits. The results were carried out to the full nine digits. How the percentage figures were obtained is not indicated. The State Statistical Bureau gave figures representing the population by sex for the mainland and Taiwan for year end 1949, 1953, and 1957 in its *Ten Great Years*, which have since been repeated each year by the *People's Handbook*. The figures were apparently calculated by applying assumed percentage figures by sex in four significant digits to the total population figures to the nearest 10,000. The percentage figures for 1949 differ by exactly 0.1 per cent from the figures for 1953 in the direction of a greater surplus of males. The percentage figures for 1957 assume a continuation of the trend toward a balance of the sexes, but only enough to round the percentage figures to the next tenth of one per cent. The 1953 year end percentage figures by sex imply a change in the wrong direction when compared with the percentage figures by sex for the population 'directly surveyed' by the census as of the middle of 1953.[98] The over-all rate of change in the sex ratio implied by these figures is too slow for a country in which mortality levels were declining as rapidly as they are presumed to have declined in China between 1949 and 1957. Thus, it must be inferred that the percentage figures by sex for year end 1949, 1953, and 1957, at least, and perhaps the census figures as well, were the products of a very crude method of estimating.

Ethnic composition, According to the 1953 census, 6 per cent of the mainland population were members of ethnic and religious minorities. Most of the minority peoples are located around the land borders of China in regions that are sparsely populated but increasingly penetrated by migrants of the Han majority from other parts of China (see Map 10). Of the 35,320,360 non-Han people reported during the census, more than four-fifths were members of one or another of the ten largest minorities:

Chuangs	6,611,455	Miaos	2,511,339
Uighurs	3,640,125	Manchus	2,418,931
Hui	3,559,350	Mongols	1,462,956
Yi	3,254,269	Puyi	1,247,883
Tibetans	2,775,622	Koreans	1,120,405

The remaining 6.7 million were distributed among some forty other minority groups, some of which contained only a few hundred persons.[99]

The presentation of these figures to the last digit is another of the many anomalies of the population data from the P.R.C., since it was admitted when the census results were published that parts of some minorities could not be directly enumerated and that the numbers had been completed by supplementary estimates. Presumably the difference between the 'directly surveyed' population and the reported mainland total, about 8.4 million, represents the estimated portion, in which case it would

---

[98] The 1953 census sex ratio given by Tai differs slightly from that reported for the 'directly surveyed' population in the 1953 census, but it coincides exactly with that implied by the State Statistical Bureau's figures for year end 1953.

[99] A more complete list of minority population figures is given in Fang Jen, 'Wo-kuo Shao-shu Min-tsu te Jen-k'ou yü Fen-pu (The Populations and Distribution of the National Minorities in China),' *Ti-li Chih-shih*, No. 6, June 14, 1958, pp. 258–59. Many of the figures in this article seem to be rounded versions of the 1953 census figures, but a few are apparently intended to be later estimates.

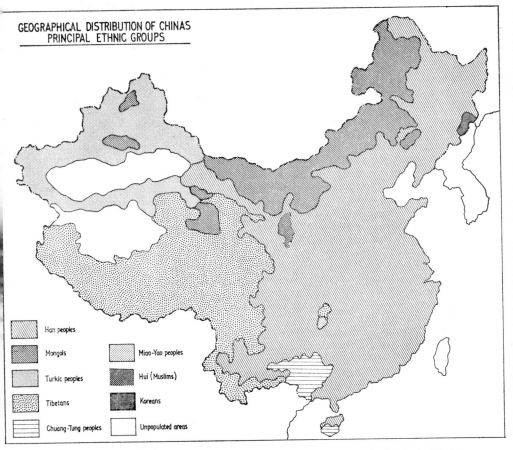

GEOGRAPHICAL DISTRIBUTION OF CHINAS PRINCIPAL ETHNIC GROUPS

Han peoples

Mongols

Turkic peoples

Tibetans

Chuang-Tung peoples

Miao-Yao peoples

Hui (Muslims)

Koreans

Unpopulated areas

Map 10   Geographical Distribution of Mainland China's Principal Ethnic Groups

Source: Adapted from S. I. Bruk, *Karta Narodov Kitaya MNR i Korei* (*Map of the People's of China, the Mongolian People's Republic, and Korea*) (Moscow: Akademiya Nauk SSSR, 1959).

amount to something less than one-fourth of the minority population total. However, the estimated portion was probably greater for some minorities, such as the not wholly pacified Tibetans and Kazakhs, than for others more completely under Han domination in 1953. Moreover, census registrars were instructed to let heads of households decide how they wanted their minority status recorded. In the case of minority residents of urban areas, at least, there may have been both reason and opportunity to conceal minority status for purposes of public record. Hence no great confidence should be placed in the number or relative size of minority groups as officially reported.

Since the census, a few more recent figures for particular minorities have appeared in the mainland press. Some of these may be based on local population reports, but the rest appear to be very rough estimates. One such estimate, for the Tibetan population (not including the Han Chinese) in the Tibet Autonomous Region, gives figures for 1960 and 1965 that were evidently calculated by assuming a base total and an annual increase rate of exactly 2 per cent, the official national increase rate as of

1953.[100] Estimates employing such crude methods and improbable assumptions are virtually worthless.[101]

POPULATION DATA IN PERSPECTIVE

The data discussed above are the official population data for mainland China currently available. By international standards, the collection is modest. Some subjects are missing from the list altogether. There are no data for the entire country on such subjects as occupation, employment, educational attainment, literacy, marital status, marriages, divorces, internal migration, or immigration, nor have there been any attempts to collect such data on a national scale, possibly excepting the 1964 investigation. The record systems set up during the First Five-Year Plan period were theoretically capable of compiling some of these types of data and might have done so if their development had continued after 1957. Several special surveys and censuses of limited scope gathered data on some of these subjects, notably on particular types of nonagricultural employment,[102] but the data yield from even these investigations is extremely limited.

The published demographic data cover only a limited span of years and are often incomplete within that span. The most complete series, the State Statistical Bureau's total, urban, and rural population figures, consists to a considerable extent of estimated or partially estimated instead of reported figures. The methods of estimating are uniformly crude and sometimes rest on implausible assumptions. There is every reason to suspect that the detailed data from the 1953 census, the population registers, and the vital registration experiments would show many defects that cannot be detected in the summary data, and that the failure of official agencies to publish demographic data in detail is due in part to the fear of exposing their shortcomings to the critical view of domestic and foreign scholars. If this is so, it is unlikely that the full record of past demographic investigations will ever be revealed, as long as the Chinese Communist authorities are able to prevent their disclosure.

Nevertheless, there is some reason to believe that the population data collected by the P.R.C. during the First Five-Year Plan period came much closer to demographic reality than did any previous population figures. Granted that the technicians who designed and supervised the investigations and reporting systems were inexperienced, the cadres who executed their orders poorly trained, and the population whose cooperation was required for the success of these efforts remained distrustful of their stated purposes, still, compared with previous regimes, the Chinese Communists had a fairly well-disciplined administrative apparatus during the early years and much seriousness of purpose. Though their methods of data-collecting were not unlike many that had failed in the past, the Chinese Communists were certainly in a position to make them serve better than they had ever served before. In a country that has never known statistical accuracy, even approximation to reality is a signal achievement.

If the population data are compared with other kinds of statistical data for mainland China for the same period, the population figures appear to be better than some,

---

[100] 'Tibet's Population Increases,' NCNA (English), August 20, 1965; in *Survey of China Mainland Press*, No. 3525, August 25, 1965, p. 22.

[101] For further discussion of ethnic groups in the P.R.C., see John S. Aird, 'Population Growth and Distribution in Mainland China,' *An Economic Profile of Mainland China*, 2 (Washington, D.C.: U.S. Government Printing Office, February, 1967): 391–401.

[102] For a review of official data on nonagricultural employment in mainland China and the investigations and reporting systems that produced the data, see John Philip Emerson, *Nonagricultural Employment in Mainland China: 1949–1958*, U.S. Bureau of the Census, International Population Statistics Reports, Series P-90, No. 21 (Washington, D.C.: U.S. Government Printing Office, 1965), 240 pages.

worse than others. This is partly because, in the nature of things, some types of data are more easily collected than others. Activities of a relatively specialized nature or a relatively limited scope carried on within a relatively few institutions, structures, channels, or localities—such as heavy industry, rail or air transport, state finance, or foreign trade—are often continuously recorded as a matter of functional necessity or, if not, can be enumerated without too much difficulty by special surveys. The primary sources of information for mass phenomena—such as population, health, agriculture, and the production, distribution, and consumption of widely utilized consumer goods and services—are comparatively inaccessible. Among the latter, demographic data are by no means the most difficult to collect. Human beings are at least conveniently countable units; because they must be fed, clothed, and housed, the signs of human habitation are not readily concealed from a determined search.

Moreover, biological human nature imposes rather narrow limits of plausibility on demographic measures, whereas the possible magnitudes and trends of many other kinds of phenomena are intrinsically less circumscribed. Bad population data can often be recognized at a glance for what they are and summarily rejected. Other kinds of data are more likely to be accepted uncritically because they are not obviously defective. Demographic data may also be analyzed for internal consistency; other types of data offer fewer opportunities for consistency checks. It is therefore easier to assess the probable biases and margins of error in demographic data than in many other kinds of social statistics. This difference sometimes gives rise to a 'double standard' of data evaluation when population factors are related to other social, economic, or political parameters. Whatever the difficulties, it is important that all data from the P.R.C. be subjected, insofar as possible, to an equivalent standard of statistical evaluation.

For many purposes, it may be better to leave officially reported figures alone and make use instead of estimated and projected figures. So far as demographic estimates and projections are concerned, these at least have the virtue of internal consistency, and the methods and assumptions used in generating the figures are usually described in detail in the accompanying text. The most elaborate series of estimates and projections of the mainland China population currently available are those prepared by the Department of Economic and Social Affairs of the United Nations and the Foreign Demographic Analysis Division of the U.S. Bureau of the Census.[103] Both series include a number of alternate models based on various assumptions about past and future demographic trends, from among which the user may make his own selection according to his assessment of the relevant general conditions of life in mainland China.

SELECTED BIBLIOGRAPHY

AIRD, JOHN S. *Estimates and Projections of the Population of Mainland China: 1953–1986.* U.S. Bureau of the Census, International Population Reports, Series P–91, No. 17. Washington, D.C.: U.S. Government Printing Office, 1968, pp. 1–73. Detailed tables of model population estimates and projections for mainland China by age and sex in five-year age groups and in various functional age groups, together with components of change and vital rates,

---

[103] For the United Nations series, see Department of Economics and Social Affairs, United Nations, *World Population Prospects as Assessed in 1963*, Population Studies, no. 41 (New York, 1966), pp. 51–58. The Bureau of the Census series are presented in John S. Aird, 'Population Growth,' Chapter 4 of Eckstein, Galenson, and Liu, eds., *Economic Trends in Communist China* (note 30, above), pp. 183–327, and in more elaborate tabulations in John S. Aird, *Estimates and Projections of the Population of Mainland China: 1953–1986*, U.S. Bureau of the Census, International Population Reports, Series P–91, No. 17 (Washington, D.C.: U.S. Government Printing Office, 1968).

from January 1, 1953, through January 1, 1986. Text discussion covers the underlying methods and assumptions, demographic developments since the models were constructed in 1965, and some implications and uses of the figures.

———. 'Estimating China's Population,' *The Annals of the American Academy of Political and Social Science*, 369 (January, 1967): 61–72. A brief summary of the problems of evaluating demographic evidence, making current estimates of China's population, and using the estimates properly.

———. 'Population Growth,' Chapter 4 edited by ALEXANDER ECKSTEIN, WALTER GALEN-SON, and TA-CHUNG LIU, eds., *Economic Trends in Communist China*. Chicago: Aldine Publishing Company, 1968, pp. 183–327. A review of evidence and scholarly argument over population growth in China from the Ch'ing dynasty to the present time, with emphasis on differing evaluations of the data collected by the Chinese Communist authorities. Model estimates and projections of the population by age and sex from 1953 through 1985 are presented in summary tables, with a discussion of the underlying methods and assumptions.

———. 'Population Growth and Distribution in Mainland China,' *An Economic Profile of Mainland China*. Washington, D.C.: U.S. Government Printing Office, 1967, pp. 341–401. A short analysis of demographic information from the P.R.C., with summary tables giving estimates and projections of the population. The distribution of the population by age and sex, by province and region, by rural and urban residence, and by ethnic status, is also discussed.

———. 'Population Growth: Evidence and Interpretation,' *The China Quarterly*, No. 7, July–September, 1961, pp. 44–56. A general statement of the problem of interpreting the evidence on population growth in China, its implications for professional differences of opinion and for would-be users of population figures for China.

———. 'The Present and Prospective Population of Mainland China,' *Population Trends in Eastern Europe, the U.S.S.R., and Mainland China*. New York: Milbank Memorial Fund, 1960, pp. 93–140. A review of official data on the size, age-sex structure, and rate of growth of the population of the P.R.C., with an evaluation of the methods and inherent biases of the 1953 census, and a discussion of China's demographic prospects as envisioned in 1959.

———. *The Size, Composition, and Growth of the Population of Mainland China*, U.S. Bureau of the Census, International Population Statistics Reports, Series P–90, No. 15. Washington, D.C.: U.S. Government Printing Office, 1961. An analysis of the 1953 census, the population registers, and other sources of population data from the P.R.C., with estimates of the population by age and sex for 1953 and 1958.

DURAND, John D. 'The Population Statistics of China, A.D. 2–1953,' *Population Studies*, 13, No. 3 (March, 1960): 209–56. A review of all available figures for the total population of China from the earliest historical records through the 1953 census. An effort is made to relate the trend of the official figures with other information and general demographic knowledge to produce an overview of the course of population growth in China during the twentieth century.

EMERSON, JOHN PHILIP. 'Employment in Mainland China: Problems and Prospects,' *An Economic Profile of Mainland China*. Washington, D.C.: U.S. Government Printing Office, 1967, pp. 403–69. A summary evaluation of employment data from the P.R.C., review of the sources of the labor supply, and the size and distribution of nonagricultural employment by sector and branch. Discussion of level of skill and of educational and professional attainment in selected specialized branches.

———. *Nonagricultural Employment in Mainland China, 1949–1958*, U.S. Bureau of the Census, International Population Statistics Reports, Series P–90, No. 21. Washington, D.C.: U.S. Government Printing Office, 1965. A detailed analysis of the sources of official employment data, definitions of terms and concepts, evaluation of data on nonagricultural employment, total and by sector, branch of the economy, branch of industry, and in handicrafts, with summary tables, full documentation, and special appendixes.

HO, PING-TI. *Studies on the Population of China, 1368–1953*. Cambridge, Mass.: Harvard

University Press, 1959. A historical study of the nature of population figures for China and of the administrative systems that produced them from the time of the Ming Emperor T'ai-tsu to the 1953 census. Major attention is directed to historical records of social, political, and economic changes that affected population growth, including catastrophic occurrence.

ORLEANS, LEO A. 'The Population of Communist China,' in RONALD FREEDMAN, ed., *Population: The Vital Revolution*. Chicago: Aldine Publishing Company, 1964, pp. 227–39. A short statement of recent trends in Chinese demographic development and population policy.

———. 'Population Redistribution in Communist China,' *Population Trends in Eastern Europe, The U.S.S.R., and Mainland China*. New York: Milbank Memorial Fund, 1960, pp. 141–56. A discussion of the directions and causes of the major movements of population in mainland China, both interregional and rural-urban.

———. *Professional Manpower and Education in Communist China*. Washington, D.C.: U.S. Government Printing Office, 1961. A review of the development of education in Communist China, including policies and practices relating to organization, staffing, enrollment, curricula, and the training of a skilled labor force.

TAEUBER, IRENE B., and NAI-CHI WANG, 'Questions on Population Growth in China,' *Population Trends in Eastern Europe, the U.S.S.R., and Mainland China*. New York: Milbank Memorial Fund, 1960, pp. 263–310. A critical survey of historical and recent population figures for China. Technical reasons for doubting the validity of official population data.

———. 'Population Reports in the Ch'ing Dynasty,' *The Journal of Asia Studies*, 19, No. 4 (August, 1960): 403–17. Evaluation of Ch'ing dynasty population reports and reporting procedures. Anomalies in the figures and criticisms by contemporary authorities.

TIEN, H. YUAN. 'The Demographic Significance of Organized Population Transfers in Communist China,' *Demography*, 1, No. 1 (1964): 220–26. The development of various aspects of official policy regarding rural-to-urban migration, including relocation of the migrants and surplus urban population in rural areas and in sparsely populated frontier regions, where land reclamation projects were under way. Concludes that the demographic effect of these programs thus far has been minimal.

United Nations, Department of Economic and Social Affairs. *Future Population Estimates by Sex and Age: Report IV, The Population of Asia and the Far East, 1950–1980*, New York, 1959, pp. 24–28, 76–99. Population projections for the P.R.C. and a discussion of methods and assumptions, including a case for subdividing China into two major regions having different traditional fertility levels.

———. *World Population Prospects as Assessed in 1963*, Population Studies No. 41. New York, 1966, pp. 51–58. Presents the rationale behind the United Nations' most recent population estimates for the P.R.C.

6

THE CHINESE COMMUNIST PARTY: HISTORY AND DOCTRINES

MICHAEL LINDSAY

The Beginning

Leninist origin. Most of the Communist Parties that were founded within a few years of the Russian Revolution started through a split in an established socialist party, so that their Leninism developed from a previous background of Marxism. The Chinese Communist Party, however, was Leninist from the start.

Marx was not entirely unknown in China before 1917, but he was certainly not well known. In 1915, even Ch'en Tu-hsiu, who later became the leader of the Chinese Communist Party, was writing of Marx and Lassalle as Germans who had developed the French socialist theories of Babeuf, Saint-Simon, and Fourier. This relative lack of interest is quite understandable. Marxism is primarily a theory about the development of capitalism, while China before 1920 was a country in which capitalism had barely started to develop. A revolutionary Chinese intellectual would naturally be inclined to dismiss Marxism as a theory relevant for the industrialized West and perhaps for Japan but not for his own country. When Western ideas really started to spread among Chinese intellectuals from the 1890's on, anarchism was more attractive to those who wanted to be most revolutionary and most up-to-date; and, until about 1920, anarchism had a wider following than Marxism.

The attractiveness of Leninism is also understandable. By 1917 most patriotic Chinese intellectuals had become disillusioned and frustrated. The revolution of 1911 had only produced the dictatorship of Yüan Shih-k'ai, and Yüan's death in 1916 started the period of the warlords, leaving China's problems even worse than before. Europe, which had seemed to offer a model for development, was involved in a destructive war. The Kuomintang (Nationalist Party) still had a fairly large membership, but Sun Yat-sen's rival government at Canton depended on the favor of local warlords and seemed unlikely to become an effective force in Chinese politics.

While real power was in the hands of soldiers, the intellectuals still had prestige based on the traditional Chinese respect for education. The intellectual center of China was Peking. Ts'ai Yüan-p'ei was able to maintain a high degree of academic freedom at Peking University, which the intellectuals used for bitter criticism of traditional Chinese society and heated debates about what new system could solve the problems of their country. Leninism offered a technique through which a highly disciplined party could organize the masses who had remained outside Chinese political life and thereby win power to reconstruct society. It also offered a plausible diagnosis of China's troubles in terms of imperialist exploitation and class conflict.

Western versus Soviet influence. The democratic West offered little competition in the realm of ideas. John Dewey and Bertrand Russell gave lectures in Peking, which roused great interest and won some permanent followers (Hu Shih, for example, always considered himself a disciple of Dewey). But it would be hard to find in the ideas of either man the basis for any program of action applicable to China in the warlord period. And the actions of Western statesmen turned Chinese opinion against the West. President Wilson's declarations had had considerable appeal, but the actual results of the Versailles Conference seemed to show that these principles had no operational meaning. The Western powers showed no signs of willingness to renounce their imperialist privileges in China and even supported the claims of Japanese imperialism.

Soviet policy combined enthusiasm for the world revolution with opportunistic maneuvers to safeguard the national interests of the Soviet Union. The Karakhan Declaration of July, 1919, tried to win the support of Chinese public opinion by renouncing all the rights and privileges Tsarist imperialism had acquired in China. At this time, the Soviet position in the Far East was very weak, and the Karakhan Declaration was renouncing rights that the Soviet Government was not in a position to exercise. When the Soviet envoys—Yurin, Joffe, and then Karakhan himself—came to China for negotiations that led to the establishment of diplomatic relations in 1924, the Soviet Government was not willing to give up Russian rights on the Chinese Eastern Railway or the control of Outer Mongolia, which the Soviet Union had acquired by the end of 1921. And the Soviet envoys were willing to deal with all forces in China, the warlord-controlled government in Peking and Chang Tso-lin in Manchuria, as well as Sun Yat-sen in Canton. There was, however, enough difference between Soviet policy and that of the Western powers to have a favorable effect on Chinese public opinion.

A new Comintern strategy for Asia. Meanwhile, there had been a very important shift in Comintern strategy at the Second Comintern Congress in 1920. By that time, the Bolshevik leaders had seen the failure of their hopes that the Russian Revolution would touch off revolutions in other parts of Europe on the regular Marxist pattern based on the industrial proletariat. Communist revolutionary efforts in Germany and Hungary had failed, and by the end of the Congress Soviet forces in Poland had been defeated. This led to the development of a new strategy for Asia.

Lenin's *Imperialism* argues that the bourgeoisie of the advanced industrial countries are able to delay the development of revolutionary conditions at home, as predicted by Marx, by bribing their workers with the proceeds of exploiting colonial areas. (Mao Tse-tung still used this argument to explain the rising living standards of British workers during a discussion with a British Labour Party delegation in 1954.) Thus, an anti-imperialist revolution in the colonial and semicolonial areas would lead to a breakdown of capitalism in the advanced industrial countries. This anti-imperialist revolution need not be based on the industrial proletariat, which was very small in all Asian countries except Japan, and it could include large sections of the bourgeoisie who also suffered from imperialist exploitation.

In the following years, there came an increasingly clear realization that a Communist-led revolution in Asia could only be based on the peasants. A 'Resolution on the Eastern Problem,' issued by the Fourth Comintern Congress at the end of 1922, states that the revolution in the East must be based on the strength of the peasants. A declaration of the Chinese Communist Party of April 22, 1927, is even more explicit:

> In order to repel the combined forces of imperialism and its instrument, native militarism, the national government must rely on full and class-conscious support from the masses whose power of self-sacrifice is the only defense of the revolution. . . . This means that the national revolution must first of all be an agrarian revolution. The peasants make up 80 per cent of the Chinese population; hence a revolutionary-democratic power can be established only by means of an agrarian revolution.[1]

---

[1] Robert C. North and Xenia J. Eudin, *M. N. Roy's Mission to China* (Berkeley and Los Angeles: University of California Press, 1963), p. 179.

Comintern and Chinese Communist directives or declarations have often stressed the need to develop proletarian leadership or proletarian hegemony in the revolutionary movement because the proletariat is the only fully reliable revolutionary class. But to understand the practical meaning of these phrases, one must bring in the unquestioned assumption of those who use them that the Communist Party represents the proletariat.

These questions of doctrine have been discussed at some length because it is important to realize that a Communist-led agrarian revolution based on the peasants was an accepted part of the Comintern strategy for Asia, as opposed to the original Marxist type of revolution based on the proletariat in the advanced industrial countries. *This strategy may have been unorthodox Marxism, but it was not unorthodox Leninism.*

Ch'en Tu-hsiu and the study of Marxism. In 1918, Li Ta-chao, Professor of History and Chief Librarian at Peking University, and Ch'en Tu-hsiu, Dean of the College of Arts and Letters, became seriously interested in Marxism. From then on, they argued for Marxism in such Chinese periodicals as *Hsin Ch'ing-nien (New Youth).*

A great stimulus to revolutionary development in China came from the May Fourth Movement of 1919 which grew out of a demonstration by university students in Peking against the government for instructing the Chinese delegates at the Versailles Conference to yield to Japanese demands. This was one of the earlier cases in which the educated elite tried to bring wider segments of the population into political activity. As the movement spread, the protesters tried to organize shopkeepers for a boycott of Japanese goods and to organize strikes in Japanese-owned factories.

The official formation of the Chinese Communist Party. The actual organization of the Chinese Communist Party was largely the work of agents sent to China by the Comintern. A special department of the Far Eastern secretariat of the Comintern was set up in Irkutsk, and in the spring of 1920 the Comintern sent to China G. N. Voitinskii and Yang Ming-chai, a native of Shantung living in the Soviet Union. They were followed some months later by Hendricus Sneevliet (alias Maring) who had been a left-wing member of the Dutch Socialist Party and had tried to organize revolutionary activities in the Dutch East Indies.

In May, 1920, Ch'en Tu-hsiu organized a new Society for the Study of Marxist Theory, with branches in Shanghai, Peking, Hunan, Kwangtung, Shantung, Chekiang, Anhwei and Hupei. It is likely that much of the Marxism studied was highly simplified. Men like Ch'en Tu-hsiu, who had a good knowledge of Western languages, could read the fairly complete sources on Marxism available in Western Europe, but in 1920 only a very few Marxist works had been translated into Chinese and thus made available to revolutionaries who knew no foreign languages, such as Mao Tse-tung, who by that time was active in revolutionary politics in Hunan.

It took some time for the Comintern organizers to sort out from the general left-wing revolutionary movement a hard core of genuine Communists ready to accept Comintern discipline. The Chinese Communist Party officially dates its foundation from July 1, 1921, when twelve or thirteen delegates representing about one hundred members met for a First Party Congress (sources differ about the exact dates of the meeting and the number of delegates). The program adopted was simple and showed no influence from the newly developing Comintern strategy for Asia. The Party committed itself to working for the dictatorship of the proletariat and the overthrow of the private ownership of the means of production. It defined the main work of the Party as the organization of labor unions and said that the Party 'should allow no relationship with other parties or groups.'[2]

---

[2] Ch'en Kung-po, *The Communist Movement in China*, edited by C. Martin Wilbur, East Asian Institute Research Series No. 7, Columbia University, 1960, pp. 108–9.

At the end of 1921, a First Congress of the Toilers of the Far East met first at Irkutsk and then in Moscow and Leningrad in early 1922. This was attended by delegates from both the Chinese Communist Party and the Kuomintang, and the Comintern representatives urged them to cooperate.

The Second Congress of the Chinese Communist Party was held in the summer of 1922 (sources differ on the date and place of meeting). The new program placed more emphasis on opposition to imperialism and advocated temporary cooperation with Nationalists against the common enemies, imperialism and militarism.

Membership Recruitment in Europe

Meanwhile, members of the Chinese Communist Party had been recruited among Chinese students in Europe. To many people in the Chinese revolutionary movement, France had appeared to be the most advanced and revolutionary society of the West. In 1912, Ts'ai Yüan-p'ei (then Minister of Education) and some like-minded associates had organized a Society for Frugal Study in France which sent about 120 students to France during the next year. The original society was dissolved by Yüan Shih-k'ai but was reconstituted in France and developed plans for combined study and work. In 1916, a Societé Franco-Chinoise d'Éducation was organized by Ts'ai Yüan-p'ei and his French and Chinese friends; by the end of 1919, it had brought some 400 students to France. The next year brought a large contingent of about 1,200.[3] Agents of the Comintern succeeded in recruiting a number of these students, and several who joined the Communist movement in this way now hold leading positions in the People's Republic of China, such as Chou En-lai, Ch'en Yi, and Nieh Jung-chen. Of these, Nieh Jung-chen was among the few who followed the program of combined work and study. He worked in a factory and studied chemistry for two years in a workers' college at Charleroi. Chou En-lai is said to have obtained a job at the Renault factory but soon gave it up as impossibly hard work and devoted most of his time to Chinese student politics. Ch'en Yi was deported after about two months in France for organizing a demonstration against the French Government's plans for the Chinese students. Still others who later became important in the Chinese Communist movement, such as Liu Shao-ch'i, went to the Soviet Union for study and training in the early 1920's.

Alliance with the Kuomintang

The Chinese Communist Party showed only a small increase in membership between the First and Second Congresses, though it had made a start in the organization of trade unions. The rapid growth in membership and influence began after the formation of an alliance with Sun Yat-sen's Kuomintang.

Sun Yat-sen had been provisional President of the Republic of China immediately after the 1911 Revolution. However, Yüan Shih-k'ai, who then commanded the best army in China and had been given plenary powers by the Manchus to defend the dynasty, first demonstrated his ability to defeat the revolutionaries and then bargained to join them if he were made first President of the Republic. Sun, therefore, resigned in Yüan's favor. By 1913, it had become clear that Yüan was trying to establish his personal dictatorship, and Sun's followers revolted against him. Yüan quickly crushed the revolt, and Sun went into exile. In 1917, after Yüan's death, Sun was able to set up a rival Chinese government at Canton in alliance with local warlords.

Sun Yat-sen had a firm belief in his own mission as the rightful leader of the Chinese revolution and had an unusual power of inspiring personal devotion in his

---

[3] See Chow Tse-tsung, *The May Fourth Movement* (Cambridge: Harvard University Press, 1960), pp. 36–37.

followers. Many of his ideas on basic issues were wise and farsighted, though he was often extremely confused on practical details. His education had been largely Western —a missionary school in Hawaii and medical training at Hong Kong—and he had spent a long time in the United States and Western Europe. His natural sympathies were with the Western democracies, and he tried on a number of occasions to get help from the Western powers.[4] Unfortunately, however, most Western statesmen, who prided themselves on being 'realistic,' were impressed by the obvious military power of Yüan Shih-k'ai and his warlord successors and were inclined to dismiss Sun Yat-sen as an impractical dreamer or troublemaker. The Comintern leaders were farsighted enough to see that, though Sun had little immediate power in the early 1920's, he was potentially more powerful than the Northern warlords. The Kuomintang, which had about 150,000 members, was by far the largest political organization in China, and Sun Yat-sen, unlike the warlords, could win the support of enthusiastically nationalistic Chinese youth.

A Comintern representative, Adolph Joffe, first approached Sun Yat-sen in 1921. At this time, however, Sun was hoping to extend his power by a military offensive and showed little interest. In June, 1922, Ch'en Chiung-ming, the primary military power in Kwangtung, expelled Sun Yat-sen, who was compelled to take refuge in the foreign concessions in Shanghai. (Ch'en had little sympathy with Sun's plans for unifying China and favored a loose federation of provinces, which would enable him to retain his personal power in Kwangtung.) At this low point in Sun Yat-sen's fortunes, Joffe approached him again, and an agreement was reached in January, 1923, whereby the Soviet Union agreed to furnish Sun with military supplies and military and political advisers and agreed that Sun's Three People's Principles rather than Communism was best suited for China. Sun accepted the Soviet alliance and agreed that members of the Communist Party could become members of the Kuomintang without giving up their Communist Party membership. Later in January, 1923, Ch'en Chiung-ming was defeated by a Kwangsi army and had to retire from Canton, which enabled Sun Yat-sen to return there in February.

In June, 1923, the Chinese Communist Party, by that time more than 300 strong, held its Third Congress at Canton, which accepted the policy of allowing Communists to join the Kuomintang. According to some sources, Ch'en Tu-hsiu was reluctant to accept this policy and only did so when the Comintern adviser invoked Comintern Party discipline. Membership in two parties was in conflict with the Communist doctrine of a one-to-one correspondence between political parties and classes: The Communist Party was part of the proletariat, while the Kuomintang was clearly bourgeois. Stalin got around this difficulty by citing as a precedent Lenin's argument to justify Communists' joining the British Labour Party: The Labour Party (or the

---

[4] The autobiography of Sun's bodyguard, 'Two-Gun Cohen,' describes a visit to Hong Kong during which Sun asked the Governor for advisers to help him reorganize his government at Canton. The Hong Kong Government favored the plan, but it was turned down by the Colonial Office in London. It is interesting to speculate what the history of China would have been had the Kuomintang been reorganized by advisers from the British Colonial Service instead of by advisers from the Comintern. (Charles Drage, *Two-Gun Cohen* London: Cape, 1954). The British records confirm that the Government of Hong Kong proposed the loan of advisers to Sun Yat-sen in 1923 and that the Foreign Office rejected the proposal on the ground that Britain recognized the Chinese Government in Peking and should not take action in China without the cooperation of other powers. Information from paper read at the 1969 Conference of the Association for Asian Studies, 'Sun Yat-sen, Hong Kong and British Policy,' by Walter Gourlay.

A more scholarly account of Sun's attempts to get Western aid is given in Norman Palmer and Leng Shao-chuan, *Sun Yat-sen and Communism* (New York: Praeger Publishers, 1961).

Kuomintang) was not really a party at all in the Communist sense of the term but only a loose alliance of different groups.[5]

In August, 1923, Sun Yat-sen sent Chiang Kai-shek on a military inspection trip to the Soviet Union, where he remained for several months. In October, Mikhail M. Borodin, the chief Soviet political adviser, arrived in Canton. He was followed by military advisers under Vasilii K. Blücher (alias Galen), later Soviet Commander-in-Chief in the Far East.

In January, 1924, the Kuomintang held a national congress and adopted a new constitution largely drafted by Borodin, which followed the Leninist principle of 'democratic centralism.' The newly elected Central Executive Committee of twenty-four included Li Ta-chao and three other Communists with Kuomintang membership, while Mao Tse-tung, Ch'ü Ch'iu-pai, Lin Pai-ch'u, and another Communist were among the seventeen alternate members. Communists became heads of the Organization Bureau and the Peasant Bureau.

On January 27, Chiang Kai-shek was appointed to a seven-member committee to organize a new officers' training school, which opened in May at Whampoa near Canton. Chiang Kai-shek became Commandant, Chou En-lai Deputy Political Commissar, and Yeh Chien-ying Deputy Chairman of the Instruction Department. With the assistance of Soviet advisers, this school began the task of building a loyal and politically indoctrinated army. Russian arms supplies began to arrive in the latter part of 1924.

To begin with, Sun Yat-sen's new regime in Canton was in a rather weak position. Even within Canton, it faced opposition from the Merchants' Volunteers, an armed organization financed by Canton big business and receiving assistance from Hong Kong. Ch'en Chiung-ming still controlled parts of Kwangtung and made efforts to recapture Canton. Many of the troops at the disposal of the Canton government were unreliable forces of minor allied warlords. The Whampoa cadets played an important part in the early fighting, until the First Army under Chiang Kai-shek was organized as a politically indoctrinated loyal force. It was not until the end of 1925 that the Kuomintang controlled the whole of Kwangtung Province.

At the time of its Fourth Party Congress in January, 1925, the Chinese Communist Party had nearly 1,000 members, with about 2,000 in the Communist Youth League. During the next two years, the Party grew at a spectacular rate. By the beginning of 1927, Chinese Communist Party membership had risen to about 50,000 and that of the Communist Youth League to about 30,000. There was an equally rapid growth in mass organizations. At the height of its power in early 1927, the Party claimed to control about 2.5 million organized workers and 9 million or 10 million organized peasants.

The growth of communist influence. The atmosphere of the Canton regime in 1925 was one of revolutionary enthusiasm. Anti-imperialist agitation played an important part and helped to spread Kuomintang-Communist influence over the rest of China. The Canton government supported a Hong Kong seamen's strike. Demonstrations in various foreign concessions were fired on by police or foreign troops, which further exacerbated antiforeign feeling. Foreign missions and schools came under attack, and the newly organized trade unions staged strikes in foreign-owned factories. A great deal of this agitation was under Communist leadership and produced new recruits for the Communist movement.

Within the Kuomintang, some members opposed the Communist alliance and charged that the Communist members of the Kuomintang were acting not as individuals but under Communist Party Central Committee orders. Sun Yat-sen, however,

---

[5] See Conrad Brandt, *Stalin's Failure in China* (Cambridge: Harvard University Press, 1958).

supported the alliance and argued that, if he found that the Communists were trying to subvert the Kuomintang and take over control, he would personally call for their expulsion. Given Sun Yat-sen's prestige and his power of inspiring personal loyalty, he was probably right in believing that he had the power to win in any showdown with the Communists. There is also some evidence that Sun did not really understand the Communist position. While he did not entirely trust the Chinese Communists, he thought that he could rely on the Soviet advisers to restrain them. This was the period of the Soviet New Economic Policy, and Sun was inclined to believe that, having tried Communism and found that it did not work, the Russians were turning to policies much closer to his own Three People's Principles and that he could, therefore, rely on the Russians to observe the 1923 agreement that the Chinese Revolution should be based on his principles.

So long as Sun Yat-sen was alive the alliance did, in fact, work fairly smoothly. His authority restrained any serious challenge to the alliance from the Kuomintang side, and his general prestige in China was so high that the Communists would have found it hard to eliminate him. In March, 1925, however, Sun Yat-sen died, of cancer of the liver, in Peking, where he had gone for negotiations. (Feng Yü-hsiang, a 'left-wing' warlord, had taken Peking from Wu P'ei-fu and organized a new government, which proposed an alliance with the Kuomintang; actually, no agreement was reached.)

There was no single successor to Sun Yat-sen as leader of the Kuomintang, though four men had special prestige. Hu Han-min, associated with the moderate right wing of the party, had been appointed by Sun as Deputy Generalissimo when he left for Peking. Wang Ching-wei, associated with the left wing of the party, had been chosen by Sun to accompany him to Peking. Liao Chung-k'ai belonged to the extreme left wing of the party and was most closely associated with the Communists. Chiang Kai-shek had so far avoided any clear political commitment but was generally considered to be left wing and was important because of his military position.

In August, 1925, Liao Chung-k'ai was assassinated, and there was some evidence that Hu Han-min's brother had instigated the assassination. It was decided that Hu Han-min should leave Canton, and he went to Moscow as the Chinese delegate to a Congress of the International Peasant Movement, where he gave fervent revolutionary speeches to great applause.

This curious episode raised the question of how deeply the Soviet advisers really understood Chinese politics. They may have been as confused as their American counterparts twenty years later. Few, if any, of them seem to have known Chinese, to say nothing of Cantonese, and some of them actually had to work through two interpreters, Russian-English and English-Chinese. Borodin, who had lived in the United States, spoke fluent English and so could communicate directly with Sun Yat-sen and some other leaders, though not with Chiang Kai-shek, whose only foreign language was Japanese. The impression one gets from reading the documents of the time is that the Russians were far too ready to fit Chinese politics into a neat Marxian system of class interests. Wang Ching-wei, for example, is nearly always said to 'represent' the petty bourgeoisie, though there seems to be no evidence that he had any special connections with or concern for the people whom Communist analysis placed in that category.

The Communists could claim that they had a special concern for the interests of the workers and poor peasants, but few, if any, leading Communists came from worker or poor peasant families. Mao Tse-tung's family, for example, would certainly be 'rich peasants' by Communist classification, which would have been a political liability for anyone trying to join the Communist Party after 1949. Other Communist leaders came from families even farther removed from worker or poor peasant status.

The latter part of 1925 saw a consolidation of Communist influence. The army was brought under more effective political control. Two of the less reliable warlord generals were defeated and expelled, and the warlord character of the remaining forces was reduced by increased centralization of finance and supplies. Even more important was the introduction of the political commissar system. Although the Communists were a minority on the Central Executive Committee of the Kuomintang, their control of the Organization Bureau enabled them to put Communists in effective control of a large proportion of the local and subordinate Kuomintang organizations. Communist control of the Peasant Bureau enabled them to control the rapidly developing peasant organizations. The Soviet advisers acquired more power and took an active part in directing the campaign that finally cleared Ch'en Chiung-ming's forces from Kwangtung.

The shift toward the left in Canton intensified opposition in the right-wing Kuomintang. In December, 1925, right-wing members held a meeting in the Western Hills near Peking and issued a call for the removal of Communists from the Kuomintang and the dismissal of Borodin. However, the Second National Congress of the Kuomintang, which met at Canton in February, 1926, expelled the leaders of the Western Hills group and warned the others. Three-fifths of the 256 delegates attending the congress were Communist Party members, seven Communists were elected to the thirty-six-man Central Executive Committee, and seven among the twenty-four alternates were Communists. A Communist, T'ang P'ing-shan, became head of the Organization Bureau. Another Communist, Lin Pai-ch'u, became head of the Peasant Bureau. Mao Tse-tung became deputy head of the Propaganda Bureau, and because the head, Wang Ching-wei, was busy with other duties, Mao was actually in control.

Thus, at the beginning of 1926 everything seemed to be going according to plan for the Communists. They had successfully infiltrated the Kuomintang and were establishing positions from which they could hope to control it. They were using the alliance to build up the worker and peasant organizations, which would be the basis for the next stage of the revolution. The Communist Party itself was expanding very rapidly and, while many of the new recruits must have had more enthusiasm than discipline, effective organization would be only a matter of time. The Canton regime had won effective control of Kwangtung, and Communist-led mass organizations were expanding in other parts of China. The northern warlord regimes still had to be defeated, but the Communists and the Soviet advisers had every reason to hope that, within a few years, they would control the major part of China.

The alliance with Feng Yü-hsiang. The prospects for the revolution were also improved by an ally among the northern warlords, General Feng Yü-hsiang. Feng was plausible as a 'revolutionary warlord.' His father had been a common soldier and he himself had joined the army at an early age and risen from the ranks. He made some efforts to educate and indoctrinate the men under his command, and his main armies had a reputation for good discipline in relations with the civilian population, which was unusual in the warlord period. At one time, Feng had been known as 'the Christian general,' but he seemed to be prepared to switch from Christianity to Communism. In 1925, he accepted Soviet advisers and started to receive Soviet arms through Outer Mongolia, which bordered on the area he controlled. On his side, he allowed Communists to start the organization of mass movements.

At the end of 1925, Feng Yü-hsiang was defeated by Chang Tso-lin and lost his influence in the area around Peking. He then took a more clearly pro-Communist line, expressing revolutionary sentiments, and announcing his intention to study Marxism, and he visited the Soviet Union in 1926. Some of his Soviet advisers had doubts about his reliability as an ally of the revolution. They were, for example, shocked to find that Feng also had a Japanese adviser, though they reported that he seemed to be inactive. However, he continued to receive Soviet assistance, and Borodin apparently placed hopes on him until Borodin's expulsion in July, 1927.

In fact, Feng Yü-hsiang was primarily a warlord and only secondarily a revolutionary. His interest in the revolution and an alliance with the Kuomintang and

Communists was greatest when his military position was weak and declined when he seemed to have a good chance at power based on his own resources. The Japanese adviser was part of the normal warlord strategy of keeping options open. If the Soviet alliance broke down, an accommodation with the Japanese would have been a possible alternative.

The role of the army. The weakest point in the Communist position was the army. Here the officer training program and the political commissar system were the vital issues. There was little hope that the older officers from warlord armies would ever become reliable allies of the Communists, but if the army could be infiltrated by well-trained younger Communist officers, these could expect to rise rapidly in command. If the troops could also be indoctrinated, it would be only a matter of time before the older officers could be eliminated. One of the advisers with Feng Yü-hsiang's army proposed such plans quite frankly in a private report: Use the officers' training program to feed in competent and reliably Communist junior officers and, as far as possible, leave the senior officers untrained and incompetent.[6]

The allegiance of the officers in training at Canton was still in question at the beginning of 1926. Rival organizations existed among the Whampoa cadets: the League of Military Youth for the Communists, and the Sun Yat-sen Society for the Kuomintang. Here Chiang Kai-shek's position was crucial. He was known as a very loyal follower of Sun Yat-sen, and the Soviet advisers were inclined to classify him as left wing. He had played an important part in defeating several right-wing military threats to the regime. He had expressed strongly anti-imperialist sentiments, and the Second National Congress of the Kuomintang had left him sharing the leadership with Wang Ching-wei, who was associated with the left wing of the Party. His relations with some of the Soviet military advisers began to deteriorate at the beginning of 1926, but nothing serious had yet developed when Borodin left Canton in February for a conference with Feng Yü-hsiang.

Chiang Kai-shek's coup of March, 1926. There is still no clear published evidence from which to determine the facts of or the responsibility for the events of March 18–26, 1926, involving the gunboat *Chungshan.* It is claimed on one side that Chiang Kai-shek acted to frustrate a plot against him—perhaps to kidnap him—and, on the other side, that Chiang staged an incident to give himself an excuse for acting against the Communists.

Whatever the origins of the incident, Chiang Kai-shek declared martial law, put the Soviet advisers under house arrest, disarmed the workers' militia in Canton, and arrested many Communists, including those at Whampoa and in the First Army, which he commanded. Wang Ching-wei, who had been ill at the time of the incident, denounced Chiang Kai-shek's actions as illegal and soon afterward retired to France.

With the advantages of hindsight, Communist statements from 1927 on describe the incident as Chiang Kai-shek's break with the revolution, but this was not clear to the Communists at the time. Chiang helped to produce the uncertainty. He professed his desire for a continuation of the Communist alliance, explained that he had only personal objections to a few of the Soviet advisers (who left for Russia a few days later), and invited Borodin to return. Soon after, he issued strong denunciations of the Kuomintang right wing and dismissed some right-wing supporters in Canton.

When Borodin did return at the end of April, the Kuomintang-Communist alliance was continued but on terms that greatly weakened Communist power. In May, 1926, the Second Plenum of the Kuomintang Central Executive Committee passed a set of resolutions severely limiting Communist influence in the KMT. For example, no Communist could be the head of any organization, nor could Com-

---

[6] C. Martin Wilbur and Julie Lien-ying How, *Documents on Communism, Nationalism and Soviet Advisers in China, 1918–1927* (New York, Columbia University Press, 1963), p. 343.

munists hold more than one-third of the seats on any committee. They were required to report the names of all their members who were also members of the Kuomintang. Any Communist pronouncements had to be approved by a joint committee with five Kuomintang and three Communist members. Chiang Kai-shek himself became chairman of the Organization Bureau, with Ch'en Li-fu, a close associate, as his deputy. Soon after this, Chiang recalled all Communist political officers in the army and announced that, in future, all political training must be based on Kuomintang principles. This started a prolonged struggle in which Chiang Kai-shek and his associates tried to remove all influential Communists from the Kuomintang organization, particularly the army.

After these changes, though Communist membership and Communist-controlled mass organizations continued to grow, the Communist Party had lost its best chance of taking over or defeating the Kuomintang, because it had lost the means to take over the army. The developments of 1927 showed that some army units had been won over to the Communist side but, after May, 1926, any further introduction of Communist officers or Communist indoctrination could only be a clandestine operation.

The idea expressed in Mao Tse-tung's aphorism that political power grows out of the barrel of a gun was not original. It had been the practical rule for every successful Chinese politician since the formation of the Republic in 1912. The original element that Mao later introduced into Chinese politics was a demonstration that one gun in the hands of a politically indoctrinated soldier with an organized population behind him is worth several guns in the hands of mercenaries or unwilling conscripts.

For the world as a whole, the countries in which military power does not determine political power are the exception rather than the rule, and under the conditions of Chinese politics, 100,000 soldiers controlled by the Kuomintang were a much stronger political force than 10 million organized peasants and workers controlled by the Communists, so long as the latter had few arms and no military training.

The Comintern's 'Theses on the Chinese Situation.' A few weeks before the Chungshan incident, the Sixth Enlarged Plenum of the Executive Committee of the Comintern had issued 'Theses on the Chinese Situation' strongly supporting the alliance with the Kuomintang.[7] The authors of the 'Theses' did not envisage the events of a few weeks later, which completely surprised even the Soviet advisers on the spot. However, it would have been awkward for anyone in the Comintern organization to suggest that the situation in China had changed drastically because of developments that a Central Executive Committee plenum had failed to foresee or even to consider as a possibility. The natural reaction was to belittle the importance of what had happened. Voitinskii, head of the Far Eastern Bureau of the Comintern, published an article in *International Press Correspondence* of May 6, 1926, claiming that reports of a *coup d'état* in Canton were 'an invention of the imperialists.'[8] This reaction explains a serious weakness in subsequent Comintern strategy, an unwillingness to admit that the Communist chances of taking over or controlling the Kuomintang had declined from good to poor.

The alternatives. There is evidence that the Communist regional committees in both Kwangtung and Shanghai advocated resistance to Chiang Kai-shek, including, in one plan, the supplying of Soviet arms to organized peasants in Kwangtung. It could very reasonably have been argued that a fight with Chiang was inevitable in the long run and that the Communists had a better chance if they acted quickly than if they allowed Chiang the time to reduce the Communist infiltration of the army.

The case against such action comes from its further implications. Had the Communists won, they would have been left in control of Kwangtung with an army

---

[7] See *ibid.*, p. 225; and North and Eudin, *Roy's Mission to China*, pp. 22–23.
[8] Wilbur and How, *Documents on Communism*, p. 221.

seriously weakened by the internal strife. In time, a new reliable army could have been recruited from the worker and peasant organizations, but in the interim Kwangtung would have had very weak defenses. And it is unlikely that the Kuomintang's warlord allies in neighboring provinces would have continued their alliances with a Communist-controlled regime. Even before March, 1926, the Canton regime had been concerned about a real danger that Wu P'ei-fu would attack Kwangtung from Hunan and also about a largely imaginary danger that the British would cooperate with Wu P'ei-fu by launching an attack from Hong Kong. It could have been argued, therefore, that the end result of an attack on Chiang Kai-shek might well be the conquest of Kwangtung by warlord armies, eliminating both the Communists and the Kuomintang as parties with an army and a territorial base.

Ch'en Tu-hsiu later claimed that he had suggested that the Communists should immediately withdraw from the Kuomintang and form a two-party alliance, which would allow the Communists to follow an independent policy and to win the confidence of the masses. The obvious weakness of this proposal was that a Kuomintang dominated by Chiang Kai-shek would have been unlikely to accept terms that allowed the Communists to develop independent power.

A possible policy that no one in the Communist movement seems to have suggested would have been to admit that the Communists had been outmaneuvered in their attempt to take over the Kuomintang and to observe the terms of the original Sun-Joffe agreement. Genuine cooperation with the members of the Kuomintang who wanted to develop and implement Sun's principles of Democracy and People's Livelihood, as well as his principle of nationalism, might have produced some real social and political reforms. Many officers in the army who eventually sided with the right-wing Kuomintang when the alternative was Communist power would have supported this reformist program. However, such a policy would have defied the Comintern's warning against 'right-wing liquidationism' and would have required a radical change in Communist strategy and style of work. Also, if moderate reforms had improved conditions for the masses, the result would have been an indefinite postponement of a Communist-led revolution.

Thus, if one looks at the possibilities open to the Communists, the decision to continue the Kuomintang alliance, even on the terms reached in May, 1926, is understandable.

The Northern Expedition. Another concession that Borodin made to Chiang Kai-shek was approval for an early start of the Northern Expedition. The conquest of the rest of China from the revolutionary base in Kwangtung was a fully agreed objective, but the Communists had a strong case for wanting first to consolidate the gains of the revolution in Kwangtung. Subsequent developments showed that it was easy for General Li Chi-shen to become a new warlord in Kwangtung, and, because the Kuomintang had organized only a few units of a new-style army with good training and political indoctrination, it was not able to destroy the warlord system, but only became a new and rather stronger player in the game of warlord politics.

Military operations started in May, 1926, to aid a warlord ally, T'ang Sheng-chih, in Hunan. The Northern Expedition officially started two months later, with Chiang Kai-shek as Commander-in-Chief. The left flank, driving directly north, had very rapid success. By the beginning of September, the Kuomintang forces had captured Hankow and Hanyang and were besieging Wuch'ang. The mass movements organized by the Communists gave very important help. Wu P'ei-fu's forces were disorganized by disturbances and strikes in their rear, and a number of places fell to local uprisings before the arrival of the Kuomintang army. The fighting also showed that the politically indoctrinated and well-trained units of the Kuomintang army were far superior to normal warlord soldiers.

The right flank, directly under Chiang Kai-shek, made much slower progress. Chiang first negotiated with Sun Ch'uan-fang, who controlled the provinces of

Kiangsu, Chekiang, Anhwei, Kiangsi, and Fukien, offering to leave him as Commander-in-Chief in the same five provinces if he would accept the authority of the Kuomintang government. Fighting did not start until September, and it was only after the breakdown of negotiations at the end of October that the Kuomintang army started a serious offensive. It had conquered Kiangsi by the end of November and Fukien by the end of December, though with heavier fighting than in the Hunan-Hupei sector.

These military developments had political consequences. It was a common practice in Chinese civil wars for generals to switch from the losing to the winning side as soon as they felt sure of defeat, and their troops were normally incorporated into the victorious army. Consequently, the army of about 100,000 that had started the Northern Expedition had swollen to 260,000 by December, with the early increases accruing largely to T'ang Sheng-chih, who became Commander-in-Chief for Hunan and Hupei.

At the end of November, 1926, it had been decided to move the government and the Kuomintang Central Executive Committee from Canton to Wuhan. In the middle of December, a preliminary joint council of the government and the Central Executive Committee started to operate in Wuhan. The council included two Chinese Communists, Borodin, and mostly left-wing Kuomintang members. At the end of December, the main group of the government and the CEC reached Nanchang, then Chiang Kai-shek's headquarters, on the way to Wuhan.[9] Chiang had already had difficulties in obtaining funds to pay his troops from the joint council at Wuhan and was naturally reluctant to have government and Party authority centered in a place dominated by his main military rival and his political opponents. He persuaded the members of the Central Executive Committee in Nanchang to hold a meeting and decide that Nanchang was most convenient as a temporary capital. The result was a split in the Kuomintang between a Wuhan group and a Nanchang group, each claiming that it had legitimate authority.

This issue was mixed up with a dispute over the strategy of the Northern Expedition. Borodin and the Soviet military advisers thought that the Northern Expedition should by-pass the lower Yangtze valley and drive straight to the north from Wuhan to link up with Feng Yü-hsiang's army. (Feng was now considered a reliable revolutionary warlord.) Chiang Kai-shek wanted first to capture Nanking and Shanghai and argued that Nanchang was a more convenient base for operations toward the lower Yangtze valley.

Communist problems at Wuhan. This background is necessary to understand the problems that faced the Communist Party, particularly relations with the Kuomintang and the land revolution. A series of Comintern directives had stressed that the Communist Party should maintain its association with the Kuomintang and should work to strengthen the Kuomintang left. The attempts to find and strengthen the left-wing Kuomintang had not been successful at Canton, but the left did seem to be stronger at Wuhan and was further strengthened by the return of Wang Ching-wei to Wuhan on April 10, 1927. However, while the political leaders at Wuhan could be considered left wing, Communist strategy overlooked the importance of military power in Chinese politics. Some army units in the forces of the Wuhan regime were under Communist leadership, and more important ones could be classified as left-wing Kuomintang, but these were a minority compared with the troops, which were primarily warlord units. It should have been obvious that the willingness of T'ang Sheng-chih' former warlord turned KMT Commander-in-Chief for Hunan, and

---

[9] At this time the Hankow–Canton railway only extended to a point slightly south of Changsha, and there was no road passable for motor traffic. The quickest means of travel was by steamer and, with the lower Yangtze under enemy control, the journey by way of Nanchang gave the shortest distance of very slow overland travel.

Hupei, to cooperate with the Communists, or even with the Kuomintang left, was purely opportunistic and based only on his rivalry with Chiang Kai-shek. So long as he was the main military leader, any left-wing power at Wuhan had an insecure foundation. It could not take any action that would seriously weaken what the Communists called the 'militarist-feudal order.'

Communist agrarian policy and the Comintern. In spite of the repeated stress in Comintern directives on the importance of the peasants, the Chinese Communists were slow to work out an agrarian program, except for announcing an ultimate objective of nationalizing all land. They organized peasant associations without clear plans of what these associations should try to do. Eventually, in July, 1926, the Second Enlarged Plenum of the Chinese Communist Party adopted 'Resolutions on the Peasant Movement,' which set out a very mild policy.[10]

The government was to fix a maximum rent of 50 per cent of the crops and a maximum interest rate of 3 per cent. (This was, presumably, 3 per cent per month, which would have been a mild reduction in usury comparable to the mild reduction in rent.) Other demands were for an honest and regular tax system, unified weights and measures, and the prohibition of hoarding. The political demands were for freedom of assembly and for popularly elected *hsien* (county) magistrates and village governments. The peasant associations could include small landlords and should exclude only large landlords and usurers. (This was realistic, for both small landlords and peasants suffered from the onerous, irregular, and dishonest taxation system.

The greatest weakness of the program was its failure to deal with the question of real power in the countryside. It was impossible to implement reforms so long as armed force in the countryside—the local militia or *min-t'uan*—was controlled by the vested interests opposing reform. The resolutions admitted this problem but refused to face it.

The very mild program may have been influenced by Borodin, who seems to have been comparatively uninterested in agrarian revolution. He gave first priority to the anti-imperialist aspect of the revolution, and, given this preoccupation, the agrarian revolution was a distraction, because many people who opposed imperialism had vested interests against agrarian reform.

The 'Theses on the Situation in China' produced by the Seventh Plenum of the Executive Committee of the Comintern in November–December, 1926, proposed a far more radical land program. The theses included:

(a) Reduce rents to a minimum;
(b) Abolish the numerous forms of taxes imposed upon peasantry and substitute them with a single progressive agricultural tax;

....

(d) Confiscate the monasterial and church lands and the lands belonging to the reactionary militarists, landlords, and gentry who are waging civil war against the Kuomintang national government;
(e) Guarantee the tenant farmers perpetual leases of the land they cultivate and the fixing of maximum rent jointly by the peasant unions and representatives of the revolutionary authority;

....

(g) Disarm the *min-t'uan* and other armed forces of the landlords;
(h) Arm the poor and middle peasants and subordinate all armed forces in the rural districts to the revolutionary authorities;

....

The Communist Party must see to it that the Canton government enforces these measures as a transition to a more developed state of agrarian revolution. This

---

[10] Wilbur and How, *Documents on Communism*, Document 29, pp. 296–302.

very important task will be accomplished by creating the peasant committees under Communist leadership. As the revolution develops, the peasant committees will not only assume the authority and power to enforce the above demands, but also will intensify the struggle by putting forward more radical demands. The peasants' committees will be the basis of the people's government and the people's army in the rural districts.[11]

The drafting of these 'Theses' was influenced by M. N. Roy, an Indian Communist, who then went to China as Comintern representative. The completely unrealistic point in this agrarian policy was the phrase, 'The Communist Party must see to it that the Canton government enforces these measures . . .' Even the more clearly left-wing government at Wuhan was quite certainly unable and almost certainly unwilling to enforce such a program.

The land program of the Comintern 'Theses' would have had a strong appeal for the peasants' committees that had appeared over much of the area recently conquered by the Kuomintang army. Mao Tse-tung's 'Report on an Investigation of the Peasant Movement in Hunan,' based on an investigation trip in five *hsien* from January 4 to February 5, 1927, reported that peasants' committees had seized local power, eliminated opposing forces, were executing 'local bullies and bad gentry,' and were demanding an extremely radical agrarian program.

It is not clear whether or not Mao was aware of the Comintern 'Theses' when he produced his report in March, but there was no conflict between the two, and the fact that a translation of Mao's report was published in the Soviet Union would seem to confirm its orthodoxy. If anything, the defect of Mao's writings on the agrarian problem was that they were too orthodox, trying to fit the society of the Chinese countryside into class categories worked out by Lenin for Russia. In Russia, where the peasants had been serfs until the 1860's, there was a marked social and cultural distinction between landlords and peasants. Later, especially as a result of Stolypin's reforms, a fairly clear distinction started to develop between the rich peasants and the rest. In China, on the other hand, though there was a very wide range in wealth between rich landlord and poor peasant, there were no such clear points of discontinuity to mark sharply defined classes. And relationships in an extended family might link together people differing widely in economic status.

The dilemma posed by cooperation with the Kuomintang. The dilemma for Communist strategy was that the Communist Party could not support the revolutionary peasant movement and also keep up its alliance with the Kuomintang. By trying to pursue two mutually incompatible objectives, the Communists failed in both.

At the beginning of 1927, the Chinese Communist Party decided to give priority to cooperation with the Kuomintang, though only after some controversy.[12] For a time, this policy seemed to be successful. The Third Plenum of the Kuomintang Central Executive Committee was held at Wuhan in the middle of March and consolidated the position of the left against Chiang Kai-shek. New ministries of agriculture and labor were created, headed by Communists. In fact, the apparent Communist gains had little substance. The Communists' policy of 'allaying the fears of the Kuomintang' forced the Communist Minister of Agriculture, T'an P'ing-shan, to try to restrain the peasant movement rather than to promote it. And he was unable to stop action by officers of T'ang Sheng-chih's army against local peasant associations.

Meanwhile, Chiang Kai-shek's forces had captured Nanking on March 24. In the course of this action, attacks on foreigners led to a bombardment by American and British gunboats. On March 21, Shanghai workers, who had already made two unsuccessful revolts against Sun Ch'uang-fang, staged a third and successful revolt.

[11] North and Eudin, *Roy's Mission to China*, pp. 139–40.
[12] Wilbur and How, *Documents on Communism*, p. 433.

Kuomintang troops under Pai Ch'ung-hsi, a Kwangsi warlord, then entered Shanghai, and Chiang Kai-shek arrived there on March 26. This created another crisis for Communist strategy. Should the Communist-led armed workers of Shanghai oppose Chiang Kai-shek? The decision was that they should not but should conceal their arms. However, Chiang Kai-shek took the initiative. Having established relations with the financial community in the foreign concessions, which assured him money for his troops, he acted on April 12 to suppress the Communists and executed a large number of them.

This took the Comintern by surprise. While the Communist relations with Chiang Kai-shek had been steadily worsening, the Moscow analysts believed that he was helping the revolution by waging a campaign that was weakening foreign imperialism and that the Communists could choose their own time to discard him.

The disagreement between Roy and Borodin at Wuhan. Meanwhile, on April 2, M. N. Roy, an Indian Communist from the Comintern, had arrived at Wuhan. He soon became involved in a dispute with Borodin, which was argued at the Fifth Congress of the Chinese Communist Party, meeting at the end of April, 1927. One main issue was the resumption of the Northern Expedition, with Borodin this time favoring an early renewal of the offensive while Roy argued for consolidation of the revolutionary base.

Borodin still placed great hopes on Feng Yü-hsiang. He wanted an offensive northward from Wuhan to join Feng for a drive on Peking. This plan involved maintaining the Kuomintang-Communist alliance, which, in turn, involved confining the agrarian revolution to a minimum program of rent reduction and local self-government. Wang Ching-wei thought that agrarian reform should be postponed until after the capture of Peking.

Roy argued that all warlord allies, including Feng Yü-hsiang and T'ang Sheng-chih, were unreliable and that a Northern Expedition would increase their strength relative to any revolutionary forces in the Kuomintang. He maintained that Chiang Kai-shek's defection had simplified the situation, because it showed that the landowning classes, with which it formerly had been necessary to compromise, had deserted the revolution. 'Therefore, there are no longer tactical or other considerations which could interfere with the development of the class struggle in the villages.' The left-wing Kuomintang was bound to accept Communist leadership and the hegemony of the proletariat, because 'the petty-bourgeois Left cannot return to Chiang Kai-shek: This would be political suicide. Politically, perhaps, the petty bourgeoisie may not be particularly shrewd, but it understands this.' His proposals were, therefore:

First, and at the basis of all, the agrarian revolution.

Second, the arming of the peasants for defending the gains of the revolution.

Third, the organization of rural self government for destroying the power of feudal lords in the village.

Fourth, the creation of a state machinery through which the democratic dictatorship will be realized.

Fifth, the creation of a revolutionary army, not by converting militarists into revolutionaries, but by organizing a revolutionary army on a firm, social basis.

Having consolidated Hunan and Hupei, the revolution could then recover Kwangtung and spread into the areas controlled by Chiang Kai-shek.[13]

---

[13] This is summarized with quotations from Document No. 10 in North and Eudin, *Roy's Mission to China*, pp. 188–208. This document is given as a speech by Roy to the Fifth Congress and dated April 30. However, it refers to the revolt of Hsia Tou-yin against the Wuhan government, which occurred on May 18. It seems likely that the document is a revised version of Roy's arguments based on his actual speech to the Congress.

This would have been an excellent strategy for the Communists had there been a remote possibility of carrying it out. The basic fallacy in Roy's argument came from the ingrained Communist habit of thinking about Chinese politics in terms of standard Marxian class analysis. Whatever the difference in class interests between the big and petty bourgeoisie, it was not political suicide for the left-wing Kuomintang leaders to return to Chiang Kai-shek. Most of them decided a few months later that this was preferable to Communist leadership; most of them continued to hold public office under Chiang Kai-shek; and a few survivors still hold positions in Taiwan. Also, even if the left-wing Kuomintang had followed Communist leadership, there would still have been a hard-fought struggle to eliminate T'ang Sheng-chih and other warlord allies.

In any case, the Fifth Congress approved the Northern Expedition after some hesitation and also passed a radical agrarian platform, though with the qualification that land belonging to small landowners and to officers of the revolutionary army should not be confiscated.

The renewed Northern Expedition had the results predicted by Roy: Feng Yü-hsiang and T'ang Sheng-chih were strengthened, and the forces primarily loyal to the left wing of the Kuomintang were weakened. At the same time, the needs of the campaign provided an excuse for refusing demands by peasants or workers in the Wuhan government area, while T'ang Sheng-chih's subordinates intensified their repression of the peasant movement.

Roy appealed to Moscow for support and received this answer by telegram on June 1:

> Without an agrarian revolution victory is impossible. . . . We are decidedly in favor of the land actually being seized by the masses from below. . . . A large number of new peasant and working class leaders from the ranks must be drawn into the Central Committee of the Kuomintang. . . . It is necessary to liquidate the dependence on unreliable generals. Mobilize about 20,000 Communists and about 50,000 revolutionary workers and peasants . . . and organize your own reliable army before it is too late. . . . Organize a revolutionary tribunal headed by prominent non-Communist Kuomintangists. Punish officers who maintain contact with Chiang Kai-shek, or who set soldiers on the people. . . . If the Kuomintangists do not learn to be revolutionary Jacobins, they will be lost both to the people and to the revolution.[14]

The expulsion of Communists from the Kuomintang. The Chinese Communist leaders and Borodin realized that it was completely beyond their power to carry out the June 1 Moscow directive. Roy, however, gave a copy to Wang Ching-wei, perhaps because he believed that the Kuomintang left wing had no alternative to the Communist alliance. Wang and his associates naturally concluded that the Communists were trying to eliminate them from leadership and turned against the Communists.

On June 12, the Wuhan leaders and Borodin had a conference with Feng Yü-hsiang at Chengchow. Feng showed that he was warlord first and revolutionary second. He demanded control of the newly conquered province of Honan and a large payment for his army and advised the Wuhan leaders to come to terms with Chiang Kai-shek's rival government at Nanking. Feng himself then went to Hsüchou for a conference with Chiang Kai-shek.

The Comintern finally directed the Communists to leave the Wuhan government but to remain in the Kuomintang. However, on July 15 the Kuomintang left wing expelled the Communists. By the end of the month, Communists were being executed at Wuhan, and the leadership had gone underground, operating mainly from the Japanese and French concessions at Hankow.

---

[14] *Ibid.*, pp. 106–7.

On July 27, Borodin left Wuhan to return to the Soviet Union. Roy followed shortly afterward. A disillusioned Borodin remarked to Anna Louise Strong, who accompanied him, 'When the next Chinese general comes to Moscow and shouts, "Hail to the World Revolution," better send at once for the GPU. All that any of them wants is rifles.'[15]

Borodin survived in Russia, holding minor positions. Roy was made a scapegoat for the failure in China by the Ninth Plenum of the Central Executive Committee of the Comintern in February, 1928. He escaped to Germany and later returned to India, where he died in 1954.

Uprisings and Return to Illegality

New Comintern representatives, Besso Lominadze and Heinz Neumann, took over from Borodin and Roy. Lominadze called a conference on August 7 of such Communist leaders as could be collected and secured a denunciation of Ch'en Tu-hsiu and T'an P'ing-shan for their opportunistic and compromising policy. Ch'ü Ch'iu-pai became the new Party leader.

The Chinese Communists have continued to blame Ch'en Tu-hsiu for the mistakes of this period. He was expelled from the Party in 1929 and, denounced for Trotskyism, finally became a Trotskyist. Actually, he seems always to have obeyed Borodin and followed the Comintern line as he understood it.

Lominadze brought a new Comintern line, which stressed insurrections against the Kuomintang leadership, though the directive also stressed that one should not 'play at insurrections' and should only stage them when they had a good chance of success.[16] Apart from any Comintern directives, the situation by July, 1927, was such that Communists unwilling to wait passively for liquidation by the Kuomintang had to choose between fighting and going underground.

The Nanchang Uprising. The first important uprising was at Nanchang, where there were some army units with Communist commanders. Planning started in July, though there was some controversy—a Comintern message favored dispersal of Communist forces into the countryside. The military leader was Yeh T'ing, a division commander in the Eleventh Army. Other Communist participants who later became prominent included Chu Te, Lin Piao, and Hsiao K'o. Ho Lung joined the Communist Party at the time of the uprising.

The uprising started on the night of August 1, which is still celebrated as the birthday of the Red Army. The Communists captured Nanchang and proclaimed a new revolutionary government, without consulting most of the people whose names they announced as members of the government. These included Chang Fa-k'uei who was in command at Nanchang and soon attacked to recover the city.

On August 5, the Communist forces abandoned Nanchang and started a retreat to Kwangtung, where they hoped to revive the original revolutionary base area. They still claimed to be Kuomintang revolutionaries and, though their policy included the agrarian revolution, they fixed a limit on landholdings, which exempted all but the largest landlords from confiscation. Toward the end of September, they captured the port of Swatow but could not hold it and soon suffered serious defeats.[17]

---

[15] Anna Louise Strong, *China's Millions*, New York Coward-McCann, 1928, p. 242. The section on China in Louis Fischer, *The Soviets in World Affairs* (New York: Vintage Books, 1960), gives a strong defense of Borodin and may have been based on information from him. It argues that Borodin could have succeeded but for Roy's interference.

[16] For details see Hsiao Tso-liang, *Chinese Communism in 1927: City vs. Countryside* (Hong Kong: The Chinese University of Hong Kong, 1970).

[17] For details see C. Martin Wilbur, 'The Ashes of Defeat,' *The China Quarterly*, No. 18, April–June, 1964.

The Autumn Harvest Uprising. The next in the series of uprisings was the Autumn Harvest Uprising in Hupei and Hunan in the first half of September. The movement in Hupei only managed to raise very small forces, which were quickly defeated. Mao Tse-tung, in charge of the uprising in Hunan, planned to capture Changsha, the provincial capital. He had at his disposal two army units, one of which proved completely unreliable; one peasant force with a secret society basis; and one unit of miners from Anyüan, who proved to be the best fighters. The uprising was defeated in about a week, and Mao retired with the remnants of his forces to Chingkangshan, a mountainous region on the Hunan-Kiangsi border that had long been a refuge for bandits.[18] Mao was later criticized for excessive reliance on military force and neglect of mass organization.

Some remnants of the Communist forces from Nanchang supported the Hailufeng Soviet. Haifeng and Loufeng were two *hsien* in Kwangtung where peasant organization had been started in 1922 by P'eng P'ai, a Communist from a local rich landlord family. A soviet government was proclaimed in November and managed to hold out until February, 1928.[19]

The Canton Commune. The final episode in the series of uprisings was the Canton Commune, which was proclaimed on December 11. A struggle between Chang Fa-k'uei and Li Chi-shen for control of Canton seemed to offer an opportunity to seize the city. A cadet regiment, which had been infiltrated by the Communists, was about to be disbanded, and the 1,200 cadets were reinforced by about 2,000 armed workers. The revolt was poorly planned and was defeated by December 13, and 7,000 or 8,000 Communists were killed. There is evidence that the Communist leadership in Shanghai did not know of the plans for the uprising.[20] Some members of the Soviet consulate were involved, and the new National Government made this an excuse for breaking off diplomatic relations with the Soviet Union, which were not resumed until 1932. Thus, by the beginning of 1928 the Chinese Communists were reduced to an underground organization in the cities and a few small guerrilla groups in the countryside.

The reasons for Communist failure. There has been a great deal of controversy over this period of Chinese Communist history. Many accounts place the main responsibility for Communist failure on Stalin's policies in 1927. The account given here argues that the Communists lost their best chances of taking over the Chinese Revolution in March and April, 1926. Stalin may be responsible for the long delay in switching from cooperation with the Kuomintang to armed insurrection. Uprisings, especially in the countryside, would have had a much better chance of success early in 1927, when local peasant associations were at the height of their power. The Communists might have started in 1927 with larger base areas in South and Central China than those they later acquired in the early 1930's. Whether they could have gone on to conquer the whole of China is highly speculative, because there are so many possible lines of development.

The other thesis that has been argued above is that the Communist failure came not so much from particular mistakes in Comintern directives as from certain basic weaknesses in Communist thinking. The Communists in this period always exaggerated their ability to manipulate other people. They failed to see that, without the apparatus of a totalitarian state, people can be manipulated for purposes with which they do not agree only so long as they do not realize that they are being manipulated.

---

[18] For details see Roy Hofheinze, Jr., 'The Autumn Harvest Insurrection,' *The China Quarterly*, No. 32, October–December, 1967.

[19] For details see Eto Shinkichi, 'The Hailufeng Soviet,' *The China Quarterly*, Nos. 8 and 9, October–December 1961, and January–March, 1962.

[20] For details see Hsiao Tso-liang, 'Chinese Communism and the Canton Soviet,' *The China Quarterly*, No. 30, April–June, 1967.

Even more important was the habit of thinking about Chinese politics in terms of a Marxian class analysis taken from the West, except for the category of 'compradores' (Chinese big bourgeoisie allied with foreign imperialism). This habit produced the persistent delusions about 'revolutionary warlords.' The Communists would have been the first to ridicule the concept of 'revolutionary landlords' or 'revolutionary capitalists' (except for a purely anti-imperialist bourgeois-democratic revolution), because a revolution was bound to liquidate both landlords and capitalists. A more common-sense Marxism would have shown them that warlords formed a class peculiar to China and were bound to be antirevolutionary so long as they remained warlords. Even the most bourgeois nationalist revolution would try to restore the authority of regular government and to create a national army, producing a society in which warlords had no place.

Again, the real differences within the Kuomintang came not from representing different classes but from different hopes for the future of China. The right wing emphasized Sun Yat-sen's principle of nationalism. It wanted a fully independent, strong, and modernized China, but with minimum disturbance to the values of traditional Chinese society. The moderate left placed more emphasis on Sun's desire for democracy and constitutional government; and those farther to the left emphasized Sun's principle of people's livelihood.

One could draw some comparisons between the Comintern advisers of the 1920's and the American advisers of the 1940's, who were equally confused by thinking about Chinese politics in terms of an equally inappropriate system—American politics. Just as the Comintern advisers always tried to find a strong Kuomintang left wing, so the American advisers looked for democratic individualists. In both cases, the individuals they found to fit their desired category had no real influence in Chinese politics, because they controlled no armed force.

Communist strategy for China was debated at the Fifteenth Congress of the Communist Party of the Soviet Union in December, 1927; the Ninth Plenum of the Executive Committee of the Comintern in February, 1928; the Sixth Congress of the Chinese Communist Party, which met in Moscow in June–July, 1928; and the Sixth Congress of the Comintern, which met from July to September, 1928. Lominadze, Neumann, and Ch'ü Ch'iu-pai argued almost to the end for attempts to overthrow the new Kuomintang government as soon as possible. This line was supported by theoretical arguments that the bourgeoisie was extremely weak in China, so that the revolution was already developing from the bourgeois-democratic to the socialist stage. These arguments were rejected by Stalin and the Comintern leadership. An official Comintern line was indicated at the Ninth Plenum and given more detail at the Sixth Congress of the Chinese Communist Party. The main emphasis was on guerrilla warfare in the countryside, gradually building up areas under Communist control and gradually developing local forces into a Red Army. Elsewhere, the Communist Party was to strengthen its organization, restore its influence in the trade union movement, and discredit any popular support for the Kuomintang.[21]

Insurgency in Central and South China

The next phase of the history of the Chinese Communist Party was the rise and fall of peasant-based insurgency in South-Central China. The beginnings were on a very small scale. In October, 1927, Mao Tse-Tung's forces at Chingkangshan had only 120 rifles in bad repair, and Chu Te had only about 1,000 men under his command. Chu Te moved north, picking up some strength on the way, and Mao increased his forces

---

[21] For details see Richard C. Thornton, *The Comintern and the Chinese Communists, 1928–1931* (Seattle: University of Washington Press, 1969).

by incorporating some local bandit units. When they joined at Chingkangshan in April, 1928, they had about 10,000 men and about 2,000 rifles. In the winter of 1928–29, they moved to southeastern Kiangsi. Other remnants of the Nanchang uprising under Ho Lung and Hsiao K'o made their way to western Hunan near the borders with Hupei, Szechwan, and Kweichow. Another Communist force operated on the borders of Hupei, Honan, and Anhwei. Within a few years, these small forces had multiplied many times, and by January, 1932, National Government sources estimated that the Red Army had grown to a total of 200,800 men with 152,600 rifles and some heavier weapons.[22]

Information is most complete about the area in which Chu Te and Mao Tse-tung operated, partly because this contained the Communist capital, Juichin in southeastern Kiangsi, and partly because General Ch'en Cheng, who commanded in some of the major campaigns against this area, followed the Chinese tradition of respect for historical source material and instructed his troops to collect all the Communist documents they could find. There was a period in which the Hupei-Hunan-Anhwei region, where Hsü Hsiang-ch'ien was military commander and Chang Kuo-t'ao, political leader, was perhaps even stronger, but much less information about it is available.

Guerrilla war strategy. Writing at the beginning of 1930, Mao Tse-tung summed up the tactics that had been evolved and had proved successful:

> The tactics we have derived from the struggle of the past three years are indeed different from any other tactics, ancient or modern, Chinese or foreign. With our tactics, the masses can be roused for the struggle on an ever broadening scale, and no enemy, however powerful, can cope with us. Ours are guerrilla tactics. They consist mainly of the following points:
>
> Divide our forces to arouse the masses, concentrate our forces to deal with the enemy.
>
> The enemy advances, we retreat; the enemy camps, we harass; the enemy tires, we attack; the enemy retreats, we pursue.
>
> To extend stable base areas, employ the policy of advancing in waves; when pursued by a powerful enemy, employ the policy of circling around.
>
> Arouse the largest numbers of the masses in the shortest possible time, and by the best possible methods.
>
> These tactics are just like casting a net; at any time, we should be able to cast or draw it in. We cast it wide to win over the masses and draw it in to deal with the enemy. Such are the tactics we have used for the past three years.[23]

It is clear from the writings of Mao Tse-tung that there was a lot of controversy about guerrilla strategy and tactics. Some people envisaged guerrilla warfare as very widespread operations by small units. Mao insisted that the guerrilla movement must try to build up base areas in which it could function as a government and must be able to concentrate its forces for battles. Other people advocated concentration on building up the regular army. Mao insisted that the Red Guards (local village militia) had an important function in harassing small enemy forces and assisting the Red Army by providing intelligence of enemy movements and guides fully familiar with the country. Also, when strong enemy forces were not engaged in an offensive, the Red Army should help the expansion of the area under Communist control by splitting into small units capable of defeating local *min-t'uan* and similar forces. Another

---

[22] T'ang Leang-li, *Suppressing Communist-Banditry in China* (Shanghai: China United Press, 1934), Appendix II, pp. 114–15. (The table gives a total of 125,600 rifles, but this is a wrong addition of the individual items in the column.)

[23] *Selected Military Writings of Mao Tse-tung* (Peking, Foreign Languages Press, 1963), p. 70.

controversial issue was defense of the base area. There was an obvious temptation to try to hold territory that was under firm Communist control. Mao argued, however, that the correct strategy against an enemy offensive was to retreat into the base area and to decide on a terminus for retreat at which the Red Army would concentrate for an attack, either on the weaker enemy units in the base area or else into the enemy areas, which would force the enemy to withdraw for the defense of their own bases.

Another very important general principle was to avoid battle except when there was a good chance of annihilating an enemy force. The Red Army depended entirely on capture for its arms and ammunition. A battle that merely forced the enemy to retreat, even with heavy losses, left the Red Army in a worse situation than before, if it had not captured at least as much ammunition as it had expended.

Very great emphasis was placed on political indoctrination. Many Red Army recruits came from prisoners or deserters from the opposing armies, especially warlord armies. It proved possible to turn most such men into reliable Communist soldiers. Living conditions in the Red Army were very hard, but the soldier would find that he was treated with a degree of personal respect that no one had given him under the old system, and that he was given education and a chance to rise on his own merits. Above all, he was taught to believe that he was fighting for the liberation of his country and for the building of a new society. This indoctrination not only gave the army high morale but also made it possible to maintain a high standard of discipline toward the civilian population.

Factors favoring insurgency. Mao Tse-tung's writings show a clear recognition that Communist insurgency depended on the weakness of its opposition. While the events of 1927 had nearly destroyed the Communist Party, they had also prevented the Kuomintang from completing even a nationalist revolution by ending the warlord system. Although by 1929 the new National Government had nominally unified China, it had fully effective authority only in the lower Yangtze valley. Elsewhere, its power depended on varying degrees of accommodation with remaining warlords, who often challenged its authority or quarreled among themselves. Consequently, operations against the Communists were frequently distracted by civil wars and also, from 1931 on, by Japanese attacks.

Between 1927 and 1937, the National Government was building up a new and stronger army whose primary loyalty was to the central government. But it needed its best troops to maintain its superiority in the system of warlord politics and was, therefore, reluctant to commit them to operations against the Communists. At first, operations against the Communists were conducted by low-quality provincial troops. Even when the National Government took direct charge of anti-Communist operations from 1930 on, it was inclined to use its second-rate troops. This was strongly counterproductive. The Red Army was able to defeat National Government offensives by concentrating against the weaker units taking part in them and to build up its own strength from captured arms and ammunition and by incorporating prisoners. At times, whole units on the National Government side deserted to the Communists. For example, according to Communist sources, 20,000 National Government troops came over to them on December 11, 1931, in the Chingkangshan area.

Another factor in the Communists' favor was the lack of communications in South China. In mountainous country with no roads, the lightly armed Communist forces with local guides could move much faster than the National Government forces. A major road-building program, which started in 1932, contributed to the final success of the National Government.

Communist policies. The Communists' policy in the area they controlled was based on class war in the countryside, confiscating the land of class enemies, and redistributing it. This left room for a number of doctrines on detailed application. The Communists attached great importance to drawing the correct line between friend and enemy (*fen ti wo*). Landlords were clearly enemies, and poor peasants and landless laborers were clearly friends, but there were difficult intermediate cases. For example, a prosperous tenant farmer who employed labor was exploited as a tenant and was therefore a 'friend' but, as an employer, he was also an exploiter, and was therefore an 'enemy.' There was also the practical problem, which Communist theory ignored, that efficient farmers tended to be rich peasants. Too strong a line against the rich peasants caused a fall in production. The policies of different groups in the Communist leadership differed appreciably in the point at which they drew the line between friend and enemy among the rich and middle peasants.

A sign of continuing Comintern influence is that Chinese Communist policy turned more strongly against the rich peasants when Stalin started his drive against the kulaks in Russia. One can also see why Li Li-san was condemned for both rightist and leftist deviations. The land policies he sponsored were rightist in being lenient to rich peasants but leftist in distributing only the right to cultivate the land and not the land itself, which showed that the policy of land distribution was only temporary. (Within the Party leadership, it was accepted that the next stage of land policy would be collectivization, but it was a leftist deviation to make this public too soon.)

Another issue was whether confiscated land should be distributed equally per individual among the favored classes or according to 'labor power,' the number of people capable of taking part in cultivation. Again, some Communists, including Mao Tse-tung, favored a more general rearrangement of landholdings so that all families would have fair shares of both good and bad land. This was one of the few points where Mao diverged from the official Comintern line.[24]

While Communist policy was committed to class warfare in the countryside, it did not, in this period, advocate class warfare against the bourgeoisie. There were some cases in which Communists confiscated the property of merchants and shopkeepers in the small towns they controlled, but these were condemned as leftist deviations. The announced Communist policy for the cities was a moderate reformist one.

These doctrinal differences were mixed up with bitter factional disputes. In 1928, Ch'ü Ch'iu-pai lost the leadership of the Party because of his disagreement with the Comintern line at the Sixth Congress. (He was retained in less important positions until he was captured by the Kuomintang and executed in 1935.) The effective leadership of the Party then passed to Li Li-san until the latter part of 1930, though Hsiang Chung-fa had nominal authority for the early part of the period.

While the Red Army and the areas it controlled were expanding in the countryside, the Central Committee remained as an underground organization in Shanghai. However, the strength of the Communists in the cities steadily weakened. They gradually lost control of the trade unions to rival organizations sponsored by the Kuomintang, because they continued to call for strikes for political ends when they had no chance of success. Although the leaders of Kuomintang unions may not have been as militant as many of their members would have liked, if they did call a strike, it would have a good chance of winning better wages or working conditions. Also, the Kuomintang police organizations were increasingly successful against the Communist underground.[25]

Attacks on the cities. A crisis came in 1930. Li Li-san seems to have had some sympathy for the views of Ch'ü Ch'iu-pai and Lominadze, and his own strength in the Party organization lay in the cities. Comintern analysis predicted a rising tide of revolution in China, and the National Government was weakened by a series of wars against its warlord associates.

The result was a decision to use the Red Army for the capture of major cities. The

---

[24] For details of Communist land policy in this period, see Hsiao Tso-liang, *The Land Revolution in China* (Seattle: University of Washington Press, 1970.)

[25] For an interesting account of these operations by a man who was in charge of them, see U. T. Hsu, *The Invisible Conflict* (Hongkong: China Viewpoints, 1958).

main target of the offensive was Wuhan, and preparations started in April, 1930. On July 29, the Third Red Army managed to capture Changsha, mainly because National Government troops had moved to North China for a war against Feng Yü-hsiang and Yen Hsi-shan, who had set up a rival government with Wang Ching-wei as political leader. However, the Red Army met with little response from the workers in Changsha and had to withdraw on August 9. An attack on Nanchang on August 1 was a failure. The Central Committee called for a renewed attack on Changsha, which was staged at the beginning of September. By that time, its defenses had been reinforced, and Chu Te and Mao Tse-tung soon called off the attack.

Finally, in November, 1930, Li Li-san was attacked in a letter from the Comintern and was ordered to Russia, where he had to make a self-criticism before an investigating committee. (He remained in Russia until 1945, when he returned to Manchuria with the Soviet Army.)

Meanwhile, Pavel Mif, director of the Sun Yat-sen University in Moscow, had become the chief China expert of the Comintern. Some of his students, the Returned Students Group, took over leadership from Li Li-san in a period of very bitter factional disputes. In the Kiangsi base area, there was some fighting—the Fut'ien incident—between Mao Tse-tung's forces and a group sympathetic to Li Li-san. And there is evidence that a number of Communists in the cities were betrayed to the Kuomintang police by opponents in the Party.

The National Government campaigns. The attacks on Changsha alerted the National Government to the seriousness of the Communist threat. A special anti-Communist headquarters for the provinces of Hupei, Hunan, and Kiangsi was set up at Hankow for an 'encirclement and suppression' campaign, which started at the beginning of November, 1930. This and a second campaign in February, 1931, failed completely by the end of the year, leaving the Communists stronger than before through captured supplies and prisoners.

A third campaign, under the command of Chiang Kai-shek himself, started in July, 1931, using still more troops, including some of the good National Government divisions. This was a less complete failure, but it ended after about three months during which the National Government forces suffered severe losses. The Japanese seizure of Manchuria and the fighting at Shanghai then interrupted operations against the Communists until the summer of 1932.

On the Communist side, the First National Soviet Congress was held at Juichin in southeastern Kiangsi, which set up a Chinese Soviet Republic on December 11, 1931. Mao Tse-tung became chairman of the government. Sources disagree widely on the date at which the Central Committee of the Chinese Communist Party moved from Shanghai to Juichin. A possible explanation for the disagreement is that there was no single date but a gradual shift in units of the Central Committee organization, extending over a year or so.

On April 15, 1932, the Chinese Soviet Republic declared war on Japan. The move had no operational significance, since there was no point of contact with the Japanese, but it was very effective as a propaganda gesture. After September, 1931, the National Government got into an increasingly difficult position because it followed a policy toward Japan that it could not explain to the Chinese public. (There are good arguments on both sides of the question as to whether or not this policy was wise): The longer the National Government, intent on building up a strong central government army with the help of German advisers, could postpone full-scale hostilities with Japan, the stronger its position would become. However, in order to postpone full-scale hostilities, it had to follow a policy of appeasement in the face of continued Japanese encroachments on Chinese sovereignty. If it had told the Chinese people that it would resist Japan when it became strong enough to do so, the Japanese Army would naturally have taken this as the signal to take everything it wanted from China, while the balance of power was in its favor. The National Government, therefore, incurred increasingly bitter criticism for its appeasement of Japan, and the Communists won increasing support by the advocacy of resistance, especially from strongly nationalist groups, such as the students.

Meanwhile, the civil war continued. The early campaigns against the Communist areas had aimed at a quick victory. In August, 1931, Chiang Kai-shek had talked of eliminating the Red Army within three months. At the end of 1932, plans were started for a long-term counterinsurgency effort. An officers' training school for counterinsurgency was set up. A large-scale road-building program was started. Measures were taken to strengthen local government in the areas surrounding the Communist bases, with strict control of the population and the organization of local militia to prevent Communist infiltration and with control of trade to enforce an economic blockade of the Communist bases. Finally, at the end of 1933, a fort and blockade line strategy was adopted, involving gradual encroachment on the Communist-held areas with lines of forts and consolidation of the recovered area outside each line of forts before beginning a fresh advance.

The Communists had no effective counter strategy, and their base areas suffered from the increasingly effective blockade. They lacked such staples as salt.

Within the Communist Party, the Returned Students Group consolidated its power, and Mao Tse-tung's position weakened. In the summer of 1932, he lost his position as political commissar in the army to Chou En-lai. In 1933, he was still strong enough in the government to put through a reinvestigation of classes in the countryside, which reflected an intensification of class warfare, but he lost further power in February, 1934, and in March his land policy was denounced by Chang Wen-t'ien.

Communist histories of this period written under Mao's leadership blame the Returned Students Group for doctrinaire attitudes and mistakes in strategy causing the Communist defeat. They are blamed in particular for failing to make a closer alliance with a rival Kuomintang government, set up in Fukien in November, 1933, by the Nineteenth Route Army, and had fought very well against the Japanese at Shanghai in 1932. It is doubtful, however, whether Mao could have prevented the Communist defeat if he had been in control. In his 'Strategy in China's Revolutionary War,' he argues that the Red Army should have conducted an offensive into the main Kuomintang base area in the lower Yangtze valley, which would have aided the 'People's Government in Fukien.' This would have been a risky gamble. If it had succeeded, it might have produced a collapse of the National Government and a great increase in Communist power. On the other hand, if Communist aid had failed to prevent the defeat of the Fukien government, the National Government could have concentrated against the Red Army in an area where Kuomintang organization was strong and where the Communists had not had time to build up mass organization, where the terrain was relatively unfavorable for guerrilla warfare, and from which the Red Army could only have retreated to its original base by again breaking through the National Government blockade lines.

In fact, the Fukien government had collapsed by the end of January, 1934, and the situation of the main Communist base area became increasingly difficult. In July, the government of the Chinese Soviet Republic and the Red Army issued an announcement about moving north to oppose the Japanese. In October, the Red Army started a general retreat from its bases in South and Central China—the famous Long March.

The Long March. After breaking through the blockade lines, the main force of the Red Army from Kiangsi moved into Kweichow, where it was joined in January, 1935, by the Red Army units from other bases south of the Yangtze. In the middle of January a conference was held at Tsuni, which chose Mao Tse-tung as the Party leader. The Returned Students Group had been discredited by their military failure, and Mao had retained strong personal connections in the army.

Meanwhile, the Red Army units from bases north of the Yangtze moved west into

Szechwan. There is some evidence that they had hoped to establish a new base in Szechwan—a province in which the National Government had little authority and in which local power was disputed among several warlords. In fact, they were not able to inflict a decisive defeat on local forces and continued their move westward.

The Red Army south of the Yangtze divided and moved by several routes on a long detour to the west and then to the north through very wild mountainous country west of Szechwan. They had to contend with local warlord forces and hostile non-Chinese tribesmen and were pursued by National Government forces. On several occasions, important units narrowly escaped being caught between an impassable river and pursuing National Government troops, which would have meant annihilation. The crossing of the Tatu River, for example, is rightly celebrated by the Communists as an example of extreme heroism in the capture of a bridge that offered the one hope of escape. Other stages of the march included the crossing of very high passes, where lack of air caused many deaths from exhaustion, and areas of grassy marsh, where anyone who left the narrow path sank in the mud.

The Red Army units from bases north of the Yangtze followed a much easier route across Szechwan and, when the two sections of the Red Army made contact, the forces under Chang Kuo-t'ao and Hsü Hsiang-ch'ien were stronger than those under Mao Tse-tung and Chu Te. A conference was held in June, 1935, at Maoerhkai in northwestern Szechwan. There is still no satisfactory account of the proceedings, but there seems to have been a dispute between Chang and Mao over the final goal of the Long March.

Chang Kuo-t'ao apparently favored a move into Sinkiang or an area bordering on Sinkiang. At that time, the Russians had a dominant influence in Sinkiang, and this move would have enabled the Red Army to get arms from the Soviet Union and gained the big advantage of contact with territory under Soviet control. However, such a base, while safe, would have been too remote to have had much influence on Chinese affairs.

Mao Tse-tung favored a move into northern Shensi, where a small area of Communist insurgency had formed in 1931. This was a gamble on the early outbreak of war with Japan. While the Long March was a remarkable accomplishment, it was also a serious defeat for the Red Army. Losses had been extremely heavy, not so much from fighting as from exhaustion, disease, starvation, and desertions.[26]

Since the National Government, with the strategies it finally evolved, had been

---

[26] Edgar Snow has reported an interview with Chou En-lai on September 26, 1936, about losses during the Long March. According to Chou, 188,000 men had left the base areas in South and Central China. Of these, about 10,000 had already reached northern Shensi, where the Red Army strength was about 35,000, including about 10,000 from the original Communist forces in the area and about 15,000 newer recruits. Chou estimated the strength of the Second and Fourth Front armies then on their way to the new base area at 40,000 to 50,000. Edgar Snow, *Random Notes on Red China, (1936–1945)* (Cambridge: Chinese Economic and Political Studies, Harvard University Press, 1957), pp. 100–101.

In fact, the Second and Fourth Front Armies suffered heavy losses before they reached northern Shensi.

A footnote to *Selected Military Writings*, p. 151, gives the strength of the Eighth Route and New Fourth armies as 'only a little more than 40,000 men when the War of Resistance began in 1937.' Since the New Fourth Army, formed from the Communist forces remaining in South and Central China, had an initial strength of about 10,000, this would leave only a little over 30,000 for the Red Army in Shensi-Kansu-Ninghsia. This seems improbably small.

At the other extreme, Chalmers Johnson estimates the Communist forces in North China at 90,000 for the same date. Chalmers A. Johnson, *Peasant Nationalism and Communist Power* (Stanford, Calif.: Stanford University Press, 1962), pp. 72–77. This seems improbably large unless it includes village militia, because the base area, with a population of less than 1 million, was still extremely poor and could hardly have supported an army of this size.

able to defeat the Red Army when it had a strength of 200,000 to 300,000, holding base areas with a population of several million, it could almost certainly have defeated a Red Army of perhaps 50,000 in a base area with a population of less than 1 million if it had been able to continue full-scale anti-Communist campaigns. If the Japanese had relaxed their pressures on China for a few years, thus allowing the civil war to continue, the Red Army might have been reduced to a few scattered bands of guerrillas.

After the Maoerhkai conference, Mao Tse-tung moved to northern Shensi with part of the Red Army. In February, 1936, his forces started a move into Shansi, which was proclaimed as an offensive against the Japanese. The National Government moved large forces to assist the defense of Shansi and the Red Army withdrew in May.

A larger part of the Red Army under Chang Kuo-t'ao made an unsuccessful attempt to set up a base area in Sikang and Chinghai and finally retreated through Kansu, suffering heavy losses in the process. It was not until the beginning of 1937 that the whole Red Army was concentrated in the new base area, which had expanded to include parts of Kansu and Ninghsia.

The Second United Front

In 1935, there was an important change in Comintern strategy. In the early 1930's, the policy had been 'united front from below.' The Chinese Communists appealed for a united front against Japan but excluded the Kuomintang leaders, whom they denounced as traitors who had sold out to Japanese imperialism. Similarly, in Europe, the Communists had appealed for a united front against Fascism and Nazism but denounced the leaders of the Social Democrats and other non-Communist parties. In 1935, the line changed to 'united front from above.' The Communists announced their readiness to cooperate with the leaders of non-Communist parties. In the case of China, the Soviet Union had additional motives for wanting better relations with the Kuomintang. The Soviet Union faced a real danger of attack from Japan, and the increasing strength of the National Government armies made China a desirable ally. In 1936, Soviet publicity ceased to attack Chiang Kai-shek and denounced opposition to him as inspired by Japanese imperialism, even when the slogan of the opposition leaders was, 'Oppose Japan and save the country.'[27]

The Chinese Communists did not immediately follow the new Comintern line but, by August, 1936, were appealing to the Kuomintang leadership for a united front. According to some sources, Chinese Communist representatives went to Nanking for secret negotiations.

These attempts to secure a 'united front from above' were not successful, and the National Government continued to assert its determination to eliminate the Red Army. However, the 'united front from below' was increasingly successful. As the Japanese strengthened their forces and increased their demands in North China, the National Government found it steadily harder to restrain popular demands for united national resistance to Japan and made itself steadily more unpopular by suppressing student demonstrations and arresting advocates of resistance to Japan.

In operations against the Red Army, the National Government repeated its earlier mistake of using unreliable troops, in this case the former Manchurian army under Chang Hsüeh-liang. This army, which had been driven from its home area by the Japanese, was, naturally, especially susceptible to Communist appeals for an end to the civil war and a united front against Japan. On the Manchurian army's front,

---

[27] For details see Charles B. McLane, *Soviet Policy and the Chinese Communists, 1931–1946* (New York: Columbia University Press, 1958).

operations against the Communists declined into an informal truce. Chang Hsüeh-liang had a secret meeting with Chou En-lai, and increasing friction developed in Sian between the Manchurian army and National Government organizations, such as a gendarmerie regiment, which wished to maintain the anti-Communist policy.

The Sian Incident. On December 8, 1936, Chiang Kai-shek went to Sian to try to revive operations against the Communists and to restore his authority over the Manchurian army. Four days later, he was seized by Chang Hsüeh-liang and Yang Hu-ch'eng. Some people in the National Government advocated an attack on the rebels, including the bombing of Sian where Chiang was held. The Soviet press denounced the incident as a Japanese-inspired plot against Chiang Kai-shek. The Chinese Communists came in as mediators and secured his release. Chiang left Sian on December 24, and Chang Hsüeh-liang accompanied him to Nanking. Chang was arrested on arrival and kept prisoner for thirty years.

There is still no definitive account of the Sian Incident. Some sources maintain that Stalin ordered the Chinese Communists to work for Chiang Kai-shek's release. It is not clear why Chang Hsüeh-liang agreed to go to Nanking or whether Chiang Kai-shek made any explicit agreement to end the civil war. In fact, though the Kuomintang continued to issue strongly anti-Communist statements, the civil war was not resumed and desultory Kuomintang-Communist negotiations continued.

As part of the move for a new united front, the Communists enforced a less extreme land policy in their new base area. There was still confiscation of land, but landlords were allowed to share in the distribution and to survive as farmers.

The year 1936 marks the beginning of contacts between the Chinese Communists and non-Communist foreigners. A few foreign missionaries had previously been captured and held for varying periods, but an American, Edgar Snow, was the first foreign journalist to visit the Communist base area and interview the leaders. During the following year, several other foreigners visited Yenan, which the Communists took over in December, 1936. The Communist leaders at that time seem to have been waiting for the outbreak of war with Japan and were, therefore, relaxed and willing to talk about their past experiences.[28]

War with Japan. War with Japan began on July 7, 1937, with an incident involving Japanese troops on maneuvers near Peiping. For several weeks, fighting was confined to the Peiping-Tientsin area and attempts were made to negotiate a local settlement. Chinese Communist publications showed a fear that the National Government would yield to avoid a general war, but the National Government was not willing to tolerate any further increase of Japanese power in North China. At the end of August, the Japanese started offensives along the Peiping-Suiyüan and Peiping-Hankow railways. It was only after this that the National Government and the Chinese Communists reached agreement for a new united front.

On September 22, the Communists issued a statement in which they proposed three common objectives: a campaign of resistance to recover lost territory and restore the integrity of China, the enforcement of democracy, and measures to improve the well-being of the Chinese people. They then declared:

1. Dr. Sun Yat-sen's Three People's Principles constitute the needs of China today, and our Party is willing to work for their complete realization.

2. Our Party is to abandon its policy of armed uprisings against the Kuomintang regime, and its Communization movement, and cease its policy of forced confiscation of the landlord's land.

---

[28] The accounts of Chinese Communist Party history that Edgar Snow recorded in *Red Star over China* contain some serious inaccuracies. At the time, Snow could not have detected this, because the first documented study in English, Harold Isaacs's *Tragedy of the Chinese Revolution*, was not published until 1938.

3. The present Soviet Government is to be abolished and democratic rule is to be enforced so as to achieve unification of government throughout the country.

4. The Red Army is to drop its title and identity and reorganize itself into National Revolutionary Forces placed under the command of the National Military Council of the National Government, and it shall wait for orders to move out to shoulder front line duties in the anti-Japanese war.[29]

This Communist statement met demands that the Kuomintang Central Executive Committee had made in February, 1937.[30] In return, the National Government recognized the Red Army in North China as the Eighth Route Army (later Eighteenth Group Army) with three divisions, the 115th, the 120th, and the 129th. The remnants of the Communist forces in South and Central China were recognized as the New Fourth Army. (It took some months to assemble these small scattered units, so the New Fourth Army with about 10,000 men under Yeh T'ing did not start operations until 1938.) The area under full Communist control was recognized as a special local-government area, and a wider area surrounding this was assigned to the Eighth Route Army as its recruiting and garrison area.[31] This larger area had a population of about 1.5 million.

Expansion of the Eighth Route Army. The Eighth Route Army moved into Shansi at the invitation of the Second War Zone commander, Yen Hsi-shan. The 115th Division successfully ambushed a Japanese column at P'inghsingkuan, but the Japanese captured Taiyüan at the beginning of November, 1937, and continued their advance. This left the Communist forces behind the regular front in areas where the prewar Chinese administration had largely disappeared. The Communists proceeded to organize these areas and to recruit local forces.

By the end of 1938, the Eighth Route Army had expanded to 156,000 men. This expansion was greatly helped by two serious Japanese mistakes. The first was the long delay in trying to get control of the countryside in North China. Because the Japanese army had not expected a major war in China in 1937, they did not have the forces available both to establish control in the North China countryside and also to defeat the main National Government regular forces. They chose to concentrate on the latter objective and could only spare the 110th Division under General Kuwaki to hold their lines of communication in North China. Consequently, after their initial sweep through the countryside against the regular Chinese armies, the Japanese only held the railways and made occasional raids from them. It was only after the fall of Wuhan and Canton in September, 1938, that large forces were shifted to North China for attempts to establish full control.

An insurgency movement is weakest in its early stages. It takes time to turn a new recruit into an effective soldier, to build up mass organizations, and to win popular support for the new insurgent government. Over large parts of North China, the Communists had nine or ten months almost undisturbed to train their new recruits and to organize the countryside. The importance of this can be illustrated by comparison with the one area where the Japanese acted quickly against Communist-led

---

[29] Quoted in Warren Kuo, *Analytical History of the Chinese Communist Party*, book three (Taipei: Institute of International Relations, 1966 *et seq.*), p. 324.

[30] *United States Relations with China*, Department of State Publication 3373, Far Eastern Series 30, 1949, p. 49.

[31] After the united front had broken down, the Kuomintang issued maps showing the illegal expansion of the Communist area while the Communists put out maps showing Kuomintang encroachment on their area. In different senses, both were correct. The Communists took over full control in the Eighth Route Army garrison area, removing officials appointed by the National Government; while the National Government drove Communist forces from parts of the area originally assigned to the Eighth Route Army as garrison area.

insurgency. In July, 1938, Eighth Route Army units penetrated into East Hopei (the Peiping-Tientsin-Shanhaikuan triangle) and produced a general uprising which, for a week or so, eliminated Japanese control. Because this was a key strategic area, the Japanese reacted quickly with large numbers of troops from Manchuria and subsequently regained control. It was not until the latter part of 1942 that the Communists were able to revive guerrilla operations and set up a small base area in the mountains on the Hopei-Jehol border. And even this would have been more difficult if there had not been a secure base area west of Peiping from which organizers could penetrate.

The other, more lasting Japanese mistake was the failure to maintain discipline toward the civilian population. At the time of the Russo-Japanese war, the Japanese army had won general admiration for its good discipline, but its standards had collapsed by the 1930's. Everywhere it went, it aroused violent anti-Japanese feelings. In the summer of 1938, a Communist officer told me that it was hard to develop anti-Japanese organization in areas where the Japanese Army had not been. This lack of discipline antagonized even the groups whose support the Japanese tried to win, such as the conservative gentry who were naturally inclined to be anti-Communist.

In the first months of the war there was a proliferation of small anti-Japanese self-defense units, and a large part of the early Communist expansion came from absorbing them. The Communists could offer such local units the obvious advantages of belonging to a larger force with political organization and a regular supply system behind it, and also training and advice from the cadre of old Red Army soldiers with long experience of guerrilla warfare. To begin with, arms were fairly plentiful, large amounts having been abandoned by the Chinese regular forces in their retreat. While the Communists took most advantage of this situation, a number of areas of Kuomintang guerrilla operations also developed.

Communist-Kuomintang relations. Communist-Kuomintang relations during the war are a very complicated subject. Almost all the available material is propagandistic, and a good deal of it is demonstrably false even from internal evidence.

Several sources report disagreement among the Communist leaders in 1937, with Chang Kuo-t'ao and Wang Ming in favor of close cooperation with the Kuomintang, and Mao Tse-tung favoring a high degree of independence of action for the Communists.[32] (The charges against Liu Shao-ch'i during the Cultural Revolution include advocacy of close cooperation between the New Fourth Army and the Kuomintang.)

In 1938, the united front seems to have worked quite well. Communists helped run a training school for guerrilla warfare at Wuhan, and a number of Kuomintang units adopted something like the Communist style of organization. Each side was willing to make concessions to the other. The National Government recognized a new local government set up under Communist leadership in Shansi-Chahar-Hopei, and the Communists allowed General Lu Chung-lin, appointed as governor of Hopei, to move his troops and officials through Communist areas to take over southern Hopei, where Communist forces had been operating.

The united front began to break down in 1939. Once the Japanese had started serious attempts to control the countryside, only a high degree of mutual trust could have prevented trouble in regions where both Communist and Kuomintang forces

---

[32] The often quoted statement that Mao advocated a division of effort—70 per cent to expansion, 20 per cent against the Kuomintang, and 10 per cent against the Japanese—is doubtful, because expansion and action against the Japanese were not really alternatives. A large part of Communist expansion was into areas where they were opposed only by the Japanese. Also, the quotations do not give a reference to an original Communist document. The best answer the author could get to inquiries about the original source was that a Communist prisoner captured by the Kuomintang said that he had heard this statement in a lecture by Mao Tse-tung before he left Yenan.

were operating. Base areas were not interchangeable, because no Kuomintang units went so far as the Communists in mass organization and reform of local government, taxation, and agrarian policy. If the Japanese started an offensive against an area, the guerrilla forces operating there would move to avoid a positional battle. The move might take them into an area held by guerrillas of the other party, where they would certainly be an extra burden on resources and might rouse suspicions that they wanted to take control. When the Japanese offensive ended the newcomers might be better placed to take control for their party than the forces that had operated there before the offensive and would be tempted to do so if the area had strategic importance.

Once clashes between Communist and Kuomintang forces had started, mutual trust declined and made future clashes more likely. Mutual trust was also decreasing at the higher levels of the parties, and by the end of 1939 extra causes for mutual suspicion had appeared. In December, 1938, Wang Ching-wei fled from Chungking to Hanoi, whence he issued an appeal to the National Government to make peace and started his own negotiations with the Japanese. He finally emerged as leader of a new Japanese-sponsored Kuomintang government at Nanking in March, 1940. The National Government did not seem wholehearted in denouncing him and maintained contacts with his organization. The Communists suspected that some elements in the Kuomintang were considering the possibility of coming to terms with Japan, and these suspicions were almost certainly correct. Official American documents from 1941 on record a number of occasions on which high-ranking Kuomintang officials reacted to American pressure for reforms by threatening to make peace with Japan. The continued contacts with Wang Ching-wei were simply a reversion to the normal warlord practice of 'keeping options open.'

On the other side, Mao Tse-tung provided grounds for suspicion of the Communists by his completely uncritical support for the Soviet line during the period of the Nazi-Soviet nonaggression pact. In a speech at Yenan on September 14, 1939, he argued that Chamberlain was as much responsible as Hitler for starting the war, that England had become the most reactionary and most imperialist power in the world, and that the people of Poland must join with the Soviet Union to resist German aggression.[33] On September 28, he made another speech justifying the Soviet invasion of Poland.[34] Finally, in On New Democracy, published in January, 1940, he argued that an alliance between China and the United States or England could only be directed against the Soviet Union and not against Japan.[35] While not many people on the Kuomintang side would have read these particular statements by Mao, the line they laid down was reflected by the Communist newspaper in Chungking, which made frequent vituperative attacks on the British and French governments but only occasionally applied terms of mild disapproval to Hitler.

This Chinese Communist line in international affairs provided the more extreme

[33] 'Ti erh-tz'u ti-kuo-chu-i chan-tou chiang-yen t'i-kang (Main Points of a Lecture on the Second Imperialist War),' in Mao Tse-tung Hsüan Chi (Selected Works of Mao Tse-tung, hereafter Hsüan Chi) (Harbin: Tung-pei Shu-tien, 1948), pp. 442–44.
[34] 'Su-lien li-i yü jen-lei li-i i-chih (The Identity of Soviet Interests with the Interests of Mankind),' in Hsüan Chi, pp. 459–61.
[35] Hsin min-chu-chu-i (On New Democracy), Chapter 10, 'Chiu san-min-chu-i yü hsin san-min-chu-i (The Old Three People's Principles and the New Three People's Principles),' Hsüan Chi, p. 257. The 1948 edition is the last to reproduce the original text of Mao's writings. Some of the passages cited have been cut from later editions. The English-language edition of On New Democracy, which Earl Browder published in the United States in 1945, used a translation prepared by the Eighteenth Group Army Liaison Office in Chungking, which cut out passages referring to the international Communist line of 1940 that had become embarrassing after 1941.

anti-Communists in the Kuomintang with a persuasive argument for their contention that the Chinese Communist Party was controlled by the Soviet Union.[36] It also discouraged the groups in the Kuomintang that would have been inclined to favor a united front in China but whose sympathies in international affairs were pro-Ally and anti-Nazi.

Most of the Communist-Kuomintang clashes in 1939 seem to have been between local units. The first important Communist-Kuomintang fighting, which involved headquarters rather than local commanders, seems to have occurred in the winter of 1939–40 between the Eighth Route Army in southeastern Shansi and General Chu Huai-ping's Ninety-Seventh Army. According to General Chu Huai-ping, he visited Chu Te's headquarters to discuss orders from Chungking for a joint offensive against Shihchiachuang.[37] Chu Te and P'eng Te-huai refused to discuss any joint military plans until agreement had been reached on the case of Wang Ching-wei and on the correct international line, in the face of which Chu Huai-ping pointed out that such general issues of policy were beyond his competence and should be discussed in Chungking, where Chou En-lai headed the Eighth Route Army Liaison Office. He later ordered the Ninety-Seventh Army to move north on its own, which took it into Communist territory, and the Communists fought against it.

This Communist behavior could have been an evasive way of refusing to obey orders from Chungking whose primary objective was to weaken the Eighth Route Army. Shihchiachuang was a major Japanese base with excellent communications. An attacking Chinese force would have had a very long supply line, with the last 150 miles or so through roadless mountain country dependent on porters or pack animals. The almost certain outcome of an offensive would have been the destruction of the Chinese attacking force at very small cost to the Japanese.

The Eighth Route Army did launch its one major offensive, the Hundred Regiments Campaign, in August, 1940. The motives for this were almost certainly political —to encourage Chinese opinion against surrender after the formation of Wang Ching-wei's government—and perhaps also to disprove Kuomintang propaganda that the Communists had stopped fighting the Japanese. The Communists captured many Japanese positions and put the Shihchiachuang-Taiyüan railway out of commission for a week or so, but the gains were only temporary. Within a few months, the Japanese had recaptured all their previous positions and rebuilt their forts more strongly. Communist officers would later refer to the campaign as a military failure. The temporary gains had cost very heavy casualties and had used up nearly all reserves of ammunition.

Conflicts between Communist and Kuomintang forces were frequent in 1940, especially in Shantung and in Kiangsu and Anhwei, where the New Fourth Army was operating. Also in 1940, the National Government started a blockade of the original Communist base area around Yenan.

At the end of 1940, the New Fourth Army was ordered to move north of the Yangtze, which could have been part of a sensible plan to assign clearly separated areas to Kuomintang and Communist forces. However, as the headquarters unit was moving, it became involved in a battle with Kuomintang forces and was almost completely wiped out. General Yeh T'ing was captured. Accounts of the incident are completely conflicting, though the Communist version seems the more plausible, as it is unlikely that the New Fourth Army would have chosen its headquarters unit, with a high proportion of noncombatants, to make an attack on Kuomintang forces.

---

[36] This argument was still used in 1944 by General Ho Ying-ch'in in a letter to General Hearn and, within the American organization, by General Chennault in a letter to President Roosevelt. See *Foreign Relations of the United States, 1944*, Vol. VI, *China* (Washington, D.C.: Department of State, 1967), pp. 402, 159.

[37] Interviewed by the author in Taiwan.

Although the National Government then officially abolished the New Fourth Army, the Communists appointed Ch'en Yi to replace Yeh T'ing, with Liu Shao-ch'i as his political commissar, and the New Fourth Army continued to operate south of the Yangtze. Its main efforts were directed to building up a strong Communist base area in northern Kiangsu.

A number of books on this period describe the New Fourth Army incident as the first battle between Communist and Kuomintang forces and the event that caused the breakdown of the united front. In fact, the breakdown was gradual, and the New Fourth Army incident was merely the first clash to which both sides gave wide publicity.

Communist-Kuomintang clashes declined from 1943 on, because a practical separation developed between the two forces. The Japanese objective at the end of 1941 was to restore 'public order' in an area east of the Yellow River, which then flowed south of the Shantung peninsula, and extending along the coast to south of Shanghai.[38] In the resultant fighting, the Communists proved able to survive Japanese 'mopping up' campaigns, while most Kuomintang units were forced to withdraw or to surrender. And many of those that surrendered accepted new positions in the army of Wang Ching-wei's Nanking government. Thus, in this part of China after 1943, the forces opposing the Japanese were almost entirely Communist.

Some Kuomintang guerrilla units held out in Shantung until 1945, when the Communists destroyed them. These had an organization with many similarities to that of the Communists, similarities determined by the requirements for effective guerrilla warfare. It may well have been their remoteness from Chungking that allowed them to maintain a type of organization that was necessary to resist the Japanese but that had become highly unorthodox and suspect by Kuomintang standards.[39]

Japanese operations against the Communists. The Japanese operations against the Communists followed a pattern similar to that of National Government operations in earlier years. Until 1940, the typical Japanese offensive against a Communist area was a converging attack. The Communist counterstrategy was to evade the encirclement and to concentrate against one of the attacking columns or to attack the Japanese base areas. By the end of 1939, the Japanese had captured most of the *hsien* cities and held motor roads connecting them, but Communist strength continued to grow in the countryside. In 1940, the Eighth Route army had grown to about 400,000 and the New Fourth Army to about 100,000, and the population under Communist control was about 60 million.[40]

In 1940, the Japanese in North China changed to the fort and blockade line strategy that had finally defeated the Communists in South China. A fort and blockade line system that had been started to protect the railways was extended to cut down the Communist base areas. After the temporary setback as a result of the Hundred Regiments Campaign, the fort system was steadily expanded. At one time there were about 30,000 Japanese forts, about 60,000 miles of blockade ditch, and nearly 8,000 miles of blockade fence. Large-scale offensives into the Communist base areas continued, but their objective was not so much to annihilate the main Com-

---

[38] See the Japanese map reproduced in Charles F. Romanus and Riley Sunderland, *Stilwell's Mission to China* (Washington, D.C.: Chief of Military History, 1953), facing p. 55.

[39] Information from interviews in Taiwan. See also Laurance Tipton, *Chinese Escapade* (London: Macmillan, 1949). Mr. Tipton escaped from the Weihsien internment camp and joined one of the more successful Kuomintang guerrilla units.

[40] Many accounts of the period continue to describe the Communist areas as the 'Northwest.' This applied to the original base area around Yenan, but from 1938 on the newer areas had much larger populations. For China excluding Manchuria, 'Communist Northeast' would be more appropriate.

munist forces as to make the base areas unable to support them. Villages were burned, farm animals and stocks of food seized or destroyed, and many civilians deported for labor in Manchuria.

As a result of this strategy, the Japanese were gaining in North China from 1940 to the end of 1943. The strength of the Eighth Route Army fell from 400,000 to 305,000 at the end of 1941 and only recovered to 339,000 at the end of 1943, although it was operating over a larger area. The population under Communist control fell from 60 million to about 40 million.[41]

The Communists had no fully effective counter to the Japanese strategy, because they had no artillery to use against the forts and were very short of ammunition. They were receiving no supplies from outside and had to depend for ammunition on what they could capture or what they could make in small local arsenals. The Japanese took increasing precautions to prevent the capture of ammunition, so even the best Communist units might have only about 100 rifle cartridges per man, and these would have to last for several months. The only items in fairly good supply were hand grenades and land mines, which could be made locally. The most effective developments on the Communist side were the widespread use of land mines by the village militia and the development of a tunnel system on the North China plain.

The weakness of the fort and blockade line strategy was that it required very large numbers of troops. The Japanese garrisoned a large proportion of their forts with locally recruited Chinese troops, but these were quite unreliable without a considerable stiffening of Japanese. When Japanese forces in North China were reduced by the demands of the war in the Pacific and for the offensives of 1944 in Honan and South China, their control started to crumble with increasing rapidity. By the end of 1944, the Eighth Route Army had grown to more than 500,000 men and held more than forty *hsien* cities, as against one at the end of 1943, while the New Fourth Army numbered slightly more than 250,000, compared with 125,000 at the end of 1943. By the end of the war, the Japanese controlled little more than the railways, while the Communist regular forces numbered about 1 million and the population under Communist control nearly 100 million.

The wartime Communist organization. The ability of the Communists to resist the Japanese attempts at pacification depended very largely on the organization that gave them mass support. The striking contrast between the Chinese Communist insurgency of this period and later Communist insurgency in Southeast Asia is that the Chinese Communists did not need to use terrorism, because they had genuine popular support.

During this period, many people called the Chinese Communists 'agrarian reformers,' and the term was quite appropriate for their practical policies, as distinct from their theoretical pronouncements. The basis of Communist land policy from 1937 to 1946 was a law that the National Government had issued in July, 1930, but never implemented, outside of a few experimental areas, until it withdrew to Taiwan. Maximum rent was limited to 37.5 per cent of the main crop, and the tenant had good security and some technical assistance. The postwar experience of both Taiwan and Japan has shown that this type of agrarian reform, based on family farms, can win strong peasant support and produce a large increase in productivity. This was equally true in the wartime Communist areas.

Another change whose importance is often neglected was reform of taxation and government finance. The prewar tax system had been both inequitable and inefficient. (The efficiency of a tax system is measured by the ratio between what the govern-

---

[41] 'Population under Communist control' is a rather indefinite concept, because there were no sharply defined boundaries between Communist-controlled and Japanese-controlled areas.

ment gets and what is taken from the public.) The main Communist system was apportionment of a total levy on the basis of estimates of ability to pay. The regional government apportioned quotas to the *hsien*, the *hsien* governments to the villages, and the village councils among the families in the village. This system was quite efficient and reasonably equitable.[42]

Taxation and government finance were increasingly reckoned in terms of units of grain, with money playing a subsidiary role. This meant that the whole public sector in the Communist regions was hardly affected by depreciation of the currency, and most of the private sector was subsistence agriculture, which was equally unaffected. By contrast, in the Kuomintang areas, inflation played a major part in demoralizing the government organization.

In Communist areas, each village was responsible for its tax quota. Troops or government employees on the move would carry 'grain tickets' in multiples of half a day's ration (normally 11 ounces of millet) and could present these at any village. The village preferred to account for its tax quota by turning in 'grain tickets,' because otherwise it had to deliver the grain at a *ch'ü* (*hsien* subdivision) government depot. This arrangement eliminated a possible source of conflict between the army and the people.

There was an effective transfer of power to elected village councils, because the village militia replaced all former local armed forces, such as the *min-t'uan* or *pao-an-tui*. When armed force was in the hands of a fairly representative sample of the population, no one could challenge the village council in carrying out reforms that had popular support.

In principle, elected government continued up through the *hsien* (county) to the region, but in most regions the military situation only rarely permitted the meeting of regional councils. Even at the *hsien* level, there was a large element of political tutelage in the system.

Communist control was complete in the army, but the government system in most regions included many non-Communist officials who often held responsible positions. Also, it was Communist policy to confine Communist membership to one-third of the elected bodies. The position of non-Communist officials in this period was quite different from what it became after 1949. It was possible for a non-Communist official to retain his independence of judgment and to cooperate with the Communists, because he agreed with their policies. It is unfortunate that the Communist leaders of the post-1949 period never fully realized how important this kind of non-Communist cooperation was for the efficient working of the system.

The region around Yenan was always depicted as a model area directly under the top Communist leadership, and it is true that material conditions in this area, where the Japanese had never penetrated, were much better than those in other regions that were frequently fought over. However, the efficiency of administration was much lower. People coming to Yenan from the front-line areas would complain in private conversations of the low standards of efficiency at Yenan and the completely unnecessary bureaucracy and red tape. This inefficiency could have been related to the fact that Yenan had a more nearly pure Communist organization. Party discipline and the principle of democratic centralism prevented any open criticism of anything that seemed to have the authority of the Central Committee behind it, even though the defect was one that the Communist leaders were perfectly willing to correct, once it had been brought to their attention, for instance, by visiting foreign journalists. In Shansi-Chahar-Hopei and probably in other front-line regions, non-Communist officials were not inhibited by Party discipline from arguing about Party directives

---

[42] See Michael Lindsay, 'The Taxation System of the Shansi-Chahar-Hopei Border Region, 1938–45,' *The China Quarterly*, No. 42 (April–June, 1970), pp. 1–15.

when they seemed to be producing undesirable results. The comparison that it was possible to make at this period can explain a lot of what happened after 1949, when almost all criticism was suppressed.

Divergence from normal Communism. The experience of the wartime system had a great effect, not so much on Communist doctrine as on Communist attitudes. A great deal of normal Communist behavior can be explained by the wide gap between what Communists like to think of themselves as doing and what they are actually doing. This wide gap between 'ego ideal' and 'reality principle,' to use Freudian terms, can be maintained only by an emotionally charged refusal to consider certain questions or face certain evidence. During the period of the war against Japan, this gap was unusually small, and the Chinese Communists could think freely and reasonably without disturbing their beliefs. The Communists claimed to be leading national resistance to the Japanese, and the performance of their armies was remarkable, considering the complete absence of supplies from outside. They claimed to represent the masses and to serve the interests of the masses; the reformist policies they were following really improved the conditions of the masses and won their genuine support.

This difference in attitude from that of the normal Communist was specially noticeable in the front-line areas, where the survival of the army during a Japanese offensive or the survival of an official or mass-movement organizer in the guerrilla areas depended on active support from the people. The typical doctrinaire Communist who believes that, because he understands Marxism-Leninism, he knows what the masses want better than they know themselves is unlikely to inspire this kind of support. There was, therefore, a strong process of natural selection against doctrinaire Communists. The proportion of doctrinaires was higher among people with only headquarters experience and higher still at Yenan, but even at Yenan there was a great deal of quite untypical reasonableness. A very noticeable change between the Chinese Communists in the early 1940's and in 1949 or 1954 was the steady shrinkage of the range of topics about which it was possible to have a reasonable discussion.[43]

There is some evidence to suggest that the Chinese Communists were beginning to think about a question that is completely subversive for the orthodox Communist system of beliefs, namely: How can one be sure that the Communist Party does really represent the masses? (In the orthodox system, the claim of the Communist Party to represent the masses is taken as an *a priori* truth that cannot be disproved by empirical evidence.) An editorial in April, 1942, defended the policy of confining Communist representation on elected bodies to a minority by arguing that only these conditions could compel the Party either to persuade other people of the correctness of its policies or else to modify its policies to take account of objections from people outside the Party. The concluding paragraph started by saying: 'Only when a party is functionally separate from the government can it be fitted into a system of democracy.[44]

Unfortunately, these ideas were not developed further. Mao Tse-tung later defended the limitation on Communist membership with arguments about the multi-class nature of the national resistance to Japan.[45]

CHINESE COMMUNIST DOCTRINE DURING THE YENAN PERIOD

In the four-volume edition of Mao Tse-tung's *Selected Works* published in Peking in 1961, Mao's writings before 1936 fill only half of the first volume, while his writings

---

[43] For a more complete treatment of this topic, see Michael Lindsay, 'Changes in Chinese Communist Thought,' in E. F. Szczepanik, *Economic and Social Problems of the Far East* (Hong Kong: Hong Kong University Press, 1961).

[44] Hsu Yung-ying, *A Survey of the Shensi-Kansu-Ninghsia Border Region* (New York; Institute of Pacific Relations, 1945), Part I, pp. 75–77.

[45] *Ibid.*, Part I, p. 77.

between 1936 and the end of the war with Japan fill two and a half volumes. The later writings include important works on military strategy, on politics—such as *On New Democracy* and *On Coalition Government*—and on more philosophical topics, e.g., *On Practice* and *On Contradictions*. During the same period, Liu Shao-ch'i produced some important works on Communist Party organization and discipline. One can, therefore, take 1936 as the year in which the Chinese Communist Party started to produce its own material on Marxist-Leninist doctrine.

While the practical policies of the Chinese Communists during this period were very far from orthodox Stalinism, the divergence in their more theoretical writings was much less marked. An orthodox Soviet theoretician might well have found tendencies and matters of emphasis in Chinese Communist theoretical works with which he felt dissatisfied, but he would not have found many points that he could have attacked as clearly and explicitly unorthodox. For example, in the 1950's, Mao Tse-tung drew conclusions from his theory about the universality of contradictions which did produce disagreement in Moscow, but these were not explicit in Mao's original essay.[46]

The one work by Mao Tse-tung that was almost certainly unorthodox was his small book on dialectical materialism. This had been withdrawn from circulation by 1949, and Mao later denied that he had ever written it. My impression from reading it in 1943 was that Mao had started with the assumption that dialectical materialism should make sense and had, therefore, produced something that seemed much more sensible than orthodox works on the subject to a reader who had been teaching a course on Logic and Scientific Method.

One factor that almost certainly influenced the development of Chinese Communist thinking was the cutting of contacts with the Soviet Union, except by radio. In an article written on the occasion of Stalin's seventieth birthday, Ch'en Po-ta explained that Mao Tse-tung had been out of touch with Stalin's thought for much of the Yenan period. Travel between Yenan and the Soviet Union had been fairly easy via Sinkiang until the Kuomintang blockade was imposed in 1940, but it became extremely difficult after 1942, when Sheng Shih-ts'ai, the Sinkiang warlord, turned against the Communists and executed Mao Tse-tung's brother. By 1944, the only Russians at Yenan were two Tass correspondents who spoke no Chinese and two doctors at the Central Hospital.

There is nothing surprising in the fact that the Chinese Communists did not adjust their theory to correspond to their unorthodox practice during the Yenan period. Even in cases of a permanent change in policy, there is usually a time lag in theoretical analysis. For instance, the Yugoslavs only started to produce a new theoretical analysis two years after their actual break with the Soviet Union, while the German Social Democrats clung to Marxist theory for decades after they had become in practice a reformist trade-union party. In the long run, the interaction between theory and practice is very important, and it will be argued below that later developments of Chinese Communist policy were greatly influenced by their failure to work out the theoretical implications of their practical success during the Yenan period.

The cheng-feng *Movement.* The membership of the Chinese Communist Party expanded very rapidly from about 40,000 in 1937 to about 800,000 in 1943, and a large part of the increase in membership was in the new base areas. The new members had widely differing backgrounds. The largest group numerically came from the local population of the base areas, many of which were in mountainous regions with a very low level of education and literacy. A smaller but very important group came from the students and intellectuals who left the Japanese-occupied cities to join in the

---

[46] While the official Chinese Communist dating of *On Contradictions* is August, 1937, Arthur Cohen, in his *The Thought of Mao Tse-tung* (Chicago: University of Chicago Press, 1964), argues that it must have been written later.

resistance movement and who, because of their education, filled a high proportion of the administrative positions in the new regional governments and in the mass organizations. The former group had a very low level of theoretical knowledge. The latter group had mostly read a number of Marxist works and, in the tradition of Chinese intellectuals, were inclined to believe that this knowledge of books was a sufficient qualification for practical action.

The leadership at Yenan faced the problem of maintaining the greatly expanded Party as a highly disciplined organization with a clear body of agreed doctrines. In February, 1942, it therefore started a movement whose full name was *Cheng-tun san-feng* (Correcting the Three Winds) directed against the three wrong tendencies of subjectivism, sectarianism, and formalism. (Subjectivism was subdivided into empiricism and dogmatism, of which dogmatism was considered the more important and more dangerous.) Members of all Party organizations were to devote a period of two or three months to the study and discussion of a selection of material that included some extracts from the works of Lenin and Stalin, some pieces by Liu Shao-ch'i and Ch'en Yün or Party organization, and a larger number of speeches and articles by Mao Tse-tung. The study was combined with self-criticism, and at its conclusion all organizations reported to higher levels on the standards attained by their members.[47]

The workings of the movement varied in different regions. At Yenan it was used to discredit the group that had held power in the Party before Mao's rise to leadership. Wang Ming and others who had been trained in the Soviet Union could be identified as the target of attacks on 'Party formalism' and the uncritical application to China of theories worked out for Russia. Also, Mao's lecture on literature and art, which formed part of the *cheng-feng* material and took the orthodox Stalinist line, formed the basis for an attack on writers who wanted some independence in literature.[48]

In Shansi-Chahar-Hopei, which was going through the most difficult period of the war against Japan, independence for literature and factional disputes in the Party leadership were not practical issues. The main emphasis of the *cheng-feng* movement was the criticism of dogmatism and of the tendency to attach more importance to book learning than to knowledge of practical Chinese problems, because these defects had immediate practical relevance to the conduct of the war and the retention of mass support.

When Sino-Soviet disagreements intensified during the Cultural Revolution in 1965–68, Soviet writers took the *cheng-feng* movement as the point at which the Chinese Communists started clearly to diverge from Communist orthodoxy. The element of truth in this is that the *cheng-feng* movement did show a very strong emphasis on the need to adapt Marxism-Leninism to Chinese conditions and on the uselessness of erudition in Communist theory not adapted to China. Also, though the *cheng-feng* material included some writings by Lenin and Stalin, it made Mao Tse-tung and, to a lesser extent, Liu Shao-ch'i the main sources of doctrine for the Chinese Communist Party.

COMMUNISTS, KUOMINTANG AND THE UNITED STATES

The united front between Kuomintang and Communists had really broken down by 1941, though neither side openly denounced it and some attempts were made to reach a new agreement. In the winter of 1942–3, General Lin Piao went to Chungking and had some interviews with Chiang Kai-shek, but without results.

In the summer of 1943, there seemed to be a serious risk of civil war. Large

---

[47] For details see Boyd Compton, *Mao's China: Party Reform Documents, 1942–44* (Seattle: University of Washington Press, 1952).
[48] See Merle Goldman, *Literary Dissent in Communist China* (Cambridge: Harvard University Press), 1967.

numbers of National Government troops were moved to intensify the blockade of the Yenan area, while the Communists moved General Ho Lung's army to the south of Yenan and started open denunciations of the Kuomintang to prepare the people of their areas for possible civil war. In fact, the crisis passed over, though important sections of both armies remained tied up in a mutual confrontation.

Negotiations were resumed at Sian in May, 1944, but the results only revealed basic disagreement. The position of the National Government was that it had only authorized the Communists to have a local government in the Yenan area and an army of three divisions. (The New Fourth Army had been officially abolished in 1941.) The regular provincial governments should, therefore, take over all regional governments set up by the Communists outside the Yenan area. The National Government would recognize a Communist army of ten divisions, which should be 'concentrated for use' and come under the orders of the local war zone commanders, but troops in excess of ten regular-sized divisions should be disbanded.

The Communists' position was that they had actually organized an army of 470,000, which had shown a good record against the Japanese but had received nothing from the National Government since 1940, while the new regional governments were necessary for the war effort and were based on Sun Yat-sen's principles. They asked the National Government to recognize and supply sixteen divisions of their army and to accept all the new regional governments as 'legally constituted.'[49]

With the Pacific War, the United States became an unwilling participant in Chinese internal politics, because the Kuomintang-Communist hostility was an obvious hindrance to an effective war effort against the Japanese in China. Until 1944, the American authorities had little information about the Communists. In 1937 and 1938, a number of foreign observers had visited the Communist areas, including Captain Evans Carlson of the U.S. Marine Corps. However, from 1940 on, the National Government blockaded the Communist areas and cut off almost all contacts except for the Eighteenth Group Army Liaison Office in Chungking under Chou En-lai, and Chou had only very limited information about the military situation.

National Government spokesmen claimed that the Communists had ceased to fight the Japanese and that Hopei Province was entirely under Japanese control. The Americans were skeptical about these claims, because the Japanese news services reported widespread fighting against the Communists, but it was not until 1943 that they received information from an American observer. G. M. Hall, manager of the National City Bank in Peiping, escaped from Japanese internment in 1942 and spent more than six months in Communist front-line base areas before reaching Chungking via Yenan. He reported large areas under well-organized Communist control and active operations against the Japanese.

Finally, in February, 1944, President Roosevelt sent a message to Chiang Kai-shek asking for an American observers' mission to northern Shensi (the Yenan area) and other parts of North China. Chiang's reply ruled out the Communist areas, but pressure was renewed when Vice President Henry A. Wallace visited China in June, 1944, and this secured Chiang's permission.

The U.S. Army Observers' Section (USAOS) arrived at Yenan in the latter part of July, 1944. It was commanded by Colonel David D. Barrett, and the chief political

---

[49] For details see *United States Relations with China* (Washington, D.C.: Department of State, 1949), pp. 533–36. Both sides showed ineptitude in the negotiations. The National Government strengthened the Communist suspicion that it was much more interested in destroying the Communists than in fighting the Japanese because its proposals implied abandoning large parts of North China to undisputed Japanese control. The Communists never used the strong argument that the National Government in 1938 had recognized the largest of the new regional governments, Shansi-Chahar-Hopei.

officer was John S. Service. Both had lived a long time in China and spoke excellent Chinese. To begin with, relations were very cordial. The Americans found that a great deal of useful intelligence could be obtained from the Communist areas and were impressed by the high morale of the Communist organization and the good physical condition of the soldiers, which were in marked contrast to the conditions they knew in the Kuomintang areas. The Communists welcomed the Americans as allies against Japan and hoped that these first contacts would develop into fuller cooperation. From December, 1944, however, relations deteriorated as the result of General Patrick J. Hurley's policies.

During Vice President Wallace's visit, Chiang Kai-shek asked for a personal representative of President Roosevelt in China. General Hurley was appointed in August and reached Chungking in September. His letter of appointment said: 'Your mission will be to promote harmonious relations between General Chiang and General Stilwell [the American commander of the China-Burma-India Theater] and to facilitate the latter's exercise of command over the Chinese armies placed under his direction.'[50] The background to his appointment was a serious deterioration in the position of the National Government. In the middle of April, the Japanese had launched an offensive in Honan, and the Honan front had collapsed by the end of May. They then moved to gain control of the Hankow-Canton railway and to eliminate American air bases in South China. Changsha fell on June 18, and the main air base at Kweilin on November 2. Meanwhile, the Communists had been gaining against the Japanese, and their increasing strength produced wider demands for a settlement with the Kuomintang. Communist publicity increasingly stressed that the situation in China could be saved only by a coalition government and a coalition high command.

General Hurley traveled via Moscow, where V. M. Molotov, in an interview:

> explained that in parts of China, the population was extremely impoverished, half starved, miserable. Some of these people called themselves 'Communists' but they had no relation whatever to communism. They were merely expressing their dissatisfaction at their economic condition by calling themselves Communists. However, once their economic conditions had improved, they would forget this political inclination. The Soviet Government could not be blamed in any way for this situation nor should it be associated with these 'Communist elements.'

General Hurley not only believed this but also believed that he had managed to convince Chiang Kai-shek that 'the Russian Government does not recognize the Chinese Communist Party as Communists at all.'[51]

During September, 1944, the disagreements between General Stilwell and Chiang Kai-shek came to a head and culminated in October with Stilwell's recall at Chiang's request. General Wedemeyer, who succeeded Stilwell, tried to confine himself to technical military affairs, and Ambassador Gauss resigned in November. This left all political issues in the hands of General Hurley.

On November 7, General Hurley went to Yenan, taking with him his own draft for a new Kuomintang-Communist agreement and a draft prepared by the Kuomintang. He astonished the Communists by giving Indian war whoops at the airfield and at the banquet that evening.

The Communist leaders took violent exception to the Kuomintang draft, but the meeting settled down to an 'amicable discussion by all parties,' which produced a five-point 'Agreement Between the National Government of China, the Kuomintang of China, and the Communist Party of China.' Clause 2 stated:

---

[50] *Foreign Relations of the United States, 1944*, VI: 250.
[51] *Ibid.*, VI: 255, 746-47.

The present National Government is to be reorganized into a Coalition National Government embracing representatives of all anti-Japanese parties and non-partisan political bodies. A new democratic policy providing for reforms in military, political, economic, and cultural affairs shall be promulgated and made effective. At the same time, the National Military Council is to be reorganized into the United National Military Council consisting of representatives of all anti-Japanese armies.

Clause 4 read: 'All anti-Japanese forces will observe and carry out the orders of the Coalition National Government and its United National Military Council and will be recognized by the Government and the Military Council. The supplies acquired from foreign powers will be equitably distributed.' Clause 1 was an expression of general good intentions. Clause 3 contained passages from the Gettysburg Address, the Bill of Rights, and the Atlantic Charter. Clause 5 recognized the legality of all anti-Japanese parties.[52]

Foreign Relations of the United States prints these proposals with only Mao's signature and blank spaces for Chiang Kai-shek's and for Hurley's as a witness. However, Hurley himself later wrote, 'I was at least co-author of them and had signed them as a witness to Mao's signature.'[53] According to Colonel Barrett, Hurley proposed that both he and Mao should sign the proposals to indicate their agreement that they were fair and just.[54]

On returning to Chungking, accompanied by Chou En-lai, Hurley gave a copy of the proposals to T. V. Soong requesting that a translation should be given to Chiang Kai-shek. Soong and Wang Shih-chieh then came to see him and told him that he had been tricked by the Communists, and Chiang Kai-shek later rejected the proposed agreement. The National Government then produced a series of three counter-drafts. The third of these offered to incorporate the Communist forces in the National Army with equal treatment, after reorganization; to recognize the Communists as a legal party; and to designate some high-ranking officer from the Communist forces to membership of the National Military Council, but it required the Communists to give over control of their troops to the National Government. General Hurley pressed Chou En-lai to accept this offer, but Chou returned to Yenan and sent a message on December 8 that the Central Committee had decided that there was no common ground between the two sets of proposals and that it would be pointless to continue negotiations.

Mao Tse-tung and Chou En-lai expressed their views at an interview with Colonel Barrett. They argued that reorganization by the National Government could be used to destroy the Communist forces and that one seat on the National Military Council, which had not met in full session for a long time, afforded no power or influence. Generals Hurley, Wedemeyer, and McClure had urged Chou to accept the Kuomintang terms. The Communists responded: 'The United States, however, offers us absolutely no guarantee of our safety under these terms. . . . We cannot trust the good faith of the Generalissimo.' They expressed their willingness to serve unconditionally under an American general and their determination to continue the fight against Japan even without American help. They were puzzled by General Hurley's behavior.

> We understood perfectly that General Hurley did not guarantee that the Generalissimo would accept the 'five points.' We know that he said only that the terms were fair and he would do his best to get them accepted. But after Chiang

---

[52] *Ibid.*, VI: 687–88.   [53] *Ibid.*, *1945*, p. 206.
[54] David D. Barrett, *Dixie Mission: The United States Army Observer Group in Yenan, 1944.* (China Research Monograph No. 6 (Berkeley: University of California, Center for Chinese Studies, 1970), p. 64.

Kai-shek refused these fair terms, we did not expect General Hurley to come back and press us to agree to a counterproposal which requires us to sacrifice ourselves.

Finally, they announced their intention to set up a 'United Committee' for all the Communist areas as the first step toward the formation of a separate government. During the interview, Mao Tse-tung furiously abused Chiang Kai-shek while Chou En-lai 'backed up in calm, cold language everything that Chairman Mao said.'[55]

In a memorandum of January 4, 1945, to President Roosevelt, Secretary of State Stettinius commented that, 'The gap between Chiang and the Communists is wide and fundamental.' He suggested an American military command for all Chinese forces, which both sides in China had said they would accept.[56] General Hurley, however, remained optimistic. He considered that the primary objectives of his mission were to prevent the collapse of the National Government and to sustain Chiang Kai-shek.[57] In pursuit of these objectives, he insisted that 'any aid from the United States to the Chinese Communist Party must go to that party through the National Government of China.'[58] He came to believe that his efforts to secure submission of the Communists to the National Government were unsuccessful only because his policies were being sabotaged, at first by other diplomatic missions,[59] then by a scheme of General McClure's for direct cooperation between the American army and the Communists,[60] and finally by disloyal Foreign Service officers.[61]

On January 20, 1945, Hurley sent a message to Mao in which he said, 'I am convinced that the National Government is now ready to make such important and concrete concessions as to make a settlement really practicable,'[62] and Chou En-lai returned to Chungking. The National Government offered (1) a policy-making 'war cabinet' in which the Communists would be represented; (2) a three-man Communist-Kuomintang-American committee to recommend reorganization of Communist troops for approval by the Generalissimo, and (3) an American officer appointed by and responsible to the Generalissimo as immediate commander of Communist troops who 'shall insure the observance and enforcement of all Government orders, military or non-military, in the area under his control.'[63] Later, the National Government offered a Political Consultation Committee to discuss the ending of a political tutelage.

To anyone with some understanding of the situation, it should have been obvious that these terms would not produce a settlement. The second clause failed to meet the strong Communist argument that it was the National Government forces rather than theirs that needed reorganization, while the third implied complete submission of the Communists, with the American commander merely an agent for transmitting the Generalissimo's orders.

Chou returned to Yenan on February 16, and Hurley left for consultations in Washington on February 19. The Communists acted to strengthen their military position against the Kuomintang and, in March, informed Hurley that it was futile to continue negotiations.

Thus, General Hurley's efforts over four months had, if anything, exacerbated tensions between Communists and Kuomintang and had produced Communist mistrust of American good faith. Chou En-lai, reporting to a meeting at Yenan at which I was present, asked rhetorically, How can one deal with a country whose ambassador pledges his word and puts his signature to it and then repudiates his promises a few weeks later?

---

[55] *Foreign Relations of the United States, 1944*, VI: 727–32.   [56] *Ibid., 1945*, p. 154.
[57] *Ibid., 1944*, p. 745.   [58] *Ibid., 1945*, p. 196.   [59] *Ibid., 1944*, pp. 748–49.
[60] *Ibid., 1945*, pp. 175–76.   [61] *Ibid., 1944*, pp. 722–26.   [62] *Ibid., 1945*, p. 180.
[63] *Ibid., 1945*, pp. 185–86.

Meanwhile, General Hurley's policies had had a disastrous effect on direct Communist-American relations at Yenan. Members of the USAOS could see very clearly that cooperation with the Communists could make important contributions to the war effort against Japan. They proposed a number of schemes, which, in several cases, involved the Communists in commitment of scarce resources, but then the American share of the scheme would be withheld.[64] The Communist reaction was counterproductive. If they had made open complaints of bad faith and threatened to withdraw from their share of a joint scheme, it would have produced strong pressure to overrule General Hurley. (For instance, the Air Force would have reacted strongly to a threatened loss of weather reports from large parts of North China.) Instead, the Communists became sulky and uncooperative, which alienated the Americans who favored cooperation.

The situation was made worse by Hurley's removal of Colonel Barrett in December, 1944. This left the USAOS under a Lieutenant Colonel Peterkin, who knew no Chinese and had little understanding of the situation. The military attaché, Colonel de Pass, occasionally visited Yenan but spent much of his time there shooting pheasant. Members of the USAOS found themselves almost completely boycotted, and some of them took to drink.

Finally, in May, 1945, the Americans realized that they had almost completely lost contact with the Communists. A new commander of the USAOS, Colonel Ivan Yeaton, was appointed and made real efforts to improve relations. His task was made more difficult by an incident that occurred about the time of his appointment. An American team parachuted into a Communist area near Shihchiachuang without prior notice and at first tried to resist when approached by Communist troops. The Americans admitted that their mission had been to train Chinese troops in Japanese service in the use of American equipment so that they could change sides and be re-equipped when National Government or American forces approached the area.[65] Thus, while the Americans refused cooperation to the Communists, they were, apparently, willing to work with troops in Japanese service fighting the Communists, in a scheme which made more sense as preparation for a civil war than as part of the war effort against the Japanese. In spite of this, Colonel Yeaton managed to produce an improvement in relations at Yenan and the USAOS played a useful role in contacts until 1947.

The Communists still hoped for good relations with the United States. In an interview with John Service on March 13, 1945, Mao Tse-tung complained that America did not seem to understand the issues in China and that American policy was 'still an enigma.' However, he went on to say:

> Between the people of China and the people of the United States, there are strong ties of sympathy, understanding, and mutual interest. Both are essentially democratic and individualistic. Both are by nature peace-loving, nonaggressive,

---

[64] For instance, very soon after reaching Yenan, the USAOS proposed a network of American-equipped radio stations throughout the Communist areas to send the weather and intelligence reports they wanted. They asked the Communist army network to handle the traffic until the American equipment could be delivered. In fact, American equipment only reached Yenan in June, 1945, and the sets were useless for their intended purpose because of limited frequency range and excessive weight. The Americans had been told at an early stage that this type of set was useless, and the Communists had asked for much lighter components from which they could quickly have built suitable sets. In the American army, portable equipment was normally carried by jeep and used only for short distances. In the Communist army, the crew of a radio station had to carry their equipment on their backs and to communicate up to several hundred miles with power from a hand generator.

[65] Information from the officer of the Shansi-Chahar-Hopei Public Safety Bureau who interrogated the Americans.

and nonimperialistic. China's greatest postwar need is economic development.
... America is not only the most suitable country to assist this economic development of China; she is also the only country fully able to participate. For all these reasons, there must not and cannot be any conflict, estrangement, or misunderstanding between the Chinese people and America.

Mao denounced the Kuomintang proposals as a propagandist maneuver, but he added, 'We are glad to accept American command, as the British have in Europe. But it must be of all Chinese armies.'[66]

In a later memorandum, Service reports that he discussed with the Communist leaders the possibility that their policy might become more radical, especially if there were a civil war, because peasants might demand a confiscation of landlords' property. 'Without exception, the Communist leaders vigorously and emphatically rejected this possibility of their policy becoming more radical.'[67]

In relation to the actual developments of Chinese Communist policy, these views expressed in 1945 are interesting.

General Hurley returned to China via Russia and had an interview with Stalin and Molotov on April 15. He mentioned Molotov's earlier statement that the Chinese Communists were not Communists at all, and Molotov agreed that it was correct. He then went on to outline his view of the objectives of American policy in China and understood that Stalin expressed full agreement with them.[68] A memorandum from George Kennan on April 23 suggests that Hurley had failed to realize 'that words mean different things to the Russians than they do to us.' Kennan felt sure that Russian objectives would include the effective recovery of the rights of Tsarist Russia, the maximum possible exclusion of other foreign influences in North China, and the domination of Chinese provinces adjoining Russian Central Asia.[69]

Meaningful Communist-Kuomintang negotiations had ended in March, and during the following months the two sides clashed repeatedly, while Communist publicity made increasingly violent attacks not only on Chiang Kai-shek and the Kuomintang but also on General Hurley and 'American imperialists.'

General Hurley then put his hopes on the Soviet Union and the treaty that was to result from the Yalta Conference. In a dispatch to the Secretary of State on July 10, he argued that the Chinese Communists were expecting support from the Soviet Government against the National Government. 'Nothing will change their opinion on this subject until a treaty has been signed between the Soviet and China in which the Soviet agrees to support the National Government.' Once the Communists realized that they would not receive Soviet support, they would become willing to reach a settlement, if the National Government offered reasonable terms. General Hurley then argued that 'State Department officials, Army officers, newspaper and radio publicity' had largely accepted statements by the Communist leaders exaggerating their military and political strength and concluded: 'Nevertheless, with the support of the Soviet, the Chinese Communists could bring about civil war in China. Without the support of the Soviet the Chinese Communist Party will eventually participate as a political party in the National Government.'[70]

In fact, most Chinese Communists at Yenan believed that they could win a civil war on their own. The general Communist expectation was that a civil war might last ten or twelve years, so everyone wanted to avoid it if possible, but Soviet aid was not a factor in the Communists' confidence that they could win in the end.

State Department officials and Army officers had based their estimates of Communist strength on reports from American observers. Members of the USAOS had visited the Communist areas as far east as central Hopei and had been impressed by

---

[66] *Foreign Relations of the United States, 1945*, pp. 273–78. [67] *Ibid.*, p. 404.
[68] *Ibid.*, pp. 338–40. [69] *Ibid.*, pp. 342–44. [70] *Ibid.*, pp. 430–33.

what they had found, while rescued American airmen had traveled through all the main Communist areas except Shantung.[71] On the other hand, it would have been correct to say that General Hurley had in large measure accepted the statements of Kuomintang leaders, which exaggerated the military and political weakness of the Communists.

With the Japanese surrender, events moved rapidly toward civil war. Chiang Kai-shek ordered Communist forces to remain in their positions and ordered the Japanese to surrender only to National Government forces, while General Chu Te asserted the right of Communist forces to accept the surrender of the Japanese forces in the areas where they were operating. Nearly all the Chinese troops in Japanese service proclaimed their allegiance to the National Government and were accepted into its forces. At first, the Japanese started to retreat toward their main bases, leaving only these ex-puppet troops to oppose the Communists, who rapidly extended their control in North and Central China. The Japanese were then ordered to hold their positions and to resist the Communists. Also, the Americans started to move National Government troops to several of the main cities of North China. As a result, the Communists captured only two important cities, Kalgan (Hsüanhua) and Chefoo (Yent'ai), though they took almost all the *hsien* cities off the railways and some sections of railway. During this period of confusion, Captain John Birch was killed by a Communist unit, and the episode merits a footnote.[72]

The Sino-Soviet Treaty was signed on August 14, 1945, and General Hurley invited Mao Tse-tung to Chungking for negotiations with the Kuomintang. There was a good deal of discussion among the leaders at Yenan as to whether Mao should accept this invitation. Finally he went to Chungking on August 28, accompanied by General Hurley, who guaranteed his safety. The negotiations produced a joint statement on October 10. This recorded agreement on a few points, of which the most immediately important was an undertaking by the Communists to withdraw their troops to areas north of the Lung-Hai railway plus northern Kiangsu and northern Anhwei. On other points, the statement merely recorded disagreement. The most important was the status of the Communist regions. The Communists first proposed official recognition of the existing regional governments and then offered other formulas, including free elections with an elected provincial government, where half the *hsien* in the province had elected *hsien* governments. (This was Sun Yat-sen's plan for all China, which had never been implemented.) The National Government throughout insisted on restoration of the provincial governments it had appointed.[73]

Mao Tse-tung returned to Yenan on October 11 and was criticized for having made real concessions in return for nothing but promises from the Kuomintang, which he should have known to be worthless. He defended himself by arguing that civil war would be so disastrous for China that it was worth taking considerable risks to avoid it and finally won a vote of confidence.[74]

---

[71] For example, a USAOS observer reported in February, 1945: 'Evidence of popular support of the Communists in north China is so widespread that it is impossible to believe that it is a stage setting for the deception of foreign visitors.' *Ibid.*, p. 201. Another report in March said: 'All evidence verifies Communist claims of controlling substantially all the countryside of "occupied" China.' *Ibid.*, p. 287.

[72] Robert Welch, in his *The Life of John Birch* (Chicago: Regnery, 1954), complains that the War Department was not willing to reveal the purpose of John Birch's last mission. However, he reports that the party included Koreans. According to the noncommissioned Americans in the party, who were returned to Yenan, it also included a Chinese officer in Japanese uniform. It is, therefore, extremely likely that Captain Birch's mission was to recruit forces that had been in Japanese service for the Kuomintang side in the civil war.

[73] *United States Relations with China* (Washington, D.C.: Department of State, 1949), Annex 49, pp. 577–81.

[74] I heard this account of a Party meeting at Yenan from a friend who had attended it.

Although the joint statement of October 10 had an agreed first clause about avoiding internal strife, heavy fighting resumed at the end of October, when three Kuomintang divisions were defeated in northern Honan as they tried to push north along the Peking-Hankow railway. The Communists considered this clear evidence of Kuomintang bad faith. According to Chou En-lai,[75] besides the published joint statement, there had been an informal understanding by which the Communists agreed that they would not oppose Kuomintang troop movements to take over areas actually held by the Japanese but made clear that they would fight if Kuomintang troops tried to enter areas actually held by the Communists. (The Kuomintang would probably have replied that Communist troops had no right to be on the Peking-Hankow railway, because they had been ordered to remain in the positions they held on V-J Day).

Though negotiations continued during November, the situation steadily deteriorated. It became clear that the Soviet Union was not acting in good faith in regard to its promise in the Sino-Soviet Treaty to support only the National Government. The Russians refused to allow Kuomintang troops to land at Dairen to take over Manchuria and timed their withdrawal from the ports of Yink'ou and Hulutao to allow immediate takeover by Communist forces. While they refused to allow regular Communist units to move into their area of occupation,[76] they did not prevent plainclothes Communist infiltration and the build-up of local Communist forces. On the other side, the Americans transported Nationalist troops to North China and American Marines were landed to assist the disarmament and repatriation of the Japanese. In messages of November 23 and 26 to Washington, General Wedemeyer pointed out that the National Government forces were not disarming and repatriating the Japanese because (1) they were involved in fighting the Communists; (2) they were using the Japanese to guard their lines of communication; and (3) they did not want the Japanese to withdraw from areas that would then be taken over by the Communists. (In fact, the last units of the Japanese Army fighting in China were only eliminated in 1949, when the Communists captured Taiyüan.) Wedemeyer complains, with good reason, that his orders were impossible. He could not carry out his orders to assist the deployment of National Government forces to key areas of China and to assist the disarmament and repatriation of the Japanese without becoming involved in fratricidal warfare, which he had been ordered to avoid.[77] The response from the Joint Chiefs of Staff was to restate the 'impossible' orders.[78]

After the complete failure of his plans and hopes, General Hurley resigned as Ambassador on November 26, with a letter blaming his failure on 'colonial imperialism' and 'Communist imperialism' and on the disloyalty of State Department officers.[79]

The features of American policy that gave the Chinese Communists good reasons for distrusting the United States were almost entirely the responsibility of General Hurley. The material published in *Foreign Relations of the United States* shows an extraordinary situation of bureaucratic paralysis in decision-making, which allowed

---

Stalin told Yugoslav leaders in January, 1948, that he had advised the Chinese Communists to come to terms with Chiang Kai-shek and dissolve their army. Vladimer Dedijer, *Tito Speaks* (London: Weidenfeld & Nicolson, 1954), p. 331. Such Soviet advice would explain Chinese Communist efforts to reach an agreement, but it is not clear exactly when this advice was given.

[75] In a statement he made to me.

[76] A Russian plane with a party of Soviet officers visited Yenan in early September, and the general rumor was that they asked the Communists not to send troops into areas held by the Russians.

[77] *Foreign Relations of the United States, 1945*, pp. 662–65, 679–84.

[78] *Ibid.*, pp. 698–99.   [79] *Ibid.*, pp. 722–26.

policy to be decided by one strong-willed, vain, and opinionated man who was almost totally ignorant of China and who believed that anyone who disagreed with his estimates of the situation or doubted the wisdom of his policies must be plotting against him for sinister motives. A study prepared by the State Department in May, 1945, probably represents a fairly general view within the Department. It recommends a coalition government and war council, an American commander for all Chinese armies, release of all political prisoners, and so forth, and so meets all the Communist conditions for a settlement.[80] Had the State Department decided policy, a settlement could have been reached.

The Communists did not understand the importance of bureaucratic confusion in American policy, and they were clearly wrong in diagnosing American motives as 'imperialist.' All the American documents that argue that postwar Communist control of all or part of China would be against American interests do so on anti-imperialist grounds, a fear that the Chinese Communists would be agents of Soviet imperialism. There was a noticeable shift in the official U.S. general viewpoint from the spring of 1945, when there was clear evidence of Soviet bad faith and imperialist ambitions in Europe. One memorandum by the Chief of the State Department's Division of Chinese Affairs in November, 1945, argues against permitting a Communist regime to control North China and Manchuria, because 'the creation of such a Communist state would seem, in effect, to bring about a situation which in many important particulars would be little different from that obtaining before the defeat of Japan. Instead of a Japanese-dominated puppet regime we should probably find in its place one dominated by the U.S.S.R.'[81] A more rational American policy would have given the Communist leaders strong evidence that they need not fear American hostility if they made clear that their loyalty as Chinese patriots was stronger than their loyalty to the Soviet Union as leader of world Communism.

The Seventh Congress of the Chinese Communist Party. The Chinese Communist Party held its Seventh National Congress at Yenan from April to June, 1945. The Congress consolidated Mao Tse-tung's position as leader of the Party and his claims of authority in interpreting Marxism-Leninism. The preamble to the new Party Constitution, which was adopted on June 11, says, 'The Communist Party of China guides its entire work by the teachings which unite the theories of Marxism-Leninism with the actual practice of the Chinese revolution—the Thought of Mao Tse-tung—and fights against any dogmatist or empiricist deviations.' Article 2a says that the duty of a Party member is 'to understand the fundamentals of Marxism-Leninism and the Thought of Mao Tse-tung.'[82] Liu Shao-ch'i's speech introducing the constitution is also full of flattering references to Mao. An Enlarged Plenary Session of the Central Committee adopted a 'Resolution on Some Questions in the History of Our Party,' which claims that Mao Tse-tung had always followed a correct line and which criticizes the mistakes of other leaders.[83]

Those who were criticized were not purged but remained on the Central Committee. Po Ku (Ch'in Pang-hsien), who was strongly criticized, remained in charge of the New China News Agency. Even Li Li-san, who was still in the Soviet Union and had been denounced for years as a bad example in the newspapers of the Communist areas, was still listed as a member of the Central Committee.

The key policy statement was Mao Tse-tung's 'On Coalition Government,' a good deal of which is a comparison of the performances of the Communists and the Kuomintang in the struggle against Japan, with violent denunciations of the Kuomintang leadership. The program for the future follows the general lines of the earlier

---

[80] *Ibid.*, pp. 879–82.   [81] *Ibid.*, p. 633.

[82] Liu Shao-ch'i, *On The Party* (Peking: Foreign Languages Press, 1950), pp. 157, 163.

[83] Mao Tse-tung, *Selected Works* (New York: International Publishers, 1956): 171–218.

'New Democracy.' China was not yet ready for the transition to socialism but needed a period of development under a coalition of several classes, though with the working class as leaders. For this period, the Communists should accept Sun Yat-sen's principles as their minimum immediate program.

The Marshall mission. With the retirement of General Hurley, President Truman appointed General George C. Marshall as his Special Representative in China. General Marshall's instructions were the subject of a good deal of discussion in Washington. At a meeting on December 10, 1945, with Secretary of State Byrnes, Under Secretary Dean Acheson, and John Carter Vincent, General Marshall asked what he should do if the Communists offered reasonable concessions for a settlement, and the National Government did not, and vice versa. Byrnes replied that, if the Communists were reasonable and the Nationalists not, then the latter should be informed that the United States would not give them any assistance and would deal directly with the Communists to secure the evacuation of the Japanese from North China. If the National Government was reasonable and the Communists not, then full support should be given to the National Government, and its troops would be moved to North China as required.[84] However, at a meeting the next day with Truman, Byrnes, and Admiral Leahy, Marshall said that, if Chiang Kai-shek proved unreasonable and caused the failure of a political settlement, and if the United States then withdrew support from him, 'there would follow the tragic consequences of a divided China and of a probable Russian resumption of power in Manchuria, the combined effect of this resulting in the defeat or loss of the major purpose of our war in the Pacific.' Truman and Byrnes agreed that the United States must, in any event, assist the movement of National Government troops to North China to complete the evacuation of the Japanese. It was agreed that the decision to give unconditional aid to the National Government should be kept secret to give Marshall some leverage in the negotiations.[85] In his personal statement of January 7, 1947, Marshall complained that, 'The reactionaries in the Kuomintang have evidently counted on substantial American support regardless of their actions,'[86] but this was a natural consequence of his own decision of December 11, 1945, that made his leverage against the Kuomintang only a bluff that could be called.

Insofar as one can judge Soviet objectives from Soviet actions, it would seem that support for the Chinese Communists was a secondary objective of Soviet policy. If it had been a primary objective, the Soviet Government could simply have kept to the assurances that Stalin had given to T. V. Soong on July 11, 1945, that Soviet forces would begin to withdraw from Manchuria within three weeks after the defeat of Japan and would complete the withdrawal in two or three months.[87] If the Soviet Government had kept to this timetable the Communists could have taken over the whole of Manchuria with a large armament industry in working order. The National Government was not ready to land troops in Dairen until near the middle of October and, before this, could only have opposed the Communists in Manchuria with small numbers of airlifted troops.

In fact, Soviet forces did not complete their withdrawal from Manchuria until the beginning of May, 1946, though some of the delay was with the agreement of the National Government. They used this delay to remove very large quantities of industrial equipment under the pretext of war booty. The Soviet Government also tried to negotiate with the National Government, offering assistance in return for extra economic privileges in Manchuria.[88] It would, therefore, seem that the primary objec-

---

[84] *Foreign Relations of the United States, 1945*, pp. 762–63.

[85] *Ibid.*, pp. 767–69.　　[86] *United States Relations with China*, p. 688.

[87] *Foreign Relations of the United States, 1945*, pp. 612–13.

[88] Tang Ts'ou, *America's Failure in China* (Chicago: University of Chicago Press, 1963), pp. 335–37.

tives of Soviet policy were economic gains for Russia and a desire to weaken China, which they expected to remain under the National Government.

No patriotic Chinese could approve the Soviet wrecking of Manchurian industry, which could have been very valuable for the postwar economy of China. Equally, no patriotic Chinese could approve the bad discipline of Soviet troops toward the civilian population, with very widespread looting and rape.

Thus, either the Americans or the Kuomintang could have used Russian behavior in Manchuria as an issue that would have forced the Communists to make a clear choice between loyalty to China and loyalty to the Soviet Union. One can only speculate as to what would have happened had they been forced to choose. My guess, based on nearly four years as an adviser in the wartime Communist organization, is that there would have been a split in the Party leadership, with such doctrinaires as P'eng Chen and Liu Shao-ch'i taking the Soviet side and most of the military leaders, Chou En-lai, and probably Mao Tse-tung taking the Chinese side. Even if the leadership as a whole had come out on the Soviet side, there would have been a great weakening of loyalty to the Party among a very high proportion of the lower ranks in the Communist organization who had joined it during the war out of patriotic motives.

For their part, the Communists failed to use an issue that could have forced the United States to make a choice between impartial mediation and support to the Kuomintang and that would have been highly embarrassing to the extreme anti-Communists in the Kuomintang. The Americans had repeatedly and publicly stated that American troops were in China only for the disarmament and repatriation of the Japanese, and in the joint statement of October 10, 1945, the National Government had agreed in principle to the disbandment of ex-puppet troops. In fact, important sections of the Kuomintang lines near main American troop concentrations were still held by Japanese units as late as February, 1946, while ex-puppet troops were an important part of Kuomintang strength in North China. Suppose that, when the Communists declared their willingness to accept a ceasefire, they had insisted on an exception to it, with a short time limit, in the case of Japanese units that retained their arms and Chinese units that had served under the Japanese. They could have argued, very cogently, that willingness to disarm the Japanese was a test of American good faith and that willingness to disband units that had served the Japanese was a test of Kuomintang good faith. Given American public opinion at the beginning of 1946, it would have been hard for the U.S. Government to continue assistance to the Kuomintang, if a peaceful settlement in China had failed because the National Government insisted on using Japanese troops and troops that had been in Japanese service. I asked a number of Americans involved in China policy at that time what the reaction would have been to such a Communist challenge. The most usual reply was that it would have forced a major reconsideration of American policy in China.

In spite of General Marshall's weak position, it seemed for a few months as if his mission might succeed. A ceasefire agreement was reached on January 10, 1946, and an Executive Headquarters, with truce terms to supervise the ceasefire, was set up on January 14. The agreement allowed the National Government to move troops into Manchuria and south of the Yangtze River, though all movements were to be reported to Executive Headquarters. On January 31, the Political Consultative Council produced agreements on (1) Government Organization, (2) Program for Peaceful National Reconstruction, (3) Military Problems, (4) Agreement on the National Assembly, and (5) the Draft Constitution. The first provided for an interim State Council of forty members, of whom half were to be Kuomintang. Major changes in policy required a two-thirds majority, and subsequent argument turned on whether or not the Communists and their allies would have the number necessary for veto power. On military problems, the emphasis was on civilian control, with a provision that no officer on active status could hold a civilian position. The last two agreements provided for an enlarged National Assembly to meet on May 5 to inaugurate constitutional government.[89]

The high point of agreement came on February 25, with a Military Reorganization Agreement that provided for demobilization to ninety National Government and eighteen Communist divisions within twelve months and to fifty National Government and ten Communist divisions within the following twelve months. Units that had been in Japanese service were to be completely disbanded within three months.[90]

On paper, a settlement had been obtained, except for a serious weak point in Manchuria, where the National Government did not allow truce teams to operate until the end of March, and where National Government commanders were trying to eliminate Communist forces. The settlement proved to be extremely fragile and largely collapsed during General Marshall's visit to Washington between March 11 and April 18. Controversy became more heated over the composition of the State Council. Chiang Kai-shek made a speech suggesting that the agreements made by the Political Consultative Council might be unconstitutional. There were allegations of cheating over the demobilization agreement, and violations of the ceasefire increased on both sides.

From May on, negotiations became increasingly futile. Chiang Kai-shek conducted military operations to extend National Government holdings and demanded Communist withdrawal from important areas, in the belief that the Communists would make more concessions as their military position weakened. In fact, the Communists ended by refusing any settlement that did not include a return to the military positions of January 13, when the ceasefire had come into operation. Communist publicity became more and more violently anti-American, and, still more important, Communist agrarian policy shifted from moderate reformist lines toward class war against landlords.

General Marshall considered withdrawing in October but was persuaded to stay on and seems to have put his hopes in the new constitution that was to emerge from the National Assembly, which met on November 15. However, on November 16 Chou En-lai asked for transport to evacuate Communist personnel, and his departure on November 18 ended the negotiations.

General Marshall finally withdrew on January 7, 1947, and issued a personal statement the next day in which he attributed his failure to 'the dominant group of reactionaries who have been opposed, in my opinion, to almost every effort I have made to influence the formation of a genuine coalition government' and to 'the dyed-in-the-wool Communists [who] do not hesitate at the most drastic measures to attain their end.'[91]

Since General Marshall's mission actually failed, many people argue that the objective of a genuine coalition was impossible to begin with. In fact, there would have been a basis for cooperation between the less doctrinaire Communists and the moderates in the Kuomintang so long as the Communists retained the reformist policies they had followed from 1937 to 1946. The policies that the Kuomintang later carried out on Taiwan were substantially the same as the Communist policies of this period—a land reform based on family farms, which eliminated landlordism by peaceful economic means, encouragement of cooperatives and farmers' associations, and elected local governments.

Marshall's view that there were moderates among the Communists at that time was shared by some competent Chinese observers.[92] What follows from the analysis of

---

[89] *United States Relations with China*, pp. 609–21.

[90] *Ibid.*, pp. 622–27.   [91] *Ibid.*, pp. 686–89.

[92] For example, Chang Kia-ngau, in a conversation with me, expressed his belief that the negotiations had been influenced by the accidental death of Po Ku and Wang Jo-fei, because

his final message is that he needed to split both parties in order to succeed in his mission.

Had Marshall been in a position to make clear that failure to remove power from the reactionaries would mean the end of American aid to the Kuomintang, he would have secured the implementation of the Political Consultative Council agreements. Had he then been able to offer American support to the coalition State Council for a protest against Russian behavior in Manchuria, the Communists would have faced the choice between joining in denunciation of the Soviet Union or else resigning from the coalition and resuming the civil war over an issue on which Chinese public opinion would have been universally against them. The most likely result would have been a continued coalition with at least part of the Chinese Communist Party. In time, the Communists might have come to dominate the government, but it would have been a very different Communist Party with very different policies.

The Civil War

A computer analysis based on quantitatively measurable factors would almost certainly have predicted that the Communists would lose the Civil War. The Kuomintang started in 1946 with a superiority of about 3:1 in regular troops and a very great superiority in equipment, as well as a fairly large air force, while the Communists had none. The actual Communist victory depended on intangible factors. The most important was superior leadership. For Party members, promotion in the army had depended largely on merit. Most Communist generals were, therefore, men of real ability, who could adjust to changing types of warfare. Because the primary loyalty of all commanders was to the Party, the Communist high command could be confident that its orders would be obeyed, even if they involved heavy losses for particular units.

Many Kuomintang generals, on the other hand, owed their positions to political influence. There were many cases where generals continued to hold important commands after repeated demonstrations of incompetence or disobedience to orders, while men with records of military success received only limited support if they belonged to a political faction that was out of favor. Also, many Kuomintang generals tended to think of their armies as their personal property on which their power depended and were unwilling to risk their troops to help other generals. Finally, the Kuomintang failed to provide the degree of honest and competent government that could have won popular support. This was especially so in the former Japanese-occupied areas.

In November, 1948, General Barr of the Joint U.S. Military Advisory Group reported that only American troops and American control could prevent a Kuomintang defeat.

No battle has been lost since my arrival due to lack of ammunition or equipment. Their military debacles, in my opinion, can all be attributed to the world's worst leadership and many other morale-destroying factors that lead to a complete loss of will to fight. The complete ineptness of high military leaders and the widespread corruption and dishonesty throughout the Armed Forces could, in some measure, have been controlled and corrected had the above authority and facilities been available. Chinese leaders completely lack the moral courage to issue and enforce an unpopular decision.[93]

In a book based on a visit to China in 1940, Paul Linebarger argued that the

---

they had been among those in the Communist leadership most desirous of a peaceful settlement.

[93] *United States Relations with China*, p. 358.

Kuomintang had the opportunity to compete successfully with the Communists.[94] The year 1940 may have already been too late. The defeat of the Kuomintang can be traced back to a failure to use the patriotic enthusiasm of the early war years to make essential reforms in taxation and land tenure and to eliminate warlord traditions from the army. Having missed the best opportunities, the Kuomintang became involved in a system of interacting vicious circles, which became steadily harder to break. It was only after the psychological shock treatment of complete defeat that the Kuomintang leaders became willing to carry out on Taiwan the reforms that could have prevented their defeat on the mainland.

The course of the war. In the fighting of 1946 and early 1947, the Kuomintang greatly increased the area under its control and captured most of the railway network in North China. It failed, however, to inflict serious losses on the Communist army, which increased slightly during this period. The expansion left the Kuomintang over-extended, with a large proportion of its troops tied down in garrison duties. The Communist forces, on the other hand, remained mobile, could concentrate superior forces for local offensives, and were able to harass Kuomintang communications.

The Communist counteroffensive started in Manchuria and, by the middle of 1947, had surrounded the Kuomintang-held cities north of Mukden. In the summer, a Communist force under General Liu Po-ch'eng moved into the area between the Lung-Hai railway and the Yangtze River, compelling the Kuomintang to withdraw from some of its gains in Shantung to defend the Lung-Hai railway.

During 1948, the initiative lay almost entirely with the Communists. By that time, they had captured enough artillery for assaults on defended cities. According to some reports they decided, against the advice of Stalin, to shift to a strategy of positional warfare and assaults on cities. At the beginning of the year, Mukden was surrounded and Kuomintang forces in Manchuria could be supplied only by air. In the spring, the Communists captured Loyang and K'aifeng on the Lung-Hai railway. They then staged an offensive in Shantung and captured the provincial capital, Tsinan, in September. The decisive battle of the Manchurian campaign was fought in October. The Kuomintang had been hoping to relieve Mukden by an offensive from the port of Chinchou, but the Communists captured Chinchou and defeated a belated breakout by the garrison of Mukden, which surrendered at the beginning of November. The Kuomintang thus lost almost all its troops in Manchuria, some 300,000, which had included most of its best-trained and best-equipped divisions. Another major battle in November destroyed the Kuomintang forces round Hsüchou, blocking a Communist advance to the lower Yangtze.

A feature of the fighting in 1948 was increasingly large-scale defection of Kuomintang units to the Communists. In January, 1949, the U.S. Military Attaché at Nanking estimated that about 200,000 former Kuomintang troops had been integrated into the Communist fighting forces, with perhaps 400,000 more employed in service units.

The end of the Manchurian campaign freed Communist forces for an offensive in North China. They captured Tientsin in the middle of January, and Peiping was surrendered at the end of the month. Taiyüan fell in March, 1949. In April, the Communists crossed the Yangtze River, captured Nanking, and moved on Shanghai, which fell on May 25. This marked the end of large-scale military operations, because much of the remaining Kuomintang strength had been moved to Taiwan. Fighting continued in the west of China, where Chungking was not captured till the end of December and some outlying areas continued resistance into 1950.

Li Tsung-jen's peace efforts. On January, 21, 1949, Chiang Kai-shek announced his

---

[94] Paul M. A. Linebarger, *The China of Chiang Kai-shek* (Boston: World Peace Foundation, 1941), pp. 174-75.

retirement as President of the Republic of China and the Vice President, Li Tsung-jen, took over as Acting President. Li at once started discussions with the Soviet Embassy in Nanking and offered strict Chinese neutrality in any international conflict, the elimination of American influence in China, and real cooperation between China and Russia.[95] He then started negotiations with the Chinese Communists.

The Communists published peace terms that amounted to unconditional surrender for the Kuomintang—strict punishment of war criminals, abolition of the constitution, abolition of the Kuomintang legal system, reorganization of Kuomintang troops on democratic principles, confiscation of bureaucratic capital, reform of the land system, abolition of treasonous treaties, and a Political Consultative Conference excluding 'reactionary elements.' These terms would establish a democratic coalition government that would take over all authority.[96] Negotiations continued until April, but the Kuomintang representatives could only secure quite minor changes in the Communist terms. Finally, the Communists presented an ultimatum for the acceptance of their terms and started the crossing of the Yangtze on April 20 when it expired.

The National Government started to move to Canton in February, and Li Tsung-jen followed in April. In October, the capital was moved to Chungking. At the end of November, Li Tsung-jen flew to Hong Kong and then retired to the United States. Finally, the National Government moved to Taipei in December, and Chiang Kai-shek announced his resumption of the Presidency in March, 1950.

These final peace negotiations are strong evidence against the view that the Chinese Communist leaders were really very clever and Machiavellian. By making some face-saving concessions to Li Tsung-jen, they could almost certainly have secured a settlement that left them in dominant military position and with strong influence in a new government. Because Li Tsung-jen was the legal Acting President, the new government would have been the legal government of the Republic of China and would have remained so, even if the Communists had established complete dominance during the next few years. Thus, the Communists would automatically have succeeded to the Chinese seat in the United Nations and to diplomatic recognition by all countries. Any government that Chiang Kai-shek set up in Taiwan would have been a new regime that could have obtained diplomatic recognition only from countries willing to break off diplomatic relations with the Republic of China. It is unlikely that even the United States would have been willing to do this in 1949 or 1950. Thus, the Communists forfeited very important possible gains through intransigence and failure to understand the conventions of the international system.

Similar misunderstanding and intransigence showed in the treatment of foreign diplomats, and there is some evidence here of disagreement within the Communist Party. When the Communists occupied Mukden, the new mayor first acted with diplomatic correctness toward the foreign consular corps and produced a very good impression. However, after about ten days he reversed his policy and declared that they had no diplomatic status.[97] The subsequent ill-treatment of the staff of the American Consulate had an important influence in deciding the American Government against recognition of the People's Republic of China. Again, only the Soviet Embassy followed the National Government to Canton. When the Communists captured Nanking, they followed their newly established practice of refusing to recognize the diplomatic status of the remaining diplomats. However, Communist representatives had discussions with the American Ambassador, Dr. J. Leighton Stuart, and invited him to visit Peking.[98]

I obtained very clear evidence that the Communists did not understand the con-

---

[95] *United States Relations with China*, p. 293.   [96] *Ibid.*, p. 293.
[97] Information from the British Vice Consul in Mukden at the time.
[98] Information from Dr. Stuart.

ventions of diplomacy from a conversation in the summer of 1949 with members of the Foreign Affairs Bureau of the North China Regional Government. They asked why Great Britain had not recognized them. I replied by asking them to say what they wanted the British Government to do, when they had only set up a number of regional governments. Until they had recognized themselves by setting up a new government of China, what was there for any foreign country to recognize? It at once became clear that the members of the Foreign Affairs Bureau had never thought about the problem in those terms.

The shift in Communist agrarian policy. Meanwhile, in 1946, the Communists had begun to change their moderate agrarian policy. During the war against Japan, a handbook for cadres in the rural areas had suggested a standard answer to peasants who asked: If rent can be reduced to 37.5 per cent, why can it not be reduced to zero? The answer was that it was necessary to leave the landlords in a tolerable position so that they would not be compelled to go over to the Japanese.

While nearly all landlords preferred the Communists to the Japanese, they were not so likely to prefer them to the Kuomintang. A Kuomintang victory would be likely to restore their prewar rents and their dominant position in local society. The Communists, had, therefore, less reason to conciliate the landlords and more reason to make sure of the support of the poorer peasants.

So long as negotiations continued, the shift in policy kept technically within the terms of the National Government land reform law of 1930. With the breakdown of negotiations, policy became much more radical and by mid-1947 had reverted to the extremist, class-warfare policy of the Chinese Soviet Republic. There were confiscation and redistribution of land and directives for 'struggle meetings' against a certain percentage of the population and for the execution of a certain percentage as 'wicked landlords.'

This program caused a great deal of injustice and dissatisfaction, especially in the older Communist regions, where many former landlords had sold out to their tenants as a result of the rent reduction and taxation policy. In some villages, the local Communist cadres could only meet their prescribed quota of people to be struggled against by ruling that anyone who had a landlord grandparent should be counted as a landlord.

These policies secured a firm commitment of the poorer peasants to the Communist side. However, by 1948 Communist publications admitted 'leftist errors' in their agrarian policy of 1947, which had unnecessarily alienated a large number of middle peasants. Refugee movements provide evidence of this loss of peasant support. For example, A. Doak Barnett, reporting on a visit to Taiyüan in March, 1948, described the area ruled by Yen Hsi-shan as 'a police state ruled by an iron hand, and a place of near starvation, fear, and despair,' but he also reported that a stream of refugees, including former Communist Party members, was coming into these bad conditions because conditions in the Communist areas were even worse.[99]

It seems likely that the extreme policies of 1947 reflected a shift of power within the Party. The failure of negotiations had discredited moderate views. Doctrinaires could argue that it should have been obvious from the beginning that negotiations were futile, because it followed from Marxist-Leninist principles that reactionaries would never yield except to force, and that the United States, as a capitalist power, could not possibly be an honest mediator.

The People's Republic of China. As the Communists extended their control of China, they set up a series of Regional Governments—Northeast (Manchuria), North China, Central China, and so forth. With the end of serious military operations, they started

---

[99] A. Doak Barnett, *China on the Eve of Communist Takeover* (New York: Praeger Publishers, 1963), pp. 157–80.

to organize a new central government on the lines of their peace terms of early 1949. A People's Political Consultative Council was set up, including members of the parties in the Democratic League, which had been centered in Hong Kong since 1947, and defectors from the Kuomintang, who formed the Revolutionary Committee of the Kuomintang. This Council then proclaimed the People's Republic of China (P.R.C.) on October 1, 1949.

THE DEVELOPMENT OF CHINESE COMMUNIST THOUGHT, 1949–69

Victory in the Civil War left the Communists in practically unchallenged control of the Chinese mainland and, therefore, with far fewer restraints on their freedom of action than before 1949. They have had options for choice within a wide range of possible policies, and to explain actual developments it is necessary to consider the reasons that made the Chinese Communist leaders choose some possible lines of development and to reject others.

This leadership has operated with a high degree of secrecy, only partially lifted by the Cultural Revolution. The result has been widely differing speculations about the motives of the Chinese Communist leaders. Some people have argued that they have been greatly influenced by traditional Chinese culture, that the P.R.C. is equivalent to a new dynasty; others have argued that the Communists represent a complete break with traditional culture. Some people have described the Chinese Communist leaders as doctrinaire and reckless; others have portrayed them as pragmatic and cautious. The motives behind the Sino-Soviet dispute have been variously diagnosed as conflicting national interests, competition for leadership of the world Communist movement, disagreement over Communist doctrine, and so forth.

What this section will try to show is that the development of Chinese Communist policies and doctrines has manifested a certain logical consistency and that some of the conflicting interpretations can be at least partly reconciled by consideration of the way in which ideology influences decisions.

Ideology, rationality, and unstable beliefs. Any considered decision is based on an estimate of its consequences, and the estimate will usually depend on an analysis with theoretical as well as factual premises. In decisions involving a complex system, such as human society, and especially in decisions concerned with long-term consequences, it is impossible to estimate the consequences of any decision except by using some theory of how the system works. The decision will produce its expected results only if its theoretical basis is correct. When people act in terms of a theory that is incorrect, the results of their actions may be entirely contrary to their intentions.

Though some people claim to be entirely empirical and pragmatic and to despise theory, an analysis of their actions nearly always shows that they act in terms of implicit theoretical assumptions. The pragmatist cannot avoid the use of theoretical assumptions; he can avoid the use of any coherent system of theory only by concentrating on immediate and short-term results and by ignoring the indirect and long-term consequences of his decisions. The pragmatist, consequently, is likely to show what might be called 'muddle-headed' irrationality.

The Chinese Communists denounce pragmatism and empiricism as errors to be avoided. They like to think of themselves as operating in terms of a universal 'scientific' theory of society. People who operate in terms of a universal general theory place far more emphasis than pragmatists on long-term objectives and are likely to act with a greater degree of logical consistency.

Some Western commentators have identified rationality with logical consistency and have, therefore, argued that the Chinese Communist leaders are highly rational. However, people who act with logical consistency in terms of some general theory are likely to show a different type of irrationality, which might be called 'pig-headed.' They persist in acting according to the logical implications of their theoretical beliefs, even when there is clear empirical evidence that the system of theory upon which they are acting is incorrect.

An irrational position of either kind cannot be defended under reasoned criticism or examination. Such criticism or examination will show that the position is logically inconsistent or else that it depends on theories or factual assumptions incompatible with empirical evidence. Someone who was completely rational would modify his views whenever they proved to be indefensible, but complete rationality is a theoretical limiting case. In practice everyone has a number of 'unstable beliefs,' that is, beliefs that can be maintained only by failing to consider certain evidence, to ask certain questions, or to follow up certain lines of reasoning.

Some people have 'unstable beliefs' that are very far removed from rationality and also very persistent, because they are protected by 'psychological blocks' that produce a strong emotional distaste for considering the evidence, asking the questions, or following up the lines of reasoning that would destroy the 'unstable belief.' They can also be protected at a more logical level by various subsidiary theories to explain away conflicting evidence. Finally, when 'unstable beliefs' form part of an official orthodoxy, they can be maintained by the force of group opinion and procedures of indoctrination and repression.

The Chinese Communist position. A good analogy for the Chinese Communist position is provided by the often quoted slogan: 'Navigating the ocean, rely on the helmsman; making revolution, rely on the thought of Mao Tse-tung.' The Chinese Communist leaders could be compared to helmsmen who persist in guiding the Chinese ship of state according to a chart with very serious inaccuracies—Marxist-Leninist doctrine as interpreted by Mao. When their chart gives them no guidance, they show themselves to be very skillful sailors. When their chart has led them into clearly visible dangers, they show great skill in avoiding a shipwreck and will ignore their chart so long as the dangers remain clearly visible. (It is their behavior in such situations that leads some people to call them pragmatists.) However, they are extremely reluctant to admit that there are errors in their chart.

The reluctance to modify the chart has not been absolute. By the 1960's, the Chinese Communists had abandoned the orthodox Communist doctrine of giving the development of heavy industry complete priority over agriculture. Until the mid-1950's, they maintained the orthodox Marxist-Leninist position that a problem of over-population is theoretically impossible, but, after some fluctuations, they seem finally to have adopted measures to limit the growth of population. On world politics, they have finally admitted that the Soviet Union is an imperialist power. However, the modifications have been slow and limited.

The conflicting reports about progress in the People's Republic of China can be at least partially explained by the generalization that the Chinese Communists have usually been quite successful in fields where their Communist doctrine is irrelevant and have often done a very poor job when guided by doctrine. So far as I know, there is nothing in the works of Marx, Engels, Lenin, Stalin, or Mao about how to make nuclear weapons, how to organize relief for areas hit by natural disasters, how to run a railway system, how to stabilize the currency, how to organize a public health service, and so on through a list of technical fields in which the Chinese Communist regime has been remarkably successful. In these fields, Communist leadership has contributed enthusiasm and organizing ability, has used common sense, and has been willing to make full use of advice from technical experts and of suggestions and criticism from people in the lower ranks of the organization. It is likely that some operations of the Chinese Communist regime would compare favorably with the best in advanced Western countries.

However, in fields where Communist doctrine has prevailed, it has overruled common sense, expert advice, and criticism. Enthusiasm and organizing ability have been directed toward trying to force the real world into conformity with what Communist doctrine says the world should be, or to keeping up a pretense that the two do conform. The most extreme example was the Great Leap Forward of 1958, when doctrinally inspired policies produced a setback in the Chinese economy of the same order as the decline in the American economy between 1929 and 1933, though, as usual, the Chinese Communist leaders saved themselves by pragmatic adjustments when complete disaster was imminent.

The People's Democratic Dictatorship. The Communists in 1949 acted skillfully to deal with the immediate problems left by the war. In such things as restoring public utilities and the transportation system, they located competent experts, took their advice, and gave them effective backing. To end the financial chaos and runaway inflation, they used procedures based on those of the wartime Communist regions. Wages and salaries were paid in commodity units, and taxes were collected rapidly in the cities by assessing quotas on guilds and trade associations, which were made responsible for dividing the assessment among their members. Initially, the policy toward former political opponents was very moderate. It was announced that people who confessed to previous association with Kuomintang organizations would not be penalized so long as they cooperated with the new regime.

These moderate and sensible policies won the Communists a great deal of support in the cities, even from people who had been afraid of the Communist takeover. A government that provided efficient and honest administration and started a process of economic recovery was an attractive contrast to the confusion and declining standards of Japanese and postwar Kuomintang rule.

However, the period of moderate policies proved to be transitional. The guidelines for future policy were laid down in Mao Tse-tung's *On People's Democratic Dictatorship*, which was published on June 30, 1949. This document began by stating the ultimate objective: Communist society and the withering away of the state and all political parties. It then went on to argue that, ever since the Opium War, the Chinese had been trying to learn from the West how to reconstruct their country but without success until the Russian Revolution, when 'the Chinese obtained Marxism-Leninism, this universal, wholly correct and general truth; the face of China then became changed.'[100]

World politics was described as a system of implacable struggle. China must 'join the Soviet Union, join the people's democracies and join the proletarian class and the broad masses in every other country to establish an international united front.' It was necessary to choose the side of socialism or the side of imperialism. 'Sitting on the fence is impossible. There is no third road.' Then follows a passage, quoted again and again in later statements, about dealing with imperialists and reactionaries. 'For these sorts of people, the question of being provocative or not does not arise. If you provoke them they are like that, if you do not provoke them they are like that, because they are reactionaries.' The Chinese revolution could not win or be consolidated without the help of the international revolutionary movement. China could not expect help from the capitalist countries, even though the Communist Parties and progressive people in them were pressing their governments to start trade and diplomatic relations.

Internally, there was to be a united front of workers, peasants, the petty bourgeoisie of the towns, and the national bourgeoisie to establish a democratic dictatorship based on the worker-peasant alliance, always under the leadership of the working class. Only the members of this united front were to count as 'people' and to have rights. The state apparatus must be strengthened to exercise dictatorship over the reactionaries and provide protection against imperialism. The reactionary classes were to be given land or work as a means of living and would be re-educated,

---

[100] Quotations translated from *Hsüan Chi* (1960), 4: 1473–86.

provided they did not cause trouble. Any signs of opposition would be severely repressed. The national bourgeoisie would also be re-educated.

Although Mao made the peasants one of the partners in the democratic dictatorship, they were also objects for re-education. 'A serious question is the education of the peasants. The peasants' economy is scattered. From the experience of the Soviet Union, it required long and careful work to socialize agriculture. If agriculture is not socialized, then socialism is not consolidated.'

'The people's democratic dictatorship needs the leadership of the working class because the working class is the most far-sighted, most public-spirited and richest in thorough revolutionary spirit. The whole history of revolution tells us that, without the leadership of the working class, revolution fails; with the leadership of the working class, revolution is victorious.' 'The Communist Party of the Soviet Union is our best teacher, we must learn from them.'

It can be argued that the unusual characteristics of the Chinese Communists as compared to normal Communists during the war against Japan—their reasonableness and willingness to engage in meaningful discussion—came from the fact that there was only a small gap between what they claimed to be doing and what they were actually doing. In other words, they were not then committed to maintaining highly unstable beliefs on issues of practical importance. The statement that has just been summarized shows that this situation had drastically changed by 1949, that the Chinese Communists, like most other Communists, had committed themselves to highly unstable beliefs.

The claim that Marxism-Leninism is a 'universal, wholly correct, and general truth' is incompatible with the claim that it is a scientific system, and many points in the Chinese Communist position can be explained by a failure to understand the nature of scientific knowledge. The characteristic of a scientific theory is that it can be tested by new evidence and is, therefore, potentially disprovable. What one learns from the procedure of scientific method is not any final and certain knowledge but only what is reasonable to believe on the available evidence. One finds again and again in Chinese Communist statements the assumption that a process of investigation and discussion must end with unanimous agreement. In fact, the available evidence is often compatible with a number of alternative hypotheses. All that can be expected is agreement that only a limited number of hypotheses are reasonable and agreement about the kind of new evidence needed to decide among them.'[101]

The important practical corollary of the belief that discussion should end with unanimous agreement is that honest disagreement is impossible, that anyone who questions the absolute truth of Marxism-Leninism as applied to some particular issue by the Party line can do so only if he is really a reactionary or imperialist.

Another highly unstable belief was that world politics was a clear-cut struggle between the evil forces of reaction and imperialism and the forces of good headed by the Soviet Union under Stalin. The belief was protected by a subsidiary theory that prevented consideration of evidence. When I was in China in the summer of 1949, I argued that completely uncritical admiration for the Soviet Union was foolish, because there was very clear evidence from the Soviet-occupied areas of Europe to show that the Soviet NKVD was the same sort of brutal and corrupt organization as the Japanese Kempetai. The usual reply to this was: 'You ought to know that these accounts you give of Soviet behavior in Europe cannot be true, because it is theoretically impossible for the agents of a socialist power to behave in the ways you describe.' Only one high-ranking Party member was rational enough to say that, if

---

[101] This Chinese Communist view of truth is rather less irrational than that of many Western intellectuals who believe in cultural relativism or some determinist form of behaviorism, implying that truth is simply a matter of opinion.

the Chinese Communists found from their own observers that such accounts of Soviet behavior were correct, they would then have the duty to denounce the Soviet Union for disgracing the good name of socialism.

The uncritical Communist attitude toward the Soviet Union implied approval for Soviet actions in Manchuria, and this was an obstacle to getting full support from the intellectuals in North China. In 1949, the large student population in Peking strongly supported the Communists on most issues, but many were informed about Soviet behavior in Manchuria, the looting of industry, and bad discipline toward the civilian population.

It is understandable in the light of their experience that the Chinese Communist leaders should have concluded that they faced the irreconcilable hostility of the United States and had no alternative to reliance on the Soviet Union, but to explain a belief does not show that it is correct. In fact, the hostility between the Chinese Communists and the United States is an extremely good illustration of positive feedback between mutual suspicions.

On internal affairs, 'democratic dictatorship' provided the basis for another set of highly unstable beliefs. It is possible to have societies with a high degree of freedom and democracy for one part of the population and no rights for another part. Classical Athens, with its large slave population, was an obvious example. However, it was obviously contrary to the evidence to claim that China in 1949 was ruled by the workers and peasants, because the great majority of Communists in responsible positions were not workers or peasants. Even those from worker or peasant families had had long careers as Party cadres, and many had no worker or peasant background at all. When a British Labour Party delegation visited China in 1954, Sam Watson of the Northumberland Miners' Union continually embarrassed his hosts by asking about the background of the groups which the delegation met, trade union executives, town councils, and others. The great majority proved to be people with middle school or university education, which in China at that time implied at least middle-class family background. Sam Watson would then ask why he seemed never to meet any workers or peasants among the officials of a regime that claimed to represent them.[102]

On People's Democratic Dictatorship promised freedom of speech, assembly, and association to the classes forming the united front—workers, peasants, the petty bourgeoisie of the towns, and the national bourgeoisie. If such freedom had actually been allowed, there would have been serious criticism of the pro-Soviet line from the intellectuals and of agrarian policy from the peasants.

In the countryside, as the previous section has shown, the return to the agrarian policies of the Chinese Soviet Republic was less effective in winning general peasant support than the reformist policies of the Yenan period. The class war in the countryside, which formed the basis of Communist policy, was not completely unreal. There were landlords who fitted the Communist stereotype of the wicked and oppressive landlord and whom the ordinary peasant considered to be enemies. However, in large segments of Chinese agrarian society, the class divisions were not sharp, and the proportion of landlords who could reasonably be classified as enemies of the peasants varied not only among regions but even among villages in the same *hsien*. One bit of evidence of the unreality of the policy based on general class warfare is that the Communists found it necessary to make elaborate regulations to deal with cases of intermarriage between families classified as 'people' and families classified as enemies of the people. Frequent intermarriage between two groups is evidence that the degree of real hostility between them is not very high.

---

[102] In the British delegation, only Attlee and Summerskill were middle-class intellectuals. The other six were men from working-class families who had gone straight into industrial jobs from elementary school. Aneurin Bevan, for example, had started underground work as a coal miner at the age of twelve.

In this situation, the application of rules for struggle against a certain proportion of the population inevitably caused a great deal of suffering and injustice. It also made the cadres in charge of the agrarian policy into village bosses who quite often abused their powers. This was especially serious in the newly conquered areas of South China, where Communist policy was enforced by rather hastily trained cadres from the older Communist areas in North China, even though the degree of class warfare may have been higher in the South, where the ratio of tenants to landowning peasants was higher.

C. K. Yang's study of a village in South China up to 1951[103] shows that, though the poorest groups in the village gained from Communist policy, the village as a whole became worse off. The taxes paid to the Communist regime were greater than the previous total of taxes plus rent paid to absentee landlords, and also the supply of credit dried up. In this particular village, the one rich landlord family whom the peasants genuinely hated had escaped to Hong Kong, and the Communist cadres did not enforce the parts of official policy that would have been most unpopular.

It is possible that the Chinese Communist leaders were sincere when they promised freedom to the workers and peasants, but the inevitable consequence of their determination to maintain a set of highly unstable beliefs was the destruction of this freedom. The actual result of Communist policy was a 'dictatorship' of the Communist Party, while anyone who criticized Communist policy was classified as a 'reactionary' to be suppressed, regardless of actual class status. A series of campaigns, culminating in a drive against 'counterrevolutionaries,' produced a general fear of expressing any criticism without official approval. At the same time, a very elaborate program of indoctrination was organized that tried, with a good deal of success, to secure universal acceptance of the Communist position.

Totalitarian society. One cannot understand the Chinese Communist position without understanding the real attractions of a totalitarian model for society. The Chinese Communist regime has never been satisfied with simple obedience from its subjects but has tried to obtain their enthusiastic support. Insofar as it succeeds in obtaining enthusiastic and unanimous support from its subjects, a totalitarian regime can be far more efficient than an authoritarian regime that only requires obedience.

In a system that simply demands obedience, all initiative must come from the ruling group at the top. This is a serious disadvantage for a regime that wishes to produce rapid social change. Also, an authoritarian system will be most stable when the rulers have some obvious superiority over the ruled. In traditional China, for example, the rulers were educated, and the masses were not. However, a complex industrialized society requires an educated population, and an educated population is much less likely to give simple obedience to its rulers than a population of illiterates.

The ideal totalitarian society avoids all these difficulties by being a system in which the people actively want what their rulers want them to want, in which everyone agrees with the rulers about the objectives of society and about the best means to attain these objectives. In a totalitarian society, as depicted by its own publicity or the accounts of highly sympathetic visitors, all right-minded people are unanimous and enthusiastic about the building of a new social order and support the rulers because they provide inspiration and leadership for this common purpose. Disagreement comes only from a minority who have been corrupted by the evil influences of the old society or subverted by alien enemies, which implies that opposition will fade away as the new society develops.

People who share the objectives of the rulers and who analyze the situation from the same theoretical basis as the rulers will naturally tend to do what the rulers would

---

[103] C. K. Yang, *A Chinese Village in Early Communist Transition* (Cambridge: The MIT Press, 1960).

have ordered if they had known the detailed circumstances of any case. The rulers can announce a general directive and can then rely on people at the lower levels of the organization to do what is necessary to carry it out, and it is noticeable that the Chinese Communist system tends to work through directives rather than through detailed laws and regulations.

In an organization where everyone shares a common purpose, people will not merely obey orders but will add efforts of their own to carry out the purpose behind the orders and may even try to anticipate the wishes of their rulers. The rulers can allow and encourage a great deal of initiative at the lower levels with confidence that it will be used in ways of which they approve. Here again, one finds in the Chinese Communist system many instances of orders being carried out with enthusiasm and an unusual degree of initiative at the lower levels of the organization.

All this means that a totalitarian society, insofar as it approximates its ideal, can be extraordinarily efficient in carrying out its policies. Everyone works with enthusiasm for the common purposes of the system; initiative is encouraged at every level; and leadership is exercised by those of the greatest ability. Membership in an efficient organization is attractive, and this can explain the fascination of totalitarian organization and the determination to produce what is required for it, namely, enthusiastic unanimity throughout the whole of society.

This ideal totalitarian society is what a free society would become if all its members were in unanimous agreement about a set of objectives that gave first priority to collective aims and about the system of theory on which they based their practical action to attain these aims. The relevance of this ideal for Chinese Communist thought is that, if the entire population had really been convinced of the truth of Marxist-Leninist doctrine and Mao Tse-tung's thought, totalitarianism in its most attractive form would then be self-sustaining without an apparatus of repression and indoctrination to maintain unanimity based on unstable beliefs.

By the mid-1950's, the People's Republic of China seemed to be a rather successful totalitarian state. The extremes of repression had relaxed after the end of the Korean War, and it appeared that the elaborate program of indoctrination had been fairly successful in producing general support for the regime. There was almost no intellectual freedom, and most people had to spend much of their time at meetings that formed part of the indoctrination program. However, the system of detailed controls and mutual surveillance brought some positive advantages, such as the almost complete elimination of ordinary crime. (It was extremely difficult to gain anything by theft or robbery, when the local residents' association, to which everyone had to belong, would ask any member to explain how he had acquired any new possessions.) Agriculture had been collectivized without producing the violent opposition and disruption that had resulted from collectivization in the Soviet Union, even though there was a good deal of evidence to suggest that it did not have the degree of peasant support that was claimed in official propaganda.

There was evidence of enthusiasm behind many of the regime's projects, and progress had been rapid in many fields. Industrialization was developing rapidly, the railway network was being extended and improved, and so on. Progress in agriculture was less rapid, but food production was running slightly ahead of population growth.

Peaceful coexistence. In foreign policy, there was a shift in attitude from 1954 on that could be related to this internal progress. In the early 1950's, the foreign policy line had been intransigent, denouncing Asian neutralists such as Nehru. The Geneva Conference of 1954, the meetings between Chou En-lai and Nehru, and the Bandung Conference of 1955 showed a shift to a new line tolerant of neutralism and advocating peaceful coexistence.

This shift did not mean that the Chinese Communist leaders had abandoned their long-run hopes for the spread of Communism, but only that they had changed their view about the way in which it could develop. From their Marxist-Leninist principles, they could expect that the bourgeois neutralist regimes in Asia would fail to solve the economic and social problems of their countries. When the failure became clear, China would provide a model to show that rapid social and economic progress was possible for an underdeveloped Asian country under Communist rule. The people of India and other neutralist countries would therefore be likely to follow the Chinese model on their own initiative. There was even some change in policy toward Taiwan, based on the hope that the People's Republic of China could attract the refugee population in the Republic of China.

Another change was in the attitude toward foreign contacts. The changes in this attitude have been a good indicator of the extent and strength of contradictions within the society under Chinese Communist control. During the Yenan period, the Chinese Communists welcomed foreign visitors. In the early years of the People's Republic of China, during the campaigns against class enemies and counterrevolutionaries, the policy on foreign contacts was very restrictive. Restrictions were then relaxed, and there was a minimum of them by the end of 1956, when the Peking authorities even invited visits by American correspondents.[104] Restrictions increased from mid-1957 to another maximum during the economic difficulties of the early 1960's. There was another relaxation in the mid-1960's, followed by a great tightening of restrictions during the Cultural Revolution. The variation has been greatest in the attitude toward foreign visitors qualified to obtain information. It has been much less for visitors with no background knowledge of China who could make contacts only through officially provided interpreters, or else visitors whose political attitudes at the outset almost guaranteed favorable reports.

The attitude to the Soviet Union also started to change. Khrushchev's denunciation of Stalin in 1956 produced an open disagreement. The attack on the cult of personality was embarrassing for Mao Tse-tung. More important, the disagreement showed that the Chinese Communists took their Marxist-Leninist doctrine more seriously than the Russian Communists. The Chinese Communists argued, quite logically, that it was contrary to basic Marxist doctrine to explain important historical developments by the character of an individual, that a Marxist explanation must be in terms of social forces. They therefore developed Mao's theories on contradictions into an explanation that allowed for the existence of continuing contradictions, even in a socialist society. Mao Tse-tung made a distinction between antagonistic contradictions arising from conflicts of class interest and nonantagonistic contradictions, which could develop in a socialist society. Conflicts arising from differences in class interest could not be reconciled and could only be ended by the complete victory of one side and the suppression of the other. Nonantagonistic contradictions, on the other hand, might be serious but could potentially be reconciled by a process of discussion and compromise.

Disagreements within the Chinese Communist Party. From 1936 to 1958, the Chinese Communist Party leadership showed a degree of unity that contrasted sharply with the purges in other Communist Parties. The only exceptions were the escape of Chang Kuo-t'ao in early 1938 and the action against Kao Kang and Jao Shu-shih in 1953-54. The latter case was unusual in Communist purges, because even before Kao Kang was denounced within China for a power struggle against the existing leadership, foreign analysts had suggested that he was trying to build up his own personal power in Manchuria.

However, the material that became public during the Cultural Revolution suggests

---

[104] The failure to use this opportunity is one of the obvious blunders of U.S. policy. The State Department took so long to reach a decision that the Chinese Communist line had changed before any correspondents had obtained passports valid for travel to the People's Republic of China. Subsequent American attempts to secure an exchange of correspondents were rejected by the Chinese side.

that the divisions that became serious in the later 1950's had started soon after the establishment of the People's Republic of China.

In the attacks on Liu Shao-ch'i during the Cultural Revolution, he was accused of having opposed the collectivization of agriculture and of having favored an agrarian economy in which the majority of peasants would be 'rich peasants' and the continuation of a capitalist sector in the industrial economy. He was also accused of originating the slogan, 'Learn to be a willing tool of the Party,' which at one period had official approval, and of spreading reactionary ideas from neo-Confucian philosophers in his book, *How to be a Good Communist*. (On this last point, Western scholars had traced neo-Confucian influences in Liu's writings many years before these Chinese criticisms.)

The hypothesis that can explain the disagreements between Mao Tse-tung and Liu Shao-ch'i as representatives of opposing factions is that they have differed in their vision of the long-range future of China. This also explains their earlier cooperation, because the disagreement would have practical significance only when the Communist Party had attained power and was in a position to influence the long-run future.

Liu's writings suggest that his major interest has always been in securing a strong and highly disciplined Communist Party, an outlook epitomized by the slogan, 'Learn to be a willing tool of the Party.' This slogan implies a vision of the future rule of a highly organized Communist bureaucracy, a system with similarities to the traditional ideal of neo-Confucianism, which was imperfectly realized by the ruling bureaucracy of the Chinese Empire. For this ideal, a collectivized agriculture was unnecessary. In the course of Chinese history, peasant revolts had been dangerous only when a dynasty was declining, when bad government had made the condition of the peasants intolerable. Once Communist agrarian policy had equalized land holding and eliminated any concentrations of power in the countryside, a scattered peasant economy of family farms would have presented no danger for a ruling Communist bureaucracy. Collectivization, on the other hand, might arouse serious peasant opposition and, by hindering the growth of production, would slow down the development of Chinese power. A limited capitalist sector in the economy would also have been no threat to a ruling Communist bureaucracy. Merchant power had never been a danger to the ruling bureaucracy of the empire.

Developments from 1957 on suggest that Mao Tse-tung has been strongly motivated by a vision of the ideal future society of Communist theory and that he has, therefore, wished to transform Chinese society into something totally different from the past. When Mao wrote, 'If agriculture is not socialized, then socialism cannot be consolidated,' it is likely that he took this entirely seriously and believed that collectivization was an essential step in the transformation of China toward the ideal Communist society. He may have maintained an unstable belief in the rationalizations of official publicity that collectivization was demanded by the peasants and that it would be more productive than family farming, but it is likely that he would have pressed for it even had he realized that, for a long time to come, it would be unpopular with most peasants and less productive than family farms.[105] Similarly, to tolerate capitalism and private trade beyond a limited transitional period would have compromised the transition to socialism.

---

[105] To give one sample of the evidence, when pressure on the peasants was relaxed because of the economic crisis of the early 1960's, the Communist authorities became alarmed by the growth of what was called the 'household contract system.' A group of peasants who were supposed to be a collective farming team would make a mutual agreement under which each household contracted to supply its share of the common obligation to the government—taxes and compulsory sales to state purchasing agencies—and would then go back to family farming. This would not have happened on a large scale if collective farming had really been popular and more productive.

The experiment in free criticism. The pressures for conformity of the early 1950's had completely intimidated most intellectuals. Eminent scholars wrote articles that they must have known to be nonsense. The pressure on intellectuals was relaxed in 1956. Academic salaries were raised threefold; the load of indoctrination meetings was reduced; and greater freedom of expression was allowed in some fields. Sections of the Party leadership disliked any relaxation of control. In December, 1956, two members of the Army Political Department published an article in the *People's Daily* criticizing the relaxation of controls over literature as likely to confuse the public; and criticism of an actual official policy could hardly have been published without very high-level support.

In fact, liberalization continued in China, although a move back toward Stalinism had started in the Soviet bloc after the suppression of the Hungarian revolution. At the end of February, 1957, Mao Tse-tung gave a speech calling for very wide freedom of criticism. The audience of several thousand was chosen to be broadly representative. The speech was recorded and reproduced for similar audiences in other centers, and some duplicated copies of the text were circulated. It was not until the middle of June that what purported to be the text of Mao's speech appeared in the press, and there is much evidence to indicate that this published version differed appreciably from the actual speech and put much greater qualifications on the freedom to criticize.

After the event, Communist statements claimed that the whole episode had been a trick to induce opponents of the regime to reveal themselves, but the weight of evidence is against this explanation. A much more likely explanation is that Mao Tse-tung misjudged the extent to which expressions of support for the regime represented an unstable belief maintained by Communist pressure and indoctrination. It was easy to judge wrongly on this point. The foreign visitors admitted in 1956 included a fair number with background knowledge of China, and the impression they got from their Chinese friends was that they gave general approval to the regime though they were critical on a number of minor points.

It is understandable that Mao Tse-tung should have believed that the contradictions remaining in Chinese society at the beginning of 1957 were nonantagonistic. Almost all industry and trade had been taken over by the state, and almost all agriculture collectivized. The hostile classes, landlords and bourgeoisie, had either been liquidated or else re-educated to a point at which they appeared to accept the new society. Antagonistic contradictions based on class conflict should therefore have disappeared. If the remaining contradictions had really been nonantagonistic, the freedom of criticism would greatly have strengthened the regime.

The previous section has shown that, in the wartime Communist areas, standards of administration were lower where criticism was inhibited by Party discipline. Such inhibition was almost universal in the People's Republic of China. The Communists have always prided themselves on criticism and self-criticism but the criticisms that appeared in the Chinese press were always made on the initiative of the Party authorities. There were many reports of cases in which the higher levels of the Party had discovered that mistakes were being made, that directives were not producing their intended results, or that local cadres were abusing their powers. These defects would be criticized, and the Party would claim the credit for remedying them. However, it was often clear from these reports that the defects had continued a long time before the Party leaders discovered them, or that they were only discovered by chance. What the reports of criticism revealed but ignored was that the ordinary citizen could not normally initiate criticism of defects, even though they might seriously affect him.[106]

---

[106] To give one instance, which appeared in the *People's Daily* in 1954: A soldier who was still in the hospital received a decoration for bravery in the Korean War. The Communist cadres in his home village suggested to his family that they celebrate the decoration by giving

If freedom of criticism had produced criticism mainly directed against defects that the Party leadership would have been willing to remedy, then the freedom of criticism would greatly have increased the efficiency of the system and made the regime more popular.

Another motive may have been competition with the Soviet Union. If Mao Tse-tung had been able to claim that he could allow freedom of criticism, while the Soviet Union was increasing restrictions on it, this would have shown the superiority of the Chinese model of Communism to the Soviet model. If the experiment in free criticism had worked as Mao hoped, China would have become the ideal totalitarian society, which is also a free society.

The slogans of the movement were: 'A hundred flowers bloom together, a hundred schools of thought contend,' and, 'The speaker without guilt, the hearer satisfied to accept.' It was some time before contention started. The Communists had to call meetings at which they actively elicited criticism. However, once a few people had spoken out without being penalized, criticism started to increase exponentially in both volume and severity.

The Soviet Union was attacked for its niggardly help to China. It was argued that the Chinese Communists had not done nearly enough to improve the living conditions of the masses and that the city workers had been made a privileged group as compared to the peasants. It was charged that many people had been quite unjustly penalized during the various campaigns against counterrevolutionaries. There were demands for the abolition of Party control in the universities, and students demanded greater freedoms, such as the right to read foreign publications. Members of the minor parties in the nominally coalition government demanded that the united front should be made a reality, that the other parties should supervise the Communists as the Communists had supervised them.

The most common criticism, and the most unwelcome to the Communist leaders, was that the Communist Party did not represent the masses but had become a new privileged ruling group. The complaint was often particular. People would say that, in their organization, the nominal head, who was technically expert, had no authority, while the Party representatives claimed personal privileges and gave orders, though they did not understand the work. Other critics generalized by comparing the position of the Communist Party to that of the imperial bureaucracy in traditional China, and some even compared the Communists to the Manchus in the Ch'ing dynasty or the Mongols in the Yüan dynasty.

The Communist leaders would not have been seriously worried if the strongest critics had been the older intellectuals. They would merely have argued that re-education had not succeeded in eliminating their bourgeois prejudices. What made the period a traumatic experience for the Communist leaders was that much of the most bitter criticism came from the groups that they believed to be their most loyal supporters, the students of worker or peasant origin, the industrial workers, and even some Communist Party members of long standing. Criticism was more serious at People's University, which specialized in training students of worker or peasant origin as cadres, than from the more middle-class student body at Peking University. One of the leading critics at People's University, a Miss Lin Hsi-ling, had joined the People's Liberation Army at the age of fifteen and served in it for several years.

---

a feast for the village. The family protested that they were poor people and that such a celebration would ruin them. The cadres then threatened to classify the family as unpatriotic. Luckily the family was able to communicate with the soldier, whose hospital was in a city and who was able to complain to people at higher levels in the Party. The local cadres were then reprimanded and publicly criticized. What the report implies but ignores is that the family might have been ruined if the soldier had been discharged from the hospital before receiving the decoration.

Free criticism was ended at the beginning of June. Because of the slow start, it had only been effective for about six weeks. An 'antirightist' campaign attacked and penalized the critics, though it was milder than previous campaigns against counter-revolutionaries. Few people were executed, but many were sent for 'reform through labor.' Indoctrination programs were resumed with increased vigor, and ceremonies were started at which people gave their hearts to the Party, presenting large paper hearts to a Party representative after appropriate self-criticism and professions of loyalty.

The Communist leaders apparently concluded that no ruling Communist Party could safely allow any criticism that might touch on Party doctrine. They increasingly denounced the dangers of 'revisionism.' In world politics, Yugoslavia was attacked as a focus of infection from which dangerous thoughts might spread to other Communist-ruled countries.

The Great Leap Forward and the communes. Given his doctrinal assumptions, Mao Tse-tung's next experiment was a logical development from the failure of the experiment in free criticism. The outburst of criticism challenging the basis of the Communist system showed that antagonistic contradictions remained in Chinese society, and antagonistic contradictions come from class conflict. Therefore, the changes in Chinese society had not been sufficient to eliminate class conflict, at least in the form of evil influences from the old society. It followed that what was needed to move toward the ideal Communist society was much more radical social change.

The programs of 1958 were aimed at starting China on the transition from socialism to Communism. In the countryside, the collectives were amalgamated into people's communes, each containing thousands of farming families, which were also to become the lower levels of government organization. The program called for communal living and the abolition of material incentives. The individual was supposed to put himself at the disposal of the commune and, in return, would receive a guaranteed livelihood, which covered not only food and clothing but also details such as so many baths and so many haircuts. Individual family dwellings were to be replaced by communal housing, with mess halls and nurseries. Women, freed from the duties of cooking and looking after children, would be able to join the communal labor force.

It was recognized that the organization of communes in the cities would be more difficult, but some preliminary steps were taken, and there was a shift in industry away from such incentive schemes as piecework payment. The aim was to implement the old Marxist slogan about a Communist system, 'From each according to his ability, to each according to his needs.'

Only a few communes had made the full transition to communal living before the program was abandoned, but there was a general shift to the communal organization of agricultural labor. The slogan was, 'Collectivize production, militarize organization, democratize administration.'

The other part of the program was the Great Leap Forward, which got underway in May 1958. Here, the basic slogan was, 'Politics in command.' It was believed that sufficient enthusiasm and sufficient organization of the masses could solve China's basic economic problems within a few years. The masses were told that, if they would join with enthusiasm in a few years of austerity and hard work, they would then have 'rich clothes and sufficient food.'

Another slogan of the time was, 'Walking on two legs,' that is, expanding production not only in highly capitalized modern factories but also by the development of all kinds of small-scale industry. Up to a point, this was a rational economic development. There was a great deal of underemployed labor in the Chinese countryside that could not be shifted permanently from agriculture, because it was needed at periods of peak demand for labor. The use of this labor at other periods in small-scale local industry gave a clear gain in production, even if the productivity per man-hour was much less than in a modern factory.

In fact, the whole program was distorted by the absolute priority given to rousing enthusiasm. An extreme example was the small-scale production of iron. Handicraft production of iron had been going on for centuries in parts of China with easily available iron ore and coal, and it would have been sensible to expand this. What actually happened was that Communist cadres came to believe that the Party line required them to organize iron or steel production even if the raw materials were not locally available and even if labor was diverted from other important work.

An even more serious consequence of the absolute priority for enthusiasm was the ruin of the statistical system. Accurate statistics are essential for efficiency in a planned economy, and the Chinese system had been steadily improving since 1949. However, in 1958 statistical workers who tried to make accurate reports were attacked for damping the enthusiasm of the masses and were told that the function of statistics should be to arouse enthusiasm.

The result was an extraordinary process of mutual deception between the top and bottom levels of the organization. The leaders in Peking issued two sets of target figures, one that should certainly be attained and another giving what they hoped for, if the masses showed enough enthusiasm in production. The provincial authorities, wishing to show enthusiasm, passed down targets based on the high figures from Peking as what must be attained and added a still higher set of targets as what was hoped for. In some cases, this exaggeration was repeated again at the *hsien* level. The cadres actually responsible for production found themselves faced with impossible demands that they dared not criticize as impossible for fear of being denounced as conservatives. They could avoid immediate trouble only by making false reports of huge increases in production. The Party leadership, having claimed that the Great Leap Forward would produce wonderful results and having penalized objectivity in their statistical service, could hardly treat with skepticism the reports from below that the results were wonderful. Some time elapsed before it became quite clear that the extra production was imaginary.

For example, most foreign analysts considered that the reports of the grain harvest in 1957 as 185 million tons were fairly accurate. In 1958, however, the grain harvest was first reported as 375 million tons, and a target of 525 million was announced for 1959. Finally, the 1958 figure was officially revised down to 250 million tons, and even this seems to have been an exaggeration. By 1960, a serious food shortage was developing and was made worse by bad weather conditions. The distribution and rationing system remained efficient enough to prevent extensive deaths from starvation, but serious malnutrition was general.

The Great Leap Forward did manage to arouse a great deal of enthusiasm, especially in many of the younger cadres, some of whom seem to have become even more utopian than the Party leaders. For instance, one journal devoted a long article to criticizing the view that, because money and accounting were features of a capitalist economy, they should therefore be abolished in a socialist economy. There was almost certainly a considerable increase in the number of man-hours worked in the Chinese economy. This failed to produce its hoped-for results, because 'politics in command' proved incapable of directing the efficient use of labor.

The general intellectual atmosphere of the period was highly irrational. For example, though the Party leaders had admitted in 1956 that China had a population problem and had started a birth control campaign, in 1958 they returned to the belief that overpopulation was impossible and said that China needed a much larger population. Many articles in the Chinese press denounced diminishing returns in agriculture as a 'bourgeois fallacy' and argued that there was no limit to what could be raised from a given area of land, provided only that enough labor was applied to it.

The claim that the communes marked the beginning of the transition from socialism to Communism was a challenge to the Russians, who considered themselves to be still in the stage of socialism. It implied that the Chinese had made more revolutionary progress in nine years than the Russians had in forty. There was also increasing Sino-Soviet disagreement on world politics. With the launching of the first Soviet satellite, Mao Tse-tung had produced the slogan, 'The East wind prevails over the West wind' and had argued that the socialist bloc now had clear technical superiority over the imperialist bloc and should therefore pursue a more active foreign policy in supporting revolutions all over the world. The Chinese moved toward a position that might be called 'Marxist-Leninist fundamentalism.' They emphasized Lenin's most simple and uncompromising statements about the inevitability of violent conflict between socialism and capitalism and the natural tendency of monopoly-capitalist imperialism to resort to war. They refused to admit that the development of nuclear weapons might have invalidated Lenin's analysis and argued that talk of the possible destruction of mankind by nuclear war only served to weaken the will of the masses in resisting imperialism. These trends in the Chinese position were unwelcome to the Soviet leadership, which, in the late 1950's, was moving toward accommodation with the Western powers. The Russians tried to bring the Chinese into line by economic sanctions and, in 1960, recalled their technical advisers and cancelled their contracts for delivery of equipment. This had no effect on the Chinese position except to exacerbate Sino-Soviet disagreement.

Both sides had an attachment to the principle of Communist unity. This produced a curious period during which the Chinese concentrated their attacks on Yugoslavia, though often with obvious reference to the Soviet Union, and the Russians concentrated their attacks on Albania, though often with obvious reference to China.

Power struggle in the Chinese Communist leadership. Up to the mid-1950's, the Chinese Communist leadership was kept united by a common purpose. One can trace some competition for power, but, except in the Kao Kang case, it was subordinated to the attainment of aims about which all the Communist leaders agreed. Up to 1949, they all agreed in wanting the Communist Party to rule China, and for the next few years disagreements were minor compared to the agreed program of reconstruction and social change.

The power struggle became serious only when different groups in the Party leadership wanted to use the power of the Party for different purposes. One section of the leadership, later identified with Liu Shao-ch'u, envisaged Chinese development on the same sort of lines as Soviet development. They wanted to use the powers of the Communist Party to restore China's position as a great power in world politics, to produce rapid economic progress and prosperity, and to maintain the Communist Party as a ruling group, with a position something like that of the traditional Confucian bureaucracy, which also claimed to be ruling China in the interests of the people. They did not reject the Marxist-Leninist vision of the ideal future Communist society, but, like the Communist Party of the Soviet Union, they were willing to postpone it to the indefinite future. One could apply Saki's aphorism: 'It is one of the consolations of middle-aged reformers that the good they inculcate must live after them if it is to live at all.' This did not necessarily make them pro-Soviet, because they could compete with the Soviet Union for leadership of the world Communist movement, they could quarrel over national interests, and they could criticize revisionist ideas in the Soviet Union that might threaten the power of ruling Communist Parties.

Another section of the leadership, with Mao Tse-tung as its leader, wished to use the power of the Communist Party to realize the ideal society of Marxist-Leninist doctrine as rapidly as possible. For this end, they were prepared to risk slowing the development of China or weakening the control of the ruling Communist Party. This willingness to take risks was evident in the series of experiments for which Mao Tse-tung seems to have been the strongest advocate.

There is evidence of disagreement over the experiment in free criticism, but the experiment was over too quickly for disagreements to become serious. The communes and the Great Leap Forward provoked much more serious disagreement. Even at the time, there were references in the Chinese press to 'highly placed conservatives,' and it became clear after the event that disagreements had been bitter.

The failure of this experiment seems to have ended with a compromise. Mao Tse-tung lost influence when he resigned as President of the People's Republic of China and was replaced by Liu Shao-ch'i, but some of the strongest critics of the experiment, such as P'eng Te-huai, were purged. (There is evidence that P'eng's most serious offense was that he had negotiated for Soviet support.)

Liu Shao-ch'i's group seems to have taken control of practical economic and social policy. The communes were decentralized back to the equivalent of the old collectives, and the peasants were allowed private plots and more freedom in other ways, while many programs of the Great Leap Forward were abandoned.

On the other hand, the communes still retained a formal existence, and official publicity continued to claim that the Great Leap Forward had been a success. (It is not likely that the Chinese Communists would ever have admitted publicly that the Great Leap Forward had been a mistake, but, if the leadership had agreed in private that it was a mistake, one would have expected it simply to disappear from official publicity.) Mao Tse-tung's influence remained strong in cultural affairs, in foreign affairs, and in the army, where a trusted follower, Lin Piao, replaced P'eng Te-huai as Defense Minister.

This division of effective authority can be seen during the period from 1960 to 1965. The economic system recovered from the setback caused by the experiments of 1958 under cautious policies that avoided any radical experiments and allowed greater freedom for the peasants, including the development of markets for surplus produce, and more initiative for factory managers. In education, there was a stress on the importance of standards and of technical competence. Intellectuals had somewhat greater freedom and started some cautious criticism by traditional Chinese methods, such as historical analogy. For instance, criticism of the dismissal of P'eng Te-huai was implied by a play about the dismissal of a Ming dynasty official for advocating policies that proved to be correct.

On the other hand, cultural policy became more radical from 1963 on. For instance, there was a campaign for the reform of Peking opera, a traditional art form that enjoyed wide popularity. It was argued that the traditional plots about emperors and their ministers and generals were reactionary and should be replaced by new ones emphasizing proletarian virtues. Again, an old Party theoretician, Yang Hsien-chen, was attacked for favoring the concept 'two combine into one' over the concept 'one divides into two.' This philosophical dispute was taken to involve the issue of whether the class struggle in China would die out or become sharper. The class struggle was emphasized in articles that denied that there was any common human nature independent of class status and identified all virtues with the proletariat. In 1965, ranks and badges were abolished in the army. (This was a return to an earlier practice of the Chinese Communist army, when there were no badges of rank and officers were called only by the titles of their commands—battalion commander, regiment commander, and so on.)

Mao Tse-tung made several statements about the danger that the younger generation would lose its revolutionary fervor and that this might cause a return to capitalism. (This was unorthodox Marxism, because the basic Marxist view of history is of an inevitable development toward socialism and finally Communism, which conscious human efforts can speed up or slow down but cannot reverse.)

Foreign policy remained fairly cautious in practical action but extremely intransigent in words. American imperialism was the worst enemy of mankind, with revisionism a close second. Any revolutionary action had Chinese support, including the groups in the former Belgian Congo who killed anyone who could read and write.

From 1963 on, the Sino-Soviet dispute developed to the stage of open mutual attacks. A great deal of the dispute was over the correct international line, but the Chinese criticisms of Soviet society are of special interest, because they showed what Mao Tse-tung believed to be wrong with Communism in the Soviet Union and, therefore, what he hoped to prevent in Chinese Communism. It was charged that Soviet Communism had lost its revolutionary beliefs and was interested only in material gains; that the Communist Party of the Soviet Union had degenerated into a privileged bureaucracy exploiting the masses; that the children of higher Party members got special privileges in education and the whole Soviet educational system was organized to produce a stratified society; that the Soviet ruling group used secret police terrorism against its own citizens; and that the Soviet Union had become an imperialist power exploiting its satellites. There is a great deal of evidence from other sources to show that this set of criticisms was well founded.

However, it was also argued that these defects in the Soviet Union had developed only since the death of Stalin and that the post-Stalin Soviet leadership was returning to capitalism. These criticisms show the weak points in Mao Tse-tung's thinking. He was apparently unwilling to admit that the Chinese Party had been mistaken in its former uncritical support of the Soviet Union, and the determination to defend Stalin made it impossible to make a correct diagnosis of the developments in Soviet society responsible for the defects that were rightly criticized.

The charges that the Soviet Union was returning to capitalism show an unwillingness to question the Marxist-Leninist doctrine that there is only one possible line of historical development. It follows that the only possible directions of movement for a socialist society are forward toward Communism or backward toward capitalism. It is not possible to move sideways toward a society that is neither the Communist ideal nor capitalism.[107]

The effects of Marxist-Leninist doctrine in inhibiting clear thinking also show in the violent attacks on the Soviet claim to have become a 'state of the whole people.' In a common-sense view, it would seem reasonable to argue that class conflicts from Tsarist society could no longer be of any importance in the Soviet Union after the regime had been liquidating the bourgeoisie for fifty years. If one accepts the Marxist-Leninist-Maoist doctrine that antagonistic contradictions can arise only from the class conflicts considered by Marx and Lenin, then these conflicts should have disappeared in the Soviet Union, and the claim to be a 'state of the whole people' should be correct. If one accepts the evidence that antagonistic conflicts remain in Soviet society, then it follows that there must be other sources of conflict not considered by Marxist-Leninist doctrine but arising within the type of society established by Lenin and Stalin. The Chinese Communist position refused to accept either conclusion but argued that bourgeois influence in the Soviet Union produced continuing class conflict.

Another criticism showed Mao Tse-tung's lack of interest in technical economic efficiency. The experiments in the Soviet bloc in using competitively determined profit as a 'success indicator' were not seen as a technical device for handling a technical economic problem in the efficient allocation of resources. They were denounced as evidence of a return to capitalism, and Chinese statements claimed that, in a socialist economy, all prices should be determined by the central planning authority, even though this principle was not being followed in the Chinese economy.

The Great Proletarian Cultural Revolution. By the latter part of 1965, Mao Tse-tung seems to have felt strong enough to reassert his power and to have come to believe that the bureaucratic organization of the Communist Party was a major obstacle to realizing his ideals for Chinese society. To attack the ruling bureaucracy, he had to find a reliable source of support. He did have support in the army as reorganized by

---

[107] While some Western scholars argue that there is convergence between the Soviet and American systems, they see the convergence as a move toward a system different from both orthodox socialism and orthodox capitalism.

Lin Piao, but the army was not a suitable basis for a cultural revolution. The students, however, were a group that would still respond to a call for new revolutionary enthusiasm, and the army was used to help start the Cultural Revolution. A number of students were sent from the army into the Chinese universities. They concentrated on activity in student organizations rather than on academic study and laid the basis for the Red Guards.

As a hypothesis, one can suggest a process of reasoning underlying the emphasis on culture. In the traditional Marxist view, ideas are a superstructure dependent on the mode of production. The experiments of 1958 had tried to make a radical change to a new type of society by starting with a radical change in the mode of production. These experiments had failed, and Mao Tse-tung must have wondered why. A possible cause would be that the thinking of the masses had not changed rapidly enough to allow them to adjust to the requirements of the new mode of production.

There is clear evidence that Mao Tse-tung had come to question the simple Marxist doctrine that ideas are merely superstructure. An article in the *Peking Review* quotes him as saying: 'While we recognize that in the general development of history the material determines the mental and social being determines social consciousness, we also—and indeed must—recognize the reaction of mental on material things, of social consciousness on social being, and of the superstructure on the economic base.'[108] This recognition of a two-way reaction between ideas and the structure of society is common sense, even though it is unorthodox Marxism. It would be quite logical to conclude from this view that it was necessary to change the thinking of the masses before making a new attempt to change the economic base of Chinese society.

In fact, the Cultural Revolution has not led to a revival of the communes and the Great Leap Forward, but there were a number of indications of intention to revive them. It seems likely that, if the Cultural Revolution had developed in accordance with Mao Tse-tung's original hopes for it, it would have been followed by a new attempt to make a radical transformation of the 'economic base.'

It is easy to understand the attractiveness of the Red Guard movement for the students. They were offered the opportunity to make history by the reformation of their country. For most of their lives, they had lived under tight control by Communist cadres, and a high proportion of Party *apparatchiki* in a Communist-ruled society are unpleasant characters. When the highest authority in the Party declared an open season on cadres, the response was naturally enthusiastic. Also the positive goal of the movement, the ideal of a utopian participatory democracy, had a real power of attraction for youth, as the growth of the New Left in other countries shows. Some of the pronouncements issued by the Revolutionary Rebel organizations in China put the general case for the New Left much more convincingly than those of their counterparts in the United States.

The claims that the 'little red book,' *Quotations from Chairman Mao Tse-tung*, offered inspiration and guidance for every situation and problem are harder to understand but are not entirely inexplicable. It has been pointed out that many of the quotations from Mao are sound common sense expressed in traditional proverbs; people who would have rejected common sense if it came from tradition could accept it when it came from Mao Tse-tung. Also, just because there is nothing in the little red book that is relevant to many actual problems, its operational message was, 'Think for yourself.' The most serious defect of traditional Chinese education, which the Communists had not eradicated, was its emphasis on authority. Under the empire, all Chinese students were taught to look to the Confucian classics for the justification of any decision; under the Republic, they were taught to follow the authority of Sun Yat-sen's writings or of foreign textbooks; under the People's Republic of China, the

---

[108] *Peking Review* (June 10, 1966), p. 7.

Marxist classics replaced the Confucian classics. When students and others were told to reject all authority, except that of a small book that provided common-sense maxims but no detailed guidance on most problems, they had to use their own intelligence. In a great many situations, the best decision was likely to result from the practical message of the little red book, namely, 'Use common sense; think for yourself; do not be bound by what you have been previously taught to respect as authority.' Mao's authority would give self-confidence in following this advice.

One can also understand why the Cultural Revolution would be opposed not merely by entrenched bureaucrats trying to preserve their power and privileges but also by genuinely public-spirited Party members. A Communist official could have reasoned that the experiments of 1958 had caused serious suffering to the Chinese people; that the recovery and progress during the subsequent years had benefited the people; and that he would be acting in the interests of the people by trying to frustrate a new experiment by Mao at making a radical transformation of Chinese society, because the most likely result would be not a better society but another breakdown.

The development of the Cultural Revolution was very complicated, because no one dared to make an open counterattack against Mao Tse-tung. Those in the Party apparatus whom he was attacking could defend themselves only by the tactics described as 'waving the red flag to oppose the red flag,' organizing groups that used the slogans of the Cultural Revolution but that actually opposed it.

The high point of the Cultural Revolution came in the first half of 1967, after the army had been ordered to support the left. The result was an effective destruction of the Party apparatus. The victory of the left-wing Red Guards and 'Revolutionary Rebels' was short-lived, because they proved incapable of providing an alternative administration. There were statements about a new system of government following the principles of the 1871 Paris Commune, and some steps were taken to organize a Shanghai Commune, but the Paris Commune, however important in Marxist mythology, does not really provide a model for a system of government. In a situation of continued confusion and factional struggles among revolutionary organizations, the army was called on to restore order, and it could find competent administrators only among the old officials.

A new program called for the organization of revolutionary committees representing the army, the revolutionary movement, and cadres from the old administration who had not been followers of the 'power-holders taking the capitalist road' or who had been reformed. The organization of these committees proceeded slowly, and factional struggles continued. Though the revolutionary movement made several partial recoveries, the trend was against it. Mao Tse-tung finally expressed his disappointment with the students and, at the beginning of August, 1968, gave his approval to the 'worker-peasant teams,' which were being sent into the universities to restore order.

The organization of revolutionary committees speeded up, and it became clear that the dominant partner was the army, with the reformed former cadres in second place, and the new revolutionaries having the least power. The radical revolutionary groups were attacked as anarchists, and anarchism was denounced as reactionary.

By the end of 1968, a movement was starting that finally destroyed the power of the revolutionary student groups by exiling their members to the countryside. It has been estimated that about 20 million people were eventually moved out of the cities. Official publicity had many stories of revolutionary students nobly volunteering for work in the countryside, where they were welcomed by the peasants. However, there were also many reports of peasant resentment at an inflow of people with no experience in agricultural work and of those sent to the countryside making their way back to the cities, even though they could only lead an illegal existence there.

The goals of the Cultural Revolution were set out very attractively by Joan

Robinson in a book written after a visit to China in the latter part of 1967.[109] She argues that Liu Shao-ch'i and his followers wanted development on the same general lines as, the Soviet Union. She sums up Mao Tse-tung's view very succinctly:

> He wanted the succession to go to the people, that is to a Party who had been broken in to serving, not ruling them, and to a public that had learned to watch the Party, at every level, for signs of ambition, corruption and privilege sprouting again. The slogan 'Rebellion is justified,' which sounds strange in the mouth of the leader of an established government, becomes the equivalent of: The price of freedom from Party bosses is eternal vigilance.

She argues that the social goal was to replace selfishness with a desire to serve the community in a system based on cooperation, rather than competition, with an educational system that would train its students to serve the people rather than to qualify themselves for superior jobs and incomes as in the Soviet Union. She ends her introduction by saying, 'None of the great religions has succeeded in producing a satisfactory society. The purpose of the Thought of Mao Tse-tung is to create a setting in which the claims of the ideal are not at variance with the necessities of daily life.'

Thus, the goals of the Cultural Revolution were very attractive, but it was predictable from the start that the movement would not attain its goals, because it was based on a wrong diagnosis of the evils to be attacked and on theories with very serious deficiencies.

No society has really solved the problem of how to keep a large bureaucracy under the effective control of the people, but it was hopelessly confusing to present the problem as preventing the revival of capitalism. The ideal of laissez-faire capitalism, which was approximated in early nineteenth-century England and late nineteenth-century America, is a society with almost no bureaucracy. Engels showed a far sounder understanding of the problem of keeping popular control of a revolution when he described the rule of law for every citizen against any official as 'the first condition of all freedom.' Unfortunately, Mao Tse-tung has always despised the rule of law as a bourgeois concept.

The anarchist tendencies of the revolutionary organizations were a natural result of Mao Tse-tung's emphasis on contradiction and struggle. The anarchist position depends on the assumption that, once the forces of evil have been defeated and their regrowth prevented, a functioning society based on natural cooperation will emerge.

Mao Tse-tung's attitude to freedom was inevitably equivocal, because he retained his belief that a process of free discussion must end by producing unanimity. When he encouraged free discussion, it produced disagreements which he refused to accept.

Finally, the movement failed because it was utopian. As against the position of many Western liberals, there is a very strong case for holding that any satisfactory 'invisible hand' does not operate to produce a satisfactory society from a set of individuals and pressure groups motivated by self-interest. However, while the encouragement of public spirit is an essential part of any realistic program for the improvement of society, it was completely unrealistic to aim at a society that required public spirit to be the dominant motive for the great majority of its citizens.

The Cultural Revolution was successful in breaking the power of the Party apparatus and of Liu Shao-ch'i and his associates in the Party leadership. This success at least postponed the development of China toward something like the Soviet model or traditional China, with the Communist Party as a ruling bureaucracy.

It has also apparently been successful in making a drastic reduction in the size of the bureaucracy. There have been numerous reports of organizations reducing their

---

[108] Joan Robinson, *The Cultural Revolution in China* (London: Pelican Books, 1969).

administrative personnel, in some cases by 90 per cent. This is a remarkable contrast with the failure of would-be reformers in other countries to resist the workings of Parkinson's Law and the inefficiencies of a growing bureaucracy increasingly occupied with its own internal paperwork.

The future. In 1970, it seemed that the Cultural Revolution had left the army as the dominant power in China. The army representatives held the leading positions in the provincial revolutionary committees while, at the center, Lin Piao had been officially designated as Mao Tse-tung's chosen successor.

In 1971, it became clear that this situation had been unstable. Lin Piao and several other prominent military leaders disappeared from public life. Later, a campaign of criticism started that appeared to be directed against Lin Piao though not actually mentioning his name. (It had only been in the later stages of the campaign against Liu Shao-ch'i that his name was introduced.) By the end of 1971, it seemed clear that Chou En-lai had become the dominant leader. Since the Cultural Revolution, the Chinese Communist Party had returned to its practice of conducting its internal affairs with a high degree of secrecy. Thus, while there has been a plethora of rumors and speculations, there are no reliable sources for an explanation of recent developments or an estimate of contending views within the Party.

The one prediction that can be made with a high degree of confidence is that there will be major changes in the Party leadership during the next ten years. Up to now, leadership has been concentrated in the hands of a group who started their political careers in the 1920's and are now in their seventies or late sixties. Simply on actuarial grounds, it is likely that a large proportion of this group will be dead by the 1980's.

On other points, the reliable information now available is enough to identify some influences likely to be important in the future and to justify some speculation but is not enough to justify prediction. One can envisage several widely diverging lines of possible development.

SELECTED BIBLIOGRAPHY

BARNETT, A. DOAK. *Communist China: The Early Years, 1949–1955.* New York, Praeger, Publishers, 1964. A reprint of a selection of reports made from Hong Kong during the period.

BRANDT, CONRAD. *Stalin's Failure in China, 1924–1927.* Cambridge, Harvard University Press, 1958. Very readable account of Comintern policy and the Chinese Communist Party during this period, though some conclusions have been invalidated by later studies of Comintern material.

CHASSIN, LIONEL M. *The Communist Conquest of China: A History of the Civil War, 1945–1949.* Cambridge, Harvard University Press, 1965. One of the very few books on this subject, though it contains many inaccuracies such as mistakes on Chinese geography.

CHEN, THEODORE H. E. *Thought Reform of the Chinese Intellectuals.* Hong Kong: Hong Kong University Press (Oxford University Press), 1960. A good account of the pressures to secure conformity from 1949 on, the experiment in free criticism in 1957, and the subsequent antirightist campaign.

COHEN, ARTHUR A. *The Communism of Mao Tse-tung.* Chicago: University of Chicago Press, 1964. A detailed study of Mao's more theoretical writings.

HSIAO, TSO-LIANG, *Chinese Communism in 1927: City vs. Countryside.* Hong Kong: The Chinese University of Hong Kong, 1970. The best account of the relation between Chinese Communist and Comintern policies during this critical period.

ISAACS, HAROLD R. *The Tragedy of the Chinese Revolution.* Stanford, Calif.: Stanford University Press, 1961. This is a revised edition of a book that first appeared in 1938 and was the first documented study in English of the Chinese Communist movement up to 1928. Because the author met many of the people involved in the events he describes, its descriptions are more vivid than those of later studies, though the reader should remember that it is written from the standpoint of a strong supporter of Trotsky and that some of its conclusions have been disproved.

JOHNSON, CHALMERS A. *Peasant Nationalism and Communist Power: The Emergence of Revolutionary China, 1937–1945.* Stanford Calif.: Stanford University Press, 1962. A good account of the development of Chinese Communist military power during the war against Japan, based largely on Japanese sources. According to informants from the History Section of the present Japanese National Defense Force, the accounts on which this book relied exaggerated the success of the Japanese pacification program in Central China.

LEWIS, JOHN W. *Leadership in Communist China.* Ithaca, N.Y.: Cornell University Press, 1963. An interesting study of Chinese Communist doctrine on leadership.

LIFTON, ROBERT J. *Revolutionary Immortality: Mao Tse-tung and the Cultural Revolution.* New York: Vintage Books, 1968. A very interesting study of the motivations behind the Cultural Revolution, by an author who is both a Sinologue and a psychiatrist.

LINDSAY, MICHAEL. *China and the Cold War.* Melbourne: Melbourne University Press, 1955. An analysis of Chinese foreign policy and the influence of Communist doctrine.

MARCUSE, JACQUES. *The Peking Papers.* New York: E. P. Dutton & Co., 1967. The author was correspondent of the Agence France-Presse in Peking from 1962 to 1965 and had lived in China before the Communist takeover. The book is often very amusing and gives a good idea of the frustrations of a journalist in the Chinese People's Republic.

MEHNERT, KLAUS. *Peking and the New Left.* Berkeley: University of California, Center for Far Eastern Studies, 1969. A very interesting study of the Cultural Revolution that reproduces many of the Red Guard documents.

NORTH, ROBERT C. *Chinese Communism.* New York: McGraw-Hill, 1966. A good short history up to 1964 with interesting photographs.

SCHRAM, STUART. *Mao Tse-tung.* Baltimore: Penguin Books, 1966. A good general study of Mao and the Communist movement up to the mid-1960's.

SCHURMANN, FRANZ. *Ideology and Organization in Communist China.* Berkeley and Los Angeles: University of California Press, 1966. Interesting study of Chinese Communist ideology and doctrines of organization. Its weakness is that it tries to present the ideology as the Chinese Communists themselves see it and therefore fails to differentiate between true and false parts of the doctrine.

SNOW, EDGAR. *Red Star over China.* New York: Grove Press, 1961. A new edition of a book first published in 1937. Mr. Snow was the first foreign journalist to visit the Chinese Communist areas and found the Chinese Communist leaders willing to talk about their experiences. It should be remembered that some of the statements made to Mr. Snow have since been proved false by documented studies and that the account of the Long March is incomplete, because some groups, taking different routes, had not reached northern Shensi at the time of his visit.

SCHWARTZ, BENJAMIN. *Chinese Communism and the Rise of Mao.* Cambridge Harvard University Press, 1951. An interesting study of the development of the Chinese Communist Party up to 1932, though his main thesis—that Mao's strategy of peasant-based revolution was unorthodox—ignores the difference in Comintern strategy for Asia and for the West.

THORNTON, RICHARD C. *The Comintern and the Chinese Communists, 1928–1931.* Seattle: University of Washington Press, 1969. A good study of the influence of the Comintern on the Chinese Communist Party, showing that the strategy of the Chinese Communists was not unorthodox but followed Comintern directives.

TSOU, TANG. *America's Failure in China, 1940–1950.* Chicago: University of Chicago Press, 1963. Probably the best study of American-Communist-Kuomintang relations during this period, through the author is too inclined to assume that hostility between the Communists and the Americans was inevitable.

VAN SLYKE, LYMAN P., ed. *The Chinese Communist Movement: Report of the United States War Department, July, 1945.* Stanford Calif.: Stanford University Press, 1968. This gives some of the information obtained mostly from the U.S. Army Observers Section at Yenan about the wartime Communist regions.

7

THE CHINESE COMMUNIST PARTY: STRUCTURE, MEMBERSHIP, AND MASS ORGANIZATION

JOYCE K. KALLGREN

INTRODUCTION

As China entered the 1970's, no one could deny that there had been changes in the structure and membership of the Party. Some observers, noting the chaos of the Cultural Revolution and attendant changes in top Party personnel, contended that the Party not only had suffered deeply in the tumultuous years 1966–68 but still remained weak and impotent. Others, seeing economic progress and finding familiar Party faces in government ministries, were less quick to pronounce the Party ailing. By 1971, it was undeniable that efforts to reconstitute the Party were under way, though problems of intra-Party relationships had not yet been solved. The leadership and structure of the Party, which had been attacked from the beginning of the Cultural Revolution, still seemed to be evolving.

Leadership stability, which had seemed to distinguish the Chinese from other Communist Parties, came under open attack in August, 1966, with Mao's slogan: 'Bombard the Party headquarters.' Since 1949, there had been only two major purges: the removal of Kao Kang and Jao Shu-shih in 1953–54 (which was not widely known until 1955) and the replacement of P'eng Te-huai in 1959. But between the ouster of P'eng Chen, head of the Peking Party Committee, in the spring of 1966 and the Party Congress in the spring of 1969, few Party leaders emerged entirely unscathed. Members who had been prominent in Chinese Communist politics since the beginning of the Party in 1921 were attacked and branded as traitors. In some cases, well-known Party officials seemed to disappear. With the sole exception of Mao Tse-tung (there were even some reports of anti-Mao statements), few Party leaders escaped Red Guard accusations.

It was to be expected, therefore, that the Ninth Party Congress would bring to light changes in the leadership. The large number of military men in the final listing suggested a possible new role for the PLA, and the length of the Party Congress (more than three weeks) caused many to wonder what problems remained, even while the Congress was to signal a new stage in Party history.

The changes in structure and organization appeared to be sweeping. The alterations in the Party structure necessitated by the Cultural Revolution were formalized in the 1969 Party Constitution. Previously, the implementation of Party rules had always been flexible, but the content of the Party Constitution had presented the orientation and procedures within which flexibility was permitted. The new tone of the 1969 document, the sparsity of its formal content, would raise a number of questions about the day-to-day operations of the Party.

Party goals had been restructured, and some formal organizational features that had contributed to Party strength had been deleted. The relatively specific parameters of authority had been replaced by generalized statements emphasizing the thought of Mao Tse-tung, though there is little specific direction as to how that thought should be asserted and carried forward through the Party mechanism.

Along with leadership and structure, the Ninth Congress documents indicate a third major change that the Cultural Revolution brought about. It concerned the role of the 'mass organizations.' Since its establishment, the Party has been related to, worked with, and laid great stress on its leadership of, a variety of mass organizations in Chinese society. The organizations have provided activists for Party membership, vehicles for specific functional tasks in the nation, and mechanisms for support of domestic and foreign interests. Prominent among these groups have been the Young Communist League (YCL), the All-China Federation of Trade Unions, and the Democratic Women's Federation. All of these furnished activists for policy campaigns, channels for Party programs, and specific services to segments of the society. Yet in the first year of the Cultural Revolution, these organizations and their publications came under attack by radical student groups. They were accused of supporting revisionism or disgraced leaders. Their publications were suspended and eventually discontinued. The organizations themselves entered into a state of limbo, neither disbanded nor actively participating in political life. The new Party Constitution mentions 'mass organizations' but speaks of the groups upon which they might draw—not specific organizations.

Thus, despite the quotations of Chairman Mao reaffirming the importance of the Party (which were prominently featured in the literature accompanying the Party Congress), one had to wonder whether, in fact, 'our Party is now more united, more consolidated than at any time in the past,'[1]—or, indeed, whether this was the same Party. It is to these questions of structure, membership, and mass organization that this chapter now turns.

PARTY STRUCTURE

Analysts of the Chinese Communist Party have recognized the importance of its structural and organizational capabilities. Changes in short-range goals or the restructuring of priorities depends upon the capacity of the Party and its members to undertake the tasks; hence, it is important to understand the scope and strength of the Party's organization. One of the best ways to undertake this study is through analysis of the basic documents, principally the Party Constitution in its changing versions. Though it is true that the provisions are not always carried out and that some articles are ignored or unenforced, the thrust and direction of each document as a whole reflect the priority of the drafters, the consensus of the Party leadership, and the structures deemed appropriate for their implementation. Since the end of World War II, there have been three Party constitutions, those of 1945, 1956, and 1969.[2] The similarities and differences between them are instructive.

[1] *Peking Review*, Vol. 12, No. 17 (April 25, 1969), inside front page.
[2] The 1945 Constitution is to be found in Conrad Brandt, Benjamin Schwartz, and John K. Fairbank, *A Documentary History of Chinese Communism* (London: George Allen & Unwin Ltd., 1952), pp. 419–39. (The American edition is Cambridge: Harvard University Press, 1959.) The 1956 Constitution (Chinese and English versions) is in E. Stuart Kirby, ed., *Contemporary China* (Hong Kong: Hong Kong University Press, 1958), pp. 105–42. The 1969 document is included in this volume as Document No. 2. The original was published in *Peking Review*, 12, No. 18 (April 30, 1969): 36–39.

The format, length, and general tone of the Party constitutions, in addition to their obvious provisions, are useful indicators of Chinese Communist state of mind, perception of tasks, and the lessons learned from immediate history. In 1945, the Party, however murky its future, had reason for some confidence in its work. In the face of, and perhaps because of, the Sino-Japanese War, Party membership had grown and could be expected to expand even further if the Party was successful in its anti-Kuomintang efforts. This growth would pose, however, all manner of problems in terms of recruitment, discipline, and organizational expansion. Consequently, the provisions of the 1945 document reflect the need increasingly to centralize the control of the Party (particularly since World War II strategy and tactics had resulted in a higher degree of unit independence than might be proper or desirable for the Party); yet there remains a curious emphasis upon individual protection, particularly in terms of individual discipline, where the provisions specifically call for care and temperate judgment. Another feature of the 1945 provisions was the recognition of the increased importance of the rural areas in terms of Party strength.

The 1956 document represents a party in power and the need for a meshing of formal Party organizations with the political divisions of the Chinese state. By 1956, the earlier details about Party recruitment, length of membership for recommendation purposes, and the like, were no longer deemed necessary, and the formal provisions for differing probationary periods were deleted. Furthermore, the differing circumstances of the Party are apparent, particularly in the striking emphasis in 1956 on the construction of a strong and powerful state. This is not to deny the importance of ideology but rather to emphasize the consequences of industrial development and the importance of the worker class.

The 1969 Party Constitution and democratic centralism. The content of the 1969 document, and hence the present direction provided for the hitherto most important organizational entity in China, can only be described as sketchy. The Constitution of the Ninth Party Congress (adopted in April, 1969) devoted approximately one-third of its text to the General Program. This is a unifying statement of the present role of the Party in the Chinese revolution, its hierarchy of tasks, and the necessary work style for their achievement. The document contains only twelve articles, a reduction of thirty-nine from the prior documents and of well over 50 per cent in word count (see Chart 7–1). Even accepting that the highly stylized language of Party documents, directives, and the like has special meaning to the Chinese elites, the 1969 message is certainly limited in its manifest content.

Chart 7–1—Chapter Headings and Articles of the Constitutions
of the Chinese Communist Party

1945	*1956*	*1969*
		Chapter 1 :
Introduction	General Program	General Program.
Chapter 1 :	Chapter 1 :	Chapter 2 :
Membership.	Membership.	Membership.
Articles 1–13	Articles 1–18	Articles 1–4
Chapter 2 :	Chapter 2 :	Chapter 3 :
Organizational Structure	Organizational Structure	Organizational Principles
of the Party.	and Principles of the	of the Party.
Articles 14–28	Party.	Articles 5–7
	Articles 19–30	

1945	*1956*	*1969*
Chapter 3: Central Organization of the Party. Articles 29–38	*Chapter 3:* Central Organization of the Party. Articles 31–37	*Chapter 4:* Central Organization of the Party. Articles 8–9
Chapter 4: Party Organizations in Provinces and Border Regions. Articles 39–45	*Chapter 4:* Party Organizations in Provinces, Autonomous Regions, Municipalities directly Under Central Authority, and Autonomous *Chou.* Articles 38–42.	*Chapter 5:* Party Organizations in the Localities and Army units. Article 10
Chapter 5: Party Organizations in Localities, *Hsien,* Municipalities, and Districts. Articles 46–48	*Chapter 5:* County, Autonomous County, and Municipal Party Organizations. Articles 43–46	*Chapter 6:* Primary Organizations of the Party. Articles 11–12
Chapter 6: Basic Organizations of the Party. Articles 49–53	*Chapter 6:* Primary Organizations of the Party. Articles 47–51	
Chapter 7: Underground Organizations of the Party. Articles 54–55	*Chapter 7:* Control Organizations of the Party. Articles 52–54	
Chapter 8: Control Organizations of the Party. Articles 56–59	*Chapter 8:* Relations between the Party and the YCL. Articles 55–58	
Chapter 9: Party Nuclei in Organizations Outside the Party. Articles 60–62	*Chapter 9:* Leading Party Members of Groups in Non-Party Organizations. Articles 59–60	
Chapter 10: Rewards and Punishments. Articles 63–67		
Chapter 11: Finances. Articles 69–70.		

Sources: 1945 Constitution: Conrad Brandt, Benjamin Schwartz, and John K. Fairbank, *A Documentary History of Chinese Communism* (London: George Allen & Unwin Ltd., 1952), pp. 419–39; 1956 Constitution (Chinese and English versions): E. Stuart Kirby, ed., *Contemporary China* (Hong Kong: Hong Kong University Press, 1958), pp. 105–42. The 1956 and 1969 documents are also included in this volume; the original 1969 one was published in *Peking Review,* 12, No. 19 (April 30, 1969): 36–39.

Since the establishment of the Party, its basic principle for organization has been 'democratic centralism.' This is a descriptive term for a highly structured, pyramid-shaped political organization. Its definition implies that the leading organs of the Party are elected (the democratic element) but that the 'individual is subordinate to the organization, the minority . . . to the majority, the lower organization . . . to the higher level, and the entire Party . . . to the Central Committee' (the element of centralism).[3]

Though the phrase seemed important in 1969, and the chain of command implied above is by and large intact, there are additional aspects to the actual 'democratic centralism,' which must now be considered. For example, there is the problem of elections. In discussing the selection of representatives to the Ninth Party Congress, the Chinese media referred to democratic consultation. The relevant article of the Constitution, Article 5, uses the same term, thus indicating that the pre-Congress practice was not an exception or solely a matter of convenience in view of the turmoil in China. Yet the term 'election' is still found in the document.[4] The assumption, therefore, is that consultation with a range of politically acceptable individuals now occurs and may be expected to continue, and that the historically more customary election procedures will be limited in use.

While elections have given way to 'democratic consultation,' the provisions of the new Constitution enhance the position of the top-level organizations, specifically the Central Committee and its ancillary staff. This reflects one aspect of Cultural Revolution political change. The condemnation of the revisionism of political leaders and the activism of Chinese students and youths who had not yet experienced their revolution have resulted in an anomaly. On the one hand, the Party seeks broad symbolic participation; on the other hand, the functional arrangements seem to intensify the power of central organs involved in the daily activities of the Party.

There is another aspect to the problem of 'democratic centralism.' This relates to the implementing of general directives in a highly diversified country. The need is to reconcile the view of an individual with the requirement for central unity and discipline. In 1945 and 1956, the emphasis was upon the Party. Although the individual or group was provided an opportunity to express his or its views, the Party was clearly concerned with the problem of anarchy and the need for discipline.[5] The 1969 emphasis is different, as Article 5 graphically demonstrates, particularly in the light of our knowledge of the Cultural Revolution. While the organizations of state power and the revolutionary mass organizations must accept the leadership of the Party, the situation of individuals is different:

> If a Party member holds different views with regard to the decisions or directives of the Party organizations, he is allowed to reserve his views and has the right to bypass the immediate leadership and report directly to higher levels up to and including the Central Committee and the Chairman of the Central Committee.[6]

This is a direct reflection of Cultural Revolution incidents during the early struggles against entrenched Party authorities. Specifically permitted in Article 5 is the type of action reportedly taken by dissident students from Peking University in 1966, who made direct contact with Chairman Mao.

There are other indications of the experience of the Cultural Revolution to be found in the present Constitution. Party committees at all levels are directed, when

---

[3] Article 5, Paragraph 3 of the 1969 Constitution.
[4] Articles 10 and 11 of the 1969 Constitution.
[5] Article 22 and 23 in the 1945 Constitution, as cited in Brandt et al., *Documentary History of Chinese Communism*, pp. 429–30.
[6] Article 5, Paragraph 4, in the 1969 Constitution.

establishing their administrative units, to take due care for the principles of 'unified leadership, close ties with the masses, and simple efficient structure' (Article 7). Certainly the years since the last Party Constitution had provided a background for some of these terms. Maoist criticisms of the Party prior to 1966 had reflected the difficulties of an expanding bureaucracy, and emphasis upon the mass line has been a long-standing characteristic of Chinese political literature. However, the phrase noting the necessity of 'unified leadership' takes on added significance in view of the divisive forces that emerged in the Party during the Cultural Revolution. When PLA units were charged with establishing order at various points in the upheaval, it was clearly difficult to decide whom to support, let alone create a unified leadership group.[7] The delays in establishing Revolutionary Committees in the provinces, or Party provincial organs, testifies to this very fact. The 1969 Constitution reflects both the uncertainty regarding Party organization and the unresolved relationships that are a legacy of the Cultural Revolution.

Locus of political power. Because the 1969 document is so limited in explicitness and data about the actual Party operations, fragmentary conclusions about structure remain very tentative. Piecing together what has been published with some estimates based upon past experience, one can offer comments on political power. The Chinese refer to the National Party Congress as the highest leading body. In April, 1969, it was composed of 1,512 delegates and had a higher percentage of workers and lower-middle and poor peasants than any previous Congress.[8] As indicated above, the 1969 Congress must have confronted some important issues, because the meetings were unexpectedly lengthy. There are similar Congresses known to exist in the 'localities,' army units, and various 'departments.' But in view of the fact that the National Party Congress is to be convened every five years (a rule rarely observed in the past) and the local congresses every three years, the latter cannot serve as the locus of ongoing power.

In China, as in other Communist countries, the principal function of the Party Congress has been neither legislative nor even supervisory. The Congress serves the purpose of maintaining Party unity—or of reaffirming it. It reviews developments since the last meeting and perhaps approves a new direction that has been agreed upon in preceding and more restricted discussions.

Of course, the central position of the Party requires that it function on a continuing basis. Decision-making is a daily necessity and there must be mechanisms for Party officials to decide on or to concur in policy matters. These ongoing demands have been met through the selection and election by the Party Congress of a Central Committee and the election by the Central Committee of a Political Bureau and a Standing Committee. In the interim between congresses, these committees (and similar ones at the provincial, city, *hsien*, and commune levels), have the responsibility to decide and act. At all levels below the Party Congress, actions of the Party organs are subject to review by the next higher body. There is thus an effective higher control —one important purpose of which is to guard against the possibility of the Party's capture by particularistic interests.

But the problem in exercising control also exists at the level of the Central Committee, which has usually been convened only infrequently. For example, during the thirteen years of the Eighth Party Congress, there were only twelve Central Committee plenums (though there were several other gatherings involving large segments of

---

[7] John Gittings, 'Army-Party Relations in the Height of the Cultural Revolution,' in John Wilson Lewis, ed., *Party Leadership and Revolutionary Power in China* (Cambridge: Cambridge University Press, 1970), pp. 399–403.

[8] 'Press Communiqué of the Secretariat of the Presidium of the Ninth National Congress of the Communist Party of China,' *Peking Review*, 12, No. 18 (April 30, 1969): 40.

the top political leadership). These Central Committee plenums dealt, it is true, with important issues of the particular time.[9] Examples are the Sixteen Points to serve as guidelines in the Cultural Revolution, which were passed in 1966, or the new economic policies adopted at the plenum in 1962. The fact remains that, although the Central Committee is more involved than the Party Congress in decision-making, the infrequent scheduling of its meetings can only mean that the Committee itself is unable to carry out administrative supervision and ongoing control of the Party and the nation. In addition, the sheer size of the Committee would seem to hamper effective discussion and review: The old committee (as of 1966) was composed of 91 members and 89 alternates.[10] It is interesting to note, then, that the new (1969) Central Committee has 170 regular members and 109 alternates.

The inevitable consequence of this situation is that the Political Bureau and its Standing Committee (both of which are elected by the Central Committee) have been —and must be expected to continue to be—the locus of power. Twenty-one members were elected to the Political Bureau, of whom five constituted the Standing Committee. The structural framework and division of power specified in the Party Constitution, together with the actual development of pragmatic methods for handling problems, have ensured that these small bodies carry on the important work of the Party and are the true vehicles of power in China.

The Secretariat and subordinate and local organs. The top political elite was assisted in the past by a number of departments with responsibility for substantive areas of Party work. In addition to the Party Secretariat, the Organization Department was responsible for the myriad personnel needs of the Party; the Propaganda Department for ideological programs; the United Front Work Department for relations with the many organizations coordinated, directed, and supervised by the Party; and the Social Affairs Department for matters of internal security. In published accusations during the Cultural Revolution, it became clear that the Maoists believed that Liu Shao-ch'i and his associates had used these organs for their own power ends. However, despite their importance, these were subordinate staff organizations; the persons holding office in them were therefore subject to scrutiny, particularly during the Cultural Revolution. One practical example of this was the meteoric rise and equally rapid eclipse of T'ao Chu.[11] In the confusion that has prevailed since 1966, it has been unclear what has happened to these organs, or who now holds positions in them. It seems prudent to view each organization with caution.

For example, the Central Committee's Military Affairs Committee had been assumed to be the locus of decision-making power in military policy matters. Prior to the Cultural Revolution, the membership was thought to be a select group of the Party's hierarchy. With the upheavals of 1966–68 and the importance of military leadership since the Cultural Revolution, one might have expected it to continue to be an important organization. Yet the list of members that was made public in May, 1969, includes Party members who are either too old or too suspect to wield political power. The logical question, then, is whether the role of the committee itself has

---

[9] H. Franz Schurmann, *Ideology and Organization in Communist China* (Berkeley and Los Angeles: University of California Press, 1966), pp. 141–42, lists the meetings of the Central Committee from March, 1949, through September 1962, and the main topics of discussion.

[10] See 'Who's Who in Peking,' *Current Scene*, 4, No. 15 (August 8, 1966): 10, for a list of the Central Committee, and p. 13 for a list of the alternates.

[11] T'ao Chu was a former senior Kwangtung Party official. In 1966, he replaced Lu Ting-i as Director of the Central Committee's Propaganda Department and 'assumed a seat on the small but powerful Central Secretariat,' but last appeared in the late 1966 and has been denounced in Red Guard and official press statements. See Donald Klein and Anne Clark, *Biographic Dictionary of Chinese Communism, 1921–1965*, 2 (Cambridge: Harvard University Press): 812.

changed. Because the organization met recognized functional needs of the CCP, it seems likely that, in one or another guise, it—and others like it—will have a continuing existence.

Below the Central Committee and administrative staff of the Party was a set of provincial central committees with ancillary organizations to meet provincial needs. It has never been completely clear whether all local-level—provincial, city, *hsien*, etc.

Chart 7–2—Organization of the Communist Party of China
(1945 Constitution)

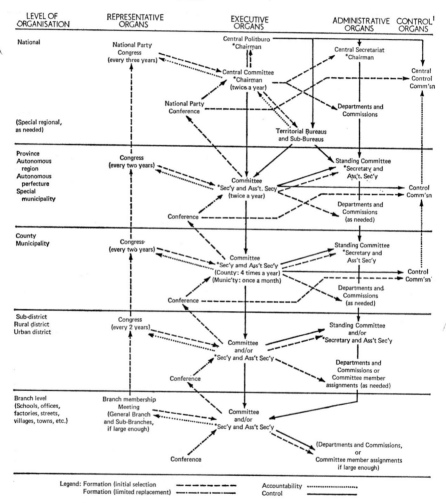

[1] For the control organs, the lines of formation, accountability and control follow the National Party Conference resolution of March 31, 1954, rather than Chapter VIII of the Party Constitution.

Source: Peter S. H. Tang, *Communist China Today: Domestic and Foreign Policies*, Vol. I, revised edition (Washington, D.C.: Research Institute on the Sino-Soviet Bloc, 1961).

—organizations maintained duplicate sets of administrative departments. Prior to the Cultural Revolution, it was possible to diagram the organization units involved, as Professor Peter Tang has done (see Charts 7–2 and 7–3). With the new Constitution, this attempt is no longer productive. The provisions in 1956 were comparatively explicit, and with the passage of time Party publications permitted the observer to gain some knowledge of developing bureaucratic organs that serviced Party units. The vagueness of the 1969 Constitution suggests that, while the former local-level organizations are no longer effective and perhaps no longer appropriate in post-Cultural Revolution China, the task of developing successful and acceptable substitutes has yet to be completed. Thus, the provisions of Chapter 5 speak merely of 'Party organizations' in the localities and army units.

There remains, of course, the continual problem of knitting together the various local Party organizations. In 1961, the Chinese announced the existence of six regional bureaus, which cross provincial boundaries and are similar to earlier Party organs abolished in 1954.[12] The regional bureaus and their staff organizations indicated a continuing concern with the possible parochialism of provincial organizations and the need for better liaison between the Center and outer organs.

At the very onset of the Cultural Revolution, it became clear that the problems responsible for the establishment of the regional bureaus had not been solved. Red Guard criticisms threw a spotlight on the continuing power of the provincial Party committees and the close relationships that existed between them and local military commanders. The purges of Party committees and the attacks on personnel of regional bureaus rendered them impotent. What institution should supplant them was a more difficult problem.

One answer was the so-called Revolutionary Committees, which have appeared at the provincial level. They were designed to bring together representatives of revolutionary cadres, poor and lower-middle peasants, workers, and rehabilitated or acceptable Party members. In 1969 and 1970, the army membership in these committees was important. However, in a situation where various contending groups all claimed to be supporting Mao and the Cultural Revolution, the formation of such committees presented a serious problem. As finally formed in 1968, they reflected the difficulty of reconciling diverse interests, and the large PLA representation was apparently one of the costs of reconciliation. In the aftermath of the 1969 Party Congress, efforts went on to re-establish the Party framework and organization working from the bottom up. This was a difficult task, and the reconstitution of the Party provincial committees was not completed until September, 1971.

Relations between the Party members and the Party Center remained unclear. To some extent, the PLA served as a transmission belt. But by training, function, and size, the army is not fitted to be a permanent substitute in running the country or in substituting for the leadership efforts of the Party.[13] By 1971, it seemed possible that the Party reorganization efforts were making substantial progress and that the Chinese leadership was itself calling upon the PLA to slowly phase out of leadership roles.

What of Party organization below the province level? So-called 'primary organizations' are formed in 'factories, mines, and other enterprises, people's communes, offices, schools, shops, neighborhoods, companies of the People's Liberation Army; and other primary units . . . may also be set up where there is a relatively large membership or where the revolutionary struggle requires.'[14] These organizations are

[12] Shih-fei Li, 'The Party's Middlemen, the Role of the Regional Bureaus in the Chinese Communist Party,' Current Scene, 3, No. 25 (August 15, 1965): 1–15. This article includes a map of the areas of each regional bureau.

[13] Gittings, 'Army-Party Relations,' is very interesting on this point.

[14] Article 11 in the 1969 Party Constitution.

Chart 7–3—Organization of the Communist Party of China
(1956 Constitution)

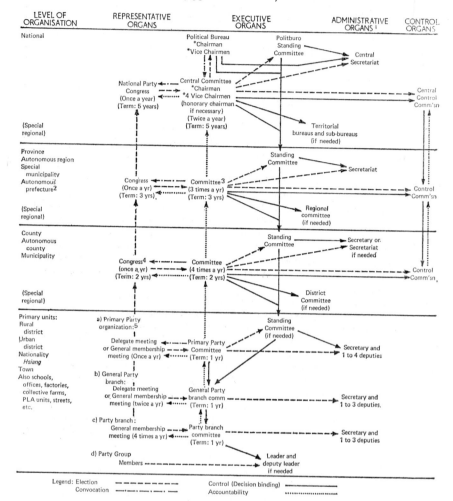

| LEVEL OF ORGANISATION | REPRESENTATIVE ORGANS | EXECUTIVE ORGANS | ADMINISTRATIVE ORGANS ¹ | CONTROL ORGANS |

Legend: Election — — — — — — — — —
Convocation —·—·—·—·—·—·—
Control (Decision binding) ▬▬▬▬▬▬
Accountability ·················

Source: Peter S. H. Tang, *Communist China Today: Domestic and Foreign Policies*, Vol. I, revised edition (Washington, D.C.: Research Institute on the Sino-Soviet Bloc, 1961).

of crucial importance for the Party. It is here that the new member is recruited and Party discipline enforced. It is here that the close ties with the masses are to be maintained. It was here that many of the struggles of the Cultural Revolution were fought out. But in the aftermath of the struggle, there is little information on how these units are developing. Certainly this set of 'Party Rules'[15] is much less directive than previous ones in terms of the organizational apparatus at the lowest level.

---

[15] Schurmann, *Ideology and Organization*, p. 118. The author indicates his preference for the term 'Party Rules.' In some ways this is an appropriate term for the 1956 document, but not for the 1969 Constitution, which clearly is less of a series of prescriptions for organization and more of an ideological statement that also includes some rules.

Thus, an institutional view of the Party leaves a number of unresolved issues. The Party organization in China, reaching from the Political Bureau down to the small Party branch, was a structure that paralleled the government and other organizational units. This facilitated close scrutiny and effective direction of all activities of concern to the Party. The study of local organizations through intensive interviewing of refugees has produced some detailed and thoughtful analyses of Party work at ministry, *hsien*, and commune levels. These studies have demonstrated the capacity of the Party to influence all decision-making and the expectation of non-Party members that policy decisions are to be made by the Party.[16]

It is still not clear how Party control and surveillance is or will continue to be carried out. During the Cultural Revolution, the PLA sometimes moved into factories and mines in a quasi-directive capacity. In the aftermath of the Cultural Revolution, worker's teams in the cities and poor and lower-middle-class teams in the countryside are presumably mechanisms for transmitting Party objectives to those segments of the society. In schools, hospitals, factories, and other organizations, representatives of the PLA or workers will often be the 'responsible person in charge.' Once Party provincial committees were established, there appeared to be continued effort to revive or strengthen Party committees throughout the country. By the spring of 1972, the more traditional Party organizations were to be seen in parts of China.

PARTY MEMBERSHIP

Eligibility and duties. Considering the importance of the CCP and the elite nature of the Party, requirements for membership are rather simple. The 1969 Constitution states:

> Article 1. Any Chinese worker, poor peasant, lower middle peasant, revolutionary army man, or any other revolutionary element who has reached the age of eighteen, and who accepts the Constitution of the Party, joins a Party organiza, tion and works actively in it, carries out Party decisions, observes Party discipline- and pays membership dues may become a member of the Communist Party of China.

The content of the paragraph has some important similarities to preceding versions: The age of eighteen has remained the lower boundary; all must be willing to pay dues and to accept and work for the programs of the Party. The provisions on age and fiscal responsibility have not been important. Refugee accounts indicate that membership was seldom attained much before the middle twenties and usually substantially later. The progress of youth through the ranks of the YCL seems to have gone far beyond the age of eighteen. Since the Cultural Revolution, there has probably been pressure to admit younger members; some of the student activists must have attained the minimum age limit. But data on the post-1965 experience is too limited to see whether the pattern of admission has altered.

The change, over the years, has been in the explicit way that class status has been handled. The actual composition of the Party will be discussed later in this section; at this juncture, it is important to note changes in the manifest ways that the issue is covered. In 1945, there were certainly assumptions about who should join, as reflected in differing probationary periods, the need for recommendations and the like; but the assumptions behind such requirements were unstated in the document.[17] By

---

[16] A. Doak Barnett, with a contribution by Ezra Vogel, *Cadres, Bureaucracy, and Political Power in Communist China* (New York: Columbia University Press, 1967). For a specific example, see the comments on pages 18–37.

[17] See Articles 4–9 in the 1945 Constitution, Brandt, *et al.*, *Documentary History of Chinese Communism*, pp. 425–29.

1956, the Party not only had formalized more clearly the procedures for membership, but also had tried to describe the potential member as 'any Chinese citizen who works and does not exploit the labor of others,'[18] a broadly based definition. In 1969, the article is orientated in a different direction (though it would probably still include many of those eligible in the 1956 version). Certainly the intellectuals, and all those not classified as a poor or lower-middle peasant, will have to become 'revolutionary elements' in order to obtain membership.

There were tacit assumptions in the three constitutions in regard to requirements or characteristics of the duties of the Party member. The differing emphasis on duties in the three documents reflects the differing work styles and concerns of the Party over a historical span. In 1969, the member should 'study and apply Marxism-Leninism-Mao Tsetung Thought in a living way' (Article 3, section 1). Clearly, the study requirement, no matter how heavy the emphasis upon application, has an inherent educational component. The injunction to work for 'the interests of the vast majority of the people of China and the world,' to 'consult with the masses when matters arise,' and to 'be bold in making criticism and self-criticism' (Article 3, section 5) resonate with provisions of earlier years. However, the 1956 article, with its citizenship requirement, had more of a tone of nationalism; in 1969, the term 'people of China' is used. Unique to the 1969 document is a hortatory injunction that seems addressed more to present members than to prospective candidates. This is a call for unity with the majority (including those who have been in error and opposition but 'are sincerely correcting their mistakes') and vigilance against 'careerists, conspirators, and double-dealers' (who might repeat the usurpation of Liu Shao-ch'i) in order to 'guarantee that the leadership of the Party and the state always remains in the hands of Marxist revolutionaries' (Article 3, section 3).

While the explicit requirements for Party membership seem modest, the procedures have been quite rigorous. The requirement includes completion of a detailed application form supported by the recommendation of two Party members, the serving of a probationary period, and close examination of the personal history and attitudes of the individual by the Party branch membership. The branch approval of the application requires confirmation by the next higher Party level. It is interesting to note that the 1969 document no longer makes it possible for a higher level to admit an individual directly, perhaps a change occasioned by the experience since 1965 with the excessive power of Party committees.

Refugees interviewed on application procedures confirm the impression derived from published data. Detailed investigations require close analysis of the candidate's background, family, attitudes, and friends. The present Constitution calls for the seeking of opinions of the broad masses 'inside and outside the Party,' and the work of the individual, both as to substance and work style, is subjected to careful study. Although in the past there must have been some individuals who achieved Party membership with only minimal attention to procedures, all available data seems to indicate that they were few, and that membership in the Communist Party of China has always been a rigorous matter indeed.

The vitality and integrity of the Party was also maintained through various standardized practices for members. All Party documents assert the necessity of freshness and innovative application of directives; but they also require continual criticism and self-criticism. In the past, all members participated in the intimate personal contact of small group sessions that reviewed the work and goals of the Party and the activities and contributions of the group's members. In addition, the Party has occasionally embarked upon a Partywide campaign of rectification designed to weed out those who had fallen into ideological lassitude or error, and to punish those

---

[18] Article 1 in the 1956 Constitution, in *Contemporary China*, 1958, p. 113.

who had succumbed to the temptations of power. While the Party up to 1965 had not undergone the purges that had characterized the Soviet Communist Party in the 1930's, there were many reports of Party discipline for members whose conduct and work style did not measure up to expectations. All the Party constitutions have provided penalties for infractions of discipline. Until 1969, the Party constitutions devoted considerable attention to the mechanisms and organizational units that were to administer this discipline; Article 4 of the 1969 Constitution sets out in relatively brief fashion the disciplinary measures to be applied to members violating Party discipline.

Size and composition. Because the Communist Party is the key element in contemporary China, the composition of its membership is obviously a subject of great interest. Unfortunately, hard data are scarce and difficult to evaluate. Biographical analysis is frequently thwarted by the unavailability of information. Except in the cases of individuals who have been criticized, CCP comment in papers and radio is usually only fragmentary—and since 1966 has been almost nonexistent. These limitations must be kept in mind when considering the present level of research.[19]

The CCP is the largest Communist Party in the world; its estimated membership in 1961 was 17 million. At the same time, it has the smallest ratio of members to total population of any ruling Communist Party. Numerous efforts have been made to chart the growth of the Party over the years; the following figures probably are indicative of the pattern:[20]

	Million
1945	1.2 plus
1947	2.7
1949	4.5
1951	5.8
1953	6.0
1955	9.3
1957	12.7
1959	13.9
1961	17.0

No figures for total membership have been available since 1961. Estimates arrived at by Professor John Lewis of Stanford University indicate that there may have been an average annual increase of approximately 1.5 million.[21] This would mean that the Party membership in 1965, on the eve of the Cultural Revolution, was 23 million, but this is probably on the high side. The upheavals since 1965 make it impossible to estimate present membership with any confidence. In any case, as compared with China's total population of 750 million or more, it is clear that the CCP is an elite group.

The membership figures are interesting both for their totals and for the light they throw on relative rates of expansion. Growth during certain periods reflects contemporary needs such as for leadership cadres in agriculture and collectivization campaigns. The toll of a rectification campaign can be seen in the more modest increases of other periods, such as 1957–58. For the purpose of summary, it can be

---

[19] Despite this caution, the long-awaited publication of Klein and Clark, *Biographic Dictionary of Chinese Communism*, represents a great achievement and real contribution by bringing together available information on CCP leaders.

[20] Schurmann, *Ideology and Organization*, p. 129; and John Wilson Lewis, *Leadership in Communist China* (Ithaca, N.Y.: Cornell University Press, 1963), p. 116. Both have charts derived from published Chinese sources. The charts are in substantial agreement. The figures cited here are an abbreviated version of those charts.

[21] Lewis, *Leadership in Communist China*, p. 111.

noted that, as of 1961, '80 per cent [of Party members] have joined the Party since the founding of the People's Republic of China, and 70 per cent since 1953.'[22] Forty per cent have entered since the Eighth Party Congress in 1956.[23]

There is only fragmentary data about the class background of Party members. Party figures for 1957[24] may be considered indicative:

	Per Cent
Intellectuals	14.8
Peasants	66.8
Workers	13.7
Others	4.7

It was clear, eight years after the Party had returned to the cities, that the Party was representative of the workers, but workers were in a minority in China. With the ensuing emphasis on agriculture, it does not seem likely that these percentages were substantially changed in the years prior to the Cultural Revolution.

Judgment about the distribution of Chinese Communist Party members within the country is even more difficult. First of all, the distribution of Party members between urban and rural China and among provinces is uneven. In the post-1949 period, the effort to expand Party membership in factories and among intellectuals probably added to the urban concentration. An apparently high ratio of Party membership in the military obviously has ramifications for important garrison areas. Policies of sending students and intellectuals to the countryside and efforts to increase the population in border regions presumably also have consequences in distribution.[25] Finally, as Schurmann has noted,[26] the requirement for educational tasks most likely results in uneven recruitment patterns in the country.

*Leadership characteristics.** In view of the consequences of 'democratic centralism' (that is, the concentration of power at the Central Committee level), the charactersitics of Party leadership are important. The available data are, of course, partial but very interesting. Given the information available, the groups most suited for study are the Party Central Committee, the Politburo, and its Standing Committee. John Lewis[27] and Donald Klein[28] have been responsible for much of the work based on these membership lists.

Prior to the Cultural Revolution, the leadership of the Party had worked and aged together. All members and alternates of the Central Committee between 1945 and 1958, with perhaps one exception, had joined the Party prior to 1938. Both Klein and Lewis agree that this top leadership was well educated (primarily in China), though Klein has noted the larger incidence of foreign (Western) training among the old Party members.[29] As Lewis wrote: 'The Party is led by men and women (four are

---

[22] *Jen-min Jih-pao (Peoples Daily*; hereafter *JMJP*), July 1, 1961.

[23] *Ibid.*, October 17, 1961.

[24] Teng Hsiao-p'ing, *Report on the Rectification Campaign* (Peking: Foreign Languages Press, 1957), p. 45.

[25] Mr. Lynn White, doctoral candidate in political science, University of California, Berkeley, is preparing a dissertation on the city of Shanghai. In his work, he has noted the fact that students who were *hsia fang* (sent down) to border regions often believed they had an opportunity for Party membership.

[26] Schurmann, *Ideology and Organization*, p. 138.

[27] Lewis, *Leadership in Communist China*, pp. 120–32, section on 'The Policy Apparatus and Senior Party Leaders.'

[28] Donald Klein, 'The "Next Generation" of Chinese Communist Leaders,' in Roderick MacFarquhar, ed., *China Under Mao* (Cambridge: MIT Press, 1966), pp. 69–86.

[29] *Ibid.*, p. 75.

* See also Chapter 9.

women) who bring to their posts long service, common sacrifice, and extensive education and training in China.[30]

As for province of origin, the very top levels of leadership (those elected to the Central Committee in 1945) came from the Central-South provinces. This concentration was diluted with the election of members in later years but is still marked.

Regarding tasks, Klein concluded that there were some differences between the older and younger (post-1945) Central Committee members that may have reflected relative age and experience. Younger members, as a whole, seemed to have had less military experience and to be assigned more frequently to work in the provinces. By 1962, the Party elite, as compared with elites in other countries, showed a high degree of stability, long tenure in office, and high average age. This situation means that the second echelon of leadership faces a problem of promotional opportunity.

In attempting to answer the question of the extent to which characteristics of the Central Committee membership may be common to those at the second level, the problem of limited biographical data becomes increasingly serious. The work of Michel Oksenberg,[31] focusing upon ministers, governors, and provincial Party secretaries, suggests that they also show the characteristics described above. There is a high degree of stability, and the average age is high. Vertical mobility is much less marked than lateral mobility. The Central-South geographical origins of the Chinese Communist revolution continue to be clearly reflected at this leadership level. Oksenberg suggests that it may require two or three decades for substantial modification.

The third level for analysis is that of local-level leadership. Here microsocietal studies by political scientists have contributed to knowledge about the characteristics and patterns of leadership. The information comes primarily from Party versus non-Party comparisons and is not directly comparable to the data cited above. The work of Y. M. Kau on Wuhan (an urban center), and that of Oksenberg on rural local leaders,[32] offer some important data. Among the rural leadership, Oksenberg comments, there was a tremendous increase in activist and Party work in the post-1949 period. He notes the aging process at work in comparing leaders between the mid-1950's and the early 1960's; the presence of Party or YCL members in the more central positions of power; a rather low level of educational background (not unexpectedly); and the fact that, in terms of tasks, the older man or Party member was more likely to have a position of authority and/or to come from outside the region to which he has been sent to implement social change. In the city study, Kau finds some comparable data. In urban Wuhan, the Party member had a generally high level of education (though less than a non-Party man who had achieved a high post), but was often not technically trained. Party members held the more powerful and politically sensitive posts. In Wuhan, as in the Party nationally, the CCP still reflected the middle- and upper-middle-class socio-economic groups, though some members of the Party had lower-class backgrounds.

In 1965, the Central Committee of the CCP, the Political Bureau, the Standing Committee, and the Party organs were still controlled by the men who had won the revolution. Below these top levels of power at the center, the provinces, cities, and countryside, there had been a dramatic expansion of total Party membership; some newer leadership was emerging; and some of the characteristics of the first generation

---

[30] Lewis, *Leadership in Communist China*, p. 123.

[31] Michel Oksenberg, 'Paths to Leadership in Communist China: A Comparison of Second Echelon Positions in 1955 and 1965,' *Current Scene*, 3, No. 24 (August 1, 1965): 1–11.

[32] Both Oksenberg and Kau have contributed to the volume *Chinese Communist Politics in Action*, edited with an introduction by A. Doak Barnett (Seattle: University of Washington Press, 1969). The volume itself is the product of a Social Science Research Council conference on the microsocietal study of Chinese politics.

of leaders were being diffused. Yet, in large measure, the personnel remained unchanged. The transfer of power to a younger elite was being delayed.

The Party, through its Organization Department, had tremendous power and was willing to use it. It could accept or reject individual candidates; it could control rates of recruitment and even the sectors of the population from which recruitment would occur. This organizational power, backed by the attractiveness of Party membership with its elite nature, was confronted by the modernization needs of China, the problem of competitive demands for technical training, and the pressure of Party members for upward mobility. Thus, there might well have been interesting tests for the cohesiveness of the Party. But the Cultural Revolution intervened, and with it came upheavals in the leadership ranks.

The Ninth Central Committee. The fact that the Party Congress of 1969 elected the Ninth Central Committee in the course of what appears to have been a long meeting points toward some degree of uncertainty. This delay, and the postponement that had occurred in the calling of the Congress itself, reinforces the need for scrutiny of the membership. Clearly, the years since the Eighth Congress in 1956 would have resulted in some new personnel. The convening of the Ninth Congress represented a leadership belief that a decision on political leadership was possible. But the delays required for the final result suggest that differences still remained up to the very selection of individuals and that consequently some compromises must have been made.

During 1969, the Central Committee comprised 170 members and 109 alternates; the Politburo of twenty-one members and four alternatives;[33] and the Standing Committee of five members, namely, Mao Tse-tung (Chairman of the Central Committee), Lin Piao (Vice-chairman of the Central Committee), Chou En-lai (Premier), Ch'en Po-ta (Chairman of the Cultural Revolution Group), and K'ang Sheng (Adviser to the CRG). Prior to 1969, as with other socialist countries, Western analysts had many cases, the Chinese have seemed to substantiate this view. In the immediate aftermath of the Ninth Congress, with the exception of Chairman Mao, Vice-chairman Lin, and Premier Chou, the practice was changed to list names in the Chinese equivalent of alphabetical order (by the number of strokes in the surname).

A first question concerning the new Central Committee was the extent of political continuity in its membership. To be sure, changes cannot be solely attributed to the Cultural Revolution, for it had been thirteen years since the last election. But of the 279 members and alternates of the new committee, only 53 individuals were carried forward from the Eighth Central Committee; in other words, only 18.9 per cent are survivors of the Cultural Revolution. Of these 53, moreover, 18 have been relatively inactive because of health, age, or political disfavor, so that only 35 really represented ongoing political leadership. In the Politburo, 12 individuals were carried forward from the pre-1966 era;[34] that is, 57 per cent of the most important policy-making group were individuals who had retained their former posts, and 43 per cent were new.

Another view of political power may be derived from a rough estimate of those individuals who appear to have been outside the circle of political power, despite their membership on the Central Committee. Of the 279 total, 29 were totally unknown, that is, they were people about whom there were no biographical data; 28 may be classified as relatively unimportant because of age, health, and political status; and 46 seemed to hold relatively low ranks in provincial activities. This total of 103 individuals, comprising 37 per cent of the Central Committee, would appear therefore, on the basis of biographical data, to be outside of effective political power. This group reflects, therefore, an attempt to build a consensus—if not a compromise—committee,

---

[33] The list of members is to be found in the *Peking Review*, 12, No. 18 (April 30, 1969): 47–49.

[34] Mao Tse-tung, Lin Piao, Ch'en Po-ta, Chou En-lai, K'ang Sheng, Yeh Chien-ying, Liu Po-ch'eng, Chu Te, Li Hsien-nien, Tung Pi-wu, Hsieh Fu-chih, Li Hsüeh-feng (alternate).

as well as the emergence of 'radical' heroes who must, for the present at least, possess limited power. We can assume that there has always been a ranking in the Central Committee that reflects internal Party judgments about power. In view of the turmoil of the Cultural Revolution, the existence of such a substantial group that appeared, even on this rough scale, to be relatively powerless, must have enhanced the political power of the other members.

The circle of real power was even further narrowed with the removal from public view of Lin Piao, named successor to Chairman Mao in the 1969 Party constitution, along with Ch'en Po-ta, and the equivocal position in 1972 of K'ang Sheng. Thus only two members of the five-man Standing Committee could be said to remain clearly in political power. In the Politburo similar occurrences were to be found. Within three years of election only twelve members appeared to remain politically active. Though in 1972 the cause of this purge remains unclear, it is safe to assume that relations with Lin Piao and hence the PLA played an important role, as well as the changing foreign policy of the Chinese vis-à-vis the United States.

The role of the military. An important issue looming large since the Cultural Revolution is the present and future role of the military. The number of individuals now at the top levels of power in China who hold military positions is very large. More than 40 per cent of the identifiable new members of the Central Committee are from the military forces. On the Central Committee, there are thirty-two PLA headquarters officials and seventy-five officials drawn from provincial military assignments. Of the ten new members of the Politburo (excluding alternates), six were primarily military figures. They were the commanders of the Nanking and Shenyang military districts, the Commissar of the Navy (also a member of the Military Affairs Committee), the air force chief, the director of the General Rear Services Department, and the Chief of Staff (former commander of the Canton Military Region).[35] It should be noted that all three regional commanders are from areas with large troop concentrations.

The purge of Lin Piao had ramifications for the military leadership. Many of those purged from the Politburo were military men. Li Tso-peng (Navy Commissar), Wu Fa-hsien (Air Force Chief); and Huang Yung-sheng (Chief of Staff) all disappeared. Despite this shift at the very top level, regional military figures remain quite prominent. In the aftermath of Party rebuilding, men associated with the PLA concurrently hold the positions of Party First Secretary and Chairman of the Revolutionary Committee in seventeen of the twenty-six provinces of China.

Care should be exercised in interpreting this military data. While one cannot ignore the increase in individuals with primarily military assignments, this fact does not necessarily suggest military control, nor is it incompatible with Party control. The PLA is not in size a competitor of the CCP. The large military representation does, however, have implications for issues with a high military component, such as national security and the like. Furthermore, the fact that many of the provincial representatives on the Central Committee are themselves commanders or political commissars of military districts raises questions about provincial leadership and the possibility of regionalism—two characteristics of traditional Chinese politics.

In any case, the incidence of 'unknowns' and the increase in those with military standing means that the number of individuals representing the bureaucratic departments or available for the bureaucratic needs of the nation is more restricted.

---

[35] Hsü Shih-yu, Commander, Nanking Military Region; Ch'en Hsi-lien, Commander, Shenyang Military Region; Li Tso-p'eng, Navy Commissar; Wu Fa-hsien, Air Force Chief; Ch'iu Hui-tso, Director, General Services Department; Huang Yung-sheng, Chief of Staff and former Commander, Canton Military Region.

MASS ORGANIZATIONS

In their efforts to create a Marxist-Leninist society and a modern industrial state, the CCP obviously had personnel needs that exceeded those of the Party membership. The programs of land reform, labor organization, public health, and the Marriage Reform Law all required large numbers of cadres committed to the values of the specific program as well as to generalized support of the major goals of the Party. The Party itself, in its ideological slogan of the mass line, needed to have a means for on-going contact with the masses. The emphasis on physical labor in agriculture or industry for each Party member would provide some of this contact. In addition, however, the mass line assumed ways and means for continual dialogue and insurance of mass support for policies that were to be implemented. Finally, in the years just after 1949, the Party, for both domestic and international programs, tried to enlist and insure the explicit support and presence of leading political figures and groups in Chinese life. The development of the so-called mass organizations provided the means for achievement of many of the above tasks.

James Townsend defines the term 'mass organization' in the following way:

> The term 'mass organization' sometimes refers to all forms of organization in China that give political direction to large numbers of people at the basic level. In this sense, it includes cooperatives, communes, resident committees, and basic level congresses. For the purposes of this discussion, however, the term is used in a much more limited sense to refer to those secondary associations that recruit their members on the basis of common interests, characteristics, or occupations and have national as well as local organizations.[36]

This limited sense is the one that is acceptable to the widely diverse interpretations of such authors as K. C. Chao, Peter Tang, and Richard Walker[37] and is the meaning most commonly implied when discussing the organizations active in China in late 1965. It is useful to consider the range of activities covered under this rubric: One can find in the 1966 Directory of Chinese Communist Officials the following titles: The Afro-Asian Solidarity Committee of China, the All-China Federation of Trade Unions, the Chinese People's Committee for World Peace, the Political Science and Law Association of China, the twenty-six friendship associations, such as the Sino-Cuban or the Sino-Ceylonese friendship associations, and such issue-oriented groups as the Chinese People's National Committee in Defense of Children.[38] All of these are classified under the subheading 'Mass Organizations.' In addition, one might well wish to include the youth organizations of the CCP—the YCL, the Red Scarfs, and the Young Pioneers.

Certain characteristics were shared by these organizations to a greater or lesser degree. First, the membership of most, but not all, of the organizations was large. Those organizations based upon professional or occupational criteria were obviously limited, such as the All-China Journalist Association. Still, for many of the associations, the membership figures were impressive. For example, the Sino-Soviet Friendship Association had 68 million members (1953), the All-China Federation of Trade

---

[36] James R. Townsend, *Political Participation in Communist China* (Berkeley and Los Angeles: University of California Press, 1967).

[37] K. C. Chao, 'Mass Organizations in Mainland China,' *American Political Science Review*, 48, No. 3 (September, 1954): 752–65; Peter Tang, *Communist China Today: Domestic and Foreign Policies* (New York: Praeger Publishers, 1957), pp. 324–35; and Richard Walker, *China Under Communism* (New Haven Conn.: Yale University Press, 1955), pp. 34–42.

[38] U.S. Department of State, *Directory of Chinese Communist Officials*, Washington, D.C., March, 1966, pp. 383–424.

Unions (ACFTU) had 20.8 million (1965), the Democratic Women's Federation (DWF) had 76 million (1953), and the CYL had 25 million (1964).

A second characteristic pertains to the structure and leadership of these groups. Most of the organizations had structures based upon the principle of 'democratic centralism,' in that the top levels of their bureaucracies had a high percentage of high-ranking CCP leaders. As in the CCP, most of the larger mass organizations had local branches and an ascending pyramid of committees, congresses, and the like that culminated in national organizations. Yet the local units of the YCL, the DWF, and the ACFTU were also pledged to maintain local discipline in accordance with central directives. The mass organizations, with the exception of those directly affiliated with the Party, such as the YCL, did have a large number of non-Party members and leaders at all levels. At the top echelons, as early as 1953, the director was frequently a Party member and most certainly was sympathetic to Party leadership and programs.[39] To the extent that such joint leadership was a form of the 'united front' politics of the post-1949 years, it was decreasing in form and reality by the mid-1960's.

Third, all the mass organizations served as active vehicles for the policies of the Party and the state structure, though the means employed by each group were often individually determined and appropriate for the membership characteristics of the group. For example, the DWF was intimately involved in the implementation of the Marriage Reform Law. It arranged meetings for its members and other groups, explaining the provisions of the law, the necessity and advantages of it, the role of women and children in its provisions. In the ACFTU, the importance of labor discipline was a constant emphasis in group literature. The All-China Federation of Industry and Commerce provided the opportunity to implement Party goals through individuals who, by profession or past economic status, might not be sympathetic toward or enthusiastic about the new China. In addition to the domestic programs, there were organizations, often with more limited membership, that served to aid foreign-policy objectives. The friendship associations are a prime example of this type. The Sino-Burmese Friendship Association could provide a nongovernmental welcoming group for foreign visitors sensitive to political neutrality. The associations could select potentially friendly visitors for tours to China. They could serve as channels for communication through propaganda statements and contact with foreign guests, political leaders, and potential activists. The professional groups did provide avenues for China to broaden its international reputation and possibly political recognition. They sought to participate in international conferences of experts. They could serve as nongovernmental units espousing governmental goals. The Chinese Medical Association invited foreign visitors to tour and report on Chinese medical achievements. After the outbreak of the Sino-Soviet dispute, many of these organizations could become means for seeking moral support or for access to other countries.

It would be a misreading of the mass organizations' function to see their activities solely as conveyor belts of Party goals, particularly for the larger mass organizations functioning primarily in China itself. A number of the organizations provided important services to their members, and this very fact provided a reservoir of support when they were engaged in the implementation of Party goals. Furthermore, a number of Party goals and programs were popular. Some examples will illustrate the complexity of this issue. In the postliberation years, the Chinese initiated and carried on efforts in public health, such as mass inoculation, control of pests, and related programs. Such programs were often genuinely popular in the country, and the role of the mass organization was an important one. Some organizations served as quasi-

---

39 Chao, 'Mass Organizations,' p. 753.

governmental agencies in the provision of services. Thus, the trade unions were charged with providing welfare services to their members. Labor insurance, sanatoriums, and the like required labor union membership for full enjoyment of the service. The problem of 'economism' that played such a role in the domestic upheavals in China's cities of 1967 is evidence that some labor unions did indeed carry out their tasks but apparently placed the separate interests of their constituents above those of the Party.[40] The youth organizations' programs were not only the implementing of directives but also the provision of socialization training for their members. The recreational and some of the instructional activities of the Red Scarfs, the Young Pioneers, and, to a lesser extent, the YCL, have similarities to the Boy Scout programs in the United States and England. In sum, an important element in mass organization success was a skillful mixture of politics with the interests and characteristics of the membership. In functional terms, the mass organizations were responsive to the direction and goals of the Party but also met other needs common to most societies.

From the point of view of Party membership and ideology, the mass organizations performed important functions. That is, their tasks should not be seen as primarily short-run in nature. The YCL, the ACFTU, and the DWF were specific attempts to politicize and organize those segments of Chinese society that had traditionally suffered from discrimination or economic privation. In this respect, the mass organizations were means for changing social status and roles in a CCP-approved direction.

Furthermore, because the largest of the mass organizations embraced important segments of the society, they could and did play an important role in terms of Party membership, recruitment, and growth. The Party recruited a large number of its new members from the political activists who came to the fore in various campaigns. Certainly, a great many of these eligible individuals were on the rosters of the YCL. Because its members ranged in age from the late teens through the middle twenties, scrutiny of their activities could provide an opportunity to see the style and quality of the work of potential Party members. But activists were found in other mass organizations, most certainly the ACFTU and the DWF.

In addition, the publications of the large groups, that is, the YCL and the ACFTU, provided channels for the guidance of these groups and opportunities to learn about the concrete realities and problems they faced.[41] The publications usually provided some type of 'letter to the editor' column through which the Party could learn about administrative difficulties and the faulty performances of cadres and Party members and respond by directing and reinforcing values and programs that were of specific interest.

Despite the impressive size and activity of the groups described above, not all Chinese were effectively linked to the state and Party through their organizations. To the nonemployed housewives in urban China, the resident committees seem to have been the major access. In the countryside, the cooperatives and the communes offered the most available mechanism for the Party to reach each individual.

With the onset of the Cultural Revolution, almost all of these organizations seemed to fall into disfavor. Their newspapers and magazines were suspended. Though the Chinese Party leaders indicated that the organizations would eventually re-emerge in some form, the specific form and direction that they would take is still not clear. This is certainly not a minor matter. In Chinese cities, there are buildings for labor unions and sanatoriums that were presumably under labor union directions; the YCL

---

[40] This argument is suggested by the author in a chapter in Barnett, ed. and intro., *Communist Chinese Politics in Action*, pp. 540–73. See also the analysis by The Editor, 'Sources of Labor Discontent in China: The Worker Peasant System,' *Current Scene*, 6 Nos. 5 and 6 (March 15 and April 15, 1968).

[41] James R. Townsend, *The Revolutionization of Chinese Youth*, China Research Monograph No. 1 (Berkeley: University of California, Center for Chinese Studies, 1967).

had similar facilities. These organizations served important functions. The labor unions, for example, administered various welfare programs. Even into 1970, refugees would speak of such ongoing facilities, though they did not report organizational ties outside of a given factory.

The Party's policy of reliance upon and use of the mass organizations was similar to that of other Communist countries and based upon an assumption of the importance of total organization throughout the society, both to convey messages of the Party and to bring about maximum participation. So it would seem mandatory for the eventual development of similar entities. In some areas this has occurred. The YCL has reappeared, and Red Guard organizations in the schools appear similar to pre–Cultural Revolution student organizations. The Chinese Medical Association is now inviting guests. Certain binational friendship associations seem active. But some mass organizations, specifically the labor unions, have not reappeared. Many organization journals have not yet been reissued.

Although the 1969 Party constitution mentions mass organizations, it does so without saying much about their nature. Clearly satisfactory resolution of Party organizational problems will have to precede the full-scale development of many of these mass organizations.

Relations Between the CCP and Foreign Communist Parties

Given the former size, vitality, and power of the Chinese Communist Party and the potential strength of the Chinese state, what have been the relations of the CCP with foreign Communist Parties?

In the pre-1949 years, the most important relationship was between the CCP and the Communist Party of the Soviet Union (CPSU), but there is considerable dispute about its nature. Was the CCP led by and/or dominated by the CPSU or the Comintern? Was the CCP relatively independent in its growth and policies? Was there indeed a basic conflict between the long- and short-range interests of the CCP and CPSU? While it is unlikely that the total picture will ever be known, the available evidence points toward the important role of the Soviet representatives, not only for the Kuomintang, but also for the CCP. In the 1920's and, to a lesser extent, the 1930's, there was a close and sometimes strife-torn relationship, although the entire leadership professed commitment to Marxist theory and allegiance to the Comintern. But the evidence from the leadership of Ch'en Tu-hsiu, Li Li-san, and the Twenty-Eight Bolsheviks shows varying degrees of compliance. Furthermore, some have argued that the rise of Mao Tse-tung would seem, at points, to have run counter to the prevailing policy of the day.[42]

In addition, however, to the CCP-CPSU relations, there is also a hidden story of relationships between the CCP and other nascent Communist Parties in Asia. In the travel and education experiences of CCP leaders in China and Moscow, there were contacts between such individuals as Ho Chi Minh, founder of the Indochinese Communist Party, and the CCP. Korean Communists were apparently in contact with some CCP leadership. In the history of the Korean Communists, there appears to have been a so-called Yenan wing of the Party. In present-day North Vietnamese

---

[42] The problem is one that has received a great deal of scholarly attention. The classic in the field is Benjamin Schwartz, *Chinese Communism and the Rise of Mao* (Cambridge: Harvard University Press, 1951). In addition, there are other very interesting accounts that deal with various facets of the problem, specifically Robert North, *Moscow and the Chinese Communists* (Stanford, Calif.: Stanford University Press, 1953), and Harold Isaacs, *The Tragedy of the Chinese Revolution* (London: Secker & Warburg, 1938). A new book by Richard Thornton, *The Comintern and the Chinese Communists, 1928–31* (Seattle: University of Washington Press, 1969), adds valuable data.

politics, there also seems to be a pro-Chinese and a pro-Soviet wing of the Party, whose emergence is based upon ideological considerations but also derives from the interrelationships of individuals, which may date back to classes at the Whampoa Military Academy, which was established in 1924.

In the first few years of the People's Republic, particularly during the postwar reconstruction period, 1949–52, and the First Five-Year Plan period, 1952–57, Party relations mirrored the closeness of state operations as the Russians provided aid and technical assistance. At a time when Chinese students were trained in Russia and the Soviet Army was the model for Chinese military reorganization, there were obviously close ties between members of both Parties. Some Chinese may well have cultivated, for their own purposes, Soviet friends. Suspicion about Kao Kang's relations with Soviet leaders may have been involved in his purge in 1953–54.

With the emergence of the Sino-Soviet dispute after 1956, outward indications of a close relationship with Soviet Party leaders vanished and indeed became a liability for CCP leaders. At various times during the Cultural Revolution, 'some Chinese' were accused of having relationships with the Russians. However the dispute itself is analyzed, it is clear that an important aspect of it centers upon the problem of inter- Party relations as well as tactics and strategy. In addition, the importance of nationalism has colored the Party view. Since the Soviet Army played no role in the winning of China, and indeed Soviet advice may have hindered Party development, it is not surprising that the Sino-Soviet dispute has resulted in a high level of animosity and the use of the CCP for Chinese national purposes.

A consequence of the dispute has been the development of Russian and Chinese wings in every national Communist Party. The Chinese have pursued an active policy of enlistment of foreign Communist Party members in the support of their position. Examples of this may be seen in the Japanese and Indian Communist Parties. In most cases, this division within a Party almost always weakens it politically, at least in the short run. Those who accept and support the Chinese position are encouraged by appropriate publicity in such Chinese publications as *Peking Review* and by some financial support, though there is little information about the extent of it.

In state relations with other Communist governments, the Chinese have shown the capacity to maintain policies that apparently contradict the policies enunciated by the CCP, depending upon their view of long-range Chinese national interests. In the realm of Party relations, however, there has been a more clear and unequivocal emphasis upon the Chinese ideological position, with less concern for the unity of worldwide Communist interests.

CONCLUSION

The Ninth Party Congress was an act of confidence on the part of the Maoist leadership, a reaffirmation of the basic principles they saw as central to the Chinese revolution, and an attempt, in the designation of Lin Piao, to provide for Chairman Mao's successor. But the outcome of the Congress and events since then have left many issues of Party structure and strength unresolved.

Our central question is how management and decision-making occur. Prior to the Cultural Revolution, the so-called united front policy was being eroded as Party members in both government and mass organizations were rising at the expense of non-Party cadres. Once the turmoil of the Cultural Revolution ended, it might have been expected that the Ninth Party Congress or the Party constitution would indicate the means or mechanisms for future evolution of policy. While participation is emphasized, they provide little guidance on Party structure from 'branch' to Central Committee, nor is the relationship between province and center made clear.

In terms of the individuals selected for the Ninth Central Committee, we see an internal 'united front' including older and disfavored (that is to say, heavily criticized)

Party members within the circle of honor, if not of power. Such a policy is, of course, consistent with the emphasis of Chairman Mao on reconciliation. In the Cultural Revolution, few were deemed beyond redemption and the majority of the Party elite was encouraged and permitted to remain with the Party and to retain their positions. It may well be true that many Party members have recognized their errors; but, in view of the factionalism revealed in the Cultural Revolution struggles, it seems difficult for the Party to be both generous in its membership policies and effective in the implementation of Maoist policies.

Evidence of continued division remained into 1972. Those identified with extreme leftist policies were largely removed from the political arena. Policies that seem more practically oriented than those of the Cultural Revolution are emerging. There has been continued change with the disappearance of members of the Central Committee, Politburo, and Standing Committee. All of these suggest that leadership problems remain.

Some scholars have argued that the military constitutes an alternative to Party leadership at least at the top levels of the Party. Many recent visitors to China have met members or veterans of the PLA in positions of leadership in schools, factories, and the like. At the top level of the Party, there are unquestionably a high number of military figures. But, as yet, it would be a mistake to see this as military leadership. Some of the major military commanders have clearly been affected by the fall from power of Lin Piao. In local organizational units, military representatives may dominate, but this is by no means clear or universal. Furthermore, it has yet to be demonstrated that the military/Party leader has indeed a policy difference with the nonmilitary/Party leader. In sum, until further evidence is available, we should be cautious about drawing conclusions as to the consequences of military presence in the top leadership of the Chinese Communist Party.

The status of mass organizations also remains opaque. Some of the organizations, particularly professional ones like the Chinese Medical Association, seem to be functioning. Other units with larger membership, such as the trade unions, have yet to reappear. Instead, there are occasional references to emerging factory organizations but apparently without the nationwide hierarchy.

Three years after the formal end of the Cultural Revolution, the anomaly of China remains. The country appears stable. But, with the exception of an exceedingly small number of highly visible officials, there is still much uncertainty about the organization and the leaders who direct the nation.

SELECTED BIBLIOGRAPHY

BARNETT, A. DOAK, ed. and intro. *Chinese Communist Politics in Action*. Seattle: University of Washington Press, 1969. Collection of articles is the product of a 1967 SSRC Conference on the Microsocietal Study of Chinese Politics. Of particular relevance to this chapter are the articles by M. Oksenberg on local leaders in rural China and Y. M. Kau on the urban bureacratic elite.

BARNETT, A. DOAK, with a contribution by EZRA VOGEL. *Cadres, Bureaucracy, and Political Power in Communist China*. New York: Columbia University Press, 1967. Based upon intensive refugee interviewing, a detailed statement of the operation of the bureaucracy in a ministry, county, and commune. An extremely useful supplement to the more theoretical descriptions.

CHAO, K. C. 'Mass Organization in Mainland China,' *American Political Science Review*, 48, No. 39 (September, 1954): 752–65. Though dated, still a good statement on the role and function of large-scale non-Party organizations.

Current Scene Developments in Mainland China. Hong Kong: Green Pagoda Press (Vol. 1, No. 1 dated May, 1961; irregular). Two and occasionally three issues appear each month, dealing with current developments in China. A majority in recent years have dealt with Party developments and the Cultural Revolution.

KLEIN, DONALD, and ANNE CLARK. *Biographic Dictionary of Chinese Communism 1921–1965.* Vols. 1 and 2. Cambridge: Harvard University Press, 1971. An extraordinarily valuable collection of biographical data, well organized and well written. Essential for any serious scholar in the field.

LEWIS, JOHN W. *Leadership in Communist China.* Ithaca, N.Y.: Cornell University Press, 1963. A solid piece of scholarship bringing together much of the data on Party membership, recruitment, and the like. It includes an extended discussion of Party ideology and training. Chapters on the mass line, cadre training, and rural activities.

LEWIS, JOHN W., ed. *Party Leadership and Revolutionary Power in China.* Cambridge, England: Cambridge University Press, 1970.

NEUHAUSER, CHARLES. 'The Chinese Communist Party in the 1960's: Prelude to the Cultural Revolution,' *China Quarterly,* No. 32 (London: Congress for Cultural Freedom, October–December, 1967), pp. 3–36. Good summary of leading trends and developments in the Party on the eve of the Cultural Revolution.

SCHURMANN, H. FRANZ. *Ideology and Organization in Communist China.* Berkeley and Los Angeles: University of California Press, 1967. A particularly interesting chapter on the Party offers a number of provocative hypotheses as well as an idealized discussion of Party organization.

TANG, PETER. *Communist China Today: Domestic and Foreign Policy.* New York: Praeger Publishers, 1957. Though somewhat dated, the chapter 'The Party Machine,' pp. 95–159, is a detailed description of the Party up to the Eighth Party Congress in 1956. A chart on Party organization reflects changes in 1956.

TOWNSEND, JAMES R. *Political Participation in Communist China.* Berkeley and Los Angeles: University of California Press, 1967. A careful analysis of the crucial question of how the individual in China participated in the political process and the role of the Party in leadership. Has an excellent brief statement on the organization and function of mass organizations.

———. *The Revolutionization of Chinese Youth: A Study of Chung-kuo Ch'ing-nien.* China Research Monograph No. 1. Berkeley: University of California, Center for Chinese Studies, 1967. An analysis of the process and issues confronting Chinese youth prior to 1966, based upon YCL publications.

U.S. Department of State. *Directory of Chinese Communist Officials.* Washington, D.C., March, 1966. Based entirely on published sources, this publication provides a listing of individuals in leadership positions in China. It includes a section on Party leadership, governmental positions, and the mass organizations. No post-Cultural Revolution issue has yet been issued.

8

CONSTITUTION AND GOVERNMENT

FRANKLIN W. HOUN

BACKGROUND

SINCE the founding of the People's Republic in 1949 the Communist government—as opposed to the Party (discussed in the preceding chapters)—has operated under two constitutions. The first 'constitution' comprised the Common Program of the Chinese People's Political Consultative Conference (CPPCC), the Organic Law of the People's Republic of China (P.R.C.), and the Organic Law of the CPPCC and was provisional in nature. Adopted by the CPPCC in September, 1949, this provisional constitution remained in force until September 20, 1954, when it was superseded by the present Constitution.

According to official theory, the new Constitution was designed to 'consolidate and legalize the achievements of the People's Democratic Revolution' (that is, the revolution against imperialism, feudalism, and bureaucratic capitalism) in the preceding years and to open a new era of transition to socialism, during which the main task of the state was, and still is, to bring about, step by step, the socialist industrialization of the country and the socialist transformation of agriculture, handicrafts, industry and commerce.[1]

The enactment of the new Constitution began with the adoption by the Central People's Government Council, on January 13, 1953, of a resolution relating to the convocation of a National People's Congress (NPC) and of local people's congresses at various levels. The resolution provided for the appointment of a twenty-six-member committee, with Mao Tse-tung as chairman, to draft a constitution for the country. On March 23, 1954, Mao, on behalf of the Central Committee of the Chinese Communist Party (CCP), submitted a 'Preliminary Draft' to the Committee. After 'consulting' more than 8,000 people from all walks of life, the committee accepted the draft on June 11 and immediately thereafter submitted it to the Central People's Government Council for action.

Three days later, the Council decided by unanimous vote to publish the draft 'so that the people throughout the country [could] discuss it and make suggestions for its improvement.'[2] During a period of more than two months, more than 150,000,000 people reportedly took part in the nationwide debate, lending their 'support' to the draft constitution and suggesting 'many amendments and addenda.' After considering

---

[1] See the preamble to the Constitution. An English text may be found in *Documents of the First Session of the First National People's Congress of the People's Republic of China* (Peking: Foreign Languages Press, 1955), pp. 131–63.

[2] Liu Shao-ch'i, 'On the Draft Constitution of the People's Republic of China,' *Current Background*, No. 294, U.S. Consulate General, Hong Kong, September 20, 1954, p. 1.

the suggestions, none of which contradicted the basic spirit and provisions of the draft, the Constitution Drafting Committee presented a slightly revised draft to the Central People's Government Council, which, on September 9, resolved to submit it to the First Session of the First NPC for final examination and adoption. On September 20, the 1,197 NPC delegates who had been elected during the preceding two months by the people's congresses of the various provinces and by other electoral units, including the armed forces, gave their unanimous approval to the document without proposing any changes whatsoever.

The Functions and Principles of the Constitution

Although it is the thought of Mao Tse-tung, rather than any legal document, that has been the principal determinant of the national life of Communist China, the Constitution nevertheless has performed, and may continue to perform, many of the usual functions of a national constitution. For example, it (1) legalizes the existing social order and sets forth its ideological principles, (2) establishes a formal structure of government, (3) prescribes certain basic rules governing social and institutional behavior, and (4) expresses the normative goals and aspirations of the state. Some of the ideological principles that find expression in the Constitution have since been fully implemented. Among them are the hegemony of the CCP in the state; the socialist transformation of industry, commerce, handicrafts, and agriculture; the nationalization of natural resources; and centralized economic planning.

Ideological principles and normative goals that have been only partially realized include the right to work; the right to assistance in old age, illness, or disability; the right to education; special attention to the physical and mental development of young people; the socialist industrialization of the country; and the economic and cultural development of the minority nationalities.

Among the rules governing social and institutional behavor are: (1) All organs of the state shall practice 'democratic centralism'; (2) discrimination against, or oppression of, any nationality is prohibited; (3) work is a matter of honor for every citizen able to work; (4) all organs of the state must adhere to the 'mass line'; (5) all state employees and citizens shall be loyal to the 'people's democratic system' and observe the Constitution and the law; (6) all treasonable and counterrevolutionary activities shall be suppressed and punished; (7) feudal landlords and bureaucratic capitalists shall reform themselves through labor and thereby become citizens who earn their livelihood by their own labor; (8) equality between men and women shall be established in all spheres; (9) citizens have the right to bring complaints against any person working in organs of the state for transgression of law or neglect of duty; (10) public property shall be held inviolable; (11) no one may use his personal property to the detriment of the public interest; and (12) all citizens shall, according to law, pay taxes, defend the homeland, and perform military service. The regime has endeavored to enforce these rules energetically.

Like the basic laws of many other lands, however, some principles of the Constitution merely express the political ideals and myths of the regime and therefore are not always in complete accord with reality. Among them are the assertions that 'the P.R.C. is a people's democratic state led by the working class and based on the alliance of workers and peasants,' that 'all power in the P.R.C. belongs to the people,' that 'the NPC is the highest organ of state power,' and that 'in administering justice the people's courts are independent, subject only to law.'

Another category of principles deals with 'the fundamental rights of citizens': the right of suffrage and eligibility for office; freedoms of speech, of the press, of association, and of assembly, processions and demonstrations; inviolability of the person and his home; privacy of correspondence; freedom in choosing residence and freedom of travel; freedom of religion; freedom of scientific, literary, and artistic expression. In accordance with Mao Tse-tung's theory on the people's democratic dictatorship, which calls for 'democracy' for 'the people' (consisting of workers, peasants, the petty bourgeoisie, and the national bourgeoisie) and 'dictatorship' over 'enemies' of the people (including landlords, 'bureaucratic capitalists,' and lackeys of foreign imperialism), the Constitution unequivocally states that the 'fundamental rights' are not to be enjoyed by all citizens regardless of their political convictions but only by those who support the sociopolitical system that the Constitution provides.

THE NATIONAL PEOPLE'S CONGRESS

The greater part of the Constitution deals with the organs of the state. Like the constitutions of other Communist-dominated states, which, following Lenin's teachings,[3] discard the principle of separation of powers in setting up organs of state power, the Chinese document designates a unicameral body—'the National People's Congress'—as the supreme organ of state authority.

Organization. The members of the NPC are elected indirectly by citizens of the People's Republic and overseas Chinese, in accordance with the procedure established by the electoral law. According to the electoral law promulgated on March 11, 1953, members of the First (1954–59), Second (1959–64), and Third (1964–present) congresses were elected not by the citizens directly but by the people's congresses of the provinces, of the municipalities directly under the central authority (Peking and Shanghai), as well as 'industrial municipalities' under provincial jurisdiction with a population exceeding 500,000, and of autonomous regions, and by the armed forces and Chinese residents abroad. There is no way of knowing the exact procedures used by the armed forces during the last three elections, but there have been indications that delegates supposedly representing Chinese residents abroad were designated each time by the regime 'in consultation with' returnees from Chinese communities overseas. According to Chinese Communist leaders, the indirect system is necessary so long as the mass of voters cannot be expected to have much familiarity with names and policies on a national scale; they indicate, however, that eventually all elections will become direct.[4]

The NPC term is four years, but it may prolong its own term, presumably indefinitely, until circumstances permit election of a new congress. In conformity with the general pattern of constitutions of Communist-dominated countries, members of the NPC are accountable to their respective constituencies, which have the right to recall their representatives at any time in the manner prescribed by law. In fact, after the 'Hundred Flowers' episode in 1957, the regime invoked this provision in dismissing many delegates to the NPC who had been stigmatized as 'rightists' for their unbridled criticism of the regime and its basic policies.

The sessions of the NPC are either regular or extraordinary and are convened by the NPC Standing Committee. Although the Congress is supposed to be convened in regular session once a year, since the early 1960's this requirement has not been met. The latest session was held in late December, 1964, and early January, 1965. No extraordinary session has been held up to this writing.

Powers and Functions. Designated as the 'highest organ of state power,' in theory at least, the NPC is to perform, in some cases by itself and in others through its Standing Committee, not only legislative functions but also constituent, executive, and judicial ones. Within the direct competence of the Congress fall the functions of (1) amending the Constitution; (2) enacting laws; (3) supervision of enforcement of the Constitu-

---

[3] Vladimir Ilyich Lenin, *State and Revolution* (New York: International Publishers, 1932), pp. 40–42.
[4] Teng Hsiao-p'ing, 'Kuan-yü Hsüan-chü-fa ti Chiai-shih (An Explanation of the Electoral Law),' *Jen-min Jih-pao,* March 3, 1953.

tion; (4) election of the chairman and vice-chairmen of the People's Republic; (5) appointing the premier on the nomination of the chairman of the People's Republic, and appointing the vice-premiers and other members of the State Council on the nomination of the premier; (6) appointing the vice-chairmen and members of the National Defense Council on the nomination of the chairman of the People's Republic; (7) election of the president of the Supreme People's Court; (8) appointing the procurator-general; (9) adopting national economic plans; (10) review and approval of the state budget and final accounts; (11) approval of the establishment of autonomous regions and municipalities directly under the central authority; (12) granting amnesty; (13) declaring war and peace; (14) dismissal of (a) the chairman and vice-chairmen of the People's Republic, (b) the premier, the vice-premiers, ministers, chairmen of the various commissions, and the secretary-general of the State Council, (c) the vice-chairmen and members of the National Defense Council, (d) the president of the Supreme People's Court, and (e) the procurator-general; and (15) other functions that the NPC may deem appropriate.

In reality, however, handicapped as it is by an unwieldy membership (the present Congress has more than 3,000 members) and by infrequent and brief sessions, the NPC, is in no position to exercise these powers, even had the CCP not taken into its hands the authority to make ultimate decisions. As the records of the Congress show, the actions of the assembled delegates were essentially formalistic: They heard reports on various phases of the work of the government, held discussions on programs of future action, gave approval to what had been done or was anticipated, and elected various state officials designated by the CCP top leadership 'in consultation with' the delegates themselves. Prior to the antirightist campaign in 1957, however, the regime did seem to have experimented with the idea of making the NPC a 'ventilating shaft' for the Chinese people by requiring members of the Congress to make tours of inspection in various parts of the country before attending each session of the Congress, by calling upon the public to file complaints with members and the secretariat of the NPC, and by encouraging members of the NPC to speak freely at sessions of the Congress on administrative shortcomings and inadequacies at various levels of government. This policy was gradually abandoned after the campaign.

A real use of the NPC is to focus the attention of the whole nation on the programs and policies unfolded at its meetings. Enthusiasm among the rank and file for the implementation of new programs and policies is whipped up by meetings of the Congress, which are usually held amid great fanfare with top leaders of the nation appearing in full force to add luster to the proceedings. Because the delegates are leaders or model workers in various fields, their close identification with the regime is apt to help strengthen the latter's hold on the nation. The regime has attempted to make ample use of membership in the NPC as a means of rewarding activists and soliciting popular support, as witness the fact that before the election of the Third NPC in 1964, the regime decided to make its membership more than twice as large as its two predecessors'.

The Standing Committee of the NPC. Operating under the NPC are several committees, dealing respectively with nationalities, bills, the state budget, credentials of members, and other matters. Although they operate even when the Congress itself is not in session, they have seldom done so in practice. The body that is intended to function regularly after the adjournment of the NPC is its Standing Committee, which consists of a chairman,[5] about a dozen vice-chairmen, a secretary-general, and more than sixty members. The Standing Committee is elected by the NPC and continues to serve until the Standing Committee of a new Congress is elected. The Standing Committee is theoretically responsible to the NPC, to which it submits reports on its work.

---

[5] Liu Shao-ch'i held this post from 1954 to 1959; it has since been held by Chu Te.

The NPC may recall the members of the Standing Committee even before the end of the term for which they have been elected.

Charged with conducting state affairs between sessions of the NPC, the Standing Committee has played a more important role than has the National People's Congress itself, not only in legislation but in executive, judicial, and administrative matters as well. Specifically, its functions are (1) to conduct the elections of the members of the NPC; (2) to convene the NPC; (3) to interpret the laws; (4) to issue decrees; (5) to supervise the work of the State Council, the Supreme People's Court, and the Supreme People's Procuratorate; (6) to annual decisions and orders of the State Council and of the people's councils at lower levels if they do not conform to the Constitution, the laws, or the Standing Committee's decrees; (7) to appoint and dismiss, during the NPC recess, the vice-premiers (but not the Premier of the State Council), the ministers, the chairmen of the various commissions of the State Council, and its secretary-general; (8) to appoint and dismiss the vice-presidents of the Supreme People's Court; (9) to appoint and dismiss the vice-procurators-general; (10) to appoint and dismiss diplomatic representatives; (11) to ratify and denounce international treaties of the People's Republic; (12) to establish military titles, diplomatic ranks, and other special titles; (13) to grant pardons; (14) to declare, in the intervals between sessions of the NPC, a state of war in the event of military attack on the state or, when necessary, to fulfill international treaty obligations concerning mutual defense against aggression; (15) to order general and partial mobilization; (16) to proclaim martial law in specific localities or throughout the nation; (17) to guide the proceedings of the various committees of the NPC when the NPC is not in session; and (18) to perform such other functions as the NPC may designate. In 1965, the NPC also authorized the Standing Committee to enact certain laws during any NPC recess.

Although the Standing Committee resembles the Presidium of the Supreme Soviet of the Soviet Union in many respects, there are some important differences between them. Under the Constitution of the Soviet Union, the president of the Presidium of the Supreme Soviet is technically the chief of state, over whose signature laws passed by the Supreme Soviet are published and who, on behalf of the Presidium, receives the credentials and letters of recall of diplomatic representatives accredited to the Presidium by foreign states. Under the Chinese Constitution, these functions are performed by the chairman of the People's Republic who, as mentioned before, is elected by the NPC, without necessarily being a member of the Standing Committee of the NPC. Second, the Presidium of the Supreme Soviet, at least theoretically, has the power to control the armed forces through appointing and removing the high command of the armed forces of the U.S.S.R., whereas, under the Chinese Constitution, the armed forces are commanded by the chairman of the People's Republic, who is concurrently the chairman of the National Defense Council, although, in reality, the Chinese armed forces are under the control of the Military Affairs Committee of the CCP Central Committee, headed by Mao Tse-tung, with Yeh Chien-ying as his principal deputy, since 1971. Third, the Presidium of the Supreme Soviet stands alone between the Supreme Soviet, 'the highest organ of state power,' and the Council of Ministers, 'the highest administrative and executive organ,' whereas under the Chinese Constitution, between the NPC and the State Council are, besides the Standing Committee of the NPC, the chairman of the People's Republic and the Supreme State Conference (whose composition and functions will be discussed below). This comparison does not imply, however, that the Standing Committee of the NPC is designed to play a less important role in the Chinese political system than the Presidium has played in the hierarchy of the U.S.S.R. In addition to the fact that the Standing Committee of the NPC has some powers that are not given to the Presidium by the Soviet Constitution of 1936, including the power to revise and annul inappropriate decisions of the provincial people's congresses, the role of the Standing

Committee in the formal exercise of legislative and supervisory powers has been enhanced by the fact that until the onset of the Cultural Revolution the Standing Committee normally met at least twice a month to hear reports from officials of the State Council and other agencies and to discuss and approve various measures submitted by the latter. Furthermore, since the adoption of the national Constitution the Standing Committee has been the principal agency where leaders of the 'democratic (noncommunist) parties' and independent personages take part more regularly in the apparatus of the state.[6]

THE CHAIRMAN OF THE PEOPLE'S REPUBLIC

The chairman of the People's Republic, as already noted, is elected by the NPC for a term of four years. Allowing for certain distinctions, the chairman of Communist China bears a general resemblance to the president under the constitution of Nationalist China. In neither case is the office designed for the actual ruler, nor is its holder simply a titular figure. While the Executive Yüan in the case of the Republic of China and the State Council in the case of Communist China are charged with 'the highest administrative and executive responsibilities,' the two constitutions give the president of Nationalist China and the chairman of Communist China, respectively, quite important roles to play. In both cases the office is that of a national leader, standing comparatively aloof from day-to-day administrative affairs and having the authority and prestige to play his part in state affairs of the highest importance. Specifically, the P.R.C. Constitution stipulates the following powers and functions for the chairman. First, he represents the Chinese nation in its foreign relations. In that capacity, he may receive diplomatic representatives from foreign countries and may, in pursuance of the decisions of the Standing Committee of the NPC, appoint and recall diplomatic representatives of China and ratify treaties with foreign countries. Internally, the chairman is charged with the duty of organizing the executive branch of the government. He is invested with the right to nominate the premier who, in turn, is to nominate members of the State Council. With the approval of either the NPC or its Standing Committee, he may formally appoint and dismiss these officials, promulgate laws and decrees, award orders and medals, confer titles of honor of the state, proclaim amnesty, grant pardons, proclaim martial law, proclaim a state of war, and order mobilization.

These, however, are not the most important powers stipulated for the chairman in the Constitution. What makes the chairman of the People's Republic a legally important figure in the government are the provisions of Articles 42 and 43. Under Article 42, the chairman is technically the commander-in-chief of the armed forces and the chairman of the National Defense Council. The chairman's position is further strengthened by the provisions of Article 43, according to which a Supreme State Conference, composed of the vice-chairmen of the People's Republic, the chairman of the Standing Committee of the NPC, the premier, and other officials, may, if necessary, be called by the chairman of the People's Republic into sessions to discuss, under the latter's chairmanship, important state affairs. The Conference's opinions are to be presented by the chairman to the NPC, or to its Standing Committee, or to the State Council, or to other agencies concerned, for consideration and decision. Thus the chairman may use the Supreme State Conference as an exalted forum to voice his views on important matters of state. Through this forum he may be better

---

[6] The 'democratic parties' are the Kuomintang Revolutionary Committee, the China Democratic League, the China Deomocratic National Construction Association, the China Association for Promoting Democracy, the Chinese Peasants and Workers Party, the China Chih Kung Party, the Chiu San Society, and the Taiwan Democratic Self-Government League.

able to influence the work of the various branches of government and to mold public opinion, *provided his views represent those of the top leadership of the CCP*. When Mao Tse-tung (September, 1954—April, 1959) and Liu Shao-ch'i (April, 1959—probable suspension from office in the fall of 1966)[7] were successively serving as chairman of the People's Republic, they actually made use of the more than twenty sessions of the Supreme State Conference for that purpose. For example, Mao's famous speech 'On the Correct Handling of Contradictions among the People' was delivered at a session of the Conference on February 27, 1957.

From September, 1954, to April, 1959, the chairman of the People's Republic was assisted by a vice-chairman, Marshal Chu Te. In April, 1959, the Second NPC decided to add another vice-chairman to the People's Republic, and elected Soong Ch'ing-ling (Madame Sun Yat-sen) and Tung Pi-wu (an elder statesman of the CCP) to the two vice-chairmanships, while transferring Chu Te to the chairmanship of the NPC Standing Committee. In December, 1964, the Third NPC re-elected them to their respective offices. The vice-chairmen are to act in the place of the chairman, if the latter is prevented by illness or other reasons from exercising his functions. Since late 1966, Tung Pi-wu and Soong Ch'ing-ling have been performing many of the ceremonial functions of the chairman of the People's Republic, though Tung appears more active than Soong, and since February 1972, Tung has been identified as the Acting Chairman of the P.R.C.

THE STATE COUNCIL

Organization. Aside from the executive functions performed by the Standing Committee of the NPC and by the chairman of the People's Republic, the 'highest executive and administrative organ of state power' is the State Council, which consists of the premier, the secretary-general, and a number of vice-premiers, ministers, and chairmen of commissions. The number in the last three categories is laid down by law or by decision of the NPC Standing Committee. With the approval of the Standing Committee, the State Council may establish a certain number of agencies directly subordinate to it for the purpose of handling special affairs but whose heads are not members of the State Council. Chou En-lai has occupied the premiership since its inception. Before the Cultural Revolution, there were as many as sixteen vice-premiers and more than forty ministers and chairmen of commissions. Like Premier Chou, most of the vice-premiers were concurrently members of the CCP Politburo. All but a few of the vice-premiers also headed ministries or commissions of the State Council. For example, Ch'en Yi was Minister of Foreign Affairs; Li Hsien-nien, Minister of Finance; and Lu Ting-i, Minister of Cultural Affairs. With the death of K'o Ch'ing-shih in 1965 and the purge of Teng Hsiao-p'ing, Ho Lung, Ulanfu, T'an Chen-lin, Po I-po, Lu Ting-i, Lo Jui-ch'ing, and T'ao Chu during the Cultural Revolution, there were in the spring of 1967 only seven vice-premiers: Lin Piao, Ch'en Yün, Ch'en Yi, Li Fu-ch'un, Li Hsien-nien, Nieh Jung-chen, and Hsieh Fu-chih. Since then the ranks of vice-premiers seem to have been further depleted. For more than three years, Nieh Jung-chen has not been officially identified as a vice-premier but as a vice-chairman of the CCP Military Affairs Commission. On January 6, 1972 Ch'en Yi died of cancer following several years of unsuccessful medical treat-

---

[7] The enlarged twelfth plenum of the CCP Eighth Central Committee, held in Peking in October, 1968, decided to expel Liu Shao-ch'i from the party 'once and for all' and to 'dismiss him from all posts inside and outside the Party.' Undoubtedly this decision affected Liu's chairmanship of the Republic, but his formal dismissal from that particular post still must be acted upon by the NPC if the constitutional procedure is to be adhered to. Be that as it may, the CCP Central Committee's decision was definitive and final for all practical purposes.

ment. In March, 1970, Hsieh Fu-chih was taken ill, and he passed away two years later. Although the official press continues to identify Ch'en Yün and Li Fu-ch'un as vice-premiers on infrequent ceremonial occasions, since 1968, it has not linked their names with other activities. This fact, coupled with their failure to be re-elected in April, 1969, to the new CCP Politburo, has led observers to believe that their present role in the State Council is essentially nominal. Even if Lin Piao never ceased to perform the functions of a vice-premier after his elevation in 1966 as Mao's principal deputy and potential successor in the CCP, his eclipse in the fall of 1971 unquestionably brought to an end all his political roles. Thus, the only one who still functions actively as a vice-premier is Li Hsien-nien.

Legally, the State Council reports to the NPC. Between NPC sessions, the State Council is accountable to the Standing Committee of the NPC. The premier presides over the meetings of the State Council and directs its work. The importance of the premiership has been greatly enhanced by the prestige and influence of Chou En-lai in the Party. The ministers and chairmen of the various commissions of the State Council direct their respective branches of the administration and, within the limits of the jurisdictions of their respective agencies, issue orders and instructions on the basis of the laws and decrees in operation and also of decisions and orders of the State Council.

Powers conferred upon the State Council as a whole are supposedly exercised by it in its collective capacity. According to its Organic Law,[8] the State Council is to make decisions at either a plenary session or an administrative session. Prior to the Cultural Revolution, a plenary session, composed of the premier, the vice-premiers, the ministers, the chairmen of the commissions, and the secretary-general, usually met at least twice a month. Since then, and as of May, 1972, no more such meetings have been reported. The administrative meetings, attended by the premier, the vice-premiers, and the secretary-general, have never been reported in the press. Nor has there been any information on the demarcation between the jurisdiction of the meetings and the plenary sessions. However, the composition of the administrative meetings seems to indicate that they are more important in the decision-making process than the plenary sessions. Those who attend the administrative sessions apparently constitute a steering committee of the State Council, resembling somewhat the informal inner circle of a British Cabinet.

In directing the various ministries and commissions, the State Council, in the years prior to the Cultural Revolution, relied heavily on six 'administrative offices': Foreign Affairs, Internal Affairs, Agriculture and Forestry, Industry and Communications, Finance and Trade, and Cultural and Educational Affairs. Headed in most cases by one of the vice-premiers, each of these 'staff agencies' actually supervised and coordinated the work of a number of the ministries and commissions on behalf of the State Council, although they were not officially defined as 'line agencies.' Because most of the vice-premiers in charge of the six offices were purged during the Cultural Revolution, it was not clear in the middle of 1972 whether the offices themselves were still functioning.

Powers and functions. Powers formally conferred upon the State Council include: (1) undertaking administrative measures in pursuance of the Constitution, the laws, and the decrees; (2) issuing orders, promulgating decisions and supervising the execution thereof; (3) proposing bills to the NPC or its Standing Committee; (4) coordinating and directing the work of all the ministries and commissions; (5) coordinating and directing the work of the local people's councils at all levels; (6) revising or annulling inappropriate orders and instructions of the ministers and the chairmen of the various

[8] An English text of the Organic Law of the State Council may be found in *Current Background*, No. 298, American Consulate General, Hong Kong, October 12, 1954, pp. 4–6.

commissions; (7) revising or annulling inappropriate decisions and orders of the local people's councils at all levels; (8) taking steps to carry out the national economic development plan and the budget; (9) regulating external and internal trade; (10) exercising general guidance in (a) cultural, educational, and health affairs, (b) affairs concerning the various nationalities, (c) affairs concerning overseas Chinese, and (d) foreign relations; (11) adopting measures for the protection of the interests of the state, the maintenance of public order, and the safeguarding of the rights of the citizens; (12) assuming leadership in building up the armed forces; (13) appointing and dismissing administrative officials in pursuance of the law; and (14) performing such other functions as the NPC and its Standing Committee may assign.

Despite this impressive list of powers and functions, the State Council is not intended to be a body capable of carrying out its own policies, for it is required by unwritten law and open injunctions to be extremely alert to the Chinese Communist Party line and its oscillations. Except for the premier and vice-premiers who take part in the deliberations of the highest councils of the CCP, members of the State Council appear to be merely high-level technical advisers and administrators—executors of the will of the Politburo of the ruling Party. They undoubtedly have plenty of opportunities to render expert advice, draw up initial plans, suggest policies that may be adopted, and administer their execution, but the definite word on all fundamental courses of action still lies with the central authority of the CCP, with Mao Tse-tung as the supreme leader.

LOCAL GOVERNMENT

Local administrative divisions. There are rather complicated local administrative divisions in the country even after the abolition of the six 'greater administrative regions,' which existed from 1949 to 1954 as an intermediate level of government between the central authorities in Peking and the more than twenty provinces and their equivalents.[9] The highest and largest local administrative areas now are the twenty-one provinces (*sheng*), five autonomous regions (*tzu-chih-ch'u*; Inner Mongolia, Sinkiang, Tibet, Ninghsia, and Kwangsi), and three municipalities directly under the central authority (*chih-hsia-shih*; Peking, Tientsin, and Shanghai).[10] The provinces and

---

[9] The six 'greater administrative regions' were established in 1949 to enable the new regime to achieve centralization of administration while taking regional peculiarities into consideration in handling day-to-day affairs. They were the Northeast region, the North China region, the East China region, the Central-South region, the Northwest region, and the Southwest region. Each region comprised several provinces, and the principal leaders in charge of them wielded enormous powers over Party, government, and military affairs in their respective areas. In many respects, the regional establishments became replicas of the Party, government, and military organs at the national level. This state of affairs soon gave rise to centrifugal tendencies. On November 15, 1952, the Central People's Government Council at its nineteenth meeting adopted a resolution calling for a reduction of the authority of the various regional governments. The measure, however, failed to check the trend of decentralization. At the fourth plenum of the CCP Seventh Central Committee, held in February, 1954, one of the most influential national leaders complained that some of those who were in charge of regional governments even regarded the region under their leadership as their 'personal property or independent kingdom.' Finally, on June 19, 1954, two months before the adoption of the national Constitution, a decision calling for the complete abolition of regional administrations was passed by the Central People's Government Council. Under the new Constitution the highest territorial-administrative subdivisions of the country are the provinces, the autonomous regions for minority nationalities, and a few municipalities directly under the central authority.

[10] The number of provinces and municipalities directly under the central authority have undergone several changes since 1949. So have their boundaries. For example, in 1949, there

the autonomous regions are, in turn, divided into either autonomous prefectures (*tzu-chih-chou*), counties (*hsien*), autonomous counties (*tzu-chih-hsien*), or else municipalities (*shih*). Under the counties and autonomous counties are the *hsiang* (an administrative area comprising several villages), the nationality *hsiang*, and the town (chen). The muncipalities directly under the central authority and the large ordinary municipalities have administrative subdivisions known as *ch'ü* (districts), whereas the autonomous prefectures are divided into counties, autonomous counties, or municipalities. The autonomous regions, autonomous prefectures, and autonomous counties are designed to enable national minorities to practice 'self-government' in areas where they are concentrated.[11] Thus, in some cases there are only two levels of government; in others four; and in most cases three.

Local People's Congresses. Except for the various autonomous bodies. the Constitution provides a uniform pattern of governmental arrangements for all local units ranging from town and *hsiang* to province and municipality directly under the central authority. In all cases, there is a people's congress and a people's council. The people's congress is made up of members chosen by the same organ at the next lower level, except at the lowest level of the administrative subdivisions. All congresses are elected for two years except the provincial, regional, and municipal (those directly under the central authority) people's congresses, which serve for a four-year term. Under a supplementary law enacted in 1954, local people's congresses at all levels except the lowest are normally to meet twice a year, and the people's congresses of the *hsiang*, nationality *hsiang*, and towns are to hold their sessions once every three months.

Designated as the local organs of state power, the local people's congresses at all levels are responsible for executing and observing all laws and decrees handed down from above; preparing and executing plans for local economic and cultural development and public works; approving local budgets and receiving reports on them; protecting public property; maintaining public order; and safeguarding the rights of citizens and the equal rights of the national minorities.

They are also entrusted with the power to issue orders in pursuance of existing laws and the decisions of the people's congresses of higher levels and to annul or revise inappropriate decisions and orders of the people's councils at their own levels. The people's congresses at the county level and upward have the additional right to elect and recall the presidents of the local people's courts at the same level and to revise or annul inappropriate decisions and orders of the people's congresses and councils of lower levels. Members of all people's congresses are accountable to the

---

were thirty-two provinces and four municipalities directly under the central authority and eleven municipalities under the supervision of regional governments. The present number of territorial-administrative subdivisions immediately under the national level is a result of a series of amalgamations, regrouping, and other developments in the ensuing years. Perhaps the most significant change was the establishment of the five autonomous regions: the Inner Mongolia Autonomous Region (first created in May, 1947, before the founding of the Peking regime itself, and then enlarged in 1954 and 1955), the Sinkiang Uigur Autonomous Region (created in 1955), the Kwangsi Chuang Autonomous Region (March, 1958), the Ninghsia Hui Autonomous Region (October, 1958); and the Tibet Autonomous Region (September, 1965). Although the Sinkiang Uigur Autonomous Region and the Kwangsi Chuang Autonomous Region were established simply by changing the legal status of the former provinces of Sinkiang and Kwangsi respectively, without altering their boundaries, the formation and enlargement of the other three regions entailed the dismemberment of several existing provinces. For example, the Inner Mongolia Autonomous Region today is made up of the former Suiyüan Province in its entirety plus large slices of territory from Liaoning and Heilungkiang and the now defunct provinces of Ninghsia and Jehol.

[11] For more information on Peking's policy toward national minorities, see Franklin W. Houn, *A Short History of Chinese Communism* (Englewood Cliffs, N.J.: Prentice-Hall, 1967), pp. 195–202.

bodies that have elected them and are subject to recall. As with the NPC, however, the real function of the local people's congresses is to engender a sense of involvement in public affairs on the part of political activists and the citizens in general.

Local people's councils. Designated as the executive branch of the local people's congresses as well as the local organs of state administration, the people's councils at every level are elected by, and responsible to, the respective local people's congresses and hold office for a like term; they may also be recalled at any time. Each of the provincial, county, and *hsiang* people's councils is headed by a provincial governor, a county magistrate, or a *hsiang* head, who is assisted by a number of vice-governors, vice-magistrates, or deputy *hsiang* heads, together with a large appointed staff organized into departments, bureaus, and sections.

The local people's councils are to carry out local administrative activities in accordance with the laws. Emphasis is placed upon their responsibility at all levels for the full execution of the decisions and orders of the superior congresses, councils, and central administrative organs of the state. In pursuance of the laws, they may make decisions and issue orders. People's councils at the county level and upward are, furthermore, given the authority and duty to direct the activities of the same organs at lower levels and to appoint and dismiss administrative officials. They are also accorded the right to suspend the execution of inappropriate decisions of the people's congresses of lower levels and to revise or annul inappropriate decisions and orders of their subordinate departments and of lower-level people's councils.

The local people's congresses and local people's councils have two common characteristics, so far as their status is concerned. The first is their dual responsibility to the local bodies that elect them and to the organs of state at higher levels. The second is their subordination at all times to the CCP local organizations at the corresponding levels, especially the first secretaries of such organizations, who also direct and oversee the local 'people's organizations' (such as urban residents' committees, trade unions, and women's federations) and the armed forces stationed in their respective territories. Although the local people's organizations are not a part of the formal governmental structure, they have been vital to both the government and the Party by assisting them in explaining official policies to individuals within their respective groups, in remolding the ideology of their members, and in rousing their members to collective action for the construction of a socialist new China. These organizations also serve as the regime's eyes and ears, reporting to it on the sentiments and behavior of their members and helping it in suppressing dissident elements.

Mention should be made, at this juncture, of the merger in 1958 of the *hsiang* people's governments with the newly established communes. As a result of the merger, communal membership meetings and communal management committees assumed the functions of the former *hsiang* people's congresses and councils. The merger was designed to simplify rural administration and to avoid overlapping of functions. However, since the reorganization of the communes in 1959, the authority of the communal membership meetings and communal management committees now differs only slightly from that of the former *hsiang* people's congresses and councils.

PEOPLE'S COURTS AND PEOPLE'S PROCURATORATES

People's courts. The Constitution provides for a Supreme People's Court, a series of local people's courts, and special people's courts. The local people's courts operate at three levels: higher people's courts, at the provincial level; basic-level people's courts, at the county level; and intermediate people's courts, sitting between them. The special people's courts are the military courts, railway transportation courts, and water transportation courts.

The president of the Supreme People's Court is elected for a four-year term of office by the NPC. The vice-presidents and judges of the Supreme People's Court are appointed and dismissed by the Standing Committe of the NPC. Presidents of the local people's courts are appointed and dismissed by the people's congresses of the corresponding levels, and the vice-presidents and judges of the various local people's courts of every level are appointed and dismissed by the corresponding people's councils. With the exception of the special courts, the system is composed of four tiers of courts with a judicial procedure permitting two trials.

As in the Soviet system, people's assessors sit with a collegium of judges of the court in cases tried for the first time, and they enjoy the same rights as the judges, while cases on appeal are reviewed by a collegium of judges only. All citizens who possess electoral rights and have reached the age of twenty-three are entitled to be elected as judges or people's assessors. Unlike the judges who work in the courts day in and day out, people's assessors perform their functions only on an *ad hoc* basis. The system of people's assessors is an application of the 'mass line,' which calls for popular partic-ipation in all phases of government work. In reality, there is a strong functional resemblance between people's assessors in a Communist state and jurors in an American or British court.

Although the Constitution states that judges at all levels are independent and subject only to the law, one of the important legal doctrines of the CCP obliges them to discharge their duties in the interest of socialism and the proletarian dictatorship.

The principle of 'control from the top' is applied to judicial procedures. The people's courts of higher levels are empowered to supervise the work of those of lower levels, while the highest organ, the Supreme People's Court, supervises all the local and special people's courts. In addition, the people's courts at the respective levels are accountable to the people's congresses of the corresponding levels.

People's procuratorates. The all-pervading supervisory authority of the state over public agencies and private citizens is also exercised through a system of 'procura-torates.' The chief organ in the hierarchy is the Supreme People's Procuratorate, charged with 'the highest supervision of the exact observance of all law by all agencies of the State Council and all local administrative organs of the state, as well as obser-vance by individuals holding official posts and also by citizens of the People's Repub-lic.' Each of the provinces, autonomous regions, and municipalities directly under the central authority also has a people's procuratorate, directly appointed by the Supreme People's Procuratorate for four years (subject to removal), and each of the counties, municipalities, autonomous prefectures, and autonomous counties has a similar office, to which members are appointed by either the provincial or the re-gional people's procuratorate with the approval of the Supreme People's Procura-torate at the top. The organs of prosecution at all levels perform their functions under responsibility only to the superior procuratorates and the Supreme People's Procura-torate; they are in no way dependent upon the local authorities at the various levels. Insofar as formality is concerned, the procurator-general of the People's Republic is accountable solely to the NPC, which elects him for a term of four years. In intervals between sessions of the NPC, he is supposedly accountable to the latter's Standing Committee. In reality, like all other key officials of the government, including the chairman of the People's Republic, the premier of the State Council, and the president of the Supreme People's Court, he is designated for the office by the CCP Politburo, which guides him in his work and may cause him to be removed or suspended.

Generally speaking, the courts and the procuratorates seem to have discharged their duties conscientiously and effectively. Unlike the people's tribunals (*jen-min fa-t'ing*) in the early years of the regime, which often meted out summary justice to 'landlords' and other 'counterrevolutionaries' in response to 'the demand of the masses,' most of the judicial personnel since the adoption of the Constitution in 1954 have demonstrated considerable professionalism in their work. Despite constitutional and doctrinal injunctions holding that the courts and the procuratorates are but parts of the apparatus of the proletarian dictatorship and therefore must perform their

232

functions from a class point of view, many of the judges and procurators in the decade preceding the Cultural Revolution actually differed very little in attitude and work style from their counterparts in a non-Communist country. Indeed, during the Cultural Revolution some Red Guard wall posters attacked such judicial personnel as well as 'those top party persons' overseeing the judicial organs such as Liu Shao-ch'i and P'eng Chen for enforcing a 'feudal, capitalist, and revisionist legal line.'[12] Among other things, they were accused of preaching the concepts that 'everyone is equal before law,' that 'justice must be administered independently,' and that 'cases must be adjudged solely on the basis of facts and law.'[13] They were also said to have clamored for 'strengthening the legal system' at the expense of the hegemony of the Party and the working class as a whole.[14] To Liu Shao-ch'i and P'eng Chen were attributed the principal responsibility for 'the wholesale adoption of the feudal, capitalist, and revisionist sets of lawyers and notary public system, legal procedure, judicial proceedings, etc.'[15]

Regardless of how the courts and the procuratorates have really functioned, their impact on the Chinese people appears to have been relatively limited. This stems in part from the fact that the judicial organs handle only a comparatively small percentage of all civil disputes. In keeping with the Chinese tradition, the Peking regime has endeavored to encourage settlement of such disputes by mediation. As a result, most private conflicts of a noncriminal nature are settled out of court, often through the good offices of the CCP basic-level secretaries, communal officials, or cadres of people's organizations, especially those of the urban residents' committees. Even in ordinary criminal cases and cases involving political offenses, the likelihood that the judicial organs will impose inordinately severe penalties is minimized by the Maoist precept that, except for the incorrigible, the preferable way of treating a wayward person is to remold him. Mao Tse-tung has characterized this policy as one of 'curing the disease to save the patient.'[16]

The Relationship Between the Government and the CCP

As has been noted, the governmental structure is largely formal, and therefore no description of it can adequately show how political power in Communist China is actually exercised. For a more realistic knowledge, one must examine further the relationship between the formal government and the controlling force behind it, the CCP.

In the first place, the CCP regards the formal governmental apparatus, along with the armed forces and the 'people's organizations' in various fields, as nothing more than necessary tools with which to maintain its hegemony, enact its programs and policies, and realize its ideals. In the meantime, the Party considers itself to be the leader and hard core of both the state and society.[17] As a Communist commentator has explained, the Party fulfills its paramount role in the state in at least five major ways.[18] First, it formulates all important policies to be executed by the government and guides the latter in its operations. Second, it trains and designates the personnel of the government at all levels, especially the more important ones. Third, it checks on the performance of the various governmental agencies and takes steps to rectify any short-

---

[12] 'Completely Smash the Feudal, Capitalist and Revisionist Legal Systems,' *Selections from China Mainland Magazines*, No. 625, American Consulate General, Hong Kong, September 3, 1968, pp. 23–28.

[13] *Ibid.*, p. 27.   [14] *Ibid.*, p. 23.   [15] *Ibid.*, pp. 23–25.

[16] Mao Tse-tung, *Selected Works*, 3 (Peking: Foreign Languages Press, 1965): 50.

[17] Houn, *Short History of Chinese Communism*, p. 77.

[18] Chou Fang, *Wo-kuo Kuo-chia ti Chi-kou* (*Our Nation's State Apparatus*), revised edition (Peking: China Youth Press, 1957), pp. 55–58.

comings and deviations that may occur. Fourth, it requires its members in the various governmental agencies to provide 'forceful and correct leadership' and make themselves shining examples for the non-Party personnel, so as to ensure the dynamism and proper functioning of the government as a whole. Finally, the Party gives immense assistance to the government in the implementation of massive social reform measures and nation-building programs by mobilizing popular support for them through its all-pervading propaganda and organizational networks. This working relationship between the CCP and the government has been greatly facilitated by two facts: The Party's pyramidal structure is nationwide, roughly resembling the territorial tiers of the administrative hierarchy of the government, and in many instances the device of interlocking leadership is employed. But the Party's most important instrument for controlling the various governmental agencies are the 'leading Party members' groups' within each agency.

However, the relationship between the Party and the government is more subtle than the above description indicates. For example, those who work primarily in the various governmental agencies are not always merely executors of the will of the Party. By recommending new policies, by drawing up concrete plans for carrying out the policies that the Party has decided upon, and by simply resorting to artful evasion, procrastination, or other devious means, many government officials often have ample opportunities to influence the Party's policy decisions at the outset or to subvert them in the course of execution, provided they do not openly and consistently violate the basic tenets of Mao Tse-tung's 'revolutionary line.'

The Cultural Revolution and the Governmental Apparatus

Although the governmental organs have their ways of influencing the Party, the fact remains that the government as a whole is subordinate to the CCP or, to be more accurate, to Mao Tse-tung and his thought. Perhaps nothing else better illustrates this point than does the Great Proletarian Cultural Revolution. To begin with, despite its broad dimensions and far-reaching consequences, the Cultural Revolution was launched by Mao without even going through the formality of securing a resolution of endorsement by the NPC or its Standing Committee, although he deemed it desirable to have the CCP Central Committee put a stamp of approval on the decision at a plenary session. More significantly, there is no indication whatsoever that the 'sanctity' of the Cultural Revolution was compromised in the minds of the Chinese people because of Mao's failure to seek a formal authorization from the 'highest organ of state power.' It is therefore clear that even the legitimizing role of the governmental apparatus in the current Chinese political system is not indispensable. Indeed, Mao himself has recently stated, in effect, that what really legitimizes his leadership is the support given to his ideals and programs by the overwhelming majority of the Chinese people. Publicized as one of his 'latest instructions,' Mao's illuminating statement deserves to be quoted in full:

> Who is it that gives us our power? It is the working class, the poor and lower-middle peasants, the laboring masses comprising over 90 per cent of the population. We represent the proletariat and the masses and have overthrown the enemies of the people, and therefore the people support us. Direct reliance on the revolutionary masses is a basic principle of the Communist Party.[19]

Second, the Cultural Revolution reveals Mao's enormous authority over the personnel of the government. Upon the unfolding of the movement, millions of Red Guards and 'revolutionary rebels,' ardently responding to Mao's call to 'criticize and

---

[19] 'Chairman Mao's Latest Instructions,' *Peking Review*, No. 43, October 25, 1968, p. 2.

repudiate those who have taken the capitalist road,' and allowing no constitutional or legal procedures to impede their struggle to 'defend Chairman Mao and his thought,' quickly set out to 'bombard' and 'drag out' from all governmental agencies (as well as Party organs) 'revisionists,' 'rightists,' and 'other anti-Party elements.' In addition to Liu Shao-ch'i and eight vice-premiers, references to whose cases have already been made, victims of this unprecedented drive to purge the government included the majority of the ministers and chairmen of commissions of the State Council, the President of the Supreme People's Court, the mayors of Peking and Shanghai, all but a handful of the provincial governors and vice-governors, and countless lesser officials throughout the country. Judging by the enthusiastic support that Mao apparently enjoys from various segments of the Chinese people, the latter seem to prize his leadership more than constitutional formalities. Because of his towering achievements during the Chinese revolution, Mao, in the eyes of his faithful followers, has become the source of all wisdom and the infallible guardian of the Party and the country.

Third, as the Cultural Revolution also directed its spearhead against 'revisionists' in the Party, the movement to seize power by the pro-Mao 'revolutionaries' in the Party and the government led to the scrapping of the Party-government duality below the national level in favor of a unified provisional organ known as the 'revolutionary committee,' which is composed of representatives of the 'revolutionary masses' (Red Guard and 'revolutionary rebel' organizations), the 'revolutionary cadres' of the abolished Party and government organs, and local units of the army, thus constituting the 'three-in-one-alliance.' The establishment of revolutionary committees at the provincial, county, and communal levels was an arduous and time-consuming task, necessitating the imposition in each locality of an interim military control commission, formal or otherwise. The task was completed at long last on September 5, 1968, with the inauguration of revolutionary committees in Sinkiang and Tibet.[20]

At the national level, the various governmental organs that were in existence on the eve of the Cultural Revolution have not been abolished thus far. As has been alluded to earlier, however, they have undergone drastic changes in personnel and operations. For example, several ministries of the State Council have been operating under the control of formal or de facto revolutionary committees, composed of 'revolutionary rebels' and army representatives. In response to Mao's call that the government should be reorganized so as to achieve 'better troops and simpler administration,' there have been reductions in the staffing of all state agencies and mergers of some ministries. One such merger occurred between two machine-building ministries. Another involved two light-industry ministries. Still another affected the Ministry of Agriculture and the Ministry of Forestry. Consolidation has also taken place between the Coal and Chemical Industry ministries and between the Ministry of Railways and the Ministry of Communications. There is also some evidence that the Ministry of Textile Industry has become a part of the new Ministry of Light Industry. As for the over-all direction of the day-to-day business of the entire government during the Cultural Revolution, the responsibility seems to have been given to Premier Chou En-lai, who not only has survived the political storm but appears to have gained in influence since 1967 as a result of the purge of many other veteran leaders of the Party and because of his great contributions to the Cultural Revolution. Indeed, he once was hailed in Red Guard posters as 'the Chief of Staff to Chairman Mao and Vice-Chairman Lin Piao.'

---

[20] For an official exposition of the functions and merits of the revolutionary committees, see Ting Hsüeh-lei, 'Revolutionary Committees Are Fine Indeed,' NCNA (in English), May 17, 1968.

THE NEW DRAFT CONSTITUTION

In the wake of all the changes mentioned above, the second plenum of the CCP Ninth Central Committee met in late August and early September, 1970. Before adjournment on September 6, it issued a communiqué, which, among other things, called for the convocation of the Fourth NPC 'at an appropriate time.' presumably to give constitutional sanctions to all the structural, operational, and personnel changes that had been made in the government during the Cultural Revolution and to introduce new ones. About two months later, on November 4, the Central News Agency in Taipei released the text of a new draft constitution for the People's Republic, which the Chinese Nationalist authorities asserted had been approved by the latest CCP plenum and was being circulated in mainland China for discussion by key cadres pending its final approval by the promised Fourth NPC.

Assuming its authenticity, the draft document consists of thirty articles in a little more than 3,400 words—a much shorter charter in comparison to the present Constitution, which contains 106 articles and 14,000 words. The draft's brevity is due mainly to the fact that it shuns more specific provisions concerning the powers and organization of various state organs as well as their mutual relations. Specifically, the draft devotes only ten articles to 'the state structure,' whereas the present Constitution deals with the same matter in as many as sixty-four articles. Despite the contrast, the draft stipulates essentially the same governmental structure as does the present Constitution, although it makes no mention of the Supreme State Conference and the National Defense Council. Marking a departure more in nomenclature than in substance, the draft refers to executive bodies of local government at various levels as 'local revolutionary committees' instead of 'local people's government councils,' as does the present Constitution. Like the local people's government councils before the Cultural Revolution, the local revolutionary committees are to be elected by the local people's congresses at the corresponding levels. As has been noted above, during the Cultural Revolution, local revolutionary committees were not formed in accordance with this procedure.

What really distinguish the draft from the present Constitution are its provisions that define the nature of the Chinese political system, that assign lifetime leadership roles in the state to Mao Tse-tung and Lin Piao, and that give clear and emphatic expression to Mao's thought in proclaiming fundamental national policies and in prescribing norms of social and institutional behavior. The serious disagreements that had developed between Mao and the 'revisionists' in the CCP over policies and norms in the years prior to the Cultural Revolution eventually promoted Mao to launch the Cultural Revolution against the revisionists and their policies.

Unlike the present Constitution, which defines the P.R.C. as a people's democratic state, because, at the time of its adoption, the socialist transformation of industry, commerce, and agriculture had yet to be carried out and the country was still in a period of transition from 'people's democratic dictatorship' to socialism, the draft, taking cognizance of the fact that the socialist transformation has long since been completed, characterizes the P.R.C. as a 'socialist state under the dictatorship of the proletariat, led by the working class (through the CCP) and based on the alliance of workers and peasants.' By describing the P.R.C. not simply as a socialist state but as one under the dictatorship of the proletariat, the draft obviously seeks to stress the Maoist line that the economic dethronement of the bourgeoisie does not mean the end of class struggle, that it is absolutely necessary to consolidate the dictatorship of the proletariat so as to carry through the socialist revolution and the socialist construction, and that the theory of 'the dying out of class struggle' and the clamor for the substitution of 'a state of the whole people' for a state under the dictatorship of the proletariat are nothing but subterfuges used by the bourgeoisie to prepare public opinion for the restoration of capitalism.

With regard to Mao's role in national affairs, the draft declares, 'Chairman Mao is the great leader of the people of all nationalities, head of state under the dictatorship of the proletariat, and supreme commander of the whole nation and the whole army.' The document describes Lin Piao as the 'close comrade-in-arms of, and successor to, Chairman Mao and deputy supreme commander of the whole nation and the whole army.' The assignment of pre-eminent roles in the state to the two men is a natural outgrowth of what has been provided in the CCP Constitution adopted in April, 1969. The present Constitution of the P.R.C., it is to be recalled, merely stipulates that the NPC shall elect the chairman and vice-chairmen of the P.R.C. and does not directly name specific persons to those posts.

Also in keeping with the new CCP Constitution, but in contrast to the present Constitution of the P.R.C., which makes no mention of Mao's thought, the draft proclaims that Mao's thought is the 'guiding principle of all work carried out by the people of the whole country.' 'The most fundamental rights and obligations of the citizens,' says the draft, 'are support of Chairman Mao and his close comrade-in-arms, Vice-Chairman Lin, support of the leadership of the Communist Party of China, support of the dictatorship of the proletariat, and support of the socialist system.' Prominence is also given to Mao's thought in other articles of the draft, especially those of Chapter I, which is entitled 'General Provisions.' Article X describes political work as the 'life-blood of all work' and calls upon the nation to 'grasp revolution, promote production, step up preparations for war, and develop the socialist economy in a planned and well-balanced manner so as to improve gradually the people's material and cultural life and consolidate the nation's security and independence.' Signifying a determination to continue Mao's fight against bureaucratism and to promote mass participation in government, Article XI of the draft enjoins 'all the personnel of the state organs and other organizations to study and use Mao's thought in a living way, to give prominence to politics of the proletariat, and to oppose bureaucratism.' It also states that all personnel must maintain close contact with workers and peasants and other laboring masses, must serve the people wholeheartedly, and must participate in collective labor. With regard to governmental organization, the principle of 'simple administration' is to be followed. The leading bodies of all state organs shall effect two three-in-one combinations. The first combination requires the presence of representatives of the masses, cadres of the state organs concerned, and representatives of the army. The second combination means that the leading body of each state organ must comprise 'old, middle-aged, and young people.'

Embodying Mao's cultural and literary policy, Article XII declares that the proletariat shall exercise all-round dictatorship over the bourgeoisie in the realm of the superstructure and that all cultural, educational, literary, artistic, and scientific activities must serve the political interests of the proletariat, stimulate production, and meet the needs of workers and peasants. Formally legitimizing some of the devices used during political campaigns, Article XIII describes 'big contending, big blooming, big debate, and big-character wall posters' as 'new tools of the popular masses for carrying on the socialist revolution,' and therefore guarantees their use by the masses with the objective of creating 'a lively political atmosphere that fosters democracy and centralism, combines discipline with freedom, and ensures unity of purpose while providing individuals with plenty of opportunities to express themselves freely.' Incorporating Mao's principles of army-building, Article XV states that 'the People's Liberation Army and the militia, composed of the sons of peasants and workers and led by the CCP, is not only a combat unit but also a working unit that engages in economic production and mass campaigns.' The military tasks of all the armed forces are 'defense of the socialist revolution, defense of the fruits of the socialist construction, defense of national sovereignty and security and territorial integrity, and defense against subversion and invasion by imperialism, social imperialism, and their lackeys.' The reference to 'social imperialism' as a possible source of external threat reflects Chinese leaders' continuing concern about Soviet intentions, though lately both Peking and Moscow seem to have shown a desire not to allow their ideological differences to 'hinder the two countries from maintaining and developing normal state relations.'

The draft's provisions concerning the people's communes should be of particular interest to many foreign observers who have thought that the eruption of the Cultural Revolution signaled, among other things, a Maoist attempt to seek a thoroughgoing overhaul of the rural communes by reviving those 'radical' measures that originally prevailed in those organizations in the late 1950's and that quickly 'made a mess of the Chinese countryside.' The draft is in keeping with Mao's policy enunciated at the very beginning of the Cultural Revolution, which, insofar as agriculture was concerned, sought to check further dilution of the socialist nature of the communes (as would be brought about by such measures as 'extension of the rural fairs, extension of the private plots, and even return to individual farming'). It does not rescind those necessary and fruitful changes in the communes' organization and operations that did not repudiate the socialist principle of income distribution and that were made during the period of 'economic readjustment' (late 1958–62) apparently with Mao's acquiescence, if not positive approval. Instead, the draft constitution reaffirms the principles that the communes shall 'generally adhere to the 'three-level ownership system,' with the lowest units or the production teams (above which are the communal management committees and production brigades) assuming the primary responsibility for organizing agricultural production,' that small private plots shall be preserved 'so long as they do not endanger the supremacy of the collective economy,' that members of the communes, like other citizens, shall be compensated according to their work, and that the state shall protect the citizen's right to his labor income, savings, house, and the means of life.

In conclusion, the proposed constitution is designed to consolidate and legalize the achievements of the Cultural Revolution. In the meantime, it provides an institutional framework and sets forth some of the most basic principles according to which China, during the lifetimes of Mao and Lin, will carry on the 'stupendous' task of industrialization and self-strengthening, while continuously remolding man and society. However, before this document can be formally adopted, at least its references to the question of succession in general and to the now politically eclipsed Lin Piao in particular will have to be amended

SELECTED BIBLIOGRAPHY

BARNETT, A. DOAK. *Cadres, Bureaucracy, and Political Power in Communist China*. New York: University Press, 1967. Based on information provided by Chinese refugees in Hong Kong, the book describes in detail the organization and operations of the government at the ministry, county, and village levels.

BARNETT, A. DOAK, ed. *Chinese Communist Politics in Action*. Seattle: University of Washington Press, 1969. Written by eleven scholars, the thirteen essays of this book deal with a great variety of subjects, including leadership characteristics and problems at the local level of the Party and government apparatus.

COHEN, JEROME ALAN. *The Criminal Process in the People's Republic of China, 1949–1963: An Introduction*. Cambridge, Mass.: Harvard University Press, 1968. With the bulk of its space devoted to translated texts of relevant documents, this book gives a competent description and analysis of the subject matter.

GINSBURGS, GEORGE, and ARTHUR STAHNKE. "The Genesis of the People's Procuratorate in Communist China, 1949–1951,' *The China Quarterly*, No. 20 (London: The Congress for Cultural Freedom), October–December, 1964, pp. 1–37.

——. 'The People's Procuratorate in Communist China: The Institution Ascendant, 1954–1957,' *The China Quarterly*, No. 34, April–June, 1968, pp. 82–132.

——. 'The People's Procuratorate in Communist China: The Period of Maturation, 1951–1954,' *The China Quarterly*, No. 25, October–December, 1965, pp. 53–91.

HOUN, FRANKLIN W. *A Short History of Chinese Communism*. Englewood Cliffs, N.J.: Prentice-Hall, 1967, Chapters VI, VII, and VIII. A concise and comprehensive survey of the Chinese Communist movement and the Peking regime today.

——. 'Communist China's New Constitution,' *The Western Political Quarterly*, 8 (Salt Lake City: University of Utah, June, 1955): 199–233.

LENG, SHAO-CHUAN. *Justice in Communist China*. Dobbs Ferry, N.Y.: Oceana Publications, 1967. A careful study of the legal institutions and procedures.

LEWIS, JOHN WILSON. *Major Doctrines of Communist China*. New York: W. W. Norton, 1964. Contains excerpts of official Chinese pronouncements on the basic principles of the political system in mainland China.

LIU SHAO-CH'I. 'Report on the Draft Constitution of the People's Republic of China,' *Current Background*, No. 294 (Hong Kong: American Consulate General), September 20, 1954, pp. 1–26. The most authoritative official statement on the background and contents of the Constitution.

MAO TSE-TUNG. 'On the People's Democratic Dictatorship,' in *Selected Works*, 4: 411–24. Peking: Foreign Languages Press, 1961. The most authoritative exposition of the theoretical foundation of the present Chinese political system.

SCHURMANN, FRANZ. *Ideology and Organization in Communist China*. Revised edition. Berkeley and Los Angeles: University of California Press, 1968. In the introductory chapters, the author provides a theoretical framework for understanding the Chinese Communist system, but fails to adhere to the framework in discussing various phases of that system in subsequent chapters. A much-praised book, marred by a number of factual errors.

STEINER, H. ARTHUR. 'Constitutionalism in Communist China,' *American Political Science Review*, 69 (Washington, D.C.: The American Political Science Association, March, 1955): 1–21. The article emphasizes the socio-economic programs stipulated in the Constitution.

TANG, PETER S. H., and JOAN M. MALONEY. *Communist China: The Domestic Scene, 1949–1967*. South Orange, N.J.: Seton Hall University Press, 1967, Chapter V. Discusses 'the political order and state apparatus' of mainland China.

TOWNSEND, JAMES R. *Political Participation in Communist China*. Berkeley: University of California Press, 1967. A detailed and systematic study of the evolution of the theory and practice of the CCP's mass line on political participation.

9

THE RULING ELITE

THOMAS J. WEISS

WITHIN the Chinese People's Republic at large, the ruling elite group is the Chinese Communist Party (CCP). Within the Party, the elite group is the Central Committee. Within the Central Committee, it is the Political Bureau (Politburo) of the Central Committee; and within the Politburo, it is the Standing Committee of the Politburo.[1] The incumbents within this Party hierarchy fill the most important positions within the Party's own executive apparatus, the state bureaucracy of the P.R.C., and the People's Liberation Army (PLA).

The Ninth Central Committee of the CCP was selected[2] by the Ninth National Party Congress in session, April 1–24, 1969. That congress, the first held since 1956 (a second session of the Eighth Congress was held in 1958), expanded the Central Committee from 97 full and 96 alternate members to 170 full and 109 alternate members. Of the 171 full and alternate members of the former (Eighth) Central Committee living at the time of the Ninth Congress, only 54 (31.6 per cent) were named to the Ninth Central Committee. Thus, more than 80 per cent of the full and alternate members of the much larger Ninth Central Committee were newly selected to that body in 1969.

The first plenum of the Ninth Central Committee on April 28, 1969, elected a Politburo of twenty-one full and four alternate members, including a five-man Standing Committee.

Not all members of the Central Committee, nor even of the Politburo, can, from an operational point of view, be considered part of the ruling elite. Some of the individuals on those bodies hold their positions more as an honor than as a responsibility

---

[1] For a discussion of the various usages and meanings of the term 'elite,' see Harold Lasswell, 'The Study of Political Elites,' in Lasswell and Daniel Lerner, eds., *World Revolutionary Elites* (Cambridge, Mass.: MIT Press, 1966), pp. 4–28.

[2] The method of selection was described as follows: 'In accordance with the rules laid down by the presidium of the congress, candidates for membership and alternate membership of the Central Committee were first nominated by the delegations freely. The presidium, after collecting the opinions of the delegations, proposed a preliminary list of candidates and handed it back to the delegations, and a list of candidates was worked out after full consultation. A preliminary selection by secret ballot was then conducted. After such repeated, full democratic consultation from below and from above, a final list of candidates was decided upon, and it was submitted by the presidium to the congress for final election by secret ballot. The process of the election of the Ninth Central Committee of the Chinese Communist Party was a full manifestation of the Party's democratic centralism and mass line.' 'Press Communiqué of the Secretariat of the Presidium of the Ninth National Congress of the Communist Party of China,' *Peking Review*, No. 18, April 30, 1969, p. 44.

and fill no important posts connected with the making or implementation of national policy. In functional terms, China's ruling elite consists of the organizational network of 'cadres' (*kan pu*). The cadre is an individual who fills any responsible position within the organizational apparatus of the Party, government, army, or local administrative units, at any level from the highest to the lowest. Those cadres who have leadership roles within their particular units of the organizational hierarchy are called 'leading cadres' (*ling-tao kan-pu*). Thus, the first secretary of a Party branch at the level of the production brigade and a member of the Politburo of the Central Committee are both leading cadres, one at the Party branch level and the other at the Central Committee level. Not all cadres in government and administrative organs are CCP members, but the most important positions at all levels are virtually monopolized by Party cadres, in order to assure complete Party control over the making and implementation of policy down to the grass roots level.[3]

Channels of social mobility in China have always been pre-eminently political. This is still true today; Party membership and status as a Party cadre, whether in a state, Party, or military organizational unit, are the obvious career goals for able and ambitious Chinese. The life of a Party cadre is in many respects not an enviable one, especially at the lower levels. It is characterized by long hours, hard work, incessant political indoctrination, slow promotion, frequent (temporary or even permanent) downward mobility, and vulnerability to political attacks. Cadre morale is a chronic problem for the regime. Nevertheless, there is no other career pattern that can hold promise of as many rewards as that of the Party cadre. Consequently, it is in many respects a simpler matter to discuss the ruling elite of Communist China than it would be to discuss that of Western and most other countries. There are no coexisting or competing informal 'power elites' based on wealth, birth, or tradition, or even, to any significant extent, on technical knowledge or expertise. This does not mean, of course, that there are no conflicting interests and perspectives within the ruling elite, but rather that all members of the elite, including high military commanders, are comprehended within a single organizational hierarchy, which has hitherto successfully maintained a complete monopoly of political power. Rival groups or individuals may compete for control of the Party, but no politically influential forces exist that the Party itself cannot control. Even the non-Party Red Guards during the Cultural Revolution, for instance, were politically powerful only while one section of the Party chose to use them as a weapon against another section. When Mao Tse-tung decided in the summer of 1968 that he had no further use for the Red Guards, they were quickly and forcefully suppressed.

THE CENTRAL PARTY ELITE

The top elite of the central Party organization in 1971 still consisted largely of a group of men who had been active and influential Party members at least since 1928 and frequently as early as 1921, when the Party was founded. They have dominated Party policy-making since 1935, when Mao Tse-tung achieved the paramount position within the Party that he has held ever since. They are predominantly from China's interior, especially from the South-Central provinces. (About 20 per cent of the original full members of the Ninth Central Committee elected in 1969 were natives of Mao's home province of Hunan.) Many of them lived abroad for a time when they were young, studying or working in either Japan, Europe (especially France), or the

---

[3] See the discussion of the meaning of 'cadre' in John W. Lewis, *Leadership in Communist China* (Ithaca, N.Y.: Cornell University Press, 1963), pp. 185–95, and A. Doak Barnett, *Cadres, Bureaucracy, and Political Power in Communist China* (New York: Columbia University Press, 1967), pp. 39–41.

Soviet Union. By the standards of an agrarian society, they are generally well educated, the majority having had some college, normal school, or professional training.[4] They typically had careers as political commissars, military commanders, labor organizers, or propagandists in the twenty-odd years before 1949.

Thus, for the past thirty-five years or so, Party and regime have been dominated by a group of men with a long history of shared or similar experiences and, in many cases, close personal relations. This is a very different situation from that in the Soviet Party and regime. In the Soviet Union, the 'Old Bolsheviks' who participated in the October Revolution in 1917 had largely been eliminated by Stalin before World War II began. They were supplanted by men who joined the Party after 1917, such as Khrushchev (who joined in 1919); later, leadership roles were assumed by men who reached maturity under the Soviet regime and who had risen in the aftermath of the purges of the late 1930's, such as Brezhnev and Kosygin. In China, there has been only a single generation of top leaders of the Communist Party and regime.

One of the most striking and most important manifestations of the great continuity of leadership since 1935 is that the average age of the top-level elite has tended to rise almost as rapidly as time itself has passed. The average age of the party Politburo in January, 1934, was approximately thirty-five.[5] Early in 1969, thirty-five years later, the average age of the ten active members of the Politburo of the Eighth Central Committee was about sixty-eight; Mao Tse-tung, at seventy-five, was the oldest, and Lin Piao, at sixty-one, the youngest. This fact is obviously of very great importance for the future of the regime and by itself accounts for much of the motivation behind the Great Proletarian Cultural Revolution, signs of which began in late 1965. The Politburo that emerged after the Ninth Congress was somewhat younger (see below); however, the average age of the five Standing Committee members was still sixty-eight.

Intra-elite cohesion and conflict. Before the Cultural Revolution, students of Chinese Communist affairs frequently observed that the top leadership of the CCP had for about thirty years displayed a high degree of cohesiveness and unity, which stood in striking contrast to the leadership of the Communist Party of the Soviet Union. It then appeared that there had been only one occasion on which an important Party figure attempted to conspire against or openly challenge the top authorities in the party. That was the case of Kao Kang, a Politburo member who allegedly tried to use his political base in Manchuria to form a conspiracy with Jao Shu-shih, organization department head in the Central Committee Secretariat, and other provincial leaders, hoping to replace Chou En-lai as head of the State Council of the P.R.C. Kao, Jao, and several lesser figures were officially expelled from the Party in 1955.

Evidence that became available after 1965, however, revealed much more about intra-Party conflict and rivalries, particularly since the failure of the Great Leap Forward in 1958. Red Guard newspapers and official news media accused Liu Shao-ch'i and others of having kicked Mao upstairs in April, 1959, by forcing him to relinquish the post of Chairman of People's Republic and accept honorary chairmanship. 'They treated me like a dead parent at a funeral,' Mao was reported as saying. Mao complained that thereafter he was 'never consulted' on important questions and that his

---

[4] An analysis of the age, geographical origins, education, and other social characteristics of the members of the Ninth Central Committee is contained in Jürgen Domes, 'The Ninth Central Committee in Statistical Perspective,' *Current Scene,* IX, 2 (February 7, 1971), 5–14; *cf.* data on the Eighth Central Committee in Chao, Kuo-chün 'Leadership in the CCP,' *Annals of the American Academy of Political and Social Science,* 321 (January, 1959), 40–50.

[5] Not all birth dates are known for certain: Robert C. North, 'Kuomintang and Chinese Communist Elites,' in Lasswell and Lerner, *World Revolutionary Elites,* p. 449, gives an average age of 35.2 for ten of the eleven known Politburo members in 1934.

expressed wishes were ignored.[6] Even more serious charges were made, particularly by Red Guard media, against P'eng Chen, Lo Jui-ch'ing, Lu Ting-i, Yang Shang-k'un and others. They were accused of various treasonable acts, including passing secret information to the Soviet Union and plotting (with several other high Party figures) to carry out a *coup d'état* against Mao in 1965–66. P'eng Te-huai, who had been dismissed from his position as Minister of National Defense in 1959 for his criticism of Mao's policies, was accused in 1967 of having been part of the Kao Kang and Jao Shu-shih 'anti-Party conspiracy.' Defense of P'eng Te-huai's views appears to have been a rallying point for Mao Tse-tung's opposition throughout the early 1960's. Many such charges are undoubtedly false and others greatly exaggerated or distorted, but the evidence is great that there is a strong current of truth in them. In any event, serious conflicts among the top leadership since 1958 are now undeniable.

Thus, in retrospect, the leadership of the Party was not as cohesive as it appeared to outsiders. The Cultural Revolution itself, of course, showed how precarious was the degree of unity that did exist. Despite all this, it remains remarkable that the Party leadership was able to contain the conflicts and rivalries within bounds for such a long period of time. The process of making and implementing decisions at the topmost level during that period appears to have incorporated a significant tolerance for dissent, conflict, and compromise. For example, although Mao complained that he had been deprived of real power in April, 1959, he was still able to secure the dismissal of P'eng Te-huai in August of that year and to replace P'eng with his own candidate, Lin Piao. On the other hand, P'eng, who had made himself Mao's enemy by his forthright criticism of Mao's policies, was not purged from the Party. The resolution censuring him said he would be allowed to retain his membership on the Central Committee and Politburo. Even during the Cultural Revolution, Mao, although not completely eschewing the use of force, could not—and perhaps had no desire to— carry out a bloody purge campaign. For more than a year after intense criticism and denunciation of Liu Shao-ch'i had begun, Liu continued to live in his official residence and to draw his regular salary. Although he was probably suspended from his functions in the fall of 1966, he was not explicitly removed from office until October, 1968. Before that time, the official media did not even refer to him by name when denouncing him, using instead the apellation 'China's Khrushchev.'

There are at least two reasons for such phenomena. The first is that secret police forces have always had an ambiguous status and power position within the Chinese Communist Party and regime. In Communist China there has been no single, unified, powerful secret police force comparable to the KGB and its predecessors in the Soviet Union or the Gestapo in Nazi Germany. Mao during the Cultural Revolution had no 'trusty hatchet' comparable to Stalin's in the purges of the 1930's. Police functions in the P.R.C. are primarily the responsibility of the public security forces, whose ministry was headed by Hsieh Fu-chih until his death in 1972. However, PLA and public security functions are not always distinct. For a time in 1967, the public security forces were put under PLA command. Also, Minister Hsieh himself sat on the Party Central Committee's Military Affairs Committee, the highest military authority in the nation. Intra-Party secret police functions were, until the Cultural Revolution, very likely performed by the Social Affairs Department of the Party Secretariat. Within the governmental apparatus, there is also the Ministry of Internal Affairs, which also appears to have secret police functions.

A second reason why the intra-leadership conflicts were relatively well contained for so long is that the Party's theory and practice since the early days of the Yenan period in the late 1930's have managed to routinize conflict resolution into a dialectically conceived process of 'struggle–criticism and self-criticism–transformation,'

---

[6] *The New York Times,* January 6, 1967, pp. 1–2.

in which a limited degree of conflicting opinion, or even tactical mistakes in conduct, are considered beneficial. Development is impossible without struggle, in the Chinese Communist view. The process is a blend of the textbook principles of democratic centralism and certain aspects of the thought of Mao Tse-tung, particularly his theory of contradiction and his emphasis on the importance of the Party's relationship to the masses. What is particularly important for elite unity, however, is that the process (in the form of accusations, confessions of error, and full or partial reinstatement) has been applied even at the highest levels of leadership, indicating that it is more than a cynically contrived method of control. Many Party leaders have at one time or another undergone such a process and been thus 'rehabilitated.'

The impact of the Cultural Revolution on the top elite. Within an over-all context of Party control, national political power before the Cultural Revolution flowed from three major sources: the Party apparatus, the army, and the state bureaucracy, in that order of importance. In the course of the Cultural Revolution, however, the political power of the Party as an institution declined drastically, even though the national ruling elite continued to be composed almost entirely of high-ranking Party members. The political power of the state bureaucracy also declined, from its already distinctly tertiary position. On the other hand, the PLA, having taken over many of the functions of the former Party apparatus and state bureaucracy, as well as performing the newly critical function of controlling domestic disorder, became a much more important source and locus of political power than before.

Finally, a new major source of political power arose, namely, propaganda in the form of manipulation of 'the thought of Mao Tse-tung,' the supreme symbol of political legitimacy in China. In itself, such propaganda is, of course, not new. But only in the Cultural Revolution did Mao's thought acquire its supremacy as a symbol of legitimacy; most important, control over it was divorced from the Party itself by Mao, who used it as a weapon to sanction and control mass political action and other forms of political attack against the Party and government apparatus at all levels, including the highest. This innovation was most dramatically expressed in the 'big character poster' which Mao wrote and displayed at the eleventh plenum of the Eighth Central Committee in August, 1966. It read, 'Bombard the Headquarters!'— meaning the Party headquarters, up to then the locus of supreme political authority. Thus, the most important effects of the Cultural Revolution on the composition of the top national elite could be summarized as gains in the power of specialists in violence and symbol manipulation at the expense of specialists in organization.

One result of the changes in the source of power was the decline in the importance of the Politburo as an institution. One might even say that the Politburo lost its identity between late 1966 and early 1969, when it became impossible for China-watchers to tell whether membership in the Politburo was the criterion of membership in the top power elite or vice-versa. In official and unofficial media during that time, the highest authority referred to was that of the 'proletarian headquarters headed by Chairman Mao, with Vice-Chairman Lin [Piao] as his deputy.' Although the power of the top handful of Politburo figures grew or remained stable during the Cultural Revolution, some non-Politburo figures, by virtue of their importance in military and propaganda work and the special trust Mao had in their loyalty to him, played political roles of equal importance to, or greater importance than, those of most members of the Politburo, even those who had survived the Cultural Revolution. This fact is suggested by a comparison of the National Day rostrum lineups for October 1, 1966 (the first year such extensive name lists appeared in the press), and those for subsequent National Day celebrations. In reports of the 1966 National Day celebrations, twenty-one of the first twenty-two names of 'leaders of the Party and the state' listed after Mao Tse-tung and Lin Piao as present on the rostrum were members of the Politburo (the exception was Soong Ch'ing-ling, Sun Yat-sen's widow). In reports of the 1968 National Day celebrations, the New China News Agency mentioned twelve men and women immediately after Mao and Lin, only four of whom (Chou En-lai, Ch'en Po-ta, K'ang Sheng, and Hsieh Fu-chih) were Politburo members. Seven of the remaining eight became Politburo members at the 1969 Party Congress (the exception was Wen Yü-ch'eng, a deputy Chief of Staff of the PLA). At National Day celebrations in 1969 and 1970, the restored pre-eminent status of the Politburo was reflected in the fact that all of its members present were given pride of place after Mao and Lin. However, a continuing high attrition rate among the Politburo after 1969 again made its institutional status questionable.

THE POLITBURO OF THE NINTH CENTRAL COMMITTEE

The members of the Politburo of the Ninth Central Committee selected in 1969 were:

Standing Committee	Other Full Members	Alternate Members
Mao Tse-tung	Hsieh Fu-chih	Li Hsüeh-feng
Lin Piao	Li Hsien-nien	Wang Tung-hsing
Chou En-lai	Yeh Chien-ying	Li Te-sheng
Ch'en Po-ta	Chiang Ch'ing	Chi Teng-k'uei
K'ang Sheng	Chang Ch'un-ch'iao	
	Yao Wen-yüan	
	Huang Yung-sheng	
	Wu Fa-hsien	
	Li Tso-p'eng	
	Ch'iu Hui-tso	
	Ch'en Hsi-lien	
	Hsü Shih-yu ˙	
	Yeh Ch'ün	
	Chu Te	
	Tung Pi-wu	
	Liu Po-ch'eng	

All five members of the Standing Committee, plus Li Hsien-nien, Yeh Chien-ying, and Hsieh Fu-chih, were carryovers from the previous Politburo. Chiang Ch'ing, Chang Ch'un-ch'iao, and Yao Wen-yüan are propaganda specialists. Those on the above list from Huang Yung-sheng through Hsü Shih-yu are, or were, leading figures in the central or regional apparatus of the PLA. Chu Te, Tung Pi-wu, and Liu Po-ch'eng are aged and infirm heroes of the revolution. They, along with Yeh Ch'ün, Lin Piao's wife, appear to have been selected for the Politburo largely for ceremonial and honorific reasons.

Excluding the four known inactive Politburo members, the average age of the seventeen other Politburo members whose age is known was about sixty-four at the time of their selection by the Ninth Congress in 1969. The four of unknown age are very likely somewhat younger than the average. The oldest active member of the Politburo is Mao, and the youngest is Yao Wen-yüan, who is probably in his early forties.

Even after the 1969 Congress, however, the top leadership of the Party continued to suffer a fairly rapid turnover. By mid-1972, political conflicts, as well as illness (K'ang Sheng) and death (Hsieh Fu-chih), had reduced the active Politburo members from 21 to the following 12:

Standing Committee	*Other Full Members*	*Alternates*
Mao Tse-tung	Li Hsien-nien	Wang Tung-hsing
Chou En-lai	Yeh Chien-ying	Li Te-sheng
	Chiang Ch'ing	Ch Teng-k'uei
	Chang Ch'un-ch'iao	
	Yao Wen-yüan	
	Ch'en Hsi-lien	
	Hsü Shih-yu	

The most spectacular political casualty of the post-Congress period was Lin Piao. The circumstances surrounding Lin's sudden fall from power were not known to outsiders in 1972, but the climactic events clearly took place in September, 1971. In the middle of that month, preparations for the annual October 1 National Day parade in Peking were halted and the parade itself cancelled. All aircraft in China were grounded for several days. Soviet sources reported the crash deep in Mongolia of a Chinese military aircraft the night of September 13 and said that nine charred bodies had been recovered from the wreckage. Some believed that Lin Piao, who had not been seen in public since June, was aboard this plane, attempting flight to the Soviet Union after a coup attempt against Mao. No further references were made to Lin by the national press and radio (the last mention of his name by a provincial broadcast was October 8). Pictures of Lin and works by him were removed from display in stores and public places.

With Lin disappeared several of the high officials of the central PLA apparatus who had been newly appointed to the Politburo: Huang Yung-sheng, PLA Chief of Staff since 1968; Wu Fa-hsien, Commander of the PLA Air Force; Li Tso-p'eng, Political Commissar of the PLA Navy; and Ch'iu Hui-tso, Director of the PLA General Rear Services Department. Wu, Li, and Ch'iu are known to have had fairly close ties with Lin, under whom they had served before Lin became Minister of National Defense. Huang, who had been Commander of the Canton Military Region from 1956 to 1968, was less closely identified with Lin and was thought to have more in common with the veteran regional, as opposed to central, military authorities. One theory was that the fall of Lin and Huang may have been the outcome of a clash between Mao and the regional military commanders who counted Huang as one of their number and who found Lin's prospective succession to Mao unacceptable.[7]

After the fall of Lin, the regime began to emphasize the removal of the PLA from the wide variety of nonmilitary tasks it had undertaken in the course of the Cultural Revolution. Whereas for years the people had been exhorted to 'learn from the PLA,' the PLA was now exhorted to 'modestly learn from the people throughout the country.'[8]

The remaining important Politburo member to fall from power after the Congress was Ch'en Po-ta. Ch'en had been Mao's political secretary and writer since Yenan days and had long edited *Red Flag*, the Party's theoretical journal. Ch'en had come under a cloud during the Cultural Revolution for backing the May 16 group of ultra-leftists, among whom was Ch'i Pen-yü, Ch'en's protégé on the *Red Flag* staff; this group was purged in 1967 for stirring up mass criticisms of the army and of Chou En-lai. Ch'en was not seen in public after April, 1970, and subsequently was the target of indirect and allegorical criticism for errors of line in the past.

Brief biographical details are given below for each of the recently active members of the Politburo.

---

[7] See Simon Leys, 'Downfall of a Trusting Zealot,' *Far Eastern Economic Review* (February 26, 1972), p. 20.

[8] *Peoples Daily*, January 4, 1972, p. 1.

Standing Committee. Mao Tse-tung, Chairman of the CCP, and until 1959 Chairman of the P.R.C. and of the Party's Military Affairs Committee, stands at the apex of the power hierarchy.[9] Born December 26, 1893, in Hsiang-t'an County, Hunan Province, he was educated in Changsha, where he completed normal school. In 1918 he went to Peking, where he worked as a librarian's assistant at Peking University. He was present at the founding congress of the CCP in 1921. From 1927 on, Mao led rural-based armed forces in civil war with the Kuomintang, while attempting to set up rural soviets. During that time, however, the CCP headquarters in Shanghai was giving priority to promoting revolution in the urban areas. In January, 1935, while on the Long March from Fukien to Shensi, the CCP leaders held a conference in the town of Tsuni, Kweichow Province, where they elected Mao Politburo Chairman. Since that time, he has held the supreme position within the Party uninterruptedly. Between late 1935, when the Communists arrived in Northwest China, and 1945 (the so-called Yenan period) Mao and the other top CCP leaders developed the theory and style of work that shaped the policy not only of the wartime CCP but also of the P.R.C. in the years after 1949. Mao was succeeded as Chairman of the P.R.C. by Liu Shao-ch'i in 1959, and it was then thought that Liu would ultimately succeed to Mao's Party position as well. In the period from 1959 to 1965, Mao's political power ebbed in the aftermath of the ill-fated Great Leap Forward, while that of Liu reached its apex. During the Cultural Revolution, Mao very skillfully caused all of his opponents among the top Party leadership to be deprived of political power. The chief target was Liu Shao-ch'i. For decades, Mao has from time to time been rumored dead, ill, incapable, or the captive tool of other leaders, most recently Chiang Ch'ing or Lin Piao. On one occasion in 1930, the Comintern organ *Inprecor* even printed his obituary. None of these rumors or theories has ever been verified, and most were later proved wrong. Mao is known to have been abroad only twice, visiting Moscow for negotiations in 1949 and 1957.

Mao's so-called closest comrade-in-arms until 1971, *Lin Piao,* was born in 1907 in Hupei Province. Until his fall, he was Vice-Chairman of the CCP Central Committee; member of the Standing Committee of the Politburo; *de facto* (if not *ex officio*) Chairman of the Military Affairs Committee; and Minister of National Defense. He was the sole Vice-Chairman of the Central Committee; the former four other vice-chairmen (Liu Shao-ch'i, Chou En-lai, Chu Te, Ch'en Yün) lost their positions in 1966. He was elected to the Politburo Standing Committee in 1958; his Military Affairs Committee and ministerial posts dated from 1959, when he succeeded Defense Minister P'eng Te-huai. Lin, most sources agree, was the first commander of the Chinese forces in the Korean War, during their period of greatest success against the Allied forces. In 1955 he was named one of ten Marshals of the PLA (a title that has since, along with all military ranks, been abolished). During the 1950's Lin was absent from public view for long periods and was widely believed to be seriously ill. After 1959, however, he became much more active, promoting a massive campaign within the PLA for the study, propagation, and application of the thought of Mao Tse-tung. In 1963 the campaign was held up as a model for all Chinese society, which was urged to 'learn from the PLA.' After the eleventh plenum of the Eighth Central Committee in 1966, Lin was accorded prominence and precedence second only to Mao. Thereafter, official sources gradually began to refer to him as Mao's 'best successor'; he was specifically given that status in the new constitution of the CCP. Until Lin's abrupt fall from power in 1971, his wife, Yeh Ch'ün, was also accorded

---

[9] Only brief details will be given in this and the biographical notes to follow. For more extensive biographical information on most of these figures, see the sources listed in the bibliography. For Mao Tse-tung, the most important are the works by Snow, Schram, Ch'en, and Rue.

high public status; in 1967 she was made a member of the PLA Cultural Revolution Group, and in 1969 elected to the Politburo.

Premier of the P.R.C. State Council, *Chou En-lai* was the highest official of the People's Republic active from 1966 to 1971, while the chairmanship of the P.R.C. was vacant. Born in Chekiang in 1899, he grew up in Kiangsu, which is usually regarded as his home province. He studied in Japan during World War I and in 1920 went to France under the work-study plan. He was one of the founders of the Paris branch of the CCP in 1921. After residing in France, Germany, and England, he returned to China in 1924. During the period of Kuomintang-CCP collaboration, 1924–27, he held various positions under the Kuomintang, including that of Acting Director of the Political Department at the Whampoa Military Academy. Throughout his subsequent career, Chou has functioned as a diplomat, negotiator, and liaison man, with the Kuomintang and Soviet Union before 1949, and with other countries thereafter. He has been a Politburo member continuously since 1927, a longer period than Mao himself. Premier of the State Council since 1949, Chou was concurrently Minister of Foreign Affairs from 1949 until 1958. During the Cultural Revolution, Chou became, after Mao and Lin Piao, the third most powerful man in Peking's power hierarchy. Chou is generally regarded as having been the consistent advocate of a relatively 'moderate' course during the Cultural Revolution. Unconfirmed Hong Kong reports[10] said that it was he who opposed criticizing Liu Shao-ch'i by name in the official media. (As mentioned above, Liu was always referred to as 'China's Khrushchev' until October, 1968, when he began to be denounced by name). Chou also frequently used his influence to protect various members of the top elite from criticism campaigns, particularly those reponsible for state bureaucratic functions. He even publicly defended T'an Chen-lin, former Politburo member and agricultural minister, who was accused of being the 'ringleader' of the high officials who had tried to 'reverse the verdict' on Liu Shao-ch'i, shortly before T'an was purged in the summer of 1967. In turn, Mao himself has protected Chou from criticism by extreme leftists, such as by ordering the purge of the May 16 Corps, a group of leftists within the Cultural Revolution Group who in 1967 began to instigate propaganda attacks against Chou and some PLA leaders.

Ch'en Po-ta was born in 1904 in Fukien. Joining the Party in 1927, he studied in Moscow and became a professor at China College in Peking in 1931. Going to Yenan in 1937, he became Mao Tse-tung's political secretary. He became an alternate member of the Politburo in 1956, and a member of the Politburo Standing Committee in 1966. He has been chief editor of *Red Flag*, the Central Committee's theoretical organ, since its founding in 1958. However, it is doubtful that Ch'en has served in that capacity since the Cultural Revolution began and his responsibilities were greatly increased. (The *Red Flag* post appears to have been Ch'i Pen-yü's until he was purged in early 1968.) Ch'en, personally very unprepossessing, is a prolific writer and probably has penned much of the 'thought of Mao Tse-tung' in recent years. He is probably the author of many of the so-called 'joint editorials' attributed to the editorial departments of *People's Daily*, *Red Flag*, and *Liberation Army Daily*. During the Cultural Revolution, he bore the chief responsibility for direction of the campaigns of criticism and repudiation and the selection of targeted individuals. In this capacity he worked most closely with K'ang Sheng and Chiang Ch'ing. Despite his closeness to Mao, he apparently lost his standing in 1970; he did not appear in public after August 1 of that year.

---

[10] *Star*, Hong Kong, April 7, 1967.

K'ang Sheng was born about 1903 in Shantung and joined the Party in 1924 or 1925. He spent several years in the Soviet Union in the 1930's and, upon his return to China in 1937, became director of the Social Affairs Department and the Central Intelligence Department of the Central Committee. He first became a Politburo member in 1945, was demoted to alternate member in 1956, and was again promoted in 1966, this time to the Politburo Standing Committee. At present he is responsible for relations with other Communist Parties and groups throughout the world. K'ang was one of Mao's top lieutenants in the execution of the 1942–44 Party rectification campaign and performed a similar function throughout the Cultural Revolution. He was one of the original five members of the Cultural Revolution Group under P'eng Chen in 1965 and early 1966. He managed to dissociate himself from the February, 1966, outline program for the Cultural Revolution, which this group circulated and which was condemned in May of that year as anti-Maoist. According to Soviet sources, he headed a ten-man Party Rectification and Reconstruction Group at the close of the Cultural Revolution; he had chief responsibility for deciding which high-level cadres should be reinstated, or 'liberated,' in the wake of the Cultural Revolution.

Other Full Members. Born in 1905 in Hupei, *Li Hsien-nien*, is the only member of the present Politburo whose responsibilities lie primarily in the areas of finance and economic planning. Joining the Party in 1927, Li became a guerrilla leader and later an important military commander. His posts after 1949, however, were civilian. He has been Minister of Finance since 1954, and is a vice-chairman of the State Planning Council and a vice-premier of the State Council. He is reputed to have opposed Maoist economic policies on several occasions since the Great Leap Forward in 1958. Li usually participates in international negotiations regarding economic and trade treaties and agreements. He has been a Politburo member since 1956.

Yeh Chien-ying, born in Kwangtung in 1897, is a member of the Standing Committee of the Military Affairs Committee and a former PLA Marshal. An instructor at the Whampoa Military Academy, Yeh joined the Party in 1924 or 1927. He spent 1929–32 studying and traveling in the Soviet Union and Europe. He participated in the Long March and was one of Mao's important supporters in his split with Chang Kuo-t'ao in 1935. Yeh has held a wide variety of military and civilian posts, including PLA Chief of Staff and Mayor of Peking. In the 1930's and 1940's, he worked particularly closely with Chou En-lai; like Chou, he is known for his skill as a negotiator. Yeh's status rose dramatically during the Cultural Revolution. A Central Committee member since 1945, he was raised to the Politburo in August, 1966. After the fall of Lin Piao and Huang Yung-sheng in 1971, Yeh appeared in public very frequently as the highest-ranking officer of the PLA, third in the active Party hierarchy, after Chou En-lai. A Hakka, Yeh is the only member of a minority nationality among the Politburo.

Mao's third and current wife (excluding a childhood bride with whom Mao never lived), *Chiang Ch'ing* was born in Shantung *circa* 1910–15. A minor film actress in Shanghai in the 1930's, she went to Yenan in 1939, where she soon became romantically involved with Mao. Party leaders were reluctant to approve Mao's marriage to her and to admit Chiang Ch'ing to the Party, but some important figures supported her cause, including K'ang Sheng and Li Ta-chang, now a vice-chairman of the Szechwan Province Revolutionary Committee. Among those said to have opposed her at that time was Liu Shao-ch'i, whom Chiang Ch'ing during the Cultural Revolution was most vigorous in denouncing. In the early 1960's she became politically active as an apostle of Maoist ideological purity in the performing arts; her centers of activity were the Shanghai performing arts groups and the PLA cultural units. In 1966 she began to take a much more prominent role, becoming a chief supporter of the Red Guard movement, 'adviser' to the PLA Cultural Revolution Group, and Deputy Director of the Cultural Revolution Group of the Central Committee. She was not even a member of the Eighth Central Committee, however. Her power and influence since 1966 has been less constant than that of Ch'en Po-ta and K'ang Sheng. During the periods of leftist extremism and violence during the Cultural Revolution she was frequently described by China-watchers as a possible latter-day empress. She became far less prominent during periods of relative moderation and consolidation. After the Red Guard movement fell into disfavor with Mao in the late summer of 1968, Chiang Ch'ing's power appeared to have waned considerably. One clear hint of her subsequent lower status was the great amount of public attention paid in November, 1968, to the anniversary of the execution of Mao's first wife, Yang K'ai-hui, who was killed in 1930 by a Kuomintang warlord. A commemorative poem by Mao himself was published for the occasion.

Born probably between 1905 and 1910, *Chang Ch'un-ch'iao* has had a long career in the Shanghai propaganda apparatus. Since 1949 he has been a New China News Agency executive in Shanghai, as well as managing director of the Shanghai *Liberation Daily*, and has held the posts of Director of the Propaganda Department and Secretary of the Secretariat within the Shanghai Municipal Party Committee. When Chiang Ch'ing was active in promoting ideological reform of the performing arts in 1963–64, Chang Ch'un-ch'iao gave her the support and cooperation in Shanghai that the Party authorities in Peking did not extend to her. Throughout the Cultural Revolution, Chang was the top reliable ally of Mao in Shanghai. A deputy director of the Cultural Revolution Group, he became Chairman of the newly-formed Shanghai Municipal Revolutionary Committee in February, 1967. His management of the serious threat to Maoist control over Shanghai in early 1967, when the short-lived, faction-ridden Shanghai People's Commune was proclaimed, reportedly won Mao's deep personal gratitude. Shanghai was the base from which Mao launched his attack on the Party apparatus in Peking in 1965; throughout the Cultural Revolution, the Shanghai propaganda apparatus continued to serve as the most reliable vehicle for the propagation of the central Maoist line. Thus, Chang's great influence in the Shanghai region is of more than parochial interest to Mao and makes Chang *de facto* part of the national policy-making elite. Chang became head of the newly reconstructed Shanghai Municipal Party Committee in December, 1970.

The epitome of the newly-important propaganda specialist, *Yao Wen-yüan* is the youngest member of the top elite, probably born around 1928 or 1929. He appears to have risen to prominence almost completely on the strength of his pen, which for some years has been vigorously employed in the defense of Mao's political line. Some sources have reported, however, that Yao is also Mao Tse-tung's son-in-law. Since 1955, Yao has written articles of criticism against writers and intellectuals accused of being rightist or bourgeois. Yao, too, has worked from within the Shanghai literary and propaganda apparatus and has close contacts with both Chang Ch'un-ch'iao and Chiang Ch'ing. His article attacking the play *Hai Jui's Dismissal from Office* (see Chapter 29) and its promoters within the Peking Party apparatus, published in the Shanghai press in late November, 1965, signaled the beginning of the Cultural Revolution. In 1967 and 1968 he also began to take part in international Party and government liaison work; he led a delegation of Red Guards to Albania in 1967 and has often appeared in pictures of receptions of foreign Communist leaders along with Mao, Ch'en Po-ta, K'ang Sheng, and Chou En-lai. He is also a leading member of the Shanghai Municipal Revolutionary Committee and Party Committee. Yao has written at least four books, including a biography of Lu Hsün.

Born in Hupei in 1910 or 1913, *Ch'en Hsi-lien* is the Chairman of the Liaoning Province Revolutionary Committee, First Secretary of the provincial Party Committee, and Commander of the Shenyang Military Area, a post he has held since 1959. Ch'en's Communist activities date from 1926, when he was a member of a children's arson brigade in his native province. He became an important military commander in the 1940's, serving under Liu Po-ch'eng, and later commanded an army corps in Korea.

Born in Honan in 1906, *Hsü Shih-yu* is Chairman of the Kiangsu Province Revolutionary Committee, First Secretary of the Provincial Party Committee, and Commander of the Nanking Military Area. He served as an army commander in the former Third Field Army under Ch'en Yi. Although he has previously held no civilian posts, he appears to be well connected with the top civilian Party leaders around Mao, particularly K'ang Sheng; they defended him against attacks by radical mass organizations during the Cultural Revolution.

Alternate Members. Wang Tung-hsing is a relative newcomer to the top elite. His early career is unknown. He has a history of public security work since 1949, and since 1962 has been a Deputy Minister of Public Security. He was for a brief time Mao's personal bodyguard in 1947 and appears to be on fairly close personal terms with Mao. He traveled with Mao on his 1949 Moscow trip and in 1967 was one of four men mentioned in the press as accompanying Mao on an inspection trip through several provinces in September.

Li Te-sheng is an army commander who rose from relative obscurity during the Cultural Revolution, becoming Commander of the Anhwei Military District in the summer of 1967. In April, 1968, he also became Chairman of the Anhwei Province Revolutionary Committee. In September, 1970, he was identified as the head of the PLA General Political Department. In January, 1971, Li became First Secretary of the Anhwei Province Party Committee.

Chi Teng-k'uei is the least well-known member of the Politburo. First noted as an alternate secretary of the Honan Province CCP Committee in 1965, he is the first Vice-Chairman of the Honan Province Revolutionary Committee and the third-ranking secretary of the new provincial Party committee.

In sum, our knowledge of the present Chinese Communist top elite is quite limited. Although a fair amount is known about many of the top individuals and their areas of responsibility and activity, the policy-making process at the highest level remains a mystery to outside observers. Moreover, it is clear that that process (if, indeed, it can be called a process at all) has become more fragmented and disorderly since the Cultural Revolution began. Whatever the nature and extent of pre–Cultural Revolution factional-type disputes among the top leadership, they subsequently became both more serious and less structured by the informal rules of 'inner-Party struggle.'

Leadership factions. Numerous theories or factional models have been constructed to explain shifts and changes in policy since the beginning of the Cultural Revolution. Perhaps the most popular theory during the Cultural Revolution was that the primary tension was between the extreme Maoists collected around Chiang Ch'ing and Lin Piao, and a moderate coalition of military and civilian leaders; accordingly, important shifts in policy were thought to reflect the policy preferences of the group in the superior power position at any given time. Certainly there is some validity to such an interpretation, at least to the extent that some members of the top elite—for instance, those responsible chiefly for state bureaucratic functions—did have more 'moderate' policy preferences than the members of the Central Committee's Cultural Revolution Group. However, it is very hard to believe that such relative power positions could have shifted as quickly, as markedly, and as often as did the official line and policy during the Cultural Revolution. If the top leadership were really in such a fluid and unstable state, it would be more reasonable to expect that there would be no clear direction to policy at all rather than that there would be successive sharp changes in it. It probably comes closer to the truth to suppose that the successive shifts in policy reflected Mao's own deliberate, if often reluctant, adjustments of his so-called great strategic plan in the face of intractable reality. Moreover, despite the shifts in policy, the Cultural Revolution did have a continuity to its over-all direction that was quite compatible with Mao's own power interests, values, and political style. The most important manifestation of that continuity was the persistence of extremely heavy reliance on the mass movement as the mode of politics, and the concomitant commitment of the regime to the goal of 'remolding the world outlook' of the entire Chinese population. These remained even during the periods of moderation and consolidation in the Cultural Revolution. For instance, in the fall of 1968, when a more moderate policy became the order of the day following the 'leashing' of the Red Guards, there was simultaneously launched an unprecedentedly ambitious mass campaign for cadre re-education and manual labor, for which large numbers of special farms had to be established. The scope of the campaign was such that within three months in Kwangtung Province alone there were 300 cadre school farms; more than 100,000 Kwangtung cadres were reported to be enrolled in the schools or to have been sent to do manual labor in other production units.[11]

This is not to suggest, of course, that Mao's power was absolute during the Cultural Revolution, or that the course of the Cultural Revolution was planned in detail beforehand by him. Moreover, it is reasonable to expect that in the wake of the demoralization caused by the Cultural Revolution Mao's power and influence was eroded, just as it was in the aftermath of the failure of the Great Leap Forward. It is also possible that some important initiatives during and after the Cultural Revolution were not taken by Mao, but by others, with Mao giving his approval only after the fact. The dismissal in 1967 of PLA Acting Chief of Staff Yang Ch'eng-wu, for instance, may have been at the initiative of Chiang Ch'ing (with Lin Piao's approval) rather than Mao. Nevertheless, it appears that, at least up to the Ninth Congress (April, 1969), if not thereafter, Mao's personal authority remained paramount, and that his voice was the decisive one on policy questions when he chose to make it so.

There are, however, more fundamental obstacles to arriving at a factional model of the top Chinese leadership than ignorance of the state of Mao's personal power and influence. For one thing, statements by leaders concerning controversial questions often cannot be taken as representing personal opinions or preferences. It has long been the practice within the CCP for opponents of a policy that is ultimately adopted as the official one to be given the responsibility for announcing that policy and defending it. In August, 1968, for instance, an article by Yao Wen-yüan, 'The Working Class Must Take the Lead in Everything,' appeared in *Red Flag*.[12] The article explained and defended the role of the workers' Mao Tse-tung thought propaganda teams, which had displaced the Red Guards as the chief executors of the Cultural Revolution. It was Chiang Ch'ing whose personal power and interests were most closely bound up with the Red Guard movement, and Yao was closely associated with her as a member of the Cultural Revolution Group. There is no easy way to discern whether Yao was 'sincere' in the article. Conceivably, he may have been in some degree constrained to write such an article, or he may have been switching his

---

[11] *South China Morning Post*, January 11, 1969, p. 18.
[12] *Hung Ch'i (Red Flag)*, No. 2, Peking, 1968; *Peking Review*, No. 35, August 30, 1968.

allegiance away from Chiang Ch'ing. Or he may never have been part of an extremist 'faction' in the Western sense at all.

A related point is that the value structures of the individual leaders are not necessarily determined by, or deducible from, their functional specialties; that is, the division of labor among the leadership need not lead to corresponding small group perspectives. Many of the elite members do not have deep personal roots in the areas of their present specialities. Li Hsien-nien, for instance, who has borne major responsibilities for economic planning and financial affairs as Minister of Finance is far from being a professional economist; he did not have any such responsibilities before 1949. Before then, he was a high-ranking military commander.

Finally, it is worth reiterating that the Chinese Communists have, doubtless both deliberately and unconsciously, incorporated within their own practice elements of traditional Chinese culture relating to conflict management and to interpersonal relations generally. Aside from such explicit processes as that of struggle–criticism and self-criticism–transformation, mentioned earlier, there are more subtle and informal ways in which the behavior of Peking's elite may be affected by cultural factors. Moreover, these aspects of traditional Chinese culture have been modified and distorted by the impact of the West and modernity. To say the least, these aspects of culture and their modifications are still quite imperfectly understood and are difficult to integrate into any analysis of elite behavior. Here we can do no more than mention a few such factors regarded as important by contemporary social scientists.

One of the most important factors is the traditional Chinese tendency to take kinship, or primary group, relations as the model or pattern for personal associations outside the family. Another is the traditional Chinese preference for mediation and compromise as a means of settling disputes rather than judicial-type decisions based strictly on principles of legality or justice. Still another is the traditional Chinese tendency to suppress the expression of sentiments of aggression and the modern emergence of ritualized hate and hostility in Chinese politics. Finally, there is the traditional Chinese particularistic attitude toward life experiences, and the relative lack of need on the part of the Chinese to integrate their actions into a meaningful whole or into the service of a single purpose.[13] These and other cultural variables complicate the problem of deducing likely factional divisions among the top Chinese Communist leadership.

THE REGIONAL ELITE

Before the Cultural Revolution, the ruling elite below the operational level of the Politburo occupied positions within the six regional bureaus of the Party apparatus (the North, Northeast, Northwest, East, South-Central, and Southwest China bureaus). The establishment of these bureaus was announced in 1961, in connection with a move to decentralize the execution of policy, especially in economic matters. Under each regional bureau was the apparatus for four to six provinces. Each provincial CCP committee had a first secretary and five to ten secretaries and alternate secretaries, for a national total of about 210 to 220. The provincial first secretary was almost invariably a full or alternate member of the CCP Central Committee; the remaining provincial secretaries were in most cases not Central Committee members.

---

[13] The literature on those and related topics is vast. On the role of kinship relations, see Francis L. K. Hsü, *Under the Ancestors' Shadow* (Garden City, N.Y.: Anchor Books, 1967), Chapter X; on Chinese attitudes toward aggression and authority, see Lucian W. Pye, *The Spirit of Chinese Politics* (Cambridge, Mass.: MIT Press, 1968); Richard Solomon, *Mao's Revolution and the Chinese Political Culture* (Berkeley: University of California Press, 1971); on Chinese Communist practices for resolving conflict, see Robert Jay Lifton, *Thought Reform and the Psychology of Totalism* (New York: Norton), 1961.

The provincial secretaries frequently held concurrent posts within the provincial government apparatus, such as governor or, more often, vice-governor.

Aside from their administrative functions, the six regional bureaus' chairmanships may have been conceived as posts for prospective members of the Politburo. Before the Cultural Revolution, the six chairmen were Li Hsüeh-feng, Sung Jen-ch'iung, Liu Lan-t'ao, K'o Ch'ing-shih, T'ao Chu, and Li Ching-ch'üan. Of these, only K'o and Li Ching-ch'üan were Politburo members, both having been elected in 1958. In August, 1966, or shortly thereafter, T'ao Chu was elevated to the Politburo. Only a few months later, however, he was denounced as an enemy of Mao and lost his positions. Both Sung Jen-ch'iung and Li Hsüeh-feng also appear to have been Politburo members for a time in 1966–67. After the Ninth Congress, Li was again made an alternate member of the Politburo. Liu Lan-t'ao, never on the Politburo, lost his post about the same time as T'ao Chu. When K'o Ch'ing-shih, head of the East China Bureau, died in 1965, his replacement was Chang Ch'un-ch'iao; judging by his high standing in Mao's eyes, Chang may even then have been marked by the Chairman as a future Politburo member.

The group average age of the first secretaries of the pre–Cultural Revolution provincial Party committees tended to be several years lower than that of the Politburo members or regional bureau heads but was rising at about the same rate. In 1965, the first secretaries whose age is known averaged about fifty-seven years, as compared to fifty years in 1957.[14]

From 1956 to 1966, very few of the provincial secretaries were promoted to higher positions within the central Party or government apparatus. Two became heads of regional bureaus and two became ministers in the central government; one of the latter, Hsieh Fu-chih, became a Politburo member in 1966. In 1969, the former alternate secretary of the Honan Province Party Committee, Chi Teng-k'uei, was raised to the Politburo. A significant amount of upward mobility into, if not out of, provincial secretarial positions is evident, however, especially for those secretaries below the level of first secretary of the provincial committee. Of a sample of 225 party officials who received provincial secretarial posts from 1956 to 1966, about two-thirds of the 182 whose backgrounds are known were promoted into their new positions. while about one-fourth were transferred from comparable posts.[15] It is possible that among these were a fair number of younger people whose official careers began only in the 1940's and whose personal perspectives can be expected to be significantly different from those of the 'Long March generation.'

Relations with the central elite. Despite the regime's goal of establishing and maintaining complete political control over the provinces from the capital, the regional elite has in past years always had a significant degree of operational discretion or autonomy vis-à-vis central political authority. Such discretion or autonomy is the product of three different types of causal factors. The first comprises those inherent in any large-scale organization or bureaucracy. First analyzed in detail by Max Weber, they are within the domain of modern organizational theory. A good example would be the power that naturally accrues to regional authorities through their role as centers of communication between the highest and lowest levels of the Party apparatus. By virtue of such a role, regional leaders can conceal central directives from lower authorities and can also distort or falsify communications from the lower levels to the center. The second type of factor resulting in regional discretion or autonomy is that which springs from regional differences or peculiarities, including physical, geopolitical, or cultural differences, which may make it difficult to control a particular

---

14 Frederick C. Teiwes, *Provincial Party Personnel in Mainland China, 1956–1966* (New York: Occasional Papers of the East Asian Institute, Columbia University, 1967), p. 7.

15 *Ibid.*, pp. 41–42.

region from a distant capital. The military strategic importance of a region, its rugged terrain, its hostile native population, its grain surplus or gold mines—all these are examples of regional distinctiveness that gives the regional elite a certain amount of independent power vis-à-vis the center. The third type of factor stems from the peculiar Chinese-cum-Communist heritage, culture, and style of leadership, which demands for its successful implementation a certain amount of local initiative and autonomy. To be sure, the regime has continuously sought to limit and counter-balance regional autonomy by means of various types of supervisory and control devices, but there appear to be definite limits to the potential of such techniques for success. Thus, the growth of what Peking calls 'independent kingdoms' has been a chronic problem for the regime. Beyond a certain point, centralized political control over regional authorities in Communist China can be achieved only at the cost of administrative weakness or ineffectiveness, which in turn means a clash between the regime's political goals and its economic goals. During the Cultural Revolution, many provincial elite members were accused of building up 'independent kingdoms' by means of the power accruing to them from all three of the above types of factors. Mao's own determination that political goals shall prevail over economic ones was not shared by all members of the central elite during the early 1960's, however, and this further strengthened regional autonomy during that period.

How much collusion there was between the regional elite and anti-Mao elements at the center before the Cultural Revolution is, of course, not known. Nevertheless, the ubiquitous charges that anti-Maoist regional leaders were 'agents of Liu Shao-ch'i' had some logic to them, inasmuch as the pre–Cultural Revolution central and regional elites were largely identical and had close personal relations, shared experiences, and similar perspectives. To this extent, charges of conspiracies by one top leader against another had a kind of *prima facie* plausibility. Thus, many such charges, even if false, were not as fantastic as they might have appeared to an outside observer. To illustrate, the alleged *coup d'état* plot against Mao in 1965–66 at first was said to be the work of P'eng Chen, Lu Ting-i, Lo Jui-ch'ing, and Yang Shang-k'un. Next, Ho Lung was said to be involved, making military preparations with Lo Jui-ch'ing and preparing a base area in Szechwan for possible retreat (Lo is Szechwanese; Ho, a native of Western Hunan, was a top official in the Southwest in the early 1950's). Next, Li Ching-ch'üan, Teng Hsiao-p'ing, and several others were accused of being party to the plot. Li was a protege of Ho Lung, and the Ho and Li families were reportedly on close personal terms as well. Both Ho and Li had served under Teng Hsiao-p'ing, himself a Szechwanese, when Teng was serving in the Southwest in 1949–52. At the Central Committee's tenth plenum in 1962, where Mao's policies were reportedly extensively criticized by other party leaders, Lo Jui-ch'ing and Lu Ting-i were made secretaries of the party Secretariat headed by Teng. Such net-works of informal personal and official relationships abound among the CCP elite; under some circumstances, they may be a force for cohesion, and under others a force for factionalism and conspiracy.

The provincial elite and the Cultural Revolution. During the Cultural Revolution, the apparatus of regional Party bureaus, provincial Party committees, and provincial governments was superseded by the new provincial-level revolutionary committees. These were officially described as 'provisional organs of power,' composed of rep-resentatives of the 'revolutionary masses,' local PLA authorities, and 'revolutionary cadres' united in a 'three-way alliance.' In practice, the influence of the military authorities in the committees was most often paramount; that of the 'revolutionary cadres' was secondary, while that of the mass representatives was distinctly tertiary. Although a committee had anywhere from 150 to 300 members, the leadership group, which in practice wielded power within the committees, was much smaller, usually ten to twenty people, including the chairman and several vice-chairmen, particularly the first vice-chairman. Of the twenty-nine provincial-level revolutionary committees (including those of the three special municipalities, Peking, Tientsin, and Shanghai), nineteen were chaired by leading PLA commanders; twenty of twenty-nine first vice-chairmen were PLA men. Only 14 per cent of all vice-chairmen, and those usually the lowest-ranking ones, were known to be representatives of the 'revolutionary masses.' In all areas of mainland China, the PLA took on great responsibility for political functions. Many of the PLA figures prominent on the revolutionary committees were army or divisional commanders, who formerly had been excluded from civilian posts.

Fewer than one-third of the new revolutionary committees formed by September, 1968, in the provinces had a member of the old (Eighth) Central Committee among their leaders, although most of the leaders of the revolutionary committees later became full or alternate members of the Ninth Central Committee. As the provincial-level Party committees became reinstated in 1971, they were to take precedence in authority over the provincial revolutionary committees; most commonly, however, the chairman of the provincial revolutionary committee became concurrently first secretary of the provincial Party committee. Again, this meant that, more often than not, the leading PLA commanders in the provinces were also the leading political figures.

FUTURE CHANGES IN CHINA'S RULING ELITE

Available evidence strongly suggests that the most important intra-elite cleavage is generational; until the first generation of CCP revolutionaries has largely passed from the scene, any significant ideological or functional cleavages are likely to be along generational lines. The gap, for instance, between the perspectives of the young officers and old officers in the PLA is likely to be greater than between the generality of military and civilian officials.[16] Mao, of course, hoped to bridge the generation gap among the leadership by selecting his own like-minded revolutionary successors; to promote the emergence of such successors was a major goal of the Cultural Revolution. It seems clear, however, that in this the Cultural Revolution failed. Although some such young political top elite members did emerge, they are from Mao's point of view too few, have too little power, and are of questionable sincerity in their absolute devotion to the thought of Mao Tse-tung.

Relatively rapid turnover among the top elite is inevitable in the coming years. Stability of leadership under such conditions is likely to depend on the ability of the present leaders to re-establish the authority of the Party, weakened by the Cultural Revolution and subsequent purges. If fortune grants the present regime several years to rebuild and strengthen the Party as an institution before Mao passes from the scene, prospects would seem good for an orderly transfer of power. Otherwise, a serious and prolonged succession struggle may well ensue among the most powerful military commanders.

The old system of provincial CCP committees was being reinstated in early 1971 as the most important locus of regional authority, with the leading secretaries of the committees being drawn from among the leadership of the provincial revolutionary committees. The Party probably will try gradually to return the military commanders among the new provincial elite to strictly military positions, although it will be necessary, for a time at least, to utilize the PLA administrative apparatus for civilian purposes. But if past experience is any guide, civil Party authorities in all but the border regions of China should be able to prevent the military commanders from obstructing a return to civilian predominance in provincial-level administrative organs.

---

[16] The 'generations' of PLA officers are analyzed in William Whitson, 'The Concept of Military Generation: The Chinese Communist Case,' *Asian Survey*, Vol. 8, No. 11, Berkeley: Institute of International Studies, University of California, November 1968, pp. 921–47.

The future of the six former CCP regional bureaus is doubtful. The Maoist leadership has now twice found them politically unsatisfactory. They were first abolished in 1953–54 at the time of the Kao Kang—Jao Shu-shih 'anti-Party conspiracy.' Reinstated in 1960–61, the bureaus were made organs of the Central Committee, but this did not, apparently, prevent the growth of 'independent kingdoms.'

The former Central Committee Secretariat also may not be reinstated as the Party's day-to-day executive arm, as it was the stronghold of the most powerful opponents of Mao, and Mao's successor may fear that such a secretariat would develop substantial independent power. Instead, the leadership may preserve some kind of permanent Cultural Revolution Group heavily oriented toward propaganda functions. This would mean, of course, some cost to the Party's administrative effectiveness.

As for the ultimate succession to Mao's own position, one possibility is that a kind of 'caretaker' government under Chou En-lai might well emerge. Under such an arrangement, provincial authorities would have a relatively high degree of autonomy. This kind of outcome would be more likely in the event the succession question arises in the near future. Since Chou himself, however, was 71 years old in 1970, it could not be regarded as a very stable situation.

The perspectives and values of those who succeed China's present ruling elite cannot but be very different from those of the generation of the Long March. The present primacy of the thought and person of Mao Tse-tung as a political symbol evoking solidarity and loyalty and giving over-all direction to policy cannot endure in the face of repeated costly failures of the Maoist line. Marxist-Leninist practices and concepts will continue to play an important part in Chinese politics, but the new leadership will also stress other political symbols. And while none can say for certain what these will be, the ones that most readily suggest themselves are those which spring from China's long history as a great civilization, its emerging status as a powerful nation, and the aspirations it shares with all developing countries: national wealth, power, and prestige.

SELECTED BIBLIOGRAPHY

BARNETT, A. DOAK. *Cadres, Bureaucracy, and Political Power in Communist China.* New York: Columbia University Press, 1967. A valuable description of the organization and leadership of a central ministry, a county, and a commune, based on refugee interviews.

BERTON, PETER, and EUGENE WU. *Contemporary China, a Research Guide.* Stanford, Calif.: Hoover Institution, 1967, pp. 160–73. A bibliography of materials in Chinese, English, and Japanese.

BOORMAN, HOWARD, ed. *Biographical Dictionary of Republican China.* 4 vols. New York: Columbia University Press, 1966–71. Prominent Chinese (Communist and non-Communist) between 1911 and 1949; Vol. 4 contains extensive bibliography of biographical materials.

CH'EN, JEROME. *Mao and the Chinese Revolution.* New York: Oxford University Press, 1965. The first scholarly biography of Mao Tse-tung.

CHUNG, HUA-MIN, and ARTHUR C. MILLER. *Madame Mao: A Profile of Chiang Ch'ing.* Hong Kong: Union Research Institute, 1968.

Chung-king Jen-ming Lu (Who's Who in Communist China). Taipei, Taiwan: Institute of International Relations, 1967. 2,013 entries.

HSÜ, KAI-YU. *Chou En-lai: China's Grey Eminence.* Garden City: N.Y. Doubleday and Co., Inc., 1968. Strong on Chou's personal background and early career in the 1920's and 1930's.

KLEIN, DONALD W., and ANNE B. CLARK, *Biographic Dictionary of Chinese Communism, 1921–1965.* 2 vols. Cambridge, Mass.: Harvard University Press, 1970. 433 entries.

LEWIS, JOHN W. *Leadership in Communist China.* Ithaca, N.Y.: Cornell University Press, 1963. The best general discussion published of Chinese Communist leadership techniques.

————. 'Chinese Communist Party Leadership and the Succession to Mao Tse-tung: An Appraisal of Tensions,' Washington, D.C.: U.S. Department of State, Bureau of Intelligence and Research, 1964. Analyzes characteristics and perspectives of the middle-level elite in the P.R.C.

NORTH, ROBERT C. 'Kuomintang and Chinese Communist Elites,' in HAROLD D. LASSWELL and DANIEL LERNER, eds., *World Revolutionary Elites*. Cambridge, Mass.: The MIT Press, 1966. First published in 1953, this is a comparative analysis of the social backgrounds of the Kuomintang and CCP immediate post-World War II elite; somewhat dated, but general conclusions are still valid for current CCP elite.

RUE, JOHN E. *Mao Tse-tung in Opposition: 1927–1935.* Stanford, Calif.: Stanford University Press, 1966. Examines the complicated relations between the Comintern-backed CCP headquarters and Mao, and their disputes over relative emphasis on rural versus urban revolutionary movements.

SCHRAM, STUART. *Mao Tse-tung.* New York: Simon and Schuster, 1966. The best published analysis of the evolution of Mao's political thought; some disagreements with Ch'en.

SNOW, EDGAR. *Red Star Over China.* New York: Grove Press, 1961 (paperback), 1968 (hardcover). Originally published in 1937, includes the only autobiographical interviews ever given by Mao. The 1968 revised and enlarged edition includes previously unpublished interview material and a useful appendix of biographical notes on veteran CCP leaders.

Who's Who in Communist China. 2 vols. Hong Kong: Union Research service, 1969, 1970. The most comprehensive biographical dictionary of CCP leaders published in English. 2,837 entries.

10

THE PEOPLE'S LIBERATION ARMY

ELLIS JOFFE

THE ROLE OF THE PEOPLE'S LIBERATION ARMY

THE Chinese Communist army has played a central role both in the history of the Chinese Communist movement and in the People's Republic of China. Early in the struggle for power between the Nationalists and the Communists, Mao Tse-tung realized that the Communists could not survive, let alone strive for victory, without a military force of their own. Consequently, Mao and his colleagues began to concentrate on the development of a Red Army, which was officially founded on August 1, 1927. In the last analysis, it was that army which enabled the Communists to withstand the efforts of the Nationalists and the Japanese to destroy them and finally brought them to power.

With the establishment of the Communist regime, the army, known since 1946 as the People's Liberation Army (PLA), acquired new tasks, both internal and external. First, it became the ultimate bulwark of the new regime's authority. Second, it performed pivotal duties in local administration for a few years, and later continued to fulfill significant social and economic functions. Finally, the PLA became responsible for protecting the security of the country and, in the last resort, for implementing the leadership's foreign policy objectives.

During the Cultural Revolution, the political importance of the army rose to unprecedented heights. From the start of that great upheaval, Mao Tse-tung turned to the military leadership for support in his attempt to push through his policies and to purge his opponents in the Party. Subsequently, the PLA was drawn more and more deeply into the political maelstrom until it rose to a dominant position in the provinces and greatly enhanced its influence on the national level. This new and pivotal role of the army in the Chinese power structure has had a momentous impact on Party-PLA relations as well as on politics in the PLA.

STRENGTH AND CAPABILITY

When the Communists came to power in 1949, the PLA was a massive and highly effective semiguerrilla force, but from a strictly military viewpoint it was essentially a premodern army. It had no air force or navy; its soldiers were irregulars; its command and staff structure was skeletal; and its equipment, which consisted mainly of arms captured from the Japanese and the Nationalists, was heterogeneous and largely outdated. The Chinese leadership was well aware of the need to modernize the PLA rapidly, but the country's shattered economy and backward technology were in no position to support a swift and sweeping modernization of the armed forces. It was clear to the Chinese that they needed military aid.

The Korean War, Soviet aid, and modernization. The only possible source of military aid was the Soviet Union, but there are indications, such as the primitive equipment of the Chinese when they entered the Korean War, that such aid was not immediately forthcoming. However, whatever inhibitions the Russians may have had about supplying military hardware to the Chinese were removed after Peking, convinced that the advance of the United Nations forces toward its borders was a threat to China's security, reluctantly entered the Korean War, which had been initiated by the Soviets and the North Koreans. When the poorly armed Chinese forces were faced with disaster in Korea, the Russians came to their aid with a massive infusion of military materiel.

No such aid was given to the PLA in the first stage of the war. The Chinese forces that crossed the Yalu in late October, 1950, were still inadequately equipped and poorly serviced. Confronted by a modern adversary, the Chinese strategists sought to offset their critical technical inferiority by capitalizing on their one major asset—highly motivated, disciplined, and mobile troops. This was the source of the 'human wave' assaults, a tactic designed to pit superior numbers against superior firepower in order to make penetrations at vital points.

In the first phase of the war, reliance upon the 'human element,' as well as on guerrilla tactics enabled the Chinese to rout the United Nations forces. Because of their primitive logistics system, however, they were unable to maintain the momentum of their offensives and were forced to withdraw after each attack in order to regroup and resupply. After sustaining initial defeats, the United Nations Command adopted new tactics to cope with the Chinese attacks. The concept was to confront the Chinese with a firm battle line, which deprived them of the ability to exploit their guerrilla maneuvers, and then to counterattack with concentrated firepower in order to inflict maximum casualties.

The new tactics proved highly effective. Hemmed in by fixed battle lines and subjected to terrible punishment by superior firepower, the Chinese began to suffer growing hardships and to sustain increasing casualties. Consequently, combat morale, discipline, and the political control system began to crumble. By mid-1951 the Chinese forces in Korea were in serious trouble.[1] Under these circumstances the Soviet Union came to the rescue with large quantities of military aid. This not only helped the Chinese to bring the Korean War to a stalemate but also launched the PLA on the road to modernization.

No less important was the impact of the Korean War on the thinking of Chinese military leaders. This impact was undoubtedly traumatic and sobering. It showed them that the PLA suffered from dangerous deficiencies in weapons, organization, and doctrine, and it decisively demonstrated that there were severe limitations on the extent to which the 'human element' could offset material shortcomings. Those lessons rapidly accelerated the modernization of the PLA.

Weapons and equipment. The starting point for military modernization had to be the rearming and re-equipping of the PLA. This the Chinese proceeded to do primarily with Soviet materiel, which they received in diminishing quantities from the Korean War until 1960. The materiel enabled them to increase the firepower and mobility of the PLA, to improve its logistics, to create specialized arms, service units, and technical branches, and to lay the basis for an indigenous military industry. By the late 1950's the technically primitive PLA of the Korean War had been transformed into a fairly complex professional army.

Despite its impressive progress, however, from a technical standpoint the PLA still lags far behind the conventional armies of the great powers. Aside from objective

---

[1] Alexander L. George, *The Chinese Communist Army in Action* (New York: Columbia University Press, 1967), Chapters 9 and 10.

economic and technological constraints, two interrelated reasons seem to account for the lag. In the first place, it appears that by the late 1950's the Chinese leadership had concluded that the PLA had reached an adequate level of modernization in the conventional field in terms of its strategic aims and defensive military doctrine. As a result, it decided—and this decision involved rejecting the views of professional military leaders—that additional large-scale advances would have to be preceded by further economic development, which was necessary to provide the base for long-range local military production.

That decision was sparked and strengthened by the deterioration of Sino-Soviet relations, as a result of which the Soviets refused to give China the military aid it desired, primarily in the nuclear field (all Soviet military aid was abruptly cut off in 1960). Convinced that they could not obtain a nuclear capability except through a policy of 'self-reliance,' the Chinese decided to give nuclear development first priority. Consequently, they were compelled to limit the development of their conventional forces, which, in any case, had reached a level that the leadership considered commensurate with its strategic doctrine. In line with this decision, the development of conventional forces during most of the 1960's (that is, after China overcame the crisis caused by the Great Leap Forward) was carried on slowly and selectively, with primary emphasis on weapons systems considered necessary for defense. In the last few years there has been a marked improvement in the quantity and quality of Chinese military production.

The conventional forces. Since unclassified information on China's military establishment is scanty and speculative, any attempt to describe it must take into account a wide margin of error. Nevertheless, on the basis of the available data it is possible to sketch its main features.

The ground forces number about 2.9 million men and comprise about 110 infantry divisions, which are organized into armies, and about 20 artillery, 5 armored, 3 cavalry, and 2 paratroop divisions. In addition, there are various service and technical units.[2] An average infantry division consists of 12,000–14,000 men and comprises 3 infantry, 1 artillery, and 1 tank regiment. Reconnaissance, chemical warfare, medical, transport, engineering, and communications units are all organic to the infantry division.

The armored divisions are equipped with Soviet JS-2, T-34, and T-54 tanks; a Chinese version of the T-54 (T-59) and the T-62 are produced domestically. Separate tank regiments are equipped with Soviet model JSU-122 and JSU-155 self-propelled assault guns. The artillery consists principally of 122-mm, 152-mm, 155-mm and 203-mm guns; 122-mm and 152-mm howitzers; 132-mm rocket launchers; 120-mm and 160-mm heavy mortars; 57-mm and 85-mm antitank guns; and 57-mm and 100-mm anti-aircraft guns.[3]

A considerable part of this equipment is considered obsolete by Western standards, but it undoubtedly can still be effective, especially against less advanced armies. Military experts believe the Chinese arms industry is capable of keeping the PLA supplied with high-quality light and medium infantry and artillery weapons as well as some armor. The PLA, however, is considered to be deficient in complex weapons and communications systems, as well as in mechanized transport. Strategic airlift capability is extremely limited and strategic sealift capability is virtually nonexistent.

The Chinese air force at present is not the formidable factor that it was considered to be in the mid-1950's. The extensive aid China received in the later stages of the Korean War and shortly thereafter seems to have tapered off sharply in subsequent

---

[2] *The Military Balance 1971–1972* (London: Institute for Strategic Studies, 1970), p. 40–41.
[3] *Ibid.*, and Samuel B. Griffith, II, *The Chinese People's Liberation Army* (New York: McGraw-Hill, 1967), pp. 220–21.

years. As the aircraft supplied to China became obsolete, the Russians apparently did not replenish them with their newest models, especially offensive aircraft. The Chinese air force, moreover, was closely tied to Soviet supplies, and their termination caused a drastic deterioration of China's air capability.

Since the early 1960's the Chinese have tried hard to remedy this situation. They have evidently concentrated on the production of fighter-interceptors and are known to be capable of manufacturing the MIG-19 and the MIG-21. The Chinese are also producing a close-support fighter-bomber of their own design, the F-9, which flies at about 1,400 miles an hour and has a combat radius of 300 to 500 miles. Until 1970, there was no evidence that the Chinese had made any attempt to develop long-range heavy bombers—an indication that the Chinese high command had decided to bypass the manned bomber as a strategic delivery vehicle and to focus on the development of missile delivery systems for their nuclear weapons. In 1970, however, it was reported that the Chinese were producing a twin-engine jet bomber capable of carrying nuclear weapons with a range of about 2,000 miles. The bomber is a copy of the Russian TU-16, which is considered obsolescent, but it is assumed that the Chinese have made improvements on the Russian version. It is also not known what prompted the Chinese to manufacture this aircraft. One possibility is that they decided to diversify their delivery systems. Another is that the TU-16 is intended to provide tactical atomic support to ground forces and for use against troop concentrations, primarily Soviet, close to China's borders. At any rate, the production of the bomber does not indicate any shift in China's basically defensive strategic doctrine. The Chinese are believed to have at least 30 TU-16 bombers and an estimated production capacity of about five a month.

The air force comprises an estimated total of 2,800 combat aircraft crewed and serviced by some 180,000 men. There are about 1,700 MIG-15's and MIG-17's, up to MIG-19's and a growing quantity of MIG-21's. In addition to the TU-16, the bomber force is made up mainly of some 150 Soviet IL-28 twin-jet light bombers, which is still considered a good aircraft and could be used even as a nuclear delivery vehicle in Asia. China also has some Soviet propeller-driven TU-4's, which have no strategic value because of their slowness and vulnerability.[4]

The navy at present is basically a coastal defense force, although in the long run the Chinese may use the submarine as one missile delivery system. The bulk of the fleet consists of several hundred torpedo boats and high-speed patrol boats, including some of the Soviet Komar class, which are capable of firing short-range anti-shipping missiles. There are also four destroyers and four destroyer escorts, as well as small vessels of various types. Naval personnel strength is estimated at about 150,000.

The navy's only potentially offensive weapon is the submarine. The Chinese are believed to have over thirty, mostly Soviet W-class vessels, some of which have been equipped with deck ramps for launching missiles. Western military men consider this craft obsolete. The Chinese are also known to have one or two Soviet-type G-class submarines, which were apparently built in China. Each is equipped with three missile-launching tubes with a range of about 600 km. and has long-distance cruising capability. The Chinese may be constructing more submarines of this type in the context of their missile delivery systems program.[5] They are also building destroyers armed with short-range missiles for use against ships.[6]

---

[4] *The Military Balance 1971–1972*, p. 42; Griffith, *Chinese People's Liberation Army*, pp. 224–25; *The New York Times*, February 1, 1972.

[5] *The Military Balance 1971–1972*, p. 42; Griffith, *Chinese People's Liberation Army*, pp. 226–27; and Ralph L. Powell, 'Military Affairs of Communist China,' *Current History*, 51, No. 301 (September, 1966), pp. 212–17.

[6] *The New York Times*, February 1, 1972.

From this brief sketch it is reasonable to conclude that the PLA is still not a fully modern and balanced army. It is deficient in sophisticated conventional weapons systems and equipment, and its strategic mobility is extremely limited. The PLA can undoubtedly overrun China's smaller neighbors and effectively carry out limited operations close to China's borders, as demonstrated in the Sino-Indian War of 1962. It is unlikely, however, that, barring a real threat to national security, China's leaders envisage committing the PLA to a large-scale, sustained conventional war beyond China's borders involving long supply lines subject to air interdiction. The leadership views the main mission of the PLA as defensive, and it apparently considers the army capable of carrying out such a mission without costly major technological advances, at least for the time being.

Nuclear capability. If the Chinese are not emphasizing the development of sophisticated conventional weapon systems, it is primarily because they have decided to give top priority to nuclear weapons and missile delivery vehicles. The Chinese began to conduct nuclear research in 1955, with considerable assistance from the Soviet Union, and in 1957 they launched a military nuclear program.

The program was apparently based on the assumption that advanced aid would be forthcoming from the Soviets. Such aid, however, though apparently promised, did not materialize. As Russian and Chinese views on global policy moved steadily farther apart, the Russians probably balked at helping China's nuclear program. The widening cleavage over nuclear aid and strategy, which contributed to the general deterioration of Sino-Soviet relations, convinced the Chinese both that they urgently needed an independent nuclear capability and that they would have to acquire it by themselves. In 1958 the Chinese decided to proceed with nuclear development on the basis of their own efforts.

Consequently, nuclear development clearly became the first item on the list of national defense priorities in terms of resources and manpower. The first payoff for their efforts came in October, 1964, when the Chinese carried out a nuclear test. Since then, the Chinese have conducted a dozen tests of various types, including the explosion of hydrogen devices. The speed and quality of China's nuclear program in the initial stages generally exceeded the estimates of Western experts and demonstrated a high level of technological achievement (such as, for example, in the use of Uranium-235 instead of plutonium) and professional competence. Military experts believe that China already has a modest nuclear arsenal.

Along with nuclear development, the Chinese have been working on missile delivery systems. By the end of 1970, the Chinese were known to have tested middle-range and, apparently, intermediate-range missiles. Experts believe that the Chinese have deployed about twenty middle-range (600 to 1,000 miles) missiles, which are presumably targeted on Soviet military installations along the Sino-Soviet border. The Chinese are also believed to be concentrating their efforts on the development of sophisticated intermediate-range (1,500 to 2,500 miles) missiles, which are capable of reaching the Soviet heartland. By 1972, they were said to have deployed a handful of the new missiles. Since it is assumed that the Chinese are worried first of all by the military threat posed by the Soviet Union, they are thought to be stressing intermediate-range rather than intercontinental ballistic missiles. This, however, does not preclude the development of an ICBM, and experts estimate that by the mid-1970's the Chinese will have a small number of operational ICBM's.

STRUCTURE AND ORGANIZATION

Parallel to the modernization of weaponry, the Chinese carried out fundamental and far-reaching reforms in the structure and organization of the PLA. Here, too, Soviet influence had a major impact. It was imparted by Soviet advisers, who arrived in China as the PLA began to modernize and remained, in declining numbers, until the late 1950's. At the same time, many Chinese officers were sent to the Soviet Union for study. Under Soviet influence the PLA discarded or downgraded many of its revolutionary principles and practices and by the mid-1950's began to resemble the much more professionally oriented Soviet Army, much to the chagrin of the Chinese political leaders.

The command and staff system. On the eve of modernization the command and staff structure of the PLA was still relatively rudimentary and decentralized. During the first few years of the People's Republic, over-all direction of military affairs was ostensibly the responsibility of the People's Revolutionary Military Council (basically a Party organ); more likely it rested with the Military Affairs Committee, which was subordinate only to the Party Politburo, had been the supreme military organ during the revolutionary period, and presumably had continued its existence unpublicized during those years. As there was no Ministry of Defense, the Headquarters of the PLA (General Staff) and its staff departments were subordinate directly to the People's Revolutionary Military Council. The departments were of secondary importance, because most of the important military officers did not serve on them but on the Military and Administrative Committee, which controlled the six regions into which China was divided during the initial period of Communist rule.

In 1952 the leadership began to dissolve the Military and Administrative Committees and to centralize authority at the national level. The dissolution was accompanied by the transfer of high-ranking military officers from the regional commands to the capital to head, or to serve on, the new General Staff departments or specialized arms and technical branches that were being created.

Centralization was completed smoothly in 1954. At the national level, the People's Revolutionary Military Council was abolished and a National Defense Council was set up within the government structure, but it was an organ devoid of any real power. A Ministry of Defense was established subordinate to the State Council, and it took charge of the daily direction of military affairs, in conjunction with the General Staff and its departments. The departments have been reorganized several times, and now consist of the General Staff Department, the General Political Department (which ceased functioning for a while during the Cultural Revolution), and the General Rear Services Department (Logistics). Each department oversees a variety of subdepartments within its sphere of responsibility. Below them stand the headquarters of the specialized arms and services. Cumulatively, the departments and headquarters cover a wide range of specialized functions characteristic of a complex army. Nuclear weapons development is apparently under the direction of the PLA's Scientific and Technological Commission for National Defense, while missiles seem to be the responsibility of the Second Artillery Corps.

The highest organ with responsibility for military affairs is the Military Affairs Committee; its members include all the top-ranking military leaders. During the modernization period the Military Affairs Committee remained in the background, and, although it probably continued to be the ultimate source of important decisions, the main responsibility for the daily administration of the PLA passed to the Ministry of Defense and the General Staff, which emerged as the standard-bearers of professionalism. When the leadership began to crack down on professionalism in the late 1950's, the role of the Ministry of Defense was downgraded and the Military Affairs Committee became more and more prominent. Following a major reshuffle in the army high command in the autumn of 1959, the status of the Military Affairs Committee was greatly enhanced, and since then it has become an extremely powerful body, which not only sets military policy but also supervises its execution and keeps a tight grip on the routine running of the military machine. During the Cultural Revolution, as the army became progressively more involved in politics, the political importance of the Military Affairs Committee increased greatly.

Below the central level, the military organization is divided geographically into military regions, military districts, and military garrison commands. The General Staff departments and the headquarters of the various arms and services have counterparts at, and chains of command to, the lower levels.

Conscription and training. A major step in the organizational transition of the PLA from a guerrilla to a regular army was the introduction of conscription, which began on an experimental basis in 1953 and became a permanent institution with the adoption of the Military Service Law in 1955.[7] Compulsory military service thus replaced the irregular 'volunteer' system of recruitment, whereby men were drafted through a mixture of appeals and social pressures and served for an indefinite period.

Length of service for noncommissioned officers and men was set at three years in the ground forces and the public security forces; four years in the air force and coastal defense forces; and five years in the navy. In January, 1965, the terms of service were extended to four years in the ground forces; five years in the public security forces, the air force, shore-based naval units, and 'special army units' (presumably technical units); and six years for men serving on ships.[8] Terms of service were probably extended when it became apparent that, because of the length of time required for specialization, trained soldiers were being discharged before the army could make adequate use of their skills.

The reserve service until 1957 consisted of, first, demobilized NCO's and men who served in the militia as cadres or hard-core members, and second, those eligible but not called up for active service who served in the militia as ordinary soldiers.

In theory, compulsory military service is universal; in practice it is highly selective. Of an estimated total of 7 million males who reach the age of eighteen each year, only 750,000 or so are drafted. This enables the military authorities to choose the cream of the crop. And indeed, internal Chinese evaluations that reached the West in the early 1960's, indicate that the leadership was generally satisfied with the high quality of the individual soldier: He was said to be physically fit, politically reliable, disciplined, and motivated. Western observers by and large agree with such evaluations.

The draftees undergo tough and thorough training. The military leadership clearly recognizes the need for systematic training in a modern army based on conscription, and it has generally stressed the importance of military training programs, albeit not at the expense of political work and not as intensive as the professional officers want. The nature of military training is determined by the combat doctrines as well as the equipment of the PLA. The emphasis is on short-range combat, small-unit tactics, long marches, and night fighting, but there are also combined maneuvers of several arms and probably some training in defense against tactical nuclear weapons. The type of training given the PLA can be applied both offensively and defensively.

The militia. A key component in the defensive doctrine and strategy of the Chinese leadership is the people's militia. The origins of the militia date back to the early period of the Red Army, and throughout its history the militia performed important auxiliary functions for the army. After the establishment of the Communist government, the militia continued to play a key role during the social reform campaigns and to fulfill security tasks. Its paramilitary organization remained subordinate to the PLA, and its membership was fairly selective. According to estimates, until 1957 the strength of the militia never exceeded 12 million. However, following the merging of the militia with the reserves in 1957, the number reportedly rose to 30 million.

During the high tide of Soviet-oriented modernization in the mid-1950's, the militia fell into relative oblivion, and little was heard of it. From mid-1957, as the leadership began to turn away from the Soviet example and to reassert revolutionary principles, the militia was accorded increasing attention. This was a prelude to the

---

[7] NCNA, July 30, 1955; translated in *Current Background*, No. 344, August 8, 1955, pp. 4–11.
[8] NCNA (English), January 19, 1965.

frenetic expansion of the militia during the Great Leap Forward of 1958–60. In the autumn of 1958, the militia movement burst on the national scene with unprecedented force, and a colossal campaign to make 'everyone a soldier' swept the country. The campaign caused considerable dissatisfaction among professional officers, who took an extremely dim view of the militia's military capabilities, especially since control of the militia was apparently removed from their hands.

By 1959, 220 million men and women were reportedly members of the militia. Whereas previously the militia had been limited in size and functions, now it was not only supposed to include every able-bodied person, but its role both in the defense of China and in production was greatly expanded as well. The aim of the movement, in short, was nothing less than the militarization of society.

Two major purposes lay behind this. First, the universal militia was meant to be a concrete manifestation of Mao's concept of 'people's war,' which was revived at that time and according to which China's strength lies primarily in its mobilized masses. Second, the militia was conceived as part of the commune movement and was designed to provide a tight organizational framework in which the masses could be mobilized more effectively for production.

It quickly became apparent, however, that the high hopes the leadership had placed in the militia lay shattered on the rock of reality. The results of an investigation made in 1960 by the military authorities revealed that the militia was in a monumental mess. At best, it was largely a paper organization, since only a small percentage of those formally enrolled actually received any military training. At worst, it became a heavy burden on the population, since shady elements penetrated its ranks and abused their authority. In the light of these findings, the leadership decided on a shift in militia policy.

During the next two years, little was heard of the militia, and to the extent that its activities were reported the stress was on retrenchment and reorganization. The notion of a universal militia was quietly dropped. Emphasis was placed on the distinction between the hard-core militia, whose membership is relatively small and select, and the ordinary militia, whose main tasks were said to be economic rather than military. Control of the militia was restored to the PLA.

Since 1962 there has been a renewed stress on the militia, but there have been no zealous efforts reminiscent of 1958–60. Despite the theoretical importance of a large-scale militia in Mao's military doctrine, the leadership has continued to give priority to quality rather than quantity.

A professional officer corps. The modernization of the PLA required a large number of officers specialized in modern military skills. The Red Army commanders, however, while tough, talented, and trained in guerrilla warfare, were by and large not qualified for the new tasks. It was necessary, therefore, to develop a professional officer corps. As the army stood on the threshold of modernization, the leadership made a concerted effort to meet that need.

To train officers in new skills, special schools were set up and campaigns were launched to recruit officer candidates with some educational background. In the following years the schools developed into a wide network of military academies, which cover many military subjects. The graduates of the academies, as well as the officers trained in the Soviet Union, became members of the new professional officer corps. At the same time, many veteran military leaders, who had performed both military and civil functions during the revolutionary period and for several years thereafter, were assigned solely to military duties and began to specialize in military affairs. Specialization of both the younger and the veteran officers became a prime source of the professional orientation of the officer corps.

Another principal source of professionalism has been the whole range of measures designed to put the officer corps on an institutional basis. The most important was the 'Regulations on the Service of Officers,' adopted in 1955. For the first time in the history of the army, ranks were established (they were abolished in 1965); specialized categories of officers were set up; and regular channels for entry into the officer corps and for advancement on the basis of professional criteria were introduced. Shortly after the adoption of the regulations, a differentiated pay scale was put into effect for the first time, and military honors, titles, and insignias were conferred upon officers. Cumulatively, these measures signaled the demise of the irregular, informal, and egalitarian guerrilla commander and his replacement by a regular, formal, and status-conscious professional officer.

DOCTRINE AND STRATEGY

Communist Chinese military doctrine covers three types of warfare: nuclear, conventional, and revolutionary. Nuclear and conventional doctrine, which relates to the role of the Chinese armed forces in a future war, is basically defensive. The doctrine of revolutionary warfare, on the other hand, which relates to the operation of indigenous insurgent movements in other countries, is aggressive.

The cornerstone of China's military doctrine is the concept that in war 'man' is more important than weapons. While China's political and military leaders fully recognize the importance of weapons in modern warfare, they maintain that the outcome of a war is ultimately decided not by superior material resources but by superior spiritual resources—morale, courage, and determination. Since spiritual superiority is contingent upon the level of the soldiers' political consciousness and ideological motivation, political-ideological factors are given more weight in warfare than military-technical considerations.

The leadership's steadfast attachment to this concept probably stems from both experience and expedience. On the one hand, it derives from the protracted struggle waged successfully against far better-armed enemies by relying primarily on the 'human element.' On the other hand, it provides a convenient counterweight to China's military-technological inferiority in relation to the United States and the Soviet Union.

The belief in the predominance of the human element, while always latent in Chinese Communist military doctrine, was played down during the height of the modernization period. In the late 1950's, when the Chinese began to veer away from the Soviet path and to return to their revolutionary model, it was vigorously reasserted. Despite the opposition of professional officers, it remains the dominant theme in China's military doctrine.

Nuclear and conventional doctrine and strategy. Despite Peking's claim that China's 'spiritual atomic bomb' is more powerful than the nuclear bomb, China's leaders are clearly aware of the importance and implications of nuclear weapons for modern warfare. Since China's nuclear doctrine is still sketchy, their awareness is most apparent in their actions. And their actions have been dominated by considerable caution, which stems from a realistic appraisal of China's capabilities and weaknesses. The Chinese, in short, are fully aware of the nuclear balance of forces and shape their strategy accordingly.

Until the late 1950's, Chinese strategy was based on the assumption that the United States had a decisive nuclear superiority over the Soviet Union, which put severe limitations on the Communist bloc's actions in the international arena. The limitations, Peking concluded, were removed in the autumn of 1957 following the launching of an ICBM and the orbiting of earth satellites by the Soviets. The Chinese then believed that the military-technological achievements of the U.S.S.R. gave the bloc a superiority, or at least a parity, which enabled it to launch a worldwide assault on U.S. 'imperialism' through militant support of 'national liberation' wars and the initiation of local conflicts. The Chinese neither desired nor foresaw a general war, and they maintained that such actions would not escalate into a general nuclear war because Soviet strength and determination would restrain the U.S. from taking extreme action.

The Soviet leaders, however, saw things differently. They did not claim that the military balance was tilted decisively in their favor, and they were reluctant to foment local conflicts for fear that they would escalate and draw them into a nuclear war over issues that did not involve their vital interests. It soon became apparent to the Chinese that, instead of initiating a new offensive against the United States, the Soviet leaders were more interested in reaching a détente with it. For the Chinese, this meant that their Soviet allies were not prepared to use their power either to support the attainment of China's immediate objectives—the removal of the United States from Taiwan and the reduction of the American presence in Asia—or to promote the progress of world revolution. In short, the Chinese felt that the Russians were prepared to sell them out in order to promote their own interests.

These deeply divergent views pushed China and Russia farther and farther apart. As the relations between them deteriorated drastically, the Chinese undoubtedly concluded that they could no longer rely on the Soviet nuclear shield to protect them against an attack. Because the Chinese realized that they were still far from having a credible deterrent, they found themselves in a position where, from a military viewpoint, they could do little if anything to prevent an attack by the United States. What they could do was exercise caution and restraint in order not to provoke the United States into launching an attack. That demanded a damping down of their militancy toward the United States, in actions if not in words. Nowhere was this more apparent than in China's policy toward the Vietnam war. Thus, paradoxically, the very militancy toward the United States that initially led the Chinese to quarrel violently with the Russians later led to the adoption of a cautious posture toward the United States. By 1969, moreover, the large-scale clashes on the Sino-Soviet border and the concomitant threats from Moscow probably convinced the Chinese that the Soviet Union was a more immediate and a more real threat to China's security than the United States. This means that until the Chinese develop a credible deterrent they will remain vulnerable to nuclear attack by either of the superpowers. In the absence of such a deterrent, there is little the Chinese can do militarily except to act in a cautious and nonprovocative fashion.

Such caution is clearly evident in the thinking of the Chinese leaders on nuclear war, which is dominated solely by defensive considerations. Although the Chinese do not think in terms of initiating a war, they are clearly aware that certain situations might escalate into an all-out war. In such an event, they expect the first phase to take the form of a surprise nuclear strike against China's urban centers and military installations. Unable to deter such an attack, let alone retaliate, China's immediate efforts are directed to mitigating its effects. The Chinese have emphasized the strengthening of their air defense and communications systems and have called for the hardening, camouflaging, and dispersal of military installations. Nevertheless, the Chinese are fully aware that a nuclear attack will inflict immense devastation. Yet, they maintain—and this is the crux of their strategy—while a nuclear attack can destroy urban China, it cannot defeat rural China. China, they say, cannot be subjugated by long-range nuclear strikes. An enemy bent on total victory will have to follow up such strikes with a ground invasion of the mainland, and here, the Chinese claim, they hold decisive advantages that make them virtually unconquerable.

Their advantages stem from several sources: China's vast territory and difficult terrain; the massive and mobilized population; the superior morale and motivation of the armed forces; its 'people's war' strategy and tactics. In short, in the second and conventional phase of the war, when the opposing armies are locked in ground combat, China's ultimate reliance on the human element will give it the upper hand.

That phase, as the Chinese envisage it, will take the form of a protracted war of attrition. China's strategy will be based on a defense in depth and will comprise several steps. First, the Chinese Army will abandon the urban areas and will withdraw into the interior, trading space for time. The enemy will be drawn deep into Chinese territory and will be forced to fight in unfamiliar and hostile terrain, to extend his lines of communication, and to divide his forces. In the meantime, the entire able-bodied population will be mobilized to fight a 'people's war' together with the army. Next, the Chinese will attack the enemy using time-tested guerrilla and mobile tactics, which emphasize tactical concentration of forces, close combat, night fighting, deception, and surprise. They will thereby overcome the enemy's superiority in weapons, including tactical nuclear weapons, and by destroying his forces piecemeal, will gradually erode his total strength. Finally, the Chinese will switch from a strategic defense to a strategic offense aimed at destroying the invading forces.

The whole validity of this doctrine is based on the highly dubious assumption that, in the event of a war, the United States—and now also the Soviet Union—will invade China with ground forces following a nuclear attack. Whether or not China's leaders really believe that such an invasion will take place, it is clear that, in addition to its strategic-military function, the doctrine serves at least two other purposes. First, it is meant to reassure the Chinese Army and people and to maintain their morale by portraying China as virtually invincible despite its technological inferiority. Second, it is probably aimed at deterring the Americans and the Soviets from launching an attack by trying to convince them that a nuclear attack cannot defeat China and a ground invasion will be repulsed.

Although at present China's military doctrine is dominated by defense considerations, there is some question whether this will continue to be so as China moves toward the acquisition of a nuclear capability. While predictions are hazardous, available evidence of Chinese thinking on nuclear warfare gives no reason to suppose that the development of a modest capability will radically alter the leadership's hitherto realistic appraisal of the nuclear balance of forces. The paramount factor in the balance in the foreseeable future will remain the overwhelming nuclear superiority of the United States and the Soviet Union, of which the Chinese will certainly be aware. If so, then there is no reason to assume that they will be prepared to adopt a reckless and high risk military strategy, which is likely to provoke precisely the kind of all-out war that they are at present anxious to avoid. Moreover, the detente between China and the United States and China's normalization of relations with many countries since the end of the Cultural Revolution suggests that the Chinese are not bent on pursuing militant foreign policies.

At the same time, assuming continued caution not to provoke either of the superpowers to attack China, the Chinese will undoubtedly use their nuclear capability to promote the objectives for which they are developing it. First and foremost, they will probably feel that even a small capability in relation to the superpowers will constitute a deterrent that will reduce the possibility of 'nuclear blackmail' against China and will give them greater freedom of action in the international arena than they now have. Second, they may play up both the military power that nuclear capability will give them and the technological achievements it reflects in order to consolidate their claim to great-power status. In the same way, they may try to increase their influence over other Communist Parties. Third, the Chinese may try to intimidate neighboring countries in order to increase their influence.

China's defensive posture and low-risk military policy should not by any means rule out the possibility of offensive action if its leaders come to the conclusion, as they did prior to China's entry into the Korean War, that there is a real threat to the national security or vital interests of the P.R.C.

Doctrine of revolutionary warfare. China's defensive and moderate military strategy is paralleled and, in a sense, supplemented by a militant doctrine of revolutionary warfare, designed to goad and guide revolutionaries throughout the underdeveloped world to launch armed revolts modeled on the pattern of the Chinese revolution against 'U.S. imperialism' and the local governments allied with it.

The vision of the non-Western world following the Chinese road to revolution was present in the Chinese world outlook when the Communists came to power, but in the mid-1950's it was played down, both out of deference to the Soviet Union and out of a desire to cultivate 'bourgeois' non-Western governments. When the Chinese began to challenge Soviet authority and to adopt a more militant foreign policy, the vision re-emerged. It was restated in its fullest and most systematic form by the now-purged Chinese Minister of Defense, Lin Piao, in his treatise 'Long Live the Victory of People's Wars' in September, 1965.

Lin's central theme was the extension of the Chinese revolutionary model to the world scene. As the Chinese envisaged it, each revolutionary movement in the under-developed countries would apply the Chinese model in its struggle for power against the local United States–allied government. Then all those countries would cumulatively extend the model to the world arena and would launch an assault on Western 'im-perialism.' Thus, just as during the revolutionary wars in China the 'towns,' which were the strongholds of the enemy, were encircled and overrun by the 'countryside,' from which the Communists drew their strength, so on a world wide basis the 'towns' —the capitalist countries of Western Europe and North America—would be encircled and overrun by the 'countryside,' the peoples of Asia, Africa, and Latin America.

Lin Piao's treatise, as well as Peking's subsequent pronouncements, were widely interpreted as portending Chinese military and territorial expansion in Asia and beyond. Such an interpretation was mistaken and misleading. Far from fore-shadowing the march of China's armies across its frontiers, Lin actually served notice on revolutionaries in various countries that, while China would give them guidance, encouragement, and limited material support, in the last analysis they would have to do the job by themselves. China's cardinal contribution to world revolution is a tested model for revolutionary warfare, but basically it is a do-it-yourself recipe for revolu-tion. China's military forces will not intervene in 'national liberation wars' abroad.

By fomenting insurrections and acting as the spiritual center of world revolution, the Chinese apparently hoped to achieve both military-strategic and political-ideo-logical aims. First, they expected that, by involving the United States in numerous up-risings, they would be able to strain its resources and weaken its total strength; this would force the United States to reduce its presence in the areas surrounding China. Second, they hoped that, by sparking, supporting, and supervising revolts against 'imperialism,' they would gain prestige and influence in the non-Western world, which would enable them to replace the Soviet Union as the 'true' leader of world revolution.

For most of the 1960's the Chinese, in fact, pursued a policy of encouraging anti-U.S. 'revolutionary' movements and of competing with the Russians for the leadership of such movements. On balance, however, this policy proved to be a failure. This was doubtless one of the reasons for the reappraisal of China's international posture by the post-Cultural Revolution leadership, a reappraisal that led to the rapprochement with the U.S. Although the Chinese profess to see no contradiction between their desire to maintain a revolutionary stance and their felt need to deal with 'U.S. imperialism,' as well as with other 'bourgeois' countries, it is evident that in practice both objectives cannot be pursued with equal intensity at the same time. Since the main thrust of China's foreign policy after the Cultural Revolution has been toward the normalization of state relations and toward 'peaceful coexistence' with most countries regardless of the nature of their regimes, the 'revolutionary' ingredient in China's world outlook and operations has been correspondingly de-emphasized. As long as this thrust continues, the Chinese can be expected to support 'revolutionary' movements only so long as such support does not interfere with the dominant objec-tive of improving state relations, especially with the United States. This approach hardly leaves much scope for a 'revolutionary' posture. China's failure to make any meaningful move in the face of U.S. escalation of the Vietnam war by the imposition of a blockade and the intensification of bombing in May, 1972, is a striking illustration of this approach.

PARTY-ARMY RELATIONS

'Political power,' Mao Tse-tung observed in a much-quoted statement, 'grows out of the barrel of the gun. Our principle is that the Party commands the gun and the gun shall never be allowed to command the party.'[9] The maintenance of political supremacy and control over the military has been a cardinal concern of China's political leaders from the founding of the Red Army until this day. Until recent years they have, on the whole, been singularly successful in putting the principle into practice. However, the transition of the PLA from a guerrilla to a professional army created new problems for Party control of the army, because the principal product of the transition has been a professional officer corps whose views and values differ drastically in many important respects from those of the Party leaders. This divergence of views has brought the PLA into conflict with the Party over a number of inter-related issues at the core of which lies the question of political and professional priorities.

The PLA-Party conflict is part of the broader and basic 'red versus expert' contradiction that characterizes China in a time of transition from a revolutionary to a modern society. Although it has had a disruptive effect on Party-PLA relations, it has occurred within an over-all context of Party supremacy over the armed forces. The officers themselves are by and large Party members who share the same basic political beliefs as the Party leaders and are ultimately loyal to the Party. This, however, has not prevented the development of a professional orientation, which has led the officers to oppose views of the Party leaders that have run counter to their professional judgment.

Control and conflict. In order to ensure the supremacy of the Party over the army, the Chinese leaders instituted a powerful and pervasive political control system parallel to the military chain of command. The system, which has remained in force with few modifications from the first days of the Red Army, although parts of it broke down during the Cultural Revolution, consists of Party committees, political commissars, and political departments. It functions through two separate but interrelated hierarchies, one of which is concerned primarily with supervision and control, the other with education and indoctrination.

Party control is exercised through the Party committees at each level, which direct and supervise the activities of the military commander and the political commissar, one of whom is responsible for military affairs, the other for political. Although this complex system is fraught with potential friction, it generally functioned smoothly during the revolutionary period and the Korean War. However, the development of professionalism and the growth of technical and career specialization brought the elements of friction to the fore. As a result, the professional officers assaulted the political control system on the grounds that it was cumbersome and dangerously detrimental to combat efficiency in modern warfare. What the officers advocated was the adoption of the 'single commander' system on the Soviet pattern, giving greater authority to the professional commander within a considerably looser framework of political controls. More important, the officers did not hesitate to translate their views into action and actually took steps to circumscribe the political controls severely. As a result, by the late 1950's the political control system had deteriorated drastically, especially at the critical company level.

---

[9] *Selected Military Writings of Mao Tse-tung* (Peking, Foreign Languages Press, 1963), p. 272.

The dispute over the degree of political control has been only one of several fundamental issues that have divided the Party and the PLA. Central to all the issues is a basic question: To what extent are the revolutionary-egalitarian principles and practices of the Chinese Communists relevant to the present? Concretely, the question has had several facets. How applicable is the 'man-over-weapons' concept to modern warfare and the modern army, and how far should it dominate the doctrine and organization of the PLA? Should the guerrilla tradition of 'democracy' and the 'mass line' be perpetuated at the expense of strict formal discipline and hierarchy? How should the relations between a garrison army and the population be regulated? To what extent should the army be employed for nonmilitary purposes? To what degree should the PLA follow the example of the more professionally oriented Soviet Army? What proportion of the national budget should be allocated for defense purposes?

Differences over such questions emerged in the mid-1950's, deepened dramatically during the next few years, and reached a climax in 1959. As the professional officers began to denounce or discard revolutionary principles and practices, the Party leadership made efforts to reassert political control and to crack down on the various manifestations of professionalism. In retrospect, however, it is clear that its efforts were largely unsuccessful, primarily because of resistance in the officer corps led by the Minister of Defense, Marshal P'eng Te-huai, and the Chief-of-Staff, General Huang K'o-ch'eng. By 1959, tensions between the Party and the PLA had reached a high point.

The tension was exacerbated and brought to a head by the opposition of Marshal P'eng and his supporters to the Great Leap Forward and, more important, to the growing rift with the Soviet Union. Their opposition, which P'eng reportedly communicated to the Russians, was rooted in a fear that a break with the Soviet Union would seriously harm China's army and nuclear program as well as its strategic posture. In September, 1959, Marshal P'eng, General Huang, and several other leading officers were removed from their posts; Lin Piao was appointed Minister of Defense, and Lo Jui-ch'ing became Chief of Staff.

Upon assuming command, Lin Piao took vast and rapid action to restore the political health and prestige of the PLA. By 1964, the PLA was deemed worthy of emulation by the entire nation. A 'learn from the army' campaign was launched in which the army was presented to the people as the shining model of revolutionary virtues and techniques. More significantly, military officers were transferred to economic departments to take charge of political work.

Under Lin's leadership, the army launched sustained and determined drives to reassert political and ideological control, to revive the revolutionary military model, and to remove the extreme manifestations of professionalism. The drives, while massive and relentless, were also moderate and restrained as far as the professional officers were concerned—and this explains their success. What Lin succeeded in doing, in short, was to maintain a balance between political and professional demands.

The balance was upset in 1965. The major reason, apparently, was the Vietnam war. As the war escalated, the Chinese began to consider seriously the possibility that they would have to fight a war with the United States. Questions of military strategy and policy, which had been relatively dormant, suddenly acquired a new reality and urgency and had to be thrashed out. Consequently, a debate broke out at the highest level of leadership over contingency plans for a possible war with the United States. One group, headed by Mao and Lin Piao, advocated a 'people's war' strategy, with all that it implied for political mobilization. Opposing them was a school of thought, whose main spokesman was Chief of Staff Lo Jui-ch'ing, that favored a more conventional response, more emphasis on military preparations rather than political training, and probably some sort of reconciliation with the Soviet Union, presumably in order to obtain the supplies and support that a conventional strategy required. In the face of this challenge, the leadership intensified political pressures, which in turn generated counterpressures in the officer corps. As a result, the 'red and expert' equilibrium was upset, and a renewed conflict over priorities broke out, which again led to a deterioration of Party-PLA relations. Some time after November, 1965, Lo Jui-ch'ing was dismissed and was replaced by Yang Ch'eng-wu (in an acting capacity). Yang was ousted during the Cultural Revolution.

The problem of 'red versus expert' in the PLA thus continues to wax and wane and will probably remain chronic as long as the leadership holds to its contradictory desire for an army that is both modern and revolutionary.

The army in politics. In the course of the great upheaval of the Cultural Revolution, the PLA was compelled to intervene. The consequences of its intervention have been momentous. It has catapulted the PLA to a position of political primacy in the provinces and has greatly increased its power in Peking. It has forced the army to assume a wide range of new administrative and civil functions. It has eroded the control of the Party center over regional military commanders. And it has split the army itself.

The emergence of the army as a political force began some time before the Cultural Revolution, when Mao started to turn away from the Party and to look upon the PLA as the paradigm of revolutionary purity. The reason was twofold. On the one hand, Mao began to encounter subtle but stiffening resistance in the Party to his efforts to return China to a more revolutionary course, after the relaxation that followed the disastrous Great Leap Forward. On the other hand, the PLA was proving itself to be the most revolutionary organization in China, responsive to Mao's direction and replete with such qualities as struggle, self-sacrifice, and simplicity, which the Maoists found increasingly lacking in the Party. As the power struggle among the top Party leaders intensified, Mao increasingly relied on the military leadership against the opposition in the Party. When the Maoists decided in the summer of 1966 to launch the Cultural Revolution in order to purify and rejuvenate the Party and society, the military leadership under Lin Piao became the spearhead of the new campaign.

Despite the involvement of the army high command in these events, the army itself was carefully kept out of the upheaval during the first phases of the Cultural Revolution. However, when the Cultural Revolution reached the critical stage at which the Maoists were confronted with the unhappy choice of calling off the campaign or calling in the army, they decided to bring in the PLA—with dramatic and unforeseen consequences.

That stage was reached in January, 1967, after the resistance of the Party bureaucracy had thwarted the Maoists in their efforts, first, to use the Red Guards to purge the Party and, next, to have 'revolutionary rebels' seize power from Party organizations throughout China. Faced with this resistance, the Maoists decided that the only way to break the deadlock was to use the PLA, the only remaining organization with the power and discipline to tilt the balance in their favor. Overriding the opposition of some top-ranking military leaders, the Maoist leadership ordered the army to help the 'revolutionary rebels' seize power.

What the army actually did, however, was quite different. Instead of simply installing the revolutionaries in positions of authority and thereby exacerbating the existing chaos, the army from the outset entered the political arena as a stabilizing force. While paying lip service to Maoist revolutionary goals, military commanders began to restore order and to fulfill far-reaching functions of administration, management, and control formerly exercised by the paralyzed Party. For the sake of efficiency, and also because of personal ties, they cooperated with and supported the old-line Party bureaucrats, many of whom were under attack by the revolutionaries.

The PLA's preference for stability rather than revolution quickly brought it into conflict with Maoist groups that wanted to continue the revolutionary campaign. Attacked by the revolutionaries for their actions, the army commanders responded by cracking down on them with a heavy hand. The result was a significant slowdown of revolutionary activity and a virtual stalemate in the Maoist efforts to create a new power structure.

Confronted again with the choice of acquiescing in the stalemate or intensifying revolutionary activity, the Maoists opted for escalation. Denouncing the army for suppressing the revolution, they severely curbed the powers of the PLA and urged the Maoist groups to get on with the Cultural Revolution.

Those moves had calamitous consequences. The absence of effective authority led to severe disorders, which mounted steadily. By the summer of 1967, many major cities had become battlegrounds for countless power struggles, some of which were waged with weapons looted from the army. The reaction of the military commanders was either to do nothing, in order not to get involved, or to suppress the most active Maoist troublemakers, usually by supporting moderate groups linked with the local Party machine. The most extreme example of the latter course was the July 'Wuhan incident,' in which the local military commander tried to defy Peking. Although he failed, the badly shaken Maoist leadership responded by launching an assault on the PLA.

The strife intensified as a result, and by the end of the summer it became so severe that the Maoist leadership had no choice but to damp down the Cultural Revolution drastically in order to avert total chaos. Because only the army was capable of restoring order, it was given clear and wide powers, including the use of force, to do so. At the same time, an effort was made to rebuild the prestige of the PLA, which had been damaged by the attacks of the Maoists. With its new authority, the PLA by and large succeeded in imposing order, although in many areas tensions continued to simmer, occasionally breaking out in violent clashes.

Under the aegis of the PLA 'revolutionary committees' began to be established to replace the decimated Party and government administrations. Although the process preserved the fiction that a new revolutionary power structure was being set up, in fact the committees were dominated by military men or by seasoned bureaucrats supported by the military, while Maoist representatives were given minor roles or simply ignored.

This led to a repetition of the action-reaction cycle. Stalemated again in their efforts, the Maoists counterattacked and a conflict at the highest level of leadership, which became intertwined with internal PLA rivalries, led to the removal of the Acting Chief of Staff, Yang Ch'eng-wu, in late March, 1968. Unlike the previous year, however, no assault was launched on the PLA, and Yang's replacement by Huang Yung-sheng, who had been attacked by Red Guards for his moderation and was apparently respected by the powerful provincial commanders, was also designed to reassure the military. Nevertheless, the revolutionaries were again given the green light, and an upsurge of violence ensued. Once again the Maoists were forced to pull back and to call upon the army to restore and maintain order. Convinced finally of the intractable indiscipline of the Red Guard revolutionaries, Mao personally sanctioned the dissolution of their organizations at the end of July, 1968. That was the beginning of the end of the Cultural Revolution.

With the long-sought sanction of Peking behind them, the regional commanders proceeded to discipline the Red Guards and to break up their organizations. The restoration of order was carried out with the help of newly formed 'Worker-Peasant Mao Tse-tung Thought Propaganda Teams,' probably because the Maoist leadership was reluctant to sanction publicly a full-scale military crackdown on the Red Guards. It was clear, however, that the effectiveness of the teams depended on the guidance and support of the PLA. Thus, the military again moved to the center of the stage—and there it was to remain.

In September, 1968, the last provincial revolutionary committee was established. With the military's almost complete domination of these committees, the PLA emerged as the central political and administrative authority in the localities. As a result of its pivotal political role, the army also became a major political force in national policy-making councils, although at this level the radical elements, though greatly weakened, still remained a force to be reckoned with.

The new power structure, with the army as its central pillar, was reflected in the composition of the central Party organs set up by the Ninth Party Congress, which convened in April, 1969, in effect, to wind up the Cultural Revolution. Of the 170 full members of the Central Committee, 87 were military men (about 51.2 per cent), 53 were veteran cadres (about 31.5 per cent), and 29 were representatives of mass organizations (about 17.2 per cent). In the Politburo, at least one-third of the members could be classed as having a primary identification with the military. More striking was the rise in the prominence of regional military officers: The representation of regional military organs increased from 2 per cent in the Eighth Central Committee to more than 26 per cent in the Ninth, while the representation of the central military organs remained about the same. In the Politburo, of the seven military men, two were regional commanders, while one, the now-purged Chief-of-Staff Huang Yung-sheng, was a former regional commander with close local ties. In the previous Politburo, no regional military leaders were represented. In sum, if the Cultural Revolution resulted in a far-reaching shift of political power to the army, within the army, much of this power seemed to be concentrated in the hands of the regional military commanders.

The regional commanders, however, have set strict parameters on the exercise of their newly-acquired power. Although they have used it freely to flout unacceptable directives from Peking, they have scrupulously refrained from open defiance or from taking any other step that would endanger the framework of national unity or bring into question the basic allegiance of the regions to Peking. The only exception was the outright insubordination of the Wuhan commander in July, 1967, and he was swiftly removed. In short, the fundamental adherence of the regional commanders to central authority has far outweighed the centrifugal tendencies inherent in their newly-attained power. The flexibility deriving from this power, however, has added a new dimension to the power structure in China.

Greatly compounding the complexity of this structure has been the fact that political power shifted to an army which came out of the Cultural Revolution marked by deep internal fissures. As a result of its involvement in the political struggle and of the new political role that it has assumed, the army has been subjected to unprecedented strains. These strains have exacerbated old cleavages and created new ones, laying the groundwork for the formation of cliques and coalitions along new lines.

Although such cleavages cannot be identified with any certainty, it appears that the most basic division has been between the PLA high command in Peking and the regional commands. Rooted primarily in the hectic days of the Cultural Revolution, when central and regional military leaders were laboring under conflicting pressures, this division gave rise to tensions that apparently continued to simmer after the end of the Cultural Revolution and eventually erupted in the struggle that resulted in the purge of Lin Piao and other central military leaders in the autumn of 1971. Other intra-army splits and alignments probably run along interregional, service, and professional-political lines.

Given these actual and potential sources of disunity, the army seemed to maintain an impressive outward unity until the fall of Lin Piao and his associates. Since in retrospect it is reasonable to assume that infighting was going on all the time, it appears that the internal rifts were submerged by more compelling factors.

The main factor was doubtless the common desire of the army leaders to protect and promote the interests of the army as an institution. In the provinces, this meant that the army commanders had to safeguard and solidify their power against encroachment by radical elements during the process of reconstruction of Party organizations, which began in the autumn of 1968. The radical Maoists in Peking and the localities apparently viewed this process as an opportunity for taking power from the army. The army commanders, however, clearly had no intention of accommodating them. Due to the conflicts over the distribution of positions in the new Party committees, the process of reconstruction proceeded slowly, but in the end the army won out. When the last provincial Party committee was finally established in August, 1972, it was clear that, if anything, the political power of the army had increased: Almost 60 per cent of the top leadership personnel on these committees were military men; some 35 per cent were veteran officials, generally allied with the military against the radicals; representatives of mass organizations (by no means the most radical) captured less than 6 per cent of the key posts.

As the army consolidated its regional power, it also moved, doubtless in alliance with moderate Party and government leaders headed by Chou En-lai, to 'settle accounts' in Peking. The prime targets of this move were some of the radical leaders responsible for the excesses of the Cultural Revolution, and especially for extremist attacks on the PLA. Foremost among these was Ch'en Po-ta, Mao's close associate for many years and a prominent radical leader during the Cultural Revolution. Ch'en dropped out of sight after the Second Plenum of the Central Committee in August, 1970, and subsequently an intensive, though indirect, campaign was launched against him in the press.

This trend toward what appeared to be the consolidation of power by a seemingly unified army was sharply disrupted by the enigmatic purge of Lin Piao and several top members of the PLA general staff. Whatever may have been the subterranean tensions that led to this purge, its external manifestations began to surface only in September, 1971. They included the mysterious crash of a Chinese military plane in Mongolia, presumably en route to the Soviet Union; the complete grounding of the Chinese air force for several days and its almost complete grounding for several weeks; the cancellation of the October 1 military parade; the disappearance and 'depersonalization' of Lin Piao and the disappearance of several top central military leaders; and the fantastic story given out to lower-level officials of a plot by Lin Piao and his associates to assassinate Mao. In subsequent months, the press launched an oblique campaign against Lin (now termed a 'political swindler' or 'charlatan'), accusing him, among other charges, of 'illicit relations with a foreign country' (presumably the Soviet Union), pursuing an ultra-leftist political line, manipulating the cult of Mao for his personal benefit, and masterminding conspiracies.

These puzzling developments have prompted analysts of Chinese political affairs to suggest various scenarios for the Lin Piao affair, but no one explanation is comprehensive or completely convincing. One theory is that the campaign against 'ultra-leftist' leaders was viewed by Lin and his colleagues as a threat to their position, causing them to make some move that led to their downfall. If so, the reason for this would be that, although Lin was hardly a firebrand radical, he had become identified with the radical wing of the Maoist leadership during the Cultural Revolution, with the result that regional and professional commanders, who had been harassed by the radicals during the turmoil, wanted Lin and his associates removed. Personal and factional rivalries, moreover, may have become intertwined with concrete issues of external and internal policy, namely, the detente with the United States and the question of resource allocation. One unanswered question with respect to this possibility concerns what role Mao played in the whole affair. Another related theory is that the purge of Lin was partly connected with the political role and power of the army. However, although Lin's demise was followed by a lowering of the army's profile on the Chinese political scene, there were no signs that its power had been significantly reduced. In short, the real story of this mysterious affair remains to be told.

This much, however, can be stated with certainty: The downfall of Lin Piao and his supporters was brought about by a coalition of several groups, including regional and professional elements in the army, civilian leaders headed by Chou En-lai, and, presumably, the remaining radical leaders. This coalition appears to make up the leadership in China in the post-Lin Piao period. Because of the disparate interests of its component parts, however, such a coalition has elements of instability built into it. How long these elements will be submerged by an overriding common interest remains to be seen. As of the summer of 1972, Chinese politics was still very much in flux.

SELECTED BIBLIOGRAPHY

(Translations of Chinese articles and statements can be found in the translations series put out by the American Consulate-General, Hong Kong.)

CHENG, CHESTER. *The Politics of the Chinese Red Army: A Translation of the Bulletin of Activities of the People's Liberation Army.* Stanford Calif.: The Hoover Institution on War, Revolution, and Peace, 1966. Translation of twenty-nine issues of a secret periodical covering the period January 1 through August 26, 1961.

DOMES, JÜRGEN. 'The Role of the Military in the Formation of Revolutionary Committees, 1967–1968,' *The China Quarterly*, No. 44 (October–December, 1970), pp. 112–145. A scholarly treatment of the army's political involvement during the Cultural Revolution.

GARTHOFF, RAYMOND L., ed. *Sino-Soviet Military Relations.* New York: Praeger Publishers, 1966. A useful collection of articles, some of which are very good, others less so.

GEORGE, ALEXANDER L. *The Chinese Communist Army in Action: The Korean War and Its Aftermath.* New York: Columbia University Press, 1967. An excellent analysis of the political organization and practices of the PLA during the Korean War, based on interviews with prisoners of war. Final chapter summarizes later developments.

GITTINGS, JOHN. *The Role of the Chinese Army.* New York: Oxford University Press, 1967. A first-rate political and social history of the PLA since 1946, the most comprehensive account available.

GRIFFITH, SAMUEL B. *The Chinese People's Liberation Army.* New York: McGraw-Hill, 1967. A lucid and informative, though somewhat uneven survey of the history of the Chinese army and its current capability and doctrine.

HALPERIN, MORTON H. *China and the Bomb.* New York: Praeger Publishers, 1965. A thoughtful and valuable treatment of China's nuclear strategy and its implications.

HSIEH, ALICE LANGLEY. 'China's Secret Military Paper: Military Doctrine and Strategy,' *The China Quarterly*, No. 18, April–June, 1964, pp. 79–99. An excellent analysis based on the documents cited in CHENG, above.

———. *Communist China's Evolving Military Strategy and Doctrine.* Institute for Defense Analysis, Paper P-646, June, 1970. An excellent analysis of the subject, with special emphasis on China's attitude toward the Vietnam war and the Sino-Soviet border conflict of 1969.

———. *Communist China's Strategy in the Nuclear Era.* Englewood Cliffs, N.J.: Prentice-Hall, 1962. A solid, pioneering analysis of the subject.

JOFFE, ELLIS. 'The Chinese Army in the Cultural Revolution: The Politics of Intervention,' *Current Scene*, 8, No. 18 (December 7, 1970), pp. 1 ff. An analysis of the PLA's role in the Cultural Revolution.

———. *Party and Army: Professionalism and Political Control in the Chinese Officer Corps, 1949–1964.* Cambridge, Mass.: Harvard University Press, 1965. Focuses on the conflict between military professionalism and political control.

POWELL, RALPH L. 'Maoist Military Doctrines,' *Asian Survey*, 8, No. 4 (April, 1968): 239–62. A valuable treatment of China's defense and revolutionary warfare doctrines and of internal opposition to Mao's military line.

———. *Politico-Military Relationships in Communist China.* Washington, D.C.: External Research Staff, Bureau of Intelligence and Research, U.S. Department of State, 1963. An excellent analysis of documents.

———. 'The Party, the Government, and the Gun,' *Asian Survey*, 10, No. 6 (June, 1970), pp. 441–71. A detailed account of Party–PLA relations and the army's role in the rebuilding of the Party after the Cultural Revolution.

RHOADS, EDWARD, J. M. *The Chinese Red Army, 1927–1963: An Annotated Bibliography*. Cambridge, Mass.: Harvard University Press, 1964. A comprehensive and annotated bibliography.

WHITSON, WILLIAM W., 'The Field Army in Chinese Communist Military Politics,' *The China Quarterly*, No. 37 (January–March, 1969), pp. 1–30. A provocative and original analysis.

11

EVOLUTION OF FOREIGN POLICY

HAROLD C. HINTON

Objectives of Foreign Policy

The foreign policy objectives of the Chinese Communists may be briefly defined as the deterrence or avoidance of external attack by a hostile power; unification of the country and termination of the civil war through the 'liberation' of Taiwan; and the maximization and acceptance by others of Chinese Communist influence, through revolutionary (Communist and specifically Maoist) as well as conventional means, in Asia, the developing countries, an expanding (it is hoped) international Communist movement, and, ultimately, the entire world. Since about 1958, the Chinese Communists have tried to enhance their influence on the left everywhere by posing as the most enthusiastic and effective leader of an alleged worldwide struggle against American 'imperialism,' and since about 1960 also against Soviet 'revisionism.' During 1969, when the Soviet Union appeared at times to threaten military action against Communist China, the 'social imperialists' and 'new Tsars' were often pictured as a greater enemy of China—and as certainly no better—than the Western imperialists. In addition, where the power of the Communist Chinese state could reach, meaning mainly continental Asia, they have employed it, or more often the explicit or implicit threat of its use, as a means of further enhancing their influence through the creation of a 'wave of the future' psychology and of promoting their security through working for the elimination of the threatening military presence of the United States.

The Alliance with Stalin (1949–53)

'Lean to one side.' Although the Chinese Communists, and Mao Tse-tung in particular, had had some serious disagreements with Stalin before 1949, they never produced an open break like the one between Stalin and Tito in 1948. What concerns us here is not the reasons for this fact but its result: The Chinese Communists came to power in 1949 convinced that considerations of ideology, Party history, and expediency (geographic contiguity and the need for economic and military aid and protection) all dictated that the People's Republic of China should, in Mao's phrase, 'lean to one side,' that is, toward the Soviet Union.[1] Similarly, considerations of ideology (the belief that such a thing as the 'imperialist camp' existed and that the United States was its leader), history (American support for the Chinese Nationalists during the preceding civil war), and expediency (Stalin's involvement in the cold war with

---

[1] The phrase is from Mao's 'On the People's Democratic Dictatorship,' June 30, 1949, *Selected Works of Mao Tse-tung*, 4 (Peking: Foreign Languages Press, 1961): 415.

the United States and his insistence that other Communist Parties follow his lead in it as in other matters) dictated a policy of hostility toward the United States. Presumably because a continuing American political presence in mainland China would have seemed inconsistent with such a stance and would have complicated the elimination of Western ties and pro-Western feelings from the country, an early decision was taken to have no diplomatic relations with the United States, which was forced by maltreatment of its diplomatic and consular personnel to withdraw them about the beginning of 1950.

If, for the P.R.C., the essentially friendly Soviet Union was so strong that it could best be managed through conciliation, falling short, however, of an acceptance of satellite status by Peking, and if the essentially hostile United States could best be holding it at arms length and vilifying it, somewhat greater opportunities for flexibility existed in the direction of the relatively 'soft' countries of southern Asia. Like Stalin, the Chinese Communists overestimated the revolutionary opportunities presented by the wave of decolonization that had begun in the Philippines in July, 1946, and assumed tidal proportions on the Indian subcontinent a year later. They denied that the new states were truly independent of 'imperialism' and that they were neutral in the cold war, as they professed to be. Every state, said Mao Tse-tung, and not merely China, must 'lean to one side.' In February, 1948, the Chinese Communists told the leftist Calcutta Youth Conference that 'armed struggle' (revolutionary warfare), Chinese-style, was the wave of the future for southern Asia,[2] and Liu Shao-ch'i elaborated on the same theme in a celebrated speech of November, 1949.[3] There was a clear implication in these statements that, as even Stalin seems to have conceded in mid-1949, the P.R.C. would exercise a degree of leadership over leftist revolutions in southern Asia, not only by force of example and incitement but also by virtue of strategic advice and probably arms, training, and funds as well.

Mao Tse-tung went to Moscow for the first time in December, 1949–February, 1950, to establish and formalize a viable relationship with Stalin. He was treated with great respect, and it was obvious that his regime was regarded by his host as occupying a special place in the 'socialist camp,' second to the Soviet Union but not subservient to it, and far ahead of the 'people's democracies' of Eastern Europe. The negotiations, nevertheless, were not only prolonged and secret but undoubtedly heated at times. The affairs of the major Asian Communist Parties were discussed and joint directives formulated as appropriate; the Japanese Communists, for example, were told to launch an insurrection against the American occupation authorities, and the Indian Communist leadership was told to stop criticizing Mao. In the light of subsequent developments, there can be little doubt that the planning of the Korean War, which was to be Stalin's counterpart to the Berlin Blockade in the West and his answer to American moves toward a peace treaty with, and (as Stalin and Mao saw it) the rearmament of, Japan was discussed. A thirty-year defensive alliance, directed against Japan or any power allied with it (meaning the United States) was signed and published. A Soviet economic credit of $300 million was agreed on, and there was probably a secret agreement on military aid as well. Soviet control over the major railways and ports of Manchuria, gained by virtue of the defeat of Japan and a treaty with Nationalist China in 1945, was confirmed, but that control was to be restored to China no later than the end of 1952. Four 'joint' companies, actually to be under predominantly Soviet control, were created in Manchuria and western Sinkiang.[4]

---

[2] 'Congratulations on the Opening of the Southeast Asia Youth Conference,' NCNA, February 16, 1948.

[3] Speech at Trade Union Conference of Asia and Australasian Countries, November 16, 1949 (NCNA, November 23, 1949).

[4] Cf. Max Beloff, *Soviet Policy in the Far East, 1944–1951* (London: Oxford University Press, 1953), pp. 70–78, 260–67.

Around the central core of its alliance with the Soviet Union and its hostility toward the United States, the P.R.C. constructed in the first several months after coming to power a substantial network of diplomatic relationships. It was promptly recognized by, and recognized in return, all the states of the 'socialist camp,' except that it did not reciprocate the recognition of the anti-Stalinist Tito. In mid-January, 1950, it preceded the Soviet Union in granting recognition to Ho Chi Minh's Democratic Republic of Vietnam, which had just appealed for such recognition. The P.R.C. was also recognized about the same time by four neutral Asian countries (Burma, India, Pakistan, and Indonesia) and by seven European countries (the United Kingdom, the Netherlands, Switzerland, and the Scandinavian states).

Intervention in the Korean War. In the spring of 1950, while the P.R.C. made some clumsy and ultimately ineffective preparations for an amphibious assault on Taiwan where the Nationalists were holding out without benefit of American aid or protection, Stalin proceeded to strengthen the North Korean Army for an invasion of South Korea, which was lightly armed, denuded of American troops, and (as indicated by a famous speech by Secretary of State Dean Acheson on January 12)[5] like Taiwan without American protection. Two days after North Korean forces began their invasion on June 25, President Truman not only initiated American intervention on behalf of South Korea but announced the extension of American protection to Taiwan. Increasingly, the Chinese Communist leadership seems to have seen General MacArthur as the architect and leader of a vast, coordinated operation whose ultimate target was themselves, and they were accordingly alarmed when in October his forces, after driving the North Koreans from South Korea, entered North Korea and moved toward the Manchurian frontier. Stalin, for his part, was anxious to salvage something from the unexpected defeat of the North Koreans, at least to the point of preventing a permanent 'imperialist' conquest of North Korea, but since he was still unwilling to intervene himself, he turned to the only other available proxy, the P.R.C. It seems that Mao not only accepted Stalin's views on the need for Chinese intervention in Korea but basically agreed with them. In addition, the P.R.C. apparently wanted to increase its leverage on the United States and the international community so as to increase its chances of 'liberating' Taiwan and entering the United Nations.[6]

Fortified by a pledge of prompt deliveries of modern Soviet weapons (not strategic in character, however), the P.R.C. secretly sent a sizable force of 'volunteers' into North Korea beginning in mid-October. They began to fight in earnest in late November, as soon as General MacArthur, who apparently was unaware of both the strength and the seriousness of the Chinese forces in Korea, launched his 'home by Christmas' offensive. By the end of the year the United Nations forces had been driven back approximately to the 38th parallel, but the Chinese began to suffer defeats when they tried to invade South Korea in the first weeks of 1951. Unconvinced, they launched another major offensive in late April and mid-May, apparently in order to achieve the best possible position prior to the armistice talks that, since the relieving of General MacArthur on April 11, seemed increasingly probable. The crushing of that offensive left the P.R.C. with no choice but to endorse a Soviet proposal that armistice talks get under way, as they did on July 10.

Changing policy in Southeast Asia. While its 'volunteers' were fighting a more or less conventional war in Korea, the P.R.C. was trying, with what must have been grudging consent from Stalin, to exercise at least a degree of political leadership over the Communist movements of southern Asia. For a variety of reasons, however, there

---

[5] Text in Margaret Carlyle, ed., *Documents on International Affairs, 1949–1950* (London: Oxford University Press, 1953), pp. 96–108.

[6] Cf. Allen S. Whiting, *China Crosses the Yalu: The Decision to Enter the Korean War* (New York: Macmillan, 1960).

were severe limitations on Chinese capabilities for doing so, as well as on the prospects of the local Communist movements themselves. The Malayan Party, for example, although overwhelmingly Chinese in composition and well prepared for guerrilla warfare, was too remote to be effectively directed from Peking and, worse still, was gradually crushed by a huge and well-directed British counterinsurgency campaign. The Burmese Communist Party was too divided, and the Philippine Party too remote, for Chinese influence to be very great, and the Indonesian Party's effort at a revolt was crushed in 1948, before the Chinese Communists were in power. Only in Vietnam did a Communist insurgency make significant gains, but the explanation was less Chinese aid and advice (which were provided, to be sure) than the ineptitude and colonial overtones of the French regime and the vigor and effectiveness of the Vietnamese Communist movement led by Ho Chi Minh. Chinese defeats in Korea diminished Peking's leverage with Stalin, who had felt less interest in Communist revolts in southern Asia since he had conceded a primary Chinese role in their guidance; instead of reviving his interest now that Peking's revolutionary designs were faring poorly in southern Asia, Stalin kept his eyes on other areas, notably Europe and Korea, and in the autumn of 1951 had one of his leading orientalists announce that the Chinese revolutionary model should not be regarded as a 'stereotype' for the rest of Asia.[7] Finally, as the P.R.C. realized as soon as it began to encounter defeats in Korea, the good will of Asian neutrals, India in particular, could be a valuable political asset and a restraint on possible American military designs against China.

For all the above reasons, in 1951 and 1952 the P.R.C. sharply reduced its incitement of and support for Communist revolts in southern Asia, except for the one in Vietnam, which was progressing well and in any case was being conducted against a colonial regime rather than an independent one. Clearly the Chinese leadership had begun to comprehend the independence and essential neutrality of the new Asian states, notably India, even though it did not yet say so in public. In a clumsy and tentative way, and apparently with Soviet approval, the P.R.C. began to cultivate them diplomatically while also trying to mobilize the fellow travelers of the world (as at the Asian and Pacific Peace Conference, held in Peking in October, 1952) to oppose American military pressures on China.

The Korean armistice negotiations. Although both sides in the Korean armistice negotiations continued to fight and bargain hard for the best possible position, agreement in principle seemed to have been reached by the beginning of 1952 on an armistice roughly along the 38th parallel, with foreign troops to remain in Korea. At that time, however, it became clear that the United Nations Command intended not to return a substantial proportion of the North Korean and Chinese prisoners it was holding, on the ground (true, but regarded in Pyongyang and Peking as probably false and in any case politically unacceptable) that they were unwilling to be repatriated. The injection of this politically sensitive issue delayed the armistice for another year and a half, during which tension rose drastically. In September, 1952, the P.R.C. not only persuaded Stalin to pledge additional industrial and military aid but ostensibly asked him, while withdrawing from his other positions in Manchuria, to leave a garrison at Port Arthur as a deterrent to possible American attacks on Manchuria. Late in the year, the Indian Government introduced a 'compromise' resolution on the Korean prisoner question in the United Nations General Assembly.[8] It was acceptable to the Communist side, because it stressed the right to repatriation, but the Indian Government soon modified it, presumably under Western pressure, in the opposite direction.[9]

---

[7] Cf. Charles B. McLane, *Soviet Strategies in Southeast Asia: An Exploration of Eastern Policy under Lenin and Stalin* (Princeton N.J.: Princeton University Press, 1966), p. 453.

[8] *The New York Times*, November 18, 1952.   [9] *Ibid.*, December 2, 1952.

Pyongyang and Peking now attacked it, apparently with the full support of Stalin, who in his last months was evidently not of sound mind and was in a very bellicose mood.

The Eisenhower Administration, which was pledged to achieve an armistice in Korea by whatever means were necessary, came into office in January, 1953, and promptly tried to pressure Peking by announcing that the Chinese Nationalists were now free to attack the mainland. When that produced no result, Washington began to threaten Peking, privately but explicitly and through a variety of channels, with the extension of the war from Korea to the mainland of China and the use of nuclear weapons.[10] In its extremity, the Chinese leadership turned to Stalin, apparently with a request for a prompt transfer of nuclear weapons to Chinese control, among other things, but Stalin died in March, 1953, just as the crisis was at its height. His successors, who were in a far from bellicose mood, refused the P.R.C.'s requests and left it to sink or swim.[11] Chang avoided sinking by agreeing on July 27, after an appropriate delay and further bargaining, to an armistice that did not guarantee the return of all the prisoners it had lost, about 70 per cent of whom ultimately refused repatriation.

A number of lessons were drawn from the Korean War, not always correctly, by the participants in it. The P.R.C., for its part, knew that it had enhanced its prestige by its involvement and believed it had enhanced its security by keeping American forces away from the Manchurian border and presumably deterring the United States from behaving in the same way again. On the other hand, Chinese human and economic losses had been quite heavy, and Peking knew that it had not only incurred grave military risks but had evoked against itself an American policy of military containment that was likely to prove both a threat and an obstacle in the future. *Never since has the P.R.C. chosen to confront the United States militarily in as direct and therefore dangerous a fashion as in Korea from late 1950 to mid-1953.*

The Heyday of Peaceful Coexistence (1953–55)

Cooperation with Khrushchev. The death of Stalin and the relative weakness and disunity of his successors left Mao Tse-tung in the position of the world's senior Communist and gave his regime a degree of leverage on the course of events in Moscow. The two main Soviet factions, led after mid-1953 by Malenkov and Khrushchev, competed for Chinese support; Khrushchev gained it by his relatively tough policies, which conveyed the promise of greater aid to and support of the P.R.C. than did his opponent's. The Chinese preference for Khrushchev came out clearly when he led an important delegation, minus Malenkov, to Peking in September–October, 1954; the result was a far-reaching agreement on economic, technical, and political cooperation.[12]

Vietnam and the Geneva Conference of 1954. As soon as the P.R.C. decided, in the spring of 1953, to accept an armistice in Korea, it began to step up its military aid to the Vietnamese Communists. When the latter besieged the French outpost of Dienbienphu in the spring of 1954 in order to achieve the best possible position at the peace talks that had already been agreed on by the Big Four, a Sino-American crisis began to materialize as Secretary of State Dulles threatened the P.R.C. with retaliation if it should intervene directly in support of the Vietnamese Communists.[13] In reality, the

---

[10] Dwight D. Eisenhower, *Mandate for Change, 1953–1956* (New York: Doubleday, 1963), p. 181.

[11] Harold C. Hinton, *Communist China in World Politics* (Boston: Houghton Mifflin, 1966), pp. 222–29.

[12] *The New York Times*, October 12, 1954.

[13] Melvin Gurtov, *The First Vietnam Crisis: Chinese Communist Strategy and United States Involvement, 1953–1954* (New York: Columbia University Press, 1967), pp. 81–83.

P.R.C. almost certainly contemplated no such intervention. The crisis soon passed, but it left the Chinese leaders in a nervous frame of mind and helped Dulles to create an atmosphere suitable for the formation, later in the year, of SEATO (the Southeast Asian Treaty Organization), which was to protect Southeast Asia as far as possible from Chinese or Vietnamese Communist attack or subversion.

Largely because of nervousness over American intentions, the P.R.C. gave its main attention at the Geneva Conference on Indochina (May–July, 1954) to ensuring that no American military presence would be permitted in Indochina rather than to maximizing the political position of the Vietnamese Communists. The latter, who also received much less than full support from the Soviet Union, accordingly found themselves in a political position considerably less favorable than their military victory seemed to warrant. The most important provision of the settlement was the division of Vietnam at the 17th parallel into two zones, a Communist one in the north and a non-Communist one in the south, for purposes of military regroupment. The two zones were to be reunited following general elections to be held within two years.

Dissatisfied with the outcome of the Geneva Conference and apprehensive that the growth of the military potential of the U.S. aided Chinese Nationalists, would result in a Nationalist offensive operation in the Taiwan Strait, the P.R.C. promptly turned its attention to that area. For about six months, beginning in September, 1954, a major politico-military crisis raged in the strait, one of the few concrete results being the conclusion of a defensive alliance between Nationalist China and the United States. The P.R.C. eased its pressures on the Nationalists in the spring of 1955, apparently because of some retaliatory threats by Secretary Dulles, Soviet non-support, and a desire to appear in the best possible light at the forthcoming Asian-African Conference to be held at Bandung, in Java.

The 'spirit of Bandung.' In pursuit of its decision to improve relations with neutral Asia, motivated to a large extent by anti-American reasons, the P.R.C. signed an agreement with India in April, 1954, that recognized Chinese sovereignty in Tibet and and bound both parties to abide by the principles of peaceful coexistence. Premier Chou En-lai similarly endorsed peaceful coexistence during visits to India and Burma during the course of the Geneva Conference, at which he led the Chinese delegation with great brilliance. The essence of the Chinese position was that other Asian countries could expect, for the time being at least, reasonable immunity from Chinese subversive pressures as long as they refrained from aligning themselves in any way with the United States. Chou expounded this position with great effect at the Bandung Conference (April, 1955), insisted on the P.R.C.'s desire for peace and for security from 'imperialist' threats, and even offered to negotiate with the United States on Taiwan.[14]

Sino-American ambassadorial talks actually began later in the year and have continued with some interruptions down to the present; although there has been some useful communication and even negotiation, neither side has succeeded in modifying the other's position on Taiwan or any other fundamental issue between them. The P.R.C. insists that the United States is occupying Taiwan and must stop; the United States demands that the P.R.C. promise not to use force to settle the Taiwan issue.[15]

There is no doubt that the Chinese preaching of peaceful coexistence with neutral Asia, combined with outrageous flattery of neutral leaders like Prince Sihanouk of Cambodia, greatly enhanced its influence as a state. It remained to be seen whether

---

[14] Cf. *China and the Asian-African Conference (Documents)* (Peking: Foreign Languages Press), 1955.

[15] Cf. Kenneth T. Young, *Negotiating with the Chinese Communists: The United States Experience, 1953–1967* (New York: McGraw Hill, 1968).

Peking would accept indefinitely the concomitant diminution of its effectiveness as a revolutionary influence.

THE EMERGENCE OF A HARDER LINE (1955–58)

Drifting apart from close Soviet cooperation. It is very likely that each party to the Sino-Soviet understanding reached in Peking in October, 1954, considered itself betrayed in spirit by the other during the succeeding months. The main issues were two: (1) Soviet willingness to conciliate the West without making sufficient provision for Chinese interests, as symbolized by Soviet participation in a Summit Conference in July, 1955, from which the P.R.C. was excluded; and (2) emerging Sino-Soviet rivalry in the Third World, as symbolized by Chinese participation in the Bandung Conference, to which the Soviet Union was not invited. As Khrushchev adopted an increasingly active policy in such far-flung areas as the Middle East, China's relative importance to Soviet interests declined, and Peking's leverage on Moscow's behavior was accordingly reduced.

De-Stalinization. Khrushchev's reluctance to provoke the United States and his determination to play an active role in the third world while discouraging Communist insurgency wherever there was a chance for local Parties to come to power by electoral means came out clearly in his published report to his party's Twentieth Congress (February, 1956).[16] His attitudes were basically unacceptable to the Chinese Communist leadership, or at least to Mao. Even more unpalatable was Khrushchev's famous attack, on Stalin's memory in his 'secret speech.'[17] The attack on Stalin indirectly reflected on Mao and seems to have led to some efforts by Mao's colleagues to tone down the overwhelming 'cult of personality' that had grown up around Mao in China.[18] In an effort to defend and enhance his own position against pressures from both his own colleagues and Khrushchev, as well as to demonstrate the superiority of his own system to the Soviet, Mao launched a series of dramatic policy initiatives, beginning with the Hundred Flowers campaign for greater freedom of expression in the spring of 1956 and culminating with the Great Leap Forward in 1958. All were largely unsuccessful, and all exacerbated relations with Khrushchev, who was coming to regard Mao with increasing disfavor as bumptious and unpredictable. Mao, for his part, thought the same of Khrushchev.

The 'Hundred Flowers' campaign. Having cautioned Khrushchev in April, 1956, not to push de-Stalinization too far,[19] the Chinese leadership played a constructive role in the aftermath of the Hungarian crisis by encouraging the restless East European states to accept a degree of Soviet leadership sufficient to prevent the appearance of more crises like the one in Hungary. At home, Mao reasoned that he could both ensure against an explosion of the Hungarian type and score points against Khrushchev by renewing his invitation, originally tendered in the spring of 1956 but so far not taken up to any great degree, to intellectuals and others to speak their minds freely on public issues.[20] Once convinced that they could do so safely, numerous in-

---

[16] Text released by Tass, February 14, 1956.

[17] Text in *The New York Times*, June 5, 1956.

[18] The new constitution adopted by the Communist Party of China in September, 1956; text in Peter S. H. Tang, ed., *Communist China Today*, 2 (New York: Praeger, 1958): 112–33), contained several innovations adverse to Mao and his 'cult of personality.'

[19] 'The Historical Experience Concerning the Dictatorship of the Proletariat,' *Jen-min Jih-pao*, April 5, 1956; text in *Communist China, 1955–1959: Policy Documents with Analysis* (Cambridge Mass.: Harvard University Press, 1962), pp. 144–51.

[20] An edited version of the invitation, given in a speech made by Mao on February 27, 1957, was published on June 18, 1957, as 'On the Correct Handling of Contradictions Among the People,' *Selected Readings from the Works of Mao Tse-tung* (Peking: Foreign Languages Press, 1967), pp. 350–86.

dividuals expressed some severe criticisms of the Chinese Communist regime in May, 1957. Mao promptly withdrew his invitation and punished the critics. There can be no doubt that this fiasco weakened Mao politically at home and abroad and was a profound shock to him. From that period, one can trace a rapid movement of his general political attitude in a hard and militant direction.[21]

The Great Leap Forward. In domestic affairs, the first major manifestation of Mao's new militancy was the Great Leap Forward of 1958. Of such importance was this titanic 'mass campaign,' which indeed in many ways is the most important single episode in the history of the P.R.C., that it virtually determined Chinese foreign policy from the autumn of 1957 to the autumn of 1958. Mao tried to place demands on revolutionaries everywhere in the world almost as sweeping as those he could place on the Chinese people. The Chinese people's efforts, furthermore, would seem more justifiable and more palatable if they could be portrayed as forming part of a dynamic and worldwide advance against 'imperialism.' Accordingly, in the autumn of 1957 Mao began to proclaim that, to a large extent as a result of recent Soviet successes in space and missilery, 'the East wind has prevailed over the West wind,'[22] in other words, that the revolutionary forces of the world, allegedly led by the Soviet Union, had acquired a superiority in the overall balance of power (psychological and political as well as merely material) over 'imperialism.' The clear implication was that the Soviet Union ought to act accordingly by putting politico-military pressures, which were not expected to eventuate in general war, on the United States, on behalf of China as well as of other segments of the revolutionary camp.

China and nuclear weapons. Under cover of a barrage of flattery and exhortation, the P.R.C. pressed the Soviet Union successfully, in the autumn of 1957, for major new commitments of military technical assistance. Moscow, in a complex and secret piece of negotiation, agreed to provide substantial aid in both the warhead and the delivery aspects of a Chinese nuclear weapons program that had apparently been decided on in Peking about 1956.[23] Early in 1958, probably under the impact of an American decision to base 'tactical' nuclear weapons in South Korea, the P.R.C. asked Moscow for an outright transfer of nuclear weapons and appropriate delivery systems.[24] Khrushchev responded by pressing what had become a favorite project of his, the placing of most if not all of China's armed forces under 'joint' (really Soviet) control in the manner of the forces of the Warsaw Pact allies. The P.R.C. indignantly refused.[25] It consequently did not get its nuclear weapons and felt compelled to announce in May, 1958, that it would produce them entirely on its own no matter how long the time required.[26] The Soviet Union continued its nuclear technical assistance, however, until mid-1959, when Khrushchev's growing dislike of Chinese policy, plus, perhaps,

---

[21] Cf. Donald S. Zagoria, *The Sino-Soviet Conflict, 1956–1961* (Princeton, N.J.: Princeton University Press, 1962), Chapter 2.

[22] See Mao's speech of November 18, 1957, in Moscow; excerpt in *Quotations from Chairman Mao Tse-tung* (Peking: Foreign Languages Press, 1966), pp. 80–81.

[23] Chinese statement of August 15, 1963, in William E. Griffith, *The Sino-Soviet Rift* (Cambridge, Mass.: M.I.T. Press, 1964), p. 351.

[24] The Soviet Union has stated that it rejected Chinese requests for nuclear weapons, apparently about this time. Radio Moscow broadcast, July 10, 1964, quoted in Raymond L. Garthoff, *Soviet Military Policy: A Historical Analysis* (New York: Praeger Publishers, 1966), p. 181.

[25] 'In 1958 the leadership of the CPSU put forward unreasonable demands designed to bring China under Soviet military control. These unreasonable demands were rightly and firmly rejected by the Chinese Government.' 'The Origin and Development of the Differences Between the Leadership of the CPSU and Ourselves,' *Jen-min Jih-pao* and *Red Flag*, September 6, 1963, cited in Griffith, *Sino-Soviet Rift*, p. 399.

[26] Alice Langley Hsieh, *Communist China's Strategy in the Nuclear Era* (Englewood Cliffs, N.J.: Prentice-Hall, 1962), pp. 107 ff.

a desire to improve his position for bargaining with the United States, induced him to terminate it.[27]

The 1958 Taiwan Strait crisis. Khrushchev also declined to adopt the activist stance implicitly required by the 'East wind, West wind' line. He realized that Mao was in reality urging on him a position combining maximum responsibility with minimum authority. Neither for China's nor for any one else's sake was he interested, at that time at any rate, in direct confrontations with the United States.

He made that clear, and thereby rendered himself useless for the role assigned him in Peking, by taking a fairly conciliatory line on the Middle East crisis of July, 1958. The Great Leap Forward was then at its height, and Mao promptly tried to compensate for Khrushchev's refusal to provide an appropriate backdrop by providing one of his own in an accessible and relatively controllable area, the Taiwan Strait. Over probable Soviet objections, substantial politico-military pressures were exerted on the Nationalist-held offshore islands for a period of about seven weeks, beginning on August 23. The pressures were eased when it became clear that they would not lead to the isolation and surrender of the offshore islands, much less to the 'liberation' of Taiwan, and that the United States was supporting the Nationalists in deed as well as in word, whereas the Soviet Union was supporting the P.R.C. in word only. The pressure on the islands also eased when the high tide of the Great Leap Forward began to recede with the gathering of the harvest.

In order to rationalize his odd and none too successful ploy, Mao published at the end of October a collection of his anti-American statements under the title 'Imperialism and All Reactionaries Are Paper Tigers.'[28] Under the surface, this document, seems to say that the P.R.C. should not engage in direct military confrontations with the United States because the latter is strong and dangerous militarily. Politically, on the other hand, it is a weak and declining force, which with no risk to China will be disposed of in time by the 'revolutionary people' of the world as a whole. The corollary is that the P.R.C. must be able to point convincingly to anti-American revolutionary progress elsewhere in the world, or the excuse for its policy of nonconfrontation with the United States collapses. In order to make its case convincing, Peking has sometimes tried to push revolutionary movements along, notably in some African countries, faster than the local political situation would bear, and has encountered setbacks as a result.

THE CAMPAIGN AGAINST 'KHRUSHCHEV REVISIONISM' (1959–64)

In 1959, the Sino-Soviet dispute clearly became the major item on Peking's external agenda, placed there, from its point of view, by Khrushchev's actions and policies. To be brief, he went farther than ever before in conciliating the United States (through his visit to Camp David), tried to influence Chinese domestic policy, threatened the future existence of the P.R.C.'s large and cherished conventional forces by proposing 'general and complete disarmament' before the United Nations General Assembly, advised the P.R.C. to ease its pressures on the United States and Taiwan, indicated disapproval of the P.R.C.'s behavior along its border with India, and indicated publicly that he had no intention of playing the peculiar 'leading' role in world Communism assigned to him by Peking.[29]

Beginning of attacks on Khrushchev. In April, 1960, in an important editorial entitled

---

[27] Griffith, *Sino-Soviet Rift*, p. 351.   [28] NCNA, October 31, 1958.

[29] Cf. Zagoria, *Sino-Soviet Conflict*, Part Four. The fall of the relatively pro-Soviet Defense Minister, P'eng Te-huai, in the summer of 1959 probably also tended to increase Sino-Soviet friction. Cf. David A. Charles, 'The Dismissal of Marshal P'eng Te-huai,' *The China Quarterly*, No. 8 (October–December, 1961), pp. 63–76.

'Long Live Leninism,' the Chinese opened a public polemic against Khrushchev, and against his alleged appeasement of 'imperialism' in particular, but without actually naming him.[30] The timing was shrewd, for Khrushchev was about to go to a summit meeting in Paris, and Chinese pressure along with other considerations undoubtedly contributed to his decision to torpedo the conference and take a harder line toward the West.[31] Refusing to be appeased so easily, the Chinese began to denounce him at meetings of other Communist Parties and of international front organizations. Enraged, Khrushchev withdrew all technical assistance from the P.R.C. in the summer of 1960 and thereby set back its industrialization program several years. Coming at a time of agricultural crisis caused to a large extent by the Great Leap Forward, Khrushchev's action contributed to the adoption of more moderate economic policies by Peking at the end of 1960, but it also worsened Sino-Soviet relations.

A major international conference of Communist Parties convened in Moscow in November, 1960, mainly in order to discuss the by now sensational Sino-Soviet dispute. The result was inconclusive. Neither side altered its view or succeeded in imposing it on the other, and the statement issued at the conclusion of the conference generally avoided taking a clear-cut stand on the major issues in dispute. Chief among the issues were policy toward the United States and the associated question of the risks of general war, and the issue of revolutionary strategy in the developing areas. The Chinese favored a more activist policy, one less influenced by fear of a clash with American 'imperialism,' than did the Russians.[32]

In 1961, Peking considered Moscow's line toward the Kennedy Administration to be insufficiently tough, but the chief overt issue of that year was Soviet policy toward Albania. Khrushchev's efforts to coerce the Albanians into political and economic subservience merely led them to defy him and turn for support to Peking, which for a variety of reasons was happy to provide it. After the Soviet Party's Twenty-second Congress (October, 1961), at which Khrushchev denounced the Albanians only to be politely criticized by Chou En-lai, the Chinese representative, the P.R.C., in addition to continuing to support Albania economically and politically, began to criticize Khrushchev, by name but not for publication, within China.[33] Presumably it hoped that his colleagues would overthrow him.

Laos, Indonesia, and the 1962 border war with India. There were significant developments during those years in Peking's policy toward southern Asia. Reluctant to risk a direct confrontation with the United States and convinced after 1960 that sub-Saharan Africa offered a more promising and risk-free field for revolutionary activity,[34] the P.R.C. discouraged Ho Chi Minh, with temporary success, from giving major support to the insurgency against the Diem government in South Vietnam. The P.R.C.'s economic crisis of 1960 compelled it to reduce its economic aid to North Vietnam and diluted its influence in Hanoi, however, and North Vietnamese aid to,

---

[30] Published in *Red Flag*, April 16, 1960.

[31] Cf. Michel Tatu, *Le pouvoir en U.R.S.S.: Du déclin de Khrouchtchev à la direction collective* (Paris: Éditions Bernard Grasset, 1967), pp. 44–48.

[32] William E. Griffith, 'The November 1960 Moscow Meeting: A Preliminary Reconstruction,' *The China Quarterly*, No. 11 (July–September, 1962), pp. 38–57.

[33] Jerrold L. Schecter, 'Khrushchev's Image Inside China,' *The China Quarterly*, No. 14 (April–June, 1963), pp. 212–17.

[34] 'Africa is now both the center of the anticolonialist struggle and the center for East and West to fight for the control of an intermediary [i.e., intermediate] zone, so that it has become the key point of world interest'—from a classified Chinese source, quoted in J. Chester Cheng, ed., *The Politics of the Chinese Red Army: A Translation of the Bulletin of Activities in the People's Liberation Army* (Stanford, Calif.: The Hoover Institution, 1966), p. 484.

and support of, the insurgency, contrary to Chinese advice, increased rapidly after 1960.[35]

For its relative restraint in Vietnam, the P.R.C. felt itself poorly repaid by what it regarded as an aggressive American policy in Laos, where the United States tried energetically, between 1958 and 1960, to create an anti-Communist bastion in place of the weak neutral state envisaged by the Geneva agreement of 1954. The result was a complex crisis, the overrunning of the Laotian highlands by North Vietnamese forces at the end of 1960, and a lengthy (1961–62) conference at Geneva that removed the American military presence from Laos under the guise of neutralizing the country, without actually compelling the North Vietnamese to withdraw. This crisis and the conference were probably the last major occasion on which the P.R.C. and the Soviet Union can be said to have coordinated their foreign policies with reasonable effect.[36]

The Laotian crisis was only one of several occasions during that period when the P.R.C. considered the United States to have acted aggressively. Accordingly, it tended to become more insistent that the Asian neutrals accept its own harsh view of American intentions rather than Khrushchev's somewhat kindlier one. Nehru's India, which had been central to Peking's calculations when it adopted a strategy of peaceful coexistence, refused to accept the Chinese view of the United States, on which it was heavily dependent for aid. In addition, India cheerfully accepted aid from the Soviet Union, which the Chinese suspected of wanting to build Nehru up as a counterweight to themselves, and showed an inconvenient concern for the fate of Tibet, which Peking had been dragooning ruthlessly to the point where revolts began in late 1955. Finally, there was a disagreement as to the location of the Sino-Indian border in two major areas, the frontier between eastern Tibet and the Northeast Frontier Agency, and that between western Tibet and Sinkiang and the Aksai Chin region, which the P.R.C. claimed but which India regarded as part of Kashmir.

For these reasons, and specifically because of the flight of the Dalai Lama to India in March, 1959, some minor fighting, accompanied by an exchange of letters expressing disagreement as to the location of the border, occurred in 1959, with the Soviet Union siding quietly with India.[37] The effect was not only further to enrage Peking with India and the Soviet Union but also to raise doubts about its previous relative tolerance toward the Asian neutrals in general. In the latter months of 1959, China quarreled loudly with Indonesia over discriminatory treatment of Chinese residents there. In early 1960, however, Khrushchev visited both India and Indonesia, and Peking promptly saw reason to fear Soviet political gains at China's expense. It therefore made conciliatory gestures to Indonesia on the question of the overseas Chinese and to India on the border (by offering to let India have the eastern disputed region in return for continued Chinese control of the western one). Since Sukarno was not only receptive but able to enforce his views on his colleagues, an accommodation with Indonesia was reached and soon developed into a kind of revolutionary, anti-Western alliance. Nehru, on the other hand, although interested in the Chinese offer, could not control some of his more conservative and influential colleagues, who vetoed the idea of an accommodation with the P.R.C. on the border question.

---

[35] Harold C. Hinton, 'China and Vietnam,' in Tang Tsou, ed., *China in Crisis, 2: China's Policies in Asia and America's Alternatives* (Chicago: University of Chicago Press, 1968): 203–4.

[36] Arthur Lall, *How Communist China Negotiates* (New York: Columbia University Press, 1968).

[37] China later denounced a Soviet statement of September 9, 1959, as 'the first instance in history in which a socialist country, instead of condemning the armed provocations of the reactionaries of a capitalist country, condemned another fraternal socialist country when it was confronted with such armed provocations.' 'Whence the Difference?' *Jen-min Jih-pao*, February 27, 1963.

The result was that, whereas Indonesia accepted Soviet arms with an anti-Western purpose, India accepted them with an anti-Chinese purpose. In 1961, Indian troops began to establish outposts in territory claimed by China in the Aksai Chin, in the confident belief that the Chinese forces there would eventually retire without fighting. The P.R.C. had no intention of doing so, however; it considered both the security of western Sinkiang and western Tibet and its prestige to be involved. As early as the spring of 1960 it had begun to make it difficult for India, and the Soviet Union for that matter, to exploit the border issue for political advantage by reaching a series of boundary agreements with other countries. Eventually they were concluded with Burma, Nepal, Pakistan, Afghanistan, and Mongolia. Once the P.R.C. had completed reinforcing its troops in Fukien so as to deter what it saw as a Chinese Nationalist plan in the late spring of 1962 to attack the mainland, it turned its full attention to India. Since Indian troops continued to advance in spite of Chinese warnings, the result in October and November, 1962, was a border war that produced a sharp and humiliating defeat for the poorly prepared Indian forces and created a major international crisis but otherwise left the situation on the ground little changed: India still substantially occupied the eastern disputed sector, and China substantially occupied the western sector, without agreement as to the legal location of the boundary. In essence, this situation remains unchanged.

The Cuban missile crisis and the partial test ban treaty. At first Khrushchev, who was deeply involved in the Cuban missile crisis, gave a measure of support to the P.R.C. in its border war, but, as soon as Peking began to denounce his agreement to remove his missiles as 'another Munich' and a betrayal of Castro, he reversed his stand and began to support India. The result was a further exacerbation of the Sino-Soviet dispute. In 1963, the P.R.C. launched an energetic and largely successful campaign to win the major Asian Communist Parties to its side, and a much less successful campaign to win over Parties elsewhere or to set up new 'Marxist-Leninist' splinter parties where it could not. Worse still for Sino-Soviet relations was the signature by the Soviet Union of the nuclear test ban treaty in July, 1963. The main Chinese objections to the treaty were the ideological or emotional one that it constituted a flagrant act of appeasement of 'imperialism' in betrayal of the demand of revolutionaries everywhere for struggle against it, and the more practical one that it clearly implied Soviet opposition to the idea of an independent Chinese nuclear force, to which Peking was committed for reasons both of security and of prestige.[38]

The unsettled border with the Soviet Union. After the signing of the test ban treaty, Peking became far more outspoken and detailed in its public denunciations of Khrushchev, whom it now named in public for the first time as the object of its wrath.[39] Of special importance was the fact that it confirmed the existence of a Sino-Soviet border dispute, one of whose aspects was alleged to be Soviet subversion among minorities in Sinkiang. In July, 1964, in a sensational interview with some Japanese visitors, Mao criticized the Soviet Union for having taken too much territory from its neighbors, including Outer Mongolia from China, and seemed to imply that the victims of this process should combine to work for a revision of boundaries.[40] Khrushchev, who was clearly disturbed by the interview and probably also by the prospect of the imminent emergence of China as a nuclear power, held extensive maneuvers in the Soviet Far East in 1964 and may have contemplated actual military pressures on the P.R.C. On the political front, he tried with little success to put together another

---

[38] See the Chinese Government statements of protest against the test ban treaty of August 15 and September 1, 1963; text in Griffith, *Sino-Soviet Rift*, pp. 340–53, 371–87.

[39] See documents in *The Polemic on the General Line of the International Communist Movement* (Peking: Foreign Languages Press, 1965).

[40] Excerpts in Dennis J. Doolin, ed., *Territorial Claims in the Sino-Soviet Conflict: Documents and Analysis* (Stanford, Calif.: The Hoover Institution, 1965), pp. 42–44.

international conference of Communist Parties like the one of 1960, for the purpose of condemning the Chinese. For his part, Mao denounced the project and also Khrushchev's 'revisionist' domestic policies, which he clearly regarded as a dangerous example for China and a possible source of encouragement to 'revisionist' and bureaucratic tendencies that he discerned among his colleagues.[41]

It was in this climate that Khrushchev was overthrown in mid-October 1964, probably for the excesses and ineffectiveness of his China policy, among other things. On October 16, the day after his removal was officially announced in Moscow, China conducted its first nuclear test.[42]

CHINESE FOREIGN POLICY SINCE KHRUSHCHEV (1965–68)

Intensification of rivalry with the Soviet Union. At first Mao seems to have regarded Khrushchev's fall as a triumph for himself and as the opening gun in what he hoped would be a series of dramatic foreign policy successes to complement and give additional momentum to the revolutionary initiatives in domestic policy that he was contemplating. Among the additional external successes were to be, apparently, a Communist victory in South Vietnam, a triumph for Indonesia in its Chinese-supported 'Confrontation' with Britain and Malaysia, additional gains for the Sino-Indonesian partnership at the forthcoming Afro-Asian Conference at Algiers (the successor to the one at Bandung in 1955), and at least the beginnings of a 'people's war' in Thailand.

Almost from the beginning, Mao's great expectations were confounded. Within a few weeks of Khrushchev's fall his successors made it clear that they had no intention of accepting Mao's political leadership or of reversing the essentials of Khrushchev's 'revisionist' domestic and foreign policies (as distinct from the peculiarly abrasive character of his behavior toward China) to the extent desired by Mao, and they intended to pursue a much more active Asian policy, necessarily in competition with the P.R.C. than had Khrushchev. The American escalation in Vietnam beginning in February, 1965, which Mao seems not to have expected[43] and which greatly dimmed the prospects of a Communist victory, provided the Soviet Union with an opportunity to furnish indispensable military equipment to North Vietnam and to press it to seek a solution through negotiation.

Rejection of 'united action' in Vietnam. The increased Soviet role in Vietnam and any thought of negotiations were both unacceptable to Mao; still more so was the idea, which soon began to be peddled by Moscow under the label 'joint action' or 'united action,' that the whole Communist world, including the P.R.C., should join hands, implicitly under Soviet leadership, in support of Hanoi. Evidently, to some other members of the Chinese leadership the idea seemed worth discussing, however. Notably, the outspoken Chief of Staff, Lo Jui-ch'ing, seemed interested. While a strategic debate centering on Vietnam and Sino-Soviet relations raged in Peking during the spring and summer of 1965, a limited agreement was reached with the Soviet Union to permit the transit of Soviet equipment to North Vietnam by rail, but more sweeping Soviet requests for air transit rights were rejected. The ultimately victorious Maoist view, which was officially formulated in Lin Piao's famous tract, 'Long Live the Victory of People's Wars,'[44] was that the Viet Cong and Hanoi should fight a 'protracted war' at the guerrilla level, in a manner as 'self-reliant' as possible, until eventual victory. Soviet and Chinese involvement should be kept to the mini-

---

[41] *The Polemic on the General Line of the International Communist Movement,* pp. 469–70.
[42] Text of Chinese statement in *The New York Times,* October 17, 1964.
[43] Edgar Snow, 'Interview with Mao,' *New Republic,* February 27, 1965, pp. 22–23.
[44] Text released by NCNA, September 3, 1965.

mum, and in fact the P.R.C. has substantially confined itself to shipping rice and infantry weapons and stationing military railway engineer units in North Vietnam to keep the rail lines to China open. On occasion the P.R.C. has obstructed the flow of Soviet weapons to North Vietnam, sometimes it would appear by design and sometimes involuntarily, as a consequence of the confusion attendant on the Cultural Revolution, and thereby given the Russians useful polemical fuel.

Not only in practice but also in theory, the dominant Maoist faction has rejected the Soviet call to 'united action' and has continued to carry on its strange political struggle against Moscow's 'revisionism.' One of the main reasons for its persistence is unquestionably the determination to pursue the anti-'revisionist' Cultural Revolution at home, which indeed may have been precipitated in part by the spectacle of the essentials of Khrushchev's 'revisionism' surviving his overthrow.

Foreign policy setbacks in 1965–66. It was not only in the direction of Moscow and Hanoi, but also in the Third World as a whole, that Maoist foreign policy encountered setbacks in 1965. Peking so antagonized a number of neutral states by its demands, including one for the exclusion of the Soviet Union from the Algiers Afro-Asian Conference, that they took advantage of a coup in Algeria in mid-June to postpone and ultimately torpedo the conference, much to Peking's disgust.[45] Peking's revolutionary alliance with Indonesia was destroyed when, at the end of September, the Indonesian Communist Party most unwisely attempted a coup against the army.[46] The resulting slaughter of Communists not only came close to annihilating the Party but ended the political career of Sukarno, who had known of and supported the coup in advance, and virtually eliminated the influence of the P.R.C., which had known of the plans for the coup and had assented to them. In September, the P.R.C. tried, unsuccessfully, through a variety of political pressures on India to keep its informal ally Pakistan fighting a losing war rather than agree to an armistice without having gained any concessions on the crucial issue of Kashmir. Early in 1966 the P.R.C. suffered a number of setbacks to its revolutionary plans for sub-Saharan Africa, notably the overthrow of its friend President Nkrumah of Ghana. Shortly after that, a series of editorials began to appear in the Chinese press to the effect that revolution was a 'wavelike' process with troughs as well as crests; the former could of course be made to give way to the latter by hard work under Maoist political guidance.

'Red Guard Diplomacy.' None of the setbacks just mentioned, including American escalation in Vietnam, seems to have contributed decisively to the launching of the Cultural Revolution. To the extent that the Revolution had an external cause, it was a determination on Mao's part to prevent 'revisionism' of the Soviet variety from entrenching itself in China. The Vietnamese crisis and, in particular, the alleged danger of an American attack on China and threats of Chinese military intervention in Vietnam under various vaguely defined conditions were manipulated in Maoist propaganda so as to create a 'siege mentality' and an appropriate climate for the Cultural Revolution. The latter in turn exerted a determining influence on Chinese foreign policy from the summer of 1966 to the summer of 1967 and gave rise to a phenomenon sometimes referred to as 'Red Guard diplomacy.' This included the bringing back of many diplomats from abroad for reindoctrination, violent pressures by Red Guards on the Foreign Ministry and Foreign Minister Ch'en Yi, demonstrations against the sieges of foreign embassies (particularly the Soviet), harassment of the crews of foreign ships, the creation of border incidents (notably with the Soviet Far East), and violent demonstrations on foreign soil (especially in Macao, Hong

[45] Guy J. Pauker, 'The Rise and Fall of Afro-Asian Solidarity,' *Asian Survey*, 5, No. 9 (September, 1965): 425–32.
[46] John O. Sutter, 'Two Faces of *Konfrontasi*: "Crush Malaysia" and the *Gestapu*,' *Asian Survey*, 6, No. 10 (October, 1966): 523–46.

Kong, and Burma). The rationale of such behavior, which was certainly stimulated by Maoist propaganda but was apparently not ordered or even desired by Mao—although it may have been by his wife, Chiang Ch'ing, and her Cultural Revolution Group—was that foreigners, like the Chinese, should accept the 'thought of Mao Tse-tung' and support the Cultural Revolution; if they did not, so much the worse for them. The high point of Red Guard diplomacy was an actual takeover of the Foreign Ministry by Maoist militants, including Red Guards, on August 19, 1967, followed by the sacking of the British mission compound on August 22. This was too much for nearly everyone, it appears, and on the following day control over the Foreign Ministry was resumed by Chou En-lai and Ch'en Yi. During the succeeding months, the P.R.C. moved to improve its relations with Cambodia, Nepal, and some other Afro-Asian countries, many of which had been alienated by the excesses of Red Guard diplomacy, by means of soothing diplomatic disputes, extending economic aid, and the like.

Some outstanding issues. The events of 1968 presented a mixed picture from the viewpoint of Maoist foreign policy interests. Peking was greatly encouraged by signs that the United States was tending to reduce its commitments in Asia and by serious unrest in a number of Western countries, notably the United States and France. On the other hand, it was deeply troubled that Hanoi agreed to begin talks with the United States in the absence of a revolutionary victory in South Vietnam or even a halt to American bombing of North Vietnam. It was disturbed by the growth of Soviet activity and influence in the Third World, including Asia. It was probably perturbed at the growing bellicosity of North Korea, which no one could control but over which Moscow was in a better position than Peking to exert influence. In 1966–68, all these concerns, however, apparently occupied much less of the Chinese Communist leadership's attention than did the complex and turbulent progress of the Cultural Revolution. Thereafter, however, relations with the U.S.S.R. took a threatening turn.

As Peking was bringing the Cultural Revolution to an end in the summer of 1968, the Soviet Union invaded Czechoslovakia. This development startled and frightened the Chinese leaders[47] and led to a serious increase of tension along the Sino-Soviet frontier. On March 2, 1968, counting mistakenly on continued Soviet involvement in a crisis then in progress over West Berlin, Chinese troops ambushed a Soviet patrol on a disputed island in the frozen Ussuri River. The Soviet response, both military and political, was unexpectedly strong. A number of additional border clashes soon followed, some engineered by the Soviet Union.[48] Large Soviet troop movements to the Far East, which required the closing to regular traffic of sections of the Trans-Siberian Railroad, together with other reinforcements, including tactical nuclear weapons, were supplemented by press reports of Soviet soundings in Eastern European countries about their attitudes toward a possible Soviet attack on the P.R.C. At the same time, from the end of March, Moscow paralleled its formidable military buildup along the Chinese frontier with a series of diplomatic proposals for negotiations on the settlement of the border dispute and the normalization of relations between the two states (not the two Parties). Brezhnev also spoke vaguely of the need for collective security in Asia, presumably at the expense of China.

Mao was reluctant to accept the Soviet overtures, but as Soviet pressure mounted

---

[47] 'This act of naked armed intervention has fully brought out the grisly fascist features of the Soviet revisionist clique and has fully revealed its extreme weakness; it has proclaimed the total bankruptcy of Soviet modern revisionism.' 'Total Bankruptcy of Soviet Modern Revisionism,' *Jen-min Jih-pao*, August 23, 1968.

[48] The Institute for Strategic Studies (London) listed sixteen such incidents during March–April, 1969, in its 1969 *Strategic Survey*.

the United States indicated that it would follow an 'even-handed' policy. The United States was not about to give China even the mild moral support that it had given Romania after the invasion of Czechoslovakia. Finally, as Hanoi pressed the Chinese to agree to talks, following a Chou En-lai–Kosygin meeting at the Peking airport, an agreement to hold negotiations in Peking was reached during September and early October. However, once Peking was convinced that Moscow wanted the talks to succeed, it became rather uncooperative. The main observable result of the talks to date has been an agreement to exchange ambassadors once more, but even this very limited gesture was not carried out until late 1970.

Partly to gain sympathy that might be useful in case the Soviet Union should act on its threats, and partly as an aspect of the general retreat from the Cultural Revolution, Peking began during the Sino-Soviet border crisis to normalize its foreign relations and diplomacy with a considerable number of more or less friendly countries. For a time before the Cambodian crisis, U.S.-Chinese talks at Warsaw were resumed. Despite limited American gestures, however, Peking's relations with the United States remained bad, not only on account of the usual reasons but also on account of the Cambodian crisis. Improved relations with other Western countries were marked notably by the recognition of the P.R.C. by Canada and Italy in the fall of 1970 and the U.N. vote of 51 to 49 to seat Peking and to expel Taiwan in the 1970 General Assembly, followed by the admission of the P.R.C. and the expulsion of Taiwan in October, 1971.

The Problem of Interpretation

The foregoing interpretation is of course mine. In it, I have tried to emphasize considerations relevant to policy-making and causal connections among events, and to achieve the blend between ideology and national interest that I am convinced governs foreign policy. Although most of my analysis would probably be accepted by most other students of the subject, there of course are differences of opinion as to interpretation and emphasis.

General surveys and analyses of Chinese foreign policy as a whole are rather few, perhaps because most students believe, and may be right in believing, that the subject is too complex and imperfectly known to lend itself to general treatment.

Among those students who have essayed comprehensive interpretations of Communist Chinese foreign policy, A. M. Halpern[49] has apparently accepted the widespread—but, in the writer's opinion, mistaken—opinion that Stalin prevented the Chinese Communists from concluding an armistice in Korea as long as he lived. Although he holds that a faction of 'native radicals' (presumably including Mao) acquired ascendancy in Peking late in 1957, Halpern has not connected this development closely with domestic politics (the fiasco of the Hundred Flowers) and has explained the 'East wind, West wind' line almost entirely on the basis of the conviction of the 'native radicals' that the worldwide balance of power had shifted in favor of the 'socialist camp' and a desire to export the P.R.C. revolutionary model.

Richard Lowenthal has argued that the P.R.C. began to encourage and support an intensification of Communist insurgency in South Vietnam as early as 1959–60; I believe this did not happen until 1963, when Peking wanted—and to a considerable extent temporarily gained—Hanoi's backing in the Sino-Soviet dispute.

David Mozingo has stated that Communist revolutions in southern Asia, except, of course, for Vietnam, were virtually over by the time the Chinese Communists came to power (something that is definitely not true of the Philippines and Malaya and is

---

[49] All sources referred to in this section can be readily identified under the authors' names in the selected bibliography that follows.

debatable in the case of Burma) and has minimized the Chinese role in the 'armed struggles' of that period. He assigns to the Chinese rather than the Soviet Party the priority in grasping the futility of 'armed struggle' (again, except for Vietnam) and in initiating a shift in the direction of peaceful coexistence; I would award priority to the Soviet Party. Mozingo has argued that Peking raised no public objections to Khrushchev's deprecation of 'armed struggle' at the Twentieth Congress and therefore must have accepted it; the first part of this proposition is true, but there is evidence to support the view that the question was a controversial one in Peking and that Mao, at least, was not willing to write off 'armed struggle' in more than a temporary and tactical sense. Mozingo has also interpreted the Chinese attitude toward Khrushchev's struggle with his domestic opponents in 1956–57 as one of support for him; in my view, the evidence supports the opposite conclusion.

I myself, in a book published in 1966, advanced a number of interpretations to which I no longer subscribe. In particular, I then believed that Mao, rather than Stalin, was the prime mover behind the launching of the Korean War, and I thought that the P.R.C. endorsed the revival of Communist insurgency in South Vietnam as soon as it began in the late 1950's.

William E. Griffith has advanced an interpretation with which I do not agree in arguing that Khrushchev's China policy had little or nothing to do with his fall from power.

In retrospect, it seems clear that although Chinese foreign policy has consistently sought to maximize China's security and influence, the actual pursuit of these goals has been marked by significant discontinuities. These have apparently been due in most cases to shifts in the domestic Chinese political situation (always a consideration of high priority) or to varying estimates, as well as varying realities, of China's military and other capabilities (which are gradually increasing), the degree of threat or effective competition offered by the United States and/or the Soviet Union at a particular time, or the revolutionary opportunities offered by a given situation (real or imagined) in the third world. The varying estimates, in turn, seem to have reflected, to a significant extent, the varying comparative political influence of two major schools of thought within the Communist Chinese leadership, with respect to foreign as well as domestic policy. These may be approximately identified as the Maoist, or predominantly revolutionary; and the predominantly national, which it seems safe to identify, until the Cultural Revolution, with Liu Shao-ch'i, among others. To adapt older Communist terminology, one might describe the former as a strategy operating 'from below' and the latter as a strategy operating 'from above.' At no time has either had the field entirely to itself. At present, for example, the pendulum is clearly swinging in favor of a foreign policy that is more national, or state-oriented, and comparatively less revolutionary, than was the case while the Cultural Revolution was at its height. And yet, just as China's domestic policies still include a large component of Maoist language and even of Maoist policies, so Chinese foreign policy still attempts to promote revolution in certain situations considered favorable, such as the area from Assam through Burma and Thailand into the Indochina countries.

Postscript

During 1970, the P.R.C. became sufficiently concerned over the Soviet threat and, to a lesser extent, the resurgence of Japan so that it decided, in view of the American tendency to 'wind down' the war in Indochina, to reciprocate the Nixon administration's overtures and invite President Nixon to visit China. The invitation was formally extended in July, 1971. The growing sense of common interest between the United States and China was strengthened by a joint setback suffered when India defeated and dismembered Pakistan in late 1971. The dramatic shift in Chinese policy toward the United States was accompanied by keen debate in China and probably contributed to the fall (in September, 1971) of Defense Minister Lin Piao, who until then had been Mao's heir apparent but who evidently opposed Premier Chou En-lai's diplomatic opening to the United States. Probably the main achievement of the Nixon visit to China in February, 1972, apart from an improvement of the atmosphere surrounding Sino-American relations, was to create a linkage between Taiwan and Vietnam: The United States (in the Shanghai Communiqué) promised to withdraw all its military personnel from Taiwan when peace had been restored to 'the region,' clearly including Indochina. Peking was thus given an incentive to become more cooperative in working toward a political settlement for Indochina, not necessarily on Hanoi's terms, and in fact it appeared to become at least marginally more cooperative. This developing, although limited, Sino-American relationship was only strained, but apparently not ruined, by the re-escalation of the war in Vietnam in the spring of 1972. On the other hand, the crisis in Vietnam at that time produced at least some signs of an improved relationship between China and the Soviet Union, whose forces on and near the Chinese border had risen to a level of approximately forty-five divisions. It was clear that China's relations with the three major powers (the United States, the Soviet Union, and Japan) would absorb most of its external energies, directly and indirectly; to a considerable extent, its dealings with other countries were being conducted with an eye to their utility in enhancing Peking's position with respect to these three.

SELECTED BIBLIOGRAPHY

BARNETT, A. DOAK. *Communist China and Asia: Challenge to American Policy*. New York: Harper & Brothers, 1960. A balanced and detailed analysis of Chinese foreign policy, especially in its Asian aspect, and of the problems and policy options available to the United States in this connection. It is inevitably somewhat dated by now.

GRIFFITH, WILLIAM E. *Albania and the Sino-Soviet Rift*. Cambridge, Mass.: MIT Press, 1963; *The Sino-Soviet Rift*, Cambridge, Mass.: MIT Press, 1964; *Sino-Soviet Relations, 1964–1965*, Cambridge, Mass.: MIT Press, 1967. These books all contain extensive and valuable original documentation. Griffith was the first analyst to stress in print the struggle for ideological authority as a major aspect of the Sino-Soviet dispute. He also emphasizes, occasionally with excessive detail, the role of third parties and international front organizations in the dispute. He tends to minimize the role of Soviet and Chinese domestic politics in the dispute.

HALPERN, A. M. 'Communist China and Peaceful Co existence,' *The China Quarterly*, No. 3 (London: Congress for Cultural Freedom), July–September, 1960, pp. 16–31; 'The Chinese Communist Line on Neutralism,' *The China Quarterly*, No. 5, January–March, 1961, pp. 90–115; 'The Foreign Policy Uses of the Chinese Revolutionary Model,' *The China Quarterly*, No. 7, July–September, 1961, pp. 1–16; 'Communist China's Foreign Policy: The Recent Phase,' *The China Quarterly*, No. 11, July–September, 1962, pp. 89–104; 'China in the Postwar World,' *The China Quarterly*, No. 21, January–March, 1965, pp. 20–45. These articles are valuable and interesting, but somewhat abstruse and one-sided in that the author makes heavy use of psychological reconstruction and content analysis, without much attention to the details of political and diplomatic history (or, in other words, to the actual context of the attitudes that he posits). He sees Chinese foreign policy as proceeding from successive and differing estimates of the international balance of power, with little attention to (among other things) domestic politics.

HINTON, HAROLD C. *Communist China in World Politics*. Boston: Houghton Mifflin, 1966. This work aims at comprehensiveness in both fact and interpretation. It attempts to weigh both ideology and national interest but lacks a unifying theme because of the author's belief that the subject is too complex to possess such a theme.

LOWENTHAL, RICHARD. 'Communist China's Foreign Policy,' in TSOU TANG, ed., *China in*

Crisis Vol. 2, *China's Policies in Asia and America's Alternatives*. Chicago: University of Chicago Press, 1968, pp. 1–18. With his usual brilliance and clarity, Lowenthal portrays the P.R.C. as an underdeveloped, dissatisfied power, resentful of the injuries that it suffered in the past from 'imperialism.' He grasps the influence of domestic on foreign policy. He analyzes soundly the collapse in 1965 of the P.R.C. effort to build a coalition of anti-'imperialist' Afro-Asian states under its own leadership.

Mozingo, David. 'The Maoist Imprint on China's Foreign Policy,' *China Briefing* (Chicago: Center for Policy Study, University of Chicago, 1968), pp. 23–51. Although brilliant in many ways, this paper tends to underestimate the dynamism of the P.R.C.'s foreign policy, to overestimate the degree to which it moves reactively in response to real or imagined American pressures, and therefore to underestimate the Chinese threat to Asia.

Passin, Herbert. *China's Cultural Diplomacy*. New York: Praeger Publishers, 1962. A detailed and competent study of that important arm of Chinese foreign policy sometimes called people's diplomacy.

Poole, Peter Andrew. 'Communist China's Aid Diplomacy,' *Asian Survey*, 6, No. 11 (Berkeley: Institute of International Studies, University of California, November, 1966): 622–29. A very useful summary of the role played by economic aid in Chinese foreign policy.

Whiting, Allen S. *China Crosses the Yalu: The Decision to Enter the Korean War*. New York: Macmillan, 1960. This important and pioneering study contains many valuable and interesting data and analyses, but also many of little or no relevance. The author is reluctant to formulate a clear opinion as to the role of the P.R.C. in planning the Korean War and the reasons for its intervention.

Zagoria, Donald S. *The Sino-Soviet Conflict, 1956–1961*. Princeton N.J.: Princeton University Press, 1962. This important book stresses the ideological aspect of the dispute, such as the problem of 'revisionism,' but not the aspect of authority, and emphasizes the quarrel over appropriate domestic policies and revolutionary strategy. It says little about the impact of Soviet reluctance to give the P.R.C. strategic support against the United States as a factor in the dispute from the mid-1950's onward.

12

RELATIONS WITH THE UNITED STATES

JAMES T. MYERS

INTRODUCTION

IN order properly to treat the subject of Communist China's relations with the United States, it is necessary at the outset to set forth the basic framework of attitudes, aims, and ambitions that have shaped this relationship over the years. On the Chinese side, the relationship has been marked by the desire, perhaps the overriding desire, to re-establish Chinese primacy in an area that had, in varying degrees, been under Chinese cultural influence, if not political domination as well, for more than a millennium. The desire to recapture the former greatness of Imperial China has been combined with the Communist Chinese adherence to world-encompassing Marxist-Leninist ideology, which explains, justifies, and supports the development of anti-colonial and 'anti-imperialist' revolutionary movements for the purpose of setting free the 'oppressed peoples' of the world to follow the path of socialist-Communist development. The policies and attitudes that flow from a commitment to those two aims of Chinese national reassertion and encouragement for those engaged in the 'anti-imperialist' struggle have from the outset clashed head-on with United States plans and programs for East Asia.

Since the end of World War II, the United States, for its part, has been committed primarily to the creation and maintenance of stability in the Far East. That commitment, in turn, has been combined with an adherence to the principles of self-determination (that is, the absence of 'outside' interference) and free political development for the nations on the rim of the Communist mainland. In pursuit of those aims, the United States has sought to establish friendly relations with non-Communist Asian nations and to provide military assistance and armed defense, where requested, when those nations have been threatened by external aggression. It is the polar opposition of fundamental goals—stability versus revolutionary change—that has marked the relationship between Communist China and the United States over the last twenty years. If Communist China continues to be implacably hostile to the United States in its public utterances, it is because during the more than twenty-year life of the People's Republic of China the United States military presence in the Far East has been overwhelming (viewed by the U.S. Government as a thoroughly justified presence in light of its position as a Pacific power and of its vital national security interests), and because Chinese ambitions and revolutionary aims (thoroughly legitimate and fully justified from the Chinese point of view) have nearly everywhere been thwarted by U.S. countermeasures. The belligerent attitude of the Communist Chinese toward the United States, which had already emerged in the late 1940's, was a function not only of the U.S. support for Chiang Kai-shek during the civil war but also of the very keen and accurate perception on the part of the Communist leaders that the United States, as the most powerful military force in the Pacific, would be the major roadblock to the realization of Communist revolutionary goals and to the assertion of China's traditional greatness in territorial terms. The Chinese thus correctly viewed the United States as the major enemy in a struggle of two antagonistic views of the just and proper order in East Asia at a time when the United States was only beginning to feel the political shock waves of the Chinese civil war, and when there were clearly no long-range plans of any sort toward China—Nationalist or Communist.

Given the basic conflict in aims, the hostility directed at the United States by the P.R.C. leaders was nearly inevitable.

THE FALL OF THE MAINLAND AND THE U.S. CHINA POLICY

The Nationalist defeat. The problems surrounding United States China policy that were thrust into the domestic political arena following the fall of the Chinese mainland to the Communist forces became one of the most explosive political issues of the early 1950's. The ordinary American citizen had come to know the Chinese as friends and allies. Indeed, a substantial propaganda effort had been directed toward that end during World War II. Moreover, the United States was responsible for the inclusion of China among the great powers and as a permanent member of the Security Council of the United Nations. The United States desire to bring China into the family of nations as a leading member had been expressed at the Cairo, Teheran, and Yalta conferences.[1] The key to U.S. Far Eastern policy was a strong, united, and friendly China that would fill the power vacuum created by the defeat of Japan.[2]

It was with considerable shock and dismay, therefore, that the American public discovered China to be controlled not by its Chinese allies but by a group of little-known Chinese Communists who had certain ominous connections with the Soviet Union. The Communist connections of the new Chinese regime seemed particularly menacing to many in light of the steady worsening of United States–Soviet relations and the growing animosities that characterized the East-West cold war. Indeed, the fall of mainland China to the Communist armies in 1949 was the cause of a political trauma of considerable magnitude.

The Chinese civil war. The defeat of Japan in 1945 was followed by the renewal on a large scale of fighting between Nationalist and Communist Chinese forces, which had been greatly reduced, though not entirely ended, during the war years.[3] The decades-long hostility between the two sides quickly escalated to the level of full-scale military operations, as both Nationalists and Communists raced to occupy the territories being vacated by the Japanese armies. Even before the defeat of Japan there had developed

---

[1] U.S., Department of State, *United States Relations with China* (Washington, D.C.: Government Printing Office, 1949), pp. 113–14, 519. Hereafter cited as *White Paper.*

[2] Cordell Hull, *The Memoirs of Cordell Hull*, 2 (New York, 1948): 1583. Also Tang Tsou, *America's Failure in China* (Chicago: The University of Chicago Press, 1963), pp. 33 ff; and Herbert Feis, *The China Tangle* (Princeton, N.J.: Princeton University Press, 1953), *passim.*

[3] A general account of the events of this period may be found in Franz Michael and George E. Taylor, *The Far East in the Modern World*, revised edition (New York: Holt, Reinhart, and Winston, 1964), pp. 432 ff. Also, cf. Tang Tsou, *America's Failure in China*, Parts Two and Three. The period up to the Marshall mission is also covered in Feis, *The China Tangle.* For a more detailed account of the military aspects of the struggle see F. F. Liu, *A Military History of Modern China* (Princeton, N.J.: Princeton University Press, 1956), and Lionel Max Chassin, *The Communist Conquest of China* (Cambridge, Mass.: Harvard University Press, 1965). Mao Tse-tung's analysis of this period may be found in his *Selected Works*, Vol. 4 (Peking: Foreign Languages Press, 1967).

a growing concern in Washington that the national government, seriously weakened by the long years of war, would not be able to survive a civil war with its Communist rival. A key element in United States policy, therefore, became a concern with the survival of the national government of Chiang Kai-shek. Recognizing the serious internal weakness of the Chinese government and at the same time mindful of the key role assigned to a friendly, united China in U.S. Far Eastern policy, Washington pursued efforts both to support the national government and to assist it in reaching a compromise understanding with the Chinese Communists. While the United States continued to supply both military and economic aid to Chiang and to insist that the national government provide the most 'satisfactory base for a developing democracy,' this aid and support was tied with an insistence, consistently ineffective, that the Nationalists carry out internal reforms and reach a negotiated settlement with the Communists.[4] General George C. Marshall was dispatched to China at the end of 1945 as the personal representative of President Truman to undertake the first of his several attempts to act as a mediator in a negotiated settlement.[5] Although for a brief time there appeared to be a chance that some sort of a negotiated settlement might be reached, the efforts of the United States ultimately met with no success. All attempts to reach a peaceful solution to Chinese domestic political problems proved futile, as neither side displayed a strong desire to settle differences through negotiation and compromise.[6] General Marshall's efforts continued up to January, 1947, when he refused any longer to continue as mediator, blaming the impasse in the negotiations on the 'almost overwhelming suspicion with which the Kuomintang (Nationalist Party) and the Chinese Communists regarded each other.'[7]

By late 1947, as the fighting continued in China, the condition of the national government was rapidly deteriorating. General Albert C. Wedemeyer, sent to China on a 'fact-finding' mission following Marshall's return to the United States, vigorously criticized the nationalist government for its corruption and inefficiency. Wedemeyer declared: 'To regain and maintain the confidence of the people, the Central Government will have to effect immediately drastic, far-reaching political and economic reforms. Promises will no longer suffice.'[8] By mid-1948, many observers had reached the conclusion that nothing short of massive American military intervention could stem the Communist tide, and it was clear by the beginning of 1949 that a Communist victory was only a matter of time. Peking fell to the Communist armies at the end of January, and the major cities of Nanking, Hankow, and Shanghai were in Communist hands by early spring. On August 5, 1949, the United States Department of State issued the famous 'White Paper' that effectively wrote off mainland China. The defeat of the Nationalists was blamed on the ineptitude of their own leadership rather than the failure of United States policy or lack of assistance. Secretary Acheson in his letter of transmittal to President Truman declared:

> The unfortunate but inescapable fact is that the ominous result of the civil war in China was beyond the control of the government of the United States. Nothing that this country did or could have done within the reasonable limits of its capabilities could have changed that result; nothing that was left undone by this country has contributed to it. It was the product of internal Chinese forces, forces which this country tried to influence but could not. A decision was arrived at within China, if only a decision by default.[9]

---

[4] See Secretary of State Dean Acheson's 'Letter of Transmittal,' *White Paper*, p. xiv, and, on the Marshall Mission, Chapter V.

[5] In addition to the sources cited above, an excellent chronological summary of the events of this period and of the later years up to 1966 may be found in *China and United States Far East Policy, 1945–1966* (Washington, D.C.: Congressional Quarterly Service, 1967).

[6] *White Paper*, pp. 180 ff.   [7] *Ibid.*, p. 217.   [8] *Ibid.*, p. 764.   [9] *White Paper*, p. xvi.

On October 1, 1949, the Central Government of the People's Republic of China was formally inaugurated. Little remained for the Communist armies but a military mopping-up operation. On December 8, the seat of the national government was moved to Taiwan.

United States domestic debates. It is difficult at this distance to recapture the mood and temper of the early 1950's—of the 'McCarthy Era'—and the frightened and confused response of the American public, as well as many leading political figures, to the loss of China to the Communists and to the general worsening of East-West relations. As the certainty of a Communist victory in China became increasingly clear in the early months of 1949, a mounting volume of criticism of United States policy rose on Capitol Hill. Nor was the outcry limited to members of the Republican opposition. A young Democratic Congressman and future Democratic President declared:

> Mr. Speaker, over this weekend we have learned the extent of the disaster which has befallen China and the United States. The responsibility for the failure of our foreign policy rests squarely with the White House and the Department of State.
>
> The continued insistence that aid would not have been forthcoming, unless a coalition government with the Communists were formed, was a crippling blow to the national government.
>
> So concerned were our diplomats and their advisors, the Lattimores and the Fairbanks, with the imperfection of the democratic system in China after twenty years of war and tales of corruption in high places that they lost sight of our tremendous stake in a non-Communist China. . . .
>
> This House must now assume the responsibility of preventing the onrushing tide of communism from engulfing all of Asia.[10]

The atmosphere of the domestic debates over the fall of China became increasingly bitter as the loyalty of persons involved in the formulation of American foreign policies was called into question. Many felt that a foreign policy failure of this magnitude could not have occurred without the connivance of some persons inside governmental institutions. Senator McCarthy charged that there were 'Communists' in high positions within the Department of State, and on the floor of Congress charges of stupidity, if not of treason as well, became regular fare. The complexity and high emotional content of the question of U.S. responsibility for the fall of China are indicated by the public reception of the State Department White Paper, which was roundly denounced by supporters of the Chiang government and by the Chinese Communists as well. General Patrick Hurley, former United States Ambassador to China, declared the White Paper to be 'a smooth alibi for the pro-Communists in the State Department who had engineered the overthrow of our ally . . . and aided in the Communist conquest of China,' while on the floor of the Senate the report was described as a 'whitewash of a wishful, do-nothing policy which has succeeded only in placing Asia in danger of Soviet conquest.'[11] Denunciations from supporters of the national government were matched in intensity by denunciations issuing from the Chinese Communist side; and this despite the fact that the Communists would seem to have been the beneficiary of the United States 'write-off' of the Chiang regime. A New China News Agency editorial declared the 'first and most basic revelation' of the White Paper to be 'the deep-rooted hostility of the American imperialist government toward the National interests and the People's democratic forces in China.' The editorial continued, 'The American White Paper does not in the least hide the imperialist aggressive stand of the United States Government.' The report was said by the Com-

---

[10] Speech by John F. Kennedy, January 25, 1949, *Congressional Record*, 95, Part 1, 81st Congress, First Session (Washington, D.C.): 532–33.

[11] *China and U.S. Far East Policy*, p. 47.

munists to be based on 'Hitlerite dogmatism' and to be a 'masterpiece of distortion, putting black for white and white for black.'[12]

Despite the uproar caused by charge and counter-charge and by the Congressional hearings, it was impossible to satisfy large numbers of observers as to the causes contributing to the fall of mainland China to the Communists. Though the debate became much less an emotional issue over the following years, there remain today strong differences of opinion on many of the questions of U.S. China policy originally raised in 1950. In simple terms, the debate may be reduced to an opposition of those who think nothing the United States could have done after 1945 short of a massive commitment of troops could have saved China (and perhaps not even that), and those who in varying degrees believe the United States must bear the responsibility for the loss of China.

On balance, there seems to have been little the United States could have done after 1945, given the existing conditions in China, to influence the outcome of the Chinese civil war. If one wishes to look for outside influences in the victory of the Chinese Communists, Japan is the most logical candidate. The roots of the Nationalist defeat go back to the Japanese invasion of Manchuria in 1931 and the long, debilitating years of war that followed. The growing incapacity of the KMT leadership throughout those years to deal with the internal problems of the Nationalist movement rendered it incapable of dealing effectively with the rejuvenated Communist forces. In the final analysis, it would seem to be the Chinese Nationalists who lost China to the Communists—not the United States.

As the debates over the loss of China moved into the summer of 1950, U.S. policy toward China remained in a state of suspended animation. The picture changed dramatically, however, when, on the morning of June 25, 1950, 75,000 North Korean troops poured across the 38th parallel into South Korea.

THE DEVELOPMENT OF A POLICY: CONTAINMENT AND ISOLATION

The impact of the Korean conflict. Although the Chinese Nationalists had continued to call for United States aid to prevent an invasion of Taiwan,[13] U.S. policy-makers were 'waiting for the dust to settle.' On June 27, 1950, however, two days after the invasion of South Korea, President Truman took the first step toward the development of a new China policy. The President ordered United States forces to the aid of South Korea and at the same time directed the Seventh Fleet to prevent an invasion across the Taiwan straits.

President Truman declared that it was 'plain beyond all doubt that Communism had passed beyond the use of subversion to conquer independent nations and will now use armed invasion and war.' The President continued:

> In these circumstances, the occupation of Formosa by Communist forces would be a direct threat to the security of the Pacific area and to the United States performing their lawful and necessary functions in that area. The determination of the future status of Formosa must await the restoration of the security in the Pacific, a peace settlement with Japan, or consideration by the United Nations.[14]

The status of Taiwan soon became, as it has remained, the key issue in the relationship between China and the United States. The Chinese Communists immediately reaffirmed their determination to 'liberate' Taiwan and called for a withdrawal of U.S. 'armed invading forces,' while General MacArthur urged that Taiwan be

---

[12] *China Digest*, 6, No. 10 (Hong Kong: Pong Gwan Publisher, August 24, 1949): 3 ff.

[13] Cf. *China and U.S. Far East Policy 1945–1966*, p. 51.

[14] Harry S. Truman, *Years of Trial and Hope 1946–1952* (Garden City, New York: Doubleday, 1956), p. 339.

turned into a bastion of United States defenses in the Far East.[15] The official position of the U.S. Government continued to favor the protection of Taiwan while at the same time attempting to assure the Chinese Communists that the United States had no designs on Taiwan or on any other Chinese territory. In a letter addressed to the Secretary General of the United Nations, the Administration maintained that 'the United States has not encroached on the territory of China, nor has the United States taken aggressive action against China. . . . We have no designs on Formosa, and our action was not inspired by any desire to acquire a special position for the United States.'[16]

It is here that the clash of two mutually exclusive and antagonistic views of the proper political order in East Asia may be seen clearly for the first time.

While relations between the United States and the Chinese Communists up to the summer of 1950 had not been marked by excessive warmth, the United States decision to protect Taiwan, which up to the 1970's has prevented a successful conclusion of the Chinese civil war, provided conclusive proof to the Chinese Communists of the evil and hostile intent of the United States toward their new regime. Adding to the Chinese bitterness was the fact that, dating from the early days of the Korean conflict, the U.S. Government, following a United Nations recommendation, had imposed a total embargo on trade with mainland China and had sought to make the cooperation of other nations in this effort a condition for their receipt of U.S. aid. Likewise, the outbreak of the war in Korea also saw the United States take the lead in opposing the seating of the P.R.C. in the United Nations.

From the American point of view, the neutralization of Taiwan was 'an action designed to keep the peace and was, therefore, in full accord with the spirit of the Charter of the United Nations.'[17] The Chinese, however, saw the Truman move as 'an aggressive act . . . aimed at severing Taiwan altogether from China.'[18] The Chinese reaffirmed their pledge that the 'Chinese people . . . will surely be victorious in driving out the American aggressors and in recovering Taiwan and all other territories belonging to China.'[19] Though the United States made strenuous efforts to reassure the Chinese that there was no hostile intent toward the new Communist regime, the Chinese Communists continued to respond with a combination of vitriol and denunciation that U.S. policy-makers seemed unable to comprehend. Nor, apparently, has the passage of time clarified for some U.S. officials the fundamental conflict of aims that emerged in 1950. In the late 1960's, former Under Secretary of State Nicholas deB. Katzenbach noted almost sadly, 'Although right from the beginning we made efforts to maintain contacts and avoid hostile relations, the Communist authorities left little doubt that they wanted to eliminate any American representation from the Chinese mainland and to pursue a politically hostile policy toward this country.'[20] Given the conflicting basic aims of Chinese and United States policy cited in the Introduction to this chapter—the establishment of stable, free governments and a general condition of peace and order on the one hand, and support, encouragement, and promotion of Marxist-Leninist revolutionary movements coupled with the expansion of influence beyond China's national borders on the other—the mere pres-

---

[15] Averell Harriman was sent to Tokyo in August 1950 by President Truman for a full discussion of the political situation in the Far East with General MacArthur. See *ibid.*, pp. 349 ff.

[16] *Ibid.*, p. 357.   [17] *Ibid.*, p. 357.

[18] C. K. Cheng, 'Hands Off Taiwan!' *People's China*, 2, No. 10 (Peking: Foreign Languages Press, November 16, 1950): 7.

[19] *Ibid.*, p. 9.

[20] Nicholas deB. Katzenbach, *Communist China: A Realistic View* (an address before the National Press Club at Washington, D.C., May 21, 1968) (Washington, D.C.: Government Printing Office, 1968), p. 3.

ence of the United States, with its overwhelming military strength, around the rim of the Chinese mainland was a clear indication to the Communist leaders of United States hostility toward Chinese intentions and desires, which no amount of reassurance from Washington could change.

It is important here to reiterate that the hostile posture of the Communist authorities toward the United States predates the move by the Truman Administration to neutralize Taiwan, although that move and the response it elicited were symptomatic of the deep differences between the two sides. As far back as 1947, when General Wedemeyer issued his deeply critical report on corruption in the KMT, the Communists responded by naming him an 'utter hypocrite' and a 'bloodthirsty butcher.'[21] In response to the United States White Paper in 1949, which would seem to have given Chiang Kai-shek up to his fate, the Communists declared:

> the American government is still trying to recruit saboteurs of all shades inside and outside China to undermine the sacred and beautiful fatherland of the Chinese people, to undermine the Soviet Union and the democratic forces of the peoples of the world and to undermine peace in East and West.[22]

At a time when the United States, from its point of view, clearly had not adopted a hostile posture toward the Communist government, the Communists maintained that, 'as long as America remains an imperialist country and has not been changed into a people's country, the United States Government will remain hostile to the Chinese people to the very end. . . . American imperialism is the irreconcilable enemy of the Chinese nation and the Chinese people.[23]

The question must therefore be raised whether Communist China's relations with the United States might have been more friendly, or at least less hostile, if the Truman Administration had not decided to neutralize (protect) Taiwan. In my view, the answer is that relations probably would not have been friendlier. If, however, the United States had failed to respond in Korea (no matter which view one selects to explain the Chinese role in the invasion of South Korea by North Korea), had left Taiwan and the KMT to their fate, and sounded a general retreat from East Asia, U.S. policies would no longer have clashed directly with those of the Chinese. One does not have to assume an infinitely expansionist and virulently aggressive Communist China to support the view that anything short of a virtually complete U.S. withdrawal from involvement in the affairs of Korea, Taiwan, mainland Asia, and perhaps even Japan would eventually have led the United States to a clash with Chinese policy, designs, and interests.

The hardening of Communist Chinese–United States relations. The climate of ill will in Chinese–U.S. relations became more intense as the U.N. offensive under the direction of General MacArthur rolled through North Korea toward the Manchurian border in October, 1950. Throughout August and September, the Chinese had expressed first their 'concern' over events in Korea and finally the threat that they would not 'sit back with folded hands and let the Americans come to the border.'[24] The threats and expressions of concern were either ignored or discounted, though General MacArthur was ordered to restrict his bombing in the area of the Yalu River and to insure, as far as practicable, that the spearhead of the drive toward Manchuria was manned by South Korean troops (toward whom the Chinese would presumably be less sensitive) and not by U.S. units.[25] At the same time, all demands by the Chinese

---

[21] *White Paper*, pp. 816, 817.   [22] *Chinese Digest*, 6, No. 10 (August 24, 1949): 5.

[23] *Ibid.*, p. 4. Similar sentiments were expressed in the NCNA Editorial, 'Good Bye, Leighton Stuart!' *China Digest*, 6, No. 11 (September, 1949): 3–5.

[24] Statement by the Acting Chief of the PLA General Staff, General (later Marshal) Nieh Jung-chen. See Allen S. Whiting, *China Crosses the Yalu* (New York: Macmillan, 1960), p. 93.

[25] Truman, *Years of Trial and Hope*, pp. 360, 372.

and their allies that the Communist government be allowed to participate in the U.N. debates on the Korean situation were rebuffed.[26] On October 16, the first Chinese 'volunteers' crossed secretly into South Korea.[27] By the end of the month, U.S. and South Korean troops had suffered their first serious defeats at the hands of combined Chinese-North Korean forces, and by the end of November the Chinese had begun their massive offensive, which smashed the center of the U.N. line and drove the allied forces back toward the 38th parallel. On December 4, Communist troops re-captured Pyongyang, the North Korean capital. One month later, despite calls by the U.N. for a ceasefire, the Communist armies had reoccupied Seoul.

Further U.N. appeals for a ceasefire and the opening of peace talks met with a Chinese demand that the U.N. troops withdraw from Korea and that the United States cease to protect Taiwan.[28] As the fighting continued, U.S. Ambassador to the United Nations Warren R. Austin, in response to a nearly unanimous call from the U.S. Congress, introduced a resolution to declare Communist China guilty of aggression in Korea. On February 1, 1951, despite predictions of dire consequences made by friends of Communist China and by neutral India as well, the resolution passed the U.N. General Assembly by a vote of 44 to 7, with eight abstentions.

By mid-March, a U.N. counteroffensive, which had succeeded in wresting Seoul from Communist control, placed the U.N. forces once again within a few miles of the 38th parallel. Once more U.S. policy makers were faced with deciding whether to cross the parallel into North Korea or, having repulsed the invader and regained control over South Korea, to hold fast. The view of the Administration in Washington was that 'further diplomatic efforts toward settlement should be made before any advance with major forces north of the 38th parallel.'[29] That view was opposed by General MacArthur, who in effect threatened expansion of the war to the territory of China itself should the enemy commanders not capitulate.[30] The tension between General MacArthur and the President reached the breaking point when MacArthur directed a letter to the House minority leader criticizing Administration policy in Korea, ending with the declaration, 'There is no substitute for victory.'[31] The issue was resolved on April 11, 1951, when the President, as Commander-in-Chief, relieved General MacArthur of all his commands. The dismissal of General MacArthur re-flected the decision to hold fast south of the 38th parallel—a decision that stood de-spite the uproar following MacArthur's return to the United States.[32]

If the entry of Communist China into the Korean conflict hardened the pattern of hostile relations between China and the United States, the re-establishment of the old line of demarcation at the 38th parallel and the dismissal of General MacArthur established the limitations within which these relations proceeded over numerous years. It was made clear that U.S. commitments would be confined to holding actions, as opposed to the sponsorship of counterrevolutionary, anti-Communist actions against those areas already in Communist hands. The Communists would thereafter be secure in those areas under Communist control but would not be per-mitted to expand beyond existing borders. Thus, the United States would defend South Korea, Taiwan, and eventually South Vietnam (where the United States

---

[26] Whiting, *China Crosses the Yalu*, covers this period in great detail. See especially pp. 101 ff. Also, cf. Harold C. Hinton, *Communist China in World Politics* (Boston: Houghton Mifflin, 1966), pp. 205 ff.

[27] Whiting, *China Crosses the Yalu*, p. 94.

[28] *China and U.S. Far East Policy 1945–1966*, p. 55.

[29] Truman, *Years of Trial and Hope*, p. 438.   [30] *Ibid.*, pp. 440 ff.   [31] *Ibid.*, p. 446.

[32] The record of the Congressional hearings on the dismissal of General MacArthur is con-tained in *Military Situation in the Far East: Hearings* before the Senate Armed Services and Foreign Relations Committees, 82nd Congress, 1st session (Washington, D.C.: Government Printing Office, 1951).

would soon be paying the bulk of the costs for the French war), but would not undertake military action to overthrow the governments of North Korea, mainland China, or North Vietnam—a limitation that has been repeated endlessly by the United States throughout the current Vietnam conflict. The distinction was an important one, for it marked the decision on the part of the United States to forgo an aggressive, counterrevolutionary, anti-Communist policy in favor of the creation of a defensive shield for the free governments of Asia. Despite the emotional denunciations of the MacArthur hearings, the rhetoric of the Presidential campaign of 1952, and even President Eisenhower's 'unleashing' of Chiang Kai-shek in his 1953 State of the Union Message, this broad policy has, in its basic outlines, remained unchanged. In keeping with its policy decision, the United States took the lead in the creation of the South East Asia Treaty Organization (SEATO) in 1954—a collective defense organization joined by Australia, Britain, France, New Zealand, Pakistan, the Philippines, Thailand, and the United States. A separate treaty for the defense of Taiwan was concluded with the Republic of China in December of 1954. On the Chinese Communist side, the stalemate in Korea also marked the end of what Harold Hinton has called the Chinese phase of armed struggle.[33]

The Bandung spirit. In response to a new thrust in Chinese diplomacy in early 1955, there occurred a brief thaw in Communist Chinese–U.S. relations. The Asian-African Conference held in Bandung, Java, in April, 1955, marked the beginning of a Chinese attempt to exert a leading role in forging a third political force in the Afro-Asian world. The Bandung spirit is perhaps best represented by the Chinese attempt to popularize 'five principles' of peaceful coexistence first embodied in an agreement with India signed in 1954.[34] In keeping with the over-all Chinese policy of conciliation, Chou En-lai declared in April, 1955, that China was ready to discuss the question of relaxing tensions in the Far East.[35] Chou further held out the possibility of 'peaceful' liberation of Taiwan through negotiations, an offer stemming in part at least from the fact that Communist Chinese military efforts in the Taiwan Straits early in 1955 (see below) had ended in a virtual standoff. In July, discussions between China and the United States, which had taken place from time to time in Geneva, were raised from consular to ambassadorial level. These talks were later continued between the United States and Chinese Ambassadors at Warsaw.

Initially, the talks involved the fate of a small number of U.S. civilians still in Communist China, some of whom were freed soon after the new round of talks began in July. For a time as well, both sides appeared satisfied with the progress being made toward a satisfactory solution to some of the persistent problems that had continued to plague the relationship. By early 1956, however, the atmosphere of the talks and the tone of the public exchanges had become more acrimonious, as once again the sticking point proved to be the Taiwan question. Though Secretary Dulles had lauded Chou En-lai for his substantial move in the direction of the renunciation of the use of force, the Chinese had refused to sign a joint statement committing them to such a renunciation in all cases. Specifically, the Chinese insisted on exempting from the formula such 'internal affairs' as the settlement of the Taiwan problem.[36]

In the end, though the talks continued, the short-lived period of improved relations

---

[33] Hinton, *Communist China in World Politics*, pp. 25 ff.

[34] The five principles are: mutual respect for each other's territorial sovereignty, mutual nonaggression, mutual noninterference in each other's internal affairs, equality and mutual benefit, and peaceful coexistence. Cf. Hinton, *Communist China in World Politics*, p. 103.

[35] *China and U.S. Far East Policy 1945–1966*, p. 74.

[36] The entire history of these negotiations is covered in elaborate detail by Kenneth T. Young, *Negotiations with the Chinese Communists: The United States Experience, 1953–1967* (New York: McGraw-Hill, 1968). For the exchange on the renunciation of force, see Appendix C, pp. 414–17.

gave way once again to a condition of mutual suspicion and hostility. Nor had the objective conditions governing the relations of the two states been changed in any substantial way. That is, no progress had been made toward solving the fundamental contradictions in outlook. The situation clearly was not improved by the publication in January, 1956, of an article in *Life* magazine[37] in which Secretary Dulles enunciated his 'brinkmanship' philosophy, especially with regard to the 1955 crisis in the Taiwan Straits.

Now that at least a limited settlement had reduced the level of conflict in Korea and Indochina, the focus of U.S.-Chinese differences shifted back to Taiwan and the offshore islands. The brief period of relaxation between China and the United States, which seemed initially to hold the promise of a permanent betterment of relations, foundered on the same obstacles that have continued to stand in the way of improved relations—the future status of Taiwan and the continuing basic conflict of policy aims in the Far East.

The offshore islands. In January, 1955, following renewed warnings to the United States over Taiwan and an increase in the shelling of Nationalist-held Quemoy, the Communists moved with force against the Tach'en Islands, opposite the coast of Chekiang Province and northernmost of the three groups of islands held by Nationalist Chinese forces. In response to the Communist occupation of Ichiang Island, a few miles to the north of the Tach'ens, President Eisenhower asked the Congress to give him emergency authorization to use U.S. forces to protect Taiwan and the Pescadores. The precise status of Quemoy and Matsu, the principal islands in addition to the Tach'ens held by the Nationalists, was left somewhat unclear by the resolution, although an amendment offered by Senator Hubert H. Humphrey that would have restricted the use of U.S. forces specifically to the protection of Taiwan and the Pescadores was rejected by the Senate.[38] In any case, there was clearly no intention on the part of the administration to commit U.S. forces to the difficult task of defending the Tach'ens, from which the Nationalists withdrew in February with the aid of the U.S. Seventh Fleet. Though tensions remained high in the area, no further attacks were directed at Quemoy and Matsu. The Communist leaders were probably swayed in their decision to forgo an invasion of the offshore islands by a combination of factors, including the lukewarm support for their activities by the Soviet Union, the very strong warning by Secretary Dulles that armed aggression might mean 'open war in Asia,'[39] and by the approaching opening of the Bandung Conference. The result of the 1954–55 action in the Taiwan Strait was an uneasy standoff, with the position of the United States toward the defense of the last two groups of offshore islands remaining to be precisely defined.

The confrontation in the Taiwan Strait once again reached the point of open military hostility when the Chinese Communists, in a clear attempt to test U.S. intentions with respect to the offshore islands, appeared ready to invade the islands in August, 1958. As the level of the artillery bombardment of Quemoy increased (eventually to about 8,000 rounds a day), and, as the Communist Chinese public statements became increasingly threatening, President Eisenhower was forced to take a public stand on the U.S. military commitment to Chiang Kai-shek. Once again, the U.S. position with respect to the offshore islands was somewhat ambiguous, though seeming to lean in the direction of extending U.S. support to the defense of Quemoy and Matsu. Under the provisions of the Formosa Resolution of 1955, the President was authorized to extend protection to the offshore islands if, in his judgment, an attack on the islands was the prelude to an attack on Taiwan and the Pescadores. With this

---

[37] 'How Dulles Averted War,' *Life* magazine, January 11, 1956.

[38] Cf. *China and U.S. Far East Policy 1945–1966*, pp. 72–73.

[39] *The New York Times*, March 9, 1955. Also cf. Hinton, *Communist China in World Politics*, pp. 260–63.

in mind, Secretary Dulles declared that it would be 'highly hazardous for anyone to assume' that an attempt to change the situation 'by attacking and seeking to conquer these islands . . . could be considered or held to a "limited operation." '[40] The President's concern, as he expressed it, was that 'we could not say that we would defend with the power of the United States every protruding rock that was claimed by the Nationalists as an "offshore island." On the other hand, if we specified exactly what islands we would defend, we simply invited the Reds to occupy all the others of those groups.'[41] The supplying of the Nationalist forces on Quemoy continued under the protection of the U.S. Seventh Fleet, which escorted Chinese vessels up to the three-mile international limit of the mainland, while the implications of U.S. policy statements became more direct. On September 4, Secretary Dulles declared, 'We have recognized that the securing and protecting of Quemoy and Matsu have increasingly become related to the defense of Taiwan (Formosa). . . . Military dispositions have been made by the United States so that a Presidential determination, if made, would be followed by action both timely and effective.'[42] The implications of this threat, combined with the apparent reluctance of the Soviet Union to support its Chinese comrades in an invasion of the islands[43] prompted the Chinese Communists to moderate their approach to the crisis. On September 6, Chou En-lai offered to resume talks with the United States,[44] and a new round of ambassadorial talks was begun in Warsaw on September 15.

The level of tension subsided considerably in early October, when the Communists announced a one-week suspension of their shelling—a suspension that was extended for two additional weeks immediately at its expiration. Though the shelling was renewed briefly late in October, the Communist Chinese Minister of Defense subsequently announced that thereafter the shelling would occur only on odd-numbered dates. No further assaults (except periodic shelling) have been mounted from the mainland, and the situation with regard to the reunification of Taiwan with the mainland remains a standoff. Nor has the pattern of hostile relations established by 1958 been substantially altered in other respects with the passage of years.

The Future of Communist Chinese–U.S. Relations

Communist China's 'United States problem.'[45] As indicated earlier, Peking's United States problem stems principally from the fact of the overwhelming U.S. military superiority in the Western Pacific and from the fact of the U.S. commitment to support free (non-Communist) governments on China's periphery. It is the United States that has stood in the forefront in opposing 'people's wars,' in thwarting Chinese (or at least Communist) designs in Korea, and in preventing the successful conclusion of the Chinese civil war by denying Taiwan to the Communist government. One can easily imagine the anger and frustration of the Chinese Communist leaders with their great power ambitions when confronted with the reality of their inability even to take control of Quemoy, much less the booming island province of Taiwan. Indeed, as one observer has noted, 'wherever one may look, one is confronted on every side with the frustrations of Chinese ambitions and aspirations.'[46]

---

[40] Dwight D. Eisenhower, *Waging Peace 1956–1961* (New York: Doubleday, 1965), p. 296.

[41] *Ibid.*, p. 296.

[42] *Ibid.*, p. 299. Cf. Hinton, *Communist China in World Politics*, pp. 265–70.

[43] Cf. Hinton, *Communist China in World Politics*, pp. 115, 268.

[44] NCNA, Peking, September 6, 1958.

[45] I am indebted to Professor Yuan-li Wu for this formulation. See his 'Peking and the United States,' *Modern Age*, 12, No. 4 (Chicago, Ill.: Foundation for Foreign Affairs, Fall, 1968): 361–70.

[46] *Ibid.*, p. 362.

There is, however, another dimension to Peking's problem that is less frequently noted. If the policies of the United States have failed to come to grips with the reality of the more than twenty years of Communist rule in China, as many critics insist, the failure of the Chinese leaders accurately to perceive the realities of the American situation is even more striking. The failure of the Chinese Communists to take advantage of the U.S. write-off of Chiang Kai-shek, noted above, may be attributable to an uncompromising revolutionary commitment to the desire to proceed on the road to socialism uncontaminated by contact with the leader of the 'imperialist camp.' It may, on the other hand, have been the result of a gross miscalculation of the relative strength of the 'forces of imperialism' against those of the 'people.' Of more immediate concern, however, is the fact that Peking's long-range hopes appear to hinge on the success of liberation struggles around the world, and most especially on the 'people's war' now perceived to be raging in the United States. Peking has for some time shown an interest in the black civil rights movement in the United States, but only in the last several years has the black 'liberation struggle' become a key element in the worldwide struggle of oppressed people to overcome the various evil oppressing forces. Following a number of serious outbreaks of violence in 1966, the official Communist Chinese media observed:

> In the past three years the American Negroes' struggles against racial discrimination have swept the length and breadth of the United States like a prairie fire. Since the beginning of this summer, a series of Negro people's armed struggles against tyranny have again broken out in Chicago and other big cities of the United States. The American Negroes' struggle has begun to take the road of using revolutionary violence against counterrevolutionary violence. This marks a new stage in the struggle of the American people.[47]

More recently Lin Pao, in his report to the Ninth National Congress of the Communist Party of China, observed that 'an unprecedentedly gigantic revolutionary mass movement has broken out in Japan, Western Europe, and North America, the "heartlands" of capitalism.'[48] 'Since he took office,' Lin declared, 'Nixon has been confronted with a hopeless mess and an insoluble economic crisis, with the strong resistance of the masses of the people at home and throughout the world.'[49] Lin once again declared the Chinese support for 'the proletariat, the students and youth, and the masses of black people of the United States in their just struggle against the U.S. ruling clique.'[50] As there is little evidence to suggest that statements of this sort are mere rhetorical smoke, they should probably be accepted as representing a substantially genuine picture of the perception by a key element of the Chinese leadership of conditions in the United States. In terms of the future of U.S.-Chinese relations, the United States can probably expect to find Peking relatively unyielding and inflexible if the Communist leaders really believe things are going very well for them around the world while the United States rushes toward the brink of an abyss—an 'enemy' that 'rots with every passing day.'[51]

Having noted the reality of the U.S. frustration of Chinese ambitions, one must also call attention to the positive and useful role played by the U.S. 'imperialist devils' in Chinese Communist demonology. It has been often noted that a Communist ideological movement must identify, or perhaps create, an evil presence against which to hurl its historically superior forces. There is a need to contrast the historically doomed forces of reaction with one's own progressive and inevitably victorious move-

---

[47] NCNA (English), August 8, 1966, as cited in Wu, 'Peking and United States,' pp. 366–67. Professor Wu's article contains the fullest discussion yet seen by the author of the Chinese concept of 'people's war' in the United States.
[48] *Peking Review*, 12, No. 18 (April 30, 1969): 31.   [49] *Ibid.*   [50] *Ibid.*, p. 34.
[51] *Peking Review*, 12, No. 18 (April 30, 1969): 31.

ment—the function of the chief enemy being much the same as that served by Satan in Christian dogma. It may be that the Soviet Union will eventually replace the United States as the chief enemy in Chinese propaganda,[52] but for the moment the Chinese still appear to find it useful to retain the United States in the leading role.

The Chinese Communist leaders give little indication that from their point of view their United States problem has in any way diminished. Nor, indeed, do the objective conditions of U.S.-Chinese relations, including the Chinese perception of the revolutionary situation in the United States, appear to hold out a very strong promise of basic and fundamental improvement of those relations.

The Chinese nuclear program. Despite the built-in difficulties described above, the surprisingly rapid development of the Chinese nuclear weapons program will undoubtedly force both parties to reconsider long-held positions. The program achieved its first success with the detonation of a uranium device in Western China on October 16, 1964.[53] The development of the program proceeded rapidly throughout 1965 and 1966 with the first successful detonation of a thermonuclear device occurring on December 28, 1966. A subsequent test in June, 1967 saw the Chinese detonate a multi- megaton H-bomb, probably dropped from an aircraft.[54] The Chinese announced ten successful atomic tests, the last coming in the fall of 1970, and the launching of two earth satellites. Forecasts indicate that China will shortly achieve a medium-range ballistic missile capability and within a decade, perhaps, complete development of an ICBM capable of reaching targets in the United States. Such was the concern in the United States over the prospect of this development that an anti-ballistic missile (ABM) system was proposed. The original proposal—a controversial one—envisaged a 'thin' defense against a potential Chinese missile attack. Though it seems unrealistic to imagine that the Chinese will in the foreseeable future possess the capability to challenge the United States to an intercontinental duel with thermonuclear weapons, there is no doubt that the imminent Chinese acquisition of even a limited nuclear capability carries with it the potential, at least, for substantial changes in Chinese-U.S. relations.

From a purely military point of view, the Chinese acquisition of a reliable delivery system for nuclear weapons—especially one in the ICBM range—can scarcely fail to alter the strategic balance of power in Asia, if not, indeed, on a worldwide scale. While up to the present the United States has been able to undertake military operations in the Western Pacific free of the threat of nuclear destruction on U.S. soil, the future acquisition by the Chinese Communists of the ability to inflict politically unacceptable damage on the continental United States should substantially affect the bargaining position of the Communist regime in any future confrontations with the United States, as for example in the Taiwan Strait crisis of 1958. Even the more limited capacity to inflict unacceptable damage on Taiwan, Okinawa, the Philippines, and Japan should substantially strengthen the Chinese bargaining position. The successful Chinese development of a delivery system for nuclear weapons may, however, have a more salutary consequence as well. For a nuclear threat to be credible, that threat must be communicated to the potential adversary. As Michael Yahuda observes: 'Strategic deterrence involves a process of interaction with the adversary, which necessitates minimally a two-way communication of intentions, capabilities, and, beyond that, policies and strategies.'[55] China's position of isolation

---

[52] It is interesting to note that, while Lin Piao maintained the United States in the leading position in his address to the Ninth Party Congress, the strongest language and more lengthy denunciation was reserved for the Soviet Union. Cf. *ibid.*, pp. 31–34.

[53] *Peking Review*, Vol. 7, No. 42, 1964 (Special Supplement dated October 16, 1964).

[54] Cf. Michael B. Yahuda, 'China's Nuclear Option,' *Bulletin of the Atomic Scientists*, 25, No. 2 (Chicago: Educational Foundation for Nuclear Science, February, 1969): 72–77.

[55] *Ibid.*, p. 77.

from the mainstream of world events, increasingly self-imposed through the 1960's, may have to be abandoned if China is to bargain effectively with the other nuclear powers. To quote Mr. Yahuda again:

Chinese deployment of a strategic deterrence capability may indeed serve as the primary agency by which China becomes inducted into fuller participatory membership of the international community of states in more ways than simply sitting on certain international bodies, such as the U.N. Security Council.[56]

It seems, in fact, that for the Chinese their nuclear weapons program may be as important for the political leverage it will gain them as for the military value of the weapons themselves.[57] It is clear that one of the primary aims of the Chinese nuclear program is to provide the Communist regime with a ticket to great power status and thus to an increased role in high international councils. Above all, it appears that the Chinese want to be consulted—in the same way that the United States and the Soviet Union are consulted—on any matters of importance, anywhere in the world. But consultation requires contact of a more structured sort than is available through the occasional meeting of ambassadors in a third foreign capital. Thus, while the Chinese nuclear capability may make the Chinese more difficult to deal with in some respects by providing the P.R.C. with a stronger bargaining position, it may also force Peking into increasingly structured contacts with the United States as a potential adversary.

CONCLUSION

Despite the lack of improvement in the fundamental issues underlying U.S.-Chinese relations, many see small signs of hope for increased contacts and betterment of relations in the future.

Beginning in November, 1968, Peking, moving out of the isolation of the Cultural Revolution, announced its willingness to resume the Warsaw talks. Plans for continuing the meetings, which had been in suspension for ten months, were scuttled by the defection to the United States of a Chinese diplomat in the Netherlands in January, 1969. By December, 1969, however, talks were once again under way, held this time in the Chinese Embassy in an atmosphere of unusual warmth and hospitality. The fall of 1969 also saw the U.S. Government announce that thereafter certain categories of persons could have passports validated for travel to China, and that Americans traveling abroad would be allowed to bring back up to $100 in goods from China. That was followed by the announcement of a partial lifting of the embargo on trade with China, allowing foreign subsidiaries of U.S. firms to trade with the P.R.C. in nonstrategic goods and permitting U.S. companies to buy Chinese goods for trade with third countries. Further, U.S. citizens would be allowed to purchase unlimited amounts of Chinese goods for personal use. In 1971, the United States relaxed the remaining restrictions on the validation of passports for travel to China.

On the Chinese side, signs of good intentions were seen in the release on July 10, 1970, of Bishop James Walsh, an American who had been sentenced in 1958 to twenty years' imprisonment for espionage activities. Clearly, the Soviet invasion of Czechoslovakia and the enunciation of the 'Brezhnev Doctrine' provided good reason for the leaders of the P.R.C., especially the military leaders dominating the Chinese political scene, to reconsider possible options in China's foreign relations— including closer contacts with the United States. In the United States, at least two

---

[56] *Ibid.*

[57] Cf. Henry A. Kissinger's discussion of 'The Limits of Bipolarity: The Nature of Power in the Modern Period,' in his *American Foreign Policy: Essays* (New York: W. W. Norton, 1969), pp. 59–65.

developments created an atmosphere in which a reconsideration of long-held positions may take place. First, the development of the Sino-Soviet conflict destroyed the idea of a monolithic world Communist movement. China has been increasingly seen as an independent political entity to be dealt with in its own right. Second, and perhaps more significant, China is no longer important as a domestic issue within the United States. One recent analysis suggests that 'most central to all the years of relative inaction' was the fact that China was still a hot issue in U.S. politics, and charges of 'appeasement' were still seen to be politically potent.[58] The culmination of the move toward increased contact with the P.R.C. came in 1972 with President Nixon's historic visit to China. The President's lengthy stay in the P.R.C. (February 21 to February 28) was taken by many observers as evidence of his deep concern with the betterment of Sino-American relations. The joint communiqué issued in Shanghai prior to the President's departure was likewise seen as offering guarded indications of a Chinese desire to seek a genuine improvement of relations.

Despite the note of cautious optimism sounded in many quarters, however, many of the old sticking points in the U.S.-Chinese relations remain, represented most prominently by the Vietnam war and the problem of Taiwan. The war in Vietnam remains as a manifestation of the antithetical U.S. and Chinese views of the necessary and just order of things in Asia. The conflict represents a continuation of the policy of military containment that grew out of the Korean War. To a large extent, the future of U.S. relations with the Communist governments of East Asia, China in particular, may depend on the nature of the lessons the two sides learn from that prolonged and bloody conflict. As for the Taiwan problem, there is no realistic way at present for the P.R.C. to 'liberate' Taiwan. Equally, the Nationalist Chinese have little hope of 'liberating' the mainland. At the same time, whatever developments take place in U.S.-Chinese relations, the United States appears firmly committed to honor its commitments to the Taiwan government. Thus, for the short run, at any rate, the ultimate conclusion of the Chinese civil war appears ruled out. Nor is there much chance for a real settlement of U.S.-Chinese hostilities if the leaders of the P.R.C. insist, as they may well do, on a lump settlement—all or nothing—which would involve a complete U.S. withdrawal from Asia and the U.S. abdication of any role as a Pacific power.

In the final analysis, while fundamental improvement of relations may not be forthcoming in the near future, the seeds of change have been sown: in the development of the Chinese nuclear capability, in the increased bitterness of the Sino-Soviet conflict, and in the changing domestic conditions within China and the United States. Thus, like so many other seemingly insoluble problems, the key to eventual improvement may rest simply in the passage of time.

SELECTED BIBLIOGRAPHY

BARNETT, A. DOAK. *Communist China and Asia*. New York: Vintage Books, 1961. An interesting, though now somewhat dated, discussion of the nature of Chinese Communist power in the Far East and the implications for U.S. Far Eastern policy.

BARNETT, A. DOAK, and EDWIN O. REISCHAUER, eds. *The United States and China: The Next Decade*. New York: Praeger Publishers, 1970. A variety of points of view presented at the 1969 convocation of the National Committee on United States–China Relations.

China and United States Far East Policy 1945–1966. Washington, D.C.: Congressional Quarterly Service, 1967. A very useful compendium of documents, brief descriptive essays on background material, and a lengthy, detailed chronology of events from 1945 through 1966.

---

[58] James C. Thompson, Jr., 'Will the Nixon Administration Recognize Communist China? *Pacific Community*, Vol. 2, No. 1, Tokyo: Jiji Press, October, 1970.

Department of State. *United States Relations with China*. Washington, D.C.: U.S. Government Printing Office, 1949. The famous State Department White Paper on China. An invaluable source for background on U.S.-Chinese relations up to 1949.

FEIS, HERBERT. *The China Tangle*. Princeton, N.J.: Princeton University Press, 1953. An excellent analysis of the U.S. involvement in China from 1941 to 1946.

HINTON, HAROLD C. *Communist China in World Politics*. Boston: Houghton Mifflin Company, 1966. A full and detailed treatment of the whole range of issues in China's foreign relations.

TSOU TANG. *America's Failure in China 1941–1950*. Chicago: The University of Chicago Press, 1963. Perhaps the fullest and most balanced analysis of the shortcomings of U.S. China policy.

WHITING, ALLEN S. *China Crosses the Yalu*. New York: Macmillan Company, 1960. A complete discussion of the events surrounding the Chinese Communist decision to enter the Korean War.

YOUNG, KENNETH T. *Negotiating with the Chinese Communists: The United States Experience, 1953–1967*. New York: McGraw-Hill, 1968. A complete account of the diplomatic meetings between the United States and Communist China.

13

SINO-SOVIET RELATIONS

FRANZ MICHAEL

The Strategy of National Liberation Movements

THE origin of the peculiar love-hate relationship that the Chinese and Soviet movements share can be traced back to Lenin's genius as an inventor of methods to expand the Communist revolution far beyond the orthodox Marxian concept of a proletarian revolution in the industrial countries. Having failed to extend the Bolshevik revolution into a wider proletarian revolution in the industrial countries of central Europe, Lenin turned east and devised a strategy to exploit the revolutionary potentials in the preindustrial countries. What Lenin conceived as the Communist strategy in the Afro-Asian world has little to do with proletarian revolution in the true Marxist sense, even though there was a tenuous link between the two through Lenin's doctrinal claim that imperialism, as the last phase of monopoly capitalism, could best be attacked in its colonial and quasi-colonial territorial possessions.

The idea of promoting revolution in the colonial world was not new. In the heated arguments among socialist leaders of the late nineteenth century, two schools of thought had emerged: A Western school held that the liberation of the colonial people and exploited countries of the East would result from the victory of the proletariat of the industrial countries, and an Eastern school held that these peoples could not only liberate themselves but in doing so would destroy monopoly capitalism and the capitalist system. Lenin belonged to the Eastern school.[1] He had laid the theoretical groundwork for his position in his 'Imperialism, the Highest Stage of Capitalism,'[2] and, when his hopes for a Communist revolution in Germany following World War I were disappointed, he was instrumental in organizing and relating the elements in the Asian world to be used in his revolutionary plan.

In the Bolshevik revolution, Lenin had already surprised his comrades by his use of Russian peasants in the overthrow of the Tsarist order and by their participation with the workers and soldiers in the new soviets. Turning east and inviting revolutionary representatives of the countries of Central and Eastern Asia to the Baku Conference of 1920, Lenin reversed the usual order of 'workers and peasants' and appealed to the 'peasants and workers,' or simply to the 'peasants' of those countries in which the proletariat was either small or nonexistent.[3] The peasants were thus to become a primary factor in the Asian revolution in which Lenin placed his principal hope.

---

[1] Demetrio Boersner, *The Bolsheviks and the National and Colonial Question, 1917–1928* (Paris: Librairie Minard, 1957), pp. 29 ff.

[2] V. I. Lenin, *Collected Works*, 19: 83–196.

[3] See invitations to the Baku Conference in Jane Degras, ed., *The Communist International, 1919–1943*, Vol. 1: *1919–1922* (London: Oxford University Press, 1960): 105–9.

By appealing to the masses for a revolution that was to fuse with the Communist purpose, Lenin changed the Marxist revolutionary concept. It was no longer the most advanced class, the industrial proletariat, that was to make the revolution, it was the oppressed people in general, 'the toilers' (*die werktätigen Massen*), who were to be the revolutionary force. In this wider concept of the revolutionary class, the term proletariat lost its specific meaning. It is only natural that the broad appeal to the masses, later to be emphasized by Mao Tse-tung, was to derive from Lenin's widening of the Marxist concept, and that the term proletariat was to become related to revolutionary loyalty rather than to class origin. Lenin had opened the door to what eventually became a main aspect of Chinese Communism under Mao.

The leadership of the anti-imperialist revolution in the colonial and quasi-colonial world was to be, however, in the hands of the class that represented the emerging nationalism. This was, as Lenin clearly realized, the bourgeoisie. In its nationalist phase, the national bourgeoisie was supposed to resist the imperialist control of monopoly capitalism and to fight for national independence. It was, in Communist terms, still in the progressive phase of development. As such, the national bourgeoisie and the petite bourgeoisie could be given Communist support in the leadership of the anti-imperialist struggle. This became the basis of Lenin's concept of a united front policy under nationalist leadership, in which the Communists would participate in order eventually to take over and to transform the nationalist revolution into a socialist revolution. That was Lenin's strategy as applied to China. It was expressed in the 1923 agreement between the Chinese Nationalist leader, Sun Yat-sen, and the Comintern representative Joffe, who agreed that China had first to achieve national unification and independence and that the conditions for the successful establishment of Communism did not yet exist.

It was not without difficulty that Lenin obtained Comintern support for his policy of cooperating with and supporting, in the Asian countries, the very class that was regarded as the chief enemy of the proletarian revolution in the industrial world. The debate at the second Comintern congress in 1920 was heated. To avoid the issue, Lenin agreed to a change in terminology under which the term 'revolutionary nationalism' was used in lieu of bourgeoisie, a concession that did not affect the policy itself.[4]

The support of a national bourgeoisie and support of agrarian revolution constituted the two basic elements of the strategy of 'national liberation movements,' so called by Lenin and the Comintern leaders of his time. They could be applied simultaneously, but they could also conflict when the interests of the agrarian population clashed with those of the urban bourgeoisie. In that case, a careful balancing, or phasing of the application of the two strategems was needed, as in China, where the United Front with the national bourgeoisie was first applied and, when it failed, was replaced by agrarian revolution. Both stratagems were regarded as important, but the timing of the shift from one to the other, and the form of their application, led to leadership conflicts both in China and in Moscow.

The common organizational aspect of the nationalist anti-imperialist revolution, as well as of the agrarian revolution, was their military character. National liberation movements were from the outset related to wars of national liberation. In contrast to the political organization of the proletarian revolution in the West, the nationalist and agrarian revolution in Asia was to be organized in military form and was to be accomplished through 'war of national liberation' conducted primarily by a 'revolutionary army.'

The period of the United Front. Sino-Soviet relations between 1917 and the present can be divided into two major phases: the period before the Communist takeover in 1949,

---

[4] See Boersner, *Bolsheviks and National and Colonial Questions*, p. 80; and the Lenin-Roy debate in Degras, *Communist International*, 1: 138–44.

during which the Soviet Party, through the Comintern, and the Soviet government dealt with a number of factors in the Chinese situation, and the period of the People's Republic of China after 1949, during which Sino-Soviet state relations were determined by the relations of the two Communist Parties in power in each country. The Parties were at the same time constituent members of a community of 'socialist internationalism,' or a 'socialist commonwealth,' and their relations—friendly or hostile—concerned the questions of cohesion and leadership of the commonwealth.

The first phase was characterized by the development and application of the strategy of a Communist seizure of power in a nonindustrialized country. The Communist effort to conquer China by that strategy, through a war of 'national liberation,' took many years. From the founding of the Communist Party of China in 1921 and the Comintern agreement with Sun Yat-sen in 1923 until the Communist victory in 1949, the Soviet Party and the state had to deal with a number of Chinese groups simultaneously. For a time they dealt with a nominal Chinese Government in Peking, with the nationalist movement of Sun Yat-sen based in Canton, and with the Chinese Communist Party, which was to cooperate with the Nationalists. During that period the Soviets used a three-pronged policy to promote Communist interests and eventually to gain victory in China. The CCP was the direct tool of international Communist Party policy; Sun Yat-sen was the instrument of the Soviet united front policy of the Comintern; the Chinese Government in Peking was the object of a state treaty that abolished the 'unequal treaties' of Tsarist Russia and Imperial China and served the propaganda purpose of depicting the Soviet Union as a country that had abandoned its imperialist past and was dealing with China on a basis of equality. The Soviet's also attempted to deal directly with some of the warlords in China, such as Wu P'ei-fu and Teng Yü-hsiang. This, then, was the period of the development of the strategy of national liberation, which itself went through three phases.

When Moscow, through the Comintern, offered aid to Sun Yat-sen for his national revolution in 1923, Communist influence was exerted from above through Soviet advisers and from below through CCP members. The CCP had been established with the assistance of Comintern advisers who continued to direct its policies. As a result of the agreement with Sun Yat-sen, CCP members were admitted as individuals to membership in the Kuomintang (Nationalist Party) without having to renounce their membership in the Communist Party, which continued to direct them. The goal was to have those members eventually take over the direction of the Kuomintang and the revolution, with the assistance of their Soviet comrades.

Of even greater importance was the Soviet attempt to gain control of the military core of China's national revolution, the nationalist army. From the outset, Soviet advisers had impressed Sun Yat-sen with the necessity of establishing a nationalist army in order to free himself from dependence on the regional warlord forces, whose support, in a shifting power pattern, Sun had tried to obtain up to that time. As the cradle of the new army, the Whampoa Academy was established near Canton, with Chiang Kai-shek as its president. To obtain an understanding of the concept of the new revolutionary force, Chiang Kai-shek went to the Soviet Union in the autumn of 1923 as the head of a Chinese mission and there learned about the Soviet military system. He was impressed with the Party representative system, which in each of the units separated political affairs, put under a political commissar, from military affairs, which were under the control of the commander. In his reports from Moscow and after his return, Chiang recommended, and Sun accepted, the concept of a part-army in which political orientation was to play a major part in the training of officers and men.[5] The Whampoa Academy was organized according to this concept. A

---

[5] See, among others, Mao Ssu-ch'eng, *Min-kuo Shih-wu-nien i-ch'ienchih Chiang Chieh-shih hsien-sheng* (*Mr. Chiang Kai-shek Before 1926*) (Hong Kong, Lung-men Bookstore, 1965), pp.

political department was established within the academy to supervise the program of indoctrination. Both Sun and Chiang stressed in speeches to the students that they were to be the backbone of the future revolution and that the power of the party was in the hands of the officers and soldiers, who were to become the only hope of saving China. The military was thus assigned the main role in the revolution. Beyond a broad appeal to patriotism, the substance of this revolutionary role remained, however, undefined by the Nationalist leadership. This left ample room for maneuver by the staff of the political department in the army and its hierarchy of officials, who were almost all Communist Party members. All of the training programs and propaganda publications in the army were therefore formulated within the framework of Communist doctrine. In addition, the Communist cadets within the academy were organized into the Chinese Young Soldiers' Association, which had its own magazine to influence the students.[6]

The Soviet political advisers under Mikhail Borodin and the Soviet military advisers under Marshal Galen were thus in a pivotal position to use the Chinese Communist structure within the military, which supplied the base for political power. In retrospect, it is evident that the Soviet-directed Communist strategy came close to success. The attempt to take over the army and the party was foiled in the main by the opposition of one man, Chiang Kai-shek, who, as president of the academy, began to recognize the Communist purpose and defeated it. The turning point was the so-called *Chungshan* incident on March 20, 1926,[7] which Chiang Kai-shek believed to be a kidnaping attempt against him. Chiang assumed full military power, placed the Soviet advisers under arrest, and negotiated a new agreement that greatly reduced Communist influence in the party and the army.

Chiang's aim was to extricate his Nationalist forces from the vise in which they were held by Soviet control and influence. Aside from the Russians' direct manipulation of policy and their influence as teachers at the academy, the Chinese were dependent on Soviet arms and equipment brought in by ship from Vladivostok and on Soviet financial support for the Chinese forces. To free themselves from that dependency, Chiang aimed at leaving Canton as soon as possible to begin the campaign against the warlords that was to result in the Nationalist conquest of power over all China. The Soviet advisers had hoped to delay the northern campaign until they had gained a more complete hold over the Nationalist army, but after the *Chungshan* incident they were willing to compromise and to undertake the campaign in 1926.

A second issue between Chiang and his Soviet advisers was the route of the campaign. Chiang Kai-shek aimed at Shanghai and Nanking, where he hoped to obtain access to a non-Communist–controlled arsenal and to gain the support of Chinese— and possibly Western—banking and merchant groups, essential for him to free his army from Soviet control. The Soviet advisers, in turn, hoped to keep the campaign away from the Shanghai area and to direct it instead to Central China, there to link up with the forces of the warlord Feng Yü-hsiang, whose troops they also had supplied, financed, and provided with Soviet advisers. In the political tug-of-war a compromise was reached. The First Army and a number of other units, with Chiang Kai-shek as Commander-in-Chief, marched toward the lower Yangtze area, while other units, with the KMT Central Executive Committee and the Soviet advisers, moved to

---

205–206; *Kuo Fu Ch'üan-chi (Selected Works of Sun Yat-sen)*, Vol. 2 (Taipei, 1966), Section 8, pp. 259–264; and Chiang Kai-shek, *Soviet Russia in China* (New York: Farrar, Straus & Cudahy, 1965), pp. 16–17.

[6] Mao Ssu-ch'eng, op. cit. p. 369, and Chiang Kai-shek, op. cit. p. 26.

[7] This incident was the unauthorized move of the gunboat *Chungshan* under the command of a Communist officer, Li Chih-lung, formerly director of the Communist student cadet association, to attempt a sudden coup.

Wuhan in the central Yangtze area. This led to a division between Chiang Kai-shek and the Central Executive Committee, which continued to support the Soviet alliance in cooperation with the Communists. Eventually, however, when the Communist goal was revealed to the left Kuomintang members (the Kuomintang by this time having split into 'left' and 'right' factions), they in turn turned against the Soviet advisers, who were expelled together with the Chinese Communist supporters. Thus, the way was free for a Chinese Nationalist government to be established in Nanking in 1927 under the leadership of Chiang Kai-shek.[8]

The agrarian revolution. The failure of the United Front led to a Communist shift to the second ingredient of the Communist national liberation strategy, 'agrarian revolution.' Its introduction had been well prepared. Borodin, the chief Soviet adviser, had given lectures to Chinese Communists in Canton on the tactics of agrarian revolution, attended by Mao Tse-tung, among others.[9] A training department for agrarian agitators had been established within the Kuomintang administration and placed under the direction of Mao Tse-tung. Students from the school, almost all Communists, later became agitators for the promotion of agrarian uprisings under Communist guidance. An experimental agrarian soviet under Communist leadership was established at Hailufeng in late 1927 but was abandoned in February, 1928, by its Communist leadership when the local administration regained control with the help of military forces and executed the peasant leaders.[10]

As the threat of a split with the Kuomintang came nearer, Moscow prepared to shift its policy, as indicated in the discussions of the Executive Committee sessions of the Comintern in December, 1926, and May, 1927. 'Agrarian revolution' as the new stage of the national liberation movement in China and 'a radical agrarian policy' were stressed in the resolution of 1926, which established a detailed agrarian program.[11] The stress was not only on peasant organization but also on the importance of 'the organization of armed forces into partisan detachments.' At the time of the eighth plenum of the Comintern Executive Committee in May, 1927, Stalin, anticipating the possibility of a split, advised the Chinese Communists to 'organize your own revolutionary army before it is too late.' At the same time an intensive effort was to be made to extract Communist units from the Nationalist army. The two elements, the salvaging of the Communist units in the Nationalist army and the beginning of the build-up of a peasant-based Communist army, were to be combined. It is in those two elements that the origin of the Red Army is to be found.

When the split came, the attempt had to be made to withdraw the Communist-controlled units from the Nationalist army. The attempt led to the Nanchang uprising of August, 1927. The Communist hope was to entice as many units of the Nationalist army as possible to come over to the Communist side. There was no plan to hold the city of Nanchang for any length of time. In this sense, there was no plan for an 'urban' policy, as has sometimes been maintained. The attempt by the chief Soviet military adviser to sway the Nationalist Commander, Chang Fa-k'uei, to defect failed, but the Communists succeeded in winning over one of his army commanders, General Ho Lung, along with his units, to their side. After Nanchang had been captured, the plan was to retreat into areas of potential peasant unrest and thus to link up with the agrarian revolution. The plan failed for lack of preparation.[12] Most of the units were

---

[8] For an account of the Northern Expedition and the battle against Communist control of the military, see F. F. Liu, *A Military History of Modern China, 1924–1949* (Princeton, N.J.: Princeton University Press, 1966), pp. 25 ff.

[9] Stuart Schram, *Mao Tse-tung* (New York: Simon and Schuster, 1966), p. 73.

[10] See Shinkichi Eto, 'Hai-lu-feng, the First Chinese-Soviet Government,' *The China Quarterly*, Nos. 8 and 9 (October–December, 1961, and January–March, 1962).

[11] Degras, *Communist International*, 2: 340–47.

[12] Martin Wilbur, 'The Ashes of Defeat,' *The China Quarterly*, No. 18 (April–June, 1964),

destroyed, while the commanders escaped. Only one unit, under Chu Te, went on its own and later joined up with another force, formed in a different way under the policy of peasant military organization.

That policy had been initiated under the direction of the Comintern agent Besso Lominadze at a conference on August 7, 1927, which outlined a program of peasant insurrection, the so-called Autumn Harvest uprisings in four provinces in Central and South China.[13] Only one of the uprisings got under way, in Hunan Province, where Mao Tse-tung was entrusted with its organization. That uprising was a complete failure, largely because, according to the Communist view, it relied too much on traditional military ventures and not enough on peasant organization. It was for this reason that Mao was demoted in the aftermath of the uprising by the Central Committee under Comintern direction. Mao, however, retreated with the remnants of his forces of ragtag peasant units to the mountain area of Chingkangshan where he joined forces with Chu Te to form the Chu-Mao army, the initial force of the new Chinese Red Army.

The political content of the military program for the Red Army came out in the resolution of the ninth plenum of the Comintern Executive Committee in February, 1928, restated, in Chinese terms, at the CCP Sixth Congress held in Moscow during the summer of that year.[14] The concepts of the political training of the army and of its political role can be found in the early writings of Mao Tse-tung of that time, restated by Mao in close approximation to the Comintern Resolution.[15] After his initial failure, Mao followed closely the outline of the new agrarian strategy as provided by Moscow and established himself in his leading role in Chinese Communism as a disciple of Stalin, not an opponent.

From non-alignment to the second united front (1927–36). During the first years of the strategy of guerrilla warfare, the Chinese Communists, on the advice of Moscow, were to be on their own in the sense that they were not to ally with other Chinese groups opposed to the national government. During the Kiangsi period (1927–34) they were located in an area in the south of China, remote from Soviet territory and therefore isolated from Soviet support. After their first victories against four attacks by the national government carried out in traditional manner, they were hard pressed when the government began to apply the new strategy of blockade in its fifth campaign with the purpose of depriving them of all supplies and help from the outside. The policy imposed by Moscow, which forbade an alignment with such antigovernment uprisings as the Fukien revolt in November, 1933, prevented them from broadening their base and retaining access to the coast. In retrospect, Mao himself said that this failure to exploit opposition to the national government for the Communists' purpose was a mistake,[16] but there was no attempt at the time, or later, to defy Stalin's leadership.

The Nationalist blockade made the Communist position in Kiangsi untenable, and in October, 1934, the Communists broke through the blockade of their soviet area and

---

and Chang Kuo-t'ao, 'Wo-ti Hui-i (My Memoirs),' *Ming Pao Yüeh-k'an (Ming Pao Monthly),* No. 26 (February, 1968), pp. 93–95.

[13] For an account of the conference at Wuhan, see Chang Kuo-t'ao, *op. cit.* No. 27 (March, 1968), pp. 95–97. For Stalin's policy, see Richard Thornton, 'The Emergence of a New Comintern Strategy for China, 1928,' in Milorad Drachkovich and Branko Lazitch, eds., *The Comintern: Historical Highlights* (New York: Praeger, 1966), pp. 66–110.

[14] For relevant discussions at these congresses, see Thornton, *loc. cit.*

[15] Mao Tse-tung, *Selected Works,* I (Peking: Foreign Languages Press, 1950): 74–104 *et passim.*

[16] Edgar Snow, *Red Star Over China* (New York: Random House, 1938; paperback, Grove Press, 1961), pp. 417–19. See also Ho Kan-chih, *The History of the Modern Chinese Revolution* (Peking: Foreign Languages Press, 1960), p. 250.

went on a prolonged campaign, which has since become widely known as the Long March. The Long March covered a distance of more than 6,000 miles and took the Communists through the border areas of western China to their new headquarters at Yenan in Shensi Province, where they arrived in October, 1935. By that time, Mao, who had greatly strengthened his position in the interim, had become Chairman of the Central Committee and the undisputed leader of the Party. The man who had started his career as a political commissar in the rural-based Communist army had won over the leaders of the regular Party apparatus. In retrospect, this logical development of the party-army struggle was to determine the future development of China's communism.

During the Long March, the CCP's political line was affected by a shift in Soviet policy brought about by the changing international situation. Under the threat of the recently accomplished Nazi victory in Germany, the new alignment of the Nazi leadership with Japan, and the growing specter of a two-front war for the Soviet Union, the Soviet leadership shifted back to a united front policy. The Seventh Congress of the Comintern, held in Moscow in the summer of 1935, announced this policy and initiated measures to strengthen the Soviet position by gaining as many allies as possible against the threat from Germany and Japan. All Communist Parties were instructed to cooperate with any political group or government opposed to German National Socialism or Japanese militarism. Communists everywhere were to abandon their propaganda against the 'imperialist powers,' which became the 'Western democracies'; they were to stress 'national pride' and 'national interests' in the common fight against the fascist countries. When Germany and Japan concluded their anti-Comintern pact in November, 1936, the united front policy became even more urgent to the Soviet Union and more plausible to the West.

Immediately after the Seventh Comintern Congress, the CCP, still on the march, began to clamor for an end to civil war and a common stand against the Japanese; and eventually, Chiang Kai-shek, who had been maligned as the 'running dog of Western imperialism, became the 'national leader' in the clamor for a common resistance against Japan. The slogan 'Chinese should not fight Chinese at the time of national danger' was highly effective. It took, however, a special incident to force Chiang Kai-shek to abandon his strategy of eliminating the Communist danger first before turning against the Japanese might. At Sian in December, 1936, one month after the anti-Comintern pact, Chiang was kidnaped and forced by mutinous troops to accept a truce and to prepare for armed resistance against the anticipated Japanese attack, which was to begin formally half a year later.

The Soviet and Chinese Communist role in the negotiations for the release of Chiang Kai-shek is not fully known, but from Soviet and Chinese Communist revelations at the time of the conflict[17] it can be assumed that Soviet pressure forced the Chinese Communists to cooperate in their effort to release Chiang and to accept him as the leader in the war of resistance.

The second united front was different in nature from the first. There was no true integration of Chinese Communist forces or political leadership into the Nationalist military and government framework. The Communists, who remained in control of the northwestern area held by their armies, expanded their influence during the war into the rural areas behind Japanese lines and accepted Nationalist leadership more in name than in reality. Only at the outset of the war did they coordinate their military action with that of the Nationalist forces. After the 'Hundred Regiments' campaign of the late summer and fall of 1940, in which they suffered heavy losses, they made no further sizable attempt to risk their strength in a direct confrontation with Japanese troops.[18] The Soviet leaders, on the other hand, remained faithful to their policy of

---

[17] Ho Kan-chih, *History of Modern Chinese Revolution*, p. 305.
[18] John Gittings, *The Role of the Chinese Army* (London: Oxford University Press, 1967), pp.

supporting the national government rather than their Communist allies. During the first years of the war, when China was almost completely cut off from the West and got little external help, financially or in equipment, the Soviets provided a major part of whatever outside support the Nationalists did receive, including a considerable percentage of the support that came over the Burma Road. After Hitler's attack against the Soviet Union in 1941, this support declined. The concentration of all war effort on the Western front forced the Soviets even to abandon their position of influence in Sinkiang Province, thus enabling the national government to reassert its own control.

YALTA AND THE SOVIET ROLE IN THE CHINESE COMMUNIST VICTORY

With the approaching defeat of Nazi Germany, the Russians turned their attention back to the Far East. The Yalta Agreement of February, 1945[19] provided the international basis for the Soviet re-entry into Far Eastern politics. From the American point of view, the main purpose of the agreement was to obtain Soviet assistance in the war against Japan and Soviet support for a policy of establishing the national government in China as the major peace-preserving force in the postwar Far East and as a member of the Security Council of the future United Nations. The Soviet concession on this point included the promise to maintain relations only with the national government, which would preclude any assistance to the Chinese Communists. On the surface, the Soviets maintained correct relations with the national government longer than any other power, following the latter's retreat in 1949 to Canton. In practice, they gave decisive aid to the Chinese Communists in their victory over the Nationalists in the crucial area of Manchuria. In this regard, it was the Soviet breach of the Yalta agreement rather than the agreement itself that contributed to the Communists' victory. However, the price the Soviets were promised for the policy they did not keep was the re-establishment of their position in Manchuria. They were promised a free port at Dairen, a joint Sino-Soviet naval base at Port Arthur, and railroad rights in Manchuria in exchange for their aid in defeating the Japanese in Manchuria. At the time of the Yalta conference, Soviet aid there appeared to the American Government more essential than it may have been in retrospect, in view of the collapse of Japan in August, 1945, after the effective destruction of its military potential and communication systems and, finally, the use of the atomic bombs.

The Soviet attack on Manchuria occurred only in the very last days of the war. It may well have been that with or without agreement the Soviets could not have been prevented from this move, but Yalta provided them with the international sanction by which to establish a position in Manchuria. They used that position to obstruct the Nationalist forces when they attempted to take over the Manchurian provinces from the defeated Japanese. By refusing to permit Nationalist transports to land at Dairen, they delayed the Nationalist advance long enough to give the Communists an opportunity to move into Manchuria with large numbers of troops first. In the race for territory between the Nationalists and the Communists that took place immediately after the Japanese surrender, the Communists thus had the decisive advantage in a most valuable area of the Manchurian provinces. The Nationalists eventually had to fight their way in through the Manchurian corridor. They still administered a crushing defeat to the Communist forces at Ssup'ingchieh in April and May, 1946. But when the Nationalist advance was halted by the negotiations between the Nationalists and Communists, initiated under United States auspices, the Russians assisted the

---

53 ff, and Samuel Griffith, *The Chinese's People's Liberation Army*, (New York: McGraw-Hill, 1967), pp. 70–71.

[19] U.S., Department of State, *U.S. Relations with China, with Specific Reference to the Period 1939 to 1949* (Washington, D.C.: Government Printing Office, 1949), pp. 113–14, 585 ff.

Communists in establishing in the occupied areas of Manchuria an infrastructure that enabled them to entrench themselves in the countryside and collect and recruit under their commander Lin Piao a large new military force that became the Fourth Field Army.[20]

In addition to this crucial support, the Soviet forces permitted the military equipment that they had captured from the Japanese troops in Manchuria to fall into the hands of the Chinese Communist forces, which were thus for the first time enabled to move from guerrilla warfare to massed battles and to victory.

THE MOSCOW-PEKING ALLIANCE

The political alliance. The Communist victory in China in 1949 affected the balance within the Communist bloc and movement as a whole. Communist China was a much larger country than what were then the Eastern European satellite countries and much more remote and difficult to manage by a centrally determined policy emanating from Moscow. It was also a country where Communism had come to power through a prolonged civil war and under a strategy that by intent differed from that applied by the Communists in Europe. A question was therefore immediately posed as to what role the Chinese Communists would play within the world Communist power structure.

From the outset, the relationship of Peking with Moscow differed from that of other Communist Parties in power. At that early stage, when the Communists had just come to power, there was no question that the Chinese Communists would form a part of the Communist movement and would continue to accept Soviet leadership or, in the words of Mao Tse-tung, 'lean to one side.' This inter-Party relationship could at that time be taken for granted. The state relationship was formally established by the Sino-Russian Treaty of Friendship, Alliance, and Mutual Assistance, concluded in Moscow in February, 1950, after negotiations that Mao Tse-tung personally carried on, covering every important aspect of Sino-Soviet relationships—political, economic, military, and cultural. The fact that, at the very outset of the establishment of the Communist regime in China, its leader spent six weeks in Moscow indicated the importance of the relationship for the Chinese Party and government, and perhaps the complexity and possible difficulties encountered in the negotiations. The treaty established a military alliance between the Soviet Union and China, directed officially against the possibility of a renewed attack by Japan or any other state that might 'directly or indirectly' support renewed Japanese aggression. The implication clearly was that the alliance would be directed against the United States if, in the Chinese Communist and Soviet interpretation, an act of Japanese aggression and of United States support could be established. The treaty's counterpart became the Japanese-American security pact, concluded in February, 1952, and revised in 1960. The lines were clearly drawn. The treaty's importance was further demonstrated by the questions raised after the intervention of Chinese volunteers in the Korean War regarding the problems of the Manchurian sanctuary.

On the basis of the Sino-Soviet treaty of February, 1950, Russian military advisers and technicians began to train the Chinese Communist army in the use of modern weapons provided by the Soviet Union, a development greatly intensified during the period of the Korean War. The treaty also provided for the return to China of the Manchurian railroad rights, the naval base of Port Arthur, and the Soviet free port rights in Dairen, originally obtained on the basis of the Yalta agreement in a treaty with the national government concluded in August, 1945. These rights were to be

---

[20] Carroll Wetzel, 'From the Jaws of Defeat: Lin Piao and the Fourth Field Army in Manchuria.' Unpublished dissertation, The George Washington University, May 1972.

returned at the time of the conclusion of a peace treaty with Japan or, at the latest, in 1952. In that year the Soviet Union indeed returned the rights to the Chinese Communist government, with the exception of the Soviet naval base at Port Arthur, which it retained at the 'invitation' of Peking, obviously as a guarantee of Soviet support should the Chinese intervention in Korea cause the military action to spill over into Manchuria. Finally, in 1955 Port Arthur was returned after the settlement of the Korean War. The Geneva agreement of 1954 had established the victory of Ho Chi Minh in North Vietnam, obtained with Chinese support, and the Bandung Conference in 1955 had increased the prestige of Communist China as a country whose peaceful coexistence policy was widely heralded throughout Asia. The Soviet presence in Manchuria was no longer needed. The military alliance, however, remained in force and provided for China the nuclear umbrella that protected its basic policy position.

Soviet aid to the Chinese economy. Of greater importance still was the Soviet promise of economic aid and cooperation contained in the treaty. In its initial form, the aid consisted of a five-year credit of $300 million to be used for the purchase of Soviet industrial equipment. This was to be a first and basic installment of Soviet support for the Chinese program of industrial development that was to follow the Soviet emphasis on heavy and military industries. A measure of Soviet control was indicated in the agreement to set up four joint Sino-Soviet stock companies in Manchuria and Sinkiang that were to operate airlines and shipbuilding plants and exploit oils and minerals. The general agreements[21] were followed by special arrangements concluded by Chinese delegations from Manchuria and Sinkiang, indicating a form of direct Soviet dealings with the Chinese leadership in those Chinese provinces, which in retrospect appear to be related to Soviet attempts at intervening in Chinese Communist inner-Party relations.

In 1953, when Peking initiated its First Five Year Plan, the Chinese asked for additional aid. This request and the Soviet reaction became linked with the succession struggle that followed the death of Stalin in March of that year. The first agreement of 1953, concluded during the period when Malenkov was in power, increased the number of large-scale industrial enterprises to be built or expanded with Soviet aid.

The agreement of October, 1954, was negotiated in Peking by a Soviet delegation headed by Nikita S. Khrushchev himself, which included several cabinet members. Both the site of the negotiations and concessions made in the agreement indicated the Soviet leaders' willingness to accord the Chinese leadership a higher standing in inner Communist relations than had been granted by Moscow before. Not only was the naval base at Port Arthur to be returned by May 31, 1955, but the Soviet shares in the four joint Sino-Soviet companies established in 1950 were to be sold to the Chinese Government on easy terms. The Soviets also agreed to add fifteen more major industrial plants in China to the 141 already under way and promised another long-term loan of $230 million, combined with an increase in Soviet advisers and technical assistance for a five-year period. The treaty also provided for the construction of two major railroad lines linking China with the Soviet Union through Mongolia and Sinkiang; the latter line in particular was obviously designed to relate the Soviet industrial development of Central Asia with China's development of the great potential of raw material resources and industrial opportunities in its most vital Central Asian province. If these stipulations had been carried out, the Soviet and Chinese economic development efforts in Central Asia would have grown together.

It is generally agreed that the new concessions and upgrading of China in the

---

[21] A cultural aspect of the treaty of 1950 dealt with the development of the Sino-Soviet Friendship Association and the use of Soviet literature and communications media and visiting academicians and artists to promote the Soviet model of Communism in the communization of Chinese society.

Communist world were related to the promise of Chinese support for Khrushchev in the power struggle in Moscow. The Chinese choice appears to have been based on the indications that of the two contending Soviet leaders, Khrushchev and Malenkov, Khrushchev then represented the harder line.[22]

The turning point. The partnership thus established was shaken at the Soviet Twentieth Party Congress in 1956 by the dramatic shift in Soviet policy and Khrushchev's secret speech against Stalin, which inaugurated the policy of de-Stalinization. That indeed was the turning point in Sino-Soviet relations, as well as the beginning of the internal conflict in China that escalated into the Cultural Revolution. Following the Twentieth CPSU Congress, the Eighth Congress of the CCP was held in 1956 and 1958 in two successive sessions. Although Khrushchev declared that de-Stalinization was not directed against China, Mao's position in China was affected by the denigration of Stalin and the leader cult. As a Stalinist, Mao was vulnerable to the charges leveled under the new policy, which led to purges of several Stalinist leaders in Eastern European countries.

The Chinese reaction to de-Stalinization was complex. The new Party statutes accepted at the Chinese Congress in 1956 introduced collective leadership and removed from the Preamble of the Party Statutes the official acceptance of the thought of Mao Tse-tung as the guiding spirit of Chinese Communism.[23] Mao attempted his own theoretical explanation to counter the threat but continued to follow the example of the Soviet line.[24] He introduced the 'hundred flowers' movement in a speech delivered in February, 1957,[25] but not published until June—in a modified version. Mao admitted in the speech, entitled 'On the Correct Handling of Contradictions Among the People,' that mistakes had been made and that innocent people had suffered, but he blamed those errors on the overzealousness of local cadres rather than on the Chinese Communist leadership. He could hardly 'de-Mao' himself, after all. The slogans 'Let the hundred schools of thought contend' and 'Let the hundred flowers bloom'—both taken from Chinese history—were to imply a tolerance of criticism that was meant to correspond to the Soviet 'thaw.' The Soviet thaw, however, had produced a genuine, if limited, literary protest against Stalin's police methods. The 'hundred flowers' slogan, on the other hand, was an official invitation to controlled political criticism. It caused not a literary reaction, nor the orderly regulated discussion Mao intended, but a protest movement against the CCP itself, which revealed a violent, far-reaching disaffection for the Party and its leadership even among Communists. This debacle, already presaged in the publication of Mao's speech, led to the 'anti-rightist' movement of the summer of 1957. It only confirmed Mao's apprehension about the new Soviet line and hardened the Chinese reaction. In November, 1957, Mao led the Chinese delegation to the Moscow Meeting of the Representatives of Communist and Workers' Parties of Socialist Countries to propagate, unsuccessfully, a Communist hard-line policy toward the West, in contrast to Khrushchev's policy, which had shifted to peaceful coexistence at the Soviet Congress in 1956. Mao

---

[22] George Paloczi-Horvath, *Khrushchev, The Making of a Dictator* (Englewood Cliffs, N.J.: Prentice-Hall, 1960), p. 193; cf. Richard Thornton 'China and the Communist World,' in Frank N. Trager and William Henderson, eds., *Communist China, 1949-1969: A Twenty-Year Assessment* (New York: New York University Press, 1970).

[23] The Statutes of 1945 had proclaimed, 'The CCP is guided in all its works by the thoughts of Mao Tse-tung, which is the unification of the Marxist-Leninist theory with the experience of the Chinese revolution.' For the history of the Party statutes and reference to Mao and Mao's thought, see *China News Analysis*, No. 757, Hong Kong (May 16, 1969).

[24] Donald S. Zagoria, *The Sino-Soviet Conflict, 1956-1961* (Princeton, N.J.: Princeton University Press, 1962), pp. 39-65.

[25] See 'Let a Hundred Flowers Bloom,' the complete text of 'On the Correct Handling of Contradictions among the People,' by Mao Tse-tung, with notes and an introduction by G. F. Hudson (New York: Tamiment Institute, n.d.).

also demanded a partnership of 'real, not formal, consultation' in which the new role of the Chinese leader would bar any future danger for Mao of being confronted with unpleasant policies determined by the leadership in Moscow.

Mao's policy proposal, as well as his demand for partnership, was disregarded by Khrushchev. The only conciliatory move made by Moscow was the conclusion of a weapons agreement in 1957, through which Moscow was to support the Chinese development of thermonuclear arms. While that major Soviet concession, perhaps designed to assuage the Chinese military, may have taken the edge off Mao's discontent, it did not remove the cause of his concern. Mao returned to China after the Moscow meeting to challenge the Soviet hegemony over the Communist bloc and movement. During the second session of the Eighth CCP Congress in 1958, Mao strengthened his position and at the same time initiated his strategy of the Great Leap Forward, which was to establish a radical turn in Chinese policy toward 'instant communism.'

The Great Leap launched in 1958 was an attempt to overcome, by sheer organization and will power, the problems created by Mao's acceleration of agricultural collectivization in 1955–56, and to speed up China's industrial development through its own efforts, if necessary, rather than by reliance on the Soviet Union. It was the application to China's economic advance and social transformation of the military methods of revolutionary warfare, which had been Mao's stock-in-trade during the civil war. This attempt to find a shortcut to Communism without Soviet help was also Mao's challenge to Moscow's leadership.

After the end of the Comintern and Cominform, Soviet leadership was no longer based on any formal institutional structure. It was the Soviet development itself that sanctioned Soviet hegemony. The Soviet Union was ahead of all other Communist countries on the road to Communism. In the Moscow Declaration of 1957[26] and in the Moscow Statement[27] of 1960, the Soviet Union was recognized as the 'vanguard' of the Communist world movement, leading all others on the way to Communism as a result of its experience and economic development. Communist Parties in other Communist countries would reach Communism after the Soviet Union, and there remained still the argument as to whether their arrival at the final stage would occur at 'approximately the same time' or in the somewhat undefined same 'epoch.'[28] Soviet aid could in itself be a determining factor in the rating of each Communist country. The Great Leap was not only to free China from this Soviet economic hegemony, it was also to challenge the Soviet leadership itself. China's extravagant claim that, through its own efforts, it was 'bypassing the Soviet Union on the way to communism' attacked the very foundations of the hitherto unchallenged Soviet claim to leadership of the Communist movement and arrogated it to itself.

By the end of 1958, the massive problems created by the Great Leap led to a retreat and a weakening of Mao's position. At the Central Committee meeting on December 10, 1958, the most revolutionary measures of the Great Leap were curtailed, the claim of rapid advance to Communism was abandoned, and Mao was reduced in power. He lost the position of Chairman of the Republic, which was to be taken over by Liu Shao-ch'i. The Soviet role in the retreat and in Mao's loss of the chairmanship can be surmised from the fact that immediately following the meeting Chou En-lai flew to Moscow and concluded, in January, 1959, a new aid agreement for Soviet delivery of thirty-one additional industrial plants to China.[29]

---

[26] See G. F. Hudson, Richard Lowenthal, and Roderick Macfarquhar, *The Sino-Soviet Dispute* (New York: Praeger Publishers, 1961), pp. 45–56.

[27] *Ibid.*, pp. 177–205.

[28] See Franz Michael, 'Who Is Ahead on the Way to Communism,' *Communist Affairs*, 4, No. 6 (November–December, 1966): 9 ff.

[29] *Ibid.*

From 1959 on, Liu began to dismantle, step by step, various measures taken during the Great Leap and the People's Commune experiment. Mao's program was discredited, though not officially abandoned. Six months later, an attempt was made to attack the program and, at least by implication, Mao himself. In August, 1959, at a plenum of the CCP Central Committee in Lushan, P'eng Te-huai, Minister of Defense and leading military member of the Politburo, condemned Mao's whole program as 'petit-bourgeois fanaticism.' P'eng's attack came after a military visit to Eastern Europe and a meeting with Khrushchev. It has been widely assumed, therefore, that Khrushchev had, at the very least, foreknowledge of the attack. It is also hardly accidental that the ideological denunciation of 'petit bourgeois fanaticism' used by P'eng was later used by Moscow to decry Mao's Great Proletarian Cultural Revolution.

Mao survived P'eng's attack and, though apparently reduced in power, gained a decisive advantage by having P'eng Te-huai dismissed as Minister of Defense. The position was given to Lin Piao, the most loyal supporter of Mao Tse-tung and his chief collaborator in the coming battle with Party leaders.[30] The position of Chief of Staff went to General Lo Jui-ch'ing, who, as shown by later events, was not committed to unconditional support of Mao. Lin Piao's appointment signaled the beginning of the Maoist indoctrination of the PLA, which transformed it into Mao's most reliable power base, later to be used in the Cultural Revolution for Mao's attack against the Party and government organization and the re-establishment of his leadership over China.

MAO'S BATTLE AGAINST REVISIONISM

The purge of Marshal P'eng was followed by a Soviet termination of the thermonuclear weapon agreement of 1957.[31] But both parties continued attempts at negotiation and reconciliation of the growing conflict. Khrushchev appeared in person on October 1, 1959, in Peking at the ten-year celebration of the establishment of the People's Republic and found occasion in his speech to salute the Party and the leadership of Mao Tse-tung. In 1960, a Chinese mission under Chou En-lai participated in the Meeting of the Representatives of Communists and Workers Parties in Moscow and signed the Moscow Statement in an attempt to gloss over the growing rift. On that occasion, the Russians refused to accept the role of 'center' of the Communist movement, which the Chinese tried to assign to them, the better to challenge and attack Soviet leadership in the bloc and the movement. According to the Russians, all Parties were independent and equal and should apply the general line to the specific conditions prevailing in their countries. Leadership was based only on the Soviet vanguard role as 'the universally recognized vanguard of the world Communist movement.'[32] The Chinese were given a special place after the Soviet Party in the listing of Communist Parties in power.

Because the Chinese attempt to bypass the Soviet Union on its march to Communism had failed, the stage was set for a different challenge in the battle for hegemony: the Chinese attempt to disqualify the Soviet Union altogether by accusing its

---

[30] See David Charles, 'The Dismissal of Marshal P'eng Te-huai,' *The China Quarterly*, No. 8 (October–December, 1961), pp. 64 ff.

[31] See *The Origin and Development of the Differences Between the Leadership of the CPSU and Ourselves* (Peking: Foreign Languages Press, 1963), p. 26.

[32] See 'The 1960 Moscow Statement,' *The China Quarterly*, No. 5 (January–March, 1961), pp. 51–52; William Griffith, 'The November 1960 Moscow Meeting: A Preliminary Reconstruction,' *The China Quarterly*, No. 11 (July–September, 1962); and Franz Michael, 'Khrushchev's Disloyal Opposition: Structural Change and Power Struggle in the Communist Bloc,' *Orbis*, Vol. 7, Spring, 1963.

leadership of having deviated from the road and become 'revisionists' and 'capitalist-roaders.' The Chinese alone remained the true leaders on the way to Communism. In an article entitled 'Long Live Leninism' in April, 1960, the Chinese attacked revisionism and laid the groundwork for their claim of being the proper heirs to the Leninist tradition.[33]

The battle was first carried on by proxy. Soviet accusations against 'Stalinist' Albania were in truth directed against Mao and Peking; Chinese condemnations of 'revisionist' Tito were meant for Khrushchev. Meanwhile, in view of their desperate economic situation, the Chinese, in March, 1960, abandoned their program of rapid industrialization in order to give priority to agricultural development and to pursue an economic policy of 'advancing step by step.' By implication, they were forsaking the challenge to the Soviet vanguard role. The decisive Soviet move in the intensifying dispute with China was the withdrawal, by the fall of 1960, of all Soviet economic and technical advisers from China, leaving the construction of plants unfinished and delivering a further severe blow to the already prostrate Chinese economy. Relations were not broken off altogether. In the spring of 1961 a Soviet delegation visited China for negotiations on economic assistance. An agreement on repayment of Soviet loans and credit was concluded, with little added in the way of new assistance, but the delivery of Soviet oil, most crucial for Chinese industrial development, was continued.

The temporary alleviation of the conflict ended in October, 1961, with a renewed assertion of Soviet leadership at the Twenty-second Congress of the CPSU in Moscow. At the congress, Khrushchev submitted a new Communist program designed to outline the imminent advance of Soviet society into the final stage of Communism. Together with the claim, already established at the previous congress, that the Soviet Party had become a 'Party of all the people' and the Soviet state the 'state of the whole people,' transcending the stage of proletarian dictatorship, this forecast was clearly an answer to the challenge of Soviet leadership by Peking, now in the depths of the disastrous economic crisis caused by the Great Leap. In addition, the congress renewed the attack against Stalin, whose body was removed from Lenin's mausoleum, and against the Albanian leadership. Chou En-lai, representing Peking at the congress, left prematurely, and the Sino-Soviet conflict entered a new stage.

During 1962 and 1963, Moscow and Peking accused each other in newspaper editorials and Party statements of having deviated from the Marxist-Leninist tradition. The Chinese demanded a new Communist inter-Party meeting as a forum for their attack. The Russians sought bilateral discussions to contain the argument. Both Parties agreed to meet in July, 1963. Before their meeting the Chinese publicized on June 14 a 50,000-word letter from their Central Committee to the CPSU Central Committee containing in detail the sharpest attacks against Khrushchev's policy up to that time. The Soviet Party answered in an open letter of July 14 with a rebuttal and counter-accusation from the Soviet Central Committee directed to Party organizations and all Communists in the Soviet Union. This, in turn, led to the publication of nine Chinese pamphlets of *Comments on the Open Letter of the Central Committee of the CPSU*, taking issue with it point-by-point.[34] At the same time, Peking published five

---

[33] Text in *Red Flag*, No. 8 (April 19, 1960), and *Peking Review*, No. 17 (April, 1960). See also 'Forward Along the Path of the Great Lenin,' *Jen-min Jih-pao*, April 22, 1960, translated in *Peking Review*, No. 17 (April, 1960).

[34] 'The Origin and Development of the Differences between the Leadership of the CPSU and Ourselves,' 'On the Question of Stalin,' 'Is Yugoslavia a Socialist Country?,' 'Apologists of Neo-colonialism,' 'Two Different Lines on the Question of War and Peace,' 'Peaceful Coexistence—Two Diametrically Opposed Policies,' 'The Leaders of the CPSU Are the Greatest Splitters of our Times,' 'The Proletarian Revolution and Khrushchev's Revisionism,' and 'Khrushchev's Phony Communism' (Peking: Foreign Languages Press, 1963–64).

volumes of Khrushchev's speeches and statements, aimed at discrediting the Soviet leader in the eyes of the Communist world.

The Chinese attacks, as well as the Soviet answers, contained obvious distortions of each other's doctrinal line and policy. The Soviet leaders had not abandoned revolutions or wars of national liberation, as the Chinese charged, nor had the Chinese preached thermonuclear world war, as they were accused of doing by the Russians. Both had stated that such a world war was no longer unavoidable but that, if it came to pass, such a war would lead to socialist victory. The emphasis on the Chinese side was more on violence, at least in theory, while Chinese policy remained in practice cautious. The Russians, on the other hand, tried to combine their substantial support of wars of national liberation and revolution with a greater emphasis on 'peaceful coexistence,'[35] although their actions were not always peaceful.

The fall of Khrushchev brought a short halt to the mutual accusations. It is possible to argue that one cause of Khrushchev's fall was his inability to deal with the widening gap between Moscow and Peking, and that he may even have been at the point of promoting a complete break in the Communist camp, a move unacceptable to his colleagues. His fall was followed by a short moratorium on polemics and mutual feelers about possibilities of negotiations. After a visit by Chou En-lai to Moscow in November, 1964, the attempts at reconciliation ended, and Peking renewed the attack against 'Khrushchevism without Khrushchev.' The conflict spilled over into Communist Parties, both ruling and nonruling. Mao attempted to establish himself as the leader of the true Communist tradition in contrast to the revisionist Soviet Union, which had deserted the cause of the revolution. In the bloc countries, only Albania followed fully the Chinese lead; the Communist rulers of Vietnam and Korea, dependent on support from both Soviet and Chinese contenders for Communist leadership, attempted to retain their links with both sides of the conflict. Defections of Maoist sections occurred in many Communist Parties, threatening a worldwide split of Communism.

Moscow and the Cultural Revolution. The conflict between Moscow and Peking entered a new phase in 1965, when the United States intervened in South Vietnam to prevent at the last moment a Communist takeover that seemed imminent. Both Moscow and Peking had supported the North Vietnamese Communist attack but had accused each other of interfering with or neglecting assistance to the North Vietnamese fraternal Party. When the almost certain Communist victory appeared in danger as a result of the American move, Moscow extended a new appeal to Peking for unity in view of the change in the Vietnamese situation.

The Soviet appeal found a willing echo among CCP leaders and even military men and threatened Mao's position, which by now was based on the conflict with Moscow. Liu Shao-ch'i, second in command in the Party and Mao's successor as Chairman of the Republic, indicated his favorable reaction to the Soviet appeal. So did Lo Jui-ch'ing, the Chief of Staff, who not only expressed his confidence in the Soviet people and army and in the unity of proletarian internationalism, but also belittled the conflict itself, which he called a 'debate' and which in his view had actually worked out to be a political gain for Communism as a whole. In his words: 'One aspect of the historic significance of the debate of the last few years between the two lines in the international Communist movement is that it has enabled Marxism-Leninism to spread on an unprecedented scale and has promoted the integration of the universal truth of Marxism-Leninism with the concrete practice of the people's revolution in

---

[35] See Michael, 'Khrushchev's Disloyal Opposition,' *Orbis*, Vol. VII, No. 1, Spring 1963, pp. 49–76, and Michael, 'The Struggle for Power,' *Problems of Communism*, Vol. 16, No. 3 (May–June, 1967).

every country.'[36] A shift in Chinese policy would have gravely threatened Mao's position. The threat of defections from his anti-Soviet policy may, therefore, have triggered Mao's most recent attack on the Party and government leaders in China, an attack carried out with the help of the People's Liberation Army on the basis of the leader-cult of Mao. Lo was purged at some time toward the end of 1965, just as the Cultural Revolution was beginning. A high-level attack in November, 1965, on a play written by the vice-mayor of Peking was followed in the spring of 1966 by attacks on the Peking municipal Party leadership and the news media that had been critical of Mao's personality cult. The Cultural Revolution was formally introduced in August, 1966, at the eleventh plenum of the CCP Central Committee in Peking. At the end of the year, the Party leaders were singled out as Chinese 'revisionists' and 'capitalist-roaders,' and Liu was denounced as 'China's Khrushchev.' In November and December, the Soviet newspaper *Pravda* and a Soviet Central Committee meeting, respectively, sided openly with the Chinese Party leaders and Liu Shao-ch'i against Mao.

Ever since, the Soviet position has been that Mao is no longer a Communist but a 'petit bourgeois fanatic' and that the Chinese movement under him has gone astray. The attempt to explain this phenomenon in doctrinal terms has led even to a renewed Soviet preoccupation with the Marxist slogan of 'Asiatic mode of production' as an explanation of the problems of Chinese Communist deviation.[37] The Russians have not abandoned their hope for division in the ranks of the leadership group around Mao and have particularly attempted to find signs of disunity and opposition to Mao Tse-tung among the Chinese military forces.

At the height of the Cultural Revolution, the bitterness of the anti-Soviet fervor in China found its outlet in attacks on members of the Soviet Embassy and mass demonstrations in Peking. The provocations instigated by Maoist students in turn created reactions on the Soviet side that led to an escalation of petty insults into ever larger public demonstrations. Chinese students in Moscow who demonstrated in favor of Mao in Red Square were roughly treated by the Soviet police; this in turn produced more demonstrations in Peking. An attack on a Soviet ship's captain and crew in Dairen was abandoned only when the Russians threatened to end all trade relations.

Worldwide attention was aroused by frontier incidents in Manchuria and Sinkiang. In the propaganda battle between Moscow and Peking the Chinese have pointed on several occasions to the imperialism of Moscow's Tsarist predecessors and the 'unequal' treaties by which the present Soviet-Chinese border was determined. Chinese maps continued to point to the borderline stipulated by the 1689 Treaty of Nerchinsk, which gave to China the territory east of the watershed between the Lena and Amur rivers. The 1860 Treaty of Peking, which established the present border, was condemned as an unequal treaty, and the Chinese demanded that before negotiations on minor border issues could be initiated the Russians should admit the imperialist position and injustices of their Tsarist predecessors. There has been no Chinese 'irredenta' or demand for the return of the territory in question, but the Soviet refusal to confess to the sins of the Tsars frustrated all possibilities of negotiation on actual border issues.

The most significant of the border problems was the defection at the beginning oı the Cultural Revolution of some 70,000 Uigurs from Chinese Sinkiang to Soviet territory. Since then, the frontier has been closed and heavily guarded by large military forces on both sides. These frontier incidents, as much as the economic aspects of

---

[36] See *Peking Review*, No. 36 (September 3, 1965), pp. 31–39; cf. Franz Michael, 'Moscow and the Current Chinese Crisis,' *Current History*, September, 1967.

[37] Richard Thornton, 'Soviet Historians and China's Past,' *Problems of Communism* (March–April, 1968), pp. 71–75.

the conflict, the decline of Soviet aid and trade, appear to be results rather than causes of a conflict that has centered upon the leadership struggle between Moscow and Peking and the debate over Communist strategy as seen in the two major centers of the Communist world.

The Maoist attempt of 1969 to reorganize the CCP and the new Party Statutes drawn up for this purpose were severely criticized by Moscow. In the eyes of the Soviet leaders, the constitutional draft made public at the Central Committee meeting of October, 1968, and adopted at the Ninth Party Congress in April–May, 1969, was not a Marxist-Leninist document. To them, the acceptance of Mao as a leader and of Lin Piao as his successor introduced a 'monarchical' system, no longer related to the Marxist-Leninist tradition.

The Soviet takeover in Czechoslovakia in August, 1968, opened a new phase in the relationship of the Sino-Soviet conflict to the affairs of the Communist camp. The very prototype of revisionism, Yugoslavia was suddenly treated with cordiality by Peking as a country with which China could establish new trade relations, simply because Yugoslavia had also become a target of Soviet threats. Czechoslovakia, certainly a 'revisionist' country by any Communist standards, became the object of Chinese sympathy as a victim of Soviet 'socialist imperialism.' And Romania, cautiously defiant toward the Soviet Union, was treated with great consideration. Such a disregard for ideological issues in the choice of friends or foes revealed the true basis of the Sino-Soviet conflict and the fears caused in Peking by the use of force and the new Soviet doctrine of the right of intervention to protect socialism in any country of the camp.

Leonid Brezhnev's statement of the principle that it was a Communist duty to intervene in socialist brother-countries where socialism might be threatened from within, the so-called Brezhnev Doctrine, gave the Soviet threat an ideological substance. Though Moscow later denied ever having proclaimed it in doctrinal form, the principle if applied to China would have justified Soviet military action to remove Mao, whom the Soviets in their propaganda regard not as a Marxist-Leninist but rather as a 'petit bourgeois fanatic.' A massive Soviet military build-up along the Chinese-Manchurian and Sinkiang frontiers and in Mongolia lent credibility to the possibility of Soviet action. During 1969, the Soviets assembled more than thirty-three divisions along the Chinese frontiers, backed by Soviet forces in the Mongolian People's Republic and in secondary positions in Central Asia. Even without the use of nuclear weapons, this force appeared strong enough to overwhelm any Chinese military defense in Manchuria, let alone Sinkiang, which would be geographically difficult to defend and where no strong Chinese forces were assembled. The placing of Soviet troops along the frontiers of Manchuria and in Mongolia in the positions that the Soviets had occupied before attacking the Japanese at the end of World War II made all the more ominous their threat against the crucial Chinese-Manchurian area and Peking itself.

In March, 1969, frontier incidents led to serious fighting at Damansky (Chenpao) Island in the Ussuri River, where a Soviet unit was ambushed, and at other locations along the Amur River and the Sinkiang border. An article by the Soviet journalist Victor Louis implied military action, and widespread speculation appeared both in Communist China and abroad about the possibility of military action that might range from a 'surgical' strike against Chinese nuclear sites to wholesale invasion. On June 7, 1969, at the Third International Conference of Communist Parties in Moscow, Brezhnev combined a sharp attack on Peking with a call for the establishment of a collective security system in Asia, obviously as a part of Soviet policy for a combined diplomatic-military move against Communist China. The tension, which led the Chinese to strengthen their military defenses and launch propaganda attacks against Moscow's 'socialist imperialism,' subsided with two successive developments. In September, 1969, Chou En-lai accepted the Soviet offer for negotiations and invited

Alexei Kosygin to a meeting at the Peking airport on his return flight from the funeral of Ho Chih Minh at Hanoi. An agreement for negotiations between Moscow and Peking was reached. The negotiations, which started in Peking that October, appeared to remove the immediate threat of military confrontation. The agenda for the negotiations seems to have been an issue in itself. While Moscow appeared to demand an over-all settlement, Peking stressed the need to remove the frontier tension, demanding a withdrawal by both sides from the immediate frontier lines. What progress was made, if any, remained a matter of speculation. A gradual shift in Chinese Communist policy led, however, to a decline in the cult of Mao and the disappearance of the claim of Mao's leadership of the world revolution—the most serious challenge to Moscow to come out of the conflict and the Cultural Revolution.

The new Peking trend toward Moscow was marked in April, 1970, by a major shift in Chinese foreign policy. Abandoning the self-imposed isolation of the Cultural Revolution, the Peking leadership renewed diplomatic relations with a number of Communist, neutral, and Western countries and initiated a policy of an 'Asian United Front' in Korea and Indochina, directed against the 'imperialistic' United States and the American 'lackeys' in South Korea, Taiwan, Indochina, and Israel.

This new policy was clearly led by Chou En-lai, who emerged from the Cultural Revolution as the foremost important decision-maker in domestic as well as foreign Chinese Communist policy. Following Chou's meetings with Kim Il Sung and the Communist leaders of Indochina in April, 1970, and in ensuing negotiations, the Sino-Korean and Sino-Indochinese statements indicated a new militancy against the United States and its allies and omitted mention of any attack against the Soviet Union. Most important, these statements implied the equality of Mao's position as leader of the Chinese people and Chairman of the Chinese Party with that of Kim Il Sung and other Communist leaders in their respective countries and Parties. Mao was reduced from his former position as a leader of world revolution, to one of equal status with the other Asian Communist leaders. Chou's policy implied, therefore, a retreat from the Sino-Soviet conflict and an advance against the United States—a policy that would make it more difficult for the Soviet Union to use force against China, a Communist country that was doing its duty against the 'imperialist' world of the United States.

When the new policy was initiated in April, 1970, the Peking press published a new blast against Soviet imperialism and against Brezhnev personally. The attack, so much in contrast to the foreign policy actions of Chou, almost appeared as an attempt to counter the turn of Chinese policy. In spite of continued Sino-Soviet negotiations in Peking and the re-establishment of regular diplomatic representation, the concentration of Soviet troops along the Chinese Manchurian, Mongolian and Sinkiang borders remained an ominous threat. Ideological accusations continued and so did Soviet diplomatic maneuvers in the Communist and Asian world. On Peking's side, the most drastic political shift came in July, 1971 with the secret visit of Henry Kissinger to Peking and the announcement of the invitation to President Nixon to visit the Chinese Communist capital.

The invitation to the heretofore vilified leader of the 'imperialist camp' was indeed an about-face in the so-called 'Maoist revolutionary line.' While the visit was officially to serve the purpose of 'normalization of relations' in a new age of negotiations and to decrease the danger to peace, it was clearly related to the Sino-Soviet conflict and interpreted in this way in Moscow and the non-Communist world as well as in Peking. From Peking's point of view, it could serve to break up the alleged Soviet-American 'collusion' and tend to isolate Soviet 'socialist imperialism,' regarded by now as a more immediate threat than that of American 'imperialism' believed to be retreating from Asia. The recognition of the importance of the People's Republic implied in the visit and in Peking's subsequent admission to the Security Council and General Assembly of the United Nations clearly strengthened Communist China's international standing and especially its situation vis-à-vis Moscow. It also gave backing to Premier Chou En-lai in his contest for power with Defense Minister Lin Piao for the successorship to a declining Mao in Peking. In the great purge of Lin Piao and his whole faction, which occurred in and after September, 1971, the fallen leader was accused of 'illicit relations' with a foreign power—the Soviet Union—and was reported to have died in a plane crash in Mongolia on an escape flight to Soviet territory.

The new Peking-Washington affair clearly alarmed Moscow and led to diplomatic and propaganda countermoves. When the India-Pakistan conflict over the brutal suppression of East Pakistan's autonomy aspirations and the massive flight of refugees to Indian territory led to a military crisis, the Soviet Union concluded an alliance with India and supported New Delhi in its victorious war against Pakistan, the friend of Peking. The bitter anti-Soviet tirades by the new Peking delegates in the United Nations did not affect the outcome, the independence of Bangladesh and the resulting Soviet influence on the Indian subcontinent.

The communiqué of July 27, 1972, issued at the end of President Nixon's visit to Peking, did not refer to the Soviet Union, unless the opposition to hegemony of any great power over smaller nations in the Chinese part of the communiqué is interpreted as an implied aspersion on the Soviet Union. Moscow's first reaction, as expressed in *Trud* on February 29, was to regard 'the concrete results as minimal.' However, on March 5, *Pravda* related the Peking talks to the Sino-Soviet conflict by stating:

> The U.S. decided to build a bridge with China because of the failure in its attempt to control Asia and the Pacific, and it is Peking's anti-Soviet policy that prompted Washington to take this decision. China considers it possible to find a friend in Washington when great difficulties have emerged in her relations with the Soviet Union.

In a speech on March 20 before the Congress of Soviet Trade Unions, Brezhnev reiterated Soviet policy. He questioned the basis of the Sino-American talks but repeated Soviet willingness for negotiations with China and agreed to acceptance of the principles of 'peaceful coexistence'—lowering Sino-Soviet relations to the level of state relations with non-Communist countries—since this was the Chinese wish. On this basis, proposals for nonaggression, border settlement, and improved relations could be settled. At the same time, however, Brezhnev renewed the Soviet proposal for a collective security organization for Asia, the policy designed to restrain China and expand Soviet influence in Asia.

In practice, this policy found its expression not only in India and the Indian Ocean, where Soviet naval strength was increased, but also and especially in the massive Soviet military support to Hanoi in preparation for Hanoi's invasion of South Vietnam. Hanoi's decision in March to normalize relations with India provided another link in this Soviet diplomatic-military offensive. Lastly, the Soviet efforts to normalize relations with Japan had to be regarded as another part of Moscow's answer to the Sino-American talks. In January, Foreign Minister Gromyko visited Japan, reiterating the Soviet proposal for an Asian collective security system. At the meeting of the Japan-Soviet Joint Economic Committee in February, the Russians asked for Japanese help in the development of coal mines in Yakutsk, in prospecting for oil off Sakhalin, and in the construction of a pipeline between the Tumen oil fields and the Far East region, all clearly important for the further strengthening of Soviet air and naval power in East Asia. The Peking talks between President Nixon and Premier Chou En-lai were thus closely related to a new phase of Sino-Soviet competition.

The President's visit to Moscow in May, 1972, aimed at balancing U.S. policy and finding agreements with the chief U.S. counterpart in world affairs, the Soviet

Union. It further complicated the tug-of-war between Peking and Moscow in which the Soviets continued their efforts to redirect the course of Chinese policy. On the side of the People's Republic, the decline of Mao Tse-tung, the question of the age of Chou En-lai, and the unresolved issue of successorship, provided an unstable and uncertain basis for Peking's future policy within and without the orbit of the socialist world.

SELECTED BIBLIOGRAPHY

BELOFF, MAX. *Foreign Policy of Soviet Russia, 1929–1941.* 2 vols. London: Oxford University Press, 1947–49. A standard work on Soviet policy issued under the auspices of the Royal Institute of International Affairs.

BOERSNER, DEMETRIO. *The Bolsheviks and the National Colonial Question.* Paris: n.p., 1957. A basic analytical study of the development of Communist strategy.

BORKENAU, FRANZ. *World Communism: A History of the Communist International.* New York: Norton, 1939. A standard work on the early history of the Comintern based on personal knowledge.

BRANDT, CONRAD. *Stalin's Failure in China, 1924–1929.* Cambridge, Mass.: Harvard University Press, 1958. An interpretation that ascribes to Stalin a policy of Communist urban insurrection in contrast to the strategy followed later by Mao.

BRZEZINSKI, ZBIGNIEW. *The Soviet Bloc: Unity and Conflict.* Cambridge, Mass.: Harvard University Press, 1960. An analysis by a specialist, including the early period of conflicts.

CHIANG KAI-SHEK. *Soviet Russia in China: A Summing Up at Seventy.* New York: Farrar, Straus & Cudahy, 1957. A personal account by the Nationalist leader.

Comment on the Open Letter of the Central Committee of the CPSU. Nine pamphlets: 'The Origin and Development of the Differences between the Leadership of the CPSU and Ourselves,' 'On the Question of Stalin,' 'Is Yugoslavia a Socialist Country?,' 'Apologists of New-colonialism,' 'Two Different Lines on the Question of War and Peace,' 'Peaceful Co-existence—Two Diametrically Opposed Policies,' 'The Leaders of the CPSU Are the Greatest Splitters of our Times,' 'The Proletarian Revolution and Khrushchev's Revisionism,' and 'Krushchev's Phony Communism.' Peking: Foreign Languages Press, 1963–64. The main Chinese expression of their point of view in the 'ideological battle' with Moscow.

DALLIN, ALEXANDER. *Diversity in International Communism: A Documentary Record, 1961–1963.* New York: Columbia University Press, 1963. A collection of the main documentation of the mutual recriminations during this period.

EUDIN, XENIA, and ROBERT NORTH. *Soviet Russia and the East: A Documentary Survey.* Stanford, Calif.: Stanford University Press, 1957. A useful compilation.

HO, KAN-CHIH. *The History of the Modern China Revolution.* Peking: Foreign Languages Press, 1960. An official Chinese Communist interpretation of Chinese Communist history as written before the conflict came into the open and before the Cultural Revolution.

HSIAO, TSO-LIANG. *Power Relations Within the Chinese Communist Movement, 1930–1934.* Seattle: University of Washington Press, 1961. An introduction to the documents dealing with the conflict between the Chu-Mao rural forces and the Party leadership.

HUDSON, G. F., et al. *The Sino-Soviet Dispute.* New York: Praeger Publishers, 1961. A selection of essays on the early stages of the Sino-Soviet conflict.

ISAACS, HAROLD R. *The Tragedy of the Chinese Revolution.* Rev. ed. Stanford, Calif.: Stanford University Press, 1951. A Trotskyite interpretation of the Communist failure in China in 1927 ascribing to Stalin the responsibility for it.

LAQUEUR, WALTER, and LEOPOLD LABEDZ, eds. *Polycentrism: The New Factor in International Communism.* New York: Praeger Publishers, 1962. A collection of essays on the earlier period of the conflict, seen by most as a decentralization rather than a Moscow–Peking power struggle.

LENIN, V. I. *Imperialism, the Highest State of Capitalism*. Rev. trans. New York: Little Lenin Library, 1939. Lenin's essay that formed the doctrinal basis for the Communist strategy of national liberation movements.

MAO TSE-TUNG. *Selected Works*. 5 vols. London: Lawrence and Wishart, 1954–60. The official Chinese Communist selection of Mao's works.

MICHAEL, FRANZ. 'Khrushchev's Disloyal Opposition: Structural Changes and Power Struggle in the Communist Bloc,' *Orbis*, Philadelphia: Foreign Policy Research Institute, University of Pennsylvania, Spring, 1963.

———. 'Moscow and the Current Chinese Crisis,' *Current History*, Vol. 53, No. 313, Philadelphia: Current History, Inc., Sept., 1967.

———. 'The Struggle for Power,' *Problems of Communism*, Vol. 60, No. 3, Washington, D.C.: U.S. Government Printing Office, May–June, 1967.

———. 'Who Is Ahead on the Way to Communism?,' *Communist Affairs*, No. 6, Los Angeles: Research Institute on Communist Strategy and Propaganda, University of Southern California, November–December, 1956.

MICHAEL, FRANZ H., and GEORGE E. TAYLOR. *The Far East and the Modern World*. Rev. ed. New York: Holt, Rinehart & Winston, 1964. Includes a survey of Sino-Soviet relations from the Bolshevik Revolution to the period before the Cultural Revolution.

NORTH, ROBERT. *Moscow and Chinese Communists*. 2d. ed. Stanford, Calif.: Stanford University Press, 1963. A standard study that follows the interpretation ascribing to Stalin a lack of understanding of the potential of Chinese agrarian revolution.

'Open Letter of the CPSU.' *Peking Review*, No. 30, July 26, 1963. The Soviet version of the 'ideological battle' of the basic conflicts with Peking.

THORNTON, RICHARD. 'The Emergence of a New Comintern Policy for China, 1928,' in MILORAD M. DRACHKOVITCH and B. LAZITCH, eds., *The Comintern: Historical Highlights*. Stanford, California: The Hoover Institution, 1967. A new interpretation of Stalin's role in the development of Chinese Communist strategy.

———. The Comintern and the Chinese Communists, 1928–1921. Seattle: University of Washington Press, 1969. A new analysis of Comintern strategy in China, especially the Li Li-san story.

U.S. Relations with China, 1939–1949. Washington, D.C.: Department of State, 1949. A government collection of documents with comments of the crucial period leading to the Communist victory.

WHITING, ALLEN S. *Soviet Policies in China, 1917–1924*. New York: Columbia University Press, 1954. An analysis of Soviet policies in China during the crucial years of the establishment of the first United Front.

ZAGORIA, DONALD. *The Sino-Soviet Conflict, 1956–1961*. Princeton, N.J.: Princeton University Press, 1962. An early account of the conflict, especially valuable for its analysis of China's reaction to de-Stalinization.

337

14

SINO-JAPANESE RELATIONS SINCE WORLD WAR II

LEONARD A. HUMPHREYS

HISTORICAL BACKGROUND

Before and after World War II. Generally speaking, relations between Japan and China have been poor in the modern era. From the time of the Sino-Japanese War of 1894–95 until its surrender in 1945, Japan played a dynamic, if unfortunate, role in imposing change upon a disunited China. During that period, diplomatic and military initiative lay almost entirely in the hands of the Japanese, who used it with increasing ruthlessness to force their will on the Chinese.

From 1945 until 1952 there was a hiatus in relations, during which great changes took place in both nations. After seven years of U.S. military occupation, Japan re-emerged as an independent nation, military impotent, shorn of empire, economically weak, and spiritually chastened. China's metamorphosis was equally traumatic, but in an opposite direction. Communist China came upon the world scene in the decade of the 1950's as a nation born in battle and bloodshed, united, dynamic, confident, and motivated by a revolutionary zeal.

Japan in 1952 could no more ignore China than China could Japan in the prewar period. The time when either nation could afford the luxury of isolation from its neighbor had passed a century before, and it seemed that U.S. Secretary of State Robert Lansing's often criticized statement of 1917 that 'territorial propinquity creates special relations among nations,'[1] albeit unwelcome, was as true as ever.

The history of Sino-Japanese relations spans a millennium and a half, and contact between mainland Asia and the Japanese archipelago dates back to remote antiquity. Japan owes a great cultural debt to the civilizing influence of Imperial China, for it was the example of the magnificent T'ang dynasty that brought the Japanese onto the stage of history. Not surprisingly, therefore, China's traditional attitude toward Japan was one of condescension and benign superiority. As the great Middle Kingdom, radiating its civilizing influence and culture to the lesser states on its periphery, China showed no inclination to deal with Japan, or any other client state, on a basis of equality, even though Japan's dependent status might in some cases have been more imagined than real.

With the coming of the modern age, the roles of the two nations were suddenly reversed. It was not the great Chinese empire but Japan that survived and overcame

---

[1] A phrase used by Lansing in a note to the Japanese on November 2, 1917, which recognized that geography gave Japan a peculiar interest in China. Lansing was roundly condemned for that admission, and the note was rendered null and void in 1923.

the fury of the West's physical and intellectual assault. Transformed politically, cloaked in nationalism, and in command of the machines and weapons of the industrial revolution, Japan eventually laid claim to leadership in East Asia. China, on the other hand, was by the early twentieth century powerless and divided; its traditional system of government was in disrepute, and its effectiveness destroyed. After more than 2,000 years of service, Chinese institutions proved unable to cope satisfactorily with the onslaught of 'Westernization,' in which Japan, ironically, played a major part. China, however, never really acquiesced in what it considered to be Japan's usurpation of China's traditional role. The Chinese attitude toward Japan in the 1930's was one of helpless rage and resentment. China resisted Japanese military aggression as best it could, but it was probably not China's opposition to the encroachment of Japanese power, but Japan's own audacious simultaneous challenge to the United States and the West in the 'Pacific War' (1941–45) that reversed Japan's course of conquest in China.

When Communist Party Chairman Mao Tse-tung, as victor in the Chinese civil war that followed Japan's collapse, proclaimed in October, 1949, that China had 'stood up,' it quickly became clear that the new unified Chinese state would test the mettle of Japan in any future contest for leadership in East Asia. For the defeated and occupied Japan of 1949, however, no thought could have been farther from its mind than a trial of strength with the Chinese. To rebuild a morally and physically shattered nation and to regain independence and self-respect were Japan's chief goals.

Japan's post–World War II situation was a natural consequence of the military operations conducted against it, but its enemies did not leave to the chance of military campaigns the final disposition of the Japanese empire. In December, 1943, Roosevelt, Churchill, and Chiang met at Cairo to discuss the disposition of Japanese territory once victory was achieved. They decided then that they would strip Japan of all its imperialist gains at China's expense, that it would be deprived of 'all other territories which she had taken by violence and greed,' and that Korea would be free. The three countries agreed to prosecute the war until Japan's unconditional surrender. Later, at the Yalta Conference in February, 1945, Churchill and Roosevelt reached an agreement with Stalin to return Southern Sakhalin and to transfer the Kurile Islands to the Soviet Union. These accords, subsequently enforced, defined the territorial limits of postwar Japan. The Potsdam Declaration of July, 1945, confirmed the Cairo agreement, broadly hinted at the Yalta decisions, and communicated to the Japanese the demand for their unconditional surrender. The general deterioration of Japan's ability to prosecute the war, the impossibility of victory, the impact of two atomic bombs, and the entry of the Soviet Union into the war provided sufficient inducement to Japan to accept the demand on August 14, 1945.[2] The San Francisco Peace Treaty of 1951 embodied the decisions of Cairo and Yalta in its provisions, though neither Communist China nor the Soviet Union was party to the treaty. The treaty added the Ryukyu Islands to the list of lost territories for an indefinite period by placing them under the United States for administration and disposition. Two years later, the United States conceded to Japan 'residual sovereignty' in the islands, including Okinawa, and with it the promise of their eventual return.

The crushing finality of Japan's defeat and the Japanese public's nearly unanimous repudiation of its former military leaders made easy the Allied occupation's avowed task of reorienting Japan's attitude and relationship to the world. The occupation reinforced and institutionalized Japan's new-found, but heartfelt, pacifism by inserting the remarkable 'no war' clause in the Japanese Constitution of 1947. In the early days of the occupation, the Supreme Commander of the Allied Powers (SCAP)

---

[2] Robert J. C. Butow, *Japan's Decision to Surrender* (Stanford, Calif.: Stanford University Press, 1954), provides a detailed account of the events leading to the end of the war.

overlooked no means to convince the Japanese people of their collective war guilt and of the necessity and desirability for Japan to remain forever neutral and at peace.

Unfortunately, the Japanese-American congruence of interest could not last. By the end of 1947, the United States had become involved in the Cold War with the Soviet Union, and China was clearly falling to the Communists, who by this time, if ideological differences were not enough, had become thoroughly hostile to the United States as a result of its aid and support for their Nationalist enemies. The United States, imbued with a sense of mission to preserve the free world from Communist encroachment, desperately needed a strong ally on whom it could anchor its position in East Asia, and Japan was the only promising candidate. Yet Japan was economically weak and psychologically unprepared for such a crucial role. Nor was it 'socially acceptable' to many other nations of Asia that had suffered at Japanese hands during the war.

The Sino-Soviet Treaty of 1950. The Chinese Communists had quickly transferred their hostility from Japan to the United States in the immediate postwar period. By 1949, however, the U.S. effort to turn Japan from defeated enemy to friend and ally caused the Chinese to view Japan, weak as it was at the time, with grave suspicion. The People's Republic was only four months old when Communist China signed, in February, 1950, the thirty-year Treaty of Friendship, Alliance and Mutual Assistance with the Soviet Union, which promised mutual military aid if either party were attacked by Japan or any nation allied to it.[3] Thus, there was no mistaking the Sino-Soviet attitude toward any eventual revival of Japan as a military power.

The Korean War and the Japanese rearmament. However, in that very year, it was the Communists themselves who forced a reluctant Japan to take its first hesitant step toward rearming. When China's North Korean Communist comrades attacked South Korea,[4] an apprehensive Japan, stripped of all U.S. combat troops, hastily formed a 75,000-man army at the order of the SCAP, General of the Armies Douglas A. MacArthur, under the pretext of organizing a police reserve force. This precautionary measure might even have been dispensed with, had not Japan's own Communist Party been forced by Moscow—with a sharp second from Peking—to opt for a line of revolutionary militancy in early 1950,[5] dropping the guise of moderation under which it had made rapid strides. At any rate, those were the circumstances of Japan's first step toward rearmament, a process that has continued slowly and inconspicuously to this day under conditions that many Japanese feel are a violation of their Constitution.

When North Korea's armies were being destroyed by U.S., South Korean, and U.N. military power, China intervened in October, 1950, to prevent Korea from being unified on U.S. and South Korean terms. The act not only caused the United Nations to brand China an 'aggressor' but also alarmed many Japanese and did much to arouse first doubts in Japan about the peaceful character of its new giant neighbor to the west. The Chinese invasion also served to reinforce earlier Japanese misgivings about the Sino-Soviet alliance.

Japan's peace treaties with the United States and Nationalist China. Since 1947, the United States, in pursuit of a secure strategic position in the Western Pacific, had been discussing with its allies the possibility of a peace treaty for Japan. With the Korean War, the United States became extremely anxious to end Japan's status as an occupied country and to build up an American-Japanese alliance. The Soviet Union now had

---

[3] See *United Nations Treaty Series*, Vol. 226, 1956, No. 3103.

[4] The part played by the Chinese Communists in the North Korean attack is obscure. It is conceivable that they had nothing to do with the planning or execution of the initial campaign and perhaps no more than limited advance knowledge that it was to take place. See Allen S. Whiting, *China Crosses the Yalu* (New York: Macmillan, 1960), p. 45.

[5] Robert A. Scalapino, *The Japanese Communist Movement, 1920–1966* (Berkeley and Los Angeles: University of California Press, 1967), pp. 60–78.

the atomic bomb; the Chinese Communists had swept China into the Communist camp; Communist-inspired revolutionary wars were raging in Vietnam, Laos, Cambodia, Burma, Indonesia, Malaya, and the Philippines; and finally, the Korean invasion posed a direct military threat to Korea and an indirect one to Japan. The time had come for the United States to consolidate its power in the Western Pacific on a more or less permanent basis.

As a result of U.S. initiative, Japan signed a peace treaty with forty-eight non-Communist World War II belligerent nations[6] on September 8, 1951, at San Francisco. In return for a formal peace and independence, Japan also signed on the same day a bilateral security treaty with the United States. Under the latter agreement Japan received assurance of American protection from the threat of any Communist attack, but it had to grant to the United States the unrestricted use of a great number of bases, as well as the continued stationing of large numbers of American troops on Japanese soil. Following the completion of the two treaties, Japan concluded in April, 1952, a separate treaty of peace with the Government of the Republic of China on Taiwan, recognizing the Nationalists as the sole Government of China.

The Character of the Developing Sino-Japanese Relationship

The Chinese view of Japan. It is this complex of treaties firmly linking Japan with the United States, Taiwan, and the non-Communist world that shapes the fundamental attitude underlying Communist China's specific foreign policy toward Japan. The inherent threat to Communist China in the Japan–U.S. mutual security relationship, with American military bases in Japan and Okinawa, and the affront to Peking's sensibilities arising from Japan's perversity in continuing recognition of the Nationalist 'rump' state on Taiwan are, in the eyes of Peking, ever present obstacles to any normalization of relations between the two countries. In fact, both countries realize that the greatest single inhibiting factor in their relations, economic or political, is Japan's tie with the United States. The Chinese, quite naturally, see no advantage in Japan's continuing an alliance with China's proclaimed enemy; for most Japanese, however, the value of the relationship with America is apparent. Japan's trade with the United States and the Western world accounts for a preponderant share of its total trade, and most Japanese (including many of Communist China's staunchest supporters) value highly the country's democratic political institutions, which are a tangible legacy of the West, while they are skeptical of Communist Chinese political and social experiments.

Beneath the surface of the Chinese attitude toward Japan one detects an undercurrent of hostility born of war memories and a determination to prevent Japan from ever again posing a military threat to China. There is also still a touch of the traditional Chinese superiority complex, the propensity to regard the world with ethnocentric eyes—in the feeling that the Japanese, like all 'barbarians,' cannot be the true equal of the Han race. Besides, the strongly Marxist-Leninist-Maoist ideological stand of the first-generation revolutionary leaders in China strongly colors their attitude. Japan, after all, is a capitalist country, and hence capable of imperialism, as it has demonstrated in the past. The Japanese people, on the other hand, suffer under the yoke of monopoly capitalism and must be liberated. While the principle of peaceful

---

[6] The Soviet Union, Poland, and Czechoslovakia attended the San Francisco Peace Conference but refused to sign the treaty. Neither Communist nor Nationalist China was invited; India and Burma declined to attend. In spite of the recognized danger of the Communist encroachment in Asia, several of America's World War II allies were reluctant to make peace until the United States undertook to guarantee their defense against a resurgent Japan. The ANZUS pact and the U.S. bilateral agreement with the Philippines were thus preconditions for the San Francisco Peace Treaty.

coexistence with states of divergent social systems may be tactically applicable to Japan, true proletarian friendship and solidarity can be reached only when the Japanese people overthrow their capitalist masters.

The influence of ideology in China's relationship with Japan is periodically diluted, however, by a strong infusion of pragmatism when it comes to economic relations between the two countries. The Chinese would like to use the lure of trade as an incentive for the Japanese to change foreign and domestic policies unfavorable to China and to the cause of revolution. On the other hand, with the dramatic modernization and progressive strengthening of Japanese industry, and as Chinese relations with the Communist world have deteriorated, China has felt the attraction of trade with Japan for the economic and technical advantages it can provide. Waves of Chinese political pressure—the withdrawal of or threat to withdraw trade privileges unless political concessions are granted—have tended to ebb in the face of real Chinese interest in Japanese goods for their own sake.

The Japanese view of Communist China. Japanese attitudes toward Communist China seem to be motivated by a quite different set of factors. Japan pays relatively little heed to the ideological differences that separate Tokyo from Peking, accepting the latter's political system as purely a matter of Chinese concern. Some Japanese are inclined to color their attitudes with a tinge of emotion, which can be attributed to a feeling of guilt for having caused the Chinese so much distress and unhappiness in the recent past. This feeling manifests itself in sympathy for the Chinese people, a sense of sharing in China's postwar successes, a sentimental and nostalgic view of China, and a deep appreciation for Japan's Chinese inheritance. Much is made of cultural affinity, a common writing system, and similar racial origins. The prewar competition with China for historical equality is gone; the Japanese no longer extend their history back a millennium beyond historical records to rival China in the antiquity and continuity of their civilization.

Another ingredient in Japan's attitude is the emphasis on its own economic development that has stirred it to such a high pitch of activity in the postwar period. Coupled with the nostalgia for, and sentimentality toward, China, there has been a tendency to envision a vast Chinese market for Japanese manufactures. That attitude was especially prevalent among Osaka businessmen who profited from the large prewar China trade and whose businesses suffered most from its termination. However, the trend of the 1960's has been to view the China market more pragmatically and to recognize its practical limits, without, however, dampening the Japanese businessman's enthusiasm for customers in China.[7]

The political opposition in Japan. Unlike China, which at any given time presents a unified foreign policy position toward Japan, the Japanese display a broad range of opinions on the proper course for Japan's relations with China. The official position of the most important opposition party in Japan is almost diametrically opposed to that chosen and adhered to since 1952 by the government and, since its formation in 1955, by the ruling Liberal Democratic Party (LDP). The Japan Socialist Party (JSP) contends that there is inherent danger in Japan's close ties to the United States and in the country's Western orientation. The JSP still looks at the world through ideological lenses ground to a Marxist-Leninist prescription. It is an old-fashioned socialist party with strong populist and farmer-labor roots.[8] Suppressed, harassed and isolated in the prewar era, the JSP has never outgrown many of the orthodox Marxist-Leninist concepts long since discarded by Western social democratic parties. As a consequence, it still accepts the Leninist dictum that imperialism is the highest and final stage of capitalism.

---

[7] See Chapter 23, below.

[8] Scalapino, *The Japanese Communist Movement*, pp. 32–33, and George M. Beckmann, 'Marxism in Japan's History,' *Asia*, No. 8 (Summer 1967), p. 42.

According to the JSP, the menace of imperialism today is embodied in the United States, the world's greatest capitalist power. The party professes the belief that U.S. imperialism will attempt desperately to maintain or strengthen its hold on the under-developed areas of the world and that it will inevitably clash—as in Vietnam—with the peoples of these colonial and semicolonial lands struggling for national liberation. Tied to the United States by instruments such as the Security Treaty, Japan runs the grave risk of being dragged into the colonial wars and is *ipso facto* a party to U.S. imperialist adventures in Asia. The Security Treaty is in fact nothing more than a means for imperialist America to fasten its talons on Japan, reducing it to a less than independent status. Thus, the JSP feels compelled to lead the struggle against U.S. imperialism in Japan and considers China and the Soviet Union its allies in the struggle.

The JSP attitude is always that Japan's conservatives are more of a menace to Japan than foreign Communists. No member of the JSP has served in the government since 1948, before the establishment of the People's Republic of China. The party has, therefore, lived in the frustrating situation of permanent opposition for twenty years. The Marxist-Leninist inclination of its leaders, coupled with their divorce from responsibility and the realities of international politics, is often advanced by the JSP's critics as one reason for its steadfast adherence to a doctrinaire and unrealistic foreign policy. Since there is such a wide gulf between the opinions of the conservatives, as represented by the ruling LDP, and the radicals in Japan, and since the LDP has dominated the national government for so long, the foreign policy–making process has come to be largely an intraparty function of the LDP.[9] It goes without saying that a bipartisan foreign policy has not been possible.

The JSP foreign policy platform, largely unchanged over the years, holds that Taiwan is a Chinese domestic problem and that Japan should abrogate its treaty with the Nationalists and recognize Communist China; they approved Communist China's entry into the U.N. The JSP would conclude trade agreements with Peking on a government-to-government basis immediately, as a prelude to a full-scale adjustment of relations. Considering this program in conjunction with the JSP's stated policy on relations with the United States, which includes abolition of the Security Treaty and revision of the San Francisco Peace Treaty, many Japanese conservatives consider the JSP program tantamount to capitulation to Communist China. Certainly there is a striking parallel between China's Japan policy objectives and the JSP foreign policy platform. In addition, the JSP would disarm Japan by abolishing its armed forces[10] and seek a guarantee for national security through a quadripartite treaty with China, the U.S.S.R., and the United States, a scheme attacked by the LDP as naive, foolhardy and impossible to attain. The JSP program, nevertheless, appeals to the many Japanese who are inclined toward pacifism and neutralism, and has in the past found support among liberals, intellectuals, students, and women.

The Japan Communist Party (JCP) position on China was similar to the program of the JSP until it broke with the Chinese Communist Party in 1966. Since then, the Japanese Communists have had an 'independent Communist' foreign policy, while the JSP has tended to assume a more important role as the intermediary between the Chinese Communists and the Japanese 'people.' The JCP favors unarmed neutrality as long as Japan is a bourgeois capitalist state, but would arm Japan were it 'socialist.' Two other opposition parties—the Democratic Socialists (DSP) and the *Kōmeitō* (Clean Government Party), the political arm of the militant religious group *Soka Gakkai*—take stands between those of the LDP and JSP on foreign policy matters.

---

[9] Donald C. Hellmann, 'Japan's Relations with Communist China,' *Asian Survey*, 4, No. 10 (October, 1964): 1087.

[10] These military forces—collectively, the Japan Self Defense Forces—are technically not an army, navy, and air force. They are a relatively small but competent military organization, numbering approximately 250,000 officers and enlisted men, all volunteers.

Although most Japanese reject the JSP view, they desire normal ties with Communist China and consider it a matter of necessity to establish them. Nor is that feeling restricted to Japanese of radical political views. It would be no exaggeration to say that a considerable majority of the Japanese people feel that Japan should normalize relations with China.

China's Japan policy. China's policy toward Japan is shaped within the larger context of its general foreign policy, which includes defensive and offensive aspects motivated by both Chinese nationalism and the ideological assumptions of China's leaders. The defensive vector of China's over-all foreign relations seeks protection for China from both physical and intellectual assault, shielding the territorial and systemic integrity of the state from outside forces and influences. The offensive aspect attempts to project Chinese political and economic influence abroad in order to create an atmosphere congenial to the development of the Chinese conception of socialism, and, in doing so, to increase the security of the Chinese state. Its goals include the promotion of national and social revolutions in the non-Communist world and, more recently, the reversal of the 'revisionist' tendency among the socialist states, recovery of lands outside China's present borders that it feels rightfully belong to it or the creation of buffer zones to enhance the PRC's defensive capability, and the establishment of China as a major world power with a leading role in Asia and beyond.

In the present world situation Peking's Japan policy must of necessity remain subordinate to more vital concerns—China's relations with the U.S.S.R. and the United States. In a very real sense, China's policy toward Japan from 1950 to the present is a corollary to the problem of mutually hostile relations between China and the United States. The primary thrust of Chinese diplomacy toward Japan, whether employing the carrot or the stick, has been to separate Tokyo from close military, economic and political relations with Washington.

After relations between Peking and Moscow had attained a state of unprecedented crisis in 1963, the Soviet Union showed increasing concern for the security of its eastern provinces, and, as a consequence, Moscow has come to seek improved relations with Japan. The Soviet Union continues its efforts to secure a treaty of peace with Japan. Moscow has agreed to return two small islands, Habomai and Shikotan, as part of a peace agreement, but treaty talks have bogged down over the Russian refusal to discuss the retrocession of Kunashiri and Etorofu, the southernmost of the Kuriles. The Russians have generally been more conciliatory on matters relating to fishing in the Sea of Okhotsk; they have recently made a reciprocal agreement with Japan that allows Japan Airlines to fly through the Soviet Union and service Soviet cities en route to Europe (the first such concession made to a foreign airline); and they have had discussions with the Japanese, unproductive so far, on the use of Japanese capital and technology for the economic and industrial development of Siberia. In view of the sensitivity of Sino-Soviet relations, closer Soviet-Japanese ties will also have an influence on China's Japan policy.

Although the nature of China's world position relegates Japan to the secondary rank in Peking's diplomatic scale of values, for geographic, demographic and historical reasons the Japanese nation nonetheless stands second only to the great powers in Chinese foreign policy planning. Within the memory of millions of living Chinese, Japan posed a grave physical and, to a lesser extent, ideological threat to China. Accordingly, shortly after they assumed power, the Chinese Communists took steps to protect themselves, at no small cost, from the possibility of resurgent Japanese militarism by means of a Sino-Soviet alliance. The effectiveness of the alliance has gradually declined to almost nothing from the time of the Taiwan Strait (Quemoy) crisis of 1958;[11] however, in the interim, Japan has shown little or no interest in rivaling

---

[11] The effect of the Soviet refusal to give China full backing in the Taiwan Strait crisis is covered in Raymond L. Garthoff, ed., *Sino-Soviet Military Relations* (New York: Praeger,

Communist China militarily, nor has it been in serious economic or political competition with Peking. Therefore, China has, in the case of Japan, been able to disregard to a large extent the defensive aspect of Chinese diplomacy and concentrate its energy on the offensive.

Whether China will continue to view Japan as a negligible threat is at present open to conjecture. Japan's remarkable re-emergence as a world power in the decade of the 1960's, its ever widening search for raw materials and markets, and its increasing determination to exercise independent economic and political influence in regional affairs has caused China again to consider Japan a threat. Operating within the comfortable assurance of the Marxist-Leninist-Maoist system of universal truth, the Chinese Communists can predict the eventual downfall of capitalism and imperialism with confidence, but even so they must be disturbed to see capitalist Japan re-enter the arena as a serious contender for economic and perhaps even political leadership. A strong Japan in alliance with either of China's major rivals—the United States or the Soviet Union—could do much to thwart Chinese aspirations to leadership in Asia and to the exercise of international power.

It is true that Japan is in no sense a strong military power. But ironically, China's development of atomic weapons has caused the Japanese public for the first time since the Pacific war to make a positive review of their own military situation, and China cannot forget that Japan has the potential for developing atomic weapons of its own relatively quickly and cheaply.[12]

Although Communist China has long abandoned any idea it may have entertained during the early years of the People's Republic that Japan could easily be turned from a capitalist course, it would be naive to assume that Peking has given up the game. To speed Japan on its foreordained socialist destiny would obtain for China the distinct advantage of weakening the capitalist-imperialist position in the Far East (and in the world) dramatically. However, the conversion of Japan to socialism has become an increasingly formidable task. Japan has prospered under a conservative capitalist regime while the Communist world has split into openly competing factions, but the Chinese have labored persistently for a socialist Japan, aligned with Communist China in the recent past.

A serious point at issue between the two countries is the status of Taiwan. Taiwan is a Chinese province—on this both can agree—but the island was also a Japanese colony for fifty years, and the Japanese still feel a vague sense of responsibility for its welfare. But much more important is the fact that Tokyo chose to recognize the American-backed Nationalist government in Taipei as the ruling government of China when Japan made the decision to align with the West, and the Japanese Government has consistently refused to modify its attitude since. The Chinese Communists feel strongly that Japan's official recognition of the Nationalists reinforces Taipei's claim to sovereignty and helps also to sustain a rival of Peking to the governance of China.

A strategy of protracted conflict. The struggle to alter Japan's international and domestic political orientation follows two separate but complementary lines of attack, one aimed at the Japanese Government, the other directed through mass organizations and propaganda organs to the Japanese public. A general principle is to separate the rulers from the ruled. Toward 'the Japanese people,' the invariable line professes

---

1966). Especially illuminating is the contribution that deals specifically with that event, John R. Thomas, 'The Limits of Alliance: The Quemoy crisis of 1958.'

[12] For a discussion of Japan's military potential, see Sherwood S. Cordier, 'Japan: Present and Potential Military Power,' *United States Naval Institute Proceedings*, 93, No. 11 (November, 1967): 70–78, and James H. Buck, 'The Japanese Self-Defense Forces,' *Asian Survey*, 7, No. 9 (September, 1967): 597–613. A condensed version appears in *Military Review*, 48, No. 3 (March, 1968): 19–30.

sincere 'friendship,' but 'the Japanese people' is an elastic term never defined in detail. The attitude toward the Japanese Government, on the other hand, is one of flexibility designed to suit the specific situation. Each new phase of the diplomatic offensive against Japan is calculated to put the Japanese Government on trial before its own public, to embarrass it, to force it into a defensive posture, and to create the impression that it is thwarting the wishes of the Japanese people. Thus, when Communist China was actively pressing its bid for the restoration of diplomatic relations with Japan in 1955, the Japanese Government, unwilling and unable to accept the Chinese terms, was forced into a defense of its foreign policy before a hostile, pro-Chinese Communist opposition in the Diet. Simultaneous attacks were mounted by Peking and by the opposition political groups and Communist front organizations in Japan. The government was depicted as a puppet of the United States and the chief obstacle to the normalization of relations, ignoring the ardent desire of both the Chinese and the Japanese peoples. Variations of this theme have been played before the Diet time and again. In this way Japan's nostalgic and sentimental postwar view of China, reciprocated neither by the Chinese people nor by their government, is exploited by Peking in its intercourse with Japan.

Several of the front organizations through which Peking often conducts its 'people's diplomacy' have attained prominent positions on the Japanese political and cultural scene, because their objectives appear to fulfill certain sincere aspirations of many Japanese. Perhaps the best examples of such front organizations are the *Gensuikyō* (the Japan Council against Atomic and Hydrogen Bombs) and the *Zengakuren* (commonly used abbreviation of the All-Japan Federation of Student Self-government Associations).

Since World War II, the Japanese have had a deep emotional commitment to the furtherance of world peace and the prevention of atomic war. After 1954, this influential peace sentiment found its most fervid expression in *Gensuikyō*, which soon became an important vehicle in the presentation of these ideas to the world.[13] Its annual conferences, held in August to commemorate the anniversaries of the dropping of the atomic bombs on Hiroshima and Nagasaki by the United States in 1945, used to attract considerable attention in the international press, as well as peace delegations from more than fifty nations. The JCP quickly maneuvered itself into a position of control in this mass organization, and the *Gensuikyō* degenerated into a partisan sounding board for anti-imperialist, anti-American, and pro-Communist propaganda. As a result, moderates, including many government party members, lost interest and withdrew their support. The disengagement was offered by the JCP as proof that the Japanese Government had no real interest in peace and the prevention of nuclear war and that it was in fact bent on the remilitarization of Japan and was working hand in glove with the United States in plotting a nuclear conflict. Those arguments were easily reinforced by pointing to Japan's 'illegal' and unpopular self-defense forces and to the presence of United States bases in Japan. In this way, for more than ten years the *Gensuikyō* served the interests of Communist China in Japan until the JCP broke with the CCP in 1966.

The *Zengakuren* has also served the cause of China. A notoriously activist group, it has long injected a note of turbulence into Japan's political scene. Rent by factionalism since its foundation, the original *Zengakuren* split permanently after having played a vanguard role in the 1960 disturbances against the Kishi government and the renewal of the Security Treaty with the United States. The resultant factions each claim to be *the Zengakuren*. The largest has remained under JCP control, but it has not performed the function of a pro-Peking front since 1966 because of the CCP–JCP split. Other more radical factions have, however, continued to act in a manner that

---

[13] See George O. Totten and Tomio Kawakami, 'Gensuikyō and the Peace Movement in Japan,' *Asian Survey*, Vol. 4, No. 5 (May, 1964).

serves Peking's interest, although there is little evidence that Communist China or the pro-Peking defectors from the JCP control them.

The CCP–JCP split has caused a violent shift in the orientation of several other front organizations subject to the influence of the Chinese Communists, but not all of the splits within the groups have worked to the disadvantage of Communist China, as in the case of the *Gensuikyō* and the *Zengakuren*. The Japan-China Friendship Association, for example, purged its JCP members and reconstituted the association as the Japan-China Friendship Association (Orthodox). This new JCFA is under the control of Communists sympathetic to China, who in turn have been purged from the JCP itself, but the membership also has a large number of JSP adherents. By 1967 it had become the leading organ of the pro-Peking Communist movement in Japan. By the simple expedient of refusing to deal with any organization that the JCP controls or participates in, the Chinese Communists have similarly purged the Japan International Trade Promotion Association (JITPA) and its member firms of JCP followers. JCFA and JITPA continue to act in consonance with Peking's wishes. The former appears to represent Peking more through conscious ideological preference, while the latter does so more for profit, performing a ritual kowtow to the Peking line and the thought of Mao Tse-tung in return for the privilege of trade.

The lure of trade. Actual and prospective trade has been China's most promising lever in its campaign to move Japan in a direction favorable to Peking's interests. Among the Japanese, trade with Communist China evokes almost universal interest and approval. The Japanese Government, in its attempt to deal with Communist China while maintaining formal relations with Taiwan, has from the time of Yoshida's premiership affirmed the principle of 'separation of politics and economics' where Communist China is concerned. Finding such a formula most distasteful, the Chinese Communists can often embarrass the Japanese Government by injecting political demands into trade negotiations. If a private trade agreement founders as a result of the Japanese Government's opposition to its political aspects, as was the case in 1958 (see below), the government is made to bear widespread criticism for having spoiled a relationship with China that is approved by a very broad range of public opinion. The conservative government has had difficulty in preserving internal unity on trade relations when political demands are introduced. The Ministry of International Trade and Industry, backed by business interests, tends to support the China trade and to treat political concessions lightly, while the Foreign Office argues to uphold Japan's formal diplomatic position.

Today, while the temptation is strong for China to continue the same pressure on Japan, the Chinese Communists also realize that Japan is now their most important trade partner and that the China trade is proportionally far less significant to Japan. This may serve to reduce Peking's propensity to use trade as a means to induce changes in political relations. On the other hand, a cut in Sino-Japanese trade still causes a public furor in Japan's open, pluralistic society, while in China the whole matter is handled within the Party and government with no fear of popular repercussions.

Japan's China policy. Until quite recently, and in contrast to China, Japan has placed little emphasis in its postwar diplomacy on the attainment of world, or even regional, leadership. It has also expressed far less concern for its national security in terms of external threat. The main thrust of Japanese foreign policy has been to advance Japan's domestic economic position through foreign trade. That attitude has given Japan a vested interest in world political stability, while Communist China sees no virtue in peace and tranquility so long as the struggle between socialism and capitalism has not been decided.

Challenged continuously since 1952, the postwar foreign policy of Japan has proved remarkably durable. It is based on support for the United Nations; alignment with the free world, which includes Taiwan; participation in the Asian community of nations; and reliance on the United States for security, but it also includes the establishment of relations with the Communist nations on the basis of noninterference and mutual respect. The inherent contradiction that follows from this dichotomy gives rise to the specific policy toward Communist China of separating political from economic matters.

In spite of the fact that successive Japanese Governments have all supported the above policy, the Japanese people have shown a good deal of interest in changing Japan's security ties with the United States. The Security Treaty, liberalized in 1960 in Japan's favor, can be brought up for renegotiation at any time since June, 1970, although both Japan and the United States have agreed to continue the treaty in its present form for the time being. However, the Japanese feel an increasing need for greater independence in foreign policy, and the government is under some pressure to have the country take on greater responsibility for its own defense. To many Japanese the Security Treaty, a symbol of a client relationship to the United States, has become an affront to Japan's surging national pride. The desire to end dependence on the United States has been sharpened by years of Communist Chinese propaganda and by the opposition parties in Japan, which are in agreement with Peking on this matter in principle and find in it an issue on which they can exploit Japan's new nationalism to their own advantage.

Until recently the Japanese have shown little concern about Communist China's military power. The majority of Japanese saw no threat from China, except, perhaps, for a short time during the Korean War. To the conservative majority, Russia has posed the threat; to the radicals, the United States. For most Japanese, China was neither geographically nor militarily in a position to hurt Japan, and their postwar feelings toward China effectively ruled out any view of the Chinese as an enemy. However, Communist China's development of nuclear weapons has brought about a noticeable change in Japan's previously sanguine attitude.[14] More Japanese can now conceive of Communist China as a potential enemy, and their uneasiness may increase as China's nuclear potential grows.

The diplomatic defense. From the foregoing it would seem that Communist China and Japan are engaged in an unequal struggle, the advantages lying heavily with the revolutionary, dynamic, and militant Chinese. The appearance is deceptive, however, for the Japanese have displayed surprising strength and fortitude in dealing with Communist China. They have successfully resisted Chinese blandishments and pressures for more than fifteen years and are now in a relatively stronger position vis-à-vis Communist China than before.

It has been the lot of six successive conservative Japanese Governments to absorb the shock of the Chinese foreign policy offensive against Japan and still live in the world with China. Ideologically, the conservative rulers of Japan abhor the Chinese Communist form of government. In that feeling they are supported by a majority of the Japanese people. Private enterprise rules Japan, and the Japanese people, while not necessarily sympathetic to the capitalist oligarchs who dominate the country, have prospered in cooperation with the system. They certainly would not care to trade their open society for the enforced regimentation of Chinese contemporary life. Too many Japanese can remember life under their own totalitarianism. The Japanese Government is well aware of the fact that the popular desire for good relations and

---

[14] Kei Wakaizumi, 'Japanese Attitudes Toward the Chinese Nuclear Programs,' in *Sino-Soviet Relations and Arms Control*, Vol. 20, Harvard University, East Asian Research Center, Center for International Affairs, 1966. Wakaizumi deals only with the Japanese reaction to China's first two tests. Indications are that later tests have had a similarly disquieting effect. For a general discussion of the problem posed for Japan in Chinese nuclear armament see Asahi Shimbun, Anzen Hosho Mondai Chosakai, *Chukoku no kakusenryoku* (*China's Nuclear Military Power*) (Tokyo: Asahi Shimbunsha, 1967).

trade with China does not reflect any general admiration for the Chinese social and political structure. In fact, public opinion polls continue to show Communist China to be one of the least popular nations among the Japanese. This can be interpreted as a judgment of the Chinese Communist regime and the system it imposes on China, for the Japanese have a warm regard for the Chinese people in general.

Cooperation in the free world market system has given Japan the environment in which to develop its industrial society on an unprecedented scale. The Japanese position has certain serious disadvantages, however. In spite of Japan's ardent and growing desire for an 'independent foreign policy'—which in this day of complex inter-relationships between nations can be no more than a relative term—the true strength of Japan's position in dealing with Communist China has lain in its ability to retreat to the alliance with the United States and its commitment to the 'free world'—hardly a mark of total independence.

Furthermore, for the Japanese, government-to-government relations with the Chinese Communists constitute only half the problem. The government must, as we have seen, also face the thrust of China's 'people's diplomacy.' In this respect it is at a distinct disadvantage, because the Chinese allow no reciprocity, and the Japanese Government has no means to present its case before the people of China. Even if it could, it is doubtful that the Japanese would be able to penetrate the general indifference and, among many Chinese, hostility toward Japan.

The Japanese Government's best defense against people's diplomacy is a passive one; it lies in partial retreat, in delay, and in agreement in principle that is then not acted upon. For example, the Japanese Government does not renounce the idea of having diplomatic relations with Communist China; it takes a positive long-term view, but the goal is always expressed as an eventuality. The single positive defensive weapon available to the Japanese Government for combating the effects of Chinese people's diplomacy is to charge Communist China with interference in the affairs of the Japanese nation and, as a corollary, to attack opposition groups in Japan that sympathize with Chinese viewpoints as tools of Communist China. Against flagrant Chinese attempts to interfere in Japanese politics, the weapon has been effective.

A HISTORICAL REVIEW OF SINO-JAPANESE RELATIONS: 1949–68

The preceding discussion of Sino-Japanese relations has been confined to general concepts and trends. In reality, both China and Japan have, from time to time, changed their respective tactics and interpretations of their own, as well as each other's, policies. While both Chinese and Japanese foreign relations can be divided into recognizable periods—which do not coincide—Sino-Japanese relations as a whole have their own phases on which most observers basically agree. For the purposes of this chapter the phases of Chinese foreign policy have been chosen as the frame of reference in order better to place certain crucial events in Sino-Soviet relations in the perspective of Chinese relations with Japan.[15]

Phase I: Defiance and hostility, 1949–51. The years 1949–51 were bellicose years for the P.R.C. The Communists came to power after more than twenty years of incessant war. Their painstakingly devised and tested formula for revolutionary warfare had proved successful; they now recommended it to colonial and semicolonial peoples struggling for independence. In February, 1950, after declaring partisan support for Russia in the cold war, Mao Tse-tung agreed in Moscow to a thirty-year treaty of friendship and alliance with the U.S.S.R., which was directed primarily against Japan and secondarily against the United States. Before the year was out, China had

---

[15] For the Chinese Communist foreign policy phases and the description of their events and characteristics, I have relied on Harold C. Hinton, *Communist China in World Politics* (Boston: Houghton Mifflin Company, 1966), Chapter 2. See also Chapter 11, above.

plunged into a war with the United States and the United Nations in order to save the beaten North Koreans from destruction and to protect China's own vital interests in Manchuria, which were threatened by the presence of hostile forces on the Yalu.

Phase II: The transition, 1951–55. China's ordeal in Korea and the general failure of the several Communist uprisings in Southeast Asia caused Peking to reappraise its attitude toward the non-Communist world. Moscow, too, may have had misgivings about Chinese ascendancy among Asian Communists, as Mao Tse-tung's theory of guerrilla warfare had found broad application in the 'wars of national liberation.'

By July, 1954, both Peking and Moscow were willing to sacrifice some of the hard-won gains of the Vietnamese Communists in order to bring about a negotiated compromise on Indochina at Geneva—a settlement that appears to have been accepted only reluctantly by Ho Chi Minh. Up until then, nations that had declared neutrality in the cold war were still regarded as members of the enemy camp in Moscow and Peking. A change, however, was to take place. Becoming aware of the opportunity presented by a U.S. foreign policy that discouraged neutralism and attempted to coerce neutrals into cooperation with the United States and the West, the Communist bloc, and especially the Chinese, began to woo and support the neutrals.

As Japan was still an occupied country, and Communist China was at war with the occupying powers, there could be no direct contact between them before 1952. However, in August, 1951, the Chinese Communists, who were not invited to the San Francisco conference, decried the Japanese Peace Treaty as illegal and hostile to China.[16] On May 5, 1952, only one week after Japan had become a sovereign and independent nation again, Chou En-lai condemned the Japanese treaty with Taiwan.[17] Such beginnings did not augur well for future official relations between China and Japan.

As the Japanese had opted for relations with Nationalist China, the Chinese Communists realized that they would not be able to deal with the Japanese Government but had to appeal directly to the Japanese 'people.'[18] Thus, the future pattern of relations with Japan was already determined at that early date. Japan was heavily committed to an official course of solidarity with the West; China to one intent upon breaking the entente. The Chinese moved quickly to exploit the only means of contact open to them, using 'people's diplomacy' to negotiate, in June, 1952, the first of four unofficial 'people's trade' agreements with interested private Japanese citizens who were invited to Peking for the purpose.[19] Because of Korean War restrictions on trade with Communist China placed by the United States on the governments of countries receiving American foreign aid and the complicated counter-restrictions imposed by the Chinese Communists, the first trade agreement went largely unfulfilled.[20] The agreement was nevertheless a beginning, and subsequent agreements were to become more effective.

The next important Chinese initiative came within the same year. On December 1, the Chinese announced their willingness to repatriate 30,000 Japanese citizens who,

---

[16] See *Oppose the Revival of Japanese Militarism* (Peking: Foreign Languages Press, 1960), pp. 5–17.

[17] *Ibid.*, pp. 18–24.

[18] James W. Morley, *Japan and Korea: America's Allies in the Pacific* (New York: Walker & Co., 1965), p. 16. Yoshida's decision prior to the San Francisco conference to enter into relations with Taiwan rather than Communist China resulted in the Communists' resorting to 'people's diplomacy.'

[19] The dates of the other three people's trade agreements are October 1, 1953; May 4, 1955; and March 5, 1958. These are not to be confused with the Liao-Takasaki, or Memorandum, Trade Agreement, which was concluded at a later date. See below.

[20] A good explanation of the COCOM and CHINCOM trade restrictions and Chinese countermeasures is contained in Harold S. Quigley, 'The Chinese-Japanese Courtship,' *Current History*, Vol. 33, No. 196 (December, 1957).

for various reasons, were still held in China. With the Japanese Red Cross as their principal representative, the Japanese began negotiations with China, finally reaching an agreement in March, 1953, the month of Stalin's death. Although the number of persons returned was disappointingly small to the Japanese, the total impact of the repatriation was probably to China's advantage. Some of the repatriates had been converted to Communism; many agreed that the Communists and the Chinese people had treated them humanely; most confirmed the fact that substantial changes for the better had indeed taken place in China.[21] In June, the Japanese National Diet passed a resolution favoring the promotion of trade with China; the Korean War ended officially in July.

The Sino-Indian agreement, recognizing Chinese hegemony in Tibet and the enunciation of the 'Five Principles of Peaceful Coexistence,' signed by Chou En-lai and Nehru in April, 1954, followed closely by Peking's participation in the Geneva Conference, was a clear indication to the world that China was assuming a more active role in world politics and a more flexible attitude in dealing with its Asian neighbors.

In October, 1954, China and the Soviet Union, acting in concert, made a specific offer to improve relations with Japan, at the same time exploiting the controversy then raging in Japan over nuclear tests and American bases. First, in March, 1954, as a result of a U.S. test of a thermonuclear device at Bikini, a Japanese fishing vessel was dusted by fallout, and the crew became ill with radiation sickness. One of the men aboard subsequently died. The incident unleashed an anti-American torrent in Japan, which quickly became entangled with the whole subject of U.S. bases and the Security Treaty arrangements. It was a situation worth exploiting from the Communist point of view. Second, the Geneva agreements had been followed by a new confrontation between Communist China and the United States over the Nationalist Chinese–held offshore islands of Quemoy and Matsu, which were then being brought under artillery attack from Communist Chinese batteries on the mainland. The new tension in Asia hastened the formation of the Southeast Asia Treaty Organization (SEATO), specifically devised by the United States, Great Britain, and France in support of strongly anti-Communist governments of Southeast and South Asia to halt any Chinese Communist aggression into that area.

The Sino-Soviet proposal to Japan came in the form of a joint declaration that Soviet and Chinese relations with Japan be based upon 'the principle of peaceful coexistence of states with different social systems.'[22] The declaration also stated the willingness of the two countries to assist Japan in establishing normal political and economic relations with them and in securing a 'peaceful and independent' development. The joint declaration preceded the Bandung Conference by six months and may be regarded as presaging Bandung, a generally recognized turning point in Communist China's foreign policy.

Phase III: The Bandung period, 1955–57. China's policy of 'peaceful coexistence,' dating from the Asian-African Conference at Bandung, Indonesia, in April, 1955, was marked by some spectacular diplomatic gains. For the first time, Communist China was able to make its presence felt outside Asia. Bandung brought China into contact with the Middle Eastern and African states, and subsequent events in Poland and Hungary in 1956 made the P.R.C., for a short time at any rate, the arbiter of Soviet–East European satellite relations. Communist China entered into discussions with the United States at Geneva in the summer of 1955. In contrast to the belligerent attitude toward the Chinese Nationalists in the Taiwan Strait crisis of 1954–55 the Com-

---

[21] For details of the repatriation program, see Shao-chuan Leng, *Japan and Communist China* (Kyoto: Doshisha University Press, 1958), pp. 72–85.

[22] See *Oppose the Revival of Japanese Militarism* (Peking: Foreign Languages Press, 1960), p. 27.

munists took a surprisingly conciliatory position with regard to Taiwan, calling for the 'peaceful liberation' of the province.

. In keeping with the peaceful coexistence policy made explicit toward Japan in 1954, and in development since 1952, Japan continued to receive overtures from China. More than thirty agreements were concluded between the two countries from 1952 to 1958, and they were all the result of 'people's diplomacy' and were therefore unofficial from Japan's point of view. On the other hand, they were consciously developed government- and Party-sponsored activities on the part of Communist China. The total effect of China's people's diplomacy in Japan cannot, however, be measured in the dry content of those agreements alone.

There is no doubt that there was a 'China boom' in Japan in the years 1954–57, even though much of it may have been due to the natural curiosity of the Japanese about their enigmatic neighbor. During 1956, the peak year in that period, 1,243 Japanese went to mainland China. The visitors almost invariably traveled as delegates to meetings or at the invitation of some sponsor sanctioned by the Chinese Communists. They included 'peace groups,' Diet member delegations, youth and women's groups, labor unions, businessmen, religious groups, friendship delegations, and others too numerous to list. The first Chinese trade fairs in Japan were presented in Tokyo and Osaka in 1955; the first Japanese trade fair was held in China in 1956.

Japanese newspapers, magazines, and movie houses were flooded with the stories, recollections, and impressions of Japanese visitors. China provided Japanese newsstands and bookstalls with a stream of propaganda material in Japanese designed to cater to widely varying tastes. Japan's thirst for information on China seemed insatiable. To be sure, the flow of visitors was not all one way. Chinese visited Japan, too, though the net effect always seemed to redound to China's propaganda advantage. The carefully selected Chinese visitors to Japan (who numbered about one-eighth of the Japanese visitors to China) extolled the accomplishments of China's revolution, while Japanese visitors to China likewise tended to paint a bright picture of the New China. There were, of course, significant exceptions to this general rule on the Japanese side, but their voices were often drowned in the tumult of praise and wonder.

It was during this period that Japan underwent significant internal political changes. Yoshida Shigeru, the man who had completed Japan's postwar treaty system with the United States and Taiwan and whose term in office had been longer than any previous prime minister, was forced out at the end of 1954. He was succeeded by Ichirō Hatoyama, who dedicated the new government to the task of tying up the loose ends of World War II by bringing to an official end the state of war with the Soviet Union and Communist China. He was partly successful with the Soviet Union in that the two countries terminated the state of war and restored diplomatic relations, but no treaty was possible because of the territorial issue, which could not be settled. With the improvement in relations with the U.S.S.R., Japan's entry into the United Nations in the fall of 1956, previously barred by Soviet veto, was assured. When Japan entered the United Nations, a cherished desire of the Japanese nation was achieved.

With China, Hatoyama made no headway. Actually, the Chinese had taken the initiative, inundating the Japanese with offers for the improvement of relations. On one point, however, Peking would make no concession: There would be no agreement as long as Japan continued its relations with Taiwan. For the Japanese Government the price was too high; a break with Taiwan would have jeopardized the whole fabric of Japan's affiliation with the West. It was at this point that Communist China and the Soviet Union parted company over policies toward Japan, for now the Soviet Union had a *de jure* entry into Japan, while Communist China still had none.[23] Hato-

---

[23] A. Doak Barnett, *Communist China and Asia* (New York: Vintage Books, 1961), p. 270.

yama left office at the end of 1956 and was succeeded shortly afterward by Nobusuke Kishi, a strongly anti-Communist conservative who, because of his unbending attitude toward the Chinese Communists, came to be detested by them.

Phase IV: A renewed hard line, 1957–60. The Bandung phase of Chinese foreign policy began to change rapidly to a new harder line after the summer of 1957. The reasons are not fully clear, although several interesting theories are available.[24] The policy shift seemed to follow Mao Tse-tung's 'Hundred Flowers' campaign of May, when, for the first time, intellectuals were invited to criticize publicly the government and the Party, as well as their policies. The breadth, depth, and vehemence of the eventual response rocked the Communists and forced Mao to a hasty termination of the experiment in June. Taken aback by the violent reaction and unwilling to accept the criticism, the Communist regime was left with no recourse but to conclude that the intellectuals themselves were at fault. A new campaign to rectify the thinking of the Chinese intelligentsia followed. Whether or not the soul-searching aftermath of the 'Hundred Flowers' period was directly related to the change in foreign policy cannot be proved, but the peaceful coexistence policy was on the way out.

The Soviet Union's success in launching the first earth satellite in October, 1957, helped set the tone for China's foreign policy switch. After 'Sputnik,' Mao Tse-tung, speaking in Moscow in November, 1957, indicated that the world's strategic balance had changed, expressing himself in the quaint metaphor 'the east wind prevails over the west wind,' a judgment in which the Soviet Union apparently did not concur. Mao's remarks appeared to imply to many observers that the Communist bloc had moved into a permanent and increasing psychological and, possibly, military ascendance over the West. He seemed to sense in the world situation the opportunity for an offensive against imperialism. Whatever Mao may have meant, Khrushchev, better informed, more realistic, and less inclined to interpret the situation in terms of Marxist dogma, did not respond.

The Russians had made a commitment to the Chinese in October, 1957, to help them in the development of a nuclear capability. It was not long after the Moscow meeting that the Soviet Union showed reluctance in either honoring the letter of the original commitment or in giving further aid to China's nuclear program.[25] Other factors also contributed to the strain on their alliance. For example, the Chinese showed signs of disillusionment with the Soviet Union as a model for the industrialization and modernization of China, and the Russians looked upon China's Great Leap Forward economic program of 1958 as a great mistake. China disapproved of Soviet inaction in the Middle East crises of 1958. But perhaps the most telling blow to their relations was the Soviet refusal in September, 1958, to back China in the Taiwan Strait crisis. That act spelled the beginning of the end for the Sino-Soviet military

[24] See, for example, Donald S. Zagoria, *The Sino-Soviet Conflict, 1956–1961* (Princeton, N.J.: Princeton University Press, 1962), Chapter 2; Alice Langley Hsieh, *Communist China's Strategy in the Nuclear Era* (Englewood Cliffs, N.J.: Prentice-Hall, 1962), pp. 62–119; Vidya Prakash Dutt, *China and the World: An Analysis of Communist China's Foreign Policy* (New York: Praeger, 1966), Chapter 1; A. M. Halpern, 'China in the Postwar World,' in Roderick MacFarquar, ed., *China Under Mao: Politics Takes Command* (Cambridge, Mass.: The MIT Press, 1966), pp. 498–503; and idem, 'The Chinese Communist Line on Neutralism,' *The China Quarterly*, No. 5 (January–March, 1961).

[25] Details on the agreement and its implementation are obscure. In a statement protesting against the Soviet decision to sign the partial nuclear test ban treaty in 1963, the Chinese alleged that on June 20, 1959, the 'Soviet Government unilaterally tore up the agreement on new technology for national defense between China and the Soviet Union on October 15, 1957, and refused to provide China with a sample of an atomic bomb and technical data concerning its manufacture'; quoted in *Documents on Disarmament, 1963*, United States Arms Control and Disarmament Agency Publication 24, October, 1964 (Washington, D.C.: Government Printing Office, 1964), p. 363.

alliance. The next year saw new and wider differences in the policies of the two great Communist powers, which finally culminated in an open split in 1960.

Communist China's policy toward capitalist Japan began to exhibit some of the hostile spirit reserved for the American imperialists in the Bandung period. Under Prime Minister Kishi, Japan's China policy continued to be based on the principle that Japan would deal with both Taiwan and the Chinese mainland, separating trade from politics. Elsewhere, Kishi aimed his principal diplomatic effort at the improvement of relations with the non-Communist Asian nations.[26] Under the circumstances, in the summer of 1957 the Chinese Communists began to label Kishi as hostile, likening him to Yoshida. He was accused of collusion in the 'imperialist plot to establish two Chinas.' His visits to neighboring Asian states (including Taiwan, where he had discussions with Chiang Kai-shek) and his public utterances were reported in Peking as anti-Chinese and anti-Communist.[27]

Japanese businessmen negotiated a fourth 'private' trade agreement in Peking in March, 1958, with the usual tacit approval of the Japanese Government, but Taiwan, whose apprehension was aroused by the increasing *de facto* relationship between Peking and Japan, launched vigorous protests against the agreement. The Nationalists were especially exercised over the article that allowed Chinese trade representatives to fly the Chinese Communist flag in Tokyo. During the complicated events following Taipei's protest, Communist China and the Kishi government each took increasingly firm positions, which exhausted the other's patience. The matter was brought to a climax on May 2, 1958, when a young Japanese ultranationalist tore down a small Chinese Communist flag displayed at a stamp exhibit in a Nagasaki department store. On the basis of that trivial incident, and perhaps buoyed up by the euphoric atmosphere of the Great Leap Forward economic program then under way, Communist China protested the 'desecration' of its flag, cancelled the trade agreement, and went on to prohibit business contacts and sever cultural agreements with Japan. It was as if the Chinese Communists had deliberately set out in a fit of pique to destroy the strong psychological position they had gained by dint of careful planning and labor over a span of several years.

The Japanese reaction was sharp. The electorate gave Kishi a resounding vote of confidence and a victory over the Japan Socialist Party in lower house elections, which were held, coincidentally, later in the same month. The Liberal Democrats turned the Chinese denunciations of the Japanese Government to political advantage by charging Communist China with an attempt to influence the elections in favor of the pro-Peking JSP.[28] Peking's demonstrated unpredictability vindicated for the moment the long-standing official policy of nonrecognition.

When the Chinese Communists terminated 'all' contact with the Japanese Government, they did not completely sever their connections through people's diplomacy. Soon after the Nagasaki flag incident, the JSP, the JCP, and the great *Sōhyō* labor federation began agitation to reopen communications with Communist China, con-

---

[26] See James W. Morley, 'Japan's Position in Asia,' *Journal of International Affairs*, 17, No. 2 (1964): 146.

[27] For examples in English see *Survey of the China Mainland Press*, American Consulate General, Hong Kong, No. 1582, August 1, 1957, p. 21, 'Premier Chou En-lai's Interview with Japanese Press and Radio'; p. 24, '*Jen-min Jih-pao* on Kishi Cabinet's China Policy'; and No. 1588, August 12, 1957, p. 34, '*Ta Kung Pao* on Kishi's Attitude Towards China.' A book of documents presenting China's view of the world conspiracy to establish 'two Chinas' and Japan's implication in this 'plot' was compiled by the Chinese People's Institute of Foreign Affairs at the time of the Taiwan Strait crisis in *Oppose U.S. Occupation of Taiwan and 'Two Chinas' Plot* (Peking: Foreign Languages Press, 1958).

[28] Ivan I. Morris, 'Foreign Policy Issues in Japan's 1958 Elections,' *Pacific Affairs*, Vol. 31, No. 3 (September, 1958).

demning the Japanese Government policy as the root cause of the break. Not unexpectedly, they found that support was forthcoming from business and manufacturing firms doing business with Peking. As a result, a JSP Diet member, Tadataka Sata, was dispatched to China to see what could be done. The Sata Report, published upon his return from Peking in August, included three basic political demands to which the Japanese Government would have to acquiesce in order to improve relations with China.[29] First, Japan must immediately cease all actions and statements hostile to China; second, it must stop all plots to establish two Chinas; and third, the Japanese Government should no longer obstruct the normalization of relations between Japan and China.

In November, 1958, Japan and the United States entered negotiations for revision of the Security Treaty. For Communist China, the act of negotiation alone was further evidence of Kishi's hostility toward China. The Chinese Communists renewed their attacks on the prime minister, and they never ceased until 1960, when Kishi left office.[30]

Phase V: The Sino-Soviet and Sino-Indian conflict, 1960–63. The worsening Sino-Soviet dispute erupted in a major crisis in April, 1960, when the P.R.C. launched the bitterest attack yet on Khrushchev and the Soviet Union.[31] From that time on, the Sino-Soviet dispute became a topic of open discussion throughout the world, including the Communist countries, while Sino-Soviet rivalry in trying to win the backing of other Communists intensified. Without warning, the Soviet Union withdrew all its military and technical advisers from China, thus virtually ending Soviet aid. A conference of world Communist Parties in Moscow in November, 1960, completely failed to heal the breach, though Communist China and the Soviet Union did cooperate at the long Geneva Conference on Laos from May, 1961, to June, 1962.

The open br̄ak with Moscow was accompanied by the pursuit of a strongly antiimperialist forㄴgn policy on the part of Communist China, in conscious contrast to the 'soft' policy of the 'modern revisionists' in Moscow.

The slowly mounting crisis in relations between China and India after 1958, which culminated in the Sino-Indian border war, came to a head at precisely the same time as the Soviet-American confrontation over Russian ballistic missiles in Cuba. The concurrent crises of October, 1962, involving China in India and the Soviet Union in Cuba, gave both sides cause for further mutual recrimination. The Soviets refused to condone or support the Chinese action against India, and the Chinese regarded the Soviet pullout from Cuba as a latter-day 'Munich.' The stage was set for an even more serious disruption of Sino-Soviet relations in 1963.

Japan was a chief beneficiary from the worsening Sino-Soviet relations. The Chinese were exultant over Kishi's ouster in July, 1960, following the prolonged rioting in Tokyo that preceded the Diet's approval of the renegotiated Japan–U.S. Security Treaty and caused the cancellation of President Eisenhower's planned visit

---

[29] Ryozo Kurai, 'Present Status of Japan-Communist China Relations,' *Japan Annual of International Affairs*, No. 1, 1961, p. 106. An abridged version of the Sata Report appears in Japanese in *Gekkan Shakaitō*, No. 17 (October, 1958), p. 18.

[30] As the negotiations for treaty revision got under way in Tokyo, Ch'en Yi, the Communist Chinese Foreign Minister, stated: 'The Kishi government, which is the concentrated expression of latent imperialism in Japan, imagines that by further collaborating with the United States, it will be able to revive Japanese militarism, suppress the dissatisfaction and resistance of the Japanese people, save Japan from its ever more serious economic crisis, and realize the ambitions of Japanese monopoly capital to have a finger in Taiwan and to expand in the direction of Southeast Asia.' 'Statement on the Revision of the Japan-U.S. "Security Treaty" Issued by Ch'en Yi, Foreign Minister of the People's Republic of China, November 19, 1958,' in *Oppose the Revival of Japanese Militarism* (Peking: Foreign Languages Press, 1960), p. 48.

[31] 'Long Live Leninism,' *Red Flag*, April 16, 1960.

to Japan.[32] However, in spite of the violent upsurge of antigovernment and anti-American feeling, the Liberal Democrats, who held a large majority in both houses of the Diet, maintained control and chose Hayato Ikeda, a moderate conservative politician of high standing, as successor to Kishi. Ikeda was returned to office in the November lower house elections, when the LDP won yet another victory. Ikeda's elevation to the prime ministership signaled a change of emphasis in Japan's China policy.

In the first months of Ikeda's term of office the Chinese were quite active in people's diplomacy through the JSP. The Japan-China Friendship Association and other front organizations regarded Ikeda's government as a mere extension of Kishi's 'anti-Chinese' regime. On November 11, 1960, Ikeda's foreign policy was publicly criticized in the *Jen-min Jih-pao* as indistinguishable from that of his predecessor. In January, 1961, Mao Tse-tung himself commented on the state of Sino-Japanese relations in an interview with a group of JSP politicians. According to Mao, the late JSP Secretary-General Asanuma had grasped the heart of the problem when he called American imperialism the common enemy of the Chinese and Japanese peoples.[33] Mao made no direct reference to Ikeda, but he did say that it was necessary for China to distinguish between relations with the Japanese people and relations with the Japanese Government, that there were waves and troughs in the flow of any battle, that Japan's struggle against U.S. imperialism was at the moment in a trough, and, lastly, that people's diplomacy between China and Japan must expand to a greater extent than ever before.[34] Mao also referred to one faction in the ruling LDP that favored relations with China as an indirect ally. His statements reveal clearly the broad united-front tactics of Chinese diplomacy and Peking's constant effort to isolate the Japanese Government from the largest possible segment of the Japanese public.

In spite of Peking's hasty conclusion that Ikeda was just another Kishi, the new prime minister set about to change the image of the Japanese Government in both his domestic and his foreign policies. He adopted a 'low posture' toward opposition in the Diet, deferring at times to minority views so as to ameliorate somewhat the feeling engendered among Socialist Diet members during the Kishi Administration that they were being tyrannized by the majority. Ikeda sought to make Japan's foreign policy more independent of the United States, stressing autonomy within the alliance. The new low posture was reflected in his attitude toward Communist China. By 1962, the Chinese were ready to respond, although only the emphasis, not the basic tenets, of Japan's foreign policy had changed.

To Communist China, the altered trade relations between China and the rest of the Communist bloc and the terrible agricultural collapse that followed the Great Leap Forward made commercial exchange with Japan once more seem desirable, even if it had to be at the cost of tacit submission to Japan's stipulation on politics.[35] Ikeda's low-posture policy, however, made such a shift easier for China.

Japan's trade with China had dropped to virtually nothing after the Nagasaki flag

---

[32] The events of that period in Japan are thoroughly and lucidly covered in George R. Packard III, *Protest in Tokyo: The Security Treaty Crisis of 1960* (Princeton, N.J.: Princeton University Press, 1966).

[33] Inejirō Asanuma led two groups of JSP Diet members to Communist China, one in 1957 and one in 1959. Both groups were cordially received by Chinese Government leaders, including Mao Tse-tung. The joint communiqués issued at the termination of these visits reveal the wide range of policy agreement between the Chinese Communists and the JSP. Asanuma's famous and controversial statement about American imperialism was made during a speech in Peking on March 12, 1959. He was stabbed to death in Tokyo in October, 1960, as he spoke in a nationally televised political debate.

[34] Shigetoshi Kasama, *Dainiji sekai taisengo nitchū kōryūshi* (Tokyo: n.p., 1961), pp. 138–41.

[35] See Shigeharu Matsumoto, 'Japan and China, Domestic Influences on Japan's Policy,' in A. M. Halpern, ed., *Policies Toward China: Views from Six Continents* (New York: McGraw-Hill, 1965), pp. 134–40.

incident. In 1960, however, a few Japanese trading firms deemed 'friendly' to Peking were allowed by Communist China to carry on limited trade with the Chinese mainland. The Japanese Government saw no reason to interfere wich such 'friendship trade'—the term owes its origin to the fact that the trade was permitted out of China's 'feeling of friendship toward the Japanese people'—and it was the only trade link between the two countries until 1962.

The break in the Chinese attitude came in September, 1962, when Chou En-lai invited the respected Liberal Democratic politician Kenzō Matsumura to Peking to discuss the possibility of resuming trade on a more formal, albeit still private, basis. Matsumura's trip had the blessing of both the Japanese Government and the LDP, and the outcome of the talks was favorable. Matsumura was followed to Peking by a trade delegation led by Tatsunosuke Takasaki, who negotiated the first long-term trade agreement (1963–67) between the two countries. The agreement provided for barter trade totalling $180 million each year, in addition to a specific protocol for the first year. Takasaki's opposite on the Chinese side was Liao Ch'eng-chih, a high-ranking Communist Party member long connected with Sino-Japanese affairs. From the initials of the two negotiators, the memorandum became known as the L-T Trade Memorandum and the trade itself as L-T trade. The new agreement did not directly affect 'friendship trade,' which continued as before.

Japan and China embarked upon the period of closest contact since World War II. Trade rose sharply, so that by the end of 1964 Japan's trade with Communist China exceeded its trade with Taiwan for the first time since 1956. Visitors between the two countries increased to an unprecedented level after 1962; cultural exchanges, trade fairs, and the like multiplied. All these expanded activities were carried on within the framework of basically unchanged policies in both Peking and Tokyo.

Phase VI: Sino-Soviet relations at a new low, 1963–66. If we accept Moscow's adherence to the partial nuclear test ban treaty of July 25, 1963, as a key point in the worsening relations between Moscow and Peking, we can date China's classification of the Soviet Union as an enemy from about that time. Peking bitterly opposed the partial nuclear test ban treaty, primarily because the treaty would put its own nuclear development program in jeopardy. That the Soviet Union would deliberately sign the treaty knowing this ended any shred of fraternal feeling the Chinese still could have for Moscow and proved that the U.S.S.R. was not only revisionist but also clearly a traitor to the cause of socialism in Chinese eyes. From that time, the struggle for the loyalty of world Communist Parties sharpened, while new instances of Communist Party splits into pro-Moscow and pro-Peking factions multiplied in non-Communist nations. As trade with other bloc nations decreased, China became more interested in dealing with the non-Communist industrial nations of the Western world, excluding the United States.

The improvement in Sino-Japanese relations of the previous period continued in the beginning of the present period, as Ikeda pursued his low-posture policy and as China sought new trade partners outside the Communist bloc. Improving economic conditions in China now added new impetus to Japan's interest in the China trade. On the Japanese side, although Ikeda maintained his predecessor's policy in separating politics and economics, he vigorously pushed Sino-Japanese economic relations. Ikeda was convinced that Japan should not lag behind the nations of Europe in seizing new opportunities for trade made possible by the Sino-Soviet split. To do so would not only be bad business but would also be inexcusable to many Japanese conservatives as well as radicals. He even made it clear that his Administration was prepared to offer China deferred payments against Chinese imports on terms equal to those given by European countries. That decision was, however, to be the source of new complications.

In August, 1963, the Japanese Government approved a transaction of $20 million for the sale of a complete vinylon plant to China with payments pro-rated over five years. The extension of credit to Communist China was denounced by the Chinese Nationalists, who made it clear that Taiwan was prepared to do everything in its power to stop long-term credits for the Communists.[36] After long negotiations between Tokyo and Taipei, matters still remained at an impasse. The Nationalists had in the meantime taken several retaliatory steps against Japan, including the withdrawal of senior staff members from the Chinese Embassy in Tokyo and a staged mob invasion of the Japanese Embassy in Taipei. Finally, in February, 1964, the venerable former Prime Minister Yoshida, still a very powerful figure behind the scenes in Japanese conservative political circles and highly respected in Taiwan, visited Chiang Kai-shek at Ikeda's request. Yoshida succeeded in smoothing the matter over by giving a letter to President Chiang, assuring him that no additional deferred credit deals would be offered Communist China.[37]

One of the most influential Chinese Communist visitors to Japan in that period was the financial expert Nan Han-ch'en, a man already well known to Japanese businessmen, both because he had once lived in Japan as an exile and because of his former position as president of the People's Bank of China. While visiting in April, 1964, Nan made a tremendous impression on Japanese businessmen and among Liberal-Democratic politicians. Enthusiasm for contacts, especially trade, with the New China swept Japanese conservative circles as never before. Japanese trade with Communist China continued to rise as Japan became China's most important trade partner,[38] although the 'friendship trade' continued to be the most important component of the exchange, notwithstanding the quasi-official nature of the L-T trade agreement.

The new boom in relations was not destined to last, however, for Ikeda left office in November, 1964, for reasons of health, and Kishi's brother, Satō Eisaku, replaced him. Satō's determination to restore relations with the Republic of Korea (R.O.K.), with whom talks had been proceeding without result for years, immediately caused trouble between Japan and Communist China. In the spring of 1965, Communist China challenged the Yoshida letter to Chiang Kai-shek by cancelling a $30-million contract for a second vinylon plant and another for a 10,000-ton freighter, and by breaking off negotiations for a urea fertilizer plant for which no Japanese credit was forthcoming on the basis of the Yoshida letter. The setback in trade relations with China took place as Japanese negotiations with the R.O.K. entered their critical stage. The Japan–R.O.K. treaty was signed in June, 1965, and ratified by Japan in November. The completion of the treaty occasioned a renewed barrage of Chinese propaganda attacks against the Japanese Government and Prime Minister Satō. By 1966, a new period of deteriorating relations between Communist China and Japan had set in.[39]

---

[36] In 1962–63, Japan's trade with Taiwan was still twice that with Communist China; the Japanese had a generally favorable balance in the trade; and the Taiwan trade had not been subject to the anxieties and pressures that Communist China's political meddling imposed upon its trade with Japan. Taiwan was, therefore, in a position to be heard. See Ryozo Kurai, 'Current Developments in Sino-Japanese Relations and Japanese Attitudes Toward Communist China,' *Japan Annual of International Affairs*, No. 3, 1963–64 (Tokyo: Japan Institute of International Affairs), pp. 95–99, and Douglas H. Mendel, Jr., 'Japan's Taiwan Tangle,' *Asian Survey*, Vol. 4, No. 10 (October, 1964).

[37] While Japan was beset by difficulties with the Nationalists, France recognized Communist China in January, 1964, thus increasing popular pressures on the Japanese Government for the normalization of Sino-Japanese relations.

[38] With the possible exception of the Soviet Union, whose trade with Communist China was estimated to be approximately equal to that of Japan. See 'China in World Trade,' *Current Scene*, Vol. 4, No. 3 (February 1, 1966).

[39] See Arthur J. Dommen, 'In Northeast Asia: Dragon and the Dove,' *Current Scene*, Vol. 4, No. 1 (June 1, 1966).

Phase VII: The diplomacy of the Cultural Revolution, 1966–68. It could hardly be expected that Japan, so long a prime target for Chinese ideological warfare, would escape the effects of the changes wrought in the style of Chinese diplomacy by the Cultural Revolution, which made undiplomatic behavior common practice in 1967.[40] As it was, Japan in 1966 gave the Chinese more than usual cause for annoyance. The attacks on Japan over the Japan–R.O.K. Treaty had hardly subsided when, in the spring of 1966, the Japanese Government began negotiations with the hated Soviet revisionists to increase trade. Japan also pursued an active diplomatic course of its own in Asia. All this activity was scored by Peking as Japanese economic expansion into Southeast Asia and further evidence of Japan's collusion with the U.S. imperialists on Vietnam. By the end of 1966, the Chinese Communist press was directing vigorous attacks against Satō by name. On December 14, 1966, Foreign Minister Ch'en Yi told the Japanese that they could expect no great increase in trade without recognition and that Japan had to recognize the inseparability of economics and politics. He also added gratuitously that Satō was the worst among the last three prime ministers in Japan—a list that included China's old antagonist, Nobusuke Kishi.

It was also in 1966 that the Japan Communist Party and the Chinese Communists moved toward an open break. By the end of 1967, all that was left of CCP–JCP relations was the polemics between them. The front organizations remaining in Communist Chinese control, such as the Japan-China Friendship Association (Orthodox), a few small pro-Peking Communist splinter groups, and the Japan Socialist Party, were now the chief spokesmen for the Chinese line in Japan.

The Chinese Communists' attack against the Japanese prime minister heightened in 1967, reaching a crescendo in the fall, when Satō visited Taiwan, Southeast Asia, and the United States.[41] The pressure from below was equally intense. The L-T trade agreement was to expire at the end of 1967, and Japan proposed negotiations for renewal as early as July. The Chinese demurred, citing Japan's 'hostility' toward China, finally agreeing to negotiate only in January, 1968. The negotiations proved a humiliating experience for the Japanese, who were forced to accept in writing the principle of inseparability of trade and politics, as well as China's three political principles for normal relations with Japan. The Chinese also refused to sign a memorandum effective for more than one year, thus underlining their disapproval of Japan's foreign policy and the delicate state of Sino-Japanese relations.[42] As the negotiations were 'unofficial,' the Japanese Government quietly disavowed the political concessions and accepted the trade. Again, in April, 1970, in order to extend

---

[40] See Harold C. Hinton, *Policymaking and the Power Struggle in Communist China During the Cultural Revolution* (Washington, D.C.: Institute for Defense Analysis, February, 1968), pp. 35–38, and Robert A. Scalapino, 'The Cultural Revolution and Chinese Foreign Policy,' *Current Scene*, 6, No. 13 (August 1, 1968): 6–11.

[41] One example of the type of verbal assault upon Mr. Satō follows: 'With the heinous collaboration between the United States and the Soviet Union and archbetrayal of Soviet revisionism, Japan not only is trailing more and more closely behind the United States but has come to terms at an increasingly rapid pace with the Soviet Union, its former "imaginary" enemy," and a U.S.-Soviet-Japanese anti-Chinese alliance has been formed. With this tremendous change in the situation, Japanese monopoly capital has a free hand in its all-out drive for expansion in Southeast Asia. This is one of the important reasons why Eisaku Satō dares to carry out brazenly his sinister activities in Southeast Asia and the Pacific region for realization of his imperialist ambitions.' NCNA (English), October 21, 1967. English-language articles in the *Peking Review* reveal the vehemence of the Chinese Communist official attack on Satō. See 'The Satō Government is Treading Tojo's Old Road,' No. 38, September 15, 1967; and 'Strip Eisaku Satō of His Disguise,' No. 45, November 3, 1967.

[42] Trade under the one-year agreement signed on March 6, 1968, is known now as Memorandum Trade, not L-T trade, since Liao was purged in the Cultural Revolution.

memorandum trade for one more year, a Japanese delegation was forced into the humiliating position of signing a joint communiqué that openly criticized the Japanese Government's foreign policy and virtually accepted Peking's charge that there had been a revival of Japanese militarism. That time the Japanese Government attempted a mild reply, which was a 'clarification' of Japanese foreign policy rather than a direct answer to the charges in the communiqué. Before and after the event, Peking maintained a steady barrage of propaganda charging Prime Minister Satō and his government with a revival of militarism and with planning aggression in China and other places in collusion with the United States and other countries.

Eighteen Years of Sino-Japanese Relations

China's apparent advantages not decisive. Through the years, Communist China has enjoyed several advantages in dealing with Japan. These might be classified as psychological, organizational, and positional. As a dynamic, rising, revolutionary power in Asia, Communist China early gained the psychological initiative in foreign affairs over the guilt-ridden, defeated Japanese, whose spectacular economic recovery did not really begin until the mid-1950's and impressed the Japanese themselves but little until the mid-1960's. Although the Japanese people retained after the Pacific war their qualities of diligence and perseverance, which proved invaluable assets for rebuilding Japan, their aggressive nationalism was replaced by internationalism, and their militarism by pacifism. That change in outlook, admirable though it may have been, was not the stuff necessary to defend the nation from the perils of China's zealous, ideologically sustained diplomatic assault.

Communist China's psychological dominance has been reinforced by its organizational advantages. The dictatorial CCP and Peking government presented a face of monolithic unity and strength in dealing with Japan. Even in times of great internal stress, as during the eclipse of Party rule during the Cultural Revolution, there was no change in this appearance. All policy decisions with regard to Japan were, and still are, made outside the public gaze, and the policies are specifically designed to cause dissension and fissures in Japan's pluralistic society where men can, and do, express diverse opinions. Communist China can find some support in Japan for almost any proposal. Conversely, all communication from Japan to China must be directed to the ruling group, which makes all decisions uninfluenced by contrary public opinions or objections. The Chinese people are effectively shielded from any Japanese statement not specifically approved for repetition in China's controlled mass media.

The third, or positional, advantage for Communist China stems from the relative importance of the two countries to each other. For China, political relations with Japan are not generally of first importance; the Soviet Union and the United States far outweigh Japan on China's scale of foreign policy values. Japan is an interesting and challenging problem for Chinese diplomacy, but relations with Tokyo have lacked the urgency of relations with the great powers. On the other hand, Japan has found China to be its most persistent and vexing diplomatic problem in the postwar era, just as before the war.[43] China has posed a dilemma for every Cabinet, contributing directly to the fall of one. For that reason, China can usually afford to take its time in dealing with Japan, while many Japanese clamor for an early solution to the China problem, often to the embarrassment of their reluctant government.

In spite of the imperative nature of Japan's China problem, the organizational monolith Japan faces in the Chinese state structure, and the disadvantageous psychological attitudes inhibiting it in dealing with China, the Japanese Government has managed to persist without ever changing its conservative format or its basic policy toward China. It is apparent that the Japanese people's expressed sympathy for and

---

[43] See Hellmann, 'Japan's Relations with Communist China,' p. 1085.

interest in Communist China have not, so far, greatly affected their decision at the ballot box. Domestic issues and perhaps habit are of more importance. Thus, Japan has held its own and is likely to continue to do so in the future.[44]

The umbrella of U.S. military strength has been a psychologically uplifting factor for the Japanese Government in facing both the Soviet Union and China—a fact that many Japanese might be reluctant to admit. The Japanese could indulge in the belief that China was no threat to Japan only as long as the United States was standing by.[45] With the passage of time, Japan has gathered strength of its own, and the Chinese have revealed weaknesses not so clearly seen before. Not only has the myth of Communist world unity been shattered, but so has that of China's internal unity. The psychological advantages that once lay with China have begun to assume less importance, either through Chinese actions that have disillusioned the Japanese or through the slow revival of Japanese nationalism. Even after years and years of glowing reports about the New China from the lips and pens of thousands of admiring visitors, most of them carefully selected by their hosts, enough contrary evidence has filtered through, especially during periods of turmoil in China—the Hundred Flowers, the Great Leap Forward, and the Cultural Revolution periods—to cast serious doubt about the suitability of China's socialist system for Japan or the necessity of really close political relations with China's turbulent revolutionary society.

One difficult problem the Chinese face in their policy toward Japan is their inability to be consistent. Contradictions arise when Chinese action toward nations more important to them flatly belie the attitudes and images they wish to convey to the Japanese. One example was the Chinese attitude toward establishing a nuclear-free zone in the Asian and Pacific region.[46] The Japanese generally approved this Chinese proposal, but in 1964, when China detonated its first atomic device, which served to announce its intention to enter the nuclear arms race with the United States and the Soviet Union, the nuclear-free zone concept had to be abandoned in spite of any effect that might have on Japanese opinion.

PROSPECTS

Although there is little evidence of any basic change in the policies of either China or Japan with regard to each other at present, there are several factors bearing on their relationship that may well affect the attitudes of each in time.

For China, the tumultuous period of Cultural Revolution has ended; Chinese leaders, more absorbed in domestic concerns between 1966 and 1969, are now able to re-evaluate their neglected foreign affairs, and a new course is being charted. Certainly a reassessment of China's position in, and relationship with, Japan is an important part of the general review. Affecting the review would be the Soviet Union's

---

[44] 'If mass opinion is to effect a change in Japan's China policy, it would surely have to be conjoined with a broader political challenge from the Left to the conservative government itself—a challenge that would certainly involve considerations beyond the single issue of Japan-China relations. Indeed, that the Chinese attempt to foster mass support primarily through the Japanese left-wing parties implicitly acknowledges this fact. Consequently . . . any rapprochement with China from within Japan will come from the conservative politicians, bureaucrats, and businessmen who presently dominate the foreign policy formulation process.' *Ibid.*, pp. 1086–87.

[45] 'The single most important fact about Japanese foreign policy since 1945 is that it has enjoyed maximal gains with minimal risks. . . . No nation in the world approaching Japan's stature and strength has scored so many economic and political advances at such a low cost. . . . The essential element has been the United States–Japan alliance.' Robert A. Scalapino, 'In Search of a Role: Japan and the Uncertainties of Power,' *Encounter*, 27, No. 6 (December, 1966): 21.

[46] *Documents on Disarmament*, 1963, p. 272.

more conciliatory attitude toward Japan and its recent interest in arrangements with Japanese industry for accelerating the economic and industrial development of Siberia against a possible Chinese threat. Another crucial point for consideration would be the changes in the U.S. position in the western Pacific. The alteration of the status of Okinawa, the impermanent nature of the extended Japan-U.S. Security Treaty since June, 1970, the changing U.S. role in Southeast Asia, the reduction of U.S. forces in the Republic of Korea, and, most important, any rapprochement between the People's Republic and the United States, will all affect China's Japan policy. But the vital consideration for China must turn on Japan's rather sudden emergence as a power in its own right. With the U.S. military presence in East Asia receding and Japan's having become the world's third industrial power, China will probably tend to think of Japan less as an adjunct to U.S. imperialism and more as an independent economic and military competitor for power in Asia.

Peking's anti-Japanese propaganda seems to reflect this view by emphasizing Japan's resurgent militarism, the renewed threat of Japanese imperialist aggression, and the Japanese Government's hostility toward China in league (almost incidentally) with China's enemies, the 'U.S. imperialist aggressors' and the 'Soviet revisionists.' Recent renewed interest in, and public discussion of, the defense problem in Japan, in connection with the changing relationships among the powers of the north Pacific basin, has prompted China again to accuse Japan of militarism and imperialist aggressive designs in Asia. The mere discussion of nuclear weapons as a possible alternative in Japan's defense has greatly increased the vehemence of Peking's propaganda barrage, even as China resumes its own nuclear test program. However, if one considers China's continuing perception of a very serious military threat from both nuclear superpowers, it is conceivable that Japan may be able to break out of its constrained and defensive foreign policy position and to seize the diplomatic initiative with regard to China for the first time since 1945. But in the meantime, China continues its long-standing dual policy of denouncing Japan's conservative government while proclaiming 'friendship' for the Japanese people.

Within Japan, a new surge in the relationship with the United States is in the making. Much of the impetus of the movement comes from the political left, in which a large segment is sensitive and sympathetic to certain Chinese Communist viewpoints, but the Chinese actually exercise little control over such people. Politically, the pro-Mao party in Japan is inconsequential, and the fronts that Peking controls have no political power. The ailing Japan Socialist Party, which has paid dearly for its doubtful friendship with Peking, may sympathize with China and even espouse a foreign policy consistent with Chinese goals in Japan, but this is far different from being a puppet of the Chinese. The JSP has always stopped short of permanent cooperation with Communists at home or abroad. There are, of course, major ideological differences and also disagreements in policy between Peking and the JSP. China's development of nuclear weapons, for example, has never been accepted by the JSP, although the party concedes that U.S. imperialism forced China to take that regrettable step. Radical students have great potential for disruption and violence in Japan, and they will undoubtedly continue their fight for changes in the Japan-U.S. security arrangements, but they are to no significant degree manipulatable from Peking. Because China has no means to control the instruments that might force desired internal changes within Japan, and because the changes taking place so rapidly there are not necessarily to Peking's advantage, it is possible that the Chinese may in time abandon their dual diplomatic policy, which seems to hold so little promise. Should that happen, Japan may have its first opportunity for an active and positive role in diplomacy with China, depending, of course, on China's revised policy. Peking's options might range from implacable hostility toward the Japanese nation (which could include the threat of nuclear attack) to a policy of increased trade, acceptance of Japanese technological assistance, and compromise on the issue of the separation of trade and politics (which China has done before). At first glance, the former may seem the more likely course for the Chinese, but internal changes within China, or U.S. or Soviet pressures from without, might make the latter policy more attractive from the Chinese view.

Resurgent nationalism is one of the ingredients in Japan's thrust for separation from what many Japanese consider a demeaning status of dependency upon the United States. Nationalism may direct Japan away from its former intimate relations with the United States and make the idea of new and closer ties with Japan more palatable to China. A relaxation of tension between Japan and China could lead to recognition and to mutually advantageous economic agreements, but this does not necessarily mean that there will be any appreciable increase in Chinese political influence in Japan's internal affairs. It is more likely that Japan, already an established Asian power, will continue to exercise its new freedom of foreign policy action by the careful selection of options for relations with any or all of the three other competitors for power in East Asia. Closer relations between Tokyo and Peking would not preclude future rivalry for raw materials, markets, or even political influence in East Asia and beyond.

SELECTED BIBLIOGRAPHY

DOMMEN, ARTHUR J. 'In Northeast Asia: Dragon and the Dove,' *Current Scene*, Vol. 4, No. 1, June 1, 1966. Communist China's reaction to the Japan–Republic of Korea Treaty of 1965·

HELLMANN, DONALD C. 'Japan's Relations with Communist China,' *Asian Survey*, Vol. 4, No. 10, October, 1964. Short over-all survey of relations from 1949 until 1964. Particularly good on Liberal Democrat–Japan Socialist confrontation over Japan's policy toward Communist China.

KAMIYA, FUJI. 'Toward the Take-off Stage of a Japanese Diplomacy,' *Journal of Social and Political Ideas in Japan*, Vol. 4, No. 1, April, 1966. Critical of both Liberal Democrats and Japan Socialists on foreign policy views.

KENNAN, GEORGE F. 'Japanese Security and American Policy,' *Foreign Affairs*, Vol. 43, No. 1, October, 1964. Japan's reaction to the 'cloying exclusiveness' of its American ties and the effect on relations with Communist China.

KURAI, RYOZO. 'Current Developments in Sino-Japanese Relations and Japanese Attitudes towards Communist China,' *Japan Annual of International Affairs*, No. 3, 1963–64. Detailed accounts of relations during Kishi and Ikeda cabinets.

———. 'Present Status of Japan–Communist China Relations,' *Japan Annual of International Affairs*, No. 1, 1961.

LANGER, PAUL F. 'Japan's Relations with China,' *Current History*, Vol. 46, No. 272, April, 1964. Stresses Japan's difficulty in implementing dual policy of close ties with United States and trade without political implications with Communist China.

LENG, SHAO-CHUAN. *Japan and Communist China*. Kyoto: Doshisha University Press, 1958. The one book in English devoted to the problem of Sino-Japanese relations since the establishment of the People's Republic of China.

MATSUMOTO, SHIGEHARU, 'Japan and China: Domestic and Foreign Influences on Japan's Policy,' in A. M. HALPERN, ed., *Policies Toward China: Views from Six Continents*. New York: McGraw-Hill Book Company, 1965. General coverage of relations to the end of Ikeda Cabinet. Viewpoints of each political party toward China policy noted briefly.

MENDEL, DOUGLAS H., JR. 'Japan's Taiwan Tangle,' *Asian Survey*, Vol. 4, No. 10, October, 1964. Japan's dilemma over Taiwan and the mainland. Covers 1963 Japanese attempt to extend long-term credits to Communist China.

MORLEY, JAMES W. 'Japan's Position in Asia,' *Journal of International Affairs*, Vol. 18, No. 2, 1963. Broad outlines of each prime minister's foreign policy from Yoshida to Ikeda; Japan's changing view of itself as an Asian power.

PASSIN, HERBERT. *China's Cultural Diplomacy*. New York: Praeger Publishers, 1963. How China applies 'people's diplomacy' against Japan.

QUIGG, PHILIP W. 'Japan in Neutral,' *Foreign Affairs*, Vol. 44, No. 2, January, 1966. A U.S. view of Japan's neutralist tendencies.

SCALAPINO, ROBERT A. 'In Search of a Role,' *Encounter*, Vol. 27, No. 6, December, 1966. Japan's attempt to bring its newly acquired world power status to bear in foreign policy.

TERASAWA, HAJIME. 'The "Two Chinas" Myth,' *Journal of Social and Political Ideas in Japan*, Vol. 4, No. 1, April, 1966. A Japanese intellectual's view of the China relations problem.

UEDA, TOSHIO, 'The Outlook for Relations with Communist China,' *Japan Quarterly*, Vol. 13, No. 3, July–September, 1966. Japanese Government viewpoint on Communist China well explained.

VINACKE, HAROLD M. 'The Growth of an Independent Foreign Policy in Japan,' *Pacific Affairs*, Vol. 38, No. 1, Spring, 1965. Historical perspective on whole problem of Japanese foreign policy.

WAKAIZUMI, KEI. 'Japanese Attitudes Toward the Chinese Nuclear Program,' *Sino-Soviet Relations and Arms Control*, Vol. 2. Cambridge, Mass.: East Asian Research Center, Center for International Affairs, Harvard University, 1966. Japan's changing attitude toward Communist China as China develops nuclear armaments.

WATANABE, SEIKI. 'Three World Strategies and Japan,' *Japan Quarterly*, Vol. 13, No. 13, July–September, 1966. Japan as the focal point of struggle among three great powers: Communist China, U.S.S.R., and U.S.A.

WILBUR, C. MARTIN. 'Japan and the Rise of Communist China,' in HUGH BORTON *et al.*, eds, *Japan between East and West*. New York: Harper & Brothers, for the Council on Foreign Relations, 1957.

15

RELATIONS WITH THIRD WORLD
AND 'INTERMEDIATE ZONE'
COUNTRIES

KING C. CHEN

The Third World and 'Intermediate Zone' Countries

In its early view of world politics, Communist China envisaged no 'third world' or 'intermediate zone,' although the origin of Mao Tse-tung's concept of the 'intermediate zone' could be traced back to 1946.[1] The Chinese Communist world outlook in the late 1940's was a variation on the Soviet 'two camp' theory as pronounced by Andrei Zhdanov in September, 1947.[2] In 1948, Liu Shao-ch'i, in reaffirming the significance of the Soviet theory, emphasized that the two camps actually included 'all the peoples of the world—of all countries, classes, sections of the population, parties and groups.'[3] Shortly before the inauguration of the Peking regime in 1949, Mao Tse-tung asserted that 'all Chinese without exception must lean either to the side of imperialism or to the side of socialism. Sitting on the fence will not do, nor is there a third road.' And Communist China leaned 'to the side of the anti-imperialist front headed by the Soviet Union.'[4] Thus, initially, Communist China adopted a rigid policy toward the outside world, strongly opposing a third road, or noncommitment, in its struggle against imperialism.

On January 21, 1964, *Jen-min Jih-pao* carried an editorial recognizing the existence of two 'intermediate zones' between the Communist bloc and the United States. It said:

> This vast intermediate zone is composed of two parts. One part consists of the independent countries and those striving for independence in Asia, Africa, and Latin America; it may be called the first intermediate zone.
>
> The second part consists of the whole of Western Europe, Oceania, Canada, and other capitalist countries; it may be called the second intermediate zone.[5]

---

[1] See Mao Tse-tung, 'Talk with the American Correspondent Anna Louise Strong,' *Selected Works*, 4 (Peking: Foreign Language Press, 1961): 99.

[2] A. Zhdanov, 'The International Situation,' *For a Lasting Peace, For a People's Democracy* (Belgrade: Information Bureau of the Communist Parties, November 10, 1947), pp. 2–4.

[3] Liu Shao-ch'i, *Internationalism and Nationalism* (Peking: Foreign Languages Press, 1949), p. 32.

[4] Mao Tse-tung, 'On the People's Democratic Dictatorship,' *Selected Works*, 4 (Peking: Foreign Languages Press, 1961): 415, 417.

[5] *Jen-min Jih-pao* (People's Daily), (editorial), January 21, 1964, and *Peking Review*, No. 4, Peking, January 24, 1964, p. 7.

What made Communist China shift its world outlook over a period of fifteen years? A principal factor was the change in the world situation. As early as the Korean War years, Communist China took note of the presence of a noncombatant medical team from India with the United Nations forces. In the interval of the Geneva Conference in 1954, Chou En-lai took time in June to visit India and Burma, proclaiming together with Nehru the 'five principles of peaceful coexistence.'[6] Then, at the Bandung Conference in 1955, China began skillfully cultivating support from the third world, emphasizing a common opposition to imperialism. In the Soviet Union the 'two camp' theory was officially buried in February, 1956, by Krushchev, who launched the deStalinization campaign and recognized the emergence of the third world.[7]

The countries of the third world and 'intermediate zones' overlap. In the Western concept, the third world, different from the West and the Communist world, comprises more than ninety independent countries and some fifty colonial territories in Asia, Africa, and Latin America that are generally referred to as 'underdeveloped' or 'developing.'[8] This is Peking's first 'intermediate zone.' Countries or regions in Peking's second 'intermediate zone' generally do not belong to the 'third world'; some are Western and capitalist in nature. To avoid confusion, this chapter will discuss the 'third world' (underdeveloped) as the West conceptualizes it, because it is better known to the West than the first 'intermediate zone.' The five countries in the second 'intermediate zone' (developed and capitalist)—Britain, France, West Germany, Australia, and Canada—will be discussed in accordance with Peking's terminology, because Communist China, and not the West, professes to regard them as a uniform category.

Peking's Objectives

On the whole, Peking has taken the initiative vis-à-vis the third world and second intermediate zone. As the situation varies considerably from region to region and country to country, generalization is difficult, but certain prevailing common characteristics can be traced. In general, Peking's approach to these areas has been based on a certain theory and on objectives that it seeks to realize through complex but flexible strategies and tactics. The operation of its foreign policy has been conditioned by the response from local situations as well as by important international problems.

In theory, the Chinese Communists have been inspired by the belief that the 'truths' distilled from the experience of the Chinese revolution, as directed by Mao Tse-tung's thought, are relevant for the colonial and semicolonial countries in Southeast Asia, because their political, social, and economic conditions resemble those of China.[9] Since 1949, men like Liu Shao-ch'i, Ch'en Po-ta, Lu Ting-i, Wang Chia-hsiang, and Lin Piao have stressed the international significance of the Chinese revolutionary experience, calling it the classic type of revolution for underdeveloped areas. As the demand in the third world for independence and freedom has waxed,

---

[6] Mutual respect for each other's territorial integrity and sovereignty, nonaggression, nonintervention in each other's internal affairs, equality and mutual benefit, and peaceful coexistence.

[7] See N. S. Khrushchev, 'The Central Committee Report,' Leo Gruliow, ed., *Current Soviet Policies II: The Documentary Record of the 20th Party Congress and Its Aftermath* (New York: Praeger, 1957), p. 33. For Soviet views on the 'third world,' see Thomas Ferry Thornton, ed., *The Third World in Soviet Perspective* (Princeton, N.J.: Princeton University Press, 1964).

[8] See Cyril E. Black and Thomas P. Thornton, eds., *Communism and Revolution* (Princeton, N.J.: Princeton University Press, 1964), p. 432. In the author's view, there were ninety-seven independent countries in the 'third world' as of January, 1971. See Table 15-1.

[9] Anna Louise Strong, 'The Thought of Mao Tse-tung,' *Amerasia*, 11, No. 6 (June, 1947): 161-62.

Peking has tried to exploit anti-imperialist sentiment by encouraging and assisting armed revolution on the Chinese model. The 'intermediate zone' concept is used to distinguish the area from both the West and the Communist bloc, so that Peking can identify itself more meaningfully with the underdeveloped countries and help promote their revolution in accordance with Chinese experience. The concept is but a new aspect of Peking's project for a worldwide struggle against United States 'imperialism'—a case of ideological dogmatism accompanied by political flexibility.

Peking has short-, middle-, and long-range objectives to attain in its policies toward the underdeveloped countries. The short-range objectives are to strengthen and promote China's security, power, prestige, and economic welfare, fundamental goals that are similar to those of any nation in modern times.

The middle-range objectives are to gain recognition as a powerful nation, a model for national independence and revolution, and a leader in the 'third world.' These goals are very much in the Peking leaders' mind. As Mikhail A. Suslov correctly perceived in 1964:

> The Chinese leaders represent matters as though the interests of the peoples of Asia, Africa, and Latin America were especially close and understandable to them, as though they were concerned most of all for the further development of the national-liberation movement. . . . In the light of the Chinese leaders' practical activities in recent years the true political meaning of the slogan they have advanced—'The wind from the east is prevailing over the wind from the west' —has become especially clear. . . . This slogan is nothing but an ideological and political expression of the hegemonic aspirations of the Chinese leadership.[10]

The long-range objective is the overthrow of the existing rule of 'world imperialism' and the establishment of world Communism. That goal had long been proclaimed by the Chinese Communists. When the Provisional (Chinese) Soviet Government was founded in 1931 in Kiangsi, it declared that its final objective was not only to overthrow imperialism in China but also 'to unite with all the oppressed peoples in the world to overthrow the rule of world imperialism.'[11]

STRATEGIES AND TACTICS

In order to achieve the above objectives, Peking's first strategy is to label the United States as the enemy of the whole world and to urge all the peoples to encircle and isolate it. 1946, Mao predicted that the U.S. 'reactionaries' would be 'opposed by the people of the whole world.'[12] In 1964, *Jen-min Jih-pao* proposed the formation of an international anti-American united front by all peoples and all forces in the world, because

> despite the different political beliefs among the peoples and the different social systems in various countries, there is not a single country or people in the world today which is not subjected to the aggression and threats of U.S. imperialism. . . . The socialist countries should vigorously support the anti-U.S. struggle in the intermediate zone and energetically expand the united front against U.S.

---

[10] Suslov's report to the February, 1964, plenum of the Central Committee of CPSU, *Pravda*, April 3, 1964, in *The Current Digest of the Soviet Press*, 16, No. 13 (April 22, 1964): 14–15.

[11] 'Declaration to the World' of the Provisional Government of the Chinese Soviet Republic, in *Red Flag Weekly* (Chinese Communist organ), November 27, 1931, reprinted in excerpts in Wang Chien-min, *Chung-kuo kung-ch'an-tang shih-kao* (*History of the Chinese Communist Party*), 2 (Taipei: 88 Hwa Nan Sheng Tsing, 1965): 289.

[12] *Ibid.*

imperialism so as to isolate it to the greatest extent and deal it the heaviest blows.[13]

In the worldwide united front against U.S. 'imperialism,' the vital area, Peking argues, is the 'third world,' which is the 'most vulnerable' region under imperialist rule. The anti-imperialist revolutionary struggle in Asia, Africa, and Latin America today is 'undermining the foundations of the rule of imperialism and colonialism,' and the whole cause of the 'international proletarian revolution hinges on the outcome of the revolutionary struggle of the peoples of these areas.'[14] As a global strategy against the United States, Lin Piao proposed in 1965 the encirclement of North America and Western Europe (world cities) with Asia, Africa, and Latin America (world rural areas).

In the course of the Sino-Soviet dispute, Peking's strategy of opposing U.S. 'imperialism' has been accompanied by its struggle against Soviet 'revisionism.' Peking argues that the United States and the Soviet Union are 'collaborating' in 'redividing the world.' In an effort to damage Soviet prestige throughout the world and erode its position in Communist areas, Peking has accused the Soviet Union of collusion with the United States on every major international issue—from the Cuban missile crisis to the invasion of Czechoslovakia. In attacking Moscow, Peking has also scornfully described Soviet-American relations as relations between two imperialist countries and angrily labeled the Soviet 'revisionists' as a group of 'social imperialists' and 'social fascists.'[15]

Events in the late 1950's in Asia, Africa, and Latin America had helped Peking and Moscow shape a new strategy of two revolutionary stages for those areas: the national-democratic revolution and the socialist revolution. Their relationship, as Lin Piao put it, is that

the national-democratic revolution is the necessary preparation for the socialist revolution, and the socialist revolution is the inevitable sequel to the national-democratic revolution. . . . The more thorough the national-democratic revolution the better the conditions for the socialist revolution.[16]

Peking generally went along with Moscow on the definition of 'national democracy' as laid down by the Moscow Statement of 1960.[17] However, it departs from the statement in two significant ways: First, it always uses the term 'national-democratic' to describe revolutions, movements, or united fronts and, unlike the U.S.S.R., does not use this term for states; second, unlike Moscow, it stresses that the national-democratic revolution should definitely be supported by the worker-peasant alliance and

---

[13] *Jen-min Jih-pao* (editorial), January 21, 1964; in *Peking Review*, No. 4 (January 24, 1964), p. 8.

[14] The Central Committee of the Communist Party of China, *A Proposal Concerning the General Line of the International Communist Movement* (Peking: Foreign Languages Press, 1963), p. 13.

[15] 'Total Bankruptcy of Soviet Modern Revisionism,' *Jen-min Jih-pao*, August 23, 1968; 'Deal Made at Bayonet Point,' *ibid.*, August 30, 1968; 'Diabolical Social-Imperialist Face of the Soviet Revisionist Renegade Clique,' *Peking Review*, No. 43, October 25, 1968, pp. 8–10.

[16] Lin Piao, 'Long Live the Victory of People's Wars,' *Peking Review*, No. 36, September 3, 1965, p. 25.

[17] Although it might have been different in meaning, Peking employed the term 'national and democratic' revolution as early as 1955 at the Bandung Conference. See Chou En-lai's supplementary speech at the Conference as reprinted in George McTurnan Kahin, *The Asian-African Conference* (Ithaca, N.Y.: Cornell University Press, 1956), p. 54. For the definition of a 'national-democratic' state as laid down by the Moscow Statement of 1960, see the Statement as reprinted in G. F. Hudson, *et al.*, *The Sino-Soviet Dispute* (New York: Praeger, 1961), pp. 194–95. For a good summary of views on 'national democracy,' see William T. Shinn, Jr., 'The "National Democratic State": A Communist Program for Less-Developed Areas,' *World Politics*, April, 1963, pp. 377–89.

the alliance of the working people with the bourgeoisie and the nonworking people.[18] The first approach adapts 'national democracy' to various conditions in a more flexible way, and the second advocates a definite strategy for the doctrine. On this ideological basis, Peking underlines the great significance of the national-democratic revolution in the 'third world.' At the height of the Sino-Soviet polemics in 1963–64, the Chinese pointed out to the Russians that the outcome of 'the national-democratic revolution in these areas' would decide the future of the whole cause of world revolution. During a tour of Africa in 1964, Chou En-lai praised many newly independent African countries and forecast a bright future for them if they would carry the national-democratic revolution through to the end. In 1968, two years after the Cultural Revolution had begun, Peking used several different terms for the 'national-democratic revolution.' In Latin America, Peking called it the 'national-democratic' revolution, movement, and united front; in Africa, the 'national liberation movement' and 'anti-imperialist and anticolonialist' struggle; in Asia, the 'national-democratic' revolution and united front, the 'patriotic struggle,' as well as the 'national liberation' war.[19] Thus, Peking's strategy has defined the national-democratic revolution in the 'third world' as (1) a people's revolution for national salvation, national liberation, independence, and democracy; (2) a nationwide united front or movement, with the worker-peasant alliance as its hard core; (3) a revolution that is antifeudal, anti-reactionary, antidictatorial, anti-'imperialist,' and anticolonialist in character; and (4) a long and tortuous struggle with either peaceful means or violent rebellion leading to socialist revolution.

Peking regards the establishment of a cordial and firm relationship with the third world and the 'zone' countries as an extremely important strategy that will enable China to isolate the United States, to exclude Soviet influence, and to introduce the Chinese 'model' to the underdeveloped areas. To promote the relationship, Peking has employed not only diplomacy, trade, and economic aid in conventional fashion, but also has used front organizations, cultural exchanges, military assistance, and party apparatus in revolutionary ways. Its tactics in operation combine hard with soft lines, fanaticism with caution, aggressiveness with flexibility, straightforwardness with retreat, and moderation with abrupt shifts of policy.

RELATIONS WITH THE THIRD WORLD

After his agreement with Nehru on the 'five principles of peaceful coexistence' in June, 1954, Chou En-lai said in New Dehli:

> All the nations of the world can peacefully coexist, no matter whether they are big or small, strong or weak, and no matter what kind of social system each of them has. The rights of the people of each nation to national independence and self-determination must be respected. . . . Revolution cannot be exported.[20]

The above statement, the 'five principles,' and the Geneva settlement on Indochina of 1954 effectively paved the way for Peking's participation in the Bandung Conference of 1955, which, in turn, served as a most helpful stepping stone for China's approach to the third world.

The Bandung Conference and its offshoots. The Bandung Conference marked the beginning of an era of the resurgence of Asia and Africa. Among the twenty-nine parti-

---

[18] Lin Piao, 'Long Live Victory of People's Wars,' p. 14.

[19] *Jen-min Jih-pao*, June 18, 1968, p. 1; June 19, p. 1; July 10, p. 1; July 12, p. 1; July 13, p. 6; July 31, p. 1; September 1, p. 6; September 5, p. 6; and October 16, 1970, p. 5; *Christian Science Monitor*, October 9, 1968, p. 6.

[20] As quoted in *Jen-min Jih-pao*'s editorial of July 2, 1954, in *The Survey of the China Mainland Press*, No. 841, July 3–4, 1954, p. 2.

cipants, fifteen were anti-Communist, twelve neutral, and two (China and North Vietnam) Communist.[21] A strong anti-Communist sentiment prevailed at the meeting, and Chou En-lai and his delegation faced a generally hostile situation. But through his artful diplomacy, Chou appeared to be reserved, moderate, and friendly and acted first as a listener, and later as a mediator between the disputing neutralists and anti-Communists. His statement that China came to Bandung to seek 'unity' and 'not to quarrel,' to seek the 'common ground' of anticolonialism and 'not to create divergence' was surprisingly impressive and overwhelmingly welcomed by the participants. He performed successfully as a man of good will, promoting friendship, mutual understanding, conciliation, peace, and unity. The delegates were convinced of his sincerity, and his success had far-reaching effects. It facilitated diplomatic recognition by Nepal (1955), Egypt, Syria, and Yemen (1956), paved the way for Chou's good will tour in South and Southeast Asia in 1956–57, and won China an entrée in Africa.

   The Afro-Asian People's Solidarity Council and conferences. In an attempt to influence the outcome of the meeting at Bandung, the Communist-led World Peace Council sponsored an unofficial and much less influential 'Asian Conference for the Relaxation of International Tension' in New Delhi on the eve of the Bandung gathering. Soviet delegates took part in the meeting, along with the Chinese. The meeting's only significant result was the resolution to establish an 'Asian Solidarity Committee,' which arranged to hold an 'Asian Writers' Conference' in New Delhi in December, 1956. Encouraged by the 'Bandung spirit' and the rise of Nasser, the Writers' Conference succeeded in urging the committee to expand from the area of Asia to Africa and to rename itself the 'Afro-Asian Solidarity Committee.'[22]

   As later events developed, the new committee (changed into the 'Afro-Asian People's Solidarity Council' in 1957) held its first 'Afro-Asian People's Solidarity Conference' in Cairo in December, 1957. It was attended by delegates from thirty-seven nations and regions, including China and the Soviet Union. The central theme was anticolonialism. It elected Anwar el-Sadat (now President of the United Arab Republic) as its president, and located its headquarters in Cairo. In its three succeeding meetings in (Guinea in April 1960, with seventy-two delegations; in Tanganyika in February, 1963, with sixty delegations; in Ghana in May, 1965, with seventy delegations), the Conference was characterized first by anticolonialism and later by the effect of the Sino-Soviet split rather than by Afro-Asian unity.

   The Tricontinental Conference. The Third Afro-Asian People's Solidarity Conference of 1963 in Moshi, Tanganyika, passed a resolution calling for a 'Tricontinental Conference.' When it was convened in January, 1966, in Havana, at a time when China had cut its trade with Cuba, the Conference was attended by eighty-two nationalist and Communist delegations from Asia, Africa, and Latin America. Among them, twenty-one came under the name of the 'Afro-Asian Solidarity Committee,' eighteen under the name of 'national committee' for the Havana conference (mostly from Latin America), and forty-three as revolutionary parties, fronts, or movements.[23] The

---

[21] The participants were Turkey, Pakistan, Iraq, the Philippines, Thailand, Japan, Ceylon, South Vietnam, Iran, Jordan, Lebanon, Libya, Gold Coast, Sudan, Liberia, India, Burma, Indonesia, Afghanistan, Laos, Cambodia, Nepal, Egypt, Saudi Arabia, Yemen, Syria, Ethiopia, Communist China, and North Vietnam.

[22] See Robert H. Bass, 'Communist Fronts: Their History and Function,' *Problems of Communism*, September–October, 1960, pp. 14–15. For general development of the organization, see Charles Neuhauser, *Third World Politics: China and the Afro-Asian People's Solidarity Organization* (Cambridge, Mass.: East Asia Research Center, Harvard University, 1968), pp. 3–73.

[23] U.S., Senate, 89th Congress Second Session, Subcommittee to Investigate the Administration of the Internal Security Act and Other Internal Security Laws of the Committee on the Judiciary, *The Tricontinental Conference of African, Asian, and Latin American Peoples* (Washington, D.C.: Government Printing Office, 1966), pp. 49–61.

main target was 'U.S. imperialism.' In the Russian-Chinese competition for influence at the conference, the Soviet delegation emerged as the undisputed controlling force, although several delegates endorsed Maoist violent ideology. Castro's siding with the Soviet Union contributed significantly to the failure of China.[24]

While these indirect offshoots of the Bandung Conference were gradually turning against China, plans for a second Bandung Conference also miscarried. The Soviet Union strongly wanted to participate, but China as strongly opposed it. In addition, several nations, like India and the U.A.R., wanted the conference to be one of non-aligned countries so as to exclude China, while China and several other nations favored an Afro-Asian conference of delegations sympathetic to China. Although these differences presaged a split among Afro-Asian nations, China nevertheless wanted the conference to convene on schedule. Peking had opposed its first postponement until November, 1965, but, by October, 1965, support for China's views had declined, and Peking proposed an indefinite postponement of the meeting so as to avoid an open split among Afro-Asian countries.[25] This was, for Peking, a diplomatic failure.

Thus, in one decade, China's triumph at the Bandung Conference had deteriorated to the point where it could no longer make effective use of similar meetings and organizations. Peking cannot rely on such forums any longer.

Diplomacy, aid, trade and voting at the United Nations. Whereas Communist China's diplomatic relations and aid to the third world are limited to Asia and Africa, Chinese trade is extended to Latin America as well. Peking's approach is generally based on the 'five principles of peaceful coexistence' of 1954 and the ten principles of the Bandung Conference. Chou En-lai's 'five principles' toward Africa in 1964 were basically a revision and development of the original principles,[26] while Ch'en Yi's assertion in May, 1964, that China was both an 'aligned and nonaligned' nation[27] was simply a tactical pronouncement to woo more friends from the growing number of nonaligned countries.

Peking's diplomatic relations with the third world can be divided into three phases: one of growth (1955–65), one of decline (1965–69), and one of re-establishment (1969 to the present). During the first phase, which was characterized by a strong and comparatively successful diplomatic drive, foreign aid began to be employed as an instrument of national policy, while trade was expanding from Asia to Africa and Latin America. From May, 1950, to July, 1955, no new nations recognized the People's Republic. Then, in August, 1955, four months after the Bandung Conference, Nepal recognized China. It was followed by Egypt and eighteen other Afro-Asian nations over a period of eight years (1956–64). Apparently, the Suez Crisis of 1956 and the wave of the African independence in the early 1960's provided China with a golden opportunity to enter the Middle East and Africa. France's recognition in early 1964 influenced the Congo (Brazzaville), the Central African Republic,

---

[24] *Ibid.*, pp. 1–38; *The New York Times*, January 4, 1966, p. 4; and *New York Herald Tribune*, January 9, 1966, p. 2.

[25] See the statement of the Chinese Communist Government and Chou En-lai's letter in *Peking Review*, No. 44, October 29, 1965, pp. 5–7.

[26] The five principles were (1) support to the African peoples in their struggle against imperialism and neocolonialism and in safeguarding their national independence; (2) support for their policy of peace, neutrality, and nonalignment; (3) support for their desire to achieve unity and solidarity; (4) support for the settlement of their disputes through peaceful consultation; and (5) respect for their sovereignty and opposition to encroachment and interference, *Peking Review*, No. 7, February 14, 1964, p. 7.

[27] On May 3, 1964, Ch'en Yi was reported to have said to a group of foreign journalists visiting Peking: 'Some countries call themselves aligned, but aren't. Some call themselves nonaligned but are nothing of the kind. Some are both aligned and nonaligned at the same time, China is one of these.' *The Economist* (London), May 9, 1964, p. 574.

Senegal,[28] and Dahomey to shift their ties from Taiwan to Peking. Meanwhile, Peking invited numerous foreign officials to visit China. Chou En-lai also made several extensive tours in Asia (1956–57, 1960) and Africa (1963–64, 1965). Many foreign observers even preferred the Chinese 'model' to that of Russia. Sukarno, for instance, told his countrymen in April, 1957, after he had visited China in 1956, that China was the best example of 'grand reconstruction' for Indonesia. Shortly after a tour of China in 1957, Prince Sihanouk participated in road-building in his own country so as to encourage his people to undertake the extensive manual labor that the reconstruction of the country required.[29] Among the elite of black Africa, 'there are numerous and conclusive proofs that Red China has [had] a fascinating effect' on their nation-building.[30] Many Latin American leftist intellectuals, too, 'feel closer to poor, struggling China than they do to rich, powerful, bourgeois Russia.'[31] To reinforce its drive, Peking also employed a racist line against the white peoples (including Russians) at the Afro-Asian Writers' Conference in Cairo in March, 1962; the Afro-Asian People's Solidarity Conference in Moshi, Tanganyika, in February, 1963;[32] and during the Congo (Kinshasa) rebellion in 1963–64.[33]

During the second phase (1965–69), Peking's influence declined. Beginning with the Burundi Government's suspension of diplomatic relations with Peking in January, 1965, because of suspected Chinese involvement in Burundi's internal affairs, which culminated in the assassination of Premier Pierre Ngendandumwe, Communist China suffered a series of setbacks. In early February, 1965, two African presidents (Hamani Diori of Niger and Maurice Yameogo of Upper Volta) warned their neighbors against Communist Chinese 'invasion' of Africa. President Felix Houphouet-Boigny of the Ivory Coast gave similar strong advice one year later.[34] Yet another loss of face involving the same kind of message was suffered directly by Chou En-lai in June, 1965, when President Julius K. Nyerere of Tanzania in a welcoming speech said:

> Neither our principles, our country, nor our freedom . . . are for sale. . . . From no quarter shall we accept direction or neocolonialism, and at no time shall we lower our guard against the subversion of our government or of our people.[35]

By the mid-1960's, African leaders had reached a stage of maturity in judging the value of Chinese Communist activities in Africa. In Malawi, Prime Minister Hastings Kamuzu Banda reported in mid-1965 that the Chinese had thrice offered him a gift of 6 million pounds for Malawi's recognition of Peking,[36] Banda refused it. In January, 1966, the Chinese Communists were expelled from the Central African Republic after Colonel Jean Bedel Bokassa took over the government. Dahomey shifted its ties from

---

[28] Senegal recognized both Peking and Taiwan in 1961, withdrew its recognition of Taiwan in 1964, but never established diplomatic ties with Peking.

[29] For Peking's policy toward Cambodia and Indochina, see King C. Chen, 'Peking's Strategy in Indochina,' *The Yale Review*, June, 1965, pp. 550–66.

[30] As quoted in Stefan C. Stolte, 'The Soviet Union, Communist China and the Under-developed Countries,' *Bulletin*, 7 (Munich, Germany: Institute for the Study of the U.S.S.R., August, 1960): 33.

[31] U.S., Senate, 89th Congress, First Session, Hearing before the Subcommittee to Investigate the Administration of the Internal Security Act and Other Internal Security Laws of the Committee on the Judiciary, *Red Chinese Infiltration into Latin America* (hereafter: *Red Chinese Infiltration*) (Washington, D.C.: Government Printing Office, 1965), p. 57.

[32] Brian Crozier, 'The Struggle for the Third World,' *International Affairs*, July, 1964, p. 443.

[33] See C. L. Sulzberger in *The New York Times*, February 5, 1965, p. 30.

[34] *The New York Times*, April 10, 1966, p. 17.

[35] *The New York Times*, June 5, 1965, p. 7.

[36] *The Christian Science Monitor*, August 6, 1965, p. 6.

Peking to Taiwan in April, and Ghana, under a new regime, suspended its relationship with China in October of the same year. In September, 1967, Peking withdrew its personnel and closed down its embassy in Tunis because of Habib Bourguiba's siding with 'American imperialism' and with 'Soviet revisionism.' Meanwhile, Kenya threatened to break with China in retaliation for Peking's 'gross interference' in Kenya's internal affairs.[37] In Indonesia, the Chinese have suffered a series of setbacks since the September, 1965, coup attempt; Sino-Indonesian diplomatic ties were suspended in October, 1967. In September of the same year, Sihanouk's angry order to withdraw Cambodian diplomats from Peking as a reaction to Chinese subversive propaganda in Phnompenh was reversed only after Chou En-lai had apologized to the prince. In October, 1967, Peking withdrew its aid mission from Burma as a result of Burma's riots against Chinese propaganda for the Cultural Revolution in Rangoon. In fact, during the Cultural Revolution, all the ambassadors, except Huang Hua in Cairo, were recalled to Peking for 'consultation.' Diplomatic activities reached a low ebb.

The damping down of the Cultural Revolution in 1969 marked the beginning of the third phase (1969–72), a period of re-establishment. Since May, 1969, Peking has refilled most of its ambassadorial posts and adopted a generally soft policy toward third world nations, except Cambodia and South Vietnam. For example, Peking's radio has softened its anti-India propaganda, and Mao, at a May Day reception in Peking in 1970, asked the Indian Charge d'Affaires, B. C. Mishra, to convey his good wishes to President V. V. Giri and Prime Minister Gandhi. Moreover, despite China's continuous support for Burmese rebels, Peking's NCNA reported on November 16, 1970, the arrival of Burma's new Ambassador, U Thein Maung, in the Chinese capital and hinted at the possibility of establishing a new Sino-Burmese relationship. In Africa, China is making steady progress on the Tan-Zam railroad project and has gained recognition of Equatorial Guinea and Ethiopia in October and November, 1970, respectively. Chile's recognition of Peking in January, 1971, is a new Chinese gain in Latin America. If Communist China could maintain its soft policy for two or three years, it would enter a new diplomatic era.

Aid. The use of foreign aid as an instrument of national policy is not unique to China. Without exception, China's aid is employed to help achieve its political goals. Although its first offer to four 'third world' countries (Cambodia, Egypt, Nepal, and Indonesia) came in 1956, Peking's general policy of economic aid and technical assistance was not pronounced until 1964, when Chou En-lai toured Africa.[38] In practice, Peking's aid program has several characteristics: no strings are attached; loans are interest-free or at low interest; light industrial and quick-result projects are chosen; and the hard-working Chinese technicians who are assigned abroad adopt the local standards of living.

It would be naive, however, to suppose that Communist China's foreign aid is

[37] *The New York Times*, November 4, 1966, p. 1; September 3, 1967, p. 15; September 24, 1967, p. 14; *Free China Weekly*, April 24, 1966, p. 1; *Central Daily News*, Taipei, September 28, 1967, p. 1; October 15, 1967, p. 4.

[38] The policy comprises eight principles: (1) the principle of equality and mutual benefit that regards aid as something mutual and helpful to economic cooperation; (2) respect for the sovereignty and independence of the recipient countries with no conditions attached; (3) the provision of interest-free or low-interest loans with a possibility of the extension for repayment; (4) the principle of self-reliance and independent economic development for the recipient countries; (5) the buildup of low-investment and quick-result projects; (6) the provision of the best quality equipment and material of China's manufacture; (7) the requirement of full ability to operate special technical assistance by the recipient nations; and (8) the same standard of living for Chinese technicians as that of their counterparts in the recipient country. See Chou En-lai's speech at Mogadishu mass rally, *Peking Review*, No. 7, February 14, 1964, p. 8.

Table 15-1—China's Aid to, and Diplomatic and Trade Relations with, the Third World, 1949–April 1972
(Trade and Aid as of January, 1970)

Nation	Recognition	Diplomatic Relations	Total Economic Aid (millions of U.S. dollars)	Trade	Present Changes in Diplomatic Relations
Burma	Dec., 1949	June, 1950	88 (1958, 1961)	yes	
India	Dec., 1949	April, 1950	109 (1964, 1967, 1968)	yes	
Pakistan	Jan., 1950	May, 1950	62.5 (1957–58, 1963–64)	yes	
Ceylon	Jan., 1950	Feb., 1957	28 (1965)	yes	
Afghanistan	Jan., 1950	Jan., 1950		yes	
Indonesia	April, 1950	June, 1950	105 (1956, 1958–59, 1964)	yes	suspended in Oct., 1967
Nepal	Aug., 1955	Aug., 1955	62 (1956, 1960, 1966, 1968)	n.a.	
UAR	May, 1956	May, 1956	106 (1956, 1964, 1967)	yes	
Syria	July, 1956	Aug., 1956	16 (1963)	yes	
Yemen	Aug., 1956	Aug., 1956	40 (1958, 1964)	yes	
Cambodia	July, 1958	July, 1958	50 (1956, 1960, 1965)	yes	severed in May, 1970. Peking recognized Sihanouk's exile regime
Iraq	July, 1958	Aug., 1958	—	yes	
Morocco	Oct., 1958	Nov., 1958	—	yes	
Sudan	Nov., 1958	Dec., 1958	25 (1960)	yes	
Guinea	Oct., 1959	Oct., 1959	40 (1961, 1964)	yes	
Ghana	July, 1960	July, 1960	23 (1961, 1964)	yes	suspended in Oct., 1966
Mali	Oct., 1960	Oct., 1960	22 (1963)	yes	
Somalia	Dec., 1960	Dec., 1960		yes	
Senegal	March, 1961			yes	no relations
Tanzania	Dec., 1961	Dec., 1961	53 (1963, 1966)	n.a.	
Laos	June, 1962	June, 1962	—	yes	
Algeria	July, 1962	July, 1962	50 (1963)	yes	
Uganda	Oct., 1962	Oct., 1962	15 (1965)	yes	
Kenya	Dec., 1963	Dec., 1963	18 (1964)	yes	
Burundi	Dec., 1963	Dec., 1963	—	yes	suspended in Jan., 1965
Tunisia	Jan., 1964	Jan., 1964		yes	suspended in Sept., 1967
Congo (Brazzaville)	Feb., 1964	Feb., 1964	25 (1964–65)	yes	
Central African Republic	Sept., 1964	Sept., 1964	(1964)		

			Taiwan	
Mauritania	July, 1965	4 (1967)	n.a.	
South Yemen	Jan., 1968	12 (1968)	yes	
Mauritius	March, 1968	—	n.a.	
Equatorial Guinea	Oct., 1970	—	n.a.	no relations
Ethiopia	Nov., 1970	—	yes	
Chile	Jan., 1971	—	yes	
Nigeria	Feb., 1971	—	yes	
Kuwait	March, 1971	—	yes	
Cameroon	April, 1971	—	yes	
Sierra Leone	July, 1971	—	yes	
Iran	Aug., 1971	—	yes	
Peru	Aug., 1971	—	yes	
Lebanon	Nov., 1971	—	yes	
Rwanda	Nov., 1971	—	n.a.	
Argentina	Feb., 1972	—	yes	
Malta	Feb., 1972	—	yes	
Mexico	Feb., 1972	—	yes	

Total $974.5 million

Note: In addition to these nations, there are twenty-nine other third world nations that do not recognize China but have trade relations with Peking as of December, 1970: Lebanon, Aden, Iran, Jordan, Kuwait, Malta, Nigeria, Libya, Malagasy, Niger, Rhodesia, Sierra Leone, Cameroon, Chad, Ivory Coast, Togo, Malaysia, Singapore, Argentina, Mexico, El Salvador, Venezuela, Uruguay, Guyana, Ecuador, Jamaica, Bolivia, Peru, and Honduras. Moreover, there are thirty-two countries that neither recognize nor trade with Communist China: Barbados, Botswana, Brazil, Colombia, Congo (Kinshasa), Costa Rica, Dominican Republic, Gabon, Gambia, Fiji, Tonga, Guatemala, Haiti, Lesotho, Liberia, Malawi, Nicaragua, Panama, Paraguay, the Philippines, Rwanda, Saudi Arabia, Swaziland, Thailand, Upper Volta, Cyprus, Western Samoa, Nauru, Maldive Islands, Trinidad-Tobago, South Korea, and South Vietnam. There are ninety-seven independent third world nations. Seven of them (Aden, Rhodesia, Nauru, Western Samoa, Tonga, South Vietnam, and South Korea) are not United Nations members.

Communist China agreed to assist in constructing both the Tan-Zam and Guinea-Mali railroads. Peking's aid credit for the 1,116-mile Tan-Zam railroad, which was under construction by November, 1970, is approximately $412 million. A loan of $43 million was granted to South Yemen in 1970 for the construction of a 380-mile road from Aden to the port of Mukalla. Neither figure is included in this table. Communist China has also agreed to finance the projected Guinea-Mali railroad, but the amount of aid is not yet known. According to the U.S. State Department, China's aid in 1970 totaled $709 million (not included in this table).

Sources: U.S. Department of State, Bureau of Intelligence and Research, *Communist States and Developing Countries: Aid and Trade in 1969*, July 9, 1970, pp. 1–3, 14–27; U.S. Department of State, Bureau of Intelligence and Research, *Diplomatic Relations of the Republic of China and the People's Republic of China*, June 13, 1968, pp. 1–6; U.S. Department of Commerce, International Trade Analysis Division, *Value Series: Free World—Imports and Exports* (1965–69), pp. 1–2; *Free China Weekly*, Taipei, April 24, 1966, p. 1, and May 1, 1966, p. 4; *Central Daily News*, Taipei, July 13, 1966, p. 1; *The New York Times*, 1966–1970; *Far Eastern Economic Review*, January 19, 1961, pp. 81, 84–87; Alexander Eckstein, *Communist China's Economic Growth and Foreign Trade* (New York: McGraw-Hill, 1966), pp. 280–85, 307.

really offered with no strings attached. Clear evidence is the suspension of Chinese aid of $84 million to Burma in November, 1967, after Burma's riots against the Chinese. The halt in Peking's aid to Indonesia under Suharto's government is another case in point. As Chou En-lai put it, 'You cannot separate economic relations from politics.' Thus, the claim of 'no conditions attached' refers only to the absence thus far of any requirement for military bases or military alliances; it does not include Peking's political line.

Between 1956 and 1969, Peking pledged $974.5 million in grants and loans to twenty-three third world nations. Table 15-1 summarizes China's aid program as well as its diplomatic and trade relations with the 'third world' countries.

The geographical distribution of the total aid—$572.5 million for Asia and $402 million for Africa—indicates the priority given to Asia. Among the recipients, Pakistan ($109 million), the UAR ($106 million), Indonesia ($105 million), and Burma ($84 million) have received the largest amounts, indicating Peking's assessment of those four nations as strategically the most important countries to China. As of December, 1970, four recipients (Burma, Indonesia, Ghana, and the Central African Republic) have either suspended or severed their aid programs or diplomatic relations with Peking. Apparently, Chinese aid to those countries has failed to buy friends.

It must be noted that of the $974.5 million in promised aid, only slightly more than $200 million had been disbursed by the end of 1969. The total aid promised went from $54.7 million in 1956 to $300 million in 1964, then dropped to $48 million in 1965, $56 million in 1968, and none at all in 1969. The shrinking of the figures is due to (1) the deterioration of diplomatic relations, as previously discussed; (2) the Cultural Revolution of 1966–69—which has prevented China from offering more aid; (3) the inability of some recipients to absorb and utilize loans for economic development effectively, such as Burma before 1967; (4) Peking's decision to restrict its concrete aid to those forces that could launch the 'proletarian revolution' in the third world;[39] (5) Taiwan's rivalry in Africa, which has offered an alternative to Peking's aid.

But Peking still tries to keep in good faith its pacts of economic and technical cooperation with Pakistan, Guinea, Nepal, Mali, Yemen, Somalia, Tanzania, and Zambia. Peking's technical assistance programs include textile factories, power plants, sugar refineries, paper mills, plywood mills, small steel mills, hydroelectric plants, bicycle tire plants, farming programs, radio stations, railways, highways, bridges, police training, and so forth. In 1968, for instance, Peking kept its (Chinese-built) highway maintenance team in Nepal. Several hundred Chinese engineers and laborers are working in Yemen, building textile mills and highways and seeking water sources. By November, 1970, 5,000 Chinese technicians and workers had already begun construction in Tanzania of the 1,116-mile Tan-Zam railroad. This is China's largest single aid project. In addition, Peking signed in May, 1968, a pact with Guinea and Mali, agreeing to build a railway between those two nations.[40] As of December, 1970, no further action had been taken on that railroad project.

Trade. Less spectacular but, in the long run, of greater significance than aid is Peking's trade with the third world. Because foreign trade is dealt with in another chapter of this volume, only a brief account is given here. In 1956, China's trade with eight Asian nations and regions (excluding Japan, with which trade amounted to $151 million) totaled $469.2 million. In 1969, trade with 39 third world nations and

---

[39] *The New York Times*, April 26, 1966, p. 5; *Christian Science Monitor*, November 23, 1968, p. 14.

[40] *Jen-min Jih-pao*, August 19, 1968, p. 5, and October 30, 1970, p. 5; *Peking Review*, No. 36, September 6, 1968, pp. 27–28; *The New York Times*, February 1, 1968, p. 5; May 25, 1968, p. 2; May 30, 1968, p. 3; October 27, 1970, p. 2; and November 16, 1970, p. 18; *Christian Science Monitor*, February 25, 1970, p. 2; August 22, 1970, pp. 1–2.

regions totaled $1,093.9 million; of that amount, $134.1 million was with the Middle East, $105.4 million with Africa (not including South Africa), $784.1 million with the Far East (not including $624 million in trade with Japan), and $8.4 million with Latin America.[41] Although the figures declined slightly after 1965 (1965: $1,098 million; 1967: $1,031 million; 1969: $1,093 million), Peking's trade with the third world as of December, 1969, was gradually recovering from losses during the Cultural Revolution.

Voting in the United Nations. Communist China had repeatedly charged that the United Nations was under the 'control and manipulation of the imperialist countries, headed by the United States.'[42] And Ch'en Yi declared in the fall of 1965 that Communist China was not interested in such a United Nations organization. But, despite Peking's efforts in cultivating friendship through diplomatic, aid, and trade relations, it is significant to ascertain the degree of third world support for Peking in the world organization. Table 15–2 gives a clear indication.

The trend as shown in Table 15–2 is self-explanatory. (1) The total third world membership has increased since 1955 from thirty-six nations (60 per cent) to ninety nations (70.85 per cent) of the world body; should all the third world member nations act unanimously, they could easily decide the China issue. (2) Third world member nations that support Peking increased from 5 per cent (three nations) in 1955 to 23.62 per cent (thirty nations) in 1970, while those for Taiwan dropped from 46.7 per cent (twenty-eight nations) to 30.70 per cent (but thirty-nine nations). (3) If Communist China could maintain friendly relations with foreign countries for two years, the increasing third world nations' support (as well as that of other nations) for Peking would inevitably place China in a favorable position in the United Nations.

Table 15–2—Third World Nations' Support of Peking's Seating
in the United Nations, 1955–70

Year		For Peking, Vote	%	For Taiwan, Vote	%	Abstain/Absent, Vote	%	Total, Vote	%
1955	U.N. general	12	20.0	42	70.0	6	10.0	60	100.0
	Third world	3	05.0	28	46.7	5	08.3	36	60.0
1959	U.N. general	29	35.37	44	53.66	9	10.97	82	100.0
	Third world	14	17.1	28	34.1	5	06.1	47	57.3
1962	U.N. general	42	38.2	56	50.9	12	10.9	110	100.0
	Third world	25	22.7	41	37.3	7	06.3	73	66.3
1965	U.N. general	47	40.2	47	40.2	23	19.6	117	100.0
	Third world	29	24.78	32	27.35	19	16.24	80	68.37
1968	U.N. general	44	34.92	58	46.03	24	19.05	126	100.0
	Third World	26	20.63	44	34.9	19	15.07	89	70.6
1970	U.N. general	51	40.16	49	39.58	27	21.26	127	100.0
	Third world	30	23.62	39	30.70	21	16.53	90	70.85

Note: Figures given are percentages of total vote. For the ninety third world nations in the United Nations, see Table 15–1 and its note.

Sources: *Yearbook of the United Nations* (New York: Columbia University Press, in cooperation with the United Nations, 1955–66); *The New York Times*, 1959–70.

[41] U.S., Department of Commerce, International Trade Analysis Division, *Value Series: Free World—Imports and Exports* (1965–69), pp. 1–2.
[42] *Jen-min Jih-pao* (editorial), December 18, 1963, p. 1.

Cultural exchanges and people's diplomacy. One of the most effective instruments of Communist China's foreign relations is the nongovernmental cultural exchange program—'people's diplomacy.' Peking's operation of the program has been extremely successful, particularly with those nations and regions with which it has no diplomatic ties. Through front organizations and professional associations, Peking has actually built up its nonofficial relations not only with the third world, but also with almost all major capitalist nations. Such cultural diplomacy is effective for three basic reasons. (1) It covers a broad spectrum that formal diplomatic or Party relations may not cover in countries that have diplomatic ties with Peking. (2) It substitutes for formal diplomacy or Party connections in countries that have no such ties with China. (3) It promotes mutual understanding and friendship between peoples much more successfully than can be done through formal and rigid governmental channels.

Friendship associations and cultural exchanges. In addition to Moscow-sponsored international front organizations, such as the World Peace Council and the World Federation of Trade Unions, Communist China has, since 1952, formed thirteen 'Friendship Associations' with the third world.[43] Numerous similar associations or societies established in various countries serve as their counterparts (for instance, there are twelve such societies in Latin America). Moreover, Communist China has founded, as a result of the Sino-Soviet dispute, associations of Afro-Asian journalists, writers, lawyers, and women, along with a Youth Solidarity Association and a Movie Association, in opposition to their respective rival international organizations that are primarily under Soviet control. Their exchange programs include meetings, visits of personnel in various professions, cultural missions, opera companies, song and dance troupes, acrobatic teams, exhibitions, fairs, and so forth. In the past fifteen years, the trend of mutual visits and tours ran on a similar pattern as that of diplomatic relations—a rapid increase in the first ten years (1956–65), a drastic decline during the Cultural Revolution, and a resumption since 1970. To make it easier to understand, a table of actual delegation exchanges (both governmental and nongovernmental) with the third world and other areas is given in Table 15–3.

Table 15–3—Delegation Exchanges* Between Communist China
and the Third World, 1958–70
(numbers of delegations)

Year	Third World		Other Areas		Total		
	To China	From China	To China	From China	To China	From China	Grand Total
1958	142	32	212	108	354	140	494
1960	264	74	391	133	655	207	862
1963	284	91	336	156	620	247	867
1965	394	230	465	233	859	463	1,322
1967	106	21	59	19	165	40	205
1968	29	13	26	6	55	19	74
1969	19	5	32	10	51	15	66
1970	45	23	83	30	128	53	181

* Including trade and aid missions.
Sources: *Jen-min Jih-pao* and Radio Peking, 1958, 1960, 1963, 1965, and 1967–70.

[43] The Sino-Burmese (1952), Sino-Indian (1952), Sino-Indonesian (1952), Sino-Pakistani (1956), Sino-Nepal (1956), Sino-United Arab Republic (1958), Sino-Iraqi (1958), Sino-Cambodian (1958), Sino-Latin American (1960), Sino-African (1960), Sino-Ceylon (1962), Sino-Laotian (1963), and Sino-Afghan (1964) friendship associations.

Under the effects of the Cultural Revolution, the total number of delegations exchanged dropped drastically from 1,322 (1965) to 66 (1969). Equally striking is the fact that, when the exchange program reached its height in 1965, an average of more than two delegations would arrive in mainland China every day. The result of the exchanges has been generally favorable to Peking, as a few outstanding examples will demonstrate. In 1956, Chinese cultural missions visited Egypt, Sudan, Morocco, Tunisia, and Ethiopia, stirring up enthusiasn for similar exchanges of various kinds from those countries. In 1957 and 1958, at the Casablanca and Tunis fairs, Peking gave North Africans a good impression of its products and industrial techniques as an example of the achievement possible for developing countries. In 1961, Liu Ch'ang-sheng, president of the Sino-African Friendship Association, visited eight African states: Guinea, Mali, Ghana, Niger, Upper Volta, Senegal, Togo, and Dahomey. His delegation helped strengthen relations and paved the way for later establishment of diplomatic ties with Senegal and Dahomey. Sino-Mali relations 'have prospered as a result of extensive interchanges' of cultural missions and exhibitions.[44] This approach, undoubtedly, was particularly attractive to the African youth.

In Asia, the exchanges achieved even greater success. Numerous delegates admired and learned from China as a developmental model. In recent years, Pakistani visitors regarded a trip to China as not only a way to promote mutual understanding and friendship but also 'a pilgrimage of discoveries' of what was successful and promising in that country.[45]

To Latin America, where Peking maintains limited diplomatic relationships, the cultural exchanges are of extreme importance. Peking's approach is first to send in New China News Agency correspondents, who engage in various activities. Through mutual arrangements, Peking has been able to send in various delegations, ranging from trade missions (one, in 1961, was led by Nan Han-ch'en, governor of the Bank of China and chairman of the Commission for the Promotion of International Trade) to acrobatic teams. A great number of Latin American delegations have been invited to visit China. The visitors in general have been former government officials, legislators, Communist Party leaders, workers, intellectuals, newsmen, artists, students, and leaders of labor unions. Some of those who had a chance to talk with Mao Tse-tung were particularly impressed and remarked that, in Moscow, they 'had never had the honor of being received even by the most obscure member of the Central Committee.'[46]

Radio broadcasts. Apart from countless propaganda materials (pamphlets, periodicals, books, fliers, and so forth) that were exported along with the cultural exchanges, Peking has also made a massive effort in radio broadcasting. It hires young people from third world nations to work for Radio Peking and increases broadcasting hours on a yearly basis. Prior to 1957, for instance, there were no Spanish or Portuguese radio broadcasts from Peking to Latin America. Beginning with seven hours weekly in December, 1957, a Spanish-speaking program has increased to thirty-five hours in December, 1969 (the Voice of America broadcasts eighty-five and a half hours), railing at U.S. imperialism, urging violent revolution, and sniping at the Soviet Union.[47] To Asia and Africa, according to the British Broadcasting Corporation's 1964 report, Soviet and Chinese broadcasts took the lead over those of the United States and Britain.[48]

---

[44] Colin Legum, 'Africa and China: Symbolism and Substance,' in A. M. Halpern, ed., *Policies Toward China: Views from Six Continents* (New York: McGraw-Hill, 1965), p. 421.

[45] Dai Shen-yu, 'Peking and the Third World,' *Current History*, September, 1965, p. 144.

[46] Ernst Halperin, 'Peking and the Latin American Communists,' *China Quarterly*, No. 29, January–March, 1967, p. 119.

[47] U.S., Senate subcommittee hearing (1965), *Red Chinese Infiltration*, p. 57; Radio Peking, 1969.

[48] *The New York Times*, November 24, 1965, p. 65.

REVOLUTIONARY ACTIVITIES AND PARTY ALIGNMENT

It is no longer a secret that Peking has engaged in revolutionary activities to help local opposition forces overthrow existing governments in the 'third world.' Its involvement has been primarily with armed struggle on the Chinese model, and its commitment has been aggressive and adamant regardless of its diplomatic victories or setbacks.

Revolutionary bases and wars of national liberation. In order to engage effectively in revolutionary activities, China has employed Mao's 'revolutionary base' strategy. In Asia, Peking has tried to build up bases mainly in Vietnam and Indonesia. Its support to North Vietnam is crucial, because Vietnam is a vital base for revolution in the Southeast Asian continent, the focus of the Chinese policy of opposing the United States and the Soviet Union, a testing ground for the Chinese model of the 'national liberation war,' and a highly important factor in China's efforts to swing the third world to the Chinese side. For all those reasons, China must fully support, as it has, the Vietnamese Communists until victory. In Indonesia, Peking's supply in 1965 of 100,000 small arms to the Indonesian Communist Party (PKI) was intended to further Sukarno's 'grand design' of outflanking the United States in Asia by forming a Pyongyang-Peking-Hanoi-Phnompenh-Djakarta axis. Since the failure of its 1965 coup, the PKI has issued documents through Chinese news media, attributing its failure in the establishment of an Indonesian Communist regime to its former 're-visionist' policy and calling for a program of armed struggle and 'people's war' in conformity with Mao's theory.[49] In an editorial in the July, 1967, issue, *Red Flag*, theoretical journal of the CCP, 'firmly supports' the PKI in leading the Indonesian people to 'overthrow' the 'fascist' regime of Generals Suharto and Nasution. In Burma, two months after the break of Sino-Burmese friendship in June, 1967, the Central Committee of the CCP formally endorsed, and promised full support to, the White Flag Communists' proclamation of the formation of a National Democratic United Front to 'overthrow' the 'reactionary' and 'fascist' Ne Win government.[50] In fact, several hundred Chinese military personnel in civilian clothes had infiltrated into upper Burma in late 1967 to assist the insurgent Kachin Independence Army, which has established links with Shan insurgents to the west, the White Flag Communists to the south, and Karen insurgents in the Irrawaddy River delta. Many Kachins, Shans, Karens, and White Flag Communists have been trained in China and sent back to Burma with arms and ammunition as insurgent cadres to train other insurgents at home. In 1970, the rebels, using China as a sanctuary, fought battles against the government army in northeastern Burma, inflicting heavy casualties on the government side.[51] Similarly, the Chinese Communists have continued their support to the Malay and Thai Communist armed struggles as well as the Palestinian Liberation Movement, despite their various setbacks.[52] The Cambodian crisis in the spring of 1970 brought Peking a good opportunity to back up substantially the new, coordinated efforts of the armed revolution in Indochina. So influential was Peking's violent strategy in the area that even Moscow found it necessary to issue an unusual warning to the Indochinese Communists and national liberation revolutionists that

---

[49] Statement (August 17, 1966) and Self-Criticism (September 1966) of the Politburo of the Central Committee of the PKI, in *Red Flag*, No. 11, July 9, 1967, pp. 18–35; *Jen-min Jih-pao*, July 19, 1968, p. 3.

[50] *Peking Review*, No. 28, July 7, 1967, pp. 21–22, No. 34, August 18, 1967, p. 5.

[51] *The New York Times*, January 18, 1968, p. 7; July 25, 1969, p. 4; August 31, 1970, pp. 1 and 5; *Christian Science Monitor*, July 3, 1968, pp. 1 and 3.

[52] *Jen-min Jih-pao*, June 19, 1968, p. 1; July 16, 1968, p. 6; July 31, 1968, p. 6; September 28, 1970, p. 5; *The New York Times*, October 2, 1968, p. 3; January 26, 1969, p. 17.

they not let Peking dictate their actions, or else they would be led to 'defeat.'[53] As of early 1971, however, the Indochinese rebels seemed to be gaining, particularly in Cambodia.

In Africa, Peking has tried to establish bases in Egypt, Algeria, Somalia, Mali, Guinea, Burundi, Ghana, the Congo (Kinshasa), and Tanzania, but with little success. A major reason is the absence of an active Communist Party that could effectively direct revolution in Africa. Peking's revolutionary engagement, nevertheless, takes two basic forms: training and weapon supplies. Since 1960, Peking has trained several hundred leftist Africans from the Congo (Kinshasa), Cameroon, Ghana, Guinea, South Africa, Mozambique and Tanzania. The main training center is the Military Academy in Nanking. The Chinese Embassy in Bujumbura, Burundi, and the Obenemase Training Camp near Konogo, Ghana, also served as temporary training centers before 1966. Their main programs were Mao's theory and tactics and techniques of guerrilla warfare. Numerous propaganda materials were made available to the trainees and rebels.[54]

In supplying weapons, Peking's heaviest involvement was the Congo rebellion in 1963–64. Communist Chinese military material was shipped through Tanzania to Bujumbura and then across the Ruzizi River to the rebels in eastern Congo (Kinshasa), headed by Gaston Soumialot, Christophe Gbenye, and Pierre Mulele.[55] The Chinese Embassy in Bujumbura served virtually as the center to direct the shipments and advise the rebels, who also had a liaison office in the same city. At a critical point in late 1964, Peking pledged 'all possible measures' to help the Congolese rebels, and Liu Shao-ch'i even predicted in late September, 1964, the defeat of the Kasavubu regime. The turning point was the suppression of the rebels by the white mercenaries in late 1964, followed by Burundi's suspension of Chinese diplomatic ties in January, 1965. At the training center in Ghana, Peking also supplied weapons for instruction and for equipping graduated cadres. In Mozambique, rebels with limited Chinese-supplied arms are recently reported to have followed closely Mao's theory in armed struggle against the present government.[56]

In Latin America, Peking's revolutionary activities were limited by its lack of diplomatic relations. The only 'base' China has been able to establish is in Cuba, but a decline of the Sino-Cuban relationship from 1966 to 1970 because of Cuba's pro-Soviet stand and Peking's drastic cut of Sino-Cuban trade in late 1965, has considerably blunted the edge of Peking's subversive drive in the area. Prior to 1965, Peking generally made gains in Latin America, except in Brazil, where the government expelled NCNA 'correspondents' in 1964. It was able to deliver some small arms to Cuba, increase its personnel in that country from 216 in 1959 to 9,000 in early 1965, and distribute propaganda material advocating violent revolution throughout the continent. The Chinese 'specialists' trained Castro's militia in guerrilla theory and techniques; many subversive agents from other parts of Latin America came as

---

[53] M. Ukraintsev, 'Asia and the Peking Empire-Builders,' *New Times* (Moscow), No. 23, June 9, 1970, p. 15.

[54] *Free China Weekly* (Taipei), July 5, 1964, p. 2; October 25, 1964, p. 4; May 2, 1965, p. 4; May 1, 1966, p. 4; *The New York Times*, August 5, 1964, pp. 1, 6; September 8, 1964, pp. 1, 5; October 10, 1968, p. 3; *New York Herald Tribune*, August 5, 1964, p. 2; August 9, 1964, p. 2, August 10, 1964, p. 2; and Richard Lowenthal, 'China,' in Zbigniew Brzezinski, ed., *Africa and the Communist World* (Stanford, Calif.: Stanford University Press, 1963), p. 192.

[55] Pierre Mulele, Parliament member and Minister of Education in Patrice Lumumba's Cabinet, was a Chinese-trained rebel leader. He was executed in Kinshasa on October 9, 1968.

[56] NCNA, November 27, 1964; *Jen-min Jih-pao*, July 31, 1968, p. 6; September 5, 1968, p. 6; *Free China Weekly* (Taipei), March 7, 1965, p. 1; May 1, 1966, p. 4; *The New York Times*, June 24, 1964, p. 6; June 25, 1964, p. 11; November 18, 1964, p. 3; November 27, 1964, p. 1; and *New York Herald Tribune*, January 17, 1965, p. 5.

'students' to join the training programs and have returned to their countries of origin. One such training center was at a base at San Julian.[57] Since 1965, the deteriorating Sino-Cuban relations and the Sino-Soviet conflict have affected Latin American leftists' attitudes toward Peking. However, the Maoist theory of armed revolution is still accepted by many of them as expressed at the Tricontinental Conference in January, 1966.[58] Thus, Peking's involvement continues. In May, 1967, for instance, Peking praised the Dominican Communists for the significant shift of their revolutionary base from urban to rural areas and for their successful establishment of worker-peasant guerrilla forces.[59] Communist China, according to the Mexican Government's formal announcement in July, 1967, had financed a foiled plot (with thirteen important Communists arrested) of the Mexican Communists to establish a 'popular Socialist' regime through armed rebellion. Chinese support was supplied through the Mexican branch of NCNA at the rate of $1,680 a month.[60] Conceivably, that commitment was only one of many such Chinese plans in Latin America.

Alignment of Communist Parties. In view of the Sino-Soviet conflict, a brief look at the alignment of the Communist Parties of the third world will be helpful (see Table 15-4). While those Parties basically share the characteristics of small membership, low ideological level, and loose discipline, they generally recognize that Peking's militant revolutionary strategy for quick accession to power offers them more advantages than does Moscow's doctrine of gradualism through economic competition. However, after the Sino-Soviet conflict became public, many Parties split or took a neutral position.

Table 15-4—Attitudes of the Communist Parties of the Third World Toward the Sino-Soviet Conflict as of Late 1970

Country	Membership	Pro-Soviet	Pro-Chinese	Split	Neutral	Unknown
ASIA						
Afghanistan	400	X				
Burma	5,000			X		
Cambodia	400					X
Ceylon	2,300		X			
India	125,000		X			
Indonesia	150,000		X			
Laos	2,000		X			
Malaysia	2,000		X			
Nepal	9,000			X		
Pakistan	1,500				X	
Philippines	2,000				X	
Singapore	200		X			
South Vietnam	30,000		X			
Thailand	1,450		X			
MIDDLE EAST						
Iran	500	X				
Iraq	2,000	X				
Jordan	700	X				
Lebanon	1,500			X		
Syria	3,000			X		

[57] U.S. Senate subcommittee hearing (1965), *Red Chinese Infiltration*, pp. 49–53.
[58] U.S. Senate subcommittee hearing (1966), *Tricontinental Conference*, p. 2.
[59] NCNA, May 12, 1967.
[60] *The New York Times*, July 21, 1967, p. 9.

Country	Membership	Pro-Soviet	Pro-Chinese	Split	Neutral	Unknown
AFRICA						
Algeria	1,000	X				
Egypt (U.A.R.)	1,000			X		
Lesotho	100					X
Malagasy Republic	100	X				
Morocco	500				X	
Nigeria	1,000	X				
Sudan	8,000	X				
Tunisia	200	X				
LATIN AMERICA						
Argentina	55,000	X				
Bolivia	6,000			X		
Brazil	16,000			X		
Chile	45,000	X				
Colombia	9,000			X		
Costa Rica	600	X				
Dominican Republic	1,300			X		
Ecuador	1,600			X		
El Salvador	200	X				
Guatemala	750	X				
Haiti	(very small)	X				
Honduras	300	X				
Mexico	5,250			X		
Nicaragua	200	X				
Panama	250	X				
Paraquay	5,000			X		
Peru	5,000			X		
Uruguay	20,000	X				
Venezuela	8,000	X				
		20	6	15	3	2

Note: Except in the cases of India, Thailand, and Argentina, figures for Party membership are estimated. Countries that have individual Communists without organized Communist Parties are not included.

Sources: U.S., Department of State, Bureau of Intelligence and Research, *World Strength of the Communist Party Organizations* (1970 edition); *Jen-min Jih-pao*, 1968–70; *The New York Times*, 1965–70.

Table 15-4 seems to warrant certain tentative conclusions. First, of the forty-six Communist Parties on the list, only six are pro-Chinese, while twenty are pro-Soviet. Second, all six supporters of Peking are from Asia. While this shows the significance of the geographical factor in alignment, it also indicates that Communist China, as the strongest Communist power in Asia, is unable even to rally half of the other Communist Parties from the same area to its support. Third, whereas the Maoist theory of armed revolution has attracted many third world Communists, the majority of the Parties in the Middle East, Africa, and Latin America still adhere ostensibly to the Soviet doctrine of 'peaceful competition.' In the case of Latin America, this situation is of great practical significance. Fidel Castro has time and again denounced Latin American Communists for their refusal to embrace armed struggle to promote revolution.[61] Finally, the fifteen split parties show partial support of Peking, while three parties are neutral, as are the three in power in North Korea, North Vietnam,

[61] *The New York Times*, July 2, 1968, p. 1.

and Cuba. Together they present an unpleasant and even embarrassing posture for Communist China. Undoubtedly, Peking is far less happy with North Korea and North Vietnam than with Cuba and the other three neutral parties, because of its centuries-old historical relations with the two Asian countries and its decisive and generous assistance to them since 1950. Ironically enough, the sophistication and independence of these three small Communist nations is at least in part a result of the development of China's own defiant and independent action against the Soviet Union.

RELATIONS WITH 'SECOND INTERMEDIATE ZONE' NATIONS

In Chinese Communist terminology, the second 'intermediate zone' covers nations in Western Europe, Oceania, and other parts of the world, except the Communist countries, the United States, and the third world. While a complete study of the 'intermediate' nations is beyond the scope of this chapter, the following discussion of five arbitrarily selected countries (Britain, France, West Germany, Australia, and Canada), will epitomize China's relationship with the 'zone' as a whole.

Acting within the framework of its global strategy of opposing the American 'imperialists,' Communist China has directed its relations with those five capitalist countries with the aims of first driving a wedge between them and the United States and then winning them over to the Peking-centered anti-American international united front. However, because the countries and the United States have many interests in common, Peking's relations with them have consisted of limited diplomacy and trade, supplemented by some cultural exchanges and Party activities. It has been involved in no significant revolutionary engagements thus far. President Nixon's visit to China in February, 1972, has not significantly changed Peking's relations with those countries.

DIPLOMACY

The United Kingdom. Britain recognized the People's Republic of China in January, 1950, and opened up the office of the chargé d'affaires in June, 1954. London and Peking have not exchanged ambassadors although agreement on such exchange was reached in early 1972. One of the chief reasons was British dealings with Taiwan. The British Government kept a consulate in Taipei and has never ruled out the possibility that Taiwan might become an independent non-Communist entity. Peking regarded the British decision as improper and had rejected British requests for the exchange of ambassadors. In the United Nations, Britain supported proposals for the admission of Communist China. British enthusiasm, however, had worn thin because of the Sino-Indian border conflicts, Chinese diplomats' clashes with the police in London in 1967, and the Red Guard harassment (to the extent of setting the British mission aflame) of British diplomats in Peking. On the nongovernmental level, various delegations have been exchanged since 1950, ranging from goodwill delegations led by Liu Ning-i (1950) and Lord Clement Attlee (1954) to a Chinese theater company (1950) and a British Royal Society mission (1962). Members of Parliament and prominent individuals (including former Prime Minister Harold Wilson and Field Marshal Bernard Law Montgomery) were invited to visit China; newsmen from both sides have been permitted to visit or stay. Such exchanges, nevertheless, did not create as much excitement as those between China and several third world nations, such as Pakistan, Tanzania, Indonesia (until late 1965), and Cambodia (until spring, 1970). China wants to exploit Anglo-American differences on many issues, but there has been little significant opening. Even the disturbance of 1967 in Hong Kong, when the Cultural Revolution spilled over into the British colony, was skillfully and firmly headed off by the local British authorities.

France. Prior to 1964, Peking regarded France as an imperialist and colonialist power. When General de Gaulle offered his plan for a settlement of the Algerian problem in 1959, the Chinese Communists denounced it as 'nothing but a sugar-coated poison pill' and 'a trick.'[62] However, when de Gaulle recognized Peking in early 1964, he was described as a friend of world peace. As Chou En-lai commented, the recognition was 'not only in the interests of the Chinese and French peoples, but also helpful to . . . the realization of peaceful coexistence between countries with different social systems, and the cause of world peace.'[63]

Many Frenchmen have sought the role of bridge-builder between Communist China (and Russia) and the United States. Peking really hopes, however, that France will serve as a bridge between Communist China and capitalist countries other than the United States and be definitely independent from the 'domination' of the United States. This observation is supported by a *Jen-min Jih-pao* editorial:

> As a great power in the capitalist world, France will never let herself be placed under American tutelage. . . . What France wants at present is to get rid of American hegemony and to seize for herself an equal part in the direction of the Western world.[64]

There are several issues on which Peking would like to have the cooperation of France: French influence on former French Africa, France's refusal to subscribe to the partial test ban treaty, de Gaulle's disapproval of United States Vietnam policy, promotion of an increasingly powerful role for both France and China in world affairs, and trade between the two countries. General de Gaulle's 'disappointment' with his relations with the United States, the Soviet Union, and Britain motivated him to suggest a 'European Europe' and an unconventional Europe 'from the Atlantic to the Urals' in order to exclude American and limit Soviet influence on that continent. His goal was to restore France's glorious past. To that end, he defied the United States and befriended China. He hoped that China would eventually become a serious threat to Moscow that would lead one day to the partition of the U.S.S.R. A territorially split Soviet Union would play a weaker role in Europe. Such, according to one observer, was de Gaulle's fascinating global strategy.[65] Therefore, when André Malraux, the French Minister of Culture, was able to have a three-hour discussion with Mao Tse-tung in China in August, 1965, de Gaulle thought there was a good chance to realize his dream.[66] But there was no further development afterward. Instead, the Red Guards' attacks in early 1967 on Robert Richard, a French Embassy official in Peking, constituted a serious embarrassment to de Gaulle's diplomacy. In May, 1968, Peking's 'firm' support for the 'revolutionary actions by the French workers and students and the broad masses' against the 'imperialist and reactionary' de Gaulle government[67] must have been another source of unhappiness for the General.

The Pompidou government has inherited de Gaulle's China policy without his ambitious global strategy. In July, 1970, it sent a special envoy, Planning Minister André Bettencourt, to visit Mao in Peking in order to promote trade and broaden cultural exchanges. Ironically, the French Government is facing an annoying problem of French Maoist riots, which in May, 1970, led to 937 arrests and approximately

---

[62] NCNA, October 17, November 12, November 30, 1959.
[63] *Peking Review*, No. 10, March 6, 1964, p. 21.
[64] *Jen-min Jih-pao* (editorial), March 7, 1964, p. 1.
[65] C. L. Sulzberger, 'De Gaulle, Mao and Russia,' *The New York Times*, August 22, 1965, p. 10 E.
[66] For Malraux's interview with Mao, see André Malraux, *Anti-Memoirs*. Translated by Terence Kilmartin. (New York: Holt, Rinehart and Winston, 1968), pp. 356–77.
[67] *Jen-min Jih-pao* (editorial), May 27, 1968, p. 1.

$200,000 in damage in Paris.[68] The number of the Maoists is growing. Admiring the Chinese revolution but maintaining no connection with Peking, they are determined to use violence to change their social system.

Sino-French cultural exchanges began before French recognition. Newsmen, writers, students, opera singers, artists, musicians, businessmen, legislators, and others have paid reciprocal visits. The French heard much of the Chinese high opinion of French art and literature; the Chinese took note of the thunderous French applause for the Peking opera. In 1965, the Chinese pavilion at the Paris Fair and a French exhibition in Peking both received favorable public comments from the host countries. After three years' of diplomatic isolation during the Cultural Revolution, the exchange program gradually resumed. In October–November, 1970, Couvé de Murville, former French Foreign Minister, paid a three-week visit to China. He was impressed by what he saw and came out with a confirmed conviction that relations with Peking were essential.

West Germany. Peking does not have diplomatic relations with West Germany or Australia. To West Germany, recognition is out of the question as long as Peking maintains full diplomatic relations with East Germany. Meanwhile, West Germany is eager to strengthen its alliance with the United States and has no intention of adopting a China policy that runs counter to Washington. Since the Sino-Soviet dispute, China has suffered serious attacks from East Germany at various international Communist conferences, but they have been neither bitter nor strong enough to prompt Peking to shift its ties from East Berlin to Bonn. The Bonn-Moscow and Bonn-Warsaw rapprochements in 1970 have not yet led to an attempt to bridge the gulf between Bonn and Peking.

Australia. Prior to the Korean War, Australia was about to establish diplomatic relations with Peking. Since then, it has instead cooperated with the United States in containing Communist China. Peking regards Australia as a 'lackey' of American 'imperialists' because of Australian participation in the ANZUS pact and, especially, the Vietnam war. Occasional proposals of individuals for a revision of the non-recognition policy and the impact of French recognition have not changed Australian policy toward China. Prior to October, 1965, a Communist Indonesia supported by Peking was a more real fear to Australia than any direct threat from the Chinese Communists. Since 1965, cultural exchanges have not been particularly effective. Instead, Peking has resorted to trade and the Party apparatus to maintain contacts with the largest power in Oceania.

Canada. Canada recognized the Peking government in October, 1970, after twenty months of negotiations. Peking had worked long on the issue. Aware of the strategically significant location of this 'intermediate zone' country and the close Canadian-American relationship, Peking tried to drive a wedge between the two nations. It had invited members of the Canadian Parliament (including Pierre Trudeau), newsmen, writers, artists, and others to visit China; allowed favored correspondents of the *Toronto Globe and Mail* to stay in Peking; and, most impressive, included Mao's eulogy for a Canadian, 'In Memory of Norman Bethune,' as one of the three carefully selected articles in the widely circulated *Quotations from Chairman Mao.* Meanwhile, Chinese trade missions, an opera company, and other cultural groups toured Canada. The official CCP journal *Red Flag* urged the Canadians not to tolerate too long United States 'control and intervention' but to embark on 'the anti-American patriotic struggle' that had already been inspired by the brilliant Cuban example.[69]

The new Ottawa-Peking diplomatic ties indicate Canada's independent policy from the United States, as proposed by Prime Minister Trudeau in May, 1968. Its impact is far-reaching. Canada broke relations with Taiwan and noted Peking's

[68] *The New York Times,* May 30, 1970, p. 3, and June 7, 1970, p. 27.
[69] *Red Flag,* No. 12, June 30, 1964, pp. 33–38.

claim to Taiwan as an 'integral part' of the territory of Communist China. In November, Italy and Ethiopia followed Canada's step. Then, from January, 1971, to February, 1972, Chile and sixteen other countries from the third world and the 'second zone' areas recognized China. It can be expected that more countries will grant recognition to Peking. But Mao's long-range strategy is to erode U.S. 'imperialism' in a protracted struggle through various cultural activities, trade, and possible revolutionary support from a new position in Canada.

TRADE

In its trade with the 'second intermediate zone' countries, Peking has generally employed a policy of 'trade without diplomatic relations' even though Britain, France, and recently Canada established diplomatic ties with Peking in order, partly at least, to promote trade.

Table 15–5—China's Exports to, and Imports from, Five
'Intermediate Zone' Nations, 1965–69
(in millions of dollars)

	1965			1966			1967		
	Ex-port	Im-port	Total	Ex-port	Im-port	Total	Ex-port	Im-port	Total
Britain	83.2	72.3	155.5	94.6	93.6	188.2	81.5	108.0	189.5
France	43.7	60.0	103.7	53.8	92.1	145.9	48.1	93.2	141.3
West Germany	72.7	78.9	151.6	92.5	129.4	221.9	76.5	206.5	283.0
Canada	13.3	97.5	110.8	19.0	171.0	190.0	23.1	84.4	107.5
Australia	26.8	167.7	194.5	26.3	83.4	109.7	27.8	191.2	219.0
Total			716.1			855.7			940.3

	1968			1969		
	Ex-port	Im-port	Total	Ex-port	Im-port	Total
Britain	82.3	69.8	152.1	90.5	130.8	221.3
France	53.3	87.7	141.0	76.0	44.4	120.4
West Germany	85.3	174.1	259.4	88.2	157.9	246.1
Canada	21.7	151.0	172.7	25.4	113.2	138.6
Australia	30.5	89.3	119.8	34.7	119.0	153.7
Total			845.0			880.1

Sources: U.S. Department of Commerce, *Value Series: Free World*; Letter containing figures of Chinese–West German trade from Ostasiatischer Verein E. V. (East Asia Association, Hamburg) to the author, October 10, 1968.

Table 15–5 invites the following observations: (1) Trade with the five countries listed increased from 1965 to 1967 and declined in 1968 and 1969. The decline was apparently due to the Cultural Revolution. But the 1969 figure shows the beginning of a return to normal trade in the post–Cultural Revolution era, and it may be assumed that, in 1970, trade was on the rise again. The trend is compatible with the pattern of diplomacy during the same period. (2) Peking's imports exceed its exports. Imports from Australia and Canada are mainly in grain, while those from West Germany, Britain, and France (since 1965) are predominantly manufactured goods needed for Chinese industries, such as iron and steel, nickel, machinery, and heavy motor vehicles. (3) The largest amount of trade in each year goes to West Germany or

Australia, which maintain no diplomatic relations with China. Although this fact is evidence of China's industrial and food needs, it is also significant testimony to the political implications of the 'trade without diplomatic relations' policy. Peking is paving the way for future diplomatic ties, as Canada's case suggests.

In the Sino-Soviet dispute, the Communist Parties of Great Britain and Canada are pro-Soviet, while those of France, West Germany, and Australia are divided. At the beginning of the open dispute, the British Communist Party joined with the Parties of Indonesia, New Zealand, Sweden, and North Vietnam in mediating the conflict. As events developed, the British and Canadian Parties sided with Moscow, while Peking endeavored to cooperate with the pro-Chinese groups in the other three nations. Throughout the years of the dispute, the two divided Parties from Australia and New Zealand have occupied a most important position in Peking among the splinter parties in the second intermediate zone.

PROSPECTS AND PROBLEMS

Apparently, the Communist Chinese 'model' does offer several attractions to at least some of the third world countries, such as the experience of the national liberation revolution for colonial and semicolonial countries, the example of sporadically rapid nation-building from a backward technological base through hard work, and the 'no-strings-attached' foreign aid and self-reliance principle. To Asian countries like Pakistan, Cambodia, Burma, and Indonesia (before 1966), Communist China appears to be more dynamic and attractive than India both in nation-building and in the rivalry for Asian leadership. To African countries like Guinea, Mali, and Tanzania, China has acted as a helpful friend and challenged U.A.R. leadership in the uncommitted, neutral black continent. The left-wing opposition forces throughout the third world have made the Chinese experience their choice. To unite with the poor (peoples as well as nations) against the rich is Mao Tse-tung's cherished and powerful strategy. If the poor third world were to unite in an attempt to encircle the rich West at all, the prospect for China's position in the third world would be excellent, but the forging of such unity would be extremely difficult and seems unnecessary.

At the same time, Communist China faces serious problems that may prevent it from achieving its goals. First of all, Western colonialism has disappeared in most parts of the third world. The end of colonialism has almost completely removed the possibility of conducting the national liberation revolution as it is generally understood on the Chinese pattern. Except for Portuguese Africa and the special situation in Vietnam, there are almost no more 'Algerias' of 1958–59 in the third world. This is why Kenyatta refuted Chou En-lai's assertion in 1964 that 'Africa is ripe for revolution.' Reality has disproved Peking's propaganda on the emergence of 'neo-colonialism.' Consequently, the chance for a Chinese-style revolution is very limited in the third world and essentially negative in the 'second zone' areas.

Second, nationalism and the sophisticated leadership in the third world have turned against Chinese Communism. Peking's policies are self contradictory. On the one hand, Peking proclaims the 'five principles of peaceful coexistence' and revolution not for export; on the other hand, it disturbs international peace by financially or militarily supporting national liberation movements elsewhere. Leaders in most third world nations have developed their own course for nation-building. Their nationalism and sophistication in leadership have guided them to welcome foreign aid but not Chinese Communism, to allow political participation by the people but not subversive activities by local Communists. Nonalignment and neutralism seem to be the safest path for developing nations, while most 'second zone' countries keep their alignment with the United States. Peking's diplomatic setbacks in Asia and Africa in the late 1960's indicate that local nationalism, supported by either military or civilian leaders, has developed strong resistance to the advance of Chinese Communism.

Third, in competition with the Soviet Union and the United States, Peking's smaller effort in foreign aid appears insignificant, while the possible American-Soviet détente limits the area of Chinese maneuver in the international arena. It is true that Peking has offered larger amounts of aid to several nations, such as the Congo (Brazzaville), Tanzania, Zambia, Burma, Cambodia, Ceylon, and Nepal, than has the Soviet Union. But the sizable Soviet aid to Algeria, Indonesia, Afghanistan, Syria, the U.A.R., and other nations (see Table 15–6) overshadows the Chinese offer. American aid is even more impressive in scale.

Fourth, Chinese foreign relations are still under the heavy influence of uncertain domestic politics and Sino-Soviet relationship. As previously pointed out, the great convulsions of the Cultural Revolution led to serious diplomatic isolation, and the Sino-Soviet dispute has compelled many former friends either to turn away from China or to remain neutral. It is hard to gauge whether the newly restored diplomacy will progress well for a period of time before new domestic troubles arise. Possible power struggles or new forms of revolution before or after Mao's death and sporadic Sino-Soviet conflicts may well again interrupt its re-established diplomatic order.

For the above reasons, it is fair to comment that should Peking continue to pursue its militant policies abroad, the future of its relations with the third world nations will not be bright. The possibility of the so-called third wave of world revolution in the near future would be greatly in doubt. On the other hand, should 'neocolonialism' appear and prevail in the third world, which seems quite unlikely, or should Peking abandon its policy of revolutionary and subversive engagements, adopting a genuine 'Bandung spirit' line instead, the future would be promising. In light of Peking's revolutionary cause and its past international behavior, it remains to be seen whether Peking will maintain its peaceful policy for long.

Table 15–6—Comparison of Soviet and Chinese Aid to Selected
Third World Nations, 1954–69
(in millions of dollars)

Country	Soviet Aid	Chinese Aid
Algeria	232	50
Congo (Brazzaville)	9	25
Ghana	89	40
Guinea	165	25
Kenya	44	18
Mali	56	23
Somalia	66	22
Tanzania	20	53
Uganda	16	15
Zambia	6	17
Burma	14	84
Cambodia	25	50
Indonesia	372	105
Afghanistan	697	28
Ceylon	30	41
Nepal	20	62
Pakistan	265	109
Syria	233	16
U.A.R.	1,011	106
Yemen	92	40

Source: U.S. Department of State, Aid and Trade in 1969.

SELECTED BIBLIOGRAPHY

BARNETT, A. DOAK, ed. *Communist Strategies in Asia: A Comparative Analysis of Government and Parties*. New York: Praeger Publishers, 1963. A work by nine specialists first comparing the Soviet and Chinese revolutionary models and then the Communist movements in six Asian nations, including Japan, India, and Indonesia. Good comparison and analysis.

CHEN, KING C. *Vietnam and China, 1938–1954*. Princeton, N.J.: Princeton University Press, 1969. A scholarly work on China's relations to Vietnam with a comparison of Peking's positions on the peace movement in the late 1960's with that of 1954. It contains never before published Chinese documents. The first comprehensive book on the subject.

HALPERN, A. M., ed. *Policies Toward China: Views from Six Continents*. New York: McGraw-Hill Book Company, 1965. Examines policies of sixteen countries and regions toward China. This volume by sixteen specialists from various countries is a most comprehensive study on the subject, a 'must' volume for those who are interested in China's relations with the third world and the 'intermediate zone.'

HINTON, HAROLD C. *China's Turbulent Quest: An Analysis of China's Foreign Relations Since 1945*. New York: Macmillan, 1970. A clear, comprehensive review of the historical record and a good assessment of Chinese foreign policy since 1949. A second volume on the subject by the same author, it is a useful work on Chinese relations with the third world and other areas.

JOHNSON, CECIL. *Communist China and Latin America, 1959–1967*. New York: Columbia University Press, 1970. A timely book, dealing with subjects ranging from an ideological framework for Chinese policy to Sino-Cuban relations and pro-Chinese Communist parties of several countries in Latin America. A fine study.

KAHIN, GEORGE MCTURNAN. *The Asian-African Conference*. Ithaca, N.Y.: Cornell University Press, 1956. A brief but good account of the first international conference held by twenty-nine Afro-Asian powers. Good for reference.

LARKIN, BRUCE D. *China and Africa, 1949–1970*. Berkeley, Calif.: University of California Press, 1971. The first single volume on the subject, covering the areas of economic relations, revolutionary model, liberation movements, as well as Chinese setbacks and prospects in Africa. A scholarly work.

LOWENTHAL, RICHARD. 'China,' in Z. BRZEZINSKI, ed., *Africa and the Communist World*. Stanford, California: Stanford University Press, 1963. A scholarly study on Chinese Communist activities in Africa on various levels: diplomacy, cultural missions, and revolutionary assistance.

NEUHAUSER, CHARLES. *Third World Politics: China and the Afro-Asian People's Solidarity Organization, 1957–1967*. Cambridge: East Asian Research Center, Harvard University, 1968. A monograph dealing exclusively with this subject. Good for reference.

SCALAPINO, ROBERT A., ed. *The Communist Revolution in Asia: Tactics, Goals and Achievements*. Englewood Cliffs, N.J.: Prentice-Hall, 1965. Contributions by thirteen specialists, this study deals with the Communist movements in twelve Asian nations including Laos, Burma, Malaysia, Indonesia, India, Nepal, Ceylon, and Japan, with the first chapter as introduction as well as conclusion. Broad in scope and good in analysis.

TSOU, TANG, ed. *China in Crisis*, Vol. 2: *China's Policies in Asia and America's Alternatives*. Chicago: The University of Chicago Press, 1968. A collection of fifteen fine articles and thirteen comments dealing with Chinese foreign policy and its position in Asia. A very useful volume.

VAN NESS, PETER. *Revolution and Chinese Foreign Policy: Peking's Support for Wars of National Liberation*. Berkeley and Los Angeles: University of California Press, 1970. A fine work on the theory and practice of Peking's support for wars of national liberation in Asia, Africa, and Latin America. It also discusses the effect of the Cultural Revolution on Chinese policy toward the national liberation movement.

16

CONCEPT AND PRACTICE OF INTERNATIONAL LAW*

HUNGDAH CHIU

UNDOUBTEDLY Communist China recognizes the existence of international law. Evidence is found in Peking's conduct of foreign relations and, specifically, in its reference to principles of international law in treaty texts, its condemnation of the actions of other states as violations of international law in the texts of its diplomatic statements or notes, its justification of its own positions in international disputes in terms of international law, and its teaching of international law in universities and colleges. However, Communist China's international behavior has itself always raised controversial questions of international law. The purpose of this chapter is to examine some important problems of international law in the light of Communist conception and practice of it.

THE NATURE OF INTERNATIONAL LAW AND THE PROBLEM OF A UNIVERSAL SYSTEM

The role of international law. In the Soviet Union, law is viewed as an instrument of state policy: Law must be the servant of the state. A similar view is held in Communist China. According to a prominent Communist Chinese jurist, law is 'a sharp weapon for carrying out class struggle in the hands of the broad masses of laboring people led by the proletariat.' The primary task of law is to suppress the enemy, protect the revolutionary order, and insure the success of socialist construction.[1]

The role of international law is, in the words of a Soviet textbook on the subject, 'as a special form of law [that] has all the general features characteristic of the conception of law.' The same text also concedes, however, that international law has, *inter alia*, 'special features as regards the fulfillment of its role as aid or weapon.' Thus, international law does not 'express the will of the ruling class of any particular State,' but 'the agreed will of a number of States.'[2]

Writers in Communist China appear generally to agree with the Soviet view that international law, in addition to being a body of rules that must be observed by every

---

* The author wishes to express his sincere thanks to William Butler, Frank Gniffke, and R. R. Edwards for their assistance in the course of preparing this chapter.

[1] Chou Hsin-min, 'Fa-lü shih Chieh-chih Tou-cheng ti Chien-jui Wu-ch'i (Law is a Sharp Weapon of Class Struggle),' *Jen-min Jih-pao*, October 28, 1964.

[2] F. I. Kozhevnikov, ed., *International Law* (Moscow: Foreign Language Publishing House, n.d.), pp. 10–11. The Russian version was published in 1957. According to R. R. Baxter, the English version was published in 1961. See Baxter's review of the English version in *American Journal of International Law*, 56, No. 4 (October, 1962): 1131.

state, also functions as an instrument of a state's foreign policy. However, a Communist Chinese writer, Chu Li-lu, has gone even farther by arguing:

> International law is one of the instruments for settling international problems. If this instrument is useful to our country, to socialist enterprise, or to the peace enterprise of the people of the world, we will use it. However, if this instrument is disadvantageous to our country, to socialist enterprises, or to peace enterprises of the people of the world, we will not use it and should create a new instrument to replace it.[3]

Definition of international law. Before the 1950's, there was a general tendency among Western writers to define international law as a body of legally binding rules governing relations among *civilized* states. The limitation of the application of international law to 'civilized states' is severely criticized by writers in Communist China. Such a definition, in their view, excludes weak and small states in the Orient or even in the West from the protection of international law by classifying them as 'uncivilized states.'[4]

In recent years, treatises published in Western states generally omitted the reference to 'civilized states' in their definition of international law. Most of them, moreover, have departed from the old formula in their definition by also including international organizations and individuals, which is also quite unacceptable to writers in Communist China, who have continued to maintain that international law is a law among states.

In the late 1950's, writers in Communist China appeared to accept the definition of international law given in a Soviet textbook:

> the aggregate of rules governing relations between States in the process of their conflict and cooperation, designed to safeguard their peaceful coexistence, expressing the will of the ruling classes of these States, and defended in case of need by coercion applied by States individually or collectively.[5]

Since the 1960's, no Communist Chinese writer seems to have discussed the problem of the definition of international law, and the present position of Communist China on the question is ambiguous.

The problem of a universal system of international law. A cardinal principle of Communist theory is that the superstructure of the state, including all laws, reflects the economic base of the society and serves the interests of the ruling class. All laws, in this view, must possess class character. It is impossible, however, to apply the principle literally to a system of international law, which purports to govern the relations between states with different social systems. Yet it is undeniable that the recognition of the existence of such a system of international law is necessary to the relationships between non-Communist and Communist states.

In the Soviet Union, this theoretical difficulty has led some jurists to deny the existence of a general international law binding on all states, Communist or non-Communist. Since the mid-1950's, Soviet jurists have taken a theoretically weak but

---

[3] 'Po Ch'en T'i-ch'iang Kuan-yü Kuo-chi-fa ti Miu-lun (Refute the Absurd Theory Concerning International Law by Ch'en T'i-ch'iang),' *Jen-min Jih-pao*, September 18, 1957.

[4] See Ying T'ao, 'Ts'ung Chi-ke Chi-pen Kai-nien Jen-shih Tzu-ch'an Chieh-chi Kuo-chi-fa ti Chen Mien-mu (Recognize the True Face of Bourgeois International Law from a Few Basic Concepts),' *Kuo-chi Wen-t'i Yen-chiu (Studies in International Problems)*, No. 1 (Peking: Shih-chieh Chih-shih Ch'u-pan-she, January, 1960), p. 44. The article says that the bourgeois 'criterion for the so-called "civilized" or "uncivilized" is neither long history nor culture. Even though China has 5,000 years of excellent culture, she was not included in the group of "civilized states." '

[5] Kozhevnikov, *International Law*, p. 7.

pragmatic stand in regard to the dogma-reality dilemma, maintaining that 'although International Law, like any other branch of law, has a class character and pertains to the superstructure, it cannot express the will of the ruling class of any particular State.'[6] They express belief in a single system of international law that 'is the expression of the agreed will of a number of states in the form of an international agreement or custom which has grown up over a long period.'[7]

There seems to be no clear consensus among writers in Communist China on that question. Early in 1957, Professor Ch'iu Jih-ch'ing of Futan University in Shanghai wrote about the existence of two systems of international law—one socialist and the other general.[8] Socialist international law adjusts relations among socialist states, while general international law adjusts relations between socialist states and bourgeois states and among bourgeois states themselves. In Ch'iu's view, the general international law is inappropriate for the adjustment of relations among socialist states, because 'the basic principles of general international law are the five principles of peaceful coexistence, which only include those Leninist principles relating to the equality of nations, not those principles of proletarian internationalism [that are the foundation of relations among socialist states].'

According to a different viewpoint, submitted by Lin Hsin in 1958, there are a bourgeois system of international law and a socialist one, which exist side by side.[9] Lin viewed international law as a reflection of common ideological values shared by the states subject to its rules. Since few common values exist between socialist and capitalist states, there accordingly can be no uniform rules of international law equally binding upon both. Admitting that relations do exist between socialist and capitalist states, Lin still managed to avoid conceding the existence of a common system of international law adjusting such relations: All treaties and agreements concluded between capitalist and socialist states are reached only after a fierce struggle between the two parties resulting in a compromise, which reflects not common value but the realities of the power balance between them. The degree to which agreements are possible depends upon the extent to which the two systems of international law are capable of incorporating the new rule. The situation is one of 'sleeping in the same bed but dreaming different dreams.' By this Lin meant that the two interpretations of the same document of international law are radically different.

Lin's article drew severe criticism by Chou Fu-lun in an article published a few months later.[10] Chou gave an affirmative answer to the question as to whether or not there is a single system of international law binding upon all states alike. He arrived at this conclusion by first stating that during a period of peace, political, economic and cultural relationships are bound to arise among all states, whatever their system may be. He insisted that 'a certain degree of agreement must be reached in order to resolve international questions.' Chou avoided the dilemma created by a strict application of Marxist-Leninist dogma concerning the state's superstructure by distinguishing international law from municipal law. He wrote:

International law should not be confused with municipal law. The major unique characteristic of international law is that its standards are formulated not by a

---

[6] Kozhevnikov, *International Law*, p. 11.

[7] *Ibid.*, p. 11.

[8] See Ch'iu Jih-ch'ing, Hsien Chieh-tuan Kuo-chi-fa ti T'i-hsi (Systems of International Law at the Present Stage),' *Fa-hsüeh (Science of Law)*, No. 3, June 1, 1957, pp. 16–19.

[9] Lin Hsin, 'Lun Ti-erh-ts'u Shih-chieh Ta-chan hou ti Kuo-chi-fa T'i-hsi (On the System of International Law after the Second World War),' *Chiao-hsüeh yü Yen-chiu (Teaching and Research)*, No. 1, January, 1958, pp. 34–38. The terms 'bourgeois' and 'capitalist' have been used interchangeably by Communist writers.

[10] Chou Fu-lun, 'Shih Lun Hsien-tai Kuo-chi-fa ti Hsing-chih (On the Nature of Modern International Law),' *Teaching and Research*, No. 3, March, 1958, pp. 52–56.

super-legislature but through agreement reached by the process of struggle, cooperation, compromise, and consultation.

In February, 1958, a joint conference was sponsored by the Shanghai Law Association and the East China Institute of Political Science and Law to discuss the question of the systems of international law. The majority of the participants opposed Lin Hsin's view, but they could not agree among themselves on the question of whether there were, or should be, two (socialist and general) or three (socialist, general, and bourgeois) systems of international law. According to some participants, bourgeois international law still plays the role of adjusting relations among bourgeois states. Others, however, hold that the term 'bourgeois international law' is nothing but a synonym for 'illegality,' which cannot even adjust relations among bourgeois states. In their view, the relations among bourgeois states should also be adjusted by general international law.[11]

Since 1958, apparently, no writer in Communist China has discussed the problem of the systems of international law. However, several writers in the early 1960's did severely attack the idea of 'world law' or 'common law of mankind' as an attempt to transform international law into a universal system of supranational law. Such an idea was criticized by Communist Chinese writers as merely serving the ambition of the United States to dominate the world.[12]

The official Communist Chinese position is far from clear. In 1962, Vice-Premier and Foreign Minister Ch'en Yi stated that 'socialist countries [had] the principles of Marxism-Leninism and proletarian internationalism as their common ideological foundation and the building of their socialism and Communism as their common goal.' He also pointed to seven major principles governing international relations purportedly followed by socialist states:

1. The imperialists engage in subversive activities, whereas socialist countries do not.

2. The imperialists always try to impose their will upon other countries, whereas socialist countries maintain that consultations should be held on an equal footing and no country should impose its will upon another.

3. The imperialists use economic aid as a disguise to realize their true aim of political control over and interference in the internal affairs of other countries; socialist countries stand for equality and mutual support so as to bring about a common upsurge in their economies and culture and are opposed to interference in the internal affairs of other countries.

4. The imperialists pursue a policy of setting up military bases in other countries, and their troops, once stationed in a foreign country, will hang on there, whereas socialist countries are opposed to the policy of military bases and withdraw on their own initiative the troops they have sent abroad.

5. The imperialists enmesh many countries in various military pacts, making them pull the chestnuts out of the fire for them, whereas socialist countries stand for the abolition of all military blocs.

6. The imperialists do not respect but undermine the peace and neutrality of other countries; socialist countries, on the contrary, respect and support all countries that follow a policy of peace and neutrality.

7. The imperialists suppress the national liberation movement, whereas socialist countries support national independence and the national liberation movement.[13]

---

[11] See *Science of Law*, No. 3, March 16, 1958, pp. 39–54.

[12] E.g., see Chiang Yang, 'Mei-kuo Fa-hsüeh Chung ti Shih-chieh Ch'u-yi Fan-tung Ssu-ch'ao (The Reactionary Thought of "Universalism" in American Jurisprudence), *Jen-min Jih-pao*, December 17, 1963.

[13] Enunciated by Ch'en Yi at a reception given by the Bulgarian Ambassador to Communist China on September 8, 1962. See *Peking Review*, 5, No. 37 (September 14, 1962): 11.

The above statement seems to imply the existence of a socialist system of international law. However, subsequent development of the relationship between Communist China and most Communist countries does not corroborate the statement.

Since the early 1960's, Communist China's relations with the Soviet Union, most East European Communist states, and Mongolia have deteriorated significantly. Communist China has labeled many Communist states 'revisionist.' What system of international law should govern relations between Communist China and 'revisionist' Communist states is a question to which no definite answer has been given. In diplomatic exchanges concerning some disputes between Communist China and 'revisionist' Communist states, both sides, in addition to citing the socialist principle of 'proletarian internationalism,' have frequently referred to 'universally recognized norms of international relations,' 'elementary norms of international law,' and others. The terminology appears to suggest that their relations are, to some extent at least, governed by general international law, which binds all states—Communist, 'revisionist,' and bourgeois.[14]

Sources of international law. The exact attitude of Communist China toward the formal sources of international law is not clear, but recognition of treaties and customs as the principal sources of international law seems beyond doubt, inasmuch as treaties and customs are frequently invoked in diplomatic notes, government statements, and publications. Occasionally, reference is made by Communist Chinese writers to general principles of law, judicial decisions, authors' opinions, and resolutions of public or nongovernmental international organizations. It is not always clear, however, whether the sources referred to are regarded merely as 'evidence' of the existence of certain rules of international law or as 'sources' of international law.[15]

BASIC PRINCIPLES OF INTERNATIONAL LAW

It is neither possible nor necessary to discuss within this chapter every principle or rule of international law advocated or practiced by Communist China. The discussion will be confined to the 'five principles of peaceful coexistence,' which Communist China considers to be the basic principles governing relations between Communist and non-Communist states.

Development of the five principles of peaceful coexistence. The concept of peaceful coexistence was first developed by Lenin. While he was convinced that Communism was bound to triumph in the end, Lenin concluded that the prolonged coexistence of

---

[14] On August 20, 1968, the armed forces of the Soviet Union, East Germany, Hungary, Poland, and Bulgaria suddenly invaded Czechoslovakia and immediately occupied the entire country. On August 23, 1968, Premier Chou En-lai severely condemned the occupation of Czechoslovakia. He denounced the 'Soviet revisionist clique' as 'discarding all its fig leaves, its so-called "Marxism-Leninism," "internationalism," etc. and brazenly resort[ing] to direct armed aggression and intervention.' He also branded the Soviet invasion of Czechoslovakia as 'exactly the same as Hitler of the past in his aggression against Czechoslovakia.' See *Peking Review*, 11, No. 34, Supplement (August 23, 1968): 3.

[15] For instance, Professor Chou Keng-sheng maintained that the United Nations' 'resolutions in general have only the character of a recommendation (with the exception of Security Council decisions to maintain peace, taken under Chapter VII of the Charter) [and] the United Nations definitely does not possess legislative power.' *Hsien-tai Ying-mei Kuo-chi-fa ti Ssu-hsiang Tung-hsiang (Trends in the Thoughts of Modern English and American International Law)* (Peking: Shih-chieh Chih-shih Ch'u-pan-she, 1963), p. 66. On the other hand, Li Hao-pei cites United Nations General Assembly Resolution 626 (VIII) on permanent sovereignty over natural resources as support for the view that no rule of international law requires a nationalizing state to make compensation to dispossessed foreigners. 'Kuo-yu-hua yü Kuo-chi-fa (Nationalization and International Law),' *Cheng-fa Yen-chiu (Studies in Political Science and Law)*, No. 2, April 2, 1958, p. 10.

the two systems of Communism and capitalism was historically inevitable and that peaceful cooperation and competition between them was necessary and desirable. The concept was supported by Stalin and his successors.[16]

The concept of peaceful coexistence received worldwide attention in 1954, when it was formulated, in terms of five principles, in the Agreement between [Communist] China and India on Trade and Intercourse between the Tibetan Region of China and India, dated April 29, 1954,[17] and in a joint statement by Prime Minister Jawaharlal Nehru of India and the Premier Chou En-lai of the P.R.C. on June 28 of the same year.[18] The five principles are: (1) mutual respect for each other's territorial integrity and sovereignty; (2) mutual nonaggression; (3) mutual noninterference in each other's internal affairs; (4) equality and mutual benefit; and (5) peaceful coexistence. Communist Chinese sources did not claim sole credit for the initiation of the principles; they appeared to associate Nehru of India, U Nu of Burma, and Chou En-lai of Communist China with the initiative.[19]

The five principles were soon incorporated in many international documents concluded by Communist China. On June 29, 1954, one day after the above-mentioned Sino-Indian joint statement, Prime Minister U Nu of Burma and Chou En-lai of the P.R.C. approved the same principles as the guiding precepts governing Sino-Burmese relations.[20] In a joint declaration issued by the Soviet Union and Communist China in Peking on October 11, 1954, it was asserted that the two governments would strictly observe the five principles in their relations not only with states in Asia and the Pacific but also with other states.[21] Although a Declaration on the Promotion of World Peace and Cooperation adopted by the 1955 Bandung Conference listed ten principles and did not refer to peaceful coexistence, Chou En-lai later told the Standing Committee of the National People's Congress on May 13, 1955, that, 'in actual fact, for countries of different social systems to live together in peace [as mentioned in the Bandung Declaration] is the same as peaceful coexistence.'[22]

The nature of the concept of peaceful coexistence. While considering the five principles of peaceful coexistence as the guide to proper relations between states of different social systems, Communist China has nevertheless placed several limitations on their application. In a joint editorial of the authoritative *Jen-min Jih-pao* and *Red Flag* of December 12, 1963,[23] three questions concerning the nature of peaceful coexistence were raised:

1. Is it possible through peaceful coexistence to abolish the antagonism and struggle between socialism and imperialism?

2. Can peaceful coexistence be made the general line of foreign policy for socialist countries?

3. Can the policy of peaceful coexistence of the socialist countries be the general line for all Communist Parties and for the international Communist movement? Can it be substituted for the people's revolution?

The editorial answered all three in the negative and severely criticized the Soviet Union for taking an affirmative attitude toward them.

---

[16] Kozhevnikov, *International Law*, p. 15.

[17] *United Nations Treaty Series*, 299 (New York: United Nations, 1958): 57.

[18] Denise Folliot (ed.), *Documents of International Affairs, 1954* (London: Oxford University Press), p. 313.

[19] See Li Kao, 'China and Panch Shila,' *People's China*, No. 14, July 16, 1957, p. 10. See also Russell H. Fifield, 'The Five Principles of Peaceful Coexistence,' *American Journal of International Law*, 52, No. 2 (April, 1958): 504–10.

[20] Folliot, *Documents of International Affairs, 1954*, p. 314.

[21] *Ibid.*, p. 323.

[22] *Current Background*, No. 328, May 17, 1955, p. 4.

[23] Translated in *Peking Review*, 6, No. 51 (December 20, 1963): 6–18.

With respect to the first question, the editorial reasoned that 'imperialists' are by their nature 'aggressive,' and it is 'only owing to unfavorable objective causes that the imperialists dare not risk starting war against the socialist countries, or are forced to agree to an armistice and to accept some sort of peaceful coexistence.' Therefore, only through struggle against imperialists can socialist states maintain peaceful coexistence with them.

As to the second question, the editorial concluded that 'peaceful coexistence' is only *one aspect* of the general line of foreign policy for socialist states. In its view, the content of the general line of foreign policy for socialist states should include: (1) developing relations of friendship, mutual assistance, and cooperation among the states of the socialist camp in accordance with the principles of proletarian internationalism; (2) striving for peaceful coexistence on the basis of the five principles with states having different social systems and opposing the imperialist policies of aggression and war; and (3) *supporting and assisting the revolutionary struggles of all the oppressed peoples and nations.*

Concerning the third question, the editorial maintained that 'by directly hitting and weakening the forces of aggression, war, and reaction, the people's revolutionary struggles against imperialism and its lackeys help the cause of world peace and human progress, and therefore help the socialist countries struggle for peaceful coexistence with countries having different social systems.'

The above limitations on the application of the five principles of peaceful coexistence are in fact practiced by Communist China in its foreign relations. For example, Communist China does not consider its use of force in the Sino-Indian border dispute a violation of the fifth principle of peaceful coexistence.[24] Nor does it think of the encouragement of, or assistance to, armed rebellion in India, Burma, Indonesia and other states as violation of the third principle of peaceful coexistence.[25]

On the other hand, Communist China has denounced the alleged Indian support of armed rebellion in China's Tibet as violation of the principle of noninterference in internal affairs (the third principle of peaceful coexistence).[26] Similarly, the United States' support of the Nationalist government in Taiwan has also been repeatedly denounced as interference in China's internal affairs.

The principle of sovereignty. The first of the five principles of peaceful coexistence refers to 'mutual respect of sovereignty.' The importance of sovereignty as the most fundamental principle of international law is explained by two Communist Chinese writers as follows:

> The principle of sovereignty is one of the most important principles in international relations and in the whole system of international law. It is the core of all fundamental principles of international law. The principles of non-interference in internal affairs, mutual non-aggression, equality and mutual benefit, etc. are all based on the principle of mutual respect for sovereignty. At the same time, the principle of sovereignty also has important links with other norms of international law which are, in different degrees, related to the principle of mutual respect for sovereignty. . . . Therefore, in many problems of international law, the principle of sovereignty becomes a legal criterion for judging the legality or illegality of a given act.'[27]

---

[24] *Ibid.*

[25] E.g., see 'Spring Thunder Over India,' *Peking Review*, 10, No. 29 (July 14, 1967): 22–23; 'Chinese Communist Party Greets 28th Anniversary of Burmese Communist Party,' *Peking Review*, 10, No. 34 (August 18, 1967): 5; 'People of Indonesia, Unite and Fight to Overthrow the Facist Regime,' *Peking Review*, 10, No. 29 (July 14, 1967): 15–17.

[26] See 'The Truth About How the Leaders of the CPSU Have Allied Themselves with India Against China,' *Peking Review*, 6, No. 45 (November 8, 1963): 19.

[27] Yang Hsin and Ch'en Chien, 'Chieh-lu ho P'i-p'an Ti-kuo Chu-yi-che Kuan-yü Kuo-

The principle of sovereignty is frequently invoked in Communist China's official statements and diplomatic notes and is also widely used as a criterion for condemning 'imperialist aggression' against Communist China and other underdeveloped or Communist states.

THEORY AND PRACTICE OF INTERNATIONAL LAW WITH RESPECT TO SELECTED ISSUES

Territorial waters. The extent of territorial waters claimed by the pre-1911 Imperial Government of China was unclear. An 1899 treaty with Mexico provided a distance of nine nautical miles as 'the limit of their [China and Mexico] territorial waters for everything relating to the vigilance and enforcement of the custom-house regulations and the necessary measures for the prevention of smuggling.'[28] At the 1930 Hague Conference on Codification of International Law, the Nationalist government took the position that the breadth of the territorial waters should be three nautical miles, measured from the low-water marks along the coast (the 'normal baseline method').[29] The Nationalist government has maintained this position ever since.

Before 1958, relatively little was known about the Communist Chinese position on the scope of territorial waters (Communist Chinese sources use the term 'territorial sea'). On September 4, 1958, Communist China issued a declaration on the territorial sea,[30] extending it for China (including Taiwan and its surrounding islands) to twelve nautical miles. Furthermore, the territorial sea 'takes as its baseline the line composed of the straight lines connecting base-points on the mainland coast and on the outermost of the coastal islands; the water area extending twelve nautical miles outward from this baseline is China's territorial sea.' The water areas inside the baseline include the Po Hai Bay, the Chiungchow Strait, Tungyin Island, Kaoteng Island, the Matsu Islands, the Paich'üan Islands, Wuch'iu Island, Greater and Lesser Quemoy islands, Tatan Island, Erhtan Island and Tungting Island—all but the first two of which are still held by the Nationalists.

The United States strongly denounced the 'unilateral' extension of territorial waters by Communist China and use of the straight baseline method to delimit Chinese territorial waters.[31] Communist China, however, considered the extension and delimitation of Chinese territorial waters its own affair, an exercise of sovereignty not requiring the consent of other states. Recently, Communist China expressed its support for Certain South American states that had extended their territorial waters to 200 nautical miles.[32]

Airspace and outer space. Peking's practice has left no doubt that it claims territorial sovereignty over airspace above both land and territorial waters belonging to China. The Communist Chinese Government has repeatedly protested intrusions by foreign

chia Chu-ch'üan ti Miu-lun (Expose and Censure the Imperialist's Fallacy Concerning the Question of State Sovereignty),' *Studies in Political Science and Law*, No. 4, November 5, 1964, p. 6.

[28] Article 11 of the Sino-Mexican Treaty of Friendship, Commerce and Navigation, December 14, 1899. *Hertslet's China Treaties*, 3d ed., 1 (London: His Majesty's Stationery Office, 1908): 403-4.

[29] See *American Journal of International Law*, 24, Supplement (1930): 25, 27, 234, 254.

[30] *Peking Review*, 1, No. 28 (September 9, 1958): 21.

[31] See Ely Maurer (Assistant Legal Adviser for Far Eastern Affairs, Department of State), 'The Legal Considerations Affecting the Status of Taiwan and the Offshore Islands,' *American Foreign Policy: Current Documents, 1958* (Washington, D.C.: Government Printing Office, 1962), pp. 1197-99.

[32] 'China's Stand on Question of Rights Over Seas and Oceans,' *Peking Review*, 15, No. 10 (March 10, 1972): 15.

aircraft, including high altitude reconnaissance planes and weather balloons,[33] and the air force of Communist China has frequently shot down foreign aircraft over Chinese land and territorial waters.[34]

The attitude of Peking toward the law of outer space is not clear. Peking's failure to protest against artificial earth satellites orbiting through that part of outer space above its territory may suggest that Communist China does not regard outer space as subject to state sovereignty. It launched its own first space satellite on April 24, 1970.[35] It passes over the space above many cities of the world, and Peking has made no attempt to seek prior permission from the states concerned to orbit its satellite above those cities. Thus, it is far from clear what Peking may regard as the dividing line between air space and outer space.

On December 19, 1966, the General Assembly of the United Nations adopted Resolution 2222 (XXI), unanimously approving the 'Treaty Governing the Exploration and Use of Outer Space, Including the Moon and Other Celestial Bodies.' On January 28, 1967, a commentary entitled 'Another Fraud in the U.S.-Soviet Conspiracy' appeared in *Jen-min Jih-pao*, which sharply condemned the treaty on two specific points. First, it said that the treaty imposes no restriction on the criminal activities of 'American imperialism' in using outer space to serve its policy of aggression such as the use of spy satellites to collect military intelligence about other countries. Second, it said that in the guise of 'international cooperation,' the Soviet Union has agreed freely to provide 'American imperialism' with intelligence on its own activities in outer space.[36]

Taiwan and the question of 'two Chinas.' The island of Taiwan (Formosa) was ceded to Japan in 1895 under the Treaty of Shimonoseki. On December 9, 1941, China declared war on Japan and denounced all the treaties concluded between the two countries before that date. On December 1, 1943, the United States, the United Kingdom, and China issued the Cairo Declaration, which stated that 'all territories Japan has stolen from the Chinese, such as . . . Formosa and Pescadores, shall be restored to the Republic of China.' On July 26, 1945, the same three states issued the Potsdam Proclamation, which states, *inter alia*, that 'the terms of the Cairo Declaration shall be carried out.' Later adhered to by the Soviet Union, the proclamation was accepted by Japan in the Instrument of Surrender signed on September 2, 1945. On October 25, 1945, Taiwan was restored to China and was soon designated as the country's thirty-fifth province. As a result of the triumph of Communist forces in the Chinese civil war, the Nationalist government removed its seat to Taiwan 'temporarily' on December 8, 1949.

Since the outbreak of the Korean War in mid-1950, the United States has refused to recognize Taiwan as *de jure* Chinese territory. At the arrangement of the United States, both the 1951 San Francisco Peace Treaty and the 1952 Republic of China–Japan Peace Treaty merely provided the renunciation by Japan of all its claims to Taiwan, without mentioning the return of Taiwan to China. The United States has since then also maintained that the legal status of the island is 'undetermined.'

It is not clear whether or not the United States may have changed this position in

---

[33] E.g., see 'China Protests Against Spy Flight of an American U-2 Plane,' *Peking Review*, 5, No. 38 (September 21, 1962): 6; 'Protest Against Intrusions by Indian Military Aircraft,' *ibid.*, 10, No. 32 (August 4, 1967): 54–55; 'Law Expert Hsu Tun-chang on U.S. Launching of Balloons,' *Survey of China Mainland Press*, No. 1241, March 6, 1956, p. 13.

[34] E.g., see 'Red Chinese Down Straying U.S. Jet,' *The New York Times*, June 27, 1967, p. 1; 'Chinese Air Force Downs U.S. Imperialist Unmanned Reconnaissance Plane,' *Peking Review*, 11, No. 4 (January 26, 1968): 5, 8.

[35] *The New York Times*, April 26, 1970, pp. 1–2. The satellite orbits the earth every 114 minutes along a trajectory whose perigee is 263.4 miles and apogee is 1,430 miles.

[36] For a study of this question, see Hungdah Chiu, 'Communist China and the Law of Outer Space,' *International and Comparative Law Quarterly*, 16, No. 4 (October, 1967): 1135–38.

the Nixon-Chou Joint Communiqué issued in Shanghai on February 28, 1972, in which the United States said that it 'does not challenge' the Chinese position that 'there is but one China and that Taiwan is a part of China.'[37]

Since mid-1950, Communist China has severely denounced the United States position as violating both the Cairo Declaration and the Potsdam Proclamation and has considered Taiwan *de jure* Chinese territory.[38] The Communist Chinese writer Shao Chin-fu has argued that, since Taiwan 'has always been Chinese territory, it is a matter of course for China to take it back [in 1945] like a thing restored to its original owner,' and that 'it is not a case of China's taking a new territory from Japan, which must be affirmed by a peace treaty.'[39]

As Taiwan is *de jure* a part of Chinese territory, Peking has always maintained that the 'liberation of Taiwan is an internal Chinese affair in which no foreign state can interfere.' It also holds the view that the United Nations is not competent to consider the Taiwan question. Moreover, it has strongly opposed any 'two Chinas' or 'one China and one Taiwan' proposal as a solution to the Taiwan question.[40]

In line with the policy of opposing any 'two Chinas' or 'one China and one Taiwan' proposal, Communist China has always maintained that any state willing to establish diplomatic relations with Peking must sever its ties with Taipei. Although Britain recognized Communist China in early 1950, the latter had refused to exchange ambassadors until Britain closed its consulate in Taiwan, which Britain did in March, 1972. Communist China has also protested to many states with which it has diplomatic relations against their alleged acts promoting 'two Chinas' or 'one China and one Taiwan,' such as allowing governmental or parliamentary missions to visit Taiwan.

Unequal treaties. There is general agreement among Western international lawyers that a treaty obligation should not be at variance with recognized principles of international law. This view is also endorsed by Communist scholars. However, when we come to the question of what constitutes such 'recognized principles,' disagreement arises. One important area of disagreement is the concept of 'unequal treaties.' Regarded by all Communist Chinese scholars as an important principle of international law, the concept is not even discussed by most Western scholars.

The Communist Chinese concept of 'unequal treaties' has not been clearly defined, officially or otherwise. According to an article published in 1958, 'treaties can be classified into equal treaties and unequal treaties, and the latter undermines the most fundamental principles of international law—such as the principle of sovereignty; therefore, they are illegal and void, and states have the right to abrogate this type of treaty at any time.'[41] Communist Chinese writers also maintain that verbal reciprocity alone does not make a treaty 'equal' if important political and economic facts are not taken into consideration.

---

[37] *Peking Review*, 15, No. 9 (March 3, 1972): 5.

[38] For a collection of important Communist Chinese statements on this question, see *Oppose the New U.S. Plots to Create 'Two Chinas'* (Peking: Foreign Languages Press, 1962).

[39] Shao Chin-fu, 'The Absurd Theory of "Two Chinas" and Principles of International Law,' in *ibid.*, p. 91.

[40] The Nationalist government also maintains that Taiwan is *de jure* Chinese territory and strongly opposes the 'two Chinas' or 'one China and one Taiwan' proposal to solve the Taiwan question. Among the various 'two Chinas' proposals, Peking is particularly hostile to the 'Taiwan independence' idea. Before Dr. Thomas Wen-yi Liao dissolved his 'Provisional Government of Taiwan Republic' and returned to Taiwan in 1965, he was always called by Peking a 'Han-chien' (traitor to the Han) or a 'Min-tsu P'ai-lei (disgraceful element of the nation),' both terms being used by Peking to denounce the lowest form of traitors.

[41] Shih Sung *et al.*, 'Tui Kuo-chi Kung-fa chung ti Chiu-fa Kuan-tien ti Ch'u-pu Chien-ch'a (An Initial Investigation into the Old Law Viewpoint in the Teaching of Public International Law),' *Teaching and Research*, No. 4, April 1958, p. 15.

The concept of 'unequal treaties' is not limited to bilateral treaties. An example of a multilateral treaty considered by Communist China to be unequal is the 1963 partial test-ban treaty. An article in the August 10, 1963, *Jen-min Jih-pao*, signed 'Observer,'[42] a pen name believed to signify that the author is a senior Communist Chinese official, severely criticized the treaty because it placed the three nuclear powers—the United States, the United Kingdom, and the Soviet Union—in a privileged position and did not create 'identical and reciprocal obligations among all contracting parties.'[43] The article complained that other states are induced to undertake an unconditional obligation not to test any nuclear weapons in the atmosphere while the big powers can continue underground testing. Since the testing of nuclear weapons must begin with atmospheric tests, it would be impossible for other states ever to manufacture nuclear weapons if the treaty provisions were observed. Thus, states other than the three big powers are relegated to a position of permanent inferiority.[44]

Succession to treaties concluded by former Chinese Governments. It is a generally accepted principle of international law that changes in the government or in the constitution of a state have no effect upon the continued validity of its international obligations. That principle was first challenged by the Russian Communists soon after they came to power in 1917. The Soviet Government unilaterally repudiated some treaties concluded by the Tsarist regime.

When they took over mainland China in 1949, the Communist Chinese applied a similar principle to treaties concluded by earlier Chinese governments. Article 55 of the 1949 Common Program of the Chinese People's Political Consultative Conference provides that the Communist Chinese Government 'must study the treaties and agreements concluded by the Kuomintang government with foreign governments and, depending on their contents, recognize, annul, revise or reconclude them.' While Article 55 refers to 'Kuomintang' treaties only, the practice of Communist China indicates that the article is also applicable to treaties concluded by all former Chinese governments. It is not clear, therefore, what the status of any particular pre-1949 Chinese treaty might be prior to a public declaration by the Communist Chinese Government.

Communist China apparently regards treaties relating to the establishment of international organizations as continuing in force. Such a position can be inferred from the fact that, shortly after the establishment of the regime on October 1, 1949, it immediately demanded to be seated in the United Nations and its specialized agencies, an act necessarily predicated on the recognition by Communist China of the continued validity of the treaties establishing those organizations.

Peking has also recognized the validity of several agreements concluded by the Nationalist government during World War II, including the 1942 Declaration of the United Nations, the 1943 Cairo Declaration, the 1945 Potsdam Proclamation, and the 1945 Japanese Instrument of Surrender. Recognition can be inferred from its

---

[42] 'Wei She-ma San-kuo T'iao-yüeh yu Pai-pi erh wu I-li (Why the Tripartite Treaty Does Only Harm and Brings No Benefit),' translated in *Peking Review*, 8, No. 33 (August 16, 1963): 20–24.

[43] It should be noted that this principle is not always followed by Communist Chinese scholars. For instance, the United Nations Charter accords special veto power to the Big Five (including China) in the Security Council and in regard to Charter amendment. However, Communist Chinese scholars have never maintained that such features of the Charter make it an 'unequal treaty.'

[44] The treaty on nonproliferation of nuclear weapons, adopted by United Nations General Assembly Resolution 2373 (XXII) on June 12, 1968, was also considered by Communist China an 'unequal treaty.' See Commentator, 'Mei Su Ho-mou ti Heh P'ien-chü (A Nuclear Fraud Jointly Hatched by the United States and the Soviet Union),' *Jen-min Jih-pao*, June 13, 1968.

invocation of those agreements in connection with the question of Taiwan and the Japanese peace treaty.

As for other multilateral treaties, Communist China has so far recognized the following treaties signed or adhered to by the Nationalist government before 1949: (1) the four Geneva Red Cross Conventions of 1949;[45] (2) the Geneva Protocol of 1925 on Poisonous or Other Gases and Bacteriological Methods of Warfare;[46] (3) the Convention on Load Line of 1930;[47] and (4) the International Regulations for Preventing Collisions at Sea of 1948.[48]

With respect to bilateral treaties, Communist China appears to have recognized the continued binding force of all boundary treaties concluded by Chinese Governments before 1949. But this does not mean that 'unequal' boundary treaties will be continued in force forever. The recognition of the continued validity of such treaties, as stated by Premier Chou En-lai in connection with the Sino-Burmese boundary question in 1957, 'by no means excluded the seeking by two friendly countries of settlement fair and reasonable for both sides through peaceful negotiation between their governments.[49] Thus, for instance a new boundary treaty was concluded between Communist China and Burma in 1960 to replace all former Sino-Burmese boundary treaties.[50]

Among other bilateral treaties, Communist China has not yet expressly 'recognized' any treaty concluded by former Chinese governments, though it did 'reconclude' several treaties covering identical or similar subjects to those covered in earlier treaties. The status of those treaties pending 'reconclusion' is not clear. In its reconclusion of two former 'Kuomintang' treaties—with the Soviet Union in 1950 and with Afghanistan in 1960—Communist China exchanged notes with its treaty partners providing for the abrogation of the earlier treaties. This indicates that the two earlier treaties were not *ipso facto* terminated by Article 55 of the Common Program. Nevertheless, it is still unclear whether the other contracting parties to treaties with pre-Communist China could invoke those treaties in their relations with

---

[45] *United Nations Treaty Series*, 75 (New York: The United Nations, 1949): 31 (wounded and sick in armed forces in the field), p. 85 (wounded, sick, and shipwrecked members of armed forces at sea), p. 135 (prisoners of war), p. 287 (civilian persons in time of war). Peking's statement of recognition was issued by Foreign Minister Chou En-lai on July 13, 1952. See *People's China*, No. 15, August 1, 1952, p. 33.

[46] *Ibid. People's China*, No. 15, August 1, 1952, p. 33.

[47] Chung-hua Jen-min Kung-ho-kuo Wai-chiao-pu Pien, *Chung-hua Jen-min Kung-ho-kuo T'iao-yüeh-chi (Compilation of Treaties of the People's Republic of China)*, 6 (Peking: Fa-lü Ch'u-pan-she, 1958): 294.

[48] *Ibid.*, p. 313.

[49] Chinese People's Institute of Foreign Affairs, *A Victory for the Five Principles of Peaceful Coexistence* (Peking: Foreign Languages Press, 1960), p. 24. The Sino-Indian boundary question does not involve the problem of recognizing a treaty concluded by an earlier Chinese Government. The 1914 Simla Convention, which includes the so-called McMahon Line as the Sino-Indian boundary, was never ratified by any Chinese Government. Therefore, Communist China does not accept the McMahon Line as the Sino-Indian boundary. As to the validity of the 1914 exchange of letters between Britain and Tibet recognizing the McMahon Line, Communist China argues that Tibet, being a part of China, had no right to conclude such an agreement without the approval of the central Chinese Government. See Communist China's note to the Indian Embassy in China, December 26, 1959, in *The Sino-Indian Boundary Question* (Peking: Foreign Languages Press, 1962), pp. 57–61.

[50] In a statement issued by the Information Department of the Communist Chinese Foreign Ministry on March 10, 1969, concerning the March 2, 1969, Sino-Soviet armed border conflict on Chenpao Island (Damansky Island in Russian), Communist China charged the Soviet Union with refusing to negotiate the Sino-Soviet boundary question on the basis of the 1858 Aigun and 1860 Peking treaties, both regarded as 'unequal treaties' by Communist China. See *Peking Review*, 12, No. 11 (March 14, 1969): 15.

Communist China. In 1949, Communist China disregarded the United States' invocation of the 1943 Sino-American Treaty for the Relinquishment of Extraterritorial Rights when it took over the American consular property in Peking.

THE UNITED NATIONS AND OTHER PUBLIC AND NONGOVERNMENTAL INTERNATIONAL ORGANIZATIONS

The United Nations. The Chinese Communist Party went on record as early as April 24, 1945, in support of the United Nations.[51] Since the establishment of the P.R.C. on October 1, 1949, the Communist Chinese regime has, until recently, frequently issued statements expressing firm support for the United Nations Charter. Moreover, it has also cited the Charter with approval in a number of friendship treaties, declarations, joint statements and communiqués.

However, Communist China has never been happy with the actual practice of the United Nations, viewing most of its operations as a steady series of Charter violations under the manipulation of the United States. On the other hand, throughout the 1950's and into the early 1960's, official statements from Peking constantly reiterated the hope that the United Nations would 'return to the Charter and fulfill its original purposes.' Following the Indonesian withdrawal from the United Nations in January, 1965, Communist China appeared to abandon hope for the world body. At that time, it even said that the United Nations must be thoroughly reorganized and that, if it were not, a separate 'revolutionary' U.N. organization must be established. Such proposals were muted with Indonesia's return to the United Nations, following Sukarno's fall from power, and the aborted development of a hoped-for Afro–Asian–Latin American bloc.

Since the establishment of the regime in 1949, Communist China has maintained that the question of China's representation in the United Nations concerns the 'restoration of the rightful position of a Charter member' and that it is not a matter of 'admission.' Furthermore, Peking has always insisted that the question of Chinese representation in the United Nations General Assembly is a procedural matter to be decided by a simple majority. As for Chinese representation in the Security Council, a prominent Communist Chinese jurist has argued that the big power 'veto' cannot be used in this case.[52]

With respect to the Nationalist delegation to the United Nations, Communist China consistently demanded its 'expulsion,' contending that Peking alone can appoint the sole legal representative of China in the United Nations.[53] This is in consonance with its uncompromising attitude toward any type of 'two Chinas' or 'one China and one Taiwan' arrangement, whether in the United Nations or in any other international organization,[54] public or nongovernmental.

Before 1965, Communist China's only condition for participation in the United

---

[51] See *Selected Works of Mao Tse-tung*, 3 (Peking: Foreign Languages Press, 1965): 306.

[52] See Chou Keng-sheng, 'China's Legitimate Rights in the United Nations Must be Restored,' in *Oppose the New U.S. Plots to Create 'Two Chinas,'* pp. 55–75.

[53] It should be noted that any other delegation from Taiwan to the United Nations would be equally unacceptable to Peking. In October, 1960, Premier Chou En-lai stated to the American writer Edgar Snow very clearly: 'If the so-called Taiwan clique is to appear in the United Nations, under whatever form and in whatever name—be it the Chiang Kai-shek clique or some other clique—we shall definitely refuse to take part in the United Nations.' Edgar Snow, *China, Russia and the U.S.A.: Changing Relations in a Changing World* (New York: Marzani & Munsell, 1962), p. 760.

[54] In 1950, Communist China was willing to accept *ad hoc* participation in the United Nations' discussion of certain particular issues concerning China; it did not insist on the prior solution of the Chinese representation question; however, this attitude was abandoned in 1955.

Nations was the expulsion of the Nationalist delegation. On September 29, 1965, however, additional conditions for Communist China's participation were unexpectedly advanced by Vice-Premier and Foreign Minister Ch'en Yi in a press conference. The new conditions were:

The United Nations must rectify its mistakes and undergo a thorough reorganization and reform. It must admit and correct all its past mistakes. Among other things, it should cancel its resolution condemning China and the Democratic People's Republic of Korea as aggressors and adopt a resolution condemning the United States as the aggressor; the U.N. Charter must be reviewed and revised jointly by all countries, big and small; all independent states should be included in the United Nations; and all imperialist puppets should be expelled.[55]

After the end of the Cultural Revolution, however, and particularly with Peking's establishment of diplomatic relations with Canada, Italy, and other countries during 1970, there were frequent reports in the Western press of Peking's renewed interest in joining the United Nations. On October 25, 1971, the General Assembly of the United Nations adopted a resolution to seat the Communist delegation and to 'expel' the Nationalist delegation. Communist China accepted the United Nations decision without mentioning its 1965 conditions. On November 15, a Communist delegation formally took the Chinese seat in the General Assembly.

The specialized agencies of the United Nations. In addition to the United Nations, Peking in 1949–52 also demanded to be seated in various specialized agencies of the United Nations, such as the International Labor Organization, the Universal Postal Union, and others. It did succeed in replacing the Nationalist delegation in the Universal Postal Union in 1950 but was expelled in 1951. After its replacement of the Nationalist delegation in the United Nations in 1971, it also took the Nationalist seat in most specialized agencies.

Communist international organizations. Communist China has participated in four Communist international organizations: (1) the International Organization for the Cooperation of Railways; (2) the Organization for the Cooperation of Posts and Telecommunication among Socialist States; (3) the Joint Institute of Nuclear Research;[56] and (4) the Fisheries Research Commission for the Western Pacific. At least through 1965, Communist China also sent observers to the Council on Mutual Economic Aid and, before the early 1960's, to the Warsaw Treaty Organization.

Nongovernmental organizations. Communist China has participated in many nongovernmental international organizations, such as the World Federation of Scientific Workers (London) and the International Electrotechnical Commission (Geneva). An uncompromising condition for its participation in nongovernmental organizations is the absence of any concurrent participation of the Nationalist delegation whether under the name 'Republic of China' or 'Taiwan.' Thus, in 1960, when the International Law Association decided to admit a Nationalist delegation, Communist China's Political Science and Law Association promptly withdrew and severed all relations with the Association.[57] In 1967, Communist China's Red Cross Society refused to attend the twenty-ninth session of the Board of Governors and the 1967 meeting of the League of Red Cross Societies on the ground of the latter's admission of a delegation from the Republic of China.[58]

---

[55] *Peking Review*, 8, No. 41 (October 8, 1965): 7.

[56] It was reported in 1967 that Communist China had withdrawn from the Institute. See *Izvestia* (Moscow), July 19, 1967.

[57] See 'Firm Opposition to "Two Chinas" Plot,' *Peking Review*, 3, No. 32 (August 9, 1960): 24–25.

[58] See 'Chinese Red Cross Society Decides Not to Attend the Hague Meeting,' *Peking Review*, 10, No. 38 (September 15, 1967): 39–40.

RELATIONS WITH FOREIGN POWERS

Treatment of foreigners and foreign properties. Since the establishment of the regime in 1949, a number of foreigners have been imprisoned on charges of espionage and other antiregime activities. Many imprisoned foreigners have reported experiencing mistreatment while in prison.[59] Moreover, Communist China's criminal process has rejected the concepts of presumption of innocence and *nullum crimen sine lege* as unsuitable to 'people's justice.'[60] Subjecting foreigners to such a criminal process may be considered falling below the 'international standards' generally recognized by Western states and jurists. Such treatment of foreigners also would appear to violate the 1948 United Nations Declaration on Human Rights.

In addition to formal criminal charges, Peking has also practiced harassment of foreign businessmen by way of refusal to grant them exit visas. An extreme case is that of a Belgian bank official, Frank von Roesebrook. Peking claims that his bank owes it a large sum of money and has refused to permit him to leave China since 1949. For more than two years it denied von Roesebrook's wife and children permission to visit him. In the late spring of 1968, he was arrested by the security police[61] and was not heard from until October, 1971, when Belgium established diplomatic relations with Communist China.[62]

As for foreign properties, on December 28, 1950, Communist China issued an order to control all United States public and private properties in China.[63] Since then, all American properties in China have been under the control of Communist Chinese authorities and no compensation for any property under control has been offered. Nor can property-owners obtain a hearing before Communist Chinese authorities or seek relief in the courts of Communist China.[64]

Communist China also confiscated or requisitioned many British assets in China and apparently has not paid or offered to pay any compensation to the British owners.[65] Nor does it appear that Communist China has paid any compensation to other Western countries for the confiscation of their assets in China.

In addition to outright 'control' or 'confiscation,' Communist China used a number of techniques to harass foreign businesses in China, making their continuing operation economically unfeasible. The techniques included extremely high taxes, fines, artificially inspired labor troubles, and so forth. In 1954, the British Foreign Minister acknowledged that Communist China had reduced the British assets in China from 300 million pounds to less than 40 million pounds. He pointed out that 'the reduction in assets is mainly due to the Chinese authorities' forcing British firms into debt by

---

[59] E.g., see the report summarized in Peter Calvocoressi, *Survey of International Affairs, 1952* (London: Oxford University Press, 1955), pp. 341–43.

[60] For a study of this question, see Jerome Alan Cohen, *The Criminal Process in the People's Republic of China 1949–1963: an Introduction* (Cambridge, Mass.: Harvard University Press, 1967); Shao-chuan Leng, *Justice in Communist China* (Dobbs Ferry, N.Y.: Oceana, 1967).

[61] See 'Traveller's Tales,' *Far Eastern Economic Review*, 61, No. 31 (August 1, 1968): 223.

[62] 'Peiping to Free Belgian Banker,' United Press International—Brussels, October 26, 1971, in *The China News* (Taipei), October 17, 1971, p. 1. Mr. Von Roesebrook was released on April 29, 1972. See *ibid.*, April 30, 1972, p. 2.

[63] *Survey of China Mainland Press*, No. 38, December 28, 1958, pp. 1–2. The order was issued to retaliate against the United States order of December 16, 1950, for controlling all Communist Chinese assets within the jurisdiction of the United States. The United States order was issued after the Communist Chinese intervention in the Korean War.

[64] See U.S., House of Representatives, 89th Congress, 2d Session, Committee on Foreign Affairs, *Claims of Nationals of the United States Against the Chinese Communist Regime* (Washington, D.C.: Government Printing Office, September 29, 1966).

[65] E.g., see Calvocoressi, *Survey of International Affairs, 1953*, pp. 252–53.

restrictions, regulations, and taxes, et cetera, so that they have been unable to carry on, and in order to be able to liquidate and leave China they have had to surrender all their assets to the Chinese authorities.'[66]

Attitude toward foreign trade. Communist China has consistently taken a positive attitude toward foreign trade, and its record of compliance with trade agreements or contracts has been generally good, except during the period of the Cultural Revolution.

To settle trade disputes, in 1954 Peking's then Government Administrative Council established a Foreign Trade Arbitration Commission within the China Council for the Promotion of International Trade, an institution purporting to be nongovernmental, though its chairman until 1965 had been the director-general of the Chinese People's Bank, Nan Han-ch'en, and its First Vice-Chairman has since then been the First Vice-Minister of Foreign Trade, Lei Jen-min. As of 1960, the commission was reported to have been called upon to hand down rulings in sixty-one cases involving disputes between Chinese enterprises and their capitalist business partners from Britain, Switzerland, Finland, Greece, the United Arab Republic, India, Ceylon, Canada, and Singapore.[67]

During the Cultural Revolution, Peking's record of compliance with foreign trade agreements or contracts became less satisfactory. Thus, for instance, in 1968, a Communist Chinese court unilaterally cancelled a contract with a British firm for alleged 'espionage activities' and 'fraud' on the part of the British firm,[68] despite the fact that the contract provided for arbitration in case of dispute.[69]

Diplomatic and consular immunities and privileges. Generally speaking, the accepted practice of diplomatic and consular immunities and privileges was respected in Communist China throughout the 1950's and the early 1960's.[70] During that period, Communist China also concluded bilateral consular treaties with East Germany, the Soviet Union, and Czechoslovakia, providing for the immunities and privileges of consular personnel. The contents of consular immunities and privileges provided in those treaties do not seem to differ essentially from accepted Western practice.

However, during the Cultural Revolution reports of violations of diplomatic or consular immunities and privileges in Communist China were numerous. Thus, it was reported that on January 27, 1967, on one of the streets of Peking, Communist Chinese demonstrators detained a car belonging to the Hungarian Embassy, in which the Hungarian Ambassador and some embassy staff members were riding. The demonstrators surrounded the car, ripped off the flag, broke the flagstaff, and smashed

---

[66] *House of Lords Debates, 5th Series,* 189 (London: Her Majesty's Stationery Office, 1953–54): 50, cols. 3–4.

[67] See Gene T. Hsiao, 'Communist China's Foreign Trade Organization,' *Vanderbilt Law Review,* 20, No. 2 (March, 1967): 314–16.

[68] The court ordered the British firm to pay 650,000 pounds to the Chinese party to the contract. See 'Verdict in British Vickers-Zimmer Ltd. Fraud Case Pronounced in Peking,' *Peking Review,* 11, No. 28 (July 12, 1968): 4, 29.

[69] See 'Traveller's Tales,' *Far Eastern Economic Review,* 61, No. 31 (August 31, 1968), p. 223.

[70] But in 1948–49, several incidents involving violation of American consular rights in Communist Chinese controlled areas of China were reported. The case of Angus Ward is an example. When Communist Chinese forces overran Mukden in late 1948, American Consul Ward continued to stay in Mukden. From November 20, 1948, until June 6, 1949, Ward and all the consular staff and their families were placed under house arrest. On October 24, 1949, the Communist Chinese authorities arrested Ward and four members of his staff on a charge of beating a discharged Chinese employee of the consulate. On November 22, 1949, Ward and his staff members were released after a 'trial,' which found them all guilty and sentenced them to imprisonment, but the sentences were commuted to deportation. For the Ward case and other incidents, see Herbert W. Briggs, 'American Consular Rights in Communist China,' *American Journal of International Law,* 44, No. 2 (April, 1950): 243–58.

408

the windows. In the same year, several diplomats of the Soviet Union, Britain, and India were reportedly beaten up by Red Guards.[71] On June 13, 1967, Communist Chinese judicial authorities tried *in absentia* the second secretary of the Indian Embassy in Peking, K. Raghunath, and sentenced him to immediate deportation.[72] On August 22, Red Guards invaded the Office of the British chargé d'affaires at Peking. British diplomatic staff members were 'lined up, punched, kicked, and spat at in an attempt to make them "bow their heads" to a portrait of Mao Tse-tung.' Some British diplomats 'were taken outside and made to run several times up and down the street between ranks of Red Guards who kicked and struck them as they staggered up and down the gauntlet.' Inside the office, Red Guards smashed furniture, crockery, porcelain, and pictures and even broke up bathrooms and toilets before they set the office afire.[73]

During the same period, Communist China lodged protests with several states, including Britain, Indonesia, and India, protesting mob attacks against the Chinese embassies in those states.[74] Since late 1968, there does not appear to have been any significant dispute between Communist China and other nations concerning violations of diplomatic or consular immunities.

The problem of overseas Chinese. There are some 15 million Chinese residing abroad, most of them living in Southeast Asia. Both in the 1949 Common Program of the Chinese People's Political Consultative Conference (Article 58) and the 1954 Constitution (Article 98), Communist China claims the right to protect the 'proper rights and interests' of overseas Chinese. One of the important problems for Communist China in the exercise of the right of protection is to decide who are Chinese. In order to solve this problem with respect to overseas Chinese in Indonesia, Communist China concluded a dual nationality treaty with Indonesia on April 22, 1955 (effective January 20, 1960). The treaty adopted the free-option principle, that is to say, every person with dual nationality can voluntarily choose his or her nationality.[75] Those Chinese who choose another state's nationality are deemed no longer to possess Chinese nationality, though their ethnic and inherent cultural ties continue to exist.[76]

Communist China has lodged many diplomatic protests against various 'infringements' of the rights of overseas Chinese in many states and has always claimed that it has the right to send ships or aircraft to bring back to mainland China all 'persecuted' overseas Chinese.[77]

Concluding Observations

In many areas Communist China's conception and practice of international law do not differ widely from those of the West. In other areas the difference is most pro-

---

[71] See 'Izvestia Report on Diplomatic Irresponsibility,' September 13, 1967; Mohr, 'Peking's Xenophobia,' *The New York Times*, August 25, 1967.

[72] See *Jen-min Jih-pao*, June 14, 1967; reported in *American Journal of International Law*, 62, No. 1 (January, 1967): 205.

[73] Derek Davies, 'Twisting the Lions' Tails,' *Far Eastern Economic Review*, 61, No. 31 (August 1, 1968): 229.

[74] E.g., see Chinese note to India reported in *Jen-min Jih-pao*, August 7, 1967; and Chinese note to Indonesia reported in *Jen-min Jih-pao*, August 6, 1967.

[75] For a study of this question, see Tao-tai Hsia, 'Settlement of Dual Nationality between Communist China and Other Countries,' *Osteuropa-Recht*, 11, No. 1 (March, 1965): 27–38. Diplomatic relations between Communist China and Indonesia were 'suspended' in October, 1967. In April, 1969, Indonesia abolished the dual nationality treaty. See United Press International dispatch, Djakarta, April 19, 1969.

[76] See Chou En-lai's talk concerning the nationality of the Chinese in Singapore, *Jen-min Jih-pao*, October 9, 1956.

[77] E.g., see Chinese Foreign Ministry's note to the Indonesian Embassy, June 29, 1966, in *Peking Review*, 9, No. 28 (July 8, 1966): 41–42.

found. This is especially apparent, for instance, in the problems of unequal treaties, succession to treaties concluded by a former government, and the taking of foreign properties without compensation.

Throughout the 1950's, Soviet influence on Communist China's conception and practice of international law was relatively significant. However, with the deterioration of Sino-Soviet relations since the early 1960's, such influence has markedly diminished.

There is no convincing evidence that traditional Chinese concepts of foreign relations, such as the Sinocentric hierarchical system of world order and the tributary system, have exerted any influence on Communist China's concept and practice of international law. That, however, is not to say that China's past experience has no influence at all. The bitter Communist Chinese attack on the view that international law is a law among *civilized* states, for instance, is partially a reaction to the oppressive measures (such as consular jurisdiction) that Western states imposed on China in the past. Another important example is Peking's uncompromising opposition to the concept of 'two Chinas' or 'one China and one Taiwan.' In addition to the legal arguments presented, such an attitude is clearly formulated under the strong influence of the time-honored Chinese conviction that there can be only one China. As one American historian has observed:

> Chiang and Mao, though deadly rivals, agree that there is only one Chinese realm. Since 200 B.C., it has embraced all the Sons of Han in a single entity. Occasionally it has been divided, only to be reunited bigger and stronger than ever. It is coterminous with Chinese culture. . . . Recognition of the independence of Taiwan as a state is thus an idea thinkable only . . . by non-Chinese who are 'anti-Chinese.' Labeled (quite inaccurately) the Two Chinas Policy, this concept is anathema to Peking and Taipei alike. One hesitates even to put it in print. Though second nature to most Americans, it is evil to *all* Chinese. . . . Here is a real cultural-political confrontation. It is not just an old man's crotchet.[78]

SELECTED BIBLIOGRAPHY

CHENG, T'AO. 'Communist China and the Law of the Sea,' *American Journal of International Law*, Vol. 63, No. 1, January, 1969, pp. 47–73. Washington, D.C.: American Society of International Law. Discusses Communist Chinese view on various problems of the law of the sea such as territorial waters, contiguous zone, internal waters, and strait.

CHIU, HUNGDAH, *The People's Republic of China and the Law of Treaties*. Cambridge, Mass.: Harvard University Press, 1972. Analyzes Communist China's view on various problems of the law of treaties, such as contracting parties of treaties, form and classification of treaties, the procedure of concluding treaties, unequal treaties, and the suspension and termination of treaties.

———. 'Communist China's Attitude Toward International Law,' *American Journal of International Law*, Vol. 60, No. 2, April, 1966, pp. 245–67. Discusses Communist China's attitude toward some basic problems of international law, such as the role, definition, nature, systems, and sources of international law; the relation between international law and municipal law; and the science of international law in Communist China.

CHIU, HUNGDAH, assisted by R. R. EDWARDS. 'Communist China's Attitude Toward the United Nations: A Legal Analysis,' *American Journal of International Law*, Vol. 62, No. 1, January, 1968, pp. 20–50. This paper examines Communist China's attitude toward some important legal problems of the United Nations such as its legal status, the binding force of

---

[78] John K. Fairbank, *China: The People's Middle Kingdom and the U.S.A.* (Cambridge, Mass.: Harvard University Press, 1967), pp. 76–77.

its resolutions, its role in maintaining international peace and security, and the Chinese representation question.

COHEN, JEROME ALAN, and HUNGDAH CHIU, *The People's Republic of China and International Law: A Documentary Study*. 2 vols. Cambridge, Mass.: Harvard University Press, forthcoming. A comprehensive collection of cases and materials, with historical and explanatory notes, on China's law and practice of international law.

DOOLIN, DENNIS J. *Territorial Claims in the Sino-Soviet Conflict: Documents and Analysis*. Stanford, Calif.: The Hoover Institution, 1965. Contains important recent documents, with author's analysis of Communist China's view on Mongolian People's Republic, certain parts of Soviet territory, and other territorial claims.

HSIA, TAO-TAI. 'Settlement of Dual Nationality between Communist China and Other Countries,' *Osteuropa-Recht*, 11, No. 1 (West Germany: Deutsche Gesellschaft Für Osteuropakunde e. V., March, 1965): 27–38. Examines Communist China's dual nationality treaties with Indonesia and Nepal. It also discusses Communist China's general attitude toward the nationality problem of Overseas Chinese.

JOHNSTON, DOUGLAS N., and HUNGDAH CHIU, *Agreements of the People's Republic of China, 1949–1967: A Calendar*. Cambridge, Mass.: Harvard University Press, 1968. A chronological listing of all reported international agreements concluded by Communist China up to September 30, 1967, including not only the more formal documents but also communiqués, minutes, executive plans, and some important contracts.

LEE, LUKE T. 'Treaty Relations of the People's Republic of China: A Study of Compliance,' *University of Pennsylvania Law Review*, 116, No. 2 (Philadelphia: University of Pennsylvania Law School, December, 1967): 244–314. Examines the problem of Communist China's treaty compliance with respect to trade, cultural, and other technical agreements.

LENG, SHAO-CHUAN, and HUNGDAH CHIU, eds. *Communist China and Selected Problems of International Law*. Westport, Conn.: Greenwood Press, 1971. A collection of nine essays dealing with Communist China's attitude toward some important problems of international law, such as the law of the sea, the legal status of Taiwan, the United Nations, and nuclear arms control.

MORELLO, FRANK P. *The International Legal Status of Formosa*. The Hague: Martinus Nijhoff, 1966. Studies Western, Communist Chinese and Nationalist Chinese views toward the legal status of Formosa.

Oppose the New U.S. Plots to Create 'Two Chinas.' Peking: Foreign Languages Press, 1962. Collects selected important statements of Communist China on the problem of 'two Chinas' or 'one China and one Taiwan.' It also includes an article by CHOU KENG-SHENG on Chinese representation question in the United Nations and an article by SHAO CHIN-FU on legal aspects of 'two Chinas.'

17

OVERSEAS CHINESE

CHUN-HSI WU

INTRODUCTION

CHINESE migration to Southeast Asia started in pre-Christian days, but there was no large exodus until the advent of European colonialism in recent centuries stimulated trade activities and provided opportunities for a more or less secure living. Those developments coincided with the introduction elsewhere of Chinese as cheap laborers for plantations, railroads, and mines. Thus, sizable Chinese racial minorities are present not only in Southeast Asia, where their concentration is the highest, but also scattered through the Americas, Europe, the Middle East, and even India. Wherever they have gone, the Chinese have aroused suspicion and racial hostility in the host population. The hostility has, in turn, tended to weld Overseas Chinese into cohesive communities in which not only their racial separatism is maintained but also their customs and language.

Since the fall of the Chinese mainland into Communist hands in 1949, necessitating the removal of the Republic of China Government to Taiwan, the Overseas Chinese have been faced with two rallying points, one in Peking and the other in Taipei.

Chinese Communist views of the Overseas Chinese. Peking has regarded the Overseas Chinese as more than a potential prestige symbol. The Overseas Chinese can also help alleviate the mainland's economic difficulties by sending cash remittances to their relatives. Overseas Chinese have always been a source of income for those at home. They provided the financial support that enabled Dr. Sun Yat-sen to conduct his revolutionary activities. In recent years, the remittances have furnished a diminishing but still sizable portion of the Chinese mainland's foreign exchange income. To assure the continuous flow of funds, the Chinese Communists have been using mixed tactics of coercion and persuasion. Highhanded approaches alone might antagonize the Overseas Chinese, who might then employ their funds elsewhere. The loss of remittances, in turn, would upset mainland dependents and increase economic discontent.

More important, if maneuvered effectively, the Overseas Chinese can be powerful agents to spread the teachings of Mao Tse-tung, establish and maintain links with the Communists of various countries who favor Mao's line, and cause disturbances that will advance Chinese Communist ambitions for world power.

The high concentration of Overseas Chinese in Southeast Asia, the region's economic and strategic value, its closeness to mainland China, and its receptiveness to revolutionary ideas are of particular concern to Peking. Thus, the Chinese Communists have shown special interest in the Overseas Chinese of that region.

In the past, when Overseas Chinese were persecuted, China had to stand by helplessly. Now, however, the Communist regime feels better able to rectify injustices and leaps to the defense of any 'friendly' Overseas Chinese community that has been

413

wronged. This application of the principle of protecting one's own, however, may simply serve as a rationale for the assertion of Peking's 'right' to a voice in the affairs of the region.

Problems presented by the Overseas Chinese. While it is in Peking's interest to gain the sympathy and support of Overseas Chinese communities, the advantages of Overseas Chinese loyalty to Peking are not unqualified.

Most Overseas Chinese fall into the class the Communists call petty bourgeoisie. Ideologically, they are viewed as corrupt and dangerous elements. While their bourgeois traits may be tolerable and advantageous to the regime as long as they remain abroad, when they return they must be isolated from the Chinese masses to prevent the spread of their ideas. The returned Overseas Chinese find themselves outside the main community not only physically but also in terms of their way of life. Efforts to convert them to the austere Communist ways, however, generally serve only to incur their resentment, with the result that they cease to return, and, more important, cease to sympathize and send remittances. The quandary presented to Peking by the Overseas Chinese may be seen through the fluctuations in Peking's policy toward them over the years.

The Overseas Chinese also pose an external dilemma for Communist China. Often the interests of Peking conflict with those of the various national governments and ruling majorities of nations in which large numbers of Overseas Chinese reside. At other times, the traditional anti-Sinicism in Southeast Asia has brought the Chinese minorities there into violent conflict with the host population—in which case, Peking is confronted with the predicament of having to choose between gaining the sympathies of the local racial majority or of protecting the expatriates it claims to cherish. The situation is especially complex in countries which Peking hopes to win over and with which it has been on the warmest of terms, such as Indonesia before the attempted coup of September, 1965.

Serious problems thus exist in the realm of Overseas Chinese affairs, and they must be faced. The P.R.C.'s recognition of the importance of these problems is evidenced by the large and comprehensive organizational structure of governmental and non-governmental institutions designed to deal with Overseas Chinese (see below).

THE OVERSEAS CHINESE COMMUNITY

Definition of Overseas Chinese. The definition of Overseas Chinese varies from scholar to scholar, reflecting diverse points of view. Moreover, countries vary in their policies regarding nationality and the acquisition of citizenship for both native-born and immigrant, and the definitions of terms used in published statistics are therefore not standardized. Generally speaking, the policies can be classified in the following five categories:[1]

(1) Citizenship is granted only after application for naturalization, as in the case of the Philippines.

(2) Compulsory naturalization is enforced, as, for example, in Vietnam under Ngo Dinh Diem. (Since the November, 1963, *coup d'état*, the Saigon government has allowed Chinese immigrants and native-born Chinese to choose between Vietnamese and Republic of China citizenship.)

(3) Free choice between Chinese nationality and naturalization is permitted.

(4) Citizenship is granted only to applicants meeting certain requirements, such as length of stay and competence in the national language, as in Singapore and Malaysia.

---

[1] Victor Purcell, *The Chinese in Southeast Asia* (London: Oxford University Press, 1965), pp. 164–65, 215–16, 347, 483–84, 493.

(5) Assimilation of the Chinese minority is promoted, as, for example, in Thailand.

Traditionally, China and the Chinese people have regarded all Chinese living abroad as Overseas Chinese, whether or not they have given up Chinese citizenship and become naturalized citizens of another country. The nationality law promulgated by the Chinese Government[2] on February 5, 1929, adopted a policy that combined *jus sanguinus* and *jus soli*, thus recognizing dual nationality. However, there are exceptions to this rule of thumb. For example, persons of pure Chinese blood who have been naturalized as foreign citizens but have not renounced Chinese nationality and participate in local political activities as citizens of the country of residence (the majority falling in this category live in Malaysia and Singapore) are not regarded as Overseas Chinese by Taipei. Alternatively, the Overseas Chinese in Indonesia who did not choose between Indonesian nationality and Communist Chinese nationality under the terms of the treaty of 1955 tacitly accepted Communist Chinese citizenship if their fathers were Chinese. As the Republic of China did not and does not maintain diplomatic relations with Indonesia, those who did not specify a preference were and still are regarded by Indonesia as foreign persons without nationality.

The definition given by Wu Chu-hui is the most acceptable for our purposes. Wu classifies Overseas Chinese as those Chinese emigrants who continue to maintain contact with either Peking or Taipei. This means that (1) legally, they retain Chinese nationality; (2) they maintain economic relations with China; or (3) they maintain ties with the Chinese community of their place of residence or with China.[3]

Regarding the problem of nationality of the Overseas Chinese, the Government of the Republic of China allows free choice by the Overseas Chinese. In contrast, the P.R.C. Government adopts the policy of separate negotiation with each country that has a significant Chinese community.[4]

Distribution of the Overseas Chinese population. According to the official statistics of the Republic of China at the end of 1969, Overseas Chinese, including those claiming dual nationality, totaled some 18,800,339, of whom 96 per cent lived in Asia, 3 per

Table 17–1—Geographical Distribution of Overseas Chinese
(in mid-1968)

Place of Residence	Overseas Chinese[a]	Total Population[b]
Total	18,800,339	3,483,263,000
Africa	57,460	335,916,000
America (South & North)	603,186	489,351,000
Asia (including U.S.S.R.)	18,007,913	2,184,620,000
Europe	68,092	454,866,000
Oceania	63,688	18,510,000

Sources: [a] Overseas Chinese Affairs Commission, Republic of China, 1970. [b] *The World Almanac and Book of Facts,* 1970.

[2] Because of the nature of the subject matter of this chapter in the period after 1949, it must be carefully specified whether the Republic of China or Communist China is being referred to, as there are three possibilities for allegiance open to the Overseas Chinese: the country of residence, the Republic of China, and Communist China.

[3] Wu, Chu-hui, *Kakyo honshitsu no bunseki* (*The Essence of the Overseas Chinese Community*) (Tokyo: Institute of Social Science, Toko University, 1959), pp. 17–19.

[4] In September, 1954, Chou En-lai expressed the readiness of his government to resolve the question of nationality of 'some 12 million Chinese' residing outside the country by mutual negotiations with the governments concerned.

Table 17-2—Geographical Distribution of Overseas Chinese
in Southeast Asia (1966)
(Nanyang Chinese)

Place of Residence	Overseas Chinese[a]	Total Population[b]
Total	17,256,036	249,164,000
Burma	400,000	24,732,000
Thailand	3,500,000	30,561,000
Laos	46,830	3,000,000
Cambodia	260,000	6,200,000
Vietnam (South & North)	1,115,944	32,000,000
Malaysia		
Malaya	3,076,229	8,076,232
Sabah	110,000	498,031
Sarawak	282,073	809,737
Singapore	1,427,000	1,865,000
Brunei	21,795	101,000
Indonesia	3,000,000	105,000,000
Philippines	115,501	32,345,000
Hong Kong	3,739,900	3,804,000
Macao	160,764	172,000

Sources: [a] Overseas Chinese Affairs Commission, Republic of China, 1967. [b] *The World Almanac and Book of Facts*, 1967.

cent in the Americas, 0.36 per cent in Europe, 0.34 per cent in Oceania, and 0.31 per cent in Africa.

Before World War II, Chinese residents in Hong Kong and Macao were not counted as Overseas Chinese. For political and economic reasons, the Republic of China recognized the Chinese in Hong Kong and Macao as Overseas Chinese after the war. From 1945 to 1955, 1,057,000 mainland Chinese took refuge in Hong Kong. From 1956 to 1964, an annual average of 45,000 Chinese refugees went to Hong Kong.[5]

Traditionally the Overseas Chinese aspired to return to his native village upon retirement. Now an Overseas Chinese might return home occasionally to visit relatives or even to engage in business, in which case he is known as a 'returned Overseas Chinese.' The relatives of Overseas Chinese who reside in China are referred to as 'dependents' because of the remittances they generally receive. An early 1965 estimate from the Republic of China places the number of 'returned Overseas Chinese' remaining on the Chinese mainland at 382,000, while 'Overseas Chinese dependents' were estimated at 10,000,000. In addition, about 50,000 Overseas Chinese students were said to be studying on the mainland.[6]

Places of origin. Most Overseas Chinese originated in the South China coastal region, mainly Fukien and Kwangtung. This can be ascribed partly to the geo-

---

[5] Kazuma, Egashira, 'Gekido no Kakyo Sekai (Upheaval of Overseas Chinese Communities),' *Economist Weekly*, Tokyo: Mainichi Shimbun, December 8, 1964, p. 38

[6] Hsüan Ts'ai, 'Kung-fei Tang-ch'ien ti Ch'iao-chuan ho Kuei-ch'iao Kung-tso (Chinese Communists' Work on Overseas Chinese Families and Dependents),' *Fei-ch'ing Yen-chiu (Research on Communist China)*, Taipei, Taiwan: Intelligence Bureau, Ministry of Defense, February 28, 1965, pp. 44–45.

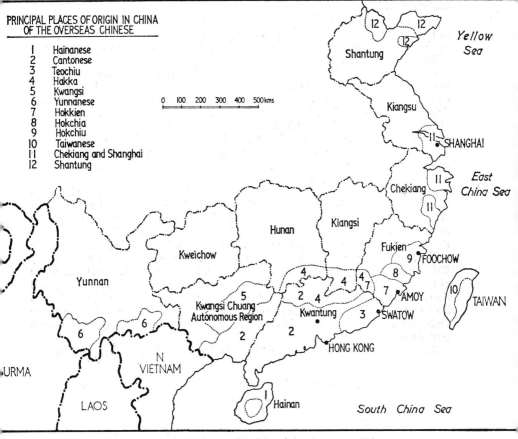

PRINCIPAL PLACES OF ORIGIN IN CHINA
OF THE OVERSEAS CHINESE

I	Hainanese
2	Cantonese
3	Teochiu
4	Hakka
5	Kwangsi
6	Yunnanese
7	Hokkien
8	Hokchia
9	Hokchiu
10	Taiwanese
11	Chekiang and Shanghai
12	Shantung

Map 13   Principal Places of Origin of the Overseas Chinese

graphic propinquity of that area to foreign lands and partly to the fact that Hong Kong, Canton, and Amoy were the centers for contract labor recruitment in the early coolie trade (1830–74).

The Overseas Chinese, contrary to the opinion of some writers, are not a homogeneous group. They are divided into groups along the lines of their various dialects. The Overseas Chinese of Southeast Asia originated predominantly from Fukien and Kwangtung, 37 per cent being Hokkiens, 24 per cent Cantonese, 21 per cent Hakkas (Keh), 15 per cent Teochius, and 3 per cent Hainanese.[7] Before 1949, the Overseas Chinese in America hailed chiefly from four counties in Kwangtung: T'aishan, Hsinhui, Enp'ing and K'aip'ing. Overseas Chinese from Chekiang, Kiangsu, and Kiangsi have established communities in the big cities of Japan, Europe, and America and are sometimes called the 'three Kiang congregation.' Overseas Chinese in Korea are overwhelmingly natives of Shantung.

Since World War II, Overseas Chinese from Taiwan have formed a new group; in fact, in Japan, they are referred to by the Chinese community as 'newcomers.' Overseas Chinese from Yünnan and Kwangsi have settled mostly in Southeast Asia. A

---

[7] Wu, *Kakyo honshitsu no bunseki*, p. 75.

small number of Muslims from the northwestern provinces are now living in the Middle East.

With the introduction of Mandarin in Overseas Chinese education and the cut-off of new immigrants from the mainland, the importance of dialect groups will gradually diminish. However, at present they remain a significant factor in the Overseas Chinese communities.

Economic activities and occupational groupings. Historically, Chinese governments from the T'ang dynasty until the early Ch'ing discouraged emigration and occasionally enacted laws prohibiting it. For that reason, the early Chinese settlers in Southeast Asia were few in number, mostly businessmen, shopkeepers, farmers, and artisans. However, in the era of the coolie trade, the Overseas Chinese population increased rapidly, and Chinese people could be found in most of Southeast Asia and Latin America. Although their chief occupation was manual labor, they gained a foothold in commerce and, in many places, came to dominate trade between the colonial countries and their colonies.

In the present century, the economic activities of the Overseas Chinese have become greatly diversified; their occupations now include virtually all walks of life. However, in each area the various Chinese dialect groups have their own special occupations. For example, in Thailand the Teochius occupy a significant position in the rice trade, finance, jewelry, hardware, and retail business, while the Hokkiens are active in the rubber industry and the tea trade. In the Philippines, traditionally Chinese were chiefly engaged in retail business, but since 1954, the situation has changed greatly.[8] In Malaysia, the Chinese concentrate on the rubber industry and tin mining, while a majority of Singapore's international trade is in Chinese hands. Table 17–3 shows that 40 to 50 per cent of the Overseas Chinese in Thailand, the Philippines, and Japan engage in commerce on some scale. Generally speaking, this is also true in other areas.

Since World War II, Overseas Chinese in Southeast Asia have made consider-

Table 17–3—Principal Occupations of Some Overseas Chinese,
1954 and 1968

Occupation	Thailand[a] 1954 %	Philippines[b] 1954 %	Japan[c] 1968 %
Government	0.02	—	—
Professions	1.59	40.00	15.80
Commerce & finance	50.84	41.00	40.00
Industry & artisans	19.41	11.00	14.40
Domestic & service	9.75	—	19.00
Agriculture	1.19	—	—
Unskilled	17.21	8.00	2.50
Others	—	—	7.40
	100.00	100.00	100.00

Sources: [a] G. William Skinner, *Chinese Society in Thailand* (Ithaca, New York: Cornell University Press, 1957), p. 303. [b] According to an investigation made by the Federation of Filipino-Chinese Chamber of Commerce in 1954. [c] *Overseas Affairs Monthly*, No. 193, Taipei, Taiwan, September 16, 1968, pp. 24–25.

---

[8] The reason for the change was chiefly the Philippine Government's promulgation of the Retail Nationalization Act (Republic Act No. 1180) in 1954, the objective of which was the eventual elimination of aliens from the retail trade of the country.

able advances in the fields of commerce, industry, mining, and communications. At the same time, their numbers have increased in personnel training, technology, and management. The achievements of the Chinese communities constitute one of the important factors contributing to the modernization of Southeast Asia. It is estimated that Overseas Chinese capital invested in that area in 1965 amounted to $3 billion,[9] which undoubtedly augments its economic development. However, the activities of Overseas Chinese in Southeast Asia have been, and remain, severely limited by nationalistic legislation in their host countries. Laws not only close certain occupations to Chinese but in some cases even determine their place of residence.

Table 17–4—Estimate of Overseas Chinese Capital Investments in Southeast Asia (in millions of U.S. dollars)

	1930	1940	1965
Total	744	594	3.000
Area			
Malaysia & Singapore	200	150	1.000
Thailand	150	100	600
Philippines	100	—	400
Indonesia	200	150	300
Vietnam	80	—	50
Burma	14	—	50
Hong Kong	—	—	600

Source: Kuo-chi Ching-chi Tzu-liao Yüeh-k'an (International Economic Information Monthly), Vol. 17, No. 3, Taipei, Taiwan, September, 1966.

Social structure. The Overseas Chinese live in racially and culturally complex societies. Their ability to resist outward political pressure depends on the strength of the social organizations that ensure their security and on the educational and cultural enterprises that perpetuate their cultural identity.

The Overseas Chinese generally form local organizations to meet their different needs. The organizations can be roughly divided into two groups: family and regional 'friendship associations' and professional and cultural organizations. According to a survey by the Overseas Chinese Affairs Commission of the Republic of China, there were, in 1969, 8,099 Overseas Chinese organizations, of which 1,335 were commercial and industrial organizations, 1,205 regional friendship associations, and 1,020 social organizations. The remaining 4,539 were clansmen's, religious, cultural, recreational, professional, welfare, youth, women's, anti-Communist, people's diplomacy, and miscellaneous organizations. Some 71 per cent of the organizations were in Asia, 23 per cent in America, 3 per cent in Africa, 2 per cent in Oceania and less than 1 per cent in Europe.[10]

Educational and cultural activities. Overseas Chinese educational and cultural establishments have shown remarkable development since World War II despite the assimilation policies of various host governments, which have severely restricted such activities. For instance, the Thai Government has stipulated that Chinese children in Thailand can receive only four years of Chinese education at the elementary level.

[9] See Table 17–4, 'Estimate of Overseas Chinese Capital Investments in Southeast Asia.'
[10] T'ung-Chi Tzu-Liao (Statistical Data), Taipei, Taiwan: Overseas Chinese Affairs Commission, 1968, pp. 8–12. Also Ch'iao-Wu T'ung-Chi (Overseas Affairs Statistics) of the same commission, 1970, p. 2.

The Indonesian Government has ruled that only non-Indonesian Chinese children may enroll in Chinese schools and that Indonesian language and Indonesian history are required courses for those studying in Chinese schools. In contrast, the Philippines has adopted a rather flexible policy toward Chinese schools.

Table 17-5—Overseas Chinese Cultural and Educational Institutions, 1969

A. Schools

Total	4,341[a]
Colleges and universities	34
Vocational schools	23
High schools	553
Primary schools	3,731

B. Publications

	Newspapers	Periodicals
Total	165	141
Anti-Communist	90	84
Pro-Communist	40	17
Independent	35	40

C. Other Facilities

Total	528
Libraries	87
Supplementary schools	139
Radio broadcasting stations	16
Others	286

[a] Includes 141 pro-Communist schools (138 primary, 3 secondary) in Cambodia, since closed down by the Lon Nol government.
Source: Overseas Chinese Affairs Commission, Republic of China, 1970.

Attitudes of host countries. The Communist takeover of the Chinese mainland in 1949 influenced the attitudes of various countries toward the Overseas Chinese. In Southeast Asia, the postwar assertion of nationalism caused various governments to adopt stern or even hostile policies toward the Overseas Chinese. Fear of Communist Chinese aggression caused them to attempt to sever ties between Overseas Chinese and the Chinese mainland.

Restrictions imposed upon Overseas Chinese can be divided into the following three categories:

(1) Restraint of Overseas Chinese economic activities is a common policy of Southeast Asian countries. In Thailand, for example, a Royal Decree of June 2, 1942, reserved twenty-seven occupations to Thai nationals. The Philippines, South Vietnam, and Indonesia have similar laws.

(2) Some countries outlaw Chinese immigration or set quotas for Chinese

immigrants. In addition, some countries levy a residence tax. For instance, the Philippines limited Chinese immigrants to fifty a year from 1951 through 1959; subsequently, no Chinese immigration has been officially permitted. Vietnam limited the duration of residence by those of Chinese citizenship and taxed them at the yearly rate of 1,000 dong per capita. Indonesia, Malaysia, Singapore, and Thailand forbid Overseas Chinese students educated on the Chinese mainland to return.

(3) Suppression of 'national consciousness' as Chinese is effected mainly through the closing of Chinese schools and periodicals. The Philippines has forbidden the establishment of new Chinese schools. In 1947, Thailand closed down a great number of Chinese schools, leaving only primary schools, two junior high schools, and four Chinese newspapers in operation. After the 1965 coup attempt, Indonesia suspended publication of all Chinese newspapers.

In the United States and Canada, Overseas Chinese communities have enjoyed relative stability. In 1959, Fidel Castro's introduction of Communism into Cuba caused 2,000 wealthy Cuban Chinese to seek refuge elsewhere. Nevertheless, Cuba's Overseas Chinese community is still the largest in Latin America. Cuban influence and Communist subversion have greatly disturbed Chinese communities elsewhere in Latin America.

COMMUNIST CHINESE POLICIES AND OVERSEAS AFFAIRS

Communist Chinese policies toward Overseas Chinese. Over the past century, the attitudes and economic power of the Overseas Chinese exerted great influence on the course of the Chinese revolution and national reconstruction. Often they affect the China policy of their host countries. Thus it is not surprising that the Chinese Communists have regarded it as a primary task to win over the Chinese abroad with the ultimate objective of exploiting them politically and economically. That objective has necessitated the large organizational structure discussed later.

Policy toward Overseas Chinese is in essence a part of Communist China's socialist policy. Peking asks the Overseas Chinese to submit to proletarian leadership and to serve the cause of socialism.

Because of the different way of life of the Overseas Chinese, Peking obviously had to formulate special policies toward their dependents on the mainland, returned Overseas Chinese, and Chinese communities abroad. Generally speaking, in order to attract the political and economic support of their relatives abroad,[11] Peking claims to treat Overseas Chinese dependents leniently, giving them 'proper care' and 'privileges' at the expense of partial violation of its austere policy. On the other hand, in order to carry out the 'general line for socialist construction,' it expects dependents of the Overseas Chinese to join the masses in participating in ideological reform, class struggle and production.[12] Toward Overseas Chinese communities abroad, Peking

---

[11] The Common Program adopted at the Political Consultative Conference in September, 1949, called for 'every effort to be made with a view to protecting the legitimate rights and interest of Overseas Chinese.' Ho Hsiang-ning, the first chairman of the Overseas Chinese Affairs Commission, in a broadcast on January 1, 1950, called for 'concern over the living conditions of Overseas Chinese and their dependents.' *Ch'iao-wu Fa-kuei Hui-pen* (*Compendium of Laws, Regulations and Statements on Overseas Chinese Affairs*), 1 (Peking: Overseas Chinese Affairs Commission, 1951): 1–2.

[12] In November, 1958, a 'National Overseas Chinese Affairs Work Conference' held in Canton urged intensified ideological education for returned Overseas Chinese and their dependents and treating 'all people on an equal footing' by abolishing all privileges. *Ch'iao-wu Pao* (*Overseas Chinese Affairs Journal*), No. 12, Peking: Ch'iao-wu Pao-she, 1968, p. 2. In September, 1964, at the third session of the enlarged Third Conference of the Overseas

puts forth the slogan 'united front of patriotic Overseas Chinese,' calling for the uni-fication of all Chinese abroad to promote its political efforts. However, it regards Overseas Chinese as 'minority nationalities' in their countries of residence, asking them to unite with the proletariat of those countries and participate in their Com-munist movements in waging an 'anti-imperialist' and 'anti-feudalist' struggle.[13]

Control over returned Overseas Chinese and their dependents. During the past ten years and more, 10 million Overseas Chinese dependents, returned Overseas Chinese, and Overseas Chinese students on the mainland have suffered under a series of Com-munist campaigns such as agrarian reform, the 'three antis,' the 'five antis,' Com-munization, and the 'three red banners.' Communist authorities, however, maintain that in spite of this, the 'bourgeois ideology' of the Overseas Chinese has become more 'complicated and prominent.' The Communists have pointed out that, in violation of government policies and regulations, they have supported *san-tzu i-pao*[14] and *san-ho i-shao*.[15] Moreover, they have advocated the 'four freedoms': to import commodities, to sell properties, to be promoted to higher schools, and to go abroad and return.[16] In their daily life and habits, they have inclined toward individualism; in their relations with the state, they look down on manual labor and refuse to join in productive labor in rural areas.

According to Communist Chinese publications, the following factors caused the 'bourgeois deviation' of dependents of Overseas Chinese, of returned Overseas Chinese, and Overseas Chinese students:[17]

(1) After living overseas in capitalist society for an extended period, their way of living, habits, and outlooks toward 'objective things' had changed.

(2) Those who returned to their fatherland more recently did not have the benefit of such important political movements as agrarian reform in rural areas and socialist and democratic reforms in urban areas.

(3) They have relatives abroad and, through contact with their relatives, may have been influenced by 'bourgeois thought.'

For the purpose of encouraging Overseas Chinese remittances, the Peking govern-ment conceded to returned Overseas Chinese and to dependents some special privi-leges, such as higher commodity rations, which enabled them to enjoy a higher living standard than their fellow villagers. This policy caused peasant antagonism toward them, which in turn led to conflict between dependents of Overseas Chinese and the peasants.[18]

On January 6, 1965, members of the Overseas Affairs Commission, deputies to the

---

Chinese Affairs Commission, Liao Ch'eng-chih declared that the general policy for Overseas Chinese affairs in the future would be to lead Overseas Chinese dependents at home to participate with the masses in the three great revolutionary movements of 'class struggle,' 'production struggle,' and 'scientific experiment.' *Ch'iao-wu Pao*, No. 6, 1964.

[13] Liao Ch'eng-chih, in a Spring Festival broadcast to Overseas Chinese in 1964, called on them to 'thoroughly carry out the foreign policies of the general line and support the revolu-tionary struggle in various countries under proletarian internationalist principles.'

[14] Extension of plots for private use, the extension of free markets, an increase in the number of small enterprises with sole responsibility for their own profits and losses, and the fixing of output quotas on the basis of individual households.

[15] The liquidation of struggle in Communist China's relations with imperialism, modern revisionism, and all reactionaries and reduction of assistance and support to the revolutionary struggle of other people.

[16] *Ch'iao-wu Pao*, No. 1, 1965, p. 4.

[17] *Ch'iao-wu Pao*, No. 4, 1965.

[18] Jen Yu and Chung K'e, 'Lun Ch'iao-nung Kuan-hsi ti Hsin-chih chi ch'i Yen-hua (On the Nature and Evolution of the Relationship between the Overseas Chinese Dependents and Peasants),' *Ch'iao-wu Pao*, No. 10, October 20, 1957, pp. 2–4.

Third National People's Congress, and members of the Fourth Chinese People's Political Consultative Conference held a symposium at which they advocated the 'timely use of proletarian socialist ideology to educate the returned Overseas Chinese and correct their bourgeois ideological deviation.' The symposium resolved to use Mao Tse-tung's thought as the guiding principle and to employ class struggle as the medium for such education; to organize the returned Overseas Chinese, dependents, and the overseas students to study Mao Tse-tung's works; and to urge them to apply Mao Tse-tung's thought to their daily lives in the course of class struggle, and to take Mao's stand, views, and methods as expressed in his works to remold their ideology, their work, and their subjective and objective worlds.[19] In brief, the aim of the ideological reform of returned Overseas Chinese and dependents was to tighten control over them.

Another main topic discussed at that meeting was how to mobilize the returned Overseas Chinese and dependents to participate in collective production. The Chinese Communists stated emphatically that they

> should be content in the rural life and production work, should be zealous in labor and collective work, and should improve the public morals, practice frugality at home, persist in socialist orientation, contribute to the reconstruction of their native places, obey arrangements made by higher authorities, and concentrate on their study and duties.[20]

Most returned Overseas Chinese and dependents live in rural areas. According to a P.R.C. survey conducted during the agrarian reform, of the total number of Overseas Chinese returnees and dependents in villages in Kwangtung Province, 65 per cent were poor and tenant peasants, 25 per cent middle peasants, 8 per cent nonagrarian laborers, and 2 per cent landlords.[21]

In the southeastern coastal provinces, villages with large numbers of Overseas Chinese dependents and returnees (30 to 50 per cent of the population) are called 'Overseas Chinese villages.' After the agrarian reform, dependents, like other Chinese, were given land. During the Communization movement, 90 per cent of the dependents and returnees, who so far had depended to some extent on remittances from abroad, were organized into communes. The aim was to ease the labor shortage and to make it easier to implement socialist ideological reform among the hitherto scattered and unorganized 'petty bourgeois' elements.

Resettlement of returned Overseas Chinese and state-owned Overseas Chinese farms. Every year a number of Overseas Chinese voluntarily return to the mainland. They may have lost their jobs, become invalids through old age and lack of care by their relatives, or been deported by the governments of the countries where they resided. According to statistics, some 300,000 Overseas Chinese returned to the mainland in the ten-year period from 1949 to 1959.[22] Of these, 80 per cent returned to Kwangtung and the rest to Fukien, Kwangsi, Yünnan, and Chekiang. To meet the influx, Peking early adopted a policy of 'settling according to their native places with emphasis on the rural areas and employing according to their skills.'[23] For example, in the period

---

[19] 'Jen-chen Hsüeh-hao Mao-chu-hsi ti Chu-tso (Earnestly Learn Chairman Mao's Works),' *Ch'iao-wu Pao*, No. 4, August, 1965.

[20] Fang Fang, 'Ying-chieh She-hui chu i Ke-ming ho She-hui Chu-i Chien-she ti Hsin-kao-ch'ao (Welcome the New High Tide of Socialist Revolution and Socialist Reconstruction),' *Ch'iao-wu Pao*, No. 1, February, 1965, p. 4.

[21] *Nan-fang Jih-pao (Southern Daily)*, Canton, October, 22, 1952.

[22] Ti Ch'in, 'Chung-kung ti Chiao-wu Kung-tso (Communist Work Concerning Overseas Chinese Affairs),' *Tsu-kuo (China Monthly)*, No. 1, Hong Kong: Union Research Institute, February 1, 1965, p. 6.

[23] Chung-kuo Hsin-wen T'ung-hsin (China News Service), Peking, December 13, 1956.

1949–56, of the 200,000 Overseas Chinese returning to Kwangtung who were given employment, 22 per cent were resettled in industrial and mining enterprises and in schools and cultural institutions, or handicraft workshops, 30.5 per cent on specially opened 'overseas farms,' and the remaining 47.5 per cent were sent to their native districts to participate in agricultural production.[24]

In late 1959, an anti-Chinese storm broke out in Indonesia. Although the Peking regime had friendly relations with Indonesia at the time, it could do nothing to protect its nationals there. However, in February, 1960, a Committee for Reception and Resettlement of Returned Overseas Chinese was established under the State Council.[25] The Committee was headed by Liao Ch'eng-chih. Under him were four vice-chairmen: T'ao Chu and Yeh Fei, governors of Kwangtung and Fukien provinces, respectively; Wang Chen, Minister of State Farms and Land Reclamation; and the late Tan Kah Kee, a former member of the Overseas Chinese Association and wealthy rubber planter of Malaysia. The Commission also established provincial reception organs in Kwangtung, Fukien, Yünnan, and Kwangsi, headed by Wen Min-sheng, Lin I-hsin, Li Yu-chiu, and Liu Cho-fu, then secretaries of the CCP committees of the provinces and autonomous region, respectively. In addition, it set up reception stations in Canton, Swatow, Amoy, Chanchiang, and Haik'ou to receive the returning Overseas Chinese. According to the Directive on Reception and Settlement of Returned Overseas Chinese issued by the State Council on February 2, 1960, the principles for resettling returned Overseas Chinese are as follows:[26]

(1) Suitable jobs will be arranged for the returned Overseas Chinese in accordance with the needs of the state and the preference of the individuals.

(2) Schooling will be arranged for those students and young men who are in a position to carry on their studies corresponding to their age and level of education.

(3) Proper arrangements will be made by the various local people's councils and people's communes concerned for those who wish to return to their native villages and join their relatives.

Communist Chinese reports indicated that in one year's time, Peking resettled about 94,000 Overseas Chinese from Indonesia. More than 90 per cent of them were 'staff and workers,' peasants, individual laborers, and their families. With the exception of a small number of students sent to Overseas Chinese schools in various areas, most of them were resettled in the twenty-five newly established or expanded 'state-owned Overseas Chinese farms' in Kwangtung, Fukien, Kwangsi, Yünnan, and Kweichow. A small number of them were sent back to their native districts and joined agricultural communes.[27]

In 1962, Peking clashed with India along the Sino-Indian border. Consequently, virtually all Overseas Chinese in sensitive areas of India were thrown into concentration camps. Peking evacuated about 2,300 of them in May, 1963. Resettlement of the repatriates from India was based on 'group arrangement as the primary means and individual arrangement as the secondary means.' Most were resettled on the 'state-owned Overseas Chinese farms,' and only a few went into other lines of business.

There are two primary reasons for the practice of centralized resettlement of Overseas Chinese in 'state-owned Overseas Chinese farms.' Wang Chen, then Minister of

---

[24] *Kuang-chou Jih-pao (Canton Daily)*, January 6, 1957.
[25] This committee was reorganized in September, 1966, with Liao Ch'eng-chih as chairman, and Fang Fang, Chao Tse-yang, Wei Kuo-ch'ing, Yen Yen-hung, Ch'en Man-yüan, Lin I-hsin and Lin Hsiu-te as vice-chairmen; Fang Fang was appointed the secretary-general, with Lin Hsiu-te and Wu Chi-sheng as deputy secretaries-general.
[26] *Jen-min Jih-pao (JMJP)*, February 3, 1960.
[27] *JMJP*, February 28, 1961.

State Farms and Land Reclamation, explained, 'Overseas Chinese farms are an important force on the agricultural front.' Aside from the plain manpower factor, the new knowledge and techniques brought back by the returned Overseas Chinese, particularly those experienced in tropical agriculture, obviously had attracted Peking's attention.

The thinking and way of life of the returnees are different from those of the local peasantry. In order not to aggravate 'contradictions' between the returnees and the peasants, Overseas Chinese have to be isolated and kept under centralized control, thus facilitating ideological reform. Their isolation further ensures the regime that the masses will not be exposed to the 'bourgeois thoughts' of the returnees.

In the period from 1950 to 1952, several 'Overseas Chinese farms' were established on a trial basis to settle some of the returned Overseas Chinese and those 'reactionary' dependents of Overseas Chinese who had been purged in their native places. The early farms were small and poorly equipped and were not even self-sufficient. From 1952 to 1959, eight 'state-owned Overseas Chinese farms' capable of absorbing 12,000 Overseas Chinese returnees and dependents were set up in Kwangtung and Fukien at a total investment of 7.8 million yüan. Subsequently, twenty-five additional state farms for settling those evacuated from Indonesia and India were constructed or expanded.[28]

According to a China News Service report, the thirty-three state farms mentioned above comprised a total land area of 1,300,000 *mou*, of which 320,000 *mou* were cultivated land or orchards. They employed a staff of 103,000 returned Overseas Chinese, had 754,000 square meters of housing space, and owned 300 tractors of various types, irrigation machinery of 4,200 horsepower, and 175 trucks.[29] *Ta-kung Pao* in Hong Kong reported that, up to 1964, there were thirty-eight 'state-owned Overseas Chinese farms' with a total investment of 69.8 million yüan (approximately U.S. $29.1 million).

Table 17–6—State-owned Overseas Chinese Farms, 1964

Region	Number of Farms	Number of Members, Staff, and Workers[a]	Cultivated Land (mou)	Housing Space (square meters)
Kwangtung Province	12	30,000	100,000	300,000
Fukien Province	12	20,000	—	100,000
Yünnan Province	7	14,000	56,000	170,000
Kwangsi Autonomous Region	6	12,000	91,000	170,000
Kweichow Province	1	1,000	—	—

a This column shows returned Overseas Chinese members, staff, and workers, but not the total population of the farms.

Source: Ch'iao Chien-shen, 'Communist China's Overseas Chinese Affairs in 1964,' *Tsu-kao* (*China Monthly*) No. 5, May 1, 1965, p. 55.

'State-owned Overseas Chinese farms' are agricultural enterprises with 'socialist all-people ownership.' From the point of view of settlement, organization, and ideological reform, however, they are, at the same time, Overseas Chinese enterprises, and

[28] *Ta-kung Pao* (*Workers' Daily*), Hong Kong, February 20, 1960.
[29] Chung-kuo Hsin-wen T'ung-hsin (China News Service), December 26, 1963.

the returned Overseas Chinese on the farms are urged to integrate their living with production and to undergo socialist education through patriotism.

An Overseas Chinese Farms Conference was held in mid-February, 1964, under the sponsorship of the Overseas Chinese Affairs Commission at the Hsing-lung Farm on Hainan Island. The conference determined the following primary tasks for Overseas Chinese farms: (1) step up ideological education, organize the staff and workers to study Mao Tse-tung's works, and promote 'ideological revolutionization' of the staff and workers; (2) unfold the 'emulate the advanced elements, learn from the advanced elements, surpass the advanced elements, and help the lagging elements' movement in order to improve operation and management; and (3) boost production in order to increase reserve products for the government, thoroughly carry out the 'three big revolutionary movements'—class struggle, production struggle, and scientific experiments—and cultivate 'new blood.'

Measures against returned Overseas Chinese students. As a rule, ardent patriotism prevails in all Overseas Chinese communities abroad. Hence, where there are Chinese communities, there are Chinese newspapers and schools that serve to perpetuate the Chinese cultural tradition abroad. Well-to-do Overseas Chinese encourage their children to return to the fatherland for education so that they may better learn the Chinese way of life and become thoroughly immersed in Chinese culture.

However, immediately after the Chinese Communist takeover, Overseas Chinese students displayed little enthusiasm for returning to the mainland to study. That led to the adoption of a series of measures by the Peking regime to encourage the return of Overseas Chinese students, including the Interim Regulations Governing Preferential Treatment to Returned Overseas Chinese Students. Promulgated in 1950 and 1952, the regulations provided scholarships for students with financial difficulties,[30] established three middle schools and a college for overseas students, initiated a campaign to recruit more Overseas Chinese students, and outlined other measures for the preferential treatment of such students. All in all, they had a pronounced effect. From 1953 to 1955, there was a flood of returning Overseas Chinese students. However, it began to abate in 1958, when Peking changed its policy to encourage only high school graduates to return for education. After the establishment of the people's communes, the fever of enthusiasm was completely dissipated. According to statistics compiled in 1961 by the Immigration Bureau of Singapore, 389 Chinese students from that area returned to the Chinese mainland in 1957; the number dropped to 212 in 1959 and to 102 in 1960. On the other hand, the number of Overseas Chinese students on the mainland who applied for 'vacation grants' to Hong Kong was increasing annually. Statistics showed that the number was 11,000 in 1962, and 20,000 in 1963. Only a few hundred of them returned to their studies in China. This indicates that overseas students as a whole have been disappointed with the Peking regime. Another factor contributing to the trend was the refusal of some Southeast Asian countries, such as Singapore, Malaysia, Indonesia, and Thailand, to permit the return of Overseas Chinese students who had gone to the homeland without the required permission.

The most important factor discouraging Overseas Chinese students, however, was Peking's educational policy toward them. Communist policy dictates that 'education must serve the proletariat, and education must be integrated with production.' Under this policy, overseas students were required to study politics and the socialist movement, and their daily lives and choice of subjects were under strict control. The Communists urged the returned overseas students to 'weed out the residual bourgeois' spirit, put themselves on the production front, and 'settle down' on the farms. Through 'five gates' of 'ideology, family, society, life pattern, and labor,' they should go to 'the countryside, the basic level and the frontier,' where they are most needed

---

[30] *Ta-kung Pao*, June 13, 1953.

by the fatherland. These measures, as the Chinese Communists expounded, were designed to assist the returned overseas students to become 'red and expert Communist successors.' Instead, they deterred overseas students from returning.

Communist China has never publicized the number of returned overseas students. *Tsu-kuo* in Hong Kong gave the following statistics: 1,176 in 1950; 2,600 in 1951–52; 40,000 in 1953–55; 3,000 in 1956; 10,000 in 1957–59; and 13,000 in 1960.[31] According to a report by Fang Fang, vice-chairman of the Overseas Chinese Affairs Commission, the number of returned overseas students in 1960 included 10,000 evacuated from Indonesia. Fang Fang also revealed that 'in 1962 there were 50,000 overseas students studying in colleges and high schools in twenty-five provinces, municipalities and autonomous regions.'[32] 'In 1964', he said, 'there were 39,000 overseas students studying in various schools. Besides, in the same year, more than 10,000 graduates from institutes of higher learning went to reside in the countryside with their relatives.'[33]

To accommodate those overseas students from 'capitalist society,' Communist China has established three types of institutions:

(1) Universities and colleges: Chi-nan University, moved to Canton in 1958; enrollment, 3,000. The Overseas Chinese University, established jointly by the Overseas Chinese Affairs Commission and the Ministry of Education in 1960, located in Ch'üan-chou, Fukien; President, Liao Ch'eng-chih; enrollment, 2,300. The Peking Institute of Foreign Languages, established jointly by the Overseas Chinese Affairs Commission and the Peking Municipal Bureau of Education in 1964, located in Peking; enrollment, 230.

(2) Short-term middle schools of four to twelve months for returned Overseas Chinese: Currently there are eight, located in Peking, Canton, Chimei, Swatow, Kunming, Nanning, Nanchang, and Ch'üan-chou. In addition, there is a short-term school for returned Overseas Chinese high school graduates in Peking, In all, they have about 500 staff and faculty members and an enrollment of some 6,000. About 50,000 Overseas Chinese students have attended them.

(3) Technical middle schools: Special institutions established on the thirty-eight 'state-owned Overseas Chinese farms.' They are half study–half work schools and offer a three-year course with emphasis on farming techniques.[34]

International payments and overseas remittances. Before World War II, China relied principally on overseas remittances to meet the deficit in its balance of international payments. As the U.N.'s *Economic Survey of Asia and the Far East* of 1950 pointed out, 'The estimated annual amount of remittances from the Chinese communities abroad in 1931 to 1936 ranged from 232 to 420 million Chinese dollars (equivalent to $80 to $100 million in U.S. currency, and constituted 30 to 130 per cent of the annual import surplus of China during the same period.'[35] From 1945 to 1949, the annual volume of overseas remittances was estimated at $60 million to $87 million, not much lower than in prewar years.[36] However, the U.S. dollar had depreciated considerably,

---

[31] Ch'iao Chien-shen, 'Chung-kung ti Hua-ch'iao chiao-yü (Education of Returned Overseas Chinese Students),' *Tsu-kuo*, No. 2, February, 1965, p. 18.

[32] *Ch'iao-wu Pao*, April 1, 1962.

[33] Fang Fang, 'Report to the Third Enlarged Meeting of the Overseas Chinese Affairs Conference,' *Ch'iao-wu Pao*, October, 1964.

[34] *Ch'iao-wu Pao*, No. 5, October, 1964.

[35] United Nations, *Economic Survey of Asia and the Far East*, 1950, p. 59. The apparent disproportion between the two currencies is explained by the depreciation of the Chinese dollar relative to the American dollar.

[36] Chun-hsi Wu, *Dollars, Dependents and Dogma: Overseas Chinese Remittances to Communist China* (Stanford, Calif.: Hoover Institution, Stanford University, 1967), p. 83.

so that its purchasing power in 1949 was equivalent to about 70 per cent of its prewar value. Thus, the importance of overseas remittances to China had gradually declined. After the Communist takeover, overseas remittances decreased more rapidly. In the past decade or so, the average annual overseas remittance has been less than half that of the prewar years, but it still constitutes an important factor in Peking's balance of international payments.[37]

Definition of remittances. Overseas remittance generally refers to money from Overseas Chinese to support their families and dependents, to purchase land or houses for the remitter or his family, or to invest in industrial or commercial enterprises. During the prewar years, 84.5 per cent of the overseas remittances went for supporting families and dependents and 15.5 per cent for investment or other uses.[38] After 1949, the situation changed significantly. According to the *Ch'iao-wu Pao* of Peking, remittances to the mainland for family support have exceeded 90 per cent of total remittances; funds for investment have accounted for only 2 per cent, the remaining 8 per cent being for other purposes.[39]

Policy shifts and remittance fluctuation. The official policy is basically to encourage remittances; however, actual measures taken in the past two decades to that end have been constantly changing. From 1950 to 1952, the attitude toward Overseas Chinese and their dependents was generally hostile and oppressive; remittances were extracted by compulsion and threat. From 1953 to 1957, when Communist China implemented its First Five-Year Plan and the economic support of Overseas Chinese was welcomed, the official policy was moderated. In 1955, the State Council promulgated the Directive on the Policy of Thoroughly Protecting Overseas Remittances and formulated methods to open an Overseas Chinese Investment Company to encourage remittances.

In the Second Five-Year Plan, beginning in 1958, with the initiation of the people's commune movement, dependents of Overseas Chinese and returned Overseas Chinese were forced to participate in productive labor, thus increasing the 'contradictions' between Communist China and the Overseas Chinese and discouraging remittances. The failure of the 'three red banners' movement (general line of the Party, Great Leap Forward, and people's communes), and the consequent decline of the mainland economy caused a serious shortage of commodities. As a result, Overseas Chinese sent goods instead of cash. Various measures were adopted by the Communists to increase overseas remittances, but to little avail.[40] After the Cultural Revolution began in 1965, remittances dropped even further.

Foreign policies toward remittances. After World War II, most countries instituted foreign exchange controls. Thailand limited the maximum amount of remittances for family support to 1,000 baht (50 U.S. dollars) a month per family. Malaya and Singapore restricted the monthly remittance to a maximum of M/S $45 (U.S. $15). With the outbreak of the Korean War, the United States and the Philippines forbade all remittances to the Chinese mainland.

Hong Kong is the center of transmission of remittances for several reasons: (1) Hong Kong is the most prominent free-exchange market in the Far East. (2) After the Communist takeover, the dependents of many Overseas Chinese emigrated to Hong Kong. The livelihood of a great many Hong Kong residents still depends to a large extent upon overseas remittances. (3) The postwar economic stability of Hong Kong has attracted large quantities of Overseas Chinese investments. Annual Overseas

---

[37] *Ibid.*, pp. 82–83.

[38] *Ibid.*, p. 22.

[39] *Ch'iao-wu Pao*, No. 2, February 20, 1957, p. 10.

[40] Wu, *Dollars, Dependents and Dogma*, pp. 50–53.

[41] Po-shang Wong, *The Influx of Chinese Capital into Hong Kong Since 1937* (Hong Kong, 1958), p. 10.

Chinese remittances to Hong Kong amounted to HK $550 million to $700 million in 1956–57, of which 30 per cent was transferred to the Chinese mainland.[41]

According to a U.S. report, Overseas Chinese remittances to the Chinese mainland annually average $80 million.[42] Professor Jan S. Prybyla estimated that annual remittances for 1965–68 amounted to only $75 million.[43] Financial circles in Hong Kong place the average annual remittances for the same period at $30 million.[44] I have surveyed this problem on a more comprehensive basis; my estimate for the 1950–64 period is summarized in Table 17–7. The relative importance of these remittances in China's supply of free world currencies may be seen in Table 17–8.

Absorption of remittances. Overseas Chinese were encouraged to invest in projects of local economic reconstruction through their remittances. To facilitate this, a Steering Committee for Overseas Chinese Investment was established in Fukien in 1952 and another in Kwangtung in 1955. Early in 1955, the people's councils in Fukien and Kwangtung promulgated the following regulations for the Overseas Chinese investment companies: (1) No change of class status was to result from such investments; (2) Dividends for such investments should be guaranteed at 8 per cent per annum; (3) Investors should retain ownership of their capital *even after socialization*; and (4) Employment should be arranged in accordance with requirements of the enterprise and the circumstances of the investor.

In June, 1956, at its fourth plenary meeting on overseas affairs, the Overseas Chinese Affairs Commission resolved to organize immediately a head office of the Overseas Chinese Investment Company, under which the company became a trust of the regime. Later, on August 2, 1957, the State Council promulgated its Regulations on Preferential Treatment of Overseas Chinese Investments in State-owned and -operated Overseas Chinese Investment Companies. During that period the dependents of Overseas Chinese on the mainland who had invested in such companies demanded that profit-sharing be accorded the investors, that dividends and principals be paid in foreign exchange, and that all shares and stocks of such companies could be used as collateral for loans. The government responded by agreeing to pay in foreign exchange one-half of the dividends payable to the investors.

Up to May, 1964, 12,000 remittance-receiving households had participated in the Kwangtung Overseas Chinese Investment Company and 10,000 in the Fukien Company. By the end of 1964, branch investment companies had been established in thirteen provinces and municipalities, and some 100 plants and factories were set up under the management and supervision of the companies. Under the regulations, investors are allowed to withdraw their capital after a period of twelve years. When, in 1963, investments in some of the companies had reached maturity, a new set of Rules for Withdrawal of Capital after a Twelve-Year Period and for Continual Investment was issued to prevent an outflow of capital. The new rules offered investors a choice between continuing their investments for twelve more years at 8 per cent per annum, half of which would be paid in ration coupons, and continuing for six years at dividends of 7 per cent per annum, a quarter of which would be paid in ration coupons.

---

[42] United Press International gives the following estimates (in millions of U.S. dollars): 1950, 120; 1952, 148; 1959, 36; 1960, 52; and an average for the period 1961 to 1964 of 62. (UPI, Washington, March 8, 1967.)

[43] Jan S. Prybyla, 'Communist China: The Economy and the Revolution,' *Current History*, September, 1968, p. 139.

[44] An Associated Press dispatch from Hong Kong datelined February 19, 1970, quoted Chinese Communist banking sources in the Crown Colony to the effect that Overseas Chinese cash remittances to the mainland from and through Hong Kong had totaled $17 million (HK $102 million) in 1969, up about 20 per cent from 1968, and that the flow was expected to reach another new high in 1970. It ought to be noted that since most mainland-bound cash remittances have to go through Hong Kong, the $17 million is close to the total the mainland received in cash from the Overseas Chinese in 1969.

Table 17–7—Overseas Chinese Remittances to Communist China, 1950–64
(in millions of U.S. dollars)

Year	Remittances via Hong Kong	Remitted by Hong Kong Residents	Foreign Currency Carried by Returning Overseas Chinese and Direct Remittances from Areas Other than Hong Kong	Total
1950	32.80	25.00	2.30	60.10
1951	29.73	25.00	2.08	56.81
1952	26.68	12.50	1.87	41.05
1953	30.69	12.50	2.15	45.34
1954	30.11	9.00	2.11	41.22
1955	35.06	9.00	2.43	46.49
1956	34.44	9.00	2.41	45.85
1957	34.04	9.00	2.38	45.42
1958	30.55	9.00	2.14	41.69
1959	25.28	9.00	1.77	36.05
1960	30.56	9.00	2.13	41.69
1961	27.94	9.00	1.95	38.89
1962	28.94	9.00	1.83	39.77
1963	27.96	12.50	1.96	42.42
1964	27.96	15.00	1.96	44.92

Source: Chun-hsi Wu, *Dollars, Dependents and Dogma, Overseas Chinese Remittances to Communist China* (Stanford, Calif.: Hoover Institution, Stanford University, 1967), p. 142.

The capital of the Overseas Chinese Investment Company was derived primarily from overseas remittances. A large portion of the capital probably came from dependents of Overseas Chinese who were forced to invest their remittances. Other investments came from the transfer of deposits placed in credit cooperatives in the home towns of Overseas Chinese. Some overseas residents directed that their funds be invested with dividends to be made payable to their dependents on the mainland to save the difficulties of remitting regularly. Before 1963, those who had invested up to 10,000 JMP could ask the company to employ one of their dependents and the Overseas Chinese University to admit one of their children. After 1963, the minimum was raised to 20,000 JMP.

No estimate of the total sum of Overseas Chinese capital invested in such companies has ever been attempted. However, we may take Ch'iao Chien-shen's estimate of capital invested in the Kwangtung Investment Company as an example of Overseas Chinese investment companies in general.

Work within Overseas Chinese communities. Since the fall of 1949, the Chinese Communists have advocated an Overseas Chinese Patriotic United Front to exert political and economic control over Overseas Chinese communities. At the same time they have stressed the need of 'thoroughly carrying out the nation's general line on foreign affairs' and 'educating Overseas Chinese to support local nationalist and democratic movements.'

United front work. Peking's united front efforts in Overseas Chinese communities have been characterized by flexible employment of political, economic, and cultural means. Political maneuvers have included, first, formation of a nucleus organization for united front work of either cadres sent directly by Peking or of designated local cadres to lead the workers' movement, student movement, youth movement, women's movement, and so forth. Second, pro-Peking Overseas Chinese leaders have or-

Table 17-8—Annual Total Chinese Communist Disposal of Free World
Currencies from Net Export Balance and Overseas Remittances, 1950–67

Year	Total Remittances (million U.S. dollars)	Total Free World Imports Surplus (Chinese Exports Surplus)[a] (million U.S. dollars)	Chinese Total Disposal (million U.S. dollars)	Total Remittance Relative to Total Chinese Disposal (per cent)
1950	60.10	82.6	142.70	42.1
1951	56.81	78.5	135.31	42.0
1952	41.05	95.4	136.45	30.1
1953	45.34	145.3	190.64	23.8
1954	41.22	85.5	126.72	32.5
1955	46.49	169.8	215.99	21.45
1956	45.85	207.2	253.05	18.1
1957	45.42	96.2	141.62	32.1
1958	41.69	—15.1	26.59	156.8
1959	36.05	47.3	83.35	43.3
1960	41.69	106.7	148.39	28.1
1961	38.89	—6.5	32.39	120.1
1962	39.77	117.8	157.57	25.2
1963	42.42	120.2	162.62	26.1
1964	—	218.0	—	—
1965	—	231.8	—	—
1966	—	381.4	—	—
1967	—	345.8	—	—

[a] Figures taken from *The Battle Act Report*, 1965, Seventeenth Report to Congress, Department of State, U.S.A., Table 2, February, 1966, p. 100; and *ibid.*, 1969, Twenty-second Report to Congress, Table 2, March, 1970, p. 36.

ganized various groups through which Communist influence has been expanded. In areas where Peking had no formal diplomatic establishments, such activities were designed both to enhance the position of pro-Communist elements and to neutralize and assail anti-Communist forces. Third, prominent leaders in Overseas Chinese communities were invited to serve on the Chinese People's Political Consultative Conference (CPPCC) and the Overseas Chinese Affairs Commission, or as vice-mayors or vice-magistrates. Finally, such organizations as 'democratic parties' or the All-China Federation of Returned Overseas Chinese are employed to spread propaganda for Peking. The Communists style themselves 'nationalists' and assert that all 'patriots' are 'brothers' and will be given 'equal treatment.' Peking's propaganda against 'U.S. imperialism,' 'Soviet revisionism,' and nuclear weaponry also seem to have an impact on Overseas Chinese youth.

Among the economic maneuvers are offers of cheap commodities, high commissions, and low interest loans. These measures are used to induce Overseas Chinese leaders to act as political agents for the Communist Party. (Such methods have been effective in Hong Kong, Macao, Japan, Canada, and Central and South America.) Communist banks and pro-Peking banks overseas offer a select clientele loans at low interest rates.[45] Trade benefits were used to entice businessmen to sponsor exhibitions of

[45] Furthermore, the overseas branch of the Peking-controlled Bank of China generally serves as headquarters for united front work. In the Hong Kong 'May storm' of 1967, for

Table 17–9—Capital Invested in the Kwangtung Overseas Chinese
Investment Company, 1955–63

Year Invested	Amount Invested[a]	
	Jen-min-pi (1,000 yüan)	U.S. Equivalent[b] ($1,000)
1955	13,760	5,856
1956	21,135	8,073
1957	23,500	8,977
1958	32,500	10,915
1959	39,000	14,898
1960	43,290	16,536
1961	48,212	18,422
1962	51,350	19,512
1963	78,616	30,040

[a] Estimated on the assumption that the company pays dividend on shares at the rate of 8 per cent annually.

[b] Based on the conversion rate of one U.S. dollar to 2.617 JMP.

Sources: Table from Ch'iao Chien-shen, 'Communist China's Overseas Chinese Affairs in 1964,' Tsu-kuo (China Monthly), No. 5, May 1, 1965, p. 54. Figures from Nan-fang Jih-pao (Southern Daily), Canton, January 7, 1957; Chung-kuo Hsin-wen T'ung-hsin (China News Service), January 21, 1958; December 20, 1959; January 8, 1961; January 7, 1962; and January 4, 1963; Wen-hui Pao (Wen-hui Daily), Hong Kong, January 9, 1959; and Yang-ch'eng Wan-pao (Yangch'eng Evening News), Canton, January 5, 1964.

Communist Chinese products (clear examples have occurred in Hong Kong and Singapore). Part of the money obtained through trade is channeled back into subsidizing united front work and local Communist movements.

Culturally, schools, publications, movie studios, and theaters spread Peking's propaganda. The Communists have bought out several newspapers in Hong Kong; in addition, they control Ta Kung Pao and Wen Hui Pao. Sixty-nine publishing institutions distribute a total of 129 publications, 104 of which originate on the Chinese mainland. Statistics compiled in December, 1964, showed a combined circulation of 730,000 copies throughout Southeast Asia.[46] Broadcasts aimed at Overseas Chinese communities have been increased. In 1962, the hours totaled 22.5 a day in various Chinese dialects and Mandarin. The seven special broadcasting areas were Southeast Asia; Australia, New Zealand, and the Philippines; Eastern North America; Western North America; India and Pakistan; North African and Asian areas; and Europe.

As a part of 'people's diplomacy,' cultural, artistic, athletic, and religious groups are dispatched to Overseas Chinese communities for visits, performances, or the sponsorship of various displays. Furthermore, visits to the mainland for homecoming, sightseeing, or various celebrations are normally encouraged. During the Cultural Revolution, however, such visits decreased greatly in number. The February 3, 1968, issue of Hong Kong's Hsin Wan Pao (New Evening News) reported that only about

example, the local Bank of China provided the base for the Communists' Struggle Committee Against Persecution by the British Authorities in Hong Kong.

[46] Yu Chung-chien, 'Kung-fei tsai Hsiang-kang Ch'u-pan-chieh Huo-tung Kai-k'uang (Outlines of Chinese Communist Activities in Hong Kong's Publishing Circles),' Kung-fei Huo-kuo Chen-hsiang (The Reality of Calamities Visited upon China by the Communists) (Taipei, Taiwan: Overseas Chinese Affairs Commission, February, 1966), pp. 272–87.

50,000 people from the Hong Kong–Kowloon area had just visited the Chinese mainland for the lunar New Year, as compared with the estimated 110,000 returnees two years before. The paper also mentioned that Peking had invited sixty-seven Overseas Chinese (mostly traders with mainland connections) to the May Day and October 1 celebrations in 1966 but cut down the number to thirty in 1967.

Subversive activities. At the third enlarged session of the Overseas Chinese Affairs Commission in September, 1964, Commission Chairman Liao Ch'eng-chih advocated expanding and strengthening the Overseas Chinese Patriotic United Front. According to Liao, 'Overseas Chinese should be educated to become interested in international affairs.'[47] In subsequent years, the Chinese Communists stepped up their subversive activities in Southeast Asia and Latin America through the Overseas Chinese communities. As early as February 24, 1959, the Malayan government issued a white paper entitled 'Communist Threat to Malaya,' which pointed out that the Chinese Communists were concentrating their propaganda on Southeast Asia in an attempt to win over non-Communist countries in the area. To achieve that goal, the Communists took advantage of the large numbers of Overseas Chinese in certain nations.

A considerable number of Overseas Chinese in Southeast Asia and Latin America have obtained citizenship in their countries of domicile. Hence, in law, they are local people, thus constituting a special minority group. This is advantageous to Peking in its effort to undertake political activities. Normally, Communist Chinese policy in overseas work has been flexibly formulated to meet a variety of situations:

(1) In countries with which Peking has no diplomatic relations but where the Communist Party organization is fairly strong, Peking works through the local Party.

(2) In countries with which Peking has diplomatic ties (such as Burma), it lends a secret hand to the local Communist movement while concentrating on united front work among the Overseas Chinese.

(3) In anti-Communist countries like the Philippines and those of Central and South America, Peking's activities are primarily covert.

Organizations and Personnel for Overseas Chinese Affairs in Communist China

Party organization. On the surface, the executive policy structure for Overseas Chinese affairs includes three separate systems: Party organizations, government organizations, and 'people's associations.' In reality, however, the leading organ is always the Party, which exercises control over all Overseas Chinese affairs.

Before the Great Proletarian Cultural Revolution, the Politburo and the Secretariat of the Central Committee were the supreme policy-making bodies of the Party. Since the Cultural Revolution, the Central Cultural Revolution Group and the Military Affairs Committee of the Central Committee have taken substantial policy-making power from the Politburo. Accordingly, some changes can be found in the Party units responsible for Overseas Chinese affairs both at home and abroad. Basically, the Overseas Work Committee of the Party is the primary functioning organ, while the United Front Department and the Social Department share partial responsibility.

The Overseas Work Committee. The Overseas Work Committee is responsible for the efforts of Chinese Communist Party branches in Overseas Chinese communities abroad and for the coordination of, as well as control over, underground work. Under the committee are many departments organized on a regional basis.[48] Furthermore, in

---

[47] *Ch'iao-wu Pao*, No. 4, August, 1964.

[48] The departments are in charge of Overseas Chinese affairs relating to the following

large Overseas Chinese communities both at home and abroad, there are some work-ing units that lack any permanent designation in the local Party organization. Until some time during the Cultural Revolution, the First Secretary of the committee, Liao Ch'eng-chih, had been concurrently Chairman of the State Council's Overseas Chinese Affairs Commission. His dual function was a result of the monolithic leader-ship of Party and government in Overseas Chinese Affairs.

United Front and the Social departments. As mentioned above, the Central Committee's United Front and Social departments shared in responsibility for Overseas Chinese affairs. In 1956, the Party placed internal united front work under the CPPCC; simultaneously, external united front work was increasingly emphasized. The objec-tive was to take advantage of the Overseas Chinese to seize leadership and control over schools and associations in their communities.

In addition, the Propaganda Department, the Foreign Affairs Department, the International Liaison Department, and other related overseas working units were more or less involved in Overseas Chinese affairs. The hierarchy of the Party organi-zations in charge of Overseas Chinese affairs prior to the Cultural Revolution is set forth in Chart 17-1.

Chart 17-1—Party Organizations Responsible for Overseas Chinese Affairs (before the Cultural Revolution)

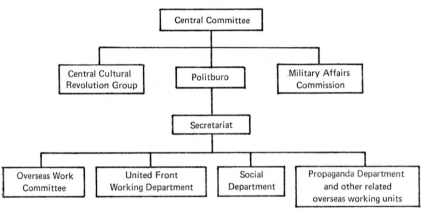

Government organizations. The National People's Congress (NPC) is the supreme organ of state power and officially the sole legislative body in Communist China. Article 23 of the 1954 Constitution provides a quota of thirty representatives of Overseas Chinese residents abroad to the NPC. The representatives of Overseas Chinese at the first NPC were designated by consultative means at an enlarged con-ference of the Overseas Chinese Affairs Commission held in 1954, while those at the third were elected at the Third Enlarged Conference of the third session of the Overseas Chinese Affairs Commission. Although the total number of representatives at the third NPC (3,037) was almost double that of the first, representation of Over-seas Chinese remained at thirty.

regions: The Philippines; Vietnam, Thailand, and Burma; Indonesia; Malaysia and Singa-pore; India, Pakistan, and Ceylon; the Arab countries; Africa; Hong Kong and Macao; Japan; The United States and Canada; Latin America, Europe; and others. Chang Hsi-ch'e, *Kung-fei Ch'iao-wu Cheng-ts'e yü Ch'iao-wu Kung-tso* (*Chinese Communist Policy and Activities To-ward the Overseas Chinese* (Taipei, 1962), pp. 163–64.

In order further to win the friendship of Overseas Chinese by offering them at least a symbolic voice in government, the P.R.C. Government has either invited or designated certain prominent Overseas Chinese as members of the CPPCC. At the fourth National Committee Conference of the CPPCC, held in Peking on December 20, 1964, Overseas Chinese held 17 of the 1,071 seats.[49] In addition, the Chih-kung Party, which is composed of Overseas Chinese returnees and dependents, is represented in the CPPCC. Through the CPPCC, united front work among Overseas Chinese has been extended.

The Overseas Chinese Affairs Commission. On October 1, 1949, when the Peking regime was formally established, the Overseas Chinese Affairs Commission was set up under the Government Administrative Council (reorganized as the State Council in September, 1954). The main task of the Commission was to work through government organs in carrying out united front work among Overseas Chinese communities both at home and abroad. Ho Hsiang-ning was the first chairman of the commission; after the first conference of the third NPC in 1959, she was replaced by her son, Liao Ch'eng-chih. A new roster of officers was then drawn up and approved by the ninety-first and ninety-second plenary sessions of the State Council in August, 1959.[50]

Four important working departments were provided in the Overseas Chinese Affairs Commission, which assumed full responsibility for Overseas Chinese affairs abroad. The First Department was in charge of work in Soviet Russia and the Communist bloc; the Second, Asia; the Third, America and Europe; and the Fourth, the West Asian Islamic countries and Africa.

Chart 17–2—Organization of Overseas Chinese Affairs Commission
(before the Cultural Revolution)

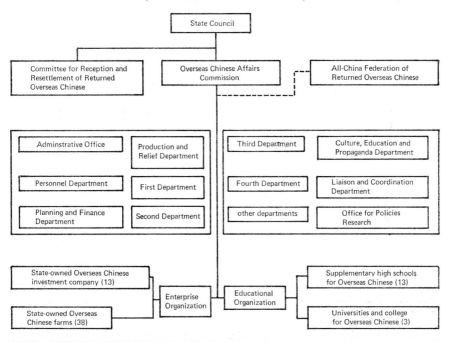

[49] *Jen-min Shou-ts'e* (*People's Handbook*) (Peking: Ta-kung-pao Ch'u-pan-she, 1965), pp. 25–39.

[50] *JMJP*, September 18, 1959.

Two other types of organization that also came under the leadership of the commission were educational organizations (two universities and one college) and business organizations (thirteen state-owned Overseas Chinese investment companies and thirty-eight state-owned Overseas Chinese farms). (See Chart 17–2.)

In addition, many other units were in charge of internal Overseas Chinese affairs, such as administrative personnel, finance, production and relief, education and propaganda, coordination, and research organs.

Chart 17–3—Organization of Local Committees for Overseas Chinese Affairs
(before the Cultural Revolution)

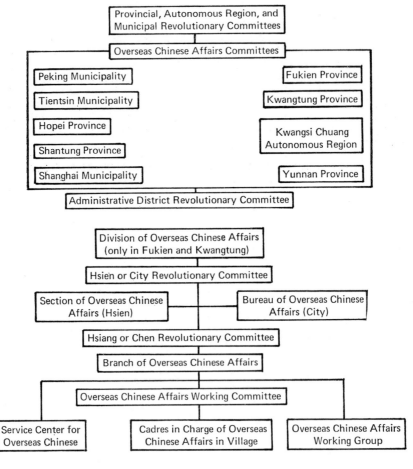

Local organizations. According to decisions made by the Fourth Enlarged Conference of the Overseas Chinese Affairs Commission, held on June 8, 1955,[51] various local working organizations were established as follows:

> (1) Based on demonstrated needs, various provinces and cities set up departments for handling Overseas Chinese affairs.

---

(2) In cities directly under provincial control, special districts, and counties with large concentrations of returned Overseas Chinese, bureaus or sections for Overseas Chinese affairs were organized or specially commissioned personnel were designated.

(3) In small cities with concentrations of returned Overseas Chinese, working committees or working groups for Overseas Chinese affairs were established as a core organization of the Resident Committee. (For the organizational system of local organizations at various levels, see Chart 17–3.)

In foreign countries with which Peking had diplomatic relations, specially commissioned staffs were assigned control of Overseas Chinese affairs. Where no diplomatic relations were maintained, service departments or correspondence sections were established in businesses run in behalf of Peking.

The Committee for Reception and Resettlement of Returned Overseas Chinese. In order to handle the reception and resettlement of returned Overseas Chinese from Indonesia and India, a Committee for Reception and Resettlement of Returned Overseas Chinese was organized under the State Council in February, 1960. Simultaneously, organizations of the same nature were established at the provincial level as noted earlier.

'People's Associations.' In the early period after 1949, many cities and counties with large populations of returned Overseas Chinese organized such societies as the Returned Overseas Chinese Association. In October, 1956, the All-China Federation of Returned Overseas Chinese was established in Peking. At the same time, the name of the returned Overseas Chinese Association was changed to Federation of Returned Overseas Chinese, and the local units were placed under the control of the All-China Federation in Peking. At present, there are such organizations in Kwangtung, Fukien, Shantung, Yünnan, and Shanghai, as well as in some autonomous regions. In small cities and counties where returned Overseas Chinese are concentrated, there are corresponding city or county units of the various associations of returned Overseas Chinese.

The main tasks of the All-China Federation of Returned Overseas Chinese are as follows:

(1) To organize and educate the returned Overseas Chinese and their dependents to make them actively join in socialist construction.

(2) To direct a comprehensive propaganda program toward the returned Overseas Chinese to promote 'their consciousness of socialism and patriotism.'

(3) To reflect opinions of the Overseas Chinese residents both at home and abroad and make suggestions to the appropriate government units.

(4) To unite with the Overseas Chinese in a 'patriotic alliance.'

(5) To help the returned Overseas Chinese develop educational and other public service careers.[52]

The Cultural Revolution and Overseas Chinese Affairs

Policy revision at National Overseas Chinese Work Conference. A conference of responsible cadres at various levels was convened by the Communist Chinese Overseas Affairs Commission in the summer of 1966, when the Cultural Revolution was in full swing. Called the National Overseas Chinese Work Conference, it revised the policy for Overseas Chinese affairs by stressing 'the factor of positiveness, self-consciousness in revolution, the necessity of triumphing over bourgeois ideologies and the gradual establishment of the proletarian world outlook.' The meeting also demanded that leading elements in Overseas Chinese affairs at various levels pay special attention to:

---

[52] *JMJP*, October 9, 1956.

(1) 'Giving prominence to politics,' putting the 'living study and application of Mao Tse-tung's thought' above all things and using 'Mao Tse-tung's thought' to improve work;

(2) penetrating deep into the masses and basic echelons, going down to the countryside and farms, and conducting experiments at selected points to obtain firsthand data;

(3) participating in the 'three great revolutionary movements' ('class struggle,' 'production struggle,' and 'scientific experimentation') and practicing the system that requires cadres to engage in labor;

(4) cultivating and promoting young cadres who are faithful to 'Mao Tse-tung's thought' and who work wholeheartedly for the Communist Party to strengthen the 'leading body.'[53]

On the basis of the above resolutions, a vigorous campaign was launched on the mainland in 1967 to establish 'cultural schools' in the home towns of the Overseas Chinese and on state-owned Overseas Chinese farms. In the span of one year, the state-owned Hsing-lung Overseas Chinese Farm alone opened 180 such schools to take charge of the campaign for the study of Mao Tse-tung's works. In addition, study groups were organized on the basis of production teams, and study classes were set up in the home towns of the Overseas Chinese. For example, the state-owned Chang-shan Overseas Chinese Farm mobilized a total of 30,000 returned Overseas Chinese to join in the study movement.[54]

'Power-seizure struggle.' During the Cultural Revolution, hundreds of Red Guard organizations were formed by returned Overseas Chinese and their relatives through-out the mainland. Almost all such 'rebel organizations' shouted pro-Mao slogans and engaged in 'power seizures' against government agencies and 'class struggles' against other Overseas Chinese.

During the struggle within the Overseas Chinese Affairs Commission of the State Council, two rival organizations appeared: the Joint-Power-seizure Committee of Proletarian Revolutionaries of the Overseas Chinese Affairs Commission, which supported the 'power-holders,' and the Revolutionary Rebel General Command of the Overseas Chinese Affairs Commission, a pro-Mao unit. The targets of the Maoist organization were Liao Ch'eng-chih, chairman of the Overseas Chinese Affairs Commission; Fang Fang and Lin Hsiu-te, vice-chairmen; Wu Chi-sen, commission member and concurrently department director; and Chen Man-yin, deputy department director.[55] At a 'liquidation rally' held on April 6, 1967, the Maoists demanded the dissolution of the commission. The major charges against Liao Ch'eng-chih and Fang Fang were:

(1) Implementation of Liu Shao-ch'i's policy of 'capitulation to the imperialists, the modern revisionists and the reactionaries of different countries and stamping out the flames of revolution in the world';

(2) opposition to Mao's instructions that 'class struggle is also needed in the Overseas Chinese work';

---

[53] *Hsiang-kang Shih-pao (Hong Kong Times)*, August 13, 1966.

[54] China News Service, No. 4654, Peking, January 4, 1967.

[55] Other important cadres involved in the struggle included Chang Fan, commission member and concurrently holding responsible post in the China News Service; Chou Chien-chih, head of the Shanghai Branch of the China News Service; Chang Chih-ping, head of the Overseas Chinese Affairs Division of the Shanghai Municipal Government; Liu Hsiang-wen, deputy head of the division; Huang Ching-shu, chairman of the Shanghai Municipal United Association of Returned Overseas Chinese; and Pao Kuang-hung, head of the Shanghai Municipal Cultural Revolution Group.

(3) disbanding of 'Mao Tse-tung's thought study groups' and prohibition of the study of politics by the Overseas Chinese; and

(4) 'shielding capitalist-roaders, attacking revolutionary masses and turning the Commission into independent kingdoms.'

Liao Ch'eng-chih subsequently was purged, but the vacancy has remained unfilled because appointment of a person of his rank has to be decided by the Standing Committee of the National People's Congress, and the committee has not been functioning properly since the outset of the Cultural Revolution. However, external dealings of the commission had to continue, and these were handled by Li Ch'u-li, director of the commission's International Liaison Department.

In May, 1967, when all the State Council's ministries and commissions were placed under the watchful eyes of soldiers, the Military Control Committee created for the Overseas Chinese Affairs Commission came under the direction of Kuo Shih-yung, known to outsiders only as a former deputy commissar.

Chou En-lai remained silent at the height of the power struggle, when no one could discern the qualities, intentions, and prospects of the contending factions. When the heat had somewhat subsided, Chou as an innocent go-between asked the two sides to forge a 'great alliance.'[56] His aim was eventually to bring both sides firmly under his control so as to strengthen and elevate his own position. In November, 1969, the State Council started shuffling its agencies in an effort to simplify and streamline operations. The Overseas Chinese Affairs Commission was merged into the Foreign Ministry under the State Council in July, 1970.

To the Red Guards, the returned Overseas Chinese and their relatives are the 'remnant force of the bourgeois elements.' A movement to 'remold their spiritual outlook' had to be pushed in earnest along with the Socialist Education Movement and the 'three big revolutionary movements' of class struggle, production struggle, and scientific experiments. This was followed by a series of stern actions, including reinvestigation of the backgrounds of Overseas Chinese in their countries of residence and a temporary ban on their exit from China. Some of them were subjected to 'struggle' under the charges of being 'revisionists,' 'capitalists,' and 'feudalists.' Strict control was exercised over their financial activities, and kidnaping and blackmail were used to extort remittances from overseas relatives. Thus Communist persecution of Overseas Chinese during the Cultural Revolution period is reminiscent of the 1950–53 excesses. Later, recognizing that these and other tyrannical measures actually did more harm than good throughout the mainland, Peking felt compelled to criticize the Red Guards for committing serious mistakes of 'infantilism.'

Red Guard expansion into Overseas Chinese communities. The communiqué of the eleventh plenary session of the Eighth Central Committee of the CCP, adopted on August 12, 1966, stated:

> Proletarian internationalism is the supreme principle guiding China's foreign policy. The session warmly supports the just struggle of the Asian, African, and Latin American peoples against imperialism headed by the United States and its stooges and also supports the revolutionary struggles of the people of all countries.

Thus, the expansion of the Red Guards was the vanguard of Communist China's 'revolutionary exporters'; Peking attempted to 'export' the 'violent thought of Mao Tse-tung' to foreign soil by openly promoting the study of Mao's works in Overseas Chinese communities.

Macao became the first target of the Red Guards abroad. In early December, 1966, when the Portuguese government of Macao refused to permit pro-Peking elements to open a school, Red Guards staged demonstrations and organized a 'struggle

---

[56] *Hsing-tao Jih-pao (Hsing-tao Daily)*, Hong Kong, May 22, 1967.

committee against persecutions,' finally forcing the Portuguese authorities to yield. Later, the 'struggle committee' was reorganized as the Representative Conference of Compatriots from All Walks of Life in Macao for the purpose of controlling the entire Overseas Chinese community in the colony.

In May, 1967, Red Guards began to organize in Hong Kong. On May 16, a 'struggle committee' to lead riots was established for Hong Kong and Kowloon. By November, there were eighty-seven 'struggle committees' organized by students and hundreds of 'fighting corps.' On November 8, the struggle committees issued a 'struggle program' calling on the people in the British colony 'to grasp tightly the invincible ideological weapon of Mao Tse-tung's thought and develop the Red Guard spirit that dares to launch struggles and score victories.'[57] However, after a short period of time, the British Government, with the strong support of the anti-Communist Overseas Chinese community, was able to regain control of the situation.

Immediately after the 'May storm' in Hong Kong, Peking's Red Guards began to extend their activities into Southeast Asia. An Associated Press dispatch of May 21, 1967, reported that Red Guard-type turmoil had broken out in Malaysia. Soon Chinese students appeared in Singapore, holding aloft copies of *Quotations from Chairman Mao Tse-tung* and wearing Mao's badges. On June 22, Red Guards demonstrated in Rangoon in defiance of an order of the Burmese Government and thus came into conflict with local authorities. On June 26, Burmese students reacted by launching a campaign against all Overseas Chinese in that country regardless of political sympathies. Peking's political subversion also touched off anti-Chinese movements in Indonesia and other Southeast Asian nations.

Future developments. The Great Proletarian Cultural Revolution has, for the time being at least, dealt a severe blow to Peking's Overseas Chinese work. For example, the Communists have always regarded the encouragement of Overseas Chinese remittances as of prime importance. However, since the launching of the Cultural Revolution, Overseas Chinese have become hesitant to send money back to the chaotic mainland. Overseas Chinese students are equally unwilling to subject themselves to possible ordeals under the 'Mao Tse-tung's thought propaganda teams' in the schools.

The Cultural Revolution adversely affected Peking's foreign trade in Southeast Asia. For example, the Canton-Kowloon Railway Bureau reported that foodstuffs bound for Hong Kong via the railroad between May, 1967, and March, 1968, dropped 45.75 per cent from the corresponding period in the preceding year.[58] The number of tourists to the mainland also decreased. Statistics released by the Hong Kong Immigration Bureau showed that Chinese going to the Chinese mainland totaled only 276,700 in 1967, compared with 431,000 in 1966.[59]

Since the National Overseas Chinese Work Conference in the summer of 1966, no similar meeting has been possible because of the ravages of the Cultural Revolution. Like all the other administrative organs of Peking, the system in charge of Overseas Chinese activities still remains crippled. But that does not mean the Chinese Communists are no longer attaching importance to the Overseas Chinese. Quite the contrary, the 'carrot and stick' tactics for the Overseas Chinese, including returnees and dependents on the mainland, must now be put to intense use because of the regime's current diplomatic 'offensive of smiles' and the need to have Overseas Chinese representation for the long-pending Fourth National People's Congress.

Mergers and personnel reshuffling under the State Council also have to be completed before the Congress. If Peking cannot find some one better qualified than Liao Ch'eng-chih to direct Overseas Chinese affairs, the deposed chairman of the Overseas

---

[57] *Ta-kung Pao*, Hong Kong, November 28, 1967.

[58] *Ch'iao-hsin (Overseas Chinese Correspondence)*, No. 378, Taipei: Federation of Overseas Chinese Associations.

[59] *Hsing-tao Jih-pao*, December 15, 1967.

Chinese Affairs Commission may have to be employed again. Hong Kong's *Nan-hua Wan-pao* (*South China Evening Post*), in its March 5, 1971, issue, quoted mainland sources as saying that Liao was getting ready for a comeback with Chou En-lai's assistance. Earlier, in February, 1971, Aiichiro Fujiyama, who headed the Japanese trade mission to Peking, reportedly saw Liao in that city. Liao's connections in Hong Kong, Macao, and Southeast Asia, not to mention other areas, will have to be exploited if Peking wants to intensify its united front campaign abroad

The joint editorial of Peking's three major organs—*Jen-min Jih-pao, Liberation Army Daily,* and *Hung Ch'i* magazine—on New Year's Day, 1971, stated that the regime externally would 'stanchly fulfill its obligations toward the proletariat of the world and resolutely support the revolutionary struggles of peoples in various countries' and internally would 'carry out an over-all ideological and political re-education for the Party, further strengthen unity on the basis of Mao Tse-tung's thinking, and more efficiently safeguard and follow the Maoist line of proletarian revolution.' Even though the joint editorial did not refer directly to Peking's Overseas Chinese policy, it suggested a dynamic external policy. As regards the Overseas Chinese, the following trends appear likely:

First, returned Overseas Chinese and their dependents will be subjected to intensified ideological indoctrination in keeping with Mao's thought. They will be forced to participate in 'productive labor.' Privileges formerly available for Overseas Chinese returnees, dependents, and students will be cancelled so as to close the gap between these 'petty bourgeois elements' and the economically less privileged masses.

Second, Peking-incited subversion in Overseas Chinese communities abroad will increase the vigilance of local governments against Communist ambitions and inevitably lead to more anti-Chinese campaigns. The Maoists probably will go all out for the implementation of their policy of 'exporting revolution' despite considerations of the security and welfare of the Overseas Chinese.

The Chinese Communists claim to be protectors of Overseas Chinese interests, but there is a lot of truth in the frequent Radio Moscow declarations that Peking seeks politically to exploit the Overseas Chinese in Southeast Asia. A Chinese-language broadcast from the Russian capital on October 23, 1970, for instance, said: 'Peking's policy has been to win over the majority of Overseas Chinese to its side as reserves for the struggle to elevate its international position and political status.'

SELECTED BIBLIOGRAPHY

Books and Monographs

NAOSAKU, UCHIDA. *The Overseas Chinese.* Stanford, Calif.: Hoover Institution, Stanford University, 1959. A bibliographical essay with supplementary bibliography by EUGENE WU and HSÜEH CHÜN-TU.

OEY GIOK PO. *Survey of Chinese Language Materials on Southeast Asia in the Hoover Institution and Library.* Ithaca, N.Y.: Cornell University Press, 1953.

PURCELL, VICTOR. *The Chinese in Southeast Asia.* 2d ed. London: Oxford University Press, 1965. A fairly comprehensive study of the Overseas Chinese in each of the countries of Southeast Asia.

SKINNER, GEORGE WILLIAM. *Chinese Society in Thailand: An Analytical History.* Ithaca, N.Y.: Cornell University Press, 1957.

WILLIAMS, LEA E. *The Future of the Overseas Chinese in Southeast Asia.* New York: McGraw-Hill Book Company, for the Council on Foreign Relations, 1966.

WU, CHUN-HSI. *Dollars, Dependents and Dogma: Overseas Chinese Remittances to Communist China.* Stanford, Calif.: Hoover Institution, Stanford University, 1967. A comprehensive work on Overseas Chinese remittances to Communist China.

WU, CHU-HUI. *Kakyo honshitsu no bunseki (The Essence of the Overseas Chinese Community).* Tokyo

Institute of Social Science, Tokyo University, 1959. A fundamental study of the Overseas Chinese.

Collections and Periodicals

Ch'iao-wu Fa-kuei Hui-pien (*Compendium of the Laws, Regulations and Statements on Overseas Chinese Affairs*), Peking, 1951. Communist China's policy on Overseas Chinese.

Ch'iao-wu Pao (*Overseas Chinese Affairs Journal*), Peking: Ch'iao-wu Pao-she, 1957–66. Bimonthly organ of Communist China's Overseas Chinese Affairs Commission. Contains reports on Overseas Chinese activities, official statements, and essays on policy.

Tsu-kuo (*China Monthly*), Hong Kong: Union Research Institute, 1950. A monthly publication discussing current conditions in Communist China.

18

POPULATION PROBLEMS, THEORIES, AND POLICIES*

JOHN S. AIRD

Is China today merely another example of an underdeveloped country whose development is impeded by the multiplication of its human liabilities, or is it the unique case of a wholly self-made nation that has discovered a way to maximize the potential of its human assets? The answer to this question has such far-reaching implications that it should not be derived from popular impression or from the more articulate but equally prejudiced assertions of interpreters of the Chinese scene who have ideological axes to grind and are determined to make China their whetstone. Yet, unfortunately, the kind of information needed for more scholarly approaches and more definite answers is not available.

The Chinese Communist leaders themselves do not have it, and therefore they have not been able to decide once and for all whether population growth is a great danger, a minor obstacle, or a positive contribution to the realization of their hopes for China. In the course of their two decades as masters of China's destiny, they have held all three views, though they do not seem ever to have taken the position that China needs a still greater population or a still more rapid population growth rate.

When they came to power in 1949, the Party leaders accepted an obligation, for both humanitarian and political reasons, to improve public health and sanitation and to mitigate famine and undernutrition among the Chinese masses as rapidly as possible. Even though reliable statistical evidence is lacking, there can be little doubt that they succeeded to a certain extent, particularly in the early years, and that, as a result, death rates in China declined sharply and natural increase rates rose.

Mao and his colleagues were slow to grasp the implications of changes. They were distrustful of the demographic evidence, and not without some reason. As doctrinaire Marxists, they should have been undismayed by rapid population growth, but they were also well aware of China's backwardness and by no means confident, despite what Marx said, that population growth had nothing to do with it. They tried very hard to maintain their faith in the promise of Marxism, but, when confronted with adverse circumstances that Marxism could not rationalize, they reacted with deep anxiety, plunging into a crash program of family limitation. When conditions seemed to ease, they reverted to revolutionary optimism once more. When official population policy was not at one end of its swing or the other; it hung indecisively between. The instability of population policy meant that family limitation programs had little

---

* The opinions expressed in this chapter are those of the writer and do not necessarily coincide with the official views of the United States Government.

chance of realizing their potential effectiveness. Hence the variable course of population policy cannot be closely linked with demographic phenomena in China, either as cause or as effect. It seems more directly tied to varying perceptions by Party leaders of China's problems and prospects and to alternating currents of dogmatism and pragmatism within the Central Committee. The study of population policies in the P.R.C. is useful mainly for what it reveals about decision-making by an authoritarian leadership without firm ideological or empirical reference points.

The commitment of the Party leaders to Marxist ideology was not completely rigid, nor was it so loose that they could readily turn to other value systems for reasons of expediency or convenience. Marxism provided the arguments that legitimized their claim to power. It also sustained their hopes of transforming China into a modern, industrial nation within their own lifetime, thus consolidating their revolution and confirming their own place in history. Marxist theorists had rather little to say specifically about how population growth might affect China's transition to socialism, but they denounced Malthus with great vehemence and, in the process, virtually denied the possibility of population problems in a socialist society. According to Marx, there was no such thing as 'absolute overpopulation' in the Malthusian sense. A state of 'relative overpopulation' emerged in capitalist countries as the capitalists, taking advantage of their control of the 'means of production,' used technology to displace labor and create a surplus of unemployed workers the better to exploit the working class. But under socialism, with the 'means of production' in the hands of the workers through state ownership, no such displacement could occur. Instead, the working classes, inspired by their new political dispensation, would achieve a far higher level of production and productivity than was possible under capitalism, enabling socialist society to develop technologically without unemployment and to raise living levels at the same time. For each stage in the evolution of society there was a specific 'law of population,' according to Marx. Just what the socialist 'law of population' consisted of he did not specify, but it seemed to include the proposition that, since labor is the source of wealth and the key to economic development in a socialist society, a large and growing population must inevitably be not a liability but an asset.

A POSTURE OF MARXIST OPTIMISM

Consistent with the above views, Peking's position on population policy from 1949 through 1953 was ostensibly an unshakeably optimistic one. The official view was set forth in a New China News Agency release on September 16, 1949, the text of which subsequently turned up among the collected works of Mao:

> It is a very good thing that China has a big population. Even if China's population multiplies many times, she is fully capable of finding a solution; the solution is production. The absurd argument of Western bourgeois economists like Malthus that increases in food cannot keep pace with increases in population was not only thoroughly refuted by Marxists long ago, but has also been completely exploded by the realities in the Soviet Union and the Liberated Areas of China after their revolutions.

> . . . .
> . . . . Of all things in the world, people are the most precious. Under the leadership of the Communist Party, as long as there are people, every kind of miracle can be performed. . . . We believe that revolution can change everything, and that before long there will arise a new China with a big population and a great wealth of products, where life will be abundant and culture will flourish. All pessimistic views are utterly groundless.[1]

---

[1] 'The Bankruptcy of the Idealist Conception of History,' September 16, 1949, *Selected*

With such prospects, birth control was unnecessary. More than that, it was an alien, inhumane idea, a foreign plot to 'kill off the Chinese people without shedding blood.' Contraceptives could not be imported into China even for medical reasons. Those who expressed concern over population growth were denounced as Malthusians.

Yet there were some signs that the Party leaders were not as confident of the ultimate self-solution of population problems as they pretended to be in public pronouncements. When the urban police and rural 'land reform' investigations reported larger population totals than had been expected, the new figures were received with skepticism instead of enthusiasm, as if a large population total were not such a good thing after all. The decision to discontinue vital registration work by the Ministry of Public Health in order to discourage Malthusian ideas seems to owe as much to anxiety as to ideology. When the preliminary census total was announced on June 19, 1954, by Teng Hsiao-p'ing, who had been secretary of the General Election Committee, no ideological context was supplied to let the Party cadres and the people know what was the officially approved attitude toward the new figure. Teng merely said that the figure was accurate and could be used for economic planning.[2] A Jen-min Jih-pao editorial the next day noted briefly that the figures showed a 'marked increase in the country's population' but ventured nothing further.[3] Not until August 7, 1954, was an effort made to assure readers of the Party's leading newspaper that the unexpectedly large total was good news, despite what foreign Malthusians might say. The August article affected an air of jubilation, but its undertone was somewhat defensive.[4]

Malthusian Seedlings

The first public indication of a change in China's population policies appeared on September 18, 1954, between the preliminary and final census announcements. Shao Li-tzu, a non-Communist intellectual and a deputy to the newly convened First National People's Congress, rose to deliver a speech before that body calling for a national family limitation campaign. Shao argued that, although a large population was still a 'good thing' and a point of national pride, it could also cause temporary difficulties while China remained a backward country, and that contraceptive practices should be propagated to speed the pace of socialist transformation and industrialization. Shao's speech was printed the same day in Jen-min Jih-pao.[5] Neither the speech nor its instant publication could have been accidental; both must have had the highest sanction. Such an inference is further supported by the fact that, although Shao received many letters criticizing his views from a traditional Marxist standpoint,

---

Works of Mao Tse-tung, 4 (Peking: Foreign Languages Press, 1961): 453–54. The original article was a critique of views attributed to U.S. Secretary of State Dean Acheson that the Chinese revolution was the result of the failure of previous regimes to solve China's population problem and that the new regime would also be unable to find a solution. Mao granted that this view sounded plausible 'to those Chinese who do not reason clearly,' and his article was apparently intended to allay their doubts.

[2] 'Census and General Election Completed in China: Population of China Over 600 Million,' NCNA, June 19, 1954; translated in Survey of China Mainland Press, No. 832, June 19–21, 1954, p. 2.

[3] 'Greeting the Completion of the Basic Level Elections Throughout the Country,' Jen-min Jih-pao, June 20, 1954; translated in Survey of China Mainland Press, No. 832, June 19–21, 1954, pp. 5–7.

[4] Jo Shui, 'Six Hundred Million,' Jen-min Jih-pao, August 7, 1954; translated in Survey of China Mainland Press, No. 890, September 17, 1954, pp. 31–33.

[5] 'Deputy Shao Li-tzu Speaks on Birth Control at National People's Congress,' Jen-min Jih-pao, September 18, 1954; translated in Survey of China Mainland Press, No. 920, November 2, 1954, pp. 3–5.

the hard-line Marxist position, which had until then been national policy, was without a public champion for the next four years. This too was no accident.

When the final census results were released on November 1, 1954, a suitable ideological setting had been prepared. It included many of the same protestations and reassurances that had been given out in August, but it dealt more specifically and at greater length with Malthusian fears. A census official, Pai Chien-hua, denounced the 'fantastic rumor' that China could not feed its large population, arguing that the rate of increase in food production was higher than the rate of increase in population. But Pai admitted that 'in an economically underdeveloped country, rapid increase in population may cause difficulties in living,' among which he mentioned problems of unemployment. Although he insisted that the development of socialism would ultimately eliminate such problems, the admission that they could occur even temporarily was a step closer to Malthusianism.[6]

In December, 1954, Shao wrote for another Peking paper an article that he described hopefully as a 'prelude to the dissemination of knowledge about contraception.' In it he disclosed that in July, 1954, the Ministry of Public Health had drafted some proposals concerning the 'problem of contraception and birth control.'[7] He may also have been aware of the fact that, as was subsequently revealed, the State Council had instructed the Ministry of Public Health as early as August, 1953, to 'help the masses exercise birth control' and that Mao's then heir apparent, Liu Shao-ch'i, had scheduled a symposium on birth control in Peking for December 27, 1954,[8] but no word of these developments appeared in the press until more than two years later. Those signs of official endorsement, though covert, may have led Shao to suppose that official action was imminent, but he was mistaken. A directive issued by the Party Central Committee in March, 1955, gave qualified support to birth control, but again there was no public disclosure of even that modest gesture until a year and a half later.[9] At the second session of the First National People's Congress in July, 1955, Shao requested a 'strengthening' of the still very feeble propaganda campaign for contraception and a relaxation of restrictions on surgical sterilization. Shao's motion was passed on to the Ministry of Public Health by the State Council, but little else happened.[10] Reviewing the ministry's achievements at the third session of the Congress in June, 1956, Health Minister Li Te-ch'üan admitted in two sentences that birth control propaganda had been neglected and needed further strengthening.[11] Shao professed satisfaction with Madame Li's statement but showed his impatience with official foot-dragging by inviting other deputies to join him in 'paying close attention' to the ministry's future actions.[12]

Finally, on August 3, 1956, an editorial in a Peking paper criticized public health organs for failing to take an active role in promoting contraception and declared that

---

[6] Pai, Chien-hua, '600 Million People: A Great Strength for Socialist Construction of China,' *Jen-min Jih-pao*, November 1, 1954; translated in *Survey of China Mainland Press*, No. 926, November 11–12, 1954, pp. 32–34.

[7] Shao Li-tzu, 'Concerning the Problem of Dissemination of Knowledge About Contraception,' *Kuang-ming Jih-pao (Enlightenment Daily)*, December 19, 1954; translated in *Survey of China Mainland Press*, No. 976, January 28, 1955, pp. 26–31.

[8] 'Exercise Appropriate Birth Control' (editorial), *Jen-min Jih-pao*, March 5, 1957; translated in *Survey of China Mainland Press*, No. 1487, March 12, 1957, p. 6.

[9] 'Speech by Comrade Ts'ai Ch'ang,' *Eighth National Congress of the Communist Party of China*, 2 (Peking: Foreign Languages Press, 1956): 286.

[10] Shao Li-tzu, 'The Problem of Birth Control,' NCNA, June 26, 1956; translated in *Current Background*, No. 405, July 26, 1956, p. 17.

[11] Li Te-ch'üan, 'New Tasks for the Protection of Public Health,' NCNA, June 18, 1956; translated in *Current Background*, No. 405, July 26, 1956, p. 15.

[12] Shao Li-tzu, *loc. cit.*

henceforth this task must be regarded as 'the order of the day.'[13] Ten days later, the same paper disclosed that the ministry had delivered essentially the same message to all provincial and municipal public health departments and bureaus throughout the country in a directive issued on August 6. The directive instructed local health officials to set up clinics, train and reassign medical and propaganda cadres, improve the supply of contraceptive devices and drugs, and provide whatever leadership was needed to assure conscientious work.[14]

From August, 1956, onward, the campaign began to move, and the press contained much evidence of the accelerated activity. Local birth control guidance committees were appointed, with high Party officials as members or nominal chairmen. The production of contraceptives was given a new priority by pharmaceutical and rubber goods enterprises. Research institutes were set up to test Chinese herbalist contraceptive formulas. Posters, film strips, films, pamphlets, and physiological models were produced and distributed; lectures, exhibits, and discussion meetings were held. The mass organizations were activated to bring pressure on their members. Party and health cadres took the campaign into factories, shops, and private homes. If the people would not come to contraception, contraception would go to the people.

But, as the tempo of the campaign quickened, many obstacles loomed that had not been apparent in its earlier stages. Some were purely technical. As might have been expected, contraceptive propaganda could be produced more quickly than contraceptive devices. The modest stocks carried by the local pharmacies were promptly depleted and could not be immediately replenished. In the rush to meet the new demand, the pharmaceutical and rubber industries turned out defective products: Condoms and diaphragms were perforated when purchased or ruptured in use; spermicides had toxic side effects; inadequate instructions were issued with the devices, and they were sometimes inappropriately used. The Chinese Communist penchant for herbalist medicine led to the promotion of untested herbalist contraceptive formulas, some of which were later found to be ineffectual and even dangerous.[15] When the legal restrictions on sterilization and abortion were relaxed by the Ministry of Public Health in recognition of the new priorities for family limitation after August, 1956, many practicing surgeons were not technically capable of performing the operations, and some operations were done badly.

There were also major political obstacles to the campaign. Traditional prejudices gave rise to widespread popular resistance, which took many different forms. The older generations still regarded numerous offspring as a proof of the beneficence of heaven and a guarantee of security in their old age. Some parents thought that childbearing was a matter of fate that should not be tampered with. Others felt that contraception was immoral. Still others were embarrassed by the open publicity about

---

[13] 'For Active Dissemination of Contraceptive Knowledge' (editorial), *Kuang-ming Jih-pao*, August 3, 1956; translated in *Survey of China Mainland Press*, No. 1352, August 17, 1956, pp. 2–4.

[14] 'Wei-sheng-pu Fa-ch'u Kuan-yü Pi-yün Kung-tso Chih-shih (Ministry of Public Health Issues Directive Concerning Contraceptive Work),' *Kuang-ming Jih-pao*, August 13, 1956.

[15] Shao himself was implicated here. At the third session of the First National People's Congress he repeated a formula related to him by the herbalist Yeh Hsi-chun, also an NPC deputy, which promised remarkable contraceptive results from swallowing live tadpoles. Shao was criticized by doctors of Western medicine, who insisted that such formulas should not be broadcast until they had been subjected to proper clinical testing. When the tests were finally carried out nearly two years later, it was discovered that tadpoles had no effect on human fertility, but some tadpoles were found to harbor ascaris and other parasites in their intestines. (See Shao Li-tzu, 'Problem of Birth Control,' p. 18, and 'Test of Chekiang Research Institute of Chinese Medicine Proves that Tadpoles Are Useless for Contraceptive Purposes,' *Jen-min Jih-pao*, April 14, 1958; translated in *Survey of China Mainland Press*, No. 1759, April 28, 1958, p. 17.)

intimate details of domestic life. Some people thought contraception was too much bother, or that it would inhibit sexual enjoyment, or that it was likely to cause sterility, or that it would not work. As the pressures of the campaign mounted, there was increasing evidence of public resentment at government interference in private affairs.

Among doctors and other public health personnel there was considerable resistance to some aspects of the campaign, particularly the liberalization of regulations on sterilization and abortion. The China Medical Association fought a vigorous rear guard action against the Party policy of unrestricted abortion, and the Ministry of Public Health was caught in the crossfire. In the end, the Party triumphed, but at the expense of alienating some key figures in medical circles.

Other opposition came from within the Party. Traditional Marxists were not ready to accept the need for a reduction of population growth rates. Though they could not openly attack the new policies in the press, they could ask questions privately as to whether or not the program would reduce population growth, whether it contradicted the Marxist idea that manpower was the source of all wealth, and whether it was not liable to encourage bourgeois ideas about economic self-advancement. Some asked pointedly why China must discourage childbearing while the Soviet Union encouraged it. All of these arguments were patiently answered in the press. The difference between Malthusian and Chinese Marxist birth control programs was carefully spelled out: Though they might appear to be alike, the former expressed an anti-humanitarian attitude and were motivated by the desire to exploit the people, whereas the latter were humane and intended to benefit the people. But the Party hard-liners were not easily persuaded.

Convincing the orthodox Marxists was made all the more difficult by the doctrinaire line taken by the Party leaders in the past and by the lack of any good Marxist peg on which to hang the rationale for a family limitation campaign. The Party theoreticians, finding little support in the works of Marx, scoured the writings of Engels, Kautsky, Lenin, and others in search of suitable texts, but the gleanings were meager. Lenin had written that medical propaganda and the protection of democratic rights were one thing but neo-Malthusianism was another, that the working class had no use for neo-Malthusianism, but that this did not prevent a socialist country from abolishing Tsarist laws against abortion or from propagating medical 'theories' on contraception.[16] Engels, in a letter to Kautsky, allowed the possibility that population growth in a socialist country might make it necessary to control the birth rate, but he was confident that, should that need arise, a socialist country could meet it without the slightest difficulty.[17] At best, these statements were equivocal.

MALTHUSIANISM IN FULL FLOWER

Nevertheless, the Party theoreticians did what they could to evolve a 'proletarian population theory.' During the late phases of the Hundred Flowers period in the spring of 1957, they were joined, at the invitation of the Party leadership by a number of non-Communist academicians. In May, 1956, Mao had proclaimed the policy of 'letting a hundred flowers bloom and a hundred schools of thought contend.' Originally the Hundred Flowers policy applied only to literature, art, and science, not explicitly including the social sciences or the sphere of political action.[18] Its avowed

---

[16] These two statements, taken from Lenin's essay 'The Working Class and the Neo-Malthusian Theory,' were widely quoted in China from 1954 until early 1958.

[17] Cited from a Chinese translation of Engels's letters by Wang Cho, 'Way to Solve Population Problem in China,' *Jen-min Jih-pao*, February 1, 1958; translated in *Survey of China Mainland Press*, No. 1721, February 28, 1958, p. 3.

[18] Mao's original speech, made to the Supreme State Conference early in May, 1956, was not published. The Hundred Flowers policy was elaborated by Party propaganda chief Lu

purpose was to stimulate new ideas for solutions to China's problems by opening up a forum for intellectual debate. As 1956 wore on, the public debate in the press dealt increasingly with food shortages, the backwardness of agriculture, and the question of what, if anything, had been accomplished by the agricultural producers' cooperatives. But it was Mao himself, in his famous speech to the Supreme State Conference on February 27, 1957, who vitalized the Hundred Flowers and placed population problems in the center of the intellectual ferment.

Among others, the sociologists Ch'en Ta and Wu Ching-ch'ao and the economist Ma Yin-ch'u accepted with apparent enthusiasm the invitation to enter the discussion of the population question. Though they were obliged to observe the conventions of Marxist anti-Malthusianism, they were much less doctrinaire in examining China's population problems and much freer in citing the demographic experience of other countries than were their Marxist colleagues. In setting forth their theories, the academicians cut through some Marxist Gordian knots while tying a few of their own that the Party theoreticians were not able to loose.

In an article for the magazine *New Construction* in March, 1957, Wu began by demolishing the Marxist argument that a large labor force was an asset to national economic development. He pointed out that to increase the rate of economic accumulation it was not enough to increase gross output if per capita output did not also increase. A surplus of labor power was of little value for this purpose without a rise in the productivity of labor. To raise the productivity of labor, it was necessary to increase the level of investment per worker in mechanization, but investment in mechanization was impeded by large labor force increments, which could be reduced only by lowering the birth rate. Wu made it clear that lowering the birth rate would take a long time, and that it would not solve the problem of how to dispose of the present labor surplus left over from the 'old society.' For that problem, Wu concluded disarmingly, he had no solution.[19]

Ch'en Ta joined the discussion in May, 1957, with an article in the same magazine in which he noted that the problems of reducing unemployment and reducing the birth rate 'urgently require solution.' As a demographer, he confined his attention to the second problem. He confirmed Wu's contention that birth rates fall slowly. The experience of Western countries showed that reduction of the birth rate to a more reasonable level took anywhere from twenty to thirty-nine years, that socialist countries were no more successful in this respect than capitalist countries (he made no reference to Engels's blithe prediction), and that abortion, which had been quite effective in Japan, was not appropriate for China. Instead, he recommended that young people be encouraged to marry at a later age. Ch'en was aware that this would require a major change in established customs and would take some time. His views, like those of Wu, were somewhat pessimistic.[20]

Ma Yin-ch'u, the distinguished president of Peking University and long-time friend of Chou En-lai, presented his own population theory in a written statement to the fourth session of the First National People's Congress on July 3, 1957. He declared

---

Ting-i in a speech to a group of writers, artists, and scientists in Peking on May 26. This group did include social scientists, but all the concrete references to science in Lu's speech concerned only the natural sciences. See Lu Ting-i, 'Let All Flowers Bloom Together; Let Diverse Schools of Thought Contend,' *Jen-min Jih-pao*, June 13, 1956; translated in *Current Background*, No. 406, August 15, 1956, pp. 1–18.

[19] Wu Ching-ch'ao, 'A New Treatise on the Problem of China's Population,' *Hsin Chien-she* (*New Construction*), No. 3, March 3, 1957; translated in *Extracts from China Mainland Magazines*, No. 78, April 15, 1957, pp. 1–16.

[20] Ch'en Ta, 'Wan-hun Chieh-yü hsin Chung-kuo Jen-k'ou Wen-t'i (Delayed Marriage, Birth Control, and China's Population Problems),' *Hsin Chien-she*, No. 5, May 3, 1957, pp. 1–15.

that the 'contradiction' between social classes in rural China had been resolved by 'land reform,' only to be replaced by a new 'contradiction' between economic development and the supply of capital under conditions of overpopulation. Because of the large population, there was overconsumption in rural areas, leaving too little surplus capital for accumulation. The essential problem for China was how to raise productivity, particularly among the peasants, when the capital for investment in technological development was insufficient. Ma went beyond Wu and Ch'en in tying the population problem to the problem of food supply and the limited quantity of arable land, a connection most non-Communist scholars hesitated to make for fear of offending the Party's known sensibilities on this point.

Ma had wanted to make his views known at the second session of the First National People's Congress Session in 1955 but had been discouraged by some of his fellow deputies from Chekiang Province, who regarded his position as Malthusian.[21] However, he felt that by 1957 the climate of opinion in official circles had changed.

THE ROOTS OF MALTHUSIANISM

What had brought about the change? Probably a number of different factors were involved, but among the most compelling was surely the new and rather pessimistic evaluation of the prospects for China's agriculture being made in official circles in 1956. Recognition of the backwardness of agriculture was nothing new for the Party leaders. One of the primary political aims of 'land reform' had been the 'mobilization' of the peasant masses to raise their 'productive zeal' and increase agricultural productivity.[22] While collectivization was the ideal, it was necessary to advance it with caution because many of the peasants had only recently become landowners for the first time in their lives and were not ready to surrender their newly acquired land to collective ownership. But in 1953 and 1954, official data showed population increasing more rapidly than food production. As food shortages and famines occurred and became more acute, the Party found it necessary to use somewhat stronger means of 'persuading' the peasants to join cooperatives.

Coercion proved costly, as the peasants, angry at being herded into the cooperatives, sabotaged agricultural production with various forms of noncooperation. The collectivization drive vacillated. In the brief periods of relaxation, the rural cadres were charged with 'commandism,' some cooperatives were disbanded, and new assurances about landownership were given to the anxious peasants. By the middle of 1955, the peasants, the cadres, and the Party leaders were all, for various reasons, unhappy with the situation in rural areas. The food problem was apparently becoming more serious. On July 31, 1955, in a report to a conference of local Party committee secretaries, Mao likened those cadres who were resisting the cooperative drive to women with bound feet who walk 'in an unsteady manner,' complaining all the while that others are going too fast. He called for a moderate speed-up of cooperativization during 1955–56, which would have increased the proportion of peasant

---

[21] Ma Yin-ch'u, 'A New Theory of Population,' *Jen-min Jih-pao*, July 5, 1957; translated in *Current Background*, No. 469, July 25, 1957, pp. 1–18. One of Ma's colleagues, the anthropologist Fei Hsiao-t'ung, had gone much farther, declaring that denunciations of Malthus could not eliminate the phenomena that Malthus was trying to explain. (Quoted in Li P'u, 'The Rightists Shall Not Be Permitted to Take Advantage of the Population Problem for Political Scheming,' *Jen-min Jih-pao*, October 14, 1957; translated in *Survey of China Mainland Press*, No. 1644, November 4, 1957, p. 6.)

[22] Teng Tzu-hui, 'The Political Significance of Agrarian Reform,' *Ch'ang-chiang Jih-pao* (*Yangtze Daily*), Hankow, December 27, 1950; translated in *Current Background*, No. 212, September 25, 1952, p. 6.

households in cooperatives from 14 per cent in June, 1955, to about 30 per cent by October, 1956.[23] By the fall of 1955, however, the all-out drive for socialization of the entire economy was under way, and all former timetables were scrapped. The private sector was virtually eliminated in both urban and rural China. By June, 1956, 91.7 per cent of all peasant households were reportedly in cooperatives.[24]

Meanwhile, the subject of population and food shortages had entered for the first time into overt discussions of rural socialization by officials. Just three weeks before Mao's order on cooperativization, Vice-Premier Li Fu-ch'un noted that the population was large but cultivated land limited and that this problem made it necessary to plan for fuller land utilization.[25] Mao also cited the large population, shortage of cultivated land, frequency of natural calamities, and backwardness of agricultural techniques to explain the lack of prosperity in rural areas.[26] At that stage, official statements did not treat those problems in public as matters of critical urgency, but the July, 1955, decision on cooperativization suggests that they were so regarded within the Party Central Committee.

In 1956, food shortages became a major preoccupation of the Chinese Communist press. At the beginning of the year, the official posture was that the widespread complaints of lack of food were unjustified. In February, Ch'en Po-ta, Mao's personal secretary and spokesman, expressed confidence that China showed 'no sign of overpopulation' but could support 'at least another 600 million people' and that China's agriculture had provided 'proof' that Malthusian population theory was 'nonsense.'[27] In April, Chou En-lai reportedly told a group of foreign visitors that population increase posed no problem, because population was increasing by only 2 per cent annually whereas 'production' was increasing by 10 per cent, and that China needed

---

[23] Mao Tse-tung, 'On the Cooperativization of Agriculture,' NCNA, October 16, 1955; translated in *Current Background*, No. 364, October 19, 1955, p. 3. As of June, 1955, Mao said, there were 650,000 'semisocialist' cooperatives in China, with some 16,900,000 peasant households as members. This would mean that 14.2 per cent of the officially reported total of 119,201,000 peasant households in China in 1955 were in cooperatives. Tentatively, Mao indicated, it had been decided to increase the number of cooperatives to 1,000,000 by October, 1956, in order to have at least one cooperative in each rural *hsiang* throughout the country. Mao added that he himself thought it possible to reach a total of 1,300,000, or double the June, 1955, figure, within the fourteen-month period from August, 1955, to October, 1956. This would imply a membership of about 28 or 29 per cent of all peasant households, if the official 1956 total of peasant households is used. However, Mao also took some pains to assure his listeners that the completion of agricultural socialization was to be accomplished gradually. 'Semisocialist' cooperativization was not to be completed until 1960, and 'fully socialist' cooperativization not until the end of the Third Five-Year Plan period in 1967. From its initiation in 1949, Mao pointed out, the whole transition would require eighteen years. *Ibid.*, pp. 10–14.

[24] Of these, 62.6 per cent were said to be in 'fully socialist' cooperatives, which were larger than the 'semisocialist' cooperatives and marked the end, for all practical purposes, of individual ownership of the land, draft animals, and implements contributed by the peasants on joining the cooperatives. Legally, the peasants still retained the option of withdrawal from the 'fully socialist' cooperatives, but in actuality they could not get out. The June, 1956, figures were given in 'The Gigantic Achievements in Socialist Construction and Transformation. During the First Half of 1956,' *T'ung-chi Kung-tso t'ung-hsin (Statistical Work Bulletin)*, No. 15, August 14, 1956; translated in *Extracts from China Mainland Magazines*, No. 55, October 29, 1956, p. 3.

[25] Li Fu-ch'un, 'Report on the First Five-Year Plan for the Development of the National Economy,' NCNA (English), July 6, 1955; also in *Current Background*, No. 335, July 12, 1955, p. 33.

[26] Mao Tse-tung, 'On the Cooperativization of Agriculture,' *loc. cit.*

[27] Ch'en Po-ta, 'The Socialist Transformation of China's Agriculture,' NCNA, February 2, 1956; translated in *Current Background*, No. 377, February 15, 1956, p. 44.

population but had no need for birth control.[28] Official figures for 1955 had shown food grain production increasing more rapidly than population. In an address to the third session of the First National People's Congress in June, Food Minister Chang Nai-ch'i cited the same figures to show some improvement in the food situation, but he admitted that the amount of grain available per capita was 'not really much.'[29]

From that point on, pessimistic statements about the food situation were heard from all levels. Chou En-lai remarked to a visiting Indian agricultural delegation in September, 1956, that China and India were alike in having too many people and too little arable land.[30] In the same month, the press carried statements about the 'famine situation' developing in parts of China.[31] Official figures for 1956 again showed grain production rising more rapidly than population, but less grain reserves had been added to the stocks in government granaries in 1956 than was distributed as emergency rations during th e winter of 1956–57. In January and February, 1957, despite what had been said about how the cooperatives raised agricultural productivity, it was admitted that the living levels of the peasants were low and would remain so for a long time to come because of the pressures of increasing population on arable land and agricultural production.[32] Most press accounts reiterated the official line that all the difficulties were bound to disappear in due course, but a mood of uncertainty and pessimism pervaded many of the articles. Mao's revolution seemed to be losing its way.

MAO AMONG THE MALTHUSIANS

Then, in February, 1957, Mao made a dramatic, apparently extemporaneous four-hour speech to the Supreme State Conference. The original text of his speech was never published. Apparently, Mao's remarks were declared off the record and not to be quoted directly. Yet it is obvious, from oblique references, that he depicted China's economic situation as grave and issued a clear call for the Chinese people to practice birth control 'in a planned manner.'[33] Ma Yin-ch'u noted that Mao's speech had

---

[28] W. R. Geddes, *Peasant Life in Communist China*, Monograph No. 6, Society for Applied Anthropology (Ithaca, N.Y.: Cornell University Press, 1963), p. 16.

[29] Chang Nai-ch'i, 'The Food Situation in China,' NCNA, June 26, 1956; translated in *Current Background*, No. 407, August 17, 1956, pp. 25–26.

[30] Government of India, Ministry of Food and Agriculture, *Report of the Delegation to China on Agricultural Planning and Techniques* (New Delhi: Government of India Press, 1956), p. 22.

[31] For example, see 'Central Relief Committee Spokesman on Current Famine Situation,' NCNA, September 3, 1956; translated in *Survey of China Mainland Press*, No. 1372, September 18, 1956, pp. 3–4.

[32] P'an Ching-yüan, 'How to View the Living Standard of Peasants,' *Chung-kuo Ch'ing-nien (China Youth)*, No. 1, January 1, 1957; translated in *Extracts from China Mainland Magazines*, No. 74, March 18, 1957, p. 29; Wen Hou-hua, 'What Is the Real Position of Agricultural Cooperativization During the Past Year?' *China Youth*, No. 3, February 1, 1957; translated in *Extracts from China Mainland Magazines*, No. 76, April 1, 1957, p. 22; Ho Wei, 'A Review of the 1956 Grain Work,' *Liang-shih (Grain)*, No. 2, February 25, 1957; translated in *Extracts from China Mainland Magazines*, No. 80, April 29, 1957, pp. 5–11; and Wang Tan-sheng, 'What Is the Major Contradiction in the Present Stage of Development of China's Agriculture?' *Cheng-chih Hsüeh-hsi (Political Study)*, No. 1, January 13, 1957; translated in *Extracts from China Mainland Magazines*, No. 74, March 18, 1957, pp. 25–28.

[33] A Chinese doctor who was present at the conference spoke later of 'the wise directive of Chairman Mao concerning the need of planned birth control' to regulate population growth in China and urged medical workers to 'respond warmly to the call of Chairman Mao.' See Chung, Hui-lan, 'Population and Birth Control' (speech to the third session of the Second Chinese People's Political Consultative Conference National Committee, March 14, 1957), *Jen-min Jih-pao*, March 17, 1957; translated in *Current Background*, No. 445, April 5, 1957, pp. 14–21.

'mentioned definitely the population problem in China.'[34] A report circulating in Warsaw later in the year attributed to Mao a statement that, while the large number of births in China was a sign of medical progress,

> this figure must also be of great concern to us all. . . . The increase in grain harvest in the last two years has been 10,000,000 tons a year. This is barely sufficient to cover the needs of our growing population. . . . Steps must therefore be taken to keep our population for a long time at a stable level, say, of 600,000,000.[35]

A delegate to a provincial people's congress said that Mao had warned that when the Chinese population reached 6 billion, it would hasten its own extinction.[36] Whatever Mao actually said greatly stimulated the family limitation campaign. As one writer later remarked, birth control, once considered to be 'a Malthusian type of weed,' was now 'recognized as a scented flower.'[37] Mao had come a long way from his New China News Agency statement of 1949. He had taken a position close to that of the despised Malthus.

Other official spokesmen were not slow to follow suit. In April, Public Health Minister Li Te-ch'üan described China as a 'large, populous country' whose high rate of population growth must be reduced if China was soon to escape poverty and 'satisfy adequately the requirements of the increased population.[38] Vice-Premier T'an Chen-lin declared that China's 'basic difficulty' was overpopulation.[39] Wang Kuang-wei, chief agricultural planner on the State Planning Commission, said, 'The main feature of our backward agricultural country is that the population is large and the

---

[34] Ma Yin-ch'u, 'A New Theory of Population,' *Current Background*, No. 469, p. 4.

[35] Quoted in 'Communist China: The Population Problem,' *Current Notes on International Affairs*, 29, No. 11 (November, 1958): 717.

[36] K'ung Hsi-wu, 'Chien-i Chao-k'ai Chieh-yü Kung-tso Hui-i (Birth Control Work Conference Proposed),' *Hei-lung-chiang Jih-pao* (*Heilungkiang Daily*), Harbin, June 11, 1957. This incredible figure was also cited, without attribution to Mao, in a letter to the editor of another provincial paper, in which the time period for reaching the total was given as 'another fifty years.' The item is entitled: 'T'i-ch'ang Chieh-yü Shih-pu-shih p'a Mei-yu Ch'in-te (Is the Advocating of Birth Control Caused by Fear of Not Having Enough Food?),' *Yün-nan Jih-pao* (*Yünnan Daily*), Kunming, June 4, 1957. Evidently this figure was current in birth control discussions at that time, and it is quite likely that Mao had used it, as K'ung, in a breach of security, revealed. Dr. Chung Hui-lan had given a series of long-range population projections at rates of 2, 3, and 4 per cent per year in her speech to the National Chinese People's Political Consultative Conference on March 14, 1957, the highest of which gives a total above 5 billion in fifty-four years. Dr. Chung heard Mao's address at the Supreme State Conference on February 27, and it is not impossible that her projection of population growth at 4 per cent was intended to provide mathematical justification for Mao's sensational statement. See Chung Hui-lan, 'Population and Birth Control,' *Jen-min Jih-pao*, March 17, 1957; translated in *Current Background*, No. 445, April 5, 1957, p. 16.

Neither the constant population at 600,000,000, a figure already exceeded by the official total for year end 1956, nor the projection of 6 billion in fifty years, which would require a sustained increase at a rate exceeding 4.5 per cent per year, would make any sense demographically, but this fact would not necessarily have deterred Mao from using one or both of them. Mao's use of figures in other contexts is sometimes rather free.

[37] Hsiao Te, 'Why Should We Boldly "Bloom?" ' *China Youth*, No. 9, May 1, 1957; translated in *Extracts from China Mainland Magazines*, No. 95, August 19, 1957, p. 14.

[38] Li Te-ch'üan, 'Birth Control and Planned Families,' *Jen-min Jih-pao*, March 8, 1957; translated in *Current Background*, No. 445, April 5, 1957, pp. 2–3.

[39] T'an Chen-lin, 'A Preliminary Study of the Income and Living Standard of the Peasants of China,' *Jen-min Jih-pao*, May 5, 1957; translated in *Survey of China Mainland Press*, No. 1555, June 21, 1957, p. 32.

amount of farmland is relatively small.'[40] Yang Po echoed both T'an and Wang in citing 'overpopulation, inherent impoverishment, and backwardness' as dominant characteristics of the Chinese economy.[41] The views expressed by leading contenders both inside and outside the regime unquestionably reflected the new ideological guidelines issued by Mao in his February speech.

Why was that speech classified off the record? Partly, no doubt, because it was so pessimistic that it would have given much gratification to enemies of the regime at home and abroad.[42] But Mao's caution may also have stemmed from a desire to retain the option of retrospective revision, not necessarily in reference to his remarks on population, but perhaps to those on general economic conditions and to his invitation to critics of the Party to enter without reservation into the spirit of the Hundred Flowers.

This should have warned the wary that Mao might betray the trust of those who took him at his word and expressed their views too openly. Apparently some scholars were dubious. Fei Hsiao-t'ung wrote in March, 1957, that, although the 'gentle winds' of spring were blowing, early spring weather was changeable, hence the older intellectuals had 'many reservations.'[43] In May, 1957, with the Hundred Flowers at last profusely in bloom, there were still reportedly 'many people' who regarded the policy as 'a temporary measure which they think will immediately be followed by a policy of restraint.'[44] By the middle of June they were proved right. The Hundred Flowers wilted in the chill wind of the 'great rectification,' among them the incautious population theorists, including Wu, Ch'en, and Fei, who, despite his doubts, had not been cautious enough to conceal his views.[45]

The edited version of Mao's February speech that was finally published on June 18, after the start of the rectification, contained few of the new ideas that had caused such excitement at the Supreme State Conference. There was no mention of birth control. Moreover, the discussion of the Hundred Flowers policy included six criteria for 'blooming and contending,' which sound more like June than February.[46] Mao's revised statement on population was equivocal and contained some non sequi-

---

[40] Wang Kuang-wei, 'How to Organize Agricultural Labor Power,' *Chi-hua Ching-chi (Planned Economy)*, No. 8, August 9, 1957; translated in *Extracts from China Mainland Magazines*, No. 100, September 23, 1957, p. 11.

[41] Yang Po, 'A Study of Distribution of China's National Income,' *Ching-chi Yen-chiu (Economic Research)*, No. 6, December 17, 1957; translated in *Extracts from China Mainland Magazines*, No. 122, March 10, 1958, p. 12.

[42] Before Mao had assumed his Malthusian position, one Chinese Communist theoretician had written that some people, on discovering the new stand on birth control, were 'gleefully' saying 'Look! The Communists too need Malthus no less than they need Marx.' See Yang Shih-ying, 'On the Malthusian Theory of Population,' *Hsüeh-hsi (Study)*, No. 10, October 2, 1955; translated in *Extracts from China Mainland Magazines*, No. 16, November 28, 1955, p. 11.

[43] Fei Hsiao-t'ung, 'Chih-shih Fen-tzu te Tsao Ch'un T'ien-ch'i (Early Spring Weather for the Intellectuals),' *Jen-min Jih-pao*, Peking, March 24, 1957, in *Hsin Hua Pan-yüeh-k'an (New China Semi-monthly)*, No. 8, August, 1957, pp. 109–12.

[44] Hsiao Te, 'Why Should We Boldly "Bloom"?' *Extracts from China Mainland Magazines*, No. 95, p. 16.

[45] Ma alone of the 'bourgeois rightist' scholars refused to wilt. He said he was used to cold showers and did not mind the attacks of the Party theoreticians who were trying to overwhelm him. In fact, their hot invective was no match for his cold ridicule in the exchange of views that lasted until the spring of 1960. Ma's confidence owed something, however, to his friendship with Chou En-lai. When even this resource failed him in April, 1960, he was dismissed from his position as president of Peking University, and his spirited counterattacks against his critics were no longer published.

[46] Robert Loh, who heard a recording of the original speech, says the six criteria were not in it but were added to the published version. See Robert Loh, *Escape from Red China* (New York: Coward-McCann, 1964), p. 331.

turs. In all its planning, he said, China must proceed from the fact that it has a population of 600 million. This is an objective fact and an asset. 'We have this large population,' he continued. 'It is a good thing, but of course it also has its difficulties.' Progress and difficulties were a contradiction, but one that could be solved with planning. Whether it was a matter of food, natural calamities, employment, education, intellectuals, minorities, or any other question, the necessary arrangements must be made. There should be no grumbling that there were too many people, that people were backward, or that things were troublesome and hard to handle.[47] Mao had backed off.

Still, there was no abatement of the family limitation campaign or of the debate in the press over food shortages and problems in the agricultural economy during the rest of 1957, and the first several months of 1958. During the winter of 1957 and spring of 1958, a determined drive was initiated to get the birth control movement under way in the countryside, where it had been largely neglected.[48] In both urban and rural areas, however, strong popular resistance continued.

As the spring of 1958 wore on, the pressures behind the family limitation campaign mounted. Public health cadres in Shanghai were giving 'guarantees' that they would limit their childbearing during the Second Five-Year Plan period and challenging other units to match their pledges.[49] In Shanghai cotton mills, women workers were required to fill out a 'birth plan' form; those who failed to do so were threatened with public exposure through big-character posters.[50] Little wonder some people began to ask whether birth control was 'compulsory.'[51] The reasons for exercising compulsion must also have seemed compelling to the Party leaders. Though the need to 'protect the health of mothers and children' was mentioned more often in official explanations, it is more likely that it was the need to improve the health of the Chinese economy that was the driving force behind the family limitation campaign. Evidently that need was still perceived as acute in the spring of 1958.

ESCAPE INTO MAOISM

Then came the Great Leap Forward, and with it another major change in official population policies. The underlying cause of the change may have been the frustration of the Party leaders at the continuing pessimistic reports from the agricultural front in the fall in 1957. At least, that seems to have been the reason for the 'reforms' of statistics instituted from April, 1958, onward, under which statistical cadres were directed to stop striving for objectivity in their data and to produce instead figures that would help to inspire the masses to greater feats in production. To their objection that the accuracy of statistical work would suffer, the Party replied that obedience to

---

[47] Mao Tse-tung, 'On the Correct Handling of Contradictions Among the People,' NCNA (English), June 18, 1957; in *Current Background*, No. 458, June 20, 1957, p. 16.

[48] Even some of the major cities had not yet initiated a formal drive. Wuhsi did not establish a birth control guidance committee until the end of January, 1958. See 'Wu-hsi-shih Ch'eng-li Chieh-yü Wei-yüan-hui (Wuhsi Municipality Establishes Birth Control Committee),' *Hsin-hua Jih-pao (New China Daily)*, Nanking, February 7, 1958. Propaganda activities were announced as 'starting' in Foochow municipality in April, 1958. See 'Chi-hua Sheng-yü Hao-ch'u To (Planned Childbirth Has Many Advantages),' *Fu-chien Jih-pao (Fukien Daily)*, Foochow, April 19, 1958.

[49] 'Contraception and Planned Childbirths Must Be Practiced,' *Wen-hui Pao (Wen-hui Daily)*, Shanghai, January 23, 1958; translated in *Survey of China Mainland Press*, No. 1721, February 28, 1958, p. 7.

[50] 'We Don't Want to Turn a Good Thing into a Bad Thing,' *Chung-kuo Fu-nü (Women of China)*, No. 104, June 1, 1958. As the title implies, this article warns against such excesses.

[51] 'Carry Out Birth Control Work with Great Effort to Improve the Health and Prosperity of the Nation,' *Liao-ning Jih-pao (Liaoning Daily)*, Shenyang, June 9, 1958.

Party cadres would set their minds 'free' and would 'encourage the Communist spirit of thinking, speaking, and acting with courage and daring,'[52] which would make their figures more accurate than ever.[53]

What the 'reforms' really meant for the accuracy of agricultural statistics was soon apparent. In May, Hsüeh Mu-ch'iao, Director of the State Statistical Bureau, told his staff that targets for food grain production in 1958 had recently been raised and that an increase of 15 per cent or more over 1957 was now considered possible.[54] Also in May, T'an Chen-lin told the second session of the Eighth National Party Congress that the increase could amount to 'more than 10 and perhaps 20 per cent.'[55] In August, T'an reported that summer grain crops in various areas had increased by between 40 and 100 per cent.[56] By the end of the year, Agriculture Minister Liao Lu-yen estimated that the over-all increase in grain crops during 1958 was more than 100 per cent.[57]

Long before the Great Leap Forward figures on grain production had reached their maximum inflation, the Party leaders had received them eagerly as glad tidings that put an end to all Malthusian fears. At the Party Congress, Liu Shao-ch'i declared that the Leap had completely undermined the pessimistic view that agricultural development could not keep pace with population growth and 'blown sky high' the notion that a large population impedes capital accumulation. He ridiculed scholars for underestimating the 'revolutionary peasants of our country' and for failing to see that men are producers as well as consumers. 'Their views,' he added, 'obviously run counter to Marxism-Leninism.'[58] Mao himself, explaining the upsurge of revolutionary fervor in the first issue of the Party's new journal Red Flag, said that the decisive factor, besides Party leadership, was the 600 million people. The more people there were, the more views and suggestions and the more fervor and energy. Though China's millions were 'poor and blank,'[59] this was not a bad thing but a good thing, because 'poor people want change, want to do things, want revolution.' Buoyed by the 'leap' statistics and the wild reports that politically inspired peasants were transforming the countryside overnight, Mao had abandoned Malthusianism and reverted to his earlier convictions. By September, 1958, a New China News Agency dispatch exultantly declared that the 'almost incredibly high yields' in food grains had

---

[52] Ch'en Chien-fei, 'Big Leap Forward in Statistical Work in Heilungkiang,'Statistical Work, No. 14, July 29, 1958; translated in Extracts from China Mainland Magazines, No. 145, October 13, 1958, p. 45.

[53] 'All Party and People To Engage in Statistical Work' (editorial), Jen-min Jih-pao, August 13, 1958; translated in Survey of China Mainland Press, No. 1839, August 25, 1958, pp. 28-29.

[54] Hsüeh Mu-ch'iao, 'T'ung-chi Kung-tso Ju-ho Yo-chin (How to Leap Forward in Statistical Work),' Statistical Work, No. 5, March 14, 1958, p. 2.

[55] T'an Chen'lin, 'Explanatory Report on the Second Revised Draft of the 1956–1967 Program for Agricultural Development,' NCNA (English), May 27, 1958; in Current Background, No. 508, June 4, 1958, p. 3.

[56] T'an Chen'lin, 'Strive for a Bountiful Life in 2–3 Years,' Red Flag, No. 6, August 16, 1958; translated in Extracts from China Mainland Magazines, No. 144, October 6, 1958, p. 1.

[57] Liao Lu-yen, 'The Task for 1959 on the Agricultural Front,' Red Flag, No. 1, January 1, 1959; translated in Extracts from China Mainland Magazines, No. 158, February 16, 1958, p. 14.

[58] L'iu Shao-ch'i, 'The Present Situation, the Party's General Line for socialist Construction, and Future Tasks,' NCNA (English), May 26, 1958 (speech originally given on May 5); in Current Background, No. 507, June 2, 1958, p. 17.

[59] Mao's use of 'blank' was a figurative reference to the cultural condition of the Chinese people as a blank sheet of paper awaiting his political inscription. He added, 'A clean sheet of paper has nothing on it, and so the newest and most beautiful words can be written and the newest and the most beautiful pictures painted on it.' See 'Chairman Mao Tse-tung's Article for Red Flag,' NCNA (English), May 31, 1958; in Survey of China Mainland Press, No. 1784, June 4, 1958, p. 9.

'smashed the idealistic theory of diminishing yields of the soil and put the final nail in the Malthusian coffin.'[60]

After the first week of June, 1958, the press campaign for family limitation dwindled. The obligatory 'birth plans' were dropped. The posters, lectures, films, and exhibits came to an end. Contraceptives disappeared from the display cases in the state pharmacies. Manufacture of contraceptive medicines and devices was cut back. The birth control guidance committees languished. There was no formal declaration that the campaign had ended; it was simply left to wither away gradually. Birth control, that fragrant flower, had survived the cold blast of the rectification only to succumb to the hot blast of the Leap Forward.

Retreat from Maoism

By the end of 1958, some of the ardor of the Great Leap Forward was beginning to cool. Rumors circulated that Leap agricultural statistics and many of the production 'miracles' reported in the press were fraudulent. In the spring of 1959, the 'miracles' were on the wane, and an undercurrent of skepticism was stirring even within Party circles. The Party leaders felt its backlash and fought desperately to protect Leap illusions against incredulity and anxiety. Despite mounting criticism from professional statisticians at a conference in Peking in April, 1959, the Leap grain and cotton figures for 1958 were made official and astronomical targets were announced for grain production in 1959. By August, however, the rising tide of disillusionment had dampened enthusiasm in the Central Committee. At the eighth plenum of the Eighth Central Committee, the 1958 figures and 1959 targets were scaled down and renewed attacks were directed against 'rightists' who were trying to deny the achievements of the Great Leap, the people's communes, and other Party policies, all of which were said to have been 'correct.'

By the end of 1959, natural calamities and food shortages were again under discussion. It was discovered that food supplies were insufficient, that agriculture was backward, that wild animals and wild plants were needed to supplement the diet, that the communes were too advanced for 'the ideological state of the peasants,' and that statistics must reflect the 'objective situation.' The communes were partially dismantled, and the fallow land program, which had contributed to the food shortages in 1959, was scrapped. Official claims about agricultural production became more vague. By 1961, the food crisis was at its worst. Industry at last was directed to serve agriculture as a first priority, and national investment was reallocated accordingly. In 1962, the weather also took a turn for the better, and the outlook for agriculture began to improve for the first time in three years. Agricultural specialists commented euphemistically that the dark years had yielded a rich 'harvest of experience.' One added hopefully that 'failure is the mother of success.'[61]

Renaissance of Malthusianism

In the spring of 1962, the family limitation campaign was quietly reborn. When the decision was taken is not indicated in the evidence available, but in January, 1962, the Canton Customs Office announced that no duty would henceforth be charged on imports of contraceptive goods,[62] and by April the press campaign had started. By midsummer of 1962, the new campaign seemed to be in full swing.

---

[60] 'China's Rice Harvest: Second Major Food Crops Success in 1958,' NCNA, September 30, 1958; translated in *News from Hsinhua News Agency*, No. 283, October 2, 1958, p. 44.
[61] Shih Hung, 'Several Problems Relating to the Summing Up of Experiences about Agricultural Production,' *Shih-shih shou-ts'e (Current Events)*, No. 15, August 6, 1962; translated in *Extracts from China Mainland Magazines*, No. 334, October 8, 1962, p. 10.
[62] 'Canton Customs Office Announces Revision of Tariff on Travelers' Personal Effects and

In many respects it was quite different from its predecessor. The press picked up the subject with less hesitation but never gave it as much urgent attention as in 1957-58. The propaganda was more disciplined and internally consistent and showed little evolution over time. The new drive attached somewhat greater importance to late marriage and sought to popularize an ideal family size of not more than two or three children. For the first year, abortion was discouraged, but in the spring of 1963 there seems to have been a change toward a more liberal official attitude, this time without any audible demurrers from the China Medical Association. Sterilization received favorable publicity from the start and even the personal approbation of Chou En-lai.[63] Intrauterine devices, which had been introduced on an experimental basis in 1957, were made generally available for the first time.

The rationale for the new campaign was essentially the same as before, but the emphasis was quite different. Much more attention was given to specific and personal arguments. The health of mothers and children was said to be a prime consideration of the Party and Chairman Mao. For health reasons, women were advised not to get married and begin childbearing too early. Until the age of twenty-five, their bones were not fully calcified and their reproductive organs were not 'mature.' The physical burden of the 'ten months' of gestation (!), the pain and loss of blood at delivery, and the drain of nutrients from the mother's body during lactation were described in harrowing detail, along with a host of special problems for the too-young mother, including ovarian disorders, menstrual irregularities, difficult labor, and cancer of the cervix.[64] Young men who married too early were also in grave danger. They were warned that because their physical and neurological development was incomplete before the age of twenty-three to twenty-five, they lacked self-control and would be unable to avoid excessive sexual indulgence, which would cause malfunctioning of the central nervous system, 'sexual neurasthenia,' impotence, low spirits, headaches, and 'discomfort all over the body.'[65] Besides all this, the children of early marriages were weak, sickly, and difficult to nurse and did not develop satisfactorily,[66] and the mar-

---

Goods Delivered by Post' (Canton dateline), *Ta-kung Pao*, Hong Kong, January 21, 1962; translated in *Survey of China Mainland Press*, No. 2670, January 31, 1962, p. 12.

[63] Wang Po-ch'ing, 'Ch'in-ch'ieh te Kuan-huai, Jeh-ch'ing te Ku-li (Intimate Concern and Warm-hearted Encouragement),' *China Youth*, No. 17, September 1, 1963, p. 15.

[64] Yeh Kung-shao, 'What Is the Most Suitable Age for Marriage?' *Chung-kuo Ch'ing-nien Pao* (*China Youth Daily*), April 12, 1962; translated in *Survey of China Mainland Press*, No. 2745, May 24, 1962, pp. 17–19; Ta Yü, 'What Are the Disadvantages of Early Marriage?' *Kung-jen Jih-pao* (*Worker's Daily*), June 28, 1962; translated in *Survey of China Mainland Press*, No. 2777, July 13, 1962, pp. 10–11; 'Early Marriage Is Harmful, Not Beneficial,' *Nan-fang Jih-pao* (*Southern Daily*), Canton, May 15, 1962; translated in *Survey of China Mainland Press*, No. 2757, June 13, 1962, p. 11; Yeh Kung-shao, 'My Views on the Problem of Young People's Marriage, Love, and Children,' *Chung-kuo Ch'ing-nien Pao*, July 21, 1962; translated in *Survey of China Mainland Press*, No. 2795, August 9, 1962, pp. 13–15; T'ao Ch'eng, 'A Talk with Young Friends about the Question of Marriage,' *Kung-jen Jih-pao*, July 28, 1962; translated in *Survey of China Mainland Press*, No. 2800, August 16, 1962, pp. 11–12; Yeh Kung-shao, 'What Benefits Will Youths Get by Getting Married a Little Later?' *Chung-kuo Ch'ing-nien Pao*, Peking, May 9, 1963; translated in *Survey of China Mainland Press*, No. 2989, May 29, 1963, pp. 5–7.

[65] Yeh Kung-shao, 'What Is Most Suitable Age for Marriage?' *Survey of China Mainland Press*, No. 2745, p. 17; Yang Hsiu, 'For Late Marriage,' *Chung-kuo Ch'ing-nien*, No. 11, June 1, 1962; translated in *Extracts from China Mainland Magazines*, No. 322, July 16, 1962, p. 24; and Ta Yü, 'What Are Disadvantages of Early Marriage?' *Survey of China Mainland Press*, No. 2777, p. 11.

[66] Yeh Kung-shao, 'What Is Most Suitable Age for Marriage?' *loc. cit.*; Early Marriage Is Harmful, Not Beneficial,' *loc. cit.*; and Wang Wen-pin, 'A Talk About the Question of Age for Marriage from the Physiological Angle,' *Kung-jen Jih-pao*, Peking, November 15, 1962; translated in *Survey of China Mainland Press*, No. 2871, December 3, 1962, p. 11.

riages themselves were beset by emotional upsets, mental anguish, and quarrels, and likely to end in divorce.[67] All of these terrors of early marriage and early prolixity could be avoided by marrying after the age of thirty and using birth control religiously.

On the positive side, young people who had not committed themselves to wedded agony were invited to put education and career ahead of marriage, not only for their own personal advantage but in the interests of the state as well. They were urged to recognize a new definition of happiness that consisted not of love, marriage, material comforts, and the pleasures of the 'small family,' but in working hard and enduring privation for the sake of the revolution, the people, and the state (the 'large family'). As the propaganda line developed, it increasingly emphasized the spiritual joys of material hardship, self-sacrifice, and even martyrdom.

By the end of 1963, there were some indications that greater pressure was about to be brought to bear in the family limitation campaign. A local press item warned that birth control was not merely an individual matter, because the state must shoulder responsibility for food, clothing, housing, transportation, schooling, and employment for the new generation.[68] Reports began to circulate that cloth rations would not be allowed for additional children born to families that had already had the approved maximum of three.[69] On the other hand, statements attributed to Chou En-lai suggested that the regime did not expect immediate results from its family limitation efforts, but hoped to reduce the population growth rate to about 1 per cent in perhaps another twenty years.[70] So far as the press propaganda campaign is concerned, there was no acceleration during 1964. Instead, the coverage seems to have been confined increasingly to publications for women and youth. The few items available during 1965 contain no hint of an intensified campaign, just the usual discussion of achievements, obstacles, and the need to exert more 'leadership.'[71] In the spring of 1966, only one publication, *Women of China*, continued to devote much space to family limitation.

THE MAOIST-LIUIST STRUGGLE

Then, in June, 1966, the tensions of the Cultural Revolution, which had been building up since late fall, 1965, erupted in a violent intra-Party struggle for power. Instantly, the family limitation campaign, along with most other nonpolitical mass programs, went into limbo. With government agencies and Party organs paralyzed by Maoist and anti-Maoist violence and intimidation, it was no time to conduct business as usual. Moreover, there was reason to doubt whether family limitation, with its inherently sober and rational implications, was more closely linked with the 'revisionism' and 'economism' of Liu Shao-ch'i or with Mao's demands that youth forgo

---

[67] 'Is It Desirable to Get Married Early?' *Kung-jen Jih-pao*, Peking, October 5, 1962; translated in *Survey of China Mainland Press*, No. 2845, October 24, 1962, pp. 8–10; and Chou Hsin-min, 'On the Encouragement of Late Marriage and Statutory Marriage Age,' *Kung-jen Jih-pao*, November 7, 1962; translated in *Survey of China Mainland Press*, No. 2871, December 3, 1962, pp. 13–14.

[68] Chung Cho-huan, 'This Is Not an Embarrassing Thing or an Unimportant Matter,' *Nan-fang Jih-pao*, December 1, 1963; translated in *Survey of China Mainland Press*, No. 3128, December 30, 1963, p. 12.

[69] Jacques Marcuse, 'Birth Control in China by Cotton Rationing,' *The Sunday Times* (London), November 17, 1963. Other reports implied that food rations were also withheld; see Seymour Topping, 'Peking Urges Birth Curbs; Big Families Are Penalized,' *The New York Times*, April 27, 1966.

[70] Edgar Snow, 'Halte aux Naissances,' *Candide*, Paris, No. 209, 1965, p. 22.

[71] See, for example, 'Kwangtung Province Convenes Conference to Exchange Experiences in Work on Planned Childbirth,' *Nan-fang Jih-pao*, April 14, 1965; translated in *Survey of China Mainland Press*, No. 3446, April 29, 1965, pp. 19–20.

the satisfactions of marriage and family and practice revolutionary asceticism. Both Liu and Mao had blown hot and cold on the issue in the past, and no wary cadre would have ventured to guess in whose precincts it now lay when a wrong guess could be so costly.

At first there were some signs that family limitation was one of Liu's ideological appurtenances. In June, 1966, the editor of *Women of China*, Tung Pien, had been denounced as a 'black gang element' on the grounds that she had opposed the 'thoughts of Mao' and 'disseminated reactionary viewpoints' in her magazine. The specific charges against her did not mention her support of the family limitation movement but said that she had slipped into 'bourgeois humanism' by relying too much on the contributions of experts on such subjects as 'knowledge of life,' love, marriage, and childbirth.[72] Tung Pien was purged, and, in the pages of *Women of China*, the 'thoughts of Mao' replaced thoughts about vasectomies, late marriages, and the happy home life of the planned family. In September, 1967, the Tsingtao radio station carried charges by a local 'revolutionary' that 'China's Khrushchev' and his agents in Shantung Province had been spreading the 'poisonous stuff of revisionism' in connection with the women's movement, marriage, family planning, and children's education.[73] It was not clear in context whether there were non-poisonous approaches to family planning, or whether all such ideas were now politically contaminating.

Evidently many Maoists drew the latter conclusion. Later on in the fall of 1967, however, it was rumored that a high Maoist official in Peking had insisted that birth control and late marriage were Maoist, not Liuist, ideas. On January 15, 1968, a 'Notice on Strengthening Planned Birth and Advocating Late Marriage' was issued by the Municipal Revolutionary Committee in the Maoist stronghold of Shanghai. It called upon all 'revolutionaries' to 'strengthen their leadership,' intensify 'ideological education for the masses,' and get the propaganda machine rolling again.[74] An editorial in a Shanghai paper in April sought to explain the previous confusion as due to the efforts of a 'handful of class enemies,' who had tried to 'sabotage the patriotic health movement' and, more specifically, had 'even distorted late marriage and planned birth as "a measure of the bourgeois reactionary line." '[75] Be that as it may, the Maoists left no doubt in the spring of 1968 that they were again committed to family limitation.

There was an unaccountable lapse in press coverage on the campaign from May, 1968, to November, 1969, when the Shanghai Revolutionary Committee urged that birth control work be linked with 'the patriotic health movement' and designated the elimination of schistosomiasis and the promotion of birth control as the 'two big tasks' for health workers in the rural areas around the city.[76] Early in December, a meeting

---

[72] Federation of Women, Meng *Hsien*, Shansi, '*Chung-kuo Fu-nü* Will Become a Red Periodical, We Hope,' *Chung-kuo Fu-nü* (*Women of China*), No. 7, July 10, 1966; translated in *Selections from China Mainland Magazines*, No. 542, September 19, 1966, pp. 5–7; 'The Big Plot of False Discussion and Real Release of Poison,' *Chung-kuo Fu-nü*, No. 8, August 10, 1966; translated in *Selections from China Mainland Magazines*, No. 548, October 31, 1966, pp. 22–25; and *Chung-kuo Fu-nü*'s Whole Body of Revolutionary Workers, 'Expose the Crimes of Black Gang Element Tung Pien,' *Chung-kuo Fu-nü*, No. 7, July 10, 1966; translated in *Selections from China Mainland Magazines*, No. 543, September 26, 1966, pp. 4–10.

[73] Tsingtao radio, Shantung, September 13, 1967.

[74] 'Go Quickly into Action to Carry Out the Patriotic Public Health Movement with Elimination of the Four Pests as Key,' *Wen-hui Pao*, April 22, 1968; translated in *Survey of China Mainland Press*, No. 4179, May 16, 1968, pp. 8–9.

[75] 'Paper Boats and Bright Candles Light the Way to the Skies' (editorial), *Wen-hui Pao*, April 22, 1968; translated in *Survey of China Mainland Press*, No. 4179, May 16, 1968, p. 11.

[76] Radio Shanghai, November 27, 1969. The broadcast cites an article in *Chieh-fang Jih-pao*, November 28, 1969, claiming 'splendid results' in birth control and preventive health work but calling for sustained efforts 'until success is achieved.'

of representatives from four suburban counties around Shanghai was convened to 'exchange experiences' in their drive to set up 'cooperative medical services,' develop herb medicines, control schistosomiasis, and promote birth control, at which the latter two tasks were again cited as 'two important matters' for medical and health work during the winter.[77] In January, 1970, Shanghai declared a 'shock week' for propaganda on birth control and late marriage in combination with a drive to eliminate flies and mosquitoes and improve environmental hygiene.[78] Occasional reports of propaganda efforts in other areas have been carried in news dispatches during 1971 and 1972. The campaign seems to have a firm though not extremely high priority.

The commitment to birth control is indicated by the fact that the campaign is currently rationalized by reference to quotations from the works of Mao. Birth control is sanctioned as in accord with Mao's command: 'Be prepared against war, be prepared against natural disasters, and do everything for the people.' Late marriage is said to have been encompassed in Mao's directive, 'Show concern for the growth of the younger generation.' Birth control and late marriage are said to be 'of exceedingly great significance in changing habits and customs and transforming the world,'[79] 'a major event bearing on the national economy,'[80] and an aspect of 'the all-out struggle waged against the class enemy in the political, ideological, and economic fields.'[81] In May, 1971, Chou En-lai told a Canadian newsman that his government planned to lower population growth to 'about 1 per cent in the 1970's' and added, 'If we can make it even lower than 1 per cent in the 1980's, it will be even better.'[82] A somewhat greater sense of urgency is conveyed by Vice-Premier Li Hsien-nien during an interview with an Egyptian newsman in November, 1971, in which he said that 'we have been racing against time to cope with the enormous increase in population,' but he also noted that 'despite the enormous population' China had been able to guarantee that 'no citizen will die for lack of food or clothing.'[83]

Although the current birth control campaign seems to lack the urgency that marked the first campaign, the technical development of contraception is far more advanced than in either of the previous campaigns and has been sustained with great seriousness of purpose. In the first and second campaigns, contraceptive techniques were borrowed from the West and were not of the latest type. There was some experimentation with contraceptive rings during the first campaign, but little was said about them in the press and they were not generally available. Steroid pills were tested during the second campaign without public comment. Now the medical and pharmaceutical agencies in China have taken the initiative in conducting research on the frontiers of contraceptive technology. In the winter of 1970–71, Edgar Snow was told by Dr. Lin Chiao-chih in Peking that Chinese researchers were testing a once-a-

---

[77] Radio Shanghai, December 6, 1969.

[78] Radio Shanghai, January 24, 1970.

[79] 'Practice of Planned Birth and Late Marriage Is Formed at State Cotton Mill,' *Kung-jen Tsao-fan Pao* (*Worker Rebel Paper*), Shanghai, February 1, 1970.

[80] Shanghai Municipal No. 1 Health Clinic for Women and Infants, 'Planned Birth,' in 'Planning Childbirth and Promoting Late Marriage,' *I-liao Wei-sheng Tzu-liao* (*Medical and Health Data*), No. 5, July, 1970.

[81] Liuli Commune Revolutionary Committee, Ch'uansha *Hsien*, 'Under the Guidance of Mao Tse-tung Thought, Do a Good Job to Promote Late Marriage of Young People,' in 'Planning Childbirth and Promoting Late Marriage,' *I-liao Wei-sheng Tzu-liao* (*Medical and Health Data*), Shanghai, No. 5, February, 1970.

[82] Canadian Broadcasting Corporation, 'A Conversation with Chou En-lai,' aired on July 28, 1971.

[83] Mamduh Rida, 'Days in China—an Interview with the Number Three Man in China,' *Al-Jumhuriya*, Cairo, November 18, 1971.

month pill, that other experiments were going forward on a once-in-three-months pill, and that a once-a-year pill or vaccine was contemplated.[84]

Meanwhile, two oral contraceptives utilizing synthetic progesterone and oestrogen are apparently in general use in at least some areas and seem to be supplanting the contraceptive rings. There are still some problems in getting users of the pills to adhere to the regular regimen of pill-taking necessary to provide protection, yet the pills are said to be more than 99.9 per cent effective. A once-a-month contraceptive injection is also advertised for general use, but it is said to be only 98.6 per cent effective, despite the fact that it does not require daily self-administered doses.[85] A New China News Agency Dispatch of February, 1972, on the development of China's pharmaceutical industry notes briefly that 'good results have been obtained in research and trial production of contraceptive drugs' and that 'some contraceptives taken orally are being supplied free of charge in towns and in the countryside.'[86] Sterilization is again encouraged, and the suction abortion machines seem to be in general production, though the official attitude toward abortion is that it is a 'passive' approach to family limitation that can adversely affect health, even though the operation is simple, and that contraception is preferable.[87] Perhaps the most significant sign of the serious intent of the birth control campaign is the fact that, despite the great emphasis on traditional medicine in the rural health movement, and particularly on the economy of substituting Chinese medicines for Western medicines wherever possible, not a word is said about the Chinese traditional contraceptive formulas so much publicized during the first campaign. Chinese medicine may be good enough for the prevention of disease and death, but it is not good enough for the prevention of births.

Evidently, the campaign for late marriage and birth control is still encountering significant popular resistance. In Shanghai in April, 1968, a 'wave of getting married now' appeared in some factories and some cadres were afraid to oppose it lest they 'say the wrong things' and be subjected to 'denunciation.' Cadres who tried to discourage youthful marriages were sometimes told to 'mind your own business and teach yourself!' There were also other persons, not specifically identified, who talked 'rubbish,' asserting that efforts to promote late marriage were a manifestation of 'the "bourgeois reactionary line." '[88] In July, 1968, an editorial in a Shanghai paper noted that the 'evil wind of falling in love and getting married early has prevailed not only among literary and art circles but in factories, villages, and schools.'[89]

The evil wind was still blowing in December, 1969, when Radio Shanghai observed that 'a handful of class enemies' were advancing the 'reactionary theories' of Confucius, Mencius, and Liu Shao-ch'i in support of early marriage and other 'old ideas.'[90] In 1970, Liu Shao-ch'i was charged with having insisted that there be 'no interference in one's marriage and love affairs nor with early marriage' and with

---

[84] Edgar Snow, 'Population Care and Control,' *The New Republic*, May 1, 1971, pp. 21–22.

[85] Shanghai Municipal No. 1 Health Clinic, 'Planned Birth.'

[86] NCNA, Peking, February 15, 1972.

[87] Shanghai Municipal No. 1 Health Clinic, 'Planned Birth.'

[88] 'Revolutionary Youths Should Care for the Affairs of State and Oppose Early Marriage; Revolutionary Cadres Should Boldly Guide Youths to Attain Healthy Growth,' *Wen-hui Pao*, April 23, 1968; translated in *Survey of China Mainland Press*, No. 4181, May 20, 1968, pp. 17–18; Chu Yung-hsing, 'Revolutionary Youths Should Take the Lead in Changing Prevailing Bad Practices and Customs,' *Wen-hui Pao*, April 23, 1968; translated in *Survey of China Mainland Press*, No. 4181, May 20, 1968, pp. 15–16.

[89] 'Stem the Evil Wind of Falling in Love and Getting Married Early Among Literary and Art Circles,' *Wen-hui Pao*, July 28, 1968; translated in *Survey of China Mainland Press*, No. 4250, September 4, 1968, pp. 17–18.

[90] Radio Shanghai, December 27, 1969.

advocating the establishment of a 'match-making agency.' In some cases, 'barefoot doctors' were directed to watch for the 'signs of early love' among young people, to make inquiries among teammates about urban youths in rural areas, and bring pressure to bear on those who persist in the 'evil customs and habits of the bourgeoisie.'[91] Still another gust of the evil wind of early marriage blew up 'suddenly' in January, 1971, in a production team in Honan Province, proof that 'the class struggle has not yet ended yet.'[92] The persistence of the older traditions in spite of all efforts to eradicate them during and since the Cultural Revolution indicates the limited effectiveness of mass propaganda campaigns and systematic indoctrination even among the young people of China.

Liu Shao-ch'i was also charged with the 'towering crime of sabotaging planned birth' at a Shanghai cotton mill, because 'some people with ulterior motives' had spread rumors that oral contraceptives would cause sterility, obesity, and loss of memory and had thus dealt a setback to contraceptive work at the mill, where some of the workers 'dreaded the trouble involved' in contraceptive practice or had 'incorrect thoughts' about birth control.[93] In March, 1971, the comrades in a rural revolutionary committee thought that they had no time to promote birth control until they studied Mao's 'great instruction' on war and calamities and 'unified their thoughts.'[94] In the autumn of 1971, a visitor in Canton was told that traditional desires to have children of both sexes sustained high fertility in rural areas.[95] Even in the Tachai production brigade in Shansi, the family planning propaganda program at first elicited 'little positive response' because there were 'misgivings clouding the minds of the women.' By September, 1971, it was said that 98 per cent of the Tachai women of childbearing age had 'joined the family planning program,' but the fact that such resistance could be evident in a model brigade of national renown suggests that the cultural inhibitions against late marriage and family planning have not been eliminated in rural areas.

Some foreign travelers in China during 1971 and the spring of 1972 gave accounts of conversations with local officials in which both progress and difficulties in the birth control campaign were mentioned, and others reported only local claims of phenomenal success. Some visitors quoted urban birth rates as low as 6 per 1,000 population and rural rates of 18 to 20 per 1,000; others cited rates as high as 18 per 1,000 for Peking and 30 per 1,000 for Kwangtung Province. It is not clear whether these divergences reflect differences in the way their tours were conducted or differences in the attitudes of the visitors themselves. It should be noted that the Chinese leaders, who are not averse to celebrating successes they believe they have attained, have not made any sweeping claims for their family planning efforts thus far. In fact, in several instances they seem to have been embarrassed by the testimonials of their more enthusiastic guests. When Edgar Snow talked with Mao in December, 1970, he remarked that popular attitudes toward birth control had changed greatly in China compared with five or ten years earlier, but Mao countered that Snow had been 'taken in' by Chinese propaganda. Mao cited peasant preferences for male children

---

[91] Tung Yin-ti, 'For the Revolution's Sake, Insist on Late Marriage,' *Nan-fang Jih-pao*, February 6, 1970; Liuli Commune Revolutionary Committee, 'Promote Late Marriage'; and 'Vigorously Encourage Late Marriage for the Revolutionary Cause,' *Jen-min Jih-pao*, January 30, 1971; translated in *Survey of China Mainland Press*, No. 4831, February 4, 1971, pp. 122–23.

[92] 'Vigorously Encourage Late Marriage,' *Jen-min Jih-pao*.

[93] 'Practice of Planned Birth and Late Marriage Is Formed at State Cotton Mill,' *Kung-jin Tsao-fan Pao*.

[94] 'Wei T'i-kao Fu-nü Chien-k'ang Shui-p'ing erh Tou-cheng (Struggle to Raise the Level of Health of Women),' *Jen-min Jih-pao*, March 3, 1971.

[95] Ross Terrill, 'The 800,000,000,' *The Atlantic Monthly* (November, 1971), p. 110.

as one cause of high rural fertility and said that it would take time to change these attitudes.[96] In a similar vein, Vice-Premier Li Hsien-nien told an Egyptian correspondent in November, 1971, that economic development in China had made 'some progress' but that the Chinese leaders did not regard it as very great progress. 'When we hear from our friends that it is great progress,' he added, 'we look at such talk as something bigger than reality, or as courteous talk.'[97]

PROSPECTS FOR POPULATION POLICY

The prospects for population policy in the P.R.C. depend upon how the leaders perceive the relationship between population growth and economic development. Despite the charges now made against Liu, there is no evidence from the public record that Liu, Mao, and Chou differed greatly in their views on population. The first birth control campaign was supported by all three and especially endorsed by Mao. The second campaign was begun when, according to statements issued during the Cultural Revolution, Liu was in virtual command of the country. The third campaign now has the blessing of both Mao and Chou. While Chou holds power, population policy will probably be stable.

How long the central authority will remain stable is another question. It was only during the Cultural Revolution that the outside world learned the extent of internal dissension at times when outwardly the P.R.C. appeared unified and calm. Recent efforts to rebuild the Party and reaffirm the principles of national unity and 'democratic centralism' evidently have not yet fully restored the degree of central control that existed prior to the Cultural Revolution. A change in administration in the near future is therefore a possibility that cannot be ruled out. However, even if the country is seized by another political convulsion, the chances of a reversion to old-style Marxist or Maoist dogmatism seem to have been lessened by the failure of such expedients to cope with China's problems during their previous applications. So far as population is concerned, there seems to be no rational alternative to encouraging family limitation.

The priority assigned to family limitation would probably be much higher if the pressure of population on food supplies felt so acutely during the First Five-Year Plan period were still continuing. It was anxiety about food that made Mao a Malthusian, and it was confidence in Leap grain figures that restored him to the Marxists again. The post-Leap food crisis reinstated Malthusian views, and, with a brief interruption early in the Cultural Revolution, they have prevailed ever since. For some ten years, there has been no general food shortage in China, though the population is now some 300 million larger than it was in 1949. To feed a population that has grown this rapidly is no mean feat, and it was accomplished without the aid of most of the agricultural technologies associated with the 'green revolution' in other parts of Asia. However, the feat was no doubt due in part to a more effective system of procurement and emergency distribution of food surpluses and in part to multiple cropping and other practices that cannot be indefinitely reduplicated. If the margin between food production and consumption were to narrow once more, family limitation could become once again as urgent as it was in 1957–58.

Even a highly urgent priority would not assure success in family limitation so long as the Party and the government lack the administrative means to make late marriage and birth control compulsory for a significant proportion of the population. Central authority in the P.R.C. seems to have reached its peak of effectiveness during the latter part of the First Five-Year Plan period, when the first birth control campaign

---

[96] Edgar Snow, 'A Conversation with Mao Tse-tung,' *Life*, Vol. 70, No. 16 (April 30, 1971), p. 47.
[97] Mamduh Rida, 'Days in China,' *Al-Jumhuriya*.

was at its height. Yet the few claims of success publicized at that time related to women workers in highly organized industrial establishments and women Party cadres, both of whom were much more susceptible to political pressure than were other groups in the population. These claims may also have been exaggerated for propaganda purposes.

Whether the current campaign will be more effective remains to be seen. There has apparently been some increase in positive economic incentives in urban areas because of increased consumer goods, but the magnitude is not great. In some areas, denial of welfare services to families that do not restrict their childbearing may constitute a negative incentive. In both urban and rural areas, propaganda efforts are obviously being concentrated on married women in the childbearing ages, and the message is being transmitted through many different channels—maternal and children's health clinics, itinerant medical teams, 'barefoot doctors,' local revolutionary committees, and Party cadres. However, the claims of miraculous success currently presented in the press and to foreigners on guided tours have the same stereotyped quality that characterized the claims put forward during the Leap and the Cultural Revolution, many of which were subsequently discredited. Past experience should have taught us by now that reality never quite measures up to the illusions created for propaganda purposes. If this were not sufficient basis for caution, other warning signs may be read in the purposefully obscure press references to popular 'criticism' of the 'barefoot doctors,' to their feelings that their lot is a 'misfortune,' to their fear of 'offending people,' to their need for 'ideological revolutionization,' and to public rejection of their methods, and also in the comments on the convictions among some cadres that 'a needle and a bunch of herbs' cannot cure illness and that public health work is 'antagonistic to revolution and production.' There is evidently much more to these comments than meets the eye. If there can be doubt as to whether peasant attitudes toward the rural health movement, which should involve no fundamental value conflicts, have been transformed, then assumptions that peasant attitudes toward family limitation have been 'revolutionized' must be premature. It would seem wiser to defer judgment on the unofficial statements about sharply falling birthrate until such trends are confirmed by reasonably reliable demographic evidence.

SELECTED BIBLIOGRAPHY

AIRD, JOHN S. 'Population Policy in Mainland China,' *Population Studies*, 16, No. 1 (July, 1962): 38–57. Developments in official policy on fertility control from 1949 through the collapse of the Great Leap Forward and the relationship of these developments to official population data, Marxist ideology, and problems in agricultural development and food supply.

FREEBERNE, MICHAEL. 'Birth Control in China,' *Population Studies*, 18, No. 1 (1964): 5–16. The early stages of population policy and developments from the start of the second campaign in spring, 1962, up to July, 1963.

ORLEANS, LEO A. 'Birth Control: Reversal or Postponement?' *The China Quarterly*, No. 3 (London: Congress for Cultural Freedom), July–September, 1960, pp. 59–73. Developments in population and related policies from the start of the first birth control campaign in 1954 through its remission in the latter half of 1958, and the debate between Ma Yin-ch'u and Party spokesmen that continued into 1960.

——. 'Evidence from Chinese Medical Journals on Current Population Policy,' *The China Quarterly*, No. 40, October–December, 1969, pp. 137–46. An attempt to assess the trend of official policy on birth control, abortion, and sterilization from articles appearing in medical journals during the years 1963–66.

——. 'A New Birth Control Campaign?' *The China Quarterly*, No. 12, October–December, 1962, pp. 207–10. A short note on the resumption of birth control propaganda in 1962.

TIEN, YUAN H. 'Birth Control in Mainland China: Ideology and Politics,' *The Milbank Memorial Fund Quarterly*, 41, No. 3 (New York, July, 1963): 269–90. Political factors relating to the origin and the abatement of the first birth control campaign, including the ideological arguments between the non-Communist academicians and the Party spokesmen.

——. 'Induced Abortion and Population Control in Mainland China,' *Marriage and Family Living*, 25, No. 1 (February, 1963): 35–43. Official attitudes on abortion during the first birth control campaign and the arguments against abortion by the China Medical Association in 1957, in the context of Chinese demographic developments and the Japanese experience with abortion.

——. 'Sterilization, Oral Contraception, and Population Control in China,' *Population Studies*, 18, No. 3 (March, 1965): 215–35. Efforts to promote sterilization and oral contraception, including herbalist formulas, during both birth control campaigns, and their relationship to population policy in general.

19

NATIONAL INCOME*

K. C. YEH

THE development of the Communist economy on the Chinese mainland can best be summarized by the movement of the total and per capita national product since 1949. The national product encompasses the results of all economic activities conventionally defined as contributing to the total annual output available for consumption and investment. If reasonably full employment of human and other resources prevails, it also indicates the national capacity to produce.

Several important reservations must be made immediately. First, the total capacity to produce should not be confused with the capability to achieve a specific aim. The national product of a nation may be small on a per capita basis. Nevertheless, success in a particular endeavor is possible if sufficient resources are concentrated on it. In a totalitarian state, the authorities are free to devote a disproportionately large amount of resources to purposes that contribute neither to the material well-being of the people nor to the productive capacity of the economy.

Second, the national product, as computed on the conventional framework, is inadequate as an indicator of human welfare, especially in the case of the Communist Chinese economy. There have been many radical changes in the social and political environment on the Chinese mainland. There has been a reduction of personal liberty for all classes of people, including the peasants, throughout the period under study. The adverse effects on human welfare of the Communist effort at regimentation found no expression in the national product. Nor are all the costs incurred in producing monetary and imputed incomes (those not represented by market transactions, e.g., rental values of owner-occupied houses) recognized in national income accounting. This is especially true of the Great Leap Forward years (1958–59). For instance, we have no way of estimating the proper depreciation charges for the resources wasted in constructing the backyard furnaces, let alone the deterioration of the health of the people and of the quality of land that must have followed the hardship and abuses inflicted upon them during the Great Leap. A proper evaluation of the tempo of development must supplement the purely economic analysis presented in this paper with sociological and political studies, a task beyond the competence of an economist.

---

* This chapter draws heavily from two earlier works: Ta-chung Liu and K. C. Yeh, *The Economy of the Chinese Mainland: National Income and Economic Development, 1933–1959* (Princeton, N.J.: Princeton University Press, 1965), and Ta-chung Liu, 'Quantitative Trends in the Economy of the Chinese Mainland, 1962–1965,' in Walter Galenson, Alexander Eckstein, and Ta-chung Liu, eds., *Economic Trends in Communist China* (Chicago: Aldine Publishing Co., 1968). The reader is referred to these two publications for more detailed data, computation, and analysis.

Third, the basic Communist data are inadequate and inaccurate. For this reason, several independent estimates of national product have been made by scholars in the United States, especially for 1952 and the First Five-Year Plan period, 1953–57.

The Communist data deteriorated in quality precipitately during 1958–60, and they have practically vanished since 1961. Only an exploratory estimate of the movement since 1958 can be attempted. There are reasons to believe, however, that this estimate represents a reasonable approximation of the main trend in the economy during these years. A crude reconstruction of the Communist estimate of the domestic product for 1958–65 will also be presented.

My analysis will deal with the following three periods separately: the rehabilitation period (1949–52); the period of relatively steady growth (1952–57); and the Great Leap Forward and its aftermath (1958–65).

THE PERIOD OF REHABILITATION, 1949–52

As the economy recovered from the devastation of twelve years of war, production in all fields increased greatly from 1949 to 1952. The statistics during the period of rehabilitation, however, are very unreliable for the simple reason that the Communists did not have an effective national statistical reporting system of their own until the establishment of the State Statistical Bureau on August 8, 1952. The rate of growth of national income and the gross value of output of industry and agriculture given in Table 19–1 are the official Communist data. It is impossible to say how much of the 70 per cent increase in national income from 1949 to 1952 represented genuine recovery and how much was merely a reflection of the gradual improvement in statistical coverage during this period. It is, however, possible to compare the economy in 1952 with the relatively normal prewar year of 1933. As the data in Table 19–2 show, the total and per capita products in 1952 exceeded those in 1933, indicating that by 1952 the economy had completed the phase of rehabilitation.

Table 19–1—Communist Data on National Income and Production
During the Period of Rehabilitation, 1949–52

Year	National Income (1949 = 100)	Combined Gross Output Value of Industry and Agriculture (billions of 1952 yüan)
1949	100.0	46.6
1950	118.6	57.5
1951	138.8	68.3
1952	169.7	82.7

Source: P.R.C. State Statistical Bureau, Ten Great Years (Peking: Foreign Languages Press, 1960), pp. 16, 20.

THE PERIOD OF STEADY GROWTH, 1952–57

For the period 1952–57, relatively good economic statistics became available in increasing volume. This period roughly coincides with the First Five-Year plan period (1953–57). Because recovery from war damage had been completed by 1952, it becomes possible to evaluate a large portion of the Communist data for this period on the basis of what little is known about the normal productivity of agriculture in China. Taking advantage of the relatively abundant Communist data, several scholars in the United States have made independent estimates of national product for this period.

Table 19-2—Total and Per Capita Product, 1933 and 1952

	Net Domestic Product (billions of 1952 yüan)		Per Capita Product (1952 yüan)	
Year	Reconstructed Communist Estimate* (1)	Liu-Yeh Estimate (2)	Reconstructed Communist Estimate (3)	Liu-Yeh Estimate (4)
1933	—	59.5	—	119
1952	68.6	71.4	121	126

* Reconstructed Communist estimate represents an effort by Liu and Yeh to reconstruct or rederive the Communists' own estimates on the basis of Communist data without making adjustments for suspected inaccuracy in the data.

Sources: Net domestic product from Liu and Yeh, Economy of Chinese Mainland, pp. 66, 221; per capita product computed from population data given in ibid., pp. 102, 171.

Available estimates of national product. The different estimates of national product for 1952 and 1957, expressed in constant 1952 yüan, are presented in Table 19-3, together with the estimated average annual rates of growth.

While discrepancies exist among the different estimates for 1952, the reasons for the differences are now fairly clear.[1] The main difference between the Communist estimate of the net material product, 61.1 billion yüan, and the Liu-Yeh reconstructed estimate of net domestic product, 68.6 billion yüan, lies mainly in the omission, from the former, of the contribution of the service sectors, following a well-known Communist convention in estimating national income. Eckstein's estimate of the gross national product, 71.3 billion yüan, and the Liu-Yeh estimate of the net domestic product, 71.4 billion yüan, can be almost completely reconciled.[2] Hollister's and Li's estimates will be discussed presently in connection with the discussion of the rate of growth. Wu's estimate is close to the Liu-Yeh estimate. The net domestic product for 1952 can be put at around 71 billion yüan without running a serious risk of misrepresenting the actual level of total product.

Of more importance than the absolute magnitude of the national product in 1952 are the differences in the growth rates implied in the different estimates during 1952-57. According to the Communist estimate (Table 19-3, column 1) and in terms of the constant 1952 yüan, the average annual rate of growth of the net material product during 1952-57 is 9 per cent. In all likelihood, this is an overestimate of the over-all growth rate of the economy for several reasons.

First and more important, there is general agreement among scholars in the United States that the Communist data on agricultural production during the early years in this period underestimated the actual output so that the rate of growth of this sector was overstated for the period as a whole.[3]

The second source of upward bias in the growth rate lies in the way the value of industrial production was computed by the Communists. The 1952 (third quarter) prices were used as weights in computing the official gross values of production for

---

[1] For a detailed analysis of the differences between the estimates, see Liu, 'Quantitative Trends,' Section II.

[2] See Liu, 'Quantitative Trends,' pp. 99–108.

[3] See the following pages in the sources cited in Table 19-3: Eckstein, p. 32; Hollister, pp. 19 and 29; Li, p. 63; Liu and Yeh, pp. 43–46; Wu, p. 185.

Table 19–3—National Product Estimates of the Chinese Mainland, 1952–57
(billions of 1952 yüan)

| Year | Communist (Net Material Product)* (1) | Eckstein (Gross National Product) (2) | Hollister (Gross National Product) (3) | Li (Net National Product Reconstructed Communist Estimate) (4) | Liu-Yeh | | Wu (Net National Product) (7) |
					Net Domestic Product Reconstructed Communist Estimate (5)	Authors' Estimate (6)	
1952	61.1	71.3	67.9	72.9	68.6	71.4	72.4
1957	93.5	—	102.4	111.8	104.2	95.3	94.8
Average Annual Growth Rate	9.0	—	8.6	8.8	8.8	6.0	5.6

Terms: Net domestic product is gross domestic product net of depreciation. It is different from the net national product in that the latter includes net factor incomes from abroad. Net material product is a concept used mainly in Communist countries; it includes certain 'service items' from the domestic product.

Sources: (1) Liu and Yeh, *Economy of Chinese Mainland*, p. 220; (2) Alexander Eckstein, *The National Income of Communist China* (Glencoe, Ill.: The Free Press, 1961), p. 56; (3) W. W. Hollister, *China's Gross National Product and Social Accounts, 1950–57* (Glencoe, Ill.: The Free Press, 1958), p. 2; (4) C. M. Li, *Economic Development of Communist China* (Berkeley and Los Angeles: University of California Press, 1959), p. 106; (5) Liu and Yeh, *Economy of Chinese Mainland*, p. 213 (this estimate was reconstructed from basic Communist data without corrections for reliability, but was computed on the standard Western concept of net domestic product); (6) *ibid.*, p. 66; (7) Y. L. Wu, F. P. Hoeber, and M. M. Rockwell, *The Economic Potential of Communist China* (Menlo Park, Calif.: Stanford Research Institute, 1964), p. 241.

years prior to 1957. Consumer goods prices were depressed in the fall of 1952 because of the 'Five-Anti' campaign against private enterprises, but prices of producer goods were little affected. Thus, producer goods were 'overvalued' relative to consumer goods. Because producer goods increased faster than consumer goods after 1952, the official rates of growth of industrial production were upward biased. The valuation of new products at trial-manufacturing expenses, the so-called 'new-product effect,' also exaggerated the increasing trend. In addition, as will be shown later, there are indications of exaggeration in the reported increase in consumer goods production.

Another important source of upward bias is the omission from the estimate of employment of workers in many traditional, small, and scattered producing units in the handicraft, trade, and transportation sectors.[4] Because the output of these workers hardly increased, if it did not actually decline, during 1952–57, the omission would result in an exaggerated over-all rate of growth.

Fourth, there are admissions by the Communists themselves that local units deliberately falsified reports and overstated output in order to fulfill and overfulfill quotas.[5] It is reasonable to assume that the pressure to expand output intensified during 1952–57, and hence attempts to falsify reports may also have increased.

Finally, the concept of 'net material product' excludes many so-called nonproductive sectors (trade, passenger transportation, and so forth), which expanded apparently less rapidly than the sectors included. This is reflected in the difference between the Communist estimate of a 9 per cent rate of growth and the 8.8 per cent computed from the estimate (Table 19–3, column 5) reconstructed by Liu and Yeh from Communist data without correction for reliability but on the standard Western concept of domestic product, which includes incomes originating in the nonproductive sectors.

The reconstructed Communist estimates by Li (Table 19–3, column 4) and Liu and Yeh (column 5) naturally yield a rate of growth, 8.8 per cent per year, almost as high as the Communist estimate. The Hollister estimate (column 3), 8.6 per cent per year, is not free from the sources of the upward bias in the Communist estimate discussed above, except the last one.

Attempts to correct the apparent defects in the Communist statistics on food crops and consumer goods and to supplement the deficient Communist data on the traditional and small enterprises were made in deriving the Liu-Yeh estimate given in column 6 of Table 19–3.

That the Communist figures on the production of food crops for the early years during 1952–57 are underestimates of the actual output is no longer in question.[6] The difficult problem is to correct this bias. The procedure followed by Liu and Yeh is briefly outlined here.

First, the Communist figure for the per capita consumption of food crops in 1957 was accepted as roughly correct. It is unlikely that the Communist figure for 1957 is a clear-cut underestimate of the actual output, because the per capita consumption figure implied for that year is as much as 14 per cent higher than the estimated average ration allowed by the Communist regime. It is reasonable to assume that the Communists, knowing that rationing and control regulations could not be completely enforced, would fix the ration at a lower level than the actual amount of consumption. But the Communist rationing and control systems were probably effective enough for actual consumption not to have been more than 10 to 15 per cent higher than the ration amounts allowed.[7] On the other hand, it is also unlikely that the 1957 per

---

[4] See J. P. Emerson, *Nonagricultural Employment in Mainland China: 1949–1958* (Washington, D.C.: Bureau of the Census, 1965), p. 69.

[5] See, for instance, *Jen-min Jih-pao* (*People's Daily*, hereafter: *JMJP*), Peking, September 12, 1953.

[6] See Liu and Yeh, *Economy of Chinese Mainland*, pp. 47–51.   [7] *Ibid.*

capita figure overestimates the actual output, for the calorie intake implied in the 1957 per capita figure is 5 or 6 per cent power than the estimated 1933 level, and there is no evidence that the per capita food consumption level in 1957 was much smaller than in 1933.

Second, the per capita consumption of food crops during 1952–56 must be estimated. This is an exceedingly difficult task; at the very best, we could give no more than an educated guess. There is no reason to assume that per capita consumption of food crops had been increasing during 1952–57. In fact, the control of food consumption had been gradually tightened throughout the period, and this would have been unnecessary had there been increases in per capita supply of food crops. On the other hand, there is no evidence that per capita consumption was reduced during this period. It seems that the only reasonable assumption one can make is that it was more or less constant throughout 1952–57.

This assumption enabled us to estimate the production of food crops for all the years 1952–57. Crops were increasingly used for food, and Communist data are available on the annual percentage used for food in total food crop production, including quantities exported. Assuming that the importation of food crops during this period had been negligible and that there had been no change in the amount in storage, the output was easily computed for 1952–57 on the basis of the population data. The increase in total production therefore reflects mainly the growth of population, modified only by the increasing percentage of crops used for food.[8]

Another adjustment was made in the Communist figure for hog production in 1957. It was reported by the Communists that the number of hogs increased by as much as 47 per cent during 1957, a claim that is not only improbable but also contradicted by a number of events.[9] First, there is no evidence of increases in either exports or domestic consumption of pork subsequent to 1957. Second, animal feeds actually decreased from 1956 to 1957. For the lack of a better alternative, it seems reasonable to assume a percentage increase in the number of hogs equal to the rate of growth of population in 1957.

While it is clear that the particular price weights used, the 'new-product effect' (inflated valuation of new products due to inclusion of trial-manufacturing expenses), and the tendency to exaggerate performance all point to an upward bias in the Communist data on the output of producer goods, no adjustments were made in the Liu-Yeh estimate because of the lack of a reasonable procedure for doing so. There is, however, an increase of 200 per cent in the production of a group of unidentified consumer goods from 1952 to 1957 in the Communist statistics, much higher than the 45 per cent increase of the output of identified and essential consumer goods during the same period.[10] The latter increase is already fast, reflecting, as it did, not only the increase in actual consumption but also, to an unknown extent, a shift from handicraft output and consumption goods processed at home to modern factory production. Such a fast rate of increase (200 per cent over five years) of consumer goods of unknown identity, at a time when the rate of investment was not only high but also increasing rapidly, cannot be accepted at face value without further scrutiny. An effort must be made to examine what commodities they could have been.

From 1952 to 1956 the Communists published some aggregate data on daily con-

---

[8] A number of possible criticisms of this procedure have been discussed and answered in *ibid.*, pp. 43–54. They include such questions as whether the recovery from war damage could have been largely completed by 1952; whether the effects of increasing use of fertilizers and mechanized implements and of the completion of certain irrigation and flood-control projects have been taken into consideration; and whether the rationing controls were not imposed to prevent higher consumption of food crops in response to higher income, implying that per capita consumption of food crops may have been increasing during 1952–57.

[9] *Ibid.*, pp. 54–55.   [10] *Ibid.*, p. 60.

sumer items, including china and earthenware; consumers' metal products; leather and fur products; glass products; furniture; soaps and cosmetic products; cultural, educational, and 'technical' products; and an unspecified 'others' category, which varied in size from one-fifth to one-third of the total. The gross value of output of this aggregate group of consumer goods increased 44 per cent, from 3.7 billion yüan in 1952 to 5.3 billion yüan in 1956. This is about equal to the rate of increase of the identified portion of the total value of consumer goods, but is a great deal less than the 200 per cent increase reported for the unidentified portion from 1952 to 1956. This information fails to support the claim made for the rate of increase of the global total output of consumer goods. At the risk of duplicating some of the items already covered in the daily-consumption items mentioned above, we have put together some fragmentary data on such 'luxuries' as fountain pens, radios, clocks, hot water bottles, pencils, bicycles, and antibiotics. The total value of these goods (in 1952 yüan) cannot have exceeded about 1.1 billion in 1957, but there was a total value of 9.6 billion yüan worth of unidentified consumer goods (again in 1952 yüan). However fast the rate of increase of these 'luxury' items may have been, their increased production could not possibly explain a 200 per cent increase from 1952 to 1957 of the unidentified portion of the gross value of consumer goods to a total of 9.6 billion (1952) yüan.

The 200 per cent increase in the unidentified portion of consumer goods from 1952 to 1957 is therefore inexplicable. Actually, even an increase of 45 per cent in the identified portion of consumer goods from 1952 to 1957 is probably too high, in view of the fact that resources were being channeled increasingly to investment. The nature of the identified consumer goods is largely known, and we have no reasonable basis on which to make an adjustment in the data; but there can be no doubt that the rapid rate of increase reported for the unidentified portion is exaggerated. To use the Communist data on the value of production of consumer goods without adjustment would result in an overestimate of the rate of growth of the national product. We have recomputed the total annual value of consumer goods production from 1953 to 1957 by assuming that the unidentified portion increased at a rate equal to that of the identified portion. If that assumption is wrong, it overstates the increase in unidentified goods and our estimate errs in the upward direction.

The Liu-Yeh estimate given in column 6 of Table 19-3 was derived after adjustments were made in Communist data on agricultural output and consumer goods production, together with the consequent modification in the other sectors of the economy.[11] The average annual rate of growth according to this estimate is 6 per cent. While substantially lower than the Communist estimate of 9 per cent, it is by no means a low over-all rate of growth compared to many other nations.[12]

All the adjustments described above can be criticized as more or less arbitrary. But, given the weaknesses in the Communist statistical system, the tendency of local producing units to exaggerate achievements, the known underreporting of crop production in the early 1950's, and the inexplicable 200 per cent increase of unidentifiable consumer goods over a short period of five years, it would be even more arbitrary to accept the Communist statistics without adjustment. The question is whether the adjustments made are reasonable and plausible.

There are, of course, weaknesses in the adjustments made by Liu and Yeh. In particular, the year-to-year change in the Liu-Yeh estimate of the value added by agriculture is unlikely to be as reliable as the average rate of change during the six years as a whole. For one thing, weather conditions have not been taken into consideration—it is indeed very difficult to calculate the effects of floods and drought on

---

[11] A smaller amount of production of agricultural products and consumer goods would reduce the incomes of the trading, transportation, and finance sectors and would reduce the flow of raw materials to the handicraft sector.

[12] See under heading 'The Great Leap Forward and Its Aftermath, 1958–1965,' below.

crop production. The adjustments made, however, are based on a detailed evaluation of the basic Communist statistics; and in all likelihood they have reduced the margins of error in these data. A better knowledge of the economy of the Chinese mainland can be obtained only by improving the adjustments in the Communist statistics; it cannot be achieved by accepting the Communist data without correcting the known defects.

THE GREAT LEAP FORWARD AND ITS AFTERMATH, 1958–65

With the announcement of the Great Leap Forward in December, 1957, the central Communist regime exerted tremendous pressure on local Party members, directors of communes, and managers of local enterprises to expand production at a pace practically impossible to achieve. The accomplishments of a few pilot projects using concentrated technical skill and scarce resources under the most favorable conditions and closest supervision were expected to be duplicated by producers all over the country. Soon enthusiastic reports were received from one locality after another claiming that the targets were being fulfilled and overfulfilled. When the 'Communiqué on Economic Development in 1958' was issued in April, 1959, the regime announced that the output of such important products as food crops, cotton, and iron and steel had more than doubled during 1958 and that the gross value of agriculture and industry had increased by about 65 per cent.[13]

It soon became apparent that these announced increases could not be true, as there was neither improvement in the food rations nor evidence of sufficient increases in the supply of industrial goods to sustain the claims. A drastic downward revision of the claims was announced in August, 1959, reducing the estimated production of food crops and cotton in 1958 by one-third. The claimed increase in iron and steel production was scaled down in a more subtle way. It was admitted that roughly 30 per cent of the iron and steel produced in 1958 was 'native' and not really usable for modern industrial purposes. It is difficult to say what the native iron and steel were good for, but it is significant that the backyard blast furnaces were soon abandoned. As the output of iron and steel was not really reduced in the revised announcement, the total value of industrial production remained unchanged. The increase in agricultural production announced for 1959 was more restrained, but the increase claimed for steel and industrial production in general was high.

Some existing estimates of the post-Leap national product. Because of the 'statistical fiasco' brought about by the Great Leap Forward in 1958, it has become extremely difficult to estimate Communist China's national product and its components since that year with a reasonable degree of confidence. Some of the existing estimates of the post-1957 total product are presented in Table 19–4, together with the estimates for 1957.

The Communist estimate and the reconstructed Communist estimate by Liu-Yeh for 1958 and 1959 were based on the extravagant Communist claims of increase of agricultural and industrial output. An over-all rate of growth as high as 34 per cent in a single year, from 93.5 billion yüan in 1957 to 125.3 billion yüan in 1958, does not seem to belong in the realm of possibility. Hollister's estimate of an increase of 23 per cent (from 102.4 billion yüan in 1957 to 126.2 billion yüan in 1958), while lower than the Communist claim, appears also to be quite unprecedented.

Now that the dust of the Great Leap has settled, it is certain that all the estimates for 1959 (including the conjectural estimate by Liu-Yeh and Wu's estimate of a modest increase of 7 per cent, from 104.8 billion yüan in 1958 to 112.0 billion yüan in 1959) will be seen to be overestimates. A basic reason for this conclusion is that agricultural production not only did not increase from 1958 to 1959 but, as will be shown later (Table 19–6), it actually declined substantially.

---

[13] See *Peking Review*, 2, No. 17 (April 21, 1959): 33–36.

Table 19-4—National Product Estimates of the Chinese Mainland, 1957-62
(billions of 1952 yüan)

| Year | Communist (Net Material Product) (1) | Hollister (Gross National Product) (2) | Liu-Yeh (Net Domestic Product) | | Wu (Net Domestic Product) (5) | Wu (Gross Domestic Product) (6) |
			Reconstructed Communist Estimate (3)	Authors' Estimate (4)		
1957	93.5	102.4	104.2	95.3	94.8	—
1958	125.3	126.2	145.0	108.0*	104.8	—
1959	152.9	142.6	176.8	125.0 *	112.0	—
1960	—	158.1	—	—	112.5	—
1961	—	—	—	—	73.2	82.1
1962	—	—	—	—	—	109.0†

* Conjectural estimate.

† Without taking into consideration possible 'investment limitations and waste.' If possible 'investment limitations and waste' were taken into account, the figure would be 101.4.

Sources: (1) Liu and Yeh, *Economy of Chinese Mainland*, pp. 116, 220; (2) Hollister, *China's Gross National Product and Social Accounts, 1950-57*, p. 2; (3) Liu and Yeh, *Economy of Chinese Mainland*, pp. 218, 660; (4) *ibid.*, p. 66; (5) Wu, *The Economic Potential of Communist China*, 1: 241; (6) *ibid.*, 3: 120-22.

A reconstructed Communist estimate of the domestic product, 1958-65. While it is admittedly difficult to derive a reliable estimate of the national product for the post-Leap years, the importance of having even a crude picture of the recent economic trends compels us to make such an attempt. Before doing so, it is desirable to reconstruct from scattered Communist information the Communists' own estimate of the domestic product for these years. The Liu-Yeh reconstructed estimates for 1958-59 are presented in column 3 of Table 19-4. A very crude reconstruction for later years is possible on the basis of some Communist observations on food crops and on the total value of industrial production.

For the output of food crops, there is the report by Lord Montgomery after his visit to the mainland that the total output for 1960 was 150 million tons.[14] Since that time, it has been reported in Communist sources that the 1962 output was 'better than 1961,' that the 1963 output was 'better than 1962,'[15] and that the 1964 output was 'larger than 1957.'[16] Finally, the Communists claimed that the 1965 output was about 200 million tons.[17] By linear extrapolation on the 1960 and 1965 figures, the Communist 'claims' for 1961, 1962, 1963, and 1964 may be put at 160, 170, 180, and 190 million tons.[18] On the assumption that the ration of value added by agriculture to the output of food crops during 1960-65 is the same as in 1957,[19] agricultural net value added may be estimated at 32.6 billion, 34.7 billion, 36.9 billion, 39.1 billion, 41.2 billion and 43.4 billion 1952 yüan, respectively, for the six years 1960-65.

[14] *The Sunday Times* (London), magazine section, Oct. 15, 1961.

[15] *Jen-min Shou-ts'e* (*People's Handbook*) (Peking: Ta-kung Pao-she, 1964), p. 6.

[16] Report by Chou En-Lai, *JMJP*, December 31, 1964.

[17] *Chinese News Summary*, April 28, 1966, p. 1.

[18] The 1964 estimate, 190 million tons, is thus larger than that for 1957 (185 million tons). See the report by Chou En-Lai, *JMJP*, December 31, 1964.

[19] The 1957 ratio is computed from the data given in Liu and Yeh, *Economy of Chinese Mainland*, p. 223.

The net value added by manufacturing industries can be reconstructed in a similarly crude way. It has been reported by the Communists that the gross value of industrial output (manufacturing factories and handicrafts) increased by 18.4 per cent from 1949 to 1950.[20] Applying this percentage increase to the Liu-Yeh reconstructed Communist estimate of the net value added by manufacturing factories and handicrafts for 1959,[21] the net value added in 1960 is estimated at 61.9 billion 1952 yüan. In a paper by Chao,[22] the Communist estimate of the gross value of output of manufacturing factories and handicrafts has been reconstructed at 79.8 billion, 88.6 billion, 101.9 billion, and 113.1 billion yüan for the four years from 1962 to 1965. The net value added for the same years may be estimated at 23.4 billion, 26.0 billion, 29.9 billion, and 33.1 billion yüan on the 1957 ratio of net value added to the gross value of output.[23] All sources are in agreement that industrial production declined from 1960 to 1962. The 1961 net value added is therefore estimated at 42.6 billion yüan, the average of the 1960 and the 1962 figures (61.9 billion and 23.4 billion yüan, respectively).

Applying the 1957 ratio of net domestic product to the sum of agricultural and industrial value added,[24] we derived the reconstructed Communist estimate of net domestic product for 1960–65 (presented in Table 19–5) from the estimates of the net value added by agriculture and industry given above for these years.

Table 19–5—Reconstructed Communist Estimate of Net Domestic Product (Total and Per Capita) Compared with Exports of the Following Year, 1957–65

| | Reconstructed Communist Estimate* | | | Percentage of Exports in Domestic Product of Preceding Year |
Year	Net Domestic Product (in billions of 1952 yüan) (1)	Per Capita Product (in 1952 yüan) (2)	Exports of the Following Year (in billions of 1952 yüan) (3)	(4)
1957	104.2	164	4.65	4.5
1958	145.0	222	5.31	3.7
1959	176.8	267	4.74	2.7
1960	155.9	232	3.59	2.3
1961	127.5	187	3.59	2.8
1962	99.5	144	3.67	3.7
1963	107.4	153	4.55	4.2
1964	117.3	165	4.91	4.2
1965	126.2	165	—	—

* The figures given for 1958–65 are a very crude reconstructed estimate.

Sources: (1) and (2) for the 1957–59 figures of net domestic product, see Liu and Yeh, Economy of Chinese Mainland, pp. 213, 660; for the 1960–65 estimates, see text; for the per capita estimates, the 1957–58 population figures used in the computation are the official Communist data (ibid., p. 102); and for those for the later years, see text; (3) supplied by F. H. Mah.

[20] This percentage is given by Edwin F. Jones from a published Communist source.
[21] See Liu and Yeh, Economy of Chinese Mainland, p. 660.
[22] Kang Chao, 'Policies and Performance in Industry,' in Galenson, et al., eds., Economic Trends, Section 3b.
[23] The 1957 ratio is calculated from data given in Liu and Yeh, Economy of Chinese Mainland, p. 223.
[24] This ratio is calculated on the data given in ibid.

It is desirable to have an approximate picture of the rough order of magnitudes of the per capita product during this period. The rates of growth of population during the post-Leap years, as given in various Communist sources, contradict one another. On the one hand, an estimate of 700 million, probably for 1965, is given in a *Jen-min Jih-pao* editorial of June 8, 1966. The average rate of growth during 1959 to 1965 implied in this estimate is only about 1 per cent per year. On the other hand, Chou En-Lai mentioned a 2 per cent rate of growth for 1960–62.[25] In reconstructing the per capita product, an average rate of growth of population of 1.5 per cent, the average of the two Communist estimates, is used. It should be noted that, if this percentage rate of growth of population is an underestimate, the reconstructed Communist estimate of the per capita product would be correspondingly overstated. The estimated per capita product during 1957–65 is given in Table 19–5.

The plausibility of the reconstructed Communist estimate of the domestic product must be evaluated. While the Communists have assigned a high priority to the allocation of resources for exports, the level of exports attainable is basically constrained by domestic output. To account for the time lag between domestic production and the arrival of exports at foreign ports, domestic product of a given year and exports of the following year are compared in Table 19–5. The reconstructed Communist estimate of the domestic product increased very greatly from 1957 to 1959, but the percentage of exports in domestic product declined sharply from 4.5 per cent for 1957 to 2.7 per cent in 1959. Moreover, while the reconstructed Communist estimates of the domestic product for 1960 and 1961 (respectively, 155.9 billion and 127.5 billion 1952 yüan) are a great deal higher than that for 1957 (104.2 billion yüan), the 1960 and 1961 percentages (respectively, 2.3 per cent and 2.8 per cent) are substantially smaller than that for 1957 (4.5 per cent). This indicates that the reconstructed Communist estimates of the domestic product for 1958–61 are likely to be overestimates.[26] Because the reconstructed Communist estimates of the domestic product for 1963–65 are based on claimed increases of agricultural and industrial production over the exaggerated estimates for the preceding years, they are also likely to be overestimates.

An exploratory estimate of the domestic product, 1958–65. In spite of the practically total blackout of statistics on commodity output from Communist sources on the mainland since 1960, there has emerged a set of rough but educated estimates of the output of food crops and cotton during 1959–65. These data, prepared by the U.S. Consulate General in Hong Kong on the basis of piecemeal information on acreages and yields, are the most generally accepted estimates of the recent trend of output by qualified sources in Hong Kong and are given in Table 19–6.

Agricultural output declined precipitously from 1958 to 1960. Recovery in food crops production began in 1961. The output of cotton, the major commercial crop, lagged behind and did not start to recover until 1963. As late as 1965, neither food crops nor cotton had regained the 1957 level.[27]

The movement in heavy industrial output may be typified by the output of steel. Estimates of steel output by sources in Hong Kong are given in Table 19–7, together with the estimate made by the U.S. Bureau of Mines and some other data. The figures given for 1958–60 in columns 1 through 4 are Communist claims, and all non-Communist sources are in agreement that these data are highly inflated. Starting with

---

[25] *JMJP*, December 26, 1963.

[26] Because the export data used are compiled from the import data of countries having trade relations with Communist China, they are fairly reliable data. While during the difficult years 1961–62 the percentage of exports in domestic product may be expected to be smaller than the more normal years 1957–58, the decline was too sharp to be plausible, especially as the reconstructed estimates of the domestic product for those years are substantially higher in absolute terms than that for 1957.

[27] See Liu, 'Quantitative Trends,' pp. 149, 179.

Table 19–6—Estimates of the Output of Food Crops and Cotton, 1957–65

Year	Food Crops (million metric tons)	Cotton (million bales)
1957	185	1.6
1958	194	1.9
1959	168	1.8
1960	160	1.4
1961	167	0.9
1962	178	0.9
1963	179	1.0
1964	183	1.2
1965	180	1.3

Source: Reported in R. F. Emery, 'Recent Economic Development in Communist China,' *Asian Survey*, June, 1966, pp. 303–4. Estimates are those of the Agricultural Officer, U.S. Consulate General, Hong Kong.

1962, the scattered data in columns 1 through 3 begin to converge to a fairly uniform pattern. The estimate made by the U.S. Bureau of Mines (column 4) differs rather sharply from those given in columns 1 through 3. It is explained by the Bureau of Mines, however, that its figures may be 'grossly exaggerated by perhaps one-fifth or more.'[28] No opinion is expressed on how much 'more' than one-fifth. If the exaggeration were from one-fourth to one-third, the estimate by the Bureau of Mines for 1962–64 would be quite close to those in the first three columns. It is clear that steel production fell substantially from 1959 to 1962 and then recovered from 1962 to 1965.

A model of sixteen structural relationships was developed in a previous paper[29] for estimating domestic product and investment for 1959–65, together with the value added by the two main branches of the economy (the traditional sectors and the relatively modern ones), on the basis of the data given in Tables 19–6 and 19–7. The parameters in most of the structural relationships were estimated from the input-output relationships observed during the statistically more reliable years 1952–57. The derivation of these equations will not be discussed here;[30] the main feature of the model, however, can be outlined by explaining these relationships as follows. The value added by modern factories is determined by the agricultural and mining raw materials consumed. Agricultural raw material consumed is assumed to be a function of the output of the agricultural sector of both the current and the preceding years. The total amount of mining raw materials consumed by modern factories is extrapolated on the basis of the quantities of coal and iron ore produced by modern mines. However, because the data on the latter two items are rather confused during recent years, a relationship is derived for estimating these quantities from the data on steel. The value added by all traditional sectors is related to the value added by agriculture; and that by the relatively modern sectors as a whole is determined by the value added by modern factories. The domestic product is obtained as the sum of the value added by the different sectors. The levels of employment in these sectors are then estimated

---

[28] This qualifying statement was originally given for the 1959–60 estimates in the *Minerals Yearbook, 1963* (Washington, D.C.: U.S. Government Printing Office, 1963), Table 2, p. 1282, but in later mimeographed sheets distributed by the Bureau of Mines, it is given for the estimates for all the years 1959–64.
[29] Liu, 'Quantitative Trends,' Section V.2.
[30] For a full explanation of the model, see *ibid.*

Table 19-7—Scattered Data on Steel and Electric Power, 1957–65

| | Steel (million metric tons) | | | | | Data Used in This Chapter | | Electric Power, Emery | |
| | Current Scene (1) | Emery (2) | Far Eastern Economic Review (3) | U.S. Bureau of Mines (4) | Liu-Yeh (5) | Quantity (6) | Index (1957 = 100) (7) | Quantity (Billions) kwh (8) | Index (1957 = 100) (9) |
Year									
1957	5.35	5.2	5.35	—	5.35	5.35	—	19.0	—
1958	8.00*	8.0*	11.08*	—	6.3	6.3	—	27.5*	—
1959	13.35*	13.4*	13.35	13.35*	8.9	8.9	—	41.5*	—
1960	18.45*	18.5*	18.45*	18.45*	—	8.4	—	58.0*	—
1961	7–8	—	11–12	9.5	—	7.9	—	—	—
1962	7–8	—	7–8	10.0	—	7.5	—	—	—
1963	7–9	7.0	8–9	12.0	—	8.0	149.5	30.0	157.9
1964	8–10	—	10	14.0	—	9.0	—	—	—
1965	—	10.0	12	—	—	10.0	186.9	33.0	173.7

* Communist claims.

Sources: (1) Current Scene, April 15, 1965, p. 9; (2) Robert F. Emery, 'Recent Economic Developments in Communist China,' Asian Survey, June, 1966, p. 307; (3) Far Eastern Economic Review, March 31, 1966, p. 623; (4) mimeographed sheet obtained from the U.S. Bureau of Mines; (5) Liu and Yeh, Economy of Chinese Mainland, pp. 454, 681–83 (the 1958 and 1959 figures are obtained, respectively, by dividing the value figures of 3.8 billion and 5.36 billion yüan by the price of 600 yüan per ton); (6) for 1957–59, the data given in (5) are used; the 1962 figure is the midpoint of the range given in (1) and (3); the figures for 1960–61 are obtained by linear extrapolation on the 1959 and 1962 data; the 1963 and 1964 data are the midpoints of the ranges given in (1); the 1965 figure is taken from (2), (it is seen from (7) and (9)) that the steel figures for 1963 and 1965 bear relationships to that for 1957 similar to the data on electric power); (8) Asian Survey, June, 1966, p. 307.

on the basis of the value added by the respective sectors. Per capita consumption is then related to per capita productivity. Finally, domestic investment is derived by subtracting consumption from the total product.

With this system of equations obtained, the domestic product and investment for 1959–65 can be calculated in a straightforward manner on the basis of the estimates of food crops, cotton, steel and some other data. For the estimates on food crops and cotton, the figures presented in Table 19–6 are accepted. The data on steel used in the computation are presented in column 6 of Table 19–7. The estimates of net domestic product and investment are given in Table 19–8.

The decline of the domestic product from 1958 to 1961 confirms the deepening difficulty encountered by the economy during those years. The domestic product in 1961, 92.2 billion 1952 yüan, was 15 per cent lower than the 1958 peak of 108 billion 1952 yüan. The economy began to recover in 1962. The annual rate of recovery, as measured by the percentage growth in domestic product, increased from 2 per cent in 1961–62 to 6.2 per cent in 1963–64. The rate, however, slackened to 3.7 per cent during 1964–65, mainly because of the drought in North China.

Table 19–8—Estimate of Net Domestic Product and Investment, 1957–65

Year	Net Domestic Product (billions of 1952 yüan)	Net Domestic Investment (billions of 1952 yüan)	Proportion of Net Domestic Investment in Net Domestic Product (in per cent)
1957	95.3	18.2	19.1
1958	108.0	23.6	21.9
1959	104.4	20.0	19.2
1960	95.9	17.1	17.8
1961	92.2	15.6	16.9
1962	94.0	15.7	16.7
1963	98.1	16.7	17.0
1964	104.2	18.1	17.4
1965	108.1	19.5	18.0

Source: Liu, 'Quantitative Trends,' Tables 24 and 25.

The 1957 level of domestic product was regained during 1962–63, and the 1965 product was about the same as in 1958. The economy in 1965 stood where it was in 1958, a 'loss' of seven years of growth.

Net domestic investment decreased by 34 per cent, from 23.6 billion 1952 yüan in 1958 to 15.6 billion in 1961. The proportion of investment in total product declined fairly consistently, from 21.9 per cent in 1958 to 16.7 per cent in 1962. By 1965, however, investment exceeded the magnitude reached in 1957, but the 1957 proportion of investment in domestic product had not yet been fully regained.

The plausibility of the post-1958 estimate must be investigated. The product estimate can be checked against the data on exports, and the investment estimate examined in the light of certain Communist policy pronouncements.

As shown in Table 19–9, the ratio of exports to the domestic product of the preceding year rose fairly consistently from 1952 to 1959, within a range of 3.6 to 4.9 per cent. This proportion fell from 4.9 per cent in 1959 to 3.7 per cent in 1960, reflecting the increasing difficulty experienced by the economy.[31] It recovered thereafter quite

---

[31] The drop, however, is much less drastic than the implausible decline reflected in the reconstructed Communist estimate (see Table 19–5).

consistently to 4.7 per cent in 1964. The post-1960 range of this proportion, 3.7 per cent to 4.7 per cent, is close to the one observed during 1952–57, but the ratios for the most difficult years, 1960–62 (3.7 per cent to 3.9 per cent), are lower than those in the best years before the Leap, 1956–57, and those attained in 1958–59 under the initial impetus of the Leap. The picture reflected by these data appears plausible. While the foreign-trade data are also subject to a substantial margin of error, they are derived from the statistics of countries having trade relations with the Chinese mainland and are more reliable than our exploratory estimate of the domestic product. That a reasonable relationship exists between the data on exports and the product estimate lends credibility to the latter.

Table 19–9—Net Domestic Product Compared with Exports
of the Following Year, 1952–65

Year	Net Domestic Product (billions of 1952 yüan)	Exports of the Following Year (billions of 1952 yüan)	Percentage of Exports in Net Domestic Product of Preceding Year
1952	71.4	2.59	3.6
1953	75.3	2.82	3.8
1954	79.3	3.36	4.2
1955	82.3	3.98	4.8
1956	92.1	3.89	4.2
1957	95.3	4.65	4.9
1958	108.0	5.31	4.9
1959	104.4	4.74	4.5
1960	95.9	3.59	3.7
1961	92.2	3.59	3.9
1962	94.0	3.67	3.9
1963	98.1	4.55	4.5
1964	104.2	4.91	4.7
1965	108.1	—	—

Source: Liu, 'Quantitative Trends.' Net domestic product is drawn from Table 31, p. 164; the middle and right-hand columns are derived from Table 33, p. 165.

Liu's estimate of net domestic investment (Table 19–8) indicates a very substantial decline from 1958 to 1961–62. Investment in 1963–65 was still low in its ratio to the total product as compared to 1957 and the Great Leap Forward years, 1958–59. The magnitudes of investment during 1962–65 (15.7 billion to 19.5 billion 1952 yüan), however, remain substantial. This may seem to contradict certain policy pronouncements of the Communist regime.

When the agricultural crises continued into 1960, the Ninth Plenum of the Central Committee decided early in 1961 that, 'since there had been tremendous development in heavy industry in the last three years, its output of major products already far in excess of the planned level for 1961 and 1962, the scale of basic construction should therefore be appropriately reduced.'[32] Moreover, it is known that in December, 1961, the Communist Party issued a secret document to cadres in the field directing that 'all basic construction should be suspended, all those enterprises that had been operating regularly at a loss be shut down, and the practice of recruiting labor from

---

[32] Choh-ming Li, ed., *Industrial Development in Communist China* (New York: Praeger Publishers, 1964), p. 10.

rural areas be abandoned for at least three years.'[33] Then, on March 27, 1963, Chou En-lai again reported the decision to reduce basic construction.[34]

In view of the apparently firm decision to cut down capital construction since 1961, it may be questioned whether investment in 1961–65 could have been as high as Liu's estimate indicates. It is possible, of course, that the investment estimate presented in Table 19–8 is unreliable. Yet there are grounds to believe that the actual investment may not have been significantly below Liu's estimate.

According to Liu's estimate, the average level of investment during 1961–63 (16 billion 1952 yüan) was lower than that during 1957–59 (20.6 billion 1952 yüan) by 4.6 billion yüan. In view of the large number of construction projects known to be under way at the end of 1959, the momentum might have been such that a more drastic curtailment was unenforceable—despite the announced policy of entrenchment. By 1964 the domestic product exceeded the 1957 level (Table 19–8), and the policy of curtailing investment may have been relaxed. Moreover, while the 1965 product was virtually the same as in 1958, Liu's estimated investment for 1965 is substantially smaller than that for 1958.

Also, while basic construction in general may have been reduced, it is known that the Communist regime increased investment in the petroleum and fertilizer industries and significantly expanded the production of tractors and other farm equipment. Investment relating to the production of atomic weapons must have been quite substantial. It is not possible, however, to make a quantitative estimate of the investment in these areas at the present moment.

Another possible explanation of the substantial amount of investment during 1961–65 is an excessive increase in the stock of inventory. Steel, machinery, and other producer goods were perhaps actually produced in quantities compatible with the investment estimate, but they were merely being piled up. They had not been installed and put to use. A degree of confusion in the management of economic affairs may have existed after the agricultural crises during 1959–61. Orders were issued to curtail basic construction—but there was no corresponding reduction in the production of those producer goods that did not rely upon agriculture as the major source of raw materials. In fact, the regime may have been more anxious to avoid the difficult problem of excessive unemployment, already serious because of a slowdown of activities in such industries as textiles and food processing, than concerned with the problem of excessive stockpiling.

SUMMARY

An estimate of the domestic product and per capita output during 1952–65 is reproduced in Table 19–10. According to the reconstructed Communist estimate, the rate of growth of the net domestic product during 1952–57 was 8.8 per cent. The per capita product also grew at a fast rate (6.5 per cent net). As I have explained, strong reservations must be made as to the credibility of such a picture. Indeed, one would seriously question why the Communist leaders, however ambitious they may have been, would have been so eager to institute as radical a change in their economic policies as the Great Leap Forward in 1958 if everything was indeed making such great progress, unprecedented not only in China but also in the entire world.

The growth history represented by the Liu-Yeh estimate seems more in accordance with reality. The over-all growth rate (6.0 per cent net) is by no means low.[35] But population was expanding much faster (2.3 per cent) than employment (1.5 per cent).[36]

---

[33] *Ibid.*, p. 11.   [34] *Ibid.*

[35] For the data on population, investment, consumption, and capital-output ratio used below, see Liu, 'Quantitative Trends.'

[36] Liu and Yeh, *Economy of Chinese Mainland*, pp. 69, 102.

The rate of investment (23.8 per cent at 1952 prices), while high, was not sufficient to absorb the fast-growing population into employment. Per capita consumption was rising at a much more modest rate (1.9 per cent, excluding communal services) than that indicated by the reconstructed Communist estimate (5.2 per cent); but the pre-war 1933 level had not been regained even at the end of this period (1957). The capital-output ratios were reasonably low. But an incremental capital-output ratio of 3.9, coupled with an investment proportion of 23.8 per cent, yielded a growth rate of the gross product of 6.2 per cent per year which, while quite high, failed to bring about an increase in employment and consumption satisfactory to the regime. Even the picture represented by the Liu-Yeh estimate for 1952–57 was very good; but to a leadership having extraordinary ambitions, both domestic and international, and an unusual confidence in its ability to put through radical reorganizations of the economy, a prospect of growth on the 1952–57 pattern might have been considered unsatisfactory. A radically different program, which might promise to utilize the increasingly underemployed human resources to the fullest extent without having to divert capital resources from large-scale modern projects, would have appeared attractive to the Communist leadership. In the light of the Liu-Yeh estimate, the motivation underlying the Great Leap Forward (1958–59) seems more understandable.

Table 19–10—Net Domestic Product of the Chinese Mainland,
Total and Per Capita, 1952–65
(total product in billions of 1952 yüan;* per capita product in 1952 yüan)

Year	Reconstructed Communist Estimate		Liu-Yeh Estimate		Exploratory Estimate	
	Total (1)	Per Capita† (2)	Total (3)	Per Capita (4)	Total (5)	Per Capita† (6)
1952	68.6	121	71.4	126	—	—
1953	73.3	126	75.3	130	—	—
1954	77.8	131	79.3	133	—	—
1955	83.3	137	82.3	135	—	—
1956	96.4	155	92.1	148	—	—
1957	104.2	164	95.3	150	—	—
1958	145.0	222	—	—	108.0	166
1959	176.8	267	—	—	104.4	158
1960	155.9	232	—	—	95.9	143
1961	127.5	187	—	—	92.2	135
1962	99.5	144	—	—	94.0	136
1963	107.4	153	—	—	98.1	140
1964	117.3	165	—	—	104.2	146
1965	126.2	165	—	—	108.1	150

* For well-known reasons, the use of the 1952 exchange rate of 1 U.S. dollar = 2.343 yüan to obtain estimates of total and per capita product in U.S. dollars will give misleading results.

† The figures given for 1958–65 are very crude estimates.

Sources: (1) and (3): figures for 1952–57, Liu and Yeh, Economy of Chinese Mainland, pp. 213, 660, 66; for 1958–65 estimates, see Table 5. (2), (4), and (6): population data used in obtaining per capita estimates for 1952–58 are Communist official data given in ibid., p. 102; for population data used for years after 1958, see under heading 'A Reconstructed Communist Estimate of the Domestic Product, 1958–65,' in this chapter, and Table 19–5; (5): Liu 'Quantitative Trends,' Tables 26 and 31.

The Great Leap Forward was based on a sound diagnosis of the basic weakness of the mainland economy but a serious misconception of the proper way to deal with it. There was a tremendous amount of surplus labor and a serious shortage of capital and of highly trained manpower as late as 1957, in spite of the significant degree of industrialization achieved during 1952–57. Communes were organized in 1958. Life in the villages was almost completely regimented. Peasants were marched to the field to work impossibly long hours, and terrific pressure was imposed on industrial enterprises to expand production at unprecedented paces. The output of almost everything was to double in a single year from 1957 to 1958.

Because the reconstructed Communist estimate of the domestic product for 1958–65 is very unreliable, the exploratory estimate in Table 19–10 will be the basis of the summary discussion. Under the initial stimulus of the Leap, there was perhaps a 13 per cent increase in the total product from 95.3 billion (1952) yüan in 1957 to 108 billion in 1958. But the excessive regimentation in the communes, the denial of work incentives through the abolition of private plots and the change to equalitarian distribution systems for the peasants, the total miscalculation of technical possibilities in introducing the backyard furnaces and unworkable agricultural techniques (for example, deep plowing, close planting, and the poorly designed irrigation and flood control systems), and the exhausting pace imposed on the population, together with bad weather conditions, brought disaster to agriculture. Farm output declined sharply from 1958 to 1960. The supply of agricultural raw materials to the industrial sectors diminished severely. The whole economy suffered a serious leap backward from 1958 to 1961. The domestic product in 1961 (92.2 billion 1952 yüan) was 15 per cent lower than the 1958 peak (108 billion). The per capita product dropped perhaps 19 per cent from 1958 to 1961, roughly back to the 1955 level.

As the agricultural crisis deepened and industrial production slackened, the Communist regime relaxed the worst features of the Leap (for example, it abolished such unworkable schemes as the commune mess halls and the 'miracle techniques of cultivation,' and made a limited restoration of private plots and incentive payment schemes) and sharply cut back the investment program. The economy began to recover in 1962. The total product in 1965 probably regained the 1958 level, with the per capita product perhaps back to the 1957 level. A total of seven years, however, was lost without any growth during a period (1958–65) when practically all other nations experienced a significant measure of growth and development.

For the 1952–65 period as a whole, the relatively impressive record of development during the earlier years 1952–57 was marred by the poor performance during 1958–65 following the Great Leap Forward. The average annual rates of growth of total and per capita product during 1952–65 amounted to 3.3 and 1.4 per cent, respectively. Following the considerable achievement of roughly the First Five Year Plan period, 1952–57, the Communist regime pursued a 'big push' policy, which resulted in a cycle of peak and trough, with practically no growth from 1958 to 1965.

Because of the absence of detailed statistical information on sectoral output, no real attempt can be made to estimate China's national income after 1965. However, it is generally agreed that the Cultural Revolution, which began in the fall and winter of that year, had the effect of significantly lowering Communist China's industrial output in 1967 and 1968.[37] Industrial production began to recover in 1969 and apparently continued its upswing in 1970. On the other hand, agricultural production, which was not as seriously affected by the Cultural Revolution, is believed to have registered only small gains during the period. For these and other reasons, such projections of the Chinese GNP as have been made by others are significantly divergent and are

---

[37] According to a study by the Japanese Foreign Ministry, 'the scale of industrial and agricultural production last year (1968) is estimated at only slightly above the levels of 1965.' The study was reported in *The New York Times*, May 19, 1969, p. 10.

cited here only for illustration. For instance, a Tokyo estimate attributed to the Japanese Foreign Office and reported by KYODO gave the Chinese GNP for 1970 at 75 billion dollars. (There is no information on the basis of pricing and the rate of conversion into dollars.) On the other hand, Werner Klatt gives a rough estimate of 160 billion yüan for the same year.[38]

SELECTED BIBLIOGRAPHY

ECKSTEIN, ALEXANDER. *The National Income of Communist China*. Glencoe, Ill.: The Free Press, 1961. Contains a careful estimate of the national income for 1952.

HOLLISTER, W. W. *China's Gross National Product and Social Accounts, 1950–57*. Glencoe, Ill.: The Free Press, 1958. Presents estimates of national product constructed on the basis of Communist data with little evaluation and adjustment.

LI, CHOH-MING. *Economic Development of Communist China*. Berkeley and Los Angeles: University of California Press, 1959. The first postwar attempt to estimate the national income of the Chinese mainland.

LIU, TA-CHUNG. 'Quantitative Trends in the Economy of the Chinese Mainland, 1952–1965,' in WALTER GALENSON, ALEXANDER ECKSTEIN, and TA-CHUNG LIU, eds. *Economic Trends in Communist China*. Chicago: Aldine Publishing Company, 1968, pp. 87–182. Presents national income estimates and analysis of growth pattern.

LIU, TA-CHUNG, and KUNG-CHIA YEH, *The Economy of the Chinese Mainland: National Income and Economic Development, 1933–1959*. Princeton, N.J.: Princeton University Press, 1965. Both the reconstructed Communist estimate and an independent estimate are presented.

WU, Y. L., F. P. HOEBER, and M. M. ROCKWELL. *The Economic Potential of Communist China*. Menlo Park, Calif.: Stanford Research Institute, 1963. Contains estimate of national income and evaluation of growth potential.

---

[38] Werner Klatt, 'A Review of China's Economy in 1970,' *The China Quarterly*, No. 43 (July–September, 1970), pp. 100–20

20

AGRICULTURAL POLICIES AND PERFORMANCE

K. C. YEH

INTRODUCTION

ONE of the basic goals of the Communist regime is to accelerate economic growth. To do so with virtually no recourse to foreign financing, it is generally necessary to rely heavily on the agricultural sector for resources to supply additional imports and to finance a higher level of investment. The extent to which the agricultural sector can fulfill its role is therefore critical to the rate of economic growth. A slowdown in agriculture would retard the growth process. That was precisely the situation in Communist China during the early phase of its development. As Mao Tse-tung himself succinctly summed up the problem: 'The levels of grain marketings and production of industrial raw materials in China today are very low. Yet the state's demand for these items grows year by year. This is a sharp contradiction.'[1] To resolve this contradiction, the regime must strive to increase agricultural production and to extract a larger share of the agricultural output for development uses. To increase output is by no means simple, mainly because China's agricultural resources, relative to its enormous and rapidly expanding population, are far from abundant. Nor is the problem of extraction any less complicated because of the possible conflict between the twofold objective of maximizing output and maximizing extraction, since output is not entirely independent of the amount collected from the peasants. The history of Communist China's agricultural development in the last two decades is essentially a record of the regime's continuous struggle to achieve a major breakthrough in production and to strike a proper balance in distributing output between the state and the peasants. This chapter reviews the major agrarian policies adopted by the regime and examines their impact on agricultural production and economic growth during the period 1949–68.

Broadly speaking, one can distinguish five phases in Communist China's agricultural development: (1) land reform and rehabilitation, 1949–1952; (2) the collectivization movement and the First Five Year Plan, 1953–57; (3) the Great Leap and the communes, 1958–59; (4) the agricultural crisis and recovery, 1960–65; and (5) the Cultural Revolution, 1965–68, and its aftermath. The following five sections discuss the major problems, policies, and performance in the agricultural sector in these periods. A summary is given in the final section.

---

[1] Mao Tse-tung, 'The Question of Agricultural Cooperativization,' *Hsin-hua Yüeh-pao* (*New China Monthly*, hereafter: *HHYP*), No. 11, November, 1955, p. 5.

LAND REFORM AND AGRICULTURAL REHABILITATION, 1949–52

The most important single event during the period of rural rehabilitation was the nationwide land reform. In June, 1950, the government promulgated the Agrarian Reform Law, formally launching the land redistribution program.[2] There were two major factors that impelled the Chinese Communists to push forward with land reform at the time. The first was political. In 1949 the military campaign ended far ahead of the Party's own schedule, thus creating the immediate need to institute effective political control of the vast, newly occupied rural areas. Land reform was the device designed primarily for that purpose. Through land reform the Party intended to destroy the landed class, which was closely tied to the traditional power structure, and to replace it with a new group of community leaders more responsive to the directives of the state. Moreover, by satisfying the peasants' long-pent up hunger for land, the Party hoped to secure the popular support of the poor peasants, who constituted by far the majority of the rural population.

The second purpose of land reform was economic. When the Communists came to power in 1949, the rural economy was badly torn by many years of war. The maintenance of dikes and irrigation works had been neglected. After the Sino-Japanese War ended, the civil war began. The continuous internal strife not only made rehabilitation in many areas impossible but also seriously disrupted trade and transportation. There were considerable losses in farm tools, implements and draft animals during the war.[3] As a result, agricultural output in 1949 had fallen below the prewar level.[4] Meanwhile, the demand for agricultural output in the early years of the regime was rapidly expanding, in part because grain and other food products were badly needed to control inflation, and in part because many textile plants formerly dependent on imported cotton were forced to turn to agriculture for raw materials. The situation was further aggravated by Communist China's entry into the Korean War in late 1950. The most pressing agricultural problem for the regime, therefore, was to restore production as quickly as possible. Thus, the Agrarian Reform Law stated that the fundamental objective of abolishing the landed class and establishing a system of peasant proprietorship was 'to set free the rural productive forces, develop agricultural production, and thus pave the way for New China's industrialization.'[5] By redistributing land to the tenant farmers and farm laborers, the Party hoped to stimulate their will to work and save and thereby to increase output. At the same time, the Party adopted the policy of preserving the class of rich peasants, who were generally the more enterprising and efficient producers.

---

[2] For the Agrarian Reform Law and other related documents including Liu Shao-ch'i's report on the agrarian reform law, see *Agrarian Reform Law of the People's Republic of China* (Peking: Foreign Languages Press, 1953). For an account and analysis of the land reform program, see Kuo-chün Chao, *Agrarian Policy of the Chinese Communist Party, 1921–1959* (London: Asia Publishing House, 1960), pp. 94–146; Li T'ien-min, *Chung-Kung Yü Nung-min (CCP and Peasantry)* (Hong Kong: Union Press, 1958), pp. 81–102; Yuan-li Wu, *An Economic Survey of Communist China* (New York: Bookman Associates, 1956), pp. 113–53. Actually, the Communists had begun confiscating and redistributing land in areas under their control as early as 1946.

[3] According to one report, the number of draft animals was 16 per cent, and of farm tools 30 per cent, below the prewar level. Li Shu-ch'eng, 'New China's Great Achievement in Agricultural Production in the Past Three Years,' *San-nien-lai Hsin-chung-Kuo Ching-chi ti Ch'eng-chiu (New China's Economic Achievements in the Past Three Years)* (Peking: Jen-mi ch'u-pan-she, 1953), p. 128 (hereafter: *San-nien-lai*).

[4] According to Communist statistics, grain output in 1949 was only 78 per cent, and cotton 52 per cent, of the respective pre-1949 peak levels. See Table 20–6.

[5] See *Agrarian Reform Law*, cited above, p. 1.

Because the intent of the policy was political, the process of land redistribution took the form of an intensive class struggle. A work team was first dispatched to the villages to initiate a propaganda and indoctrination campaign to arouse the 'class conciousness' of the peasants. The activists were urged to form peasant associations. The second step was to organize mass meetings to accuse and punish the evil landlords and despots and to define the class status of the villagers. The farm households were classified into five categories: landlords, rich peasants, middle peasants, poor peasants, and farm laborers. The criteria were as follows. A landlord lived on rent and other nonlabor income; a rich peasant worked on the farm but also hired labor; and a middle peasant worked his own land with no hired labor or rented land. Poor peasants and farm laborers had no land and worked as tenants or hired hands. The final stage was the confiscation of the 'surplus properties' and the 'surplus land' of landlords and certain rich peasants, and their distribution among the poor peasants and farm laborers. A victory celebration, with more propaganda and the issuance of new title deeds, concluded the process.

The nationwide land reform movement was completed in 1953. According to Communist reports, more than 300 million peasants who owned little or no land received in the process 115 million acres of arable land and other properties, such as draft animals, farm implements, and houses.[6]

The land reform movement was perhaps a success in terms of the Party's political objective. The landlords as a class were virtually eliminated.[7] As a result, the traditional power structure was completely torn down. The economic impact on output, however, was not clear. The Communists claimed that output increased very sharply and that by 1952 the output of grain, cotton, and other major crops reached or surpassed the pre-1949 peak level.[8] While the reliability of the Communist statistics for the period is open to question, there seems to be little doubt that a substantial increase in output had taken place. However, whether or not land reform had been the major contributing factor is not clear, for two reasons. First, there had been other favorable factors, such as the restoration of law and order, rehabilitation of transportation and trade, increase in the supply of means of production, and repair of irrigation works. The last item was perhaps of particular importance. According to Communist reports, 20 million people took part in water conservation work during the period.[9] Consequently, the area of farm land suffering from natural disaster declined sharply from 16 million acres in 1949 to 3 million acres in 1952, while irrigated areas expanded from 40 million acres to 53 million acres over the same period.[10]

The second reason was that while the redistribution of land might have had stimulating effects on the peasants' incentive, there were also two disadvantages. One was the fragmentation of land. Traditionally, farm land was already highly fragmented.[11] Land reform broke it up into even more numerous small parcels. Frag-

---

[6] State Statistical Bureau, *Ten Great Years* (Peking: Foreign Languages Press, 1960), p. 34 (hereafter: *TGY*).

[7] In many areas, the treatment of the landlords was harsh, apparently a deliberate move to destroy their social and political image. How many were killed during the struggle is not known. Estimates range from half a million by Dick Wilson to two million by Chow Ching-wen (including bandits and despots). Dick Wilson, *A Quarter of Mankind* (London: Weidenfeld and Nicolson, 1966), p. 25. Ching-wen Chow, *Ten Years of Storm* (New York: Holt, Rinehart & Winston, 1960), p. 105. According to the 'Warsaw' version of Mao's speech in 1957, a total of 800,000 enemies of the state were liquidated. *The New York Times*, June 13, 1957, p. 8. The lower figure of 500,000 was cited in Mu Fu-sheng, *The Wilting of the Hundred Flowers* (New York: Praeger, 1963), p. 128.

[8] See Table 20–6.

[9] Fu Tso-i, 'Great Achievements in China's Water Conservation,' *San-nien-lai*, pp. 133–42.

[10] *Ibid.*, p. 133; *TGY*, p. 130.

[11] Buck's survey shows that two-thirds of the farms had one to five parcels per farm and

mentation generally lowers output, because the scattered fields are more difficult to manage and irrigate, and more tillable land is wasted in uncultivated strips between parcels. Another unfavorable outcome of land reform was that, with the elimination of the landlord class, a major source of credit in the villages also disappeared.

One important effect of land reform not publicized by the Communists was the benefit to the state in the collection of grain and other agricultural products. During this period, the state relied mainly on taxation in kind to secure a substantial share of the agricultural output. Taxation in kind accounted for more than 90 per cent of the total agricultural tax in 1950–52.[12] One distinctive feature of the tax system was that the tax was calculated on the basis of 'normal' instead of actual output. In the old 'liberated' areas of North and Northeast China, the tax was levied at a fixed proportion of the normal yield; in the newly 'liberated' areas, progressive tax rates were used. The basic purpose of using the normal yield to assess the tax was to guarantee the state a constant amount of the farm produce and at the same time to increase the peasants' incentive to produce more. To a certain degree, the information on actual yields and cultivated acreage made available during land reform probably provided a more solid basis for determining the normal yields than the pre-1949 crop estimates. Moreover, the integration of the village organization with the state administrative machinery as a result of land reform probably increased the efficiency in tax collection.

More important than the ease of tax administration was the impact of the employment of 'normal yield' on the volume of tax collected. According to official statistics, the agricultural tax rose from 13.5 million tons to 19.4 million tons of fine grain equivalent during 1950–52, an increase of more than 40 per cent in two years. The official figures also show only a slight increase in the percentage of output collected, from 12.3 to 13.2 per cent.[13] Because of the likelihood of a higher degree of understatement of output in the earlier years, the percentage probably rose more sharply than the official figures would indicate. In any event, it seems clear that the agricultural sector contributed substantially to the pool of resources at the disposal of the state. The agricultural tax, together with a relatively small amount of other taxes paid by the peasants, accounted for about 30 per cent of the total government revenue in 1950–52.[14]

Two major factors have made possible the rapid increase in the agricultural tax. The first was the rehabilitation of production noted above. The second was a marked change in the redistribution of output that accompanied land reform. A considerable part of the agricultural tax represented land rent formerly paid by the tenants to the landlords. The following statistics of relative income and tax payments by different groups based on a survey of 130 localities in six southern provinces illustrate this point (see table opposite).[15]

The figures clearly show that prior to land reform the landlords were the most important single group of taxpayers. In the post–land reform period, the poor peasants contributed the largest share of the total tax. It would appear that the poor peasants who were given the land of the former landlords also took over a larger part of their tax burden. Actually, the shift of burden was more imaginary than real. The income of the former landlords declined sharply because they no longer received any rental

---

more than one-fifth had six to ten parcels per farm. John Lossing Buck, *Land Utilization in China* (Chicago: University of Chicago Press, 1937), p. 181.

[12] Li Cheng-jui, *Chung-hua-jen-min-kung-ho-kuo Nung-yeh-shui Shih-ko (A Draft History of Agricultural Taxation in the P.R.C.)* (Peking: T'sai-cheng, 1959), p. 116.

[13] See Table 20–7.

[14] *Ibid.*

[15] Li Cheng-jui, *Nung-yeh-shui Shih-ko*, p. 161. Note that the data in the third column, taken directly from the original source, do not add up to 100.

| | Before Land Reform | | After Land Reform | |
	Income as % of Total Output	Tax Levy as % of Total Tax	Income as % of Total Output	Tax Levy as % of Total Tax
Landlord	18	50	4	4
Rich peasants	12	20	10	15
Middle peasants	35	20	36	39
Poor peasants	35	10	45	42
Total	100	100	100	100

income, and their share of the taxes was also greatly reduced. What was formerly the rental income and taxes paid by the landlords were now largely paid by the poor peasants to the state, thus increasing their share of the total tax from 10 to 42 per cent. In a revealing statement in 1955, the Chairman of the State Planning Commission readily admitted that the former land rent had become one of the major sources of financing capital formation.[16]

The result of the survey also suggests that land reform had reduced the degree of inequality in the distribution of income among the different groups. About the time of the survey, the relative sizes of the four groups in total farm population were as follows: landlords, 3 per cent; rich peasants, 4 per cent; middle peasants, 36 per cent; and poor peasants, 57 per cent.[17] Before land reform the smallest group (landlords) was not the one with the smallest income share. Nor was the largest group (poor peasants) the one that had the largest income share. However, after land reform the ranking of the various groups by size corresponded to the ranking by income share.

The transfer of land rent from the hands of the landlords to the state was at best a nonrecurrent source of revenue. Over the long run the amount of resources that could be extracted from the agricultural sector necessarily depended on output and consumption of the peasants. By 1952, the regime was confronted with serious problems in both consumption and production. Despite rapid recovery, the per capita consumption of the peasants remained low. The average per capita income after taxes in 1952, a year of bumper harvest, was said to be only 58 yüan, slightly below the Communists' official minimum living standard of 60 yüan.[18] Further reduction would be difficult and would probably have serious disincentive effects on output. This meant that any significant increase in state collection could be achieved only by increasing output. But by then the regime had about exhausted the opportunities for output expansion through rehabilitation. How to generate and sustain a high rate of growth output was one of the most pressing problems confronting the leaders as they embarked on their First Five Year Plan.

[16] *Chung-hua-jen-min-kung-ho-kuo fa-chan Kuo-min Ching-chi ti Ti-i-ko Wu-nien-chi-hua 1953–1957* (*The First Five Year Plan for the Development of the National Economy of the P.R.C.*) (Peking: Jen-min ch'u-pan-she, 1955), p. 183 (hereafter: *FFYP*).

[17] Tung Ta-lin, *Agricultural Cooperation in China* (Peking: Foreign Languages Press, 1958), p. 11. The figures are based on a survey of 14,334 households in twenty-one provinces that presumably covered the 1949–52 period. The geographical coverage is different from that of the other figures. However, the pattern for the southern provinces is not likely to be much different from the one given here.

[18] Li Cheng-jui, *Nung-yeh-shui Shih-ko*, p. 200. Both the per capita income and minimum standard are Communist figures. There are reasons to believe that actual output in 1952 was higher than the Communist estimate. See T.C. Liu and K. C. Yeh, *The Economy of the Chinese Mainland* (Princeton, N.J.: Princeton University Press, 1965), pp. 43–47. However, raising the income figure by, say, 10 per cent still would not affect our conclusion here.

THE FIRST FIVE YEAR PLAN AND THE COLLECTIVIZATION MOVEMENT, 1953–57

The First Five Year Plan was essentially an investment plan designed primarily to accelerate industrial development. Accordingly, agriculture ranked rather low in the leaders' scale of preference in resource allocation. The Plan provided only 8 per cent of the state capital investment for agriculture, as compared to 58 per cent for industry and 19 per cent for transportation and communications.[19] More significantly, heavy industry, to which was alloted the lion's share of state investment, was oriented almost exclusively to the needs of defense and its own growth. Industries producing for agriculture, such as chemical fertilizers and farm equipment, were not among those most favored.

The relatively low priority assigned to agriculture is also reflected in the planned investment in human capital. The plan called for 283,000 college graduates and 888,000 graduates from middle and technical schools during 1953–57. Only 7 per cent of the former and 9 per cent of the latter total were to be students majoring in agriculture and forestry.[20]

While the agricultural sector received a minor share of total state investment, it was called upon to contribute heavily to the development program. First, the peasants were to increase agricultural output by 23 per cent in five years, a modest but nonetheless significant increase in view of the resource constraints noted in Chapter 3. Furthermore, they were to provide a major portion of the savings for the plan.[21] Finally, they were to supply food and other goods for the growing urban labor force, raw materials for the expanding light industries, and exportable products to exchange for industrial equipment and technology from abroad.[22]

In sum, the leaders deliberately minimized agriculture's role as a user of resources while assigning to it the task of supplying the bulk of resources needed for industrialization. This asymmetrical policy was apparently based on several considerations. The leaders' overriding concern at that stage was the construction of the Soviet-aided projects. The capacity of the agricultural sector itself to absorb new industrial inputs was still rather limited. At the same time, the leaders anticipated a substantial amount of private investment by the peasants. But perhaps the most important factor was that, in their view, the key to agricultural growth was collectivization and not state investment.[23] Their strategy for the plan was to increase agricultural output through reorganization and then to convert the agricultural resources into industrial capital with as little resource feedback to the agricultural sector as possible. The crucial assumption underlying the strategy was, of course, that agriculture could generate and sustain its own growth by organizational means alone.

Let us now turn to the organizational changes that had been made and their effect on agricultural production during this period.

The collectivization movement. Long before the Communist Party came to power, Mao had pointed to collectivization as the only solution to the peasants' poverty problem.[24]

---

[19] *FFYP*, p. 23.   [20] *Ibid.*, pp. 120, 123.

[21] Mao Tse-tung, 'The Problem of Agricultural Cooperativization,' *HHYP*, No. 11, November, 1955, p. 5.

[22] Li Fu-ch'un, 'Report on the First Five Year Plan,' *FFYP*, p. 196. In terms of Kuznets's three concepts of agricultural contribution to economic growth, the agricultural sector was expected to make a product contribution, a factor contribution, and a market contribution. S. Kuznets, 'Economic Growth and the Contribution of Agriculture: Notes on Measurements,' in C. Eicher and L. Witt, eds., *Agriculture in Economic Development* (New York: McGraw-Hill, 1964), pp. 100–19.

[23] *FFYP*, p. 82.

[24] Mao Tse-tung, 'Get Organized,' *Mao Tse-tung Hsüan-chi* (Selected Works of Mao Tse-tung, hereafter: *Selected Works*), 4 (Peking: Jen-min Ch'u-p.an-she, 1960): 934. For his earlier views

In 1949, as Communist control of the entire mainland was imminent, Mao restated his intent to carry out a positive program to organize cooperatives in the villages.[25] But, while the determination to collectivize was there from the very beginning, it was also recognized that socialized agriculture was a goal for the distant future. For reasons noted above, the Party's immediate concern was land reform, a form of rural reorganization diametrically opposite to collectivization. It was not until late 1951, when the land reform program was well under way, that the Central Committee quietly launched the collectivization movement on an experimental basis.[26] By 1953, land reform was completed. In December 1953, the Party adopted the Resolution on the Development of Agricultural Producers' Cooperatives, formally opening the drive toward collectivization.[27] In the subsequent years of the plan period, the transformation of agriculture went through the following stages: a gradual transition from individual farming to mutual aid teams in 1953–55, an upsurge in the formation of 'lower' cooperatives in 1955–56, and the formation of 'higher' cooperatives in 1956–57. A mutual aid team involved labor-sharing and individual ownership of land and other properties, but joint use of tools and animals on a seasonal or permanent basis. A lower cooperative involved joint ownership and management of land, tools, and animals, and sharing of output according to the peasants' contribution of labor and land to the cooperative. A higher cooperative had the same features as a lower cooperative, except that landowners no longer received a share of the output as rental income.

Table 20–1 shows for 1950–57 the total number of farm households, the percentage of farm households organized, the number of mutual aid teams and cooperatives, and the average size of mutual aid teams and cooperatives. Two interesting features in the collectivization movement are worth noting. First, the pace of development was extremely rapid. Within a period of six years the Party had completed what took the Russians seventeen years to accomplish. By 1957, the traditional system of individual farming that had dominated Chinese agriculture for thousands of years virtually disappeared. In fact, the speed of reorganization far exceeded even the leaders' own expectations. Originally, in 1953, the official target date for complete socialization was 1967.[28] In 1955, it was moved forward to 1960 and later to 1958 by Mao.[29] But collectivization was actually completed in 1957, with 97 per cent of the peasant households organized in cooperatives.

Second, the path of the movement was by no means a smooth one, suggesting some undercurrents within the Party that opposed rapid collectivization. Mao was strongly committed to rapid collectivization, and no one in the Party was strong enough to oppose him openly. As shown in Table 20–1, the percentage of households in mutual aid teams declined by more than the increase in the percentage of households in cooperatives in 1953, and there were cutbacks in the number of cooperatives in some

---

on collectivization, see Ch'en Po-ta, 'Explanation of the Draft Decision on the Question of Cooperativization,' *HHYP*, No. 11, November, 1955, p. 14.

[25] Mao Tse-tung, 'Report Before the Second Plenum of the Seventh Central Committee,' *Selected Works*, 4: 1433.

[26] Central Committee, CCP, 'Resolution on Mutual Aid and Cooperation in Agricultural Production,' *Hsüeh-hsi* (*Study*, hereafter: *HH*), No. 5, 1953, pp. 3–6.

[27] *Cooperative Farming in China* (Peking: Foreign Languages Press, 1954).

[28] Mao Tse-tung, 'Problem of Agricultural Cooperativization,' *HHYP*, No. 11, November, 1955, p. 5.

[29] *Ibid.*, p. 7; *Hsin-hua Pan-yüeh-k'an* (*New China Semimonthly*, hereafter: *HHPYK*) Peking: No. 4, February, p. 1.

[30] *HH*, No. 12, 1955, p. 13; Central Committee, CCP, *Chung-kuo Nung-ts'un She-hui-chu-yi Kao-chao* (*The High Tide of Socialism in China's Countryside*, hereafter: *High Tide*) (Peking: Jen-min ch'u-pan-she, 1956), p. 569; Mao, 'Problem of Agricultural Cooperativization,' *HHYP*, No. 11, November, 1955, p. 3.

Table 20-1—The Collectivization Movement, 1950-57

	1950	1951	1952	1953	1954	1955	1956	1957
Number of farm households (thousands)	105,536	109,273	113,809	116,325	117,326	119,201	121,523	122,556
Percentage of total organized	10.7	19.2	40.0	39.5	60.3	64.9	91.9	97.0
In mutual aid teams	10.7	19.2	39.9	39.3	58.4	50.7	—	—
In cooperatives	—	—	0.1	0.2	2.0	14.2	91.9	97.0
Lower	—	—	0.1	0.2	1.9	14.2	28.7	3.7
Higher	—	—	—	—	—	—	63.2	93.3
Number of teams or cooperatives (thousands)								
Mutual aid teams	2,724	4,075	8,026	7,450	9,931	7,147	—	—
Lower cooperatives	—	—	4	15	114	633	682	84
Higher cooperatives	—	—	—	—	—	1	312	668
Average number of farm households per team or cooperative								
Mutual aid teams	4	4	6	6	7	8	—	—
Lower cooperatives	10	12	16	18	20	27	51	54
Higher cooperatives	32	30	184	137	59	76	246	171

Note: Dashes signify none or negligible.

Sources: Shih Ching-tang et al. eds., *Chung-kuo Nung-yeh Ho-tso-hua Yün-tung Shih-liao* (*Historical Materials on the Agricultural Cooperative Movement in China*), 2, No. 3 (Peking: San-lien Bookstore, 1959): 989–99, 992–98. Helen Yin and Yi-Chang Yin, *Economic Statistics of Mainland China* (Cambridge, Mass.: Harvard University Press, 1960), pp. 37–38. Totals for 1950–56 refer to totals at the end of June. That for 1957 refers to total at the end of March, 1957.

provinces in 1955.[30] There were also three abrupt increases in the percentages of peasant households organized in 1952, 1954, and 1956. Each surge was preceded by a major decision at the highest levels to push ahead, which indicates that the movement was largely initiated at the Party center and was not a spontaneous development from below. The growth of cooperatives was especially dramatic. Up to mid-1955, only 14 per cent of total farm households were in the cooperatives. In July, 1955, before a conference of provincial Party secretaries, Mao made known his momentous decision to press ahead with full speed. Six months later, the households organized rose to 80 per cent.[31] The increase was so rapid that many higher cooperatives were organized without going through the stage of mutual aid teams and lower cooperatives.[32]

Why did Mao decide to accelerate the collectivization movement? The rationale can perhaps be best understood by considering the problems that had emerged in the 1950's and how, in Mao's view, collectivization could effectively resolve these problems. One major problem was the rapid and spontaneous growth of capitalistic elements in the villages. Immediately after land reform, many peasants again engaged in trade, money lending, and buying more land.[33] As the years went by, such activities became more rampant. Quite naturally, the more enterprising and capable peasants prospered, while others lost their land and remained poor.[34] At the same time, many cadres came under the sway of capitalistic ideas and were more concerned with their own economic benefits than with the state's interests.[35] In short, the countryside had become a battleground for socialism and capitalism—and capitalism was gaining fast. As Mao saw it, a laissez-faire policy would only intensify the tendency of the peasants to gravitate toward the two extreme poles of wealth and poverty. The wealthy middle peasants would never be satisfied unless the Party followed the capitalist road indefinitely. The poor peasants would complain of the Party's passivity with respect to their destitution. In the end, the Party would lose the support of all.[36] The political implication of the rampant capitalistic development in the villages was perhaps the most compelling reason for the big push. The burning issue was not a fear of peasant revolt but the pressing need to reorient and reorganize the peasants' efforts toward the goals set by the Party. This emphasis on the ideological aspect of the movement was clearly reflected in the Central Committee's statement that elimination of capitalistic exploitation was the first major objective of the big push.[37]

A second major problem that beset the regime in the days before collectivization was the slowdown in agricultural production in 1953–54. The emerging gap between the supply of and demand for agricultural products can be seen from the following indices for 1953 and 1954, with 1952 as a base of 100:[38]

---

[31] Shih Ching-tang *et al.*, eds., *Chung-kuo Nung-yeh Ho-tso-hua Yü-tung Shih-liao* (*Historical Materials on the Agricultural Cooperative Movement in China*), 3, No. 3 (Peking: San-lien Bookstore, 1959): 991.

[32] This is evidenced by the much higher percentage of households in higher cooperatives in 1956 than the percentage of households in lower cooperatives in the previous year. See Table 20–1.

[33] Mao Tse-tung, 'Problem of Agricultural Cooperativization,' *HHYP*, No. 11, November, 1955, p. 6; Ch'en Po-ta, 'The Socialist Transformation of China's Agriculture,' *HHPYK*, No. 5, March, 1956, p. 28.

[34] Tung Ta-lin, *Agricultural Cooperation in China* (Peking: Foreign Languages Press, 1959), pp. 10–20.

[35] The Party readily admitted that these 'rightist-leaning opportunists within the Party ... could be found almost anywhere.' Central Committee, *High Tide*, p. 729.

[36] Mao Tse-tung, 'Problem of Agricultural Cooperativization,' *loc. cit.*

[37] *HHYP*, No. 12, 1955, December, p. 141.

[38] The indices are computed from data given in: Table 20–6, below; N. R. Chen, ed., *Chinese Economic Statistics* (Chicago: Aldine, 1966, pp. 127, 210; A. Eckstein, *Communist China's Economic Growth and Foreign Trade* (New York: McGraw-Hill, 1966), p. 95.

Output of crops and animal products	1953	1954
Output of crops and animal products	102	105
Grain output	102	104
Urban population	108	115
Imports	124	142
Industrial output: consumer goods	127	145

On the supply side, agricultural production, particularly grain output, increased rather slowly at an annual rate of about 2 per cent in 1952–54, compared to about 13 per cent in 1949–52. Meanwhile, the demand for food in the cities, for exportable agricultural products, and for raw materials expanded much faster. The slowdown in agricultural production apparently caused some concern. In September, 1954, Chou En-lai pointedly remarked that for two consecutive years since 1952 output fell short of the annual planned targets.[39] In March, 1955, Liao Lu-yen, the Minister of Agriculture, admitted that in the past two years the supply of not only grain and cotton, but also of other major products such as oil seeds, tea, tobacco, animal and marine products, was lagging behind demand.[40]

In part, the slowdown was due to poor weather conditions in 1953 and 1954. But more fundamentally, crop yields had apparently reached a plateau under the existing institutional and technical conditions.[41] To solve this problem, the regime accelerated collectivization in the belief that reorganization of the system could raise output substantially. In principle, the cooperative had three distinct advantages over individual farming. First, the size of the production unit was much larger, and there were considerable economies of scale. As shown in Table 20–1, a lower cooperative comprised about fifty households, and an average higher cooperative about two hundred and fifty households, in 1956. In terms of cultivated area, the average size of the cooperative in 1956 was 249 acres, compared to the average land holding per household of less than 3 acres in 1952.[42] A larger organization under unified management made it possible to use the available resources more fully and efficiently. For example, the elimination of boundaries between the numerous small parcels of land could increase total acreage by 4 per cent, or about 11 million acres.[43] Land of different qualities could be used to plant crops most suitable to the soil. There could be 'collaboration between the middle peasants with more means of production and poor peasants with more labor.'[44] Labor could be organized to work on projects too large for a single household to tackle. Second, under centralized management, technical reforms could be introduced with greater ease. Third, the cooperative provided a built-in mechanism for compulsory savings. The cadre could set aside a substantial portion of the current output for capital accumulation. He could mobilize farm labor to undertake investment projects, such as roadbuilding, water conservation, and terracing of new land.

For these reasons, the leaders strongly believed that collectivization could increase production, although these seemed to be no consensus as to how superior the cooperatives were. The State Planning Commission estimated that the cooperatives could

[39] Chou En-lai, 'Report on Government Work,' Chung-kuo Nung-pao (China's Agricultural Journal, hereafter: CKNP), No. 19, 1955, p. 16.
[40] Liao Lu-yen, 'Report on the Basic Conditions of Agricultural Production in 1954 and Current Measures to Increase Output,' HHYP, No. 4, 1955, p. 115.
[41] Teng Tzu-hui, 'Rural Work During the Transitional Period,' Current Background, No. 306, November 22, 1954, pp. 1–2.
[42] For data used in calculating the average size, see Table 20–1; Jen-min Shou-ts'e (People's Handbook, hereafter: JMST) (Peking: Ta-kung-pao She, 1958), p. 456; TGY, p. 128.
[43] Buck, Land Utilization, p. 173.
[44] Teng Tzu-hui, 'Rural Work During Transitional Period,' p. 4.

increase output by 10 to 12 per cent within one or two years.[45] Others, like Ch'en Po-ta, were more optimistic and expected a 100 per cent increase in about four or five years.[46] Still others were more pragmatic and suggested a positive but diminishing increase over time.[47] Whatever the result might be, the state had yet to extract the increase in output from the peasants—which brings us to the third major problem confronting the regime in 1953–54.

The problem was that, as output expansion began to slow down, the collection of grain became increasingly difficult. As noted above, the main collecting device in the early 1950's was the agricultural tax. The tax burden in 1949 was probably quite heavy relative to the peasants' income, although the exact proportion is hard to determine.[48] In the 1950–52 period, the annual rate of increase in agricultural tax consistently exceeded that of agricultural production, indicating that the tax burden was on the rise.[49] Probably because the agricultural tax had reached a level that began to dampen the incentives of the peasants, the state announced in 1953 that in the three succeeding years the tax would remain unchanged at the 1952 level.[50] While the decision might give the peasants an incentive to produce, it also compelled the state to resort to other measures to secure an increasing amount of the farm produce.

Up to late 1953, state purchase of farm products at the market had been used extensively to supplement taxation in kind. During 1950–53 the amount of grain purchased by the state rose rapidly but at a decreasing rate.[51] By mid-1953, the program ran into difficulty, mainly because the peasants were reluctant to sell.[52] It became clear to the leaders that, when the decision to sell was left almost entirely to the peasants, the amount they released was highly uncertain. To assure adequate supply, the state therefore resorted to coercion. In November, 1953, the system of planned purchase and supply of grain was introduced. Planned purchase simply meant obligatory sale of a prescribed quota of grain to the state at government procurement prices. Planned supply was essentially a rationing system for the urban population. Under the new system, the free market for grain was replaced by state monopoly. Subsequently, edible vegetable oils, oil seeds, cotton, and cotton cloth also came under the planned purchase and supply system.

The effect of the new system on grain collection was immediate and drastic. Total grain purchase during 1953–54, a poor crop year, exceeded that of the preceding year by 70 per cent.[53] The sharp increase, however, also created other problems. It resulted directly in a shortage of food in the villages, generated considerable discontent among

---

[45] FFYP, p. 82.

[46] Ch'en Po-ta, 'Socialist Transformation of China's Agriculture,' HHPYK, No. 5, 1956, p. 30.

[47] Cheng Chao-chien, 'Several Keys to Increasing Grain Output,' CKNP, No. 5, 1954, p. 14.

[48] This is indicated by the peasants' violent reaction to tax collection in 1949–50 and by Po I-po's admission that the progressive rates were too high. Po I-po, 'The Problem of Adjusting the Tax Revenues,' San-nien-lai, p. 61. Po reported that more than 3,000 cadres were killed in the process of collecting grain from the peasants.

[49] For annual rates of increase in agricultural production, see TGY, p. 118. Those for agricultural tax are based on data given in N. R. Chen, Chinese Economic Statistics, p. 441. Note that the former is in constant 1952 prices and the latter in current prices. But the difference is not likely to affect the conclusion.

[50] 'Directive of the State Council on Agricultural Taxation Work in 1953,' in Chung-yang Jen-min-cheng-fu Fa-ling Hui-pien (Compendium of Laws and Decrees), 4 (Peking: Jen-min-ch'u-pan-she, 1955): 140–43.

[51] Ta-kung Pao, September 19, 1955.

[52] Ho Wei, 'The Achievements in Planned Purchase and Supply of Grain Must Not be Belittled,' Ta-kung Pao, August 7, 1957.

[53] Li Sze-heng, 'The Effect of Planned Purchase of Grain on National Construction and the Socialist Transformation of Agriculture,' HH, No. 9, 1954, p. 11.

the peasants, and caused a reduction in the number of livestock in certain areas.[54] By the spring of 1954, *Jen-min Jih-pao* reported that 100 million peasants were short of grain.[55] Peasants flowed into the cities. The situation was no better in early 1955.[56] The adverse effect of planned purchase on the peasants' incentive was apparently quite profound, for *Jen-min Jih-pao* candidly admitted that the peasants' loss of incentive was a major cause of the grain shortage.[57] In the spring of 1955 the state adopted the 'three-fixed' policy, designed especially to stimulate production. The normal yield, the quota of compulsory purchase, and state supply of grain to the peasants were to remain unchanged at approximately the 1953–54 level for the following three years.[58]

The effectiveness of the new device was contingent upon reasonably accurate estimates of the normal yields and the consumption needs of the peasants. Here, the cooperative functioned as a piece of administrative machinery, facilitating the implementation of the three-fixed policy in the following ways. First, the cooperative was in a better position than other government agencies to gauge the output and requirements of the peasant households.[59] Moreover, since the cooperatives were generally managed by cadres loyal to the Party, the regime could control the distribution of output and make sure that the state got its maximum share. Finally, as the peasant households merged to form cooperatives, the number of units from which to collect grain would be drastically reduced, from more than 110 million to less than 1 million. Thus, it was with good reason that the Minister of Finance expected state revenues to go up after collectivization.[60]

To sum up, the decision to accelerate collectivization in 1955 was in response to three major problems that emerged after land reform: rampant capitalism in the countryside, the slowdown in agricultural output, and the increasing difficulty of grain collection. Collectivization was deemed necessary to curb the revival of a rich peasant economy and to reforge the peasants' ideology, to increase output without having to divert resources from industrial development, and to regulate the peasants' consumption. Of the last two economic objectives, increasing output was clearly the more fundamental.

For reasons noted above, the leaders relied heavily on the peasants' own effort to increase output. Table 20–2 shows four major developments in that direction. The first is the more intensive use of land. Total cultivated area increased by about 2 per cent during 1952–57, but the sown acreage expanded by 11 per cent, indicating a considerable increase in the multiple cropping index. Second, there was an expansion in irrigation work. The percentage of cultivated area under irrigation rose from 20 per cent in 1952 to 31 per cent in 1957. Third, the use of improved seeds was more widespread, particularly in the production of grain and oil seeds. Fourth, the period also witnessed a sharp increase in the afforested area. In all the statistical series, a marked increase in 1956 over 1955 is discernible, indicating that the impact of collectivization on the mobilization of labor was quite profound.

---

[54] Ch'en Yün, 'The Problem of Planned Purchase and Supply of Grain,' *HHYP*, No. 8, 1955, p. 51; Liao Lu-yen, 'Report on Basic Conditions,' p. 116.

[55] *Jen-min Jih-pao* (*JMJP*), February 10, 1954, p. 1.

[56] Ch'en Yün, 'Problem of Planned Purchase,' p. 50.

[57] *JMJP*, August 29, 1955, p. 1.

[58] Only when the state needed grain for disaster relief would it purchase any output in excess of the normal output, and then only up to 40 per cent of the excess. The surplus grain would be subject to purchase at a proportionate instead of a progressive rate. 'Provisional Measures of Unified Purchase and Supply of Grain in the Villages,' *HHYP*, No. 9, 1955, pp. 160–62.

[59] Teng Tzu-hui, 'The Cooperativization Movement in the Past Year and Tasks for the Future,' *HHPYK*, No. 24, 1956, p. 58.

[60] *HHYP*, No. 12, 1955, p. 165.

Table 20-2—Selected Indicators of Direct Investments, Technological Improvements, and Supply of Industrial Goods and Services, 1952–57

	1952	1953	1954	1955	1956	1957
Cultivated area (million hectares)	107.9	108.5	109.3	110.1	111.8	111.8
Sown area (million hectares)	141.3	144.0	147.9	151.1	159.2	157.2
Irrigated area (million hectares)	21.3	22.0	23.3	24.7	32.0	34.7
Percentage of cultivated area irrigated	19.7	20.3	21.3	22.4	28.6	31.0
Percentage of area fertilized	70	—	—	—	—	85
Percentage of area sown with improved seeds						
Grain	4.7	7.4	14.9	20.6	36.4	55.2
Cotton	50.2	61.4	67.7	89.5	93.9	97.0
Oil seeds	1.9	2.4	2.9	4.0	31.5	47.7
Afforested area (million hectares)	1.1	1.1	1.2	1.7	5.7	4.4
Sales of producers' goods to agriculture (million yüan)	1,410	1,920	2,500	2,820	3,700	3,260
Chemical fertilizer (1,000 tons)	318	592	802	1,255	1,608	1,944
Insecticides (thousand tons)	15	19	41	67	159	149
Insecticide sprayers (thousands)	251	198	315	429	1,308	647
Two-wheeled shear ploughs (thousands)	1	15	23	426	1,086	95
Power equipment (thousand horsepower)	13	14	22	45	189	265
Tractors	2,006	2,719	5,061	8,094	19,367	24,629
Agricultural technical stations	232	3,632	4,549	7,997	14,230	13,669

Source: TGY, pp. 128, 130–31, 133, 170–71, and 135–36; Ministry of Agriculture, 'China's Grain Production during the First Five Year Plan Period,' HHPYK, No. 9, 1958, p. 81.

Table 20–2 also shows the increase in the supply of industrial producers' goods and services to agriculture. Total supply rose from 1.4 billion yüan in 1952 to 3.3 billion yüan in 1957. The supply of chemical fertilizers, insecticides, and other industrial input was increasing at very rapid rates. Again the increase in farm expenditures on those products and services were especially marked after collectivization was completed. But despite the rapid increase, the availability of industrial input per acre of cultivated land remained minuscule. For example, chemical fertilizer consumption in 1957, in terms of plant nutrients, amounted to about 4 kg. per hectare of arable land, compared to about 200 kg. in Taiwan, and 300 in Japan.[61] Furthermore, not all the investments were productive. A classic example is the case of double-wheeled, double-bladed plows, which the authorities decided in 1956 to popularize on a large scale. Production plans were raised from 400,000 to 5 million units but later scaled down to 2 million units. By mid-1956, 1.4 million units were produced and 800,000 sold. But less than half were actually used, because the plow was not suited to the conditions in most areas. In 1957, only 95,000 were sold, less than one-tenth of total sales in 1956.[62]

Agricultural performance. How well has the agricultural sector performed? Table 20–3 presents the rates of growth of actual and planned output for total agricultural production and twenty-one products both in the First Five-Year Plan period (1952–57) and in the two sub-periods (1952–55 and 1955–57), in order to contrast the achievements before and after the big push in collectivization in 1955.[63] For subsequent discussion of the changing conditions of supply and demand, the rate of growth of sales of agricultural products to the nonagricultural sector is also shown. I focus on rates of growth, because the leaders had repeatedly stated that the pace of development was their primary concern.[64] The figures in Table 20–3 are drawn from Communist sources, as the purpose here is to present the picture as the Communist leaders themselves saw it.

Turning first to the growth of output for the period as a whole, one notices a rising trend in all cases except for two minor products. Total output grew at 4.5 per cent per annum, a modest but respectable growth rate when compared to a decline in the Soviet Union during its own First Five-Year Plan period.[65] It should be noted that the official statistics probably understate the grain output in the earlier years, so the rates of growth of grain production and total output are somewhat exaggerated.[66] However, the distortions are not likely to affect the broad observation that agricultural production had expanded moderately during 1952–57.

The rates of growth of the individual products are rather uneven. Several major changes deserve mention. The first is the shift within the grain crops from coarse grain to other grains. To some extent the shift reflected the regime's emphasis on higher-yield crops, such as rice and potatoes. The second was the relatively stagnant growth of soybean and oilseeds, two important crops in total food supply. The third

---

[61] Liu Jung-chao, 'Fertilizer Supply and Grain Production in Communist China,' *Journal of Farm Economics*, Vol. 47, No. 4, November 1965, pp. 925–26. Note that the figures for Taiwan and Japan refer to consumption in 1960–61.

[62] *Chi-hua Ching-chi* (*Planned Economy*, hereafter: *CHCC*), No. 9, 1956, pp. 1–4.

[63] The gross value of the products included in the table accounted for about 85 per cent of the gross value of agricultural products. See Liu and Yeh, *Economy of Chinese Mainland*, pp. 397–99.

[64] See, for example, editorial in *JMJP*, January 1, 1953; Liu Shao-ch'i, 'Report on the Work of the Central Committee,' *HHPYK*, No. 11, 1958, p. 7.

[65] D. Gale Johnson and Arcadius Kahan, 'Soviet Agriculture: Structure and Growth,' in U.S. Congress, *Comparisons of U.S. and Soviet Economies*, Part I (Washington, D.C.: Government Printing Office, 1959), p. 204.

[66] See Table 20–8 for independent estimates of grain and total agricultural production. For an incisive appraisal of official statistics, see Wu, *Economic Survey*, pp. 136–47.

Table 20–3—Average Annual Rates of Growth: Agricultural Output,
Planned Targets, and Supply to Industry, 1952–57
(per cent per year)

	Actual Increase in Output			Planned Increase in Output	Increase in Supply to Industry
	1952–55	1955–57	1952–57	1952–57	1952–57
Agricultural production	4.7	4.2	4.5	4.3	9.8
Grain	4.2	2.9	3.7	3.3	12.2
Rice	4.5	5.5	4.9	3.6	—
Wheat	8.2	1.5	5.5	5.5	—
Coarse grain	2.2	—2.1	0.4	1.2	—
Potatoes	5.0	7.7	6.1	5.5	—
Soybean	—1.4	5.0	1.1	3.3	—
Oilseeds	5.4	—7.0	0.2	—	6.2
Cotton	5.2	3.9	4.7	4.6	2.3
Jute and hemp	—5.6	18.4	3.3	3.7	5.0
Cured tobacco	10.4	—7.3	2.9	12.1	14.5
Sugar cane	4.5	3.2	7.9	13.1	12.1
Sugarbeet	49.4	—3.0	25.7	34.8	33.0
Tea	9.4	1.6	6.3	6.3	8.2
Silk cocoon, domesticated	2.6	0.8	1.7	8.5	—
Silk cocoon, Tussah	1.6	—16.6	—6.1	0.2	—
Marine products	14.8	11.3	13.4	11.0	—
Livestock					
Cattle	5.2	—1.8	2.4	5.4	10.5
Horses	9.2	—0.1	3.5	6.4	—
Donkey	1.6	—6.4	—1.6	3.8	—
Mules	1.6	—1.2	0.5	3.4	—
Sheep and goats	10.9	8.2	9.8	12.9	9.3
Hogs	—0.7	28.8	10.2	9.1	2.5

Source: FFYP, pp. 80–81, 88–89; Niu Chung-huang, *Wo-kuo Ti-i-ke Wu-nien-chi-hua Shih-chi Ti Sheng-chan Ho Hsiao-fei Kuan-shih* (*The Relation Between Production and Consumption During China's First Five Year Plan Period*) (Peking: Ts'ai-cheng, 1959), p. 23. See also Table 20–6, below.

is the more rapid growth of most 'technical crops' relative to grain.[67] Finally, among livestock, the population of large draft animals expanded much more slowly than sheep and goats or hogs.

A comparison of the rates of increase in the two sub-periods, 1952–55 and 1955–57, shows no discernible improvement in the growth rates after collectivization.[68] Actually, total output expanded less rapidly while the growth rates of all but five of the twenty-one products declined. Of particular significance is the decline in the case of large draft animals, largely the result of slaughtering by the peasants during collectivization. In the case of grain, by far the most important, the drop in growth rate is rather

---

[67] Technical crops are cotton, jute, hemp, tobacco, sugar cane, and sugarbeet.

[68] For an analysis of the economic impact of collectivization, see Yuan-li Wu, 'Some Economic Effects of Land Reform, Agricultural Collectivization and the Commune System in Communist China,' in Walter Froehlich, ed., *Land Tenure, Industrialization and Social Stability* (Milwaukee: Marquette University Press, 1961), pp. 17–37.

marked. Allowances for possible downward biases in the output statistics for the first sub-period probably will narrow the differences but are not likely to reverse the situation. In any event, it is safe to conclude that the post-collectivization years did not witness the dramatic increase so enthusiastically anticipated by some leaders prior to 1956.

When measured in terms of what the leaders expected to accomplish, the result was a success. Table 20–3 shows that, by and large, the agricultural production plans had been fulfilled. Although thirteen of the twenty products failed to reach their targets, grain and cotton, by far the most important items, just about exceeded the planned output. In the case of hogs and marine products, production plans were overfulfilled by a considerable margin. For agricultural production as a whole, actual output in 1957 was slightly above the projected level.

Despite the slight upward trend and over-all fulfillment of the planners' expectations in terms of official statistics, agricultural growth lagged far behind the rising demand for agricultural products. The lag and its impact can be clearly seen in the sharp disparity between the rate of agricultural growth and the growth rates of industrial production, population, and exports, in the stationary share of agricultural products marketed, and in the declining saving ratio in the agricultural sector.

Table 20–4 contrasts the growth rates of industrial production, output of industrial consumer goods, and agricultural production. While industrial production surged forward at 19 per cent per annum, agriculture grew at the much slower rate of about 4 per cent. The consumer goods industry, which relied heavily on agriculture for input, expanded at a rate three times that of agriculture. The emerging disparity between industrial consumption and the output of raw materials can be more vividly seen in Table 20–3, which compares the increase in industrial consumption of eleven agricultural products with their growth rates in 1952–57. In all but three cases, the former exceeds the latter. The total supply of agricultural products to industry increased at about 10 per cent per year, more than twice as fast as agricultural production.

A second major gap existed between the production and consumption of grain. According to the official statistics summarized in Table 20–4, grain production rose at 3.7 per cent per year. However, official data for the earlier years may well be too low, so that the true rate was probably somewhat below 3.7 per cent. On the demand side, consumption rose at more than 5 per cent, considerably faster than output. The increase in grain consumption was due in part to rapid population growth and in part to an increase in per capita consumption. The latter, in turn, was the result of two developments: (1) a rise in per capita consumption in the rural areas from 218 kg. to 259 kg., while that in the urban areas remained unchanged at 285 kg., and (2) a rapid structural shift in total population from the rural to the urban sector.[69] Because of the substantial increase in rural consumption, the amount of grain available for other uses actually declined.

A third major gap was that between the output and exports of agricultural products. As Table 20–4 shows, imports expanded at 9 per cent per year during 1952–57, or twice as fast as agricultural production, and clearly faster than most individual products that entered into foreign trade. To finance the rising imports, agricultural exports also rose much faster than agricultural production. The sharp disparity indicates that a diversion of agricultural output from domestic uses to exports had

---

[69] For per capita consumption, see *T'ung-chi Kung-tso* (*Statistical Work*, hereafter: *TCKT*), No. 19, 1957, p. 28. A note of caution is in order. It is possible that the official statistics of grain consumption exaggerate the rate of increase. But the difference between the rates of increase in output and consumption is so wide that even a sizable margin of error, say a reduction of 25 per cent in the growth rate of consumption, would not affect the conclusion here.

Table 20-4—Comparative Economic Performance in Agriculture and Related Sectors, 1952–57

		1952	1957	Annual Rate of Growth (%)
(1) Industrial and agricultural production:				
Industrial production	(%)	100	241	19.2
Output of consumer goods	(%)	100	188	13.5
Agricultural production	(%)	100	125	4.5
(2) Population and grain consumption:				
Total population	(millions)	569	637	2.3
Urban population	(millions)	69	91	5.6
Rural population	(millions)	500	546	1.8
Grain output	(million tons)	154	185	3.7
Grain consumption	(million tons)	129	167	5.3
Urban consumption	(million tons)	20	26	5.5
Rural consumption	(million tons)	109	141	5.3
Output less rural consumption	(million tons)	45	44	− 0.5
(3) Imports and agricultural exports:				
Imports	(million yüan)	2,332	3,644	9.4
Agricultural exports	(million yüan)	1,622	3,029	13.3
(4) Peasant income and consumption:				
Index of income	(%)	100	128	5.0
Index of consumption	(%)	100	130	5.5
(5) Labor force and employment:				
Labor force	(millions)	338	380	2.3
Nonagricultural employment	(millions)	59	64	1.6

Sources: See Table 20-6; Liu and Yeh, *Economy of Chinese Mainlands*, p. 490. Industrial production refers to the output of modern industry and handicraft workshops at 1952 prices. (2) For population and grain output, see Liu and Yeh, *Economy of Chinese Mainland*, p. 212, and Table 20-6. Grain consumption is derived from population in 1952 and 1957 and per capita grain consumption in 1953–54 and 1956–57, respectively, given in *TCKT*, No. 19, 1957, p. 28. (3) Eckstein, *Foreign Trade*, p. 120; *TGY*, p. 176. Agricultural exports include processed and unprocessed products of agriculture and side occupations. (4) For index of peasant income, see *TGY*, p. 216. Index of consumption is actually that of material consumption of the rural population based on data from *Ching-chi Yen-chiu* (*Economic Research*, hereafter: *CCYC*), No. 6, 1957, p. 10; Liu and Yeh, *Economy of Chinese Mainland*, pp. 212, 232; Niu, *op. cit.* (see Table 20-3), p. 38. (5) For labor force, see Yeh, *Industrialization Strategies*, p. 343. For nonagricultural employment, see Liu and Yeh, *Economy of Chinese Mainland*, p. 69.

been taking place. However, toward the end of the period such diversion was becoming increasingly difficult, and the growth of output set a limit to the rate at which agricultural exports could expand. Thus, exports increased abruptly in 1956 following the bumper harvest in 1955 but dropped sharply in 1957, mainly as a result of the agricultural slowdown in 1956.[70]

As a direct consequence of the relatively slow agricultural growth, the share of total agricultural output marketed not only did not increase but actually declined slightly after 1954.[71] The marketing ratio for grain and soybean shows a similar trend. Total collection of grain and soybean rose from 33 million tons in 1953 to 45 million tons in 1955 but remained stable at about 42 million tons in the subsequent ten years. Apparently, with output hardly increasing, grain collection approached a ceiling so that even the more efficient control mechanism of the collectivized system failed to raise the marketing ratio. Meanwhile, urban population continued to rise. By 1957, the state had to curb the inflow of peasants into cities by decree and simultaneously cut exports and dip into stockpiles in order to meet the rising demand for grain.[72]

The relative slow agricultural growth created yet another problem. Table 20–4 shows that the peasants' consumption increased faster than their income, which implies that the saving-to-income ratio had declined. To the extent that agricultural savings contributed significantly to total capital formation, the declining saving ratio constituted another drag on economic growth.

To sum up, the economic performance of the agricultural sector was fair when measured in terms of official indexes of output and the degree of plan fulfillment. But output was grossly inadequate to meet the needs of rapid industrial and population growth, and consequently agriculture had become a limiting factor in Communist China's economic growth. The crucial problem became how to close the gap between the growth rates of industrial and agricultural production. Two choices were open to the leaders. One would be to adjust the industrial growth rate downward to reduce the demand for agricultural products and to release some resources for agricultural development. The advantage of such a policy was that, with greater emphasis on technical change and an inflow of industrial resources into agriculture, an increase in agricultural output could be almost assured. But the price would be a lower rate of industrial growth. An alternative choice would be to adjust the agricultural growth rate upward by more intensive and efficient use of resources within the agricultural sector. This alternative would have the advantage of maintaining and perhaps even raising the over-all growth rate. But it was highly uncertain how effectively it could be done. Labor was about the only resource in the agricultural sector that could be put to more intensive use, and the brief episode of mobilizing rural labor in the post-collectivization years had failed to produce any significant effect on output.

There were sharp differences of opinion among the leaders over which course of action to follow. Some were in favor of the first alternative, more material support of agriculture, as evidenced by the changed targets of chemical fertilizer output for the Second Five-Year Plan (SFYP) period. In 1956, when the first draft of the SFYP was prepared, the output target set for 1962 was 3 million to 3.2 million tons.[73] In mid-1957, it was reset at 3.2 million to 5 million tons.[74] In late 1957, both *Jen-min Jih-pao* and the State Planning Commission proposed greater support of agriculture by in-

---

[70] U.S., Department of Agriculture, *Trends and Developments in Communist China's World Trade in Farm Products 1955–1960* (Washington, D.C.: Government Printing Office, 1962), pp. 22, 24.

[71] See Table 20–7.

[72] Yeh Chi-chuang, 'On Foreign Trade,' *HHPYK*, No. 16, 1957, p. 91; Sun Wei-tsu, 'Principles for Drawing Up the Grain Circulation Plan,' *CHCC*, No. 2, 1958, p. 25.

[73] *HHPYK*, No. 1, 1957, p. 86.

[74] *HHPYK*, No. 16, 1957, p. 99.

dustry,[75] and the target was then raised further to 7 million tons.[76] However, others took the opposite view that 'peasants whose political ideas have been liberated can increase agricultural output very rapidly even without the support of large quantities of tractors and chemical fertilizers.'[77]

Apart from the serious difficulty presented by the emerging agricultural gap, the leaders faced another fundamental problem: the employment gap, that is, the gap between the supply and employment of labor. In sharp contrast to the agricultural gap, the problem with respect to labor was one of overabundance. Underemployment of labor was a serious problem even before the FFYP was launched.[78] The problem became more acute because of two developments during the FFYP period. On the supply side, rapid population growth added large numbers of able-bodied men annually to the already huge reservoir of labor supply. On the demand side, employment in the nonfarm sector increased rather slowly, mainly as a result of the regime's investment policy that emphasized capital-intensive technology. As Table 20–4 shows, nonagricultural employment expanded by about 1 million a year, while the total labor force increased by about 8 million annually. Toward the end of 1957, there was growing concern among the leaders over the underemployment situation.[79] The question was how to utilize fully and productively the enormous labor supply. This problem had several dimensions: Should the incentive system be based primarily on ideology or material reward? To what extent were capital and technology needed to utilize the surplus labor? Should the leaders emphasize agricultural or industrial employment, rural or urban employment? Over the long run, should the regime actively push a population control program? Again, there were disputes among the leaders over the two distinctly different policies. It was in late 1957 and early 1958 that Mao formulated a solution to the agricultural and the employment gap. The solution was the program for a Great Leap Forward.

THE GREAT LEAP AND THE COMMUNE MOVEMENT, 1958–59

As a national goal, the Great Leap referred to a sharp upsurge in output at a rate substantially higher than in the FFYP period. According to Chou En-lai, an annual rate of increase of 10 per cent or more in agricultural production is a leap, an increase of more than 15 per cent is a great leap, and an increase of more than 20 per cent is an extra-great leap.[80] Exactly when the leaders decided to increase output by leaps and bounds was not clear. But signs of a big push were discernible after the third plenum of the Eighth Central Committee in September, 1957. The plenum adopted a revised draft of the ambitious National Agricultural Development Program. Thereafter, a series of conferences on rural work were held. Numerous directives and editorials were issued, specifying the various tasks and calling upon the peasants to implement the policies laid down in the program. In the winter of 1957 and early spring of 1958, water conservation projects were undertaken on a large scale. As the big push gathered momentum, the output targets escalated. In February 1958, Po I-po, Head of the State Economic Commission, presented the annual economic plan for 1958 before the People's Congress, which set the production goals for agricultural output

---

[75] *JMJP*, October 1, 1957; *CHCC*, No. 10, 1957, p. 4.

[76] *JMST*, 1958, p. 26.

[77] Sung P'ing, 'Recognize and Utilize the Law of Planned, Proportionate Development of the National Economy,' *CHCC*, No. 12, 1958, p. 2.

[78] See *HH*, No. 6, 1952, p. 35; *JMJP*, April 17, 1953.

[79] *HHPYK*, No. 11, 1957, p. 90; *HH*, No. 12, 1957, p. 25.

[80] Chou En-lai, 'Report on the Adjustment of the Major Targets for the National Economic Plan of 1959 and Further Development of the Campaign to Increase Production and Economize,' *HHPYK*, No. 17, 1959, p. 22.

at 6.1 per cent above the 1957 level and grain output at 196 million tons, or 5.9 per cent over 1957.[81] Subsequently, the target for grain was reset at 212 million tons.[82] In June, it was raised even higher to 250 million tons, or 35 per cent above the 1957 level.[83] Thus, by Chou's standards, the leaders were aiming not at a great leap but at an extra-great leap.

How was the extremely high rate of increase to be achieved? The question can best be discussed in terms of Mao's grand strategy of the Great Leap. Mao's development strategy was based on a simple dualistic model. The two sectors in the model comprised the traditional and the modern, roughly corresponding to agricultural and industrial, sectors. The basic concepts underlying the strategy were: (1) parallel development of both agriculture and industry, of large and small plants, using both modern and indigenous technologies; (2) a labor theory of growth for the self-supporting traditional sector, and (3) a capital theory of growth for the modern sector, with continuous support from agriculture.

Mao rejected outright the alternative of increasing agricultural output at the expense of industrial expansion. Growth of agriculture was to be achieved not by redistributing the investment resources from industry to agriculture, but by a more or less direct transformation of labor into output and capital through: (1) the use of highly labor-intensive techniques in agricultural production, such as close planting and deep plowing; (2) large-scale investment in kind, such as building irrigation systems, soil conservation, and afforestation; and (3) massive development of small industrial workshops in the villages—such as small furnaces and shops for the manufacture of farm tools, fertilizers, and construction materials—which employed indigenous methods and local supplies and produced primarily for the traditional sector.

Mao's notion of mass mobilization of rural labor was not new. What was unique in his scheme was the important role of ideology, the tremendous scale of the effort, and the concept of *rural industrialization*. The crucial role of ideology stemmed from Mao's fundamental belief that political consciousness, rather than material reward, should and could provide the drive behind the human effort. The gigantic scale of the labor utilization projects was characteristic of Mao's approach to almost all problems— total commitment and mass participation in the form of a nationwide campaign. The rural industrialization program was designed to minimize the diversion of industrial resources from the modern sector and to solve the underemployment problem at the same time.

The development policy for the modern sector was quite different from that for the traditional sector. Here, capital, instead of labor, was the key. The goal of rapid development of heavy industry remained unchanged. As before, the investment program centered upon the Soviet-aided projects, which were relatively large, highly capital-intensive, and primarily oriented toward furthering industrial growth. An important feature of the policy was that investment was largely financed by savings in the traditional sector. Moreover, the export of agricultural products remained a major channel through which modern technology was acquired from abroad.

In short, labor would generate growth in the traditional sector, which in turn would provide the capital to sustain growth in the modern sector. The implication of this asymmetric relationship was that, if the strategy for the modern sector failed, the

---

[81] Po I-po, 'Report on the Draft National Economic Plan for 1958,' *HHPYK*, No. 5, 1958, p. 15.

[82] Choh-ming Li, 'China's Agriculture: A Great Leap in 1958?' in E. F. Szczepanik, ed., *Economic and Social Problems of the Far East* (Hong Kong: Hong Kong University Press, 1962), p. 28.

[83] T'an Chen-lin, 'Strive for Abundant Supply of Food and Clothing in Two or Three Years,' *Hung-ch'i* (*Red Flag*, hereafter: *HC*), No. 6, 1958, p. 8.

economic system would be disrupted but not seriously, partly because that sector was relatively small and partly because the traditional sector was more or less independent of development in the modern sector. However, if the strategy for the traditional sector failed, the whole system would collapse, because the modern sector depended heavily on the traditional sector. Because the very cornerstone of the strategy was the labor utilization scheme, the central task was to mobilize fully the available labor and utilize it effectively in both agricultural and nonagricultural activities. It was mainly for this purpose that the communes were organized.

The commune movement. As early as 1955, while the collectivization movement was still in progress, Mao had made known his preference for organizations larger than the newly established cooperatives.[84] In March, 1958, at a conference in Chengtu, he proposed combining the cooperatives into larger units. The proposal was later adopted by the Party. In June, 1958, Mao decided upon a name for the new organization: the people's commune. Meanwhile, in response to the call of the Party, more and more mergers took place. In early August, after an inspection of the communes in Hopei, Honan, and Shantung, Mao openly gave the commune his blessing: 'It is better to organize communes. It has the advantage of combining the management of industry, agriculture, trade, education, and military affairs [under a single administrative unit] and thus facilitates control and direction.'[85] On August 29, 1958, the Politburo adopted the 'Resolution on the Question of Organizing Communes in the Villages,' formally launching the movement.[86] At the time, about 30 per cent of the total farm households had already joined the communes.[87] As in the case of collectivization, the movement was extremely rapid. Hardly one month after the resolution was promulgated, participation rose to 98 per cent. By the end of the year, there were 26,578 communes, with more than 99 per cent of the farm households participating.

What distinguished a commune from a cooperative? According to Mao, the commune had two principal features: It was larger in size, and it represented an organization in a higher stage of socialism.[88] In the winter of 1957, large-scale development in water conservation had created the need for massive deployment of labor. During that three-month period, about 100 million peasants were mobilized. The cooperatives were apparently too small to cope with problems of this magnitude. In anticipation of the demand for manpower for the new techniques of cultivation and the development of rural industries, the leaders decided to amalgamate the cooperatives to form larger organizations. In terms of resources under its control, a commune was many times larger than a cooperative. On the average, there were 4,600 farm households in a commune, compared to 150 in a cooperative in 1957, and each commune had about 4,000 hectares of cultivated land, compared to 140 hectares in a cooperative.[89] Quite apart from the differences in size, the scope of activities of the commune was far broader. It was a social, economic, and administrative unit engaged in both agricultural and nonagricultural activities, including trade, education, and military training, whereas the cooperative was almost purely an agricultural organization. The Communist leaders argued that the new organization enjoyed tremendous economies

---

[84] 'Small cooperatives have fewer members, less land, and not much money. They cannot operate on a large scale or use machinery. The development of their forces of production is still hampered. They should not stay in this position too long, but should go on to combine with other cooperatives step by step.' See *High Tide*, 2: 611.

[85] *HC*, No. 8, 1958, p. 8.

[86] *HHPYK*, No. 18, 1958, pp. 1–2.

[87] Teng Tzu-hui, 'Socialist Transformation of China's Agriculture,' *CKNP*, No. 20, 1959, p. 4.

[88] Chih-p'u, 'From Cooperatives to Communes,' *HC*, No. 8, 1958, p. 8.

[89] Figures are based on Teng Tzu-hui, 'Socialist Transformation'; see also Table 20–1.

of scale.[90] First, the larger size provided more opportunities in the deployment of labor. Many projects too large for a single cooperative to undertake could now be carried out by the commune. The integration of the local administration and commune management released labor from administrative work. More important, the establishment of child-care centers and public dining halls freed an enormous volume of female labor for more productive work. Second, the larger area under a single management would permit a higher degree of crop specialization and more rational use of water or other resources. Finally, there were economies of scale in the utilization of technology, such as agricultural experimentation, extension service, and schooling.

The commune was said to be more socialistic in character in several respects than the cooperative. Certain elements of ownership by the whole people had been added to the collectively owned economy.[91] Private ownership of means of production had been completely eliminated. The distribution of output among the members was now based partly on the principle of 'to each according to his need.' Furthermore, not only production activities were collectivized, but the peasants' daily lives were to some extent communized. For these reasons, the commune movement was considered a major step in the advancement toward the Communist society. In a burst of optimism, the Party confidently predicted in 1958: 'In our view the realization of Communism in China is no longer an event of the distant future.'[92]

At that utopian stage, the basic characteristics of a commune[93] were as follows: (1) The organization of the commune was in three levels: the commune, the production brigade, and the production team. A commune comprised a number of brigades, and under each brigade there would be some five to ten teams. In size, the brigade and the team corresponded to the former higher and lower cooperatives. The team was the unit for labor organization; the brigade for production management; and the commune for over all administration. The decision-making power was centralized at the commune level. (2) Ownership of all means of production belonged to the commune. Private plots, houses, and orchards, which the peasants were permitted to own under the cooperatives, were now placed under collective ownership. The peasants, however, could retain 'small numbers' of the poultry and animals they raised. (3) The total gross revenue of the commune, after allowing for production cost, depreciation of commune properties, and state taxes, was distributed as follows: food expenditures for the members; wages; the welfare fund; the accumulation fund. The welfare fund did not in general exceed 5 per cent of the total gross revenue and might be regarded as a form of collective conscription. The accumulation fund represented internal savings of the commune. The peculiar feature was the dual income distribution system. A part of the peasant's income consisted of food supply as determined by the state grain rationing schedule, which bore no relationship to the individual's labor

---

[90] T'an Ch'i-lung, 'It is Better to Organize Communes,' *HC*, No. 9, 1958, pp. 21–24; Wu Chih-p'u, 'From Cooperatives to Communes'; Li Ching-ch'uan, 'The Commune Is the Inevitable Product of China's Social Development,' *HC*, No. 20, 1959, pp. 16–23.

[91] 'This is because the people's communes and the basic organizations of state power have been combined into one; because the banks, stores and some other enterprises owned by the whole people, originally existing in the countryside, have been placed under the management of the communes; because the communes have taken part in establishing certain undertakings in industrial and other construction which are by nature owned by the whole people; because in many counties the county federations of communes, exercising unified leadership over all the people's communes in these counties, have been formed and have the power to deploy a certain portion of the manpower, material, and financial resources of the communes and undertake construction on a county or even bigger scale and so on.' CCP, 'Resolutions of the Sixth Plenary Session,' *HHPYK*, No. 24, 1958, p. 5.

[92] CCP, 'Resolution on the Question of Organizing Communes in the Villages,' *HHPYK*, No. 18, 1958, p. 2.

[93] *HC*, No. 7, 1958, pp. 16–22.

contributions. This was known as the supply system. Another part of the income was paid in monthly wages. The specific wage level for an individual depended on the nature of his job, his physical strength, his technical skill, and his attitude toward labor. (4) The commune set up nurseries and public dining halls for its members.

Almost from the very beginning the communes ran into serious difficulties. The peasants reacted strongly against the more or less egalitarian system of distribution. There were wastes and mismanagement due to overcentralization. To cope with such problems, a series of Party conferences were held.[94] In December, 1958, the Central Committee laid down the following new guidelines for the organization and management of the communes:[95] (1) Private ownership of properties for personal use was permitted.[96] The peasants were allowed to engage in household subsidiary work, provided such activities did not interfere with collective production. (2) Some decision-making power over such matters as organization of production, capital construction, finances and welfare was passed from the commune to the brigade and team in an attempt to bring their initiative into full play. (3) A larger proportion of the output was to be distributed through the wage system, which linked together income and the amount of work done. Wage scales were divided into six to eight grades to allow for differences in skills and effort. (4) The Party conceded that the transition from collective ownership to ownership by the entire people would take longer than expected and that the transition from socialism to Communism would be even more remote.

However, there was no wavering in the leaders' determination to push ahead with the Great Leap program. Several radical measures in the commune movement were retained. For example, the resolution called upon the cadres to organize the county federation of communes, to build rural industries on a large scale, and to increase the saving ratio of the communes. There was no change in the Party's policy toward public dining halls and nurseries.

Immediately after the sixth plenum ended in December, 1958, the Party launched a campaign to rectify the defects and mistakes in the commune structure and management. However, the new measures were apparently ineffective. In February, 1959, the Politburo issued further instructions to modify the commune system. Six months later, at the eighth plenum of the Eighth Central Committee at Lushan, a heated debate took place between some Party members, notably P'eng Te-huai, who were critical of the Great Leap and the communes, and Mao, the chief architect of the entire program.[97] The bitter debate ended with the purge of Mao's opponents. Mao's victory was, however, somewhat hollow so far as the commune movement was concerned. For by then, one year after the Party adopted its first resolution on organizing people's communes in Peitaiho, the commune had already lost most of its original characteristics. First, the peasants were now permitted to have their private plots.[98] Second, much of the control and ownership of the means of production was turned over from the commune to the brigade. The team also had limited ownership of certain properties. As of August, 1959, there were 24,000 communes, 500,000 brigades, and 3 million teams, each with about forty households. The brigade, as the basic accounting unit, directed production and distributed the output. The pre-1958

---

[94] The Politburo convened in Chengchow in November, 1958. This was followed by a conference of the Party first secretaries of the provincial committees in Wuch'ang.

[95] 'Resolution on Some Questions Concerning the People's Communes,' *HHPYK*, No. 24, 1958, pp. 3–11.

[96] Specifically, these included: houses, clothing, bedding and furniture, bank deposits, trees around houses, small farm tools and instruments, and small domestic animals and poultry. *Ibid.*, p. 8.

[97] For documents relating to the clash between Peng and Mao, see Union Research Institute, *The Case of Peng Teh-huai, 1959–1968* (Hong Kong: n.p., 1968).

[98] Ch'en Cheng-jen, 'On the Ownership and Distribution System of the People's Communes,' *CKNP*, No. 20, 1959, p. 11.

system of 'three guarantees and one reward' was re-established. Under this system the brigade entered into contracts with the teams that guaranteed a predetermined volume of output, the level of cost, and the number of labor days. The team would receive a reward if the output target was overfulfilled. Third, the income distribution system had been drastically modified in order to stimulate individual incentives. The dual system still existed, but the emphasis was on the wage system. That part of output to be distributed under the wage system was to be maintained at 70 per cent and was not to fall below 60 per cent of the total available for distribution.[99] To some extent total wage payments varied with the number of labor days the peasant contributed.[100] Finally, the leaders no longer insisted on 'living in a collective way.' Peasants participated in the public dining halls on a voluntary basis. Beginning with the summer harvest of 1959, grain rations were distributed to the individual households instead of to the public dining halls.[101] In effect, the commune system had retrogressed to the stage of the higher cooperatives.

Technological changes and other developments. During the commune movement in 1958–59, the leaders also introduced new production techniques and intensified the use of certain traditional ones. The measures to increase agricultural output, summarized by Mao as the eight-point charter, included soil improvement, increased application of natural fertilizers, more irrigation works, seed selection, close planting, pest control, field supervision, and farm tool improvement. During these two years, tremendous efforts were made to implement the measures, particularly in deep plowing, use of fertilizers, irrigation, and close planting. About one-half of the total area under cultivation was deep-plowed.[102] It was claimed that more than ten tons of fertilizers were applied to each *mou* of cultivated land.[103] Irrigated area in 1958 increased by 92 per cent over 1957;[104] 1,800 medium and large dams were built in 1958–59.[105] Close planting was practiced throughout the country. Extensive work on the other measures was also carried out. In addition, the state supplied the peasants with large quantities of chemical fertilizers, insecticides, and power machines. The amount of producers' goods purchased from the nonagricultural sector doubled in 1958.[106]

The development of rural industries was also unprecedented in pace and in scale. In September, 1958, shortly after the Central Committee formally had launched the commune movement, Mao spoke out strongly for the construction of small plants.[107] By the end of 1958, some 6 million small industrial plants had been established in the rural areas.[108] The Communists claimed that the gross value of output of the commune industries totaled 5.8 billion yüan, or roughly 9 per cent of the gross value of industrial output in 1958, and that it rose further, to 10 billion yüan, in 1959.[109]

Communist sources also reported a substantial rise in the savings ratio during that period. According to a survey of 228 better-managed cooperatives in 1957, the accumulation rate was about 22 per cent.[110] It was increased to 30 per cent in 1958.[111]

[99] *Ibid.*, p. 12.　　　　[100] *HHPYK*, No. 17, 1959, p. 39.
[101] Teng Tzu-hui, 'Actively Manage Well the Public Dining Halls and Follow the Voluntary Principle,' *HHPYK*, No. 12, 1959, p. 107.
[102] *TGY*, p. 115.　　　　[103] *HHPYK*, No. 18, 1958, p. 11.　　　　[104] *TGY*, p. 130.
[105] Liao Lu-yen, 'A Decade of Glorious Achievements on the Agricultural Front,' *CKNP*, No. 19, 1959, p. 7.
[106] *TGY*, p. 170.　　　　[107] *HHPYK*, No. 19, 1958, p. 1.　　　　[108] *TKP*, December 31, 1958.
[109] Li Fu-ch'un, 'Report on the Draft Economic Plan for 1960,' *Chi-hua yu t'ung-chi (Plan and Statistics*, hereafter: *CHYTC*), No. 4, 1960, p. 11.
[110] *HHPYK*, No. 18, 1959, p. 95. For comparability we have recalculated the accumulation rate as follows. Accumulation is defined as the sum of the cooperatives' reserve fund, agricultural taxes and investment in kind. Total income refers to total gross receipts plus investment in kind less production expenses. The accumulation rate is the ratio of accumulation to total income.
[111] Ch'en Cheng-jen, 'On Ownership and Distribution System,' p. 14.

Agricultural production, 1958–59. Despite the dramatic changes in rural organization, the tremendous expansion in the agrotechnical programs, and the rise in compulsory savings in the communes, the Great Leap in agricultural production failed to materialize. As noted above, the State Planning Commission originally set a target of increase in agricultural production of 6 per cent in 1958 over 1957, along with a grain output target of 196 million tons and a target output of 1.75 million tons for cotton.[112] As the pressure on the cadres to increase output continued to mount and the regular statistical reporting system broke down, high yields in a small number of experimental plots led cadres to report greatly exaggerated results all over the country. In September, 1958, the authorities estimated a total grain output of 300 million to 350 million tons, 60–90 per cent above the 1957 level, and cotton output at 3.5 million tons, or double the output of 1957.[113] In April, 1959, Chou En-lai reported before the People's Congress that agricultural production in 1958 had increased by 64 per cent over the last year instead of the 6 per cent as planned.[114] Grain output reached 375 million tons, more than double that of 1957, and cotton output totaled 3.3 million tons, also twice that of 1957.[115] In short, the bumper harvest of 1958 had far exceeded not only the planned targets but also Chou En-lai's criterion of an extra-great leap.

Fantastic as the claim might be, there were indications that the leaders really believed that they had achieved a phenomenal breakthrough in agricultural production. As early as June, 1958, greatly encouraged by reports of extremely high yields, Mao proposed an output target of 0.75 tons of grain per person, which a *Jen-min Jih-pao* editorial called definitely attainable in 1959.[116] With a total population of 650 million, this would imply a total grain output of 487 million tons, another 30 per cent increase over the incredibly high output of 1958. In August, 1958, Mao actually expressed concern over what to do with the surplus grain.[117] In fact, he considered the agricultural problem completely resolved and directed the Party cadres to reorient their major effort toward industry.[118] Thus, in December, 1958, the Central Committee openly dismissed the problem of over-population as nonexistent.[119] In April, 1959, Chou En-lai proudly announced that the economic upsurge in 1958 really began with the Great Leap in agriculture.[120] The economic plan for 1959 presented before the People's Congress at that time was based on the unrealistic claims for 1958. The plan called for a 39 per cent increase in agricultural production.[121] Grain output was to reach 525 million tons, higher than the goal set by Mao. Targets for other products were no less fantastic.

But shortly after the People's Congress, the leaders became aware of the unreliability of their estimates, possibly because the collection of grain ran into difficulties. The first sign of their awakening was the reversal of an early plan to reduce the sown acreage.[122] By August, 1959, it was clear that fulfillment of the 1959 plan formulated only four months before was beyond the realm of possibility. Accordingly, the leaders drastically revised their estimates for 1958 and scaled down the targets for 1959. As shown in Table 20–5, downward adjustments were made in the output of grain, cotton, soybean, peanuts, cured tobacco, hemp and jute, and in the total number of hogs for 1958. The extent of overreporting is indicated by the wide margin between the preliminary and revised estimate of grain output: The former is 50 per cent above the revised figure. A similar comparison of the two estimates of total agricultural

---

[112] *HHPYK*, No. 5, 1958, p. 15.

[113] *JMJP* editorial: 'Strive for a Great Leap in Agriculture in theComing Year,' *HHPYK*, No. 18, 1959, p. 9.

[114] Chou En-lai, 'Report on Government Work,' *HHPYK*, No. 9, 1959, p. 3.

[115] *1958 Communiqué*, p. 53.   [116] *HHPYK*, No. 18, 1958, p. 9.

[117] *HHPYK*, No. 16, 1958, pp. 36–37.   [118] *HHPYK*, No. 18, 1958, p. 14.

[119] *HHPYK*, No. 24, 1958, p. 7.   [120] *HHPYK*, No. 9, 1959, p. 4.

[121] *HHPYK*, No. 9, 1959, p. 15.   [122] *HHPYK*, No. 12, 1959, p. 118.

Table 20–5—Planned Targets and Official Estimates of Agricultural Production, 1957–59

	1957 Actual 8/59 (1)	1958			1959		
		Plan 2/58 (2)	Claim 4/59 (3)	Revised 8/59 (4)	Target 4/59 (5)	Revised Target 8/59 (6)	Claim 1/60 (7)
Agricultural production (billion 1957 yüan)	53.70	68.83	88.00	67.10	122.20	73.80	78.30
Grain (million tons)	185	196	375	250	525	275	270
Cotton (thousand tons)	1,640	1,750	3,319	2,100	5,000	2,310	2,410
Soybean (thousand tons)	10,050	10,500	12,500	10,500	15,000	—	11,500
Peanuts (thousand tons)	2,517	3,085	4,000	2,800	6,000	—	3,058
Rapeseed (thousand tons)	887	1,154	1,100	1,100	1,600	—	—
Cured tobacco (thousand tons)	256	379	—	380	—	—	422
Hemp and jute (thousand tons)	360[a]	—	325	371[b]	500	—	—
Sugar cane (thousand tons)	10,392	13,250	13,750	13,525	20,000	—	13,931
Sugarbeet (thousand tons)	1,501	1,943	2,900	2,900	5,500	—	3,683
Tea (thousand tons)	111	—	—	140	—	—	151
Large animals (millions)	83.82	88.27	85.06	85.06	90.00	—	—
Sheep and goats (millions)	98.58	—	108.86	108.86	120.00	—	112.53
Hogs (millions)	145.90	150.00	180.00	160.00	280.00	—	180.00

[a] Taken from Table 20–6.
[b] Taken from *HHPYK*, No. 17, 1959, p. 69.

Sources: (1) and (4), *TGY*, pp. 118–19, 124–25, 132. (2) Po I-po, 'Report on the Draft National Economic Plan for 1958,' *HHPYK*, No. 5, 1958, pp. 15, 19. (3) State Statistical Bureau, 'Communiqué on the Economic Development in 1958,' *HHPYK*, No. 8, 1959, p. 53; Li Fu-ch'un, 'Report on the Draft National Economic Plan for 1959,' *HHPYK*, No. 9, 1959, pp. 16–17. (5) Li Fu-ch'un, *ibid.* (6) *HHPYK*, No. 17, 1959. p. 22. (7) 'Press Communiqué on the National Economic Development in 1959,' *CHYTC*, No. 1, 1960, p. 1; Huang Chien-to, 'Great Leap in Agricultural Production,' *CHYTC*, No. 1, 1960, p. 27.

production shows a gross overstatement of more than 30 per cent. According to the official explanation, output was overreported because of a lack of experience in crop estimates under conditions of bumper harvests over large tracts of land, because of inadequate deployment of labor for the autumn harvest, so that the reaping, threshing, and storage were handled rather carelessly, and because of underestimation of the effect of natural disasters that affected 25 per cent of the cultivated area.[123]

The cutback in the targets for 1959 was no less dramatic. Planned grain output was reduced from 525 million tons to 275 million; cotton output from 5 to 2.3 million, and total agricultural production from 122 billion yüan to 73.8 billion yüan. The revised targets were still quite high compared to the 1957 levels. In fact, they were about the same as the targets for 1962, the final year of the SFYP period. In early 1960, official reports showed that output came close to or surpassed the revised targets, thus fulfilling also the SFYP three years ahead of schedule.[124] If true, the achievements in 1959 were still a leap, if not a Great Leap, by Chou's standards.

As will be discussed later, there were political reasons for Chou En-lai's insistence that a Great Leap did take place in 1958–59. Nonetheless, reports on grain consumption sharply contradicted his claims. Chou himself admitted that the supply of food was short in some localities in 1959.[125] In 1960, the situation worsened and the state tightened control of grain and cotton cloth rationing.[126] The poor performance in 1959 was also reflected in the sharp decline of agricultural exports in 1960. Exports of agricultural products to the Soviet Union and the free world dropped by 30 per cent.[127] The reports suggest that the revised figures are still very much on the high side. Moreover, it seems most unlikely that grain output and total agricultural production in 1959 could have exceeded the 1958 levels, if only because the weather conditions were much worse and sown acreage considerably smaller in 1959. The actual levels of output during the Great Leap years, however, cannot be determined precisely. Independent estimates of grain output range from 175 to 210 million tons for 1958, and 154 to 192 million tons for 1959. Even the highest estimates are much lower than the revised official claim of 250 and 270 million tons.[128] In all likelihood, there had been a good harvest in 1958, but far below the level of 250 million tons. For 1959, there seems to be a consensus among Western observers that it was lower than the 1958 level. Some believe it fell below the 1957 level. In any case, it is clear that the Great Leap had failed to bring about a breakthrough in grain production.

Why did the Great Leap fail? The causes were many. First and foremost, the remuneration system apparently failed to provide adequate incentives for the peasants to exert their best effort. The authorities had relied heavily on the political consciousness of the peasants to provide the drive for the Great Leap. The economic interest of the individual was therefore de-emphasized. Private plots were confiscated, rural free markets abolished, and output distributed partly on an egalitarian basis. To the peasants, ideology was evidently a poor substitute for material reward. The disruption of family life, the mismanagement of the public dining halls, and the cadres' abuse of power further aggravated the peasants' discontent. Consequently, the intensive effort the leaders had anticipated was not forthcoming, and the commune system had to undergo almost continuous readjustment to restore 'productive activism.'

Even when labor was effectively mobilized, the authorities ran into additional

---

[123] *HHPYK*, No. 17, 1959, p. 22.   [124] *CHYTC*, No. 4, 1960, pp. 1–2.

[125] *HHPYK*, No. 17, 1959, p. 21.

[126] *The New York Times*, June 10, 1960, p. 26; *Washington Post*, August 7, 1960, p. A-5.

[127] U.S., Department of Agriculture, *Trends and Developments in Communist China's World Trade in Farm Products, 1955–1960* (Washington, D.C.: Government Printing Office, 1962), pp. 22, 24.

[128] See Table 20–9.

R

difficulties. The increase in labor input did not always increase output. In their fanatical drive to achieve a Great Leap, technology was grossly neglected. Untested farming techniques were adopted uniformly over large areas, irrespective of differences in local conditions and without proper technical guidance. Close planting, the key measure in Mao's eight-point charter, was an example. In many localities, the crops were planted too densely, resulting in a decline in output.[129] Another example was irrigation. Two-thirds of the total irrigated area was unproductive because the water resources were inadequate or because of the lack of proper equipment to utilize the water resources.[130] Worse still, some irrigation systems were defective in design or in construction. At times, reckless digging caused alkalization of the soil.

Moreover, the deployment of labor was badly managed. Millions were drafted to work on backyard steel furnaces and water conservation projects while labor on the farms at harvest time was in short supply.

A fourth factor was the failure of the rural industries to provide industrial input for the agricultural program. At the end of 1958, there were about 6 million rural industrial plants.[131] Some were producing fertilizers, farm tools, and building materials to serve agriculture production, while others processed the agricultural products. However, partly because they competed with agriculture for resources, partly because many were technically inefficient or economically costly to operate, the number of these plants fell to some 200,000 by the end of 1959.[132]

Finally, the decline in 1959 was partly due to a serious planning error. Misled by greatly inflated claims, Mao believed that the peasants had really broken through in raising the crop yields. In late 1958, he adopted the policy of 'plant less, increase yields, and harvest more.'[133] Specifically, he proposed that China eventually needed only one-third of the current cultivated area for crop production, leaving one-third in fallow and the remaining one-third afforested.[134] As a first step toward this goal, the leaders reduced sown acreage from 386 million acres in 1958 to 346 million acres, and that for grain, from 300 million acres to 264 million acres, in 1959.[135] In mid-1959, it was discovered that the Great Leap had been largely a mirage. Mao hurriedly reversed his policy and instructed the cadres to plant more.[136] The peasants were even encouraged to plant on tiny strips of land around houses and ponds and on the hills. But by that time the damage to the summer harvest had already been done.

AGRICULTURAL CRISIS AND RECOVERY, 1960–65

By the end of 1959, the leaders had probably realized that an agricultural crisis was in the making, although official statements never for once admitted the Great Leap to be a blunder. They adopted a new development policy that was different from past ones in several respects. First, there was a subtle shift of emphasis toward agriculture from other sectors. Agriculture was to be the 'foundation of the economy,' whereas industry was to be the 'leading sector.'[137] Accordingly, acceleration of agricultural

---

[129] Teng Tzu-hui, 'Implement Fully the Eight Point Charter and Strive for High Yields and Stable Harvest,' *HHPYK*, No. 12, 1959, p. 118.

[130] *Ibid.*, p. 119. [131] *TKP*, December 31, 1958.

[132] Li Fu-ch'un, 'Raise High the Red Flag of the General Line and Continue to March Forward,' *HC*, No. 16, 1960, p. 3. See also *HHPYK*, No. 12, 1959, p. 127.

[133] CCP, 'Resolution on Certain Problems of the People's Communes,' *HHPYK*, No. 24, 1958, p. 7.

[134] Liao Lu-yen, 'The Task for the Agricultural Front in 1959,' *HHPYK*, No. 1, 1959, p. 88.

[135] Li Fu-ch'un, 'Report on the Draft Economic Plan for 1959,' *HHPYK*, No. 9, 1959, p. 16; *TGY*, pp. 128–29.

[136] *HHPYK*, No. 12, 1959, pp. 118 and 126–27.

[137] Li Fu-ch'un, 'Welcome the New Leap of 1960,' *HC*, No. 1, 1960, pp. 3–5; Li Fu-ch'un, 'Report on the Draft Economic Plan for 1960,' *CHYTC*, No. 4, 1960, p. 6.

development became the central problem; an important task for all other sectors, including industry, trade, and transportation, was the support of agriculture. The new theme marked a notable departure from the FFYP, which assigned to industry the highest priority, and from the Great Leap program, which called for simultaneous development of industry and agriculture, with agriculture more or less self-supporting.

Within the agricultural sector, the focus was on grain, because it concerned the subsistence of all the people, and also on hogs, because of the need for fertilizer. The leaders called for a large-scale expansion in hog-raising in an attempt to increase the number of hogs from 180 million to about 650 million in a few years. The abrupt shift of emphasis to hogs suggests that the small fertilizer plants had failed to become an important source of supply.

A third notable change was the new farm mechanization program, which called for moderate mechanization in four years beginning in 1959, semimechanization by 1967, and complete mechanization by 1970.[138] For this purpose, the economic plan for 1960 provided for the supply of large quantities of steel, tractors, machines, irrigation pumps, trucks, and small farm implements.[139]

Despite the reorientation of effort toward agriculture, the harvest in 1960 failed again, and a severe food crisis developed. In late 1960, the authorities admitted grave difficulties in grain supply but attributed the shortage to abnormally serious natural disasters.[140] The acute shortage can be seen in the Communists' own internal reports of thousands of military servicemen afflicted with malnutrition, widespread discontent among the servicemen, and peasants stealing grain from the troops.[141] The crop failure also brought a sharp drop in exports in 1961.

In November, 1960, the Party issued an 'Emergency Directive on Rural Work' granting further concessions to the peasants.[142] Subsequently, the twelve articles in the emergency directive were expanded and restated more specifically in the 'Draft Regulations Governing the Work of the Rural People's Communes,' promulgated by the Party on May 12, 1961.[143] Several significant changes in the commune organization were made: (1) The brigade, instead of the commune, now owned the land, draft animals, and farm implements. It handled production planning and management and distributed output. The management committee of the commune could not force a production plan upon the brigades. The earlier method of centralized management at the brigade level was formally replaced by the contractual relationship between the brigade and the team, with the team permanently in possession of the means of production. (2) As the decision-making power shifted from the commune to the brigade, the scale of the operating unit became smaller both in size and in the scope of its activities. On the other hand, the number of units increased from 24,000 to about 500,000. The purpose was partly to facilitate management by decentralization of responsibility, and partly to reduce the conflict between brigades with widely different per capita incomes. Nonagricultural activities, including rural industries, were also severely restricted. The use of labor for these purposes by the brigade was not to exceed 3 per cent of the labor of the teams. (3) A larger share of the output was distributed to the members. Moreover, a minimum of 70 per cent of this portion of

---

[138] *CHYTC*, No. 4, 1960, p. 6.   [139] *Ibid.*, p. 9.

[140] *Kung-tso T'ung-hsün* (*Bulletin of Activities*—hereafter: *KTTH*—house organ of People's Liberation Army), No. 1, 1961, p. 7.

[141] *KTTH*, No. 1, 1961, p. 20; No. 7, 1961, p. 18; No. 11, 1961, p. 19; No. 15, 1961, pp. 10, 17.

[142] The directive was monitored from a broadcast from the Kiangsi People's Broadcasting Station on November 3, 1960.

[143] The draft regulations are reprinted in *Jen-min Kung-she Tzu-liao Hsüan-chi* (*Special Collection of Materials on People's Communes*), No. 6 (Taipei: publisher unknown, 1961): 136–59.

output was to be distributed according to the wage system. (4) To supplement the income of the peasants, 5 per cent of the cultivated area was given to the peasants as private plots for an indefinite period. The produce from the private plots belonged entirely to the peasants. Farm subsidiary occupations were encouraged. Orders were issued that the peasants should be given some spare time to work on their small plots or on handicrafts. Except for commodities that came under the unified purchase system, output of the peasants' subsidiary occupations could be sold in the 40,000 rural markets.

But neither the new policy of 'all people to support agriculture' nor the reorganization of the communes had produced a significant rise in output. A *Jen-min Jih-pao* editorial reported that the harvest of 1961 was only slightly better than that of the preceding year.[144] As the grain output in 1960 was disastrously low, a slightly higher volume could hardly bring relief to the near-famine situation. The poor performance was due partly to the poor weather conditions in 1961 and partly to the vicious circles generated by the crop failures of the earlier years. Food shortages compelled the authorities to tighten control over consumption, which led to discontent and lowered the peasants' incentives and physical capabilities, and that in turn affected output adversely. One manifestation of the peasants' loss of incentives was the widespread overgrowing of weeds in the crop fields. The agricultural crisis also set in motion another vicious circle between feed for the draft animals and hogs, on the one side, and output, on the other. Because of the lack of food and proper care, large numbers of draft animals died.[145] The loss of domestic animals again added to the difficulties of restoring production.

The impact of three successive years of crop failures was profound. According to a Communist source, Liu Shao-ch'i was reported to have said in 1961 that there were more people who died than were born.[146] Whatever the effect on population growth, there seem to be little doubt that malnutrition was quite prevalent. To provide some relief, the authorities had to import grain on a sizable scale for the first time since the regime came to power, even while total exports and imports both fell very sharply. A retrenchment in investment was made in 1961. In short, the agricultural failure degenerated into an economic crisis. The abrupt and complete withdrawal of all Soviet technical assistance in 1960 compounded the difficulties further.

Toward the end of 1961, the commune system underwent further reorganization.[147] First, the team replaced the brigade as the basic accounting unit. The team owned the major means of production (land, draft animals, and farm tools), planned production, and distributed its output among its members. The transfer of ownership and authority from the brigade to the team signified a further reduction in the size of the farming unit. Second, there was no longer any restriction as to what part of the output had to be distributed on a per capita basis, thus permitting the entire output to be distributed according to the quality and quantity of work done. The specific formula of distribution was to be decided by the members themselves. Third, private plots could be increased to 7 per cent of the team's cultivated land. Together with the land for fodder crops and reclaimed land, land made available for the peasants' own use could total in area the equivalent of 15 per cent of the cultivated area of the team.

In sum, by 1962, the commune system existed only in name. It had lost completely

---

[144] *JMJP*, January 1, 1962.

[145] One commune in Fukien lost 80 per cent of its draft animals between 1958 and 1961. Chin Fang-chun, 'Report on the Actual Conditions in the Red Star Commune in Kuang-tse County, Fukien,' *Chin-jih Ta-lu* (*Mainland Today*, or *CJTL*), No. 176 (Taipei, 1963), p. 9.

[146] Ting Wan, *Chung-kung Wen-hua Ta-ke-ming Tzu-liao Hui-pien* (*A Compendium of Documents on Communist China's Great Cultural Revolution*), 1 (Hong Kong: Ming-pao Monthly, n.d.): 314.

[147] 'Revised Draft of the Regulations Concerning the Work in the People's Communes' (n.d., reprinted in Taiwan).

its principal features of being large and socialistic. In 1958, there were 26,000 communes, which were combined into 24,000 communes in 1959, comprising 550,000 brigades and 3 million teams. By 1961, there were 50,000 communes, 700,000 brigades and 4.6 million teams.[148] The reduction in size was accompanied by successive steps of decentralization. In 1958, management of most activities was centralized at the commune level. In 1962, the team operated as a more or less independent unit. Equally significant were the almost complete replacement of material for ideological incentives, the disappearance of public dining halls, and the reopening of rural markets. The commune had retrogressed to the stage of the lower cooperatives. From 1962 on, up to the Ninth Party Congress in 1969, no major change in rural organization had apparently been made.

How effective the decentralized system was in raising output is difficult to judge. There were, however, indications that agricultural production has been on the road to recovery since 1960. As can be seen from Table 20–9, most independent estimates of grain output show a rising trend since that year. Exports and imports have also turned steadily upward since 1961. Apart from the more rational incentive system, two other factors probably contributed significantly to the recovery. The first was a rapid increase in the use of chemical fertilizer from 2.7 million tons in 1958 to 9.5 million tons in 1967.[149] The second was the extensive use of water pumps in the high-yield areas in the Yangtze and Pearl River delta regions. The new program was far less ambitious than Mao's grand scheme proposed in 1960, but it was much more pragmatic. Given the objective to maximize the volume of grain delivered to the state, the concentration of investment in the delta regions rather than in the remote low-yield areas can be justified on economic grounds. In general, there were existing facilities, such as power lines, railroads, and irrigation canals, which were necessary for effective use of the new investment. Furthermore, transportation costs from the producing to the consuming centers might be lower. Finally, the income elasticity of demand for food in the poorer regions might well be higher than in the rich delta regions. Rising income resulting from rising productivity in those regions might result in a smaller share of the increment released to the state.

The struggle between the two roads. While the economy gradually moved upward, a political storm was brewing. It began with the intra-Party dispute over the Great Leap and subsequently developed into a struggle between the capitalist and socialist roads in the countryside. Then came serious disagreements over the Socialist Education Movement, culminating in confrontation during the Cultural Revolution. The origin of the storm was the bitter dispute over the Great Leap and the communes, which broke out at the eighth plenum of the Eighth Central Committee at Lushan in August, 1959. On one side were Mao and his stanch followers, who held to the more radical views. On the other side were P'eng Te-huai, Liu Shao-ch'i, Teng Hsiao-p'ing, Ch'en Yün, and others, who opted for more pragmatic measures. Three related questions were at issue: Was the Great Leap an error? Why did it fail? What remedial measures should be taken?

On the first question, Mao admitted that the Great Leap and the commune movement had created some difficulties but insisted that the difficulties were temporary, and localized, and could be overcome, that the achievements were more significant than the losses.[150] Mao was particularly adamant about the 'correctness' of the commune movement. He argued: 'In social struggle, the forces representing the advanced class sometimes suffer defeat not because their ideas are incorrect but because in the balance of forces engaged in struggle they are not as powerful for the time being as the

---

[148] The number of communes in 1961 was attributed to Liao Lu-yen in an interview with a Japanese correspondent, quoted in *CJTL*, No. 176, 1963, p. 17.

[149] See Table 20–9.

[150] Union Research Institute, *Case of Peng Teh-huai*, pp. 402, 423.

forces of reaction.'[151] Thus, he maintained that the commune was a natural development and would not collapse.[152] 'The dining hall is a good thing. . . . The number of
dining halls may be increased.'[153] Those who thought otherwise were sick with rightist
ideas.[154]

The opposition contended that the commune movement was premature, that the
Great Leap had been an impulsive move and had caused serious economic disloca-
tions, and that the gains could not compensate for the losses.[155] The basic issue, as one
opponent put it, was 'that Mao and the Party Central had committed a strategic
error.'[156]

The views of the two groups on the causes of the economic setback also varied. The
Maoist, or official, explanation was that three consecutive years of natural disasters in
1959–61, abrupt withdrawal of the Soviet technicians, and certain shortcomings of
the cadres had been responsible for the economic difficulties.[157] The implication was
that Mao's policies had been basically correct. However, others like Liu Shao-ch'i and
Ch'en Yün, had their misgivings. Liu was reported to have said that the weather
could account for only 30 per cent of the failure and that the rest must be attributed
to human errors.[158] By human errors, he obviously was not referring to the shortcomings of the cadres. For the policies that Liu adopted in the post-Leap period were
directed more toward reversing Mao's Great Leap program than reforming the
cadres, although a rectification campaign was also carried out during that period.

The controversy was actually more than a dispute over what happened to the
Great Leap. It represented a clash of two diametrically opposite views on how to
organize rural economic activities so as to generate and sustain growth in the agricultural sector. Four major issues were involved. First, there was the question of what
should be the incentive to motivate the peasants to work. Mao emphasized ideology.
Hence, 'let politics take command.' Income should be distributed, at least in part, on
the principle, 'to each according to his need.' Liu emphasized material reward. Let
'work-points' take command. Output should be distributed on the principle, 'to each
according to his work.' Second, with respect to property rights, Mao would opt for
complete elimination of private ownership. The peasants should not only work collectively but also live collectively. In contrast, Liu would preserve some private
ownership. Third, in Mao's view, the optimum rural organization should be large in
size, its management should be highly centralized, and its operation under the direct
control of the state. To Liu, the functioning unit should be small, with considerable
autonomy with respect to production planning and distribution, and free markets
should be permitted to exist in order to introduce some flexibility into the planning
system. The relationship between the state and the farming unit should be placed on
a contractual basis. Some, like Teng Hsiao-p'ing, even went as far as to advocate
contracts for production directly between the state and the individual households.
Fourth, concerning the method of increasing output, Mao emphasized organization
rather than technology, indigenous inputs rather than modern industrial inputs, and

---

[151] CCP Central Committee, 'Draft Resolution on Some Problems of Current Rural Work,'
in Richard Baum and Frederick C. Teiwes, *Ssu-ching: The Socialist Education Movement of
1962–1966* (Berkeley and Los Angeles: University of California Press, 1968), p. 59.

[152] *Ibid.*, pp. 410, 485; Mao Tse-tung, 'On Mei Sheng's "chi-fa," ' in *ibid.*, p. 494.

[153] 'Mao's Speech before the Eighth Plenary Session of the Central Committee,' in *ibid.*,
pp. 22 and 24.

[154] Mao Tse-tung, 'Comment on the Report on the Implementation of the Central Committee's Directive to Oppose Right Deviation in Liaoning,' in *ibid.*, p. 323.

[155] 'P'eng Teh-huai's Speech before the Eighth Plenary Session,' in *ibid.*, p. 420; 'P'eng
Teh-huai's Testimony,' in *ibid.*, p. 446; *JMJP*, August 16, 1967; *Kuang-ming Jih-pao (Enlightenment Daily*, or *KMJP*), August 9, 1967.

[156] *KMJP*, August 9, 1967.   [157] *HC*, No. 1, 1965, p. 4.

[158] *Ming Pao*, Hong Kong, April 7, 1967, p. 4.

labor rather than capital. Thus, Mao contended that collectivization must precede mechanization. One of the basic purposes of his rural industry program was to provide agriculture with more fertilizers. When that failed, his alternative was to produce more organic fertilizer through hog raising. To Mao, political dedication was more important than expertise. Liu, however, favored mechanization before collectivization, the extensive use of chemical fertilizers, and heavy reliance on technology. On the specific issue of mechanization, Mao wanted to push ahead once collectivization was completed. But Liu advocated a more conservative program with emphasis on small farm tools and irrigation equipment. In sum, the dispute was one of politics versus professionalism—between ideology, organization, and massive labor, on the one hand, and technical skills, industrial inputs, and economic incentives, on the other, as the major factors to increase output.

Reportedly, there had been a shift of power after the Lushan conference in 1959. Mao was said to have given up most of the economic decision-making power to Liu Shao-ch'i and Teng Hsiao-p'ing, but it is not clear whether he did so voluntarily or was forced to do so. In any case, the period 1960–2 witnessed a marked change of policy from the radical to the more pragmatic approach. The basic tenets of Mao's Great Leap program were dropped one by one, until all that remained was a few slogans and the commune in name only. To Mao, the revisionist policies were perhaps acceptable as temporary emergency measures. What was clearly intolerable to him was the erosion of the revolutionary spirit of the rural cadres through such bourgeois ideas as letting profits take command. In 1962, when the economy began to show signs of recovery, he made his countermove. At the tenth plenum of the Eighth Central Committee in September, 1962, Mao reminded the cadres of the importance of class struggle and called for a socialist education movement to consolidate the collective economy in the countryside.

The socialist education movement. The socialist education movement began in late 1962. Its specific purpose was to clean away bourgeois influence, cadre corruption, and other malpractices through propaganda and education of the peasant masses and the basic-level cadres.[159] The emphasis was on cleaning up the cadres' undesirable work style in handling the 'accounts, granaries, properties, and work-points.'[160] In May, 1963, the Party adopted a 'Draft Resolution on Some Problems in Current Rural Work,' which laid down two major guidelines for the movement: (1) the establishment of poor and lower-middle peasant organizations at the commune, brigade, and team levels, as a subsidiary of the Party, to supervise the work of the basic-level cadres, and (2) the systemization of cadre participation in farm labor to guarantee sound direction of production and to prevent the alienation of the cadres from the masses.[161] The document, known during the Cultural Revolution as the First Ten Points, was reportedly drafted by Mao.

After four months of experimentation, the Central Committee issued a new directive: Some Concrete Policy Formulations Concerning the Rural Socialist Education Movement (Draft).[162] This was known as the Later Ten Points, reportedly drafted by Liu Shao-ch'i. The draft shifted Mao's original focus of the movement in a subtle way. It assigned a leading role to the work teams formed by cadres from provincial or county levels to direct the movement. The reliance on the work teams tended to overshadow to some extent the influence of the poor peasant organizations. The new directive also instructed the cadres to be more lenient toward those who erred and to coordinate socialist education work with production. In effect, it ignored Mao's call for class struggle. The emphasis on moderation was perhaps understandable, for the

---

[159] For an excellent account of this movement see Baum and Teiwes, *Ssu-ching.*
[160] Hence the name, 'four clean-up movement.'
[161] For a translation of the document, see Baum and Teiwes, *Ssu-ching,* pp. 58–71.
[162] For a translation of the document, see *ibid.,* pp. 72–94.

upper-middle peasants were generally the ones with the strongest capitalist tendencies, but at the same time they were the more capable producers, and alienation of this class might reduce output.

In June, 1964, Mao apparently made an attempt to reorient the effort by listing six criteria for evaluating the success or failure of the movement.[163] At the top of the list was mobilization of the poor and lower-middle peasants. To supplement Mao's directive, the Party laid down some concrete rules for setting up the poor and lower-middle peasant organizations.[164] Three months later, in September, 1964, the revised Later Ten Points, allegedly drafted by Liu, was issued.[165] The new directive indicated a turn to the left. There was a hardening of the class lines in dealing with the masses, and fewer restraints against attacking the basic-level cadres or cadres of the higher-level organizations. Subsequently, the cadres came under heavy fire. They were mainly accused of economic corruption, such as mishandling of public funds, acceptance of bribes, extravagance, misappropriation of work-points, and permitting spontaneous capitalist activities to flourish at the expense of collective undertakings.

Beginning in 1965, the movement underwent a sharp change in its nature. In a twenty-three point directive promulgated in January, 1965, the Party checked the indiscriminate attacks against the basic-level cadres. But it also broadened the scope of the movement. The Party declared that the principal contradiction was the antagonistic contradiction between socialism and capitalism, much more fundamental than the nonantagonistic contradiction between the corrupted cadres and the peasants.[166] 'The key point of the movement is to rectify those people in position of authority within the Party who take the capitalist road and to progressively consolidate and develop the socialist battlefront in the urban and rural areas.'[167] Toward the end of 1965, the movement turned upward, focusing on the 'bureaucratism, conservatism, and commandism' of cadres at the county level. About the same time, the Maoists launched the Cultural Revolution with an attack against the leading cadres in the Peking Municipal Party Committee. The attack soon turned into a stormy campaign that completely overshadowed the socialist education movement in the countryside.

The Cultural Revolution, 1966–68, and Its Aftermath

The Cultural Revolution had many ramifications, among which was the political purge of Liu and other opponents of Mao, motivated in part by broad policy differences, particularly differences in economic policies. The immediate goal was to seize power from Liu Shao-ch'i and to purify the Party of all those elements that 'followed the capitalist road.' The long-term goal was to get rid of all revisionist ideas and institutions and to rekindle the revolutionary spirit of the whole nation, particularly that of the younger generation. The revolution began in late 1965 with Mao's seizure of the propaganda machinery and the purge of the Peking Party Committee in 1966. It then led to a reshuffle of the top leadership, the rampage of the Red Guards, and the spread of the purge in the latter part of 1966. Beginning in 1967, the workers, the army, and, in some areas, the peasants were involved in the struggle. For three years the political turmoil continued. Finally, in the fall of 1968, Liu was formally dismissed from his posts in the Party. By late 1968, Revolutionary Committees had been

---

[163] *Ibid.*, p. 27.

[164] 'Organization Rules of Poor and Lower-Middle Peasant Association,' pp. 95–101.

[165] CCP, 'Some Concrete Policy Formulations Concerning the Rural Socialist Education Movement (Revised Draft),' in *ibid.*, pp. 102–17.

[166] CCP, 'Some Problems Currently Arising in the Course of the Rural Socialist Education Movement,' in *ibid.*, pp. 118–26.

[167] *Ibid.*, p. 120.

established in all the twenty-nine provinces, municipalities, and autonomous regions. In the spring of 1969, Lin Piao declared before the Ninth Congress that the Cultural Revolution had achieved a great success.

During that period, the peasants had their share of the ordeal, although the political struggle was, for the most part, confined to suburban communes, and, by and large, the conflict was less stormy than in the urban areas.[168] As early as August, 1966, Red Guard activities began to spread from the cities to the suburban communes.[169] About the same time, the urban cadres mobilized the peasants from nearby communes to go to the cities and fight the students.[170] The Party center, however, soon decided to curb the revolutionary activities for the time being for fear that the spread of the Cultural Revolution might interfere with the autumn harvest. The Party's instruction was to 'grasp revolution and promote production,' with the accent on production.[171] It was not until November, 1966, that the Party tacitly removed the ban on revolutionary activities.[172] From then on, numerous revolutionary organizations sprang up in many suburban communes and production brigades, clashing with the local cadres and, at times, with each other. In December the Party issued a ten-point directive that formally sanctioned organized political struggle in the countryside.[173] The directive called upon the rebels to rectify the cadres and peasants with capitalistic tendencies and to reorganize the leadership in charge of production and distribution.

Subsequently, rural cadres in many localities were attacked almost indiscriminately, resulting in a temporary state of leadership paralysis and labor indiscipline. As the political struggle intensified, the local cadres resorted to many tactics in their counterattack, the most effective of which was perhaps 'economism,' that is, the use of economic benefits to incite people to resist the Cultural Revolution. The resistance took many forms: Peasants were instigated to leave their production posts to go to the cities to demand various welfare benefits. Others illegally distributed a large portion of public grain reserves. Still others divided, slaughtered, or sold their draft animals. Youths who had settled in the countryside were urged to return to the cities. Apparently such practices were widespread enough to alarm the Party leaders, who hastily issued a series of directives in January, 1967, to curb the development.[174] At the same time the army was ordered to support and help the revolutionary masses.[175]

As the spring planting season approached, the chaotic struggles had to be stopped. Accordingly, in an open letter to the poor and lower-middle peasants, the Central

---

[168] For an in-depth study of the Cultural Revolution in the countryside during 1966–68, see Richard Baum, *The Cultural Revolution in the Countryside: Anatomy of a Limited Rebellion* (forthcoming).

[169] *JMJP*, February 20, 1967.

[170] *Chinese Communist Party Documents of the Great Proletarian Cultural Revolution 1966–1967* (Hong Kong: Union Research Institute, 1968), p. 74 (hereafter: *CCP Documents*).

[171] 'Regulations of the CCP Central Committee Concerning the Great Proletarian Cultural Revolution in the Countryside below the County Level,' *CCP Documents*, pp. 77–78; *JMJP*, September 7, 1966.

[172] *JMJP*, November 10, 1966.

[173] 'Directive of the CCP Central Committee Concerning the Great Proletarian Cultural Revolution in the Countryside (draft),' *CCP Documents*, pp. 137–38.

[174] 'Document of the CCP Central Committee, the State Council and the Central Military Commission, January 11, 1967,' 'Circular of the CCP Central Committee Concerning the Opposition to Economism, January 11, 1967,' and 'Document of the CCP Central Committee, the State Council and the Central Military Commission, January 19, 1967,' *CCP Documents*, pp. 139, 163–64.

[175] 'Decision of the CCP Central Committee, the State Council, the Central Military Commission, and the Cultural Revolution Group of the Central Committee Concerning the Resolute Support of People's Army for the Revolutionary Masses of the Left, January 23, 1967,' *ibid.*, pp. 193–94.

Committee called upon them to mobilize immediately all forces to prepare for spring cultivation and to support the majority of the cadres who were 'good or basically good.'[176] However, the factional violence in many localities continued. It was not until the Party leaders categorically prohibited further power seizures in production brigades and teams during the spring planting season that the factional conflicts subsided somewhat.[177]

In the period between late spring and winter of 1967, the army began to play an increasingly important role. The military had been assigned to mitigate the confusion in the countryside and to participate actively in farm work. Partly as a result of the army's intervention, there had been a general decline in revolutionary activities in most areas, with the exception of some suburban communes. In November, 1967, the Party reoriented the direction of the struggle toward attacking Liu Shao-ch'i's capitalist-individualist principles and practices of agrarian organization and administration.[178] In December, the Party laid down the guidelines for rural Cultural Revolution in the coming slack season of 1967–68.[179] The new directive emphasized the repudiation of self-interest and revisionism, and unity among the various factions in the villages. All peasants were instructed to participate in Mao Tse-tung Thought Study Classes. However, the current commune organization, with the production team as the basic unit, and the system of private plots were to remain unchanged. Seizing power in the production teams was generally not permitted.

In the spring of 1968, a drive was launched to establish revolutionary committees at the commune and brigade levels. Despite the Party leaders' effort to maintain peace and order and to forge revolutionary alliances, the first half of 1968 witnessed an upsurge of factional conflict. Again the military was called in to suppress the leftists. In the late summer and autumn of 1968, a massive campaign of 'struggle-criticism-transformation' was launched in the villages. Meanwhile, millions of urban youths and others were sent to the countryside for 're-education.' By the end of 1968, the violent conflicts diminished as the nature of the Revolution shifted from local power struggles to an ideological struggle. Since late 1968, there have been indications that Mao was moving in the direction of reorganizing the local leadership and reforming certain institutions. First, following the rural 'struggle-criticism-transformation' campaign, the Party leaders ousted the conservative cadres to make way for a leadership of poor and lower-middle peasants, who were more radical in outlook and who had less to lose if the regime again pushed forward with Mao's aggressive policies.[180] Second, there were signs of the growing importance of the brigade at the expense of the team. The management of rural primary education and the medical care system were assigned to the brigades, in part to expand collective activities within the commune and in part to reduce state expenditures, as the responsibility of financing those programs was also transferred to the brigades. In some localities in Kiangsi, mergers of teams and brigades into larger units were reported. Third, there was a greater emphasis on political work. Along with the 'struggle-criticism-transformation' campaign, the propaganda effort to induce the peasants to 'learn from

[176] 'Letter from the Central Committee of the CCP to the Nation's Poor and Lower-Middle Peasants and Cadres at All Levels in Rural People's Communes, February 20, 1967,' *ibid.*, pp. 329–30.
[177] 'Circular of the CCP Central Committee Concerning the Undesirability of Seizure of Power in Rural Production Brigades and Teams During the Spring Period, March 7, 1967,' *ibid.*, pp. 347–48.
[178] *JMJP*, November 1967.
[179] 'Directive of the CCP Central Committee Concerning the Great Cultural Revolution in the Countryside in the Coming Winter and Next Spring, December 4, 1967,' *CCP Documents*, pp. 627–29.
[180] Colina MacDougall, 'The Cultural Revolution in the Communes: Back to 1958?' *Current Scene*, Vol. 7, No. 7, April 11, 1969.

Tachai' was intensified.[181] Included in Tachai's lessons were hard work, ideological purity, and a new work-point system based on the political consciousness of the peasants. In some areas, handicraft workers were absorbed into the commune. Finally, there was a renewed emphasis on small factories in the countryside.[182] But, while the direction of change was clear, the pace was deliberate. Except for the campaign to consolidate the leadership of the poor and lower-middle peasants and the emphasis on small rural factories, the new developments were not carried out on a national scale. As yet there has been no indication of any change in the Party policy toward the private plots, the stronghold of private enterprise in the countryside.

In 1969 and 1970, two major developments in the countryside are worth noting. The first was the continuation of the 'to-the-countryside' movement. In early 1969, about 20 million youths were sent to the farms.[183] There were three main reasons for such a policy: (1) There were insufficient facilities in the cities to provide college education or employment for all. In the villages, even unskilled labor can be fully utilized in construction projects and during the busy farming seasons. (2) The movement was designed to close the cultural gap between city and the countryside. The urban youths, for their part, were to experience physical hardship and learn to tackle all problems with little more than their bare hands, as the revolutionaries had once done. In this sense, it was a training program. On the other hand, it was a program for a 'domestic peace corps.' The youths brought with them some formal education, which most peasants lack, and they could provide useful services as teachers, barefoot doctors, workers in rural factories, accountants, and new cadres. (3) Finally, there was the economic reason. Because the standard of living was higher in the cities than in the villages, a sizeable shift of population from the urban to rural areas would result in some savings.

The other major development was the construction of numerous small rural factories and electric power stations, in part 'to prepare for war,' but mainly to support agriculture.[184] The industries included iron and steel, coal, machinery, electric power, cement, chemical fertilizers, and nonferrous metals. The factories were built with local funds and generally run by cadres at the county level. The current program of rural industrialization seemed to be more orderly and more pragmatically carried out than the Great Leap. Whether it would contribute substantially to agricultural expansion remained to be seen.

How well did the agricultural sector perform during those years? According to official reports, it had never performed better. In 1966, the first year of the Cultural Revolution, the harvest was hailed as the best in seventeen years.[185] On November 14, 1967, Chou stated that grain output in 1967 increased by 5 to 6 per cent over 1966. Hsieh Fu-chih also claimed that grain output increased by 9 million to 10 million tons until 1967.[186] In 1968, Communist China claimed to have gathered another rich harvest, but an increase in grain output was reported for only part of the country.[187] Taken together, these official reports indicate: (1) a continuously rising trend since 1965, and (2) that the increase in 1967 over 1966 was rather small. The semiofficial estimates of grain output (200 million, 220 million, and 230 million tons in 1965–67, respectively) seem consistent with the reported trend.[188]

---

[181] Tachai refers to the Tachai Brigade of Tachai Commune in Shihyang County, Shansi Province. In February, 1964, Mao called upon all peasants to learn from Tachai, which had followed closely Mao's line.

[182] TKP, October 25, 1969: *The New York Times*, November 2, 1967.

[183] *Economist* (London), March 1, 1969, p. 31. [184] *JMJP*, August 24, 1970.

[185] NCNA, December 27, 1966. [186] *Current Scene*, 6, No. 12 (July 17, 1968): 5.

[187] *Peking Review*, No. 50, 1968, pp. 13–15.

[188] For sources of the semiofficial estimates, see Table 20–9. I have termed these estimates semiofficial because they are from secondary sources.

It is difficult to judge whether the level of output and the trend suggested by the Communists reports reflect the situation accurately, for data available for independent estimates of agricultural production in the period are virtually nil, and whatever tentative estimates of grain output there are differ with respect to both the trend and the absolute level.[189] In any case, two observations are perhaps worth making. First, the semiofficial estimates of grain output for 1966 and 1967 are higher than all the independent estimates. Second, weather conditions in 1967 were reportedly much more favorable than in 1966, and the supply of fertilizer also increased by 1 million tons in 1967.[190] Yet, according to Chou En-lai, grain output in 1967 was only 5 to 6 per cent above that of 1966, a strikingly small increase in view of the favorable weather conditions. It will be recalled that the revolutionary activities in 1967 were much more widespread and violent than in 1966. If Chou's estimate was accurate, then it can only mean that the Cultural Revolution indeed had serious adverse effects on grain production in 1967.

How good the harvests were in 1968–70 one can only guess. Official sources claimed another rich harvest for all kinds of crops in 1968, a better grain harvest in 1969, and that total grain output exceeded the previous records in 1970.[191] The various independent estimates of grain output (in millions of tons) are as follows:[192]

	1967	1968	1969	1970
(1)	190	180–85	190	
(2)		182	187–90	
(3)	220	187	210	
(4)		180	195	
(5)			200	
(6)				200 +

While these estimates vary, they all indicate a drop in output in 1968 and an increase in 1969 over the preceding year. Whether or not the drop and subsequent rise were due to an increase and then decrease in political turmoil in those years is not clear. In any event, if one compares the most optimistic estimate of 210 million tons in 1969 with the official grain output of 154 million tons in 1952 and 185 million tons in 1957, the average annual rates of growth of grain production are, respectively, 1.9 and 1.1 per cent per annum, a rather grim performance relative to the average annual rate of population growth of about 2 per cent.

CONCLUDING REMARKS

At this juncture, Mao faces the same fundamental problem he faced before he launched the Great Leap: how to achieve a breakthrough in agricultural production by harnessing the enormous energy of the peasants with organizational means and ideological indoctrination. The setting of the problem, however, is considerably different from what it was in 1957. In the first place, total population in 1970 is undoubtedly much larger than in 1957. No one, perhaps not even the leaders, knows for sure the size of China's population today. Peking has referred loosely to a total of

---

[189] See Table 20–9. [190] See Table 20–9.
[191] *Peking Review*, No. 40, October 4, 1968, p. 33; *TKP*, November 17, 1969, p. 1; *Peking Review*, No. 2, January 8, 1971, p. 6.
[192] The sources for these figures are: (1) *The New York Times*, January 19, 1970, p. 49; (2) *Economist*, December 13–19, 1969; (3) *Far Eastern Economic Review, 1970 Yearbook*, 1970, p. 110; (4) Economic Intelligence Unit, *Quarterly Economic Review*, No. 1, 1970, p. 7; M. R. Larsen, 'Mainland China's Economy: An Upsurge But No "Leap," ' *Foreign Agriculture*, May 25, 1970, p. 3; (6) *The New York Times*, October 4, 1970, p. 9. *Ming Pao*, Hong Kong, February 28, 1971, p. 4.

700 million. One independent estimate presents a range of 754 million–933 million for 1968.[193] Official population figures released during the Cultural Revolution suggest a total of 730 million to 750 million in 1968.[194] In any case, there seems to be little doubt that total population increased substantially over the last decade, even though there had been a slowdown in population growth during the lean years of 1960–62. In all likelihood, the age structure of the total population has also changed, as the initial upsurge in population in the early 1950's has now turned into a new crop of teen-agers and young adults. As a result of these changes, a larger volume of agricultural output would have to be used to feed and clothe the increase in population, the savings ratio is likely to be lower, and the regime would have to provide productive employment for a larger labor force. In particular, the grain situation probably remains critical, for, even if we take the lower estimate of 754 million people in 1968, grain output would have to increase to about 220 million tons just to maintain the same level of per capita output in 1957.

Second, in recent years, Communist China's defense expenditures might well have risen considerably for a number of reasons. The rather impressive record of nuclear development since 1964 indicates that Communist China has embarked on an ambitious military program. The internal strife during the Cultural Revolution and the tensions along the Sino-Soviet border probably increased the need to maintain a high level of military preparedness. The predominance of the military in the new power structure since the Ninth Congress further suggests the likelihood of a larger military program. All this means that, unless total output increased faster than personal consumption and defense expenditures, resources for investment would be lower—and the pressure for the agricultural sector to generate savings greater—than in 1957. In sum, a breakthrough in agricultural production is much more imperative and no less difficult than ever before.

In the light of the experience of the past two decades, the prospects of a breakthrough will depend largely on the availability of nonconventional inputs, particularly chemical fertilizers; on the volume and effectiveness of agricultural investment; and, above all, on the size of the farm unit and the incentive system. Mao's thought can provide the zeal and dedication, but it is no substitute for material reward, technology, or capital. Ironically, it is by intensifying rather than eliminating the revisionist policies that the Maoists will have the best chance to break through.

---

[193] J. S. Aird, *Estimates and Projections of the Population of Mainland China, 1953–1968* (Washington, D.C.: Government Printing Office, 1968), pp. 44–49. Figures refer to totals in January 1 of the year.

[194] *Far Eastern Economic Review*, September 12, 1968, p. 498.

Table 20-6—Agricultural Production, 1949-59

	Pre-1949 Peak	1949	1950	1951	1952	1953	1954	1955	1956	1957	1958	1959
Gross value of output[a] (billion yüan)	—b	32.59	38.36	41.97	48.39	49.91	51.57	55.54	58.29	60.35	67.10	78.30
Output (in thousands of tons) of:												
Grain	138,698	108,095	124,690	135,055	154,395	156,900	160,435	174,810	182,512	185,000	250,000	270,050
Rice	57,341	48,645	55,100	60,555	68,425	71,270	70,850	78,025	82,480	86,825	113,700	—
Wheat	23,295	13,808	14,495	17,230	18,125	18,280	23,335	22,965	24,801	23,650	28,950	—
Potatoes[c]	6,331	9,842	12,390	14,000	16,325	16,655	16,980	18,595	21,851	21,900	45,400	—
Coarse grain	51,731	35,800	42,705	43,270	51,520	50,695	49,270	54,925	53,380	52,650	61,950	—
Soybean	11,307	5,086	7,435	8,630	9,520	9,930	9,060	9,120	10,234	10,050	10,500	11,500
Peanut	3,171	1,268	1,739	2,096	2,316	2,127	2,767	2,926	3,336	2,571	2,800	—
Rapeseed	1,907	734	683	778	932	879	878	969	923	887	1,100	—
Sesame		326	—	—	481	521	229	464	339	312	—	—
Cotton	849	444	692	1,031	1,304	1,175	1,065	1,518	1,445	1,640	2,100	2,410
Jute and hemp	109	37	79	250	305	138	137	257	258	360	390	—
Cured tobacco	179	43	56	242	222	213	232	298	399	256	380	420
Sugar cane	5,652	2,642	3,133	4,629	7,116	7,209	8,592	8,116	8,655	10,392	13,525	—
Sugarbeet	329	190	245	360	479	505	989	1,596	1,646	1,501	2,900	—
Tea	225	41	65	79	82	85	92	108	120	111	140	—
Fruits		—	—	—	2,443	2,969	2,977	2,550	3,105	3,247	3,900	—
Domesticated cocoons		31	33	47	62	60	65	67	72	68	84	—
Tussah cocoons		12	25	26	61	12	26	64	62	44	57	—
Marine products		448	912	1,332	1,666	1,900	2,293	2,518	2,648	3,120	4,060	—
Livestock[d] (million head)												
Cattle	45.27	43.94	48.10	52.09	56.60	60.08	63.62	65.95	66.60	63.61	—	65.43
Horses	6.48	4.88	—	—	6.13	6.51	6.94	7.31	7.37	7.30	—	7.60
Donkey	12.15	9.49	—	—	11.81	12.21	12.70	12.40	11.69	10.86	—	—
Mules	4.60	1.47	—	—	1.64	1.64	1.72	1.72	1.71	1.68	—	—
Camels		0.25	—	—	0.28	0.30	0.32	0.36	0.36	0.36	—	—
Sheep and goats	62.52	42.35	46.73	52.87	61.78	72.02	81.30	84.22	91.65	98.58	108.86	112.53
Hogs	78.53	57.75	64.01	74.40	89.76	96.13	101.72	87.92	84.03	145.89	160.00	180.00

a Totals for 1949–57 are in 1952 prices, and those for 1958–59, in 1957 prices.
b (—) means not available.
c Output of potatoes in grain equivalent weight, i.e., one-fourth of natural weight.
d Totals refer to midyear totals.

Sources: TGY, pp. 100, 118–19, 124–25, 127; JMJP, January 23, 1960, p. 1; TCKT, No. 3, 1957, p. 33; No. 14, 1957, pp. 9, 11; CHYTC, No. 1, 1960, p. 27; Chen, Chinese Economic Statistics, p. 340; Government of India, Report of the Indian Delegation to China on Agricultural Planning and Techniques (Delhi: Government of India Press, 1956), pp. 97, 103; Economic Intelligence Unit, Three Monthly Review, Annual Supplement, June, 1962, p. 4.

Table 20-7—Agricultural Taxation and Marketing, 1950–57

	1950	1951	1952	1953	1954	1955	1956	1957
(1) Crop production (million tons of fine-grain equivalent)	109.8	124.7	147.0	144.0	149.4	164.8	170.5	173.8
(2) Agricultural tax (million tons of fine-grain equivalent)	13.5	18.1	19.4	17.2	18.6	19.2	18.3	19.7
(3) Ratio: tax/output (%)	12.3	14.5	13.2	11.9	12.4	11.6	10.7	11.3
(4) Government revenue (million yüan)	6,519	12,967	17,560	21,762	26,237	27,203	28,743	30,702
(5) Taxes paid by peasants (million yüan)	2,854	4,030	3,777	3,596	3,767	3,738	3,526	3,704
(6) Ratio: taxes/revenue (%)	43.8	31.1	21.5	16.5	14.4	13.7	12.3	12.1
(7) Agricultural production (million current yüan)	—	—	48,390	54,950	58,690	62,870	67,970	73,870
(8) Agricultural sales (million yüan)	8,000	10,500	12,970	15,320	17,360	17,800	18,400	20,280
(9) Ratio: sales/production (%)	—	—	26.8	27.9	29.6	28.3	27.1	27.4
(10) Grain and soybean output (million tons of fine-grain equivalent)	—	—	122.9	124.3	129.3	139.0	146.1	147.9
(11) Grain and soybean marketings (million tons of fine-grain equivalent)	—	—	—	33.2	42.4	44.6	42.7	42.9
(12) Ratio: Marketings/output (%)	—	—	—	26.7	32.8	32.1	29.2	29.0

Sources: Li, *Agricultural Taxation*, pp. 112–13, 131, 156, 171, 180, 192–93; Perkins, *Market Control*, p. 248; *TGY*, pp. 118, 168, 173. Gross value of agricultural production in current prices is obtained by inflating the series in constant prices by the price index of agricultural products sold. Grain and soybean marketings in grain year have been converted to totals in calendar year. For example, the total for 1953 is the sum of three-fourths of that for 1952–53 and one-fourth of that for 1953–54.

Table 20–8—Grain Output and Agricultural Production: Ten Estimates, 1952–57

	1952	1953	1954	1955	1956	1957	Annual Growth Rate
Grain output (million tons)[a]							
(1) Official	154	157	160	175	182	185	3.7
(2) Jones & Poleman	165	168	168	175	182	185	2.3
(3) Dawson	170	166	170	185	178	185	1.7
(4) Liu and Yeh	177	180	184	186	184	185	0.9
(5) Meeker	—	160	153	175	160	170	1.2
(6) Wu	184	180	177	184	182	185	0.1
Agricultural production (%)[b]							
(7) Official	100	103	107	115	120	125	4.5
(8) Hollister	100	111	112	119	128	136	6.4
(9) Liu-Yeh	100	102	104	105	108	109	1.7
(10) Wu, et al.	100	99	99	101	105	106	1.2

[a] Output of potatoes measured in one-fourth of natural weight.

[b] Official index is based on gross value of agricultural output in constant 1952 prices. Hollister's estimate refers to gross value added in current prices. Other estimates are based on gross value added in 1952 prices.

Sources: (1) *TGY*, p. 119. (2) P. D. Jones and T. T. Poleman, 'Communes and the Agricultural Crisis,' *Food Research Institute Studies*, 3, No. 1 (February, 1962): 4. (3) *Economic Profile*, p. 93. (4) Liu and Yeh, *Economy of Chinese Mainland*, p. 132. (5) *Current Scene*, 1, No. 32 (January 22, 1962): 3. (6) Y. L. Wu, *The Economy of Communist China* (New York: Praeger, 1965), p. 146. (7) *TGY*, p. 118. (8) W. W. Hollister, *China's Gross National Product and Social Accounts, 1950–57* (Glencoe, Ill.: Free Press, 1958), p. 12. (9) Liu and Yeh, *Economy of Chinese Mainland*, p. 66. (10) Y. L. Wu, F. P. Hoeber, and M. M. Rockwell, *Economic Potential of Communist China* (Menlo Park, Calif.: Stanford Research Institute, 1964), 1: p. 241.

SELECTED BIBLIOGRAPHY

CHAO, KUO-CHUN. *Agrarian Policy of the Chinese Communist Party*. London: Asia Publishing House, 1960. A historical account of the Party's agrarian policy up to the period of the communes.

CHEN, NAI-RUENN, and WALTER GALENSON. *The Chinese Economy Under Communism*. Chicago: Aldine Publishing Co., 1969. A good summary of agriculture's contribution to economic growth, the controversy over grain output estimates in the post-1958 period and problems and policies of technical reform.

DAWSON, OWEN L. *Communist China's Agriculture: Its Development and Future Potential*. New York: Praeger Publishers, 1970.

HOU, CHI-MING. 'Sources of Agricultural Growth in Communist China,' Journal of Asian Studies, XXVII: 4, August 1968, 721–37. A lucid discussion of the factors responsible for increase in agricultural output.

Ministry of Food and Agriculture, Government of India. *Report of the Indian Delegation to China on Agricultural Planning and Techniques*. New Delhi: Government of India Press, 1956. A firsthand report on agricultural planning in China.

PERKINS, DWIGHT H. *Agricultural Development in China, 1368–1968*. Chicago: Aldine Publishing Co., 1969.

———. *Market Control and Planning in Communist China*. Cambridge, Mass.: Harvard University Press, 1966. Discusses (on pp. 21–98) Communist experiences with centralized and decentralized controls in agriculture.

SCHRAN, PETER. *The Development of Chinese Agriculture, 1950–1959*. Urbana: University of Illinois Press, 1969.

SCHURMANN, Franz. *Ideology and Organization in Communist China*. 2d. ed. Berkeley and Los Angeles: University of California Press, 1968. A stimulating study of the Party policy toward the peasants in an historical and sociological context. See esp. pp. 404–500, 576–92.

TANG, ANTHONY M. 'Policy and Performance in Agriculture,' in W. GALENSON, A. ECKSTEIN, and T. C. LIU, eds., *Economic Trends in Communist China* (Chicago: Aldine Publishing Co., 1968), pp. 459–507. A technical analysis of the sources of agricultural growth and implications.

WALKER, KENNETH R. 'Organization of Agricultural Production,' in GALENSON *et al.* eds., *Economic Trends in Communist China* (see above), pp. 397–458. A study of the cooperatives and communes in 1955–65.

WU, YUAN-LI. *The Economy of Communist China*. New York: Praeger Publishers, 1965. A concise analysis of the problems of agricultural development (pp. 130–56) and measurement of performance.

Table 20-9—Selected Indicators of Economic Change, 1958-68

	1958	1959	1960	1961	1962	1963	1964	1965	1966	1967	1968	1969
(1) Grain output (million tons)												
(a) Official	250	270	150	162	174	183	200	200	220	230	—	—
(b) Jones & Poleman	210	192	185	185	—	—	—	—	—	—	—	—
(c) U.S. Consulate	194	168	160	167	178	179	183	180	—	—	—	—
(d) Washenko	—	—	—	—	180	178	190	185	178	190	182	200
(e) Wu	175	154	130	140	160	183	—	—	—	—	—	—
(f) Dawson	204	170	160	170	180	185	195	207	205	204	—	—
(g) Japanese source	200	185	150	160	180	190	190	200	210	215	206	—
(h) FCNP	195	160	120	130	135	136	152	150	150	155	152	160
(i) 'Official' adjusted	215	193	161	189	204	219	238	258	—	—	—	—
(2) Other agricultural products (million tons)												
Cotton	1.9	1.8	1.4	0.9	0.9	1.0	1.2	1.3	—	—	—	—
Soybean	9.8	9.5	8.2	7.9	7.7	7.8	6.9	6.8	—	—	—	—
Peanut	2.7	2.3	1.9	1.7	1.6	1.9	2.3	2.3	—	—	—	—
Rapeseed	1.1	0.9	1.1	0.6	0.5	0.5	0.7	0.7	—	—	—	—
Sesame	0.4	0.4	0.3	0.3	0.3	0.2	0.3	0.3	—	—	—	—
(3) Imports (million U.S. dollars)	1,825	2,060	2,030	1,495	1,150	1,200	1,475	1,740	2,035	1,945	1,820	1,825
(4) Exports (million U.S. dollars)	1,910	2,205	1,945	1,525	1,525	1,560	1,770	1,995	2,170	1,915	1,890	2,060

(5) Grain imports (million tons)	0	0	0	4.4	6.0	4.6	6.8	5.5	6.4	4.0	4.5	4.7
(6) Fertilizer supply (thousand tons)	2,700	2,955	3,320	2,283	3,100	4,600	4,530	7,000	8,500	9,500	—	—
Output	1,244	1,765	2,460	1,400	2,100	2,900	3,500	4,500	5,600	6,000	—	—
Imports	1,456	1,190	860	883	1,000	1,700	1,030	2,500	3,500	3,500	6,000	6,000
(7) Population (millions)	650	667	682	696	706	715	727	734	749	765	781	797

Sources: (1) (a) For 1958–65, see Edwin F. Jones, 'The Emerging Pattern of China's Economic Revolution,' in *Economic Profile*, p. 93; for 1966, see Han Suyin, *China in the Year 2001* (New York: Basic Books, 1967), p. 54 (Han Suyin did not attribute these figures to any Chinese leaders); for 1967, see 'Communist China Economy at Mid-Year 1968: Eighteen Months of Disorder,' *Current Scene*, 6, No. 12 (July 17, 1968): 3. (b) P. P. Jones and T. T. Poleman, 'Communes and the Agricultural Crisis in Communist China,' *Food Research Institute Studies*, 3, No. 1 (February, 1962): 4. (c) R. F. Emery, 'Recent Economic Developments in Communist China,' *Asian Survey*, 6, No. 6, June, 1966); 303. (d) S. Washenko, 'Agriculture in Mainland China—1968,' *Current Scene*, 7, No. 6 (March 31, 1969): 8. Marion R. Larsen, 'Mainland China's Economy: An Upsurge But No Leap,' *Foreign Agriculture*, 8, No. 21 (May 25, 1970): 3. (e) Wu, *The Economy*, p. 146. (f) E. F. Jones, *Emerging Pattern*, p. 93; O. L. Dawson, *Communist China's Agricultural Development and Future Potential*, U.S. Department of State, 1968, p. 197. (g) *CJTL*, No. 294, 1967, p. 7; *Issues and Studies*, 5, No. 12 (September, 1969): 60; Ch'en Ting-chung, 'Food Production in Mainland China,' Paper presented at the First Sino-American Conference on Mainland China, Taipei, December 14–19, 1970. (h) *Fei-ching Nien-pao 1967* (*Yearbook on Chinese Communism*) (Taipei: Institute for the Study of Chinese Communist Problems, 1967), p. 979. (i) S. Swamy and S. J. Burki, 'Food Grain Output in the People's Republic of China,' *China Quarterly*, No. 41, January–March, 1970, p. 62.

(2) Emery, 'Recent Economic Developments,' p. 304.
(3), (4) R. L. Price, 'International Trade of Communist China, 1950–65,' *Economic Profile*, p. 584; 'China's Foreign Trade in 1969,' *Current Scene*, 8, No. 16 (October 7, 1970): 2.
(5) Larsen, 'Mainland China's Economy,' p. 2.
(6) M. R. Larsen, 'China's Agriculture Under Communism,' *Economic Profile*, p. 246; *Mainland China in the World Economy* (Washington, D.C.: Government Printing Office, 1967), pp. 237–38; *Current Scene*, 8, No. 16 (Oct. 7, 1970): 6.
(7) John S. Aird, *Estimates and Projections of the Population of Mainland China: 1953–1986* (Washington, D.C.: U.S. Government Printing Office, 1968), pp. 42, 44.

21

ECONOMIC DEVELOPMENT AND INDUSTRIALIZATION

LAWRENCE J. LAU*

INTRODUCTION

THE purpose of this chapter is to provide a general survey of the process of industrialization in Communist China in the two decades following 1949. First, the changing roles of the industrial sector in the different stages of Communist Chinese national development are briefly indicated. Next, the choices of specific industrialization strategies for the achievement of various economic and noneconomic objectives are analyzed. There follows an evaluation of the performance of the industrial sector on the aggregate and subsectoral levels with regard to rates of growth of output and productivity. Finally, a general evaluation of the degree of success of the industrialization program in Communist China is given, together with a brief discussion of the future prospects of development.

The two decades under consideration are commonly divided into the following five periods: (1) rehabilitation, 1949–52; (2) First Five-Year Plan, 1953–57; (3) Second Five-Year Plan,[1] 1958–60; (4) readjustment, 1961–65; and (5) Third Five-Year Plan,[2] 1966–70. The discussion in this chapter will follow this temporal division.

Before proceeding further, a word of caution needs to be said about the statistics. It is well known that official Communist Chinese statistics are of very uneven quality and comparability.[3] Many scholars of the Chinese economy have chosen to construct or reconstruct independent estimates. Both official and secondary figures are utilized in this paper. However, it should be emphasized that the figures presented are subject to unknown and possibly rather wide margins of error.

THE ROLE OF INDUSTRY

The long-run objective of the Communist Chinese regime may be taken to be the attainment of the perfect Communist society, organized in completely decentralized

* The author is grateful to Grace H. Wu and Professor Pan A. Yotopoulos for helpful suggestions, to Annabella Li for competent research assistance, and to Fram Poundstone for skillful preparation of the tables. Financial support from the East Asian Studies Committee of Stanford University for some of the research needed is gratefully acknowledged. Responsibility for errors, however, rests entirely with the author.

[1] Usually referred to as the Great Leap Forward.

[2] Generally referred to as the Great Proletarian Cultural Revolution and its aftermath.

[3] See, for instance, the excellent discussion in C. M. Li, *The Statistical System of Communist China* (Berkeley and Los Angeles: University of California Press, 1962).

and self-sufficient units and on the principle of distribution according to need. However, in the intermediate and short run, the consolidation and preservation of Communist control at home and enhancement of national power abroad must be regarded as the primary goal.

In pursuit of this latter goal, the Chinese economy is called upon to undertake certain necessary tasks, namely: (1) provision of essential consumption;[4] (2) generation of an economic surplus that may be used for investment or foreign aid; (3) production of national defense goods; (4) establishment of an industrial and technological base for research, development, and production of advanced national defense goods in the shortest time possible; and (5) maintenance of economic independence from foreign and natural influences.

Not all these five tasks are always consistent and simultaneously feasible. In different periods and under different circumstances, one or more of the tasks are stressed, while the others are relegated to secondary positions. Moreover, other considerations, ideological or political, which often remain implicit, may dictate courses of actions that are incompatible with the above economic tasks. Economic gains, therefore, may be *rationally* foregone in exchange for ideological or political gains.

It follows, both from the nature of the economic tasks and the importance of non-economic factors, that the conventional objectives of economic development, e.g., maximum growth in per capita output or per capita consumption (broadly defined), may not be applicable to the Chinese case. Hence the industrial sector may be called upon to serve roles that are different from those assigned to it in other developing countries. These roles also undergo changes as the conditions of the economy and the experiences of the Chinese decision-makers vary. I shall examine the changing role of industry in Communist China during each of five periods.

The Changing Tasks of the Industrial Sector

The period of rehabilitation (1949–52). In 1949–52, the major concern of the Chinese Communist Government was restoration of the productive capacity paralyzed and destroyed during the war, in particular the industrial base in Manchuria. A subsidiary goal was production of military goods for the Korean conflict. On the whole, the industrial sector was only called upon to perform tasks (3) and (4). By contrast, agriculture had the twofold task of providing for essential consumption—mainly food—and generating an economic surplus in the form of raw materials for industry and exports in exchange for imports of capital and military equipment. This role remained essentially unchanged all through the 1950's.

Also during this period, steps were initiated for the takeover of certain industrial enterprises by the state. However, the socialization drive did not proceed on a massive scale until the First Five-Year Plan period.

The First Five-Year Plan (1953–57). During this period, a Stalinist strategy of development was adopted after the Soviet model, in which rapid industrialization through comprehensive planning was the most important objective. Industry continued to be primarily concerned with the execution of tasks (2), (3), and (4). Priority, in terms of the allocation of investment and other resources, was decidedly given to heavy industry. Soviet aid provided the backbone of the industrialization program and partially dictated the adoption of large-scale plants using relatively capital-intensive techniques of production.

---

[4] Essential consumption is defined as the minimum level of aggregate consumption necessary for the maintenance of the existing government in effective control. It includes aggregate personal subsistence consumption and aggregate government consumption, as well as military and police expenditures necessary for the maintenance of the government in power, but excludes luxury consumption and basically offensive military expenditures.

Agriculture was subordinated to industry, especially heavy industry, and continued to execute its role as provider of essential consumption and supplier of raw materials and exports. Assertion of economic independence from foreign nations was not a feasible alternative during this period, although increasing the degree of self-sufficiency in certain commodities and equipment was one of the secondary objectives because of the possible savings of scarce foreign exchange.

This period also witnessed the almost total socialization of the industrial sector. Industrial enterprises were transformed into either state or joint private and state enterprises. Until then, private entrepreneurs who were classified as 'national capitalists,' as opposed to 'bureaucratic capitalists,'[5] had been allowed to retain ownership of their enterprises and to continue in the management of them with substantial freedom of action. However, their scope for independent action was considerably narrowed after the socialist transformation, which put both the state and joint state and private enterprises under the direct supervision of the industrial ministries in the central government. Thus, centralized control of the enterprises could be exerted through the industrial ministries in the implementation of the state plan.

The Second Five-Year Plan (1958–60). In this period, also known as the Great Leap Forward, heavy industry was still the core of the economic development program. However, as a result of the Great Leap, the actual implementation of the industrialization program took on a dualistic line—there was a parallel emphasis on large-scale, capital-intensive enterprises and the use of native methods and mainly local resources. Simultaneously, control of state enterprises was decentralized to the provincial and local levels.

The most important industrial tasks continued to be generation of an economic surplus, production of defense goods, and establishment of a base for research and development and production of defense goods, although maintenance of economic independence gained in prominence. During this period, however, it was discovered that agriculture could not continue to execute tasks (1) and (2) successfully, and that the accomplishment of task (5), where economic independence included independence from foreign control as well as independence from the influence of natural disasters,[6] without the support of industry, was also in jeopardy. A decision to develop a nuclear weapons program was also made during this period.

The Second Five-Year Plan was short-lived. Because of overly ambitious targets, poor planning and coordination, bad harvests in 1959 and 1960, and the abrupt withdrawal of Soviet aid in mid-1960, the plan was silently terminated, and a process of readjustment began in 1961.

The period of readjustment (1960–65). The readjustment period was necessitated by the failure of the Great Leap Forward. The guiding policy for economic development in this period was 'agriculture as the foundation and industry as the leading factor.' In 1962, a new order of priority—agriculture, light industry, heavy industry—was formally established. The most important tasks of industry were to support the development of agriculture and to provide essential industrial consumer goods. Consequently, the output of fertilizers, tractors, and consumer goods was greatly increased. On the other hand, investments were generally curtailed, and small-scale enterprises that were high-cost producers were phased out of operation.

Because of the deterioration of Sino-Soviet relations, tasks (3), (4), and (5) took on a new urgency. Support of the nuclear weapons program continued, resulting in the

---

[5] Bureaucratic capitalists were those who had profited from their collaboration or connections with Nationalist government officials.

[6] See the illuminating article by A. M. Tang, 'Policy and Performance in Agriculture,' in W. Galenson, A. Eckstein, and T. C. Liu, eds., *Economic Trends in Communist China* (Chicago: Aldine Publishing Company, 1968), pp. 459–508.

explosion of the first atomic device in 1964. Production of conventional armaments was also undertaken. Other measures were taken to increase the degree of economic independence. First, there was a gradual diversification of trading partners to include many of the industrialized Western nations. Second, the extractive industries, e.g., petroleum, were singled out for expansion to overcome domestic bottlenecks caused by the shortage of mineral resources. Third, synthetics were introduced as raw materials for industry to reduce industry's dependence on the vagaries of agriculture and to ease the pressure on agriculture, which also had the responsibility of providing essential consumption.

The Third Five-Year Plan (1966–70). Not much is known about the contents of the Third Five-Year Plan. At any rate, the Great Proletarian Cultural Revolution, which started in mid-1966 and swept across the country, appears to have disrupted whatever economic plans there were initially. The tasks that were emphasized during this period were (1) support of agriculture; (2) strengthening of national defense; (3) priority development of extractive industries; and (4) lowering production costs and raising the level of self-sufficiency.[7] The basic policy, however, of 'agriculture as the foundation and industry as the leading factor' appears to have been unchanged.

This period saw further nuclear tests, including the testing of hydrogen devices. It was also clear that industrial output actually declined during 1967 and 1968, the two peak years of Cultural Revolution activities. This is another example of how a short-run reduction of output may be bartered for ideological or political factors.

Industry's Position in the Aggregate Economy

Industry's share of output. In Table 21–1, the official data on the distribution of national income by major sectors are presented. In Table 21–2, estimates of the national income distribution made independently by Liu and Yeh and by Wu, Hoeber, and Rockwell are presented. These various estimates do not differ much, and the conclusion is quite clear. From 1952 to 1960, the share of industry more than doubled, from 18 per cent to 40 per cent! And mostly, it appears, at the expense of agriculture. However, with the failure of the Great Leap Forward, which brought about a sharp reduction in industrial output, the share of industry, according to Wu, *et al.*, fell back to approximately 20 per cent in 1961 and 1962. It is also significant that the share of

Table 21–1—Official Estimates of the Percentage Distribution of
National Income by Sectors at 1952 Prices, 1952–56
(per cent)

	1952	1953	1954	1955	1956
National Income	100.0	100.0	100.0	100.0	100.0
Agriculture[a]	59.2	—	—	—	48.1
Industry[b]	18.0	21.0	23.4	23.6	26.4
Construction[b]	3.0	3.8	4.1	4.3	5.6
Transportation and					
Communications[b]	4.0	4.2	4.5	4.4	4.4
Trade[a]	15.8	—	—	—	15.5

Note: (—) indicates data unavailable for those years.
Sources: [a] *Tung-chi Yen-chiu (Statistical Research)*, No. 1, January, 1958, p. 11. [b] *Chung-kuo Kung-jen (Chinese Worker)*, No. 4, February 27, 1958, p. 7.

[7] See, for instance, *Jen-min Jih-pao (People's Daily,* hereafter: *JMJP)*, February 21, 1969, and March 22, 1969.

handicrafts also declined from 1952 to 1960, although it increased slightly during 1961–62. Hence, one must conclude that the real expansion of industry came basically from the factory subsector. I shall return to this point in the next section.

Table 21-2—Percentage Distribution of National Income by Sectors,
1933, 1952–62
(per cent)

	Industry						Agriculture		Others	
	Total		Factory		Handicrafts					
	Liu-Yeh	Wu	Liu-Yeh	Wu	Liu-Yeh	Wu	Liu-Yeh	Wu	Liu-Yeh	Wu
1933	14.0	—	6.6	—	7.4	—	56.9	—	29.1	—
1952	18.1	17.9	11.5	11.3	6.6	6.6	47.9	48.5	34.0	33.6
1953	19.8	20.1	13.4	13.7	6.4	6.4	46.2	46.2	34.0	33.7
1954	21.2	21.4	14.9	15.3	6.3	6.1	44.8	44.2	34.1	34.4
1955	22.2	22.3	16.0	16.1	6.2	6.2	43.5	43.3	34.3	34.4
1956	24.7	24.6	19.0	18.9	5.7	5.7	40.1	40.1	35.2	35.3
1057	26.3	26.0	20.7	20.3	5.6	5.7	39.0	39.2	34.7	34.8
1958	30.2	28.0	24.7	22.5	5.5	5.5	35.9	36.6	33.9	35.4
1959	34.8	34.8	29.2	29.5	5.6	5.3	30.0	32.2	35.2	33.0
1960	—	40.0	—	35.2	—	4.8	—	26.9	—	33.1
1961	—	22.2	—	15.6	—	6.6	—	44.8	—	33.0
1962	—	20.9	—	14.5	—	6.4	—	47.1	—	32.0

Note: (—) indicates data unavailable for those years. Totals may not add up to 100 per cent because of rounding.

Sources: T. C. Liu and K. C. Yeh, *The Economy of the Chinese Mainland: National Income and Economic Development, 1933–1959* (Princeton, N.J.: Princeton University Press, 1965), p. 66, Table 8; K. C. Yeh, 'Capital Formation,' in W. Galenson, A. Eckstein, and T. C. Liu, eds., *Economic Trends in Communist China* (Chicago: Aldine Publishing Co., 1968), p. 532, Table A-1; and, for Wu estimates, Y. L. Wu, F. P. Hoeber, and M. M. Rockwell, *The Economic Potential of Communist China*, 1 (Menlo Park: Stanford Research Institute, 1963), 241, Table 51.

Industry's share of capital. In Table 21-3, the industrial share of the gross value of fixed assets at original cost is given. It is seen that both the absolute value of industrial assets and the share increased over time. Industrial fixed assets constituted more than half of the total value of fixed assets of the economy.

Industry's share of employment. In Table 21-4, total industrial employment and total factory employment are expressed as percentages of total nonagricultural employment. Although the percentages *do differ* among the three series, partly because of differences in coverage, the magnitudes and directions of year-to-year changes appear to be comparable. We note that the share of factory employment increased almost continuously through 1958 and at a much faster rate than total industrial employment (including handicrafts). Both the shares of industrial employment and of factory employment made a big jump during the 1958 industrialization drive, with the latter more than doubling the figure of 1957. This showed the rapid infusion of labor into industry during the Great Leap Forward period.

Industry's share of investment. In Table 21-5, the official data on industry's share of basic construction investment[8] in the economy as a whole and within the state plan

---

[8] In Chinese Communist usage, basic construction investment includes expenditures on construction, installation, purchases of machinery and equipment, and other expenditures ancillary to the process of fixed capital formation.

Table 21-3—Gross Value of Fixed Assets at Original Cost in the
Entire Economy and in Industry, 1949-59

| | Absolute Values (millions of yüan) | | Percentage Distribution (per cent) | |
	Economy as a Whole	Industry	Economy as a Whole	Industry
1949	(24,410)	12,800	100.0	52.4
1950	—	—	100.0	—
1951	—	—	100.0	—
1952	(29,680)	15,800	100.0	53.2
1953	—	—	100.0	—
1954	—	—	100.0	—
1955	(46,220)	26,300	100.0	56.9
1956	—	—	100.0	—
1957	—	35,200	100.0	—
1958	—	47,400	100.0	—
1959	—	57,840	100.0	—

Note: (—) indicates data unavailable for that year.
Source: N. R. Chen, *Chinese Economic Statistics: A Handbook for Mainland China* (Chicago: Aldine Publishing Company, 1967), p. 146, Table 3.1.

Table 21-4—Industrial Employment as a Percentage of
Total Nonagricultural Employment, 1949-58
(per cent)

| | Liu-Yeh (1) | | Emerson (2) | | Hou (3) | |
	Total	Factory	Total	Factory	Total	Factory
1949	—	—	35.8	11.6	26.6	4.0
1950	—	—	36.7	11.2	28.3	4.4
1951	—	—	34.9	12.6	27.8	6.3
1952	28.7	6.0	35.8	14.3	28.8	8.0
1953	30.5	6.9	37.0	15.6	30.0	9.4
1954	32.6	7.1	39.9	16.0	33.4	10.1
1955	31.5	7.3	38.5	15.7	32.8	10.3
1956	30.1	7.8	35.3	19.0	32.2	12.7
1957	31.2	8.6	38.1	19.9	34.6	13.7
1958	—	—	45.8	41.7	42.0	34.3

Note: (—) indicates data unavailable for that year.
Sources: (1) Annual average figures, from Liu and Yeh, *Economy of Chinese Mainland*, p. 69, Table 11. (2) Year-end figures, from J. P. Emerson, 'Employment in Mainland China: Problems and Prospects,' in Joint Economic Committee of the U.S. Congress, *An Economic Profile of Mainland China*, Superintendent of Documents, U.S. Government Printing Office, Washington, D.C., 1967, 1: 460-61, Table A-1. (3) Year-end figures, from C. M. Hou, 'Manpower, Employment, and Unemployment,' in Galenson *et al.*, eds., *Economic Trends in Communist China*, pp. 366-67, Table 15.

are presented. Again there appears to be a generally increasing trend in these shares despite some year-to-year fluctuations. The share of industry in total basic construction increased from 37.2 per cent in 1950 to 61.0 per cent in 1959. Within the state plan, the share increased from 38.6 per cent in 1950 to 51.8 per cent in 1957. It is significant to note that from 1950 to 1955 the share within the state plan was substantially larger than the share in the total. This situation is reversed after 1956. This change reflected both the acceleration and completion of the process of socialization in industry as well as the gradual increase in emphasis placed on local investments with local resources. The surge in 1958 and 1959 was due to the big industrial push during the Great Leap.

Table 21–5—Industry's Share of Basic Construction Investment
at Current Prices, 1950–59
(per cent)

Year	Grand Total	Within State Plan
1950	37.2	38.6
1951	36.2	39.9
1952	38.8	41.7
1953	35.5	42.4
1954	42.2	48.5
1955	46.2	51.2
1956	46.1	46.4
1957	52.3	51.8
1958	64.8	—
1959	61.0	—

Note: (—) indicates data unavailable for that year.
Sources: K. Chao, 'Policies and Performance in Industry,' in Galenson *et al.*, eds., *Economic Trends in Communist China*, p. 577, Table 2; Chen, *Chinese Economic Statistics*, p. 158, Table 3.21 and p. 166, Table 3.35.

Table 21–6 presents alternative estimates of industry's share of gross fixed investment. Again, the increasing trend is recognizable in all the series, and the surge in 1958 is unmistakable. Moreover, industry's share was consistently higher than those of agriculture, transportation and communication, construction and other sectors. Even in 1957, when total investment was temporarily curtailed, industrial gross fixed investment increased in both absolute and relative terms.

Finally, Table 21–7 gives industry's share of gross fixed investment within the state plan as estimated by Liu and Yeh. The within-plan shares were higher than the comparable Liu and Yeh estimates for the economy as a whole as presented in Table 21–6.

Summary. From the preceding discussion of the relative share of industry in national income, in gross value of fixed assets, in employment, and in investment, the overriding emphasis on rapid industrialization is unmistakable. During the 1950's, industry had a disproportionately large share of the capital stock, and an even more disproportionate share of total investment, in comparison with its share of total income. Industry's share of national income ranged approximately from 20 to 40 per cent; its share of total fixed assets, consistently higher than 50 per cent; and its share of investment, ranging approximately from 50 to 60 per cent. It follows that the average output per unit of gross fixed assets was probably lower in industry when compared to the rest of the economy. It is also clear that industry, especially the factory component of industry, received the largest share of resources in terms of

Table 21-6—Alternative Estimates of Industry's Share
of Gross Fixed Investment, 1950-59
(per cent)

	Official Estimates (1)	Liu-Yeh I (2)	Liu-Yeh II (3)	Hollister (4)	Yeh (5)
1950	29.7	—	—	21.0	—
1951	28.1	—	—	27.7	—
1952	36.3	32.1	34.0	28.7	35.5
1953	35.7	32.0	36.0	33.0	39.2
1954	38.3	34.3	37.9	34.4	44.5
1955	44.0	40.2	43.5	34.3	46.1
1956	43.9	41.2	45.3	37.8	47.2
1957	50.1	47.0	50.2	41.3	52.1
1958	62.0	—	—	50.9	—
1959	—	—	—	49.8	—

Note: (—) indicates data unavailable for that year.

Sources: (1) Current prices, from State Statistical Bureau, *Ten Great Years: Statistics of the Economic and Cultural Achievements of the People's Republic of China* (Peking: Foriegn Languages Press, 1960), p. 66. (2) (Includes factories, mining, and utilities but excludes construction) constant 1952 prices, from Liu and Yeh, *Economy of Chinese Mainland*, p. 239, Table 76. (3) (Includes construction) constant 1952 prices from *ibid*. (4) (Includes industry, construction, and public utilities) current prices, from W. W. Hollister, 'Trends in Capital Formation in Communist China,' in Joint Economic Committee, *Economic Profile of Mainland China*, 1: 128, Table 4. (5) (Includes manufacturing, mining, electric power generation, construction and surveying) current prices, from K. C. Yeh, 'Capital Formation,' in Galenson *et al.*, eds., *Economic Trends in Communist China*, p. 521, Table 4.

Table 21-7—Industry's Share of Gross Fixed Investment
Within the State Plan, 1952-57

Year	Factories, Mining and Utilities	Factories, Mining, Utilities, and Construction
1952	41.1	43.7
1953	43.6	48.9
1954	45.5	50.7
1955	49.6	53.0
1956	45.2	49.8
1957	50.4	54.2

Source: Constant 1952 prices from Liu and Yeh, *Economy of Chinese Mainland*, p. 239, Table 76.

capital goods, both within the state plan and without. Industry was certainly the most rapidly expanding sector of the economy in the period under consideration.

EVOLUTION OF THE STRATEGY FOR INDUSTRIALIZATION

In order to study the evolution of the Communist Chinese strategy for industrialization, one must first of all identify the control variables (or instruments) at the disposal of the government for effecting changes in the industrial sector. In a market economy, the control variables are typically prices of output and inputs, interest rates, investment licenses, tax incentives, and tariffs. During the period of rehabilitation, many of these instruments were employed by the government. However, once the fundamental ideological choice of state over private ownership of the means of production was made, the effective control variables became quantities instead of prices. They were cast in terms of the allocation of scarce resources—capital, labor, investment, raw materials, imports—to the industrial enterprises, as well as the setting of output targets for each of them.[9] Control was accomplished within the framework of a comprehensive national economic plan through direct ministerial supervision of the enterprises and through financial control exercised by the banking system.

The study of the evolution of the Chinese Communist industrialization strategy will proceed in this section by examining the actual choices made.

Choice of Ownership and Organization

Ownership. Table 21–8 presents the percentage distribution of national income by ownership of enterprises. Table 21–9 presents the percentage distribution of gross values of industrial output and factory output[10] by ownership of enterprise, as well as the industrial capital of modern factories under various kinds of ownership. From an examination of these tables, several conclusions emerge. First, by 1956, the share of private enterprises in industry had dwindled to almost zero. Socialization was complete in industry and to a great extent in the aggregate economy as well. Second, note that the socialized share of factory was consistently higher than that of industry (Table 21–9), which in turn was consistently higher than the economy as a whole (Table 21–8). This reflected the importance of industry in the economic plan and the urgent desire of the planners to bring factory and industry under more direct control more rapidly. Third, when Tables 21–8 and 21–9 are compared, it appears that

Table 21–8—Percentage Distribution of National Income
by Ownership of Enterprise, 1952–57
(per cent)

	1952	1953	1954	1955	1956	1957
National income	100.0	100.0	100.0	100.0	100.0	100.0
State	19.1	23.9	26.8	28.0	32.2	33.2
Cooperative	1.5	2.5	4.8	14.1	53.4	56.4
Joint	0.7	0.9	2.1	2.8	7.3	7.6
Capitalist	6.9	7.9	5.3	3.5	—	—
Individual	71.8	64.8	61.0	51.6	7.1	2.8

Note: (—) indicates negligible quantity.
Source: State Statistical Bureau, *Ten Great Years.*

---

[9] It is obvious that the output targets cannot be set completely independently of the input allocations. They must be related by a set of input-output (possibly variable) coefficients.
[10] Industrial output includes both factory and handicrafts output.

private ownership of industrial enterprises was tolerated much more in industry (especially factory) than in the economy as a whole. Moreover, even after the socialization drive picked up momentum in 1954, when the capitalists saw the metaphorical 'handwriting on the wall,' the proportion of joint enterprises in industry was much higher than the corresponding proportion for the economy at large. In fact, by 1956, joint enterprises accounted for 32.6 per cent of factory gross value and 27.2 per cent of industrial gross value, but only 8 per cent of national income.[11] No doubt the shortage of managerial and professional talents accounted for much of the tolerance towards capitalists.

Table 21–9 also reveals that within the modern factory subsector, the state was already the biggest owner of industrial capital in 1949. The state's share as well as the joint enterprises' share both increased gradually over time, while the private share had probably disappeared altogether by the end of 1956. It is useful to note, however, that despite their relatively small shares of industrial capital, the joint and private enterprises accounted for a more than proportionate share of the gross value of factory production. Part of this may be due to the greater degree of vertical integration[12] in the state enterprises, which affects the calculation of gross value. Another part, however, may also be attributed to managerial differences.

Organization. A recurrent controversy, partly economic and partly ideological, centers upon the desired degree of centralization. From the economic point of view, decentralized decision-making is preferable to centralized decision-making if a system of signals can be found to replace direct central control and supervision. From a Marxist ideological point of view, total decentralization of decision-making is an ultimate goal. However, the danger of a decentralized system is the potential divergence between national and local interests and objectives, which is most likely to occur if no rationalized system of 'shadow prices' exists to reflect central priorities or if there is no *independent* monitoring and evaluation mechanism to reward success and discipline failure.

These preconditions for successful decentralization did not exist in Communist China. During the First Five-Year Plan, most economic decisions were made at the central government level. Beginning in 1958, an attempt was made to shift most of the economic decision-making to the provincial and local levels. The result was chaos. After 1961, the central authorities took back part of the power that had been delegated to the provincial officials, especially that of investment. With the Cultural Revolution, however, most decisions, economic or political, seemed to be made at the provincial or local levels.

Table 21–10 demonstrates clearly the switch in industrial organization from central to local control between 1957 and 1958, in terms of both gross value of production and basic construction investment. Unfortunately, comparable data are not available for the 1960's.

Inputs for Industry

I shall examine the quantities of factors of production made available to the industrial sector as a whole. While allocation of labor and new investment are obviously under the planner's control, capital, to the extent that it is shiftable between sectors, must also be considered one of the policy instruments.

Capital. In Table 21–11, the available estimates of industrial capital in Communist China from 1948 through 1959 are presented, along with their index numbers. All

---

[11] Gross value of production and national income are not directly comparable. However, the difference in the relative shares is believed to be slight in this case.

[12] Vertical integration refers to the process in which more and more of the inputs are produced by the enterprise itself.

Table 21-9—Percentage Distribution of the Gross Value of Industrial Output at Constant Prices and Industrial Capital of Modern Factories by Ownership of Establishment, 1949–56 (at 1952 Prices)

(per cent)

	1949	1950	1951	1952	1953	1954	1955	1956
Gross value of industrial output (1)	100.00	100.00	100.00	100.00	100.00	100.00	100.00	100.00
State	26.27	32.72	34.44	41.54	43.04	47.11	51.29	54.55
Cooperatives	.46	.78	1.31	3.23	3.81	4.72	6.29	17.06
Factory	.36	.58	.80	2.51	2.72	3.07	3.92	1.62
Handicraft	.11	.21	.51	.72	1.09	1.65	2.37	15.43
Joint	1.57	2.17	3.06	3.98	4.50	11.52	13.10	27.16
Private	48.71	38.06	38.40	30.66	29.33	19.90	13.24	.04
Individual handicrafts	22.98	26.27	22.80	20.58	19.31	18.48	16.08	1.19
Gross value of factory output (1)	100.00	100.00	100.00	100.00	100.00	100.00	100.00	100.00
State	34.16	44.50	44.90	52.78	54.08	58.99	62.92	65.43
Cooperative	.46	.78	1.04	3.19	3.42	3.85	4.81	1.94
Joint	2.04	2.94	3.99	5.06	5.66	12.25	16.06	32.57
Private	63.33	51.77	50.07	38.94	36.85	24.91	16.24	.05
Industrial capital of modern factory (2)	100.00	100.00	100.00	100.00	100.00	100.00	100.00	100.00
State	75.7	—	—	75.7	—	—	82.7	—
Cooperative	0.0	—	—	0.3	—	—	0.5	—
Joint	2.2	—	—	5.8	7.5	—	11.4	—
Private	22.1	—	—	18.2	20.3	9.0	5.4	—

Note: (—) indicates data unavailable for that year.
Sources: (1) Chen, *Chinese Economic Statistics*, pp. 208–9. (2) Year-end figures, including net value of fixed assets and work capital in industry, from *ibid.*, p. 152, Table 3.8.

series show an interesting trend, which accelerated toward the end of the 1950's. With the exception of the Liu-Yeh series, which shows an exceptionally high average annual rate of growth of 28.2 per cent during 1952–57, all the other series do not differ markedly, with a range of average annual growth rates between 17.4 and 22.4 per cent. The average annual growth rate of net value of fixed assets after 1957 is 28.6 per cent.

Table 21–10—Percentage Distribution of Gross Value of Industrial Production and Basic Construction Investment in Industry by the Level of Control, 1955–59

(per cent)

	Gross Value of Industrial Production (1)		Basic Construction Investment in Industry (2)	
	Central	Local	Central	Local
1955	—	—	82.9	17.1
1956	—	—	80.7	19.3
1957	46.0	54.0	80.0	20.0
1958	27.0	73.0	77.7	22.3
1959	26.0	74.0	57.3	42.7

Note: (—) indicates data unavailable for that year.

Sources: (1) Constant 1957 prices, from C. M. Li, 'China's Industrial Development, 1958–63,' in C. M. Li, ed., *Industrial Development in Communist China* (New York: Praeger Publishers, 1964), p. 16, Table 4. (2) Current prices, from Chao, 'Policies and Performance in Industry,' p. 577, Table 2.

Labor. Table 21–12 gives alternative estimates of nonagricultural employment in Communist China. After a fairly rapid increase during the period of rehabilitation, growth stagnated during the First Five-Year Plan to slightly more than 1 per cent per annum. There was a great spurt in 1958, however, in response to the Great Leap Forward. The year 1958 also turned out to be the peak year of nonagricultural employment during the two decades ending in 1969. After 1961, there was a conscious policy of retrenchment in industry and resettlement of excess urban population in the rural areas. According to B. M. Richman, nonagricultural employment in 1964 was still far below the 1958 level.

In Table 21–13, alternative estimates of industrial employment are presented. They display dynamic characteristics similar to nonagricultural employment ones, except that their growth rates during the First Five-Year Plan are much higher— ranging from 2.8 per cent to 5.0 per cent per annum.[13] A similar spurt was observed in 1958.

Table 21–14 offers alternative estimates of factory employment in Communist China. According to all series, growth rates in factory employment exceeded those of industrial employment by a wide margin. They range from 8.4 per cent to 12.6 per cent per annum during the First Five-Year Plan. Factory employment increased threefold in 1958. However, it was subsequently reduced by one-half during the 1961–62 retrenchment and even in 1966 was only 60 per cent of the 1958 peak level. The over-all growth rate from 1949 to 1965 is estimated at 9.8–10.0 per cent per annum.

[13] Nonagricultural employment figures include all workers not engaged in agriculture and forestry. Industrial employment figures include both factory and handicraft workers.

Table 21-11—Alternative Estimates of Industrial Capital, 1948-59

	Total Industrial Capital	Factory Industrial Capital	Gross Value of Industrial Fixed Assets	Gross Value of Factory Fixed Assets	Net Value of Factory Fixed Assets	Net Value of Factory Fixed Assets (Field)	Average Net Value of Factory Fixed Assets (Field)	Net Fixed Capital (Liu-Yeh)
	(1)	(2)	(3)	(4)	(5)	(6)	(7)	(8)
Absolute Value (millions of yüan)								
1948	9,430	9,820	10,330	12,800				
1949		9,100						
1950								
1951						9,744		7,400
1952	14,770	14,320	12,790	15,800	10,140	10,140	9,942	8,740
1953		14,476				11,547	10,844	11,170
1954		21,750				13,412	12,480	14,200
1955	24,800	23,869	22,300	26,290	18,140	16,024	14,718	18,140
1956		27,325				20,223	18,124	23,930
1957			35,200	35,200		25,888	23,056	
1958			47,400					
1959			57,840					
Index Numbers (1952 = 100)								
1948	63.8	68.6	80.8	81.0				
1949		63.5						
1950								
1951						96.1		84.7
1952	100.0	100.0	100.0	100.0	100.0	100.0	100.0	100.0
1953		101.1				113.9	109.1	127.8
1954		151.9				132.3	125.5	162.5
1955	167.9	166.7	174.4	166.4	178.9	158.0	148.0	207.6
1956		190.8				199.4	182.3	273.8
1957			275.2	222.8		255.3	231.9	
1958			370.6					
1959			452.2					

Note: Blank spaces indicate data unavailable for those years.

Sources: (1) Year-end figures, includes net value of fixed assets and working capital. *Tung-chi Kung-tso (Statistical Work)*, No. 1, January, 1967, p. 31. (2) Year-end figures, from Chen, *Chinese Economic Statistics*, p. 152, Table 3.8. (3) Year-end figures, gross value of industrial fixed assets at original cost; 1949, 1952, 1955 figures from *T'ung-chi Kung-tso*, No. 1, January, 1967, pp. 31–33; 1957 and 1958 figures from State Statistical Bureau, *Ten Great Years*, p. 93; 1959 figure, a preliminary estimate from Chen, *Chinese Economic Statistics*, p. 146, Table 3.1. (4) Year-end figures at original cost, from R. M. Field, 'Labor Productivity in Industry,' Galenson *et al.*, eds., *Economic Trends in Communist China*, p. 654. (5) Year-end figures, *ibid.*, p. 153, Table 3.9. (6) Year-end figures, constant 1952 prices, from Field, 'Labor Productivity in Industry,' p. 666, Table A-3. (7) Average annual figures, constant 1952 prices, *ibid.* (8) Year-end figures, constant 1952 prices, includes only factories, mining, and utilities, constant 1952 prices, from Liu and Yeh, *Economy of Chinese Mainland*, p. 240, Table 77.

Table 21–12—Alternative Estimates of Nonagricultural Employment,
1949–64

| | Absolute Numbers (thousands) | | | | Index Numbers (1952 = 100) | | | |
	Liu-Yeh (1)	Emerson (2)	Hou (3)	Richman (4)	Liu-Yeh (1)	Emerson (2)	Hou (3)	Richman (4)
1949		26,267	34,552			71.5	77.0	
1950		30,314	38,559			82.5	86.0	
1951		34,730	42,939			94.5	95.7	
1952	59,390	36,752	44,864		100.0	100.0	100.0	(100.0)
1953	59,570	39,116	47,428		100.3	106.4	105.7	
1954	59,390	39,750	46,803		100.0	108.2	104.3	
1955	60,410	38,864	45,352		101.7	105.7	101.1	
1956	61,830	39,366	47,630		104.1	107.1	106.2	
1957	64,190	39,667	47,651		108.1	107.9	106.2	
1958		56,867	63,590	56,900		154.7	141.7	154.7
1959			62,103				138.4	
1960			62,417				138.1	
1961								
1962								
1963								
1964				45,800				124.6

Note: Blank spaces indicate data unavailable for those years.

Sources: (1) Annual average figures, from Liu and Yeh, *Economy of Chinese Mainland*, p. 69, Table 11. (2) Year-end figures, from Emerson, 'Employment in Mainland China,' 1: 460–61, Table A-1. (3) Year-end figures, from Hou, 'Manpower, Employment, and Unemployment,' pp. 356–57, Table 10. (4) Year-end figures, from B. M. Richman, *Industrial Society in Communist China* (New York: Random House, 1969), p. 523. The index is linked with the Emerson index.

Table 21–13—Alternative Estimates of Industrial Employment, 1949–58

| | Absolute Numbers (thousands) | | | Index Numbers (1952 = 100) | | |
	Liu-Yeh (1)	Emerson (2)	Hou (3)	Liu-Yeh (1)	Emerson (2)	Hou (3)
1949	—	9,414	9,206	—	71.5	71.2
1950	—	11,115	10,916	—	84.4	84.4
1951	—	12,137	11,943	—	92.2	92.3
1952	17,040	13,168	12,938	100.0	100.0	100.0
1953	18,150	14,479	14,249	106.5	110.0	110.1
1954	19,390	15,876	15,646	113.8	120.6	120.9
1955	19,000	14,946	14,866	111.5	113.5	114.9
1956	18,590	13,893	15,353	109.1	105.5	118.7
1957	20,010	15,100	16,510	117.4	114.7	127.6
1958	—	26,049	26,734	—	197.8	206.6

Note: (—) indicates data unavailable for that year.

Sources: (1) Annual average figures, from Liu and Yeh, *Economy of Chinese Mainland*, p. 69, Table 11. (2) Year-end figures, from Emerson, 'Employment in Mainland China, 1: 460–61, Table A-1. (3) Year-end figures, from Hou, 'Manpower, Employment, and Unemployment,' pp. 366–67, Table 15.

Table 21–14—Alternative Estimates of Factory Employment, 1949–66

	Absolute Numbers (thousands)				Index Numbers (1952 = 100)				
	Liu-Yeh (1)	Emerson (2)	Hou (3)	Richman (4)	Liu-Yeh (1)	Emerson (2)	Hou (3)	Richman (4)	Field (5)
1949		3,959	1,371	3,059		58.1	38.1	58.1	
1950		3,386	1,707			64.3	47.5		
1951		4,379	2,705			83.2	75.3		
1952	3,540	5,263	3,594	5,260	100.0	100.0	100.0	100.0	100.0
1953	4,120	6,121	4,460		116.4	116.3	124.1		115.7
1954	4,200	6,370	4,736		118.6	121.0	131.8		124.2
1955	4,440	6,121	4,664		125.4	116.3	129.8		121.0
1956	4,810	7,480	6,053		135.9	142.1	168.4		133.9
1957	5,500	7,907	6,510		155.4	150.3	181.1	150.3	149.5
1958		23,734	21,834	{23,000– 24,000}		451.0	607.5	451.0	
1959									
1960									
1961				{11,500– 12,000}				{218.5– 228.0}	
1962				{11,500– 12,000}				{218.5 228.0}	
1963									
1964									
1965				{13,700– 14,000}				{260.3– 266.0}	
1966				{14,600– 15,000}				{277.4– 285.0}	

Note: Blank spaces indicate data unavailable for those years.

Sources: (1) Annual average figures, from Liu and Yeh, Economy of Chinese Mainland, p. 69, Table 11. (2) Year-end figures excluding handicrafts, salt extraction, and urban public utilities, from Emerson, 'Employment in Mainland China,' 1: 460–61, Table A-1. (3) Year-end figures excluding handicrafts, from Hou, 'Manpower, Employment, and Unemployment,' pp. 366–67, Table 15. (4) Year-end figures, from Richman, Industrial Society in Communist China, pp. 600–603, Table 7-2. (5) Annual average figures, from Field, 'Labor Productivity in Industry,' p. 647, Table 3.

Investment. Table 21–15 presents official estimates of basic construction investment in Communist China. Basic construction refers to the investment which will result in an addition to the productive and nonproductive fixed assets. Also included in basic construction investment are expenditures on geological surveys and exploration, engineering design, scientific testing and research, and so forth. Once more, the more than doubling of investment effort in 1958 in industry is easily noticeable. It is worth noting that even during the 1956–57 curtailment of total investment, industrial investment posted an increase in both total and within-plan investment.

Table 21–16 reports alternative estimates of gross fixed investment in industry in Communist China. Note the sharp rise in the 1950's and the equally abrupt drop in the early 1960's.

On the basis of these figures, it would appear that industrial capital grew much faster than industrial employment during the First Five-Year Plan. This trend was reversed during the Great Leap, when industrial employment increased faster than industrial capital. After 1961, however, industrial employment was drastically reduced. There was a similar cutback in industrial investment, according to Chao's data. Industrial capital could not have grown very rapidly during the period of readjustment.

Choice of the Final Demand

Balance or unbalance? Another frequent controversy in economic planning in Communist China is the desired degree of balance in the development of the principal economic sectors and subsectors. The advocates of unbalanced growth were in control during the First and Second Five-Year Plans, in which industry, especially heavy industry, was given almost exclusive attention and agriculture was ignored. Even within industry itself, there were great disparities among the growth rates of the various branches. In the early 1960's, there was a greater regard for orderly, proportional development. This debate appears to have faded into the background during the Cultural Revolution but can become an important issue again after the political dust has settled.

Table 21–15—Basic Construction Investment, 1950–59
(millions of yüan)

Year	Total Basic Investment (1)	Total Basic Investment in Industry (2)	Total Basic Investment Within State Plan (1)	Total Industrial Basic Investment Within State Plan (3)
1950	1,130	420	1,040	401
1951	2,350	850	1,880	750
1952	4,360	1,690	3,710	1,549
1953	8,000	2,840	6,510	2,756
1954	9,070	3,830	7,500	3,634
1955	9,300	4,300	8,630	4,204
1956	14,800	6,820	13,990	6,483
1957	13,830	7,240	12,640	6,550
1958	26,700	17,300	21,440	—
1959	—	20,400	26,700	—

Note: (—) indicates data unavailable for that year.
Sources: (1) 1950–58 figures from State Statistical Bureau, *Ten Great Years*, p. 55; 1959 figures from Chen, *Chinese Economic Statistics*, p. 158, Table 3.21. (2) (Excludes urban public utilities) Chao, 'Policies and Performance in Industry,' p. 577, Table 2. (3) 1950–51 figures from *ibid.*; 1952–57 figures from Chen, *Chinese Economic Statistics*, p. 165, Table 3.33.

Heavy industry versus light industry. During the First and Second Five-Year Plans, heavy industry was the core of the economic development program, in both theory and practice. This is borne out by the available data on the distribution of gross value of industrial production (Table 21–17) and basic construction investment in industry (Table 21–18). After 1961, the official priority of development was agriculture, light industry, and heavy industry. However, on the basis of output trends of selected commodities, it appeared that heavy industry still commanded a large proportion of resources, much larger than the share of light industry in the 1950's.

Producer goods versus consumer goods. As the primary task of industry during the 1950's was the building up of an industrial and technological base for the manufacture of conventional and advanced weapons, it was not surprising to find that the share of

548

Table 21–16—Alternative Estimates of Gross Fixed Investment in Industry,
1950–63
(millions of yüan)

Year	Official Estimates (1)	Liu-Yeh (2)	Chao (3)
1950	300		
1951	500		
1952	1,130	1,340	
1953	2,340	2,430	
1954	2,820	3,030	
1955	3,530	3,940	
1956	4,900	5,790	
1957	6,470	7,580	
1958	12,370		
1959			
1960			13,505
1961			4,972
1962			1,473
1963			1,943

Note: Blank spaces indicate data unavailable for those years.

Sources: (1) Current prices, from State Statistical Bureau, *Ten Great Years*, p. 66. (2) Constant 1952 prices, from Liu and Yeh, *Economy of Chinese Mainland*, p. 239, Table 76. (3) Chao, 'Policies and Performance in Industry,' p. 588, Table 6.

Table 21–17—Percentage Distribution of Gross Value of Industrial Production
Between Heavy and Light Industries, 1957–60
(per cent)

Year	Total	Heavy Industry	Light Industry
1957	100.0	48.4	51.6
1958	100.0	57.3	42.7
1959	100.0	58.7	41.3
1960	100.0	60.5	39.5

Source: 1957 prices (1960 figure is planned figure), from Li, 'China's Industrial Development,' p. 16, Table 4.

producer goods increased continuously (Table 21–19). According to official estimates, the share increased from 26.6 per cent to 58.9 per cent in ten years. According to the value-added figures of Liu and Yeh, the contrast was even more striking: Producer goods accounted for almost 50 per cent in 1952 and almost 70 per cent in 1957.

A similar trend of increasing importance of the producer goods industries is revealed by figures on gross value of fixed assets (Table 21–20). The relative importance of producer goods over consumer goods is underscored by the fact that 85.6 per cent of industrial basic investment went to the producer goods industry during the First Five-Year Plan period.[14]

---

[14] N. R. Chen, *Chinese Economic Statistics: A Handbook for Mainland China* (Chicago: Aldine Publishing Company, 1967), p. 169, Table 3.39.

Table 21–18—Percentage Distribution of Basic Construction Investment
in Industry by Type of Industry at Current Prices, 1952–59
(per cent)

| Year | Official Estimates (1) | | Hollister (2) | |
	Heavy Industry	Light Industry	Heavy Industry	Light Industry
1952	75.7	24.3	60.0	40.0
1953	82.4	17.6	62.6	37.4
1954	82.5	17.5	71.1	28.9
1955	87.7	12.3	86.0	14.0
1956	86.2	13.8	85.1	14.9
1957	84.8	15.2	83.7	16.3
1958	87.4	12.6	87.4	12.6
1959	70.0	30.0	87.3	12.7

Sources: (1) 1952–58 figures from State Statistical Bureau, *Ten Great Years*, p. 61; 1959 figure from Chao, 'Policy and Performance in Industry,' p. 577, Table 2. (2) Hollister, 'Trends in Capital Formation,' 1: 128, Table 4.

Composition of industrial output. Tables 21–21A, B, and C present three alternative sets of index numbers of Communist Chinese industrial production by branch of industry for the period 1949–59, namely those constructed by Liu and Yeh, Chao, and Field. From these tables, one can infer the changes in the composition of industrial output over time. The three series are, on the whole, remarkably similar, although there are some differences, e.g., the machine-building industry output index was 441.1 by 1957 according to Liu and Yeh, substantially higher than either Chao's (271.5) or Field's (284.1) estimate. Field's output indices for the consumer goods industries (timber, paper, textiles, food) for 1957 are uniformly higher than Chao's and the Liu-Yeh indices.

Table 21–19—Percentage Distribution of Industrial Output at Constant Prices
Between Producer and Consumer Goods, 1949–59
(per cent)

| Year | Official Estimates (1) | | Liu-Yeh I (2) | | Liu-Yeh II (3) | |
	Producer Goods	Consumer Goods	Producer Goods	Consumer Goods	Producer Goods	Consumer Goods
1949	26.6	73.4				
1950	29.6	70.4				
1951	32.3	67.7				
1952	35.6	64.4	47.6	52.4	48.8	51.2
1953	37.3	62.7	51.6	48.4	52.8	47.2
1954	38.5	61.5	53.7	46.3	54.8	45.2
1955	41.7	58.3	59.1	40.9	60.3	39.7
1956	45.5	54.5	64.0	36.0	65.1	34.9
1957	48.4	51.6	68.3	31.7	69.2	30.8
1958	57.3	42.7				
1959	58.9	41.1				

Note: Blank spaces indicate data unavailable for those years.
Sources: (1) Chen, *Chinese Economic Statistics*, p. 210, Table 4.39. (2) Gross value added, from Liu and Yeh, *Economy of Chinese Mainland*, p. 141, Table 37. (3) Net value added, *ibid*.

Table 21–20—Percentage Distribution of Gross Value of Fixed Assets
at Original Cost Between Producer Goods and Consumer
Goods Industries, 1949–55
(per cent)

Year	Total	Producer Goods Industries	Consumer Goods Industrial
1949	100.0	64.4	35.6
1950			
1951			
1952	100.0	67.4	32.6
1953			
1954			
1955	100.0	71.5	28.5

Note: Blank spaces indicate data unavailable for those years.
Source: *T'ung-chi Kung-tso,* No. 1, January 1957, pp. 31–32.

Table 21–21A—Indices of Industrial Production, 1952–57 (Liu-Yeh)
(1952 = 100)

	1952	1953	1954	1955	1956	1957
Total industrial production	100.0	115.2	129.8	141.2	175.2	194.2
Industry	100.0	122.8	143.7	159.9	212.4	240.2
Electric power	100.0	127.0	152.2	169.0	227.9	265.9
Coal	100.0	104.8	125.8	147.3	166.7	194.0
Petroleum	100.0	142.7	181.0	221.6	266.7	334.4
Ferrous metals	100.0	130.2	157.2	200.5	306.3	354.0
Nonferrous metals	—	—	—	—	—	—
Metal processing	—	—	—	—	—	—
Machine-building	100.0	154.0	188.8	216.5	411.6	441.1
Chemical processing	100.0	120.9	160.9	188.2	236.4	277.3
Building materials	100.0	152.3	160.5	164.7	247.4	269.3
Timber	—	—	—	—	—	—
Paper	100.0	108.4	129.0	150.2	201.2	253.9
Textiles	100.0	116.0	129.5	116.9	154.2	139.6
Food	100.0	126.5	135.5	139.5	153.0	168.7
Handicrafts	100.0	101.9	105.5	108.5	111.2	114.0

Note: (—) indicates data unavailable for those years.
Source: Liu and Yeh, *Economy of Chinese Mainland,* pp. 66, 146, 573, 585. The index of total industrial production is derived from data on the value added (in 1952 yüan) by industry and handicrafts, and the value added by industry is derived from data on factories, mining, and utilities. The indexes for electric power, coal, and petroleum are derived from the data on net value added in Liu and Yeh, pp. 573, 585. The indices for all other branches of industry are derived from the data on gross value added on p. 146. Ferrous metals is the sum of pig iron, steel, and rolled steel; building materials is the sum of cement, sheet glass, and other construction materials; textiles is the sum of cotton yarn, cotton cloth, silk, silk piece goods, woolen textiles, grass cloth, and knitted goods; and food is the sum of sugar, milled rice, wheat flour, edible vegetable oils, and cigarettes.

Table 21–22 presents the ranking of different branches of industry by rates of growth in different periods and according to different authors. From an examination of the rank orderings, several general observations may be made. First, it appears that during all of the periods, the same industries—ferrous metals, nonferrous metals,

Table 21-21B—Indices of Industrial Production, 1949–57 (Kang Chao)

(1952 = 100)

	1949	1950	1951	1952	1953	1954	1955	1956	1957
Total industrial production	—	—	—	100.0	122.1	139.4	149.7	179.4	189.8
Industry	—	—	—	100.0	124.7	141.6	146.9	182.2	195.9
Electric power	59.4	62.7	79.2	100.0	126.7	151.5	169.1	228.5	266.4
Coal	48.8	64.7	79.9	100.0	104.8	125.1	147.3	166.7	197.7
Petroleum	27.8	45.9	70.0	100.0	142.7	181.0	221.6	266.7	334.4
Ferrous metals	11.3	42.3	65.9	100.0	129.3	156.0	198.8	299.9	353.7
Nonferrous metals	17.4	—	—	100.0	—	—	207.1	—	370.0
Machine-building	18.1	16.9	40.5	100.0	138.1	184.4	220.8	351.3	271.5
Chemical processing	17.8	32.8	67.9	100.0	127.4	172.4	172.2	246.6	314.2
Building materials	29.6	54.9	86.5	100.0	130.6	157.6	150.9	204.8	241.6
Timber	51.4	58.2	66.4	100.0	152.0	177.7	124.8	106.8	199.6
Paper	29.0	37.9	64.8	100.0	140.5	164.2	162.1	194.1	220.1
Textiles	48.5	65.8	77.9	100.0	117.4	129.3	113.5	150.5	136.7
Food	54.3	55.4	72.5	100.0	113.7	127.5	143.4	148.2	156.2
Daily-use commodities	57.2	70.4	95.5	100.0	133.0	131.0	142.0	151.8	174.5
Handicrafts	—	—	—	100.0	—	—	—	—	164.8

Note: (—) indicates data unavailable for that year.
Source: Kang Chao, *The Rate and Pattern of Industrial Growth in Communist China* (Ann Arbor: University of Michigan Press, 1965), pp. 88, 96.

Table 21–21C—Indices of Industrial Production, 1949–59 (R. M. Field)

(1952 = 100)

	1949	1950	1951	1952	1953	1954	1955	1956	1957	1958	1959
Total industrial production	48.47	61.27	81.38	100.0	125.1	143.0	143.9	178.4	195.1	256.5	322.9
Industry	41.11	54.38	77.58	100.0	122.7	143.0	148.3	242.6	208.8	282.0	362.1
Electric power	59.32	62.66	79.38	100.0	126.6	151.5	168.6	288.6	266.4	379.1	571.6
Coal	48.77	64.54	79.81	100.0	104.8	125.8	147.3	166.7	195.6	299.8	391.0
Petroleum	27.74	45.88	69.97	100.0	142.7	181.0	221.6	266.7	334.4	519.3	848.6
Ferrous metals	10.82	35.50	61.72	100.0	134.1	159.3	200.3	290.0	386.5	549.4	765.8
Metal processing	33.86	49.68	80.55	100.0	116.8	139.0	143.0	228.3	241.0	373.8	466.2
Machine-building	—	—	—	100.0	—	—	—	—	284.1	—	—
Chemical processing	24.59	42.66	75.88	100.0	124.6	165.5	199.2	262.2	312.9	436.1	615.0
Building materials	23.11	49.30	85.04	100.0	135.5	160.8	157.4	223.5	239.8	325.1	428.9
Timber	47.30	56.09	66.37	100.0	157.1	199.6	188.7	188.5	252.9	318.6	376.4
Paper	29.07	37.84	64.79	100.0	114.9	139.4	154.6	196.2	245.6	327.3	457.2
Textiles	40.09	56.01	73.88	100.0	122.0	139.0	126.9	163.0	153.2	190.5	242.3
Food	54.54	56.99	81.25	100.0	122.5	132.8	144.5	155.1	180.2	197.5	237.2
Handicrafts	78.71	88.80	97.11	100.0	135.5	143.6	126.3	138.4	138.7	152.5	167.9

Note: (—) indicates data unavailable for that year.
Source: Field, 'Chinese Communist Industrial Production,' pp. 283, 287.

chemical processing, machine-building and petroleum—were given high priority in development policy. On the other hand, textiles, timber, food and daily-use commodities consistently lagged behind in growth rates. This confirms both the preference of heavy over light industries and of producer over consumer goods industries. A notable development is the rising importance of electric power, which rose from the slowest-growing industry in 1949–52 to the fifth or sixth fastest-growing in 1952–57, and to the second fastest-growing in 1957–59. In the meantime, the importance of textiles was downgraded. Finally, it should be noted that the fuel industries—petroleum, electric power, and coal—were given the greatest push in 1957–59.

Composition of industrial capital. Table 21–23 contains the available official data on the gross value of fixed assets used for production in selected industries. The contrast is quite distinct: capital grew much faster in iron and steel and metal processing than in textiles and paper.

Table 21–22—Rank Orders of Branches of Industry by Rate of Growth, 1949–59

	Choa 1949–52 (1)	Field 1949–52 (2)	Chao 1952–57 (1)	Field 1952–57 (2)	Liu 1952–57 (3)	Field 1957–59 (2)
Ferrous metals	1	1	2	1	2	4
Nonferrous metals	2	—	1	—	—	—
Chemical processing	3	3	4	3	4	5
Machine-building	4	—	5	4	1	—
Petroleum	5	4	3	2	3	1
Paper	6	5	8	7	7	7
Building materials	7	2	7	9	5	8
Metal processing	—	6	—	8	—	6
Textiles	8	7	13	12	10	9
Coal	9	9	10	10	8	3
Timber	10	8	9	6		10
Food	11	10	12	11	9	11
Daily-use commodities	12	—	11	—	—	—
Electric power	13	11	6	5	6	2

Note: (—) indicates data unavailable or that year.
Sources: (1) Chao, *Rate and Pattern of Industrial Growth*, pp. 88, 96. (2) Field, 'Chinese Communist Industrial Production,' pp. 283, 287. (3) Liu and Yeh, *Economy of Chinese Mainland*, pp. 66, 146, 573, 585.

Table 21–23—Index Numbers of Gross Value of Fixed Assets Used for Production at Original Cost in Selected Industries, 1952–56
(1952 = 100)

Year	Iron and Steel	Metal Processing	Textile	Paper
1952	100.0	100.0	100.0	100.0
1953	114.2	115.1	113.0	117.8
1954	166.4	136.5	126.7	130.8
1955	198.6	163.6	138.9	139.8
1956	215.0	222.5	142.9	139.8

Source: Chen, *Chinese Economic Statistics*, pp. 150–51, Table 3.6.

Composition of industrial employment. Table 21–24 presents the employment figures available for selected branches of industry. Once again, paper, textiles, and food had the lowest rate of growth during 1952–56, whereas electric power, chemical processing and ferrous metals had the highest rates of growth.

Table 21–24—Average Number of Workers by Branch of Industry,
1952 and 1956

	Absolute Numbers (thousands)		Index Numbers (1952 = 100)		Rank
	1952	1956	1952	1956	
All industry	3,599.0	4,819.3	100.0	133.9	
Electric power	29.7	59.5	100.0	200.3	1
Coal	318.0	404.0	100.0	127.0	6
Ferrous metals	134.4	209.2	100.0	155.7	3
Metal processing	510.0	743.8	100.0	145.8	4
Chemical processing	72.6	117.5	100.0	161.8	2
Building materials	275.8	381.8	100.0	138.4	5
Paper	53.8	56.9	100.0	105.8	9
Textiles	777.5	942.0	100.0	121.2	7
Food	732.0	860.6	100.0	117.6	8
Other	695.2	1,044.0	100.0	150.2	

Source: Field, 'Labor Productivity in Industry,' p. 650, Table 5, and p. 665, Table A-2.

Composition of industrial investment. In Table 21–25, basic construction investment figures for selected industries are presented. The most striking change in investment policy was revealed by the relative position of the textile industry. During 1950–52, textiles was the leading industry. However, from 1953 through 1956, it ranked behind iron and steel, electric power, metal processing, and, most likely, coal as well. Investment in paper remained small.

A comparison of Table 21–25 with Table 21–23 reveals that the industries receiving higher investments during 1953–57 did have higher growth rates in their gross value of fixed assets for production.

Table 21–26 compares the output, capital, and employment indices for selected industries. A tentative conclusion, on the basis of the limited data, is that higher growth rates of output are associated with higher growth rates in both capital and employment. However, there exists sufficient differences in factor intensities across the industries that an industry with a faster rate of growth in either capital or output is not necessarily the faster-growing industry. In addition, there may be disembodied technical change, that is, improvement in the technology that is independent of the age structure of the inputs used. The paper industry appeared to be a notable exception. Both capital and labor in the paper industry grew more slowly than that of the textiles industry; however, the growth rate of the former is substantially higher than that of the latter. This was accomplished through a rapid increase in electric power consumption by the paper industry. Finally, high rates of growth of capital tend to be accompanied by high rates of growth in labor.

Choice of Techniques

Scale. Considerations of the economies of scale (at the plant level) and of the limited choices of the size of plants that could be supplied by the Soviet Union led the Chinese Communist planners to prefer large plants to small plants. The scarcity of managerial

Table 21–25—State Basic Construction Investment at Current Prices
in Selected Industries, 1949–57
(millions of yüan)

Year	Iron and Steel	Electric Power	Coal	Petroleum	Metal Processing	Building Materials	Textile	Paper (state-operated)
1949								
1950	87		88				36	9
1951	53						99	12
1952	190				250	380	254	22
1953	300	262	180		460		274	41
1954	282	392			660		424	39
1955	630	535			720		220	37
1956	833	724	480		950		334	122
1957	883	802				623		141
1950–52	329	196	361		262	93	389	42
1953–57	2,929	2,715	2,970	1,900	3,413			380

Note: Blank spaces indicate data unavailable for those years.
Source: Chen, *Chinese Economic Statistics*, pp. 170–71, Table 3.41.

Table 21–26—Comparison of Output, Capital, and Employment Indices
of Selected Industries, 1956
(1952 = 100)

	Production Index in 1956			Capital Index	Employment Index
	Chao (1)	Liu-Yeh (2)	Field (3)	(4)	(5)
Ferrous metals	299.9	306.3	290.0	215.0	155.7
Chemical processing	246.6	236.4	262.2	—	161.8
Electric power	228.5	227.9	288.6	—	200.3
Building materials	204.8	247.4	223.5	—	138.4
Paper	194.1	201.2	196.2	139.8	105.8
Metal processing	—	—	228.3	222.5	145.8
Coal	166.7	166.7	166.7	—	127.0
Textiles	150.5	154.2	163.0	142.9	121.2
Food	148.2	153.0	155.1	—	117.6

Note: (—) indicates data unavailable for that year.
Sources: (1) Chao, *Rate and Pattern of Industrial Growth*, pp. 88, 96. (2) Liu and Yeh, *Economy of Chinese Mainland*, pp. 66, 146, 573, and 585. The index of total industrial production is derived from data on the value added (in 1952 yüan) by industry and handicrafts, and the value added by industry is derived from data on factories, mining, and utilities. The indices for electric power, coal, and petroleum are derived from the data on net value added on pp. 573, 585. The indices for all other branches of industry are derived from the data on gross value added on p. 146. Ferrous metals is the sum of pig iron, steel, and rolled steel; building materials is the sum of cement, sheet glass, and other construction materials; textiles is the sum of cotton yarn, cotton cloth, silk, silk piece goods, woolen textiles, grass cloth, and knitted goods; and food is the sum of sugar, milled rice, wheat flour, edible vegetable oils, and cigarettes. (3) Field, 'Chinese Communist Industrial Production,' pp. 283, 287. (4) Gross value of fixed assets used for production in current prices, from Chen, *Chinese Economic Statistics*, pp. 150–51, Table 3.6. (5) Field, 'Labor Productivity in Industry,' p. 650, Table 5.

and professional skills was probably another important factor in the decision. After 1958, however, the emphasis shifted to dualistic development: Small plants were encouraged to coexist with large plants. The former were to utilize basically local resources and native methods. This period also coincided with the general down-grading of the usefulness of experts. Thus, from 1958 to 1960, there was a proliferation of small industrial enterprises. After 1961, however, most of these small enterprises, with their generally low quality of output and high cost of production, were re-adjusted out of existence.

The official distinction between large and small enterprises is as follows: A small enterprise is one with fewer than sixteen workers and salaried employees if it uses mechanical power, or fewer than thirty-one workers and salaried employees if it does not use mechanical power. All other enterprises are large enterprises.

Table 21–27 shows that both in terms of numbers of enterprises and in terms of gross value of production, the proportion accounted for by large enterprises was increasing over time. It is significant to note that although only 20 per cent of the enterprises were large, they produced approximately 70 per cent of the gross value of production.

Table 21–28 gives the distribution of state and joint enterprises[15] by size in terms of number, gross value of production, gross value of fixed assets and employment in 1955. The skewed distribution is even more striking: 1.6 per cent of the enterprises accounted for 53.1 per cent of gross value of production, 81.6 per cent of fixed assets, and 48.5 per cent of employment. It follows that the large enterprises had higher productivity than the small enterprises. The capital intensity also increased drastically with size.

Factory production versus handicrafts production. A related choice is that between factory and handicrafts production. Table 21–29 shows that from 1949 to 1958 modern factory production grew at 32.2 per cent per annum, almost twice as fast as handicraft factory production or handicrafts, which grew at 16.0 per cent and 19.4 per cent, respectively. Table 21–30 gives the percentages of gross value of total industrial production and of selected outputs produced by handicrafts. On the whole, the percentages of handicrafts production showed a decreasing trend. The proportions were fairly large in the consumer goods industries—food (edible vegetable oil, salt, sugar), paper, silk fabrics, and timber. By contrast, handicrafts production was only a very small proportion of coal and pig iron, the mainstays of heavy industry.

Table 21–27—Percentage Distribution of the Number of Industrial Establishments and Gross Value of Industrial Production at 1952 Prices, by Size of Enterprise, 1952–55

Output	1952	1953	1954	1955
Number of industrial establishments (1)	100.0	100.0	100.0	—
Large enterprises	16.4	17.8	18.6	—
Small enterprises	83.6	82.2	81.4	—
Gross value of industrial output (2)	100.0	100.0	100.0	100.0
Large enterprises	68.1	68.9	71.7	74.5
Small enterprises	31.9	31.1	28.4	25.5

Note: (—) indicates data unavailable for that year.
Sources: (1) Chen, *Chinese Economic Statistics*, pp. 182–83, Table 4.2. (2) *Tung-chi Kung-tso Tung-hsin* (*Statistical Work Bulletin*), No. 22, November, 1956.

[15] Hence it is not directly comparable with Table 21–27, which applies to all enterprises.

Table 21–28—Percentage Distribution of Number of Enterprises, Gross Value
of Production, Gross Value of Fixed Assets, and Number of Workers,
by Size of Establishment, in State and Joint Industry,
Excluding Handicrafts, 1955
(per cent)

Group Size, Number of Employees	Number of Enterprises	Gross Value of Production	Gross Value of Fixed Assets	Number of Workers
4 to 15 (30)	73.7	7.7	0.9	15.5
16 (31) to 449	24.7	39.2	17.5	36.0
500 or more	1.6	53.1	81.6	48.5
Total	100.0	100.0	100.0	100.0

Note: The distinction between size groups in lines 1 and 2 of the table coincides with the
coverage of the official concepts of 'small-scale industry' and 'large-scale industry.' An enterprise in 'small-scale industry' is one with fewer than sixteen workers and salaried employees
if it uses mechanical power, or with fewer than thirty-one workers and salaried employees if
it does not use mechanical power; in either case the number of employees must exceed three.
Source: S. Ishikawa, 'Choice of Techniques in Mainland China,' *The Developing Economies,*
Preliminary Issue No. 2, September–December, 1962, p. 27, Table 1.

Table 21–29—Official Indices of Gross Value of Industrial Production
at Constant Prices by Sector, 1949–58
(1952 = 100)

		Modern Industry			
Year	Total	Total	Modern Factory	Handicraft Factory	Handicrafts
1949	40.8	39.9	35.9	57.8	44.3
1950	55.7	52.0	49.4	63.8	69.2
1951	76.8	74.8	72.2	86.6	84.0
1952	100.0	100.0	100.0	100.0	100.0
1953	130.2	131.7	130.7	136.3	124.7
1954	151.4	153.7	154.1	151.6	143.1
1955	159.9	165.6	168.2	154.4	138.5
1956	205.0	217.1	228.3	167.6	160.0
1957	228.4	240.7	252.3	189.1	182.9
1958	379.6	—	443.3	—	—

Note: (—) indicates data unavailable for that year.
Source: Chen, *Chinese Economic Statistics*, p. 207, Table 437.

Despite the general declining trend, there were temporary ups and downs in the
ratios from year to year. In 1954, the handicrafts proportion of salt, sugar, and timber
went up. Both print cloth and edible vegetable oil showed increasing proportions
from 1954 to 1957. Even the handicrafts proportion of the gross value of production
increased from 1956 to 1957. Unfortunately, data for later years are not available for
the individual industries, but an increase in the handicrafts proportion in certain
industries during the Great Leap Forward period might be expected.

Table 21—31 demonstrates that the handicrafts sector owns an astonishingly small
proportion of the total industrial capital—slightly less than 4 per cent, but produces
more than 20 per cent of the gross value of industrial output, a disproportionately

558

Table 21–30—Percentage of Selected Outputs Produced by Handicrafts, 1949–59

Year	Gross Value of Industrial Production (1)	Coal (2)	Cotton Cloth (3)	Print Cloth (4)	Edible Vegetable Oil (5)	Paper (6)	Pig Iron (7)	Salt (8)	Silk Fabrics (9)	Sugar (10)	Gross Value of Textile Industry (11)	Timber (12)
1949	23.1	4.5	12.2	2.5	37.4	52.6	2.4	30.0	40.0	49.3		33.9
1950	26.5	4.5	9.8	2.5	37.4	63.0	2.0	30.0	39.2	49.6		32.2
1951	23.3	4.5	8.5	2.6	37.4	51.0	1.9	30.0	39.7	49.0		21.7
1952	21.3	4.5	7.9	2.6	26.4	38.4	2.6	30.0	40.0	44.8	15.0	10.5
1953	20.4	4.5	6.3	1.8	11.8	35.9	2.6	43.0	29.8	47.6	14.0	13.1
1954	20.1	5.0	5.6	1.5	11.7	39.2	2.5	32.3	23.1	49.9	12.1	19.8
1955	18.5	4.8	3.3	1.6	12.9	31.5	2.0	27.7	14.9	42.8	11.6	40.3
1956	16.6	4.0	1.3	2.6	16.8	26.9	1.0	22.4	8.4	35.8	11.2	48.7
1957	(29.4) 17.1	5.2	1.3	2.6	19.8	25.2	.8	22.4	4.1	35.4		28.2
1958	(25.5)											
1959	(25.4)											

Note: Blank spaces indicate data unavailable for those dates.

Sources: (1) Chen, *Chinese Economic Statistics*, p. 207; 1957–59 figures in parentheses from Li, 'China's Industrial Development,' p. 16, may not be comparable with the 1949–57 figures. (2) Chao, *Rate and Pattern of Industrial Growth*, p. 140, Table C–4. (3) *Ibid.* (4) *Ibid.* (5) *Ibid.* (6) Chen, *Chinese Economic Statistics*, p. 195. (7) Chao, *Rate and Pattern of Industrial Growth, loc. cit.* (8) *Ibid.* (9) *Ibid.* (10) Chen, *Chinese Economic Statistics*, p. 199; 1949–51 and 1957 figures from Chao, *loc. cit.* (11) Chen, *Chinese Economic Statistics*, p. 226. (12) Chao, *loc. cit.*

large quantity. This implies that the average productivity of capital in handicrafts is at least five times that of the rest of the industrial sector. Also the rate of growth of industrial capital in the factory sector is higher than that of handicrafts. Handicrafts production will probably be phased out eventually, but for the time being, at least, the handicrafts sector plays a significant role in industrial production, especially consumer goods production.

Table 21–31—Distribution of Industrial Capital by Method of Production, 1949–55

	Absolute Values (millions of yüan)		
Year	Total	Factory	Handicrafts
1949	9,430	9,100	330
1950			
1951			
1952	14,770	14,320	450
1953			
1954			
1955	24,800	23,869	610

	Percentage Distribution (per cent)		
Year	Total	Factory	Handicrafts
1949	100.0	96.5	3.5
1950			
1951			
1952	100.0	97.0	3.0
1953			
1954			
1955	100.0	96.2	3.8

Note: Blank spaces indicate data unavailable for those years.
Source: Year-end figures, from *T'ung-chi Kung-tso*, No. 1, January, 1957, p. 31.

Capital intensity. The choice of an optimal capital intensity for an economy ought to depend on the relative prices of capital and labor. How it should be changed over time depends on the relative supply elasticities of capital and labor. One would therefore expect that Communist China, with its abundant labor resources, would elect a strategy of industrialization that called for less capital deepening[16] but more labor absorption in industry.

However, a look at the record, which is tabulated in Tables 21–32 and 21–34 for industry as a whole and factory production, shows that for industry as a whole and for the factory sector of industry, there was continual capital deepening from 1952 to 1957, following an initial decline in the capital intensity due to fuller utilization of existing capacity during the period of rehabilitation. A reversal in trend occurred in 1958, when the concept of a dualistic development of industry was introduced and vigorously advanced. The small enterprises, with their native techniques, had typi-

[16] Capital deepening refers to the phenomenon of an increasing capital intensity over time.

cally low capital intensities. Hence there was an over-all decline in the industrial capital intensity.

This temporary decline was believed to be arrested after 1961, when efforts were made to relocate urban population in the countryside. The industrial capital intensity today is probably at the same level as in 1957. Unfortunately, there is no direct evidence bearing on this.

What explains this seemingly irrational behavior of using in relatively greater quantities the scarcer factor? Part of the reason lies in the desire to exploit economies of scale in production. These economies, however, are embodied in the capital goods. In other words, one cannot obtain large plants without obtaining capital-intensive ones. A second reason is the limited availability of labor-intensive capital goods. Most suppliers of Communist Chinese capital equipment, from the Soviet Union in the 1950's to industrialized Japan and the Western European countries of today, produce basically equipment with a high capital intensity. Without a costly indigenous research and development effort, labor-intensive capital equipment with low unit cost of production may simply be unavailable.

Table 21–32—Alternative Indices of Capital Intensity in Industry, 1949–58
(1952 = 100)

	Total Industrial Capital per Worker (1)		Gross Value of Fixed Assets per Worker (2)		Gross Value of Fixed Assets per Worker (3)
	Emerson	Hou	Emerson	Hou	
1949	89.2	89.6	113.0	113.5	
1950					
1951					
1952	100.0	100.0	100.0	100.0	100.0
1953					
1954					
1955	147.9	146.1	153.7	151.8	
1956					
1957			239.9	215.7	147.6
1958			187.4	179.4	57.5

Note: Blank spaces indicate data unavailable for those years.

Sources: (1) Total industrial capital, year-end figures, including net value of fixed assets and working capital, from *T'ung-chi Kung-tso*, No. 1, January, 1967, p. 31; industrial employment, year-end figures, from Emerson, 'Employment in Mainland China,' 1: 460–61, Table A-1; industrial employment, year-end figures, from Hou, 'Manpower, Employment, and Unemployment,' pp. 366–67, Table 15. (2) Gross value of industrial fixed assets, year-end figures: 1949, 1952, 1955 figures from *T'ung-chi Kung-tso*, *op. cit.*, pp. 31–33; 1957 and 1958 figures from State Statistical Bureau, *Ten Great Years*, p. 93. (3) Industrial employment figures from Emerson, *loc. cit.*, and Hou, *loc. cit.*; year-end figures, from Chao, 'Policies and Performance in Industry,' p. 572, Table 1.

Table 21–33 presents the gross value of fixed assets of industrial production per worker for selected industries, along with the index numbers. Like the aggregate picture, there appears to be a general tendency of capital deepening in all the industries from 1952 to 1955. For 1956, the few observations that are available seem to indicate a slight drop in capital intensity from 1955. Still, the capital intensity was substantially higher than in 1952. Consumer goods, as exemplified by textiles, were a notable exception. Their capital intensity increased only very slightly. Other industries made huge gains. It is worth noting that the capital intensity figures are

Table 21-33—Gross Value and Index Numbers of Fixed Assets for Industrial Production per Production Worker
in Selected Industries, 1952-58ᵃ

Absolute Value

(yüan)

	All enterprises							State and Joint Enterprises				
	1952	1953	1954	1955	1956	1957	1958	1952	1953	1954	1955	1956
Over-all average per workerᵇ	3,523					5,168	2,026	5,656	5,273	6,072	6,835	
Coal								5,029			5,417	
Petroleum								24,945			27,785	
Iron and steel								9,251	9,241	11,662	13,302	12,781
Iron and manganese mining								1,203	1,887	4,407	4,057	3,775
Iron and steel smelting								11,166	10,151	12,385	14,244	13,420
Mining and smelting of nonferrous metals								3,192	3,362	5,684	6,480	
Metal processing	2,996	3,139	3,538	4,357	5,037			4,750	5,029	5,528	6,035	
Chemical								8,120	9,066	9,867	11,114	
Building materials								2,431	2,291	2,531	3,641	
Rubber goods								4,725	4,714	4,372	10,688	
Paper	(5,464) 5,837	6,048	6,605	7,653	7,713			9,528	8,923	9,856	10,307	
Textiles	2,856	2,899	3,213	3,452	3,143			4,806	4,943	5,125	5,107	

Index numbers
(1952 = 100)

Over-all average per worker[b]	100.0	146.7	57.5				100.0	93.2	107.4	120.8	
Coal							100.0			107.7	
Petroleum							100.0			111.4	
Iron and steel							100.0	99.9	126.1	143.8	138.2
Iron and manganese mining							100.0	156.9	366.3	337.2	313.8
Iron and steel smelting							100.0	90.9	110.9	127.6	120.2
Mining and smelting of nonferrous metals							100.0	105.3	178.1	203.0	
Metal processing	100.0	104.8	118.1	145.4	168.1	(141.1)		105.9	116.4	127.1	
Chemical							100.0	111.1	121.5	136.9	
Building materials							100.0	94.2	104.1	149.8	
Rubber goods							100.0	99.8	92.5	226.2	
Paper	100.0	103.6	113.2	131.1	132.1			93.7	103.4	108.2	
Textiles	100.0	101.5	112.5	120.9	110.0			102.9	106.6	106.3	

Note: Blank spaces indicate data unavailable for those years.

Sources: [a] Year-end figures; unless otherwise stated, all figures are from Chen, *Chinese Economic Statistics*, pp. 260–61, Table 4.93. [b] All enterprise figures from Chao, 'Policies and Performance in Industry,' p. 572, Table 1. Figures in parentheses from Field, 'Labor Productivity in Industry,' p. 667, Table A-4.

Table 21-34—Alternative Indices of Capital Intensity in Factory Production,
1949-57
(1952 = 100)

						Net Value	
				Net Value of		of Fixed	Net Fixed
				Factory Fixed		Assets	Capital
Factory		Gross Value of		Assets (3)		per	per
Industrial		Factory Fixed		(Official		Worker	Worker
Capital (1)		Assets (2)		Estimates)		(4)	(5)
Emerson	Hou	Emerson	Hou	Emerson	Hou	Field	Liu-Yeh
1949	109.3	166.7	139.4	212.6			
1950							
1951							98.6
1952	100.0	100.0	100.0	100.0	100.0	100.0	100.0	100.0
1953	86.9	81.5					94.3	125.5
1954	125.3	115.3					101.0	150.9
1955	143.3	128.4	143.1	128.2	153.8	137.8	122.3	177.8
1956	134.3	113.3					136.1	205.2
1957			148.2	123.0			155.1	

Note: Blank spaces indicate data unavailable for those years.

Sources: (1) Factory industry capital, year-end figures, from Chen, *Chinese Economic Statistics*, p. 152, Table 3.8; factory employment, year-end figures excluding handicrafts, salt extraction, and urban public utilities, from Emerson, 'Employment in Mainland China,' 1: 460–61, Table A-1; factory employment, year-end figures, excluding handicrafts, from Hou, 'Manpower, Employment, and Unemployment,' pp. 366–67, Table 15. (2) Year-end figures at original cost, from Field, 'Labor Productivity in Industry,' p. 654; Emerson, *loc. cit.*; Hou, *loc. cit.* (3) Year-end figures, from Chen, *Chinese Communist Statistics*, p. 153, Table 3.9; Emerson, *loc. cit.*, and Hou, *loc. cit.* (4) Annual average figures, from Field, 'Labor Productivity in Industry,' p. 658, Table 8. (5) Year-end figures, including only factories, mining, and utilities, constant 1952 prices, from Liu and Yeh, *Economy of Chinese Mainland*, p. 240, Table 77.

lower for all enterprises than for state and joint enterprises alone. This can be explained by the fact that most new investments were made in the state and joint enterprises and that most large enterprises were state and joint enterprises.

Another indicator of the technological level of the various industries is the consumption of electric power per worker, which is tabulated in Table 21-35. It is seen that in every single one of the industries listed, the consumption of electricity per worker increased from 1952 to 1956.

Rates of utilization of capital equipment. Table 21-36 presents indices of utilization rates in selected industries in Communist China. As expected, utilization rates were generally rising for both producer and consumer goods industries. The reasons, however, were somewhat different. In the producer goods industries, which were also the priority industries, the output demands was always pushing against capacity, no matter how fast the latter was being expanded. With production targets increasing at an increasing rate, utilization factors would have to be stepped up to meet the demand. In the consumer goods industries, however, there was little or no new investment. Hence to meet demand, which might be considered to be growing at the same rate as population, a high utilization rate would be inevitable. An exception was the textiles industry, which showed considerable fluctuations in utilization rates, most probably caused by fluctuations in the cotton harvest.

Of course, the upward adjustments in utilization rates were made possible only by the existence of relatively low-cost labor for industrial employment. Otherwise they would not have been feasible.

Year	Industry as a Whole	Coal	Petroleum	Ferrous Metals	Nonferrous Metals	Chemical	Building Materials	Metal Processing	Textiles	Paper	Food
1952	1,430	2,577	7,847	4,174	2,753	5,665	1,113	751	1,681	6,188	839
1953											
1954											
1955		3,948						1,448	1,951	9,724	
1956	2,453	3,747	9,617	7,968	9,268	7,649	1,582	1,296	2,299	11,428	1,135
1956 Index (1952 = 100)	171.5	145.4	122.6	190.9	336.7	135.0	142.1	172.6	136.8	184.7	135.3

Note: Blank spaces indicate data unavailable for those years.   *Source:* Chen, *Chinese Economic Statistics*, p. 262, Table 4.94.

Table 21–36—Index of Utilization Rates in Selected Industries, 1949–58 (1952 = 100)

	1949	1950	1951	1952	1953	1954	1955	1956	1957	1958
Electric Power										
Generating equipment	61.3	64.5	81.1	100.0	115.8	119.2	118.7	125.3	126.3	145.2
Generating capacity	62.6			100.0			134.3			
Iron and Steel										
Iron-smelting equipment	37.4			100.0			113.0	137.4		
Steel-smelting equipment				100.0			143.2	149.7		
Open-hearth furnaces	50.7	69.1	80.3	100.0	102.7	107.9	126.9	139.5	150.8	162.8
Metal Processing										
Metal-cutting machines				100.0	120.2		120.2		132.5	169.5
Cotton Textiles										
Cotton-spinning equipment				100.0	103.7	105.2	87.5	105.7		
Cotton-weaving equipment				100.0	105.6	104.0	83.4	105.6		
Yarn capacity				100.0	105.6	108.4	92.1	112.9		
Cloth capacity				100.0	105.9	103.6	82.7	103.1		
Paper										
Paper machines				100.0			112.8			
Cigarette										
Cigarette machines				100.0			166.8			

Note: Blank spaces indicate data unavailable for those years.
Source: Chen, *Chinese Economic Statistics*, pp. 254–55, Table 4.86; p. 256, Table 4.87; and p. 258, Table 4.90.

Choice of Spatial Distribution

Coastal locations versus inland locations. Tables 21–37 and 21–38 show the distribution of gross value of factory output, gross value of industrial fixed assets, and basic construction investment between inland and coast areas. Coastal areas comprise Peking, Tientsin, Shanghai, Hopei, Liaoning, Shantung, Kiangsu, Fukien, Kwangtung, and Chekiang. The rest of the country belongs to inland areas. It is seen that, although the inland areas produced only approximately 30 per cent of the gross value of factory output, they owned more than 50 per cent of the gross value of industrial assets and received more than 50 per cent of total basic construction investment in industry. This serves to reveal the privileged position of the inland areas as against the coastal areas.

Moreover, the percentages of gross value of industrial production, gross value of industrial fixed assets, and industrial basic construction investment accounted for by the inland areas increased over time. There are at least four reasons for this strategy of spatial dispersion. First, it reduced vulnerability to a foreign attack. Second, it helped to relocate population so as to bolster the control of the northern and western border provinces. Third, it would lead to some technological spin-off. Fourth, it might be rational because of the location of the raw materials, mineral resources, or the final consumers. The decision in this instance is then based on a consideration of both national defense and economic factors.

Table 21–37—Percentage Distribution of the Gross Value of Factory Output at 1952 Prices and Gross Value of Industrial Fixed Assets at Original Cost Between Inland and Coastal Areas, 1949–57
(per cent)

Year	Total	Inland Areas	Coastal Areas
Gross Value of Factory Output at 1952 Prices (1)			
1949	100.0	22.7	77.3
1950			
1951			
1952	100.0	26.9	73.1
1953	100.0	27.7	72.3
1954	100.0	30.1	69.9
1955	100.0	32.0	68.0
1956	100.0	32.1	67.9
1957			
Gross Value of Industrial Fixed Assets at Original Cost (2)			
1953	100.0	52.0	48.0
1954			
1955	100.0	57.0	43.0

Note: Blank spaces indicate data unavailable for those years. Coastal areas consist of Peking, Tientsin, Shanghai, Hopei, Liaoning, Shantung, Kiangsu, Fukien, Kwangtung, and Chekiang. The rest of the country belongs to inland areas.

Sources: (1) Chen, *Chinese Economic Statistics,* p. 217, Table 4.43. (2) Year-end figures, excluding handicrafts, *T'ung-chi Kung-tso,* No. 1, January 1957, p. 32.

Table 21–38—Percentage Distribution of Basic Construction Investment in
Industry at Current Prices Between Inland and Coastal Areas, 1950–55
(per cent)

Period	Total	Inland Areas	Coastal Areas
1950–52	100.0	50.2	49.8
1953–55	100.0	55.2	44.8
1950–55	100.0	54.2	45.8

Source: T'ung-chi Kung-tso T'ung-hsin, No. 21, November, 1956.

Self-Sufficiency or Trade?

In the process of industrialization, a country normally has the choice of either specializing in the production and/or exports of certain commodities and importing others, or producing all commodities that are demanded domestically insofar as possible. The static comparative advantage doctrine argues strongly for the first alternative. However, other considerations tend to favor economic autarky. First, the dynamic comparative advantage may be different from the static comparative advantage. There may also be learning-by-doing effects and similar technological spin-offs. Second, not all commodities are available on the world market, and not all countries are willing trading partners at all times because of military and/or political reasons. Third, economic dependence on foreign countries either as suppliers or as customers tends to undermine national independence in political matters. Fourth, there is the balance of payments constraint. Finally, for a large country, total reliance on trade for the supply of essential commodities is not a feasible option.

For one or more of the above reasons, Communist China has from the start emphasized the importance of self-sufficiency. During the First Five-Year Plan, Communist China manufactured approximately 55 per cent of its capital equipment. This self-sufficiency rate was raised to 85 per cent during the Second Five-Year Plan. The proportion of steel products produced domestically climbed from 75 per cent during the First Five-Year Plan period to 90 per cent in the Second Five-Year Plan period.[17] The number of *above-norm* investment projects[18] that were designed and equipped domestically increased from 413 in the First Five-Year Plan to 1,013 in the Second.[19] Complete domestic self-sufficiency in petroleum was reportedly achieved in 1963.[20] More recently, a great deal of attention has been focused on domestic self-sufficiency in grains, so that Communist China would not be dependent on foreign suppliers for such a crucially important item.

For Communist China, self-sufficiency is an important national target that is consistent with its long-run objective. Insofar as trade is necessary, Communist China pursues a policy of trade diversification to minimize the dependence on any one supplier (as on the Soviet Union in the 1950's) and to increase its bargaining position in the international market. One of the aims of Chinese industrial development will remain the ability eventually to supply all of its own needs for industrial commodities.

---

[17] *Peking Review*, No. 41, October, 1963.

[18] The 'above-norm' or 'below-norm' investment refers to a standard amount of investment. When basic construction investment is greater than the standard amount, the project is subject to the direct control of the State Economic Commission and is said to be 'above-norm.' The 'norm' varies from industry to industry.

[19] *Peking Review*, No. 49, December, 1963.

[20] *JMJP*, December 4, 1963.

Table 21-39—Alternative Estimates of Indices of Industrial Production, 1949-68
(1952 = 100)

Year	Official Estimates (1)	Chao (2)	Liu-Yeh (3)	Jones (4)	Field I (5)	Yeh (6)	Soviet Union (7)	State (High) (8)	State (Low) (9)	Wu (10)	Field II (11)
1949	40.8	50.0			48.5						(48.5)
1950	55.7	63.3			61.1						
1951	76.8	81.2			81.3						
1952	100.0	100.0	100.0	100.0	100.0	100.0		(100.0)	(100.0)	100.0	(100.0)
1953	130.2	122.1	115.2		125.1	115.2				116.2	
1954	151.4	139.4	129.8		143.0	129.8				129.2	
1955	159.8	149.7	141.2		143.9	141.2				140.8	
1956	204.9	179.4	175.5		178.3	175.5				173.1	
1957	228.3	189.8	194.2	208.0	195.0	194.2		228.3	189.2	189.2	(195.0)
1958	379.4	251.5	231.7		256.3	243.1		319.6	264.9	226.2	255.5
1959	528.6	330.9	285.7		323.7	304.8		376.7	312.2	299.2	323.7
1960	681.1			417.0	336.0			410.9	340.6	346.2	315.9-319.8
1961					221.9			319.6	264.9	124.6	202.8-206.7
1962				229-250	195.4			251.1	208.1	302.9	202.8-210.6
1963	377.0				215.2			260.3	215.7	326.1	224.3-236.0

Table 21–39 (cont.)

Year	Official Estimates (1)	Chao (2)	Liu-Yeh (3)	Jones (4)	Field I (5)	Yeh (6)	Soviet Union (7)	State (High) (8)	State (Low) (9)	Wu (10)	Field II (11)
1964	433.6			292– 313	240.5			296.8	246.0	345.5	253.5–269.1
1965	481.3				263.1			342.5	283.8	360.0	286.7–310.1
1966	577.6						100.0	410.9	340.6	387.1	312.0–341.3
1967							75–80	353.9	293.3		263.3–292.5
1968	529.7						60–68	319.6	264.9		288.6–325.7

Industrial Output Index
Index (1952 = 100)

	1952	1953	1954	1955	1956	1957
	100.0	120.7	138.6	146.2	190.4	209.6

Note: Blank spaces indicate data unavailable for those years.

Sources: (1) Gross value of industrial production; 1949–58 figures from State Statistical Bureau, *Ten Great Years*, pp. 87 and 94; 1959–60, 1963–65 figures from Field, 'Chinese Communist Industrial Production,' 1: 273, Table 1 (1960 and 1965 are planned figures only); 1966 figure from *Kung-jen Jih-pao* (*Workers' Daily*), December 31, 1966, 1968 figure from NCNA, May 11, 1969. (2) Chao, *Rate and Pattern of Industrial Growth*, p. 88, Table 19. (3) Net value added in industry in 1952 prices, from Liu and Yeh, *Economy of Chinese Mainland*, p. 66, Table 8; 1958–59 figures are conjectural estimates. (4) E. F. Jones, 'The Emerging Pattern of China's Economic Revolution,' in Joint Economic Committee of the U.S. Congress, *Economic Profile of Mainland China*, p. 95, Table V. (5) Field, *loc. cit.*; note that this series is different from another series given by Field in 'Labor Productivity in Industry,' p. 647, Table 3, as follows:

(6) Net value added in industry in 1952 prices; 1952–57 figures from Liu and Yeh, *loc. cit.* 1958–59 figures from K. C. Yeh, 'Capital Formation,' in Galenson, *et al.*, eds., *Economic Trends in Communist China*, p. 532, Table A-1. (7) Moscow Radio, February 12, 1969. (8) Industrial output, from U.S. Department of State, *Issues in United States Foreign Policy—No. 4: Communist China*, Department of State Publication 8499, Superintendent of Documents, U.S. Government Printing Office, Washington, D.C., December, 1969, p. 13 (the original series starts with 1957; it is linked with the official series). (9) *Ibid.* The series is linked with the Wu series. (10) Net value added in industry in 1952 prices; 1952–61 figures from Wu, Hoeber, and Rockwell, *Economic Potential of Communist China*, 1: 24, Table 51; 1962–66 figures from unpublished work of Y. L. Wu. (11) R. M. Field, 'Industrial Production in Communist China: 1957–1968,' *The China Quarterly*, No. 42 (April–June, 1970), pp. 46–64. The new Field index is linked with the old Field index in 1957.

INDUSTRIAL PERFORMANCE

Aggregate Industrial Growth

In Table 21–39, the alternative estimates of the indices of industrial production in Communist China are presented. Despite considerable diversity in these various estimates, the general trend is similar. There was almost uninterrupted progress from 1949 to 1960, with the annual growth rates accelerated during the Great Leap Forward. Then followed a period of decline, reaching a trough in 1962. The period 1962–66 was one of steady growth, and by 1965 industrial production was probably restored to the 1959 level. After 1966, industrial production took a downturn again because of the direct and indirect disruptions of the Cultural Revolution. The decline was reportedly arrested in 1969. However, information concerning the most recent developments is extremely scarce.

Table 21–40 presents alternative estimates of the average annual rates of growth of industrial production during the different periods. One can see that the highest rate of growth was achieved in the period of rehabilitation, followed by the First Five-Year Plan, with various estimates ranging between 13.6 and 18.0 per cent. The poorest performance was during the period of readjustment, with estimated growth rates ranging from — 6.9 per cent to 0.8 per cent. The Second Five-Year Plan Period

Table 21–40—Alternative Estimates of the Annual Growth Rates
of Industrial Production, 1949–68
(per cent per annum)

Period	Official Estimates (1)	Chao (2)	Liu-Yeh (3)	Jones (4)	Field I (5)	Yeh (6)	State (High) (7)	State (Low) (8)	Wu (9)	Field II (10)
1949–52	34.8	26.0			27.3					27.3
1949–65	16.7				11.1					11.7–12.3
1952–65	12.8			{ 8.6– 9.2	7.7		9.9	8.4	10.4	8.4–9.1
1952–68	11.0						7.5	6.3		6.8–7.7
1952–57	18.0	13.7	14.2	15.8	14.3	14.2	18.0	13.6	13.6	14.3
1957–62				{ 1.9– 3.7	0.0		1.9	1.9	9.9	0.8–1.6
1960–65	—6.7		{ 6.9– 5.6	—4.8			—3.6	—3.6	0.8	—2.2––0.4
1962–66							13.1	13.1	6.3	10.3–14.0
1965–68	3.2						—2.3	—2.3		—2.4–4.3

Note: Blank spaces indicate data unavailable for those years.

Sources: (1) Gross value of industrial production. 1949–58 figures from State Statistical Bureau, *Ten Great Years*, pp. 87, 94; 1959–60, 1963–65 figures from Field, 'Chinese Communist Industrial Production,' 1 : 273, Table 1 (1960 and 1965 are planned figures only); 1968 figure from NCNA, Peking, May 11, 1969. (2) Chao, *Rate and Pattern of Industrial Growth*, p. 88, Table 19. (3) Net value added in industry in 1952 prices, from Liu and Yeh, *Economy of Chinese Mainland*, p. 66, Table 8. (4) Jones, 'Emerging Pattern of China's Economic Revolution,' p. 95, Table V. (5) Field, *loc. cit.* (6) Net value added in industry in 1952 prices; 1952–57 figures from Liu and Yeh, *loc. cit.* (7) Industrial output, from U.S. Department of State, *Issues in United States Foreign Policy No. 4: Communist China*, p. 13 (original series starts with 1957 and is linked with the official series. (8) *Ibid.* (the series is linked with the Wu series). (9) Net value added in industry in 1952 prices. 1952–61 figures from Wu, Hoeber, and Rockwell, *Economic Potential of Communist China*, 1 : 241, Table 51; 1962–66 figures from unpublished work of Y. L. Wu. (10) Field, 'Industrial Production in Communist China'; the new Field index is linked with the old Field index in 1957.

did poorly because of the failure of the Great Leap. Between 1957 and 1962, growth of industrial output was estimated to lie between 0.0 and 3.7 per cent per annum. The 9.9 per cent estimate by Wu seems to be far too high and is accounted for by a higher estimate of the rate of recovery after 1960. From the trough of 1962, industrial production grew at an average between 6.3 per cent[21] and 14.0 per cent until 1966. For 1967 and 1968 there appeared to have been annual declines of between 10 and 15 per cent per annum. Despite such short-run fluctuations, long-run growth rates are quite substantial. From 1949 to 1965, the average annual rate of industrial growth was estimated to be between 11.1 per cent and 16.7 per cent. In 1952–65, the estimated average annual rates of growth ranged from 7.7 per cent to 12.8 per cent. During 1952–68, the average growth rate lay between 6.3 per cent and 11 per cent. The official estimate, however, seems to be too high. A long-run growth rate of approximately 7 per cent per annum appears to have been achieved. To this extent, the industrialization program should be regarded as moderately, but by no means spectacularly, successful.

Table 21–41 gives alternative estimates of the indices of factory production in Communist China. A comparison between Table 21–39 and Table 21–41 reveals that

Table 21–41—Alternative Estimates of the Indices of Factory Production,
1949–63
(1952 = 100)

	Official Estimates (1)	Chao (2)	Liu-Yeh (3)	Field (4)	Yeh (5)	Wu (6)
1949	39.9	44.3		41.1		
1950	52.0	57.7		54.6		
1951	74.8	77.0		77.6		
1952	100.0	100.0	100.0	100.0	100.0	100.0
1953	131.7	124.7	122.8	122.8	124.7	125.6
1954	153.6	141.6	143.7	143.1	141.6	146.3
1955	165.6	146.9	159.9	148.4	149.6	161.0
1956	217.1	182.2	212.4	188.3	182.3	211.0
1957	240.6	195.9	240.2	209.0	195.9	234.1
1958		272.6	291.6	282.1	309.6	287.8
1959		371.4	376.7	362.3	398.6	402.4
1960						482.9
1961						139.0
1962						
1963	431.4					

Note: Blank spaces indicate data unavailable for those years.

Sources: (1) Gross value of factory production; 1949–57 figures from Chao, *Rate and Pattern of Industrial Growth*, p. 12, Table 2; 1963 figure from Field, 'Chinese Communist Industrial Production,' 1: 273, Table 1. (2) Chao, *Rate and Pattern of Industrial Growth*, p. 89, Table 20. (3) Net value added in factory production in 1952 prices, from Liu and Yeh, *Economy of Chinese Mainland*, p. 66, Table 8 (1958 and 1959 are conjectural estimates only). (4) Field, *loc. cit.* (5) Net value added in industry in 1952 prices; 1952–57 figures from Liu and Yeh, *loc. cit.*; 1958–59 figure from Yeh, 'Capital Formation,' p. 532, Table A-1. (6) Net value added in industry in 1952 prices; 1952–61 figures from Wu, Hoeber, and Rockwell, *Economic Potential of Communist China*, 1: 241, Table 51.

---

[21] Since Wu's 1962 estimate appears to be too high, the 6.3 per cent growth rate for 1962–66 is probably an underestimate.

the factory sector has consistently grown faster than industry as a whole. This is to be expected in view of the emphasis on factory production, large enterprises, and capital-intensive investment projects.

Aggregate Industrial Labor Productivity

Industrial labor productivity. In Table 21–42, alternative estimates of indices of labor productivity in industry are presented.[22] The choice of the particular series is dictated by availability and comparability of data. An attempt is made to present the upper and lower bound estimates. The estimated growth rates are presented in Table 21–43. There is a wide divergence of growth rates depending on the particular series of employment figures used.

However, the different series generally agree on an increasing trend from 1949 to 1957. On the other hand, in 1958, according to Field's index of industrial production, labor productivity declined. This appears to be consistent with figures on capital intensity, which also show an increasing trend between 1949 and 1957 but a drop in 1958.

According to all estimates, the growth rate of industrial labor productivity was substantial during 1949–57. The lowest average annual rate estimated is 8.7 per cent, quite an accomplishment.

Factory labor productivity. Table 21–44 shows alternative estimates of indices of factory labor productivity. With the exception of the Field-Hou series, all series show an increasing trend from 1949 to 1956. A slight decline occurred in 1957, followed by a drastic fall in 1958 as a result of the mass industrialization movement. Factory labor productivity in 1963, however, seemed to have once again surpassed the 1956 peak level. This could well have been the effect of closing down inefficient enterprises and reduction of superfluous workers from industrial enterprises.

The growth rates computed from the various series are given in Table 21–45. The differences among them are striking. Taking all factors into account, a long-run growth rate of 5 per cent appears to be a reasonable estimate. The 1952–57 growth rates, with the exception of the Field-Hou series, also appear consistent with the indices of growth of capital intensity in factory production.

Finally, a remarkable fact revealed by these productivity figures is that industrial labor productivity as a whole seemed to grow faster than factory labor productivity from 1949 to 1957 despite the much larger proportion of new investments going into the factory sector. This implies that the marginal productivity of capital in the handicrafts sector must have been relatively high.

Labor Productivity in Selected Industries

Available estimates of productivity in selected industries[23] indicate that, on the whole, productivity rose during the period of rehabilitation and the First Five-Year Plan, confirming the aggregate observations. The producer goods industries, e.g., iron and steel, coal, and cement, however, had much higher rates of growth of productivity, by comparison with the consumer goods, industries, e.g., textiles. Ferrous metals seemed to have enjoyed the highest rate of growth of labor productivity, followed closely by paper. The average growth rate of labor productivity in all industry is estimated to be 7 per cent per annum during this period.

---

[22] Ideally, total factor productivities should be calculated. However, data on the relative shares of capital and labor in Communist Chinese industry are not available.

[23] R. M. Field analyzes the labor productivity differential across industries in some detail. See R. M. Field, 'Labor Productivity in Industry,' in W. Galenson, A. Eckstein, and T. C. Liu, eds., *Economic Trends in Communist China* (Chicago: Aldine Publishing Company, 1968), pp. 637–70.

Table 21-42—Alternative Estimates of the Indices of Productivity
in Industry, 1949–58
(1952 = 100)

	Official Estimates (1)			Field (3)	
	Emerson	Hou	Liu-Yeh (2)	Emerson	Hou
1949	54.8	55.0	—	65.2	65.4
1950	68.7	68.7	—	75.3	75.3
1951	83.6	83.4	—	88.5	88.3
1952	100.0	100.0	100.0	100.0	100.0
1953	119.1	118.8	108.2	114.5	114.1
1954	126.2	125.6	114.1	119.2	118.7
1955	131.2	129.9	126.6	118.1	117.0
1956	179.7	168.2	160.9	156.4	146.4
1957	199.2	177.8	165.4	170.2	151.9
1958	233.3	217.7	—	157.6	147.0

Note: (—) indicates data unavailable for that year.

Sources: (1) Gross value of industrial production; 1949–58 figures from State Statistical Bureau, *Ten Great Years*, pp. 87, 94; industrial employment, annual average figures, from Emerson, 'Employment in Mainland China,' 1: 460–61, Table A-1; Hou, 'Manpower, Employment, and Unemployment,' pp. 366–67, Table 15. (2) Net value added in industry in 1952 prices, from Liu and Yeh, *Economy of Chinese Mainland*, p. 66, Table 8; industrial employment, annual average figures, from *ibid.*, p. 69, Table 11. (3) Field, 'Chinese Communist Industrial Production,' p. 273, Table 1; note that this series differs from another series given in Field, 'Labor Productivity in Industry,' p. 647, Table 3, as follows:

	1952	1953	1954	1955	1956	1957
Industrial Output Index (1952 = 100)	100.0	120.7	138.6	146.2	190.4	209.6

Industrial employment figures from Emerson, *loc. cit.*, and Hou, *loc. cit.*, respectively.

Table 21-43—Alternative Estimates of the Average Annual Rates of Growth
of Productivity in Industry During Selected Periods, 1949–57
(per cent)

	Official Estimates (1)			Field (3)	
	Emerson	Hou	Liu-Yeh (2)	Emerson	Hou
1949–52	22.2	22.1	—	15.3	15.2
1949–57	17.5	15.8	—	12.7	11.1
1952–57	14.8	12.2	10.6	11.2	8.7

Note: (—) indicates data unavailable for those years.

Sources: (1) Gross value of industrial production; 1949–57 figures from State Statistical Bureau, *Ten Great Years*, pp. 87 and 94; industrial employment, annual average figures, from Emerson, 'Employment in Mainland China,' 1: 460–61, Table A-1; Hou, 'Manpower, Employment, and Unemployment,' pp. 366–67, Table 15. (2) Net value added in industry in 1952 prices; from Liu and Yeh, *Economy of Chinese Mainland*, p. 66, Table 8; industrial employment, annual average figures, from *ibid.*, p. 69, Table 11. (3) Field, 'Chinese Communist Industrial Production,' p. 273, Table 1; note that this series is different from another series given in Field, 'Labor Productivity in Industry,' p. 647, Table 3, as follows:

	1952	1953	1954	1955	1956	1957
Industrial Output Index (1952 = 100)	100.0	120.7	138.6	146.2	190.4	209.6

Industrial employment figures from Emerson, *loc. cit.*, and Hou, *loc. cit.*, respectively.

Table 21-44—Alternative Estimates of the Indices of Productivity
in Factory Production, 1949-63
(1952 = 100)

	Official Estimates			Field (4)		
	I (1)	II (2) Emerson-Richman	Liu-Yeh (3)	Emerson	Hou	Field (5)
1949		62.8		64.7	94.5	
1950		77.8		81.7	111.7	
1951		92.9		96.4	110.9	
1952	100.0	100.0	100.0	100.0	100.0	100.0
1953	114.0	111.5	105.1	104.0	96.0	104.3
1954	124.0	118.6	119.9	110.5	98.0	111.5
1955	137.0	127.9	128.0	114.6	99.6	120.8
1956	162.0	153.9	155.6	133.4	110.7	142.2
1957	161.0	150.8	153.7	131.0	104.8	140.2
1958				86.0	62.7	
1959						
1960						
1961						
1962						
1963		$\left\{ \begin{array}{l} 168.6- \\ 175.3 \end{array} \right.$				

Note: Blank spaces indicate data unavailable for those years.

Sources: (1) Gross value of factory production per worker, from Field, 'Labor Productivity in Industry,' p. 639, Table 1. (2) Gross value of factory production; 1949–57 figures from Chao, *Rate and Pattern of Industrial Growth*, p. 12, Table 2; 1963 figure from Field, 'Chinese Communist Industrial Production,' 1: 273, Table 1; factory employment, annual average figures excluding handicrafts, salt extraction, and urban public utilities, from Emerson, 'Employment in Mainland China,' 1: 460–61, Table A-1; 1963 figure obtained by interpolation of figures from Richman, *Industrial Society in Communist China*, pp. 600–603, Table 7–2. (3) Liu and Yeh, *Economy of Chinese Mainland*, p. 93, Table 23. (4) Factory production, indices from Field, *loc. cit.*; factory employment figures from Emerson, *loc. cit.*, and from Hou, 'Manpower, Employment, and Unemployment,' pp. 366–67, Table 15; latter figures exclude handicrafts. (5) Field, 'Labor Productivity in Industry,' p. 647, Table 3.

Unfortunately, data on the indices of capital intensity are too scarce for meaningful comparison.

Other Achievements

Other notable achievements of Communist Chinese industry include the increase in the level of self-sufficiency, as discussed earlier, and the development and manufacture of nuclear weapons and delivery systems.

CONCLUSIONS AND FUTURE PROSPECTS

In this chapter I have surveyed the process of industrialization in Communist China during the two decades following 1949, insofar as the data permitted. As in any survey of this nature, I have made broad generalizations and ignored the specific details. It is also apparent that because of the scarcity and unreliability of official data and the

Table 21–45—Alternative Estimates of the Average Annual Rates of Growth
of Productivity in Factory Production During Selected Periods, 1949–63
(per cent)

| | Official Estimates | | Field (4) | | | |
	I (1)	II (2) Emerson- Richman	Liu-Yeh (3)	Emerson	Hou	Field (5)
1949–52		16.8		15.6	1.9	
1949–57		11.6		9.2	1.3	
1949–63		7.3–7.6				
1952–57	10.0	8.6	9.0	5.5	0.9	7.0
1952–63		4.9–5.2				
1957–63		1.9–2.5				

Note: Blank spaces indicate data unavailable for those years.
Sources: (1) Gross value of factory production per worker, from Field, 'Labor Productivity in Industry,' p. 639, Table 1. (2) Gross value of factory production; 1949–57 figures from Chao, *Rate and Pattern of Industrial Growth*, p. 12, Table 2; 1963 figure from Field, 'Chinese Communist Industrial Production,' 1: 273, Table 1; factory employment, annual average figures excluding handicrafts, salt extraction, and urban public utilities, from Emerson, 'Employment in Mainland China,' 1: 460–61, Table A-1; 1963 figure obtained by interpolation of figures from Richman, *Industrial Society in Communist China*, pp. 600–603, Table 7–2. (3) Liu and Yeh, *Economy of Chinese Mainland*, p. 93, Table 23. (4) Factory production, indices from Field, *loc. cit.*; factory employment figures from Emerson, *loc. cit.*; and from Hou, 'Manpower, Employment, and Unemployment,' pp. 366–67, Table 15; latter figures excludes handicrafts. (5) Field, 'Labor Productivity in Industry,' p. 647, Table 3.

diversity of unofficial estimates for the same time series, the study of the economic performance of Communist China is rather difficult. Here, an effort is made to bring all available sets of estimates together to close data gaps that exist in different series in order to give a more or less continuous description of the industrial sector for the period 1949–68 wherever possible and to provide a more balanced view. Needless to say, these findings depend on the underlying series coming reasonably close to the true values. The following is a brief summary of some of the findings.

First, industry is observed to have grown at a long-run average annual rate of approximately 7.0 per cent. Considering that agriculture only grows at 2 or 3 per cent per annum, the share of industry in national income will probably increase further in the future. This long-run rate may be compared to the prewar rate of growth for 1912–49, estimated by Chang, of 5.5 per cent per annum.[24] Between 1912 and 1936, the year before the outbreak of the Sino-Japanese War, the average annual rate of growth is estimated by Chang to be 9.2 per cent.[25] Thus, this long-run estimate appears consistent with historical evidence.

Second, the long-run rate of growth of industrial labor productivity may be estimated at approximately 5.0 per cent per annum, the rate achieved during 1952–63 in the factory sector, in the absence of an alternative. Although industrial labor productivity did grow faster than factory labor productivity in 1949–57, the long-run industrial rate is probably determined by the rate of growth of factory labor productivity because of the relative expansion of the factory sector. Part of the increase in

[24] J. K. Chang, 'Industrial Development of Mainland China, 1912–1949,' *The Journal of Economic History*, 27, No. 1 (March, 1967): 68, Table 4.
[25] *Ibid.*

productivity may be accounted for by increases in capital intensity and part may be accounted for by increases in the rate of utilization.

Third, it follows from the estimates of the long-run rates of growth of industrial production and productivity that industrial employment will grow at a long-run average rate of 2 per cent per annum, or about the same as the rate of population growth. It is therefore unrealistic to expect industry to absorb substantially increasing proportions of the total labor force.

Fourth, aside from the experience of the Great Leap, Communist Chinese industries generally increased their capital intensity and scale during the two decades under study. There is some uncertainty as to whether this policy will continue to be followed.

Fifth, Communist Chinese industry has increased its level of self-sufficiency substantially. This trend is likely to continue.

Sixth, the policy of further dispersal of industry from the coastal areas into the inland areas has produced concrete results. However, this policy appears to be under review. A goal that has received heavy emphasis recently is that of provincial self-sufficiency. This may have an impact on the dispersal policy.

Finally, one should re-emphasize that the fulfillment of the five economic tasks is not the primary objective of the Communist Chinese regime. Sometimes actions were taken that would delay, if not obstruct, the accomplishment of the economic tasks, e.g., the downgrading of the professionals and experts during the 1957 rectification campaign, the Sino-Soviet dispute with the consequent cessation of Soviet aid, and the political 'struggles' during the Cultural Revolution resulting in widespread work stoppages. In each of these instances, one or more of the tasks was adversely affected in the short run. The Great Leap Forward, on the other hand, might be considered an unfortunate but genuine attempt to overcome certain bottlenecks in the economy that were preventing the successful implementation of the economic tasks.

What does the future hold for Chinese industry? The answer depends a great deal on internal politics. If a pragmatic economic policy is adopted, such as during the First Five-Year Plan and the readjustment period, it is possible that industry will grow at a fairly rapid rate. Previous rates of growth achieved during these periods of pragmatic economic management range from 6.3 per cent[26] to 18.0 per cent. Capital intensity is likely to grow over time too. On the other hand, if politics is to take total command, a repetition of the Great Leap Forward or at least a temporary period of stagnation such as those that took place during 1966–69 appears most probable. During these periods, the growth rate of industry was either negative or negligibly small. Another 'leap' will most likely be accompanied by another movement of industrialization by the masses. Overall capital intensity will decline. The commitment for priority development of agriculture to achieve total domestic food self-sufficiency seems to be so well entrenched that it would be preserved regardless of the outcomes of the ideological and political conflicts.

One should not take it for granted, however, that a period of rapid industrial growth will automatically ensue if the pragmatists return to power. Despite on-and-off experimentation and practice in economic planning for almost two decades, an effective, functioning planning mechanism was never really developed. The statistical system, which has the task of providing the information vital for planning and control, has not yet fully recovered from the fiasco during the Great Leap Forward. Moreover, other bottlenecks, such as in coal, grains, electric power, or technical personnel, may develop. Other factors, such as increased demands for military hardware and external conflicts, may also become constraints to rapid industrial growth. Nevertheless, it is safe to conclude that the fluctuations in annual growth rates will be much less violent under the pragmatists than under the revolutionaries of the extreme left.

---

[26] As noted previously, 6.3 per cent is probably an underestimate.

Regardless of the political orientation of Mao's successors, there will be continual efforts to increase the level of self-sufficiency and to promote the establishment and development of the technological industries, such as electronics and computers. In the longer run, international trade is likely to diminish in relative importance as a source of supply of capital goods to Communist Chinese industry.

SELECTED BIBLIOGRAPHY

CHAO, KANG. *The Rate and Pattern of Industrial Growth in Communist China.* Ann Arbor: The University of Michigan Press, 1965. Employs wage-bill weights to reconstruct an index of industrial production in Communist China, 1949–59.

GALENSON, WALTER; ALEXANDER ECKSTEIN; and TA-CHUNG LIU, eds. *Economic Trends in Communist China.* Chicago: Aldine Publishing Company, 1968. Contains the following articles on Communist Chinese industrial development: K. CHAO, 'Policy and Performance in Industry'; D. H. PERKINS, 'Industrial Planning and Management'; and R. M. FIELD, 'Labor Productivity in Industry.'

Joint Economic Committee of the U.S. Congress. *An Economic Profile of Mainland China.* 2 vols. Washington, D.C.: Superintendent of Documents, U.S. Government Printing Office, 1967. Contains the following articles on industrial development: K. P. WANG, 'The Mineral Resource Base of Communist China'; R. M. FIELD, 'Chinese Communist Industrial Production'; and J. ASHTON, 'Development of Electric Energy Resources in Communist China.'

LI, CHOH-MING. *Economic Development of Communist China: An Appraisal of the First Five Years of Industrialization.* Berkeley and Los Angeles: University of California Press, 1959. Examines economic growth of Communist China during the First Five-Year Plan period, relying primarily on published Chinese Communist statistics.

LI, CHOH-MING, ed. *Industrial Development in Communist China.* New York: Praeger Publishers, Inc., 1964. A collection of eleven essays on various aspects of industrial development in Communist China, originally published in the *China Quarterly.*

LIU, TA-CHUNG, and K. C. YEH. *The Economy of the Chinese Mainland: National Income and Economic Development, 1933–1959.* Princeton, N.J.: Princeton University Press, 1965. LIU and YEH independently estimate the various components of Chinese national income based on statistics on the prices and quantities of individual commodities.

RICHMAN, BARRY M. *Industrial Society in Communist China.* New York: Random House, 1969. An account of the author's visit to Communist China; also gives assorted statistics on the various industrial enterprises visited by the author.

WU, YUAN-LI. *The Steel Industry in Communist China,* New York: Praeger Publishers, Inc., 1965. A comprehensive analysis of the Chinese steel industry and an objective evaluation of the efficiency of Chinese performance in industrial planning and development in general.

WU, YUAN-LI, with H. C. LING. *Economic Development and the Use of Energy Resources in Communist China.* New York: Praeger Publishers, Inc., 1963. A comprehensive survey of Communist China's energy resources and their role in China's economic development since 1949. Extensive data have been compiled on the major energy industries, such as coal and electric power.

WU, YUAN-LI, with H. C. LING and G. H. WU. *The Spatial Economy of Communist China.* New York: Praeger Publishers, Inc., 1967. Studies the geographical distribution of human and industrial resources as well as the transportation system in Communist China.

22

BANKING AND FINANCE

GEORGE N. ECKLUND

THE BANKING SYSTEM

Organization of Banks

BANKING in China in the early twentieth century resembled a great many independent retail merchants who operated with no unifying organization and little governmental control. The large number of banks scattered throughout the country were of varied origin and served many purposes. There were banks organized solely to finance internal trade; banks owned by central, provincial, and local government units and used primarily to support government operations; branches of foreign banks; and small private banks with miscellaneous functions. Many banks brought out their own notes to circulate as currency, but the value of the notes often fluctuated and ranged from good to worthless depending on the bank of issue.[1] The Nationalist government attempted to restrict the number of activities of private and foreign banks and to unify the government banks. Nevertheless, government banks continued to issue their own currency and to float loans for government organizations, while the private banks expanded their note issues and speculative loans. Most banks held inadequate reserves, and the periodic exhaustion of reserves led to fluctuations in the supply of funds. Because speculative loans for trade and other purposes were often more profitable and absorbed large amounts of funds, industry sometimes found it difficult to obtain loans for investment, and economic growth was thereby retarded. To bring some order and stability to the system, the government gave the Central Bank of China the sole authority to issue currency and to perform all the other functions normally entrusted to a central bank. At the same time, private and foreign branch banks were greatly circumscribed. Nationalist attempts to strengthen and unify the banking system in China were halted when the Communists overran the mainland in 1949.

In December, 1948, the Communists established the People's Bank of China, an institution that was to become the focal point for all banking policy and operations throughout the mainland. As they subsequently took over other parts of China, the Communists turned branches of the Central Bank of China into branches of the new People's Bank. Starting with fewer than 200 branches in 1950, the People's Bank had expanded within several years to include several thousand branches, sub-branches, and other offices throughout the country, with more than 300,000 employees.[2]

---

[1] Albert Feuerwerker, *China's Early Industrialization* (Cambridge: Harvard University Press, 1958), pp. 225–41.

[2] Audrey Donnithorne, *China's Economic System* (London: George Allen & Unwin Ltd., 1967), pp. 402–7.

The People's Bank. The People's Bank is administratively responsible directly to the State Council, although it works closely with the Ministry of Finance. The primary duties of the People's Bank are: (1) to issue currency and thus to regulate the amount of currency in circulation: (2) to act as the repository for all taxes and other payments made to the state; (3) to pay out the funds allocated through the government budget to state enterprises, government departments, and other agencies; (4) to loan money as working capital to state enterprises; (5) to provide the central accounting services for state enterprises, government departments, and military units, and thus to monitor the financial transactions among these organizations; (6) to hold all foreign currency and precious metals for the government.

Other banks. Subordinate to the People's Bank are several other financial institutions. These include the Bank of China, responsible for foreign exchange operations; the Bank of Communications, which provides investment funds to joint state-private enterprises; the People's Construction Bank, which channels investment funds to state enterprises; and the People's Insurance Company, which insures state enterprises and some agricultural units against property damage and loss of life. In addition, the Agricultural Bank of China existed from 1955 to 1957, primarily to extend long-term loans to farm families who were required to join the agricultural cooperatives during 1955–56. The Agricultural Bank of China was again inaugurated in 1963, but very little information is available on its operations. Agricultural credit cooperatives have performed many of the normal banking functions in rural areas that had no branches of the People's Bank.

The Communists did not immediately expropriate all private enterprises when they gained control of the mainland; instead, they closely supervised what they did not expropriate until state enterprises could assume completely the role that private businessmen had fulfilled in the economy. Banking was no exception. Private bankers were allowed to continue operating after 1949, but they were required to report all details of their assets and liabilities, directors and shareholders, ownership and capital. Their interest rates had to be approved by the People's Bank; they had to submit frequent reports to the People's Bank on their loans and deposits; and they were not permitted to accept deposits from government organizations. After 1950 they were urged to consolidate and to join with the government in establishing joint public-private banks. Gradually, as the People's Bank greatly extended its branch network, the private banks found their activities increasingly restricted. By the mid-1950's private banks were of no consequence to the economy, and in the 1960's they were no longer in existence. Nevertheless, they had served a useful purpose in the early mixed private and state economy of the People's Republic.

Monetary control. In order to overcome the monetary chaos that existed in mainland China during the late 1940's, the Communists energetically pursued a campaign to restore public confidence in the currency. As they took over large areas of China, the Communists exchanged the old currencies for new 'people's money,' or *jen-min-p'iao* (JMP). For example, in East China one JMP was exchanged for 100,000 units of the existing Nationalist currency, 'gold yüan.'[3] The new JMP, or yüan, as it is also known, became the only medium of exchange, and circulation of foreign exchange and of gold and silver as money were prohibited.

The Chinese now circulate both coins and paper money. Since the currency reform of 1955, which exchanged 10,000 old yüan for one new yüan primarily to facilitate bookkeeping transactions, the paper currency has been in various denominations. In 1964, the denominations were one, two, and five yüan; one, two, and five chiao (ten chiao equal one yüan); and one, two, and five fen (100 fen equal one yüan). In 1957, aluminum coins began circulating in denominations of one, two, and five fen. A new

---

[3] Ling Tseng, 'Do We Have Inflation Now?,' *Ching-chi Yen-chiu (Economic Research)*, No. 10 (Peking: K'u-hsüeh Ch'u-pan-she, 1957), p. 39.

ten-yüan note began circulation in 1957 but was discontinued in the early 1960's. The yüan has no official rate of exchange with Western currencies, but it is approximately the equivalent of forty-two cents U.S.

By 1950, the government had established the JMP as the only circulating currency and could move ahead with a program designed to stabilize prices and, concomitantly, the value of the JMP. The resulting 'three balances' program of 1950 sought a balance (1) between government revenues and expenditures, (2) between physical production and money incomes, and (3) between bank receipts and payments. The first balance would be accomplished by a large increase in tax collections through a revision of the entire tax structure. The second balance would come as production and domestic trade were resumed. The third balance required controls over bank credit and a stimulation of savings. In addition, the government began to assert a systematic control over prices, wages, and profits.

To supplement its positive program for monetary stability, the government used various methods of drawing cash away from private holders and into the banking system. These ranged from relatively mild pressure on individuals to buy government bonds and open savings accounts to heavy-handed 'collections' from those accused of hiding large assets and accumulating unreasonable profits.

Bond sales. The People's Victory Bond of 1950, amounting to 260 million (new) yüan and representing 4 per cent of budgetary revenue, was distributed among private business (70 per cent of the total), peasants (7 per cent), state employees (12 per cent), and all others (11 per cent).[4] Some statements in the press implied that these bonds were widely distributed, and at least some of them may have been purchased under duress. For example, redemption privileges of these bonds expired in September, 1955, but several lengthy extensions were granted because many people were said to be unfamiliar with bonds and ignorant of redemption procedures, while others lived in remote areas where cashing bonds was extremely difficult.

Substantially more funds were collected from the public by force or patriotism during the early 1950's, with no hope of return. In June, 1951, a campaign was started to 'donate' aid to North Korea. Within twelve months, private businessmen and individuals had donated more than half a billion yüan. This collection was supplemented by further drives for money during the 'three-anti' and 'five-anti' campaigns of 1950–52. The latter, for example, levied fines against thousands of private businessmen for the following 'crimes against the state': (1) bribery of government workers, (2) tax evasion, (3) theft of state property, (4) cheating on government contracts, and (5) stealing economic information for private speculation.[5] All together, it is probable that private citizens turned over to the public treasury at that time well over 1 billion yüan, or perhaps 15 to 20 per cent of the currency in circulation in 1952, thus reducing the inflationary threat of excess cash.[6] As might be expected, the campaigns also had the counterproductive effect of reducing business activity.

Interest policy. Interest rates have been used by the Communists to help achieve monetary control and to ration credit to various classes of borrowers. In the early 1950's, when private business controlled most commercial activities and about one-third of industry, interest rates were excessively high. The Communists reduced the rates substantially on several occasions in order to encourage loans and stimulate production. Nevertheless, private businessmen still paid twice as much for loans as state enterprises. For example, the rates for industrial loans discriminated as follows:

---

[4] *Survey of China Mainland Press*, No. 975 (Hong Kong: U.S. Consulate General, January 25, 1955; hereafter, *SCMP*), p. 12.

[5] Kan-chih Ho, *A History of the Modern Chinese Revolution* (Peking: Foreign Languages Press, 1960), p. 64.

[6] Tseng, 'Do We Have Inflation Now?,' pp. 35–40.

For a state enterprise, interest rates ranged from 5.4 per cent to 5.8 per cent; for a joint state-private enterprise, 5.8 per cent to 16.8 per cent; and for a private enterprise, 10.8 per cent to 19.8 per cent. Interest charges on commercial loans were about one-third higher than those on industrial loans. Interest rates on loans to agricultural cooperatives were also considerably lower than rates charged private farmers. After private business and farming had disappeared, the Communists set interest rates for all industrial, commercial, and agricultural loans at 7.2 per cent annually. Although there have been minor changes in interest rates during the 1960's, the very high rates of earlier years apparently have not been reimposed.

The interest rate paid to individuals on savings accounts has varied, apparently depending on the need, from time to time to encourage savings. For example, the interest rate on savings was 0.51 per cent per month in 1964, but was reduced to 0.33 per cent per month in 1966.

The People's Bank and its branches make loans to industry, commerce, and agriculture primarily on short terms for working capital. The government budget allocates expenditures for new investments in annual appropriations, and scarcely any long-term capital needs are financed by loans. (In turn, 90 per cent or more of the profits of industrial and commercial enterprises are surrendered to the government and form the largest single source of revenue in the budget.) As the branch banks extend working capital loans to operating enterprises, they are required by individual loan agreements to supervise operations of the borrower. Thus, a certain degree of control from the People's Bank supplements the direct control imposed on an enterprise by the government ministry to which it is directly subordinated. More than half of the funds for working capital go to various units of the state trading network, because they regularly purchase large amounts of food from the agricultural sector and raw materials and finished products from industry.[7]

Credit and cash control. The financial control mechanism for carrying out the state economic plan comprises the credit and cash plan of the state bank and the consolidated government budget. The People's Bank each year draws up a plan for the circulation of money, estimating the amount of loans and deposits during the year and the amount of currency to be paid out and returned through state enterprises and other government organizations. This bank plan, together with the budget, is designed to balance the flow of money on the one hand and the flow of commodities on the other and thus to stabilize the general level of prices. The amount of credit, primarily for working capital, is allocated by months and carefully monitored by the bank. A plan for cash payments, used primarily for wages and to purchase some agricultural products, is consolidated from local government levels up to the People's Bank in order to cover all anticipated outpayments of cash. The government collection of cash —in the form of retail sales revenue, taxes, and savings deposits—is also estimated by periods.

The Communists do not permit personal checking accounts or personal notes. Checks may be used by state enterprises and organizations for transactions of 100 yüan or less. Larger transactions are handled by clearing accounts through the People's Bank. These clearing accounts are related to the flow of commodities and services among operating enterprises. In this way, the People's Bank watches over the sale and delivery of all types of commodities as specified in the national economic plan and can detect shortcomings in the performance of a specific enterprise. For example, if an enterprise falls behind in its production plan, it consequently falls behind in its contracted deliveries, and its balance with the People's Bank declines. It may then have difficulty paying for its regular deliveries of raw or processed materials and

---

[7] Ching-wen Kwang, 'The Banking System of Mainland China and Its Functions in Economic Planning and Control,' paper presented at a Conference on Economic Trends in Communist China, Carmel, California, October, 1965, p. 36.

meeting its payroll, and it may be forced to ask the bank for additional working capital. This tight control of funds by the bank apparently brings to light many production and distribution problems that might otherwise escape immediate attention. The bank has the right to suggest solutions for a backward enterprise or to report the situation to the appropriate ministry for action.

The Government Budget and Fiscal Policies

Budget and Fiscal Policies

The Chinese Communists based their early fiscal policies on traditional criteria, modifying them where necessary to fit the transition to socialist forms of organization. The government budget, together with the credit and cash plans of the People's Bank, is designed as a financial control mechanism for carrying out the state economic plan. In order to serve effectively in this role, the budget could not carry the enormous deficits that were common during the war years. Therefore, the Communists based their revenue goals on anticipated expenditure levels, and as a consequence enlarged the revenue flow by nearly eight times between 1950 and 1959. (See Table 22–1.) Although data are not available to analyze the government budget in detail, it is apparent that deficits in the consolidated government budget since 1950 have been relatively small. As a result, the Bank has not been called on to finance large budget expenditures with new money, and inflation has been effectively controlled.

As the Communists consolidated their hold over the economy and substituted public for private enterprise. the government budget became increasingly important in relation to the state economic plan. By 1959, for example, three-fourths of all gross domestic investment in China was financed through the consolidated government budget[8] (the remainder through extrabudgetary funds of local governments and private individuals). In turn, more than 90 per cent of the net profit of state enterprises was returned to the government as budgetary revenue, which together with depreciation reserves represented about 60 per cent of budget income. Although the budget has been used in this way as an effective tool in accumulating resources and directing investment, there has been no suggestion by the Chinese that fiscal policy alone could substitute for direct controls in planning economic activity.

In the Chinese view, taxation may be used as a means of redistributing income and as an aid to rapid industrialization. It has been a Chinese policy since 1950 that taxes on industry should be lighter than those on commerce and that, in both of these categories, the lowest rates should apply to heavy industry and daily necessities as opposed to light industry and luxuries. The Chinese also have used tax differentials to encourage the public sector of their economy and to restrict the private sector.[9]

The Chinese have not attempted to build personal incentives into their tax structure, and they have never imposed a tax on individual income. The progressive tax on agriculture was levied directly on households and was designed in large part to redistribute income; it was only in the definition of the tax base that an incentive arose for increasing production. Incentives were built into a net profits tax on commerce and industry, but the effect was to discriminate sharply against nonessential production and trade rather than to encourage individual initiative.

After agricultural cooperatives had become universal in the countryside and nearly

---

[8] *Current Background*, No. 615 (Hong Kong: U.S. Consulate General, April 5, 1960; hereafter, *CB*), p. 4.

[9] Chih-ta Ko, *China's Budget During the Transition Period* (Peking: n.p. 1957), pp. 10–21 (JPRS: 591-D, Washington, D.C., March 13, 1959, pp. 79–80), and 'The Growth of the National Economy as Viewed From the State Budget,' *T'ung-chi Kung-tso T'ung-hsin (Statistical Work Bulletin)*, No. 12 (Peking: June 29, 1957).

all private enterprise had been brought under various forms of direct state control in 1956, the Chinese changed their emphasis in tax theory and policy. The elimination of private wealth and the greater equality in incomes that came with socialization made it less important to consider shifting, incidence, and relative burdens of taxes. More attention than formerly was given to the relative efficiency of various types of taxes and their suitability to the socialist forms of organization. With the disappearance of the private sector, there was no longer any need to maintain restrictive and discriminatory taxes, and the five major levies that had been imposed on business since 1950 were reduced in 1958 to a single commodity tax.[10]

With this step accomplished, the next objective was to seek a proper balance in total revenue collection between commodity taxes and other forms of government income. The Chinese favored the tax pattern long used by the Soviet Union,[11] with modifications to fit their own situation. The tax and profit income that the Chinese Government derived from industry as a whole in 1957 was composed 45 per cent of taxes and 55 per cent of profit remittances; for heavy industry, taxes were 30 per cent and profits 70 per cent of the total; for light industry, taxes were 60 per cent and profits 40 per cent. Profit remittances accounted for about 55 per cent of total budgetary revenue in 1959, and depreciation reserves for an additional 5 per cent. This distribution was quite different from that of the Soviet Union, in which profit taxes from state enterprises usually made up less than 20 per cent of total budgetary revenue. Following the Soviet pattern, the Chinese have sought since the mid-1950's to acquire a larger share of budget income from the commodity taxes and a reduced share from profits.[12]

A wide range of commodity taxes makes it easier for the Chinese Government to implement its price policies without disruptions to producing units. If commodity taxes are included in the prices of most commodities, greater latitude is obtained in making subsequent price adjustments for individual products than when commodity taxes are not used at all and goods are priced at cost (including profits). When it is necessary to raise or to lower prices of specific products, these price changes can be made by altering the commodity tax rates without disturbing established costs and profit margins. The Chinese have used commodity taxes in this way. For example, in 1958, tax rates were lowered on reprocessed wines, canned foods, soda water, and other products in order to reduce their prices and to stimulate sales.[13]

Administration of the budget. The Ministry of Finance, charged with formulating the government budget, is a component of the Office of Finance and Trade, one of the offices under the State Council that constitute the administrative structure of the Chinese Government. The annual government budget is prepared by the Ministry of Finance and reviewed by a Budget Committee of the National People's Congress (NPC). The NPC Budget Committee has regularly recommended only insignificant changes or no change at all in the annual budget submitted by the Minister of Finance. In 1958, for example, the NPC Budget Committee recommended that both revenues and expenditures in the proposed 1958 budget be raised 135 million yüan, an increase of only four-tenths of 1 per cent in the total revenue proposed by the Minister of Finance.

All taxes in Communist China are collected by a unified system of revenue agencies

---

[10] *CB*, October 27, 1958, p. 19.

[11] The Soviet Union relies principally upon heavy consumer taxes, of which the most important is the turnover tax. The Russians, compared with the Chinese, price the products of heavy industry considerably lower than those of light industry and draw a much larger proportion of government revenue from taxes than from profit earnings of state enterprises.

[12] *Extracts from China Mainland Magazines*, No. 43 (Hong Kong: U.S. Consulate General, July 16, 1956; hereafter, *ECMM*), p. 23.

[13] *CB*, October 27, 1958, p. 18.

stationed at various levels of government, with the exception of the salt tax and customs duties, which are separately administered by the General Salt Tax Administration and the Customs Administration, respectively. Taxes are paid directly into branches of the People's Bank or are received by local tax offices for immediate deposit in the bank. Agricultural taxes, primarily in kind, are collected at harvest time in summer and autumn and are stored in government granaries. Commodity taxes are paid at intervals varying from several days to a month, and miscellaneous taxes are collected by local tax bureaus according to established schedules. The tax receipts are credited by the People's Bank to the accounts of various government units (local, provincial, and national) according to fixed distribution ratios.

The jurisdiction of tax offices in Communist China extends beyond the collection of revenue, although that remains their primary function. Tax offices have been required to give assistance to industrial and commercial enterprises and to help them improve their financial and accounting systems. This assignment of accounting duties to the tax offices points up the need to establish business records that will be adequate for tax collection work, such as completion of returns and postauditing. It is also part of a larger effort to introduce more effective accounting techniques throughout Chinese industry and commerce. The tax collectors recommend improvements in the accounts of enterprises which may lead to greater operating efficiency as well as ease in tax collection.[14]

In spite of the anomalies which these activities lend to the normal functions of the tax collector, there is some rationale for his dual role. The need for accounting improvements in China has paralleled that in many other less developed countries where large sectors of the economy are non-monetary. The great economic expansion under the Communists has brought a proliferation of new industrial plants of many types, as well as cooperatives for distribution and for handicraft production. Many of them required help in establishing adequate accounting records. Tax administrators, trained to some extent in accounting, could provide much of this help to the new enterprises and thus benefit the taxpayer as well as the tax collector. Furthermore, the tax collector's contacts with all industrial and commercial activity in the district has given him a large amount of information on inventories, sales, shortages, and production problems. The tax offices have served as clearing houses in their districts for a wide range of production and marketing information, and they have suggested solutions for some of the nontax problems that confront their taxpayers.

Sources of budgetary revenue. Both the magnitude and the sources of budgetary revenue in China underwent marked changes during the first decade under the Communists, as indicated in Table 22–1. The traditional sources of government revenue—agriculture and salt taxes and customs duties—were retained and made slightly more productive, but they were greatly exceeded by such new sources of income as levies on the profits of state-operated enterprises. Additional sources of revenue were essential in order to achieve the large increases in total government revenue. Although taxes by 1959 were more than four times the level of 1950, they contributed a progressively smaller share of total budgetary income in China. Millions of Chinese peasants received much of their income in farm produce rather than in money and did not provide a monetary tax base sufficiently large to meet the growing revenue requirements of the regime's economic plans. The development of state-owned industry and commerce resulted in large profits, which accounted for the biggest single flow of funds into the budget.

The growing dominance of the socialized sector in the Chinese economy is clearly reflected in the trends since 1950 in budgetary revenue sources. Scarcely one-third of government income was obtained from state-owned and cooperative enterprises in 1950, whereas nearly two-thirds were contributed by private business and the private

---

[14] *SCMP,* June 23, 1958, p. 4.

Table 22-1—Sources of Budgetary Revenue, 1950–59
(millions of current yüan)

	1950	1951	1952	1953	1954	1955	1956	1957	1958	1959
Tax Revenue										
1. Agricultural taxes	1,910	2,169	2,704	2,711	3,278	3,054	2,965	2,970	3,260	3,300
2. Salt taxes	268	339	405	461	521	481	483	620	620	650
3. Customs receipts	356	693	481	505	412	466	542	460	580	650
4. Industrial and Commercial taxes, incl.:	2,363	4,745	6,147	8,250	8,972	8,725	10,098	11,300	14,179	15,698
5. Private business	(1,910)	(3,312)	(3,458)	(3,422)	(2,872)	(1,671)	(640)	(240)	NA	NA
6. Cooperatives	NA	NA	(190)	(534)	(925)	(1,128)	(1,580)	(2,205)	NA	NA
7. Joint public-private enterprises	NA	NA	(184)	(265)	(422)	(556)	(1,580)	(2,855)	NA	NA
8. State enterprises	(435)	(1,433)	(2,315)	(4,029)	(4,753)	(5,370)	(6,298)	(6,000)	NA	NA
9. Miscellaneous tax receipts[a]	1	167	32	40	35	19	NA	1,140	91	172
10. Total tax receipts	4,898	8,113	9,769	11,967	13,218	12,745	14,088	15,490	18,730	20,470
Nontax Revenues										
11. Profits from state enterprises			4,653	6,369	8,457	9,404	11,414	11,363	18,719	28,590
12. Depreciation reserves and other income from state enterprises	870[b]	3,050[b]	1,077	1,301	1,503	1,786	2,016	3,057	3,301	4,770
13. Receipts from foreign loans	244	625	1,305	438	884	1,657	117	23	None	None
14. Receipts from domestic bonds	260	None	None	None	836	619	607	650	790	None
15. Receipts from insurance operations	NA	NA	NA	52	70	84	NA	27	10	NA
16. Other income	247	1,179	756	1,635	1,269	908	501	410	310	330
17. Total nontax revenue	1,621	4,854	7,791	9,795	13,019	14,458	14,655	15,530	23,130	33,690
Total budgetary review	6,519	12,967	17,560	21,762	26,237	27,203	28,743	31,020	41,860	54,160

[a] Includes tax on interest income, slaughter tax, a tax on private land and houses, and entertainment taxes.
[b] Includes profits, depreciation reserves, and other income.
Source: George N. Ecklund, Financing the Chinese Government Budget: Mainland China, 1950–59 (Chicago: Aldine Publishing Company, 1966), pp. 122–24.

farms. Ten years later, however, at least 98 per cent of budgetary revenue originated in the socialized sector, including cooperative agriculture. The Chinese took advantage of this shift in sources of budgetary revenue to reduce the cost of collection of revenue. Discriminatory taxes originally levied on the private sector of the economy, partly for nonrevenue purposes, together with the early campaigns against tax evasion, required a relatively large administrative effort. With the decline of the private sector, this administrative burden decreased, and in 1958 a greatly simplified tax structure was introduced for all of industry, commerce, and agriculture.

The Communists inherited the Nationalist tax structure in both urban and rural areas when they assumed power in mainland China in 1949. The traditional forms of revenue were subjected primarily to change in rates, with only slight alterations in structure and objectives. Sharp discriminations were incorporated into the new taxes on commerce and industry, which were designed to eliminate nonessentials and to help direct resources into activities the Communists considered useful. A progressive tax was levied on agriculture to assist in the redistribution of incomes in the countryside. Minor tax revisions were made in 1953, and substantial changes in tax laws were made in 1958, when many simplifications were achieved and the entire tax structure was overhauled to reflect the dominance of socialist forms of organization.

The Chinese made numerous changes in the agricultural tax to fit the varying stages of their land reform program. During the disruptive years of the civil war, ending in 1949, when adequate data were lacking on land, population, and output, taxes were collected according to 'roughly estimated quotas.'[15] In the new areas that the Communists acquired after 1949, progressive taxes generally were imposed on the gross income from land farmed by individual households. These taxes continued in force with minor variations through 1957. Proportional tax rates on agricultural income were applied only in some areas of North China and in Manchuria, where redistribution of land had been completed. In 1958, following establishment of farm cooperatives throughout rural China, proportional rates became universal.[16]

During the first eight years of the Communist regime in China, taxes levied on commercial and industrial activity were more appropriate to the private sector than to the public sector of the economy. It was only after individual businesses had been absorbed by the state that changes were made in taxes on business and industry. The tax structure was then greatly simplified and adapted to socialist forms of organization.

A gross receipts tax was levied beginning in 1950, with rates ranging from 1 to 3 per cent on merchandise sales and from 1.5 to 15 per cent of gross receipts for services. In addition to this discrimination between sales and services, the rates gave concessions to those industries and services that the Communists considered most important in their plans for economic development. Enterprises in the following heavy industry groups paid a tax of only 1 per cent of gross receipts: (1) mining and metallurgy (consisting of iron and steel, nonferrous metals, coal, sulphur, mica, silicon, and other minerals); (2) machine-building (such as engines, machine tools, agricultural machinery, and other industrial machines); and (3) basic chemicals (including sulphuric acid, nitric acid, hydrochloric acid, caustic soda, and other basic chemicals). A rate of 2 per cent was assessed against the following: (1) rubber products (such as automobile tires and rubber products for industrial use), (2) fertilizers, and (3) drugs and medical supplies. The general retail trade bore a rate of 3 per cent, as did enterprises producing such less essential items as fans and umbrellas, clocks and watches, cosmetics, tobacco products, and 'goods for ritual use.'

The rates on gross receipts for services were applied in a similar discriminatory

---

[15] *People's Practical Economic Dictionary: Public Finances in China* (Shanghai: Ch'un-ming Publishing House, 1953), p. 61.
[16] *Ta-kung Pao*, Peking, June 5, 1958.

pattern. For example, public utilities such as water supply, electric power, gas, and telephones all paid a tax of 1.5 per cent. For storage and construction contracting, the rate was 3 per cent. A rate of 4 per cent was levied on hotels, advertising firms, story-telling tea houses, and public-catering enterprises. Intermediate rates of 4 to 8 per cent applied to pawnbrokers, employment services, and auctioneers, and the highest rate of 15 per cent was applied to stock underwriting and middleman service in commercial transactions.

Net business profits were taxed at progressive rates, with no minimum income specified and a maximum rate of 30 per cent at 10,000 yüan. A discriminatory feature of the business income tax was a series of tax reductions that applied to certain activities that the government wished especially to encourage. These reductions, stated as a percentage of the new income tax payable, ranged from 10 to 40 per cent, as follows:

10 per cent:	certain essential consumer goods
	dairy products
	hospital supplies
15 per cent:	rubber and leather products
	some construction materials
	printing equipment
	hand tools and machine repairing
20 per cent:	certain transportation items
	some chemicals
	export commodities
30 per cent:	telecommunications equipment
	certain more important chemicals
	some machine-building activities
40 per cent:	heavy machine tools, generators, farm machinery
	iron and steel, nonferrous metals
	ship and vehicle manufacturing
	electric power generation

A tax based on the wholesale price of specified commodities was first applied in Communist China in January, 1950. Resembling a manufacturers' excise tax, it was payable by producers or wholesale buyers at rates that varied from 3 to 120 per cent of the taxable value of the commodity. Although the tax was amended in 1953 and again in 1958, many of the items appearing in the original measure were carried over into subsequent regulations, some of them at approximately the same effective rates.[17]

A new consolidated industrial and commercial tax was introduced in 1958 to replace the following taxes (which were abolished): (1) the commodity tax, (2) the commodity circulation tax, (3) the gross receipts tax, (4) the net income tax, and (5) the stamp tax. The need to simplify the system of taxing business had been recognized by the Chinese for several years. There were said to be too many taxes, too many rates, and too many collection channels. Private enterprise in China had been eliminated by 1958, and practically all industrial and commercial activity was in the hands of state enterprises, joint public-private firms, and cooperatives. The Communists, therefore, recognized that the old tax structure had served its purpose and that a new concept of business taxation was required. They followed the Soviet practice of applying the turnover tax on a broad scale, including industrial products, retail sales, imports, purchases of certain farm produce, and service trades. Following the major overhaul in taxes in 1958, there have been no indications of important changes in the

---

[17] *Ch'ing-tao Jih-pao* (*Tsingtao Daily*), Tsingtao, December 24, 1950, and Ko, *China's Budget During Transition Period*, pp. 71–79.

tax structure. Aside from minor changes in rates, which have occurred from time to time, taxes changed little during the decade of the 1960's.

Receipts from state enterprises, primarily profit remittances but including depreciation reserves, have emerged as the most important source of budgetary income in China. Since 1950, when they amounted to less than 15 per cent of the total, they increased at a faster rate than over-all budget receipts and in 1959 constituted about 60 per cent of the total government income. The growth in this source of revenue was the result of (1) the construction of new state enterprises, expansion of existing enterprises, and acquisition of private facilities; (2) the growth in depreciation reserves, resulting from the large increase in physical assets; (3) the gradual reduction in some industrial costs; and (4) the state policy of maintaining prices sufficiently high to assure a large volume of profits.

The budget receipts from state enterprises are composed of (1) profits, (2) depreciation reserves for amortization of fixed assets, (3) return of surplus working capital, (4) receipts from sale of fixed assets, and (5) income from other business activities. The Communists have not released detailed figures for each of these components, but profits and depreciation reserves probably accounted for nearly all of the total.

Miscellaneous sources of government income in China have been relatively unimportant and have declined as a proportion of the total revenue during the period since 1950. Sources of income other than taxes and receipts from state enterprises represented 11.5 per cent of the total budgetary revenue in 1950 but only 2.7 per cent in 1958 and 0.6 per cent in 1959. These other sources of revenue consist of loans from abroad, domestic bond sales to the public, earnings of government insurance operations, and such miscellaneous items as fines, administrative and service fees, and supplementary income from various public projects. During the decade 1960–70, no domestic bonds were sold by the Peking government and no loans from abroad were announced.

Government Budgetary Expenditures

Expenditures through the government budget increased by nearly eight times between 1950 and 1959, as shown in Table 22–2. Following the sharp decline in the private sector of the economy, which contributed only 30 per cent of industrial output in 1953 and less than 1 per cent in 1956, an increasing share of total investment was channeled through the budget. Of the total expenditure for capital construction[18] in China during the First Five-Year Plan exclusive of farm investment, 88.5 per cent was made through the government budget, the remainder having been made by state enterprises from their own funds, by local governments with funds outside the consolidated state budget, and by private enterprises.

Growing budgetary allocations to economic construction, rising from 26 per cent in 1950 to 61 per cent in 1959, were the primary source for financing Communist China's industrial growth. Economic construction consists of allocations to state-operated enterprises for acquisition of fixed assets, for supplementary working capital, and for certain miscellaneous business expenses. Expenditures on fixed assets accounted for most of this total, about 85 per cent during 1956–59. Industry received more than one-half of the total expenditures for economic construction during 1950–59, with a preponderant emphasis on heavy industry. In 1959, for example, industry received 61 per cent of the total; railroads and communications, 16 per cent; agriculture and forestry, nearly 16 per cent; and all other sectors, 7 per cent. The ratio of investment in light industry to that in heavy industry was approximately 1 to 6 during the 1952–59 period. These extensive investments increased the value of productive

---

[18] The Chinese define 'capital construction expenditures' to include outlays for new and reconstructed buildings, industrial machinery, tools, instruments, and furniture and fixtures.

fixed assets[19] in China by 49,220 million yüan from 1952 to 1958 (equal to one-half the entire GNP for 1957).[20]

Chinese defense expenditures as reported in the budget increased sharply in 1951 because of the Korean War. In that year they reached the highest share (42 per cent) of total budgetary expenditures, but subsequently declined steadily as a share of the budget and were only 11 per cent of the total in 1959. The peak of 6.5 billion yüan in 1955 included military equipment transferred to China by the Soviet Union on credit. It is probable that other Chinese military expenditures or military-related expenditures are included elsewhere in the budget, but no data are available to show the extent or composition of such expenditures. For example, investment in plants to produce military equipment probably is included in economic construction rather than military expenditures.

Chinese allocations for social, cultural, and educational purposes increased nearly eight times during the ten-year period 1950–59, thus retaining its share (about 11 per cent) of total budgetary expenditures. Outlays on education increased about seven times, reflecting heavy emphasis by the Communists on all types of training. Science expenditures, although a small part of the total budget (less than 2 per cent in 1959), increased 100 times between 1951 and 1959.

Repayments of foreign debt (primarily to the Soviet Union) and of domestic debt (redemption of government bonds)—together with interest payments on the debt— did not become substantial until 1955. These payments were nearly 700 million yüan in that year, and they increased to nearly 1 billion yüan in 1959, when they represented about 2 per cent of total budgetary expenditures. Debt payments probably declined substantially during the 1960's, as most of the bonds were redeemed and the Soviet credits repaid.

In 1959, administrative expenditures in the Chinese budget—primarily salaries for government administrative employees—were slightly more than double the expenditures of 1950, although their share of total expenditures declined from about 20 per cent to less than 6 per cent.

The Chinese budget showed a net surplus of about 6 billion yüan during the decade of the 1950's. The annual figures as reported by the Chinese[21] were as follows (in millions of yüan):

1950	− 291
1951	+ 1,067
1952	+ 770
1953	+ 272
1954	+ 1,607
1955	+ 283
1956	− 1,837
1957	+ 2,000
1958	+ 900
1959	+ 1,390

The over-all net surplus may be accounted for partly by Chinese budgetary practices. The Chinese counted as ordinary revenue some items that are not usually included as budget income. For example, if one excludes from the 1954 budget the income items 'receipts from sale of bonds' and 'receipts from foreign loans,' the surplus of 1,607

---

[19] Productive fixed assets are defined by the Chinese as factory buildings, machinery and equipment used for production purposes, railways, highways, harbors, wharves and other transport facilities, warehouses for commercial and banking undertakings, etc.

[20] State Statistical Bureau, *Ten Great Years* (Peking: Foreign Languages Press, 1960), p. 64.

[21] See Tables 22–1 and 22–2.

Table 22–2—Expenditures from the Chinese Government Budget, 1950–59
(millions of yüan)

	1950	1951	1952	1953	1954	1955	1956	1957	1958	1959
Economic Construction										
Industry	666	1,418	2,731	4,286	5,738	5,960	8,828	8,110	—	19,600
Agriculture	199	435	915	1,191	1,375	1,498	2,284	2,090	—	5,060
Railways and communications	352	675	1,037	1,227	1,760	1,925	2,782	2,220	—	5,175
Trade and banking	383	564	1,468	1,027	1,761	3,359	940	365	—	—
Other	50	174	380	355	328	329	400	350	—	—
Total	1,650	3,266	6,531	8,086	10,962	13,071	15,234	13,135	26,270	32,170
Social, Culture, Education										
Education	491	921	1,313	2,082	2,105	2,016	2,955	2,800	—	3,340
Science	—	8	11	32	34	38	244	292	—	823
Health	71	163	374	565	490	406	489	504	—	565
Culture	61	94	126	181	190	185	263	185	—	—
Other	132	157	451	485	618	511	575	582	—	—
Total	755	1,343	2,275	3,345	3,437	3,156	4,526	4,363	4,350	5,860
National Defense	2,827	5,061	4,371	5,680	5,814	6,500	6,116	5,510	5,000	5,800
Administration	1,313	1,746	1,727	2,118	2,162	2,154	2,660	2,270	2,270	2,900
Other Expenditures										
Aid to other countries	—	—	391	1,592	628	456	404	455	275	350
Interest on domestic debt	2	10	27	42	50	118	233	260	211	225
Repayments of domestic debt	0	32	35	49	30	156	57	156	115	164
Repayments of foreign debt	0	0	0	0	120	392	432	423	579	581
Credit funds to state banks	—	—	1,000	—	990	—	—	953	1,650	4,430
Miscellaneous	263	442	433	578	437	917	918	1,495	240	290
Total	265	484	1,886	2,261	2,255	2,039	2,044	3,742	3,070	6,040
Total expenditures	6,810	11,900	16,790	21,490	24,630	26,920	30,580	29,020	40,960	52,770

Source: State Statistical Bureau, *Ten Great Years*, p. 99.

million yüan for that year would become a deficit of 113 million yüan. Similarly, the surpluses shown in the budget for 1952, 1953, and 1955 would also become deficits. Domestic bonds represented a debt of the central government, and the proceeds from their sale would not normally be considered budgetary revenue. The loans China received from the Soviet Union were used to finance the purchase of industrial and military equipment and were not extended for the purpose of budgetary support. Other items might also be excluded from Chinese revenue on the grounds they do not fit standard budgetary practice, but the Chinese have not provided sufficient detail in their budget accounts to make this feasible.

Whatever the actual budgetary balance may have been, the Chinese reported that inflation had been stopped after 1950 and that prices remained relatively stable throughout the 1950's. Stability in the official price index would be expected, however, because price control extended over a wide range of commodities in China after 1950. Many basic consumer goods, particularly food and clothing, were rationed. The Chinese used several devices to reduce the pressure on official prices (repressed inflation). The tax structure was geared to absorb an increasing share of consumer income. The proportion of consumer money income taken by taxes increased steadily from 1950 (about 17 per cent) through 1954 (about 31 per cent). After dropping slightly in 1955–56, this proportion again increased annually through 1959 (to about one-third). The diversion of consumer money income into bonds and personal savings accounted for an additional 4 to 5 per cent of money income during the 1950's.[22] The local free markets and especially the black markets that thrived at various times throughout the decade had prices considerably higher than official prices. Thus, the official price index overstated the degree of price stability, although data are not available to measure the combined movement of official and black market prices.

The Decade of the 1960's

The Chinese Communists have not published data on their budgetary receipts and expenditures since 1959. Therefore, the detail shown in Tables 22–1 and 22–2 cannot be extended into the decade of the 1960's. The serious economic reverses in China beginning in 1960 probably resulted in some decline in government revenues, although there is no evidence to substantiate this possibility. It is clear, however, that the mixed public-private economy of 1950 was fully transformed into state ownership by the mid-1950's. Major changes were then made in the tax structure to fit the socialist forms of Chinese enterprise. The system of revenues and expenditures that had emerged by 1958 probably continued with little change through the 1960's.

SELECTED BIBLIOGRAPHY

Area Handbook of Communist China. Washington, D.C.: U.S. Government Printing Office, 1967.

BOLDYREV, B. G. *Finances of the People's Republic of China*. Moscow; n.p., 1953. A description of money and banking and the government budget in the early years of the Communist regime in China (1949–52).

CHEKHUTOV, A. I. 'Budget of the People's Republic of China, 1950–57,' *Soviet Sinology*, No. 1, Moscow, May 26, 1958. Provides considerable detail of the revenues and expenditures of the Chinese Government budget.

DONNITHORNE, AUDREY. *China's Economic System*. London: George Allen & Unwin Ltd., 1967.

HOWE, C. 'Problems, Performance, and Prospects of the Chinese Economy,' *World Today*, December, 1967.

---

[22] George N. Ecklund, 'Taxation in Communist China,' Ph.D. thesis, University of Minnesota, 1961, p. 127.

Hsüeh, Mu-chiao; Hsing Su; and Tse-li Lin. *The Socialist Transformation of the National Economy of China*. Peking: Foreign Languages Press, 1960. Describes the considerable changes that took place in Chinese industry, trade, and finance as private enterprise was gradually replaced by state enterprise.

Ko, Chih-ta. *China's Budget During the Transition Period*. Peking: n.p., 1957 (translation by Joint Publications Research Service, Washington, D.C., No. 591–D, March 13, 1959). Includes information released by the government in annual reports on the budget and some additional data relating to the budget. Describes the budgetary process in China.

Kwang, Ching-wen. 'The Banking System of Mainland China and Its Functions in Economic Planning and Control,' presented to Committee on the Economy of China, Carmel, California, October, 1965.

Ling, Tseng, and Lei Han. *The Circulation of Money in the People's Republic of China*. (Translated by Joint Publications Research Service, Washington, D.C., No. 3317, June 1, 1960). Description of the monetary process in Communist China and its role in development of the national economy.

Peoples Practical Economics Dictionary: Public Finance in China. Shanghai: Ch'un-ming Publishing House, 1953. Contains descriptive and statistical information on the Chinese budget, including discussion of tax policy and administration.

Prybyla, J. S., 'Communist China's Strategy of Economic Development,' *Asian Survey*, Vol. 6, No. 10, October, 1966.

———. 'Economic Cost,' *Problems of Communism*, Vol. 17, No. 2, March, 1968.

State Statistical Bureau. *Ten Great Years: Statistics of the Economic and Cultural Achievements of the People's Republic of China*. Peking: Foreign Languages Press, 1960 (Chinese language edition was published in 1959). A collection of official statistics assembled in 135 tables with supporting text. The objective is to show China's economic and cultural development during the 1949–59 period.

23

FOREIGN ECONOMIC RELATIONS

FRED C. HUNG

INTRODUCTION

A STUDY of any country's foreign economic relations should usually cover all aspects of the international balance of payments, for example, exports and imports of goods and services, overseas remittances and expenditures (both incoming and outgoing), shipment of monetary gold, short-term and long-term capital movements, and foreign aid (both receipts and payments). However, because of the limitations of space and data, this chapter will concentrate on Communist China's commodity trade, with some discussion of its credit relationship with other countries and its foreign aid to developing nations. Readers who are interested in other items in the P.R.C. balance of payments are referred to the tables appended to this chapter, where two alternate sets of estimates for 1950–64, one by Professor Feng-Hwa Mah and the other by an official U.S. Government agency, are presented in Tables 23–1 and 23–2 and compared in Table 23–3. It is sufficient to observe here that estimates of items not included in this chapter are mostly conjectural and that these items accounted for less than 10 per cent of Communist China's international receipts and payments for the period 1950–64.

The rest of this chapter is divided into six sections. The first contains a discussion of original sources of information on Communist China's foreign trade and of the need for various adjustments, leaving room for different estimates and interpretations. The second describes and compares a number of estimates of Communist China's commodity trade. The section following summarizes the trade trends from 1950 to the present. Sections four and five deal with Communist China's international borrowings and aid to other nations, respectively. An attempt is made in the last section to look into the future of China's foreign economic relations.

SOURCES OF TRADE INFORMATION

Communist China has not published foreign trade statistics since 1959. Official figures for the total value of its trade in yüan, with no distinction between exports and imports, are available for the years 1950 to 1958 in *Ten Great Years*, published by Peking in 1959.[1] From these totals, and with the help of certain indices and ratios released by Communist China and some other sources, it is possible to estimate the value of exports and imports in yüan for those years.[2] Presumably, the yüan figures could then

---

[1] The English edition is State Statistical Bureau (comp.), *Ten Great Years* (Peking, Foreign Languages Press, 1960).

[2] See, for example, Table 68 and its accompanying notes in Yuan-li Wu, *et al.*, *The Eco-*

be converted to U.S. dollars at the prevailing exchange rates. However, during that period the yüan was overvalued in terms of U.S. dollars and undervalued in terms of Soviet rubles, hence total figures given in yüan tend to overstate the value of trade with countries that settle their accounts in rubles and understate the value of trade with countries that settle their accounts in dollars.[3] For this reason, scholars now prefer to use trade statistics of Communist China's trading partners even for years prior to 1959. When all the trade figures in their respective currencies are converted to U.S. dollars and totaled, the problem of possible overvaluation or undervaluation of each currency in terms of the dollar still remains. But there is no question that this approach tends to result in far less distortion than if the totals are given in yüan.

Statistics of trade between the free world countries and Communist China are compiled every year by the U.S. Department of Commerce and included in the Annual Reports of the Administrator of the Mutual Defense Assistance Control Act of 1951 (the Battle Act). All figures have been converted from currencies of the respective countries to U.S. dollars at prevailing exchange rates. Thus, instead of consulting the trade statistics of each individual country, a convenient and reliable source is available. One disadvantage, however, of relying on this source is that the Battle Act reports come out in the spring every year, containing preliminary information not of the previous year but of the year preceding that. These figures are then revised in later reports. Thus, there is always a time lag of more than two years. For more current information, one has either to resort to the official trade returns of each individual country or rely on other sources.[4]

The Battle Act reports include trade statistics of all non-Communist countries that exported to or imported from Communist China goods valued at U.S. $1 million or more in any one year of the period covered. Occasionally, information may be lacking for certain countries in a particular year. As a rule, the omissions are not significant. Yugoslavia is included among the free world countries in the Battle Act reports. So is Cuba for its trade with Communist China from 1959 to 1961. Adjustments can, however, be easily made to exclude those two countries from the group.

Because of the practices of the free world countries in reporting their trade statistics, a number of problems arise in using the data contained in the Battle Act reports, and adjustments are often necessary. One minor problem is the inclusion of Macao, Taiwan, and/or Mongolia by certain countries in their definition of mainland China. Usually the amounts involved are not significant. A more serious problem is that, before 1960, re-exports of goods to and from Communist China through Hong Kong were lumped together with Hong Kong's domestically produced exports, resulting in double counting if other countries report their exports by country of destination and their imports by country of origin, and in misrepresentation even if no double counting is involved. Since 1960, the U.S. Department of Commerce, taking advantage of

---

nomic Potential of Communist China, 1 (Menlo Park, Calif.: Stanford Research Institute, 1963) 306.

[3] 'The official yüan-dollar rate fluctuated from 2.2 yüan to 4.2 yüan to the dollar through 1950–52. In December, 1952, and the whole year of 1953 it was pegged at 2.46 yüan to the dollar. It was changed to 2.35 yüan to the dollar at the beginning of 1954 and remained at that level until the second half of 1957. Since then it has been fixed at 2.617 yüan to the dollar.' Kang-Chao, 'Pitfalls in the Use of China's Foreign Trade Statistics,' *China Quarterly*, July–September, 1964, p. 49. On the other hand, the yüan-ruble rate was approximately 1 to 1 and the ruble-dollar rate was four rubles to the dollar during the period 1950–58.

[4] For example, *Current Scene* and *Far Eastern Economic Review*, both published in Hong Kong; *Chinese Communist Affairs*, published by the Institute of Political Research in Taiwan; and the annual research memoranda (unclassified in recent years) on trade of NATO and European non-NATO countries and Japan with Communist countries, including China, released by the Office of the Director of Intelligence and Research, U.S. Department of State. The United Nations *Yearbook of International Trade Statistics* also has a time lag of about two years.

the practice established by the Hong Kong government in 1959 to separate Hong Kong's domestically produced exports from its re-exports to Communist China, has included only the former in Battle Act reports. Unfortunately, neither the Hong Kong government nor the Department of Commerce has adopted the practice of netting Hong Kong's re-exports to other countries out of its imports from Communist China. Another problem is that free world imports from Communist China are valued at c.i.f. (cost, insurance and freight), while their exports are valued at f.o.b. In order to be consistent and have both exports and imports on the same f.o.b. basis, it is necessary to deduct from the value of their imports the estimated costs of insurance and shipping. Opinions may differ on how such estimates are to be made.

Statistics of trade between the Soviet Union and Communist China are available from 1955 to the present in the foreign trade yearbooks of the U.S.S.R. Ministry of Foreign Trade. Information for 1950–54 is given in M. I. Sladkovsky's 'The Development of the Soviet Union's Trade with the People's Republic of China,' *Vneshnyaya Torgovlya (Foreign Trade)*, Vol. 29, No. 10, October, 1959. Both exports and imports are on an f.o.b. basis. The exchange rate between rubles and dollars was 4.0 rubles to the dollar up to the end of 1961. Since 1960, the new rubles have been valued at 0.9 new rubles to the dollar.[5]

Complete trade statistics of Eastern European and Asian Communist countries are difficult to get. In addition to the United Nations *Yearbook of International Trade Statistics* and *A Background Study on East-West Trade*, published by the U.S. Senate Committee on Foreign Relations in 1965, a number of scattered sources contain spotty information. It is often necessary to complete estimates for certain countries through interpolation or extrapolation. For more detailed descriptions of sources relating to the East European and Asian Communist countries, the readers are referred to the methodology sections of Professor Eckstein's book and Professor Mah's chapter on Communist China's foreign trade.[6]

Until 1960–61, there were re-exports of goods to and from Communist China through the Soviet Union and the Eastern countries, especially before the relaxation of the Western Strategic Trade Embargo in 1957. It is extremely difficult, however, to obtain information on such transshipments.

ESTIMATES OF COMMUNIST CHINA'S COMMODITY TRADE

Alternative estimates. Because of the nature of the statistics available, there is obviously plenty of room for disagreement with regard to estimates and interpretations of Communist China's foreign trade. Three major studies, with detailed explanation of methodology, have appeared in recent years. They are the works of Eckstein and Mah,[7] mentioned earlier, and of a U.S. Government agency.[8]

---

[5] The U.S. Department of State published in 1971 detailed commodity trade statistics of the Soviet Union for the period 1964–68 (*U.S.S.R. Foreign Trade, 1964–1968*). It includes Soviet trade with China.

[6] Alexander Eckstein, *Communist China's Economic Growth and Foreign Trade: Implications for U.S. Policy* (New York: McGraw-Hill, 1966), pp. 288–92; Feng-Hwa Mah, 'Foreign Trade,' in Alexander Eckstein, Walter Galenson, and Ta-Chung Liu, eds, *Economic Trends in Communist China* (Chicago: Aldine, 1968), pp. 726–27. See also Feng-hwa Mah, *The Foreign Trade of Mainland China* (Chicago: Aldine Atherton, 1970), pp. 190–91.

[7] Mah, 'Foreign Trade,' pp. 671–738. His full-length study *The Foreign Trade of Mainland China* was published during 1971. See also Alexander Eckstein, ed., *China Trade Prospects and U.S. Policy*, with contributions by Jerome Alan Cohen, Robert F. Dernberger, and John R. Garson (New York: Praeger, 1971). Part III, by Professor Dernberger, deals with the prospects for trade between Communist China and the United States and contains a comprehensive appendix of statistical tables. Because of time limitations, other 1971 works have not been incorporated into this handbook.

[8] Actually there are two studies using the same U.S. Government source: Central Intelli-

Eckstein's study is the most detailed of the three. He concentrated on Communist China's commodity trade, while the other two tried to cover other items in its international balance of payments as well. He adjusted the import values of the free world countries (the sole exception being Hong Kong, in which case no adjustments are necessary) with a 6 per cent deduction for insurance and shipping costs.[9] He gave two estimates of trade values of the free world with Communist China, one net of re-exports through Hong Kong for both exports to and imports from Communist China and the other without such adjustment. But for practical reasons, he made no adjustments for re-exports through other countries. His summary table on the value and direction of Communist China's foreign trade, 1952–63, has been rearranged, and presented as Table 23–4 in the Appendix to this chapter.

Mah relied on the same major sources of information as Eckstein and produced a different set of estimates. Some of the differences, however, could be explained by his applying a 10 per cent, instead of a 6 per cent, deduction for insurance and shipping costs to adjust the import values of the free world and of his making no adjustments for re-exports. As can be expected, there is generally less discrepancy in estimates of trade with the free world and the Soviet Union than in trade with the East European and Asian Communist countries. Mah's estimates of Communist China's trade with various regions of the world for the period 1950–64 are given in Table 23–5.

As explained earlier, there are two studies using the same U.S. Government source. Some slight differences in their estimates do exist, primarily because of rounding of figures. As the study by Price carries one extra year of figures and is therefore presumably more up to date, it is considered to be representative of the two. Hereafter, it will be called the Price-CIA study.

The Price-CIA study used a different procedure from the other two. For 1950–58, it used Communist Chinese reported statistics, on the assumption that Peking reported China's exports at f.o.b. and its imports at c.i.f. prices.[10] Instead of using a flat rate for the adjustment of insurance and shipping costs, the study applied differential rates according to regions.[11] It also went on the assumption that Communist China records its foreign trade to show the country of destination and origin rather than the country of payment and receipt.[12] In addition, the study converts the official trade figures in yüan for 1950–58 to U.S. dollars at a number of estimated exchange rates,[13] and considers the converted figures to be the true values of Communist China's foreign trade. Any discrepancy between these totals and the sums of exports and imports reported by China's trading partners, adjusted for (1) insurance and shipping costs when applicable and (2) time leads and lags in shipping, and converted to U.S. dollars at prevailing exchange rates, was taken as the P.R.C.'s unrecorded imports and included in the totals of imports.[14] For 1959–65, the Price-CIA study accepted the trade statistics of Communist China's trading partners but

---

gence Agency, 'Communist China's Balance of Payments, 1950–65,' in Joint Economic Committee of the U.S. Congress, *An Economic Profile of Mainland China* (New York: Praeger, 1968), pp. 621–60; and Robert L. Price, 'International Trade of Communist China, 1950–65,' in the same volume, pp. 579–608. The latter relied on the basic information of the former.

[9] Eckstein, *Economic Growth and Foreign Trade*, p. 319, note 8.

[10] Price, 'International Trade,' p. 607; CIA, 'Balance of Payments,' p. 641.

[11] CIA, 'Balance of Payments,' p. 644, Table 11, note 2, and p. 647, Table 17, note 5.

[12] Price, 'International Trade,' p. 607; CIA, 'Balance of Payments,' p. 641.

[13] '[For 1950–58], U.S. $1 equals 4 yüan in trade with Communist countries and in trade with the free world, U.S. $1 equals 3.2 yüan in 1950, 2.24 yüan in 1951, 2.1 yüan in 1952, and 2.5 yüan in 1953–58' (CIA, 'Balance of Payments,' p. 643).

[14] *Ibid.*, pp. 644–45. Special adjustments were made for trade with the Soviet Union in 1950 and 1955 (p. 645).

made the necessary adjustments to keep the estimates consistent with those it had made for the previous period.

The October, 1968, issue of *Chinese Communist Affairs*, a bimonthly review published by the Institute of Political Research in Taiwan, contained an article that gave detailed statistics of Communist China's foreign trade.[15] Unfortunately, the sources of information and the methodology of arriving at estimates were not carefully spelled out. Since it admitted in one of its tables that it relied on the Price study for the estimates of total values of trade for 1950–65,[16] it may be assumed that it followed that study's definitions and methodology. Its estimates for 1950–67, labeled CCA, are given in Table 23–7.

Professor Yuan-li Wu, in his volume *Communist China's Economic Potential, 1965–1985*, prepared for the Stanford Research Institute, provides another set of estimates for 1961–67. His figures for Communist China's exports to the free world, that is, the free world's imports from Communist China, have not been adjusted to the f.o.b. basis. And his Communist bloc countries include only Albania, Bulgaria, Cuba, Czechoslovakia, East Germany, Hungary, Poland, Rumania, and the Soviet Union. His estimates are presented in Table 23–8.

In addition to the various studies described above, there are a number of other estimates available. Five editorials in *Current Scene* gave Communist China's trade figures for 1959 and 1962–70, distributed between the free world and the Communist bloc for a number of years.[17] All the figures were adjusted for exports f.o.b. and imports c.i.f.[18] No disclosure of the sources or the methodology was made. The German publication *Wochen Bericht* also gave some estimates of Communist China's foreign trade values.[19] The two sets of estimates are included in Table 23–9.

In Tables 23–10 through 23–15, all the estimates listed in the preceding five tables are compared, according to regional distributions if the breakdowns are available and in totals if they are not. While one would expect a great deal of divergence, a general trend is clearly discernible in spite of the differences in detail.

Trend from 1950 to the present. A careful analysis of Tables 23–10 through 23–15 establishes a number of significant facts. First, the total value of Communist China's foreign trade increased rapidly and almost continually from 1950 to 1959; it about tripled during that period. Then it dipped considerably until in 1962 it was only between 60 per cent and 65 per cent of the level achieved in 1959. Its recovery was almost as rapid. By 1966, it was only slightly below the 1959 peak level. There was a sizable drop in 1967 from the previous year, probably on the order of 10 per cent. Indications are that a similar decline occurred in 1968, but trade volume recovered to the 1966 level by 1970.[20]

The above-mentioned trend is in accordance with Communist China's over-all economic development. Between 1950 and 1959, as the economy of the Chinese mainland first recovered from war damage and then expanded under the impetus of industrialization, there was a corresponding sharp increase in Communist China's

---

[15] Chi-fang Wu, 'An Evaluation of the Peiping Regime's Foreign Trade in the Last 18 Years,' *Chinese Communist Affairs*, 5, No. 5 (Taiwan: Institute of Political Research, October, 1968): 55–60.

[16] Chi-fang Wu, 'Foreign Trade in Last 18 Years,' p. 56.

[17] 'Communist China's Economy at Mid-Year 1968: Eighteen Months of Disorder,' *Current Scene*, 6, No. 12 (July 17, 1968): 8–11; 'China's Economy in 1968,' *Current Scene*, 7, No. 9 (May 3, 1969): 1–9; 'China's Foreign Trade in 1968,' *Current Scene*, 7, No. 13 (July 1, 1969), 1–14; 'China's Foreign Trade in 1969,' *Current Scene*, 8, No. 16 (October 7, 1970), 1–18; 'China's Foreign Trade in 1970,' *Current Scene*, 9, No. 8 (August 7, 1971), 1–8.

[18] 'China's Economy at Mid-Year 1968,' p. 8; 'China's Foreign Trade in 1968,' p. 5.

[19] *Wochen Bericht*, No. 27 (Berlin: Deutsches Institut für Wirtschaftsforschung, July 4, 1968), p. 163.

[20] See 'China's Foreign Trade in 1968,' p. 7; 'China's Foreign Trade in 1970,' p. 1.

foreign trade volume. The reversal in its foreign trade in 1960 was due to internal economic difficulties, which developed after the failure of the Great Leap Forward and the sudden withdrawal of all Soviet specialists from the Chinese mainland in mid-1960. Chinese foreign trade—and the domestic economy—recovered from 1963 to 1966. And, as the adverse effect of the Cultural Revolution began to be felt in 1967 and 1968, foreign trade dipped again, this time probably more because of disruption of transportation than because of reduction in production.

Second, there is a clear distinction between (1) the 1950–59 period and (2) the period from 1960 to the present in terms of Communist China's direction of trade. The first period was dominated by P.R.C. trade with the Soviet Union and other Communist countries, while the second period witnessed a complete reversal of the trend. From 1950 to 1952, China's trade with the free world dropped about one-third, but that with the Communist bloc countries more than doubled. Between 1952 and 1959, and especially after 1954, its trade with the free world improved. By 1959, the total value of China's trade with the free world was more than twice that of 1952 and more than 30 per cent above that of 1950. However, during the 1952–59 period, the total value of its trade with the Communist bloc countries increased at an even faster rate, with the result that, by 1959, out of the total value of Communist China's foreign trade, almost 50 per cent went to the Soviet Union, more than 20 per cent was with the other Communist countries, and only about 30 per cent was with the free world.

From 1959 to 1962, while the total value of Communist China's trade with the Soviet Union and the East European Communist countries dropped by more than 60 per cent, trade with the free world was relatively stable. On the other hand, trade with Cuba and the Asian Communist countries went up sharply. From 1963 on, China's trade with the East European and Asian Communist countries more or less stabilized, but that with the Soviet Union continued to drop precipitously. By 1967, the total value of Sino-Soviet trade was only about 5 per cent of the level achieved in 1959. After 1965, Sino-Cuban trade also declined. More significant, however, is the fact that as China's economy recovered from 1962 to 1967, its trade with the free world more than doubled. As a result of this shift in the relative positions of Communist China's trading partners, by 1966 and 1967, about 75 per cent of the total value of its foreign trade went to the free world, while the remaining 25 per cent was shared by the Communist bloc countries, with the Asian Communist countries taking a much more significant part of China's bloc trade than they had in 1959 (approximately 40 per cent, as compared to less than 10 per cent in 1959).

The explanation for the dominance of Communist China's trade with the Soviet Union and other Communist countries from 1950 to 1959 is quite obvious. During that period, Communist China pursued at the same time a foreign policy of 'leaning to one side' and a domestic policy of rapid 'socialist industrialization.' These two policies, reinforced by the Western countries' strategic trade embargo after the outbreak of the Korean War, dictated to a large extent the course of China's foreign economic relations. Its close political and ideological ties with the Communist bloc countries and the availability of both credit and the types of goods Communist China required as imports at that time left it very little room for behaving otherwise.

In order to carry out its program of industrialization during the 1950's, Communist China imported heavily from the Soviet Union and Eastern Europe various types of capital goods and industrial raw materials, including complete plants.[21] Some of the imports were financed by Soviet long-term economic loans, which will be discussed in the next section. Although the Soviet loans were relatively moderate in size, their availability at a time of urgent need, together with the technical assistance

---

[21] For the commodity composition of Communist China's imports, 1955–59, see Eckstein, *Economic Growth and Foreign Trade*, pp. 106–7.

that Soviet Russia and the East European countries provided, played a key role in Communist China's economic planning and industrial development prior to 1960.

The upsurge in Communist China's trade with the free world after 1954 was partly due to Peking's export drive to earn foreign exchange to help pay for imports of heavy equipment and industrial raw materials and partly due to the gradual relaxation of the Western strategic trade embargo after mid-1957. However, as discussed earlier, the share of Communist China's trade with the free world did not assume significant proportions until after the drastic changes in the 1960's.

Both the continuous worsening of the Sino-Soviet relationship, which involved many other Communist countries as well, and the gradual relaxation of the Western strategic trade embargo were, of course, crucial factors responsible for the shift in relative positions in Communist China's trading partners in the 1960's. Another factor that must not be overlooked, however, is the change in the Chinese demand for imports after 1960. First of all, prompted initially by inadequate grain production at home and later reinforced by other considerations, Communist China has found it necessary to import every year since 1961 large quantities of wheat (see Table 23–16). In addition, Peking's shift in policy from 1961–62 on, which de-emphasized investment in heavy industries and devoted more state investment funds to industries that directly or indirectly aided the agricultural sector, has also modified its import requirements.[22] Many of the import items Communist China needs are either not readily available in the Communist bloc countries or are more cheaply and conveniently purchased from the non-Communist world.

Third, in terms of total values of exports and imports, both at f.o.b., Communist China had a trade deficit every year during the early 1950's.[23] The estimates for 1955 in Table 23–15, after allowing for the adjustment of insurance and shipping costs, do not agree as to whether the balance was in the red or black. However, for twelve out of the fifteen years beginning with 1956, all the estimates agree that Communist China maintained a trade surplus. The exceptions were 1960, 1967, and 1970. All this helps to support the observation that during its early stages of industrial development, Communist China relied on long-term and short-term credits to finance its trade deficits; as its economy gradually developed, it was able to pay off its debts, even during such years of extreme hardship as 1961 and 1962. The trend in trade balance also reflects Communist China's policy shift with regard to the priority assigned to imports. Since 1960, more weight has been given to matching imports with its ability to export rather than matching exports to the need for imports for industrialization. No long-term loans were contracted.

Fourth, there are three distinctive patterns in Communist China's trade with the Communist bloc countries. With the Soviet Union, the Chinese had a sizable deficit every year from 1950 to 1955 and maintained a surplus every year from 1956 to 1964 —all large surpluses with the exception of the one for 1960.

During 1965–67, there were two years with a small surplus and one year with a small deficit. The pattern reflects the availability of long-term Soviet loans in the early period and their repayment in later years. Although detailed information is

---

[22] Eckstein offers the following breakdown of the total value of P.R.C. imports from the Soviet Union and the non-Communist world in 1959 and 1963: machinery and equipment, 40.5 per cent in 1959 and 7.3 per cent in 1963; metals, ore, and concentrates, 15.2 per cent and 6.9 per cent; fertilizer and insecticides, 2.7 per cent and 5.2 per cent; textile fibers, 5.6 per cent and 15.1 per cent; and foodstuffs, processed and unprocessed, 0.3 per cent and 36.3 per cent. *Ibid.*, 105–6. Were information available on all P.R.C. imports, the contrasts in all likelihood would be still greater. On the other hand, the proportion of foodstuffs in import values would decrease in later years.

[23] Price-CIA and Adjusted CIA show a surplus for 1950, but their figures for that particular year are questionable because of their special adjustment for imports from the Soviet Union. CIA, 'Balance of Payments,' p. 645.

lacking for 1969–70, it does seem that the over-all trend of Communist China's trade with the Soviet Union has not been reversed. Total trade between the P.R.C. and the Soviet bloc remained at slightly less than $800 million a year for both 1968 and 1969, representing around 20 per cent of the P.R.C.'s total trade in both years.[24]

With the Eastern European countries, Communist China had small surpluses in some years and small deficits in some other years.[25] This tends to confirm the supposition that no long-term loans were involved. With Communist countries other than the Soviet Union and the East European countries, Communist China maintained a surplus every year without exception. This pattern may serve as a strong indication that military and economic aid had been extended to those countries by Communist China.

Fifth and last, no clear pattern has emerged from a scrutiny of the estimates in Table 23–10 relating to Communist China's trade with the free world. The estimates, after allowance for inclusion of insurance and shipping costs in some cases, disagree for most of the years. However, the lack of consistent and sizable trade deficits or surpluses in any period is consistent with the assumption that no long-term credits were involved.

EXTERNAL CREDIT RELATIONSHIP

Foreign borrowing. In managing its foreign trade, Communist China attempts in principle to achieve bilateral balance, from year to year, in trade with individual foreign countries. In general, it is done by the signing of bilateral trade agreements. In practice, however, it is not unusual to find sizable trade deficits or surpluses with individual countries at the end of the year. Between Communist countries, a maximum 'swing credit' is often agreed on to carry over trade deficits to the following year without any penalty. An interest of 2 per cent is usually charged if the limit is exceeded.[26] Communist China's credit relationship with the East European countries has been confined to such swing credits.

The total amount of Soviet economic, military and other loans to Communist China in the 1950's is subject to different interpretations. The confusion arises from the fact that three highly authoritative persons have given three conflicting figures: Finance Minister Li Hsien-nien's 5,294 million yüan, or $2,248 million, at the official exchange rate of 2.355 yüan to the dollar; CPSU Central Committee Presidium member Mikhail A. Suslov's 1,816 million new rubles, or $2,018 million, at the exchange rate of 0.9 new rubles to the dollar; and Premier Chou En-lai's 1,406 million new rubles or $1,561 million.[27] The most reasonable interpretation to date has been offered by Professor Mah.[28] He tried to reconcile these three figures in the following way: He assumed that both the Li and the Suslov figures include the principal and the interest charges; he assumed that the Sino-Soviet loan transactions were accounted in dollars; and he believed that in order to compare the Li and Suslov figures, the devalued rate of 2.617 yüan to the dollar, adopted in 1957, could be used to convert yüan to the dollar to eliminate 'the cumulative result of the increasingly greater degree of overvaluation of the yüan vis-à-vis the dollar at the 2.355-to-1 rate, relative to the extent of overvaluation of the ruble vis-à-vis the dollar at the official rate of four old rubles per dollar (or 0.9 new rubles per dollar).'[29] With such conversion, the Li figure came quite close to the Suslov figure. Mah interpreted the

---

[24] 'China's Foreign Trade in 1970,' *Current Scene*, 9, No. 8 (August 7, 1971), pp. 1–8.

[25] With the exception of 1958. All estimates give a deficit of more than $100 million for 1958.

[26] Mah, 'Foreign Trade,' pp. 676–77.

[27] For sources and a detailed discussion, see *ibid.*, pp. 697–705.

[28] *Ibid.*   [29] *Ibid.*, p. 701.

Chou figure to stand for the Soviet debts, including principal and interest charges, outstanding at the beginning of 1958. The difference between Suslov's $2,018 million and Chou's $1,561 million was the amount of principal and interest Communist China had paid to the Soviet Union up to that point.

Mah gave the breakdown of the $2,248 million in Soviet debts as the following: economic loans, $430 million; Korean War and other loans, 1950–53, $918 million; transfer of Soviet-owned shares in four joint stock companies in 1954, $313 million; transfer of military materials in Port Arthur in 1955, $570 million; and interest charges, $17 million.[30] Of the economic loans, one of $300 million was contracted in 1950, to be received in five equal amounts of $60 million each from 1950 to 1954, and to be repaid in ten equal installments from 1954 to 1963. The interest charge was 1 per cent per annum on the borrowed balance. A second economic loan of $130 million was announced in 1954; the terms were not specified. The economic loans were to be used for the purchase of capital goods and industrial raw materials. All Soviet debts were to be paid back in deliveries of goods, gold, and/or U.S. dollars. From the above, it can be seen that the economic loans were relatively small in size and that Communist China was asked to bear a sizable share of the burden of the Korean War.

All Soviet long-term loans were exhausted by 1957. Their repayment, which began in 1954 but did not take the form of net payments until after 1956 because of off-setting loans, required Communist China under the circumstances to maintain trade surpluses either with the Soviet Union or somewhere else. As I have indicated in the previous section, the P.R.C. did manage to have sizable surpluses with the Soviet Union from 1956 to 1964.

Because of internal economic difficulties, some of Communist China's scheduled debt payments were in arrears at the end of 1960. In the following year, a moratorium was obtained from the Soviet Union to spread the payments in arrears over a period of four years. In addition, the Soviet Union gave Communist China a loan of 500,000 tons of raw sugar, to be paid back in kind between 1964 and 1967. Beginning in 1961, Communist China sped up the repayment of Soviet debts through export surpluses. By the end of 1965, all Soviet debts, with the possible exception of 300,000 tons of raw sugar, had been repaid.[31]

With the reorientation of its trade in the 1960's, Communist China began to receive commercial credits from the free world. However, the loans were all short-term or medium-term, varying from six to eighteen months on purchases of grain and fertilizer and up to five years on purchases of machinery and equipment. The interest charges on the loans were usually 5 per cent or 6 per cent per annum. According to a U.S. estimate, Communist China's total drawing of credits from the free world for the period 1961–64 were about $910 million, but the net amount after deduction of repayment was only about $210 million.[32] According to another source, China's total drawing in 1966 was $140 million.[33] Its major suppliers of credit have been Australia, Britain, Canada, France, Italy, Japan, the Netherlands, and West Germany.

---

[30] *Ibid.*, pp. 702–4. For some of the other estimates, see Kang Chao, 'Pitfalls in Use of Statistics,' pp. 54–64; Chu-yuan Cheng, *Economic Relations Between Peking and Moscow 1949–1963* (New York: Praeger, 1964), pp. 76–82; and Choh-ming Li, *Economic Development of Communist China* (Berkeley and Los Angeles: University of California Press, 1959), pp. 169–74.

[31] Mah, 'Foreign Trade,' pp. 705–11. Communist China repaid 162,780 tons of raw sugar in 1964 and 37,220 tons in 1965. *Statistical Bulletin*, 27, No. 6 (International Sugar Council, June, 1968): 28. Later issues of the *Statistical Bulletin* did not give any information on the status of the remaining 300,000 tons of raw sugar.

[32] CIA, 'Balance of Payments,' pp. 655–56.

[33] Chi-fang Wu, 'A Study of Peiping's National Income and Finance,' *Chinese Communist Affairs*, 5, No. 1 (February, 1968): 24.

Foreign aid to other nations. Excluding military and economic aid to North Korea during and immediately after the Korean War, Communist China started its program of giving aid to other nations in 1954. At the beginning, Chinese aid was rather modest in size and limited to the Asian Communist countries. Then it was broadened to include Albania, Cuba, Hungary, and many non-Communist developing countries in Asia, the Middle East, and Africa. The motive behind Peking's foreign aid program is mainly political, at first to form alliances and win friends among other nations in order to isolate the Republic of China in Taiwan, and then with the added function of winning supporters in the dispute with the Soviet Union.

Between 1954 and 1966, Communist China signed economic and technical aid agreements with twenty-seven nations, of which six are Communist and twenty-one are non-Communist countries.[34] According to one source, the total commitment of loans and grants to those countries during the period was $2,663 million, of which $1,687 million, or 63.4 per cent, went to the six Communist countries, with North Korea and North Vietnam receiving $1,286 million, or 76.2 per cent of the amount allotted to the six.[35] Of the $976 million available to the twenty-one non-Communist countries, Indonesia received a sizable portion.[36]

Of its committed total of $2,663 million, $1,580 million was extended in the form of loans, of which $800 million, or slightly more than half, went to the six Communist countries. On the other hand, of the total grants of $1,083 million, North Korea and North Vietnam alone received $843 million, or almost 80 per cent.[37]

Partly because of the inability of Communist China's aid recipients to marshal domestic resources and finance local expenses and partly because of Communist China's inexperience or unwillingness to implement aid pledges rapidly, only a portion of its committed loans and grants has been delivered. According to Mah, for the period 1954 to 1964, only about 15 per cent of Communist China's committed economic aid to the non-Communist countries was actually delivered, while more than 90 per cent of its aid to the Communist countries seems to have been delivered.[38]

Although Communist China's delivered loans and grants to the non-Communist developing nations have been rather meager,[39] their impact on the recipient countries may have been much larger than the figures would suggest. This is because (1) the terms of the Communist Chinese loans were usually very liberal; (2) Chinese technicians lived modestly among the natives of the recipient nations, reducing the cost of projects and avoiding unnecessary conflicts with the natives; and (3) China carried the image of a nonwhite nation that was rapidly modernizing its economy and therefore understood the problems of the developing nations better than the other aid-giving countries.

THE OUTLOOK

As noted above, Communist China's foreign economic relations in the 1950's were more or less dictated by its foreign policy of 'leaning to one side' and its domestic policy of rapid 'socialist industrialization,' reinforced by the Western strategic trade embargo. The Sino-Soviet dispute, the change in Communist China's policy of

---

[34] The six Communist countries are Albania, Cuba, Hungary, North Korea, North Vietnam, and Mongolia. For more recent statistics, see Chapter 15 of this book.
[35] Chi-fang Wu, 'Study of Peiping's National Income and Finance,' pp. 24–25.
[36] *Ibid.*   [37] *Ibid.*
[38] Mah, 'Foreign Trade,' p. 713.
[39] From 1956 to 1965, about $200 million was actually delivered, compared to about $2 billion by the Soviet Union and $30 billion by the United States. Milton Kovner, 'Communist China's Foreign Aid to Less-Developed Countries,' in Joint Economic Committee, *Economic Profile of Mainland China*, p. 613.

industrial development with the corresponding shift in its import demand, and the relaxation of the Western embargo have all been responsible for the changes in the P.R.C. trade pattern since 1960. If it is assumed that the Sino-Soviet relationship will not improve to any large extent in the near future, and that the free world countries will continue to relax their trade embargo against Communist China, then the crucial factor seems to be Communist China's policy of industrial development and its import demand. It is difficult to predict what will happen after the economy of the Chinese mainland has recovered from the disruptions of the Cultural Revolution. The radical Mao faction may want to start another Great Leap Forward and commune movement, although, as of late 1970, there were no indications of this. One thing is certain, however: Communist China will never again rely so heavily on one single nation in its program of industrialization as it did in the 1950's. Although Peking has imported a number of complete plants from Western Europe and Japan in recent years and probably will continued to do so, it has been, and will be, reluctant to have foreign specialists residing at the site of construction to offer technical help, as the Russians did prior to 1960. Here, political ideology tends to stand in the way of economic rationality.

At present, the short duration of commercial credits from the free world and the need for frequent refinancing tend to limit the expansion of Communist China's imports. Longer-term loans will certainly help. But a great deal depends on the availability of such loans from the free world and the willingness on the part of Communist China to seek such loans.

In 1966 and 1967, Japan, Hong Kong, West Germany, Australia, Britain, Singapore, France, Italy and Canada, in that order, were Communist China's leading trade partners; Japan, Hong Kong, and West Germany continued to lead the list in 1968 and 1969.[40] However, Communist China has been known to be a shrewd bargainer, ready to take advantage of competition in the world market and to drive the best bargain possible. When it comes to trade with the free world, economic factors seem to prevail, with very few exceptions and in spite of all the rhetoric about the importance of proper politics. There is, therefore, no assurance that the composition and ranking of the top trading partners with Communist China will necessarily remain the same. After this chapter had been written, President Nixon made his dramatic change in American policy toward China and completed his trip to Peking. But the potential for Sino-American trade is still very limited, at least for the immediate future.[41]

Communist China's foreign aid program will probably follow the pattern of the past decade—it will probably be relatively modest in size and effective in practice. It will continue to be a weapon in the international political arena, particularly in the competition with the Soviet Union and Taiwan.

---

[40] 'China's Foreign Trade in 1969,' op. cit., pp. 11, 15.

[41] For a discussion of this subject, see Robert F. Dernberger, 'Prospects of Trade Between China and the United States,' Alexander Eckstein, ed., China Trade Prospects and U.S. Policy, pp. 183–319.

Table 23-1—Conjectural Estimates of Balance of Payments, 1950–64—Alternate Estimate 1
(in millions of U.S. dollars)

Annual Estimates	1950	1951	1952	1953	1954	1955	1956	1957
1. *China's payments, total*	*915*	*1,115*	*1,058*	*1,263*	*1,568*	*1,763*	*1,913*	*1,917*
2. Merchandise imports, f.o.b.	854	1,035	989	1,188	1,301	1,307	1,446	1,407
3. Freight and insurance	46	55	43	48	53	55	70	82
4. Salary of Soviet experts	5	10	10	10	10	10	10	10
5. Expenditures of students in U.S.S.R.	—	5	5	5	5	5	5	5
6. Chinese expenditures abroad	10	10	10	10	10	10	10	10
7. Repayment of Soviet debts	—	—	1	2	62	209	200	210
8. Foreign aid	—	—	—	—	127	167	172	193
9. *China's receipts, total*	*883*	*1,277*	*1,574*	*1,351*	*1,647*	*2,204*	*1,820*	*1,740*
10. Merchandise exports, f.o.b.	699	932	940	1,099	1,197	1,425	1,691	1,651
11. Foreign expenditures in China	10	10	10	5	5	5	5	5
12. Overseas remittances	70	70	70	70	70	70	70	70
13. Receipts from food parcels	—	—	—	—	—	—	—	—
14. Soviet credits	104	265	554	177	375	704	54	14
15. *Balance, deficit (—)*	*−32*	*162*	*516*	*88*	*79*	*441*	*−93*	*−177*

Annual Estimates	1958	1959	1960	1961	1962	1963	1964
1. *China's payments, total*	*2,336*	*2,520*	*2,352*	*1,732*	*1,429*	*1,613*	*1,985*
2. Merchandise imports, f.o.b.	1,861	2,036	1,926	1,370	1,075	1,139	1,392
3. Freight and insurance	118	99	103	91	74	84	114
4. Salary of Soviet Experts	10	10	5	—	—	—	—
5. Expenditures of students in U.S.S.R.	5	5	5	5	5	5	5
6. Chinese expenditures abroad	10	10	10	10	10	10	10
7. Repayment of Soviet debts	215	211	197	150	159	269	358
8. Foreign aid	117	149	106	106	106	106	106
9. *China's receipts, total*	*2,048*	*2,330*	*2,097*	*1,685*	*1,642*	*1,659*	*2,023*
10. Merchandise exports, f.o.b.	1,973	2,253	2,011	1,523	1,525	1,557	1,930
11. Foreign expenditures in China	5	5	5	5	5	5	5
12. Overseas remittances	70	70	70	70	70	70	70
13. Receipts from food parcels	—	2	11	41	42	27	18
14. Soviet credits	—	—	—	46	—	—	—

Table 23–1 (cont.)

Five-year Aggregates	1950–54	1955–59	1950–59	1960–64	1950–64
1. *China's payments, total*	*5,919*	*10,449*	*16,368*	*9,111*	*25,480*
2. Merchandise imports, f.o.b.	5,367	8,057	13,424	6,902	20,326
3. Freight and insurance	245	424	669	466	1,135
4. Salary of Soviet experts	45	50	95	5	100
5. Expenditures of students in U.S.S.R.	20	25	45	25	70
6. Chinese expenditure abroad	50	50	100	50	150
7. Repayments of Soviet debts	65	1,045	1,110	1,133	2,244
8. Foreign aid	127	798	925	530	1,455
9. *China's receipts, total*	*6,732*	*10,142*	*16,875*	*9,106*	*25,981*
10. Merchandise exports, f.o.b.	4,867	8,993	13,860	8,546	22,406
11. Foreign expenditures in China	40	25	65	25	90
12. Overseas remittances	350	350	700	350	1,050
13. Receipts from food parcels	—	2	2	139	141
14. Soviet credits	1,475	772	2,248	46	2,294
15. *Balance, deficit (—)*	*813*	*—307*	*506*	*—5*	*501*

Note: Details may not add to the total because of rounding.
Source: Feng-haw Mah, 'Foreign Trade,' in A. Eckstein, W. Galenson, and T. C. Liu, eds., *Economic Trends in Communist China* (Chicago: Aldine, 1968), Table 17, pp. 722–23. For a revised estimate of China's balance of payments, 1950–67, which came out too late to be incorporated here, see Feng-hwa Mah, *The Foreign Trade of Mainland China* (Chicago: Aldine-Atherton, 1971), Appendix Q, pp. 248–49.

Table 23-2—Balance of Payments, 1950-64—Alternate Estimate 2
(in millions of U.S. dollars)

(A) As Originally Presented	1950-57 Credit	1950-57 Debit	1958-59 Credit	1958-59 Debit	1960 Credit	1960 Debit	1961 Credit	1961 Debit
1. *Current account (net)*	—	*180*	*265*	—	—	*50*	*90*	—
2. Merchandise trade, f.o.b.	8,995	9,615	4,120	3,780	1,945	1,980	1,525	1,430
3. Nonmonetary gold	35	—	45	—	35	—	25	—
4. Freight and insurance (net)	—	300	—	145	—	80	—	85
5. Interest payments	—	85	—	35	—	15	—	15
6. Other payments and receipts (net)	—	65	—	30	—	5	10	—
7. Overseas remittances	855	—	90	—	50	—	60	—
8. *Capital and monetary gold (net)*	*430*	—	—	*500*	—	*290*	*190*	—
9. Credit and grants extended:								
10. Drawings	—	475	—	170	—	80	—	105
11. Repayments (incl. interest)	5	—	10	—	5	—	5	—
12. Credit received:								
13. Drawings	1,405	—	—	—	—	—	490	—
14. Repayments	—	405	—	280	—	165	—	175
15. Transfer of Soviet assets	—	330	—	—	—	—	—	—
16. Changes in clearing acct. balances with free world	15	—	—	15	—	15	—	—
17. Expropriation of convertible currencies	250	—	—	—	—	—	—	—
18. Changes in holdings of monetary gold	—	35	—	45	—	35	—	25
19. *Errors and omissions (net)*	—	*250*	*235*	—	*340*	—	—	*280*

Table 23-2 (cont.)

(A) As Originally Presented	1962 Credit	1962 Debit	1963 Credit	1963 Debit	1964 Credit	1964 Debit	1950–64 Credit	1950–64 Debit
1. *Current account (net)*	440	—	445	—	380	—	1,390	—
2. Merchandise trade, f.o.b.	1,525	1,110	1,560	1,140	1,755	1,365	21,425	20,420
3. Nonmonetary gold	25	—	25	—	25	—	215	—
4. Freight and insurance (net)	—	55	—	55	—	90	—	810
5. Interest payments	—	15	—	15	—	15	—	195
6. Other payments and receipts (net)	10	—	10	—	10	—	—	60
7. Overseas remittances	60	—	60	—	60	—	1,235	—
8. *Capital and monetary gold (net)*	—	445	—	370	—	275	—	1,260
9. Credit and grants extended:								
10. Drawings	—	130	—	130	—	115	—	1,205
11. Repayments (incl. interest)	5	—	5	—	5	—	40	—
12. Credit received:								
13. Drawings	205	—	285	—	295	—	2,680	—
14. Repayments	—	495	—	490	—	430	—	2,440
15. Transfer of Soviet assets	—	—	—	—	—	—	—	330
16. Changes in clearing acct. balances with free world	—	5	—	15	—	5	—	40
17. Expropriation of convertible currencies	—	—	—	—	—	—	250	—
18. Changes in holdings of monetary gold	—	25	—	25	—	25	—	215
19. *Errors and omissions (net)*	5	—	—	75	—	105	—	130

u

Table 23-2 (cont.)

(B) With Regrouping of Years	1950–59		1960–64		1950–64	
	Credit	Debit	Credit	Debit	Credit	Debit
1. *Current account (net)*	*85*	—	*1,305*	—	*1,390*	—
2. Merchandise trade, f.o.b.	13,115	13,395	8,310	7,025	21,425	20,420
3. Nonmonetary gold	80	—	135	—	215	—
4. Freight and insurance (net)	—	445	—	365	—	810
5. Interest payments	—	120	—	75	—	195
6. Other payments and receipts (net)	—	95	35	—	—	60
7. Overseas remittances	945	—	290	—	1,235	—
8. *Capital and monetary gold (net)*	—	*70*	—	*1,190*	—	*1,260*
9. Credits and grants extended:						
10. Drawings	—	645	—	560	—	1,205
11. Repayments (incl. interest)	15	—	25	—	40	—
12. Credit received:						
13. Drawings	1,405	—	1,275	—	2,680	—
14. Repayments	—	685	—	1,755	—	2,440
15. Transfer of Soviet assets	—	330	—	—	—	330
16. Changes in clearing acct. balances with free world	—	—	—	40	—	40
17. Expropriation of convertible currencies	250	—	—	—	250	—
18. Changes in holdings of monetary gold	—	80	—	135	—	215
19. *Errors and omissions (net)*	—	*15*	—	*115*	—	*130*

Note: Data are rounded to the nearest $5 million.
Source: Central Intelligence Agency, 'Communist China's Balance of Payments, 1950–1965,' in Joint Economic Committee of U.S. Congress, *An Economic Profile of Mainland China*, Table 5, p. 638.

Table 23-3—Consolidated Balance of Payments, 1950–64—Comparison of Alternate Estimates 1 and 2
(in millions of U.S. dollars)

	1950–59		1960–64		1950–64	
	Mah	CIA	Mah	CIA	Mah	CIA
1. Merchandise imports, f.o.b.	13,424	13,395	6,902	7,025	20,326	20,420
2. Freight and insurance	669	445	466	365	1,135	810
3. Other payments and receipts (net)	175	95	55	−35	230	60
4. Repayment of debts (incl. interest)	1,110	805	1,133	1,830	2,244	2,635
5. Foreign aid (net of repayment)	925	630	530	535	1,455	1,165
6. Transfer of Soviet assets	—	330	—	—	—	330
7. Changes in clearing acct. with free world	—	—	—	40	—	40
8. *Total debits*	*16,303*	*15,700*	*9,086*	*9,760*	*25,390*	*25,460*
9. Merchandise exports, f.o.b.	13,860	13,115	8,546	8,310	22,406	21,425
10. Overseas remittances (incl. food parcels)	702	945	489	290	1,191	1,235
11. Loans from Soviet Union and free world	2,248	1,405	46	1,275	2,294	2,680
12. Expropriations of convertible currencies	—	250	—	—	—	250
13. *Total credits*	*16,810*	*15,715*	*9,081*	*9,875*	*25,891*	*25,590*
14. *Errors and omissions (net)*		*15*		*115*		*130*
15. *Balance, deficit (—)*	*506*		*−5*		*501*	

Note: Details may not add to totals because of rounding.
Sources: Compiled from Tables 23–1 and 23–2.

Table 23–4—Foreign Trade of 1952–63—Alternate Estimate 1 (Eckstein)
(in millions of U.S. dollars)

Year		Free World		U.S.S.R.	Eastern Europe	Other Comm. Countries	Comm. Bloc	Total	
		Unadj.	Adj.					Unadj.	Adj.
1952	Exports	348	290	416	147	18	581	929	871
	Imports	272	183	554	143	10	707	979	890
	Total	620	474	970	290	28	1,288	1,908	1,761
1953	Exports	414	354	475	183	27	685	1,099	1,039
	Imports	285	193	697	199	18	914	1,200	1,107
	Total	699	547	1,172	382	45	1,599	2,298	2,146
1954	Exports	353	304	578	192	45	815	1,165	1,119
	Imports	287	221	759	250	30	1,039	1,326	1,260
	Total	640	525	1,337	442	75	1,854	2,491	2,379
1955	Exports	468	416	643	231	55	929	1,397	1,345
	Imports	315	286	748	237	50	1,035	1,350	1,321
	Total	783	702	1,391	468	105	1,964	2,747	2,666
1956	Exports	606	546	764	237	65	1,066	1,672	1,612
	Imports	430	408	733	264	60	1,057	1,487	1,465
	Total	1,036	954	1,497	501	125	2,123	3,159	3,077
1957	Exports	599	537	738	249	90	1,077	1,676	1,615
	Imports	528	508	544	284	55	883	1,411	1,391
	Total	1,127	1,046	1,282	533	145	1,960	3,087	3,006

1958	Exports	725	641	881	294	95	1,270	1,995	1,911
	Imports	771	746	634	410	75	1,119	1,890	1,865
	Total	1,496	1,387	1,515	704	170	2,389	3,885	3,776
1959	Exports	664	632	1,100	354	135	1,589	2,253	2,221
	Imports	670	651	954	325	80	1,359	2,029	2,011
	Total	1,334	1,283	2,054	679	215	2,948	4,282	4,232
1960	Exports	732	698	848	316	148	1,312	2,044	2,010
	Imports	656	637	817	340	117	1,274	1,930	1,912
	Total	1,388	1,335	1,665	656	265	2,586	3,974	3,922
1961	Exports	615	588	550	163	270	983	1,598	1,571
	Imports	663	647	367	164	236	767	1,430	1,414
	Total	1,278	1,235	917	327	506	1,750	3,028	2,985
1962	Exports	676	647	516	147	287	950	1,626	1,597
	Imports	603	589	233	78	239	550	1,153	1,139
	Total	1,279	1,236	749	225	526	1,500	2,779	2,736
1963	Exports	753	712	412	154	200	766	1,740*	1,699*
	Imports	710	699	182	89	155	425	1,282*	1,271*
	Total	1,463	1,411	594	243	355	1,192	3,022*	2,970*

Notes: Details may not add to the totals because of rounding. Adjusted columns give net figures of reexports. Cuba included among free world countries prior to 1959, and among Communist bloc countries after that year.

* Data incomplete for 1963. The world totals include an allowance for some countries, e.g., Cuba and Indonesia, and are larger than the sum of the free world and Communist bloc totals.

Source: Alexander Eckstein, Communist China's Economic Growth and Foreign Trade (New York: McGraw-Hill, 1966), pp. 94–95.

Table 23-5—Foreign Trade, 1950–64—Alternative Estimate 2 (Mah)
(in millions of U.S. dollars)

Year		Free World	U.S.S.R.	East Europe	Other Comm. Countries	Comm. Bloc	Total
1950	Exports	481	191	22	5	218	699
	Imports	452	389	8	5	402	854
	Total	933	580	30	10	620	1,553
1951	Exports	472	331	114	15	460	932
	Imports	446	478	106	5	589	1,035
	Total	918	809	220	20	1,049	1,968
1952	Exports	329	414	172	25	611	940
	Imports	273	554	157	5	716	989
	Total	602	968	329	30	1,327	1,929
1953	Exports	391	475	188	45	708	1,099
	Imports	288	697	193	10	900	1,188
	Total	679	1,172	381	55	1,608	2,286
1954	Exports	342	578	197	80	855	1,197
	Imports	294	759	238	10	1,007	1,301
	Total	636	1,337	435	90	1,862	2,498
1955	Exports	438	644	233	110	987	1,425
	Imports	317	748	237	5	990	1,307
	Total	755	1,392	470	115	1,977	2,732
1956	Exports	577	764	240	110	1,114	1,691
	Imports	434	733	264	15	1,012	1,446
	Total	1,011	1,497	504	125	2,126	3,138
1957	Exports	562	738	249	102	1,089	1,651
	Imports	528	544	295	40	879	1,407
	Total	1,090	1,282	544	142	1,968	3,057
1958	Exports	680	881	289	123	1,293	1,973
	Imports	771	634	408	48	1,090	1,861
	Total	1,451	1,515	697	171	2,383	3,834
1959	Exports	617	1,100	351	185	1,636	2,253
	Imports	669	955	324	88	1,367	2,036
	Total	1,286	2,055	675	273	3,003	4,290
1960	Exports	678	848	316	169	1,333	2,011
	Imports	656	817	338	115	1,270	1,926
	Total	1,334	1,665	654	284	2,603	3,938
1961	Exports	576	551	164	232	947	1,523
	Imports	645	367	164	194	725	1,370
	Total	1,221	919	328	426	1,673	2,894
1962	Exports	592	516	147	270	933	1,525
	Imports	573	233	78	191	502	1,075
	Total	1,165	750	225	461	1,436	2,601
1963	Exports	707	413	157	281	851	1,557
	Imports	693	187	73	186	446	1,139
	Total	1,400	600	230	467	1,297	2,696
1964	Exports	1,181	314	141	294	749	1,930
	Imports	977	135	85	195	415	1,392
	Total	2,158	449	226	489	1,164	3,322

Notes: Details may not add up to totals because of rounding. 1964 figures are preliminary.
Source: Feng-hwa Mah, 'Foreign Trade,' in A. Eckstein, W. Galenson, and T. C. Liu, eds., *Economic Trends in Communist China* (Chicago: Aldine, 1968), pp. 692–93.

614

Table 23-6—Foreign Trade, 1950-65—Alternative Estimate 3 (Price-CIA)
(in millions of U.S. dollars)

Year		Free World	U.S.S.R.	East Europe	Other Comm. Countries	Comm. Bloc	Total
1950	Exports	410	190	15	5	210	620
	Imports	450	135	5	0	140	590
	Total	860	325	20	5	350	1,210
1951	Exports	315	310	140	15	465	780
	Imports	605	440	65	5	510	1,115
	Total	920	750	205	20	975	1,895
1952	Exports	270	415	165	25	605	875
	Imports	305	550	155	5	710	1,015
	Total	575	965	320	30	1,315	1,890
1953	Exports	370	480	150	40	670	1,040
	Imports	370	685	190	10	885	1,255
	Total	740	1,165	340	50	1,555	2,295
1954	Exports	295	550	130	85	765	1,060
	Imports	320	720	240	10	970	1,290
	Total	615	1,270	370	95	1,735	2,350
1955	Exports	425	645	200	105	950	1,375
	Imports	360	1,055	235	10	1,300	1,660
	Total	785	1,700	435	115	2,250	3,035
1956	Exports	590	740	205	100	1,045	1,635
	Imports	475	720	270	20	1,010	1,485
	Total	1,065	1,460	475	120	2,055	3,120
1957	Exports	530	745	230	90	1,065	1,595
	Imports	560	550	280	40	870	1,430
	Total	1,090	1,295	505	130	1,935	3,025
1958	Exports	660	881	260	110	1,250	1,910
	Imports	725	634	415	50	1,100	1,825
	Total	1,385	1,515	680	160	2,350	3,735
1959	Exports	615	1,100	333	161	1,595	2,205
	Imports	695	955	326	83	1,365	2,060
	Total	1,310	2,055	659	244	2,960	4,265
1960	Exports	625	848	301	169	1,320	1,945
	Imports	745	817	341	128	1,285	2,030
	Total	1,370	1,665	642	297	2,605	3,975
1961	Exports	560	551	160	254	965	1,525
	Imports	775	367	165	185	715	1,495
	Total	1,335	919	325	439	1,680	3,015
1962	Exports	605	516	150	256	920	1,525
	Imports	660	233	80	177	490	1,150
	Total	1,265	750	230	433	1,410	2,675
1963	Exports	740	413	155	250	820	1,560
	Imports	770	187	70	169	425	1,200
	Total	1,510	600	225	419	1,245	2,755

Table 23-6 (cont.)

Year		Free World	U.S.S.R.	East Europe	Other Comm. Countries	Comm. Bloc	Total
1964	Exports	1,040	314	160	234	730	1,770
	Imports	1,080	135	85	173	395	1,475
	Total	2,120	449	245	407	1,125	3,245
1965	Exports	1,310	226	167	252	645	1,955
	Imports	1,260	192	132	156	480	1,740
	Total	2,570	417	299	409	1,125	3,695

Notes: Details may not add up to totals because of rounding. For years 1950–57, all figures are rounded to the nearest $5 million. For later years, only the free world, the Communist bloc and the total columns are rounded to the nearest $5 million; the other columns are rounded to the nearest $1 million. No attempt has been made here to change the method of rounding in the sources. 1964 figures are preliminary for CIA; 1965 figures preliminary for Price. For further explanations, see text of this chapter, at footnote 16.

Sources: Price: Robert L. Price, 'International Trade of Communist China, 1950–1965,' in Joint Economic Committee, U.S. Congress, *An Economic Profile of Mainland China,* pp. 579–608. CIA: Central Intelligence Agency, 'Communist China's Balance of Payments, 1950–1965,' in *idem,* pp. 621–60.

Table 23-7—Foreign Trade, 1950–67—Alternate Estimate 4 (*CCA*)
(in millions of U.S. dollars)

Year		Free World	U.S.S.R.	Other Comm. Countries**	Comm. Bloc	Total
1950	Exports	410	191	19	210	620
	Imports*	450	388	5	393	843
	Total	860	579	24	603	1,463
1951	Exports	315	331	134	465	780
	Imports	605	478	32	510	1,115
	Total	920	809	166	975	1,895
1952	Exports	270	414	191	605	875
	Imports	305	554	156	710	1,015
	Total	575	967	348	1,315	1,890
1953	Exports	370	475	195	670	1,040
	Imports	370	697	188	885	1,255
	Total	740	1,172	383	1,555	2,295
1954	Exports	295	578	187	765	1,060
	Imports	320	759	211	970	1,290
	Total	615	1,337	398	1,735	2,350
1955	Exports	425	644	306	950	1,375
	Imports	360	748	552	1,300	1,660
	Total	785	1,392	858	2,250	3,035
1956	Exports	590	782	263	1,045	1,635
	Imports	475	733	277	1,010	1,485
	Total	1,065	1,515	540	2,055	3,120
1957	Exports	530	739	326	1,065	1,595
	Imports	560	544	326	870	1,430
	Total	1,090	1,283	652	1,935	3,025
1958	Exports	660	889	361	1,250	1,910
	Imports	725	637	463	1,100	1,825
	Total	1,385	1,525	825	2,350	3,735
1959	Exports	615	1,100	495	1,595	2,205
	Imports	695	954	411	1,365	2,060
	Total	1,310	2,055	905	2,960	4,265
1960	Exports	625	848	472	1,320	1,945
	Imports	745	817	468	1,285	2,030
	Total	1,370	1,665	940	2,605	3,975
1961	Exports	470	551	504	1,055	1,525
	Imports	685	367	438	805	1,490
	Total	1,155	919	941	1,860	3,015
1962	Exports	523	516	486	1,002	1,525
	Imports	571	233	346	579	1,150
	Total	1,094	750	832	1,581	2,675
1963	Exports	657	413	490	903	1,560
	Imports	697	187	311	498	1,195
	Total	1,354	600	801	1,401	2,755
1964	Exports	941	314	515	829	1,770
	Imports	999	135	341	476	1,475
	Total	1,940	459	855	1,305	3,245
1965	Exports	1,309	226	464	690	1,999
	Imports	1,244	192	395	587	1,831
	Total	2,553	417	860	1,277	3,830

Table 23-7 (cont.)

Year		Free World	U.S.S.R.	Other Comm. Countries**	Comm. Bloc	Total
1966	Exports	1,711	143	378	521	2,232
	Imports	1,434	175	338	513	1,947
	Total	3,145	318	716	1,034	4,179
1967	Exports	1,548	57	343	400	1,948
	Imports	1,605	50	439	489	2,094
	Total	3,153	107	782	889	4,042

Notes: Details may not add to the total because of rounding.

* Import figure for Communist bloc countries given as $140 million which is inconsistent with figure given for U.S.S.R. alone of $388 million. It has been corrected according to information in the Price study.

** Derived from Communist bloc and U.S.S.R. totals.

Source: Chi-fang Wu, 'An Evaluation of the Peiping Regime's Foreign Trade in the Last 18 Years,' *Chinese Communist Affairs (CCA),* 5, No. 5 (October, 1968): 55–60.

Table 23-8—Foreign Trade, 1961–67—Alternate Estimate 5 (Wu)
(in millions of U.S. dollars)

Year		Free World	Comm. Bloc	Total
1961	Exports	732	628	1,360
	Imports	739	548	1,287
	Total	1,471	1,176	2,648
1962	Exports	796	572	1,368
	Imports	678	354	1,033
	Total	1,475	926	2,401
1963	Exports	940	593	1,533
	Imports	805	313	1,118
	Total	1,744	907	2,651
1964	Exports	1,258	479	1,737
	Imports	1,045	251	1,296
	Total	2,303	730	3,032
1965	Exports	1,366	414	1,780
	Imports	1,222	354	1,576
	Total	2,588	768	3,357
1966	Exports	1,727	269	1,997
	Imports	1,422	307	1,729
	Total	3,149	577	3,726
1967*	Exports	1,508	22	1,531
	Imports	1,415	41	1,456
	Total	2,923	63	2,987

Notes: Details may not add to totals because of rounding. Included in the Communist bloc are Albania, Bulgaria, Cuba, Czechoslovakia, East Germany, Hungary, Poland, Rumania, and the Soviet Union.

* For 1967, the Communist bloc includes Czechoslovakia and Poland only.

Source: Yuan-li Wu, *Communist China's Economic Potential, 1965–1985,* Stanford Research Institute.

Table 23-9—Foreign Trade, 1959-67—Alternate Estimates 6 (*CS*) and 7 (*WB*)
(in millions of U.S. dollars)

Year		Current Scene (*CS*)			*WB* (Total)
		Free World	Comm. Bloc	Total	
1959	Exports	600	1,600	2,200	2,164
	Imports	700	1,400	2,100	1,952
	Total	1,300	3,000	4,300	4,115
1962	Exports			1,500	1,437
	Imports			1,200	1,049
	Total			2,700	2,487
1963	Exports			1,600	
	Imports			1,200	
	Total			2,800	
1964	Exports			1,700	
	Imports			1,500	
	Total			3,200	
1965	Exports			1,900	1,941
	Imports			1,900	1,646
	Total			3,800	3,587
1966	Exports	1,600	600	2,200	2,199
	Imports	1,500	500	2,000	1,844
	Total	3,100	1,100	4,200	4,043
1967	Exports	1,400	500	1,900	2,005
	Imports	1,500	400	1,900	1,977
	Total	3,000	900	3,800	3,982
1968	Exports	1,400	500	1,900	
	Imports	1,400	400	1,800	
	Total	2,800	900	3,600	
1969	Exports	1,500	500	2,000	
	Imports	1,500	300	1,800	
	Total	3,100	800	3,800	
1970	Exports	1,500	500	2,100	
	Imports	1,800	300	2,200	
	Total	3,400	800	4,200	

Note: Details may not add up to totals because of rounding. *Current Scene* figures are rounded to $100 million.

Sources: CS: 1959–66, *Current Scene*, 6, No. 12 (July 17, 1968): 9; 1959, 1966, and 1967, *Current Scene*, 7, No. 13 (July 1, 1969): 7; 1966, 1969–70, *Current Scene*, 9, No. 8 (August 7, 1971): 1.

WB: Wochen Bericht, No. 27 (Berlin: Deutsches Institut für Wirtschafts-forschung, July 4, 1968), p. 163.

Table 23–10—P.R.C. Trade with the Free World, 1950–70—
A Comparison of Alternative Estimates
(in millions of U.S. dollars)

Year		Eckstein		Mah	Price -CIA	CCA	Wu	CS
		Unadj.	Adj.*					
1950	Exports			481	410	410		
	Imports			452	450	450		
	Total			933	860	860		
1951	Exports			472	315	315		
	Imports			446	605	605		
	Total			918	920	920		
1952	Exports	348	290	329	270	270		
	Imports	272	183	273	305	305		
	Total	620	474	602	575	575		
1953	Exports	414	354	391	370	370		
	Imports	285	193	288	370	370		
	Total	699	547	679	740	740		
1954	Exports	353	304	342	295	295		
	Imports	287	221	294	320	320		
	Total	640	525	636	615	615		
1955	Exports	468	416	438	425	425		
	Imports	315	286	317	360	360		
	Total	783	702	755	785	785		
1956	Exports	606	546	577	590	590		
	Imports	430	408	434	475	475		
	Total	1,036	954	1,011	1,065	1,065		
1957	Exports	599	537	562	530	530		
	Imports	528	508	528	560	560		
	Total	1,127	1,046	1,090	1,090	1,090		
1958	Exports	725	641	680	660	660		
	Imports	771	746	771	725	725		
	Total	1,496	1,387	1,451	1,385	1,385		
1959	Exports	664	632	617	615	615		600
	Imports	670	651	669	695	695		700
	Total	1,334	1,283	1,286	1,310	1,310		1,300
1960	Exports	732	698	678	625	625		
	Imports	656	637	656	745	745		
	Total	1,388	1,335	1,334	1,370	1,370		
1961	Exports	615	588	576	560	470	732	
	Imports	663	647	645	775	685	739	
	Total	1,278	1,235	1,221	1,335	1,155	1,471	
1962	Exports	676	647	592	605	523	796	
	Imports	603	589	573	660	571	678	
	Total	1,279	1,236	1,165	1,265	1,094	1,475	
1963	Exports	753†	712†	707	740	657	940	
	Imports	710†	699†	693	770	697	805	
	Total	1,463†	1,411†	1,400	1,510	1,354	1,744	

620

Table 23–10 (cont.)

Year		Eckstein		Mah	Price -CIA	CCA	Wu	CS
		Unadj.	Adj.*					
1964	Exports			1,181†	1,040	941	1,258	
	Imports			977†	1,080	999	1,045	
	Total			2,158†	2,120	1,940	2,303	
1965	Exports				1,310†	1,309	1,366	
	Imports				1,260†	1,244	1,222	
	Total				2,570†	2,553	2,588	
1966	Exports					1,711	1,727	1,600
	Imports					1,434	1,422	1,500
	Total					3,145	3,149	3,100
1967	Exports					1,548	1,508†	1,400
	Imports					1,605	1,415†	1,500
	Total					3,153	2,923†	3,000
1968	Exports							1,400
	Imports							1,400
	Total							2,800
1969	Exports							1,500
	Imports							1,500
	Total							3,100
1970	Exports							1,500
	Imports							1,800
	Total							3,400

Note: Details may not add to totals because of rounding.
* Figures net of re-exports.
† Preliminary and/or incomplete.
Sources: Compiled from Tables 23–4 through 23–9.

Table 23–11—Trade with the Soviet Union, 1950–67—
A Comparison of Alternative Estimates
(in millions of U.S. dollars)

Year		Eckstein	Mah	Price -CIA	CCA
1950	Exports		191	190	191
	Imports		389	135	388
	Total		580	325	579
1951	Exports		331	310	331
	Imports		478	440	478
	Total		809	750	809
1952	Exports	416	414	415	414
	Imports	554	554	550	554
	Total	970	968	965	967
1953	Exports	475	475	480	475
	Imports	697	697	685	697
	Total	1,172	1,172	1,165	1,172
1954	Exports	578	578	550	578
	Imports	759	759	720	759
	Total	1,337	1,337	1,270	1,337
1955	Exports	643	644	645	644
	Imports	748	748	1,055	748
	Total	1,391	1,392	1,700	1,392
1956	Exports	764	764	740	782
	Imports	733	733	720	733
	Total	1,497	1,497	1,460	1,515
1957	Exports	738	738	745	739
	Imports	544	544	550	544
	Total	1,282	1,282	1,295	1,283
1958	Exports	881	881	881	889
	Imports	634	634	634	637
	Total	1,515	1,515	1,515	1,525
1959	Exports	1,100	1,100	1,100	1,100
	Imports	954	955	955	954
	Total	2,054	2,055	2,055	2,055
1960	Exports	848	848	848	848
	Imports	817	817	817	817
	Total	1,665	1,665	1,665	1,665
1961	Exports	550	551	551	551
	Imports	367	367	367	367
	Total	917	919	919	919
1962	Exports	516	516	516	516
	Imports	233	233	233	233
	Total	749	750	750	759

Table 23-11 (cont.)

Year		Eckstein	Mah	Price -CIA	CCA
1963	Exports	412	413	413	413
	Imports	182	187	187	187
	Total	594	600	600	600
1964	Exports		314	314	314
	Imports		135	135	135
	Total		449	449	459
1965	Exports			226	226
	Imports			192	192
	Total			417	417
1966	Exports				143
	Imports				175
	Total				318
1967	Exports				57
	Imports				50
	Total				107

Note: Details may not add to totals because of rounding.
Sources: Compiled from Tables 23-4 through 23-7.

Table 23-12—Trade with Eastern Europe, 1950-65—
A Comparison of Alternative Estimates
(in millions of U.S. dollars)

Year		Eckstein	Mah	Price-CIA
1950	Exports		22	15
	Imports		8	5
	Total		30	20
1951	Exports		114	140
	Imports		106	65
	Total		220	205
1952	Exports	147	172	165
	Imports	143	157	155
	Total	290	329	320
1953	Exports	183	188	150
	Imports	199	193	190
	Total	382	381	340
1954	Exports	192	197	130
	Imports	250	238	240
	Total	442	435	370
1955	Exports	231	233	200
	Imports	237	237	235
	Total	468	470	435
1956	Exports	237	240	205
	Imports	264	264	270
	Total	501	504	475
1957	Exports	249	249	230
	Imports	284	295	280
	Total	533	544	505
1958	Exports	294	289	260
	Imports	410	408	415
	Total	704	697	680
1959	Exports	354	351	333
	Imports	325	324	326
	Total	679	675	659
1960	Exports	316	316	301
	Imports	340	338	341
	Total	656	654	642
1961	Exports	163	164	160
	Imports	164	164	165
	Total	327	328	325
1962	Exports	147	147	150
	Imports	78	78	80
	Total	225	225	230
1963	Exports	154	157	155
	Imports	89	73	70
	Total	243	230	225
1964	Exports		141	160
	Imports		85	85
	Total		226	245
1965	Exports			167*
	Imports			132*
	Total			299*

Note: Details do not add to totals because of rounding.
* Preliminary.
Sources: Compiled from Tables 23-4 through 23-6.

Table 23-13—Trade with Communist Countries Other than the U.S.S.R. and East European Countries, 1950–65—A Comparison of Alternative Estimates (in millions of U.S. dollars)

Year		Eckstein	Mah	Price -CIA
1950	Exports		5	5
	Imports		5	0
	Total		10	5
1951	Exports		15	15
	Imports		5	5
	Total		20	20
1952	Exports	18	25	25
	Imports	10	5	5
	Total	28	30	30
1953	Exports	27	45	40
	Imports	18	10	10
	Total	45	55	50
1954	Exports	45	80	85
	Imports	30	10	10
	Total	75	90	95
1955	Exports	55	110	105
	Imports	50	5	10
	Total	105	115	115
1956	Exports	65	110	100
	Imports	60	15	20
	Total	125	125	120
1957	Exports	90	102	90
	Imports	55	40	40
	Total	145	142	130
1958	Exports	95	123	110
	Imports	75	48	50
	Total	170	171	160
1959	Exports	135	185	161
	Imports	80	88	83
	Total	215	273	244
1960	Exports	148	169	169
	Imports	117	115	128
	Total	265	284	297
1961	Exports	270	232	254
	Imports	236	194	185
	Total	506	426	439
1962	Exports	287	270	256
	Imports	239	191	177
	Total	526	461	433
1963	Exports	200	281	250
	Imports	155	186	169
	Total	355	467	419
1964	Exports		294	234
	Imports		195	173
	Total		489	427
1965	Exports			252*
	Imports			156*
	Total			409*

Note: Details may not add to totals because of rounding.
* Preliminary.
Sources: Compiled from Tables 23-4 through 23-6.

Table 23-14—Trade with the Communist Bloc, 1950–70—
A Comparison of Alternative Estimates
(in millions of U.S. dollars)

Year		Eckstein	Mah	Price-CIA	CCA	Wu	CS
1950	Exports		218	210	210		
	Imports		402	140	393		
	Total		620	350	603		
1951	Exports		460	465	465		
	Imports		589	510	510		
	Total		1,049	975	975		
1952	Exports	581	611	605	605		
	Imports	707	716	710	710		
	Total	1,288	1,327	1,315	1,315		
1953	Exports	685	708	670	670		
	Imports	914	900	885	885		
	Total	1,599	1,608	1,555	1,555		
1954	Exports	815	855	765	765		
	Imports	1,039	1,007	970	970		
	Total	1,854	1,862	1,735	1,735		
1955	Exports	929	987	950	950		
	Imports	1,035	990	1,300	1,300		
	Total	1,964	1,977	2,250	2,250		
1956	Exports	1,066	1,114	1,045	1,045		
	Imports	1,057	1,012	1,010	1,010		
	Total	2,123	2,126	2,055	2,055		
1957	Exports	1,077	1,089	1,065	1,065		
	Imports	883	879	870	870		
	Total	1,960	1,968	1,935	1,935		
1958	Exports	1,270	1,293	1,250	1,250		
	Imports	1,119	1,090	1,100	1,100		
	Total	2,389	2,383	2,350	2,350		
1959	Exports	1,589	1,636	1,595	1,595		1,600
	Imports	1,359	1,367	1,365	1,365		1,400
	Total	2,948	3,003	2,960	2,960		3,000
1960	Exports	1,312	1,333	1,320	1,320		
	Imports	1,274	1,270	1,285	1,285		
	Total	2,586	2,603	2,605	2,605		
1961	Exports	983	947	965	1,055	628	
	Imports	767	725	715	805	548	
	Total	1,750	1,673	1,680	1,860	1,176	
1962	Exports	950	933	920	1,002	572	
	Imports	550	502	490	579	354	
	Total	1,500	1,436	1,410	1,581	926	
1963	Exports	766	851	820	903	593	
	Imports	425	446	425	498	313	
	Total	1,192	1,297	1,245	1,401	907	

Table 23–14 (cont.)

Year		Eckstein	May	Price -CIA	CCA	Wu	CS
1964	Exports		749	730	829	479	
	Imports		415	395	476	251	
	Total		1,164	1,125	1,305	730	
1965	Exports			645*	690	414	
	Imports			480*	587	354	
	Total			1,125*	1,277	768	
1966	Exports				521	269	600
	Imports				513	307	500
	Total				1,034	577	1,100
1967	Exports				400	22†	500
	Imports				489	41†	400
	Total				889	63†	900
1968	Exports						500
	Imports						400
	Total						900
1969	Exports						500
	Imports						300
	Total						800
1970	Exports						500
	Imports						300
	Total						800

Note: Details may not add to totals because of rounding.
* Preliminary
† Includes Czechoslovakia and Poland only.
Sources: Compiled from Tables 23–4 through 23–8.

Table 23-15—Total Volume of Foreign Trade, 1950-70—
A Comparison of Alternative Estimates
(in millions of U.S. dollars)

Year		Eckstein Unadj.	Eckstein Adj.	Mah	Price -CIA	CCA	Wu	CS	WB
1950	Exports			699	620	620			
	Imports			854	590	843			
	Total			1,553	1,210	1,463			
1951	Exports			932	780	780			
	Imports			1,035	1,115	1,115			
	Total			1,968	1,895	1,895			
1952	Exports	929	871	940	875	875			
	Imports	979	890	989	1,015	1,015			
	Total	1,908	1,761	1,929	1,890	1,890			
1953	Exports	1,099	1,039	1,099	1,040	1,040			
	Imports	1,200	1,107	1,188	1,255	1,255			
	Total	2,298	2,146	2,286	2,295	2,295			
1954	Exports	1,165	1,119	1,197	1,060	1,060			
	Imports	1,326	1,260	1,301	1,290	1,290			
	Total	2,491	2,379	2,498	2,350	2,350			
1955	Exports	1,397	1,345	1,425	1,375	1,375			
	Imports	1,350	1,321	1,307	1,660	1,660			
	Total	2,747	2,666	2,732	3,035	3,035			
1956	Exports	1,672	1,612	1,691	1,635	1,635			
	Imports	1,487	1,465	1,446	1,485	1,485			
	Total	3,159	3,077	3,138	3,120	3,120			
1957	Exports	1,676	1,615	1,651	1,595	1,595			
	Imports	1,411	1,391	1,407	1,430	1,430			
	Total	3,087	3,006	3,057	3,025	3,025			
1958	Exports	1,995	1,911	1,973	1,910	1,910			
	Imports	1,890	1,865	1,861	1,825	1,825			
	Total	3,885	3,776	3,834	3,735	3,735			
1959	Exports	2,253	2,221	2,253	2,205	2,205		2,200	2,164
	Imports	2,029	2,011	2,036	2,060	2,060		2,100	1,952
	Total	4,282	4,232	4,290	4,265	4,265		4,300	4,115
1960	Exports	2,044	2,010	2,011	1,945	1,945			
	Imports	1,930	1,912	1,926	2,030	2,030			
	Total	3,974	3,922	3,938	3,975	3,975			
1961	Exports	1,598	1,571	1,523	1,525	1,525	1,360		
	Imports	1,430	1,414	1,370	1,495	1,490	1,287		
	Total	3,028	2,985	2,894	3,015	3,015	2,648		
1962	Exports	1,626	1,597	1,525	1,525	1,525	1,368	1,500	1,437
	Imports	1,153	1,239	1,075	1,150	1,150	1,033	1,200	1,049
	Total	2,779	2,736	2,601	2,675	2,675	2,401	2,700	2,487
1963	Exports	1,740†	1,699†	1,557	1,560	1,560	1,533	1,600	
	Imports	1,282†	1,271†	1,139	1,200	1,195	1,118	1,200	
	Total	3,022†	2,970†	2,696	2,755	2,755	2,651	2,800	

628

Table 23–15 (cont.)

Year		Eckstein		Mah	Price -CIA	CCA	Wu	CS	WB
		Unadj.	Adj.						
1964	Exports			1,930†	1,770	1,770	1,737	1,700	
	Imports			1,392†	1,475	1,475	1,296	1,500	
	Total			3,322†	3,245	3,245	3,032	3,200	
1965	Exports				1,955†	1,999	1,780	1,900	1,941
	Imports				1,740†	1,831	1,576	1,900	1,646
	Total				3,695†	3,830	3,357	3,800	3,587
1966	Exports					2,232	1,997	2,200	2,199
	Imports					1,947	1,729	2,000	1,844
	Total					4,179	3,726	4,200	4,043
1967	Exports					1,948	1,531†	1,900	2,005
	Imports					2,094	1,456†	1,900	1,977
	Total					4,042	2,987†	3,800	3,982
1968	Exports							1,900	
	Imports							1,800	
	Total							3,600	
1969	Exports							2,000	
	Imports							1,800	
	Total							3,800	
1970	Exports							2,100	
	Imports							2,200	
	Total							4,200	

Note: Details may not add to totals because of rounding.
* Net of re-exports.
† Preliminary and/or incomplete.
Sources: Compiled from Tables 23–4 through 23–9.

Table 23–16—Wheat Imports over Seven Fiscal Years
(in billions of bushels)

From	1960–61	1961–62	1962–63	1963–64	1964–65	1965–66	1966–67	Total
Argentina	—	3	4	36	22	82	12	159
Australia	47	73	79	95	84	74	80	532
Canada	31	75	62	40	70	80	94	452
France	1	7	34	8	17	5	6	78
Others	2	17	4	11	—	5	—	39
Total	81	175	183	190	193	246	192	1,260
Total in million tons	2.20	4.76	4.98	5.17	5.25	6.70	5.23	34.29

Note: For the calendar years 1968, 1969, and 1970, it was reported that Communist China imported wheat at the rate of 4.4 million, 4.5 million, and 4.5 million metric tons, respectively. 'China's Foreign Trade in 1969' (editorial), *Current Scene*, 8, No. 16 (October 7, 1970): 4–6. On the other hand, the P.R.C. exported between 500,000 and 1 million metric tons of rice a year in the 1965–67 period. The world price for rice is about three times the price for wheat, and the nutritional value of wheat is only slightly less than that of rice, hence the P.R.C. gained in terms of nutritional value by exporting rice and importing wheat. Hsiao-fu Han, 'Communist China's Foreign Trade Activities,' *Communist Chinese Affairs Monthly*, 11, No. 7 (August 31, 1968): 104.
Source: Han, 'Foreign Trade Activities,' p. 103.

SELECTED BIBLIOGRAPHY

CHAO, KANG. 'Pitfalls in the Use of China's Foreign Trade Statistics,' *The China Quarterly*, No. 19, London: Congress for Cultural Freedom, July–September, 1964, pp. 47–65. Shows that Peking's official foreign trade data (in yüan) for the period prior to 1959 are not reliable because of certain distortions resulting primarily from the unrealistic and inconsistent exchange rates used by Communist China and from the different pricing bases in its trade with the West and with the Communist countries.

CHAO, KANG, and FENG-HWA MAH. 'A Study of the Ruble-Yüan Exchange Rate,' *The China Quarterly*, No. 17, January–March, 1964, pp. 192–204. Attempts to determine and analyze the effective ruble-yüan exchanges rate from 1950 to 1960. An estimate of the ruble-yüan purchasing power parity and a brief discussion of the implication of a discrepancy between the effective exchange rate and the purchasing power parity are included.

CHENG, CHU-YUAN. *Economic Relations between Peking and Moscow: 1949–1963.* New York: Praeger Publishers, 1964. Discusses in detail four integral aspects of Sino-Soviet economic relations from 1949 to 1963: Soviet assistance to Communist China's program of industrialization, Sino-Soviet trade, Soviet financial aid to Communist China, and the prospects of future relationship between the two countries.

ECKSTEIN, ALEXANDER. *Communist China's Economic Growth and Foreign Trade: Implications for U.S. Policy.* New York: McGraw-Hill, 1966. Analyzes Sino-Soviet economic relations in the broader context of Communist China's economic development and the role of foreign trade in that development. Chapters 4 to 6 deal specifically with all aspects of Communist China's economic relations with other countries, with concentration on trade, long-term loans and foreign aid.

KOVNER, MILTON. 'Communist China's Foreign Aid to Less-Developed Countries,' in Joint Economic Committee of the U.S. Congress, *An Economic Profile of Mainland China* (New York: Praeger Publishers, 1968), pp. 609–20. In addition to giving statistics of the magnitude, nature and direction of Communist China's aid to various less-developed countries from 1956 to 1965, this paper also looks into the Sino-Soviet dialogue over foreign aid and Communist China's motive in granting aid.

LI, CHOH-MING. *Economic Development of Communist China.* Berkeley and Los Angeles: University of California Press, 1959. Chapter on Communist China's external financing up to 1957 (pp. 166–95) represents an earlier effort to reconstruct Communist China's foreign trade and Soviet loan volumes based on scattered information from Chinese sources. The chapter, especially its methodology and analytical portions, is still of great interest to students of Communist Chinese economic affairs.

MAH, FENG-HWA. 'The Terms of Sino-Soviet Trade,' *The China Quarterly*, No. 17, January–March, 1964, pp. 174–91. Tries to discover whether there are significant price or unit value differences in Sino-Soviet trade as compared with each country's trade with other partners from 1955 to 1959 and to compute indices of Communist China's comparative price advantage (or disadvantage) in trading with the Soviet Union during this period.

———. 'Foreign Trade,' in ALEXANDER ECKSTEIN, WALTER GALENSON, and TACHUNG LIU, eds., *Economic Trends in Communist China* (Chicago: Aldine Publishing Co., 1968), pp. 671–738. Investigates the changing trends in Communist China's international trade and balance of international payments for the period 1950–64. Methodology on the derivation of the various items is contained in a number of appendixes. Also contains a full discussion of the objectives, organization and planning of Communist China's foreign trade.

PRICE, ROBERT L. 'International Trade of Communist China, 1950–65,' Joint Economic Committee, *An Economic Profile of Mainland China* (see under KOVNER, above), pp. 579–608. A study of the volume, composition, and direction of Communist China's foreign trade from 1950 to 1965. Most of its statistics are similar to a part of those contained in the CIA contribution to the same volume (see below).

U.S. Central Intelligence Agency, 'Communist China's Balance of Payments, 1950–65,' in Joint Economic Committee, *An Economic Profile of Mainland China*, pp. 621–60. A summary of a study of Communist China's balance of international payments from 1950 to 1964 (although the title says to 1965). Detailed information on the derivation of items in the balance of payments are given in the appendix on methodology.

WU, CHI-FANG. 'An Evaluation of the Peiping Regime's Foreign Trade in the Last 18 Years,' *Chinese Communist Affairs*, 5, No. 5 (Taipei: Institute of Political Research, October 1968): 55–60. Contains some up-to-date information on Communist China's foreign trade. One major defect is that the original sources of information are often not disclosed. Caution must also be exercised in using this source because of certain inconsistency in data and certain typographical errors.

———. 'A Study of Peiping's National Income and Finance,' *Chinese Communist Affairs*, 5, No. 1 (February, 1968): 1–31. Contains some up-to-date information on Communist China's foreign aid to less developed countries. Original sources of information are usually not disclosed.

24

SCIENCE AND TECHNOLOGY

J. A. BERBERET

Introduction

THE development of printing in Europe in the mid-fifteenth century initiated a growth of the natural sciences in the Western world that, after a formative period of approximately two centuries, has increased exponentially ever since. Thus today vast amounts of scientific information have been accumulated in books, scientific journals, and, more recently, in the memory storage units of computers.

In the beginnings of science in the West, scientific investigators were motivated by curiosity and the desire to determine scientific truths. However, as scientific knowledge was accumulated, it became apparent that certain benefits could be derived by applying scientific principles to the solution of pragmatic problems. In the West, therefore, it gradually became commonplace to conduct scientific investigations to develop new technologies in support of economic developments, for more efficient military systems, for enhancement of national prestige, and for other purposes.

It is now generally assumed that all nations should develop scientific and technological capabilities. The extent to which such capabilities exist and are employed in a country have become a yardstick for assessing the degree of development of a nation. Even more, the state of development of a nation has almost become synonymous with its scientific and technological capability. Thus, it is conventional to refer to those nations that have advanced scientific and technological capabilities and use them extensively, such as the United States and the Soviet Union, as developed nations. Those that are just beginning to acquire such capabilities are referred to as developing nations.

The best prescription for making a developed nation out of an undeveloped nation has not yet evolved, although there is more than abundance of scientific and technological information for such a metamorphosis. The process of using that information, however, is very complicated: There must be decisions about what information will be used and how; educational systems must be designed and implemented; numerous factors, such as the culture and geography of a nation, must be incorporated into the decisions.

Far more than an information base is required. For a nation to develop scientific and technological expertise, it must have scientific and technological manpower, access to capital, equipment, and raw materials. Education extending over generations is a necessity. The process of becoming a developed nation is one that will

---

Most of the material in this chapter is based on the author's studies of Chinese science and technology extending back to 1959. The more significant writings dealing with science and technology in Communist China are given in the bibliography at the end of the chapter.

produce many cultural stresses. Many customs and indigenous methods must be abandoned and new practices adopted. It has become apparent that the process is a slow one for any nation; it has become equally apparent that the national patience is often in as short supply as capital, materials, and necessary manpower. Political strife and revolutions are common growing pains of developing nations.

Communist China, with its tremendous population, large land mass, and a cultural pattern that changed very little during the two millenniums before the twentieth century, is unique among developing nations. Like all developing nations, the acquisition of a scientific and technological capability has been strongly configured into its development program. Its success in developing a scientific and technological capability will be a significant factor in its emergence as a leading nation in the world. It is therefore important that any comprehensive analysis of China include a review of many factors involved in its efforts to achieve progress toward the development of a scientific and technological capability.

THE HISTORY OF SCIENCE AND TECHNOLOGY IN CHINA

The art of printing was invented in China prior to the nineteenth century, more than 600 years before it was known in the West. The discovery served commendably to print Chinese literature, including the classics, and government documents; however, it failed completely to support a growth of science as it did in the West. The failure cannot be attributed to a lack of interest in science in China. More probably it was due to cultural values in China, specifically the pre-eminence of those values over science.

It can be demonstrated that the earliest patterns of Chinese culture were evident in the Shang (also called the Yin) dynasty, usually dated 1766–1122 B.C. It was in that period that the deep respect for knowledge and intellectual values that have characterized the Chinese down through the ages developed. A strong emphasis on government also developed. Presumably, the need for written documents in government brought the intellectual into government, thereby initiating in China an identification of learned people with government that prevailed into the twentieth century.

Certain forms of science were also apparent under the Shang dynasty, particularly an interest in mathematics and astronomy. There is evidence that a respectable knowledge of metallurgy and the agricultural sciences existed; engineering principles were applied in the building of large structures, such as temples and palaces. Thus, a form of science and technology began in China at a very early date.

The Shang dynasty was followed by the Chou dynasty (1122–403 B.C.). The pattern of thought that was to prevail in China up to the twentieth century was crystallized during that period, as were the factors that were to affect the development of science in China. In terms of influence on the future history of China, the dominant figure during the Chou dynasty was Confucius (551–479 B.C.). Confucius emphasized human conduct, the social and philosophical aspects of man. Knowledge was to be developed by abstract thought. When the landlord-scholar-official class replaced the old feudal system under the Han dynasty (206 B.C.–A.D. 22), Confucius's thinking was wholly adopted by this class. It flourished, became a kind of official state religion, and exerted a greater than ever influence on Chinese thought. That influence, although undergoing variations in certain periods of Chinese history, has prevailed to the present. It cannot be said that Confucianism opposed the development of science, but, in its preoccupation with other intellectual pursuits, it did nothing to promote scientific development.

Lao Tzu (604?–531 B.C.), founder of Taoism, also lived during the Chou dynasty. Taoism treats the relationship of the individual to his natural surroundings and upholds a state of nature where the free expression of the individual is the end and justification for everything. It seeks to teach man how to live in harmony with the controller of the universe and advocates living in harmony with nature, shunning the seeking of wealth and social rank. Unlike Confucianism, Taoism stressed that man should immerse himself in nature and thereby directed the attention of the Chinese to their natural environment. It is thus logical that this philosophy would encourage the development of the natural sciences. Indeed, when Taoism flourished in early Chinese history, advances in medicine and botany took place.

By the time of the Han dynasty (206 B.C.–A.D. 220), scholarship in China was identified with the study of the Chinese classics. The scholars were the highest class in China, and their work was held in high esteem. It became traditional for them to do no work with their hands; their long fingernails and characteristics of their dress proclaimed their status of physical inactivity. The scientists of traditional China belonged to the scholarly class. In keeping with the privileges of their class, they did no work with their hands—hence no experimental work. They only observed and theorized. This cultural trait, prevailed down through the nineteenth century and was a major cause of the slow progress of the experimental sciences in China.

Below the scholar in the class system of traditional China was the peasant farmer, followed by the artisan and, last, the merchant. It was from the artisan class that Chinese technological devices came into being. Unfortunately, the class distinction meant that there was little interchange between the scientist and the artisan engineer. Furthermore, the class separation led to downgrading of the artisans' accomplishments, for the artisans could not embellish them with words of explanation adequate to satisfy the sophistication of the scientist-scholar. Nevertheless, over the centuries the artisan class produced numerous noteworthy devices, such as elaborate clocks. Many of the artisans' devices had ended up as mental exercises, toys, or amusements for an emperor or a high official. At no time in Chinese history were the efforts of the artisan class and the merchant class combined to expand production. Therefore, no social revolution of the kind that occurred in England in the nineteenth century ever came about in China.

Chinese science has advanced in several instances as a consequence of the diffusion of foreign religions in China. Buddhism developed in China from the first to the sixth centuries A.D. It resulted in advances in mathematics and astronomy particularly. Christianity (Nestorian and possibly Jacobite) was in China from the seventh to the tenth centuries A.D. but had little impact on Chinese scholarship at any time.

In the sixteenth century, under the Ming dynasty, the Jesuit, Dominican, and Franciscan orders went into China. Led by Matteo Ricci, the Jesuits, more than any other Christian element, were accepted by high officials and even emperors because of their scholastic ability and their knowledge of Western science, mathematics, and music. The K'ang-hsi Emperor employed the Jesuits in literary, astronomical, and geographical pursuits, the last consisting of mapping his empire. The attention the Chinese leaders paid the Jesuits was due in no small part to the fact that the Jesuits helped in the design and construction of cannon and other armaments. These strengthened China militarily and were assets in the emperor's campaign to subdue China's southern areas.

Although Western scientific and technological influence filtered into China in commercial exchanges, the entry of the missionaries represented the largest wave of Western learning and scientific influence to enter China up to that time. Some seventy Western books on mathematics, astronomy, engineering, geography, and other subjects were translated into Chinese and published. The progress of the Christian venture and its influence on the development of Chinese science was severely limited as a consequence of the Rites Controversy[1] between the Pope and the

---

[1] The Rites Controversy was a dispute between Rome and the Chinese emperors that began in 1628 and ended in 1742. The central issue was whether there were conflicts between

emperor, followed by the persecution of Chinese Christians in the early part of the eighteenth century.

Although the early Christian activity had some permanent influences on Chinese science, it did not trigger any sustained growth of Chinese science. Possibly the Chinese sense of cultural pre-eminence precluded the acceptance of intellectual developments of Western origin. Probably a more basic reason was that the Confucian cultural disposition did not stimulate scientific curiosity.

After the expulsion of the Jesuits, there were few significant developments in science in China until the nineteenth century, when China was exposed for about 100 years to Western science and technology through the invasions of Western nations, Russia, and Japan; the commerce with the West in which China was compelled to participate; and the Christian missionary movement. In desperation, the Chinese adopted some of the technology to defend themselves militarily against the foreign invaders. Some provincial leaders saw in the armaments and technology of the West a means of achieving military and economic superiority over neighboring provinces. But probably most significant of all was the intense interest in Western science that developed in large numbers of Chinese youth, even though their interest was inhibited because of an association of science with the numerous misdeeds of the West. Nevertheless, in that period Western science made permanent inroads into Chinese culture.

In the latter part of the nineteenth century, railroads, the telegraph, and modern armaments were introduced to China. Mining practices were improved, and rapid strides were made in many fields of engineering, particularly metallurgy. The British introduced mechanized forms of weaving into textile manufacture. Electricity came into use.

In 1895, the Japanese defeat of China in the Sino-Japanese war made the Chinese fully aware of the relationship between technology and military strength. The Japanese occupation of Manchuria during the 1930's brought many new industrial practices to China, as did other contacts and the assistance provided by the United States and other nations, especially after World War II, until 1949. There were attempts at expanding industrial development in China, however, civil war and political and social disruption, derived from the conflict between the Nationalist government under Chiang Kai-shek and the Communists under the leadership of Mao Tse-tung, prevented the Chinese Government from extensively utilizing the technological practices to which they had been introduced. Nevertheless, prior to 1949 China was a nation that was developing in science and technology. During the civil war period, 1945–49, there were attempts to expand educational facilities and increase the number educated in all fields of learning, including the number of scientists and engineers. Following the practice that was established prior to World War II, large numbers of Chinese were also sent to foreign nations, especially the United States, to attend colleges and universities. The takeover of China by the Communists was completed before this program could be of significant value to the Nationalist government. However, all of those efforts to enhance the number of educated people in China, especially those during the second quarter of this century, did give rise to scientific and technological advances, which have been extremely important to the development of science and technology under the P.R.C. Without them, scientific and technological progress in the P.R.C. would have been much slower than it has been to date.

Christian teachings and traditional Chinese practices and beliefs. The issues were complicated by political considerations on both sides. The controversy also involved the jurisdiction of Chinese emperors over missionaries and Chinese Christians. Ultimately, both the emperor and the Pope made decisions unacceptable to each other, and the decline of Christianity in China began.

The Development of Science and Technology in the P.R.C.

Organization of science and technology. China's intellectual progress since 1949 has been due in large measure to the extensive planning of the central government, aided, prior to 1960, by Russian officials. Those responsible for planning and policy-making, despite the fact that many of them had little scientific education and knew virtually nothing about science and technology, appreciated the value of education and science and technology to the future of China and acted accordingly. Educational institutions and curriculums were reorganized, and higher education enrollments were increased immediately. Enrollments in science and, especially, engineering were increased more rapidly than in any other field.

In November, 1949, two months after the P.R.C. was founded, the support of science was confirmed with the establishment of the Chinese Academy of Sciences through a merger of the Peking Academy of Science with the existing Academia Sinica and some lesser institutions. The new organization, which started with sixteen research institutes, was commissioned to plan, direct, and promote science and technology. It was also intended from the beginning that it would aid in the education of research personnel.

Since that first official act, which signified the importance of science to the P.R.C., the organizational structure for the planning, support, and development of science and technology has been in a state of flux. Today, the state Scientific and Technological Commission, founded in 1958 and under the jurisdiction of the State Council, has become the organization in which the Chinese Communist Party has vested the most authority for the planning and direction of scientific and technological activities in China.

Concurrent with the evolution of the State Scientific and Technological Commission and the development of the Academy of Sciences, several ministries were formed and given responsibility by scientific and technological activities. Chief among them are the ministries of Education, Agriculture, Geology, and Defense. In addition to the Academy of Sciences, separate academies were formed under the Agriculture, Public Health, Geology, and Defense ministries. Most of the research and development institutes are administered by the ministries. Additional insight into the manner in which different scientific and technological functions are carried out by different organizational sectors in the P.R.C. is given in Figure 24–1. The shaded portions give a semiquantitative ranking of the relative responsibility of different organizations for certain functions. The Academy of Sciences remains the leading organization for the conduct of science in China. It comprises five departments: (1) physics, chemistry, and mathematics, (2) biology, (3) earth sciences, (4) technical sciences, and (5) philosophy and social sciences. In May, 1965, the academy was responsible for 112 research institutes, which are administered by the departments and concentrate on project-oriented basic research. It also acts in an advisory and coordinating capacity for the ministries.

Approximately the same number of institutes are operated by the other academies. For example, in 1963 the number of institutes operated by the Academy of Sciences, the Academy of Agriculture Sciences, and the Academy of Medical Science totaled 315. At the same time the government sector (central, provincial, and municipal governments, including the Ministry of Defense) was operating 345 research institutes (exclusive of those operated by the academies, educational institutions, and industry). In summary, there were in China at that time about 800 research institutes, of which 305 were in the life sciences, 205 in the physical sciences, and 271 in engineering. Under the Scientific and Technical Association of China, there were forty scientific societies in 1962, with a membership exceeding 100,000.

Relatively little is known of the organization and activities of military research and

Figure 24-1—Functions of Scientific and Technological Sectors (amount of shading indicates relative amount of activity of sectors in various functions)

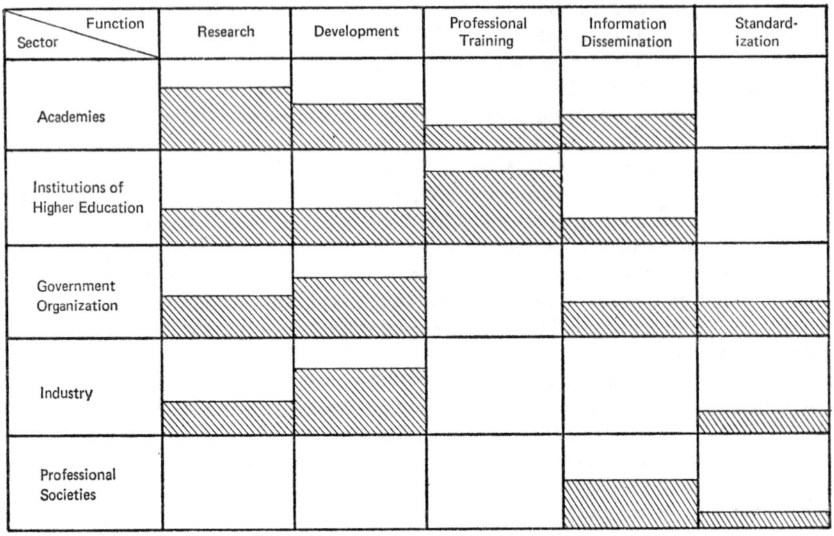

Sector \ Function	Research	Development	Professional Training	Information Dissemination	Standardization
Academies					
Institutions of Higher Education					
Government Organization					
Industry					
Professional Societies					

development, other than that the effort is large, as can be judged, for example, from the nuclear and missile testing that has been done to date. The Military Science Academy is responsible for most military research. The machine-building industries are also involved in these activities but probably do more development than research work.

Specific plans for science and technology. After the initial plans for the advancement of science and technology were laid down in 1949 and 1950, additional specific plans developed slowly for the next few years. In 1953, the First Five-Year Plan began. It emphasized scientific and technological development in China and named eleven areas to which the Academy of Sciences was to give primary attention.[2] Then, in 1956, the first formal plan for science and technology, generally referred to as the First Twelve-Year Plan, was mapped under the direction of the newly formed State Planning Commission with the aid of Soviet advisers. The plan called for China's achievement of scientific and technological equality with the leading nations of the world by 1967. It was under the same plan that atomic energy development was first emphasized. In 1963 the original plan was replaced by a new ten-year plan for science and technology about which almost no information has been released.

A Second Five-Year Plan, for the 1958–62 period, continued to emphasize science and technology, especially atomic energy, electronics, and cybernetics. The plan was largely assimilated by the Great Leap Forward, which began in 1958, and apparently lost its identity. The First Twelve-Year Plan for science was similarly assimilated. A

---

[2] Areas emphasized included atomic energy for peaceful purposes, steel mill development, petroleum prospecting and refining, seismology, multipurpose development of rivers, agricultural development, research and development of antibiotics and polymers, and national industrialization.

Third Five-Year Plan (also an economic plan) was announced in 1964, but details on its goals and objectives were never published.

A grandiose plan for the advancement of education, science, technology, and industry—Mao Tse-tung's Great Leap Forward—was initiated in 1958. The details of this movement and its collapse have been covered in various chapters of this handbook. The movement, coupled with the departure of the Russian scientific advisers in 1960, grossly disrupted the progress of research and development in China. However, by 1965 the pre-Leap status had been re-established in most areas. The Great Leap, the Russian departures, and the economic recession in the 1960–62 period appeared not to have a major effect upon the development of nuclear armaments.

Government policy and the support of science and technology.[3] If a scientific and technological capability and productive research and development programs are to exist within any nation, sources of funds greater than those that can be provided by the industrial sector must exist. They may be provided by the government, or by loans or aid from other nations.

Large Soviet loans in the 1950's helped the Chinese Communists initiate many of their research and development programs. Starting in mid-1960, these funds were cut off, making it become necessary for the Chinese to provide full support for their research and development activities.

When the government of a nation is the sole source of funds for its research and development programs, decisions must be made within the government as to the type of work that is to be done and the extent to which various programs will be supported. Hence, there must be some sort of policy toward science and technology, reflecting the attitude of a nation toward science and the roles the leaders think it will play in achieving national goals and objectives.

Accepted conventions for measuring the policies of various governments toward science and technology do not exist. However, a crude index of the scientific policy of a given nation is its financial support for research and development. A somewhat better index for many nations would be the fraction of its national budget expended in support of research and development activities. Further insight into this policy, plus some additional understanding of a nation's goals and objectives, can be gained from a knowledge of the kinds of research and development it sponsors.

In the P.R.C. all research and development projects are government-supported; in some instances the support is direct, and in others it is indirect. In the case of the former, where funds for research and development come from government agencies, the term 'government research and development' is employed. Research and development work that is financed by the state-owned and state-operated industrial and commercial enterprises (also by local and educational institutions) is referred to as 'nongovernment research and development.' Significant amounts of financial data are available for government research and development but not, unfortunately, for nongovernment projects.

It is common to discuss a nation's research and development activities in the context of defense and nondefense research and development. As demonstrated below, it is impossible to differentiate clearly between the two types of activities in the P.R.C.

The budget of the central Government of the P.R.C. is broken down into five items: (1) economic construction; (2) social, cultural, and educational activities; (3) national defense; (4) administration; and (5) other expenditures. Included in the budget for economic reconstruction is the sponsorship of the eight ministries for machine-building, whose responsibilities are:

---

[3] This discussion is based almost entirely on material presented in Yuan-li Wu, with Robert B. Sheeks, ed., *The Organization and Support of Scientific Research and Development in Mainland China* (New York: Praeger Publishers, 1970).

First: Heavy industries
Second: Nuclear Engineering
Third: Munitions
Fourth: Electronics
Fifth: Missiles
Sixth: Naval Ship Building
Seventh: Aircraft Manufacturing
Eighth: Agricultural Machinery.

As indicated by the activities associated with the above ministries, a portion of the economic construction funds support military construction and, presumably, at least a portion of the military research and development associated with those activities.

As with all nations, there is also a problem of identifying specifically what is research, development, pilot production, and full-scale production. Hence, any statements of funding of science, engineering, and so forth suffer from the same problems of semantics in China as in any other nation.

Bearing in mind that expenditure on science and technology exceeds the amount under the science budget, we may nevertheless examine the data pertaining to funds publicly budgeted for the support of scientific research by the central government for the 1950–65 period, which are given in Figure 24-2, and in Figure 24-3 as a percentage of the actual government expenditure.[4] From these and other available budget data, it may be concluded that the budget for science has been the fastest-growing item in the state budget. It has grown at an average annual rate of 116 per cent per year, whereas the corresponding average annual growth rate for the central government has been only 16 per cent per year. Thus, it must be concluded that the national government is giving high priority to research and development and sets forth a policy highly favorable for the support of science.

A portion of the state budget for science is distributed to the local governments in the provinces. The amount varies from year to year but is thought to average about 10 per cent of the amount allocated by the state for science. The local governments in turn allocate funds for local research and development. These allocations are thought to be about twice the amount provided to the local government from the national budget. Thus, on the basis of total funds of the local and central governments, about one-fourth of China's research and development work has been under the direction of the local governments, and the remaining three-fourths is directed by the agencies of the central government.

Some indication of the significance of the state budget for science, that is, for research and development activities, can be obtained by comparing the P.R.C. budget for 1960 with the corresponding expenditures by the governments of the United States and the Soviet Union. In that year the federal government of the United States spent slightly more than $12 billion for research and development. It is believed that the Soviet budget ranged between $12 billion and $14 billion. The P.R.C. budget for the same year was approximately $500 million. Thus, if we compare the U.S. *expenditure* and the Soviet and Chinese *budgets*—a rough means of comparison at best—the amount of research and development being conducted by the P.R.C. is, as expected, small compared to that under way in the United States and the Soviet Union.

---

[4] According to Orleans, the science budget is used to support research and development in the Academy of Science, in the ministries, in industry, and in educational institutions. Leo A. Orleans, 'Research and Development in Communist China: Mood, Management and Measurement,' *An Economic Profile of Communist China*, Vol. 2, *Population and Manpower Resources External Economic Relations* (Washington, D.C.: Government Printing Office, 1967), Appendix.

Figure 24-2—A Comparison of the State Budget for Science with Total
Government Expenditure, 1949-65

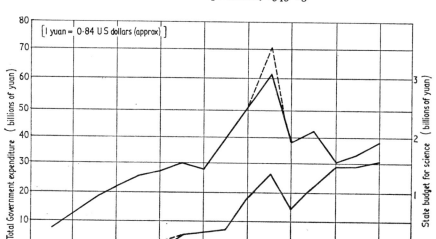

Sources: Compiled from data in Joint Economic Committee of the U.S. Congress, *An Economic Profile of Mainland China* (New York: Praeger, 1968); and Yuan-li Wu, with Robert B. Sheeks, ed., *Organization and Support of Scientific Research and Development in Mainland China*, *passim.*

As Figure 24-2 shows, the P.R.C. science budget increased each year, at least until 1965. Furthermore, analyses of total expenditures of funds for research and development have shown that, whereas total funds exceeded budget allocations by about 25 per cent in 1960, they may have exceeded the state budget by between 200 and 300 per cent in 1964. Thus, it appears that some significant changes in the funding of research and development activities took place in the post-1960 period. Further study will be necessary for an understanding of what those changes were.

Information pertaining to the expenditure of funds for science is scarce. In a broad sense, there generally has been no lack of funds for the support of scientific activities, and occasionally budgeted funds have gone unused.[5] The problem encountered most often in the P.R.C. is a shortage of professionals to conduct research and development activities.

Science funds are used to support a wide spectrum of development in China. The atomic energy and defense (including missile development) programs consume a large portion of the science funds, and agricultural and industrial development also receives heavy attention. The funding of applied research is emphasized far more than basic research.

THE BUILDING OF A SCIENTIFIC AND TECHNOLOGICAL INFORMATION BASE

An efficient information communications system is extremely important to the development and progress of almost every aspect of the P.R.C.'s activities today. The

---

[5] McGraw-Hill World News Bureau (Tokyo), 'Two Kinds of Scientists in China: Maoists Do Well,' *Scientific Research*, 2, No. 10 (October, 1967): 71.

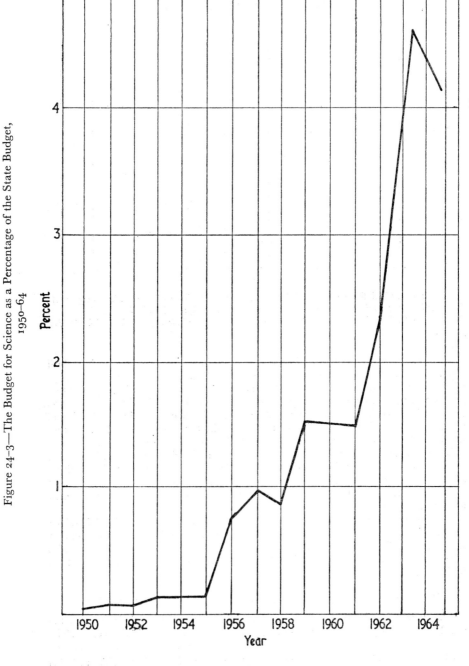

Figure 24-3—The Budget for Science as a Percentage of the State Budget, 1950-64

Sources: Compiled from data in An Economic Profile of Mainland China, op. cit.; and Wu, with Sheeks, ed., Organization and Support of Scientific Research and Development in Mainland China,

scope of the communications operation there is vast—as it would have to be for the political indoctrination alone of China's near-billion population spread over its extensive land mass. The most common means of communication are word of mouth (direct oral communication), the printed word, telephone, radio, and the telegraph.[6]

In the communication of Party propaganda, the education of the Chinese masses, and, most important of all, the development of China's scientific and technological elite, printed materials have played an extremely important role. For example, journals are the principal means whereby the Chinese learn of the latest scientific and technological developments outside of China. Because of the extreme importance of printed material, in the following discussion, attention has been given to the status of such material in China during the past decade.

In 1949, China's limited quantities of vital written material and publication capability required foreign material to support the immense information operation that had to be undertaken. Special organizations were set up to produce and distribute printed materials throughout China and continue to do so. The purchase of materials has been handled through the Chinese organization Guozi Shudian (Kuo-chi Shu-tien, or International Bookstore), where international exchanges are effected. The Institute of Scientific and Technical Information of China, an information-processing organization in the Chinese Academy of Sciences, has handled the scientific and technological exchanges; the remaining exchanges have been the responsibility of the National Library of Peking, which also has the responsibility of obtaining materials from Russia on a library loan basis.

Internal dissemination of foreign materials is a huge task and is handled by the above organizations plus another organization known as Hsin Hua Shu-tien (New China Book Company), whose primary responsibility is to assist the Guozi Shudian with the internal distribution of foreign periodicals. Thus, the Chinese Communists have set up and have in operation a highly effective system for the procurement and dissemination of foreign information within China. Reports of visitors to China concerning large amounts of foreign materials seen there indicate those organizations are doing a very effective job. Without such a system China's progress would be slow.

In 1961, China was making exchanges of printed materials with 160 countries and areas. On the exchange basis, 110,000 books and periodicals were received in China and 135,000 were exported. By far the majority of exchanges have been with Russia. In 1959 the Library of the Chinese Academy of Sciences was receiving 527 periodicals from Russia alone. (Presumably some of them were obtained on a purchase basis and others on an exchange basis.) In direct purchase, by far the greatest amount of material, amounting to many millions of volumes, has been obtained from Russia. Recent reports indicate that the Chinese are making increased use of material published in the Western nations and in Japan. The material obtained from Russia has pertained primarily to science and technology; in addition, there was also a strong interest in contemporary Russian literature.

Much of the foreign material received in China goes through a translating and abstracting process, in which primary emphasis has been placed on the translation and abstracting of materials for use by scientists and engineers. Of the material translated in 1964, 60 per cent pertained to engineering. There were three times as many Russian engineering sources as there were sources in all other languages. The materials purchased and exchanged by the Chinese include more than books and periodicals. Such items as maps, microfilms, and phonograph records are also exchanged.

China has built up a large publishing industry devoted to the publication of all its domestic propaganda materials, educational materials, and the works of its many

---

[6] Television is found in many of China's larger cities, but as yet broadcasts reach an extremely small portion of China's population and are not a major means of communication.

authors, plus all foreign materials that are translated into Chinese. Here again, the largest number of publications pertain to the fields of engineering, followed by literature, agriculture, economics, education, and the natural sciences, in that order. There is, of course, an elaborate system for publication from the national to the local level, all of which is tightly controlled by Party policies. Peking and Shanghai are the main publication centers. The widely read 'little red book,' containing excerpts from the *Selected Works of Mao Tse-tung*, was printed in millions of copies by China's publishing houses.

Through this publishing system the various scientific and engineering groups and societies were publishing 150 periodicals in 1962. Although the number may be small for more technologically advanced and research-oriented nations (Japan, China's neighbor, published 2,241 such periodicals in 1962), it is still a creditable quantity for a developing nation.[7]

Following the pattern of Chinese industry, publication activities expanded during the first ten years of the Communist regime and then began a sharp decline in 1959, which continued until 1964. The extent of the decline can be assessed when it is noted that 30,196 titles were published in 1956 and only 5,180 in 1964.[8]

The slump, caused by the failure of the Great Leap Forward, was common to all of China's industry. Most industries showed a strong recovery trend by 1962. Recovery in the publications industry appeared to have been about two years behind the rest of industry, for which there is no ready explanation.

An elaborate distribution system has been set up for distributing China's printed material. Since the most literate people are in the urban areas, it is there that most of the distribution takes place. Much of the material is distributed through the educational systems and the official Party channels. Retail distribution takes place through several thousand market-type outlets and through 20,000 rural supply outlets. Materials may also be distributed directly through the mails. According to visitors to China, there has been an active business in secondhand books in China. Considerable activity in book rentals has also been reported.

The intense interest of the Party in the intellectual training of the Chinese people can also be seen in the extensive system of libraries that have been set up in the nation. Libraries and their status in 1960 may be summarized as follows:[9]

(1) 400 public libraries with 31,000,000 volumes.

(2) 225 libraries in educational institutions with 33,400,000 volumes.

(3) 1,140 branch libraries of the Chinese Academy of Sciences with a total of 6,000,000 volumes.

(4) 182,960 rural reading rooms with 16,610,000 volumes.

(5) 35,000 trade union libraries with 34,000,000 volumes.

The main library center is the National Library of Peking, which expanded from 1,200,000 volumes in 1949 to 6,000,000 volumes in 1961, and at the beginning of the 1970's had holdings approaching 8 or 9 million volumes. By comparison, in June, 1963, the Library of Congress had 13,000,000 volumes, the New York City Public Library had 7,400,000, and the largest library of any educational institution, that at

---

[7] Following the failure of the Great Leap Forward, foreign release of all but a few of these periodicals was banned in 1959; and again in 1966 the release of essentially all periodicals was terminated as a consequence of the Great Proletarian Cultural Revolution. Presumably these actions were due to the cessation of publication of certain journals; and in other instances they were not released because of the risk of embarrassment resulting from the poor quality of the articles in the periodicals.

[8] G. Raymond Nunn, *Publishing in Mainland China*, Massachusetts Institute of Technology Report No. 4 (Cambridge, Mass: The MIT Press, 1966).

[9] *Ibid.*

Harvard University, had 7,000,000 volumes. It would be difficult to determine if all of these numbers were established on the same basis. Nevertheless, the extensive holdings of the National Library of Peking are impressive.

The system of libraries performs all the functions of a Western library, such as procurement, classification, control, and distribution of holdings. Another important activity is the preparation and publication of catalogs and indexes to aid in the use of their resources. One also frequently notes references to the use of copying facilities, presumably some type of photostating device, that are used in the libraries. Many of the holdings are in the form of such reproduced material.

CHINESE SCIENTIFIC AND TECHNOLOGICAL MANPOWER

Sources of manpower. There is no doubt that China's progress is going to depend largely upon those in China who have received an extensive amount of education. It is not a difficult task to give some good estimates of the number of people in China who have been exposed to certain types of education for certain periods of time. For instance, as of 1970, about 2 million Chinese had completed some form of college education; of those, almost one-third, or 600,000, had received some education in engineering, one-fourth in the field of education itself, and 125,000 in science. Of this last number, about 85,000 were trained in the natural sciences.[10]

These numbers may be compared with 125,000 college-trained people in China in 1949. Of this number, about 17 per cent had their education in fields of engineering, 8.5 per cent in the natural sciences, and 11.4 per cent in education. Approximately 51 per cent had received their training in finance, economics, law, social sciences, and the liberal arts in general. Only about 16 per cent of the college-trained personnel now in China have been educated in these five fields. It is interesting that in the field of agriculture, only 7 per cent of the 1949 population had received a college education, the percentage today remains virtually unchanged at 8 per cent.

Much significance can be attached to the above figures; however, they must not be viewed out of context. First of all, it must be recognized simply that the 1949 statistics are the figures for a nation that had been subjected to a century of turmoil, characterized by the colonialism of the West, armed invasions by Japan, and internal revolutions and civil wars. There was relatively little in the way of national planning for education. The disruptions also produced changes in the Chinese culture and system of values.

When considering the quality of China's intellectuals, it must be noted that many of them have been educated in nations of the West, Russia, and Japan. In the period from 1850 to 1962, about 24,300 Chinese intellectuals were trained in Western nations, such as the United States, England, Germany, and France. In the same period, 12,000 were trained in Japan. It is believed that approximately 4,500 out of both groups are still living in China today, and that 900 to 1,000 of them are holders of a doctoral degree.

According to Russian and Chinese sources, in the period from 1950 to 1960, 1,300 scientists, 1,200 instructors, 2,000 graduate students, and 5,500 undergraduate students received training of various kinds in Russia.[11] (In the same period, 8,000 technicians and 20,000 workers were also trained in Russia.) After the break-up of Sino-Soviet relations in 1960, the number of Chinese students in Russia gradually diminished until in 1966, the last 65 students were returned to China by the Soviet Government. Information as to the numbers and types of degrees granted to those

---

[10] By comparison, in 1970 the United States had approximately 300,000 natural scientists and 1,200,000 engineers with bachelor and higher degrees.

[11] John M. H. Lindbeck, 'An Isolationist Science Policy,' *Bulletin of the Atomic Scientists, 25,* No. 2 (February, 1969): 66.

educated in Russia is apparently not available. However, it is estimated that there are now in China 10,000 to 12,000 intellectuals who have received advanced degrees both in China and abroad, and that at least three-fourths of them are scientists and engineers. Thus, China has an excellent corps of highly trained intellectuals, most of whom have the scientific and technological training needed to lead China economically and intellectually.

Quality of scientific and technological manpower. Some idea of the capability of Chinese scientists and engineers can be gained from the comments of scientists and engineers of other countries who have visited China. Most frequently, visitors speak quite highly of the individuals with whom they have come in contact but reserve judgment as to whether those individuals were generally representative of those in China in their professions.

The geophysicist C. H. G. Oldham,[12] pointed out that everywhere he visited in China in 1964 there was enthusiasm for science and innovation. Although he was impressed by what had been achieved to that date, he was much more impressed by the solid educational foundation that the Chinese were laying for future development. An indication that Chinese scientists are attempting to keep abreast of the latest scientific developments was Oldham's comment to the effect that, in the laboratories he visited, 'each scientist almost always had a few of the latest English and American books pertaining to his speciality on his desk.' (In addition, almost all the scientists also had a copy of one of Mao Tse-tung's political books.) Genko Uchida, a Japanese China-watcher, expressed the opinion that China's young engineers are confident, eager, and ambitious, but their knowledge is largely theoretical and the questions they ask of foreign engineers betray their naiveté and lack of experience.[13]

Drawing upon extensive studies of Chinese professional manpower, Leo Orleans points out that many of China's engineers are overly specialized and weak in basic theory. However, he also notes that these men were intentionally trained for what China needed at that time. In short, if a reliable cost-effectiveness study of such people could be conducted, it would probably show that at that time such men better filled the national needs than men with several years more of training.

Utilization of scientists and engineers. Some estimates of the numbers of people involved in research and development work in China as of 1965 have been made. Orleans estimated that there were 450,000 engineers and 85,000 scientists in China in January, 1965, which does not include the graduating classes after 1964.[14] The employment distribution of professional manpower in engineering and the natural sciences is shown in Table 24–1.[15] Because these estimates were prepared on the basis of data from January, 1965, they should probably be increased by 15 per cent to be brought up to date. The numbers admittedly contain large uncertainties, particularly because rigorous distinctions between research and development and other activities are difficult to make. However, they do give some indication of the utilization of scientific and engineering manpower in China.

If there are significant errors in the figures in Table 24–1, I believe that those for the Academy of Sciences may be too low. Certain institutes in the academy have been called upon to support many of China's modern developments, such as those in nuclear energy and rocketry. If only the 3,500 scientists and engineers listed are doing

---

[12] C. H. G. Oldham, 'Science and Education,' *Bulletin of Atomic Scientists,* 22, No. 6 (June, 1966): 40.

[13] Genko Uchida, 'Technology in China,' *Scientific American,* Vol. 215, No. 5, November, 1966.

[14] According to present information there apparently have been no formal graduations since 1965 because of the disruption of the colleges and universities by the Cultural Revolution.

[15] See Orleans, 'Research and Development in Communist China.'

research and development work for the academy, such programs would be proceeding at a slower rate than seems likely.

The political treatment of Chinese scientists and engineers. In the literature about China, one reads about how the intellectuals are mistreated and are required to do significant amounts of manual labor. The extent to which the people in science and engineering are so treated is difficult to determine. There is little doubt that during the past two decades they have been subjected to certain types of intellectual persecution, especially in the universities, as have all of the educated in China. However, generally speaking, the interferences apparently have not resulted in gross hindrance of their activities. There is little evidence that those in the government institutes have been subjected to major political harassment. The comparatively brief period required for the Chinese to develop nuclear weapons is evidence that those who accomplished that task were not exposed to prolonged political distractions.

Table 24–1—Utilization of Scientific and Engineering Manpower in China, January, 1965

Manpower Category	Engineers	Scientists
Total	450,000	85,000
Number qualified for R & D and higher-level activities	200,000	55,000
Number involved in higher education:		
a. R & D activities	4,000	500
b. teaching and other activities	6,000	500
Number involved in Academy of Sciences		
a. R & D activities	1,500	2,000
b. other activities	—	—
Number involved in industry and miscellaneous activities		
a. R & D activities	20,000	25,000
b. other activities	168,500	27,000

Source: Orleans, 'Research and Development in Communist China.'

The compensation scientists and engineers receive for their labors allows them to live under conditions that are luxurious compared with those endured by most of China's masses. Although many of them are misplaced professionally and are not used efficiently, on the whole they are one of the few groups who get the opportunity to do work in which they are strongly interested. Very few are defecting from China. It must be concluded that their life, while far different from a scientist's life in the United States, is still comparatively good by Chinese standards.

In the planning for the Cultural Revolution there was concern that there would be gross interference with scientific and technological activities in China. To ensure that such interference would be minimal, point 12 of the sixteen-point charter for the Cultural Revolution was drafted to state:

Policy toward scientists, technical personnel and working people in general:
In the course of this movement, the policy of unity-criticism-unity should not be continued toward those scientists, technical personnel, and working people so long as they are patriotic and work actively without opposing the Party and socialism, and so long as they have no improper association with foreign countries. Those scientists and technical personnel who have made contributions

should be protected. Assistance may be rendered in the gradual transformation of their world outlook and work methods.[16]

The extent to which this policy was applied and research and development activities proceeded without interference is not known. There was some conflict in the institutes of the Academy of Sciences between the pro-Maoist revolutionaries and the pragmatist followers of Liu Shao-ch'i. The revolutionary faction, with the support of the army, is now in control of the academy, which has undergone few or no personnel changes at the highest administrative levels. Although there have been exceptions, it is believed that research and development personnel and programs were subjected to comparatively few direct abuses. However, it appears quite probable that staff personnel were disturbed emotionally by the disruptions associated with the Cultural Revolution, and the progress of their research and development programs may have suffered as a result.

The most conspicuous harm produced by the Cultural Revolution in scientific and technological sectors will be that resulting from the closing of schools in China. The extent to which schools were closed, the levels that were closed, and what schools are now back operating is not fully known. However, the general impression is that most schools were shut down for two or three years. The cessation of education will produce a gap in the manpower supply, and the gap will eventually reduce the acceleration of Chinese research, development, and production programs. If the gap is large enough, it will even cause a reduction in such activities.

It is apparent that the education of peasant youth is being stressed in the secondary schools and at the higher education level. Many of those admitted to these institutions do not have adequate preparation, and therefore the cause of education will be further retarded. Here, again, the Cultural Revolution can be detrimental to China's scientific and technological progress, at least in the immediate future.

The Progress of Science and Technology

The development of science and technology in the P.R.C. may be divided into two distinct periods, with the boundary between them in 1960. In the pre-1960 period the groundwork for the building of scientific and technological capability was laid. Priorities had to be given to planning the science and engineering programs of the future and for the education of much-needed manpower. There was a regrouping of existing engineers and scientists, who were assigned tasks involving education and reconstruction. In the latter half of the period, some new programs were started; the most significant was the atomic energy program, which eventually led to the testing of a nuclear device in October, 1964.[17]

In the latter half of the pre-1960 period, the Chinese received extended help from the Soviet Union in the form of planning assistance, equipment, and manpower training. Included in the assistance were numerous factories built and equipped by the Russians. It is estimated that between 10,000 and 20,000 Russian scientists, engineers, and technicians visited China in the 1955–60 period to participate in the aid program. Without Soviet assistance, China's level of science and technology would be far below what it is today.

The second period of Chinese scientific development began with the abrupt departure of the Soviet technical personnel from China in mid-1960. Sino-Soviet relations had become strained, and Mao decided that the P.R.C. would be the sole landlord and performer in its scientific and technological sector.

---

[16] 'Decision of the CCP Central Committee on the Great Proletarian Cultural Revolution,' adopted August 8, 1966, NCNA, August 8, 1966.

[17] See the list of Chinese nuclear tests in the Data Section of this volume.

The progress of science and technology has been more difficult to follow since that time. The cessation of Soviet assistance resulted in gross disruption of most programs. However, by 1964 it became apparent that once again progress was being made in science and engineering. China's first nuclear test in October of that year was a loud announcement to that effect. There has been continued evidence of progress since that time.

There have been numerous obstacles to progress in both periods. The Hundred Flowers Campaign and the Great Leap Forward in the first period created an environment that was not conducive to good scientific or engineering work. In the second period, the 1960–62 economic recession, the frequent harassment of intellectuals, and the Cultural Revolution had adverse effects.

The current status of science and technology in China can be judged to some extent from the activities of Chinese scientists and engineers. A review of the Chinese scientific and technological literature has shown that they are aware of and are using new approaches to the solution of problems, for example, information theory, operations research, and systems analysis. Although it is difficult to ascertain the extent of their capability in specific fields, particularly since publication of Chinese scientific journals was suspended during the Cultural Revolution, they are doing work on the frontiers of science in such fields as superconductivity, ultrahigh vacuum, lasers, electron paramagnetic resonance, nuclear magnetic resonance, semiconductors, chromatographic analysis of different types, and so forth. They are getting started in the field of microelectronics, claim to have made artificial diamonds, and have gained international recognition with their synthesis of the insulin molecule. Just as their progress in the field of nuclear weapons has been most impressive, their success in putting two satellites into orbit indicate that their accomplishments with missiles may be equally impressive.

China has held two international science meetings. The first, an international science symposium, was held in August, 1964. In August, 1966, an international physics symposium was held. These meetings, at which no Russians were present, were attended primarily by representatives from neutral and Communist nations whose stature in science was considerably less than China's.

To assist in overcoming the lack of contacts with foreign scientists and engineers, especially since their termination of scientific exchanges with the Soviet Union, the Chinese have arranged exchanges of professional personnel with France. Also, Chinese have been sent to Canada, England, France, and West Germany for study. However, many of those who were involved in such foreign study returned to China because of factors associated with the Cultural Revolution.

Not all reports concerning China's technological progress are impressive, and there are also contradictory reports of capabilities and progress. One is left with the impression from such reports that in some areas and institutes in China, the quality of work done is poor. However, when the entire scientific and technological activity is viewed collectively, the amount China has accomplished in a time span of two decades is impressive.

Within the last three or four years, numerous reports pertaining to activities in the research institutes and institutions of higher learning have been published. The reports appear to have the following features in common:

(1) Science and technology are being universally popularized in the P.R.C., and the people in China show a tremendous interest in this subject. Interest is extremely high in the educational institutions and the institutes. The Chinese are motivated to catch up with the leading nations of the world and are working hard to do just that.

(2) Research and development studies are covering a wide spectrum of activities in essentially every field of science and engineering. Applied research is being

emphasized more than basic research. Overall progress during the last four or five years has been very impressive. In some areas progress has been slow. For example, biological research lagged a few years ago but now is being emphasized.

(3) Under the totalitarian system, the Chinese can show significant progress in a limited number of specific areas by concentrating their best manpower, equipment, and material in support of those areas. It is believed that this approach has been responsible for the outstanding progress made in nuclear weapons.

(4) Most research and development work is done in the institutes of the academies and ministries. Relatively little is done at institutions of higher learning. China is obtaining many of its new technologies through the selective purchase of foreign items.

(5) Adequate funds are available for the support of most research and development activities.

(6) There is an over-all shortage of engineers and scientists. There is an acute shortage of senior scientists and engineers to plan and direct programs, accentuated by the removal of many of the Western-trained scientists and engineers from positions of responsibility because of concern over their 'redness' qualifications, that is, their political outlook.

(7) Most professional men are reasonably well informed, and keep up with the latest international events, in their own fields. Despite their familiarity with foreign technical literature, the Chinese scientists and engineers suffer from lack of contact with the leaders in their respective fields from more advanced nations.

(8) Scientists and engineers experience some political interference of fluctuating intensity. Although such interference has affected the progress of their work, it has only occasionally been a major obstacle.

(9) Laboratory equipment is good and quite adequate for the type of work being done. Most of it has been imported; some apparatus is the best that can be bought outside of the United States. The Chinese are building an increasing amount of their own equipment.

(10) There are virtually no problems with laboratory space. It is more than adequate.

(11) Libraries and sources of scientific and technical information are excellent. Soviet and U.S. sources are used most; increasing use is being made of all Western sources.

Prospects for Scientific and Technological Advancement

Before the Cultural Revolution, it appeared that the groundwork for China's technological advancement had been well laid. The prospects for progress are now clouded by the consequences of the revolution and the resulting political instability. If China's educational system continues to be disrupted, there is reason to question whether China will progress rapidly either scientifically or technologically.

Although the violence of the Cultural Revolution has passed, the emphasis on Mao's thought as the only avenue to success in any area of endeavor continues and may be an impediment to scientific and technological progress. At the very least, the time spent by scientists and engineers in ideological exercises reduces the amount of their time for professional activities. The remolding exercises to which many of them must submit can create mental tensions and diminish their productivity. The environment in which scientists must think and write is indicated by the comments of Kurt Mendelssohn, who visited China in 1967, relative to a paper presented by a

Chinese physicist at the 1966 physics symposium, when the Cultural Revolution was just beginning:

> The title of the paper is 'Research on the theory of elementary particles carried out under the brilliant illumination of Mao Tse-tung's thought.' It contains a very serious and quite impressive attempt at solving the internal structure of elementary particles in which the successive steps are copiously underlined by reference to Mao's works. The essential feature is an internal wave function describing the structure of the hadron, and the advantage of this approach is that correlation of the theory with experimental results can be made without having to make assumptions on the unknown dynamics operating inside a particle. In true Maoist language the relevant chapter is headed 'How can you catch tiger cubs without entering the tiger's lair?'[18]

The judgments of Derék Price, if applied to China's technological activities, imply that progress will be slow. Price has indicated, from his study of the relationship of nations' scientific and technological activities to their gross national product, that any nation, if it is to progress, must spend at least 0.7 per cent of its gross national product on basic research.[19] As has been pointed out, China is implementing and supporting applied research rather than basic research at this stage of its development, and it is improbable that its annual investment in basic research begins to approach 0.7 per cent of its gross national product.

In contrast to the priority given to the technologies in China, India's noted atomic scientist, H. J. Bhabha, expressed a strong belief in the support of science ahead of technology and worked for more than two decades to get extensive scientific activity under way in India.[20] Thus, the long-term progress of the two large Asian neighbors will be most interesting to watch, to gain some insight into whether a developing country should give priority to science or technology.[21]

Expressions of pessimism about China's scientific and technological progress often appear in the Western press. They may be in part an exhibition of a dangerous tendency among many Western observers to correlate all progress in China with the reported disruptions resulting from the Cultural Revolution. It must be recalled that China's scientific and technological accomplishments since 1950 have generally exceeded the estimates of Western observers, and these have been attained against a host of adversities. It would thus appear that if China remedies and expands its educational system, it may well become quite strong technologically and in time become a center of science and learning in the world. As an example of what can happen in a relatively short period, in the 1930's U.S. science was behind European science. In the 1950's it had forged ahead of European science.[22] Through the 1960's and up to the present, there has been great concern over the status of science and

---

[18] Kurt Mendelssohn, 'Science in China,' *Nature*, 215 (July 1, 1967): 10.

[19] D. J. E. deSolla Price, 'Nations can Publish or Perish,' *Science and Technology*, No. 70, October, 1967.

[20] H. J. Bhabha, 'Science and the Problems of Development,' *Science*, 151, No. 3710 (February, 1966): 541.

[21] In their approach to this problem, the Indians have been influenced by the British and presumably have given top priority to science as a consequence of that influence. It is therefore quite pertinent that the British find themselves doing very well in science, but because of shortcomings in the use of scientific information to develop new techniques, their science has been doing very little for the economy of Britain. Hence, a special Department of Technology was organized in Britain in an attempt to ensure that the sizable investment in science gives appropriate returns to the British economy. The Indians may have to resort to similar measures to reap benefits from their investment in science.

[22] J. A. Berberet, *The Measurement of the Scientific and Technological Capabilities of Nations*, 68TMP-80, General Electric, TEMPO, Santa Barbara, Calif., 1968.

technology in Europe because it is so far behind that of the United States. Thus, gross changes in scientific and technological capabilities of nations can take place in two or three decades.

Although China will progress in the sciences and technologies, it seems quite unlikely that it will have a scientific and technological capability equivalent to that of the United States or the Soviet Union in one or even two decades. On the other hand, even though it is not obvious that the Chinese will someday be successful in their efforts to achieve scientific and technological parity with leading nations of the world, it is also not obvious that they will fail.

In the last third of the nineteenth century, the West employed physical force in the treatment of China. Marshall McLuhan, a controversial figure in Western education today, has pointed out: 'Today's war is an information war.'[23] Now, in the last third of the twentieth century, it is the information from the West—especially the vast amount of scientific and technological information—that is being assimilated on the Chinese mainland. The entire scientific and technological structure in the P.R.C. has been designed not only to assimilate information from the West but also to develop and apply more information of the same type. Basic questions arise as to what will be the impact of this information on Chinese culture, what changes will result therefrom, and what implications the changes will have for the rest of the world.

SELECTED BIBLIOGRAPHY

BERBERET, J. A. *The Measurement of the Scientific and Technological Capabilities of Nations.* Santa Barbara, California: 68TMP–80, General Electric, TEMPO, 1968. It is widely accepted that a domestic S & T capability is important to the economic development of a given nation. The yardsticks for measuring such capabilities are poorly defined. This monograph is a critique of three yardsticks commonly used to measure such capabilities, namely, S & T manpower; S & T literature, including patents; and government policy toward S & T.

———. *The Prospects for Chinese Science and Technology.* Santa Barbara, Calif.: 68TMP–26, General Electric, TEMPO, 1968. Assesses the progress of Chinese S & T and points out factors both favorable and unfavorable to future development.

———. *Science and Technology in Communist China.* Santa Barbara, Calif.: RM60TMP–72, General Electric, TEMPO, 1960. Coming at the end of the first decade of Communist rule in China, this monograph was the first publication setting forth an analytical treatment of Chinese science and technology (S & T). It summarizes the main features of the Chinese educational system, particularly insofar as the latter supported the progress of S & T. It treats the status of S & T manpower and surveys the major S & T activities in China. Lastly, it demonstrates that China was capable of building an atomic bomb and presents evidence that the development of nuclear weapons was in progress.

BHABHA, H. J. 'Science and the Problems of Development,' *Science*, 151, No. 3710 (Washington, D.C.: American Association for the Advancement of Science, February, 1966): 541. Homi J. Bhabha, sometimes referred to as the father of science in India, was deeply concerned with the importance of science to underdeveloped nations. In particular, he believed that a strong basic science program was extremely important to the future of India. In this paper Bhabha discusses the science program in India, much of which he instituted directly. He also notes how this program is expected to aid India. The information presented allows some comparison of the approach to science in India with that of China.

CHENG, CHU-YUAN. *Scientific and Engineering Manpower in Communist China, 1949–1963.* Washington, D.C.: Government Printing Office, National Science Foundation, NSF 65–14,

---

[23] M. McLuhan and M. Fiore, *The Medium is the Message* (New York: Bantam Books, 1967), p. 138.

1965. By far the most comprehensive analysis of Chinese scientific and engineering manpower that has been conducted to date in the West. The education, utilization, and employment of S & T professionals are discussed at length. Government policy and planning for S & T are given a significant amount of attention. Also included are partial biographic data of 1,200 prominent scientists and engineers in China.

CHRISTIANSEN, W. N. 'Science and Scientists in China Today,' *Scientific Research* (New York: McGraw-Hill, October, 1967), p. 64. Christiansen, of Sydney University, Australia, was in Peking from May, 1966, to February, 1967, advising the Chinese Academy of Science on the construction of a radiotelescope. In this article he tells of struggles of the Chinese to develop a capability in many fields of science. He stresses that the Chinese have adopted an experimental approach to science and is optimistic about their future success.

An Economic Profile of Communist China, Vols. 1 and 2. Washington, D.C.: Government Printing Office, 1967. These two volumes, prepared for the Joint Economic Committee Congress of the United States, contain an extensive amount of information pertaining to the economy of mainland China. Included are discussions of the Chinese educational system, S & T manpower, and research and development by such students of contemporary China as Chu-yuan Cheng, Leo Orleans, and Y. L. Wu.

FUMIKO, KUSANO. *Evaluation of Comprehensive Study of Chinese Communist Science and Technology.* Tokyo: n.p., September 27, 1964; Joint Publications Research Service Translation No. 37,828. Originally written in Japanese; his book is a good description of the scientific movement in China from 1949 to 1964. Although the information it contains may be found in various journal articles about China, it serves to bring a good deal of information together in an abbreviated form. Recommended particularly for the reader who wants to obtain an overview of the development of contemporary Chinese science.

GOULD, SIDNEY H. *The Sciences in Communist China.* Washington, D.C.: American Association for the Advancement of Science, 1961. This book contains all the papers presented at a symposium on Chinese science held in December, 1960, under the sponsorship of the AAAS and the National Science Foundation. The papers cover a broad spectrum of scientific subjects in the fields of agriculture, medicine, physics, chemistry, astronomy, and others. Unfortunately, some of the source information for these papers was strongly colored by the euphoria bred by the Great Leap forward.

HARARI, ROLAND. 'The Long March of Chinese Science,' *Science Journal* (New York: Thomas Skinnul Co., April, 1968), p. 78. The comments of four French scientists who visited China are recorded by a science writer. The many facets of Chinese science and technology, ranging from significant accomplishments to ideological idiosyncrasies, are discussed.

JUNNOSUKE, KISHIDA. 'Chinese Nuclear Development,' *Japan Quarterly,* April–June, 1967, reprinted in *Survival,* 9, No. 9 (London: Institute for Strategic Studies, September, 1967): 299. A summary of China's technological advances in the nuclear field. Domestic and foreign implications stemming from the development of its nuclear technology are discussed. Special attention is given to the significance of these Chinese developments for Japan.

KLOCHKO, M. A. *Soviet Scientist in Red China.* New York: Frederick A. Praeger, 1964. Klochko spent two extended tours of duty as a scientific consultant to China for the Soviet Union in the late 1950's. His last visit was curtailed when the Soviet Union suddenly halted its scientific and technological program in China in mid-1960. Klochko writes of his many experiences with Chinese scientists and gives the reader some detailed insight into the problems the Chinese face in their scientific labors.

LINDBECK, J. M. H. 'An Isolationist Science Policy,' *Bulletin of the Atomic Scientists,* 25, No. 2 (New York: Educational Foundation for Nuclear Science, Inc., February, 1969): 66. An overview of the training, background, and activities of Chinese scientists. China's scientific exchanges with other nations and the effects of the Cultural Revolution on science are also major topics of discussion.

MARU, RUSHEKESH. *Research and Development in India and China,* Paper No. 1, The Research Policy Program, Lund, Sweden, and the Center for the Study of Developing Societies, Delhi, India (forthcoming). Maru compares many facets of research and development in

India with those in China. He shows that in the mid-1960's China was forging ahead of India in terms of S & T manpower and financial support of research and development.

MENDELSSOHN, K. 'Science and Technology,' *Discovery*, 27 (Wheaton, Ill.: Theosophical Society in America, 1966): 8. Mendelssohn went from the Physics Department of Oxford to China three times in the 1960–67 period. The quality and growth of Chinese science and technology are critically assessed on the basis of his observations. He is explicit in his view that the shortage of qualified manpower is the greatest obstacle to China's S & T progress. However, he suggests that China may someday have the largest scientific force in the world. In this article and the one listed below, he offers evidence to demonstrate that creditable scientific work is being done in China today.

———. 'Science in China,' *Nature*, 215 (London: Macmillan Ltd., July, 1967): 10.

OLDHAM, C. H. G. 'Science and Education,' *Bulletin of the Atomic Scientists*, 22, No. 6 (June, 1966): 40. A brief but excellent summary of the educational system and scientific organizations as they existed in 1966. It points out that S & T are popularized not only in the formal educational systems but in all activities throughout all of China. People are encouraged to think in terms of innovations. Oldham maintains that a solid foundation for the future of science has been laid in China; however, he notes that the progress of science will be tightly keyed to the policy of the CCP toward science.

———. 'Science for the Masses,' *Far Eastern Economic Review*, 60, No. 20 (Hong Kong, May, 1968): 353. The effects of the political struggles in China on the progress of Chinese science are discussed by the author, who argues that, if the Maoist view prevails, science in China may suffer but China's economic progress may benefit. A note of optimism for Chinese science in the twenty-first century is expressed.

———. 'Science Travels the Mao Road,' *Bulletin of the Atomic Scientist*, 25, No. 2 (February, 1969): 80. The effects of politics, particularly Maoism, on Chinese science are surveyed. Oldham points out that, despite political interference, Chinese science has been progressing. Nevertheless, his discussions demonstrate his reservations about the rate of such progress in the future.

OLIPHANT, M. 'Over Pots of Tea: Excerpts from a Diary of a Visit to China,' *Bulletin of the Atomic Scientists*, 22, No. 5 (May, 1966): 36. A professor of physics at the Australian National University, Canberra, visited China in 1964. He tells in this article about much of the S & T activity he saw. He was much impressed by portions of what he observed but does little generalizing about the current and future status of Chinese science.

———, with ROBERT B. SHEEKS, ed., *The Organization and Support of Scientific Research and Development in Mainland China*, prepared for the National Science Foundation. New York: Praeger Publishers, 1970. The title is very descriptive of the subject matter. The work is very comprehensive and detailed, treating essentially every field of science. It is well organized, and therefore highly recommended for those looking for a detailed introduction to the subject.

ORLEANS, L. A. *Professional Manpower and Education in Communist China*. Washington, D.C.: Government Printing Office, National Science Foundation, NSF 61–63, 1961. Published at the end of the first decade of Communist rule in China, this book is a comprehensive treatment of the educational system and problems of education in China during that decade. Emphasis is given to the training of scientists and engineers. A survey of China's labor force is also presented.

———. 'Research and Development in Communist China,' *Science*, 157 (Washington, D.C.: American Association for the Advancement of Science, July, 1967): 342. For the reader who desires a broad picture of the organization, goals, and support of science in China in the 1960's, it would be difficult to find better material in an abbreviated form than that provided in this article. The writer is astute in his analysis, and consequently the article may be one of the most unbiased sources of information available. Prognostications of the future of Chinese science are avoided with equal astuteness.

PRICE, D. J. DESOLLA. 'Nations can Publish or Perish,' *Science and Technology*, No. 70, New York: International Communications, Inc., October, 1967. Price has spent an extensive amount of time studying the history and character of science and its implications for the development of nations. He proposes in this study that measurements of the levels of research and development of a nation have certain implications for its future progress.

THOMPSON, H. W. 'Science in China,' *International Science and Technology,* New York: Conover-Mast Publications, June, 1963, p. 86. Thompson visited China as a member of the Royal Society of London in the early 1960's. Here he reports on many of the scientific activities he observed. He gives little support to other reports that a vigorous scientific program is under way in China. The research he saw was still at the stage of 'catching up' with Western practice and learning to use modern scientific tools. He concludes the article by observing: 'My visit was enough to show that traditions of culture and civilization may not, after all, be easy to destroy.'

UCHIDA, GENKO. 'Technology in China,' *Scientific American,* Vol. 215, No. 5, New York: Scientific American, Inc., November, 1966. This article is a survey of China's technological development, with emphasis on Chinese industry. Strengths and weaknesses in technology are pointed out. Writing just as the Cultural Revolution was beginning, the author was optimistic concerning China's future industrial progress.

WILSON, J. T. *One Chinese Moon.* New York: Hill and Wang, 1959. Tuzo Wilson, a Canadian geophysicist from the University of Toronto, was one of the first Western scientists to travel extensively through China and to visit Chinese scientific establishments. While acknowledging that much of what he saw indicated that the Chinese were just getting started in science, he was much impressed by the scientific progress already made, as well as the effort and enthusiasm exhibited for science. Many facets of Chinese scientific work are discussed in detail.

WU, Y. L. 'Expansion of the Chinese Research and Development Industry,' *The China Mainland Review,* 1, No. 2 (Hong Kong: University of Hong Kong, September, 1965): 1. Wu gives a broad review of the character and growth of research and development activities in China from 1949 to 1965. He notes that one of the main intents of Chinese research and development is the support of China's economic policies. Despite this intent, China's economy has received only modest support from such activities. This is due to the structure and performance of the research and development programs. The lack of qualified manpower is given as one of the major constraints to both the quantity and the quality of research and development performance.

25

HEALTH AND MEDICINE

ROBERT M. WORTH

ROBERT M. WORTH

HEALTH PROBLEMS INHERITED BY THE NEW GOVERNMENT IN 1949

IT is common knowledge that in 1949, when the Communists came to power in mainland China, they took over a country with crushing health problems and very limited resources to apply toward solving them. The purpose of this chapter is to outline the current medical and health situation in China against a background of the health problems inherited by the Communist government in 1949, the resources available to solve them, and significant public health events that have taken place since then.

Common diseases. Diseases transmitted by the fecal-oral route were highly prevalent throughout China, in both rural and urban populations, because of underlying population pressures that had led to deforestation, shortage of fuel for adequate cooking, the use of human feces for fertilizer, and almost universal pollution of water supplies. Enteric infections, such as typhoid fever, bacillary dysentery, and summertime cholera epidemics were among the major causes of illness and death. Stool surveys from widely scattered areas showed a tremendous variety and prevalence of intestinal parasites.

Hookworm disease was widely prevalent in areas south of the Yangtze, particularly among nightsoil-using vegetable farmers and mulberry (silkworm) workers, where 65 to 70 per cent of those surveyed in the 1930's were found to be excreting the ova in their feces.[1]

Diseases transmitted by the respiratory route were also very highly prevalent, particularly in the cities, because of severe indoor crowding. The marginal state of protein nutrition transformed normally mild diseases, such as childhood measles, into sometimes fatal epidemics. Smallpox epidemics swept across the country regularly. Diphtheria was highly prevalent, and tuberculosis was probably the greatest single cause of mortality in adults, being responsible for an estimated 10 to 15 per cent of all deaths and causing an annual death rate during the 1930's of from 208 per 100,000 in a rural, northern setting[2] to about 500 per 100,000 in an urban, southern setting.[3] Some idea of the extent of the tuberculosis problem in crowded postwar groups can be

---

[1] T. C. Chu, B. C. Liu, C. Y. Ling, and G. F. Zee, 'A Survey of Intestinal Parasites of Man in the Rural Experimental Health Area at Kao-Chiao, Shanghai,' *Chinese Medical Journal*, 50 (Shanghai: Chinese Medical Association, 1936): 1243–54. T. H. Williams, 'A Survey of Intestinal Parasites in Rural Szechwan,' *Chinese Medical Journal*, 57 (1940): 464–72.

[2] C. C. Chen, 'The Rural Public Health Experiment in Tinghsien, China,' *Chinese Medical Journal* 50 (1936): 1125–27.

[3] F. Oldt, 'Tuberculosis in Kwangtung,' *Chinese Medical Journal*, 47 (1933): 110–27.

surmised from the fact that, in 1948, 18.2 per cent of students at one Peking university were found to have active tuberculosis.[4]

Malaria was undoubtedly one of the most important of the arthropod-borne diseases, being present as far north as Manchuria, endemic south of the Yangtze River, and hyperendemic in the southeastern coastal and southwestern mountainous provinces. Another arthropod-borne disease of great importance was the parasitic disease kala-azar, which had a wide range in northern and central China, with a severely endemic zone in the plains between the Yellow and Yangtze rivers, where 4 to 5 per cent of the villagers died of Kala-azar annually, usually older children or young adults.[5] Among the parasitic diseases with an extrahuman cycle, *Schistosoma japonicum* was a major problem related to the fecal contamination of rivers and lakes from human and animal sources. The range of that parasite coincided roughly with that of its *Oncomelania* snail host, from the Yangtze delta upriver to Yünnan Province, southward along the coast and rivers to Kwangtung Province, from sea level up to as high as 6,900 feet in altitude. In heavily affected areas of Chekiang Province, 55 per cent of the men (rice farmers occupationally exposed to cercaria-infested water) and 12 per cent of the women (exposed to domestic water supplies) were found excreting *S. japonicum* ova in their feces, with about one-half of all deaths in some areas attributed to schistosomiasis or its complications.[6]

Tetanus of the umbilical cord (due to contamination of the stump) was a major cause of infant mortality.[7] Venereal diseases were quite common in cities, where there were sometimes as many prostitutes as one per 100 population, and where venereal disease was the fourth most common major diagnosis in new patients visiting hospitals.[8]

One could go on almost indefinitely with anecdotal and descriptive accounts to document the plight of the hard-pressed but amazingly resilient people of China, who had through their agricultural innovations (emphasizing grains and vegetables intensively cultivated with human feces as fertilizer) and hard work had struck a positive demographic balance that had gradually led to an enormous aggregate population. In about 1930 the crude birth rate was estimated in the neighborhood of 40 per 1,000 people per year, with a crude death rate of about 28 per 1,000 in a 'normal' year, subject to frequent increasing mortality with flood, drought, war, or epidemic.[9] Each mother averaged about 5.8 live births during her lifetime. There is no reliable estimate of maternal mortality, but the infant mortality ratio was in the neighborhood of 160 per 1,000 live births. About 30 per cent of the children died before the age of 5 years.[10]

Limited medical facilities. The forces available to fight against these manifold health problems at the time of the Communist takeover in 1949 comprised only about

[4] S. S. Fang, 'Effects of War on the Health of the People,' *Chinese Medical Journal*, 71 (Peking: People's Medical Publishers, 1953): 321–27.

[5] R. Hoeppli, 'Epidemiology of Kala-azar in China,' *Chinese Medical Journal*, 57 (1940): 364–72.

[6] H. C. Kan and J. C. King, 'Incidence of Schistosomiasis Japonica in an Endemic Area in Chekiang,' *Chinese Medical Journal*, 50, Supplement I (1936): 449–56.

[7] C. C. Chen, 'Medicine as Applied in Tinghsien,' *Chinese Medical Journal*, 47 (1933): 611–13.

[8] H. S. Gear, 'Disease Incidence in China: Analysis of Hospital Records for 1934,' *Chinese Medical Journal*, 50 (1936): 949–72.

[9] C. C. Chen, 'Medicine as Applied in Tinghsien,' pp. 611–13. C. H. Chiao and J. L. Buck, 'The Composition and Growth of Rural Population Groups in China,' *Chinese Economic Journal*, 2 (Shanghai: Bureau of Foreign Trade, 1928): 219–35.

[10] J. P. Maxwell, 'The Modern Conception of Osteomalacia and its Importance in China,' *Chinese Medical Journal*, 49, Chinese Medical Association (1935): 47–52. C. C. Chen, 'Practical Survey of Rural Health,' *Chinese Medical Journal*, 47 (1933): 680–88.

12,000 modern-trained physicians (plus a small number of nurses and auxiliary health workers) and something like 500,000 unlicensed, unsupervised, and unorganized traditional Chinese herbalist-physicians.[11] There was no communication between the two groups. In fact, throughout the Kuomintang period there had been a government policy of official neglect and nonencouragement of traditional Chinese medicine, stemming in part from the fact that Dr. Sun Yat-sen himself was one of the two men in the first graduating class in the first missionary medical college in China (Hong Kong), and in part from the 'May 4 Movement,' when young intellectuals attacked almost everything that was traditionally Chinese as being 'unscientific.' In 1949, the 12,000 modern-trained physicians were scattered in the following activities:

(1) Providing the superstructure of a modern Ministry of Public Health in Nanking that almost completely lacked the infrastructure to make it effective (except for a good foreign quarantine section at the major seaports).

(2) In private practice, caring for well-to-do people in major urban centers (accounting for the largest number).

(3) In very small numbers in missionary hospitals caring for the urban poor or in semirural hospitals at the county seat level.

The embittered traditional Chinese practitioners had thus been cut off from a majority of their well-to-do patients.

Chinese medical tradition can be traced to the classics. While the practitioner was considerably lower in status than the true Confucian scholar-official, enough of a classical aura was attributed to him for him to be regarded with due respect by the illiterate masses. Chinese medicine has ancient and honored traditions, with an elaborate system of anatomy (based, like that of Europe before Vesalius, more on theory than on dissection); rational theories of disease causation somewhat analogous to the humoral theories of medieval Europe; and a system of diagnosis based on a combination of careful palpation of the pulse, a detailed inspection of the eye, and a complicated system of numerology. Concepts of magic or evil spirits played only minor roles. Therapy was based on diet, acupuncture (the piercing with long needles of certain presumed channels of humoral flow), moxibustion (a skin counterirritant by heat), and elaborate herbal concoctions whose secret formulae were usually passed from father to son in this highly respected profession. The traditional medical practitioners were usually to be found in towns and cities, seldom out in the villages, where people were too few and too poor to support a resident practitioner, and where transportation was usually too difficult to encourage an itinerant one.

HEALTH POLICIES AND THEIR EFFECTS

Early implementation, 1949–57. As far back as October, 1944, Mao Tse-tung had said in Yenan:

Modern medicine is of course better than old medicine, but if Western-trained doctors pay no attention to the sufferings of the people, train no doctors to serve the people, and do not unite and work with the one-thousand and more old-style doctors and veterinarians in the border regions, then, in fact, they are encouraging superstition and witchcraft among the people and are indifferent to the loss of large numbers of lives, both human and animal.[12]

When the new regime set up its national headquarters in Peking, it moved the headquarters of the Chinese Medical Association from Shanghai to Peking and called

---

[11] T. C. Li, 'Every County Has Its Hospital,' *China Reconstructs*, 12 (Peking: China Welfare Institute, 1964): 6–8.

[12] Quoted by L. C. Fu, 'Why Our Western-trained Doctors Should Learn Traditional Medicine,' *Chinese Medical Journal*, 73 (1955): 363–67.

the First National Health Conference in Peking in August, 1950. The conference received the following directive from Mao: 'Unite all medical workers, young and old, of the traditional school and the Western school, and organize a solid united front to strive for the people's health work.'[13] The conference formulated the following four specific policies as a guide to all health work:

(1) Work for the improvement of the health of peasants, workers, and soldiers.
(2) Emphasize preventive medicine.
(3) Work through and participate in mass health campaigns.
(4) Join forces with traditional medical practitioners.

Except for the occasional appearance in the *Chinese Medical Journal* (the official organ of the Chinese Medical Association) of articles reviewing Chinese medical history, the last of the above four policies was largely ignored for the time being. Instead, the remnants of the former Health Ministry and Chinese Medical Association (CMA) leadership, following the first three of the above policies, designed some clear-cut programs based on modern public health practice—do first those things that can bring quick, obvious results and will gain political support from the public and from legislative bodies.

The Party apparently agreed to those initial programs, because the following things happened quickly thereafter with great pressure for popular support:

(1) By the end of 1950, all brothels had been closed, and the prostitutes had been treated for venereal diseases and were being given vocational training, thus bringing venereal diseases under control except in some aboriginal tribes, where sexual patterns militated against rapid control, but even there steady progress was being made.[14]

(2) By 1953, about 307 million people had been vaccinated, thus virtually eliminating smallpox.

(3) During 1952, charges of American bacteriological warfare in Korea and Northeast China were widely circulated through every possible medium of communication to 'arouse deep indignation in the Chinese people everywhere' and resulted in 'aid to the government antiepidemic and health work with unconditional support of all classes of the population.' This 'patriotic health movement'[15] was focused on specific tasks in each town and village to effect an improvement in environmental sanitation, and it must also have been a powerful vehicle to introduce and reinforce the concept of germ-caused disease.

(4) By 1953, more than 242,000 old-style midwives had been retrained and about 10,000 new maternity and child-health workers had been trained, cutting maternal and infant mortality rates by more than one-half.[16]

(5) Major campaigns were then launched to control the five major parasitic diseases—malaria, filariasis, hookworm, kala-azar, and schistosomiasis. In each case, there was great emphasis on 'mobilizing the masses' to do specific things about their environment, rather than having everything done for them by outside 'experts.'

In summary, during the early 1950's great emphasis was placed on public health

---

[13] Mao Tse-tung, quotation on cover of *Chinese Medical Journal*, Vol. 82, April, 1963.
[14] C. K. Hu, C. C. Chen, K. K. Yeh, K. C. Wang, H. T. Chen, and H. L. Sun, 'The Control of Venereal Diseases in New China,' *Chinese Medical Journal*, 71 (1953): 248–58.
[15] L. C. Fu, 'Achievements of the Association in the Past Ten Years,' *Chinese Medical Journal*, 78 (1959): 208–18.
[16] N. C. Kung, 'New China's Achievements in Health Work,' *Chinese Medical Journal*, 71 (1953): 87–92.

disease prevention and mass health education, with emphasis on learning by doing as well as learning by seeing and hearing.

Meanwhile, the clinical care of sick people was still largely confined to existing institutions in the cities, but these were being multiplied at a rapid rate. By 1959, there was at least one medical college in each province, which had turned out in the prior ten years about 40,000 Western-style doctors, plus auxiliary personnel. The medical curriculum for higher-level physicians consisted of graduation from senior high school, followed by four years in a curriculum similar to the American medical school sequence of courses and one year of required internship.

By about 1954 or 1955, this rational sequence of events was apparently well on the way toward alleviating many of the most serious health problems that had been present in 1949. The next logical step forward was to develop local health centers to offer for the first time routine curative and preventive services to the 85 per cent or so of the people who lived in rural districts. But how, and with whom? Five years of communication about health had undoubtedly raised great expectations, but the fact remained that there were still more than 15,000 people per Western-style doctor,[17] and to the overwhelming majority of these people, the traditional practitioner still represented curative medicine. The belief in, as well as respect for, traditional medicine was very great and could not be safely ignored. Evidently, the Communist 'mass line' policy perceived this deep faith, and the Party decided to put it to practical use. In an effort to repair the Chinese self-image, severely damaged by often highly traumatic contacts with foreigners during the previous hundred years, the government was busily building museums and reviving through theater, storytellers, and the printed word the acclaim of certain carefully selected folk heroes of the ancient past as an effort to heal the wounds and bridge the gap in identity between the 'new China' and the politically acceptable aspects of 'old China.' If traditional Chinese medicine were to be prominently held up by the Party as the equal of Western medicine—and used as part of the governmental medical services—the already existing faith in it should serve as a powerful force to the political advantage of the Party and as a step forward in healing the cultural wounds of the Chinese people. Also, a very large source of medical manpower could rapidly be brought into full partnership to fill the manpower gap, under government control and supervision.

In 1956 Fu Lien-chang, president of the Chinese Medical Association, stated that a 'tendency to disparage our medical heritage has been severely criticized,' and a 'change has finally come about after repeated instructions from the Central Committee of the Party.'[18] In other words, policy number four of the 1950 National Health Conference was now, at last, to be obeyed. He also disclosed that, while the membership of the CMA in 1952 had been 6,819, by 1956 it had risen to 15,059, including 1,037 traditional practitioners who had recently been admitted to membership.[19] Furthermore, research institutes and schools of Chinese medicine were being established, and some Peking hospitals already had traditional practitioners working in their clinics and giving lectures to their staff and students. About 5,000 Western-style doctors were studying traditional medicine part time, and 300 of them were doing so full time. It is interesting to note the appearance at the same time of a new feature in the *Chinese Medical Journal*—occasional articles describing the pharmacological analyses of traditional Chinese herbs and controlled trials of acupuncture and certain traditional treatments for fractures and burns. On the other hand, progress in modern medicine was not neglected. The development of medical specialization was encouraged, and the CMA was publishing sixteen different medical specialty journals.

---

[17] Based on the report of 40,000 Western-style doctors in 1959 (Fu, 'Achievements of the Association') and *roughly* 600,000,000 population at that time.

[18] Fu, 'Achievements of the Association,' pp. 208–18.

[19] *Ibid.*

In 1947 there had been only 66,000 hospital beds in the whole country, but by 1956 there were reported to be 262,000.

In 1957 Ho Piao, a Deputy Minister of Health, announced that there were ten schools of Chinese medicine and twenty-three refresher-training centers, with at least one hospital (all of them 'integrated' with both Western-style and traditional practitioners on the staff) in every county.

Events since the Great Leap Forward. In 1958 came the communes and the Great Leap Forward. In terms of health programs, this convulsive upheaval in the countryside meant the following:

(1) a great 'popular' intensification of the existing campaigns against the five major parasitic diseases listed earlier;

(2) the building of health centers in every commune, with smaller 'health stations' (including maternity beds) in many of the 'production brigades' (villages);

(3) an outpouring of medical workers of all kinds from towns and cities to staff the new rural health centers;

(4) a drive to induce people to divulge their home remedies and persuade traditional practitioners to disclose their secret prescriptions—an effort that reportedly produced about 1.3 million recipes to be turned over to research institutes for evaluation.

Findings from personal interviews. To get at the details of what actually went on at the time, let us depart at this point from the sequential scanning of the *Chinese Medical Journal*, which, as a semiofficial source, might be suspected of bias. During 1962, I had the privilege of meeting socially in Hong Kong nine Western-style doctors from China, all but two of whom had come out of China that same year, and was able to interview each of them individually. They were all city-dwellers but were widely scattered as to age, experience, specialty, and place of work. They had such fascinating stories to tell that it is hard to stick to the central theme here, but suffice it to say that they were firmly in agreement as to the following points:

(1) The health programs had been *genuinely* supported by the people, and had been *genuinely* effective in sharply reducing the incidence of many infectious diseases.

(2) The Great Leap Forward had left the people utterly exhausted and apathetic.

(3) There was a severe shortage of food from the fall of 1959 to the spring of 1962, but rigid nationwide rationing (to about 1,800 calories per day per adult) had limited famine deaths to a low number. Almost universal malnutrition, with widespread evidence of severe protein deprivation, had led to a lowered resistance to, and increase in the incidence of, infectious diseases.

(4) The food situation, and with it the health situation, began to improve gradually again after the spring of 1962.

The nine doctors had all gone through the 'enforced amalgamation' with traditional Chinese medicine. The six older ones, who had graduated from medical school prior to 1956, all seemed a bit apologetic about it, compared to the three younger ones, who had been given instruction in traditional medicine along with their regular Western curriculum in medical school. The younger doctors did not seem to feel the necessity of making jokes while talking about it.

When asked about the details of the amalgamation, the nine were in agreement on the following points regarding city hospitals:

(1) About 1956, certain clinics and wards had been turned over to traditional practitioners, and it was *entirely* up to each patient to choose which medical system he wanted for himself.

(2) A patient critically ill on a 'Western' ward had to have a consultation from

a traditional doctor, and the Western doctor in charge of the case felt that this advice had to be followed in order to avoid criticism from the Party secretary in the hospital. Western consultation was also mandatory for critically ill patients on a traditional ward, but the traditional practitioner felt politically secure enough to reject the advice if both he and the patient chose to do so.

(3) In the spring of 1962, at a regular staff meeting in the hospital, the Party secretary read Chou En-lai's famous 'it is as important to be expert as to be Red' speech, and instantly every Western-style doctor knew that from that day on he was free to reject the advice of the traditional practitioner if he wished to do so.

Amalgamation of traditional and Western medicine. Occasional rural clinic visits were part of every medical student's training after 1958, and two of the nine doctors interviewed had spent a year or more assigned to such centers. Every newly graduated doctor could be assigned by the authorities to such a center for up to five years (one year for each year of medical training provided by the government), but such an assignment was regarded with distaste by most, because virtually all medical students were urban people. In fact, the distaste was so great that a new graduate was not given his graduation certificate until *after* he reported for work at his assigned place. Once he arrived at his rural health center, the new graduate was likely to find that he was the only Western-style doctor there, but he would have with him a few 'modern' or retrained midwives, nurses, and other auxiliary workers, plus a young traditional practitioner as a full partner. The traditional practitioner would typically be a village boy who had become a medical corpsman in the army and upon discharge did not have the educational background to go to medical school, so had apprenticed himself to some older traditional practitioner. After two or three years he had passed an examination and had been assigned to the rural health center.

There were two doors to the health center building. Over one door was written the character *chung* (Chinese), and over the other was the character *hsi* (Western). Here, too, as in the city hospital, the patient had a free choice as to which door to enter. Consultations for serious cases were mandatory in both directions, but at no time did the poorly trained young traditional practitioner feel secure enough to disregard 'scientific' advice, as had his big-city counterpart. Whether in the city hospital or in a rural clinic, a dissatisfied patient was free at any time to file a complaint with the local Party secretary, who would conduct a hearing and then either explain things to the patient or deliver a public reprimand to the doctor, whichever seemed appropriate. This situation naturally created a considerable sense of insecurity for an inexperienced young doctor, regardless of school, so there was a lot of consultation going on. My informants also told me that the young traditional practitioners were acutely aware that their training in traditional medicine had been meager, so a large proportion of the consultation consisted of their asking the Western-style doctor to take over the case, and then sticking around to observe and ask questions. As a result, the traditional practitioner rapidly assimilated modern concepts of anatomy, physiology, disease theory, diagnostic techniques, and therapeutic practices. At the same time, because of a shortage of Western-style drugs, the Western-style doctor often found himself substituting traditional treatments in certain types of cases. Therefore, in the new institution there is rapidly developing a new pragmatic fusion of the systems of medicine into a unique modern Chinese medicine. The practical result is that the patient, whether he, being old-fashioned or more at ease with a villager, chooses to walk into the door marked *chung* or chooses to walk through the door marked *hsi*, gets about the same sort of treatment in either case, and he is also bound to perceive sooner or later that the two practitioners consult with each other and treat each other as equals.

While there appears to be real communication between, and a pragmatic amalgamation of, the two medical systems at the local level, there remain serious incompatibilities on the theoretical level, which would tend to slow down any true amalgamation between those who are very well trained in either system. But even at this high level, some progress has begun, as illustrated by the fact that acupuncture is now termed as a 'needling of the autonomic nervous system,' which is a modern equivalent of the 'humoral channels' of the classics. Over the next few decades, as the older men in both systems die and are replaced by those who have had training in both, and as careful research work continues, those aspects of traditional Chinese medical theory and practice that are incompatible with experimental evidence will undoubtedly be gradually abandoned. Those aspects that have stood up to thorough experimental testing will undoubtedly be accepted. Only then will there be unity at all levels.

It would seem from the above that the formation of the amalgamated hospital or health center has accomplished several things at once:

(1) It has become a viable channel for providing a needed and wanted technical service to rural people.

(2) It is putting traditional practitioners to constructive use in alleviating a severe shortage of medical manpower, and at the same time is providing them with valuable on-the-job training in modern techniques.

(3) Another facet of traditional China has been rescued from ignominy, thus serving to heal some of the cultural wounds of a China in rapid transition.

(4) A situation has been created in which the scientifically valuable aspects of Chinese medical tradition can gradually be identified and adopted.[20]

Through a combination of appropriate public-preventive measures and selected mass-treatment campaigns, utilizing partially trained local health center personnel it was clear from all sources of information that by the early 1960's the major parasitic diseases (kala-azar, schistosomiasis, hookworm, malaria, and filariasis) were under control. One of the emphases of the new Cultural Revolution since 1965 has been an accelerated exodus of medical personnel from the cities to rural areas and a great emphasis on training part-time peasant health workers to man health facilities all the way down to the production brigade (village) and production team, integrated with commune health centers now staffed with increasing numbers of fully-trained physicians.[21] There is evidence that smallpox vaccination and BCG immunization (indicators of a widespread local health service) are almost universal, but that the village environment was still fairly heavily polluted in 1962, as measured by the prevalence of intestinal parasitism in children.[22] By 1965, there were more than 100,000 modern-trained doctors (higher-level graduates of five-year programs and middle-level graduates of three-year programs), in addition to 450,000 qualified nurses, midwives, pharmacists, and technicians.[23] A large number of the students in the shorter medical college courses or agricultural middle school courses for part-time health workers are themselves village people.[24]

Dr. Joshua Horn has given us the best account in English of the practical aspects of

[20] The development and popularization of acupuncture anesthesia during the past few years is a spectacular example of this process.

[21] 'Medical and Health Work of Kwangtung Province Is Resolutely Directed Toward the Countryside,' (unsigned), *Yang-ch'eng Wan-pao*, Canton, September 15, 1965.

[22] R. M. Worth, 'Health Trends in China Since the "Great Leap Forward," ' *American Journal of Hygiene*, 78 (Baltimore: Williams & Wilkins, November, 1963): 349–57.

[23] W. Penfield, 'Oriental Renaissance in Education and Medicine,' *Science*, 141 (Washington D.C.: American Association for Advancement of Science, September 1963): 1153–61.

[24] 'China Directs Its Medical Service to the 500 million Peasants,' NCNA (English), September 28, 1965.

extending modern medical services into rural areas.[25] Rural medical facilities have been urged and experimented with in various ways since 1948, with added emphasis since 1958, but have been pushed in great seriousness since 1965. The usual pattern is to recruit 'volunteers' from urban hospital staffs for one-year tours in mobile medical teams. According to Horn, the goal is to organize urban hospital staffs in such a way that at any one point in time two-thirds are in the home hospital and one-third are in a mobile team, serving on an annual rotational cycle. Members of the mobile team are given a short period of preliminary training while still at their home hospital, and while in the field are given an eight-day home leave every two months and paid their normal Peking hospital salaries.

Horn describes his team of '107 nurses, laboratory workers, administrators, and doctors of all specialties and levels of seniority' as being broken down into 'medical brigades' of thirty to forty members, each based in a central clinic serving neighboring communes (about 15,000 population in his own illustrative case in northern Hopei Province). Some of the medical workers remain based at the central clinic, and the remainder are dispersed in small teams to small clinics in the villages of the region, which are all linked together by telephone. Each village is visited periodically by a doctor, who is also on call for emergencies in his area. Dr. Horn also describes specialized teams that spend a few weeks in each commune—such as EENT and dental teams, or birth control teams. He also states that an increasing proportion of the mobile teams are volunteering to settle down as permanent staff for rural clinics.

The general mobile medical teams have been given the following six tasks:

(1) to provide preventive and therapeutic services in the area, with priority given to the preventive work (including immunizations, safeguarding village water supplies, improving latrines);

(2) to train auxiliary medical personnel from among the local people (with a goal of one peasant doctor[26] for each production brigade, one voluntary sanitation worker[27] for each production team, and sufficient midwives[28] to meet local needs);

(3) to promote planned parenthood through education and the provision of free contraceptive services;

---

[25] J. S. Horn, '*Away with All Pests . . .*' *An English Surgeon in People's China* (London: Hamly Publishing Group Limited, 1969), pp. 129–46.

[26] Dr. Horn was involved in training peasant doctors and emphasizes that patterns are not yet standardized, but in his district the candidates (thirty young men and two young women with three years of secondary school) were selected by each of thirty-two production brigades. They were trained from November to April (slack farming season) at the central clinic by members of the mobile team in introductory anatomy, physiology, bacteriology, pathology, clinical medicine, and public health, focusing on the most common diseases. Each student had a specially written manual for peasant doctors, and learned to use forty drugs and fifty acupuncture points. During the next summer, these young people resumed their farm work in their own villages but also had a box of medical supplies and worked in cooperation with members of the mobile medical teams. In the following winter full-time teaching was resumed, focusing on diseases of specific organ systems and reviewing the basic science material introduced the winter before. The plan is for three successive winters of full-time study, continued stimulus from the mobile teams, and occasional refresher courses in the city hospitals.

[27] Sanitary workers have a two-week training period in water supply and latrine maintenance, and they are also taught elementary first aid and are issued a few drugs for minor ailments.

[28] They are young women who are given a few weeks' practical and theoretical instruction, who assist the doctors in prenatal and post-partum care, and who manage the uncomplicated deliveries of women who have already had normal deliveries. In case of difficulty, they call on the mobile team for help.

(4) to join with whatever traditional or modern-trained health personnel already exist in the district in a cooperative, combined effort to raise the level of medical services (meaning integration of traditional practitioners);

(5) to join with pre-existing Patriotic Health Campaign activists (circa 1954— see above) in the mass movements to eliminate pests and improve village sanitation;

(6) to utilize the one-year rural assignment to deepen their own understanding of the laboring people (through living with and periodically laboring in the fields with the farmers).[29]

Medical supplies. Judging from the accounts of foreign medical delegations that have visited China in the past few years, virtually all of the diagnostic, therapeutic, and research instrumentation they observed in clinics, hospitals, and laboratories was of Chinese manufacture. This includes even the heart-lung machines required for open heart surgery, which is performed regularly at the major university medical centers.

The Chinese have made some notable achievements in medical research in recent years, being the first to culture the trachoma virus in tissue culture, a breakthrough that has allowed experiments by many other workers in the problem of producing an effective trachoma vaccine. Likewise, the Chinese have recently been able to synthesize insulin, an objective scientists from many nations have sought for many years.

China produces its own antibiotics and other modern drugs, while traditional Chinese medicines are a major export item to supply the market in overseas Chinese communities, largely in Southeast Asia. The fact that modern drugs produced in China are not significant export items would lead one to believe that internal supply has not as yet caught up with internal demand.

THE DEMOGRAPHIC IMPLICATIONS

The doctors from China whom I have interviewed are all in agreement that the police registration of persons serves primarily political and security purposes, rather than producing vital statistical data for public health or economic planners. Such data would be available through special studies based on the local registries, but they are sure that such data are not routinely derived by anyone or reported to the central government. The entire statistical system of China was demonstrated to be very weak and politically rather than accuracy motivated at the time of the Great Leap Forward. No vital statistics have been published since then, but the account of public health services given above must inevitably have led to a rapidly increasing survival rate of infants and young children and a moderate increase in survival of adults (not to mention a general improvement of health and productivity of the adult population rid of chronic debilitating parasitic diseases). The net effect must certainly be a rapid growth of population, particularly of children who are consumers of food, housing, clothing, and education, but not yet producers.

There was a brief propaganda campaign for birth control in 1956–57, which emphasized use of mechanical contraceptives and was not well received by the country

---

[29] Dr. Horn gives a touching illustration of this process: 'Another doctor told me of a bitter lesson he had learned when he had treated a little boy suffering from meningitis. "When I arrived at the cottage, the parents were overjoyed," he said. "They looked on me as a savior and I felt like one. I assured them that I would have their son out of danger but, in spite of working all night, he died very early the next morning. . . . I wanted to shield myself. After a mental struggle I decided to tell them they had called me too late. Just then they came in and saw that their child was dead. They were terribly distressed but without hesitation they took me by the arm and started consoling me, telling me that I had worked very hard and had done my best. . . . I felt so ashamed that tears ran down my cheeks. . . . Here in the countryside we treat their physical ailments and they, without knowing it, treat our ideological ailments." ' *Away with All Pests*, p. 146.

people (who had very limited access to the devices and who did not at that time have access to local health services to care for their children). This campaign was abruptly halted in mid-1958 at the time of the Great Leap Forward, but was cautiously re-instituted in the spring of 1962, this time focused sharply on the appropriate target groups, employing face-to-face communication rather than general propaganda, and stressing postponement of marriage, the use of the intrauterine contraceptive device, and liberal availability of abortions. According to Han Suyin,[30] the commune welfare officer (usually a woman) plays a key role in the process by referring to the family-planning clinic those couples who apply for material help on the basis of too few 'work points' earned to support a large family. Evidently a visit to the clinic for advice is a prerequisite for assistance in many such cases. According to the same source, 'the two-child family is now the accepted standard in cities.' The crucial question is the reaction of the 500 million peasants. Has the official verbal activity about family planning been translated into private activity between husband and wife?

It is possible to calculate a 1961 birth rate from Jan Myrdal's account of Liu Ling commune near Yenan. It comes out very high—49 per 1,000—with a very respectably low infant mortality ratio of 28 per 1,000 (close to the U.S. figure of around 22 per 1,000). Unfortunately, he does not also give general mortality figures from the commune.[31]

From the summer of 1965 to the summer of 1966, I gathered data from 456 women arriving in Macao from southern Kwangtung Province villages in interviews standardized on 287 Hong Kong New Territories village women.[32] From these data (comparing twenty-two Kwangtung villages with twenty-four New Territories villages), I have made for these southern Kwangtung Province villages the following estimates (which should be regarded as suggestive, rather than in any way reliable, because of poorly controlled self-selective sampling biases):

Infant mortality ratio: 70–97/1,000 live births
Crude birth rate: 46/1,000 population/year
General fertility rate: 220/1,000 women age 15–49/year
Crude mortality rate: 11/1,000 population/year.

Although a very high proportion of the Kwangtung women voiced an unequivocal approval of the idea of family planning and an eager desire to learn more about it, very few of them volunteered the information that they used contraceptives themselves, and only 23 per cent of them said that family-planning services were available in the nearby health center, although 40 per cent said that abortions were available somewhere in their home districts, and 60 per cent had heard of the IUCD (intra-uterine contraceptive device) and were aware that the government was interested in people's having smaller families. Most of the women still felt that four children would be the ideal number, though a significant minority of the younger women said they thought two or three children would be ideal. There is therefore some evidence that the official message has penetrated to the village women, particularly the younger ones, but that, as of 1965–66, this message had not been translated into action. It would appear that in these few small southern Kwangtung villages the rate of re-production is still very high, and that the general medical-social conditions in these villages have improved to the point that the crude death rate and infant mortality ratio have fallen to respectably low levels. These villages, therefore, represent the most extreme form of the 'demographic gap,' with very rapid population growth. The crucial question is whether the actual reproductive behavior of these 'new China' villagers will catch up with their present verbal behavior before famine once again

---

[30] Personal communication during interview in Honolulu, 1965.
[31] Jan Myrdal, *Report from a Chinese Village* (New York: Pantheon Books, 1965).
[32] R. M. Worth. Unpublished manuscript.

returns to balance the account, as it did with great regularity in the 'old China' of my boyhood.

SELECTED BIBLIOGRAPHY

CHEN, C. C. 'Practical Survey of Rural Health,' *Chinese Medical Journal*, 47 (Shanghai: Chinese Medical Association, 1933): 680–88. One of the earliest systematic looks at health in Chinese villages.

———. 'The Rural Public Health Experiment in Tinghsien, China,' *Chinese Medical Journal*, 50 (Shanghai: Chinese Medical Association, 1936): 1125–27. More early demographic data from a rural setting.

CHIAO, C. H., and J. L. BUCK. 'The Composition and Growth of Rural Population Groups in China,' *Chinese Economic Journal*, 2 (Shanghai: Bureau of Foreign Trade, 1928): 219–35. Pearl Buck's former husband made one of the earliest attempts at a careful study of demographic patterns in rural areas in China.

FANG, S. S. 'Effects of War on the Health of the People,' *Chinese Medical Journal*, 71 (Peking: People's Medical Publisher, 1953): 321–27. An account of the devastating effects of World War II on health in China.

FU, L. C. 'Achievements of the Association in the Past Ten Years,' *Chinese Medical Journal*, 78 (Peking: People's Medical Publishers, 1959): 208–18. A systematic review of health programs during the first ten years of the Communist regime.

HORN, J. S. '*Away with All Pests . . .*' *An English Surgeon in People's China*. London: Healy Publishing Group, Ltd., 1969. A fascinating social history through the casebook of a perceptive surgeon working in North China since 1954. An excellent account of rural health work.

MYRDAL, JAN. *Report from a Chinese Village*. New York: Pantheon Books, 1965. A sensitive and systematic reconstruction of the history of one village from intensive interviews with many key people in the village.

PENFIELD, W. 'Oriental Renaissance in Education and Medicine,' *Science*, 141 (Washington, D.C.: American Association for Advancement of Science, September, 1963): 1153–61. An account of a medical tour of China by a renowned Canadian professor of neurosurgery.

26

CHINESE SOCIETY: STRATIFICATION, MINORITIES, AND THE FAMILY

WILLIAM LIU

INTRODUCTION

THERE are several reasons for the concern of the political leaders about the Chinese social system. First, in a Communist regime, the primary goal of the Party is to mobilize all of the available resources in order to transform the society for the benefit of the collectivity under the guidance of Marxist-Leninist ideology. In achieving that goal, the main problem is the effective control of, and a reasonable degree of allegiance from, the people. These interrelated problems are related to the central question of an effective *organizational weapon*. Franz Schurmann contends that a meaningful interpretation of social change lies in the understanding of the elite group and the methods of organization.[1] Like Max Weber, Schurmann emphasizes the importance of authority, charisma, and the bureaucracy in organizing society.

Aside from the *institutional* approach characterized by the *elite* and *organization* analyses, painstaking efforts to link a long historical past to the present behavior of Chinese society deserve particular attention. Some major scholars have shown that many problems of Chinese society today are neither new nor peculiar to the Communist regime. Although they regard 1949 as a historical break from the imperial past and the beginning of a new era of more effective government based on a different ideological outlook, they argue that the Communists are trying out a different solution to a complex, age-old problem. In order to do so, leaders in Peking made some quite specific assumptions about the traditional society and the roots of its illness and drew conclusions about appropriate political and economic remedies. The solution to China's problems, according to the leaders in Peking, depends on the regime's ability to replace the entire society with a new and different one. Since changes over the last twenty years still leave some of the congeries of the old society visible, it is tremendously important to investigate the changes that Peking's leaders seek and their consequences.

Although historians and other social scientists hold a number of divergent assumptions about and views toward Chinese society, some of the basic characteristics of that society can be identified. The first is that contemporary Chinese society is both Chinese and Communist. Perhaps the former adjective deserves more accent than the latter. A second is that the Chinese experience of social change comes closer to a 'conflict' than to a 'structural' model of social change. Although the analysis of

---

[1] H. Franz Schurmann, *Ideology and Organization in Communist China* (Berkeley and Los Angeles: University of California Press, 1966).

theories of social change is beyond the scope of this chapter, it is important to point out that Mao has repeatedly emphasized that conflict is beneficial to society and is not merely a *process* of the social system, but the essence of the social system itself.

Three aspects of Chinese society will be considered separately here, without investigating their interrelationships. Two of these, social stratification and minorities, have not been treated extensively in most literature on Communist China. Discussion of the third topic, the family, must still leave much to guesswork.

SOCIAL STRATIFICATION

In the writings of Mao, it is evident that social class, the basis of the Chinese revolution, is used to differentiate the 'people' from the 'enemy of the people.' For Mao, the Chinese revolution is not merely a phase in the process of breaking with the past, it is indeed life itself. As the society evolves into its endless new forms, relationships alter among and within groups. Contradictions among the various groups are perennial and are a part of the basic processes in a society.

However, the Chinese Communists have never been too precise about the class divisions in the new society, nor have they been consistent in defining *who* the 'enemy of the people' is. They have shifted the identity of the 'enemy' from one group to another. During the 'three-anti' and the 'five-anti' campaigns of 1951–52, the urban business groups were liquidated, whereas the rich peasants were the target in the collectivization phase of the land program in 1955–56. After the Hundred Flowers movement of 1956–58, the intellectuals were bitterly criticized and many were purged; in the Great Leap Forward of 1958–59, those who advocated more moderate programs were singled out as the 'enemy of the people.' Incomplete reports indicate that members of both the national bourgeoisie and the former bureaucracy still exist.[2] Other reports and recurrent attacks on the 'rich peasants' seem to indicate that they too remain, even though they may have become a politically insignificant group.

However labeled, the social classes in China have evolved during the last two decades into the general categories that exist in the Soviet Union: intelligentsia, the working class, and peasants. A wide gap separates the styles of life of broad strata of the new society. It occurs with respect to the opportunity to ascend in society and the possession of power and prestige. In the crudest terms, there is a division between the urban and rural sectors. Much of the effort of the Chinese leaders has been devoted to narrowing the gap by sending urban cadres, students, and members of the PLA to work in the rural areas.

The old Chinese division of social strata followed the occupations determined by the economic sectors of the civic society. They are: *shih, lung, kung, shang,* and *ping,* or scholar, peasant, labor, business, and soldier (the army), respectively. This usage is still prevalent in the new society to a certain extent, except that the rank order has now been altered. The new class system to be discussed below may vary in accordance with a host of factors.

First, complex political and economic factors both encourage and discourage the visible evidence of class distinction. One of these is the regime's perception of its need for trained personnel. During the First Five Year Plan (1953–57), heavy industry grew at a phenomenal and sustained rate. To support its development, the educational system was designed to give primary attention to technical subjects; technical schools and curricula on industrial and agricultural techniques dominated the scene. On-the-job training and apprenticeship were introduced everywhere. A net increase of 200 per cent of the technical and engineering personnel was reported during the

---

[2] H. Franz Schurmann, 'The Attack on the Cultural Revolution on Ideology and Organization,' in Ping-ti Ho and Tsou Tang, eds., *China in Crisis* (Chicago: University of Chicago Press, 1968): 540.

First Five-Year Plan, while industrial employment increased by only 66 per cent during the same period.[3] Upward social mobility was supplemented by a material incentive system to stimulate work output.[4] Furthermore, the Great Leap Forward, followed by the introduction of the communes in the summer of 1958, required new combinations of land resources and management, thus creating a special group in the rural areas by virtue of the need for managerial and administrative talents.[5] Despite the rise of a privileged technical and managerial class, considerable efforts to decrease the gap between the highest and the lowest wages in industry were discouraged by the failure of the Great Leap Forward. In the countryside, the restoration of limited private rural ownership and a free market in order to offset the negative effects of the Great Leap Forward once again accentuated the distinction between the rich and the poor peasants.

Secondly, there are wide variations among China's regions and between the industrial and agricultural sectors of the economy. In the rural areas, communization of the countryside has not taken place at the same pace from province to province. New experiments do not always diffuse quickly throughout the country. Many model communes, widely publicized, could not be duplicated because of variations of crops and soils. The difference between urban and rural workers, among other factors, is made apparent by a different wage structure: a piecework or wage-point system for urban workers and work points for farm workers. Consequently, the reward systems can hardly be standardized. Some of the nationally supported heavy industries, principally the Tach'ing Oilfield, which has been frequently mentioned as the industrial model since the late 1950's, has created rather affluent groups of industrial workers in comparison to other industries.[6]

Thirdly, social stratification in Communist China is determined largely by the degree to which the individual is politically involved in revolutionary activities. This has certainly been true with respect to membership in the Party and the Young Communist League (YCL). Active participation in revolutionary work has been the major factor in the recruitment of new Party members, particularly during the various 'movements' and 'campaign years' of 1955–56, 1958–60, and 1963–64, as well as during the Cultural Revolution beginning in 1966. The sources of power, therefore, are determined by the individual's ideological commitment and organizational affiliation.[7]

The class system. Political and economic demands, guided by the ultimate goals of the Communist revolution in China, had drastically altered the traditional class system by the time the First Five Year Plan began in 1953. During the reconstruction period between 1949 and 1952, a minority of businessmen, industrialists, and bureaucrats who had served in the Nationalist Government were permitted to remain because the majority of Party cadres lacked urban and industrial skills to cope with the enormous task of establishing a new industrial economy. Since 1952, the broad categories of the intelligentsia, the working class, and peasants have developed social classes within each, with Party cadres merged into these categories to form a separate elite group on each level of the strata. The social class categories are as follows:

---

[3] Choh-ming Li, 'Economic Development,' *China Quarterly*, 1 (London: Congress for Cultural Freedom, January–March, 1960): 35–50.

[4] Charles Hoffman, 'Work Incentives in Communist China's Economic Development Strategy,' *Industrial Relations*, No. 3, February, 1964, pp. 81–97.

[5] Li, 'Economic Development.'

[6] 'China's Ta-Ch'ing Oilfield: Eclipse of an Industrial Model,' *Current Scene*, Vol. 6, No. 16, September 17, 1968.

[7] Schurmann, *Ideology and Organization*; and A. Doak Barnett, with Ezra Vogel, *Cadres, Bureaucracy and Political Power in Communist China* (New York: Columbia University Press, 1967).

(1) Intelligentsia
  (a) High Communist Party ruling elites
  (b) High-ranking non-Party intelligentsia, including governmental, economic, military and cultural bureaucrats
  (c) Professional and technical specialists and high-ranking managerial personnel
  (d) The middle-ranking professional and technical personnel, the middle-ranking bureaucrats, managers of smaller enterprises, junior military officers and diplomats, and artists
  (e) The white-collar workers, including accountants, clerks, bookkeepers, technical aides
(2) Working class
  (a) The skilled workers and workers in special national industries
  (b) The rank-and-file workers with lesser skill grades or those who are not politically active
(3) Peasants
  (a) The well-to-do peasants who profit at different times either through the accumulation of greater private profit or through black marketeering. In the majority of cases, advantages are gained because of the geographical location or the nature of the crop raised, or because of some particular function they perform in the rural communes. This group may constitute about 5 per cent of the total rural population.[8]
  (b) The average peasant with several shadings of productivity and political involvement. This includes poor peasants (about 75 per cent of the rural population) and what may be called middle peasants (10 to 15 per cent of the rural population).

The rank order within the large category does not necessarily reflect the rank order of the entire list. It would be futile to attempt a precise occupational ranking without a better understanding of the complex structure of the economic and political orders. Family lineage, while favorable to the upper class in most societies in terms of property inheritance, opportunity to receive a better education, and differential access to avenues of mobility, has an inverse effect in the Communist system: Children of the former landowner class now have fewer opportunities than those of the working class, the peasants, and Party and government officials.

Membership in any of the major groups is determined not only by formal education and income level but also by the degree to which the individual is perceived as being politically active. For the young, to get on the 'right track' often meant, until recently, to become a member of the YCL, provided that the individual had the right kind of family background.[9] Aside from the political consideration, the traditional evaluation of brainwork as superior to physical labor still prevails in Communist China, especially in some economic activities. Thus, within a single industry or commune, Party cadres enjoy power and prestige derived from differences in their work assignments and the functions they perform. Yet such absolute advantage may be diluted when technical and managerial skills are needed.[10]

---

[8] Nai-kuang Hsiang, 'A Study on "Some Concrete Policy Decisions on the Rural Socialist Education Movement" Promulgated by the Chinese Communist Party Central Committee,' *Chinese Communist Affairs* (Taipei: Institute of Political Research, August, 1965), p. 24.

[9] Michael Oksenberg, 'The Institutionalization of the Chinese Communist Revolution: The Ladder of Success on the Eve of the Cultural Revolution,' *China Quarterly*, No. 36 (London, Congress for Cultural Freedom, October–December, 1968), pp. 61–92.

[10] H. Franz Schurmann, 'Organizational Contrast Between Communist China and the Soviet Union,' in Kurt London, ed., *Unity and Contradiction* (New York: Frederick A. Praeger, 1962).

Hence, it is apparent that the stratification system of the society as a whole does not simply determine the complex conditions of power and prestige within an organization, be it the bureaucracy or an industrial plant. The basic operating principle of the Chinese society seems to rely heavily on a highly developed set of organizational rules and ideological fervor, which are expected to transform the traditional social system into a modern nation-state in a few short years.

The intelligentsia and the cadre. The term 'intelligentsia' lacks precision in the Chinese context. It began to be used at the turn of the century to denote a new breed of students, in contradistinction to the old *literati*. The term became popular during the May Fourth Movement and its aftermath (1917–21) which gave birth to the 'New Intelligentsia'; the term also was associated with the early Communist Party.[11] For the Nationalist regime, the term 'intelligentsia' referred primarily to those who were graduates of universities. After assuming power, the Chinese Communists de-emphasized the superiority of the intelligentsia and sent many of its members to do manual labor.

In the current context, 'intelligentsia' can be broadly interpreted as those who work with their brains. By and large, it refers to highly educated and technically trained persons (managers, cadres, and even white-collar workers). The discussion below deals mainly with the cadre, as a representative of the intelligentsia class.

The term for 'cadre,' *kan-pu*, literally means a 'working team' or functionary. A cadre is someone who holds a formal leadership position. He is a man with prestige and authority in an organization. A cadre most likely is a Party member, a man of strict discipline who carries out orders of the Party hierarchy. He is a man that the Party leadership can depend on. He is, in short, the vanguard of the revolution.[12] The cadres form a highly stratified group and are politically and socially visible throughout the social structure of the country.

The rank of cadres is carefully defined and is published in the *pien-chih* (organizational ranking), which shows the basis of salary and promotions. Though Schurmann[13] does not specify whether a non-Party man could ever become a cadre, Barnett and Vogel explicitly note the distinction between Party and non-Party cadres in the Chinese bureaucracy.[14]

The concept of *kan-pu* can also be construed to mean the backbone of the bureaucracy, one who shapes the working policy and implements it. It follows then that the prestige and power of *kan-pu*, or the cadre, are derived from those of the organization itself. Usually the cadre in a Party organization has higher prestige and power than the cadres in a governmental organization. A national (state) cadre would, by the same token, enjoy more prestige than the local (commune) cadre. Barnett gives several basic types of cadres. The distinction between state cadres (*kuo-chia kan-pu*) and local cadres (*ti-fang kan-pu*) is whether the cadre receives his salary from the state or from the local organization.[15] The military cadres are usually officers above the rank of second lieutenant. The term may also apply to technical and professional personnel in urban areas, such as the medical corps and teaching and administrative personnel. In this sense, *kan-pu* means men in responsible positions.

While cadre stratification is well known, there is little firm information on the

---

[11] Tse-tung Chow, *The May Fourth Movement: Intellectual Revolution in Modern China* (Cambridge: Harvard University Press, 1960), pp. 278–79, 283–84, 287–89, and 293–99.

[12] John Wilson Lewis, *Leadership in Communist China* (Ithaca, N.Y.: Cornell University Press, 1963); Schurmann, *Ideology and Organization*; Barnett, with Vogel, *Cadres, Bureaucracy and Political Power*; and Ezra Vogel, 'From Revolutionary to Semi-bureaucrats: The "Regularization" of Cadres,' *China Quarterly*, No. 29, January–March, 1967, pp. 36–60.

[13] Schurmann, *Ideology and Organization*, pp. 162–72.

[14] Barnett, with Vogel, *Cadres, Bureaucracy, and Political Power*, p. 38.

[15] *Ibid.*, pp. 39–40.

topic. As Schurmann described it, 'The difficulty in obtaining information on the Chinese Communist *nomenklatura* is indicated by the fact that even Taiwan intelligence publications have little to report on the subject.'[16] In the Barnett and Vogel study, which is based on interviews with refugees, many of whom have served in various Party and governmental capacities, the information on cadre ranking suggests that a well-articulated ranking system was introduced in the early 1950's but that the system was not standardized then and was subjected to numerous criticisms. Since 1956, when the regime readjusted grades and salaries, all administrative state cadres throughout the country have been ranked.[17] Generally speaking, there are twenty-four national salary grades for cadres in urban areas and twenty-six grades in rural areas.[18] Grades and salaries of cadres of thirty grades in one county ranged from the highest grade of 13 to the lowest of 30, the salary ratio being 6:1.[19] The ranking systems of the military and certain commercial cadres (*ying yeh yuan*) also differ from the agricultural and industrial cadres.[20]

Though precise information on cadre ranking is lacking, there are some general rules that apply to the internal stratification of cadres. One factor is seniority. The founding fathers of the Party undoubtedly enjoy the highest prestige, both through involvement with Party work and by virtue of having guided the revolutionary tasks in the most difficult years of the Party's history. The land revolution cadres (who joined the Party in the 1920's in Kiangsi Province) and the cadres who survived the Long March in 1934–35 comprise almost all of the top Party elite. Among other 'old cadres,' that is, those who joined the Party prior to the liberation of 1949, there are the 'Yenan cadres,' the '1938 cadres,' the 'anti-Japanese war cadres,' and 'liberation war cadres.' The old cadres by and large have more power and prestige than newer cadres and those generally known as the 'uprising cadres' *ch'i-yi kan-pu* (former Nationalist officers and bureaucrats who switched sides in the last days of the civil war).

Numerous other conditions, in addition to the need for economic skills on the one hand, and the insistence on ideological purity, on the other, affect the power and prestige of the cadre at a given moment. First, the concept of the cadre has undergone some basic changes since Yenan days, when the Party's main objective was survival and struggle through force. A good cadre then was a leader in guerrilla combat. Since 1949, a good cadre must also be a leader in an organization. As the functions of the cadre change, so do the qualifications required to perform such functions. The obvious consequence was a change in the sources of cadre recruitment. The fact that the cadre population both before and after 1949 included new and old intelligentsia accentuated the regime's dilemma in seeking to establish a proper balance between 'expert' and 'red' in the early post-1949 period. In contrast to the Stalinist Soviet Union, where new elites among the intelligentsia who lacked revolutionary political experience were allowed to join the Party, Chinese leaders have tried to prevent the formation of a pure elite club by discouraging those who had not been politically active from becoming cadres. On that subject, Schurmann states:

> As a result of this red and expert contradiction, and the recruitment policies that derived from it, a bifurcation of elites occurred in the country. The political elite consists of the red cadres, the social elite of the intellectuals. The former derive their status from political power based on ideology, the latter from social prestige, based on education. So far, there is no evidence of a single 'new class,' in Milovan

---

[16] Schurmann cited as the best source one published in Taiwan under the title *Kung-fei Jen-shih Ts'o-shih chih Yen-chiu* (*The Study of Chinese Communist Personnel Practices*), (Taipei, 1957), particularly p. 190 ff.
[17] Barnett, with Vogel, *Cadres, Bureaucracy, and Political Power*, p. 41.
[18] *Ibid.*, p. 40.   [19] *Ibid.*, p. 191.   [20] *Ibid.*, p. 40.

Djilas' sense. The attempt to combine the two elites during the Great Leap Forward did not succeed.[21]

After the Hundred Flowers Movement of 1957, the Party intensified its campaign to transform bourgeois intellectuals into working-class intellectuals. With the aging of China's top scientific and technological personnel, the makeup of the non-Communist intelligentsia may have to undergo considerable change.[22]

The situation after the Cultural Revolution resembled the experience of the Great Leap Forward in certain ways. Students and the People's Liberation Army were encouraged to return to the countryside to work and to learn from the peasants. A new ferment of revolutionary spirit was once again stirred up in a renewed campaign against the technocratic Soviet model of revisionism. However, the campaign against moderate and technological leadership notwithstanding, no nation can afford to set aside its experienced administrative personnel and highly skilled scientists and technicians. At present, no evidence can be cited to project the emergence in the immediate future of a single elite group that combines both red and expert qualifications.

Events in the near future will probably closely follow the past pattern of protracted political efforts to emphasize the importance of political activities together with the increasing demand for technological know-how. Since 1949, CCP leaders have relentlessly guided the country's nearly 4 million intellectuals in the fields of scientific research, engineering, health, education, and literature and the arts.

The industrial workers. Next to the Party leaders and the elite intelligentsia is the broad category of industrial workers. Up to early 1956, both the wage-point system (wages were based on the volume of work done) and various multiple wage grades (based on skills) were widely used. In addition, material incentives in industry included labor insurance, special monetary rewards for innovative suggestions used in production, and benefits for the worker and his family. The system, simple as it may appear, was complicated by the variations in the prices of several staple commodities, which were related to the geographic location of industry.[23] In addition, the wage-point system placed emphasis on quota fulfillment in work. In some cases, the highest pay grade is supposed to receive roughly three times as much as the lowest.[24] Material incentives, however, were de-emphasized from 1957 to 1960. Instead, greater reliance was placed on the revolutionary fervor of the masses and on nonmaterial incentives. Collective achievement was recognized in the form of honorary prizes. In the early 1960's, a return of material awards to individual workers was made after the failure of the Great Leap. Higher pay for more work rather than for better skills was the practice until the Cultural Revolution.

In general, however, the technical complexity that existed in various industries necessitated the wide adoption of the piecework system, which constituted the basis of urban inequality among the working class. For example, in 1952, the Central South Military and Administrative Committee promulgated a wage scale that explicitly provided more pay for more work. All branches of industry were divided into eight groups, beginning with coal mining, iron and steel, and nonferrous mining, and ending with match and tobacco production. Within each group, five categories of wages were introduced according to their relative importance to the national economy. In addition, general laborers and apprentices were outside the grading system and were given three grades on a separate wage scale.[25]

---

[21] Schurmann, *Ideology and Organization*, p. 171.

[22] Chu-yuan Cheng, 'Peking's Mind of Tomorrow: Problems in Developing Scientific and Technological Talent in China,' *Current Scene*, Vol. 4, No. 6 (March 15, 1966).

[23] Hoffmann, 'Work Incentives in Economic Development Strategy,' pp. 81–97.

[24] *Ibid.*

[25] *Ch'ang-chiang Jih-pao*, August 17, 1952.

The most widely cited example of the differential reward system in Communist China prior to the Cultural Revolution was the case of the Tach'ing Oilfield in Heilungkiang Province, which came into being in 1959.[26] More than 20,000 dependents of the oil workers were employed either in agriculture or in other service jobs. The success of the Tach'ing story reflects an unequal status among industrial workers both in terms of cash reward and fringe benefits and in terms of recruitment criteria. With regard to the differential wage and other material incentives, Tach'ing workers reportedly had wages that were twice the average wage of industrial workers in the country. In addition, oilfield workers received an 'isolated area allowance' ranging from 15 per cent of base pay for office workers to 35 per cent for drillers.[27] It is clear, then, that, in spite of ideology, a basic inequality among industrial workers in relation to the reward system has always existed and can be expected to continue.

The peasant. In the vast rural areas, the peasantry is by no means a homogeneous group. After successive years of agrarian reform, collectivization, the people's commune, and the reclassification of classes, there has been a thorough alteration of the rural social structure. In some cases, the single-clan village still remains, but the basic stratification pattern has been changed. The percentage of former landlords and rich peasants has been halved, largely because of forced labor during the 'three-anti' and 'five-anti' campaigns, apart from retirement and attrition. Subjected to repeated attacks during the various movements, the rich peasants and former landlords have been reduced to minimum political significance.[28] The middle peasants, who possessed more productive facilities, constituted from 5 to 10 per cent of the rural population in the early 1950's. Even though these figures need to be carefully validated, they indicate that the large majority of the peasant population consists of 'poor peasants.'[29]

The Communists did not fail to redistribute the land. Indeed, many of those who had been poor tenant farmers under the Nationalist regime became well off after the land reform. Until 1956, a few had long-time hired hands and were accused of having exploited other peasants. The new program of land reform, however, still left only a very narrow margin of financial security for the majority of the farm population. A small-scale natural calamity, with high taxation and fluctuation of the ratio between the prices of goods sold and necessities purchased, or a misfortune of any kind would force the new landowner to sell his property, even his land. This pauperization of many new landowners made it possible for a few to get rich quickly.

Since farmers are dependent on the soil and the climate for growing crops, variation of income is inevitable. A report printed in *Jen-min Jih-pao* suggested that the variation in average per capita agricultural income in northern Manchuria can be twice that in southern Manchuria. Peasants near the great inland lakes, such as T'aihu (Kiangsu) and Tungt'ing Lake (Hunan) and in the Ch'engtu plain (Szechwan) would ordinarily enjoy better incomes than those in other regions of inland China.[30]

Freedom to sell and to purchase land after the land reform and prior to formation of the communes may have been the single most important factor in creating rural strata. *Jen-min Jih-pao* reported that, when a village in Shansi Province was 'liberated'

---

[26] 'China's Ta-ch'ing Oilfield: Eclipse of an Industrial Model,' *Current Scene*, Vol. 6, No. 16, September 17, 1968.

[27] *Current Scene*, 6, No. 16 (September 17, 1968): 3.

[28] Hsiang, 'Study on "Policy Decisions," ' p. 24.

[29] A report published by *Shansi Jih-pao* on a study of more than 5,000 Party members in 185 Party branches of Wuhsing County, Shansi, indicated that 5 per cent of the members were not in mutual aid teams and persisted in exploiting the poor peasants and that another 15 per cent were passive and politically useless and backward. These figures may have no connection with the peasant population in general, but were rather close to the proportions of rich and middle-class peasants and thus deserve attention. See *Shansi Jih-pao*, July 26, 1952.

[30] *Jen-min Jih-pao (People's Daily, or JMJP)*, July 7, 1952.

in 1947, its land was equally distributed. Five years later, however, of 126 households in the village, 'eleven are newly impoverished households and poor peasants' and '10 per cent have become upper middle peasants.'[31] After the communization in 1958, some peasants became rich through black-marketing and sales on the free market and by accumulating more work points.[32] The Cultural Revolution is expected to have changed the rural social structure again, although we do not yet have adequate data to assess the changes.

Social mobility. There were few channels for upward mobility in premodern China. A prevailing political principle of the state was to safeguard the Confucian classics. Hence, Confucian literature was the basis for bureaucratic appointment and upward mobility. This meant that social mobility was restricted to those who had access to, and a profound knowledge of, the Confucian writings. The scholar-bureaucrat elite selected candidates for admission to the power structure of the country through national civil service examinations. Political power, once acquired, became a source of prestige and a means of acquisition of wealth; it went hand in hand with authority in traditional China.[33] The stratification pattern of the civic society, therefore, was in consonance with that of the state. This legitimization of authority was further strengthened by the functions of ancestor worship[34] and by an intricate system of elaborate clan rules.[35] The precept of charity as a visible sign of virtue encouraged the bureaucrat or well-off members of the clan to give generously for the establishment and maintenance of the ritual land for ancestor worship. Subsequent returns from the ritual land were usually utilized for the education of the clan members, which thereby provided an avenue for their ascent into the scholar class and at the same time legitimized the power stronghold of the donors in clan affairs.

Prior to the turn of the present century, the civil service examination system was abolished. That change literally destroyed the main avenues of social mobility and the traditional system of control. The need to find and establish a new selection and role-allocation mechanism caused considerable confusion and conflict during the Republic period.[36] The problem was partially resolved by returning both the old and the new urban and rural bourgeoisie to bureaucratic positions.[37]

A basic aim of any kind of social revolution is bound to be the thorough alteration of the social class system and the restructuring of opportunities for those who were deprived of them in the preceding period. In Communist China, Party elites and organizational cadres replaced bureaucrats of the earlier regime as the men with power and prestige. As a result of the expansion of the national economy under the industrial and collectivization programs from 1952 on, for the majority of the middle and lower strata of the population, social mobility has been made possible by and large by the enormous shifting of population into the newly developed positions.

In order to carry out the thorough change of society it desires, the Communist Party needs trusted and capable leaders who can, through coercion, persuasion, and

---

[31] *JMJP*, July 19, 1952.

[32] Thomas P. Bernstein, 'Problems of Village Leadership after Land Reform,' *China Quarterly*, No. 36, October–December, 1968, pp. 1–22.

[33] For an illuminating discussion and summary of the current sociological thinking on authority and power, see Philip Selznick, *Leadership in Administration* (Evanston, Ill.: Row, Peterson, 1957), p. 5, and Robert Nisbet, *Community and Power* (New York: Galaxy, 1962). For a discussion on this point particularly relevant to the discussion of the Chinese case, see Schurmann, 'Attack on Cultural Revolution on Ideology and Organization,' pp. 525–32.

[34] C. K. Yang, *Religion in Chinese Society: A Study of Contemporary Social Functions of Religion and Some of their Historical Facts* (Berkeley and Los Angeles: University of California Press, 1961), pp. 164–65.

[35] Kung-chuan Hsiao, *Rural China* (Seattle: University of Washington Press, 1960), p. 323.

[36] Chow, *May Fourth Movement*, pp. 94–95.

[37] Schurmann, 'Attack on Cultural Revolution on Ideology and Organization,' p. 535.

example, mobilize the masses for participation in the Party's programs. To do the job well, the Communist Party needs experts in the more technical fields. An enormous expansion of the education system was undertaken during the First Five-Year Plan in order to meet the manpower shortage. As a result, nearly 1.2 million Chinese students were graduated from colleges and universities during the 1949–63 period. Of these, more than half majored in technical fields, including the natural sciences, agriculture, the medical sciences, and engineering.[38]

The educational ladder. Educational attainment is still an important source of social mobility in China. When the Communist Party seized power in 1949, there were slightly more than 200 institutions above the secondary level.[39] By 1953, the number reported had fallen to 182, primarily because of changes in the educational system, but then rose to about 800 after the Great Leap Forward. The sudden increase mainly reflected the hastily established institutions of the 1958 self-reliance program. Three years later, many had not survived, owing to a lack of facilities and teaching faculty.[40]

In order to increase the number of senior scientists and engineers, the Chinese Government in 1955 instituted a new associate doctoral degree (*fu-po-shih*). Though little is known about the number of persons who have benefited from the new degree, it would be safe to assume that there is still room at the top echelon of the intelligentsia stratum. Since the shortage of top scientists and engineers cannot be met in Chinese training facilities, many talented young scientists have been sent abroad to study every year. From 1949 to 1955, when China was receiving technical help from the Soviet Union on a large scale, an estimated total of 5,000 students received training in the Soviet Union and Eastern Europe. The number, however, decreased rapidly after the withdrawal of Soviet help in 1960.

Comparable advancement for the middle and lower strata of the society was possible as a result of the changes in the country's socio-economic and political structure. The enormous bureaucracy and Party organizations at other levels has created a demand for large numbers of lower-level managerial personnel and semiprofessional and skilled workers. Many of them are the product of the part-time and adult education system, which was expanded considerably shortly after the takeover, and of several varieties of work-study programs.

The political ladder. Oksenberg, in his study of the ladder of success prior to the Cultural Revolution, tentatively outlined what seemed to be the 'rules of the game' in upward mobility.[41] The perennial nature of revolutionary activities may be regarded as a permanent pattern of role allocation in the new social order, unless drastic changes take place to subordinate revolutionary fervor to the revisionist's path.

Oksenberg's material came from intensive interviews with three former college students, an accountant employed in a production brigade in Fukien, and a university professor. In broad terms, he suggests that, for some if not most young people in Communist China, the career stages are: (1) an initial response to the incessant demands of duty; (2) organizational affiliation, training, and the choice of an occupation; (3) pursuit of the accepted symbols of success in the given occupation; and, finally; (4) the tempering of ambition and pursuit of security.

---

[38] Leo A. Orleans, *Professional Manpower and Education in Communist China* (Washington, D.C.: Government Printing Office, 1960), and Chu-yuan Cheng, 'Scientific and Engineering Manpower in Communist China,' *An Economic Profile of Mainland China*, 2, Washington, D.C.: Government Printing Office, 1967): 521–47.

[39] Orleans, *Professional Manpower and Education*, pp. 521–47.

[40] By 1963, about 400 had survived. Cheng, 'Scientific and Engineering Manpower.'

[41] Michel Oksenberg, 'The Institutionalization of the Chinese Communist Revolution: The Ladder of Success on the Eve of the Cultural Revolution,' *China Quarterly*, No. 36, October–December, 1968, pp. 61–92.

The Chinese Communists invest strong hopes in youth. Political participation is, therefore, demanded in various curricular and extracurricular activities. If the individual shows a reluctance to participate in political activities, he will reduce his chances to be admitted as a student in an institution of higher learning.

The 'career track' generally demanded that a young man in his late teens or early twenties face the choice as to whether or not he wished to become a member of the YCL or the PLA. If he failed to make such a choice by his mid-twenties, his career goals would most likely be outside the political system and his chances of becoming a member of the elite group were greatly reduced. All else being equal, a Chinese youth had the same problem as youths elsewhere in pursuing a good education in the right field. Given the existing educational and political structures in China, the Chinese youth has a rather circumscribed choice as to which university or what field to enter; the ultimate decision depends on the pressure of manpower demands, as well as such factors as family connections, one's own past political participation, and the like.

Once an occupation has been chosen or assigned, vertical mobility is slow, while instances of lateral mobility may be frequent. For those who failed to have a career within the political system, it would be virtually impossible to be a political activist in the Party at a later time. Here lies the real distinction of the separate reward systems. The source of power in China has been in the Party, particularly in the Departments of Organization and Political-Legal Affairs and elsewhere in the Party Secretariats. Certain departments in the People's Liberation Army also serve as excellent avenues for social mobility. As Oksenberg observed,'—Political power had to be pursued within the organization possessing it.[42] Yet the possession of political power may well be a double-edged sword. With the cycles of 'movements' and economic relaxations over the last two decades, many cadres and Party members have been purged; new blood has been recruited into the system. Once an individual reaches the height of his career, whether in active Party work or as a peasant,[43] he turns to a life of minimal risk and some long-range security. Such goals must then be sought outside the political system. Mao's continual practice of expansion and retreat in carrying out revolutionary goals thus helps assure that there will be a sustained leadership of activists in the Party.

Sources of variations in social mobility. The interplay of political, economic, social, and educational factors at any given time produces differential probabilities that an individual will move up or fail to do so on the ladder to success. In the pattern of 'movements' every two to three years followed by 'retreats,' many succeeded and others became casualties in the fierce struggle to succeed. In the 'movement' years, young activists were recruited into the elite groups, and the number of new Party members increased rapidly. During the Great Leap Forward, many skilled workers were promoted to technical and engineering positions. During the collectivization phase, numerous former tenant farmers were elected chiefs of mutual aid teams and collective farms. In subsequent years of retreat or relaxation, the private economy was given another small chance. Black-marketeering and personal profits gained in the urban and rural sectors of the civic society. More competent and talented youths were admitted to institutions of higher learning; technical and managerial talents were given a greater role in the bureaucracy.

Aside from these *fluctuations* of chances, during campaign periods the educational ladder is biased in favour of youth with the right background. In 1957, for example, 'political quality,' measured primarily in terms of performance during the rectification and antirightist campaigns, became a prime factor in the selection of college

[42] *Ibid.*, p. 69; see also Barnett, with Vogel, *Cadres, Bureaucracy and Political Power*; and James Townsend, *Political Participation in Communist China* (Berkeley and Los Angeles: University of California Press, 1967).

[43] Bernstein, 'Problems of Village Leadership,' pp. 1–22.

entrants.[44] In addition, the Ministry of Education authorized exemptions from matriculation examinations for applicants with a working class or peasant background. In the competitive selection of students, first consideration is given to workers and peasants; next in order are demobilized PLA members, employees who have been active in revolutionary work for at least three years, and, lastly, children of war martyrs and national minority students, as well as overseas Chinese students. Rural youth seem to be in a comparatively disadvantageous position when it comes to social mobility. Since farming is their primary occupation, a great deal of energy and time must be spent in the field rather than in politics. Unless they join the Party or the Liberation Army, their avenues for success are fewer.[45]

One of the most obvious changes that has taken place on the mainland is in the status of women. Though fewer women than men pursue political careers, the demand for women's intelligence in technical and scientific fields has been evidenced by the increase in the enrollment of women in recent decades. In the 1951–59 period, the number of women students enrolled in institutions of higher learning increased from 35,000 to 180,000. Similarly, during the 1949–60 period, the number of women workers registered a twelvefold increase, from 600,000 to 8 million. In 1962, women scientists accounted for more than one-fifth of the research workers in the Chinese Academy of Sciences, which was a 42 per cent increase over a five-year span.[46] In the textile industry in Shanghai in 1962, about 1,000 women were employed as engineers and technicians; more than 500 women were reported to be managers and top administrators. In the same year, more than 600 engineers worked in a leading steel mill, where none were reported in 1949.

RACIAL AND CULTURAL MINORITIES

The Chinese Communists label cultural and racial minorities in China as 'minority nationalities.' A minority nationality comprises people of common cultural heritage who reside in politically well-defined areas and historically have a sense of minority identity vis-à-vis the Han people. In some cases, there is the added distinction of different religious beliefs, such as the Huis (Muslims) and the Tibetans (Lama Buddhists), though it is not uncommon to single out physical differences, such as those of the Uigurs of Chinese Turkestan and the Mongols of Inner Mongolia.

The Nationalist government did not systematically draw the minorities into the national political life. Since 1949, the Communists have made it quite a point in publicity that the national minorities officially enjoy equal civil and political status, including the right to retain their cultural heritage, to speak their own languages, and to practice their religions freely. All of these rights were embodied in the 'Common Program' and the 1954 Constitution.

One of the reasons for the lack of integration of the national minorities into the mainstream of Han social and political life is that most of them are distributed over a wide area in the hinterland along the southern, southwestern, and northeastern borders of the country. In the past, under both the Nationalists and the monarchies, the central government's lack of an effective political and economic machinery to bring those remote areas under its administration allowed the minority nationalities to remain more or less autonomous and separated from the Hans, although there were many historically complicated processes of migration, assimilation, and change over the years. The minority problem in Communist China is, therefore, associated primarily with efforts to draw the non-Hans into the national society.

The minority nationalities—about 6 per cent of the entire population, totaling

---

[44] Orleans, *Professional Manpower and Education*. p. 63.
[45] Oksenberg, 'Institutionalization of Revolution,' p. 77.
[46] Cheng, 'Scientific and Engineering Manpower,' p. 538.

from 40 million to 43 million people—are found mainly in Manchuria, Inner Mongolia, Sinkiang, Tsinghai, Kansu, Tibet, Szechwan, Yünnan, Kweichow, Kwangtung and Kwangsi. The ten largest groups, with numbers ranging from 1 million to 6 million each, are the Koreans in Manchuria, the Manchus, the Hui, the Mongols, the Uigurs, the Tibetans, the Miao-Yao of Yünnan, the Chuang, the Yi, and the Puyi.[47]

Traditional Communists and treatment of national minorities. Leaders of the Chinese Communist Party perceive the problem of minority nationalities in the same manner as they view religion, the family, and social classes. Ethnic differences and regional loyalties are to be subordinated to the national revolution and to Communism.

The problem of minority nationalities has had a long history. It was not until after the Communist seizure of power in 1949 that effective measures were taken to Sinicize the minorities. Two principal steps were involved. The first was to erode the solidarity of the traditional community and its culture. To do so, the Communist Party campaigned strenuously to alter the functions of what traditionally were the integrating elements in the social institutions that maintained solidarity among the various segments of the minority community. The second step was to introduce what might be regarded as Chinese, as well as Communist, institutions into the minority culture. Sedentary farming, stock-raising, and public education all have contributed to the integration of the minority society into the larger nation-state. In the course of implementing this dual policy, drastic actions were preceded by gradualism and the proclaimed policy of 'no struggle.' Perhaps the drastic actions have yielded some results. Yet the Communist Party has also paid a good price for it, as evidenced by the rebellion of the Tibetans in the 1950's and by several other uprisings in Tsinghai and Sinkiang prior to the Great Leap Forward.

In view of their professed doctrine, it is notable that the Communists have in fact followed a policy of 'divide and rule,' as did the earlier Chinese emperors. Over the centuries the emperors, who were harassed by border minorities from both the north and the south, adopted the traditional approach of (1) armed conquest by the Hans of the border peoples, (2) treaty negotiations, and (3) social and commercial intercourse. There never was any systematic plan to integrate the national minorities into the Han society in spite of the perennial problem with national minorities. Whatever short-term tactics the rulers may have followed during the imperial era, the general principle was to divide and rule. In effect, such a policy entailed the separation of the minority nationalities so that the combination of their forces against the Han people could be avoided. The Communists have tried to Sinicize the minority nationalities, but they have done so by divisive means. The way it is attempted and the effect achieved can be illustrated by the cases of Tibet and Inner Mongolia.

Social and political background of minority nationalities of Tibet and Inner Mongolia. The Chinese Communists have been uncertain and ineffective in dealing with Tibetans and Mongols because of the unique economic structure and sociopolitical history of the two autonomous regions. First, the Chinese are a race of farmers. They have neither the aptitude nor the desire to exploit the livestock potential in the hinterland of the border regions. Perhaps the lack of an effective program in dealing with nomadic Tibetans stems also from the fact that the Chinese Communists were aware of how difficult it would be to extend effective control over a large, mobile population spread over a vast and unfamiliar territory. On the Tibetan Plateau, the difficulty is compounded by high altitude. The land of the pastoral nomads is at a higher altitude than ordinary farmland. Without the potential competition of the Chinese peasant economy on the high plateaus, the Tibetans are able to raise traditional products that can be easily transported by the use of traditional energy sources. The Tibetan

[47] Josef Kolmas, 'The Minority Nationalities,' in Ruth Adams, ed., *Contemporary China* (New York: Pantheon, 1966), pp. 51–61.

economy is, and has been, under the control of the Tibetan herdsmen.[48] Control by the herdsmen is largely responsible for Tibetan resistance to Sinicization. The same may be said of the herdsmen of Inner Mongolia.

Second, the widely divergent subsistence patterns among the pastoral nomads makes it more difficult to advocate change than in ordinary farming. A poor share-cropper can own and herd a few animals of his own. He can live on the milk and cheese and use the hide to ward off the cold in the winter. Rice is not a necessity in the diet in Inner Mongolia and Tibet as it is in the southeastern part of China proper. The absence of residential permanence makes shelter and education of the young no more relevant for the nomads than are housing problems for the boat dwellers on the waterfronts of southeastern China. Trade is learned through apprenticeship within a close-knit group. Thus, the difference between the life style of the wealthy and that of the poor is not so sharp that it can be politically exploited by the Communist Party.

In addition to the special economic characteristics of the nomadic life in both Tibet and Inner Mongolia, the Tibetan religious community deserves more attention in analyzing the problem of national integration. In 1950, when the Communists seized power in Tibet, one-third of the male population belonged to the monastic community. In addition to the monastic sector of the civic society, there were nomads and sedentary farmers. Though the monastic communities also produced some of their food from the land for the use of the temples, the recruitment of monastic membership and economic support for the continuation of Lama Buddhism would have to come from the two other sectors of the society. Hence, instead of being separated from the secular society, the Tibetan religious institution actually serves as a solidifying factor in the society, imparting to it a strong sense of regional integration.

The nomadic herdsmen and their dependents must travel in groups for mutual protection. There is, therefore, a great deal of overlapping between kinship groups and self-sustaining economic units in the Tibetan society. Group solidarity is not impaired, and is in fact necessitated, by the high mobility that characterizes the life of the nomads.

In contrast to the nomadic culture, the agricultural economy gave life its stability and served as the proper place for the institutional education of the young, as well as for the care of the sick and of pregnant women. As in medieval Europe, many educated and professional people were members of the monastic community. The agricultural economy, in this respect, both served the religious community and depended upon it to survive. The social structure of Tibetan society is by no means homogeneous; with its stratification and division of labor came a high degree of solidarity. The Chinese Communist leaders, in numerous attempts to break the autonomous and religiopolitical system of Tibet, have come up with some rather original methods, albeit perhaps with only limited success.

Efforts toward national integration. In 1931, the Constitution of the Kiangsi Soviet spoke of 'the right of self-determination of the national minorities in China, their right to complete separation from China, and to the formation of an independent state for each minority nationality.'[49]

By 1949, self determination for the national minorities was rarely mentioned in official documents. In its place was the proclamation of 'administrative autonomy.'

Only a few members of the national minorities, among them Ulanfu of Inner Mongolia, reached the top echelon of the ruling elite. Because of the enormous difficulties involved in integrating minority groups into the national society, the initial policy of the regime with respect to the minorities was characterized by *gradualism*. In

[48] Robert B. Ekvall, 'Nomads of Tibet: A Chinese Dilemma,' in Francis Harper, ed., *This is China* (Hong Kong: Dragonfly Press, 1965), pp. 223–52.

[49] Conrad Brandt, Benjamin Schwartz, and John K. Fairbank, eds., *A Documentary History of Chinese Communism* (New York: Atheneum, 1966), p. 217.

more difficult cases, such as the nomads of Tibet, leaders of the CCP were hesitant to do anything. In 1959, at the third meeting of the National Committee of the Political Consultative Conference, Mao gave special emphasis to the exception of minority nationalities in the program of land reform.[50] The practice of 'gradualism' did not seem to fit the general revolutionary fervor at all, but the formulation of Party policy with respect to minority nationalities had to take into account a number of factors. Some of the considerations were historical, others were political, and some were derived from experience with the nomads of the Soviet Union in Central Asia. The most important factor may have been that few Chinese Communist leaders had had any direct knowledge of or experience with nomadic life. In Marxist guidelines there is no mention of the nomad, who does not fit into the socialist economy, and little could be done to engage the have-nots against the haves.

The practical problems associated with the integration of minorities into the national society resulted, by and large, in the rather slow integration of the autonomous regions into the national community. In Tibet, plans had been drawn up to Sinicize the nomads' land as early as 1951. However, the implementation of the plans was indefinitely postponed. The Party's plan called for dividing Tibet into two regions (eastern and western), for there are more Chinese in the eastern section of the region. Attempts to force inhabitants in eastern Tibet into the pattern of communization applied to China proper were unsuccessful. Violence was reported on the southeastern border of Tibet in 1956, in Tsinghai in 1958, and in Lhasa in 1959.[51] However, some relative successes have been recorded in Tsinghai, where monasteries were depopulated and farmers were going through the usual land redistribution, even though nomads were left untouched. Some similar successes have been reported in Sinkiang.

Political means of Sinicization. Different policies were adopted with respect to Tibet and Inner Mongolia. In the case of Inner Mongolia, with the help of Ulanfu, the Party succeeded in reducing Soviet influence in Inner Mongolia, where it could operate to separate the region from the People's Republic. Gradualism, with emphasis on teaching the Mongolian language during the late 1940's and early 1950's, caused little trouble. The political aims of the leaders in Peking were to raise Mongol political consciousness, to develop a higher standard of Mongolian culture, and to recruit young Mongolian men as cadres. In so doing, the Chinese hoped to collectivize the land and to Sinicize Mongol herdsmen.[52]

The Chinese Communist Party was able to play a greater role in implementing changes in Inner Mongolia than in Tibet, mainly because the Party apparatus in Inner Mongolia was well run and well organized, whereas that of Tibet was weak. The political groundwork in Inner Mongolia was laid by Ulanfu, who in 1945 established a 'Committee for an Autonomous Mongolia' in Kalgan,[53] forcing a rival Independent Provisional Mongolian Republic to Shangtu. By 1947, Ulanfu and the Chinese Communist Party in Peking had gained firm control of most of Inner Mongolia, with the exception of certain areas in the east and west.[54] Through a combination of political and military measures, the Chinese were able to chase Wang Te, the leader of the last remaining resistance force, out of the region and ultimately captured and imprisoned him. The control of Inner Mongolia, through an already well-

[50] Stuart R. Schram, *Mao Tse-tung* (New York: Simon & Schuster, 1966), p. 248.
[51] June Dreyer, 'China's Minority Nationalities in Cultural Revolution,' *China Quarterly*, No. 35, July–September, 1968, pp. 96–101.
[52] Paul Hyer and William Heaton, 'The Cultural Revolution in Inner Mongolia,' *China Quarterly*, No. 36, October–December, 1968, p. 116.
[53] Robert A. Rupen, 'Partition in the Land of Genghis Khan,' in Francis Harper, ed., *This is China* (Hong Kong: Dragonfly Books, 1965), p. 206.
[54] *Ibid.*

established system of command, was relatively easy. Once the organization was under control, individuals who wielded power within the organization could be purged or liquidated. The name of Sain Bayar (Pao Yueh-ch'ing), a high-ranking Party official in the early 1950's, has not been mentioned for many years. The top Party leadership has been in serious trouble in recent years, and Ulanfu, who had always been the monolithic power in Inner Mongolia, was finally forced out of the Party leadership in 1968.[55]

Aside from the political struggle within the Party, other aspects of the communization of Inner Mongolia have been less troublesome in comparison with Tibet. Collectivization of the Inner Mongolian pastoral economy apparently moved along rather smoothly after the Great Leap Forward.[56] By 1959, more than 2,000 livestock cooperatives were abruptly transformed into 150 livestock communes. The Party leaders attempted—presumably with success—to give permanent homes to herdsmen. More than 7,000 nomads in Inner Mongolia were settled in 1962.[57] More and more herdsmen are now giving up the nomadic life and becoming members of livestock-raising production brigades.

With the change of management in livestock-raising, the Communist leaders also were successful in introducing industries into Inner Mongolia to give the region's economy greater diversity. In Paotow, for instance, a steel mill employed about 37,000 former sheep-herding Mongol nomads in 1962.[58]

It would be unfair to minimize the importance of the fact that the majority of the urban population in Inner Mongolia is Chinese, making it relatively easy to control Inner Mongolia. Nevertheless, nomadic traditions, religious beliefs, racial distinctions, and the long-term influence of the Outer Mongols and the Russians in the region were all important in solidifying an intense nationalism in the 1950's and early 1960's. Ulanfu was regarded as the symbol of nationalism in the Inner Mongolia Autonomous Region. The Chinese Communists have been relatively successful in dealing with Inner Mongolian regional politics through a combination of military and political means. The situation in Tibet, on the other hand, reflects a less successful story. The leadership crisis during the Great Proletarian Cultural Revolution has altered the picture, but the current situation remains subject to speculation.

The Sinicization problem in Tibet seems perennially perplexing. In order to deal with the problem of the herdsmen's extreme mobility, attempts have been made to break up the traditional forms of economic organization and interdependence. To do this, farmland has been expanded into pastures. Confronted by the enormous task of stabilizing the herdsmen, the Party devised several rather original plans. (Such plans have also been used in Inner Mongolia and Tsinghai.)[59] First, a chain of veterinary stations or services was established. Such services answered a pressing need in the herdsmen's culture, since the pastoral economy can easily be ruined by cattle disease. Through the veterinary stations, a livestock census could be obtained. In addition, the veterinary stations serve as a focal point of community life among the nomads, thus cutting down mobility. Finally, such extension services could easily be supplemented by livestock-breeding services, thus paving the way for the eventual elimination of the nomadic way of life.[60]

Second, the Chinese Communists have established a school system in the region

---

[55] *China News Analysis*, No. 747, Hong Kong, 1968.
[56] Rupen, 'Partition in Land of Genghis Khan,' p. 209.
[57] *Ibid.*, p. 210.
[58] *Survey of China Mainland Press*, No. 280, Hong Kong: U.S. Consulate-General, January 22, 1962.
[59] Dreyer, 'Minority Nationalities in Cultural Revolution,' pp. 96–101; and Hyer and Heaton, 'Cultural Revolution in Inner Mongolia,' pp. 114–28.
[60] Ekvall, 'Nomads of Tibet,' p. 231.

which inevitably ties down the dependents of herdsmen. Education gives the next generation a sense of political consciousness that works in favor of the Communist Party in Peking.

Third, winter feed supply stations have been set up to store and manage livestock fodder. Government loans, the building of supply and storage structures, and, eventually, animal husbandry, agriculture, and handicraft production will help replace the present pastoral economy of the plateau with a diversified manufacturing and service economy.

It is more difficult to counteract the influence of the religious institution upon the Tibetan society than to stabilize the nomads in the region. On the one hand, the Communist Party must continue to proclaim the right to religious freedom. Thus, it cannot simply eliminate the religious institution; it must seek to control it.

In order to control the religious institution in Tibet and to offset its importance, a combination of economic strangulation, mob violence directed by the Party against the monasteries, and the harassment of monks has been rather successful in driving some of the religious leaders off to other parts of the region. Not all the methods were negative; material and employment inducements were also used. Rigorous campaigns have been waged to make the recruitment of new religious manpower increasingly difficult.

Other means employed to Sinicize the minority population. Aside from services and educational programs to erode the solidarity of the minority communities, the Chinese Communists have also adopted economic and other measures to disperse the minority population while increasing the number of Han Chinese in the border regions. By means of heavy taxes, fines, and sometimes enforced loans for the construction of stations and schools, the Party has managed to weaken the wealthy monasteries and to reduce the less affluent ones to a state of disability.[61] In the mid-1950's, the Tibetan Buddhists' Association was reorganized to become a part of the Chinese Buddhists' Association, thus destroying the former autonomous status of Lama Buddhism. The Communist Party used the monasteries and nunneries as vehicles for propaganda and as instruments of political control over a large portion of the Tibetan population. Many monks were organized into labor brigades or were inducted into the army.[62]

In order to alter the function of the monastery, a change of the work assignment of its members has become inevitable. Monks and nuns, like the former landowners, were first forced to participate in self-criticism sessions and later paid to perform managerial and service functions. Toward the end of the 1950's, some 56,000 monks and nuns in 1,700 monasteries and nunneries had been given political lessons, including self-criticisms.[63]

'Voluntary' but planned migration as a policy measure has served many purposes rather effectively. First, Party policy has sought to increase the cultivation of farmland in remote and previously uncultivated or undercultivated areas. Large zones of Inner Mongolia and eastern Sinkiang, as well as Tibet, have served as target areas for agricultural settlement.[64] Second, planned migration and land reclamation are regarded as ways to ease population pressure in areas of high density.[65] Third, the transfer of skilled and politically active Han people to the border regions is designed to accelerate the transformation of the national minority communities. In 1956, some 433,000 persons, out of a total of about 750,000 people who moved, resettled in the border provinces of Manchuria, Inner Mongolia, and Sinkiang.[66] Some of these movements were presumably caused by the redistribution of industries. In Sian, for

---

[61] *Ibid.*, p. 243.
[63] *JMJP*, April 10, 1960.
[65] H. Yuan Tien, 'The Demographic Significance of Organized Population Transfers in Communist China,' *Demography*, 1 (November, 1964): 220–26.
[66] *JMJP*, December 28, 1956.

[62] *Ibid.*, p. 246.
[64] *JMJP*, March 6, 1956.

example, 70,000 workers brought 60,000 relatives with them. In Lanchou, it was reported that 60 per cent of the workers had their families living with them.[67] These statistics, however imprecise, are sufficient to indicate that planned migration and the redistribution of the industrial economy in the border regions may have exerted a profound impact on the Sinicization of the minorities. The Party has also sent large numbers of youth to the countryside, particularly after the Cultural Revolution, both to avoid excessive concentrations of people in the cities and to instill correct social attitudes in the younger generation.

THE COMMUNIST REVOLUTION AND THE FAMILY

Because the family system is shaped by the social and cultural environment of the society of which it is a part, no one should be surprised that the Chinese family system has undergone considerable change in recent decades.

The family was the most important social institution in traditional China. Economically, interdependence among family members and between different nuclear units of the large clan was a common phenomenon. Socially, clan membership greatly shaped the opportunities available to its members. Mobility and career decisions of the younger members were principally subjects for collective rather than individual decision and choice. Political and religious institutions overlapped to a great extent with the family system, particularly the clan, or *tsu*. In certain parts of China, mainly the south, where villages contained persons of the same lineal descent, the family constituted the totality of one's social environment. The consequent behavior of its members generally tended to feed back to the system, reinforcing the old values and stabilizing the traditional structure.[68]

In any society, the family is the only *legitimate* social group for the procreation of new members. Through interaction between the old and the young, new members acquire socially approved ways to solve problems and to manage tensions. The family is therefore the basic intermediate institution between the individual and the larger society. What seems to be significant about the traditional Chinese family is that the functional relationships between the family and other social institutions, notably the polity and the economy, have undergone tremendous changes in recent years. Under the Communist system, the priority of family obligations over obligations of the individual with respect to the state has been reversed, at least insofar as the ideal norm is concerned.

Changes in the family. Changes in familial relations from the traditional culture to the present must be understood in terms of the distinction between the nuclear family and the kinship clan (*tsu*), which may better be called a lineage system. Changes in the first are undoubtedly related to changes in the latter since both are related to the political and economic systems of the larger society. The distinction between the *tsu* and the smaller family group, or the co-residence group, has been a frequent source of confusion for those unfamiliar with the Chinese social structure.[69]

Although the literature on family change in mainland China is rather limited,[70]

---

[67] Christopher Howe, 'The Supply and Administration of Urban Housing in Mainland China: The Case of Shanghai,' *China Quarterly*, No. 33, January–March, 1968, pp. 73–97.

[68] Francis L. K. Hsu, 'Chinese Kinship and Chinese Behavior,' in Ho and Tang, eds., *China in Crisis*, 1: 579–608.

[69] Maurice Freedman, 'The Family in China, Past and Present,' *Pacific Affairs*, No. 34, Winter, 1961–62, pp. 323–26.

[70] Important studies of the Chinese family include C. K. Yang, *The Chinese Family in the Communist Revolution* (Cambridge, Mass.: Technology Press, 1959); Morton Fried, *The Fabric of Chinese Society* (New York: Praeger Publishers, 1959); Francis L. K. Hsu, 'Chinese Kinship and Chinese Behavior,' in Ho and Tang, eds., *China in Crisis*, 1: 579–608; Freedman, 'Family in China,' pp. 323–26.

some useful hypotheses have been proposed about changes in the Chinese family under the Communist regime. These can be briefly summarized:

(1) The current legal code on marriage and divorce was promulgated in 1950, with minor changes in 1955. The new marriage law has not instituted new concepts and regulations; rather, it is an affirmation of earlier drafts of the marriage code and subsequent revisions and clarifications, which began in the early twentieth century in the Ch'ing dynasty and under the Nationalists. One important change during the Nationalist regime separated the customary *li* from the legal provisions of marriage relations and thus paved the way for more clarification of the legality of familial responsibilities and individual rights.[71]

(2) Changes in the family system had already begun during the Nationalist regime. However, such changes had taken place only in coastal urban centers, where Western influence had made some impact, and among the educated rather than the working-class population. The Communist regime has been instrumental in bringing family change throughout the country and in enforcing the 1950 Marriage Code more seriously than previous codes had been enforced. The pace of change in the urban and the rural sectors of the society has not been the same, however. Available fragmentary information indicates that resistance to change was common during the 1950's, particularly in rural areas. The discrepancy between law and custom created confusion not only among the common people but also among some of the rural cadres. After successive campaigns, reports on family difficulties with respect to marriage and divorce law enforcement became infrequent during the 1960's, an indication that the routinization of the aftermath of change had taken place. Generally speaking, freedom of choice in marriage and freedom of divorce are both recognized. Communist sources imply that marriage based on ideological factors is common, but actual occurrences of it may be limited. Romanticism is discouraged.[72]

(3) The most visible change in the area of family life has been the elimination of bigamy and concubinage, which is both a direct result of the change of the economic status of women and a socialist policy.[73]

(4) The median age for marriage may have risen because of the pressure of urban-industrial expansion, greater mobility, the higher educational attainment of women, and the increase in the legal minimum age for marriage.

(5) Under the cross pressures of successful economic planning, improvement of maternal and child health, and faith in the ideological correctness of Communism, birth control campaigns began half-heartedly in the mid-1950's, were abandoned in May, 1958, during the Great Leap Forward, and reappeared, in modified form, in the 1960's. Nevertheless, public health measures and government criticism of early marriage, together with the declining importance of kinship relations, may all have contributed to a lower fertility rate in recent years.[74] A nation that puts so much emphasis on planned change is also likely to make planned parenthood part of its planning, even if it has to rationalize its efforts as a concern for maternal health and proper spacing.[75]

---

[71] William J. Goode, *World Revolution and Family Patterns* (New York: Free Press, 1963); and Yang, *Chinese Family in Communist Revolution.*

[72] Goode, *World Revolution and Family Patterns*; and Yang, *Chinese Family in Communist Revolution.*

[73] Goode, *World Revolution and Family Patterns.*

[74] Irene Taeuber and Leo A. Orleans, 'Mainland China,' International Conference on Family Planning Programs, *Geneva, 1965. Proceedings: Family Planning and Population Programs* (Chicago: University of Chicago Press, 1966), pp. 31–54.

[75] Goode, *World Revolution and Family Patterns*, pp. 291–95; Orleans *Professional Manpower, and Education*, pp. 60–61, 69–70; S. Chandrasekhar, *China's Population: Census and Vital Statistics* (Hong Kong: Hong Kong University Press, 1960), pp. 122–68.

(6) The declining importance of authority of family elders, which began at the conclusion of the imperial era, was a common phenomenon limited to only the urban population during the Nationalist regime. A concerted Communist effort has visibly reduced their authority.[76] The campaign against the aged is not so much an attempt to break down family authority as an effort to remodel citizens' attitudes. Until the Cultural Revolution, Communist leaders invested much hope in youth and instinctively distrusted the older generation, and the tactic of encouraging youth to denounce their elders was widely reported. Youthful disorders during the Cultural Revolution raised questions about the political maturity of young people, however, and a great many of them were sent to farms and factories and instructed to learn from peasants and workers.

(7) Divorce has generally been thought to be rare in traditional China. The importance of relatives and the subordinate position of the married woman to her parents-in-law made both marriage and divorce a family and clan affair, rather than an individual one. With the declining importance of the kinship structure, there is evidence that divorce has increased during the Communist period. Several authors have reported that divorces had already begun to increase during the Republic period.[77]

(8) Freedom of choice of marriage partners should, in theory, lead to greater romanticism and the manifest expression of love between the sexes. Communist educational themes, folk songs, and reading material, on the contrary, stress the importance of correct ideology as a basis for love and marriage, rather than romantic attachment. In actual practice, the importance of affection in binding a couple together may have increased under the Communists, as the family has lost most of its traditional functions to other institutions. At the same time, kinship pressures and economic considerations may have become less important motivations for marriage.

Francis Hsu describes the absence of manifest love themes, as reported by various observers, as characteristic of Chinese behavior. Moreover, one would not expect an emphasis on romantic love in a socialist society; it would be regarded as ideologically incorrect, for it disrupts work and weakens group morale.[78] At any rate, the elimination of concubinage, the freedom of choice in marriage and freedom of divorce, and the weakening of kinship ties have all provided a new institutional framework within which a new content of conjugal interaction is taking place within the Chinese family. Such change is undoubtedly more visible in urban centers than in rural areas.

Changes in the clan or lineage system. The tendency to stress the *tsu* as a basic social unit in traditional China is correct but exaggerated. For the individual, the clan provided social status and prestige. For the wider community, it was associated with geographic regions in China and specific dynastic periods.[79]

The regional importance of the clan system is exemplified in the widespread pattern of single clan villages in Southeastern China.[80] Clan rules became one of the

---

[76] Richard H. Solomon, 'Educational Themes in China's Changing Culture,' *China Quarterly*, No. 22, April–June, 1965, pp. 154–70; Lucy Jan Huang Hickrod and H. Hickrod, 'Communist Chinese and the American Subcultures,' *China Quarterly*, No. 22, April–June, 1965, pp. 171–80; Ezra Vogel, 'From Friendship to Comradeship: The Change in Personal Relations in Communist China,' *China Quarterly*, No. 21, January–March, 1965, pp. 46–60; Yang, *Chinese Family in Communist Revolution*; and Goode, *World Revolution and Family Patterns*.

[77] Goode, *World Revolution and Family Patterns*, p. 316.

[78] Hsu, 'Chinese Kinship and Chinese Behavior,' pp. 592–93, 600, 604; and Yang, *Chinese Family in Communist Revolution*.

[79] Hsiao, *Rural China*; and Hui-chen Wang Liu, *The Traditional Chinese Clan Rules* (Locust Valley, N.Y.: J. J. Augustin, 1959).

[80] Maurice Freedman, *Chinese Lineage and Society: Fukien and Kwangtung*, London School of Economics Monographs on Social Anthropology, No. 35, 1966.

most effective agents of social and even political control.[81] There was, paradoxically, a delicate balance between the family and state in regard to the loyalty of the individual. Filial piety was the core of all interpersonal ethics. Its binding power extended from the family to the state; Confucian precepts were used by powerful dynasties to assert control over members of clans and localized lineages.

Because the clan was the best *organizational weapon* for state control over the rural population, many other local social and welfare institutions, organized around a host of needs, came under the framework of the local clan organization. To this point, Freedman perceptively states:

> Given the nature of the capital market, given a legal system which offers little protection to business, given the tendency to rely on people with whom there is some preceding tie, we should expect that kinsmen would be associating with one another in economic affairs.[82]

The observation summarizes the functional relationships between the clan as a social institution and the wider society, including the business community. At the same time, the satisfactions derived from clan associations had become such stable parts of the traditional society that legal codes of business behavior, social welfare legislation, and other politicoeconomic developments, already occurring in Europe, had not developed in traditional Chinese society in spite of the fact that there had existed, as early as the beginning of Ming in 1368, a complex of interregional economic integration that was associated with clan organization.[83]

The Communist regime did not have to depend on the *tsu* to extend its political control over the population in vast rural areas. On the contrary, the leaders of the new regime wished to destroy the delicate balance of power between the state and the clan and to have absolute control over every citizen in the country without the interference of the family. The family has been stripped of its political function. Furthermore, the leaders in Peking were quite aware of the enormously important functions that the traditional clan system had so long performed. Thus, when the physical evidence of the clan organization was removed during the 1950's, the symbolic displays of kinship relations and every aspect of interpersonal relations also underwent drastic transformations.[84] By the 1960's, little was said in the press and other media about the clan and kinship aspects of Chinese society.

Chinese Communist leaders cannot possibly have totally transformed the basic personality structure of the people in China since 1949. This period could barely produce one generation of new citizens who have been inculcated with the socialistic value system. The new Chinese citizen has not grown up in a cultural or value vacuum. No matter how chaotic conditions were at the beginning of the Communist period or how consistently changes have been implemented, the young citizens of China have still had to interact with older generations and with their parents. Most older people are products of the traditional value system. It is inconceivable that kinship relations can have been totally abandoned. Nor could the majority of the younger generation have assimilated in so short a time all the new meanings and cultural symbols. Moreover, the lag would probably be greater in rural areas, where the separation between younger and older generations is less pronounced, than in the urban centers.

Perhaps all the social structural requisites for maintaining a strong and cohesive clan or lineage system have been removed in the new society. If so, then the important

---

[81] Hsiao, *Rural China*; and Liu, *Traditional Chinese Clan Rules*

[82] Freedman, 'Family in China,' p. 326.

[83] Ping-ti Ho, 'Salient Aspects of Chinese Heritage,' Ho and Tang, eds., *China in Crisis*, 1: 33–35; and Hsu, 'Chinese Kinship and Chinese Behavior,' pp. 588–89.

[84] Vogel, 'From Friendship to Comradeship,' pp. 46–60.

functions of the kinship system for the individual and other wider institutions have been tremendously reduced. With industrialization came the freedom of choice of marriage partners, freedom to dissolve marital ties, and egalitarianism in domestic life. There seems to be little possibility of reversing this trend, even if politics were not involved.

SELECTED BIBLIOGRAPHY

BARNETT, A. DOAK (with EZRA VOGEL). *Cadres, Bureaucracy and Political Power in Communist China*. New York: Columbia University Press, 1967.

CHOW, TSE-TUNG. *The May Fourth Movement: Intellectual Revolution in Modern China*. Cambridge: Harvard University Press, 1960.

LEWIS, JOHN WILSON. *Leadership in Communist China*. Ithaca. N.Y.: Cornell University Press, 1963.

ORLEANS, LEO A. *Professional Manpower and Education in Communist China*. Washington, D.C.: U.S. Government Printing Office, 1961.

SCHURMANN, H. FRANZ. *Ideology and Organization in Communist China*. Berkeley and Los Angeles: University of California Press, 1966.

TOWNSEND, JAMES. *Political Participation in Communist China*. Berkeley and Los Angeles: University of California Press, 1967.

YANG, C. K. *The Chinese Family in the Communist Revolution*. Cambridge, Mass.: The Technology Press, 1959.

27

EDUCATION

THEODORE HSI-EN CHEN

EDUCATIONAL PHILOSOPHY

The strategic role of education. The Chinese Communists call their regime a democratic dictatorship. According to Mao Tse-tung, the dictatorship is directed toward the 'enemy,' that is, those who oppose the Communist revolution, while democracy is applied to the 'people.' The methods of dictatorship are suppression and coercion, while the democratic methods used to win over the people are 'education and per‑ suasion.'[1] To be sure, there are different degrees of persuasion, which at times become quite coercive, but the Communists prefer, whenever possible, to hold force in abeyance while education and persuasion are given a chance to produce the desired results. Education, therefore, occupies a strategic role in both the ideology and the practice of the Chinese Communists.

From another point of view, education must be considered an essential part of the Communist program. That program goes far beyond economic and political changes. It demands no less than the establishment of a new society and calls for new customs, new habits, and new patterns of thought and behavior, even new emotions. It calls for a 'new type of man.' Changing man and the remolding of heart and mind are essentially the work of education.

A broad concept of education. Because education is considered to be synonymous with persuasion, it is far broader than what goes on in the schools. Indoctrination and propaganda are forms of persuasion and are inseparable from education. Whatever makes an impact on the hearts and minds of people performs an educational task. There is, therefore, no distinction between formal education and informal education. The important thing to note is that all agencies of education, indoctrination, and propaganda are centrally directed to pursue the same general goals and the same immediate objectives. The museum, the theatre, the storyteller, the cinema, the newspapers, the novel, the play, and all products of art and literature, as well as parades, demonstrations, and mass campaigns of all sorts, are all designed to serve the same purposes.

Thus, there is no hesitation to suspend regular school work in order to send students and faculty to the farm or factory for the ideological benefits to be obtained by partic‑ ipation in labor and production. There is no feeling of loss when classes are dis‑ missed to enable students to take part in the fertilizer (manure) collection campaign or in anti-imperialism parades and demonstrations. It is deemed as educational to engage in political tasks inside the schools or outside as it is to sit in the classroom or

---

[1] See Mao's 'Report to the Party Plenum,' *People's China* (Peking: Foreign Languages Press, July 1, 1950).

to study in the library. Education, it is maintained, goes on everywhere; its value is not to be judged merely in terms of academic learning or of knowledge alone. Indeed, there are times when the 'bourgeois' concept of academic learning must be set aside in favor of practical experience in 'revolutionary work' or character-molding in the process of the class struggle.

This is a revolutionary concept of education. Past traditions are not important. Scholarship 'divorced from politics' goes out of the window. Students are promoted on the basis of their ideological fervor and political activism, rather than book knowledge or what is valued in 'bourgeois society' as systematic scholarship. Education is a direct instrument of the revolution, and its success is judged according to its direct and immediate contributions to the revolutionary program.

SPECIFIC OBJECTIVES

The guidelines for education spell out the three P's, namely, politics, production, and Party control. First, politics is the soul of all educational activities in and out of the schools. Political subjects dominate the curriculum; political activities are expected of all students and teachers; even in literacy classes and technical institutes, political study occupies a central place. Second, production and labor must be an integral part of the school program.[2] Third, all education must be under the firm control of the Communist Party.

Promotion of literacy. As soon as the new regime was established, its leaders turned their attention to education. Three tasks were undertaken without delay. The first was the reduction of illiteracy. The success of indoctrination and propaganda depended in large part on a literate population. In order that they might be more easily reached by the extensive network of mass media carrying the messages of the state to the towns and villages, as well as the cities, the masses had to be taught to read posters, handbills, propaganda sheets, and even newspapers. The reduction of mass illiteracy became a task of paramount importance. The political purpose of education was not forgotten even in the literacy classes. Political indoctrination went hand in hand with reading and writing. There was no time for organized programs in the schools. Instruction was given in special classes conducted in temples, neighborhood meeting places, and bare rooms without any resemblance to a classroom. No standards were set, no length of course prescribed. The central aim was to bring as many people as possible out of complete illiteracy.

Training of cadres for nation-building. A second urgent task was to produce the cadres and personnel needed for the numerous phases of nation-building and social reconstruction. The new agricultural reform and industrial development projects required hundreds of thousands of trained workers and administrative personnel. In all these undertakings, the Communists wished to place in responsible supervisory positions specially trained cadres who were politically loyal and ideologically motivated. The ordinary schools could not provide them. New agencies, in the form of short-term institutions and training classes, had to be created.

Ideological remolding. Third, ideological remolding aimed to change ideas, attitudes, and loyalties and to establish patterns of emotionally motivated behavior befitting the valiant warriors of the proletarian revolution. The entire population had to be remolded, but a major target of ideological remolding was the intellectuals, who were (and still are) distrusted as products of 'the old society' and condemned as transmitters of 'bourgeois ideology.' What was attacked as bourgeois ideology consisted of such ideas and attitudes as 'individualism,' 'liberalism,' aloofness from politics, aversion to the all-important class struggle, lack of class consciousness, and pro-

---

[2] See Lu Tingi, 'Education Must Be Combined with Productive Labor,' *Peking Review*, September 9, 1958, pp. 5-12.

Americanism. The intellectuals were publicly denounced and required to make public confessions of their guilt. They were pressured to practice 'criticism and self-criticism,' to examine their past, and to pinpoint their specific errors. It was hoped that through the process of 'thought reform' the intellectuals would be remolded and made fit to serve the new society.

Labor was believed to have a therapeutic value in ideological remolding. Many intellectuals, as well as capitalists and other doubtful elements, were sent to labor camps for 'reform through labor.' The Common Program of 1949[3] specifically provided that 'reactionary elements . . . shall be compelled to reform themselves through labor so as to become new men.' 'Labor service for reform' was performed in detention houses, in prisons, on farms, in mines and industries, and at other production enterprises.[4] Making 'new men' is certainly a process of education, and labor is considered a valuable vehicle for bringing it about.

THE SCHOOL SYSTEM

Under the broad concept of education described above, what happens outside the schools is often more important than class instruction in the schools. The role played by various agencies of propaganda and indoctrination at times overshadows the schools on the broad scene of 'persuasion' and the changing of people. The schools, however, still have a strategic role to play: the special task of reaching and remolding the young generation and providing a planned environment for learning.

It is difficult to describe the school 'system,' because there is no stable system that the Communists have found to be satisfactory. Old schools are being changed and new schools are added and dropped according to their usefulness in meeting what the Communists recognize as their tangible needs. Types of schools, length of schooling, the nature of the schools on various levels, and the relations between schools are subject to constant change.

The schools in existence at the beginning of the Communist regime were in their external features much like the American system. School age was supposed to be six, and the six-year elementary school was followed by the three-year junior middle school and the three-year senior middle school. Also on the secondary level were vocational schools and normal schools of junior and senior grades. Higher education consisted of the four-year college followed by postgraduate study in the university; there were also two-year institutes of various types on a level comparable to the American junior college. This system was condemned as the product of feudal and bourgeois society, and a new system was proposed in 1951, as shown in Chart 27–1.

The proposed system was not put into practice completely. Communist leaders seem not to have too much regard for system as such, nor do they hesitate to make changes as they see fit. Furthermore, they are guided by their immediate needs or ideological dogmas rather than long-range planning. In the early 1950's, higher education underwent significant changes under the tutelage of Soviet advisers, when 'Learn from the Soviet Union' was the slogan. Russian replaced English as the most important foreign language, Soviet theories dominated all studies, and the content of courses of study was reorganized along the lines of Soviet syllabuses and textbooks. Since the Sino-Soviet split, Soviet influence on Chinese education has declined, and English has been reinstated as the first foreign language.

---

[3] A statement of principles and major policies that served as the basic law of the land until the adoption of a Constitution in 1954.

[4] See 'Regulations Governing Labor Service for Reform,' promulgated by the Central Government in August, 1954. Translated text in Theodore H. E. Chen, *The Chinese Communist Regime: Documents and Commentary* (New York: Frederick A. Praeger, 1967), pp. 299–311.

Chart 27-1—The School System of the People's Republic of China, 1951

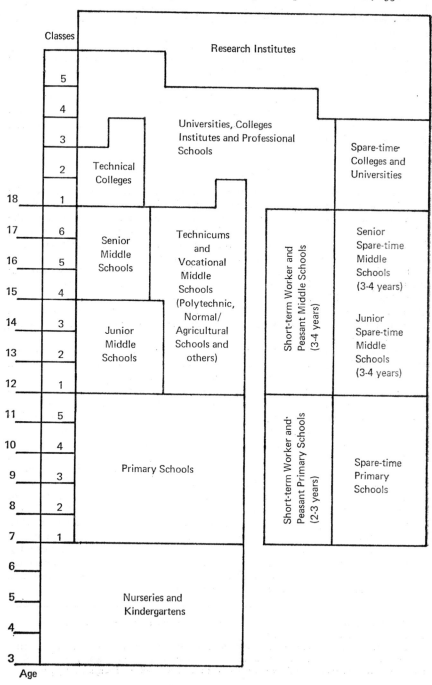

Take as another example the length of courses of study. The trend of Communist thinking is to shorten the period of schooling. The 1951 system reduced elementary education from six to five years. It was argued at the time that the lengthened course of six years was a deliberate scheme of bourgeois society to prevent the broad masses from getting a complete elementary education, because the longer course discouraged many and prevented them from gaining further education. It did not prove easy, however, to effect the change. After two years, the government issued an order to postpone the five-year school plan on account of 'inadequate preparation of teachers and teaching materials.'

The idea of shortening the period of schooling, however, continues to appeal to the Communist leaders. Proposals have been made to reintroduce five-year elementary education and to reduce the length of secondary education. The most recent development was a directive from Mao Tse-tung in the heat of the Cultural Revolution ordering that 'the period of schooling should be shortened.'[5] In compliance with the directive, proposals have been made to reduce secondary education to four years, with two levels of two years each, and higher education to two or three years.

Private education has disappeared. All education is controlled by the state and the Party; administration is highly centralized. The thirteen 'Christian Colleges,' established and supported before 1949 by mission boards and the interdenominational Protestant Board of Trustees in New York, were taken over by the state and merged into state-supported and state-controlled universities. Yenching University, for example, has become a campus of the enlarged Peking University.

New schools. Even with modifications, the schools were considered inadequate for the new needs. New schools were devised to achieve the desired objectives. Mention has been made of various short-term institutes established to produce trained personnel for different fields of work. The fields were narrowly and specifically defined, with each program serving a specific purpose. For example, there were specific institutes to produce workers and administrative personnel for newly established industries and the various government offices. There were short-term institutes to train cadres for the enforcement of the Agrarian Law, others to supervise the implementation of the Marriage Law, and still others to publicize the Electoral Law and insure its proper enforcement.

Special schools were established for the benefit of workers and peasants. In the early years of the regime, the worker-peasant short-term middle school combined the idea of abbreviated courses of study with that of education for the proletariat. Academically, the requirements for admission were flexible; ideologically, only workers, peasants, and worker-peasant cadres—in other words, the proletariat—were eligible for admission. Workers and peasants between eighteen and thirty years of age were admitted for a 'short-term' course, which tried to condense six years of secondary education into three years. It was argued that experience in production and 'revolutionary work' had given such learners a degree of maturity making possible the completion of study in a much shorter period of time. Many were admitted after barely emerging from illiteracy, but after three years of accelerated education they were supposed to qualify as 'proletarian intellectuals' and to be ready for admission into higher institutions.

The worker-peasant short-term middle schools have now been abandoned. They are no longer needed. Since the Cultural Revolution, the education of workers, peasants, soldiers, and cadres has become the central objective of education, and a scholarly elite is attacked as 'bourgeois' and 'revisionist.' The entire school system is now supposed to take over what the earlier short-term schools tried to do. All higher institutions admit workers and peasants recommended by local authorities on the

---

[5] Article 10 of 'Decision of the Central Committee of Chinese Communist Party Concerning the Great Proletarian Cultural Revolution,' *Peking Review*, Vol. 9, No. 33, August 12, 1966.

basis of their production record and political zeal. Academic prerequisites have been abolished. Formal secondary education is no longer necessary for admission into higher education.

To provide higher education for 'proletarian intellectuals,' the Chinese People's University was established in Peking in 1950 as a model of the 'new-type university,' recruiting students from among workers and worker-peasant cadres with 'advanced revolutionary experience.' Based on the proletarian ideology, it had a faculty versed in Marxism-Leninism and a curriculum of two- or three-year programs in trade, agricultural cooperatives, factory management, economic planning, foreign affairs, and the Russian language. At its early stage, Soviet advisers occupied key positions and Soviet theories dominated the educational program. Again, academic prerequisites were of little importance; the most important requirements for admission were worker-peasant class origin and a good record in production or 'revolutionary work.'

Spare-time schools. Among other new schools were 'colleges' for the ideological remolding of 'old-time intellectuals' and of industrialists and capitalists to convince them of the superiority of socialism over capitalism. The most radical innovation is what is known as spare-time education. It provides schools or classes for adults, especially workers and peasants, in their 'spare time' after work. Workers are asked to join the classes after work, peasants to attend 'winter schools' in their off season, even crew members of steamers are organized for study in their spare time. In all cases, study is not to interfere with work.

Spare-time education has proved a useful device in adult education and a major method of combating illiteracy. But spare-time education has gone beyond the level of rudimentary education and has provided technical training on 'secondary' and 'higher' levels. In line with the general policy of breaking away from 'bourgeois education' and ignoring what bourgeois education upholds as academic standards, the terms 'elementary,' 'secondary,' and 'higher' are used loosely to indicate relative levels of learning without any clear definition of meaning in terms of content or degree of mastery. It seems that any education beyond the rudimentary is classified as 'secondary' and any program that goes beyond basic training in any vocational or technical field is identified as 'higher education.' In all cases, political education is the core of the program.

According to official statistics, in 1958 there were 26,000,000 spare-time middle schools, 588,000 spare-time technical middle schools, and 150,000 institutes of higher learning.[6] Even making allowance for the inaccuracy of statistical reports and confusion of terms, one must be duly impressed with the vast growth of this phase of the educational program.

The work-study approach. There are three major types of schools: full-time schools, work-study schools, and spare-time schools. In all three types, labor is an integral part of the school program. Numerically, the full-time schools are being overshadowed by the other two types. Official policy tends toward the work-study schools, which will become the major type of the future; consequently, schools devoting full time to study will become less and less important. The work-study plan has been adopted in the lower schools as well as in colleges and universities. The development of work-study schools has received impetus from the policy of combining education with production. The work-study combination takes different forms. Work may be done on a farm, in a factory, or in a business enterprise. Labor and production are the major themes. Work and study may be scheduled on alternate days or alternate weeks or at longer intervals. Theoretically, study is to be integrated with work so that it may help solve the problems encountered in work. Education tends to be utilitarian; in line with the Communist cliché of unity of theory and action, knowledge and skills

---

[6] *Ten Great Years* (Peking: Foreign Languages Press, 1960), p. 198.

acquired in study are valuable to the extent that they are applicable to production or 'the revolutionary struggle.' One might say that utilitarianism and the domination of politics are the chief characteristics of Chinese Communist education.

School texts. The major themes of labor, production, and politics are evident in the content of the textbooks used in the lower grades as well as on the upper levels. For example, Book One of a set of primary school readers published shortly after the establishment of the new regime by the Lien Ho Publishing Company in Shanghai contains five lessons on labor and the use of the hands and six lessons on farming and vegetable planting. These themes are carried through the other books. In Book One, we find, 'I have hands, you have hands, everybody has hands, everybody should use hands.' Book Three says: 'From the glowing east rises the sun; from China comes Mao Tse-tung; he leads us in production; with increased production, there is food and clothing and no poverty.'

There are stories of labor heroes who excel in production, and many lessons are devoted to the praise of Mao Tse-tung and stories of his exemplary childhood. The army is glorified, while landlords, Chiang Kai-shek, and American imperialism are objects of derision. One book tells the story of a rich landlord who does no work all day long but enjoys good food, good clothing, and good housing and becomes fat. On a hot day he lies on a reclining chair and asks a servant to fan him. 'Look,' he says, 'My perspiration has all disappeared.' 'Yes,' answers the servant, 'It has come to my body.'

Exaltation of the Communist Party goes with the praise of Mao Tse-tung. Ideological concepts are introduced early to accompany political indoctrination. Science and nature study—birds, bugs, flowers, the sun, the wind, and so forth—are given attention because the Marxist ideology is supposed to be scientific. Evolution is considered essential; a lesson titled 'Our Ancestor' tells in an oversimplified manner how man evolved from the ape. Superstition is attacked as unscientific; so is 'belief in the spirit.'

In another series of readers, published by the Kai Ming Company in Shanghai, one finds the following description of the United States: 'The skyscrapers of New York belong to the rich. . . . The workmen who build them live in the slum district. . . . The rich in America own their own automobiles and yachts and travel in chartered trains and planes. . . . America is a paradise for the rich and hell for the poor.'

Education and the proletarian revolution. The Communist revolution is a class revolution. A major aim of political education is to 'heighten and sharpen' class consciousness and to foster a firm determination to carry on the class struggle. Much is said about 'class education.' Its purpose is to use various means to remind old and young that class enemies continue to exist and plot against the revolution, that it behooves all good revolutionaries to be alert and ever ready to wage a relentless war against them. It is the aim of class education to impart the knowledge and develop the emotions that make valiant warriors of the class struggle.

Education also contributes directly to a change in the class structure of Chinese society. By means of a positive program of worker-peasant education, it raises the position of the proletarian elements and qualifies them for leading positions in society. Communist leaders point with pride to the fact that the percentage of students of worker-peasant class origin in the school population has steadily increased in the last two decades. Before the Cultural Revolution (1966) they reported that children of worker-peasant origin constituted 90 per cent of the total enrollment in the primary schools and kindergarten, 77 per cent in secondary schools, and more than 50 per cent in institutions of higher learning. Inasmuch as worker-peasant students are given priority in opportunities for further education, the percentage is likely to be even higher in the years to come.

Hand in hand with the policy of producing a large number of 'proletarian intellectuals' is the policy of requiring the 'old-type intellectuals' to engage in labor and production. Teachers, professors, scientists, and engineers, as well as capitalists, industrialists, and government personnel are required to spend time on the farms, and in the mines and factories to become a part of the laboring class. Intellectuals and white-collar workers, as well as the landlords and urban bourgeoisie, have been stripped of their former prestige and social status. The rich are condemned and despised. The poor peasants who constitute the backbone of the peasants associations and the workers who sit in government councils and congresses as 'deputies' have been accorded a new status of political and social importance. Peasants and workers with good production records have been invited to teach and lecture in technical institutes and 'higher institutions.' Education has, indeed, played a direct role in uprooting the old class structure and opening the way for new social values.

ACHIEVEMENTS AND PROBLEMS

Programs and numbers. The expansion of educational facilities under the Communist regime is truly impressive. The increase in the types of educational programs offered and the extension of educational opportunity to workers and peasants inevitably result in more education for more people. The expansion is especially significant in the lower schools and for the adult population.

Increase in literacy. Much progress has been made in teaching more people to read and write, though it is not easy to assess the degree of progress. Statistical data on the increase of literacy are indicative only in a general way, because they report short-term progress of crash programs in selected small areas and do not tell the story for the whole country or even for large areas of the country. Moreover, even in selected areas with crash programs, what is optimistically reported as a high percentage of 'basic literacy' often proves to be inaccurate information, partly because it is easy for people who have barely attained 'basic literacy' to slide back into illiteracy. One of the basic reasons for this is the scarcity of reading material for the 'basically literate.'

Nevertheless, it seems reasonable to conclude that illiteracy has been significantly reduced. Even more significant is the increase of political consciousness among the masses. Through its pervasive 'propaganda network,' the Party and state keep up a continuous flow of information and hortatory messages, which reach the little towns and villages and produce an impact on far more people than can be brought into literacy classes. The radio, the stage, the neighborhood 'study groups,' the organized parades and demonstrations, as well as centrally directed 'mass campaigns' for the destruction of harmful insects, for stepped-up drives to fulfil production quotas, and the like, subject the entire population to a ceaseless barrage of information concerning the domestic and foreign issues of the day. True, the people hear and read only what the Party and state want them to know and think about. Nevertheless, numerous illiterate and barely literate people who used to take no interest at all in affairs outside their immediate surroundings are today aware of happenings in remote areas and take part in slogan-shouting and mass meetings that extend their interests far beyond their little village or town. They hear about American imperialism, Soviet revisionism, Albania, Cuba, Czechoslovakia, and the production campaigns and political struggles on the domestic scene.

Enrollment in the regular schools has also leaped forward. Official statistics are not altogether reliable, but according to available figures, enrollment in institutions of higher learning stood at 117,000 in 1950–51 and jumped to 820,000 in 1962–63, and graduates of institutions of higher learning soared from 18,000 in 1950–51 to 200,000 in 1962–63.[7] A preponderance of students in institutions of higher learning are enrolled in engineering and the applied sciences, such as medicine and agriculture.[8]

---

[7] Chu-yuan Cheng, *Scientific and Engineering Manpower in Communist China, 1949–1963* (Washington, D.C.: National Science Foundation, 1965), pp. 74, 78.

[8] *Ibid.*, p. 38.

No lockstep system. Educational theorists who criticize the formality and inflexibility of traditional education would be delighted with the boldness with which Chinese Communist education experiments with new methods and institutional forms. Past traditions constitute no stumbling block. Education serves specific and immediate needs and is quickly changed if it does not produce results. There is no room for 'dead knowledge.' According to Maoist ideology, knowledge must result in action and be tested in action. Education must produce changes in behavior, and the most important behavior changes, in the Communist view, are those expressed in production, in political action, and in ideological convictions.

There is no gap between school and society. The aims of the school are the same as those of the state and society. Education is no longer the privilege of the few or a haven for the leisure class or those who shun labor. The traditional dichotomy between mental and physical labor is being abolished.

Question of standards. During the Cultural Revolution, education on the Chinese mainland fell into disarray. Long before the turmoil of 1966–68, however, serious shortcomings of Chinese Communist education was already recognizable. At the very time when the popularization of education won admiration at home and abroad, educators within the country were expressing grave concern over the quality of education. To begin with, Communist policy was more concerned with quantitative than qualitative growth. The immediate aim was to educate the proletariat; in view of the high percentage of illiteracy among the proletariat, it was more important to bring some education to the many than to give more or better education to the few. The higher levels of education thus tended to be neglected.

At the same time, the new regime was in a hurry to produce trained personnel for immediate use and had to depend on short cuts, such as abbreviated courses of study and short-term institutes. Even in the regular colleges and universities, there was pressure to provide shortened sources of study. Moreover, all institutions of higher learning were ordered to admit a minimum quota of students of worker-peasant origin, most of whom had extremely inadequate academic preparation. The worker-peasant students had leaped from illiteracy to 'secondary' and 'higher' education; while their enrollment in higher institutions was a source of ideological satisfaction to the Communists, who took pride in the progress of the class revolution in education, the worker-peasant students merely accentuated the trend of subordinating academic achievement to such nonacademic qualifications as class origin, production record, and ideological fervor.

A major source of difficulty is the lack of competent teachers. Even if all available teachers were fully utilized, there would not be enough for the expanding needs of a vast educational program. But the Communists distrust many teachers as 'old-time intellectuals' unable to shake off their 'bourgeois ideology.' They prefer to fill teaching positions with trusted cadres and those who are ideologically above suspicion. The trouble is that many of the trusted cadres have not had much schooling themselves; nevertheless, they are placed in key positions or given supervisory authority over teachers. Backed by the power of the Communist Party, the supervisory cadres regard themselves as ideologically superior to the better-educated teachers. They berate the teachers for their ideological inadequacy; they demand the 'thought reform' of teachers and pass judgment on their ideological progress. Teachers have been dismissed on the basis of unfavorable reports of cadres. Low salaries and the humiliation inflicted by domineering cadres must have discouraged many from becoming teachers. Thus, the teacher shortage presents a very acute problem.

In 1956, in response to complaints, the Ministry of Education announced a 32.88 per cent raise of salaries of elementary school teachers. According to the newly adjusted salary scale, the minimum monthly salary for elementary school teachers should be about 20 yüan, which would be about $8.40 in U.S. currency. Actually, some teachers got as little as 4 yüan a month, and 10 yüan was not considered unusual.[9] Salaries for secondary school teachers in the cities are considered high; they are about 80–90 yüan a month.

An official publication of the Ministry of Education reported in 1951 that more than half of the elementary school teachers in North China had had no more than elementary education themselves, and some were unable to read anything more advanced than the third reader.[10] A later report in the same publication stated that in Honan province, 83.4 per cent of the elementary school teachers had had no more than elementary education, and 89.2 per cent of the junior middle school teachers had not gone beyond the junior middle school.[11]

The situation is even worse in the spare-time schools, the work-study schools, and the new schools established by communes and factories, where the slogan is: 'Any capable person can be a teacher.' Teachers for the spare-time schools are usually drawn from the ranks of 'advanced workers and peasants.' In one county, it was found that, among 428 teachers of spare-time schools, fifteen were actually illiterate and 239 could only be considered semiliterate.[12]

Ideological problems. Were the decline of standards due mainly to the expansion of education and the temporary need for sacrificing quality for the sake of quantity in a land where widespread illiteracy was a major problem, it would not be a matter of grave concern. More attention could be paid to the upper levels of education after a broad foundation had been firmly laid, and such shortcomings as teacher shortage could be overcome in due time. Unfortunately, many of the difficulties of Chinese Communist education are rooted in ideology. The Communists are unwilling to admit that their program of mass education has resulted in a decline of educational standards. They refuse to accept the traditional concept of educational standards; they have no patience with 'systematic knowledge' that cannot be immediately applied; they scorn and condemn 'bourgeois scholarship.' Educators who are concerned about the quality of education are, therefore, afraid to speak out for fear of being attacked as 'bourgeois intellectuals.'

Distrust of intellectuals is another ideological obsession that has had a negative effect on the educational program. The downgrading of China's intellectuals is not merely a part of a policy to bridge the gap between the intellectuals and the masses; it springs from the Communist distrust of intellectuals as products of bourgeois education and transmitters of 'bourgeois ideology.' Even in the early years of the Sino-Japanese war, when the Communists declared that it was necessary to attract the intellectual elements before organizing the masses, they stressed in the same breath that the intellectuals must be reformed in order to correct their weaknesses.[13]

The distrust of intellectuals, which still exists in Communist thinking today, has led to a rejection of what the intellectuals value as scholarship and academic achievement. As long as that attitude remains, the neglect of quality will continue to be an unsolved problem in Communist education.

Realizing the need of science and technology to help carry out the five-year plans, the Communists launched a campaign to 'storm the gates of science.' Scientists were encouraged to submit plans for 'socialist construction.' But here again Communist ideology has obstructed the progress of what might have been a highly promising

[9] See Wu Yen-yin's speech on teachers' salaries, in *Kuang Ming Jih Pao* (*Enlightenment Daily*), August 16, 1956.

[10] Tseng Fei, 'I-nien lai Hsiao-hsüeh Chiao-shih chih Hsüeh-hsi Kai-kuang (The Year's Review of the Learning of Elementary Teachers), *Jen-min Chiao-yü* (*People's Education*), Peking: Jen-min Chiao-yü-she, September, 1951.

[11] *Jen-min Chiao-yü*, July 1, 1958, p. 37.

[12] *Jen-min Chiao-yü*, January 5, 1953, p. 19.

[13] Theodore H. E. Chen, *Thought Reform of the Chinese Intellectuals* (Hong Kong: University of Hong Kong Press, 1960), pp. 3–5.

effort to promote science. The ideologists put forth the interesting theory that one did not have to be a scholar in order to be a scientist. The official organ of the Communist Party, *Jen-min Jih-pao*, editorialized (on May 22, 1958) that 'science is no mystery' and that great inventions of history had come from the working people and the oppressed classes rather than from the scholars. Proletarian thinking, therefore, must shatter the old 'superstition' that science is difficult.

Thus began a campaign to promote 'peasant-scientists' and 'worker-engineers,' persons who in their work had shown homespun ingenuity in improving crops or devising better tools, and who were now honored with the title of scientist. These worker-peasant 'scientists' had had little formal schooling, to say nothing of scientific training, but they were given appointments to lecture or do research in universities and technical institutes. Here is another example of the crippling effects of Communist ideology on educational advance.

Ineffective ameliorative measures. Communist leaders are not altogether unaware of the practical consequences of their policy. Their attention was called to students of engineering schools who were judged as unqualified by their teachers because they had not had the basic prerequisites in science and mathematics. They heard the warnings of scholars who deplored the deterioration of academic standards. They received reports from schools to the effect that political studies and political activities had left little time for systematic academic learning, and that the demand for students and teachers to engage in political 'revolutionary tasks' had left them physically exhausted and emotionally tense and, consequently, not in good condition for study.

The warnings were not entirely unheeded. Attempts were made at different times to provide more time in schools for academic study and to reduce the required participation in political activities in and out of the schools. Students on occasion were exhorted to pay more respect to teachers and scholars. There were times when it looked as if educators might be given a chance to have an effective voice in the educational program and to restore academic study to its rightful place.

Unfortunately, the ameliorative attempts were short-lived. They occurred in brief periods of relative liberalism, which were quickly terminated by a resurgence of ideological orthodoxy and consequent intellectual stagnation. A period of moderation in 1956–57 was followed by an anti-rightist campaign, and the relative relaxation of control in 1961–63 was followed by another swing that culminated in the harsh measures of the Cultural Revolution. Two decades of the Communist regime have been marked by alternate periods of relative liberalism and dogmatic rigidity, but the emergence of liberalism has always been brief and ephemeral, and hopeful signs of change have failed to lead to any change of long-range policy. Furthermore, since the onslaught of the Cultural Revolution, the appearance of liberalism on past occasions has been denounced as revisionism, threatening to overthrow the socialist revolution.

Politics above all. The Cultural Revolution produced important changes in education. It began with an attack on intellectuals and continued with a severe condemnation of the educational system. From the standpoint of the hard-line ideologists, education in the last two decades had failed to achieve the desired results. The intellectuals remained unreconstructed despite intensive ideological remolding and 'thought reform.' The masses learned to read and write, but they still adhered to old patterns of thought and behavior and did not accept socialism and collectivism with enthusiasm. Even the young people, products of the new schools supposedly dedicated to the proletarian revolution, were found to hold 'selfish' ambitions, to be addicted to bourgeois concepts of 'individualism,' and to resist the demand that all personal desires and interests be subordinated to the needs of the revolution and the Party and state. A complete overhaul of the educational system was therefore ordered.

A drastic step was taken when institutions of higher learning were ordered in June, 1966, to suspend their operations pending a thorough consideration of necessary reform measures. The closure extended to lower schools, so that revolutionary youth, relieved of schooling, could join roving bands of 'Red Guards' to 'make revolution.' After months of chaos and disruption, the government, in 1967, ordered the schools to reopen, if for no other reason than to take the riotous young people off the streets. But the schools were slow to reopen. Through 1967 and 1968, the lower schools gradually reopened, but with hesitancy and uncertainty in regard to program. The universities did not officially admit new classes until the latter part of 1970.

The schools that complied with the order to reopen did not operate on a normal schedule. The government directive frankly stated that, instead of roaming around in the streets, the young people should 'return to the schools to make revolution.' Many young people had begun to enjoy the freedom of roaming around as revolutionaries and did not care to return to the classroom. Teachers who had been targets of denunciation were afraid to confront the arrogant students, who claimed to be orthodox revolutionaries competent to decide on educational matters. Official regulations stipulated that ideological study should be the central concern of the reopened schools. For such study, teachers with a background of bourgeois education found themselves in a very shaky position.

The program of the reopened schools and universities follows the educational ideas of Mao Tse-tung, especially the various 'directives' he issued in the course of the Cultural Revolution. The basic guideline for 'revolutionary education' is provided in the now famous Directive of May 7, 1966, in which Mao said:

> While their [the students'] main task is to study, they should, in addition to their studies, learn other things, that is, industrial work, farming, and military affairs. They should criticize the bourgeoisie. The period of schooling should be shortened, education should be revolutionized, and the domination of our schools by bourgeois intellectuals should by no means be allowed to continue.

There is as yet no settled program for the schools and universities. Varied attempts are made to implement Mao's ideas. To shorten the period of schooling, elementary education is being reduced to five years or less, secondary education to two levels of two years each, and higher education to specialized courses of short duration, from a few months to a few years. Academic learning as such is de-emphasized. Labor, production on the agricultural or industrial front, and the study of 'military affairs' take up a large chunk of the students' time. At the same time, politics and ideology are 'in command,' and political education occupies a position of central importance in the curriculum and in school life in general.

The study of Mao's thought constitutes the core of political education. 'Criticizing the bourgeoisie,' or ideological struggle, is a regular and required activity. One therefore notes two trends of very different nature, from the standpoint of traditional academic education. On the one hand, there is an effort to resume the operation of the schools, but, on the other hand, a stronger emphasis on politics and labor inevitably reduces the importance of academic study. Moreover, the shortening of courses of study further dilutes the academic program.

The Communists, however, dismiss misgivings about the quality of education in China as bourgeois reactionary thinking. The slogan of the day is to eliminate bourgeois scholarship and to terminate the domination of education by bourgeois intellectuals. The concern of the teachers and scholars for academic standards is brushed aside as an expression of 'bourgeois ideology,' for the new revolutionary education has its own standards conceived not in terms of academic knowledge but in terms of ability in production and in the pursuit of revolutionary tasks.

Next in importance to political education is the practical training that increases the skills and knowledge designed to boost production. The utilitarian value of education is stressed. Liberal arts, the humanities, and the social sciences are relegated to an insignificant position. A 1968 Directive by Mao gave the following instructions on higher education.

It is still necessary to have universities; here I refer mainly to colleges of science and engineering. However, it is essential to shorten the length of schooling, revolutionize education, put proletarian politics in command and take the road of the Shanghai Machine Tools Plant in training technicians from among the workers. Students should be selected from among workers and peasants with practical experience, and they should return to production after a few years' study.

Engineering colleges now admit worker-peasant students with little background in formal technical education and graduate them in one, two, or three years. Medical courses have been reduced from five to three years, and 'barefoot doctors' are sent to rural areas as the new-style proletarian doctors after short training courses of even only a few months. The work-study program means that all students spend a part of their time in production. Since 1968, in the name of the 're-education of intellectuals,' millions of students, teachers, and graduates of secondary schools and universities have been sent to the countryside and to factories for long periods of working and living among the workers and peasants to be 're-educated,' not only by learning production techniques, but also by becoming politically and ideologically 'integrated with the masses.'

There is no doubt a strong trend of anti-intellectualism and anti-professionalism in Chinese Communist education today. Specific measures are adopted to prevent the rise of old-style academicians and professionals whose long years of education set them apart from the revolution and the masses. One of the most radical measures is the dispatch of worker-peasant-soldier 'Mao Tse-tung Thought Propaganda Teams' into the schools and universities to take a leading role in the operation and management of the educational institutions. These workers and peasants, backed by soldiers from the People's Liberation Army, also resident in the schools, are vested with authority to organize and supervise the teachers and students in 'political study' to make sure that the thought of Mao Tse-tung is given a prominent place in all studies and activities. Although they have had little schooling, these new representatives of the proletarian class now exercise a controlling voice in educational institutions. They lecture in the classrooms and vote on administrative policies. Needless to say, they are under the close direction of the Communist Party. Only thus, say the Communists, can they be sure that education will not again be under the dominant influence of the bourgeois intellectuals but will be governed solely by one overriding purpose—to serve the needs of the proletarian revolution led by the Communist Party.

SELECTED BIBLIOGRAPHY

ADAMS, RUTH, ed. *Contemporary China*. New York: Pantheon Books, 1966. Contributions by American scholars and others who have visited mainland China. Two chapters on education.

BAUM, RICHARD, and FREDERICK C. TEIWES. *Ssu-Ch'ing: The Socialist Education Movement of 1962–1966*. Berkeley and Los Angeles: University of California Press, 1968. Account of educational developments on the eve of the Cultural Revolution.

CHEN, THEODORE H. E. *Thought Reform of the Chinese Intellectuals*. Hong Kong: University of Hong Kong Press, 1960. A study of the Communist policy toward intellectuals and the status of intellectuals during the first decade of the regime.

CHENG, CHU-YUANG. *Scientific and Engineering Manpower in Communist China, 1949–1963*. Washington, D.C.: National Science Foundation, 1964. Training and employment of scientists and engineers; useful statistical data.

FRASER, STEWART, ed. *Chinese Communist Education: Records of the First Decade*. Nashville Tenn.,

Vanderbilt University Press, 1965. Collection of Communist writings on education, with an introduction by the editor.

GOLDMAN, MERLE. *Literary Dissent in Communist China*. Cambridge, Mass.: Harvard University Press, 1967. Story of the conflict between writers and the Communist regime, down to 1958.

HU, CHANG-TU. *Chinese Education Under Communism*. New York: Teachers College, Columbia University, 1962.

KIRBY, STUART E., ed. *Youth in China*. Hong Kong: Dragonfly Books, 1965. Articles on the political role of youth, their frustrations and problems.

KUO MO-JO, *et al. Culture and Education in New China*. Peking: Foreign Languages Press, n.d.

MU FU-SHENG. *The Wilting of the Hundred Flowers*. New York: Praeger Publishers, 1962. Account of tribulations of Chinese intellectuals under the Communist regime, by a refugee intellectual.

ORLEANS, LEO. *Professional Manpower and Education in Communist China*. Washington, D.C.: National Science Foundation, 1960. Survey of education and professional manpower; many statistical tables.

PRIESTLEY, K. E. *Education in China*. Hong Kong: Dragonfly Books, 1961. Brief sections on various levels of education and characteristics of Communist education.

TSANG, CHIU-SAM. *Society, Schools and Progress in China*. London: Pergamon Press, 1968. Over-all view of the school system, its objectives, and educational philosophy.

28

LANGUAGE AND LITERATURE UNDER COMMUNISM

S. H. CHEN

LANGUAGE

The two aspects of language reform. The age-old problem of the Chinese language may be stated in the most general terms as one of unity. It is a problem of all national languages to a greater or lesser degree and can often be left alone, to be solved by natural evolutionary processes. The problem of unity of the Chinese language is, however, much more complex. One aspect of the problem is the unification of the spoken language, which consists of a vast number of traditional dialects, each with its own pronunciation, vocabulary, and grammar. Another aspect, even more stubborn, is the adoption of a new script that can replace thousands of characters with a minimum of phonetic symbols, like an alphabet.

The twofold problem defies any simple solution. An alphabetic script with standard sound values for its symbols cannot prevail until there is a unified national spoken language. Meanwhile, the character script will have to maintain at least a semblance of unity of the national language in order to maintain written, if not spoken, communication. The most logical solution may seem to be to concentrate on the unification of the national spoken language, and this approach is theoretically plausible. But the current situation is complicated by immediate political and social considerations, by nationalism, and by Communist zeal.

While a new alphabetical phonetic script cannot be universally enforced before there is a unified national spoken language, a common spoken language cannot take hold until there is a phonetic script to record and analytically demonstrate the standard sounds for all to learn. Furthermore, while the advancement of the common spoken language has to contend with the stubborn habits of many dialects, to become 'common' it must succumb to some of the dialect elements. And while the alphabet script is eventually supposed to supersede the logographic characters, to the extent that the alphabet has been used its primary effect has been to help more people learn more characters, because the characters still constitute the index of literacy. Furthermore, the national cultural heritage has been deposited in millions of old documents written in the classical style and in ancient characters. Any reduction of them into phonetic script, or even into simplified characters, would impair their intelligibility. As the classics are kept alive by Communist government policy for national need as well as pride, they are taught from high school up, thus helping to perpetuate the old characters. As education spreads, classical phraseology enters the spoken language, complicates modern spoken Chinese grammar, and defies expression in alphabetical spelling.

Policy and program. The Communist Chinese Government has nevertheless attempted a totalistic program to deal with all the above problems. After five years of intensive study, planning, and debate, the program took shape after two national conferences in 1955. The first, the National Conference on Language Reform of October 15–23, was summoned by the Ministry of Education and the Committee on Language Reform and was attended by 207 representatives of all twenty-eight provinces, many municipalities, 'self-governing districts,' departments of the central government, military establishments, and civilian organizations. The second, held October 25–31 and known as the Scientific Conference on the Problems of Standardizing Modern Spoken Chinese, was sponsored by the National Academy of Sciences. It was attended by 122 members engaged in linguistic studies and language teaching from all over the country and by professionals in creative writing, translation, dramatic and operatic arts, radio broadcasting, news services, the publishing industry, and stenography, with Russian, Polish, Rumanian, and North Korean linguistic experts also participating.

Early in 1956, some forceful measures were promulgated by the highest governmental and intellectual authority. That winter, *Jen-min Jih-pao* published three documents with the State Council's sanction: the 'Scheme (*Fang-an*) of Simplified Characters' with three lists of standard forms on January 31; the State Council's 'Directions with Respect to the Promotion of *p'u-t'ung hua* (common spoken language)' on February 6; and the 'First Draft of the Scheme of Phonetic Spelling for the Chinese Language,' intended for public discussion, on February 12. The draft was not formally accepted until much later and after many debates in high official circles, for reasons I shall discuss later. It was finally approved with major revisions by the First National Congress of People's Representatives on February 11, 1958, as the officially adopted 'Scheme of Phonetic Spelling.'

The p'u-t'ung hua. A study of the essentials of these three documents and their known results may fairly represent the recent situation of the Chinese language on the mainland. First, the State Council's 'Directions' contain the over-all guiding principles and designate their general procedures. Central emphasis is on the *p'u-t'ung hua,* or common spoken language. This term officially superseded all earlier terms—*kuo yü, ta-chung yü, pai hua,* and *kuan hua,* which are literally translatable as, respectively, 'national language,' 'the masses' language,' 'vernacular' or 'plain colloquial,' and 'official language'—and represented the goal of earlier language reforms under several governments of the Republic. The establishment of the term *p'u-t'ung hua*[1] after much deliberation is significant for several reasons. Ideologically, it attempts to dissociate the new program from all earlier language reform movements. At the same time, the term shows the awareness of the need to accord some consideration to the languages of the minority races in China, since, fundamentally, the new movement involves only the language of the Han race. Hence the avoidance of the term *kuo yü* (national language). As for the other older terms, the Communists may have felt that *ta-chung yü* (the masses' language) was condescending or meaningless in Communist society; *pai hua* (vernacular, or plain colloquial) was too confined to a literary movement of the May Fourth period after World War I; and *kuan hua* (official language) was too pompous or 'feudalistic.' Thus, the 'Directions' of the State Council define the basis for the unification of the Chinese language in both speech and writing:

[1] Former research members who worked with the writer on the Current Chinese Language Project at the Center for Chinese Studies in Berkeley drew attention to the significance of this point: Professor Li Chi, in her *The Communist Term 'The Common Language' and Related Terms,* Studies in Chinese Communist Terminology Series No. 4, Part I (Berkeley and Los Angeles: University of California Press, 1957); and Dr. Paul L.-M. Serruys, *Survey of the Chinese Language Reform and Anti-Illiteracy Movement in Communist China,* No. 8 of the same series, 1962. I should also like to express appreciation to other staff members in the project, Mrs. Nora

The foundation for the unification of the Han language is already in existence. It is *p'u-t'ung hua*, which has as its standard pronunciation the Peking pronunciation, as its basic dialect the northern dialect, and as its grammatical model the exemplary literary works written in the modern colloquial. The principal method of achieving the complete unification of the Han language is to promote the use of *p'u-tung hua* in the cultural and educational systems and in all phases of the daily life of the people.[2]

To enhance the paramount importance of the *p'u-t'ung hua*, the Minister of Education, Chang Hsi-jo, in his report to the First National Conference on Language Reform, stressed that *p'u-t'ung* should be taken to mean the 'universality' (*p'u*) and 'common possession' (*t'ung*) of the language, not in the sense of 'ordinariness' or 'usual habits' that the term might otherwise connote.[3] Of course, *p'u-t'ung hua* is an ideal goal rather than an accomplished fact, but the 'Directions' have recognized a a none-too-pure Peking pronunciation as an acceptable norm of the *p'u-t'ung hua*, which would assimilate the most viable and potent modern literary and dialectal elements of the *pai-hua* literature produced since the May Fourth Movement in 1919. These literary works are by no means pure and uniform in their linguistic features, for they were produced by writers from very different dialectical backgrounds.

The Chinese Communists have also broadened the basis of the Peking pronunciation to the more widely spoken 'northern dialect.' A master plan recognizes Chinese dialects in eight main areas.[4] It includes the *hsi-nan kuan hua* (southwestern official speech), and the *hsia-chiang kuan hua* (the 'official speech of the lower Yangtze River region') within the 'northern dialect,' which the master plan claims is spoken by 387 million people, or more than 70 per cent of the Han population. Broadly speaking, similar linguistic features may justify such a comprehensive grouping, but the differences within the large group are often very great, and the effective unification of the language on this basis remains a tremendous task. The goal is not just minimal mutual intelligibility but a language with standard pronunciation, vocabulary, and grammar that serves as a 'common possession' for all communication in speech and—ideally, someday—in alphabetical writing.

The national dialectal survey. One of the impressive accomplishments of the government is the national dialectal survey of 1956–59 in 1,188 geographical localities in twenty-three provinces.[5] More specific studies of dialectal phonology and vocabulary in the eight main dialectal areas followed. Many useful manuals for the instruction of the Peking pronunciation by establishing general rules of correspondences with the dialects have been compiled.[6] Although the Peking dialect is the established standard, debates arise as to how far the dialects are to be 'Pekingized.' One segment of opinion, represented by the influential and active linguist Ni Hai-shu,[7] would disregard the

---

Wang and Dr. H. C. Chuang, for their assistance in locating material on both language and literature for this paper.

[2] In *Chung-kuo yü-wen* (*Chinese Language*) (Peking: Jen-min Chiao-yü Ch'u-pan-she), January, 1956, pp. 6–8.

[3] *P'u-t'ung-hua lun-chi* (*Collected Papers on the Communist Spoken Language*) (Peking: Wen-tzu Kai-ke Ch'u-pan-she, 1956), p. 46.

[4] *Hsien-tai Han-yü Kuei-fan Wen-t'i Hsüeh-shu Hui-i Wen-chien Hui-pien* (*Collected Documents of the Scientific Conference on the Problems of Modern Spoken Chinese*) (Peking: K'e-hsüeh Ch'u-pan-she, 1956), pp. 5–6.

[5] Records of the survey have been compiled by Yüan Chia-hua in *Ch'üan Kuo Han-yü Fang-yen Kai-yao* (*Essentials of Han Dialects of the Whole Nation*) (Peking: Wen-tzu Kai-ke Ch'u-pan-she, 1960).

[6] E.g., *The Han-yü Fang-yen Tzu-hui* (*A Pronouncing Dictionary of Han Dialects*) (Peking: Wen-tzu Kai-ke Ch'u-pan-she, 1962); and *Han-yü Fang-yen Tz'u-hui* (*A Wordbook of Han Dialects*) (Peking: Wen-tzu Kai-ke Ch'u-pan-she, 1964).

[7] *Hsien-tai Han-yü Kuei-fan Wen-t'i Hsüeh-shu Hui-yu Wen-chien Hui-pien*, pp. 228–29.

four Peking tonal distinctions, presumably to let the dialect speakers freely substitute their own. Though this extreme liberalization has not been put into effect, certain traditionally distinctive local features of the Peking dialect, such as the retroflex suffix *erh* and the neutral or 'lightened' tones in a large number of phrases, will probably be very much restricted in the *p'u-t'ung hua* in favor of general dialectal habits. While the 'entering tone,' characterized by *p*, *t*, and *k* endings, prevalent among many dialects but absent in the Peking dialect, is not admitted in the *p'u-t'ung hua*, the distinction between 'sharp' (*chien*) and 'round' (*t'uan*) initial consonants in specific syllables, which is not a Peking feature but characterizes many northern and southern dialects, will probably survive in the common language, at least as variant readings. Many dialectal expressions and neologisms, which have gained great popularity even among Peking dialect speakers, have been recommended for inclusion in the *p'u-t'ung hua* vocabulary, with a Peking pronunciation but with their original construction and meaning.

Ascendancy and evolution of p'u-t'ung hua. The Peking pronunciation, however modified or adulterated in practice, is being vigorously pushed; a relatively unified pronunciation of the language has been advanced and contributes to mutual intelligibility among the population. A Mandarin speaker can today communicate much more freely and widely in the country than a decade ago. But the relationship between *p'u-t'ung hua* and the dialects remains a dynamic and somewhat uneasy one. Chou En-lai, in his report to the People's Political Consultative Committee (PPCC) in 1958, had to reassure the nation: 'Our promotion of the *p'u-t'ung hua* aims at the removal of the barriers among the dialects but not at the suppression or destruction of the dialects.'[8] He emphatically declared that 'the dialects will stay for a long time.'[9] But in actual fact, as the expert Lin T'ao asserted earlier at the Scientific Conference on Problems of Standardization, 'the promotion of the *p'u-t'ung hua* will naturally reduce the use of the dialects. But the dialects themselves will still continuously develop, and in the process of development will continue to be used to produce new elements that suit the needs of life, so as to enrich the *p'u-t'ung hua*.'[10] This certainly seems to be happening. But the continuous process of enrichment, bringing forth successively new linguistic vagaries, is likely to complicate the task of standardization. A firm standard for a truly definitive common spoken language to serve as the basis for the total language reform, with alphabetic script as a goal, still seems remote.

Scheme of Simplified Characters. The measures of script reform since 1956, represented by both the Scheme of Simplified Characters and the Scheme of Phonetic Spelling, may seem to be designed to promote literacy, but in practice they appear mutually antagonistic. Previous regimes have also attacked the character script because it was both complex and difficult to learn. Since 1949, the revolutionary ideal has been to promote literacy by abolishing characters and substituting alphabetic writing. Yet the simplification of a relatively small percentage of characters is obviously a reformist rather than a revolutionary action and so needs explanation. At the First National Conference on Language Reform, which advocated the Scheme in 1955, Kuo Mo-jo, as head of the National Academy of Sciences, declared:

> For 4,000 years the characters have made very great contributions to Chinese culture and to the cultural life of the Chinese people. An absolutely major part of our extremely rich and treasurable cultural heritage has been preserved by records in the characters. Even today and for a long time to come, in our task of building socialism, we still have to depend on the characters as media for culture

---

[8] Chou En-lai, *Tang-ch'ien wen-tzu kai-ke ti jen-wu* (*The Task Confronting Us in Language and Script Reform*) (Peking: Jen-min Ch'u-pan-she, 1958), p. 6.

[9] *Ibid.*

[10] *Hsien-tai Han-yü Kuei-fan Wen-t'i Hsüeh-shu Hui-i Wen-chien Hui-pien*, p. 233.

and education and as means of communication in social life. The fact that the characters possess a brilliant, glorious history has been witnessed by all.[11]

His views were seconded by Minister of Culture Shen Yen-ping, but a language expert and high-ranking Party member, Wu Yü-chang, Chairman of the National Committee on Language Reform, added: 'The characters will be more widely used by the immense population as a means for reading and writing. There is no doubt of this.'[12] He stressed that portions of the characters were to be simplified to facilitate learning and use.

Character simplification and phonetic spelling. Confusion probably ensued as to whether phonetic spelling should be promoted under the circumstances and, if so, how the simplification of the characters and alphabetization should be related. According to the records,[13] some argued that the simplification of the characters was a wasteful, ineffectual half-way measure; they favored concentration on phonetic spelling of the language. But the opinion that prevailed was for rationalizing the concurrent adoption of both measures. It was said:

> The simplification of the characters, rather than hindering phonetic spelling, will by its success make people recognize through actual experience that the characters can and should be reformed. Because simplification cannot solve the basic problems, it will urge people to go a step further toward alphabetization. Moreover, the simplification of the characters and the reduction of their number will minimize some of the problems of the multifariousness of words for phonetic spelling and thus will not be useless.[14]

Such a statement placates the zealous advocates of alphabetization without fully resolving 'basic problems.' It reaffirms phonetic spelling as a goal and the simplification of the characters as the catalyst, playing a subsidiary role.

But in practice the roles have been definitely reversed. Premier Chou En-lai's report to the PPCC in January, 1958, announced that the simplification of the characters was to be a major effort, and phonetic spelling would have an ancillary role. To strengthen the position of the simplified characters, Chou had baited the 'rightist' opposition to the simplification of the characters during the Hundred Flowers movement of the preceding year:

> Because the simplification of the character benefits the great masses of our people, the rightists who are against the people would naturally be opposed to it. We who stand with the people must first of all make a positive decision about the work of simplifying the characters.

His conclusion made the position of the character script secure for any foreseeable future:

> There is one problem about which we all feel concerned. That is the problem of the future of the Chinese characters. Throughout our history, Chinese characters have attained great merits, which can never be obliterated. On this point, all our opinions are agreed. As for the future of the characters, will they last for myriads of years without change? Or will they change? . . . On these questions we shall be in no hurry to draw conclusions.[15]

---

[11] *Ti-yi-tz'u Ch'üan-kuo Wen-tzu Kai-ke Hui-i Wen-chien Hui-pien* (*Collected Documents of the First National Conference on the Reform of the Chinese Script*) (Peking: Wen-tzu Kai-ke Ch'u-pan-she, 1957), p. 3.

[12] *Ibid.*, pp. 11–12. [13] *Ibid.*, p. 12.

[14] Cheng Lin-hsi, *Han-tzu Kai-ke* (*The Reform of the Chinese Script*) (Shanghai: Chiao-yü Ch'u-pan-she, 1959), pp. 39–41.

[15] Chou, *Tang-ch'ien wen-tzu kai-ke ti jen-wu*, p. 12.

The eventual substitution of the Latin alphabet for the characters seems a very remote possibility, despite some ardent advocates. The Latin alphabet was first opposed as 'foreign.' In 1952, at the inauguration of the Research Committee on Script Reform, Mao Tse-tung's dictum was cited: The phonetic script 'should be national as to its form; the alphabet and its scheme should be designed on the basis of the Chinese characters.'[16] To appease nationalistic sentiments, Premier Chou En-lai, in his report to the PPCC in January, 1958, took pains to explain that the Latin alphabet should be regarded as an international possession. As for phonetic spelling, Chou emphasized:

> I must first of all make clear that the phonetic system will be one that serves as a system of notations to the pronunciation of the characters; it will also help promote the general adoption of a common spoken language. But it will definitely not be used as a phonetic script to replace the characters. The primary purpose of the phonetic system is to serve as notations to the pronunciation of the characters.[17]

Chou left open the question of a future change of the script within the formal structure of the characters themselves. The Latin alphabet was adopted at the First National Congress of People's Representatives in February, 1958.

Reform of the Chinese script. Thus, from early 1958, Chinese language policy began to face up to the problem of regaining stability in questions of script. Certain new features, which looked experimental and sometimes confusing, were to be better regulated and made permanent after correction. A number of simplified characters would stay, and an occasional unfamiliar character would also be printed in Latin letters (in accordance with the Phonetic Spelling Scheme) in parenthesis or subscripts to indicate the correct Peking pronunciation.

The following years saw the stabilization of the relative positions of the two schemes. According to a public announcement in 1963,[18] first-grade textbooks use characters in the first volume, followed by a phonetic notation. Those in the second volume are only partially so accompanied. Thus, literacy requires a knowledge of the characters, while the phonetic spelling serves as an aid. It was reported that phonetic spelling not only helped the children learn the correct Peking pronunciation, but also speeded their learning of the characters, including, of course, an appropriate number of the simplified ones.[19]

The two schemes are essentially tabulations, with appended sets of working rules. The most up-to-date guide to the simplified characters is the second edition of *Chien-hua-tzu Tsung-piao (Complete Tabulations of Simplified Characters)*, of which 5,109,000 copies were issued in 1965. The Scheme for Phonetic Spelling consists of three tables, listing the twenty-six letters of the Latin alphabet, which are arranged into twenty-one initials in another table and thirty-five finals in a third, to represent the basic phonetic elements of the *p'u-t'ung hua*, with diacritical marks to indicate the four Peking tones. Since its official approval in 1957, millions of copies of the Scheme for Phonetic Spelling have been circulated.

The total number of Chinese characters varies according to different dictionaries[20]

---

[16] Mao, cited by Ma Hsü-lun. See *Chung-kuo Wen-tzu P'in-yin-hua Wen-t'i (Problems of Phonetic Spelling of Chinese Characters)* (Shanghai: Chung-hua Shu-tien, 1954), p. 3.

[17] Chou, *Tang-ch'ien wen-tzu kai-ke ti jen-wu*, pp. 6–7.

[18] *Kuang-ming Jih-pao*, April 17, 1963.

[19] *Kuang-ming Jih-pao*, April 19, 1964.

[20] The famed *K'ang-hsi Dictionary*, completed in 1716, lists 47,035 characters. The *Great Chung-hua Dictionary*, published in 1915, contains 44,908. The *Great Chung-wen Lexicon*, published in Taiwan in 1962, raises the number to 49,999. There are naturally a large number of obsolete, rarely used characters and unusual variants in these works.

but usually exceeds 40,000. Optimum literacy requires a knowledge of some 8,000 to 10,000 characters. The new standard *Hsin-hua Dictionary*, designed for adequate practical usage, which was published in 1962, contains about 8,000 characters, of which about 2,000 have been simplified in accordance with the scheme. The simplifying process, however, by no means involves entirely new forms. In fact, half of the work was to select and regularize 'vulgar' or shorthand forms that had accumulated over the centuries in account books, pawnshop notes, medical prescriptions, crude prints of old fiction, and theatrical librettos. A number of them are revivals of archaic characters with fewer strokes than later versions; others had been stylistically simplified by the calligraphic 'running hand.' An inventory of most such 'vulgar' characters had been made under the Nationalists.[21]

The *Complete Tabulations of the Simplified Characters* of 1965 contains a large number of these familiar abbreviated forms but also includes new ones, which are formed generally according to three principles:[22] (1) adoption of a simple character to substitute for another or for several homophones; (2) reduction of a complex character to the minimum of its basic components; (3) the use of a minimal component in combination with other simple elements to create composite derivatives. But while the *Complete Tabulations* aims at legitimizing and producing a large number of simplified characters, to accomplish its normative role it must at the same time establish certain rules. Its first table contains 352 simplified characters whose use is prohibited for composite derivatives. These are strictly independent characters, which have been recently or traditionally simplified. The second table comprises 132 independent simplified characters that may be used as basic components of composite derivatives and fourteen graphs to be used only as basic components but not as independent characters. The third table gives 1,754 simplified characters as legitimate composite derivatives. The *Complete Tabulations* is laden with footnotes to indicate cases where the original complicated character should be retained because the new homophones or homographs may cause confusion in actual usage. The traditional inventory of characters is therefore not so much reduced as expanded.

The *Complete Tabulations* was issued to stabilize the Chinese script. Exhortations to simplify characters had produced a flood of new forms that would hopelessly disrupt communication if the trend were not reversed.[23] For example, the homophones *wu hui*, a 'dance party,' appeared in simplified forms that meant a 'noon party'; and the simplified forms for *fan ho*, 'food box,' were confused with 'opposition to unity.' Serious complaints came from the mail and telegraph services, For example, a place named Lingling might be addressed 'oo,' a double zero.

Despite the above difficulties, the simplified characters are undoubtedly easier for children and adults to learn. The initial literacy target set for workers is 2,000 characters, and for peasants 1,500.[24] One statistical study by Chin Ming-sheng[25] shows

---

[21] Liu Fu, *Sung-Yüan I-lai Su-tzu P'u* (*Tables of Vulgar Characters Since Sung and Yüan Dynasties*) (Peiping: Academia Sinica, 1930). In 1932, the Nationalist government began to order the adoption of *Chien-t'i Tzu-p'u* (*Tables of Abbreviated Characters*), based on the recommendations of Professors Liu Fu and Ch'ien Hsüan-t'ung. But the order was withdrawn in 1935 after only the first table of 324 simplified characters had been issued.

[22] For more detailed discussion, see Wei Ch'ueh, 'Brief Discussion of the Work of Simplification,' *Han-tzu Chien-hua Wen-t'i* (*Problems of Simplified Chinese Characters*) (Shanghai: Chung-hua Shu-tien, 1956), pp. 8–9; and Ch'en Kuang-yao, *Chien-hua Han-tzu Tzu-t'i Shuo-ming* (*An Explanation of the Forms of Simplified Characters*) (Shanghai: Chung-hua Shu-tien, 1956), p. 5.

[23] Concern about the problem was expressed, for example, in *JMJP*, November 17, 1962.

[24] Wei Ch'ueh, 'Anti-illiteracy Meeting in Pingyüan District, Shantung,' *Wen-tzu Kai-ke* (*Language Reform*), No. 20, 1959, pp. 1–3.

[25] China's statistics are contained in Chung-kuo Yü-wen Tsa-chih She, ed., *Han-tzu Chien-hua Wen-t'i* (*Problems of Simplified Chinese Characters*) (Shanghai, 1956), pp. 56–57.

that 335, or about 22 per cent, of the 1,500 'most frequently used characters' designated by the Ministry of Education have been simplified. Nevertheless, people must still master both the traditional characters and the original forms of simplified characters as alternate forms. Reprints of classical texts would not use simplified characters, according to a 1955 PPCC resolution. Although practice was inconsistent and the debate continued, a number of important scholars continued to back the resolution until 1962. Curiously, until 1967 Chairman Mao's *Selected Works*, which every educated Chinese is supposed to read, was printed without simplified characters, even during the years when the Scheme of Simplification was in full force. Perhaps they are considered classics, for 'ching tien' ('canonical tomes') is the term used for them. Alternatively, the need for frequent printings in large quantities may not have permitted resetting with simplified characters. Although there are no simplified characters in the de luxe publications of Mao's poetry, the popular *Mao Tse-tung Reader* does contain them.

The alphabet and the phonetic system. The Latin alphabet that was adopted for Chinese phonetic spelling in February, 1958, first of all has the pragmatic virtue, Chou En-lai pointed out, 'of not being so easily forgotten' as any new syllabary, even if the latter were derived from Chinese characters. The Latin letters are familiar to most Chinese of even minimal literacy through technology and science as well as the learning of European languages. Under the Chinese Phonetic Spelling system (PS) the twenty-six letters are maintained in their usual order. All except a few function with sound values similar to those in the *Gwoyeu Romatzyh* (GR) or national romanization system, which has been used in a number of leading American and European universities in teaching modern Chinese.[26]

The PS, in its preference for single-letter consonants, in comparison to the double and triple letter combinations of the GR, aims for simplicity and neatness in appearance. The PS does not employ the GR 'tonal spelling' system of changing letters in words to indicate tones, but uses four diacritical marks (macron, acute, breve, grave accents) to differentiate them. One additional mark, an apostrophe, is used to separate syllables beginning with a, e, or o from preceding syllables whose final vowels may cause confusion in meaning. The forms and rules are therefore relatively simple and easy to learn.

In practice, however, the PS also contains grammatical features. Communist grammarians strongly emphasize the polysyllabic nature of modern Chinese, with some validity, but the emphasis is tinged with passion and ideology. They contend that polysyllabism makes Chinese as advanced a language as any, that Chinese has a regular morphology and is even 'inflectional.'[27] In fact, polysyllabism and inflection, when objectively considered, are not necessarily advanced features of languages.

---

[26] The PS exceptions, as compared with their GR equivalents, are:

PS	GR
q	chi
x	hsi
z	tz
c	ts
ü	iu
er	el

Furthermore, the symbol for vocal prolongation of the preceding consonant *j*, *ch*, *sh*, *r*, *z* (*tz* in the GR), *c* (*ts* in the GR), or *s* is the letter *i* in the PS instead of *y* as in the GR. And the letter *v* in the PS is not used in Chinese but is reserved for the transliteration of foreign terms.

[27] For details, see Li Chi, *A Provisional System of Grammar for Teaching Chinese*, translated with introduction and commentary, Current Chinese Language Project, series No. 6 (Berkeley and Los Angeles: Center for Chinese Studies, University of California, 1960. This sentiment was articulated by Chinese grammarians following the lead of the Soviet philologist Konrad,

At any rate, to reflect the new grammatical concepts of Chinese, the PS has to have orthographic rules of spelling syllables jointly as words or phrases according to structural analysis of word-complexes, morphemes, and stems. The GR has made similar attempts, but the PS must cope with the still fluid condition of *p'u-t'ung hua*, especially in regard to its uneasy relationship with the dialects. The task is further complicated by the revival of terse classical phraseology or the invention of abbreviated expressions for use in current political slogans. In phonetic writing, they would be much less intelligible. In consequence, clear rules of spelling to establish the PS as anything close to a standard orthography have yet to be decided. *Han-yü P'ien-yin Tz'u-hui* (*Chinese Vocabulary in Phonetic Spelling*), published in 1963, with 59,100 entries of words, phrases, and idioms, does include up-to-date rules for phonetic spelling, but its preface stresses that the work is only 'temporary,' 'tentative,' and 'experimental.' In the meantime, the PS has been playing a subsidiary role as a guide to the Peking pronunciation in the campaigns to promote *p'u-t'ung hua* and literacy.

But the PS has limited value even in the literacy movement, as the major effort must go into teaching the characters. According to claims made in November, 1959, at the National Conference on Literacy in the Countryside and Spare-Time Education, about 50 million people had become 'literate' in 1958. But among those only 10 per cent were reported to have learned phonetic spelling.[28] The Central Committee of the Communist Party and the PPCC issued a joint directive in 1959 declaring, 'In the dialect areas, phonetic spelling was not to be employed in teaching literacy, on the grounds that the additional burden of learning *p'u-t'ung hua* might impede literacy.'[29]

Minority languages. The Phonetic Spelling Scheme aims to establish a standard unified alphabetical script for all races in China. It was reported in 1964 that, with the help of the Central Committee on Racial affairs and the Chinese Academy of Sciences, new scripts based on the Latin alphabet had been created for some ten different aboriginal languages in Southwest China. Attempts were also made to reform the scripts of other minorities on the same Latin basis.[30] But in education among the minorities, the learning of Chinese is essential. And it is the Chinese characters that they must learn,[31] with the aid of phonetic spelling. The *People's Manual*[32] of 1964 lists fifty-three minority groups, totaling more than 30.5 million people. As more of the minority population and the Han illiterates receive Chinese education, the character script, interspersed with the simplified forms, will be perpetuated and widely used. It will indeed become the 'common possession' and the medium for Chinese written literature, just as *p'u-t'ung hua* has been intended to be for national speech.

LITERATURE

Literary productivity and its sudden halt. An immense quantity of poetry and fiction poured from the Chinese Communist presses up until 1966. The quantity is all the

---

who wrote his book *On the Chinese Language* soon after Stalin's *Marxism and Linguistics* of 1951 had attacked the theory of the eminent Soviet linguist, N. Y. Marr. Konrad's book, emphasizing Chinese polysyllabism and enlarging on Chinese morphology, included caustic criticism of Marr and of such Western philologists as F. M. Fink, H. Maspero, B. Karlgren, and O. Jespersen, who held opposite or different views, even though these distinguished scientists, admirers of Chinese culture, in no way implied that the Chinese language was inferior.

[28] See *Wen-tzu Kai-ke*, No. 21, Nov. 15, 1959, back page.

[29] *Ibid.*

[30] See Wu Yü-chang, 'The Various Applications of the Phonetic Alphabet of the Han Dialect),' *JMJP*, February 19, 1964.

[31] As indicated, for instance, in Fu Mao-chi's article on phonetic spelling and promotion of the cultures of the minority races in *JMJP*, February 17, 1962.

[32] *Jen-min Shou-ts'e* (Peking: Ta-kung Pao, 1964), p. 270.

more impressive by contrast with the relative paucity of themes, all of which praise the Party leadership and its achievements. But by late 1966, when the Cultural Revolution was in full swing, the sudden halt of virtually all literary publication was just as striking. While the earlier profusion resulted from Party exhortations, the 1966 disruption seems to have been caused not only by turmoil but by the new centralization of publishing activities. Between 1966 and 1970, scarcely any creative work appeared, at least so far as is known outside China. And even the literary supplements in the leading papers practically ceased publication. Only the strident voices of the young Red Guards could be heard, but those young activists did not demonstrate any ambition to become writers. If they had, the Cultural Revolution ought to have fired their imaginations and found expression in creative writing. But their energy was diverted to the production of slogans and attacks on the revisionists and imperialists, which appeared in millions of copies of *ta-tzu pao* (big-character posters).

Mao Tse-tung's best sellers. In the meantime, with centralization, the presses—no longer directed by the Party, whose structure had been almost demolished in 1966–68 —concentrated on the publication of Chairman Mao's works. On January 2, 1969, The New China News Agency declared that from 1966 to the end of November, 1968, the number of Mao's works printed was thirteen times the total of the entire preceding fifteen years.[33] In less than three years, 150 million copies of Mao's *Selected Works* were printed in four big volumes; 740 million copies of the *Quotations* were reissued; and 140 million *Selected Readers* were issued, along with 2 billion other pamphlets and collections and 96 million copies of Mao's poetry. The total is therefore more than 3 billion! The vast Chinese population, exhorted to live frugally during those years, was reported to be standing in line to buy these publications.

Because they have dramatically engulfed all other literary publications since 1966, the mammoth editions of Mao's works are like a Saturn that suddenly and furiously devours all his children, for the other literary works since the early 1950's had in fact been spawned by Mao's own dicta on form, function, and source in his 1942 *Talks at the Yenan Forum on Literature and Arts* and in his maxims and other tracts. In literature, Mao demands that a 'national form'[34] serve the revolutionary masses of workers, peasants, and soldiers and that its source be 'the raw material of life ideologically wrought.'[35] Furthermore, literature 'is to obey the political demand of the classes and of the Party. It is to obey the revolutionary mission at any given revolutionary period.'[36] Thus, the Party not only determined whether any literary work carried out a revolutionary mission, but it could also define the task variously at different times. The shattering of the Party structure in 1966 was accompanied by the purge of the Party's literary policy-makers and administrators. Even before the Cultural Revolution, it had been hard enough for authors to conform to their shifting policies; thereafter, there were no Party guidelines whatsoever, and none seemed needed. Since 1966, virtually no literary works have been published, while the printing facilities of the entire nation have been devoted to producing more than 3 billion copies of Mao's works. In this extraordinary phenomenon of world printing history, the dictatorial power of one man's ideas have profoundly affected all aspects of China's national life. Since 1966, Mao's ideas have not only commanded all literary production, they are China's only literature. In 1966, the ever diminishing voice of literary creativity became silent. Against this background, let us review how creative literature has

---

[33] Substantiation of same news in *JMJP*, January 3, 1969.

[34] *Min-tsu hsing-shih* (national form) was a term Mao repeatedly emphasized in his Report to the Party Central Committee in October, 1938, and in his address 'Oppose the Party Eight-legged Essay,' in February, 1942.

[35] See Mao, *Yenan Wen-i: Tso-t'an-hui Chiang-hua* (Shanghai: Hua-tung Hsin-hua Shu-tien, 1949), p. 19.

[36] *Ibid.*, p. 28.

struggled under Communism and what it had accomplished before the cataclysm.

Literature and politics. Since the beginning of the Communist regime, all poetry, fiction, or drama has been declared to have a political purpose. Although literature was at first ordered to assume the appearance of art, it was in fact directed to serve politics totally under the tight control of ideology. Such direction and control are not unusual in other Communist countries, but they were particularly thorough and successful in Communist China and resulted in a large quantity of forced works of minimal quality by any normal standard of art. But these works conformed in varying degrees to the Chinese Communist definition of art, especially Mao's own.

It is perhaps more relevant here, therefore, to discuss the political and ideological role of Chinese Communist literature rather than its artistic quality, while still noting quality whenever it occurs. Emphasis will be placed on those major authors and works that have enjoyed at least a period of official blessing since 1949. The discussion will be confined to poetry and fiction, because drama will be discussed in the next chapter. Nor will literary theories or apparent controversies be dealt with here at length.[37] No matter how prolific or militant the proponents of the 'correct' line became, they were seeking to rationalize the Party's literary policy of a given period or to attack political attitudes expressed in certain individuals' works. A controversy can be genuinely meaningful only when the contending forces are somewhat equal. But the voice of the Party and state was so overpowering in China, even before 1966, that literature had virtually no defense against politics.

Poetry: Mao and others. All poetry since 1949 has been produced under the order 'politics takes command!' Mao's poetry, which was first published formally in 1957, is the single exception, because it is by the man who *commands the politics.* His poetry also contrasts sharply with almost all the rest in character and quality.

Although Mao's poetry conforms to his ideas on form, function, and source, the 'national form' that he uses is not the one advocated for the masses. His are strictly classical forms that have been refined and perfected over the centuries by the literati, whereas other current poems are generally in the modern vernacular, and are often conscious imitations of rustic folk songs or are folksy jingles on political themes. Consequently, Mao's poetry represents his individual self-expression, in contrast to the forced collective spirit of millions of characterless popular verses. His sources of inspiration, too, are evidently his personal experiences and his individual vision, and the ideological jargon that must be inserted in other published works is missing from his.

In all, thirty-seven poems[38] written between 1925 and 1963 formed the corpus of Mao's published poetry as of 1964. Some are very short poems or quatrains; the longest lyrics are no more than twenty-five lines. This slender *oeuvre* hardly signifies a productive poet. Yet only in Mao's poetry can one find quality unadulterated. Lacking rivals, it becomes all the more distinguished; it presents the untrammeled imagination of a free towering human figure, soaring above the huge quantity of popular verse produced under the Party's direction and Mao's literary dicta.

---

[37] A comprehensive survey appears in D. W. Fokkema, *Literary Doctrine in China and Soviet Influence, 1956–1960* (The Hague: Mouton, 1965). The most outstanding controversy is treated by Yang I-fan in *The Case of Hu Feng* (Hong Kong: Union Research Institute, 1956); and Merle Goldman, 'Hu Feng's Conflict with the Communist Literary Authorities,' *The China Quarterly*, No. 12, October–December, 1962, pp. 103–37.

[38] We refer to the collection published by Wen Wu Press in 1963. There is a thirty-eighth poem written in 1965, obtained by Jerome Ch'en from Japanese sources and reprinted in *The China Quarterly*, No. 34, 1968, in Ch'en's translation. Mr. Ch'en has also translated the thirty-seven earlier poems in collaboration with Michael Bullock and published them in his book, *Mao and the Chinese Revolution* (Oxford: Oxford University Press, 1965). See also Yongsang Ng, 'The Poetry of Mao Tse-tung,' *The China Quarterly*, No. 13, January–March, 1963, pp. 60–73.

Though in translation the contrast does not appear as sharp in tone and texture as in the original Chinese, the superiority of Mao's poetry to other contemporary output is still apparent in his famous poem 'Snow'[39] or his 'Loushan Pass,' in such lines as these:

> Cold is the west wind
> Far in the frosty air the wild geese call in
> the morning moonlight
> This very day in one step we shall pass its summit
> We shall pass its summit
> There the hills are blue like the sea
> And the dying sun like blood.[40]

In contrast, the two following samples are from literally millions of poems, produced during the *Pai-wan shih-ko yün-tung*, or 'multimillion poem movement,' of 1958:[41]

> Each year our farm production grows,
> Grains and cotton pile up mountain high, Hurrah!
> Eat the grains, but don't forget the sower,
> The Communist Party's our dear Ma and Pa.[42]

> We worship no god, nor temple build,
> Chairman Mao's love is greater manifold.
> Gods we destroy, and temples tear down,
> Better than gods we worship the One Man.
> Mountains may shake, earth may quake, and
> we are not afraid,
> But we dare not forget what the Chairman said.[43]

The two poems above demonstrate the politicization of poetry, in which immense quantities of jingles were manufactured, following the Party line, and exalted by literary commissars as the 'best poetry' of the people.[44] Because the official line was that the 'best poetry' had been produced by the people, individual poets had to learn from the people. From the two poems above, it is clear that, aside from the obvious homage to the Party and its Chairman, poets had to record the surrender of the self to the public cause, the transference of any private feelings for family to complete allegiance to Party and State, the redirection of religious sentiments to the adulation of Chairman Mao. They also had to recast whatever they used to feel about nature or the supernatural to suit ideological purposes.

Three poets have diligently and successfully turned their talents in the required directions and have become productive and popular: Feng Chih, Ko Pi-chou, and Li Chi.[45] Few of the poets best known before the Communist regime continued to write, and, as is true also of novelists, even some of the most celebrated Communist

[39] A number of English translations are available, the most widely circulated being in Mao Tse-tung, *Nineteen Poems* (Peking: Foreign Languages Press, 1958), p. 22.

[40] *Ibid.*, p. 16.

[41] For a study of this movement, see S. H. Chen, 'Multiplicity in Uniformity: Poetry and the Great Leap Forward,' *The China Quarterly*, No. 3, July–September, 1960, pp. 1–15.

[42] Original cited by a poet-critic, Hsiao San, in the article 'The Best Poetry,' *JMJP*, February 11, 1958.

[43] In *Chung-kuo Ko-yao Tzu-liao* (*Collected Materials of Chinese Folk Songs and Ballads*) (Peking: Tso-chia Ch'u-pan-she, 1959), p. 295.

[44] See Hsiao, 'Best Poetry,' *JMJP*, February 11, 1958.

[45] For more on these three poets and the exemplary nature of their works under Communism, see S. H. Chen: 'Metaphor and the Conscious in Chinese Poetry Under Communism,' *The China Quarterly*, No. 19, January–March, 1963, pp. 39–59.

poets were silenced shortly after 1949. Feng Chih, however, was already a highly regarded young lyrical poet in the May Fourth fashion in the late 1920's; having
studied in Germany, he was an erudite scholar of Goethe and a great admirer of
Rilke. In the early 1940's, untouched by politics, he had written a volume of 'sonnets'
in modern Chinese of extraordinary beauty with his native gift for lyricism. Although
he had never been a proponent of the 'national form' and was not a writer of proletarian origin, he has become an accepted poet under the Communist regime, in
contrast to Ai Ch'ing, a poet accepted by the Party in its early years but later rejected. Feng Chih's *Poems of One Decade*[46] (from 1949 to 1959) is the poetry of a genuinely
talented man who precariously maintains a 'particle of art' (in Pasternak's phrase)
while working under tremendous pressure to remain ideologically acceptable. In
every poem, he has to make the explicit point that his poetry 'also serves.' He no
longer writes sonnets, but his 'national form' is not of the traditional kind. It adopts
in lucid fashion the colloquial speech of the educated. He now totally avoids personal
lyricism. His subjects are all of public concern—rural construction, public works, and
other socialist successes. The poems still show some of his intellectual aptitude but
none of his warm personality, intimate tone, or individual sensitivity. One of his
poems, 'The Surveyors,' is typical:

> How high is the mountain, and how deep
> the water?
> How many cubic feet per second does it flow?
> How much weight can the rocks carry,
> How hard are they, above ground or below?

That is how the poem begins. We can only partly translate its natural fluency and
neatness of diction and rhythm to show that it promises at least competent verse. But
toward its end, the well-controlled poetic voice has to be lost in a bombastic
harangue:

> Our great task is just at the beginning
> The Yellow River has surrendered to us now.
> Whatever the sons and daughters of New China do,
> Is to the cheers of our friends, and to
> our enemies woe.

In another passage in 'The Surveyors,' who are apparently the all-conquering
warriors of Chairman Mao, the poet chants:

> In front of their concentrated attention
> Nature has lost all her mysteries.

With such loss of all nature's mysteries, no wonder poetry has to lose all its depth. In
another poem, 'Workshop,' perhaps quite aware that poetry has become slogan, the
'ideologically transformed' poet defends the change by protesting:

> Since it reflects a living reality,
> A slogan here becomes most powerful poetry.

Ko Pi-chou is another poet of unmistakable talent and great versatility. His four
poems entitled 'New Songs of Peimang Mountain, Four Pieces'[47] illustrate how a poet,
so capable of a variety of poetic devices, is reduced to a single mode of thought by the
demand that he enthusiastically advocate collective spirit and militant optimism in
transparently explicit themes. Since I have discussed this important group of poems

---

[46] Feng Chih, *Shih-hien Shih-ch'ao* (*Poems of One Decade*) (Peking: Jen-ming Wen-hsüeh
Ch'u-pan-she, 1959).
[47] First published in *JMJP*, March 24, 1962.

in detail elsewhere,[48] I shall simply summarize a few essential points here. Ko plays four variations on a theme, employing four different styles. The first poem is a mixture of the classical and the modern colloquial; the second is full of proletarian slogans; the third is a vernacular rhapsody; and the fourth is perfect classical pentasyllabic verse. The scene is the inland Peimang Mountain, near Loyang, the ancient capital, where great poets of past dynasties were wont to lament the ravages of time. Instead, Ko praises new construction under socialism. His images are deft, though often borrowed from rather hackneyed classical phrases, and his language is generally vivid and sonorous. But, in each poem, he has to end with the most obvious statement of his theme. Or, lest his individual voice should be too distinctive to suit the strongly anti-individualist ideology, he must end a poem with clear allusions to the collective spirit. The first poem ends thus:

> I see only clouds and water, and oceans
> of trees without limit
> The old dies, new life is born—life, life,
> never to end.

The second, about a tractor factory of the area that is assembling trucks for Albania, concludes:

> Even though from oceans away,
> You see clearly in this workshop
> That our hearts,
> Under the banner of Marxism,
> Are so closely to each other drawn.

Militant or revolutionary optimism infuses the landscape at the end of the third poem:

> See the immense motion of green trees,
> And jungles of smoking chimneys row after row,
> Factories stand like gunboats in battle array,
> O fighting ships one by one,
> A voyage of ten thousand li you have begun.

The fourth poem, 'To a Comrade,' is in classical form and treats a favorite traditional subject in Chinese poetry, friendship. But friendship can no longer be personal, and the poem ends with a clear allusion to the great collectivity, the 'human sea,' where individuals have no separate identity:

> All rivers will concourse in the great sea,
> How can clouds and mountains keep us apart?

A longer work by Ko Pi-chou, *The Romance of Mountain Song*,[49] is a well-known play of ten brisk scenes written in verse. The attractiveness of its poetic language is another testimony to Ko's versatility, and its choice of subject from popular legends in the remote southwest borderland adds to its freshness, though its theme, antifeudalism, comes through, perhaps inevitably, without subtlety.

Li Chi, a Communist 'bard,' is best known for his long narrative poems. He has diligently cultivated his knowledge of folk tales and folk songs and adapted their form in his long narrative verse on revolutionary themes. His early success with the form was in the mid-1940's, when his *Wang Kuei and Li Hsiang-hsiang*[50] was highly

---

[48] S. H. Chen, 'Metaphor and the Conscious,' pp. 42–47.

[49] Ko Pi-chou, *Shan-ko Chuan* (*The Romance of Mountain Song*) (Peking: Tso-chia Ch'u-pan-she, 1959).

[50] Many editions are available. A pocket edition was published by Jen-min Wen-hsüeh Ch'u-pan-she, in Peking, 1959. For excerpts in English and discussion of its merits and

acclaimed in Communist-controlled areas. After 1949, he published a few collections of shorter poems. But his representative work during the period is his *Romance of the Lamb*, or *Yang-kao Chuan*. It adopts an elementary allegorical device, with the hero's name, Yang Kao, punning homophonously with 'little lamb.' It tells of the orphan's suffering, like a deserted lamb, in the old evil society, and his adventures and eventual growth into a Communist revolutionary once he has been rescued and brought up by the benevolent Communist forces. In *Yang-kao Chuan*, Li chooses the folk idiom and the popular meter of folk ballads in a long narrative of some 1,840 lines. Such idiom and meter are prone to result in facile fluency and a general lightness of tone, which are incongruous when the poet strains to expound ideology. Yang Kao, a shepherd boy, is running away from his employer, a rich landlord, to join the Red Army. He secretly says goodbye to his sheep. But instead of expressing parting sentiment, he is actually indoctrinating the animals and making a fantastic political promise in his farewell speech:

> You are sheep and I am a man,
> But the rich men oppress us in the same way.
>
> The rich men spend money to keep you,
> That they may eat your flesh or sell you.
>
> Sheep, Sheep, do not be heartbroken;
> When the rich are overthrown, I'll herd you
>   again.
> The Red Army will march to victory;
> All cattle and sheep will belong to us
>   poor men.
> With enough pasture, plenty of water, you
>   will be fat.
> Everyone grows lots of flesh and long,
>   long wool.
> Then your small folds will become large folds;
> The hills will be full of sheep, more and more.[51]

Even the most appreciative reader cannot help asking, when the Red Army has marched to victory and the 'sheep belong to the poor men, grow lots of flesh and long, long wool,' will not the poor men eat their flesh or sell them, too?

The epoch has produced a number of other long narrative poems, but Li Chi's work has enjoyed perhaps the greatest official acclaim and widest circulation. Among others are the *White Orchid Flower*[52] by Ch'iao Lin, which celebrates the bravery, fortitude, and selflessness of a poor peasant girl who eventually became a Communist heroine and Li Chi-yeh's *Family on the Inland Seashore*,[53] telling the story of a poor family's suffering before the revolution and its happiness after liberation. Both works adopt the 'national form' of folk ballads. Both make the same effort as the *Yang-kao* to

---

shortcomings, see Cyril Birch, 'Chinese Communist Literature: The Persistence of Traditional Forms,' *The China Quarterly*, No. 13, January–March, 1963, pp. 83–86.

[51] Li Chi, *Yang-kao Chuan* (*Romance of the Lamb*), Part I: 'The Fifth of the Fifth Moon,' Section 6 (Peking: Tso-chia Ch'u-pan-she, 1959).

[52] Ch'iao Lin, *Pai Lan-hua* (*White Orchid Flower*) (Peking: Jen-min Wen-hsüeh Ch'u-pan-she, 1959). A later work of the same variety, but longer and in somewhat more lively language, is Wang Chih-yüan, *Hu-t'ao Po* (*Walnut Slope*) (Peking: Tso-chia Ch'u-pan-she, 1965), written in tribute to the sacrifice of a pre-1949 peasant heroine.

[53] Li Chi-Yeh, *Hai-ho An-shang Jen-chia* (*Family on the Inland Seashore*) (Shanghai: Wen-i Ch'u-pan-she, 1959).

achieve a smooth flow of narration with a catching appeal to the ear and are just as often spoiled when political propaganda jars the imagination. In *Seashore*, an old woman, mother of the hero, plays a large part in the poem. She has lost her eyesight. After liberation she is treated by a doctor, but the result remains unpredictable. What has sustained her strength through the whole ordeal is a 'secret thought.'

> The secret makes her whole body full
>   of strength,
> Able to bear any calamity big as heaven.

And the 'secret thought' is that, if she regains her sight one day, the first thing she will do will be to see an adored portrait:

> I only want to see the portrait of
>   Chairman Mao.
> I've said, without seeing him my heart
>   will never rest.

And she regains her sight. A long narrative on a different kind of subject is Tsang K'e-chia's biographical piece on Li Ta-chao,[54] the Communist intellectual leader executed by the warlords in 1927. Tsang is an experienced writer, and the editor of *Shih K'an* (*Poetry Magazine*), which first published Mao Tse-tung's poetry in 1957. In *Li Tao-chao*, he displayed his virtuosity by intermingling classical stanzas with vernacular ones, and polished literary diction with the plain folk idiom, alternating between lyrical passages and bombastic harangue. The biographical poem is supposedly based on research, as the author says in his postscript, and aims at authenticity. But, because Mao Tse-tung rose to prominence only after Li's martyrdom and little can be said of Mao in the heroic saga, the biographer-poet must have found it very hard in his important panegyric endeavor to pay homage to Mao. In the last section of the poem, he has to resort to fantasy. Thus, after Li's body had lain in a coffin for six years before burial, Li sees Mao:

> For six years after he died,
> Lying in a red-purple coffin,
> Li Ta-chao, he kept his eyes open wide.
>
> In his purple-red coffin
> For six whole years he reposed.
> The upsurge of the revolution
> Excited him so his eyes could not be closed,
> And he saw Mao Tse-tung's pair of hands
> Make the red flags upon Chingkang Mountain
>   stand.

It can be seen from these examples that Mao's person and 'thoughts' have dominated every creative work, submerging under it whatever quality the poem might have otherwise attained. Nevertheless, has Mao's poetry, which certainly has a distinct quality of its own, influenced the poetic writings of this period? Mao's personality, of course, includes both the idolized dictator and the individual poet, but it may be instructive here to consider the poet and the national idol as two separate forces. Mao has never held up his own poetry as a model for imitation. In fact, when his poetry was first published in *Poetry Magazine*, he wrote to its editor, Tsang K'e-chia:

> I have never wanted to make these [poems] known in any formal way, because they are written in the old style. I was afraid this might encourage a wrong

---

[54] Tsang K'e-chia, *Li Ta-chao*, Peking: Tso-chia Ch'u-pan-she, 1959.

trend and exercise a bad influence on young people. . . . Of course, our poetry should be written mainly in the modern form. We may write some verse in classical forms as well, but it would not be advisable to encourage young people to do this, because these forms would restrict their thought, and they are difficult to learn.[55]

As it turned out, the 'wrong trend' was set not by his poetry but by the adulation of Mao during the 'multimillion poem movement' and the enforced national credo that everyone must think his 'thought.' As for any apparent influence of Mao's poetry, in the late 1950's some old-style verse by Ministers Tung Pi-wu and Ch'en Yi and by the writer Kuo Mo-jo, among others, was published in newspapers and journals. But it was a temporary vogue rather than a serious effort. Kuo, in particular, remained Mao's feeble poetic echo into the early 1960's. Their works were largely slavish imitations in worn-out meters and diction, parodies, or even old-fashioned doggerel.

Good poetry: hard struggle or stunted growth. Nevertheless, in some oblique way Mao's poetry does seem to have influenced a few promising young poets prior to the Cultural Revolution, although little poetry has been available abroad since 1966. At least one exceptional poet deserves mention. He is Liang Shang-ch'uan, and the works of his that I have seen are in two slender volumes entitled *Mountain Spring* and *Long River Flowing Night and Day*.[56] In his verse, good poetry has emerged, despite the pressure to conform to ideological dictates and clichés. There is always genuine music in Liang's language and nuance in his description, whether he sings of his delight in the beauty of nature and his enthusiasm for heroic historical revolutionary deeds or praises life in a new society. The very rare mention of Mao's name or person in his poetry, contrasted with the Chairman's omnipresence in so many others, seems a spectacular characteristic. But we see in Liang the influence of Mao's poetry transmuted into modern verse. His extraordinary terseness of expression, the dynamism of his concrete imagery, and the hard contours of his bold colors and graphic description, tempered with occasionally subtle, even tender, touches, are the qualities of Mao's classical verse at its happiest moments. Liang writes in vernacular language, but every so often he uses Mao's diction, adapting Mao's classical phrases to his own expression and occasionally incarnating Mao's poetic spirit and vision. Because of its terseness, and integral musical quality, Liang's poetry is quite difficult to translate into English.

Liang apparently leads an itinerant life as a young member of the armed services. Many of his works present scenes of remote border regions,[57] north and south, as well as of communes in the interior. A poem entitled 'Snow on Mountain of Snow' not only has the grandeur of Mao's poetic vision but actually contains a whole phrase, *ts'ung tou yüeh*, that has been lifted from Mao's poem 'Loushan Pass,' quoted above. Liang adds a word, *fei*, to the phrase to suit the modern meter. The phrase, literally meaning 'to leap over the [mountain's] head,' or 'pass the summit,' may not sound like much in English but actually constitutes the keynote to the formal structure of

---

[55] English version in Mao, *Nineteen Poems*. The Chinese original is in some places more strongly worded. Rather than 'encourage a wrong trend,' and so forth, it says 'make the wrong seed perpetuate and cause the young people to err.'

[56] Liang Shang-ch'uan, *Shan-ch'uan Chi* (Peking: Tso-chia Ch'u-pan-she, 1962), and *idem, Ch'ang Ho Jih Yeh Liu* (Peking: Tso-chia Ch'u-pan-she, 1964).

[57] In the exploration of border regions, the Communists have discovered among the aborigines and minority races a great many epics and songs that had been orally transmitted or somehow recorded locally. The efforts to collect them are remarkable, though their interpretation and rendition into Chinese are of course ideologically colored. For more information, see a special number of *Wenxue Pinglun (Literary Criticism)*, No. 6, Peking, December, 1959.

Liang's poem, generating its rhymes, feeling, and dynamic movement. The phrase recalls a scene that Mao had witnessed on the Long March, at Hsüeh (Snow) Mountain in Southwest China. My translation will try to indicate the poem's rhyme and imagery and the suggestive color that Liang achieved in his lively modern verse, which is sympathetic to Mao's poetic tenor but free from the rigor of Mao's antique texture:

> Snow on Mountain of Snow
> White on white aglow.
>
> All because the Red Army marching
> Leaped over its head,
> All because the martyrs' blood
> Was here spread.
>
> Snow on Mountain of Snow,
> White on white aglow
> Now in the morning light sparkles,
> Faintly, faintly, scarlet.

Such works, struggling for excellence, were already rare in the early 1960's; their growth since 1966 has been stunted.

The two major newspapers, *Jen-min Jih-pao* and the *Kuang-ming Jih-pao*, have ceased publication of their literary supplements since 1966, and have only occasionally included doggerel praising Mao, his 'thought,' and sometimes his heir. For example:

> Not one inch shall we depart from
> Chairman Mao.
> Heaven may fall, earth may sink, we
> shall not be shaken off.
>
> Chairman Mao steers the direction;
> When Chairman Mao waves his hand, I go
> forward.
> Be sure to make the red flag fly all over
> the globe.[58]

The original is hardly literate and totally lacks artistic merit. Literary creativity was suffocated during the Cultural Revolution. The above review of the earlier years suggests the trend toward this state of affairs, though it is hard to believe it can last forever. A similar trend is evident in fiction.

Fiction and the writers' milieu. Since 1949, the status of authors, the distribution of fiction or its relation to the public, and the treatment of the most favored themes shows a new pattern, clearly distinguishable from the past. Ten of the major novels published from 1944 to 1966[59] illustrate this point.

First, none of the top novelists of previous decades, such as Pa Chin, Mao Tun, or Lao She, seems to have produced a novel in the P.R.C. period, even though they were treated rather well prior to the Cultural Revolution and in some cases even occupied high official positions. Before Lao She was persecuted and rumored dead during the Cultural Revolution, he had turned briefly to writing drama.[60] Others,

[58] Wei Tung, 'Ting chiao huan ch'iu hung-ch'i p'iao (Be Sure to Make the Red Flag Fly All over the Globe),' printed in *Kuang-ming Jih-pao*, November 3, 1968.
[59] C. T. Hsia, *History of Modern Chinese Fiction*, (New Haven: Yale University Press, 1961), pp. 473–95, discusses some of the critical issues and lists other titles published up to 1957.
[60] News of Lao She's death came out in late 1966 and has been so frequently repeated by travelers and refugees from Peking that it cannot be dismissed as hearsay. The most ominous

such as novelists Ting Ling and Hsiao Chün, have been ruthlessly criticized or entirely silenced since the early 1950's. While few if any of the earlier major novelists have published new works, new names, or authors previously of much less distinction, have emerged.

Second, the relationship between the author and his reading public has changed vastly, in that the Party and state, rather than a private company, now publish a work. The entire national cultural apparatus—the Party, the Party-controlled press, and countless discussion groups directed by the Party cadres in schools, factories, and the armed services are now available to publicize a work. The author of an approved work can expect an immediate sale of tens of thousands of copies of each printing, barring a policy change, in which the author is 'criticized' and his work prohibited. Among the major novels to be considered here, a sale of 50,000 to 80,000 copies is a modest average. From April to September, 1966, *Song of Ouyang Hai* was issued in successive printings totaling 1,301,000 copies.[61] The author could expect efficient distribution, since his books were produced according to plan. Under the circumstances, the author is no longer a lone artist who struggles to produce his best work for an unknown and unpredictable public in a free and competitive book market. Instead of expressing his personal conscience as an artist, the author must, of course, present the 'correct' ideological consciousness, but he is then guaranteed a huge reading public and faces little competition, as relatively few works serve as recommended reading for a vast, newly literate, and still undiscriminating population.

In certain respects, the Chinese literary scene after 1949 differs from that of the Soviet Union in the 1920's and early 1930's, when the great Russian novelists of the late nineteenth and early twentieth centuries were allowed to continue to influence writers and readers. In China after 1949, literary policy was more drastic; ideology dominated art, and novelists were obliged to cater to the least sophisticated readers among the peasants, workers, and soldiers—the leading classes of the new society. As a consequence, subject matter was generally restricted to the life of the peasants, workers, soldiers, and the often indistinct figure of the cadre as a man of infallible virtue, power, and dedication. Such literature finally developed the composite positive hero, with the experience of a peasant, a worker, and a soldier, who exemplifies total devotion to Chairman Mao's 'thought.' The people must not consider model heroes, like Lei Feng or Ouyang Hai, imaginary. On the contrary, the regime insists that they are real individuals, truthfully portrayed. Such 'reportage literature' (*pao-kao wen hsüeh*) is acclaimed as great art, however little it resembles fiction in form and structure.

Some exemplary early Communist novels. Among the novelists rising to prominence after 1949 is Chao Shu-li. Since his artistic sources, forms, and functions exemplified Mao's early literary policies, I shall discuss his development and career in greater detail than those of others. Chao is the son of a poor peasant jack-of-all-trades, who grew up in the impoverished rural area of Shansi, where the Communist influence reached during the late 1930's. Trained as a young cadre, he had no more than a junior high school education. He has the native gift for folk arts, such as balladry and playing rustic instruments, and has enjoyed local popularity as a sort of village entertainer. When he began to write, he was already a Communist activist. His first work, in 1943, *Hsiao-erh-hei Chieh Hun* (*Marriage of Little Darky the Second*),[62] brought him sudden fame and foreshadowed post-1949 Communist fiction in both theory and practice. In about 10,000 words, it drolly attacks deep-rooted folk superstitions and celebrates the

---

report is in Stuart and Roma Gelder, *Memories for a Chinese Granddaughter* (London: Hutchinson, 1967), pp. 191–95.

[61] The number of copies of each printing of a work is, as a rule, meticulously noted in each book.

[62] Chao Shu-li, *Hsiao-erh-hei Chieh Hun* (Peking: Jen-min Wen-hsüeh, 1962).

liberation of the young under the Communist border area government of the mountain region. The tale in the plainest folk idiom sketches with rustic humor the crude chicanery and fraud in sorcery and prophecy committed by country rogues, villains, and fools. The defrauders serve as foils for the wisdom of the local Communists, whose policies enlighten everyone and lead to the happy union of Darky the Second and his sweetheart, Hsiao Ch'in. The earth material in the 'national form' of oral folk tales is ideologically transformed to enlighten and entertain the masses.

The ideological content of this work, produced in Yenan, reflects the talks Mao had just delivered at the Forum on Arts and Literature there, and foreshadows the far more imposing slogan of the late 1950's: 'the combination of revolutionary realism and revolutionary romanticism.' In this formula, 'romanticism' is juxtaposed with and antithetical to 'realism.' When the terms are modified by 'revolutionary,' both change in character. Both terms are borrowed from the West, but when applied to populist literature for political ends, their meanings are necessarily vastly simplified. To 'romanticize,' according to the formula, means to blend the fanciful or unreal with the real in order to serve 'revolutionary' policy. The real means what the author actually sees, hears, and experiences in a Communist society, but he must mix it with the 'romantic,' that is, the ideal, however unreal or even false, to help the revolutionary cause.

Chao Shu-li's *Marriage of Little Darky*, in its thin and innocent appearance, exhibits the ideal of the 'combination.' Many of his characters, country people, are picturesquely real, and the story is also said to be partly based on real events. But the good Party workers remain shadowy personifications of abstract homilies, so that the happy ending seems more hollow than real. As the work was celebrated, extolled, and earnestly discussed, certain reports of the real background of the story came to light. According to one report,[63] though the chicanery, bigotry, and superstitions Chao observed were real, the hero, liberated by the cadres in the novelette, was in fact killed by some young cadres in collusion with the local forces because of rivalry over the hero's girl. The report gave credit to Chao Shu-li as an able Party worker, for he had discovered the true facts and brought about the punishment of the cadres. As an author, however, he not only refrained from exposing the Party but 'ideologically transformed' an ugly story in order to 'help the revolution.'

Two other works by Chao before 1949 gained great popularity in the People's Republic. The *Jingle Verses of Li Yu-ts'ai*,[64] also written in 1943, rather desultorily portrays village characters, who are praised or condemned by a local balladist in a uniform tone of low comedy. The protagonist is obviously Chao himself, now serving as observer and participant in social change. The virtues of the new and the vices of the old society are easily drawn in black and white. But Chao's sources are his own experience, and the characters are treated sometimes coarsely and sometimes with cunning. Naïve jingles are interspersed throughout his rather spirited, if random, narratives, which recall traditional Chinese episodic novels or long tales. *Changes in the Li Village*,[65] completed by 1946, is Chao's first full-fledged novel and shows his mature talent. Its theme draws on the powerful pre-1949 Communist slogan *ch'iung-jen ta fan shen*, or 'great overturn of the poor' against the rich. It is a work of violent action, and devastating attacks on evil landlords and their henchmen, ending with the vindica-

---

[63] In *Jen-wu Tsa-chih* (*The Magazine on Personages*), quoted by Ting Meau in *P'ing Chung-kung Tai-piao-tso* (*Critical Studies of the Representative Literary Works of Communist China*) (Hong Kong: The New Era Press, 1953), pp. 27–28.

[64] Chao Shu-li, *Li Yu-ts'ai Pan-hua* (Peking: Jen-min Wen-hsüeh, 1962), now is the title story of a collection including *Marriage of Little Darky*.

[65] Chao Shu-li, *Li-chia-chuang ti Pien-ch'ien* (*Changes in the Li Village*). The earliest edition generally available is that of 1949 (Hong Kong: Hsin Chung-kuo Shu-tien), containing a preface by Mao Tun dated December, 1946.

tion of the victims, who ruthlessly expose their crimes and slaughter them under Communist guidance. The work follows a formula but has distinction in comparison to two other famous novels on the same theme that were also completed before 1949: *Sun Over Sangkan River*,[66] by the once celebrated woman Communist author Ting Ling, and *Hurricane*,[67] by Chou Li-po. Both were based on experiences during the pre-1949 land reform, though their complete versions were published in 1949, winning for each author a Stalin Prize. In comparison to Chao's work, both novels may be more expansive (especially Chou's, which came out in two large volumes), better structured, and perhaps better written. The technical influence of Soviet authors is sometimes evident. But despite their superior skill and quick international recognition, Ting and Chou differ from Chao in that they are intellectuals who had been trained in the May Fourth tradition and were struggling to comply with the new literary policy. By contrast, Chao's rustic humor, folk idiom, and direct, naïve observations of local scenes and people illustrate how Chinese Communist fiction has had to become increasingly 'national' in form and content, using the 'raw material' closest to the peasants, workers, and soldiers in order to serve changing revolutionary conditions.

New directions in peasant fiction. After 1949, Chao Shu-li was hailed by the leading literary policy spokesman, Chou Yang, as a 'New Man' and by Kuo Mo-jo as one 'rising up from the earth, reaching up to the skies.' Writers were urged to aspire not so much to the intrinsic quality of his art as to its total conformity to the Maoist principles of source, form, and function. The three novels by Chao Shu-li, Chou Li-po, and Ting Ling that were published in 1949 practically marked the end of the subject of violent struggle and bloody purges of the landlords.

Chinese Communist fiction after 1949, like the Communist regime, entered a new phase. The novelists' new mission was to depict the benefits of a regimented agricultural economy and to portray new types of men and women to reflect progress and hope. Rapid social change within a single decade was reflected in the formation first of mutual aid groups, then of cooperatives for agricultural production, and finally of people's communes. Continuous intense struggle marked the process; however, the targets of attack were no longer the landlords but the former poor or middle peasants who, as beneficiaries of the land reform, had by hard work begun to taste the fruits of landownership. The revolutionary struggle against them was directed by the Party, with other proletarian elements as the vanguard forces. The struggle pitted one generation against another, the poor against the less poor, the collectivity against the individual, and, in some cases, the individual against himself in his agony to fit the new society.

Chao Shu-li's first major post-1949 novel, *Sanliwan Village*,[68] typifies the fiction of the period about struggle and transformation among the peasants. The novel is still a sketch in broad strokes, without elaborate documentation or psychological depth, but the narrative flows swiftly, with familiar portraits, especially those of old-fashioned country people. Chao has an ear for lifelike conversations, re-creating the bickerings between peasant sisters-in-law, the grumblings of a nagging mother, the rantings of a country shrew, or the quarrel between a poor farmhand and a peddler. He even manages a happy, comic fusion of their speech and their newly acquired political jargon—unlike other novelists, whose imitations of the unfamiliar often falsify their characters.

Sanliwan Village, dealing with the transition from mutual aid groups to cooperatives up to 1954, was published in 1955. Most of the important events occur in one building in a small Shansi village, formerly the mansion of a big landlord, which has been

---

[66] Ting Ling, *Tai-yang Chao Tsai Sang-ka-ho Shang* (Peking: Hsin Hua Book Co., 1949).

[67] Chou Li-po, *Pao-feng Tsou-yü* (Peking: Hsin Hua Book Co., 1949).

[68] Chao Shu-li, *San-li-wan* (Peking: Tung-su Tu-wu Ch'u-pan-she, 1955); for a synopsis, see Hsia, *History of Modern Chinese Fiction*, pp. 491–94.

converted for public use, as if to symbolize revolutionary change. It contains committee rooms, a meeting hall, club rooms, and archives. The characters are mostly chairmen, vice-chairmen, or members of some committee, though they are frequently addressed as uncles, aunts, grannies, or cousins. The whole village, liberated from the old 'feudalism,' seems to have been bureaucratized by tight Communist organization. A young villager, the hero of the novel, can no longer stand his selfish, capricious wife and his shrew of a mother-in-law and wants to run away. Told by the cadre that he cannot go anywhere else without an official recommendation, which will not be forthcoming, he realizes that he is stuck with the village and must 'struggle.' The new bureaucracy seems to have enmeshed the entire community in a magical web of common destiny—the happy future envisioned for them by the Party. To strengthen faith in this magical world, Chao Shu-li subtly revives old folk myths and weaves them into the people's speech. A woman yearning for knowledge in the new society calls it a 'magic gourd,' such as immortals in fairy tales used to carry. A recalcitrant peasant speaks of the slogans that convert him to the good cause as the 'incantations of the gold headband,' a reference to the means used to tame the nearly omnipotent Monkey Demon in the famed old novel *Pilgrimage to the West.*

Of course, the plot is thin, with no engrossing love story, since any private relationship treated in depth is anathema to the Communist policy of collectivism. Nevertheless, the novel ends happily, with the conversion of the peasants, the improved behavior of the country shrews and flirts, and the proper marriage of three young couples. There are hilarious moments, particularly for those who are familiar with the language and manners of the country people. Even those who lack rural experience will learn about country people from Chao's occasional lifelike portraits.

Despite its flaws, *Sanliwan Village* prophetically points to a larger social transformation to come. In stressing the movement toward collectivism, the bending of the individual spirit, and the demand for self-denial as regards private property or personal freedom, the novel presages the total nationwide collectivization—the formation of the people's communes—that took place three years later.

This message is communicated by one of the three newly married couples. Two of the couples set up their homes either by themselves or with their parents, since the cooperative system permitted private households to own certain personal necessities. But the third, the ideal combination of a gifted country boy and the best-educated girl, decide not to set up their own home. One asks, 'How shall we eat?' And the other replies, 'The public dining hall will open the day after tomorrow.' As they walk under the romantic moonlight, they already sound like ideal members of a people's commune.

Two other novels on early post-1949 rural reconstruction are of major importance. Although social and political change was occurring with breathtaking speed in the countryside as well as in the cities, these works are remarkable in that they focused on certain rural conditions shortly after liberation and before the establishment of cooperatives.

Chou Li-po's *Great Changes in a Mountain Village,*[69] was published in 1958, the year communes were established, and Liu Ch'ing's *Saga of the Builders*[70] appeared two years later. Despite their focus on an earlier period, Chou and Liu are no less politically conscious than Chao Shu-li and are even more explicit about political ideology. Perhaps change had occurred too rapidly for the novelists to reflect the most contemporary scenes. Also, by 1958 (and even more by 1960), the mid-1950's must have

---

[69] Chou Li-po, *Shan-hsiang Chü-pien* (Peking: Tso-chia Ch'u-pan-she, 1958).

[70] Liu Ch'ing, *Ch'uang-yeh Shih* (Peking: Chung-kuo Ch'ing-nien Ch'u-pan-she, 1968). English version, translated by Sidney Shapiro, entitles it *The Builders* (Peking: Foreign Languages Press, 1964). We have retained the word 'saga' (*shih*) as it is in the original to indicate the novel's large scope.

seemed like a golden age, when increased collectivization seemed to promise a bright future. Following the deceptions of the 'Hundred Flowers' period and the economic hardships after the Great Leap, life must have proved far harsher than anticipated. Communist novelists, as politically committed, or rather *commissioned*, writers, were not supposed to expose the harsher side of life, no matter how real or how widespread it was. As conditions in the late 1950's were painful, the novelists could meet the demands for political relevance and for literature for and about the masses only by writing about earlier periods. They could at least remind their readers that life in the past had been even grimmer and that the hard struggles of the new society must not be forgotten. At the same time, they could glorify the Party and Chairman Mao, whose power, resourcefulness, and wisdom had miraculously produced the new society and who should thus be fully trusted in the present and forever.

In Chou Li-po's *Great Changes*, Party leadership in the cooperative movement is more clearly treated than in Chao's *Sanliwan Village*. A large portion of the book depicts the stubborn resistance of the poor peasants, who have recently acquired land and now must surrender it to the cooperatives. Because Chou has more intellectual sophistication and more technique than Chao, his novel is highly literary, with graphic descriptions and meticulous documentation. In his portrayal of country people, the author shows his skill in writing realistic fiction rather in the European tradition. Most of the book is devoted to the struggle between the desperate and stubborn poor peasants and the manipulative cadre, who uses persuasion and threats to carry out Party policy. A climax comes when the peasants mass one night to cut down thousands of trees on the hills of the mountain village, rather than let them be expropriated. The loss reduces the village to utter poverty. Sobered by the fact that their folly has cost them their forest, just as they feared the cooperatives would have done, the peasants docilely and gratefully accept the organization of the cooperative —the Party triumphs. To an outside reader, the story may seem ironic. There may also be irony in the forced acceptance of the communes. Thus the propaganda message is at best crude and high-handed in an otherwise successful realistic depiction of life,[71] although the irony was not perceived by the Communist critics who applauded the novel. The message was that those who resisted the Party policy are at best comic, pathetic, and foolish, and can only harm themselves, since they must eventually surrender. For Chinese Communists, the Party was as infallible in 1958 as it had been in the early 1950's. The people must accept the communes.

A novel of quality will be of lasting interest, even though it may have different meanings for different people at different times and places. Both Chao Shu-li's *Sanliwan Village* and Chou Li-po's *Great Changes* are works of quality. No matter how obvious their political message, it is contained in characters and events that portray real life. The authors' views intrude only occasionally, and the obvious use of slogan and direct propaganda is minimal.

But the same cannot be said of Liu Ch'ing's *Saga of the Builders*. It is a work of gigantic scope, of which Part I was published in 1960. Like *Great Changes*, it harks back to the beginning of the decade immediately after the first waves of land reform. But the political conditions must have so changed that it was no longer enough to make recent history reflect the present. In dealing with the past, the novelist's propaganda message had to bear directly on the present. Liu's novel is so full of long citations of Chairman Mao, bald slogans, and praise of Communist wisdom that the narrative falls apart.

In the early part of *Saga of the Builders*, sharp conflicts divide the rich peasants from the 'backward' poor ones and the progressives. The doubt and hesitation of the former are not worked out through character development in action but resolved in

---

[71] See an analysis of Chou's novel by T. A. Hsia, 'Hero and Hero-Worship in Chinese Communist Fiction,' *The China Quarterly*, No. 13, January–March, 1963, pp. 117–19.

the author's short commentary on Chairman Mao's wisdom. Thereafter, progress can begin:

> If history were to stop in this year 1953, then, they will very quickly be returned to their pre-1949 miserable and cruel fate. The Communist Party definitely will not allow this! Chairman Mao has superb wisdom! Investigate the land, settle properties, rectify the Party in the meantime, and be ready to go forward.[72]

Few novels can avoid dealing with relations between the sexes or the subject of women. *Saga* treats the subject in an incredible way. A young widow is forced by poverty to leave her father-in-law, a poor blind peasant, to go into the service of a rich peasant. Having been raped by a thief and rogue when she was sixteen, she has since been the easy prey of other country ruffians. When the rich peasant seduces her, she feels she has taken revenge for her bitter past, for the times her father-in-law used to beat her. The attitude of this helpless victim, who one would think deserves sympathy, outrages the novelist, who cries out, 'Ah, women, women! When they have lost the noble human spirit, what destructive forces in the world they are!'[73] What she has destroyed, or what she could destroy, we are never told. To understand the author's point of view, we need to contrast her with the progressive women in the novel, who subordinate their desire for union or marriage to a total dedication to farm labor and national construction. Thus, a pure Communist spirit must prevail at every level of society and in every remote village. The hero, the most progressive villager, learns of the woman's seduction. Furious, as if possessed by Chairman Mao and the Party spirit, he directs his rage at an amazing target, her father-in-law, who is not even present:

> You blind devil! So this is the bastard way you behave? You are ungrateful to [*tui pu ch'i*] Chairman Mao! You are ungrateful to the Communist Party! Ungrateful to me, Liang Sheng-pao, myself![74]

How a poor, old, blind, and enfeebled peasant could have prevented his daughter-in-law's seduction is not explained. But the novelist was apparently grabbing every opportunity to evoke Chairman Mao's hallowed presence and the honor of the Party. The concluding chapter begins with whole pages of quotations from Mao's proclamation of October, 1953, on the 'transitional period toward socialist reform,' and the 'avoidance of rightist and "leftist" errors,' and cites Party resolutions on 'contradictions in problems of grains supply,' on the 'full measures of planned purchase and planned supply.' The climax occurs when, 'to the exultation of everyone' in the village, it is reported that 'the Central Committee has proposed to the full membership of the Party the task of carrying out propaganda among the peasants in accordance with the general directions.[75]

I have concentrated on the novels of three outstanding authors on peasant life, two of whom have managed to retain artistic quality in their works, in the belief that the revolutionary importance of rural areas and their heritage of national tradition make them the main source for art, according to Mao's dicta. Novels on other subjects also demonstrate that the harsh conditions of the late 1950's did not lend themselves to realistic descriptions of life. Novelists were still urged to glorify the present, of course, but not to depict the present reality. They must 'revolutionize' the material by romanticizing the present and forecasting a happy future. Mao's alleged formula of 1958, the 'combination of revolutionary realism with revolutionary romanticism,' was praised as 'the scientific summing-up of the experiences of all literary history.'[76]

---

[72] A translation of Liu, *Ch'uang-yeh Shih*, p. 135.   [73] *Ibid.*, pp. 333–34.
[74] *Ibid.*, p. 380.   [75] *Ibid.*, pp. 490–92.
[76] Chou Yang, 'New Folk Songs Have Opened up a New Road for Poetry,' *Hung-ch'i* (*Red Flag*), No. 3, Peking, 1958, pp. 33–39; see also Kuo Mo-jo, 'Realism and Romanticism,'

The hardship this formula must have imposed on art and artists is evident in the fact that, until the publication of *The Song of Ouyang Hai*, novelists on nonrural subjects also continued to portray the Communist past to reflect the present, rather than describe contemporary life. Their works will be discussed in three main categories: (1) war or military and political struggles against foreign or domestic enemies in the 1940's; (2) early intellectual or social activities of young Communist cadres; and (3) the life of the workers in the new society.

War novels and heroics. After 1957, a new crop of war or adventure novels celebrated early Communist military exploits before 1949. A pre-1949 Communist precedent for the genre was the *Heroes of Lu-liang*.[77] It was serialized in a northern border region newspaper before being edited and published in book form in 1952. An entertaining novel, it is said to have enjoyed great popularity among illiterate peasants to whom it was read aloud in villages. Its rustic zest and humor are in the 'national form' of the episodic traditional Chinese novels. It depicts gallant Chinese fighting against Japanese invaders. Their patriotism is genuine and simple. The source of inspiration is fresh and direct.[78]

Another work, *Three Thousand Miles of Lovely Land*,[79] also published in 1952, focused on the 'volunteer' railroad workers assisting communications in North Korea during the Korean War. The novel describes many small incidents designed to illustrate Sino-Korean friendship—the tearful gratitude of Koreans for Chinese help, the sentimental recollection of earlier Korean efforts to learn from Chinese Communist experiences, and a Korean commander's 'pride in having been Mao Tse-tung's warrior.' The little heroic military action is overshadowed by joy over victory, ridicule of American war prisoners, and hatred of, or contempt for, American weapons. The total effect is surprisingly light, with romantic heroism muted rather than glorified. The novel has human interest, and its realism, if strongly biased, is at least not falsified.

The character of war or heroic novels changed after the 1958 policy calling for a 'combination of revolutionary realism and revolutionary romanticism.' Under the new policy, Ch'ü Po's *Tracks in the Snowy Forest*,[80] published in 1957, became a favorite. Following high official commendation, it was made into a movie, and some of its episodes were adapted into plays. It is an incredible 'Superman' story that is easily adaptable to crude comic strips and appeals to the masses who must have been bored with interminable official ideological tirades and doctrinaire novels.

Snowy Forest is about the past glory of Communist guerrilla warfare. It focuses on a small military unit, each member of which fights dangerous battles and has fantastic adventures in Manchuria in 1946, where bandits supposedly in collusion with the Nationalists were entrenched. The feats of these legendary figures are semimiraculous, as a few chapter titles reveal: 'Mushroom Oldster's Wondrous Tale of the Nipples Mountain,' 'Jumping over the Ravine to Attack the Lairs of Tigers and Wolves,' 'Capture of the Demonic Priest,' and 'Great Knight-errant on Snow.'

Chao Shu-li's *Magic Spring Caves*,[81] published in 1959, deals with the guerrilla warfare of Shansi villagers, under Communist guidance, against Japanese troops and

---

Red Flag, No. 1, 1958, pp. 1–8. For more information on the subject see Fokkema, *Literary Doctrine*, pp. 196–201.

[77] Ma Feng and Hsi Yung, *Lü-liang Ying-hsiung Chuan* (Shanghai: Hsin-hua Shu-tien, 1952).

[78] For a synopsis and analysis see Chi Li, 'Communist War Stories,' *The China Quarterly*, No. 13, January–March, 1963, pp. 143–45.

[79] Yang Shuo, *San-ch'ien-li Chiang-shan* (Peking: Jen-min Wen-hsüeh Ch'u-pan-she, 1952); English version by Yüan K'e-chia (Peking: Foreign Languages Press, 1957).

[80] Ch'ü Po, *Lin-hai Hsüeh Yüan* (Peking: Tso-chia Ch'u-pan-she, 1957); English version by Sidney Shapiro (Peking: Foreign Languages Press, 1962).

[81] Chao Shu-li, *Ling Ch'üan Tung* (Peking: Tso-chia Ch'u-pan-she, 1959).

marauding Nationalist soldiers during the Sino-Japanese War. Only the first volume, so far as I know, has appeared. I do not know whether the sequel has met with official discouragement. But this work's romanticization of the glorious past fails to inspire or sweeten the present to the extent that *Snowy Forest* does. Precisely for that reason, it is a very good realistic novel.[82] Chao Shu-li is no less a conformist to Communist literary doctrine or Maoist dicta than Ch'ü Po, but his artistic talent limits his capacity for overromanticization. Inasmuch as his background and ability make him a model of the people's artist, his conformity to later literary policies remains natural. In *Magic Spring Caves*, Chao remains a master of the traditional novelistic form, which for him is both natural and integral to his fictional artistry. His language retains the piquancy and vigor of the folk idiom, and his characters are as vivid and authentic as before. His use of local myths, such as the rituals of prayer for rain, herbs for immortality, or the poisonous dragon, maintains lively humor and subtle perspectives. The fact that *Caves* has enjoyed much less official acclaim than *Snowy Forest* since 1959 may be due to the Party's overanxious efforts to make all art beautify the present regime in the most garish manner. Subtlety and realism were not enough; the Party demanded that the propaganda message be obvious.[83] 'Romanticized revolutionary realism' leaves little room for much realism.

Two other war or heroic novels should be mentioned in passing. The first, *Red Sun*[84] of 1959, is a war novel on a large scale, with a Communist army pitted in a battle of revenge against a Nationalist division in 1947. It is written in rich, masculine style and crowded with Communist military characters of all ranks, all of whom are labeled, rather than adequately described, as heroes. But as T. A. Hsia has observed, 'it is technically impossible for a novelist working within a realistic framework to present such an overabundance of heroism and make it authentic.'[85] Moreover, 'there is no surer way of debasing heroism than to multiply heroes.'[86]

The second heroic novel is *Red Cliff*.[87] It has a greater variety of characters than *Red Sun* and more intricate relationships among them. The protagonists are students, workers, cadres, and guerrilla fighters, all of whom are involved in underground work against the Nationalist government in Chungking during 1948–49. There are dramatic scenes, battles of wit, feats of jail-breaking, martyrdom, and sacrifice. It is a well-constructed, highly literate novel. Of course, the final triumph of the underground revolutionaries is assured. The novel served the early-1960's purpose of reviving fear and hatred of Nationalist secret agents, who are picturesquely described with their shadowy American allies. Certain positive characters border upon the fantastic, such as a resourceful little boy nicknamed 'little Radish,' a 'two-gun Old Grandma,' and the thoroughly selfless heroine, Chiang-chieh. These highly romanticized figures fit the revolutionary realism of the day, with villains and heroes drawn in black and white.

Novels of nostalgia for Communist intellectuals. Two other notable works, published in

---

[82] Cyril Birch, in 'Chinese Communist Literature: The Persistence of Traditional Forms,' calls the *Caves* among 'the most realistic and exciting war stories I have read,' *The China Quarterly*, No. 13, January–March, 1963, p. 79.

[83] The 'romanticized' scenes are the special favorite of Chiang Ch'ing (Mrs. Mao) in her promotion of new drama since 1964. See *Kuang-chow Hung-tai Hui Pao* (*The Kuang-chow Red Guards Representatives Daily*), October 28, 1968, Canton, reprinted in *Ming Pao*, February 5, 1969.

[84] Wu Ch'iang, *Hung Jih* (Peking: Jen-min Wen-hsüeh Ch'u-pan-she, revised edition, 1959).

[85] T. A. Hsia, 'Heroes and Hero Worship in Chinese Communist Fiction,' *The China Quarterly*, No. 13, January–March, 1963, p. 136.

[86] *Ibid.*, p. 131.

[87] Lo Kuang-pin and Yang I-yen: *Hung Yen* (Peking: Ch'ing-nien Ch'u-pan-she, 1961).

1959 and 1960, deal with the intellectual experiences or growth of the cadre of the 1930's. Liang Pin's *Keep the Red Flag Flying*[88] is about how high school students of the early 1930's from poor rural families developed Communist ardor under cadre training and carried out revolutionary activities in alliance with the awakened peasants, using their school in a northern provincial city as their base. The novel accurately records a southwestern Hopei dialect. For those who know the dialect, the novel is remarkably true to life. It is not a difficult dialect for Mandarin speakers, but the fact that five Tientsin college students, who must be very fond of the novel, collaborated on a glossary of 308 entries for its eleventh printing in 1961 indicates the purity of the dialectal usage and the difficulty non-Mandarin speakers have in reading the work. The theme of the novel is still the invincible Communist spirit with which the early cadres inspired and instructed youth in their revolutionary alliance with the peasants. But its narrative style is almost too subdued, particularly in comparison with the bombastic *Snowy Forest* or *Red Sun*. Not a profound or sophisticated novel, it nevertheless breathes into the dense literary atmosphere of the late 1950's some fresh air, with its idyllic descriptions, lifelike adolescents, and simple but wise country people.

Song of Youth,[89] on the other hand, is the personal history of a girl of petit-bourgeois background who, since her college days in the 1930's, has been emotionally and intellectually attracted to the Communist cause. In 1949, she finally realizes her dream of becoming a Party member. The many episodes of the novel depict real events among young intellectuals. Because it is autobiographical, it has psychological veracity, despite the naïveté of its female author. For T. A. Hsia, the heroine recalls Madame Bovary.[90] Sentimentality and utopian illusions fill many passages of the novel, but they are true of the state of mind of many youths and young adults of those days. Its realism and romanticism have not quite 'combined.'

Mao's *Talks at the Yenan Forum* had distinguished between literature for the masses and that for the cadre. The former could be directed at a lower level of appreciation, and the latter at a higher and perhaps more specialized one.[91] These two novels tend to serve the cadre readership and, before the Cultural Revolution, must have been especially appealing to older cadres. They would evoke strong personal identification and a comforting nostalgia, in view of the trials of the late 1950's and 1960's.

An exceptional novel about workers. Another important novel, Ai Wu's *Steeled and Tempered*,[92] deals with factory workers—a surprisingly rare topic, considering the fact that workers are supposed to form the leading proletarian class. The author is among the very few veteran novelists who continue to be productive. Unlike the episodic 'national form' of the novels on peasant life, the organic construction of plot in Ai Wu's distinguished work reveals conflicts at several levels. The conflicts occur between the expert's knowledge of factory management and the Party's ideal of proletarian discipline and education, between old experienced workers and young zealous ones, and between efficient production and time-consuming indoctrination. The central theme is the 'red and expert' contradiction. Despite the formula, Ai Wu has constructed a novel that is full of vivid concrete details. His description of the technical aspects of factory management, including the complicated machinery of the refinery and the foundry and the living conditions of workers in their dormitories and

---

[88] Liang Pin, *Hung Ch'i P'u* (Peking: Ch'ing-nien Ch'u-pan-she, 1958). Its English title is as given in the Peking journal *Chinese Literature*, No. 1, 1959.

[89] Yang Mo, *Ch'ing-chun Chih Ko* (Peking: Jen-min Wen-hsüeh Ch'u-pan-she, revised edition, 1960).

[90] Hsia, 'Heroes and Hero Worship,' p. 123.

[91] See Mao, *Yenan Wen-i*, pp. 18–19.

[92] Ai Wu, *Pai Lien Ch'eng Kang* (Peking: Tso-chia Ch'u-pan-she, 1958).

homes, is painstakingly accurate. The action takes place in the early 1950's. The steel industry is very young, and its equipment is far from perfect. Human ingenuity and self-sacrifice must make up for the mechanical deficiencies. The Party also wants to inculcate the correct ideology. The contradiction between 'expert and red' is eventually resolved in the emergence of a positive hero, a skilled smelting workman, topping everyone else in production, and thoroughly 'red' in his ideological enlightenment. *Steeled and Tempered* is a satisfying novel as a whole. The political message is implicit rather than explicit in the presentation and is well integrated into the narrative. It is one of the very few successful novels of the late 1950's.

Literature's nadir in 1966—and a hope. The jumble of slogans, the obvious heroics, and the constant homage to Chairman Mao and the Party in works such as *Saga* and *Snowy Forest* must have caused secret dissatisfaction among many readers and some compunction among high-ranking Party leaders who had any literary sensitivity.[93] But the trend was irresistible and culminated in Ching Ching-mai's *Song of Ouyang Hai*,[94] which sang only of Mao's glory. Although previous works had romanticized reality to serve the political purposes of revolution, they bore at least some resemblance to fiction, which *Ouyang Hai*, totally politicized, completely lacks. The fabrication of a new positive hero to glorify Mao's personal cult is forced upon the reader. The book is a gigantic hyperbole in which the author exalts the character and deeds of the Maoist hero yet insists that this is a real-life story.

Its narrative, which is badly marred by incongruous rhetoric, loosely and incoherently records a series of scenes and events. Yet, to the utter confusion of values in art and life, fiction and reality, this third-rate reportage is called a 'novel' in the blurb and a 'song' in the author's postscript. Perhaps the blurb is the best description of the lengthy book:

> The *Song of Ouyang Hai* is a work that raises high the great red flag of Mao Tse-tung's Thought and gives prominence to politics. It vividly reflects the brand new phenomena since the People's Liberation Army learned aptly and made apt use of Chairman Mao's written works. . . . It is the summation to a high degree of the spiritual expression of millions of revolutionary fighters since their immense learning of Chairman Mao's works.
>
> This novel describes the road that Ouyang Hai traveled in his twenty-three short years of life. The fact that he eagerly hoped to be a hero when he was not a hero but was then unconscious of being a hero when he did become one is the result of the cultivation and instruction of the Party. . . . It's the result of a revolutionary fighter's aptly learning and making apt use of Chairman Mao's works, with emphasis on 'use,' as he takes Chairman Mao's books as the most elevated guidance in reforming his subjective world, while reforming the objective world at the same time.
>
> The *Song of Ouyang Hai* is a song in homage to the great thought of Mao Tse-tung, also a song in homage to our age of socialism.

The 'novel' conveys exactly the same feeling of total infatuation as the blurb. Both say more about Mao's written works and thought than about the hero. Ouyang Hai

---

[93] For example, on October 28, 1968, a Canton Red Guard newspaper, *Kuang-chow Hung-tai Hui Pao* (*Kuangchow Red Guards' Representatives Daily*), revived its attack on Lin-Mo-han, who was concurrently Deputy Minister of Culture and Deputy Director of the Party's Propaganda Department until the Cultural Revolution. The Red Guard paper charged that when *Snowy Forest* was adapted into a play in the early 1960's, Lin wanted to balance its excessively positive characters by making more prominent such negative characters as the bandit leader, Mountain-perching Hawk.

[94] Ching Ching-mai, *Ouyang Hai Chih Ke* (Peking: Chieh-fang-chün Wen-i Ch'u-pan-she, 1966).

is a composite figure, a synthetic product of the three leading revolutionary classes. Born of a poor peasant family, he joins the PLA, masters artisan skills, and assists in farm production in the people's communes. The world in which he moves (most of China) seems physically large, but it is a world closed in by Chairman Mao's thought. At every important point, Mao's words are chanted, pages of Mao's works are turned and cited, and Mao's large portrait inspires tears of joy and devotion.

This is the world that Mao and the Maoists want to create, a world peopled with millions of heroes like Ouyang Hai, whose 'heroism' lies in total selfless devotion to Mao's thoughts and works. The hero of *Ouyang Hai* has so conquered himself as to be free from ego and to have become 'a pure man in accordance with the Chairman's instructions.'[95] He thinks the Chairman's thought at all times and 'aptly applies it,' whether he is engaged in gathering tea seeds for the commune, saving a five-year-old girl from drowning, or sacrificing his life to save the passengers of a train by getting a horse off the tracks. Yet, however forceful the insistence that this novel is true, it remains disingenuous and visionary, though the vision is so poorly constructed as to be totally unconvincing. *Song of Ouyang Hai*, the last of the propaganda novels before 1966, was closest to the point at which creative literature—in form and content— vanished with the onset of the Cultural Revolution. Its appearance marks the beginning of the ominous transition to a three-year period during which 3 billion copies of Mao's works, mostly nonliterature, engulfed the mainland. Reflecting now upon earlier decades of Chinese Communist literature, one can only say that, even under the most difficult circumstances, there was no lack of artistic talent. Poets like Feng Chih, Ko Pi-chou, and Liang Shang-chüan and novelists like Chao Shu-li, Chou Li-po, and Ai Wu are capable of maintaining what Pasternak has called 'a particle of art.' They may be too old for creative work when the present tidal wave has passed, but there is still hope that, when conditions have changed, new and healthy talent may yet spring from the now barren ground.

SELECTED BIBLIOGRAPHY

On Language

CHAO, YUEN REN. *A Grammar of Spoken Chinese.* Berkeley and Los Angeles: University of California Press, 1965. In more than a thousand pages, broadly covers and deeply probes practically all phases of grammatical analysis of the Chinese spoken language.

HSIA, T. A. *Metaphor, Myth, Ritual and the People's Commune.** Berkeley: Center for Chinese Studies, University of California, Current Chinese Language Project (CCLP) monograph series No. 7, 1961. Illustrates parts of the sociopsychological life of the Chinese people as reflected in their 'world' of language, guided by Communist policy during the establishment of the communes.

HSIA, TAO-TAI. *China's Language Reform.* New Haven, Conn.: Yale University Press, Mirror Series No. 21, 1956. A convenient reference, generally presenting the intention, discussion, and practice of the Communist language reform in its early phase.

KARLGREN, BERNARD. *Easy Lessons in Chinese Writing.* Stockholm: Naturmetodens Spakinstitut, 1958. With experience and erudition, the author fully and concisely presents the principles and practicality of Chinese writing. Of special instructive value to Western students.

LI, CHI. *'A Provisional System of Grammar for Teaching Chinese,' with Introduction and Commentary.** Berkeley: Center for Chinese Studies, University of California, CCLP Series No. 6, 1960. Translation of the full text of an important document with revolutionary ideas about

---

[95] *Ibid.*, p. 172.

* If out of print, microfilm copies are available on order from University Microfilms, Inc., 313 North First Street, Ann Arbor, Michigan.

Chinese grammar. Translator's introduction and commentary present valuable insight into the problems.

LI, CHIN-HSI. *Han-yü Fa-chan Kuo-ch'eng ho Han-yü Kuei-fan-hua* (*The Process of Development of the Chinese Language and Its Standardization*). Nanking: Chiang-su Jen-min Press, 1957. Influential statements on history of the Chinese language, presenting arguments for its reform and the problems involved.

SERRUYS, PAUL L. M. *Survey of the Chinese Language Reform and the Anti-illiteracy Movement in Communist China.** Berkeley: Center for Chinese Studies, University of California, CCLP Series No. 8, 1962. Contains historical surveys, discussion of current issues, and rich bibliographical information. (The remainder of the CCLP Series, No. 1 through 13, published from 1956 to 1968, examines significant features and changes of Chinese language in connection with sociopolitical and cultural movements as well as language reform. These studies are generally available in university libraries.)

On Literature

BIRCH, CYRIL, ed. *Chinese Communist Literature*. New York: Frederick A. Praeger, 1963. Conference papers by eleven contributors, with the purpose of 'establishing a sound basis for a critical approach to Chinese Communist literature.' The articles cited appeared originally in *The China Quarterly*, No. 13, London, January–March, 1963.

CH'EN, JEROME, and MICHAEL BULLOCK. *Mao and the Chinese Revolution*. Oxford: Oxford University Press, 1965. Translations of almost all of Mao's published poetry, with detailed notes and commentary.

CHEN, S. H. 'Artificial Flowers During a Natural Thaw,' in DONALD TREADGOLD, ed., *Soviet and Chinese Communism: Similarities and Differences*. Seattle: University of Washington Press, 1967, pp. 220–54. A critique of cultural and literary issues, contrasting with Soviet phenomena in the same areas. The companion article by Sidney Monas, 'The Revelation of St. Boris: Russian Literature and Individual Autonomy,' pp. 255–87, and Victor Erlich's introduction to this section of the book, pp. 215–19, are together recommended for reference.

————. 'Multiplicity in Uniformity,' *The China Quarterly*, No. 3, London: Congress for Cultural Freedom, July–September, 1960. A study in depth of an unprecedented literary and social phenomenon during the Great Leap Forward.

Chinese Literature. Peking: Foreign Languages Press. This monthly journal, published since 1952, is generally available abroad. Contains English translations of literary works of selected current authors, notes and reviews, and information about new publications. Editor was Mao Tun until 1966, thereafter anonymous.

FOKKEMA, D. W. *Literary Doctrine in China and Soviet Influence, 1956–1960*. The Hague: Mouton, 1965. A meticulously documented study of Chinese Communist literary theories and policies.

HSIA, C. T. *A History of Modern Chinese Fiction, 1917–1957*. New Haven, Conn.: Yale University Press, 1961. Two sections deal with Communist fiction from critical perspectives. The rest of the book contains information and discussion of pre-Communist periods, which offer a broad view on modern Chinese literature.

NUNN, G. RAYMOND. *Publishing in Mainland China*. Cambridge, Mass.: The MIT Press, MIT Report No. 4, 1966. Some useful statistics and tables. Although the book makes 'particular reference to publications in natural, applied and social sciences,' it reveals general publishing conditions, including those in art and literature, up to about 1964.

Wen-yi Pao (*Bulletin of Art and Literature*). Peking: Hsin-hua Shu-tien. Biweekly, 1949–50; weekly, 1957; biweekly since 1958, generally available until 1966 but not thereafter. Comparable to *Wenxue Pinglun* in importance and influence, though more concerned with

---

* If out of print, microfilm copies are available on order from University Microfilms, Inc., 313 North First Street, Ann Arbor, Michigan.

contemporary issues in art and literature, hence was involved in more controversies in earlier issues and later more directly reflected Party dicta. Founded by famous authoress Ting Ling, with Ch'en Ch'i-hsia and Hsiao Yin as editors in 1949–51. In 1952, editorial board was led by Feng Hsüeh-feng. Political controversies ensued, ending in purges of those named above. The editorship passed to Chang Kuang-nien in 1955.

Wenxue Pinglun (Discussion on Literature). Peking: Jen-min Wen-hsüeh Ch'u-pan-she. Bimonthly. In 1957–59, it was named *Wenxue Yanjiu (Research on Literature)*, and thereafter assumed its present name. Generally available until 1966 but not thereafter. Perhaps the most important literary journal, it contained solid articles by major literary critics and scholars on both classical and contemporary Chinese literature, although quality fluctuated with changing political circumstances and literary policy.

29

THE PERFORMING AND VISUAL
ARTS AND MUSIC

RICHARD F. S. YANG

COMMUNIST CHINESE ATTITUDE TOWARD ART

THE Communist revolution in China is a total revolution. It is a revolution on all fronts—political, social, economic, military, and ideological. Thus, there is also a revolution in the arts. As a matter of fact, to observers who watch the Communist revolution from the outside, a most interesting and spectacular show has been the revolution of art in its various forms since 1949. If there is anything in which the Chinese Communists have surpassed other members of the Communist world (including Soviet Russia), it is in the art reform that they have tried to carry out.

We must be aware of the standards and principles that the Communists have for art. To us, 'art is for art's sake.' Art itself is the final goal and purpose. There is nothing beyond or superseding art. To the Chinese Communists, art is not for art's sake at all. According to Mao Tse-tung: 'With us, literature and art are for the people. . . . Literature and art should serve . . . the millions and tens of millions of the working people. . . . The aim [of literature and art] must be to serve the masses of the people. . . . Who, then, are the masses of the people? The broadest section of the people, constituting more than 90 per cent of our total population, is the workers, peasants, and soldiers.'[1] Thus it is very clear that, to the Communists, art is not the ultimate purpose but a means to an end—service to the masses.

Furthermore, to us in the West, the source of art is the inspiration or experience of the artist himself. Art is but an expression of that inspiration or experience. To the Chinese Communists, 'works of literature and art as ideological forms are products of the reflection in the human brain of the life of a given society. Revolutionary literature and art are the products of the reflection of the life of the people in the brains of revolutionary writers and artists. The life of the people is always a mine of raw materials for literature and art.'[2]

It is of paramount importance for us that we understand the attitude of the Chinese Communists toward art before we can discuss what has happened in the various forms of art under Communist rule. In traditional China, art and literature were regarded as special privileges and skills that only a privileged class of intelligentsia could possess and enjoy. In traditional China, people were generally divided into four classes—scholars, peasants, workers and merchants—among which the scholars, or the intellectual class, occupied the highest position in the social strata. They were also

---

[1] Mao Tse-tung, *On Literature and Art* (Peking: Foreign Languages Press, 1967), p. 12.
[2] *Ibid.*, p. 18.

the ruling class, while the other three were usually the ruled. In the old days, soldiers were so low in society and so degraded that they were not worthy even to be regarded as a class. But the Communist revolution is purportedly a socialist revolution led by the proletariat. In this revolution, the proletariat, including the peasants, workers, and soldiers, has become the ruling class, and the intelligentsia has become the target of the revolution. In art and literature, the revolution is primarily aimed at denying and denouncing the privileges the intellectual class enjoyed for so long in the old society. Thus, when literature and art are designated to serve the masses in the socialist revolution, the Chinese Communists have in effect decided not only to destroy literature and art esteemed in the old society but also to destroy the lofty and esteemed positions that artists and men of literature enjoyed in the old society. So, in the art revolution, they have dealt not only with the forms and contents of art but also with the persons involved in art, namely, the artists.

As a result, in the two decades after 1949, when the various forms of art and music were subjected to 'reform,' they were utilized by the leaders of the Communist Party as powerful instruments for the implementation of the political programs they wanted to carry out in their proletarian revolution. Traditional arts, such as the Peking opera, have been given new style and new content. Individual artists, such as Ch'i Pai-shih, have fallen victim to the Cultural Revolution. The following survey outlines how the different phases of the cultural reform have affected the performing arts, the visual arts, and music, with particular attention to Chinese opera, modern drama (hua-chü), motion pictures, music, musicals and ballet, and painting.

THE CHINESE OPERA

Pre-Communist dominance of the Peking opera. Among all the art forms in China, opera is probably the most typically Chinese. Very few people in the West know that China is a land of operas. More than 700 years ago, when China was ruled by the Mongols of the Yüan dynasty, there already had developed a dramatic form known as the Yüan drama that had the elements of a modern opera, with singing, dancing, acting, and a plot. Subsequently, many different operas made their appearance in various regions and became the most welcome form of popular entertainment in rural areas as well as commercial centers.[3] Of all the operas, the Peking opera emerged as the most popular and important form and became a national pastime.

Several reasons accounted for the dominance of the Peking opera. First, it was developed in Peking, then capital of the Ch'ing dynasty, during the middle of the nineteenth century. Political patronage, including that of the royal families, not only helped promote it as the favorite entertainment at the capital but also spread it to other parts of the country, particularly the provincial capitals. Second, the Peking opera was the newest of all Chinese operas. Since it had incorporated several local tunes,[4] it had successfully crossed the provincial boundaries and thus acquired a 'national' status. Third, through their superb artistry, a group of actors and performers succeeded in making the Peking opera a widely recognized art form.[5] Thus,

---

[3] For a preliminary report on the reform of the Peking opera, see Richard F. S. Yang, 'The Reform of Peking Opera under the Communists,' *The China Quarterly,* July–September, 1962, pp. 124–39.

[4] The Peking opera was first developed in Peking during the middle of the nineteenth century by a group of professional singers from Anhwei Province who came to the capital on tour. These singers, in order to compete with the K'un-ch'ü opera then dominating the stage of Peking, mixed the arts and tunes of a few local operas, principally of Anhwei, Hupei, Shansi, and Hopei, and created a new 'sound' known as the 'Flowery Groups' of the Peking stage, later recognized as the 'Peking opera.'

[5] The Peking opera owed a great deal of its popularity to some of the outstanding actors in earlier days, such as T'an Hsin-p'ei, Liu Hung-sheng, Ch'en Te-lin, Kung Yüan-p'u, and

in spite of the domestic and international upheavals in modern China, the Peking opera survived and emerged intact.[6]

Developments since 1949. Following the Communist victory in 1949, the Peking opera, together with other art forms, was destined to be revolutionized. The first step was psychological, namely, the de-emphasis of the operatic art as the *only* leading form. The new regime, in a show of impartiality, had helped rejuvenate many local operas that had all but totally disappeared in the midst of constant warfare during the first half of the twentieth century. As a result, when the first National Exhibition of Operatic Art was held in Peking under the auspices of the Communist Party in 1952, twenty-three operas of many localities, such as Hopei, Hupei, Yünnan, Kiangsi, Hunan, Shansi, Honan, Szechwan, Shanghai, and Chekiang, including of course, Peking, were represented and more than 100 plays were performed by their leading professional troupes. During the exhibition, Chou Yang, then Minister of Propaganda and charged with the task of art and literature reforms, told of the following policies of the regime.

We demand that operas must portray the new life of the people. We must take into consideration the conflicts and contradictions between the various forms of opera and the new content they should present. Therefore, we must carry out reforms of all operas on the basis of their original forms. First of all, we shall re-arrange and preserve some of the good, old numbers. As far as their contents are concerned, we should remove the feudalistic ingredients and improve those elements favoring the people. As far as their artistic patterns are concerned, whether in music or in dancing, we must improve them so as to enrich and strengthen their abilities to express realism.[7]

Stressing the regime's impartiality toward all forms, the government spokesman stated that 'all the various operatic forms were products of the creative activities of the laboring people. They represent different nationalistic forms and rich local features. Whether in language, music or costume, they possess the characteristics of the people.'[8]

The actual reform of the Peking opera began when objections were raised by the Party to various aspects of the art that were deemed undesirable, including certain

---

Wang Yao-ch'ing. In the early years of the twentieth century, many additional famous actors contributed greatly to the increasingly popularity of this art. They included the 'four great *tan* actors,' namely, Mei Lan-fang, Ch'eng Yen-ch'iu, Shang Hsiao-yün, and Hsün Hui-sheng (all were female impersonators); the great *sheng* (male with beard) actors, including Yü Shu-yen, Ma Lien-liang, T'an Fu-ying, and Yen Chü-p'ing; the great *ching* (painted face) actors, such as Chin Hsiu-shan and Chin Shao-shan (father and son), and later Ch'iu Sheng-jung and Yuan Shih-hai; the great *wu-sheng* (young warrior) actors, such as Yang Hsiao-lou, and later Kao Sheng-lin; the great *ch'ou* (clown) actors, such as Shih Hsiao-fu, and Yeh Sheng-chang (warrior clown). All contributed greatly to the widespread popularity of operatic art in China.

[6] During the late nineteenth and early twentieth centuries, China went through a series of internal and external upheavals, such as the T'aip'ing Rebellion of the 1850's and 1860's, the Boxer Rebellion of 1900, the Nationalist Revolution of 1911, the May Fourth Movement (Modern Renaissance) of 1919 and thereafter, and the Northern Expedition of 1926. None of these earthshaking events made any dent on the Peking opera, although other art forms, as well as literature and the language, were all affected noticeably.

[7] Chou Yang, 'Kai-ke ho Fa-chan Min-tsu Hsi-ch'ü I-shu (Reform and Develop National Operatic Art),' *Jen-min Chou-k'an* (*People's Weekly*), No. 53, 1952. This was a talk delivered by Chou Yang at the First National Exhibition of Operas held on November 14, 1952, in Peking.

[8] Chou Yang, quoted in an editorial of *Ta-kung Jih-pao*, Hong Kong, October 9, 1952, entitled 'Ch'uan-kuo Hsi-ch'ü Kuan-mo Yen-ch'u Ta-hui K'ai-mu (The Opening of the National Exhibition of Operatic Performance).'

characterizations, themes, bad habits, and unhealthy practices. As a result, many were removed from the traditional repertoire of the Peking opera.[9]

In 1958, after the slogan 'let a hundred flowers bloom' had subsided and the new phrase, 'the Great Leap Forward,' had been coined, the reform of the Peking opera entered an important and exciting stage. Under the policy of 'walking on two legs,' certain good plays were to be preserved, although they had to be revised or rearranged, and the Peking opera would also undertake to portray the contemporary life and struggle of the people.

Traditions and their modification. The following developments are especially worth noting:

(1) Revision of old plays and composing of new numbers, in which nearly all the leading performers of the old opera took part. For example, Ma Lien-liang revised his well-known play *Ch'ün-ying hui* (*The Meeting of Heroes*) and changed its title to *Ch'ih-pi chih chan* (*The Battle of Red Cliff*).[10] Hsün Hui-sheng revised his interpretations of the leading heroines Hung-niang, Chin Yü-nu, and Hsun Kuan-niang.[11] Kai Chiao-t'ien rearranged his famous work *Wu-chiang hen* (*The Tragedy at the River Wu*).[12] Chou Hsin-fang staged a new play known as *Hai-jui shang-shu* (*Hai Jui's Memorial*); followed by other Hai Jui plays.[13] Mei Lan-fang changed his famous play *Mu-k'o chai* (*Mount Mu-k'o Garrison*), to *Yang-men nü-chiang* (*The Women Warriors of the Yang Family*).[14] The revisions or rearrangements of some of the old plays were aimed primarily at either eliminating certain undesirable ideas or at shifting to a new emphasis. For example, in the old version of *The Meeting of Heroes* there was a scene in which Chu-ko Liang, the Prime Minister of the State of Shu, was depicted as a demigod capable of 'borrowing' the east wind from Heaven, and with the help of the wind, the Shu-Wu alliance finally defeated the State of Wei. To the Communist reformers, the 'borrowing' of the east wind was sheer nonsense. So the actor rewrote the words of a long aria in the offending scene by replacing all the superstitious sayings in the old version with more acceptable wording. Chu-ko Liang in the new version was not a demigod possessing magic powers but a learned scholar who was familiar with astrology. In the old version, Ts'ao Ts'ao, the Prime Minister of the State of Wei, was depicted as a cunning, shrewd villain. This is contrary to the historical truth, for in history, Ts'ao Ts'ao was actually a man of destiny, an empire-builder. In the revised version, the historical depiction of Ts'ao Ts'ao was followed. Even though he and his navy were defeated by the allied forces of Shu and Wu, Ts'ao Ts'ao was allowed to be statesmanlike.

For the newly written plays, for instance, Chou Hsin-fang's *Hai Jui's Memorial*, the purpose seemed obvious. Hai Jui was characterized as a government official of decency and integrity whose concern for the common people could typify the new

---

[9] Yang, 'Reform of Peking Opera,' pp. 132–36.

[10] Ma Lien-liang was a well-known *lao-sheng* (male with beard) actor. The so-called Ma school (style) was known for its stage acting, graceful movement, and smooth dialogue.

[11] Hsün Hui-sheng is one of the four great *tan* (female impersonation) actors, famous for his portrayal of *hua-tan* roles, emphasizing acting and gesturing.

[12] Kai Chiao-t'ien is a stage name. He gained fame principally in Shanghai, where he specialized *lao-sheng* roles, with emphasis on acting and unusual singing style.

[13] Chou Hsin-fang, especially known by his nickname, Ch'i-ling T'ung (the Unicorn Kid), also gained his reputation in Shanghai, where he specialized *lao-sheng* roles, with emphasis on acting and unusual singing style.

[14] Mei Lan-fang, known as the King of Peking Opera, was the greatest of the female impersonators. His portrayal of graceful and dainty young ladies on stage was so real that the audience could not tell he was actually a male actor. Mei visited the United States in 1933, and his artistic presentation of the Peking opera won him an honorary degree from Pomona College. His last tour abroad took him to Japan in 1959. He died in 1961 at the age of 67.

regime's concern for the working class. In Mei Lan-fang's *Mount Mu-k'o Garrison*, though the military prowess of the heroine, Mu Kuei-ying, was superior to that of both her husband and her father-in-law, she was never given a chance to lead her troops to fight against the invaders. It typified the attitude in feudalistic China that women should always play a subordinate role. In his rearranged version, Mei Lan-fang, who incidentally played the heroine, had Mu Kuei-ying take over the leadership as commander-in-chief of the army and achieve final victory over the enemy.

(2) Revival of certain singing styles. Of the well-known stylists in the Peking opera circle, two great actors in particular, Yen Chü-p'eng and Ch'eng Yen-ch'iu, were regarded as great champions. Yen was the founder of the Yen school of the 'bearded *sheng*' voice, and Ch'eng was the founder of the Ch'eng school of the female (*tan*) voice. With their deaths, the two great styles suffered a temporary eclipse. During the Great Leap Forward period, both styles were revived—Yen's by his son, Yen Shao-p'eng, and Ch'eng's by a young singer named Li Shih-chi.[15]

(3) Resumption of the custom of accepting and training protégés. It had been an age-old practice among famous opera singers in China to take promising young pupils for training as personal protégés in order to perpetuate the masters' singing styles or dancing techniques. The practice was discontinued for a long time and was not revived until the Great Leap period. Such famous actors as Mei Lan-fang, Ma Lien-liang, Yeh Sheng-chang, Hou Hsi-jui, Ch'iu Sheng-jung, and Chou Hsin-fang,[16] all began to take in protégés and train them as heirs to their own art.

(4) Organization of foreign tours. As a gesture of friendship and goodwill, the Communist government accepted invitations from abroad and sent goodwill missions to other countries, where they generally received wide acclaim. Practically all the missions sent were made up of Peking opera performers.[17]

New themes. In order to promote the new political and social role of the opera, productions of new plays with modern themes, usually referred to as 'revolutionary modern plays,' were initiated. The first such play was *White-Haired Girl*, in which not only was the theme carefully chosen from an ideological point of view, but many of the old conventions that had made the Peking opera a unique art, such as makeup, costuming, gestering, dancing, stage props, and even dialogue,[18] were done away with.

---

[15] Yen Chü-p'eng, as a *lao-sheng* actor, introduced a singing style emphasizing enunciation and tonal harmonization with the tune. Ch'eng Yen-ch'iu was one of the four great *tan* actors who also introduced stylish singing to the Peking stage. He visited France in 1933, and his performance won him an honorary degree from one of the universities there. He died in 1958.

[16] In addition to those who have been identified before, Chang Chün-ch'iu is also a *tan* actor; Yen Sheng-chang was a well-known *wu-ch'ou* (warrior clown) performer famous for his acrobatic techniques; Hou Hsi-jui was a veteran *hua-lien* (painted face) actor; Ch'iu Sheng-jung is a famous *ching* (painted face, but civil) actor known for his singing style.

[17] The Communist regime sent four goodwill missions abroad during 1958–60, one to France, two to Japan, and one to Canada. The Canadian mission took place in 1960, when a troupe of song and dance performers was invited by the Canadian authorities to take part in the centennial celebration of Vancouver, B.C. The writer had the rare opportunity of viewing their performances in Vancouver. Besides a few folk dances and Western singing, the performance consisted of selections from the repertoire of the traditional Peking opera.

[18] The most important and unique feature of the traditional Peking opera as a form of art is its symbolism. Everything on the stage should be symbolic and nothing is real. As the Chinese saying goes, 'If it is real, it is not drama.' Thus, in the old Peking opera, the makeup is symbolic, and so are the costumes, dancing, gestures and dialogue. A whip represents a horse, an oar represents a boat. The entire stage is empty, but the empty stage could be a battlefield or a palace, a garden or a small hut. The performers do not eat real food on the stage; yet a gesture can signify a feast or meal. Nor would the actors shed real tears on the stage, but a certain movement will suggest a cry or weeping. No stage props are used, except a table, a couple of chairs with which different situations could be symbolized. All the move-

When the new type play was first presented on the stage, critics ridiculed it as 'nothing but spoken drama with singing.' Before long, however, other plays on contemporary themes appeared on the stage, including *The Red Storm, Capturing the Fierce Tiger Mountain with Wise Strategy* and *Chao I-man,* and criticism turned into praise. According to one veteran actress:

> With the production of *Chao I-man,* I hold a new point of view toward the Peking opera. In the past I was bothered by the thought that the Peking opera could not portray modern life, nor did I have the courage to experiment. But under the wonderful leadership of the Party, we have gathered new strength. Our Academy has staged *The Red Storm, Chao I-man,* and *Capturing the Fierce Tiger Mountain with Wise Strategy.* I have come to the conclusion that the Peking opera not only *can* portray [such heroines of the past as] Mu Kuei-ying, Ling Hung-yü, Ts'ui Ying-ying, and Lin Tai-yü, but it can also portray [heroines of modern times such as] Chao I-man, Liu Hu-lan, Hsi-erh, and Li Hsiang-hsiang. Therefore I have gained new confidence in the future of the Peking opera.[19]

By 1964, celebrations were held all over China for a 'bumper crop' of 'revolutionary operas.' For instance, in eastern China (the provinces of Shantung, Kiangsu, Chekiang, Anhwei, Kiangsi, and Fukien), 140 numbers representing more than sixty different operas were presented during the annual exhibition of operatic art.[20] In the city of Shanghai alone, during the first eleven months of 1964, more than seventy operatic and dramatic groups presented 485 different numbers of 'revolutionary contemporary drama and opera,' giving more than 6,900 shows, while the total audience reached an unprecedented record of 7 million. The new Peking opera *Capturing the Fierce Tiger Mountain with Wise Strategy,* which was given by the Shanghai Peking Opera Academy in Shanghai, gave a hundred performances during a three-month period from September to November; its audience totaled 200,000, thus breaking the records held by such popular traditional numbers as *Yü-chou feng* (*The Pretense of Insanity*), *Kuei-fei tsui-chiu* (*The Lady is Drunk*), *Chui Han Hsin* (*Pursuit of Han Hsin*), and *Ssu chin-shih* (*Four Scholars*).[21] With this kind of accomplishment in their record, the performers were greatly encouraged and sought to bring about early dominance of all stage performance by 'revolutionary contemporary opera.' Accordingly, from 1964 on, reports of traditional numbers of the Peking opera have gradually disappeared from newspapers and magazines.

The opera as a medium of political satire. The ax of reform fell on the Peking opera in 1965, when a new historical opera entitled *Hai Jui Pa-kuan* (*Hai Jui's Dismissal from Office*) was attacked by the critic Yao Wen-yüan in *Wen-hui Pao,* a newspaper in Shanghai, on November 10, 1965. Yao's article was reprinted in *Jen-min Jih-pao* on November 30, 1965, and again cited in its entirety in the November, 1965, issue of *Hsi-chü Pao* (*Drama Monthly*). Not only did this article touch off the final condemnation of the traditional Peking opera, it also led to the purge of the 'San-chia ts'un

---

ments and activities of men in real life, whether climbing a mountain, traveling to a distance, riding on a horse, or crossing a river, are all represented by symbolic actions. The differentiation between the rich and the poor is usually made with different costumes. Whether a person is good or bad is usually symbolized by the designs painted on the actor's face. All these put together had made the Peking opera a unique art.

[19] T'ung Chih-ling, 'Kuan-yü Ching-chü Chao I-man ti yen-ch'u (On the Production of the Peking Opera, *Chao I-man*),' *Ching-hu Pao* (*Peking-Shanghai Daily*), Shanghai, January 8, 1959.

[20] A news report entitled 'Hua-tung Ti-ch'ü 1964 nien Hsien-tai Hsi-ch'ü Ta-feng-shou (A Great Harvest of Modern Operas in 1964 in East China),' in *Chung-kuo Hsin-wen* (*China News*), Hong Kong: Chung-kuo Hsin-wen-she, January 17, 1965.

[21] *Ibid.,* January 6, 1965.

(Three-Family Village) clique' and heralded the Great Proletarian Cultural Revolution.

The author of this new opera was no ordinary writer. Before the Communist regime, Wu Han had been a historian and college professor. When the People's Republic was established in 1949, he was made deputy mayor of Peking and a member of the powerful municipal committee of the Communist Party. Beginning in 1959, Wu Han write a series of articles praising the historical figure Hai Jui, an official of the Ming dynasty. In 1961, after several revisions, he completed the play *Hai Jui's Dismissal from Office*, which was written in the traditional style of the Peking opera. In the story he praised the upright character of Hai Jui, whom he portrayed as 'one who gave every consideration to the people,' and as 'a savior for the oppressed, exploited, and wronged peasants.'

Yao Wen-yüan accused Wu Han of 'creating a false Hai Jui in order to express Wu's own point of view.' In the play, Hai Jui forced the wealthy landlords to return some land to the poor peasants and through his influence freed peasants who had been unjustly imprisoned. Thus, when this champion of the people was finally dismissed by the emperor, he became a hero for his fight against the feudalistic Ming Court. But according to Yao, Hai Jui was merely a faithful and loyal subject of a feudalistic regime, who firmly believed that the 'emperor is the master of all people and things of the world.' Thus, Wu's portrayal of Hai Jui as one who 'gave every consideration to the people' is parallel to the Ming court's praise of Hai Jui as 'one who loved the people as his own children.' In conclusion, Yao challenged Wu's motive in the following terms:

What is the realistic meaning of . . . *Hai Jui's Dismissal from Office*? What kind of impact does it produce on us, the people of Socialist China? To answer these questions, we must study the background under which this play was produced. As we all know, the year 1961 was the time when our country was confronted with a momentary economic setback because of three years' continuous natural calamities. Under the circumstances of a rising tide of anti-China movements of the reactionaries, of the imperialists and modern revisionists, those cow-demons and serpent-spirits within the country had also started black winds blowing such as the 'work alone wind' and the 'opening-up old cases wind.' They preached the superior quality of 'working alone' and demanded the restoration of the economy of private ownership and returning of the land to the people. They were really aiming at the destruction of the people's communes and restoration of the evil rule of the wealthy farmers and landlords. Those imperialists, landlords, wealthy farmers, reactionaries and rightists who caused many of the poor, laboring people to be imprisoned unjustly before have lost their right to create that same injustice now. They felt that their being overthrown was 'unjust' and so they shouted about 'righting the unjust imprisonment.' They hoped that someone who could represent their interest could come into the open and resist the dictatorship of the proletariat, fight for justice for them, and reopen old cases so as to enable them to climb once again on the political stage. The issues of 'returning the land' and 'righting unjust imprisonment' were the very focal points of the struggle between the capitalists and the socialist revolution of the proletariat. The class struggle is but an objective existence. It must be reflected in a certain ideological form by the pen of a certain writer. This is an objective principle that cannot be changed by the intention of a person, consciously or subconsciously. *Hai Jui's Dismissal from Office* is one such formal reflection of the class struggle. If comrade Wu Han does not agree with our analysis, then he should answer our question clearly: In 1961, what could the people learn from such a fact-distorting play, *Hai Jui's Dismissal from Office*? We conclude, therefore, that *Hai Jui's Dismissal from Office* is not a fragrant flower, but a poison ivy. It was published and produced a few years back; many people have since written articles to praise it. If similar writings were allowed to be circulated unchecked, the evil influence would certainly be great and its poison profound. If these writings were not purified, they would undoubtedly render great harm to the enterprise of the people. So we must discuss the matter openly. In our discussion, we will gain an understanding of a realistic and historical class struggle if we seriously examine it from the point of view of class struggle.[22]

This was not simply a criticism of a play but an accusation against an individual, and a prominent Party figure. The criticism of this historical play of the traditional Peking opera sounded the death knell of a traditional art. The accusation not only led to the purge of Wu Han and his clique[23] but also to the explosion of the Great Cultural Revolution in 1966.

In 1967, it was rumored that many well-known actors of the old Peking opera had either been killed by the Red Guards or had committed suicide.[24] Among those killed by the teen-age revolutionaries was the veteran actor Chou Hsin-fang, whose portrayal of Hai Jui on the stage had caused him to be branded as a 'reactionary capitalist.'

THE MODERN DRAMA (HUA-CHÜ)

Modern plays and playwrights. In China, modern drama is called 'spoken drama' to differentiate it from the traditional 'singing opera.' The spoken drama is an import from the West. It is a relatively recent development of the twentieth century, a new phenomenon that the Chinese people, mostly intellectuals, have experienced during China's modernization.

The so-called Spoken Drama Movement was an effort to popularize this new form of art, backed by a few enthusiastic playwrights and players. It gained tremendous momentum during the Sino-Japanese War. The new art was utilized by the government as an effective vehicle of propaganda to boost morale. Although the movement also spread to Yenan during the same period, no notable achievements were recorded there. Thus, when the Communist regime was established in 1949, the authors of spoken drama, such as Lao She (Shu She-yü), Ts'ao Yü (Nan Chia-pao), T'ien Han, Hung Shen, Sung Chih-ti, Hsia Yen, Ma Yen-hsiang, and Wu Tsu-kuang,[25] were veteran writers who had gained recognition during the war.

Because the old-timers controlled the 'drama movement' in the early years of the new regime, their old plays also dominated the stage. As late as 1959, the wartime

---

[22] Yao Wen-yüan, 'P'ing Hsin-pien li-shih chü Hai Jui Pa-kuan (Comment on the New Historical Play *Hai Jui's Dismissal from Office*),' *Hsi-chü Pao (Drama Monthly)*, Peking, November, 1965, pp. 7–14.

[23] The so-called *San-chia Ts'un* (Three-Family Village) case was reported in 1966 and involved the purge of Wu Han, historian, playwright, and deputy-mayor of Peking; Teng T'uo, editor of *Jen-min Jih-pao*; and Liao Mo-sha, a poet whose regular column entitled 'Yen-shan Yeh-hua (An Evening Talk at Yen-shan)' allegedly contained masked attacks on the Communist regime.

[24] It was rumored that many leading opera singers had committed suicide because of constant harassment by the Red Guards. They included Ma Lien-liang, Li Shao-ch'un, a *sheng* actor and a leader of the group who visited Vancouver in 1960; Yen Sheng-lan, a *hsiao-sheng* (young man) actor, Yü Chen-fei, also a *hsiao-sheng* actor but equally known for his mastery of the *K'un-ch'ü* (K'un-shan drama); Yü's young wife, Yen Hui-chu, daughter of the late Yen Chü-p'eng; and others.

[25] Among this group, Lao She, Ts'ao Yü, T'ien Han, Hung Shen, Sung Chih-ti, and Hsia Yen were all well-known playwrights in the field of modern drama; Ma Yen-hsiang and Wu Tsu-kuang were producers and directors. All were later purged by the Red Guards during the Cultural Revolution.

plays of Ts'ao Yü were still the favorites of modern drama lovers, though Ts'ao Yü himself did revise his *Thunderstorm* in order to play up the theme of the social contradictions in the old family system.[26] Ts'ao's *Jih ch'u (Sunrise)*, the second play of a trilogy, was staged three times between 1956 and 1958 with 129 shows given and more than 100,000 people in the audience.[27]

Among the old playwrights, Lao She (author of the famous novel *Rickshaw Boy*, or *Lo-t'o Hsiang-tzu*) probably contributed the greatest number of new plays. Right after the Communist takeover, he wrote *Dragon-Beard Ditch (Lung-hsü kou)*, a play about the completion of an open sewer called the Dragon-beard Ditch, under the leadership of the new regime. *Rickshaw Boy* was also adapted as a play and received wide acclaim.[28] A later play of his, *Ch'üan-chia Fu (The Family Reunion)*, tells about the reunion of a workingman's family following the 'liberation,' after many years' separation.

The drive for new plays. When the Great Leap Forward was launched, policymakers within the Party insisted that Chairman Mao Tse-tung's directive, 'Let One Hundred Flowers Bloom; Push the Old Away and Produce the New,' must be carried out in dramatic art. Not only should more new plays be produced, but plays depicting the life and struggle of the people must be emphasized. Thus, on the tenth anniversary of the Communist regime in 1959, more than thirty new plays were presented on the stage as an anniversary gift to the young nation. A viewer who was deeply impressed with the achievement wrote to a newspaper as follows:

> Within a short period of two years, the spoken drama has reaped an impressive harvest. During the celebration of our National Day, all the drama schools of the capital, together with various drama groups from the army and labor unions, as well as a part of the provincial and municipal drama schools, have presented a series of performances as 'birthday gifts' to our new nation. This is due entirely to the fact that they have listened to the Party. Under the Party's brilliant direction of the main line of socialist reconstruction, politics has taken command. Thus, they have made their joint effort and carried out the Party's policy on art and literature. This is also the result of our struggle against the individualistic viewpoint of the capitalists, against the capitalistic principles on art and literature, and against the conservatism of the rightists.[29]

Since 1960, many more new plays have been written and produced, such as *A Train of Heroes*, which tells the story of a young girl train conductor who saved the lives of 600 passengers during a disaster; *Comrade, You Have Gone Astray!*, depicting the struggle between the thought of Mao Tse-tung and that of rightist opportunism; *Princess Wen-ch'eng*, a historical tale of a princess of the T'ang dynasty married to a king of Tibet, a propaganda theme on Sino-Tibetan solidarity during the course of Tibet's 'liberation'; *A Single Spark Can Start a Prairie Fire*, a story about the 1928 armed revolution of the Communists in rural areas; *The Man from the North Wasteland*; a story about the people sent to cultivate the wasteland of the north, a propaganda play boosting the spirit of the Great Leap Forward movement; *A Brave Red Heart*, about

---

[26] *Thunderstorm* was first written by Ts'ao Yü in 1933 and was regarded as one of the modern classics in drama. The story concerns a large, wealthy family through which the author attacks the evils of the old family system and the old society. Ts'ao Yü gained his fame and recognition as a young, promising playwright after he had presented his 'trilogy' of *Thunderstorm (Lei yü)*, *Sunrise (Jih Ch'u)* and *Prairie (Yüan-yeh)*.

[27] From a news report in the *Wen-hui Pao*, Shanghai, July 23, 1959.

[28] The play *Rickshaw Boy* has been translated into English by Richard F. S. Yang and Herbert M. Stahl, published by Academic Readings Inc. of New York, 1965.

[29] Chou Wei-shih, 'The Speaking Drama during the Great Leap Forward,' *JMJP*, December 2, 1959.

the underground struggles of peasants in Hunan Province (Mao Tse-tung's birthplace) against the warlords and landlords; and *Memory is Still Fresh*, a story about America's involvement in the civil war and General Marshall's mission to China.

Mobile theater teams. Because art is no longer for art's sake but for the sake of the people, art must serve the workers, peasants, and soldiers. A movement to send drama and opera to the factories, villages, and army camps was initiated in 1960. To carry out such a gigantic task, more dramatic groups, both professional and amateur, were organized and trained. Solutions had to be found to many problems, such as those of building a mobile stage, costuming and makeup, props, and so forth. Of course, the ingenuity of the Communist cadres was not to be underestimated. Newspaper readers were soon regaled with stories about the invention of a portable stage and various props and devices. One rather amusing report tells how a stage hand designed a costume trunk with three functions: as a trunk when folded up, as a sofa when covered, and as a dresser when standing up.

Impact of the Cultural Revolution. Many leading artists and policy-makers fell victim to the Cultural Revolution of 1966–68. The purge of Hsia Yen, a Deputy Minister of Culture, is a typical case. Although Hsia had been closely linked to the Three-Family Village purge, the final verdict on his case was not pronounced until 1967, when he was denounced as a 'big boss of the Black Gang in the circles of art and literature' and a 'capable assistant to China's Khrushchev' (President Liu Shao-ch'i). His 'crimes' were alleged to be the following:

(1) He opposed Mao Tse-tung's instructions, believing that it would take time to 'serve the people'; (2) he was responsible for the production of the reactionary movie, *Wu Hsün Chuan* (*The Story of Wu Hsün*); (3) he opposed the Party's leadership in art and literary reform; (4) he sent a motion picture mission to capitalistic and revisionist countries and supported individualistic artistic principles; (5) he criticized the novelist Lu Hsün, a man whom Mao had called the 'great tutor of the people'; (6) he condemned the Great Leap Forward and showed sympathy toward the Kuomintang; (7) he was a member of the Three-Family Village clique headed by Wu Han and Teng T'o, who had already been purged; (8) he criticized the Party in an interview with Hong Kong reporters; and (9) he admitted in a self-criticism in 1965 that he had a capitalist viewpoint.

In addition, Hsia Yen was accused of having organized during the war years a private society called the 'Second Rate Club,' which advocated so-called national defense literature, and commended such reactionary motion pictures as *Sai Chin-hua* (a woman's name), *A Man Who Returned in a Snowstorm Night*, and *Phoenix City*. The club had a 'patriarch,' a constitution, and an insignia. Hsia Yen was the leader of the organization and was affectionately called 'Uncle Hsia' or 'Godfather Hsia' by its members. The organization remained in existence after the 'liberation,' with a revised constitution to 'follow the principle of New Democracy.' In 1956, the club members even attempted to publish a magazine called *Wan Hsiang* (*Kaleidoscope*) with the sole purpose of publishing articles that had been rejected by other journals. To look for successors, they organized another group called the 'Small Tribe,' headed by Wu Tse-kuang, a playwright and director. They regarded themselves as an 'art salon' and took absolutely no interest in politics. Their main interest was to create and spread rumors concerning leading personnel of the Communist Party in order to drive the Party off the political stage. The 'Small Tribe' was finally exposed during the anti-rightist campaign in 1958. But during the 'three difficult years,' Hsia Yen helped remove the 'rightist cap' from this organization. Later, the same organization strongly opposed the revolution of the Peking opera led by Chiang Ch'ing, Mao's wife.[30]

---

[30] An editorial entitled 'Ts'ung Liang-ke Ssu-ling-pu ti Tou-cheng k'an Hsia Yen ti Fan ke-ming Chen-mien-mu (A Look at the True Identity of Hsia Yen from the Struggle of Two Headquarters),' *JMJP*, August 23, 1967.

With the accusation of such crimes as opposition to Mao Tse-tung and opposition to the Communist Party, Hsia Yen's career was ended. In the same period, many of his friends and associates, including T'ien Han, Yang Han-sheng, and other veterans involved in the drama movement, were also driven out of the political arena. The great author, novelist, dramatist and humorist Lao She, it was reported, met a tragic death at the hands of the Red Guards in 1966.[31] With such people gone, modern drama is now controlled by the Party and used as a vehicle to carry out the socialist revolution in China.

MOTION PICTURES

Rapid expansion of the cinema. As an art form, the motion picture is also an import from the West. The May Fourth Movement of 1919, the first cultural revolution in China in the twentieth century, introduced many new ideas to China from abroad, and the motion picture was one of the imports. Before the Communist revolution, motion picture theaters had been dominated by foreign films, and the Chinese movie industry was never highly developed. Although motion pictures were made in China in the 1930's, they were primarily for entertainment. Very few pictures of the early years were intended as political propaganda, although crude attempts were made by both the Nationalists and the Communists.

During the first decade of the Communist regime, the Chinese movie industry produced 274 artistic films, 914 documentaries, 52 pictures on art subjects, and 327 scientific films, according to one newspaper report.[32] Among these, 324 pictures were produced in languages of minority peoples and 887 in the national language.

Among the thirty-two films made by 1950, a large number followed the policy of portraying contemporary events and people; representative of the outstanding ones were *Ch'iao (Bridge)*, *Pai-mao Nü (The White-haired Girl)*, *Kang-t'ieh chan-shih (Warriors of Steel and Iron)*, *Chung-hua nü-erh (Daughters of China)*, *Ts'ui kang Hung-ch'i (Red Flag on a Green Mountain Peak)*, and *Chao I-man* (the name of a heroine).

In order to meet the Party's directive that art must serve the masses of workers, peasants, and soldiers, the number of projection teams was increased from 646 in 1946 to 9,965 in 1957. The size of the audience rose accordingly, from 47,730,000 admissions in 1949 to 2,864,350,000 in 1958.[33]

Propaganda and educational films. Since the Great Leap Forward, motion pictures have served as an especially powerful tool to implement the policies of the Party because of their ability to reach large numbers of viewers. For instance, when the Party was promoting drives for accelerated production in agriculture and industry, many scientific educational films were sent to the countryside and factories. When the movement of 'Learning from Lei Feng' (a soldier-worker hero) was launched in 1965, a biographical film was produced and shown all over the country; in this case, the film may have functioned as a highly effective weapon in sharpening the political consciousness of many workers, students, and even peasants. Also, as a part of the Aid Vietnam Campaign, a series of propaganda movies has been produced and shown in all theaters in China. In the city of Canton alone, during the celebration of International Labor Day on May 1, 1965, local theaters were showing sixteen films that may be regarded as a cross-section of the kinds of movies made at present.[34] There were five features on general contemporary subjects, one musical, and ten films on the over-all theme, 'American Aggressors, Get out of Vietnam!'

---

[31] The death of Lao She was first rumored to be a suicide. But Ma Sitson, the musician who escaped from China in 1969, reported that Lao She had actually been beaten to death by the Red Guards.

[32] *China News* (Hong Kong), September 28, 1969.

[33] *China News* (Hong Kong), September 28, 1959.

[34] See *Yang-ch'eng Wan-pao (Yang-ch'eng Evening News)*, Canton, April 27, 1965.

Films during the Cultural Revolution. When the Cultural Revolution turned from opposing the four 'olds' to purging undesirables within the Communist Party, motion pictures, as well as other art forms, were used as 'evidence' of crimes against the Party and the thought of Mao Tse-tung. The following films were singled out as 'positive evidence':

Wu Hsün Chuan (The Story of Wu Hsün)—Wu Hsün, a beggar of the late Ch'ing dynasty and an illiterate himself, devoted his life to helping build schools so that others might have a chance to go to school. His only method was to beg money or assistance from the public, especially the wealthy. His life story was made into a movie in 1951. In 1954, Mao Tse-tung personally launched an attack against the film. Finally, in 1966, after it had been branded 'poison ivy to preach slavism and surrenderism,' the picture was banned. Those who had been responsible for its production, especially Chou Yang (to be discussed later) and Hsia Yen, have since been eliminated from the political scene.

Ch'ing-kung Mi-shih (The Secret History of the Ch'ing Palace)—Critics of this film about the Boxer Rebellion of 1900 charged that it sided with imperialism and feudalism in distorting the historical facts by praising the conservative faction and belittling the revolutionary movement of the masses. Thus it had clearly violated the golden principle enunciated by Mao: 'The road to Marxism is many-pronged. But it can be summarized in one phrase: Rebellions are justified.'[35]

Liang-chia Jen (People of Two Families)—In this film, a poor old peasant on the eve of the collectivization drive in 1953 recalls his past life. He remarks, 'In the world there is always the difference between the rich and the poor,' Critics charged that this statement favored the old-fashioned sentiments of agrarian capitalism, and they accused the film's producers of a criminal intent to restore capitalism.[36]

Wu-t'ai Tzu-mei (Sisters of the Stage)—In this film, describing the sorrows, happinesses, separations, and reunion of two sisters of the Chekiang opera, one of the sisters, the 'Queen of Chekiang opera,' Shang Shui-hua, murmurs before her death: 'The living will no longer suffer, and the dead will be avenged.' In the picture there is also shouting of such slogans as, 'Oppose the ruthless government!' 'Change the ways of the world!' and 'Down with the bosses!' The Cultural Revolution critics charged that the picture was a political satire and that the slogans actually echoed the shouts of the capitalist, reactionary forces within the Party headed by 'China's Khrushchev.' 'Change the ways of the world!' was, according to this interpretation, actually, 'Overthrow the government of the proletariat!' 'Down with the bosses!' became, 'Overthrow the leadership of the Party!' The ulterior objective of the slogans, according to the critics, was to oppose the revolution, to seize political power, and to restore the capitalist system.[37]

Ke-ming Chia-t'ing (A Revolutionary Family)—This was a biographical presentation of the life of a revolutionary. According to its critics, it was really produced to heap glory on 'China's Khrushchev' (Liu Shao-ch'i) under the personal direction of Hsia Yen. When Hsia Yen was purged as a capable assistant to the 'No. 1 ambitious person within the Party who chose to follow the reactionary, capitalist road,' namely, Liu Shao-ch'i, the picture was cited as evidence of Hsia's crime.[38]

---

[35] Ch'i Pen-yü, 'Ai-kuo Chu-i Hai-shih Mai-kuo Chu-i? (Patriotism or Betrayal?),' *JMJP*, April 1, 1967; see also *Red Flag*, No. 5, 1967.

[36] 'P'ing Fan-tung Ying-p'ien, Liang-chia Jen (Commenting on the Reactionary Picture *People of Two Families*),' by the Red Flag Art Corps of the Central Drama Academy, *JMJP*, June 12, 1967.

[37] Ch'i Hsüeh-hung, 'Cheng shen-mo tzu-yu? Cheng shen-mo wu-t'ai? (Fight for What Freedom? Grab What Stage?),' *JMJP*, December 2, 1967.

[38] Li Hung, 'Ch'ih Fan-tung Ying-p'ien, Ke-ming Chia-t'ing (Damn the Reactionary Picture, *A Revolutionary Family*),' *JMJP*, December 2, 1967.

Technical quality of Chinese films. The technical qualities of motion pictures made in China today bear comparison with those made in other countries. In Hong Kong in 1965–66, I saw four color films exported from mainland China: a historical picture, *Chia-wu Feng-yün* (*The Storm in 1895*), about a sea battle between the Japanese and the Manchu navies; a picture of recordings of the 'mountain songs' of Kwangsi Province, *Liu San-chieh* (*Third Sister Liu*); a musical about the Communist revolution in China, *Ying-hsiung Sung* (*A Praise of Heroes*); and a documentary entitled *Liberation of Tibet* (*Chieh-fang Hsi-tsang*), which purports to describe life in Tibet before and after the 'liberation.' Although the quality of the color was not always good, the Communist producers boasted that everything in connection with those pictures, from the celluloid to the production, was 'made in China.' Bearing in mind the industrial backwardness of old China, one cannot help but be impressed with the technical progress that has been scored in Communist China.

The historical film was sensitively done and very positive in its central theme—the heroic exploits of the Chinese people against the enemy. The folksinging film was pleasant, charming, and enjoyable. It followed almost all the folksong traditions by depicting the life of the people of that region in Kwangsi with, of course, the inescapable political overtone—the victory of the peasants and the defeat of the wealthy class. The musical was sheer propaganda, a biographical and chronological account of the growth of the Communist Party, its struggle with the Kuomintang, the Long March, its struggle with the Japanese, and its final victory. The entire film was filled with songs, chants, and dancing, a musical comparable to any film made in the West, except, of course, for its political theme. The documentary on Tibet was another piece of propaganda, stressing the suffering of the people in 'serfdom' under the rule of the Lamas, in contrast to the progress made after its 'liberation' by the Communists in May, 1951. Nonetheless, the propaganda was rather effective when the story of the oppressed and exploited was told. Technically speaking, color films made in China today, especially the four described above, are as good as films made in the West with regard to photography, thematic presentation, sound, and editing. If one takes the political and ideological standpoint into consideration, Communist Chinese movies are unquestionably superior and effective. In this connection, the Communist regime has certainly achieved its avowed purpose of utilizing motion pictures as political tools.

MUSIC, MUSICALS, AND BALLET

Traditional and modern music. In China's music, one must differentiate the traditional from the modern. Chinese traditional music was basically developed as popular, operatic entertainment. Modern music, on the other hand, came to China as an imitation of the West, a result of the impact of Western civilization since the end of the nineteenth century.

Differentiation may also be made between vocal and instrumental music. Both are played either for personal enjoyment or for public entertainment. For example, the use of the Chinese *ch'in* (a lute or zither-like instrument) goes back more than 3,000 years. Other instruments, such as the *p'i-pa* (a banjo-like instrument) and the flute (either the horizontal *ti* or the vertical *hsiao*), were basically for personal amusement, but they have come to accompany the dance and, particularly, the opera. China has never had orchestral music. When several instruments were employed simultaneously, they were primarily used to accompany dance or drama (opera).

Vocal music consists of songs and operas. Songs were primarily for personal enjoyment while operas were for public entertainment. Some Chinese songs have a very long history. The *Book of Songs*, one of the Confucian classics, is a collection of folksongs of the Chou period, some 3,000 years ago. Operas are a rather recent development, dating from the Yüan dynasty (1260–1367).

The so-called modern Chinese music, like modern drama, literature, painting, and even education, is an imitation of the West. Except for its language and flavor (or tone and tenor), instrumental and vocal music differs little from its Western counterpart. Thus modern Chinese music can be very well described as Westernized music.

Songs and propaganda. Songs, like drama and motion pictures, have been used by the Chinese Communists as a powerful instrument of propaganda. This is not a Communist innovation; for music education, primarily in singing, has been an integral part of modern education ever since China adopted the Western school system at the turn of the century. During the pre-Communist period, when popular sentiment was against the 'oppression of Western imperialism,' several popular tunes were imported from the West. For instance, the tune of 'Frère Jacques' was utilized by the Nationalist government to preach the doctrine of patriotism, with new words: 'Down with the powers! Down with the powers! And warlord; and warlord! The national revolution will succeed. The national revolution will succeed. All arise! All arise!'

During the Sino-Japanese War of 1937–45, many patriotic songs were written by such gifted composers and songwriters as Nieh Erh, Hsi Hsing-hai and An P'o, and played an important role in morale-building. 'Yi-yung-chün Chin-hsing-ch'ü (The Volunteer's March)' written by Nieh Erh in 1936–37, has since been adopted by the Communist regime as its national anthem. 'Huang Ho Ta Ho-ch'ang (The Yellow River Chorus),' composed by Hsi Hsing-hai, has been a favorite of the students of China for many years. Since its Yenan days, the Communist Party has utilized the *yang ko* (songs in sprouting time), an improvised version of folksinging and folk-dancing, as a very useful propaganda weapon.

Musicals. Perhaps the most spectacular musical composed after 1949 is *Tung-fang Hung (The East Is Red).* Written by Ho Lu-ting in praise of Mao Tse-tung, the original tune became the theme song for the musical. Today in China, every student, worker, and soldier can sing 'The East is Red. The sun has risen. In China, there rises a man named Mao Tse-tung.'[39] In popularity, the refrain has virtually replaced the phrase, 'Arise, those who are unwilling to become slaves!'[40] The musical has since been made into a motion picture.

Another musical spectacular later made into a movie is *Ying-hsiung Sung (Praise to the Heroes)*, which we have discussed before. It is a superb application of the techniques of singing and dancing for the purposes of political propaganda.

Other well-known musicals that have been staged include *Mei-tien Hsin Kung-jen (A New Worker in a Coal Store)*, *Hung Sung Tien (Red Pine Inn)*, *Hsiao Ts'un Lo Ku (Drums and Songs in a Small Village)*,[41] *I-ch'uan Hsiang-lien (A String of Pearls)*, and *Lao Pao-kuan (An Old Custodian)*. Perhaps the most popular recent musical is *Chiang Chieh (Sister Chiang)*, a story about an exemplary woman worker.

The ballet. The newest art form adopted from the West, especially from the Soviet Union during the days of Sino-Soviet friendship before 1960, is the ballet, which was virtually nonexistent in China before 1949. With the establishment of the Communist regime and the Sino-Soviet alliance, ballet became much imitated and promoted.

As Mao Tse-tung had instructed his audience in the Yenan talks of 1942: 'We do not refuse to make use of the art forms of the past. But when they come into our hands, we must reform them and add new content in order to make them into something revolutionary to serve the people.' Thus, the themes and content of traditional ballets, such as *Swan Lake, Romeo and Juliet,* and *Sleeping Beauty,* have been removed. The policy-makers of Communist China simply cannot accept the bourgeois sentiments conveyed in them. What has been retained is only the dancing technique of

---

[39] The first line of the song, 'The East is Red.'

[40] The first line of the new national anthem, formerly known as 'The Volunteers' March.'

[41] See a detailed report on these musical plays in *China Reconstructs*, Peking: China Welfare Institute, October, 1965.

ballet. Among the many ballets produced in recent years, two stand out as representative of the 'socialist ballet'; namely, *The White-haired Girl* and *The Red Detachment of Women Soldiers*. These have been acclaimed as 'good' ballet, for they have fulfilled the ultimate demand of the policy-makers, that 'art of the past can be used for the present and art of the West can be used for China.' 'These two ballets,' a critic said, 'have not only boldly presented the theme of armed revolt and class struggle, but have also thoroughly smashed the old concept that the ballet as an art could not be used to reflect present-day struggle.'[42]

Impact of the Cultural Revolution. Since the beginning of the Great Proletarian Cultural Revolution, music, musicals, and ballets, like the Peking opera and motion pictures, have been used as evidence against those who had failed to toe the Mao Tse-tung line. It is reported that even Ho Lü-ting, composer of 'The East is Red,' has been denounced as a counterrevolutionary. The miraculous escape of Ma Sitson, perhaps China's best violinist, to the United States[43] is living testimony to the violent struggles of this period. Other leading musicians, such as Chao Feng, President of the Peking Conservatory, and Ma K'o, a composer, have also fallen into the hands of the Red Guards. Ma K'o was also lucky enough to escape,[44] but Chao Feng was tortured and humiliated by the Red Guards.[45] A most tragic story was that of Liu Shih-k'un, a gifted young pianist who won second prize in competition with Van Cliburn at the 1958 Tchaikovsky Festival in Moscow. In a confrontation with a band of Red Guards in Peking in 1967, his wrists were twisted so badly that he can no longer play the piano.[46]

PAINTINGS AND GRAPHIC ARTS

From the traditional point of view, not all painters in China can be called artists. A sharp distinction has always been made between an artist and an artisan. Traditionally, artists belonged to the intellectual class, while artisans were regarded as craftsmen who made their living on art. In traditional Chinese society, only paintings by artists were considered art, and they were usually identifiable. The paintings of artisans, such as those found on porcelain or architecture, were not regarded as high art. Thus, in the old society, there were only two types of works done with a brush that were considered art, painting and calligraphy. Both were the products of the scholarly class.

This distinction is no longer valid in Communist China today. As a matter of fact, traditional art is now scorned and discouraged by Party policy-makers, because a landscape painting or a scroll of calligraphy reflects individualistic achievement and imagination. True art, according to Mao Tse-tung, must take its inspiration from the people's life and struggle. Fine art, like other art forms, cannot stand aloof but must serve the people. 'Each of us art workers,' according to one artist, 'should follow the guidelines of the Party to study Marxism, Leninism, and the thought of Mao Tse-tung. We must penetrate into the life of the people and join hands with the revolutionary generation and the masses in order to create newer, better, and more beautiful art for socialism, for the proletariat revolution, and for the people's revolution of the whole world.'[47]

---

[42] See a report in *China Reconstructs*, August, 1965.

[43] Professor Ma's escape story was published in *Life* magazine, June 2, 1967.

[44] Ma K'o's story appeared in the *Hsing-tao Wan-pao* (*Hsing-tao Evening News*), Hong Kong, April 20, 1967, in a news dispatch by Chao Hao-sheng from New York.

[45] Chao Feng's story was mentioned by Professor Ma Sitson in his report published in *Life*. A longer accusation of Chao Feng is published in the *Kuang-ming Jih-pao* (*The Kuang-ming Daily*), Peking, January 22, 1967.

[46] Liu's story is also mentioned in the *Life* magazine story about Ma Sitson.

[47] Liu K'ai-ch'ü, 'Mei-shu Ch'uang-tso yao Keng-hao ti wei Ke-ming Fu-wu (Artistic Creations should serve the Revolution Better),' *JMJP*, June 30, 1963.

Painters, old and new. All old artists were required to undergo a process of sincere and conscientious thought-remolding. However, according to one observer, as late as 1963 there were still 'some artists of the older generation in our country [who], because of the fact that they were brought up and trained in the old society, still possess the artistic viewpoint of the capitalist class.'[48] The only noticeable progress made by some of the older artists was in the category of portrait painting. According to Fu Pao-shih, a leading artist himself, while assessing the progress made by traditional painting from 1949 to 1963:

Many painters of the older generation received admiration and respect from the people. Many of them had opportunities to travel to many parts of the country to visit the people. For instance, one of the great masters of art, Ch'i Pai-shih [1863–1957], recipient of the World Peace Award, a member of the laboring class himself, had been admired and loved by the people for his long strides of achievement in art. At the time of liberation [1949], he was already an old man approaching ninety years of age. But because he came from a poor family and was, like other people of the laboring class, oppressed in the old society, he had experienced bitterness and suffering. So when the new China was born, he picked up his brush again to give praise to the new nation and its great leader. His masterpieces, including *Long Live Our Motherland* and *Long Live Chairman Mao*, have become well-known paintings in the whole world and have received favorable comment from the people. . . .

As far as portraits are concerned, the two well-known and well-liked painters of Peking, Chiang Chao-ho and Yeh Ch'ien-yü, have also received wide acclaim from the masses for their masterpieces entitled *Listen to the Words of Chairman Mao* and *The People's Lecture Hall*. A third artist, Ya Ming, was also praised for his painting *Picture of a Peddler*. In addition, P'an T'ien-shou of Hangchow, Chao Meng-ch'u of Shenyang, Liu K'uei-ling of Tientsin, T'ang Yüan of Shanghai, and Chang Hsing-chieh of Soochow have made impressive contributions in developing the traditions of the flower-and-bird category.[49]

Popularity of other types of paintings and drawings. In contrast to the slow progress of the traditional paintings, other types which were never regarded as high class art in the old days, such as cartoon-style sequential drawings, New Year's pictures, and *k'ang* (a brick platform-type bed of northern China) wall paintings, have made unprecedented progress and become quite popular. All of these types of graphic arts have one thing in common: They are vehicles for story telling.

During the early years of the Communist regime, when the movement of praising model workers was conducted, *lien-huan hua* (sequential drawings) had been used by the cadres as a powerful and effective vehicle of communication. Such drawings, for instance, were used in the 'Learn from Lei Feng' campaign. Hailing the unprecedented success of the *lien-huan-hua*, one writer commented as follows:

The sequential drawings are a unique type of art which combines pictures with narrative writings. Because the story is presented both in pictures and in words, it is easy to understand. Thus, this type of drawing can play a terrific role in educating the masses . . . and become a powerful instrument for propagating the Party's policies, for cultivating the thought of the people, and for enhancing the people's understanding of history, science, and class struggle. It is a satisfactory

---

[48] *Ibid.*

[49] Fu Pao-shih, 'Chung-kuo Hua ti Fa-chan he Ch'eng-chiu (The Development and Achievement of Chinese Painting),' news dispatch of *Chung-kuo Hsin-wen (China News)*, Canton: Chung-kuo Hsin-wen-she, December 10, 1963.

result of our insistence on the principle that art and literature must serve the politics of the proletariat.[50]

It is estimated that from 1949 to 1963 at least 12,700 different kinds of sequential drawings were produced and more than 560 million copies were printed.[51]

New Year's pictures are another popular form of art. Chinese peasants and workers traditionally purchased them during the celebration of the lunar New Year, the only holiday for the masses. In the old days, the pictures were usually color prints of stories of folklore or opera, including such favorites as the episodes of the Eight Immortals, the legend of the cowherd and the weaving damsel, the twenty-four filial piety legends, and excerpts from popular novels, especially *Romance of the Three Kingdoms*. But New Year's pictures of that sort, in the eyes of Party reformers, were either superstitious or feudalistic in nature and were therefore not suitable for use in educating the people. Since 1949 New Year's pictures have been kept as an art form, but new, contemporary, and revolutionary stories of the people—peasants, workers and soldiers—have been carefully adopted. The following comment of a writer is worth noting:

> Since the Liberation, it is estimated that more than 2 million copies of New Year's pictures are sold each year. Unfortunately, for hundreds of years these pictures had been dominated by themes and subjects of gods and ghosts, kings and ministers, and scholars and beauties, and had been used by the ruling class as tools to fool the people with feudal and superstitious ideas. Since the birth of a new China, constant reforms and improvements have been made on these pictures so that they will have a new and revolutionary content, and thus they have become an art form which the people love to enjoy. Of more than 200 different kinds of New Year's pictures published this year, 95 per cent have taken up new and contemporary themes—praising the Party, Chairman Mao, socialism, heroes of the new era, workers, peasants, and soldiers. In addition, 'good stories' from novels, drama, or motion pictures are used for these pictures, such as *Sister Chiang, The White-haired Girl, By All Means Never Forget, Li Shuang-shuang*, and so on. All of these are revolutionary and contemporary themes.[52]

'*Art of permanent value.*' A permanent display of modern Chinese art was organized in Peking in 1966. A review of it reveals what kind of art is acceptable to the Communist regime. The article reads in part:

> This new exhibition includes representative works from the time of the May Fourth Movement in 1919—the beginning of China's New Democratic Revolution—to the present time of socialist revolution and construction. What is immediately noticeable in this exhibition is that a new chapter has opened in China's art. These walls show a flourishing art that is brilliantly serving socialism, workers, peasants, and soldiers, and the liberation struggle of the people of the entire world. The years from 1919 to the present saw a gradual revolutionization of Chinese art. By the late 1920's and early 1930's, the people's revolutionary strife began to find increasingly strong expression in woodcuts and cartoons. In 1942, Chairman Mao delivered his famous Yenan talks on literature and art, which have charted the course for art to serve the people—workers, peasants, and soldiers—and ushered in a new historical era in Chinese art. In the ensuing years, pictorial art played a militant role in the revolution to overthrow im-

---

[50] Ma K'e, 'Huan-hu Lien-huan-hua ti Hsin Ch'eng-chiu (Cheers to the New Achievement of the Sequential Drawings),' *JMJP*, December 29, 1963.

[51] *Ibid.*

[52] T'an I-jen, 'P'o-chiu-li-hsin shuo Nien-hua (Breaking the Old and Establishing the New for the New Year's Pictures),' *Chung-kuo Hsin-wen* (China News), January 23, 1965.

perialism, feudalism, and bureaucratic capitalism. The works displayed here deal predominately with themes of socialist revolution and construction. They include scenes and achievements on various construction fronts, and of heroes and activists in many spheres of life. There are scenes of the agricultural cooperative movement and socialist industrialization, emancipation of the serfs of Tibet, and other historical episodes of the people's revolution. There are the expressions of the Chinese people's support to the peoples of Korea and Vietnam in their resistance against the U.S. aggression. The anti-imperialist struggle of the peoples of Asia, Africa, and Latin America is another theme that has inspired many painters and sculptors. Their works can illuminate and inspire the consciousness of the people for revolutionary action. The veteran artists shown in this exhibition have turned away from the outmoded artistic interests and sentiments and have developed bolder, fresher brush strokes to depict the life of the people of today. New compositional methods and new color harmonies are emerging. The dominant note is a fresh and new look at things. Stereotypes are out. These works show that when an artist sincerely endeavors to remold his world outlook, his style and technique—the form of his art—will undergo a fundamental change. His ideological remolding progresses in the course of his artistic practice. If an artist determines to serve the working masses, his artistic practice will become the means of bringing about the revolutionary transformation of his conscience, his ideology, and his art.[53]

Thus, the reform of the fine arts has followed the same guidelines as other forms of art discussed above. Today in China, paintings and graphic arts have become a means to an end instead of an expression of themselves, as in the past. Individual styles and traditional categories are out. Only this revolutionary art—art that serves the people and the proletarian revolution—is permissible. Artists today no longer hold their traditional status or privileges, for they are now workers—members of the laboring class.

The Cultural Revolution and the artists. Because the aim of the Cultural Revolution was not only to destroy 'old culture, old thoughts, old habits, and old customs' but even more to purge the society of certain undesirables—among them certain well-known painters, both living and dead—several leading artists were denounced. Three instances are of special interest. The first painter was Yeh Ch'ien-yü. He, together with a few less well-known people, was denounced as an antirevolutionary capitalist. The second was the veteran painter Ch'i Pai-shih, who was once praised as an old artist of the poor people. Chiang Ch'ing, wife of Mao Tse-tung and a leading spirit of the Cultural Revolution, called him an 'old miser,' because 'at the time of his death, he wrapped gold bars around his waist, hoping to take them with him into his coffin.'[54] The third was P'an T'ien-shou, a leading artist of Hangchow, of whom Chiang Ch'ing's comment was, 'I am disgusted with P'an's paintings. The bald eagle he painted looks very gloomy to me.' Yao Wen-yüan, a close associate of Chiang Ch'ing, even called P'an a secret agent and echoed Chiang Ch'ing's comments with his own. 'The painting [of the bald eagle] is indeed very gloomy. This has something to do with his activities as a secret agent. He personifies the secret agent.'[55] All three were once exalted personages.

The dance. Of all the art forms in China, dance has the weakest traditional base. This does not mean that dancing was never developed in China. Actually, it was one

---

[53] 'Permanent Display of Modern Chinese Art,' *Peking Review*, No. 13, March 25, 1966, p. 30.
[54] See a news report entitled 'Mao's Wife Keeps Control of Arts' in *The New York Times*, September 22, 1968, Section 1, p. 12.
[55] *Ibid.*

of the art forms that were carefully recorded in ancient times. There were two different trends in the ancient Chinese dance: folk dance and court dance. Unfortunately, both types faded away as time passed. In the recent past, except in local operas and on festive occasions (where such dances as the dragon dance and the lion dance were still performed), dancing had almost become an extinct art.

During their Yenan years the Chinese Communists developed a folksong and folk dance form known as *Yang-ko* (sprouting song), probably improvised from a local festive dance (like the lion dance). After 1949, however, *yang-ko* deteriorated. Occasionally exhibited abroad, *yang-ko* was performed at the Centennial celebration in Vancouver, B.C., in Canada, in 1960, which I witnessed. Two 'folk dance' numbers were given, a lotus dance and a harvest dance. Both proved to be simply improvised versions of the old court dances.

Very little has been reported on the reform of the dance during the reform of art and literature in general. Perhaps the pure dance forms have been de-emphasized; perhaps other art forms, especially musicals, ballet, and the new operas, have absorbed and incorporated some of the dancing forms so that the de-emphasis is a natural development.

A Summation

In reviewing the development of literature, music, drama, and other arts, one cannot help but conclude that the reformers and revolutionaries of China have been trying to do away with the very essence of man's creative activities, namely freedom, and that so far they have been very successful. With freedom banished, the artist cannot do what he wants or pleases; what worries him is whether his art is acceptable to the Party. Without freedom, the artist cannot truly be inspired. Without inspiration, there is no real art—at least from my point of view. This is exactly what has happened since the establishment of Communist rule in China.

What has become of art? What is considered 'art' by the Communists in China is nothing but a variety of convenient means to help achieve a final objective—the proletarian revolution. It is justifiable to conclude that real art is dead. There is, however, the matter of two different 'world outlooks.' The Communists never deny art or the value of art. What they deny is the 'old' art or the 'art of the bourgeoisie,' as they call it. Similarly, the Communists never deny democracy. What they have denied is the democracy that non-Communists understand, and they call their democracy 'New Democracy.' or 'People's Democracy.'

As politics takes command in China today, everything else is subordinate to it. Because the masses—workers, peasants, and soldiers—are the masters, everyone else is a servant, including, of course, the artist. A good servant must please his master. If he goes against the master's wishes, he will be punished or banished. Realizing this, one can understand what has happened to art and the artist in China today.

Who are the people, the real 'people'? One cannot get a really clear idea from the above discussion. Yet one can have a clear impression of the nature of the demands of the Communist Party. The people never demanded art reforms; the Party did. Even within the Party, however, not all members necessarily speak the same language. Thus, when Wu Han, one of the Party elite, wrote *Hai Jui's Dismissal from Office* (a traditional Peking opera), he thought he was serving the people because he portrayed Hai Jui, a historical figure, as a champion of the people. But Yao Wen-yüan, also a prominent member of the Party, criticized Wu for using a fake Hai Jui to further Wu's anti-Party ideas. Yao won and Wu lost. Similarly, the Party attacked Party member Hsia Yen's motion picture *The Story of Wu Hsün*. At the same time, extreme measures were sometimes taken against artists who did not directly contribute to agricultural or industrial production. The Red Guards smashed and twisted the fingers of the gifted, prize-winning pianist Liu Shih-k'un so that he could no longer play the piano but could still work as a laborer in charge of manure in the fields. And hatred of any trace of capitalism was evident in Chiang Ch'ing's denunciation of the renowned painter Ch'i Pai-shih for having died with gold bars around his waist in the hope of being buried with them.

All forms of music and art have become the means for political ends. Thus, the story of *The White-Haired Girl*, in which the crimes of the landlord class in the old society were revealed and condemned, has been made into a modern drama, a Peking opera, a motion picture, and a modern ballet. In order to destroy the old image of a hero or heroine, the reformers finally banned the performance of traditional Peking opera, which for many generations dramatized tales of kings and queens, generals and ministers, scholars and beauties, all of the elite class in a feudal society. The new Peking opera sings the praises of workers, the Liberation Army, or the oppressed class. For many generations, the Chinese people were familiar with the standards of filial piety. As a result, the so-called Twenty-Four Filial Piety stories were regarded as good moral lessons. The Party reformers branded these tales as feudalistic and removed them from New Year's pictures, one of the most popular art forms, and put in their place stories of revolutionary heroes and heroines.

Not only has the content of the arts been changed, even the forms have gone through a drastic change. Of all the art forms, the traditional opera has undergone, the most thorough revolution; only a few singing patterns and gestures remain. In fine arts, traditional styles and schools of painting, such as landscape, flowers-and-birds, beautiful women, and so on, were entirely wiped out in the process of 'reform.' Imaginary and abstract paintings are gone; realism has taken its place.

Since art has become a means, its intrinsic quality—technique, style, and approach—is no longer emphasized. Only its application to political purposes is given emphasis. Thus, an artist will never become an artist in his own right; he can be recognized only as a faithful follower of the thought of Mao Tse-tung and a worker for the cause of the proletarian revolution.

It is quite difficult for anyone to discuss quality in any art form in Communist China, for the accepted standards of truth, goodness, and beauty no longer exist. What the Communist leaders want is an idealized but also realistic presentation of the life of the people in all arts. Thus realism as the prime criterion for art has replaced the traditional criteria. In order to make a judgment of quality, the critic must have something in common with the artists. With the 'artists' in Communist China today, the non-Communist can find little in common.

As far as the dissemination of art is concerned, credit must go to the high organizational ability of the Communist Chinese regime. If the policy-makers find anything they think is useful and advantageous for propaganda, they will spread it to every corner of the country through movie projection teams and annual 'exhibitions' of art, drama, opera, painting, sculpture, or other forms. For exhibitions, China has been divided into several regions. All exhibitions are under the absolute supervision of the Party. The Party has also established a number of museums in which exemplary art works of every kind are on permanent display. Since 'professionalism' in art has been completely wiped out, all the people—workers, peasants, and soldiers—are encouraged either to organize their own creative groups or to try out their ability in any artistic field. All of these methods have effectively disseminated art.

What are contemporary Chinese attitudes toward non-Chinese art today? Mao does not necessarily object to non-Chinese art. As a matter of fact, there have been constant cultural exchanges between China and other countries (including Albania, Vietnam, Japan, and Korea). But the Chinese leaders make a sharp distinction between the art of the proletariat and the art of capitalists. Form is not too important for them. It is the content that counts. However, certain art forms of the West, especially those that are suitable merely for personal enjoyment and consumption, such as the piano, the violin, traditional ballet, and stylish painting, cannot in general be tolerated by the Communists. The persecution and purge of certain artists and musicians testifies to that fact. On the other hand, the reformers have not ruled out non-Chinese art or music altogether. In September, 1968, a newspaper account reported that Chiang Ch'ing had introduced the piano as an accompaniment for Peking opera in place of certain traditional Chinese instruments.[56] Oil painting is definitely non-Chinese, but the report mentioned a much-publicized oil painting entitled *Chairman Mao Goes to Anyüan* as a prime example of the 'new art' form of China. The ballet is fully utilized by the reformers to portray contemporary life. However, the traditional 'bourgeois,' ballets, such as *Swan Lake, The Sleeping Beauty,* and *Romeo and Juliet,* are rejected by the Communist Party.

So far, little of the new arts or music of the Cultural Revolution has been exported. Persons outside China have had slight opportunity to view or hear the new works, except indirectly through books, newspapers, magazine articles, movies and records. It is only hoped that, with Peking's new diplomatic moves and with official recognition of the Communist regime by an increasing number of nations, including Canada, Italy, Chile and Nigeria, art troupes and exhibitions will again be sent abroad, as they were before the Cultural Revolution.

SELECTED BIBLIOGRAPHY

Newspapers in Chinese

Jen-min Jih-pao (People's Daily), Peking.
Kuang-ming Jih-pao (Enlightenment Daily), Peking.
Wen-hui Pao (The Wen-hui News), Shanghai.

Magazines in Chinese

Hsi-chü Pao (Drama Magazine), Peking: Jen-min Wen-hsüeh Ch'u-pan-she.
Jen-min Chou-k'an (People's Weekly), Peking: Jen-min Chou-k'an Ch'u-pan-she.
Jen-min Hua-chü (People's Dream), Peking: Jen-min Ch'u-pan she.
Tien-ying Ch'uang-tao (Motion Picture Plays), Peking: Chung-kuo Tien-ying Ch'u-pan-she.
Wen-i Pao (Art and Literature), Peking: Jen-min Ch'u-pan-she.
Wu-tao (Dancing), Peking: Chung-kuo Wu-tao I-shu Yen-chiu-hui Wu-tao Pien-chi-pu, 1958.

Magazines in English

China Reconstructs, Peking: China Welfare Institute.
Peking Review, Peking.

Books and Articles in English

CHOU YANG. *China's New Literature and Art*. Peking: Foreign Languages Press, 1954.
———. *The Path of Socialist Literature and Art in China*. Peking: Foreign Languages Press, 1960.
KUO HAN-CHENG. 'New Development in the Traditional Chinese Theatre,' *Chinese Literature,* No. 1, Peking: Foreign Languages Press, 1960, pp. 127–39.
MAO TSE-TUNG. *On Literature and Art*. Peking: Foreign Languages Press, 1967.
MEI, LAN-FANG. 'My Life on the Stage,' *Chinese Literature,* No. 11, Peking: Foreign Languages Press, 1961, pp. 3–35.
———. 'The Traditional Theatre Today,' *China Reconstructs,* 8 (Peking: China Welfare Institute, October, 1959): 19–21.

---

[56] *Time* magazine, among others, picked up the report in its November 1, 1968, issue.

MOHR, CHARLES. 'Opera Rewritten by Mao's Wife in Rift with Liu Over Party Line,' *The New York Times*, June 2, 1967.

OU-YANG, YU-CH'IEN. 'The Modern Chinese Theatre and the Dramatic Tradition,' *Chinese Literature*, 11 (Peking: Foreign Languages Press, 1959): 102–23.

P'ENG CHEN et al. *A Great Revolution on the Cultural Front*. Peking: Jen-min Ch'u-pan-she, 1965.

SCOTT, A. C. *The Classical Theatre of China*. London: George Allen & Unwin, Ltd., 1957.

———. 'Hung Teng Chi, An Example of Contemporary Chinese Dramatic Experimentation,' *Modern Drama*, 9, No. 4 (University of Kansas, Spring, 1967): 404–11.

———. *An Introduction to the Chinese Theatre*. Singapore: Donald Moore, 1958.

———. *Literature and Art in Twentieth Century China*. New York: Doubleday & Company, 1963.

TAN, MAN-NI. 'The Red Lantern, An Example for New Peking Opera,' *China Reconstructs*, 14, No. 12 (Peking: China Welfare Institute, December, 1965): 35–38.

WANG CHAO-WEN. 'The Artist and His Audience,' *Chinese Literature*, No. 11, Peking: Foreign Languages Press, 1963, pp. 89–96.

———. 'The Modern Play and the Artistic Taste,' *Selections from China—Mainland Magazines*, No. 407, Hong Kong: U.S. Consulate General, March 9, 1964, pp. 32–35.

———. 'Some Reflections on Peking Opera with Contemporary Themes,' *Chinese Literature*, No. 10, Peking: Foreign Languages Press, 1964, pp. 101–9.

WEN YANG. 'New Life for Peking Opera,' *Chinese Literature*, No. 9, Peking: Foreign Languages Press, 1964, pp. 96–102.

YANG, DANIEL S. P. *An Annotated Bibliography of Materials for the Study of the Peking Theatre*. Madison: University of Wisconsin, 1967.

———. 'Peking Drama with Contemporary Themes,' *The Drama Review*, 13, No. 4 (T44): 167–73.

YANG, RICHARD F. S. 'Behind the Bamboo Curtain: What the Communists Did to the Peking Opera,' *Educational Theatre Journal*, 21, No. 1 (March, 1969): 60–66.

———. 'The Reform of the Peking Opera Under the Communists,' *The China Quarterly*. London: Congress for Cultural Freedom, July–September, 1962, pp. 124–39.

Books in Chinese

CHIANG CH'ING. *T'an Ching-chü Ke-ming* (*A Talk on the Revolution of the Peking Opera*). Hong Kong: San-lien Shu-tien, 1967.

Hsi-chü Lun-ts'ung (*Discussions on Drama*). Peking: Chung-kuo Hsi-chü Ch'u-pan-she, 1959.

Lun Hsi-chü Fan-ying Wei-ta Shih-tai Wen-t'i (*Discussions on the Question of the Role of Drama in Reflecting the Great Era*). Peking: Chung-kuo Hsi-chu Ch'u-pan-she, 1958.

P'AN HSIA-FENG. *Ching-chü Wu-t'ai Yen-chiu Pen* (*Texts of the Peking Opera Plays Performed on the Stage*). Peking: Wen-ta Shu-chü, 1954.

T'IEN HAN. *Chien-kuo Shih-nien Wen-hsüeh Ch'uang-tso Hsüan* (*Selections from Literature of the Past Ten Years since the Founding of the Nation*). Peking: Chung-kuo Ch'ing-nien Ch'u-pan-she, 1961.

30

SOURCES OF INFORMATION: A BRIEF SURVEY

JOHN T. MA

IT is often difficult to obtain reliable and accurate information on a Communist country. In the case of contemporary Communist China the difficulty is unusually great. For anyone who does not read Chinese, the most obvious problem since 1949 is the drastic reduction in the volume of English-language sources published in mainland China. Government control over publishing and the exportation of publication makes it all but impossible for people outside mainland China to receive English-language publications from Communist China other than those the Communist Chinese Government allows to be exported. The availability of such publications was further reduced at the beginning of the Cultural Revolution in 1966. As of the summer of 1972, we have not yet seen a substantial improvement in this situation.

Outside mainland China, however, we have witnessed during the past decade a phenomenal increase in the number of publications on China, especially in books in the English language. This 'publication explosion' has made bibliographical control rather difficult. The vast increase has involved both the quantity of materials produced and the variety of forms in which they appear, and has raised complex questions about how to locate, organize, and use these materials. This short chapter will attempt to describe some of the most helpful sources of information on mainland China, beginning with a general discussion on the utilization of library resources and reference works.

BIBLIOGRAPHICAL TOOLS

As long as mainland China remains behind a 'Bamboo Curtain' that interferes with the free movement of men and material, we are compelled to rely very heavily on printed material for our information. A reader should therefore first consult major bibliographical tools. Among the most important are the *Cumulative Book Index*, the *Reader's Guide to Pictorial Literature*, *Public Affairs Information Service Bulletin*, and the *Social Science and Humanities Index* (formerly the *International Index to Periodicals*). These standard reference works list under appropriate subject headings commercial publications, popular and scholarly books, and popular magazine articles on Communist China. These listings are comprehensive, not selective. No annotations are given. Nor is there any indication of the academic or intellectual standards of the books and articles listed. Moreover, and of particular importance for China, these standard reference works exclude government publications and many institutional reports.

The United States Government is the most prolific producer of English-language publications on Communist China. Universities, research institutions, public organizations, commercial and industrial companies, and individuals have all contributed to the enormous volume of publications on Communist China. However, many of these items in print are not published commercially and are therefore limited in distribution. To track them down, one must consult the catalogs of research libraries, specialized subject bibliographies, and other bibliographical tools.

Like standard major bibliographies, catalogs of research libraries usually have books on Communist China conveniently grouped together under relevant subject headings. Cross-reference cards are usually provided. A great advantage of research library catalogs is that, if the library has an extensive collection and an active acquisitions policy, its catalog will include many recent books not yet listed in published bibliographies.

However, for specialists in a topic, no library catalog can match a good subject bibliography on that topic. Although not many comprehensive bibliographies have been compiled on Communist China, many general bibliographies on China or Asia include materials on Communist China. Many bibliographies dealing with certain aspects of Communist China are also available.

General bibliographies on Communist China. One of the most recent bibliographies dealing specifically with English-language material on Communist China is entitled *Communist China: a Bibliographic Survey, 1971.* Compiled and published by the U.S. Department of the Army in 1971, this bibliography brings up to date two earlier bibliographies: *Communist China: a Strategic Survey,* published in 1966; and *Communist China: Ruthless Enemy or Paper Tiger,* published in January, 1962. It contains more than 650 items selected from several thousand books, magazine articles, reports, and documents available at the Army Library. Every item includes an annotation or an abstract of the contents. Both pro-Communist and anti-Communist items are included. It is a useful and convenient guide to economic, sociological, political, and military studies of Communist China.

Two recent bibliographies dealing specifically with China, though necessarily of limited coverage, are David L. Weitzman's *China Studies in Paperback,* published by the McCutchan Publishing Company at Berkeley, Calif., and *An Annotated Guide to Modern China,* compiled and published by the National Committee on United States–China Relations in New York in 1967.

Another useful source is Professor Charles O. Hucker's *China: A Critical Bibliography,* published by the University of Arizona Press in 1962, which lists more than 2,000 books, articles, and sections of books and provides short annotations. It stresses post-1940 publications and includes many English-language books on Communist China. Allan B. Cole's *Forty Years of Chinese Communism: Selected Readings with Commentary,* published by the American Historical Association in Washington, D.C., in 1962, is smaller than Hucker's bibliography and is mainly intended as a guide for teachers in secondary schools.

While there are very few comprehensive bibliographies on Communist China, most major works on China contain useful bibliographies. Peter Tang's *Communist China: The Domestic Scene, 1949–1967;* Walt W. Rostow's *The Prospects for Communist China;* Werner Klatt's *The Chinese Model;* and many other similar works all include valuable bibliographies.

Communist China forms a part of most of the leading bibliographies on China or Asia. The most comprehensive current bibliography on Asia today is the *Bibliography of Asian Studies,* which was formerly a special annual bibliographical issue of the *Journal of Asian Studies* but is now published separately. This bibliography began in 1936 in the *Bulletin of Far Eastern Bibliography* and was edited by Professor Earl E. Pritchard. Later, it became the *Far Eastern Bibliography* of the *Far Eastern Quarterly.* It began to appear under its present title in 1956. In addition to books on Asia, this bibliography selects articles from several hundred journals on Asia and many other journals with articles of interest to Asian scholars. The G. K. Hall Company of Boston combined all the bibliographies published in the *Far Eastern Quarterly* and the *Journal of Asian Studies* between 1941 and 1965 as a *Cumulative Bibliography of Asian Studies, 1941–1965*. This book has two parts in eight volumes: four volumes of the author catalog and four volumes of the subject catalog, containing more than 85,000 and 83,000 entries respectively. It is the prime reference book for any reader wishing to consult Western-language publications on East Asia. Its continuation, the *Cumulative Bibliography of Asian Studies, 1966–1970*, will be published by G. K. Hall and Co. in 1972.

The most comprehensive single-volume bibliography of Western-language books on China published between 1921 and 1957 is *China in Western Literature: A Continuation of Cordier's Bibliotheca Sinica*, compiled by the late Dr. Tung-li Yuan, formerly Director of the National Library of Peking. Published by Far Eastern Publications, New Haven, Conn., in 1958, it lists about 18,000 books and pamphlets, classified into twenty-eight groups and about 540 Western-language serials, but no articles in periodicals. The articles can be found in John Lust's *Index Sinicus: A Catalogue of Articles Relating to China in Periodicals and Other Collective Publications, 1920–1955*, published by Heffer in Cambridge, England, in 1964. This index contains about 20,000 entries selected from some 700 periodicals and 150 proceedings, symposia, memorial volumes, and so forth. It complements Dr. Yuan's book, and together they provide the basic sources of information on contemporary Western-language literature on China.

Two bibliographies published by Hoover Institution at Stanford University, *The Chinese Communist Movement, 1921–1937*, and *The Chinese Communist Movement, 1937–1949*, both compiled by Chün-tu Hsüeh, annotate all the important material on the historical background of Communist China held in the large Chinese collection of the institution. These two bibliographies constitute the most comprehensive compilation of sources on the historical background of Communist China.

Contemporary China: A Research Guide, compiled by Peter Berton and Eugene Wu and published by the Hoover Institution in 1967, is the most basic reference book for the study of Communist China. It describes many useful reference works in English, Chinese, Japanese, and other languages; it also lists many sources of information on mainland China. It should be among the first books consulted by all students of China.

Subject bibliographies. Bibliographies dealing with specific aspects of China are usually published as pamphlets or as part of a major work on the subject.

Most subject bibliographies record Chinese-language materials. However, there are a number of bibliographies that exclusively or prominently list English-language publications. For instance, in the field of economics, there is a thirty-nine page bibliography in Yuan-li Wu's *An Economic Survey of Communist China*, published by Bookman Associates in New York. Then there is Nai-ruenn Chen's *The Economy of Mainland China, 1949–1963: A Bibliography of Materials in English*, published in 1963, by the Committee on the Economy of China of the Social Science Research Council. For the period covered, Chen's compilation is the most extensive bibliography in this particular field. Part I contains references to the primary source materials originating in Communist China (official documents, laws and regulations, governmental reports, speeches and statements by political leaders, newspaper editorials, and news reports); Part II lists secondary source materials, such as books and reports published outside mainland China.

In the field of politics and government, there is George P. Jan's *Government of Communist China*, published in 1966 by the Chandler Publishing Company, San Francisco, which includes a thirty-four-page bibliography. It is intended for the general reader rather than specialist, and so lists only English-language books and articles. The books listed are annotated.

In 1958, the Bureau of the Census of the U.S. Department of Commerce published *The Population and Manpower of China: An Annotated Bibliography*. Of the 646 books, articles, official reports, and other publications listed, about two-fifths are in English and the rest in Chinese, Japanese, and other languages. It is the most important bibliography on population-manpower problems, and further editions of this volume are to be published.

The Christian churches have played a very active part in China's modernization process and international relations. Their fate in mainland China after the Communist takeover is of deep concern not only to the Christian churches outside China but also to the large number of Chinese Christians abroad. To help locate information on Christian churches and other religious institutions in Communist China, Frank W. Price, former Director of the Missionary Research Library in New York City, compiled and published in 1958 the *Selected Bibliography of Books, Pamphlets, and Articles on Communist China and the Christian Church in China*. The best source of current information on religions in mainland China is *China Notes*, which is published in New York by the East Asia Department of the Division of Overseas Ministries of the National Council of Churches, U.S.A.

Scientific and Engineering Manpower in Communist China, 1949–1963, compiled in 1965 by Chu-yuan Cheng for the National Science Foundation, contains a bibliography of Chinese- and English-language books and articles. *Mainland China Organizations of Higher Learning in Science and Technology and Their Publications: A Selected Guide*, compiled by Chi Wang and published in 1961 by the Science and Technology Division of the Reference Department of the Library of Congress, lists learned societies, universities and colleges, the Chinese Academy of Sciences and affiliated research institutes, governmental research organizations, libraries, the Chinese Academy of Medical Sciences and its branch institutes, and the Chinese Academy of Agricultural Sciences and its branches. All the publications of these institutions are listed, and those available at the Library of Congress are marked.

Another directory of research institutions in Communist China, entitled *Directory of Selected Scientific Institutions in Mainland China*, has been published by the Hoover Institution at Stanford University. This new directory lists 490 Chinese institutions engaged in scientific research, including universities, colleges, academies of sciences, governmental agencies, industrial enterprises, and professional societies. The description of each institution contains its name, location, personnel, structure, research activities, publications, and biographical information about key staff members.

For legal studies, Tao-tai Hsia, Head of the Far Eastern Division of the Library of Congress, has compiled a *Guide to Selected Legal Sources of Mainland China*, which contains lists of laws and regulations, as well as periodical legal literature and a brief survey of the administration of justice in Communist China.

Several documentary studies of Communist China's official documents exist. One of these is Theodore Hsi-en Ch'en's *The Chinese Communist Regime: Documents and Commentary*, published by Praeger in New York in 1967. *Communist China, 1955–1959: Policy Documents with Analysis*, published by Harvard University Press in 1962, with a foreword by Robert R. Bowie and John K. Fairbank, lists forty-eight key documents emanating from Communist China that illustrate its domestic policy during this period. Chao Kuo-chün's *Economic Planning and Organization in Mainland China: A Documentary Study (1949–1957)*, also published by Harvard in 1959–60, deals with documents on economic policy. *Agrarian Policies of Mainland China: A Documentary Study (1949–1956)*, by the same author, precedes the above-mentioned work in date of publication, and contains a collection of translated articles on China's agrarian policy taken from Chinese Communist publications. *Major Doctrines of Communist China*, edited by John Wilson Lewis and published in 1964 by W. W. Norton in New York, contains official documents and statements by Chinese Communist leaders or Party members as illustrations of the various doctrines and policies of the Chinese Communist Party regarding leadership, ideology, Party structure, state power, and other political aspects of mainland China.

In the field of international relations, *China and U.S. Far East Policy*, published by the Congressional Quarterly Service in 1967, presents a factual account of relations between the United States and China from 1945 through the beginning of 1967. It includes some key official documents and statements on the subject.

Important articles on several subjects are selected from Chinese-language periodicals and newspapers published in mainland China, translated, and published by the International Arts & Sciences Press in a publication called *China Series*. Its first five quarterly issues were entitled *Chinese Economic Studies*, *Chinese Law and Government*, *Chinese Education*, *Chinese Studies in History and Philosophy*, and *Chinese Studies in Sociology and Anthropology*. These translations are very helpful to subject specialists who do not read Chinese.

U.S. GOVERNMENT PUBLICATIONS

The importance of U.S. government publications as sources of information on Communist China is second to none. Numerous reports, monographs, pamphlets, and other publications put out by various governmental agencies are listed in the *Monthly Catalog of U.S. Government Publications*.

In addition, the American Consulate-General in Hong Kong, the Joint Publications Research Service in Washington, D.C., and the Foreign Broadcast Information Service provide English-language readers with comprehensive and up-to-date information on Communist China. Although some of their publications are not widely distributed, they are usually obtainable in the larger universities.

The U.S. Consulate-General in Hong Kong provides a number of very valuable information services on mainland China. It has been publishing since 1950 daily translations of selected news items and editorials from Chinese mainland newspapers as well as extracts from New China News Agency releases. The service is known as the *Survey of China Mainland Press*. It is distributed to many universities and libraries in this country. Also in 1950, the Consulate-General began to publish approximately once a week the serial *Current Background*. This provides within a single issue important translated items on a particular major development or event in mainland China. In 1955, a new serial, *Selections from China Mainland Magazines* (originally called *Extracts from China Mainland Magazines*), was added. This is a collection of articles selected from China mainland magazines and translated in full. These three serials have been indexed together since 1956. Microfilm of their back issues is now available. The three services are now among the most commonly used sources of current information on mainland China.

Another serial of the American Consulate-General in Hong Kong was started in 1962 and ceased publication in 1964. It is entitled *Extracts from China Mainland Publications* and deals with specific topics. It draws its material from extracts of translations already published in the three serials mentioned above. The *Review of the Hong Kong Chinese Press*, which was also published by the Consulate-General between 1947 and 1961, summarizes editorials and news published in pro-Communist and anti-Communist newspapers in Hong Kong. The above two serials are not indexed.

Since 1957, the Joint Publications Research Service (JPRS), which is a centralized translation service for U.S. Government agencies, began to publish its translated materials on Communist China in a number of serials. Though some of these are no longer published, they include *Communist China Digest*, *Translations from Hung-ch'i* (the leading theoretical journal in Communist China), *Translations of Political and Sociological Information on Communist China*, and translations of material on agriculture, industry, trade, science, and other aspects of Communist China. There is no comprehensive bibliography covering all issues of these JPRS serials. However, partial bibliographies are available. Richard Sorich's *Contemporary China: A Bibliography of Reports on China Published by the United States Joint Publications Research Service*, published in 1961, lists all the JPRS reports on China published from its inception in late 1957 through July, 1960. With a subject index, it greatly facilitates the use of these reports. Beginning in September, 1962, Research & Microfilm Publications in Annapolis, Md., has been publishing a monthly bibliography, compiled by Theodore E. Kyriak, entitled *China: A Bibliography and Guide to Contents of a Collection of the United States Joint Publications Research Service Translations in the Social Sciences Emanating from Communist China*. This monthly index is now called *Bibliography-Index to Current U.S. JPRS Translations: China & Asia (Exclusive of Near East)*. It has a social science subject index, a scientific-technical subject index, and a cross-reference index. Two cumulative indices are available for JPRS translations. One is the *Catalog Cards in Book Form for U.S. JPRS Translations*, which is published semiannually by Research & Microfilm Publications, and the other is the *Subject Index to U.S. JPRS Translations*, which was started in January, 1966 and appears semiannually. It is the cumulative volume of the *Social Science Subject Index* in the monthly *Bibliography-Index*.

At present, there is no bibliography which covers the JPRS reports published between August, 1960 and June, 1962. However, most of the important reports are included in the *Monthly Catalog of U.S. Government Publications*, which began to include the JPRS reports in October, 1958. All JPRS reports are now available on microfilm or microfiche.

The most up-to-date and comprehensive current information on Communist China is probably the *Daily Report*, the monitoring service of the U.S. Foreign Broadcast Information Service. It has a section on Communist China. Two obvious shortcomings of these reports are that there is no index and that they are not widely distributed.

The U.S. Library of Congress is, of course, the first library a general reader should visit in search of information on contemporary China. All government publications are deposited there. In addition to its own acquisitions, all government agencies are required by law to transfer library material they no longer need to the Library of Congress. Many of the publications acquired by various government agencies from sources in the Far East are not easy to obtain. Thus the transfer of those materials greatly adds to the uniqueness of the resources in the Library of Congress.

To facilitate research on Communist China, the Library of Congress has published a number of bibliographies and other reference works. For instance, the *Accession List of Chinese Communist Periodicals, January 1963–December 1966*, compiled by the Aerospace Technology Division of the Library of Congress in 1967, lists 274 journals and irregular serials and newspapers, with four indices. Other major U.S. Government libraries, such as the Library of the Department of Agriculture and the National Library of Medicine, have also published useful reference works on Communist China.

Among the federal agencies that are actively engaged in research on Communist China are the Department of State, the Department of Defense, the U.S. Information Agency, the Central Intelligence Agency, the Arms Control Agency, the Department of Commerce, the Department of the Interior, and the Congress. They have all published bibliographies, reports, serials, or other publications as a result of their research. Most of these can be found in any library that is designated as a depository library for U.S. government publications. Such depository libraries exist in every state and include the libraries of almost all leading universities.

Useful reference works and information reports published by U.S. Government agencies are too numerous to be mentioned here. Among the most useful of them are various editions of the directory of Chinese Communist officials, compiled by the Bureau of Intelligence and Research of the Department of State; the *Communist China Map Folio*, compiled by the Central Intelligence Agency in 1968 and the *People's Republic of China Atlas*, published by the same agency in November, 1971; the bimonthly *Problems of Communism*, published by the U.S. Information Agency since 1952; the two-volume *China: Official Standard Names Approved by the U.S. Board on Geographic*

Names, edited by the Office of Geography of the Department of the Interior in 1952; and the bibliographies of Western-language and Chinese materials dealing with various aspects of Communist China, published by the External Research Staff of the Department of State.

RESEARCH INSTITUTIONS AND THEIR PUBLICATIONS

Although the number of research institutions interested in the study of Communist China has grown tremendously during the past twenty years, no directory has yet been published that lists these institutions exclusively. The second edition of Ward Morehouse's *American Institutions and Organizations Interested in Asia: A Reference Directory*, published by the Taplinger Publishing Company, New York, in 1961, contains a number of established institutions whose research interests include Communist China. A more recent *Directory of Asian Library Resources and Area Studies Programs* was compiled by Yukihisa Suzuki and is included as an appendix in *Asian Resources in American Libraries: Essays and Bibliographies*, compiled by Winston L. Y. Yang and Teresa Yang in 1968. The directory and the essays and bibliographies in the Yangs' book will lead to some helpful information on library sources for China studies and on the publications and research interests of many China studies centers. The External Research Staff of the U.S. Department of State has published several editions of the *Language and Area Study Programs in American Universities*, which include many programs for China studies and provide detailed information on these programs.

Numerous publications, including reports, pamphlets, monographs, and serials, have been and are being published by research institutions concerned with Communist China. Many of these publications are not available through commercial channels and have a limited circulation. In other words, the bibliographic control of institutional publications is quite inadequate. It is often difficult to know what has been published by an institution unless an inquiry is made directly to the institution. A few of the leading research institutions and their publications will be described briefly in the following paragraphs.

The Rand Corporation, a semiofficial research institution in Santa Monica, Calif., produces a large number of reports on Communist China. Some outstanding studies have been published as commercial titles. They include: *Economy of the Chinese Mainland: National Income and Economic Development, 1933–1959*, by T. C. Liu and K. C. Yeh, and *Communist China's Strategy in the Nuclear Era*, by Alice Langley Hsieh. Almost all reports of the Rand Corporation can be found in depository libraries.

The American Universities Field Staff also produces a number of reports on Communist China. Most of them are included in its *East Asia Series*. They are indexed in the *Vertical File Index* and the *Public Affairs Information Service Index*.

The Hoover Institution at Stanford University is another important publisher of books on Communist China. In addition to the two basic bibliographies on Chinese Communism and contemporary China mentioned earlier, the Institution has published *inter alia*, Chester J. Cheng's *The Politics of the Chinese Red Army: A Translation of the Bulletin of Activities*; Yuan-li Wu's *Economic Development and the Use of Energy Resources in Communist China*, *The Steel Industry in Communist China*, and *The Spatial Economy of Communist China*; Dennis Doolin's *Communist China: The Politics of Student Opposition* and *Territorial Claims in the Sino-Soviet Conflict: Documents and Analysis*; and Robert C. North's *Moscow and Chinese Communists*. Some of the Hoover's recent books are: *The Chinese People's Republic, Communist China and Arms Control: A Contingency Study, 1967–1976, Rural People's Communes in Lien-chiang, As Peking Sees Us*, and *The Making of a Model Citizen in Communist China*. The Institute of Political Studies at Stanford University has also prepared several reports on Communist China. These have been published in journals or as separate monographs.

Among other American institutions that have published reports or papers on Communist China are the University of Southern California, the University of Michigan, the Center for International Studies at the Massachusetts Institute of Technology, Harvard University, the Institute for Sino-Soviet Studies at George Washington University, the University of California at Berkeley, the Research Institute on the Sino-Soviet Bloc (RISSB), and the East Asian Institute of Columbia University in New York. Some of the more comprehensive studies on Communist China published by these, in cooperation with various publishers, are *The Prospects for Communist China*, by W. W. Rostow and others (MIT, 1954); *Chinese Family in Communist Revolution*, by C. K. Yang (MIT, 1959); *Communist China Today*, by Peter S. H. Tang (RISSB, 1961); *The Rate and Pattern of Industrial Growth in Communist China*, by Kang Chao (Michigan, 1965); *Ideology and Organization in Communist China*, by Franz Schurmann (California, 1966); *China Crosses the Yalu*, by Allen S. Whiting (Stanford, 1960); *Communist China in World Politics*, by Harold C. Hinton (Houghton Mifflin Co., Boston, 1966); *Political Participation in Communist China*, by James Roger Townsend (California, 1967); *Soviet and Chinese Communism; Similarities and Differences*, by Donald W. Treadgold (University of Washington Press, 1967); *Mao and the Chinese Revolution*, by Jerome Ch'en (Oxford, 1965); *China under Communism: The First Five Years*, by Richard L. Walker (Yale, 1955); and *Economic Development of Communist China: An Appraisal of the First Five Years of Industrialization*, by Choh-ming Li (California, 1959).

A new and growing organization, which provides a great deal of bibliographical information and teaching material for international studies (including the study of mainland China) at the undergraduate level is the Foreign Area Materials Center in New York City. Among the publications of this Center are Edith Ehrman's *Guide to Asian Studies in Undergraduate Education*; Theodore Herman's *The Geography of China: A Selected and Annotated Bibliography*; L. A. Peter Gosling's *Maps, Atlases, and Gazetteers for Asian Studies: A Critical Guide*; Ward Morehouse's *The Comparative Approach to Area Studies and the Disciplines: Problems of Teaching and Research on Asia*; and the previously mentioned *Asian Resources in American Libraries*, by Winston L. Y. Yang and Teresa S. Yang. All these are particularly relevant to China studies.

The Asia Society in New York City also provides educational materials on Asia. Among its publications are some useful reference works, such as *A Guide to Films, Filmstrips, Maps & Globes, Records on Asia*; *A Guide to Paperbacks on Asia*; and *Asia: A Guide to Basic Books*.

FOREIGN PUBLICATIONS

Several foreign governments and institutions are watching mainland China at least as closely as does the U.S. Government. Having diplomatic, trade, or cultural relations with Communist China, some of these governments can benefit from the personal experience of individuals and from access to some information not normally available to American scholars. For this reason, it is useful to study their publications for any new light they may shed on our understanding of mainland China.

Hong Kong is the favorite listening post for 'China-watchers.' Apart from the U.S. Consulate-General and individual researchers, the Japanese Consulate-General, the British Government, the Chinese Nationalist Government, and many other governmental agencies are spending a great deal of effort collecting information about mainland China in Hong Kong. Some of their material is made available in British, Chinese, and Japanese publications. The United Kingdom Regional Information Office in Hong Kong, for example, publishes the *China News Summary, China News Items from the Press*, and *News from Chinese Provincial Radio Stations*. These mimeographed serials select and summarize current information on Communist China.

The *Far Eastern Economic Review* is probably the best-known of the English-language Hong Kong journals publishing material on mainland China. This weekly and its *Yearbook* are probably familiar to many readers. Less well-known is the *China Trade*

Report, a monthly that is marked 'confidential' by the publisher but is available by subscription.

Several English-language periodicals in Hong Kong are devoted almost entirely to information on Communist China. One of the most respected is the *China News Analysis*, a weekly newsletter edited by Father La Dany. Another is *Current Scene*, published by the Green Pagoda Press for the United States Information Service.

The Union Research Institute in Hong Kong is an important research institute that publishes specialized material on Communist China. Its *Communist China Problem Research Series* includes many basic reference books as well as treatises. The English-language yearbook *Communist China* is also published in this series. In addition, the URI publishes the periodicals *Union Research Service* and *Biographical Service*. The former appears twice a week and contains, in each issue, several articles translated from mainland China's newspapers and magazines. The latter includes in each issue a concise biography of a well-known person in Communist China. The library of the URI has a very valuable collection of books, magazines, newspapers, and other research materials on Communist China. To make its materials known and available to others, the URI has published several editions of the *Catalogue of Mainland Chinese Magazines and Newspapers Held by the Union Research Institute* and the *Index to Classified Files on Communist China Held by the Union Research Institute*. Two of the recent URI publications, very helpful for reference work, are *Who's Who in Communist China* and the *CCP Documents of the Great Proletarian Cultural Revolution, 1966–1967*, which includes 132 documents, of which 122 were issued by the central authorities and 10 by Peking municipal authorities.

The Continental Research Institute in Hong Kong, under the direction of Chow Chin-wen, publishes the anti-Communist periodical *Peking Informers*.

Under the auspices of the Institute of Modern Asian Studies of the University of Hong Kong, and under the editorship of Professor E. Stuart Kirby and, more recently, Professor Ronald Hsia, the journal *Contemporary China* made its debut in 1956; to date six volumes have been published. Each volume normally covers a period of two years and contains papers on economic and social studies, translations, a chronology, a selected bibliography, and indexes. Some reprints of these papers and bibliographies are also available from the institute. The institute also published, until 1967, *The China Mainland Review*, a quarterly containing scholarly articles and factual and documentary data on Communist China. A pro-Communist monthly journal entitled *Eastern Horizon* is also published in Hong Kong.

A journal devoted entirely to the study of China is *The China Quarterly*, published by the Contemporary China Institute of the School of Oriental and African Studies of the University of London. It publishes articles by leading China specialists, book reviews, and a quarterly chronicle and documentation. London is also the place of publication of two informative journals on the economy of China: *China Trade and Economic Newsletter*, a monthly published by Monitor Consultants, and the *Quarterly Economic Review: China, Hongkong, North Korea*, published by the *Economist* Intelligence Unit.

In Continental Europe, research work on Communist China is relatively new but is growing. The Oriental Institute in Prague, under the directorship of Professor Jaroslev Prusek, is outstanding in the study of language and literature in Communist China. The École Nationale des Langues Orientales Vivantes in Paris is the center of instruction for the Chinese language in France, while the Sixth Section of the Maison des Sciences de l'Homme in Paris is a major institution for social and economic research on China. The Sinological Institute in Leyden, the Netherlands, is developing interest in contemporary China. So are the Institut fuer Asienkunde in Hamburg, Germany, and the Scandinavian Institute of Asian Studies in Copenhagen, Denmark. Many of their research results appear as articles in learned journals or institutional reports. Wolfgang Bartke's *Chinaköpfe* is one of the reference works on

Communist China published in Western Europe. The international Documentation and Information Centre at the Hague publishes an English-language monthly entitled *Red China: Agitation, Propaganda, Contacts and Other Activities*, which summarizes international activities of Communist China.

In the Soviet Union, the establishment of the Institute of Far Eastern Studies in 1966 as a new institute within the U.S.S.R. Academy of Sciences emphasizes the importance of political and social studies of contemporary China. With about 150 staff members specializing in China, it is certainly one of the largest research institutions in this field. It has already published a number of research reports, some of which are in English.

For geographical, historical, economic, and many other reasons, Japan has always been deeply concerned with developments in mainland China. A number of governmental and academic bodies collect information and publish reports on China. The Center for Modern Chinese Studies at the Tokyo Bunko (Oriental Library), the Institute of Developing Economics (formerly Institute of Asian Economic Affairs), the Cabinet Research Office, the National Diet Library, and the China Section of the Ministry of Foreign Affairs are some of the major Japanese sources of information on mainland China. The K. D. K. Kojimachi Institute, under the directorship of E. Kohtani, publishes a mimeographed English-language newsletter entitled *K.D.K. Information*, which is a monthly summary of current events in East Asia, especially Communist China.

The China Study Centre in New Delhi, India, publishes a bimonthly called *China Report*, which deals almost entirely with developments in mainland China. The viewpoint of Tibetan refugees in India and abroad is represented by the journal *Tibetan Review*, published in Calcutta and distributed by the Office of Tibet in New York.

So far as the Republic of China is concerned, officially its civil war against the Chinese Communists is not over. Nothing can be more vital to it than information about the Communist-occupied mainland. There are several Taiwan Government agencies and institutes actively engaged in the study of mainland China. Among them are the Institute of International Relations, the Institute for the Study of Chinese Communist Problems, the National Security Council, the Institute of Political Research, the Second and Sixth Departments of the Kuomintang Headquarters, the National War College, the Institute of East Asian Studies of the National Chengchi University, the Bureau of Investigation, and the offices for the study of mainland China in various ministries and in the Executive Council. Although most of the publications put out by these agencies are in Chinese, some English-language material is available from the Chinese Government Information Office, the Institute of International Relations, the China Branch of the Asian Peoples' Anti-Communist League, and some other publishing agencies. The Institute of International Relations used to publish, among other things, the monthly *Issues & Studies*, the biweekly *Chinese Communist Affairs: Facts and Features*, and the bimonthly *Catalog of Current Research Publications on Modern China*. Beginning in July, 1969, *Issues & Studies* absorbed the other two but retained its original title.

The China Branch of the Asian Peoples' Anti-Communist League has published a number of pamphlets in the English language. The series *Charts Concerning Chinese Communists on the Mainland* summarizes annually the salient features in the political development of Communist China. A small new biweekly newsletter started by the China Publishing Company in Taipei in January, 1969, is called *What's Happening on the Chinese Mainland. Chinese Communist Affairs: A Biweekly Review*, published by the Institute of Political Research in Taipei, ceased publication in 1969.

The newly established Institute of East Asian Studies at the National Chengchi University in Taipei is the first academic institute in China devoted entirely to the study of mainland China. It publishes a Chinese-language journal called *East Asia Quarterly*.

Many of the Republic of China's government publications dealing with mainland affairs are not available to the general public in Taiwan. However, to make their views known to scholars abroad, some government agencies have sent selected publications to a few leading Chinese libraries in the United States. Among these publications of particular value to researchers are some of the reference works, such as yearbooks, maps, and biographical handbooks of Communist China. These reference works are usually in Chinese. There are occasional exceptions, such as the *Handbook of Chinese Communist Affairs*, published recently by the Institute of Political Research in English. *The Analytical History of Chinese Communist Party* by Warren Kuo, published by the Institute of International Relations, provides basic historical background on the CCP. Other English-language publications of this Institute include *Chinese Communist Who's Who, Chou En-lai* by Li Tien-min, *Collected Documents of the First Sino-American Conference on Mainland China, Sanzo Nosaka and Mao Tse-tung* by Chang Tung-tsai, and *Index of Research Papers Prepared and Published by the Institute of International Relations, Republic of China (October, 1961–June, 1966)*.

CHINESE COMMUNIST PUBLICATIONS

The major publisher of Western-language books in mainland China is the Foreign Languages Press. Its publications are exported by the Guozi Shudian (China Publications Center) and sold by many dealers abroad. Among these are the Peace Book Company in Hong Kong and China Books & Periodicals in San Francisco. To promote sales, the Guozi Shudian and the Peace Book Company publish periodic booklists and catalogs. The *Catalogue of Chinese Books Available in English* (1960), published by the Guozi Shudian, is a comprehensive list of about 300 English-language books, pamphlets, and journals. One of the most recent booklists is *Books on the Great Proletarian Cultural Revolution in China (in English)*.

The number of China mainland publications available outside Communist China fluctuates according to the political climate and export controls on the mainland. Once there were more than 100 journals available by subscription or exchange. More than a dozen of these are in English, and many others have tables of contents and abstracts in English. Since the Cultural Revolution, however, only five English-language periodicals are available. They are *Peking Review, China Pictorial, China Reconstructs,* and *Chinese Literature*. The *Peking Review* is an authoritative political journal. *China Reconstructs* contains popular articles on economic and social life in Communist China. The journal *Chinese Literature* includes translations from the writings of mainland Chinese authors.

There are no English-language daily newspapers in Communist China. The official New China (*Hsin-hua*) News Agency in Peking, however, issues a daily English release called *Hsinhua News Bulletin*. Until her death in China in 1970, Anna Louise Strong sent abroad for many years an irregular newsletter under the title *Letter from China*.

In Hong Kong, the leading Communist newspaper, *Ta Kung Pao*, publishes a weekly English supplement. A Communist journal, *Ching-chi Tao-pao*, has a quarterly English-language supplement known as the *Economic Reporter*. The Hong Kong Branch of the Hsinhua News Agency issues an English-language weekly entitled *Hsinhua Selected News Items*.

CONCLUDING REMARKS

The above is a brief survey of publications on China for the reader who is primarily English-speaking. For any study of mainland China in depth, a researcher must turn to Chinese-language materials. Bibliographical control of Chinese-language material is much more inadequate than that of English-language material. Even if he knows the language, it may take a researcher a long time to locate Chinese sources. Most Chinese-language material naturally comes from mainland China, Taiwan, and Hong Kong. Because of the political nature of some publications, a researcher often needs to know the background of the author or the publisher before he can evaluate the publication.

A survey of sources of information should not be limited to printed materials. Human resources, such as returning visitors and diplomats, refugees, and escapees, can often provide valuable firsthand information. Radio broadcasting from Peking can be heard in the United States. Newsreels and movies on Communist China are also available. So are records of Peking opera. Academic freedom in this country has given us access to almost any type of information. We should make proper use of it.

SELECTED BIBLIOGRAPHY

Books

American University Field Staff. *A Select Bibliography: Asia, Africa, Eastern Europe, and Latin America.* New York: American University Field Staff, 1960. 534 pp.

Asia Society. *A Guide to Films, Filmstrips, Maps & Globes, Records on Asia.* Supplement, including new sections on slides. New York: the Society, 1967, 64 pp.

Association for Asian Studies. *Cumulative Bibliography of Asian Studies, 1941–1965.* 8 vols. Boston: G. K. Hall, 1970.

BARTKE, WOLFGANG. *Chinaköpfe.* Hannover, Germany: Verlag für Literatur und Zeitgeschehen, 1966. 454 pp.

BERTON, PETER, and EUGENE WU. *Contemporary China: A Research Guide.* Edited by HOWARD KOCH, JR. Stanford, Calif.: Hoover Institution, 1967, 695 pp.

BOWIE, ROBERT R., and JOHN K. FAIRBANK, eds. *Communist China, 1955–1959: Policy Documents with Analysis.* Cambridge, Mass.: Harvard University Press, 1962. 611 pp.

CHAI, WINBERG, ed. *Essential Works of Chinese Communism.* New York: Bantam Books, 1969. 464 pp.

CHAN, WING-TSIT. *Chinese Philosophy, 1949–1963: An Annotated Bibliography of Mainland China Publications.* Honolulu: East-West Center Press, 1967. 290 pp.

CHAO, KUO-CHÜN. *Economic Planning and Organization in Mainland China: A Documentary Study*

CHEN, NAI-RUENN. *Chinese Economic Statistics: A Handbook for Mainland China.* Chicago: Aldine Publishing Company, 1967. 539 pp.

———. *The Economy of Mainland China, 1949–1963: A Bibliography of Materials in English.* Berkeley, Calif.: Committee on Economy of China, Social Science Research Council, 1963. 297 pp.

CHEN, THEODORE HSI-EN, comp. *The Chinese Communist Regime: Documents and Commentary.* New York: Praeger Publishers, 1967. 344 pp.

CHENG, CHU-YUAN. *Scientific and Engineering Manpower in Communist China, 1949–1963.* Washington, D.C.: Government Printing Office, 1965. 588 pp.

COLE, ALLAN B. *Forty Years of Chinese Communism: Selected Readings with Commentary.* Washington, D.C.: American Historical Association, 1962. 43 pp.

Congressional Quarterly Service. *China and U.S. Far East Policy, 1945–1966.* Washington, D.C.: Congressional Quarterly, 1967. 348 pp.

Guozi Shudian. *Books on the Great Proletarian Cultural Revolution in China (in English).* Peking: Guozi Shudian, 1969. 30 pp.

———. *Catalogue of Chinese Books Available in English.* Peking: Guozi Shudian, 1960. 82 pp.

HERMAN, THEODORE, ed. *The Geography of China: A Selected and Annotated Bibliography.* New York: Foreign Area Materials Center, 1957. Foreign Area Materials Center Occasional Publication No. 7. 44 pp.

HSIA, TAO-TAI. *Guide to Selected Legal Sources of Mainland China.* Washington, D.C.: Library of Congress, 1967. 357 pp.

HsÜEH, CHÜN-TU. *The Chinese Communist Movement, 1921–1937.* Stanford, Calif.: Hoover Institution, 1960. 131 pp.

———. *The Chinese Communist Movement, 1937–1939.* Stanford, Calif.: Hoover Institution, 1962. 312 pp.

HUCKER, CHARLES O. *China: A Critical Bibliography.* Tucson: University of Arizona Press, 1962. 125 pp.

Institute of Political Research. *Handbook of Chinese Communist Affairs.* Taipei: the Institute, 1968. 125 pp.

JAN, GEORGE P. *Government of Communist China.* San Francisco: Chandler Publishing Co., 1966. 684 pp.

KLATT, WERNER, ed. *The Chinese Model: A Political, Economic and Social Survey.* Hong Kong: Hong Kong University Press, 1965. 233 pp.

KUO, WARREN. *Analytical History of Chinese Communist Party.* Taipei: Institute of International Relations, 1966– . Vols 1 and 2 already published.

LEWIS, JOHN WILSON. *Major Doctrines of Communist China.* New York: W. W. Norton & Co., 1964. 343 pp.

LIN, FU-SHUN. *Chinese Law Past and Present: A Bibliography of Enactments and Commentaries in English Text.* New York: East Asian Institute, Columbia University, 1966. 419 pp.

LUST, JOHN. *Index Sinicus: A Catalogue of Articles Relating to China in Periodicals and Other Collective Publications, 1920–1955.* Cambridge, England: W. Heffner, 1964. 663 pp.

MOREHOUSE, WARD, ed. *American Institutions and Organizations Interested in Asia: A Reference Directory.* 2d ed. New York: Taplinger Publishing Co., 1961. 581 pp.

National Committee on United States–China Relations. *An Annotated Guide to Modern China.* New York: the Committee, 1967. 27 pp.

PRICE, FRANCIS WILSON. *Selected Bibliography of Books, Pamphlets, and Articles on Communist China and the Christian Church in China.* New York: Missionary Research Library, 1958. 21 pp.

SORICH, RICHARD, ed. *Contemporary China: A Bibliography of Reports on China Published by the United States Joint Publications Research Service.* Prepared for the Joint Committee on Contemporary China of the American Council of Learned Societies and the Social Science Research Council. New York: reprinted by Readex Microprint Corporation, 1961. 99 pp.

TANG, PETER S. H., and JOAN M. MALONEY. *Communist China: The Domestic Scene, 1949–1967.* South Orange, N.J.: Seton Hall University Press, 1967. 606 pp.

Union Research Institute. *Catalogue of Mainland Chinese Magazines and Newspapers Held by the Union Research Institute.* Hong Kong: URI, 1962– . Latest edition published in 1968.

———. *CCP Documents of the Great Proletarian Cultural Revolution, 1966–1967.* Hong Kong: URI, 1968. 692 pp.

———. *Index to the Classified Files on Communist China Held by the Union Research Institute.* Hong Kong: URI, 1956– .

———. *Who's Who in Communist China.* Hong Kong: URI, 1966. 754 pp.

U.S. Central Intelligence Agency. *Communist China Map Folio.* Washington, D.C., 1968. Includes 17 maps and 12 pp. of accompanying texts.

———. *People's Republic of China Atlas.* Washington, D.C., 1971. 82 pp.

U.S. Department of Commerce. *The Population and the Manpower of China: An Annotated Bibliography.* Washington, D.C.: Government Printing Office, 1958. 132 pp.

U.S. Department of State. *Directory of Chinese Communist Officials.* Various editions with slight changes in title. Washington, D.C., 1960.

U.S. Department of the Army. *Communist China: A Strategic Survey: A Bibliography.* Washington, D.C., 1966. 143 pp.

———. *Communist China: A Bibliographic Survey, 1971.* Washington, D.C., 1971, 253 pp.

U.S. Department of the Interior. *China: Official Standard Names Approved by the U.S. Board on Geographic Names.* 2 vols. Washington, D.C.: Government Printing Office, 1952.

U.S. Library of Congress. *Accession List of Chinese Communist Periodicals, January 1963–December 1966.* Washington, D.C., 1967. 99 pp.

WANG, CHI, comp. *Mainland China Organizations of Higher Learning in Science and Technology and Their Publications: A Selected Guide.* Washington, D.C.: Library of Congress, 1961. 104 pp.

WEITZMAN, DAVID L. *China Studies in Paperback.* Berkeley, Calif.: McCutcheon Publishing Co., 1968. 82 pp.

WU, YUAN-LI. *An Economic Survey of Communist China.* New York: Bookman Associates, 1956. 566 pp.

YANG, WINSTON L. Y., and TERESA YANG. *Asian Resources in American Libraries: Essays and Bibliographies.* New York: University of the State of New York, 1968. 122 pp.

YUAN, TUNG-LI. China in Western Literature: A Continuation of Cordier's Bibliotheca Sinica. New Haven, Conn.: Far Eastern Publications, 1958. 802 pp.

Serial Publications

Included in this section are some of the major periodicals that deal mainly with Communist China. Publisher's or distributor's address if necessary, is given in parenthesis. Chinese Communist publications are listed in section following.

American Consulate-General, Hong Kong, publications:

Survey of China Mainland Press. Daily translations since November, 1950.

Current Background. Approximately weekly, since June, 1950.

Selections from China Mainland Magazines. Since August, 1955.

Extracts from China Mainland Publications. Since April, 1962.

Review of the Hong Kong Chinese Press. June, 1947–May, 1961.

Bibliography-Index to Current U.S. JPRS Translations: China & Asia (Exclusive of Near East). New York: CCM Information Sciences, prepared by Research & Microfilm Publications. Since 1962, succeeding *China: A Bibliography and Guide to Contents of a Collection of United States Joint Publications Research Service Translations in the Social Sciences Emanating from Communist China,* compiled by Theodore E. Kyriak (866 Third Ave., New York, N.Y. 10022).

Charts Concerning Chinese Communists on the Mainland. Taipei: Asian Peoples' Anti-Communist League. Irregular, since 1955.

China Mainland Review. Hong Kong: Institute of Modern Asian Studies. University of Hong Kong. Quarterly, 1965–67.

China News Analysis. Hong Kong. 48 issues a year, since 1953.

China Notes. New York: East Asia Department, Division of Overseas Ministries, National Council of Churches. Quarterly, since 1962, succeeding *China Bulletin.*

The China Quarterly. London: Contemporary China Institute, School of Oriental and African Studies, London University. Since 1960.

China Report. New Delhi, India: China Study Centre.

China Trade and Economic Newsletter. London: Monitor Consultants. Monthly, since 1955.

China Trade Report. Hong Kong: Far Eastern Economic Review. Monthly.

Chinese Economic Studies. White Plains, N.Y.: International Arts & Sciences Press (IASP). Quarterly.

Chinese Education. White Plains, N.Y.: IASP. Quarterly.

Chinese Law and Government. White Plains, N.Y.: IASP. Quarterly.

Chinese Studies in History and Philosophy. White Plains, N.Y.: IASP. Quarterly.

Chinese Studies in Sociology and Anthropology. White Plains, N.Y.: IASP. Quarterly.

Current Scene: Developments in Mainland China. Hong Kong: Green Pagoda Press. Irregular, since 1961.

Eastern Horizon: Monthly Review. Hong Kong: Eastern Horizon Press.

Far Eastern Economic Review. Hong Kong. Weekly, since 1946.

Far Eastern Economic Review Yearbook. Hong Kong. Annual, since 1960.

Issues & Studies: A Monthly Journal of World Affairs and Communist Problems. Taipei: Institute of International Relations. Since 1964, superseding *Analysis of Current Chinese Communist Problems.*

KDK Information. Tokyo: KDK Kojimachi Institute. Monthly.

Modern China Studies International Bulletin. London: *The China Quarterly.*

Pacific Affairs. Vancouver: University of British Columbia. Quarterly.

Peking Informers. Hong Kong: Continental Research Institute. Twice monthly, since 1960.

Problems of Communism. Washington, D.C.: U.S. Information Agency. Bimonthly, since 1952.

Quarterly Economic Review: China, Hong Kong, North Korea. London: *The Economist* Intelligence Unit. With annual summary.

Red China Agitation, Propaganda, Contacts, and Other Activities: Monthly Review. The Hague: International Documentation and Information Centre.

Tibetan Review. Calcutta, India: Statesman Press. Since 1968, superseding *The Voice of Tibet.*

Understanding China Newsletter. Pasadena, Calif.: American Friends Service Committee, Pacific Southwest Region. Bimonthly.

Union Research Institute (Hong Kong) publications:

Biographical Service. Since 1956.

Communist China. Annual, since 1955.

Communist China Problem Research Series. Since 1953.

Union Research Service. Twice weekly, since 1966.

United Kingdom Regional Information Office (Hong Kong) publications:

China News Items from the Press. Weekly.

China News Summary. Weekly, in English and Chinese editions.

News from Chinese Provincial Radio Stations. Suspended with No. 239, dated January 4, 1968.

U.S. Foreign Broadcast Information Service, *Daily Report.* Includes a section on Communist China. Since 1941.

U.S. Joint Publications Research Service, *Translations on Communist China* (in several series).

U.S. Superintendent of Documents, *United States Government Publications: Monthly Catalog.*

What's Happening on the Chinese Mainland: A Bi-Weekly Newsletter of Facts and Analysis. Taipei: China Publishing Co. Since 1969.

Chinese Communist Serials

The serials in this section are either published in Communist China or published by the Chinese Communist agents abroad. They are all in English. All except *China's Foreign Trade* and *The Chinese Trade Union* are available as of the spring of 1971.

China Pictorial. Guozi Shudian, P.O. Box 399, Peking; or Peace Book Company, 83 Queen's Road, C., Hong Kong. Monthly.

China Reconstructs. Peking: China Welfare Institute (Guozi Shudian or Peace Book Co.). Monthly.

China's Foreign Trade. Peking: China Council for the Promotion of International Trade. Bimonthly, not available after 1966.

China's Medicine. Peking: China Medical Association (Guozi Shudian or Peace Book Co.). Monthly.

Chinese Literature. Peking: Foreign Language Press (Guozi Shudian or Peace Book Co.). Monthly.

The Chinese Trade Union. Peking: All-China Federation of Trade Unions. Bimonthly, ceased publication.

Economic Reporter, English-language supplement of *Ching-chi Tao-pao.* Hong Kong: Economic Information Agency (342 Hennessy Road, 11th floor, Hong Kong).

Hsinhua News Bulletin. Peking: Hsinhua (New China) News Agency. Daily.

Hsinhua Selected News Items. Hong Kong: Hsinhua News Agency. Weekly.

Letter from China, by Anna Louise Strong. Peking. Irregular, ceased publication in 1970.

Peking Review. Peking. Weekly.

Ta-kung Pao. Hong Kong: Ta-kung Pao Publisher. Weekly supplement.

Part Two
DOCUMENTS

THE CONSTITUTION OF THE
CHINESE COMMUNIST PARTY, 1956

[THE 1956 CPC Constitution described the Party's policies in terms of ideological, economic and political objectives. The 'General Program' excerpted below outlines the Party's policies. Additional information on Party functions and organizations also appended.]

GENERAL PROGRAM

The Communist Party of China is the vanguard of the Chinese working class, the highest form of its class organization. The aim of the Party is the achievement of socialism and communism in China.

The Communist Party of China takes Marxism-Leninism as its guide to action. Only Marxism-Leninism correctly sets forth the laws of development of society and correctly charts the path leading to the achievement of socialism and communism. The Party adheres to the Marxist-Leninist world outlook of dialectical and historical materialism, and opposes the world outlook of idealism and metaphysics. Marxism-Leninism is not a dogma, but a guide to action. It demands that in striving to build socialism and communism we should proceed from reality, apply the principles of Marxism-Leninism in a flexible and creative way for the solution of various problems arising out of the actual struggle, and thus continuously develop the theory of Marxism-Leninism. Consequently, the Party in its activities upholds the principle of integrating the universal truths of Marxism-Leninism with the actual practice of China's revolutionary struggle, and combats all doctrinaire or empiricist deviations. . . .

During the period of transition from the founding of the People's Republic of China to the attainment of a socialist society, the fundamental task of the Party is to complete, step by step, the socialist transformation of agriculture, handicrafts and capitalist industry and commerce and to bring about, step by step, the industrialization of the country.

A decisive victory in every field has already been attained in the socialist transformation of our country. It is the task of the Communist Party of China by continuously adopting correct methods to transform what now remains of capitalist ownership into ownership by the whole people, transform what remains of individual ownership by working people into collective ownership by the working masses, uproot

Source: *The Constitution of the Communist Party of China,* Supplement to the New China News Agency Release. Peking: NCNA, September 26, 1956, pp. 9–29. In this and subsequent documents, minor punctuation and stylistic changes have been made to correspond with modern English usage.

the system of exploitation and remove all the causes that give rise to such a system. In the process of building up a socialist society, the principle 'from each according to his ability, to each according to his work' should be brought into effect step by step; and all former exploiters should be reformed in a peaceful manner to become working people living by their own labor. The Party must continue to pay attention to the elimination of capitalist factors and influence in the economic, political, and ideological fields, and make determined efforts to mobilize and unite all the positive forces throughout the country that can be mobilized and united for the purpose of winning a complete victory for the great cause of socialism.

The victory of the socialist revolution has opened up illimitable possibilities for the gigantic development of the productive forces of society. It is the task of the Communist Party of China to develop the national economy in a planned way to bring about as rapidly as possible the industrialization of the country and to effect the technological transformation of the national economy in a planned, systematic way so that China may possess a powerful modernized industry, a modernized agriculture, modernized communications and transport and a modernized national defense. In order to achieve industrialization and bring about a continuous growth of the national economy, priority must be given to the development of heavy industry, and at the same time a due proportion must be maintained between heavy industry and light industry, and between industry as a whole and agriculture. The Party must do everything possible to stimulate the progress in China's science, culture and technology so as to catch up with the world's advanced levels in these fields. The basic object of all Party work is to satisfy to the maximum extent the material and cultural needs of the people. Therefore, it is necessary that the living conditions of the people should, on the basis of increased production, gradually and continually improve. This is also a requisite for enhancing the people's enthusiasm for production.

Our country is a multinational state. Because of historical reasons, the development of many of the national minorities has been hindered. The Communist Party of China must make special efforts to raise the status of the national minorities, help them to attain self-government, endeavor to train cadres from among the national minorities, accelerate their economic and cultural advance, bring about complete equality among all the nationalities, and strengthen the unity and fraternal relations among them. Social reforms among the nationalities must be carried out by the respective nationalities themselves in accordance with their own wishes and by taking steps in conformity with their special characteristics. The Party opposes all tendencies to great-nation chauvinism and local nationalism, both of which hamper the unity of nationalities. Special attention must be paid to the prevention and correction of tendencies of great-Hanism on the part of Party members and government workers of Han nationality.

The Communist Party of China must work untiringly to consolidate China's people's democratic dictatorship, which is the guarantee for the success of the socialist cause in China. The Party must fight for a fuller development of the democratic life of the nation and strive for the constant improvement of its democratic institutions. The Party must work in every way to fortify the fraternal alliance of workers and peasants, to consolidate the united front of all patriotic forces, and to strengthen its lasting cooperation with the other democratic parties, as well as democrats without party affiliations. Since the imperialists and counterrevolutionary remnants are bent on undermining the cause of the Chinese people, it is imperative for the Party to heighten its revolutionary vigilance and wage severe struggles against those forces that endanger our country's independence and security and those elements that try to wreck socialist construction in our country. The Party must work together with the people of the whole country to bring about the liberation of Taiwan.

The Communist Party of China advocates a foreign policy directed to the safeguarding of world peace and the achievement of peaceful coexistence between countries with different systems. The Party stands for the establishment and development of diplomatic, economic, and cultural relations between China and other countries of the world and for the broadening and strengthening of friendly relations between the Chinese people and the peoples of all other countries of the world. The Party is resolutely opposed to any act of aggression against China by imperialist countries and to any imperialist plans for a new war; it supports all efforts made by the peoples and governments of other countries to uphold peace and promote friendly relations between nations, and expresses its sympathy for all struggles in the world against imperialism and colonialism. The Party endeavors to develop and strengthen China's friendship with all other countries in the camp of peace, democracy and socialism headed by the Soviet Union, to strengthen the internationalist solidarity of the proletariat, and to learn from the experiences of the world communist movement. It supports the struggle of the communists, progressives, and laboring people of the whole world for the progress of mankind, and educates its members and the Chinese people in the spirit of internationalism, as expressed in the slogan, 'Proletarians of all lands, unite!'

The Communist Party of China puts into practice all that it advocates through the activity of the Party organizations and membership among the masses and through the conscientious efforts made by the people under its guidance. For this reason it is necessary to constantly develop the tradition of following the mass line in Party work. Whether the Party is able to continue to give correct leadership depends on whether or not the Party will, through analysis and synthesis, systematically summarize the experience and opinions of the masses, turn the resulting ideas into the policy of the Party, and then, as a result of the Party's propaganda and organizational work among the masses, transform it into the views and action of the masses themselves, testing the correctness of Party policy, and supplementing and revising it in the course of mass activity. It is the duty of the Party leadership to ensure that in the endless repetition of this process of 'coming from the masses and going back to the masses' the Party members' level of understanding and that of the masses of the people are continually raised and the cause of the Party and the people is constantly advanced. . . .

The organizational principle of the Communist Party of China is democratic centralism, which means centralism on the basis of democracy and democracy under centralized guidance. The Party must take effective measures to promote inner-Party democracy, encourage the initiative and creative ability of all Party members and of all local and primary Party organizations, and strengthen the lively contact between the higher and lower Party organizations. Only in this way can the Party effectively extend and strengthen its ties with the masses of the people, give correct and timely leadership, and adapt itself flexibly to various concrete conditions and local characteristics. And only in this way can Party life be invigorated and the cause of the Party advance on an ever wider scale and at an ever greater pace. Only on this basis, furthermore, can centralism and unity of the Party be consolidated and its discipline be voluntarily, not mechanically, observed. Democratic centralism demands that every Party organization strictly abide by the principle of collective leadership coupled with individual responsibility and that every Party member and Party organization should be subject to Party supervision from above and from below.

No political party or person can be free from shortcomings and mistakes in work. The Communist Party of China and its members must constantly practice criticism and self-criticism to expose and eliminate their shortcomings and mistakes so as to educate themselves and the people. In view of the fact that the Party plays the leading role in the life of the state and society, it is all the more necessary that it should make stringent demands on every Party organization and member and promote criticism and self-criticism; and in particular, it should encourage and support criticism from below inside the Party as well as criticism of the Party by the masses of the people, and should prohibit any suppression of criticism. The Party must prevent and resist corrosion by bourgeois and petty-bourgeois ways of thinking and styles of work and guard against and defeat any Rightist or 'Leftist' opportunist deviation inside the Party. In the case of Party members who have committed mistakes the Party should, in the spirit of 'curing the illness to save the patient,' allow them to remain in its ranks and receive education and help them to correct their mistakes, provided such mistakes can be corrected within the Party and the erring Party member himself is prepared to correct his mistakes. As for those who persist in their mistakes and carry on activities detrimental to the Party, it is essential to wage a determined struggle against them even to the point of expelling them from the Party.

Chapter I: Membership

Article 16
  Any decision to remove a member or alternate member of the Central Committee of the Party from the Central Committee, to place him on probation, or to expel him from the Party must be taken by the National Party Congress. In conditions of urgency, such decision may be taken by a two-thirds majority vote of the Central Committee at its plenary session, but it must be subject to subsequent confirmation by the next session of the National Party Congress.

Chapter II: Organizational Structure and Organizational Principles of the Party

Article 19
  The Party is formed on the principles of democratic centralism.
  Democratic centralism means centralism on the basis of democracy and democracy under centralized guidance. Its basic conditions are as follows:
  1. The leading bodies of the Party at all levels are elected.
  2. The highest leading body of the Party is the National Party Congress, and the highest leading body in each local Party organization is the local Party congress. The National Party Congress elects the Central Committee and the local Party congresses elect their respective local Party committees. The Central Committee and local Party committees are responsible to their respective Party congresses to which they should report on their work.
  3. All leading bodies of the Party must pay constant heed to the views of their lower organizations and the rank-and-file Party members, study their experiences, and give prompt help in solving their problems.
  4. Lower Party organizations must present periodical reports on their work to the Party organizations above them and ask in good time for instructions on questions that need decision by higher Party organizations.
  5. All Party organizations operate on the principle of combining collective leadership with individual responsibility. All important issues are to be decided on collectively, and at the same time, each individual is enabled to play his part to the fullest possible extent.
  6. Party decisions must be carried out unconditionally. Individual Party members shall obey the Party organization, the minority shall obey the majority, the lower Party organizations shall obey the higher Party organizations, and all constituent Party organizations throughout the country shall obey the National Party Congress and the Central Committee.

CHAPTER III: CENTRAL ORGANIZATIONS OF THE PARTY

Article 31

The National Party Congress is elected for a term of five years.

The number of delegates to the National Party Congress and the procedure governing their election and replacement and the filling of vacancies shall be determined by the Central Committee.

A session of the National Party Congress shall be convened once a year by the Central Committee. Under extraordinary conditions, it may be postponed or convened before its due date as the Central Committee may decide. The Central Committee must convene a session of the National Party Congress if one-third of the delegates to the National Party Congress or one-third of the Party organizations at the provincial level so request.

Article 33

The Central Committee of the Party is elected for a term of five years. The number of members and alternate members of the Central Committee shall be determined by the National Party Congress. Vacancies on the Central Committee shall be filled by alternate members in order of established precedence.

Article 34

When the National Party Congress is not in session, the Central Committee directs the entire work of the Party, carries out the decisions of the National Party Congress, represents the Party in its relations with other parties and organizations, sets up various Party organs and directs their activities, takes charge of and allocates Party cadres.

The Central Committee guides the work of the central state organs and people's organizations of a national character through leading Party members' groups within them.

Article 37

The Central Committee elects at its plenary session the Political Bureau, the Standing Committee of the Political Bureau, and the Secretariat, as well as the chairman, vice-chairmen, and general secretary of the Central Committee.

When the Central Committee is not in plenary session, the Political Bureau and its Standing Committee exercise the powers and functions of the Central Committee.

The Secretariat attends to the daily work of the Central Committee under the direction of the Political Bureau and its Standing Committee.

The chairman and vice-chairmen of the Central Committee are concurrently chairman and vice-chairmen of the Political Bureau.

THE CONSTITUTION OF THE CHINESE COMMUNIST PARTY, 1969,

as Adopted by the Ninth National Congress of the CCP on April 14, 1969

CHAPTER I: GENERAL PROGRAM

THE Communist Party of China is the political party of the proletariat.

The basic program of the Communist Party of China is the complete overthrow of the bourgeoisie and all other exploiting classes, the establishment of the dictatorship of the proletariat in place of the dictatorship of the bourgeoisie, and the triumph of socialism over capitalism. The ultimate aim of the Party is the realization of communism.

The Communist Party of China is composed of the advanced elements of the proletariat; it is a vigorous vanguard organization leading the proletariat and the revolutionary masses in the fight against the class enemy.

The Communist Party of China takes Marxism–Leninism–Mao Tsetung Thought as the theoretical basis guiding its thinking. Mao Tsetung Thought is Marxism-Leninism of the era in which imperialism is heading for total collapse and socialism is advancing to worldwide victory.

For half a century now, in leading China's great struggle for accomplishing the new democratic revolution, in leading her great struggle for socialist revolution and socialist construction and in the great struggle of the contemporary international communist movement against imperialism, modern revisionism, and the reactionaries of various countries, Comrade Mao Tse-tung has integrated the universal truth of Marxism-Leninism with the concrete practice of revolution, has inherited, defended, and developed Marxism-Leninism, and has brought it to a higher and completely new stage.

Comrade Lin Piao has consistently held high the great red banner of Mao Tsetung Thought and has most loyally and resolutely carried out and defended Comrade Mao Tse-tung's proletarian revolutionary line. Comrade Lin Piao is Comrade Mao Tse-tung's close comrade-in-arms and successor.

The Communist Party of China with Comrade Mao Tse-tung as its leader is a great, glorious and correct Party and is the core of leadership of the Chinese people. The Party has been tempered through long years of class struggle for the seizure and consolidation of state power by armed force, it has strengthened itself and grown in the course of the struggle against both Right and 'Left' opportunist lines, and it is

Source: Peking Review, 12, No. 18 (April 30, 1969): 36–39.

valiantly advancing with supreme confidence along the road of socialist revolution and socialist construction.

Socialist society covers a fairly long historical period. Throughout this historical period, there are classes, class contradictions, and class struggle, there is the struggle between the socialist road and the capitalist road, there is the danger of capitalist restoration, and there is the threat of subversion and aggression by imperialism and modern revisionism. These contradictions can be resolved only by depending on the Marxist theory of continued revolution and on practice under its guidance. Such is China's Great Proletarian Cultural Revolution, a great political revolution carried out under the conditions of socialism by the proletariat against the bourgeoisie and all other exploiting classes.

The whole Party must hold high the great red banner of Marxism–Leninism–Mao Tsetung Thought and lead the hundreds of millions of the people of all the nationalities of our country in carrying on the three great revolutionary movements of class struggle, the struggle for production and scientific experiment, in strengthening and consolidating the dictatorship of the proletariat, and in building socialism independently and with the initiative in our own hands, through self-reliance and hard struggle and by going all out, aiming high, and achieving greater, faster, better, and more economical results.

The Communist Party of China upholds proletarian internationalism; it firmly unites with the genuine Marxist-Leninist Parties and groups the world over, unites with the proletariat, the oppressed people and nations of the whole world and fights together with them to overthrow imperialism headed by the United States, modern revisionism with the Soviet revisionist renegade clique as its center, and the reactionaries of all countries, and to abolish the system of exploitation of man by man on the globe, so that all mankind will be emancipated.

Members of the Communist Party of China, who dedicate their lives to the struggle for communism, must be resolute, fear no sacrifice and surmount every difficulty to win victory!

Chapter II: Membership

Article 1

Any Chinese worker, poor peasant, lower-middle peasant, revolutionary army man or any other revolutionary element who has reached the age of 18 and who accepts the Constitution of the Party, joins a Party organization and works actively in it, carries out the Party's decisions, observes Party discipline, and pays membership dues may become a member of the Communist Party of China.

Article 2

Applicants for Party membership must go through the procedure for admission individually. An applicant must be recommended by two Party members, fill out an application form for Party membership, and be examined by a Party branch, which must seek the opinions of the broad masses inside and outside the Party. Application is subject to acceptance by the general membership meeting of the Party branch and approval by the next higher Party committee.

Article 3

Members of the Communist Party of China must:

1. Study and apply Marxism–Leninism–Mao Tsetung Thought in a living way;

2. Work for the interests of the vast majority of the people of China and the world;

3. Be able at uniting with the great majority, including those who have wrongly opposed them but are sincerely correcting their mistakes; however, special vigilance must be maintained against careerists, conspirators, and double-dealers so as to

prevent such bad elements from usurping the leadership of the Party and the state at any level and to guarantee that the leadership of the Party and the state always remains in the hands of Marxist revolutionaries;

4. Consult with the masses when matters arise;

5. Be bold in making criticism and self-criticism.

Article 4

When Party members violate Party discipline, the Party organizations at the levels concerned shall, within their functions and powers and on the merits of each case, take appropriate disciplinary measures—warning, serious warning, removal from posts in the Party, placing a probation within the Party, or expulsion from the Party.

The period for which a Party member is placed on probation shall not exceed two years. During this period, he has no right to vote or elect or be elected.

A Party member who becomes politically apathetic and makes no change despite education should be persuaded to withdraw from the Party.

When a Party member asks to withdraw from the Party, the Party branch concerned shall, with the approval of its general membership meeting, remove his name from the Party rolls and report the matter to the next higher Party committee for the record. When necessary, this should be made public to the masses outside the Party.

Proven renegades, enemy agents, absolutely unrepentant persons in power taking the capitalist road, degenerates, and alien class elements must be cleared out of the Party and not be readmitted.

Chapter III: Organizational Principle of the Party

Article 5

The organizational principle of the Party is democratic centralism.

The leading bodies of the Party at all levels are elected through democratic consultation.

The whole Party must observe unified discipline: The individual is subordinate to the organization, the minority is subordinate to the majority, the lower level is subordinate to the higher level, and the entire Party is subordinate to the Central Committee.

Leading bodies of the Party at all levels shall regularly report on their work to congresses or general membership meetings, shall constantly listen to the opinions of the masses both inside and outside the Party and accept their supervision. Party members have the right to criticize Party organizations and leading members at all levels and make proposals to them. If a Party member holds different views with regard to the decisions or directives of the Party organizations, he is allowed to reserve his views and has the right to bypass the immediate leadership and report directly to higher levels, up to and including the Central Committee and the chairman of the Central Committee. It is essential to create a political situation in which there are both centralism and democracy, both discipline and freedom, both unity of will and personal ease of mind and liveliness.

The organs of state power of the dictatorship of the proletariat, the People's Liberation Army, and the Communist Youth League and other revolutionary mass organizations, such as those of the workers, the poor and lower-middle peasants, and the Red Guards, must all accept the leadership of the Party.

Article 6

The highest leading body of the Party is the National Party Congress and, when it is not in session, the Central Committee elected by it. The leading bodies of Party organizations in the localities, in army units, and in various departments are the Party congresses or general membership meetings at their respective levels and the

Party committees elected by them. Party congresses at all levels are convened by Party committees at their respective levels.

The convening of Party congresses in the localities and army units and their elected Party committee members are subject to approval by the higher Party organizations.

Article 7
Party committees at all levels shall set up their working bodies or dispatch their representative organs in accordance with the principles of unified leadership, close ties with the masses, and simple and efficient structure.

CHAPTER IV: CENTRAL ORGANIZATIONS OF THE PARTY

Article 8
The National Party Congress shall be convened every five years. Under special circumstances, it may be convened before its due date or postponed.

Article 9
The plenary session of the Central Committee of the Party elects the Political Bureau of the Central Committee, the Standing Committee of the Political Bureau of the Central Committee, and the chairman and vice-chairman of the Central Committee.

The plenary session of the Central Committee of the Party is convened by the Political Bureau of the Central Committee.

When the Central Committee is not in plenary session, the Political Bureau of the Central Committee and its Standing Committee exercise the functions and powers of the Central Committee.

Under the leadership of the chairman, the vice-chairman, and the Standing Committee of the Political Bureau of the Central Committee, a number of necessary organs, which are compact and efficient, shall be set up to attend to the day-to-day work of the Party, the government, and the army in a centralized way.

CHAPTER V: PARTY ORGANIZATIONS IN THE LOCALITIES AND THE ARMY UNITS

Article 10
Local Party congresses at the county level and upward and Party congresses in the People's Liberation Army at the regional level and upward shall be convened every three years. Under special circumstances, they may be convened before their due date or postponed.

Party committees at all levels in the localities and the army units elect their standing committees, secretaries, and deputy secretaries.

CHAPTER VI: PRIMARY ORGANIZATIONS OF THE PARTY

Article 11
In general, Party branches are formed in factories, mines and other enterprises, people's communes, offices, schools, shops, neighborhoods, companies of the People's Liberation Army, and other primary units; general Party branches or primary Party committees may also be set up where there is a relatively large membership or where the revolutionary struggle requires.

Primary Party organizations shall hold elections once a year. Under special circumstances, the election may take place before its due date or be postponed.

Article 12
Primary Party organizations first must hold high the great red banner of Marxism–

Leninism–Mao Tsetung Thought, give prominence to proletarian politics, and develop the style of integrating theory with practice, maintaining close ties with the masses of the people and practicing criticism and self-criticism. Their main tasks are:

1. To lead the Party members and the broad revolutionary masses in studying and applying Marxism–Leninism–Mao Tsetung Thought in a living way;

2. To give constant education to the Party members and the broad revolutionary masses concerning class struggle and the struggle between the two lines, and lead them in fighting resolutely against the class enemy;

3. To propagate and carry out the policies of the Party, implement its decisions, and fulfill every task assigned by the Party and the state;

4. To maintain close ties with the masses, constantly listen to their opinions and demands, and wage an active ideological struggle within the Party so as to keep Party life vigorous;

5. To take in new Party members, enforce Party discipline, constantly consolidate the Party organizations, and get rid of the stale and take in the fresh so as to maintain the purity of the Party ranks.

THE COMMON PROGRAM, 1949

[THE first and most important document of the new Communist government was the 'Common Program' of the 'Chinese People's Political Consultative Conference,' which proclaimed the establishment of the People's Republic of China at its First Plenary Session on September 29, 1949. 'Democratic dictatorship' was established under the banner of a 'democratic united front,' and the policies and organizational forms of the government of 'new democracy' were outlined in the same instrument. Because of its historical importance, especially for comparisons between pronouncements in the period of takeover of power and subsequent practice, the Common Program is here reproduced in its entirety, minus only the preamble.]

CHAPTER I: GENERAL PRINCIPLES

Article 1

The People's Republic of China is a New Democratic or a People's Democratic state. It carries out the people's democratic dictatorship led by the working class, based on the alliance of workers and peasants, and uniting all democratic classes and all nationalities in China. It opposes imperialism, feudalism and bureaucratic capitalism and strives for independence, democracy, peace, unity, prosperity, and strength of China.

Article 2

The Central People's Government of the People's Republic of China must undertake to wage the people's war of liberation to the very end, to liberate all the territory of China, and to achieve the unification of China.

Article 3

The People's Republic of China must abolish all the prerogatives of imperialist countries in China. It must confiscate bureaucratic capital and put it into the possession of the people's state. It must systematically transform the feudal and semifeudal land ownership system into a system of peasant land ownership; it must protect the public property of the state and of the cooperatives and must protect the economic interests and private property of workers, peasants, the petty bourgeoisie and the national bourgeoisie. It must develop the people's economy of New Democracy and steadily transform the country from an agricultural into an industrial one.

Source: The Important Documents of the First Plenary Session of the Chinese People's Political Consultative Conference (Peking: Foreign Languages Press, 1949), pp. 1–20.

Article 4

The people of the People's Republic of China shall have the right to elect and to be elected according to law.

Article 5

The people of the People's Republic of China shall have freedom of thought, speech, publication, assembly, association, correspondence, person, domicile, change of domicile, and religious belief and the freedom of holding processions and demonstrations.

Article 6

The People's Republic of China shall abolish the feudal system, which holds women in bondage. Women shall enjoy equal rights with men in political, economic, cultural, educational, and social life. Freedom of marriage for men and women shall be put into effect.

Article 7

The People's Republic of China shall suppress all counterrevolutionary activities and severely punish all Kuomintang counterrevolutionary war criminals and other leading incorrigible counterrevolutionary elements who collaborate with imperialism, commit treason against the fatherland, and oppose the cause of people's democracy. Feudal landlords, bureaucratic capitalists, and reactionary elements in general, after they have been disarmed and have had their special powers abolished, shall, in addition, be deprived of their political rights in accordance with law for a necessary period. But, at the same time, they shall be given some means of livelihood and shall be compelled to reform themselves through labor so as to become new men. If they continue their counterrevolutionary activities, they will be severely punished.

Article 8

It is the duty of every national of the People's Republic of China to defend the fatherland, to abide by the law, to observe labor discipline, to protect public property, to perform public and military service, and to pay taxes.

Article 9

All nationalities in the People's Republic of China shall have equal rights and duties.

Article 10

The armed forces of the People's Republic of China, namely the People's Liberation Army, the people's public security forces, and the people's police, belong to the people. It is the task of these armed forces to defend the independence, territorial integrity, and sovereignty of China, and to defend the revolutionary gains and all legitimate rights and interests of the Chinese people. The Central People's Government of the People's Republic of China shall endeavor to consolidate and strengthen the people's armed forces, so as to enable them to accomplish their tasks effectively.

Article 11

The People's Republic of China shall unite with all peace-loving and freedom-loving countries and peoples throughout the world, first of all, with the U.S.S.R., all Peoples' Democracies, and all oppressed nations. It shall take its stand in the camp of international peace and democracy, to oppose imperialist aggression, and to defend lasting world peace.

CHAPTER II: ORGANS OF STATE POWER

Article 12

The state power of the People's Republic of China belongs to the people. The people's congresses and the people's governments of all levels are the organs for the exercise of state power by the people. The people's congresses of all levels shall be popularly elected by universal franchise. The people's congresses of all levels shall elect the people's governments of their respective levels. The people's governments shall be the organs for exercising state power at their respective levels when the people's congresses of their respective levels are not in session.

The All-China People's Congress shall be the supreme organ of state power. The Central People's Government shall be the supreme organ for exercising state power when the All-China People's Congress is not in session.

Article 13

The Chinese People's Political Consultative Conference is the organizational form of the people's democratic united front. It shall be composed of the representatives of the working class, the peasantry, members of the revolutionary armed forces, intellectuals, the petit bourgeoisie, the national bourgeoisie, national minorities, the Overseas Chinese, and other patriotic democratic elements.

Pending the convocation of the All-China People's Congress elected by universal franchise, the Plenary Session of the Chinese People's Political Consultative Conference shall exercise the functions and powers of the All-China People's Congress, enact the Organic Law of the Central People's Government of the People's Republic of China, elect the Central People's Government Council of the People's Republic of China, and vest it with the authority to exercise state power.

After the convocation of the All-China People's Congress elected by universal franchise, the Chinese People's Political Consultative Conference may submit proposals on fundamental policies relating to national construction work and on other important measures to the All-China People's Congress or to the Central People's Government.

Article 14

In all places newly liberated by the People's Liberation Army, military control shall be exercised and the Kuomintang reactionary organs of state power shall be abolished. The Central People's Government or military and political organs at the front shall appoint personnel to organize military control committees and local people's governments. These shall lead the people in establishing revolutionary order and suppressing counterrevolutionary activities and, when conditions permit, shall convene all-circles representative conferences.

Pending the convocation of the local people's congresses elected by universal franchise, the local all-circles representative conferences shall gradually assume the functions and powers of the local people's congresses.

The duration of military control shall be determined by the Central People's Government according to the military and political conditions prevailing in the different localities.

In all places where military operations have completely ended, agrarian reform has been thoroughly carried out and people of all circles have been fully organized, elections based on universal franchise shall be held immediately for the purpose of convening local people's congresses.

Article 15

The organs of state power at all levels shall practice democratic centralism. In doing this the main principles shall be: The people's congresses shall be responsible and accountable to the people; the people's government councils shall be responsible and accountable to the people's congresses. Within the people's congresses and within the people's government councils, the minority shall abide by the decisions of the majority; the appointment of the people's governments of each level shall be ratified by the people's government of the higher level; the people's governments of the lower levels shall obey the people's governments of the higher levels, and all local people's governments throughout the country shall obey the Central People's Government.

Article 16
The jurisdiction of the Central People's Government and the local people's governments shall be defined according to the nature of the various matters involved and shall be prescribed by decrees of the Central People's Government Council so as to satisfy the requirements of both national unity and local expediency.

Article 17
All laws, decrees and judicial systems of the Kuomintang reactionary government, which oppress the people, shall be abolished. Laws and decrees protecting the people shall be enacted, and the people's judicial system shall be established.

Article 18
All state organs of the People's Republic of China must enforce a revolutionary working style, embodying honesty, simplicity, and service to the people; they must severely punish corruption, forbid extravagance, and oppose the bureaucratic working style, which alienates the masses of the people.

Article 19
People's supervisory organs shall be set up in the people's governments of county and municipal level and above, to supervise the performance of duties by the state organs of various levels and by public functionaries of all types, and to propose that disciplinary action be taken against state organs and public functionaries who violate the law or are negligent in the performance of their duties.
The people or people's organizations shall have the right to file charges with the people's supervisory organs or people's judicial organs against any state organs or any public functionaries that violate the law or are negligent in the performance of their duties.

CHAPTER III: MILITARY SYSTEM
Article 20
The People's Republic of China shall build up a unified army, the People's Liberation Army and people's public security forces, which shall be under the command of the People's Revolutionary Military Council of the Central People's Government; it shall institute unification of command, system, formation, and discipline.

Article 21
The People's Liberation Army and the people's public security forces shall, in accordance with the principle of unity between the officers and the rank-and-file and between the army and the people, set up a system of political work and shall educate the commanders and rank-and-file of these forces in a revolutionary and patriotic spirit.

Article 22

The People's Republic of China shall strengthen its modernized army and shall establish an air force and a navy in order to consolidate national defense.

Article 23

The People's Republic of China shall put into effect the people's militia system to maintain local order and to lay the foundation for national mobilization. It shall make preparations to enforce a system of obligatory military service at the appropriate time.

Article 24

The armed forces of the People's Republic of China shall, during peacetime, systematically take part in agricultural and industrial production in order to assist in national construction work, provided their military duties are not thereby hampered.

Article 25

Dependents of those who have given their lives for the revolution and of members of the revolutionary forces who are in need shall receive preferential treatment from the state and from society. The people's government shall make appropriate arrangements for disabled or retired servicemen who have participated in the revolutionary war, providing them with the means of livelihood or with occupations.

CHAPTER IV: ECONOMIC POLICY

Article 26

The basic principle for the economic construction of the People's Republic of China is to develop production and bring about a prosperous economy through the policies of taking into account both public and private interests, of benefiting both labor and capital, of mutual aid between the city and countryside, and circulation of goods between China and abroad. The state shall coordinate and regulate the state-owned economy, the cooperative economy, the individual economy of peasants and handicraftsmen, the private capitalist economy, and the state capitalist economy in their spheres of operations, supply of raw materials, marketing, labor conditions, technical equipment, policies of public and general finance, and so forth. In this way, all components of the social economy can, under the leadership of the state-owned economy, carry out division and coordination of labor and play their respective parts in promoting the development of the social economy as a whole.

Article 27

Agrarian reform is the necessary condition for the development of the nation's productive power and for its industrialization. In all areas where agrarian reform has been carried out, the ownership of the land acquired by the peasants shall be protected. In areas where agrarian reform has not been carried out, the peasant masses must be set in motion to establish peasant organizations and to put into effect the policy of 'land to the tiller' through such measures as the elimination of local bandits and despots, the reduction of rent and interest, and the distribution of land.

Article 28

State-owned economy is of a Socialist nature. All enterprises relating to the economic life of the country and exercising a dominant influence over the people's livelihood shall be under the unified operation of the state. All state-owned resources and enterprises are the public property of all the people and are the main material basis on which the People's Republic will develop production and bring about a prosperous economy. They are the leading force of the entire social economy.

Article 29

Cooperative economy is of a semi-Socialist nature and is an important component of the people's economy as a whole. The People's Government shall foster its development and accord it preferential treatment.

Article 30

The People's Government shall encourage the active operation of all private economic enterprises beneficial to the national welfare and to the people's livelihood and shall assist in their development.

Article 31

The economy jointly operated by state and private capital is of a state-capitalist nature. Whenever necessary and possible, private capital shall be encouraged to develop in the direction of state capitalism, in such ways as processing for state-owned enterprises and exploiting state-owned resources in the form of concessions.

Article 32

The system of workers' participation in the administration of production shall, for the present period, be established in state-owned enterprises. This means that factory administrative committees shall be set up under the leadership of the factory managers. In privately owned enterprises, in order to carry out the principle of benefiting both labor and capital, collective contracts shall be signed by the trade union, representing the workers and employees, and the employer. For the present period, an eight- to ten-hour day should in general be enforced in publicly and privately operated enterprises, but under special circumstances this matter may be dealt with at discretion. The people's governments shall fix minimum wages according to the conditions prevailing in various localities and trades. Labor insurance shall be gradually established. The special interests of juvenile and women workers shall be safeguarded. Inspection of industries and mines shall be carried out in order to improve their safety devices and sanitary facilities.

Article 33

The Central People's Government shall strive to draw up, as soon as possible, a general plan for rehabilitating and developing the main departments of the public and private economy of the entire country. It shall also fix the scope of the division and coordination of labor between the central and local governments in economic construction and shall undertake centralized regulation of the interrelationship between the economic departments of the central and local governments. Under the unified leadership of the Central People's Government, the various economic departments of the central and local governments should give full play to their creativeness and initiative

Article 34

Agriculture, forestry, fisheries, and animal husbandry: In all areas where agrarian reform has been thoroughly carried out, the central task of the People's Government shall be the organization of the peasants and of all manpower available for allocation to the development of agricultural production and secondary occupations. The People's Government shall also guide the peasants step by step in the organization of various forms of mutual aid in labor and cooperation in production, according to the principle of willingness and mutual benefit. In newly liberated areas, every step in agrarian reform shall be linked . . . with reviving and developing agricultural production.

The People's Government shall, in accordance with the state plan and the requirements of the people's livelihood, strive to restore the output of grain, industrial raw materials, and export goods to the prewar production level and to surpass it within the shortest possible time. Attention shall be paid to construction and repair of irrigation works, to prevention of floods and droughts, to restoration and development of animal husbandry, to increasing the supply of fertilizers, to improvement of farm implements and seeds, to prevention of pest damage and plant diseases, to relief work in the event of natural calamities, and to planned migration for land reclamation.

Forests shall be protected, and forestation shall be developed according to plan.

Coastal fisheries shall be protected, and the aquatic products industry shall be developed.

Livestock-raising shall be protected and developed, and preventive measures shall be taken against murrain.

Article 35

Industry: In order to lay the foundation for the industrialization of the country, the central point of industrial work shall be the planned, systematic rehabilitation and development of heavy industry, such as mining, the iron and steel industry, the power industry, the machine-building industry, the electrical industry, the main chemical industries, and so forth. At the same time, the production of the textile industry and other light industries beneficial to the national welfare and to the people's livelihood shall be restored and increased so as to meet the needs of the people's daily consumption.

Article 36

Communications: Railways and highways shall be swiftly restored and gradually extended. Rivers shall be dredged and water transportation expanded. Postal, telegraphic, and telephone services shall be improved and developed. Various communications facilities shall be built up and civil aviation established step by step according to plan.

Article 37

Commerce: All legitimate public and private trade shall be protected. Control shall be exercised over foreign trade, and the policy of protecting trade shall be adopted. Freedom of domestic trade shall be established under a unified economic state plan, but commercial speculation disturbing the market shall be strictly prohibited. State-owned trading organizations shall assume the responsibility of adjusting supply and demand, stabilizing commodity prices and assisting the people's cooperatives. The people's government shall adopt the measures necessary to encourage the people in saving, to facilitate remittances from Overseas Chinese, and to channel into industry and other productive enterprises all socially idle capital and commercial capital that is not beneficial to the national welfare and/or to the people's livelihood.

Article 38

Cooperatives: The broad masses of working people shall be encouraged and assisted to develop cooperatives according to the principle of willingness. Supply and marketing cooperatives, as well as consumers', credit, producers', and transport cooperatives, shall be organized in towns and villages. Consumers' cooperatives shall first be organized in factories, institutions, and schools.

Article 39

Currency and banking: Financial enterprises shall be strictly controlled by the state. The right of issuing currency belongs to the state. The circulation of foreign currency within the country shall be prohibited. The buying and selling of foreign exchange, foreign currency, gold, and silver shall be handled by the state banks. Private financial enterprises operating in accordance with the law shall be subjected to supervision and direction by the state. All who engage in financial speculation and who undermine the financial enterprises of the state shall be subjected to severe punishment.

Article 40

Public finance: A budget and financial statement system shall be instituted. The spheres of financial administration of central and local governments shall be defined. Economizing and frugality shall be enforced. The budget shall be steadily balanced and capital accumulated for the country's production.

The tax policy of the state shall be based on the principle of ensuring supplies for the revolutionary war and taking into account the rehabilitation and development of production and the requirements of national construction. The tax system shall be simplified and equitable distribution of the burden effected.

CHAPTER V: CULTURAL AND EDUCATIONAL POLICY

Article 41

The culture and education of the People's Republic of China shall be New Democratic—national, scientific, and popular. The main tasks of the People's Government in cultural and educational work shall be the raising of the cultural level of the people, the training of personnel for national construction work, the eradicating of feudal, compradore, and fascist ideology, and the developing of the ideology of service to the people.

Article 42

Love of the fatherland, love of the people, love of labor, love of science, and care of public property shall be promoted as the public spirit of all nationals of the People's Republic of China.

Article 43

Efforts shall be made to develop the natural sciences in order to serve industrial, agricultural, and national defense construction. Scientific discoveries and inventions shall be encouraged and rewarded, and scientific knowledge shall be disseminated among the people.

Article 44

The application of a scientific-historical viewpoint to the study and interpretation of history, economics, politics, culture, and international affairs shall be promoted. Outstanding works of social science shall be encouraged and rewarded.

Article 45

Literature and art shall be promoted to serve the people, to awaken their political consciousness, and to enhance their enthusiasm for labor. Outstanding works of literature and art shall be encouraged and rewarded. The people's drama and cinema shall be developed.

Article 46

The method of education of the People's Republic of China shall be the unification of theory and practice. The People's Government shall reform the old educational system, subject matter, and teaching methods in a planned, systematic manner.

Article 47

In order to meet the extensive requirements of revolutionary and national construction work, universal education shall be carried out, secondary and higher education shall be strengthened, technical education shall be stressed, the education of workers during their spare time and that of cadres at their posts shall be strengthened, and revolutionary political education shall be accorded to both young and old-type intellectuals. All this is to be done in a planned and systematic manner.

Article 48

National physical culture shall be promoted. Public health and medical work shall be expanded, and attention shall be paid to the protection of the health of mothers, infants, and children.

Article 49

Freedom of reporting truthful news shall be safeguarded. The utilization of the press for slander, for undermining the interests of the state and the people, and for provoking world war shall be prohibited. The people's radio and publication work shall be developed. Attention shall be paid to publishing popular books and journals beneficial to the people.

CHAPTER VI: POLICY TOWARD NATIONALITIES

Article 50

All nationalities within the boundaries of the People's Republic of China are equal. They shall establish unity and mutual aid among themselves and shall oppose imperialism and their own public enemies, so that the People's Republic of China will become a big fraternal and cooperative family composed of all its nationalities. Greater nationalism and chauvinism shall be opposed. Acts involving discrimination, oppression, and splitting of the unity of the various nationalities shall be prohibited.

Article 51

Regional autonomy shall be exercised in areas where national minorities are concentrated, and various kinds of autonomy organizations of the different nationalities shall be set up according to the size of the respective populations and regions. In places where different nationalities live together and in the autonomous areas of the national minorities, the different nationalities shall each have an appropriate number of representatives in the local organs of political power.

Article 52

All national minorities within the boundaries of the People's Republic of China shall have the right to join the People's Liberation Army and to organize local people's public security forces in accordance with the unified military system of the state.

Article 53

All national minorities shall have freedom to develop their dialects and languages, and to preserve or reform their traditions, customs, and religious beliefs. The People's Government shall assist the masses of the people of all national minorities to develop their political, economic, cultural, and educational construction work.

CHAPTER VII: FOREIGN POLICY

Article 54

The principle of the foreign policy of the People's Republic of China is protection of the independence, freedom, integrity of territory, and sovereignty of the country; upholding of lasting international peace and friendly cooperation among the peoples of all countries; and opposition to the imperialist policy of aggression and war.

Article 55

The Central People's Government of the People's Republic of China shall examine the treaties and agreements concluded between the Kuomintang and foreign governments and shall recognize, abrogate, revise, or renegotiate them according to their respective contents.

Article 56

The Central People's Government of the People's Republic of China may, on the basis of equality, mutual benefit, and mutual respect for territory and sovereignty, negotiate with foreign governments that have severed relations with the Kuomintang reactionary clique and that adopt a friendly attitude toward the People's Republic of China, and may establish diplomatic relations with them.

Article 57

The People's Republic of China may restore and develop commercial relations with foreign governments and peoples on a basis of equality and mutual benefit.

Article 58

The Central People's Government of the People's Republic of China shall do its utmost to protect the proper rights and interests of Chinese residing abroad.

Article 59

The People's Government of the People's Republic of China protects law-abiding foreign nationals in China.

Article 60

The People's Republic of China shall accord the right of asylum to foreign nationals who seek refuge in China because they have been oppressed by their own governments for supporting the people's interests and taking part in the struggle for peace and democracy.

THE CONSTITUTION OF THE PEOPLE'S REPUBLIC OF CHINA, 1954

[THE following text is the translation published by the official Foreign Languages Press. Sections IV and V of Chapter Two, which deal with local people's congresses and councils, and the administration of autonomous areas, have been omitted. The constitution was adopted on September 20, 1954, by the First National People's Congress at its first session.]

In the year 1949, after more than a century of heroic struggle, the Chinese people, led by the Communist Party of China, finally achieved their great victory in the people's revolution against imperialism, feudalism, and bureaucrat-capitalism; and so brought to an end a long history of oppression and enslavement and founded the People's Republic of China, a people's democratic dictatorship. The system of people's democracy—new democracy—of the People's Republic of China guarantees that China can in a peaceful way banish exploitation and poverty and build a prosperous and happy socialist society.

From the founding of the People's Republic of China to the attainment of a socialist society is a period of transition. During the transition the fundamental task of the state is to bring about, step by step, the socialist industrialization of the country and to accomplish, step by step, the socialist transformation of agriculture, handicrafts, and capitalist industry and commerce. In the last few years our people have successfully carried out a series of large-scale struggles: the reform of the agrarian system, resistance to American aggression and aid to Korea, the suppression of counterrevolutionaries, and the rehabilitation of the national economy. As a result, the necessary conditions have been created for planned economic construction and gradual transition to socialism.

The First National People's Congress of the People's Republic of China, at its first session held in Peking, the capital, solemnly adopted the Constitution of the People's Republic of China on September 20, 1954. This Constitution is based on the Common Program of the Chinese People's Political Consultative Conference of 1949 and is an advance on it. It consolidates the gains of the Chinese people's revolution and the political and economic victories won since the founding of the People's Republic of China; and, moreover, it reflects the basic needs of the state in the period of transition, as well as the general desire of the people as a whole to build a socialist society.

In the course of the great struggle to establish the People's Republic of China, the people of our country forged a broad people's democratic united front, composed of

Source: *Constitution of the People's Republic of China* (Peking: Foreign Languages Press, 1954).

all democratic classes, democratic parties and groups, and popular organizations, and led by the Communist Party of China. This people's democratic united front will continue to play its part in mobilizing and rallying the whole people in common struggle to fulfil the fundamental task of the state during the transition and to oppose enemies within and without.

All nationalities of our country are united in one great family of free and equal nations. This unity of China's nationalities will continue to gain in strength, founded as it is on ever growing friendship and mutual aid among themselves and on the struggle against imperialism, against public enemies of the people within the nationalities, and against both dominant-nation chauvinism and local nationalism. In the course of economic and cultural development, the state will concern itself with the needs of the different nationalities and, in the matter of socialist transformation, pay full attention to the special characteristics in the development of each.

China has already built an indestructible friendship with the great Union of Soviet Socialist Republics and the People's Democracies; . . . the friendship between our people and peace-loving people in all other countries is growing day by day. Such friendship will be constantly strengthened and broadened. China's policy of establishing and extending diplomatic relations with all countries on the principles of equality, mutual benefit, and mutual respect for each other's sovereignty and territorial integrity, which has already yielded success, will continue to be carried out. In international affairs our firm and consistent policy is to strive for the noble cause of world peace and the progress of humanity.

CHAPTER ONE: GENERAL PRINCIPLES

Article 1

The People's Republic of China is a people's democratic state led by the working class and based on the alliance of workers and peasants.

Article 2

All power in the People's Republic of China belongs to the people. The organs through which the people exercise power are the National People's Congress and the local people's congresses.

The National People's Congress, the local people's congresses, and other organs of state practice democratic centralism.

Article 3

The People's Republic of China is a single multinational state.

All the nationalities are equal. Discrimination against, or oppression of, any nationality and acts that undermine the unity of the nationalities are prohibited.

All the nationalities have freedom to use and foster the growth of their spoken and written languages and to preserve or reform their own customs or ways.

Regional autonomy applies in areas where people of national minorities live in compact communities. National autonomous areas are inalienable parts of the People's Republic of China.

Article 4

The People's Republic of China, by relying on the organs of state and social forces, and by means of socialist industrialization and socialist transformation, ensures the gradual abolition of systems of exploitation and the building of a socialist society.

Article 5

At present, the following basic forms of ownership of means of production exist in the People's Republic of China: state ownership, that is, ownership by the whole people; cooperative ownership, that is, collective ownership by the working masses; ownership by individual working people; and capitalist ownership.

Article 6

The state sector of the economy is a socialist sector, owned by the whole people. It is the leading force in the national economy and the material basis on which the state carries out socialist transformation. The state ensures priority for the development of the state sector of the economy.

All mineral resources and waters, as well as forests, undeveloped land, and other resources, which the state owns by law, are the property of the whole people.

Article 7

The cooperative sector of the economy is either socialist, when collectively owned by the working masses, or semisocialist, when in part collectively owned by the working masses. Partial collective ownership by the working masses is a transitional form by means of which individual peasants, individual handicraftsmen, and other individual working people organize themselves in their advance toward collective ownership by the working masses.

The state protects the property of the cooperatives; it encourages, guides, and helps the development of the cooperative sector of the economy. It regards the promotion of producers' cooperatives as the chief means for the transformation of individual farming and individual handicrafts.

Article 8

The state protects the right of peasants to own land and other means of production according to law.

The state guides and helps individual peasants to increase production and encourages them to organize producers', supply and marketing, and credit cooperatives voluntarily.

The policy of the state toward rich-peasant economy is to restrict and gradually eliminate it.

Article 9

The state protects the right of handicraftsmen and other nonagricultural individual working people to own means of production according to law.

The state guides and helps individual handicraftsmen and other nonagricultural individual working people to improve their enterprises and encourages them to organize producers' and supply and marketing cooperatives voluntarily.

Article 10

The state protects the right of capitalists to own means of production and other capital according to law.

The policy of the state toward capitalist industry and commerce is to use, restrict, and transform them. The state makes use of the positive sides of capitalist industry and commerce that are beneficial to national welfare and the people's livelihood; restricts their negative sides, which are not beneficial to national welfare and the people's livelihood; and encourages and guides their transformation into various forms of state-capitalist economy, gradually replacing capitalist ownership with ownership by the whole people; this it does by means of control exercised by administrative organs of state, the leadership given by the state sector of the economy, and supervision by the workers.

The state forbids capitalists to engage in unlawful activities that injure the public interest, disrupt the social-economic order, or undermine the economic plan of the state.

Article 11

The state protects the right of citizens to own lawfully earned incomes, savings, houses, and other means of life.

Article 12

The state protects the right of citizens to inherit private property according to law.

Article 13

The state may, in the public interest, buy, requisition, or nationalize land and other means of production in both cities and countryside according to the provisions of law.

Article 14

The state forbids any person to use his private property to the detriment of the public interest.

Article 15

By economic planning, the state directs the growth and transformation of the national economy to bring about the constant increase of productive forces, in this way enriching the material and cultural life of the people and consolidating the independence and security of the country.

Article 16

Work is a matter of honor for every citizen of the People's Republic of China who is able to work. The state encourages citizens to take an active and creative part in their work.

Article 17

All organs of state must rely on the masses of the people, constantly maintain close contact with them, heed their opinions, and accept their supervision.

Article 18

All servants of the state must be loyal to the people's democratic system, observe the Constitution and the law, and strive to serve the people.

Article 19

The People's Republic of China safeguards the people's democratic system, suppresses all treasonable and counterrevolutionary activities, and punishes all traitors and counterrevolutionaries.

The state deprives feudal landlords and bureaucrat-capitalists of political rigats for a specific period of time according to law; at the same time it provides them with a way of earning a living, in order to enable them to reform through work and become citizens who earn their livelihood by their own labor.

Article 20

The armed forces of the People's Republic of China belong to the people; their duty is to safeguard the gains of the people's revolution and the achievements of national construction, and to defend the sovereignty, territorial integrity, and security of the country.

CHAPTER TWO: THE STATE STRUCTURE

SECTION I: THE NATIONAL PEOPLE'S CONGRESS

Article 21

The National People's Congress is the highest organ of state authority in the People's Republic of China.

Article 22

The National People's Congress is the only legislative authority in the country.

Article 23

The National People's Congress is composed of deputies elected by provinces, autonomous regions, municipalities directly under the central authority, the armed forces, and Chinese resident abroad.

The number of deputies to the National People's Congress, including those representing national minorities, and the manner of their election, are prescribed by electoral law.

Article 24

The National People's Congress is elected for a term of four years.

Two months before the term of office of the National People's Congress expires, its Standing Committee must complete the election of deputies to the succeeding National People's Congress. Should exceptional circumstances arise preventing such an election, the term of office of the sitting National People's Congress may be prolonged until the first session of the succeeding National People's Congress.

Article 25

The National People's Congress meets once a year, convened by its Standing Committee. It may also be convened whenever its Standing Committee deems this necessary or one-fifth of the deputies so propose.

Article 26

When the National People's Congress meets, it elects a presidium to conduct its sittings.

Article 27

The National People's Congress exercises the following functions and powers:
 1. to amend the Constitution;
 2. to enact laws;
 3. to supervise the enforcement of the Constitution;
 4. to elect the Chairman and the Vice-Chairman of the People's Republic of China;
 5. to decide on the choice of the Premier of the State Council upon recommendation by the Chairman of the People's Republic of China, and of the component members of the State Council upon recommendation by the Premier;
 6. to decide on the choice of the Vice-Chairmen and other members of the Council of National Defense upon recommendation by the Chairman of the People's Republic of China;
 7. to elect the President of the Supreme People's Court;
 8. to elect the Chief Procurator of the Supreme People's Procuratorate;
 9. to decide on the national economic plans;
 10. to examine and approve the state budget and the financial report;
 11. to ratify the status and boundaries of provinces, autonomous regions, and municipalities directly under the central authority;
 12. to decide on general amnesties;
 13. to decide on questions of war and peace;
 14. to exercise such other functions and powers as the National People's Congress considers necessary.

Article 28

The National People's Congress has power to remove from office:

1. the Chairman and the Vice-Chairman of the People's Republic of China;
2. the Premier and Vice-Premiers, Ministers, Heads of Commissions, and Secretary-General of the State Council;
3. the Vice-Chairmen and other members of the Council of National Defense;
4. the President of the Supreme People's Court;
5. the Chief Procurator of the Supreme People's Procuratorate.

Article 29
Amendments to the Constitution require a two-thirds majority vote of all the deputies to the National People's Congress.

Laws and other bills require a simple majority vote of all the deputies to the National People's Congress.

Article 30
The Standing Committee of the National People's Congress is a permanently acting body of the National People's Congress.

The Standing Committee is composed of the following members, elected by the National People's Congress: the Chairman; the Vice-Chairmen; the Secretary-General; and other members.

Article 31
The Standing Committee of the National People's Congress exercises the following functions and powers:
1. to conduct the election of deputies to the National People's Congress;
2. to convene the National People's Congress;
3. to interpret the laws;
4. to adopt decrees;
5. to supervise the work of the State Council, the Supreme People's Court, and the Supreme People's Procuratorate;
6. to annual decisions and orders of the State Council that contravene the Constitution, laws, or decrees;
7. to revise or annul inappropriate decisions issued by the government authorities of provinces, autonomous regions, and municipalities directly under the central authority;
8. to decide on the appointment or removal of any Vice-Premier, Minister, Head of Commission, or Secretary-General of the State Council when the National People's Congress is not in session;
9. to appoint or remove the Vice-Presidents, judges, and other members of the Judicial Committee of the Supreme People's Court;
10. to appoint or remove the Deputy Chief Procurators, procurators, and other members of the Procuratorial Committee of the Supreme People's Procuratorate;
11. to decide on the appointment or recall of plenipotentiary representatives to foreign states;
12. to decide on the ratification or abrogation of treaties concluded with foreign states;
13. to institute military, diplomatic, and other special titles and ranks;
14. to institute and decide on the award of state orders, medals, and titles of honor;
15. to decide on the granting of pardons;
16. to decide, when the National People's Congress is not in session, on the declaration of a state of war in the event of armed attack on the country or in fulfillment of international treaty obligations concerning common defense against aggression;

804

17. to decide on general or partial mobilization;
18. to decide on the enforcement of martial law throughout the country or in certain areas;
19. to exercise such other functions and powers as are vested in it by the National People's Congress.

Article 32
The Standing Committee of the National People's Congress exercises its functions and powers until a new Standing Committee is elected by the succeeding National People's Congress.

Article 33
The Standing Committee of the National People's Congress is responsible to the National People's Congress and reports to it.

The National People's Congress has power to recall members of its Standing Committee.

Article 34
The National People's Congress establishes a Nationalities Committee, a Bills Committee, a Budget Committee, a Credentials Committee, and other necessary committees.

The Nationalities Committee and the Bills Committee are under the direction of the Standing Committee of the National People's Congress when the National People's Congress is not in session.

Article 35
The National People's Congress, or its Standing Committee if the National People's Congress is not in session, may, if necessary, appoint commissions of inquiry for the investigation of specific questions.

All organs of state, people's organizations, and citizens concerned are obliged to supply necessary information to these commissions when they conduct investigations.

Article 36
Deputies to the National People's Congress have the right to address questions to the State Council or to the Ministries and Commissions of the State Council, which are under no obligation to answer.

Article 37
No deputy to the National People's Congress may be arrested or placed on trial without the consent of the National People's Congress or, when the National People's Congress is not in session, of its Standing Committee.

Article 38
Deputies to the National People's Congress are subject to the supervision of the units that elect them. These electoral units have power to replace at any time the deputies they elect, according to the procedure prescribed by law.

SECTION II: THE CHAIRMAN OF THE PEOPLE'S REPUBLIC OF CHINA

Article 39
The Chairman of the People's Republic of China is elected by the National People's Congress. Any citizen of the People's Republic of China who has the right to vote and stand for election and has reached the age of thirty-five is eligible for election as Chairman of the People's Republic of China.

The term of office of the Chairman of the People's Republic of China is four years.

Article 40

The Chairman of the People's Republic of China, in pursuance of decisions of the National People's Congress or the Standing Committee of the National People's Congress, promulgates laws and decrees; appoints or removes the Premier, Vice-Premiers, Ministers, Heads of Commissions and the Secretary-General of the State Council; appoints or removes the Vice-Chairmen and other members of the Council of National Defense; confers state orders, medals, and titles of honor; proclaims general amnesties and grants pardons; proclaims martial law; proclaims a state of war; and orders mobilization.

Article 41

The Chairman of the People's Republic of China represents the People's Republic of China in its relations with foreign states, receives foreign diplomatic representatives, and, pursuant to decisions of the Standing Committee of the National People's Congress, appoints or recalls plenipotentiary representatives to foreign states and ratifies treaties concluded with foreign states.

Article 42

The Chairman of the People's Republic of China commands the armed forces of the country and is Chairman of the Council of National Defense.

Article 43

The Chairman of the People's Republic of China, whenever necessary, convenes a Supreme State Conference and acts as its chairman.

The Vice-Chairman of the People's Republic of China, the Chairman of the Standing Committee of the National People's Congress, the Premier of the State Council, and other persons concerned take part in the Supreme State Conference.

The Chairman of the People's Republic of China submits the views of the Supreme State Conference on important affairs of state to the National People's Congress, its Standing Committee, the State Council, or other bodies concerned for their consideration and decision.

Article 44

The Vice-Chairman of the People's Republic of China assists the Chairman in his work. The Vice-Chairman may exercise such part of the functions and powers of the Chairman as the Chairman may entrust to him.

The provisions of Article 39 of the Constitution governing the election and term of office of the Chairman of the People's Republic of China apply also to the election and term of office of the Vice-Chairman of the People's Republic of China.

Article 45

The Chairman and the Vice-Chairman of the People's Republic of China exercise their functions and powers until the new Chairman and Vice-Chairman elected by the succeeding National People's Congress take office.

Article 46

Should the Chairman of the People's Republic of China be incapacitated for a prolonged period by reason of health, the functions of Chairman shall be exercised by the Vice-Chairman.

Should the office of Chairman of the People's Republic of China fall vacant, the Vice-Chairman succeeds to the office of Chairman.

Section III: The State Council

Article 47

The State Council of the People's Republic of China, that is, the Central People's Government, is the executive organ of the highest state authority; it is the highest administrative organ of state.

Article 48

The State Council is composed of the following members: the Premier; the Vice-Premiers; the Ministers; the Heads of Commissions; and the Secretary-General.

The organization of the State Council is determined by law.

Article 49

The State Council exercises the following functions and powers:

1. to formulate administrative measures, issue decisions and orders, and verify their execution, in accordance with the Constitution, laws and decrees;
2. to submit bills to the National People's Congress or its Standing Committee;
3. to coordinate and lead the work of Ministries and Commissions;
4. to coordinate and lead the work of local administrative organs of state throughout the country;
5. to revise or annul inappropriate orders and directives issued by Ministers or by Heads of Commissions;
6. to revise or annul inappropriate decisions and orders issued by local administrative organs of state;
7. to put into effect the national economic plans and provisions of the state budget;
8. to control foreign and domestic trade;
9. to direct cultural, educational, and public health work;
10. to administer affairs concerning the nationalities;
11. to administer affairs concerning Chinese resident abroad;
12. to protect the interests of the state, to maintain public order, and to safeguard the rights of citizens;
13. to direct the conduct of external affairs;
14. to guide the building up of the defense forces;
15. to ratify the status and boundaries of autonomous *chou*, counties, autonomous counties, and municipalities;
16. to appoint or remove administrative personnel according to provisions of law;
17. to exercise such other functions and powers as are vested in it by the National People's Congress or its Standing Committee.

Article 50

The Premier directs the work of the State Council and presides over its meetings. The Vice-Premiers assist the Premier in his work.

Article 51

The Ministers and Heads of Commissions direct the work of their respective departments. They may issue orders and directives within the jurisdiction of their respective departments and in accordance with laws and decrees, and decisions and orders of the State Council.

Article 52

The State Council is responsible to the National People's Congress and reports to it, or, when the National People's Congress is not in session, to its Standing Committee.

.　　.　　.　　.　　.　　.　　.　　.　　.　　.　　.　　.

CHAPTER THREE: FUNDAMENTAL RIGHTS AND DUTIES OF CITIZENS

Article 85
　　Citizens of the People's Republic of China are equal before the law.

Article 86
　　Citizens of the People's Republic of China who have reached the age of eighteen have the right to vote and stand for election whatever their nationality, race, sex, occupation, social origin, religious belief, education, property status, or length of residence, except insane persons and persons deprived by law of the right to vote and stand for election.
　　Women have equal rights with men to vote and stand for election.

Article 87
　　Citizens of the People's Republic of China enjoy freedom of speech, freedom of the press, freedom of assembly, freedom of association, freedom of procession, and freedom of demonstration. The state guarantees to citizens enjoyment of these freedoms by providing the necessary material facilities.

Article 88
　　Citizens of the People's Republic of China enjoy freedom of religious belief.

Article 89
　　Freedom of the person of citizens of the People's Republic of China is inviolable. No citizen may be arrested except by decision of a people's court or with the sanction of a people's procuratorate.

Article 90
　　The homes of citizens of the People's Republic of China are inviolable, and privacy of correspondence is protected by law.
　　Citizens of the People's Republic of China enjoy freedom of residence and freedom to change their residence.

Article 91
　　Citizens of the People's Republic of China have the right to work. To guarantee enjoyment of this right, the state, by planned development of the national economy, gradually creates more employment, and better working conditions and wages.

Article 92
　　Working people in the People's Republic of China have the right to rest and leisure. To guarantee enjoyment of this right, the state prescribes working hours and holidays for workers and office employees; at the same time it gradually expands material facilities to enable working people to rest and build up their health.

Article 93
　　Working people in the People's Republic of China have the right to material assistance in old age and in case of illness or disability. To guarantee enjoyment of this right, the state provides social insurance, social assistance, and public health services and gradually expands these facilities.

Article 94
Citizens of the People's Republic of China have the right to education. To guarantee enjoyment of this right, the state establishes and gradually extends the various types of schools and other cultural and educational institutions.

The state pays special attention to the physical and mental development of young people.

Article 95
The People's Republic of China safeguards the freedom of citizens to engage in scientific research, literary and artistic creation, and other cultural pursuits. The state encourages and assists creative work in science, education, literature, art, and other cultural pursuits.

Article 96
Women in the People's Republic of China enjoy equal rights with men in all spheres of political, economic, cultural, social, and domestic life.

The state protects marriage, the family, and the mother and child.

Article 97
Citizens of the People's Republic of China have the right to bring complaints against any person working in organs of state for transgression of law or neglect of duty by making a written or verbal statement to any organ of state at any level. People suffering loss by reason of infringement by persons working in organs of state of their rights as citizens have the right to compensation.

Article 98
The People's Republic of China protects the proper rights and interests of Chinese residents abroad.

Article 99
The People's Republic of China grants the right of asylum to any foreign national persecuted for supporting a just cause, for taking part in the peace movement, or for engaging in scientific activity.

Article 100
Citizens of the People's Republic of China must abide by the Constitution and the law, uphold discipline at work, keep public order, and respect social ethics.

Article 101
The public property of the People's Republic of China is sacred and inviolable. It is the duty of every citizen to respect and protect public property.

Article 102
It is the duty of citizens of the People's Republic of China to pay taxes according to law.

Article 103
It is the sacred duty of every citizen of the People's Republic of China to defend the homeland.

It is an honorable duty of citizens of the People's Republic of China to perform military service according to law.

Chapter Four: National Flag, National Emblem, Capital

Article 104

The National flag of the People's Republic of China is a red flag with five stars.

Article 105

The national emblem of the People's Republic of China [has] in the center [the Gate of Heavenly Peace] under the light of five stars, framed with ears of grain, and with a cogwheel at the base.

Article 106

The capital of the People's Republic of China is Peking.

OUTLINE OF THE FIRST
FIVE-YEAR PLAN, 1955

[THE Chinese First Five-Year Plan was a notable success and is worth examination. The following is an outline of the plan as reported on July 5 and 6, 1955, by Li Fu-Ch'un, Vice-Premier and Chairman of the State Planning Commission, at the Second Session of the First National People's Congress. For additional details see *First Five-Year Plan for Development of the National Economy of the P.R.C. in 1953–1957* (Peking: Foreign Languages Press, 1956).]

The general task set by China's First Five-Year Plan was determined in the light of the fundamental task of the state during the transition period.

It may be summarized as follows: We must center our main efforts on industrial construction; this comprises 694 above-norm construction projects, the core of which is the 156 projects that the Soviet Union is designing for us, and which will lay the preliminary groundwork for China's socialist industrialization; we must foster the growth of agricultural producers' cooperatives, whose system of ownership is partially collective, and handicraft producers' cooperatives, thus laying the preliminary groundwork for the socialist transformation of agriculture and handicrafts; and, in the main, we must incorporate capitalist industry and commerce into various forms of state-capitalism, laying the groundwork for the socialist transformation of private industry and commerce....

The total outlay for the country's economic construction and cultural and educational development during the first five-year period will be 76,640 million *yüan*, or the equivalent in value of more than 700 million taels of gold....

Investments in capital construction will amount to 42,740 million *yüan*, or 55.8 per cent of the total outlay for economic construction and cultural and educational development during the five-year period. Of the remaining 44.2 per cent, or 33,900 million *yüan*, part will be spent on work occasioned by the needs of capital construction, such as prospecting resources, engineering surveying and designing, stockpiling of equipment and materials, and so forth. Part will be spent to develop industrial production, transport, the mails, and telecommunications, including such items as overhaul of equipment, technical and organizational improvements in production, trial manufacture of new products, purchase of miscellaneous fixed assets, and the like; another part will serve as circulating capital for the various economic departments; and still another part will go to funds allocated to all economic, cultural, and

---

Source: Li Fu-Ch'un, *Report on the First Five-Year Plan for Development of the National Economy of the People's Republic of China in 1953–1957* (Peking: Foreign Languages Press, 1955), pp. 21–39.

educational departments for operating expenses and for the training of specialized personnel.

The sum of 42,740 million *yüan* for investments in the five-year capital construction program is distributed as follows:

Industrial departments, 24,850 million *yüan*, or 58.2 per cent of the total amount to be invested;

Agriculture, water conservation, and forestry departments, 3,260 million *yüan*, or 7.6 per cent;

Transport, postal, and telecommunications departments, 8,210 million *yüan*, or 19.2 per cent;

Trade, banking, and stockpiling departments, 1,280 million *yüan*, or 3 per cent;

Cultural, educational, and public health departments, 3,080 million *yüan*, or 7.2 per cent;

Development of urban public utilities, 1,600 million *yüan*, or 3.7 per cent;

Other items, 460 million *yüan*, or 1.1 per cent.

The proportion of state investments in agriculture is not large in our First Five-Year Plan, because agriculture cannot yet be extensively mechanized and it is not yet possible to undertake bigger projects in water conservation and forestry on a large scale in this five-year period. Furthermore, capital investments in the agriculture, water conservation, and forestry departments do not include relief funds for rural areas, agricultural loans, and other items, nor do they include capital invested in production by the peasants themselves. If all these items are taken into account, the total amount of capital used to develop agriculture in the five-year period comes close to the total investment in industry.

Capital investment in transport in our First Five-Year Plan is also not large, but it can, in the main, satisfy the needs of the First Five-Year Plan period and the initial stage of the Second Five-Year Plan.

There are 694 above-norm projects, including those that the Soviet Union is helping China to build, among the new projects and reconstruction projects under our five-year program of capital construction in industry. If we add to these the 252 projects in agriculture, water conservation, and forestry; the 220 projects in transport, the mails, and telecommunications; the 156 projects in culture, education, and public health; the 118 projects in urban public utilities; and the 160 projects in other spheres, the total number of above-norm capital construction projects reaches 1,600. In addition to these, there are more than 6,000 below-norm construction projects, of which about 2,300 are in industry. In industry, 455 above-norm projects can be completed within the present five-year period, or a total of 1,271 if those in other spheres are included. The bulk of the below-norm projects can also be completed in this period. The completion of these projects will vastly increase the productive force of China's industry; it will assist the development of agriculture, increase transport capacity; and expand cultural and educational work.

In the sphere of industry, we list below figures showing the ultimate increases in annual production capacity of principal industrial items when all the above-norm and below-norm construction projects started in the First Five-Year Plan period are completed; and figures showing the increases in annual capacity by the end of the First Five-Year Plan period when part of them are completed:

Pig iron: ultimate increase in annual capacity, 5,750,000 tons; increase in annual capacity by the end of the five-year period, 2,300,000 tons

Steel: ultimate increase in annual capacity, 6,100,000 tons; increase in annual capacity by the end of the five-year period, 2,530,000 tons

Electric power: ultimate increase in annual capacity, 4,060,000 kilowatts; increase in annual capacity by the end of the five-year period, 2,050,000 kilowatts

Coal: ultimate increase in annual capacity, 93,100,000 tons; increase in annual capacity by the end of the five-year period, 53,850,000 tons

Metallurgical and mining machinery: ultimate increase in annual capacity, 190,000 tons; increase in annual capacity by the end of the five-year period, 70,000 tons

Power-generating equipment: ultimate increase in annual capacity, 800,000 kilowatts All projects will be completed within the five-year period.

Trucks: ultimate annual capacity, 90,000 vehicles; annual capacity by the end of the five-year period, 30,000 vehicles

Tractors: ultimate annual capacity, 15,000, to be reached in 1959

Chemical fertilizers: ultimate increase in annual capacity, 910,000 tons; increase in annual capacity by the end of the five-year period, 280,000 tons.

Cement: ultimate increase in annual capacity, 3,600,000 tons; increase in annual capacity by the end of the five-year period, 2,360,000 tons

Cotton spindles: ultimate increase, 1,890,000 spindles; portion to be put into operation in the five-year period, 1,650,000 spindles

Machine-made paper: ultimate increase in annual capacity, 186,000 tons; increase in annual capacity by the end of the five-year period, 95,000 tons

Machine-processed sugar: ultimate increase in annual capacity, 560,000 tons; increase in annual capacity by the end of the five-year period, 428,000 tons

In the sphere of transport, more than 4,000 kilometers of new trunk railways and branch lines will be built in the five-year period. If to this is added the mileage of railways to be restored, reconstructed, or double-tracked, extended station spurs, and industrial and other special lines, the total length of the railway network will be increased by some 10,000 kilometers. Upward of 10,000 kilometers of highways will be built or rebuilt with capital provided by the Central People's Government in the five-year period, and more than 7,000 kilometers will be opened to traffic. Four hundred thousand tons deadweight of new steamships will be acquired in the five-year period.

In the sphere of agriculture and water conservation, 91 mechanized state farms and 194 tractor stations (both above-norm and below-norm) will be set up in the five-year period. During this period, thirteen big reservoirs will be built. In addition, dredging of waterways and repairing of dikes will involve 1,300 million cubic meters of earth and masonry work, and we will begin the engineering project to harness the Yellow River.

Buildings with a total floor space of about 150 million square meters will be constructed in the five-year period, including factory buildings, housing for factory and office workers, schools, and hospitals.

The industrial construction program is the core of our First Five-Year Plan, and the construction of the 156 industrial projects to be built with Soviet aid is in turn the core of the industrial construction program. Within the period of the First Five-Year Plan, work will have begun on 145 of these 156 projects, while survey and design work will have been carried out on the remaining 11 projects, which will go into construction in the period of the Second Five-Year Plan.

These industrial construction projects are large in scale and new in technique. Many of them are unprecedented in the history of Chinese industry. For example, in the eight-year period between 1953 and 1960, the integrated iron and steel works in Anshan, building on the basis of its original capacity, will complete, in the main, the construction or reconstruction of the following forty-eight major projects: three iron ore mines, eight ore-dressing and sintering plants, six automatic blast furnaces, three modern steel-making plants, sixteen rolling mills, ten batteries of coke ovens, and two heat-resistant material shops. The latest achievements of Soviet technology will be utilized to the fullest possible extent in the building or reconstruction of these plants, mines, and shops. When its reconstruction is completed, this integrated iron and steel works—the biggest of its kind in China—will increase its annual capacity to 2,500,000 tons of pig iron, 3,220,000 tons of steel and 2,480,000 tons of rolled steel. Its output of steel plates, sheets, tubes, and other rolled steel of various specifications will, on the whole, be able to meet the country's requirements for the manufacture of locomotives, steamers, motor vehicles, tractors, etc., during the period of the First Five-Year Plan and the early years of the Second Five-Year Plan. Its annual output of rails of different specifications will be sufficient to lay more than 3,000 kilometers of railways.

Simultaneously with the reconstruction of the integrated iron and steel works in Anshan, construction will go ahead on two new integrated iron and steel works in Wuhan and Paotow. Fifteen thermal power stations, each with a capacity of more than 50,000 kilowatts, are among the power plants to be built in the five-year period. After reconstruction, the Fengman Hydroelectric Power Station will have a capacity of more than 560,000 kilowatts. Completion of these projects will vastly increase the supply of electric power in various regions.

Coal-mining enterprises to be built during the five-year period include thirty-one with a projected annual capacity (counting the original capacity) of more than 1 million tons of coal each. Among these, which include those designed in China, the annual capacity of the five biggest mining enterprises will reach the following levels by 1957: mines under the Fushun Mining Administration, 9,300,000 tons; mines under the Fuhsin Mining Adminstration, 8,450,000 tons; mines under the Kailan Mining Administration, 9,680,000 tons; mines under the Tatung Mining Administration, 6,450,000 tons; and mines under the Huainan Mining Administration, 6,850,000 tons.

The First Motor Works will be completed in the present five-year period. When it reaches projected capacity, it will be able to provide transport with 30,000 trucks a year. The Second Motor Works, with double the capacity of the first, will also begin construction within the period of the First Five-Year Plan. These two plants will lay the foundation for China's automotive industry.

When the tractor plant, which will go into construction in the present five-year period, is completed in the period of the Second Five-Year Plan, China will be able to produce annually 15,000 54-hp. tractors to meet the needs of agriculture.

When the two heavy machinery plants (one designed for us by the Soviet Union and the other by ourselves) that begin construction in the present five-year period are completed, they will be able, according to their projected capacities, to produce every year a complete set of iron-smelting, steel-making, rolling mill, and coke oven equipment for an integrated iron and steel works with an annual capacity of 1,600,000 tons of steel.

When . . . the plants making power-generating equipment to be started in the five-year period are completed, China will be able to manufacture 12,000-, 25,000-, and even 50,000-kilowatt power-generating units to meet the requirements of electric power development in all branches of the national economy.

Many of our light industry plants were designed and built by ourselves, and many of these are of considerable size. The three cotton mills that have been or will be built in our capital, Peking, for instance, will be equipped with 230,000 spindles and more than 7,000 looms. In all, thirty-nine textile mills of considerable size will be built in the five-year period.

Many of these new industrial construction projects are large in scale, and so are many railway, highway, and water conservation projects.

For example, the Lanchow-Sinkiang Railway, which traverses Kansu and Sinkiang Provinces; the Paochi-Chengtu Railway connecting Northwest and Southwest China; the Yingtan-Amoy Railway linking Kiangsi and Fukien Provinces; and the

Chining-Erhlien Railway linking China, the Mongolian People's Republic, and the Soviet Union, which are being built in the present five-year period, not only have a long over-all mileage but also involve stupendous engineering feats in crossing deserts and towering mountain ranges.

The Sikang-Tibet and Chinghai-Tibet highways, construction of which was carried on in the present five-year period, were opened to traffic in 1954 and have a total length of more than 4,300 kilometers. They cut through mountain ranges rising several thousand meters above sea level, where there is scarcely a trace of human habitation. The engineering work involved was particularly difficult and massive in scale.

The project for the complete harnessing of the Huai River, which has been going ahead in the present five-year period, provides for four big reservoirs at Nanwan, Poshan, Futseling, and Meishan. These will be capable of storing more than 3,800 million cubic meters of water. At the same time, flood control and measures to deal with waterlogging will be carried out on the main tributaries of the Huai—the Hungho, Juho, Suiho, and Peifei rivers. The Kuanting Reservoir completed in 1954, with a storage capacity of about 2,300 million cubic meters of water, will play an important role in preventing floods on the lower reaches of the Yungting.

The permanent control of the Yellow River and multiple-purpose development o its resources will begin in the present five-year period. The Yellow River flows for more than 4,800 kilometers through seven provinces, with a drainage area of 745,000 square kilometers. In the past, it has caused more damage than any other river in the country. According to the master plan for its multiple-purpose utilization, dozens of dams will be built on its middle and lower reaches and on its main tributaries. Huge reservoirs capable of regulating its flow and big hydroelectric power stations will be erected at the Sanmen Gorge and four other sites. The work of drawing up the master plan for the permanent control of the Yellow River and multiple-purpose development of its resources will be completed in the period of the First Five-Year Plan, and construction will begin on the river regulation and hydroelectric power installations at the Sanmen Gorge.

Three hundred and seventy-five thousand *mou* of wasteland will be brought under cultivation at the Friendship State Farm, built with direct Soviet assistance. This farm, equipped with large quantities of modern machinery and equipment presented by the Soviet Union, will play an important role as a model farm and pioneering venture in the mechanization of agriculture in China.

It is with direct Soviet aid that China will, in the present five-year period, begin construction for the peaceful utilization of atomic energy in the service of its national economy.

The examples listed so far are sufficient to show that we are now engaged in a great undertaking to build a happy life for the whole nation and generations yet to come. The fulfillment of the tasks of industrial and other construction laid down in our First Five-Year Plan will undoubtedly play a tremendous role in advancing China's socialist industrialization, and so remedy the economic backwardness of our country. This program of socialist economic construction serves the long-term interests, the supreme interests, of the Chinese people as a whole.

During the period of the First Five-Year Plan, China's industrial productive force will be greatly enhanced by bringing into use the unused capacity of existing industrial enterprises as well as by putting new and reconstructed enterprises into operation. By 1957, the proportion of the output of modern industry in the total value of industrial and agricultural output will have risen from 26.7 per cent to 36 per cent.

The gross value of China's industrial output will increase by 98.3 per cent in 1957 compared with 1952, yielding an average increase of 14.7 per cent a year as compared with the year before. The increase in value of modern industrial output will be 104.1 per cent, with an average annual increase of 15.3 per cent. Such a rate of industrial development is obviously fairly rapid. It has never been, nor could . . . be, achieved in capitalist countries.

Markedly increased output of various industrial products will be achieved in the five-year period. The actual output of major items in 1952 and the planned output for 1957 compare as follows:

Steel: 1,350,000 tons to 4,120,000 tons (3.1 times)

Electricity: 7,260 million kilowatt-hours to 15,900 million kilowatt-hours (2.2 times)

Coal: 63,530,000 tons to 113,000,000 tons (1.8 times)

Generators: 30,000 kilowatts to 227,000 kilowatts (7.7 times)

Electric motors: 640,000 kilowatts to 1,050,000 kilowatts (1.6 times)

Trucks: 4,000 (not yet produced in 1952)

Cement: 2,860,000 tons to 6,000,000 tons (2.1 times)

Machine-made paper: 370,000 tons to 650,000 tons (1.8 times)

Cotton-piece goods: 111,630,000 bolts to 163,720,000 bolts (1.5 times)

Machine-processed sugar: 249,000 tons to 686,000 tons (2.8 times) . . .

The First Five-Year plan sets suitable targets for increased agricultural output. In the five-year period, the total value of output of agriculture and subsidiary rural production is to increase by 23.3 per cent, an average rise of 4.3 per cent a year as compared to the year before.

According to the plan, the projected output of staple farm products for 1957 and the expected percentages of increase over 1952 are as follows:

Grain: 385,600 million catties, an increase of 17.6 per cent

Cotton: 32,700,000 *tan,* an increase of 25.4 per cent

Jute and ambary hemp: 7,300,000 *tan,* an increase of 19.7 per cent

Cured tobacco: 7,800,000 *tan,* an increase of 76.6 per cent

Sugar cane: 26,300 million catties, an increase of 85.1 per cent

Sugar beet: 4,270 million catties, an increase of 346.4 per cent

Oil-bearing crops: more than 118 million *mou* will be sown, an increase of 37.8 per cent over the acreage in 1952

One of the vital tasks of the Five-Year Plan is to overcome the excessive lag in the development of agriculture as compared with the development of industry. Under reactionary Kuomintang rule, China's agriculture not only made no headway but, on the contrary, suffered heavy damage. In 1936, grain output was 300,000 million catties. From that time on, it decreased almost every year until 1949, when it fell to only 226,000 million catties. Cotton output fell to 8,800,000 *tan.* After liberation, it took only three years for our country to reach a grain output of 327,800 million catties in 1952 and a cotton output of 626 million *tan,* thus exceeding the highest preliberation annual output in both crops.

The five-year plan for agriculture now provides for further increases over the 1952 base figures quoted above. In view of actual conditions in our country at present, this growth in agriculture cannot be considered too slow, and we should strive our hardest to reach and surpass the targets set.

The agricultural producers' cooperative provides the basis for increasing agricultural output during the period of the First Five-Year Plan; it is also the only path along which the small-peasant economy can undergo socialist transformation. By 1957, about one-third of all the country's peasant households will have joined agricultural producers' cooperatives in their elementary form.

During the period of the First Five-Year Plan, transport, the mails, and telecommunications will be developed in proportion to keep pace with the expansion of industry and agriculture and the growing need for communications facilities. By 1957, railway freight mileage will reach 121,000 million ton-kilometers, or double the 1952 figure; railway passenger mileage will reach 32,000 million passenger-kilometers. or 59.5 per cent above the 1952 figure. Freight mileage of inland shipping will reach 15,300 million ton-kilometers, or 4.2 times that of 1952; passenger mileage of inland shipping will reach 3,400 million passenger-kilometers, a 78.7 per cent rise over 1952. Freight mileage of coastal shipping will reach 5,750 million ton-nautical miles, or 2.9 times the 1952 figure. Passenger mileage of coastal shipping will reach 240 million passenger–nautical miles, a rise of almost 140 per cent. Motor freight mileage will reach 3,200 million ton-kilometers, or 4.7 times as much as in 1952; motor bus passenger mileage will reach 5,700 million passenger-kilometers, or nearly treble the 1952 figure. Freight mileage of civil airlines will reach 8,050,000 ton-kilometers, or 3.3 times as much as in 1952. The total length of postal routes will reach 1.97 million kilometers, an increase of 45.2 per cent over the 1952 figure. There will be some expansion of other postal and telecommunication services.

On the basis of the growth and changes in the proportions of various branches of industry and agriculture indicated above, the total value of retail sales of commodities of all kinds will reach 49,800 million *yuan* in 1957, about 80 per cent more than in 1952. The breakdown figures show that the value of state retail trade will increase by 133.2 per cent, while that of cooperative trade will increase by 239.5 per cent. As the process of socialist transformation develops during the five-year period, more than half of the originally existing private business enterprises will be incorporated into various forms of state-capitalism and cooperative forms of small business organized by petty traders and peddlers. Taken together, the retail turnover of these two latter types of trade and of private commerce will still register a net increase during the five-year period. By 1957, state and cooperative trading operations will account for 54.9 per cent of the volume of all retail trade; various forms of state-capitalism and co-operative forms of small business, 24 per cent; and private commerce, 21.1 per cent.

There will be considerable progress in the fields of culture, education, and scientific research during the five-year period. In 1957, higher educational institutions will enroll 434,000 students, a 127 per cent increase over 1952; senior middle schools will enroll 724,000 students, a 173 per cent increase over 1952; junior middle schools will enroll 3,983,000 students, a 78.6 per cent increase over 1952; primary schools will enroll 60,230,000 pupils, an 18 per cent increase over 1952. More than 70 per cent of the country's school-age children will be attending primary school in 1957.

There will be a considerable expansion of scientific research during the five-year period. Twenty-three new research establishments will be added to the Academia Sinica alone, with 3,400 more research staff members. In the fields of publishing, broadcasting, literature and arts, the cinema, and popular cultural activities, comparatively rapid progress is also planned.

The Five-Year Plan makes appropriate provision for raising the people's material standards of living. In the five-year period, there will be an increase of 4.2 million in the number of employed; there will be a 33 per cent rise in average money-wages for factory and office workers; the funds disbursed by state enterprises and state organs for labor insurance, medical care, welfare services, and cultural and educational facilities for their personnel will total more than 5,000 million *yüan*; 46 million square meters of housing will be built by the state for factory and office workers.

Living standards of the rural population will also be gradually improved in the five years. With the expansion of agricultural output and the increased trend to commodity crop production, the purchasing power of the rural population will be nearly doubled. The state will allocate certain sums for the relief of peasants and other working people stricken by natural calamities to tide them over difficulties in production or livelihood.

Considerable headway will be made in the field of public health during the five-year period. There will be 77 per cent more hospital beds and 74 per cent more doctors. The services of doctors of classical Chinese medicine will be more fully utilized.

OUTLINE OF THE SECOND
FIVE-YEAR PLAN, 1956

[THE Second Five-Year Plan began with greater promise in view of the success of the first plan. The enthusiasm of the planners may be seen in the accelerated rates of growth exhibited by the target figures adopted for 1962. The following extracts are taken from the proposals of the Eighth National Congress of the CPC for the Second Five-Year Plan, which were adopted on September 27, 1956.]

The Second Five-Year Plan must promote our socialist construction by forward-looking and really sound measures, and must complete socialist transformation on the basis of the successful fulfillment of the First Five-Year Plan, so as to ensure that, in approximately three five-year plans, we can, in the main, build up a comprehensive industrial system and transform our backward agricultural country into an advanced socialist industrial country. Hence the principal tasks of the Second Five-Year Plan should be: (1) to continue industrial construction with heavy industry as its core, . . . promote technical reconstruction of the national economy, and build a solid foundation for socialist industrialization; (2) to carry through socialist transformation and consolidate and expand the system of collective ownership and the system of ownership by the whole people; (3) to increase further the production of industry, agriculture, and handicrafts and correspondingly develop transport and commerce on the basis of developing capital construction and carrying through socialist transformation; (4) to make vigorous efforts to train personnel for construction work and strengthen scientific research to meet the needs of the development of socialist economy and culture; and (5) to reinforce the national defenses and raise the level of the people's material and cultural life on the basis of increased industrial and agricultural production.

In order to guarantee fulfillment of these principal tasks, it is proposed that in drawing up the Second Five-Year Plan the following principles and measures be adopted in regard to development and transformation of the national economy.

1. In view of the domestic and international situation and the general trend of current events, it is necessary as well as possible to continue to maintain a fairly rapid rate in the development of our national economy during the Second Five-Year Plan period. As provided for in the First Five-Year Plan, 1957 will see an increase of 51.1 per cent in the total value of industrial and agricultural output (here and below, including that of modern industries, handicrafts, and agriculture), as compared with 1952, but this increase, it is estimated, may in actual practice be more than 60 per

Source: Supplement to New China News Agency Release, September 28, 1956, pp. 10–20.

cent. In the Second Five-Year Plan period, as newly built enterprises and enterprises undergoing reconstruction are brought successively into operation, as the productive potentialities of existing enterprises are further developed, as the productive potentialities of the equipment of private industrial enterprises are brought into play after they have come under joint state-private management or state ownership, and as the productive forces of agriculture and handicrafts are further developed after being organized into cooperatives, it is required that the total value of industrial and agricultural output in 1962 show an increase of about 75 per cent as compared with 1957 (here and below, this refers to the targets of the annual plan for 1957 set by the First Five-Year Plan). The value of industrial output (here and below, including modern industry and handicrafts) will be about double the planned figure for 1957, and that of agricultural output will increase by about 35 per cent. The rates of growth of industrial and agricultural output stated above appear to be somewhat high, because they are compared with the planned targets set by the First Five-Year Plan, and no account is taken of the possibility that those targets will be overfulfilled. If comparison is made with the actual achievements of the First Five-Year Plan, then the rates of growth laid down in the Second Five-Year Plan will, as stated above, be relatively lower.

Our First Five-Year Plan provides that in 1957, the capital goods industry will account for 38 per cent of the value of industrial output, while the consumer goods industry will account for 62 per cent; but it is expected that the share of the capital goods industry may actually exceed 40 per cent. In the Second Five-Year Plan period the rate of increase in the value of industrial output will still be faster in the capital goods industry than in the consumer goods industry. It is required that by 1962 the capital goods industry and the consumer goods industry will each be increased about 50 per cent.

2. Because of the growth of industrial and agricultural output, the increase in labor productivity, and the practice of strict economy in various branches of the national economy, it is possible to increase the national income in 1962 by about 50 per cent as compared with 1957. During the Second Five-Year Plan period, we should maintain in the distribution of the national income a correct proportion between consumption and accumulation, and the part that goes to accumulation may slightly exceed that of the first five-year period so as to speed up socialist construction and ensure gradual improvement of the people's livelihood.

With the increase of national income and the growth in the proportion of state-owned economy in the national income, state revenue will show a considerable increase during the Second Five-Year Plan period, as compared with the First. Expenditure must correspond to revenue, so that a balance is maintained, while certain reserves are set aside to meet any unforeseen difficulties. At the same time, funds for extending credits should be suitably increased to ensure a balance between credit receipts and payments.

During the Second Five-Year Plan period, while strengthening our national defenses and increasing administrative efficiency, we should as far as possible reduce national defense and administrative expenditures and increase expenditures on economic construction and cultural development so as to ensure the rapid advance of socialist construction. Under the First Five-Year Plan, about 56 per cent of total expenditure goes to economic construction and cultural development. This figure should be raised to between 60 and 70 per cent under the Second Five-Year Plan, while expenditure on national defenses and administration should be reduced from about 32 per cent of total expenditure under the First Five-Year Plan to about 20 per cent under the Second. The rest of expenditure will be allocated for the state's material reserves, for credit funds, repayments of domestic and foreign debts and general reserve funds.

On the basis of a bigger revenue, the proportion of state investments in capital construction during the Second Five-Year Plan period can be raised from about 35 per cent of all state expenditure in the first five-year period to about 40 per cent so as to speed up socialist construction. Thus, state investments in capital construction in the second five-year period may be about double what they are in the first. In order to ensure a rapid development of industry and agriculture—the two principal branches of the national economy—the proportion of capital construction investments in industry by the state should be raised from 58.2 per cent under the First Five-Year Plan to about 60 per cent under the Second; the share going to agriculture, forestry, and water conservation should increase from 7.6 per cent to about 10 per cent.

3. The central task of our Second Five-Year Plan is still to give priority to the development of heavy industry. This is the chief index of our country's socialist industrialization, because heavy industry provides the basis for a strong economy and national defense, as well as the basis for the technical reconstruction of our national economy.

It is required that the output of the main products of heavy industry reach approximately the following levels in 1962:

Product	Target for 1962	Target for 1957	Actual Output in 1952	Peak Annual Output Before Liberation	
				Year	Output
Electric power (billion kwh.)	40–43	15.9	7.26	1941	5.96
Coal (million tons)	190–210	112.985	63.528	1942	61.875
Crude oil (million tons)	5–6	2.012	.436	1943	.32
Steel (million tons)	10.5–12	4.12	1.35	1943	.923
Aluminum ingots (thousand tons)	100–120	20.0	—	—	—
Chemical fertilizers (million tons)	3–3.2	.578	.194	1941	.227
Metallurgical equipment (thousand tons)	30–40	8.0	—	—	—
Power-generating equipment (million kw.)	1.4–1.5	.164	.0067	—	—
Metal-cutting machine tools (thousand units)	60–65	13.0	14.0	1941	5.0
Timber (million cubic meters	31–34	20.0	10.02	—	—
Cement (million tons)	12.5–14.5	6.0	2.86	1942	2.293

In the Second Five-Year Plan period, we must make vigorous efforts to expand the machine-building industry, particularly that making industrial equipment, and continue to expand the metallurgical industry to meet the needs of national construction. At the same time, we should also energetically develop the electric power, coal-mining, and building materials industries and strengthen the backward branches of industry—the oil, chemical, and radio equipment industries. We should press ahead vigorously with the establishment of industries utilizing atomic energy for peaceful purposes.

No effort should be spared in this five-year period in strengthening the weak links in our industry and in opening up new fields, such as the manufacture of various kinds of heavy equipment, machine tools for special purposes, and precision machine tools and instruments; the production of high-grade alloy steels; the cold working of steel products; the mining and refining of rare metals; . . . the setting up of an organic synthetic chemical industry; and so forth. At the same time, we should also pay attention to multiple-purpose utilization of resources, particularly the over-all use of the associated nonferrous metals.

4. While giving priority to the development of heavy industry, we should suitably speed up the growth of light industry on the basis of a higher level of agricultural development, so as to meet the growing needs of the broad mass of the people for consumer goods and contribute to the state's accumulation of funds.

It is required that output of the main light industry products reach approximately the following levels in 1962:

Product	Target for 1962	Target for 1957	Actual Output in 1952	Peak Annual Output Before Liberation	
				Year	Output
Cotton yarn (million bales)	8–9	5.0	3.618	1933	2.447
Cotton piece goods (million bolts)	235–260	163.721	111.634	—	—
Salt (million tons)	10–11	7.554	4.945	1943	3.918
Edible vegetable oils (million tons)	3.1–3.2	1.794	.933	—	—
Sugar, incl. [hand-refined] (million tons)	2.4–2.5	1.1	.451	1936	.414
Machine-made paper (million tons)	1.5–1.6	.655	.372	1943	.165

In the Second Five-Year Plan period, in all . . . branches of light industry . . . needed by society and which have an adequate supply of raw materials, the productive potentialities of the existing equipment should be brought into full play; the proportion of investments in light industry should be suitably increased; and new construction should be undertaken according to needs and possibilities, so as to increase further the production of light industry goods. Efforts should be made to produce a greater variety of light industry goods, improve quality, and reduce costs, so as to produce low-priced, high-quality goods.

In order to increase the output of light industry products, efforts should be made by industrial enterprises under local authorities to make greater use of local resources and waste materials to produce more consumer goods of all kinds suited to the needs of the local population; the various areas, furthermore, should organize mutual exchange of products. We should continue to develop the handicraft industries on the basis of the cooperative system so as to satisfy the many-sided needs of the people.

5. During the Second Five-Year Plan period, we must continue to establish, or energetically prepare to establish, new industrial bases in the interior taking into account local resources as well as the principle of rationally distributing our productive forces in order gradually to achieve a balanced development of our economy throughout the country. In carrying on large-scale industrial construction in the interior, we must, however, at the same time make vigorous efforts to make full use of and suitably develop the existing industries in the coastal areas. This is not only to meet the growing needs of the state and the people, but also to support construction work in the interior. In capital construction for industry, attention should be paid to coordination among large, medium, and small-sized enterprises and to their proper dispersion geographically.

In these five years, we should continue the construction of the industrial bases in Northeast China, Central China, and Inner Mongolia with the iron and steel industry as their core; start the construction of new industrial bases in Southwest China, Northwest China, and the area around the Sanmen Gorge, with iron and steel industry and hydroelectric power stations as their core; carry on with the building of oil and nonferrous metal industries in Sinkiang; make energetic efforts to utilize the existing industrial bases in East China; bring into full play the role in industry of North and South China; and intensify geological prospecting in Tibet in order to prepare the way for its industrial development.

To ensure the completion of the above-mentioned construction projects, we must further expand and improve our geological work so as to collect all the data that economic construction needs concerning mineral deposits and geologic conditions; speed up the training of designers; and reinforce the ranks of builders and installation workers. At the same time, we should improve urban construction in accordance with the needs of industrial development.

6. We must make vigorous efforts to promote agricultural production so that agriculture and industry are developed in a coordinated way and . . . the needs of the state and the people are satisfied.

During the Second Five-Year Plan period, an increase in the output of grain should be ensured in the first place so as to propel the development of agriculture as a whole. At the same time, increased production of major industrial crops, especially cotton and soybeans, should be ensured so as to propel the development of light industry. In developing agriculture, we should encourage a diversified rural economy and bring about a considerable expansion of livestock-breeding, forestry, fisheries, and subsidiary cottage occupations so as to ensure an increase in the peasants' income and raise the living standards of the people.

It is required that the output of staple agricultural products reach approximately the following levels in 1962:

Product	Target for 1962 (ca.)	Total Output in 2d 5 yrs. (ca.)	Target for 1957	Actual Output in 1952	Peak Annual Output Before Liberation	
					Year	Output
Grain (billion catties	500	2,200	363.18	308.79	1936	277.39
Cotton (million (tan)	48	210	32.7	26.074	1936	16.976
Soybeans (billion catties)	25	110	22.44	19.04	1936	22.61

We must try our best to overfulfil the targets for the staple farm products listed above and take effective measures to ensure increased output of other oil-bearing crops and sugar crops. We must make efforts to increase the output of natural silk, tea, tobacco, jute and ambary hemp, fruits, and medicinal herbs. In the vicinity of cities and industrial and mining districts, the growing of more vegetables and increased production of other nonstaple foods to supply their needs should be regarded as an important task.

It is required that the number of the main kinds of livestock reach approximately the following targets in 1962 (in millions of head):

	Target for 1962 (*ca.*)	Target for 1957	Actual No. in 1952	Peak Number Before Liberation	
				Year	No.
Cattle	90	73.61	56.6	1935	48.268
Horses	11	8.34	6.13	1935	6.485
Sheep and goats	170	113.04	61.78	1937	62.52
Pigs	250	138.34	89.77	1934	78.53

Attention should be paid to promoting pig-breeding so as to increase supplies of meat and manure. In addition, intensive breeding of chickens, ducks, geese, rabbits, and other poultry and domestic animals should be undertaken. As the targets for the production of soybeans, and oil-bearing crops and the breeding of livestock were not fulfilled in the first few years of the First Five-Year Plan, effective measures must be adopted in the Second Five-Year Plan period to remedy this state of affairs. In conformity with the needs of the state and the people, and taking into account natural conditions in different areas, we should arrange the proportions of grains and various industrial crops as suited to the various localities and appropriately organize livestock-breeding and subsidiary agricultural occupations in order to ensure a well-coordinated development of the various branches of agriculture.

Agricultural producers' cooperatives should, in conformity with the Model Regulations for Advanced Agricultural Producers' Cooperatives and with the principle that cooperatives must be run industriously, thriftily, and democratically, check over and consolidate their organizations, train and promote various types of cadres, and strengthen management and the organization of production. On the principle of taking care of both the needs of the state and the welfare of the peasants, reasonable proportions should be worked out for distributing income as between the collective and the individual members. Where the collective work of the cooperatives is not affected, appropriate arrangements should be made to allow members the necessary time off to work in their own individual interests; they should be allowed to engage in various subsidiary agricultural occupations that are best undertaken by the peasants individually so as to further encourage their initiative in production and promote the development of agricultural and subsidiary production. In order to prevent difficulties arising in management and the organization of production that may adversely affect agricultural production, care should be taken to see that, as agricultural producers' cooperatives develop, they are not recklessly merged into large units. . . .

ON CLASS DIFFERENTIATION IN
THE COUNTRYSIDE, 1933 AND 1948

[THE differentiation of classes in the countryside and in conjunction with 'land reform' was carried out after 1949 in accordance with two documents that were first issued by the 'Democratic Central Government' in Juichin, Kiangsi, in 1933 and reissued by the CCP Central Committee in May, 1948. The two documents, to which were added a number of Supplementary Decisions Adopted by the Government Administration Council, were (1) *How to Analyze Class Status in the Countryside* and (2) *Decisions Concerning Some Problems Arising from Agrarian Reform.*

The following excerpts are taken from the two documents, respectively. They serve to demonstrate the basic nature of the differentiation process and the criteria employed. Additional complexities are contained in the illustrations given in the documents.]

FROM DOCUMENT (1)

1. Landlord

A person shall be classified as a landlord who owns land but does not engage in labor or only engages in supplementary labor, and who depends on exploitation for his means of livelihood. Exploitation by the landlords is chiefly in the form of land rent, plus moneylending, hiring of labor, or the simultaneous carrying on of industrial or commercial enterprises. But the major form of exploitation of the peasants by the landlords is the exacting of land rent from the peasants. The management of landholdings owned by public bodies and the collection of rent from school land also belong to the category of exploitation in the form of land rent. . . .

Warlords, bureaucrats, local despots, and villainous gentry are the political representatives of the landlord class and are exceptionally cruel and wicked elements among the landlords. (Among the rich peasants there are also small local despots and villainous gentry.)

Any person who collects rent and manages the landed property for landlords and depends on the exploitation of peasants by the landlords as his main means of livelihood, and whose living conditions are better than those of an ordinary middle peasant, shall be treated in the same manner as a landlord. . . .

2. Rich Peasant

A rich peasant generally owns land. But there are also rich peasants who own only part of the land they cultivate and rent the rest from others. There are others who

Source: *The Agrarian Reform Law of the People's Republic of China* (Peking: Foreign Languages Press, 1st ed., 1951; 2d ed., 1952), pp. 17–61.

own no land but rent all their land from others. Generally speaking, they own better means of production and some floating capital and take part in labor themselves but are as a rule dependent on exploitation for a part or the major part of their means of livelihood. Exploitation by rich peasants is chiefly in the form of exploiting wage labor (hiring long-term laborers). In addition, they may also let out part of their land for rent, or lend money, or operate industrial or commercial enterprises. Most of the rich peasants also manage the landholdings owned by public bodies. Some own a considerable amount of fertile land, engage in labor themselves, and do not hire any laborers. But they exploit the peasants in the form of land rent and loan interest. In such cases, they should be treated in the same manner as rich peasants. Exploitation by the rich peasants is of a constant character, and in many cases the income from such exploitation constitutes their main means of livelihood. . . .

3. Middle Peasant

Many middle peasants own land. Some possess only a portion of the land . . . they cultivate, while the remainder is rented. Some of them are landless and rent all their land from others. The middle peasants own a certain number of farm implements. The middle peasants depend wholly or mainly upon their own labor for their living. In general, they do not exploit others. Many of them are themselves exploited on a small scale by others in the form of land rent and loan interest. But generally they do not sell their labor power. Some of the middle peasants (the well-to-do middle peasants) practice a small degree of exploitation, but such exploitation is not of a constant character, and the income therefrom does not constitute their main means of livelihood. These people shall be classified as middle peasants.

4. Poor Peasant

Some poor peasants own inadequate farm implements and a part of the land they cultivate. Some have no land at all and own only some inadequate farm implements. In general they have to rent land for cultivation and are exploited by others in the form of land rent, loan interest, or hired labor in a limited degree. These people shall be classified as poor peasants.

In general, the middle peasants need not sell their labor power, but the poor peasants have to sell their labor power for limited periods. This is the basic criterion for differentiating middle peasants from poor peasants.

5. Worker

Workers (including farm laborers) generally have neither land nor farm implements. Some of them have a very small amount of land and very few implements. They depend wholly or mainly upon the sale of their labor power for their living. These people shall be classified as workers. . . .

FROM DOCUMENT (2)

2. Well-to-do Middle Peasant

Well-to-do middle peasants are part of the middle peasants. Their living conditions are better than those of the ordinary middle peasants and in general they practice a small degree of exploitation. The amount of income from such exploitation should not exceed 15 per cent of the total annual income of the whole family.

Under certain circumstances, although the income of a middle peasant from exploitation exceeds 15 per cent, but is not more than 30 per cent, of the total annual income of the whole family, he shall still be treated as a well-to-do middle peasant, if the masses have no objection. . . .

8. Intellectual

The intelligentsia should not be considered as a class in itself. The class origin of intellectuals is to be determined according to the status of their families. The class status of the intellectuals themselves is to be determined in accordance with the means they employ to earn the major part of their income.

All intellectuals who come of the landlord or capitalist class should be fully employed in work for the democratic government, provided they obey the laws of the democratic government, and they should be educated to overcome their erroneous ideas of looking down upon the laboring people. . . .

11. The Red Army Man of Landlord or Rich Peasant Origin and His Land

All Red Army men of landlord or rich peasant origin (be they commanders or fighters) and their dependents shall have the right to share in the distributions of land, provided they fight determinedly for the interest of the workers and peasants. . . .

12. Worker from Rich Peasant or Landlord Family

Workers of rich peasant or landlord origin, their wives, and their children shall retain their status as workers. The other members of their families shall be treated as landlords or rich peasants in status. . . .

13. The Class Status of Landlord, Rich Peasant, or Capitalist After Marriage with Worker, Peasant, or Poor Odd-jobber, and Vice Versa

1. The class status of landlords, rich peasants, or capitalists after their marriage with workers, peasants, or poor odd-jobbers, and vice versa, should be determined in accordance with their original class status, their living conditions after the marriage, and whether the marriage took place before or after the Liberation.

2. In cases where marriages took place before the Liberation: The women from the families of landlords, rich peasants, or capitalists who married workers, peasants, or poor odd-jobbers and have been engaged in labor as their major means of livelihood for a year shall be recognized as having the class status of workers, peasants, or poor odd-jobbers. Those who have not been engaged in labor or have been engaged in labor for less than a year shall retain their original class status.

The women from the families of workers, peasants, or poor odd-jobbers who married landlords, rich peasants, or capitalists and have lived the same life with them for three years shall be recognized as having the class status of landlords, rich peasants, or capitalists. Those who have not lived the same life as the landlords, rich peasants, or capitalists (that is, depending on their own labor as their main means of livelihood) or who have lived the same life as the landlords, rich peasants, or capitalists for less than three years, shall retain their original class status.

3. In cases where marriage took place after the Liberation: The women from the families of workers, peasants, or poor odd-jobbers who married landlords, rich peasants, or capitalists should retain their original class status. Those from the families of landlords, rich peasants, or capitalists who married workers, peasants, or poor odd-jobbers and have been engaged in labor and have depended on it as their major means of livelihood for a year shall be recognized as having the class status of workers, peasants, or poor odd-jobbers. Those who have not been engaged in labor or have been engaged in labor for less than a year shall retain their original class status.

4. The foregoing three articles apply to the children of workers, peasants, or poor odd-jobbers who were sold to landlords, rich peasants, or capitalists before the Liberation and to the sons of workers, peasants, or poor odd-jobbers who were adopted before the Liberation as sons-in-law by landlords, rich peasants, or capitalists, and vice versa.

5. As regards the adoption of the sons of workers, peasants, or poor odd-jobbers by landlords, rich peasants, or capitalists, or vice versa, which took place before the Liberation, if the sons of workers, peasants, or poor odd-jobbers were adopted by landlords, rich peasants, or capitalists as sons and have lived the same life as the

step-parents for five years, they should have the same class status as the step-parents. If they have not lived the same life as their step-parents but have continued to live the same life as their own parents, they shall retain their own class status. If the sons of landlords, rich peasants, or capitalists were adopted by workers, peasants, or poor odd-jobbers as sons and have lived the same life as their step-parents and have been engaged in labor for a year, they shall have the same class status as their step-parents. If they have not been engaged in labor, and have not lived the same life as their step-parents but have continued to live the same life as their own parents, they shall retain their original class status.

THE FIVE PRINCIPLES OF
'PEACEFUL COEXISTENCE,' 1955

[THE following passages are taken from Chou En-lai's speech at the Plenary Session of the Asian-African Solidarity Conference at Bandung on April 19, 1955. The speech was a calculated outright bid for leadership among the Afro-Asian nations.]

. . . The peoples of Asia and Africa have long suffered from aggression and war. Many of them have been forced by the colonialists to serve as cannon fodder in aggressive wars. Therefore, the peoples of these two continents can have nothing but strong detestation of aggressive war. They know that new threats of war will not only endanger the independent development of their countries but also intensify the enslavement by colonialism. That is why the Asian and African peoples all the more hold dear world peace and national independence. . . .

The majority of our Asian and African countries, including China, are still very backward economically, owing to the long period of colonial domination. That is why we demand not only political independence but economic independence as well. Of course, our demand for political independence does not mean a policy of exclusion toward countries outside of the Asian-African region. However, the days when the Western powers controlled our destiny are already past. The destiny of Asian and African countries should be taken into the hands of the peoples themselves. We strive to realize our own economic independence; nor does that mean the rejection of economic cooperation with any country outside of the Asian-African region. However, we want to do away with the exploitation of backward countries in the East by the colonial powers in the West and to develop the independent and sovereign economy of our own countries. Complete independence is an objective for which the great majority of Asian and African countries have to struggle for a long time. . . .

The Asian and African countries, opposing colonialism and defending national independence, treasure all the more their own national rights. Countries, whether big or small, strong or weak, should all enjoy equal rights in international relations. Their territorial integrity and sovereignty should be respected and not violated. The people of all dependent countries should enjoy the right of national self-determination and should not be subjected to persecution and slaughter. People, irrespective of race or color, should all enjoy the fundamental human rights and not be subjected to any maltreatment and discrimination. However, we cannot help being aware that the peoples of Tunisia, Morocco, and Algeria, and other dependent peoples who have been fighting for independence have never ceased to be suppressed with violence.

Source: China and the Asian-African Conference (Peking: Foreign Languages Press, 1955), pp. 9–20.

Racial discrimination and persecution under racialism in the Union of South Africa and other places have not yet been curbed. The problem of the Arab refugees of Palestine still remains to be solved.

One should say that now the common desire of the awakened countries and peoples of Asia and Africa is to oppose racial discrimination and to demand fundamental human rights, to oppose colonialism and to demand . . . national independence, to firmly defend their own territorial integrity and sovereignty. The struggle of the Egyptian people for the restoration of their sovereignty over the Suez Canal Zone, the struggle of the Iranian people for the restoration of sovereignty over their petroleum resources, and the demand for the restoration of the territorial rights of India over Goa and of Indonesia over West Irian have all won sympathy from many countries in Asia and Africa. China's will to liberate its own territory of Taiwan has likewise won the support of all righteous people in the Asian-African region. This proves that the peoples of our Asian and African countries understand each other and have sympathy and concern for one another. . . .

By following the principles of mutual respect for sovereignty and territorial integrity, nonaggression, noninterference in each other's internal affairs, equality, and mutual benefit, the peaceful coexistence of countries with different social systems can be realized. When these principles are assured of implementation, there is no reason why international disputes cannot be settled through negotiation. . . .

India, Burma, and China have affirmed the five principles of peaceful coexistence as the guiding principles in their mutual relations. These principles have received support from more and more countries. Following these principles, China and Indonesia have already achieved good results in their preliminary talks on the question of the nationality of the citizens of one country residing in the other. During the Geneva Conference, China also expressed its readiness to develop friendly relations with the Indochinese states on the basis of these five principles. There is no reason why the relations between China and Thailand, the Philippines, and other neighboring countries cannot be improved on the basis of these five principles. China is ready to establish normal relations with other Asian and African countries on the basis of strict adherence to these principles and is willing to promote the normalization of relations between China and Japan. . . .

LIN PIAO ON PEOPLE'S WAR, 1965

[THIS address by Lin Piao, China's Minister of Defense, was delivered in commemoration of the twentieth anniversary of victory over Japan in World War II.]

. . . In order to make a revolution and to fight a people's war and be victorious, it is imperative to adhere to the policy of self-reliance, to rely on the strength of the masses in one's own country, and to prepare to carry on the fight independently even when all material aid from outside is cut off. If one does not operate by one's own efforts, does not independently ponder and solve the problems of the revolution in one's own country, and does not rely on the strength of the masses but leans wholly on foreign aid—even though this be aid from socialist countries that persist in revolution—no victory can be won or be consolidated even if it is won. . . .

It must be emphasized that Comrade Mao Tse-tung's theory of the establishment of rural revolutionary base areas and the encirclement of the cities from the countryside is of outstanding and universal practical importance for the present revolutionary struggles of all the oppressed nations and peoples, and particularly for the revolutionary struggles of the oppressed nations and peoples in Asia, Africa, and Latin America against imperialism and its lackeys.

Many countries and peoples in Asia, Africa, and Latin America are now being subjected to aggression and enslavement on a serious scale by the imperialists, headed by the United States, and their lackeys. The basic political and economic conditions in many of these countries have many similarities to those that prevailed in old China. As in China, the peasant question is extremely important in these regions. The peasants constitute the main force of the national-democratic revolution against the imperialists and their lackeys. In committing aggression against these countries, the imperialists usually begin by seizing the big cities and the main lines of communication, but they are unable to bring the vast countryside completely under their control. The countryside, and the countryside alone, can provide the broad areas in which the revolutionaries can maneuver freely. The countryside, and the countryside alone, can provide the revolutionary bases from which the revolutionaries can go forward to final victory. Precisely for this reason, Comrade Mao Tse-tung's theory of establishing revolutionary base areas in the rural districts and encircling the cities from the countryside is attracting more and more attention among the people in these regions.

Taking the entire globe, if North America and Western Europe can be called 'the cities of the world,' then Asia, Africa, and Latin America constitute 'the rural areas of the world.' Since World War II, the proletarian revolutionary movement has for various reasons been temporarily held back in the North American and West Euro-

Source: Lin Piao, *Long Live the Victory of People's War!* (Peking: Foreign Languages Press, 1965), pp. 41–42, 47–49.

pean capitalist countries, while the people's revolutionary movement in Asia, Africa, and Latin America has been growing vigorously. In a sense, the contemporary world revolution also presents a picture of the encirclement of cities by the rural areas. In the final analysis, the whole cause of world revolution hinges on the revolutionary struggles of the Asian, African, and Latin American peoples, who make up the overwhelming majority of the world's population. The socialist countries should regard it as their internationalist duty to support the people's revolutionary struggles in Asia, Africa, and Latin America. . . .

ON MAO TSE-TUNG'S VIEWS OF THE WORLD DURING THE CULTURAL REVOLUTION, 1966

[MAO's idea of the Cultural Revolution as a means of rejuvenating the CCP and of maintaining a continuing revolution as a mode of social progress is expressed in the communiqué of the Eleventh Plenum of the Eighth Central Committee, which met August 1–12, 1966. The same communiqué, excerpted below, also summarizes Mao's view of the world in which the conspiracy between 'Soviet revisionism' and 'U.S. imperialism' is perceived to play a dominant role.]

The plenary session stresses that the series of directives by Comrade Mao Tse-tung concerning the Great Proletarian Cultural Revolution are the guide for action in the present Cultural Revolution of our country; they constitute an important development of Marxism-Leninism.

The plenary session holds that the key to the success of this Great Cultural Revolution is to have faith in the masses, rely on them, boldly arouse them, and respect their initiative. It is therefore imperative to persevere in the line of 'from the masses and to the masses.' Be pupils of the masses before becoming their teachers. Dare to make revolution and be good at making revolution. Don't be afraid of disorder. Oppose the making of the bourgeois stand, the shielding of rightists, the attack of the left, and repression of the Great Proletarian Cultural Revolution. Oppose the creation of a lot of restrictions to tie the hands of the masses. Don't be overlords or stand above the masses, blindly ordering them about. . . .

The plenary session maintains that to oppose imperialism, it is imperative to oppose modern revisionism. There is no middle road whatsoever in the struggle between Marxism-Leninism and modern revisionism. A clear line of demarcation must be drawn in dealing with the modern revisionist groups, with the leadership of the CPSU as the center, and it is imperative resolutely to expose their true features as scabs. It is impossible to have 'united action' with them.

The plenary session points out that proletarian internationalism is the supreme principle guiding China's foreign policy. The session warmly supports the just struggle of the Asian, African, and Latin American peoples against imperialism headed by the United States and its stooges and also supports the revolutionary struggles of the people of all countries.

The plenary session most strongly condemns U.S. imperialism for its crime of widening its war of aggression against Vietnam. The session most warmly and most

---

Source: NCNA, August 13, 1966, translation by Union Research Institute, *CCP Documents of the Great Proletarian Cultural Revolution, 1966–1967* (Hong Kong, 1968).

resolutely supports the 'Appeal to the People of the Whole Country' issued by Comrade Ho Chi Minh, president of the Democratic Republic of Vietnam, and firmly supports the Vietnamese people in fighting to the end until final victory is achieved in their war against U.S. aggression and for national salvation. The plenary session fully agrees to all the measures already taken and all actions to be taken as decided upon by the Central Committee of the Party and the Government in consultation with the Vietnamese side concerning aid to Vietnam for resisting U.S. aggression.

The plenary session severely denounces the Soviet revisionist leading group for its counterrevolutionary two-faced policy of sham support but real betrayal on the question of Vietnam's resistance to U.S. aggression.

The plenary session holds that U.S. imperialism is the most ferocious common enemy of the peoples of the whole world. In order to isolate U.S. imperialism to the maximum and deal blows to it, the broadest possible international united front must be established against U.S. imperialism and its lackeys. The Soviet revisionist leading group is pursuing a policy of Soviet–U.S. collaboration for world domination and has been conducting schismatic, disruptive, and subversive activities within the international communist movement and the national liberation movement in the active service of U.S. imperialism. They cannot, of course, be included in this united front.

We must unite with all the people in the world who are against imperialism and colonialism, and carry the struggle against U.S. imperialism and its lackeys through to the end. . . .

Part Three
DATA

1. NATIONAL CONGRESSES OF THE CHINESE COMMUNIST PARTY

Congress	Date	Location	No. of Delegates	Party Membership
First	July 1–5, 1921	Shanghai	12	57
Second	July, 1922	Shanghai	12	123
Third	June, 1923	Canton	27	432
Fourth	January, 1925	Shanghai	20	950
Fifth	April 27, 1927	Wuhan	80	57,900
Special Congress	August 7, 1927	Chuchiang	—	—
Sixth	June, 1928	Moscow	84	40,000
Seventh	April 23–June 11, 1945	Yenan	547 reg. 208 alt.	1,210,000
Eighth	September, 1956	Peking	1,026 reg. 107 alt.	10,700,000
Ninth	April 1–24, 1969	Peking	1,512	—

Sources: 1967 Fei-ch'ing Nien-pao (Yearbook on Communist China, 1967) (Taipei: Institute for the Study of Communist Chinese Problems, May, 1967), pp. 564–67, and *Peking Review*, Vol. 12. (1969), Nos. 14 and 17.

2. PLENUMS OF THE EIGHTH CENTRAL COMMITTEE OF THE CHINESE COMMUNIST PARTY

Central Committee Plenum	Date	Location
First	September 16–27, 1956	Peking
Second	November, 1956	Peking
Third (enlarged)	September, 1957	Peking
Fourth	May, 1958	Peking
Fifth	May, 1958	Peking
Sixth (enlarged)	November, 1958	Wuch'ang
Seventh	April, 1959	Shanghai
Eighth	August 2–16, 1959	Lushan
Ninth	January 14–18, 1961	Peking
Tenth	September 24–27, 1962	Peking
Eleventh	August 1–12, 1966	Peking
Twelfth	October 13–31, 1968	Peking

Sources: 1957 Fei-ch'ing Nien-pao (Yearbook on Communist China, 1967) (Taipei: Institute for the Study of Chinese Communist Problems, May, 1967), pp. 567–68; *Jen-min Jih-pao* (November 2, 1968), p. 2.

3. A CHRONOLOGY OF THE DEVELOPMENT OF THE CENTRAL GOVERNMENT STRUCTURE

(Dates established are shown in parentheses.)

A. 1949–53

1. Political and Legal Commission
    Ministry of Internal Affairs (1949)
    Ministry of Public Security (1949)
    Ministry of Justice (1949)
    Nationalities Affairs Committee (1949)
    Committee on Codification (1949)
    Ministry of Personnel (September, 1950)
    Bureau of North China Affairs (September, 1950)[1]
2. Economic and Financial Commission
    Ministry of Finance (1949)
    Ministry of Trade (1949)[2]
    Ministry of Heavy Industry (1949)
    Ministry of Fuel Industry (1949)
    Ministry of Textile Industry (1949)
    Ministry of Food Industry (1949)[3]
    Ministry of Light Industry (1949)
    Ministry of Railways (1949)
    Ministry of Posts and Telecommunications (1949)
    Ministry of Communications (1949)
    Ministry of Agriculture (1949)
    Ministry of Labor (1949)
    Ministry of Forestry and Land Reclamation (1949)[4]
    Ministry of Water Conservation (1949)
    People's Bank of China (1949)
    Customs Administration (1949)[5]
    Ministry of Foreign Trade (August, 1952)
    Ministry of Commerce (August, 1952)
    Ministry of Building and Civil Engineering (1952)
    Ministry of Geology (1952)
    Ministry of Food (1952)
    First Ministry of Machine-Building (1952)
    Second Ministry of Machine-Building (1952)
3. Cultural and Educational Commission
    Ministry of Cultural Affairs (1949)
    Ministry of Education (1949)
    Ministry of Public Health (1949)
    Academy of Sciences (1949)
    Directorate of Information (1949)[6]

Publications Administration (1949)
Commission on Physical Education (November, 1952)
Commission on Elimination of Illiteracy (1952)
Ministry of Higher Education (1952)
4. People's Supervisory Commission
5. Directly Under the Government Council
   Commission on Overseas Chinese Affairs (1949)
   Ministry of Foreign Affairs (1949)
   Directorate of Intelligence (1949)[6]
   Statistical Department (1949)[7]
   State Planning Commission (November, 1952)

B. 1954-58
   1. First Office (Political and Legal Affairs)
      Ministry of Internal Affairs (1949)
      Ministry of Public Security (1949)
      Ministry of Justice (1949)
      Nationalities Affairs Committee (1949)
      Ministry of Control (1954)
   2. Second Office (Cultural and Educational Affairs)
      Ministry of Cultural Affairs (1949)
      Ministry of Education (1949)
      Ministry of Public Health (1949)
      Bureau of Radio Broadcasting (1951)
      New China News Agency (1951)
      Ministry of Higher Education (1952)[8]
   3. Third Office (Heavy Industry)
      Ministry of Heavy Industry (1949)[9]
      Ministry of Fuel Industry (1949)[10]
      First Ministry of Machine-Building (1952)
      Second Ministry of Machine-Building (1952)[11]
      Ministry of Geology (1952)
      Ministry of Building and Civil Engineering (1952)[12]
      Ministry of Coal (July, 1955)
      Third Ministry of Machine-Building (April, 1955)[13]
      Ministry of Electric Power Industry (July, 1955)[14]
      Ministry of Petroleum (July, 1955)
      Ministry of Building Materials (May, 1956)[12]
      Ministry of Metallurgy (May, 1956)
      Ministry of Chemical Industry (May, 1956)
      Ministry of Electrical Equipment Manufacturing (May, 1956)[11]
      Ministry of Urban Construction (May, 1956)[12]
   4. Fourth Office (Light Industry)
      Ministry of Textile Industry (1949)
      Ministry of Light Industry (1949)
      Ministry of Labor (1949)
      Ministry of Local Machine Industry (1954)[9]
      Ministry of Food Industry (1956)[15]
      Bureau of Handicraft Industry Administration[16]
   5. Fifth Office (Finance and Trade)
      Ministry of Finance (1949)
      People's Bank of China (1949)
      Ministry of Food (1952)
      Ministry of Commerce (1952)[17]

Ministry of Foreign Trade (1952)
Ministry of Agricultural Products Purchase (July, 1955)[18]
Ministry of Urban Service (1956)[19]
6. Sixth Office (Communications and Transportation)
    Ministry of Railways (1949)
    Ministry of Communications (1949)
    Ministry of Post & Telecommunications (1949)
    Bureau of Civil Aviation[20]
7. Seventh Office (Agriculture and Forestry)
    Ministry of Agriculture (1949)
    Ministry of Water Conservancy (1949)
    Ministry of Forestry (1951)
    Central Meteorological Bureau (October, 1954)
    Ministry of Timber Industry (May, 1956)[21]
    Ministry of Aquatic Products (May, 1956)
    Ministry of State Farm and Land Reclamation (May, 1956)
8. Eighth Office (State and Private Joint Enterprises) Central Administrative
    Bureau of Industry and Commerce (1955)
9. Directly under the State Council
    Ministry of Foreign Affairs (1949)
    Commission on Overseas Chinese Affairs (1949)
    State Statistical Bureau (1952)
    State Planning Commission (December, 1952)
    Premier's Office (1954)
    State Archives Bureau (October, 1954)
    Bureau of Religious Affairs (October, 1954)
    Bureau of Standards (1954)
    Ministry of Defense (1954)
    State Construction Commission (1954)[22]
    Bureau of Experts (1954)
    Urban Construction Bureau (April, 1955)[9]
    Survey and Cartography Bureau (January, 1956)
    Scientific Planning Commission (March, 1956)[23]
    State Economic Commission (May, 1956)
    State Technological Commission (May, 1956)[23]
    Bureau of Material Supply (May, 1956)
    Bureau of Foreign Experts (June, 1956)
    Water Conservation Commission (May, 1957)
    State Capital Construction Commission (1958)
    Commission for Cultural Relations with Foreign Countries (1958)
    Bureau of Government Office Administration
    State Building Administration

C. 1959 to the Cultural Revolution
  1. Office of Political and Legal Affairs
    Ministry of Internal Affairs (1949)
    Ministry of Public Security (1949)
    Nationalities Affairs Committee (1949)
  2. Office of Foreign Affairs
    Ministry of Foreign Affairs (1949)
    Commission on Overseas Chinese Affairs (1949)
    Commission on Cultural Relations with Foreign Countries (1958)
    Foreign Economic Relations Commission (April, 1961)
  3. Office of Finance and Trade

People's Bank of China (1949)
Ministry of Finance (1949)
Ministry of Food (October, 1952)
Ministry of Commerce (1952)[24]
Ministry of Foreign Trade (1952)
Central Administrative Bureau of Industry and Commerce (November, 1955)

4. Office of Industry and Communications
Ministry of Railways (1949)
Ministry of Communications (1949)
Ministry of Posts and Telecommunications (1949)
Ministry of Labor (1949)
Ministry of Textile Industry (1949)
Ministry of Geology (1952)
Ministry of Coal (July, 1955)
Ministry of Petroleum (July, 1955)
Ministry of Metallurgical Industry (May, 1956)
Ministry of Chemical Industry (May, 1956)
Ministry of Building (1958)
Ministry of Water Conservation and Electric Power (1958)
First Ministry of Machine-Building (1958)
Second Ministry of Machine-Building (1958)
Ministry of Light Industry (1958)[25]
Third Ministry of Machine-Building (1960)
Fourth Ministry of Machine-Building (1963)
Fifth Ministry of Machine-Building (1963)
Sixth Ministry of Machine-Building (1963)
Seventh Ministry of Machine-Building (1964)
Eighth Ministry of Machine-Building (1964)
Second Ministry of Light Industry (February, 1965)

5. Office of Agriculture and Forestry
Ministry of Agriculture (1949)
Central Meteorological Bureau (October, 1954)
Ministry of Aquatic Products (1956)
Ministry of State Farm and Land Reclamation (1956)
Ministry of Forestry (February, 1958)
Ministry of Agricultural Machinery (August, 1959)

6. Office of Culture and Education
Ministry of Public Health (1949)
Ministry of Culture (1949)
Ministry of Education (1958)[26]
Broadcasting Affairs Administration
New China News Agency
Committee for Reforming the Chinese Written Language

7. Directly under the State Council
State Planning Commission (December, 1952)
State Statistical Bureau (1952)
Religious Affairs Bureau (October, 1954)
Ministry of Defense (1954)
State Archives Bureau (October, 1954)
Bureau of Experts (October, 1954)[27]
Premier's Office (1954)
Bureau of Foreign Experts (June, 1956)
Survey and Cartography Bureau (January, 1956)

State Economic Commission (May, 1956)
Physical Culture and Sports Committee

D. Identified as of August, 1971 (partial listing)
The Scientific and Educational Group of the State Council
People's Bank of China
China Civil Aviation General Administration
China Travel and Tourism Administrative Bureau
New China News Agency
Telecommunication General Administration[28]
Ministry of Foreign Affairs
Ministry of National Defense
State Planning Commission[29]
State Capital Construction Commission
Ministry of Agriculture and Forestry[30]
Ministry of Building Materials
Ministry of Light Industry[31]
Ministry of Communications[32]
Ministry of Metallurgical Industry
First Ministry of Machine-Building[33]
Ministry of Fuel and Chemical Industries[34]
Ministry of Water Conservation and Electric Power[35]
Ministry of Foreign Trade
Ministry of Public Health
Physical Culture and Sports Commission
Ministry for Economic Relations with Foreign Countries
Ministry of Commerce[36]

Notes

1. Changed into the North China Administration Committee in April, 1952.
2. Abolished in August, 1952.
3. Abolished in December, 1950.
4. Changed into the Ministry of Forestry in November, 1951.
5. Under the jurisdiction of the Ministry of Foreign Trade.
6. Abolished in November, 1951.
7. Changed into the State Statistical Bureau in 1952.
8. Merged into the Ministry of Education in 1958.
9. Abolished in May, 1956.
10. Abolished in July, 1955.
11. Merged into the First Ministry of Machine-Building in 1958.
12. Merged into the Ministry of Building in 1958.
13. Abolished in May, 1956; re-established in November, 1956; changed into the Second Ministry of Machine-Building in 1958.
14. Merged with the Ministry of Water Conservation into the Ministry of Water Conservation and Electric Power in 1958.
15. Merged into the Ministry of Light Industry in 1958.
16. Under the jurisdiction of the Ministry of Light Industry in 1958.
17. Changed into the First Ministry of Commerce in February, 1958; merged into the Ministry of Commerce in September, 1958.
18. Abolished in November, 1956.
19. Changed into the Second Ministry of Commerce in February, 1958; merged into the Ministry of Commerce in September, 1958.
20. Under the jurisdiction of the Ministry of Communications.
21. Merged into the Ministry of Forestry in February, 1958.
22. Abolished in 1958; re-established in 1958.
23. Merged into the Scientific and Technological Commission in 1958.

24. Absorbed the Ministry of Urban Service in September, 1958.

25. Changed into the First Ministry of Light Industry in February, 1965.

26. Changed into the Ministry of Education and Higher Education in 1964.

27. Abolished in 1959.

28. May be under the direct jurisdiction of the PLA. The Ministry of Posts and Tele-communication has been abolished. The section in charge of the postal service now comes under the new Ministry of Communications, and the other section is subordinate to the Telecommunication General Administration.

29. May have absorbed former Minister of Geology.

30. The former Ministries of Agriculture, State Farm and Land Reclamation, and Forestry, along with the Water Conservation Section of the Ministry of Water Conservation and Electric Power, have been consolidated into the present Ministry of Agriculture and Forestry.

31. Consolidated from the First and Second Ministries of Light Industry and the Ministry of Textile Industry.

32. Consolidated from the Ministries of Communications and Railways and the Postal Administration of the Ministry of Posts and Telecommunications.

33. Consolidated from the First and Eighth Ministries of Machine-Building.

34. Consolidated from the Ministries of Coal, Petroleum, and Chemical Industry and the Electric Power Section of the Ministry of Water Conservation and Electric Power.

35. This Ministry may have been wholly or partly absorbed by others.

36. Consolidated from the former Ministries of Commerce and Food.

844

4. COUNTRIES HAVING DIPLOMATIC RELATIONS WITH TAIPEI AND PEKING

COUNTRIES having diplomatic relations with the Republic of China (Taipei) as of October, 1971, were:

U.N. members (55): Argentina, Australia, Barbados, Bolivia, Botswana, Brazil, Central African Republic, Chad, Colombia, Congo (Kinshasa), Costa Rica, Cyprus, Dahomey, Dominican Republic, Ecuador, El Salvador, Gabon, Gambia, Greece, Guatemala, Haiti, Honduras, Ivory Coast, Jamaica, Japan, Jordan, Lebanon, Lesotho, Liberia, Libya, Luxembourg, Malagasy Republic, Malawi, Maldives, Malta, Mexico, New Zealand, Nicaragua, Niger, Panama, Paraguay, Peru, Philippines, Portugal, Rwanda, Saudi Arabia, Senegal, Sierra Leone, South Africa, Spain, Swaziland, Thailand, Togo, United States, Upper Volta, Uruguay, Venezuela

Non-U.N. members (3): Republic of Korea, Republic of Vietnam, Vatican

Countries having diplomatic relations with the People's Republic of China (Peking) as of October, 1971:

U.N. members (55): Afghanistan, Albania, Algeria, Austria, Belgium, Bulgaria, Burma, Byelorussia, Cameroon, Canada, Ceylon, Chile, Congo (Brazzaville), Cuba, Czechoslovakia, Denmark, Equatorial Guinea, Ethiopia, Finland, France, Guinea, Hungary, India, Iran, Iraq, Italy, Kenya, Kuwait, Laos, Mali, Mauritania, Mongolia, Morocco, Nepal, Netherlands, Nigeria, Norway, Pakistan, Poland, Rumania, Somalia, Southern Yemen, Sudan, Sweden, Syria, Tanzania, Turkey, Uganda, Ukraine, Union of Soviet Socialist Republics, United Arab Republic, United Kingdom, Yemen, Yugoslavia, Zambia

Non-U.N. members (5): San Marino, Switzerland, Korean Peoples' Republic, Democratic Republic of Vietnam, German Democratic Republic

Countries having no diplomatic relations with either:

U.N. members (14): Burundi, Cambodia, Fiji, Ghana, Guyana, Iceland, Indonesia, Ireland, Israel, Malaysia, Mauritius, Singapore, Trinidad and Tobago, Tunisia

Non-U.N. members (8): Andorra, Bhutan, West Germany, Liechtenstein, Monaco, Nauru, Tonga, Western Samoa

Between October, 1971, and the end of February, 1972, the following countries withdrew recognition from Taipei and recognized Peking on the dates indicated. In three cases noted below, however, recognition of Peking was not immediately followed by the establishment of diplomatic relations and Taipei's diplomatic mission remained.

1. Argentina, February 19, 1972.
2. Cyprus, January 12, 1972, but relations with Taipei remained for a period thereafter.
3. Ecuador, November 20, 1971.

4. Lebanon, November 9, 1971.
5. Libya, November 19, 1971, but relations with Taipei remain.
6. Malta, February 25, 1972.
7. Mexico, February 15, 1972.
8. Peru, November 2, 1971.
9. Rwanda, November 14, 1971.
10. Senegal, December 10, 1971.
11. Sierra Leone, July 29, 1971.
12. Togo, January 31, 1972, but relations with Taipei remain.

The following country raised its diplomatic mission to ambassadorial level:
1. United Kingdom, March 13, 1972.

The following states established or restored diplomatic relations with Peking:
1. Burundi, diplomatic relations restored, October 13, 1971.
2. Tunisia, diplomatic relations restored, October 8, 1971.
3. Iceland, diplomatic relations established, December 8, 1971.

5. CHINA'S BILATERAL AGREEMENTS AND TREATIES, 1949-70, BY STATE AND SUBJECT

State	1949–64 (1)		1965–70 (2)	
	All Categories	Economic	All Categories	Economic
Afghanistan	11	1	9	4
Albania	22	14	24	22
Algeria	8	2	2	—
Austria	2*	2*	—	—
Bulgaria	30	22	5	4
Burma	31	9	—	—
Burundi	1	1	—	—
Cambodia	25	13	9	8
Canada	—	—	1	—
Central Africa	3	2	1	1
Ceylon	20	13	5	5
Congo B.	4	1	8	5
Cuba	11	3	6	6
Czechoslovakia	39	23	7	5
Denmark	4	4	—	—
Equatorial Guinea	—	—	1	—
Ethiopia	2	—	1	—
Finland	21	21	4	4
France	3*	3*	3	3
Germany (East)	48	30	8	6
Germany (West)	4*	4*	—	—
Ghana	11	5	1	1
Guinea	8	3	14	11
Hungary	40	27	9	7
India	10	5	—	—
Indonesia	22	7	3	2
Iraq	6	5	2	—
Italy	—	—	3	2
Japan	26*	11*	22	4
Korean People's Democratic Republic	39	11	9	6
Laos	7	—	—	—
Lebanon	1	1	—	—
Mali	7	2	9	5
Mauritania	—	—	3	3

847

State	1949–64 (1)		1965–70 (2)	
	All Categories	Economic	All Categories	Economic
Mongolian People's Republic	32	18	7	5
Morocco	1	—	1	1
Nepal	18	3	10	7
Nigeria	1	1	—	—
Norway	2	1	1	—
Pakistan	9	2	15	11
Poland	35	21	8	7
Rumania	36	27	7	5
Singapore	1*	1*	—	—
Somalia	4	1	5	3
Southern Yemen	—	—	6	2
Sudan	6	4	8	6
Sweden	2	2	—	—
Switzerland	1	1	—	—
Syria	8	7	6	3
Tanzania	2	0	20	12
Tunisia	2	1	—	—
Uganda	—	—	1	1
United Arab Republic	23	17	11	9
United Kingdom	2	2	—	—
U.S.A.	1	—	—	—
U.S.S.R.	40	15	6	4
Vietnam, Democratic Republic of	47	27	18	11
Yemen	7	1	5	2
Yugoslavia	15	11	3	3
Zambia	—	—	14	11
Total	762	408	321	217

* Nongovernmental agreements.

Sources: (1) Gene T. Hsiao, compiler, Communist China's Trade Treaties and Agreements, 1949–1964 (Berkeley, Calif.: Center for Chinese Studies, October, 1968), pp. 656–58. Originally from thirteen volumes of the official collection Chung-hua Jen-min Kung-ho-kuo T'iao-yüeh-chi (Treaties of the People's Republic of China), covering the period 1949–64. (2) Fei-ch'ing Nien-pao (Yearbook on Communist China), volumes for 1967, 1968, 1969, and 1970 (Taipei: Institute for the Study of Chinese Communist Problems, 1968–71); Studies on Chinese Communism, Vol. 5, No. 1 (January, 1971); and Chugoku seiji keizai soran (Tokyo: Ajia Sei-kei Gakkai, Hitotsubashi Shobo, 1966).

6. UNITED NATIONS VOTING RECORD ON CHINESE REPRESENTATION

Year	In Favor*	Against*	Abstention	Absent or Not Participating
1960	34	42	22	1
1961	37	48	19	—
1962	42	56	12	—
1963	41	57	12	1
1964		(No Vote)		
1965	47	47	20	1
1966	46	57	17	1
1967	45	58	17	2
1968	44	58	23	1
1969	48	56	21	1
1970	51	49	25	2
1971	76	35	17	3

* 'In favor' or 'against' refers to the admission of Peking and the expulsion of Taiwan.

Sources: 1957–61, Department of State, *Research Memorandum*, RFE-17, March 29, 1962, pp. 11–14. 1962–63, *United Nations Review.* 1965–68, *UN Monthly Chronicle*, December, 1965, December, 1966, December, 1967, and December, 1968. 1969, *The Christian Science Monitor*, November 14, 1969. 1970, Associated Press, November 20, 1970. 1971, *New York Times*, October 27, 1971, p. 1.

7. PRODUCTION OF IRON AND STEEL, 1949–70
(in thousands of metric tons)

	Pig Iron		Steel Ingot			Rolled Steel	
Year	Official Estimate	K. P. Wang	Official Estimate	K. P. Wang	Robert Michael Field	Official Estimate	K. P. Wang
1949	252[a]	—	158[a]	—	—	141[b]	—
1950	978[a]	—	606[a]	—	—	464[b]	—
1951	1,448[a]	—	896[a]	—	—	808[b]	—
1952	1,929[a]	1,928[c]	1,349[a]	1,350[c]	—	1,312[b]	1,100[c]
1953	2,234[a]	—	1,774[a]	—	—	1,754[b]	—
1954	3,114[a]	—	2,225[a]	—	—	1,965[b]	—
1955	3,872[a]	—	2,853[a]	—	—	2,505[b]	—
1956	4,826[a]	—	4,465[a]	—	—	3,921[b]	—
1957	5,936[a]	5,940[c]	5,350[a]	5,350[c]	—	4,260[b]	4,260[c]
1958	13,690[a] (9,350)	—	11,080[a] (8,000)	—	8,000	6,000[a]	—
1959	20,500[a] (9,500)	—	13,350[a] (8,630)	—	10,000	9,200[a]	—
1960	(no figures)				13,000		
1961	—	15,000[d]	—	9,500[d]	8,000	—	8,000[d]
1962	—	15,000[d]	—	10,000[d]	8,000	—	9,000[d]
1963	—	17,000[d]	—	12,000[d]	9,000	—	10,000[d]
1964	—	18,000[d]	—	14,000[d]	10,000	—	11,000[d]
1965	—	19,000[d]	—	15,000[d]	11,000	—	12,000[d]
1966	—	20,000[c]	—	16,000[c]	13,000	—	13,000[c]
1967	—	14,000[c]	—	11,000[c]	10,000	—	9,000[c]
1968	—	19,000[c]	—	15,000[c]	12,000	—	12,000[c]
1969	—	20,000[c]	—	16,000[c]	15,000	—	13,000[c]
1970	—	—	18,000[e]	—	18,000	—	—

Note: Figures in parentheses refer to the output of modern mills only.

Sources: [a]*Ten Great Years* (Peking: Foreign Languages Press, 1960), p. 95, and, for 1959, *Survey of Mainland China Press (SCMP)*, No. 2186 (Hong Kong: U.S. Consulate General, February, 1960), p. 2. [b]*Major Aspects of the Chinese Economy Through 1956* (Peking: Tung-chi Chu-pan-she, 1958), pp. 14, 26. [c]See K. P. Wang's article in this handbook, Chapter 4. [d]K. P. Wang, 'The Mineral Resources Base of Communist China,' in Joint Economic Committee, U.S. Congress, *An Economic Profile of Mainland China* (Washington, D.C.: Government Printing Office, February, 1967), p. 174. [e]Chou En-lai, as cited by Edgar Snow in the *New Republic*, March 27, 1971. [f]Robert Michael Field, 'Chinese Industrial Development: 1949–70,' in Joint Economic Committee, U.S. Congress, *People's Republic of China: An Economic Assessment* (Washington, D.C.: Government Printing Office, May 18, 1972), p. 83.

8. COAL PRODUCTION, 1949-70
(in thousand metric tons)

Year	Official Estimate[a]	K. P. Wang	Robert Michael Field	Current Scene[f]	Great Soviet Encyclopedia[g]
1949	32,430	—	—	—	—
1950	42,920	—	—	—	—
1951	53,090	—	—	—	—
1952	66,490	66,600[b]	—	—	—
1953	69,680	—	—	—	—
1954	83,660	—	—	—	—
1955	98,300	—	—	—	—
1956	110,360	—	—	—	—
1957	130,000	128,000[b]	130,730[e] 131,000[h]	130,000	130,000
1958	270,000	—	226,400[e] 230,000[h]	270,000	—
1959	347,800	—	292,400[e] 290,000[h] 300,000[i]	—	347,800
1960	425,000	420,000[d]	325,000[e] 270,000[h] 280,000[i]	425,000	—
1961	—	250,000[c]	180,000[e] 170,000[i]	—	—
1962	—	250,000[c]	180,000[e]	190,000–200,000	—
1963	—	270,000[c]	190,000[e]	210,000	—
1964	—	290,000[c]	200,000[e]	220,000	209,000
1965	—	300,000[c]	210,000[e] 220,000[h]	—	—
1966	—	325,000[b]	240,000[h]	—	—
1967	—	225,000[b]	190,000[h]	—	—
1968	—	300,000[b]	210,000[h] 200,000[i]	—	—
1969	—	330,000[b]	250,000	—	—
1970	—	—	300,000[i]	—	—

Sources: [a]*Wei-ta ti Shin-nien* (*Ten Great Years*) (Peking: Jen-min Chu-pan-she, 1959), p. 84, and *Peking Review*, No. 9, March, 1960, pp. 8–9. [b]K. P. Wang's article in Part One of this handbook, Chapter 4. [c]Wang, 'Mineral Resources Base,' p. 174. [d]K. P. Wang, 'The Mineral Industry of Mainland China,' *Minerals Yearbook* (Washington, D.C.: U.S. Bureau of Mines, 1963 and 1964), and Robert Michael Field, 'Chinese Communist Industrial Production,' in Joint Economic Committee, *Economic Profile*, p. 293. [e]Field, *loc. cit.* [f]'Decision for an "Upsurge," ' *Current Scene*, Vol. 3, No. 17 (Hong Kong, April 15, 1965). [g]*Yezhegodnik bolshoi sovetskoi entsiklopedii, 1965* (*1965 Yearbook of the Great Soviet Encyclopedia*) (Moscow, 1965), p. 283. [h]Robert Michael Field, 'Industrial Production in Communist China, 1957–1968,' *The China Quarterly*, No. 42 (London, April–June, 1970), p. 56. [i]Robert Michael Field, 'Chinese Industrial Development: 1949–70,' in Joint Economic Committee, U.S. Congress, *People's Republic of China: An Economic Assessment* (Washington, D.C.: Government Printing Office, May 18, 1972), p. 83.

9. COAL CONSUMPTION, 1952-60
(in million yüan)

Year	Total Domestic Consumption	Industry			Transportation	Household
		All Industry Except Collieries	Collieries	Total		
		1. At 1952 Prices				
1952	762.10	221.36	4.04	225.40	86.41	450.30
1953	914.10	277.09	4.39	281.48	114.40	518.22
1954	1,045.02	341.16	5.49	346.65	125.32	573.05
1955	1,144.71	399.97	6.70	406.67	120.31	617.73
1956	1,296.66	501.15	7.78	508.93	145.73	642.00
1957	1,628.29	594.88	9.55	604.43	154.59	869.27
1958	2,837.34	1,545.94	19.40	1,565.34	266.90	1,005.10
1959	3,761.91	2,298.00	24.97	2,322.97	322.54	1,116.40
1960	4,354.11	2,712.60	30.50	1,753.10	370.31	1,240.70
		2. At Current Prices				
1952	762.10	221.36	4.04	225.40	86.4	450.3
1953	920.54	279.03	4.41	283.44	115.2	521.9
1954	1,052.31	343.55	5.46	349.01	126.2	577.1
1955	1,152.70	402.77	6.63	409.40	121.2	622.1
1956	1,314.67	508.17	7.70	515.87	147.8	651.0
1957	1,710.46	624.99	9.77	634.76	162.4	913.3
1958	2,997.62	1,624.20	35.92	1,661.12	280.5	1,056.0
1959	3,984.93	2,414.30	58.73	2,473.03	338.9	1,173.0
1960	4,614.23	2,849.90	71.73	2,921.63	389.1	1,303.5

Source: Yuan-li Wu, *Economic Development and the Use of Energy Resources in Communist China* (New York: Praeger Publishers, 1963), p. 122.

10. ELECTRIC POWER OUTPUT, 1949–70

(in million kilowatt-hours)

Year	Official Estimate[a]	John Ashton[d]	*Current Scene*[e]	Robert M. Field
1949	4,310	4,300	—	—
1950	4,550	—	—	—
1951	5,750	—	—	—
1952	7,260	7,300	—	—
1953	9,200	—	—	—
1954	11,000	—	—	—
1955	12,280	—	—	—
1956	16,590	16,600	—	—
1957	19,340	19,300	19,300	—
1958	27,530	27,500	27,500	28,000[g]
1959	41,500[b]	41,500	—	42,000[g]
1960	55,000–58,000 (plan)[c]	47,000	47,000	47,000[g]
1961	—	31,000	—	31,000[g]
1962	—	30,000	30,000	30,000[g]
1963	—	33,000	31,000	33,000[g]
1964	—	36,000	32,000	36,000[g]
1965	—	40,000	—	42,000[f]
1966	—	—	—	47,000[f]
1967	—	—	—	41,000[g]
1968	—	—	—	44,000[g]
1969	—	—	—	50,000[f]
1970	—	—	—	60,000[f]

Sources: [a] *Ten Great Years*, p. 84. [b] NCNA, Peking, April 9, 1960. [c] NCNA, Peking, March 30, 1960. [d] John Ashton, 'Development of Electric Energy Resources in Communist China,' in Joint Economic Committee, *Economic Profile*, p. 307. [e] 'Decision for "Upsurge," ' *Current Scene*, Vol. 3, No. 17. [f] Robert Michael Field, 'Chinese Industrial Development: 1949–70,' Joint Economic Committee, Congress of the United States, *People's Republic of China: An Economic Assessment*, May 18, 1972, p. 83. For 1967 and 1968, Field also gave estimates of 39,000 and 42,000 respectively. See f. [f] Robert Michael Field, 'Industrial Production,' *The China Quarterly*, No. 42, p. 56.

11. CONSUMPTION OF ELECTRIC POWER, 1949–60

(in million 1952 yüan)

Year	Net Domestic Consumption	Industry All Industry Except Power	Industry Power Industry	Industry Total Industry	Agriculture	Transport	Household	Export (+) or Import (−)
1949	224.2	169.9	9.9	179.8	1.2	5.7	37.5	—
1950	266.1	197.2	8.5	205.7	1.6	6.5	52.3	—
1951	356.5	278.3	9.8	288.1	2.0	6.9	59.5	− 10.9
1952	460.3	367.4	11.5	378.9	3.1	7.2	71.1	− 10.2
1953	571.4	466.8	11.6	478.4	2.9	7.8	82.3	2.6
1954	709.1	592.2	16.0	608.2	3.2	9.2	88.5	− 11.7
1955	785.8	670.0	18.6	688.6	3.6	8.6	85.0	1.5
1956	1,033.6	878.9	26.4	905.3	5.6	9.4	113.3	25.7
1957	1,255.8	1,073.5	27.5	1,101.0	15.6	10.2	129.0	− 11.0
1958	1,814.4	1,589.1	40.8	1,629.9	25.6	12.2	146.7	− 11.0
1959	2,727.6	2,438.3	69.0	2,507.3	38.7	14.8	166.8	− 11.0
1960	3,611.1	3,256.9	84.2	3,341.1	60.2	20.0	189.8	− 11.0

Source: Wu, *Economic Development and Use of Energy Resources*, p. 86.

12. CRUDE OIL PRODUCTION, 1949–70

(in thousands of metric tons)

Year	Official Estimate	K. P. Wang	*Current Scene*[f]	Robert M. Field
1949	121[a]	—	—	—
1950	200[a]	—	—	—
1951	305[a]	—	—	—
1952	436[a]	440[c]	—	—
1953	622[a]	—	—	—
1954	789[a]	—	—	—
1955	966[a]	—	—	—
1956	1,163[a]	—	—	—
1957	1,458[a]	1,440[c]	1,460	1,460[g]
1958	2,264[a]	—	2,260	2,260[g]
1959	3,700[a]	3,700[d]	—	3,700[g]
1960	5,200[a]	5,500[d]	4,500	4,600[i]
1961	—	6,200[e]	—	4,500[g]
1962	—	6,800[e]	5,300	5,000[i]
1963	—	7,500[e]	5,900	5,500[i]
1964	—	8,500[e]	6,000–7,000	6,900[i]
1965	—	10,000[e]	—	8,000[g]
1966	—	13,000[c]	—	10,000[h]
1967	—	11,000[c]	—	10,000[h]
1968	—	15,000[c]	—	11,000[h]
1969	—	20,000[c]	—	14,000[i]
1970	20,000[b]	—	—	18,000[i]

Sources: [a]For 1949–50, *Ten Great Years*, p. 95; for 1960; NCNA, March 30, 1960. [b]Chou-En-lai, as cited by Edgar Snow in the *New Republic*, March 27, 1971. [c]K. P. Wang's article in Part One of this handbook, Chapter 4. [d]Wang, 'Mineral Industry of Mainland China,' *Minerals Yearbook*, 1963 and 1964. [e]Wang, 'Mineral Resource Base,' in Joint Economic Committee, *Economic Profile*, p. 174. [f]'Decision for "Upsurge," ' *Current Scene*, Vol. 3, No. 17. [g]Field, 'Chinese Communist Industrial Production,' in Joint Economic Committee, *Economic Profile*, p. 293. [h]Field, 'Industrial Production,' *The China Quarterly*, No. 42, p. 56. [i]Field, 'Chinese Industrial Development: 1949–70,' in Joint Economic Committee, U.S. Congress, *People's Republic of China: An Economic Assessment* (Washington, D.C.: Government Printing Office, May 18, 1972), p. 83.

13. LAND AND AGRICULTURAL RESOURCES

A. Estimates of Cultivated Land in All Crops and Crop Hectares in Food Grains, Mainland China, 1928–67

| Source | | Period | Cultivated Land (millions of hectares) | | | Crop Hectares in Food Grains[3] |
			Twenty-two Provinces[1]	Manchuria, Jehol, and Sinkiang[2]	Mainland China (excl. Tibet)	
		Pre-Communist China				
Chinese Economic Journal (1)		1928	101.7	12.8	115	—
Statistical Monthly (2)		1929–32	68.5	14.7	83	83
National Agricultural Research Bureau (3)		1931–37	65.8	14.7	81	89
Land Utilization in China (4)	A	1929–33	88.0	14.7	103	111
	B	1929–33	88.0	19.7	108	117
	C	1929–33	93.8	20.9	115	124
Ministry of Agriculture and Forestry (5)		1946	76.2	16.9	93	—
Atlas of Mainland China (6)		1965	—	—	109	—
		People's Republic of China				
Ten Great Years (7)	A	1953–57	—	—	110	119
	B	1956 (peak)	—	—	112	124
Current Scene (8)	A	1962	—	—	110	119
	B	1963	—	—	110	119
	C	1964	—	—	112	121
	D	1965	—	—	112	121
	E	1966	—	—	111	120
	F	1967	—	—	111	120
O. L. Dawson (9)		1967	—	—	110	128
Monthly Research Communist China (10)		1967	—	—	109	118
Union Research Institute (11)		1967	—	—	114	123

[1] The twenty-two provinces are those for which the National Agricultural Research Bureau in Nanking computed production for 1931–37. They are listed in T. H. Shen, *Agricultural Resources of China* (Ithaca, N.Y.: Cornell University Press, 1951), p. 376, Appendix Table 3, as follows: Chahar, Suiyuan, Ningsia, Chinghai, Kansu, Shensi, Shansi, Hopeh, Shantung, Kiangsu, Anhwei, Honan, Hupeh, Szechwan, Yünnan, Kweichow, Hunan, Kiangsi, Chekiang, Fukien, Kwangtung, and Kwangsi.

[2] Figures for Sinkiang are included only in the first four sources. Source (5) records 300,000 hectares for Sinkiang, which is omitted because no production data are available.

[3] Crop hectares include cultivated land that produces more than one food grain crop in a

season. One hectare of land that produces two food grain crops in one season counts as two crop hectares. Crop hectares are computed from the index of multiple cropping in John L. Buck, Owen L. Dawson, and Yuan-li Wu, *Food and Agriculture in Communist China* (New York: Praeger Publishers, 1966), p. 56, for sources (3) and (4).

Sources: (1) D. K. Lieu and Chung-min Chen, 'Statistics of Farm Land in China,' *Chinese Economic Journal*, 2, No. 3 (March, 1928): 181–213. Lieu and Chen examined the large amount of historical data on the amount of cultivated land in China, as well as more recent data in the early years of the Republic of China. The authors checked the data province by province for accuracy in terms of population and the amount of land required to support one person. These amounts varied with the productivity of the land in various provinces. The population figure used was that of 485 million obtained by the Chinese Postal Service through its nationwide postmasters and published in the twelfth issue of the *Postal Guide*. However, no data were included by Lieu and Chen for the provinces of Chinghai and Ningsia, two of the twenty-two provinces, amounting to 520,000 and 123,000 hectares, respectively, in 1946, according to Shen, *Agricultural Resources*. These amounts have not been added to the Lieu-Chen data in this table. Lieu and Chen included Jehol in a group of provinces in the Metropolitan District of Peking for which only a total area was given. *The Statistical Monthly* gives 1.2 million hectares for Jehol; hence, 1.2 million hectares is subtracted and transferred to the Manchuria, Jehol, Sinkiang column.

(2) C. C. Chang, 'Estimates of China's Farms and Crops,' *The Statistical Monthly*, Directorate of Statistics, National Government of China, Nanking, January and February, 1932 (combined issue), and *idem, An Estimate of China's Farms and Crops* (Nanking: University of Nanking, December, 1932). The latter version contains statistics on total crop acreage, 102.5 million hectares, and food crop acreage, 83.4 million hectares. The 68.5 hectares for the twenty-two provinces omits Kwangsi and Chinghai for lack of data at the time of compilation. Shen, *Agricultural Resources*, p. 142, gives the cultivated area in 1946 as 1.8 million hectares for Kwangsi and 500,000 hectares for Chinghai, making a total, if added in, of 70.8 million hectares for the twenty-two provinces. *The Statistical Monthly* breaks down the other figure as 12.6 million hectares for Manchuria, 1.2 million for Jehol, and 900,000 for Sinkiang.

(3) John L. Buck, *Land Utilization in China—Statistics*, Chapter 2, Table 1, pp. 21–29. The 65.8 figure derives from a hsien-by-hsien check of the *Statistical Monthly* data, yielding 771,705 square kilometers, or 254,018 square miles, equivalent to 65.8 million hectares of cultivated land, including the provinces of Kwangsi and Chinghai. See *ibid.*, Chapter 6, p. 165, Table 3, headed 'Estimates of the Amount of Cultivated Area in the Eight Agricultural Areas,' item 7, where the amount 254,018 square miles, or 65.6 million hectares, is included for purposes of comparison with various estimates.

(4) Buck, *loc. cit.*, Table 3 of Chapter 6, headed 'Estimates of the Amount of Cultivated Area in the Eight Agricultural Areas.' The difference between the figure in lines A and B (88 million hectares) and that given by source (3) (65.8 million) represents unregistered land omitted from official statistics, popularly known as 'black land.' Land utilization enumerators had the task of obtaining from knowledgeable local individuals estimates of the percentage of unregistered land. The estimates of three local persons for each of 111 hsien were obtained for the area with which they were familiar and averaged. They indicate an increase over the National Agricultural Research Bureau's 65.8 by a factor of 1.337, which comes out to 88 million hectares, or 339,644 square miles. The average of all the highest estimates of unregistered land yields a factor of 1.425, which, multiplied by 65.8, gives a cultivated area of 93.8 million hectares (line C), or 362,082 square miles, which is item 1 in the table cited here. Under Manchuria, Jehol, and Sinkiang, the figure for line A is the source (2) figure, uncorrected; that in line B is corrected by the factor 1.337 for unregistered land, giving 19.7 million hectares; line C (20.9 million) results from multiplying 14.7 million by the maximum correction factor, 1.425. Crop hectares are obtained by multiplying the total cultivated land in lines A, B, and C by the index of double-cropping (1.08) in Buck, Dawson, and Wu, *Food and Agriculture*, p. 56.

(5) Directorate of Statistics, National Government of China, cited in Shen, *Agricultural Resources*, p. 142, Table 7. Figures for Taiwan have been subtracted in computing amounts of cultivated land.

(6) *Atlas of Mainland China* (Taipei: Defense Research Institute in Taiwan, 1966), data for 1965.

(7) Statistical Bureau, *Wei-ta ti Shih-nien (Ten Great Years)* (Peking: Jen-min Ch'u-pan-she, 1959). Line A is computed by the method indicated in source listing for source (8), below.

(8) John R. Wenmohs, 'Agriculture in Mainland China,' *Current Scene*, 5, No. 21 (Hong Kong, December 15, 1967): 10, Table 1. The amount of cultivated land is not given in this table but is computed from the number of crop hectares by dividing by the index of double-cropping of food grains (1.08) given in Buck, Dawson, and Wu, *Food and Agriculture* (see note 3 to this table).

(9) Owen L. Dawson, *Communist China's Agricultural Development and Future Potential* (New York: Praeger Publishers, 1968). The number of crop hectares is not stated by Dawson but can be calculated by dividing 213 million metric tons (Table 2, item 6) by 110 million hectares to get 1,936.3 kilograms per hectare of cultivated land; then 1,936.3 kilograms divided by the yield, 1,665 kilograms per crop hectare, equals 116.3 per cent, by which, finally, the cultivated land total of 110 million hectares is multiplied, yielding 127.9 million or, rounding, 128 million crop hectares. Dawson quotes the Communist writer Hsiao Yu as reporting '1.3 million hectares of cultivated lands annually as abandoned, or fallowed out, or out of use for various reasons in the borderlands of the Northwest, Northeast and Inner Mongolia.' This total may equal or exceed new lands claimed as brought under cultivation. Dawson estimates that increases over the 1958 Communist figure of 107.8 million hectares of cultivated land for new areas brought under cultivation in succeeding years would bring the 1967 total of cultivated land to 110 million hectares. Hsiao Yu claims that at least 2 million hectares during the First Five-Year Plan were reported as reclaimed but were actually previously unreported private holdings. Thus, the increases in Communist cultivated land from 97.9 million hectares in 1949 to 107.8 million hectares in 1958 may represent primarily the inclusion of land not formerly reported.

10. *Fei-ching Yüeh-pao* (*Monthly Research on Communist China*), 10, No. 10 (Taipei: Institute of International Relations, November, 1967): 43–44. Cultivated land is computed by method indicated in source listing for source (8) above.

(11) *Tsu Kuo* (*China Monthly*), No. 47 (Hong Kong: Union Research Institute, February, 1968), p. 35. Cultivated land is computed by the method indicated in listing for source (8) above.

B. Production and Yields of Food Grains in Mainland China, 1929–67

| Source | Period | Production of Food Grains (in millions of metric tons) | | | Yields per Crop Hectare (kg.) |
		Twenty-two Provinces	Manchuria, Jehol, and Sinkiang[1]	Mainland China	
		Pre-Communist China			
Statistical Monthly (1)	1929–32	119.7	16.3	136	1,639
National Agricultural Research Bureau (2)	1931–37	116	16.3	132	1,483
Land Utilization in China (3)	A 1929–33	167	16.3	183	1,649
	B 1929–33	167	21.8	189	1,615
	C 1929–33	178	23.2	201	1,621
		People's Republic of China			
Ten Great Years (4)	A 1949–58	—	—	163	1,430
Average	B 1953–57	—	—	172	1,448
The year 1956	C 1956	—	—	183	1,471
Current Scene (5)	A 1962	—	—	180	1,515
	B 1963	—	—	178	1,502
	C 1964	—	—	190	1,577
	D 1965	—	—	185	1,531
	E 1966	—	—	178	1,483
	F 1967	—	—	187	1,558
United Nations FAO (6)	1967	—	—	215	—

[1] Sikang is omitted because it has an estimated cultivated area of only 00,000 hectares (Shen, *Agricultural Resources*), and no data on yields are available.

Sources: (1) Shen, *Agricultural Resources*, Appendix Table 1; see also listing (3) below.

(2) *Ibid.*, Appendix Tables 2 and 4, pp. 347–75 and 378–79, consisting of averages of data for 1931–37 from the National Agricultural Research Bureau for the twenty-two provinces and for the same food grains as used by the P.R.C. For instance, rapeseed, soybeans, peanuts, and sesame are not included. Appendix Table 4 includes mungbeans, buckwheat, and potatoes and sweet potatoes at one-fourth their weight.

(3) Buck, Dawson, and Wu, *Food and Agriculture*, Appendix Tables 3 and 5, pp. 55 and 58. The total 181.9 million metric tons in Appendix Table 5, minus 14.9 million for Manchuria, Sikang, and Sinkiang in Appendix Table 3, equals 167 million metric tons for the twenty-two provinces as in lines A and B. The figure in line C, 178 million metric tons, is obtained by dividing 167 million by 1.337, the average factor of adjustment for unregistered lands, then multiplying the result by 1.425, the average factor of all the highest estimates of unregistered lands. Under Manchuria, Jehol, and Sinkiang, line B is obtained by multiplying the 16.3 million metric tons of line A by the factor 1.337, and line C by multiplying by the factor 1.425.

(4) Statistical Bureau, *Wei-ta ti Shih-nien*. See source listing (7) under the table marked as subsection 13A, above.

(5) Wehmos, 'Agriculture in Mainland China,' p. 10, Table 1. See source listing (8) under subsection 13A, above.

(6) *The State of Food and Agriculture* (Rome: U.N. Food and Agriculture Organization, 1968), p. 14: 'New FAO estimates for China (Mainland) of the production of "food grains" (including potatoes and sweet potatoes, converted to grain equivalent, in line with Chinese practice) were introduced in last year's issue of this report. These estimates are based on the assumption of a realistic trend in per capita consumption in line with general reports on the food situation, and on a population estimate of 780 million in 1966. On this basis, food-grain production is tentatively estimated as 215 million tons in 1967, in comparison with 206 million tons in 1966 and 208 million tons in 1965. The excellent harvest in 1967 was officially attributed both to favorable weather and to progress in irrigation, drainage, and related capital works. Apart from some disruption of the transport of fertilizers and other inputs, the cultural revolution does not seem to have interfered with agricultural production.' (Kindly supplied to the author by Dr. Leslie C. T. Kuo, Chief of the Oriental Project, the National Library, Washington, D.C.)

C. Estimates of Arable Uncultivated Land, Mainland China, Excluding Tibet, 1914–63

(in millions of hectares)

Source	Period	Twenty-two Provinces	Manchuria and Sinkiang	Mainland China
Report of Ministry of Agriculture and Forestry, Peking (1)	1914	—	—	27
O. E. Baker (2)	1927	—	—	28
Land Utilization in China (3)	1929–33	A 24	—	—
Possibly feasible for cultivation		B 15	—	—
Science Bulletin, Peking (4)	1963	—	—	27
Ministry of Reclamation and State Farms (5)	1958	—	—	18
O. L. Dawson (6)	1967	5.8	30.3	36

Sources: (1) Quoted in Buck, *Land Utilization in China*, p. 169.

(2) O. E. Baker, 'Land Utilization in China,' a paper presented at the Second Conference of the Institute of Pacific Relations, July, 1927. Author was formerly of U.S. Department of Agriculture.

(3) The major land classes of the eight Agricultural Areas, twenty-two provinces, in 1929–33 are set forth by Buck as follows:

Class	Area in Square Miles	Source
Gross area	1,358,905	Buck, *Land Utilization*, p. 163
Water area	77,458	See Buck, *Land Utilization—Atlas*, p. 33; water area figured at 5.7 per cent of gross
Land area	1,281,447	By subtraction
Cultivated land	362,082	Buck, *Land Utilization*, p. 165, Table 3, col. 2
Uncultivated land	919,365	By subtraction
Land in farms used for farmsteads, roads, ponds, and graves	42,027	Buck, *Land Utilization*, p. 172, Table 7, stating that 10.4 per cent is not in crops
Remainder of uncultivated land	877,338	By subtraction
Productive uncultivated land	460,592	Buck, *Land Utilization—Atlas*, p. 33, Table 6, stating as 52.5 per cent of uncultivated area
Arable land (line A)	93,875, or 24 million hectares	*Ibid.*, p. 31, Table 5, counting 10.7 per cent of uncultivated land as arable
Possibly feasible for cultivation (line B)	56,325, or 15 million hectares	*Ibid.*, pp. 44–46, Table 14

The reasons why uncultivated arable land was not cultivated were stated by local people in 251 localities, 172 *hsien*, 21 provinces in 1929–33 as follows, in percentages of all localities reporting reasons: lack of people and livestock, 26; lack of capital, 21; too many graves, 10; bandits, 8; too sandy, 7; used for forest, 7; elevation too high, 6; cultivation on government and private property not permitted, 6; excessive erosion, 5; too far from farmstead, 4; affected by drought, 4; disputed ownership of mountain land, 4; slopes too steep, 2; communication inconvenient, 2; salt and alkali, 1; profit from salt production is greater than from cultivation, 1; too cold, 1; farm prices decreasing, 1; nomads unwilling to cultivate, 1; and not known, 13. Percentages add to more than 100 because more than one reason was given for some localities. The reasons for about 60 per cent of the localities are institutional in character and could be remedied. Therefore, the so-called arable land of 93,875 square miles is reduced by multiplying it by 60 per cent to obtain the 56,325 square miles, or 15 million hectares, possibly feasible for cultivation (line B).

(4) *K'o-hsüeh Tung-pao (Science Bulletin)*, No. 8 (Peking, 1963), p. 1; Chao Shih-ying uses the figure of 26.7 million hectares.

(5) *China's State Farms in Galloping Progress* (Peking: Ministry of Reclamation and State Farms, 1958). Data were supplied by O. L. Dawson from a forthcoming book. The data are for wastelands such as arid, saline, and marshy wastelands in the Northwest; saline wastelands in the coastal regions; lake basin wastelands in the interior provinces; hilly red-soil wastelands in South China; and plateau wastelands in Southwest China. The total wasteland reported by twenty-four provinces was 54.8 million hectares. Actual surveys of these areas were made in the 1950's in all but three provinces—Honan, Hupeh, and Liaoning—and reached a total of 35.4 million hectares of wasteland. Estimates for the three provinces not surveyed totaled 1.9 million hectares. Sinkiang and Heilungkiang provinces contained about 45 per cent of the surveyed areas, or 15.8 million hectares. Wastelands were classified for ten of these provinces as (1) usable with no reconditioning, (2) usable with slight reconditioning, (3) usable with much reconditioning, and (4) not currently ready for cultivation. The first three categories account for 14.4 million hectares for ten provinces, of which 10.4 million hectares are in Sinkiang and Heilungkiang. Dawson has made estimates for the other fourteen provinces, chiefly with smaller amounts of wasteland, where surveys did not include a classification, totaling 3.7 million hectares of reclaimable land. Hence, there may be 18.1 million hectares of reclaimable wasteland and 6.1 million hectares not ready for current use. Apparently these wastelands do not include numerous smaller areas of uncultivated land adjacent to farm areas throughout the Eight Agricultural Areas.

(6) Owen L. Dawson, *Communist China's Agricultural Development and Future Potential* (New York: Praeger Publishers, 1968), p. 66. Dawson's estimate of 4 million for Tibet is not included.

D. Selected Cropping Systems from More than 500 Systems, 154 Localities, 149 *Hsien*, 19 Provinces in China, 1929–33

Regions Areas and Localities	Kind of Land	Soil Type Scientific	Soil Type Local	Number Assigned System	Year of Crop in System	Winter, Spring or Annual Crops	Summer Crops After Winter Spring Crops	Fall Crops After Summer Crops
WHEAT REGION:								
Spring Wheat Area								
Kansu								
Kaolan (1)	Hilly, terraced	Desert soils	—	1	1st	Spring wheat (s)	—	—
					2nd	Fallow	—	—
					3rd	Millet	—	—
					4th	Fallow	—	—
Shansi								
Ningwu	Hilly, steep	Chestnut colored earths	—	16	1st, 3rd & 5th	Oat (s)	—	—
					2nd & 6th	Field peas	—	—
					4th	Soybeans, black	—	—
Shensi								
Tingpien	Undulating, sloping gently	Chestnut colored earths	Sandy loam	28	1st	Millet (s)	—	—
					2nd	Millet, proso (s)	—	—
					3rd	Soybeans, black (s)	—	—
Winter Wheat– Millet Area								
Shansi								
Showyang	Moderately hilly	Chestnut colored earths	—	86	1st	Soybeans (s)	—	—
					3rd	Squash (s)	—	—
					5th	Beans small (s)	—	—
					2nd, 4th & 6th	Millet (s)	—	—

Regions Areas and Localities	Kind of Land	Soil Type Scientific	Soil Type Local	Number Assigned System	Year of Crop in System	Winter, Spring or Annual Crops	Summer Crops After Winter Spring Crops	Fall Crops After Summer Crops
Winter Wheat–Kaoliang Area Honan Kaifeng	Level	Calcareous alluvium	Sandy	161	1st	Wheat (w)	Soybeans, green	—
					2nd	Kaoliang (s)	Potatoes, sweet	—
					3rd	Wheat (w)	Beans, green (mung)	—
					4th	Kaoliang (s)	—	—
					5th	Wheat (w)	Proso millet, millet, broomcorn	—
RICE REGION: Yangtze Rice–Wheat Area Kiangsu Hinghwa	Level, irrigated	Non-calcareous alluvium	Silt loam	308	1st	Wheat or broadbeans (w)	Late rice	—
					2nd	Rapeseed (w)	Green manure (astragalus sinensis)	Early rice
Rice-Tea Area Chekiang Fenghwa	Level, hilly	Rice paddy soils	Clay loam	342	1st	Astragalus sinensis (w) (green manure)	Rice	—
				343	1st	Wheat (w)	Hemp or cotton	—
Kiangsi Nanchang	Undulating, flat	Rice paddy soils	Yellow soils	394	1st	Fallow (w)	Early rice	Buckwheat
					2nd	Winter radish (w)	Early rice	Soybeans
					3rd	Fallow (w)	Early rice	Sesame
					4th	Astragalus sinensis (w)	Early rice	Buckwheat

Region / Locality	Topography	Soil	No.	Crop order	Winter crop	Summer crop	Other
Szechwan Rice Area							
Szechwan							
Jenshou	—	Clay, sandy loam	430	1st	Wheat (w)	Potatoes, sweet	—
				2nd, 4th & 6th	Field peas (w)	Cotton	—
				3rd	Rapeseed (w)	Cotton	—
				5th	Wheat (w)	Potatoes, sweet, or kaoliang	—
Tahsien	—	—	445	1st	Rapeseed (w)	Rice	—
				2nd	Broad beans (w)	Rice	—
				3rd	Opium poppy (w)	Rice	—
Double Cropping Rice Area							
Fukien							
Hweian	Rolling moderately	Rice paddy soils	450	1st	Barley (w)	Early rice (or peanuts or cow-peas in time of drought)	—
Kwangsi							
Kweilin	Hilly and bottom land, terraced, irrigated	Rice paddy soils	465	1st	Broadbeans (w)	Rice	Beans, green
				2nd	Vegetables (w)	Rice	Potatoes, sweet
				3rd	Field peas (w)	Rice	—
Southwestern Rice Area							
Kweichow							
Pinchwan	Rolling sloping gently	Rice paddy soils	535	1st, 2nd or 6th	Broadbeans (w)	Millet	—
				3rd & 4th	Sugar cane (w)	—	—
				5th	Wheat (w)	Millet	—

Source: Buck, *Land Utilization—Atlas,* Table 18, pp. 253–69.

14. ESTIMATES OF GRAIN OUTPUT, 1957–70

A. 1957–60
(in millions of metric tons)

Year	Official Estimate	Owen L. Dawson[c]	Yuan-li Wu[d]
1957	185[a]	185	185
1958	250[a]	205	175
1959	270[b]	175	154
1960	150[b]	160	130

Sources: [a]*Ten Great Years*, p. 105. [b]See Edwin P. Jones, 'The Emerging Pattern of China's Economic Revolution,' in Joint Economic Committee, *Economic Profile*, 1:93. [c]Owen L. Dawson, *A Constraint on ChiCom Foreign Policy: Agricultural Output, 1966–1975* (Menlo Park, Calif.: Stanford Research Institute, February, 1967), p. 71. [d]Yuan-li Wu *et al.*, *The Economic Potential of Communist China* (Menlo Park, Calif.: Stanford Research Institute, 1963), 1:185; see also *idem*, *Arms Control Implications of Communist China's Domestic and Foreign Policies* (Stanford, Calif.: The Hoover Institution, January, 1967), Annex to Vol. 6, p. 7.

Year	Official (1)	Japan (2)	O. L. Dawson (3)	E. F. Jones (4)	Current Scene (5)	Soviet Union (6)	F. E. Econ. Review (7)	N.Y. Times (8)	Union Research Inst. (9)	Chao Kang (10)	Werner Klatt (11)	Y. L. Wu (12)
1961	162		170	162	167					160		140
1962	170–174		180	174	180					170		150
1963	183		185	183	178	185	185	185	184.5	182	190	179
1964	200		195	200	190	180	180	180	181.5	195	185	183
1965	200		207	200	185	185–190				200		
1966	180–200		205	200–210	178	180–185	175	175–180	182.5		190	
1967	190–200, 230		214		187–190, 182	180–185	190–220, 187					
1968									176.8			
1969		210							182.7			
1970	240	220–230							190.5		200	

Sources: (1) *Ten Great Years*, p. 119. Also, for 1961, 'Mao Told Viscount Montgomery,' *Sunday Times* (London), October 15, 1961; for 1962, Chou En-lai and 'an emigrant source,' quoted in *Dawn* (Karachi), April 11, 1963, and see Joint Economic Committee, *Economic Profile*, 1:93; for 1963 and 1964, Chou En-lai, quoted by Edgar Snow in *Asahi* (Tokyo), February 27, 1965; for 1966, *Peking Review*, No. 1, 1967, p. 18; for 1967, *ibid.*, and Anna Louise Strong, *Letter from China*, No. 55, January 15, 1968, p. 1; and for 1970, *New York Times*, March 13, 1971. (2) Foreign Ministry of Japan estimate; see FBIS *Daily Report: Communist China*, March 1, 1971, p. B1. (3) Owen L. Dawson, *Communist China's Agriculture: Its Development and Future Potential* (New York: Praeger Publishers, 1970), p. 18. (4) Edwin F. Jones, 'The Emerging Pattern of China's Economic Revolution,' in Joint Economic Committee, *Economic Profile*, 1:94; and *China Quarterly*, No. 33, January-March, 1968, p. 100. (5) *Current Scene*, 2, No. 27 (January 15, 1964): 4; 5, No. 21 (December 15, 1967): 10; and 7, No. 6 (March 31, 1969): 8. (6) *Yezhegodnik bolshoi sovetskoi entsiklopedii* (*Yearbook of the Great Soviet Encyclopedia*), 1964, pp. 238-84; 1965, p. 283; 1967, and 1968, p. 297. (7) *Far Eastern Economic Review: 1967 Yearbook*, p. 161; *1969 Yearbook*, p. 150; *1970 Yearbook*, p. 110. (8) *New York Times*, May 23, 1967. (9) *Tsu-kuo* (*China Monthly*), No. 3, 1966, p. 26; No. 5, 1967, p. 23; No. 2, 1968, p. 35; No. 3, 1969, p. 22; and No. 3, 1970, p. 7. (10) Kang Chao, *Agricultural Production in Communist China, 1949-1965* (Madison: University of Wisconsin Press, 1970), p. 246. (11) *China Quarterly*, No. 6, April-June, 1961, pp. 74-75; No. 31, July-September, 1967, p. 154; and No. 43, July-September, 1970, p. 118. (12) See sources for Wu (d) in table, subsection 14A, above.

15. DOMESTIC PRODUCTION AND IMPORTATION OF CHEMICAL FERTILIZERS, 1949–67, 1970

(in thousands of metric tons)

Year	Domestic Production			Imports	
	Ten Great Years (1)*	Jung-chao Liu (2)	Others, Including Official Estimates (3)	Jung-chao Liu (4)	Others (5)
1949	27	27	—	—	—
1950	70	70	—	—	—
1951	129	134	—	—	—
1952	181	188	194	137	139
1953	226	249	273	366	470
1954	298	327	361	504	650
1955	332	353	426	923	794
1956	523	623	663	1,083	1,336
1957	631	871	764	1,313	1,150
1958	811	1,462	983	1,797	1,500
1959	—	1,777	1,333	1,500	1,000
1960	—	2,000	1,675	1,134	787
1961	—	1,447	1,431	1,172	1,000
1962	—	2,170	2,050	1,318	1,150
1963	—	2,916	2,850	—	2,250
1964	—	—	4,280	—	975
1965	—	—	7,280	—	1,461
1966	11	—	8,500–10,036	—	3,110
1967	—	—	—	—	5,900
1970			(14,000		

* Excluding ammonium nitrate.

Sources: (1) *Ten Great Years*, p. 97. (2) Jung-chao Liu, *Fertilizer Application in Communist China*, Reprint No. 7 (Berkeley, Calif.: Social Science Research Council, Committee on the Economy of China, 1966), p. 32. (3) For 1952–62, see Wu *et al.*, *Economic Potential*, 3:34; the 1963 figure is estimated from a report in *JMJP*, January 1, 1964; for 1964, see *JMJP*, September 25, 1964; the 1965 figure is estimated from a report in *Ching-chi Tao-pao (Economic Bulletin)*, Nos. 951–52 (Hong Kong, January 1, 1966), p. 68; the higher 1966 figure is estimated from *JMJP*, December 30, 1966, and the lower is an estimate by Grace Wu, Hoover Institution; the 14 million tons for 1970 is as stated by Chou En-lai regarding the 'supply' in that year, quoted by Edgar Snow in the *New Republic*, March 27, 1971, but it is not clear whether the figure includes imports. (4) Liu, *Fertilizer Application*, p. 37. (5) For 1952–62, see Wu *et al.*, *Economic Potential*, 3:34; for 1963, see Dick Wilson, 'China's Trading Prospects,' *Far Eastern Economic Review*, 45, No. 8 (Hong Kong, August, 1964): 310; for 1964, see *Far Eastern Economic Review*, 46, No. 13 (December, 1964): 625 (calculation has been made in converting urea into ammonium sulphate on the basis of nitrogen content); for 1965–66, see Dawson, *Constraint on ChiCom Foreign Policy*, p. 44; the 1967 figure is compiled by Yuan-li Wu from issues of *China Trade Report*.

17. BILATERAL COMMITMENTS OF CHINESE CAPITAL TO DEVELOPING COUNTRIES, 1953-69

(in millions of U.S. dollars)

Year	Chinese Commitments	Total Commitments of All Centrally Planned Economies	Chinese Commitments as Percentage of Total
1953–63	453	4,795	9.4
1964	305	1,246	24.5
1965	77	646	11.9
1966	6	1,313	0.5
1967	40	527	7.6
1968	42	758	5.5
1969	—	776	—

Sources: U.N. Statistical Yearbook: 1968 (United Nations, 1969), p. 698, and *U.N. Statistical Yearbook: 1970* (United Nations, 1971), p. 710.

18. POPULATION ESTIMATES, 1953–65, AND PROJECTIONS, 1966–86

Total Population, Components of Change, and Vital Rates, Four Models
(absolute figures in thousands)

Item	1953	1954	1955	1956	1957	1958	1959	1960	1961	1962	1963	1964	1965
MODEL I													
Total population													
Census-based series	576,049	589,157	603,454	618,621	634,309	650,378	666,631	682,104	695,700	705,589	714,861	727,823	743,427
5% undercount series	606,367	620,165	635,215	651,180	667,694	684,608	701,717	718,004	732,316	742,725	752,485	766,129	782,555
10% undercount series	640,054	654,619	670,504	687,357	704,788	722,642	740,701	757,893	773,000	783,988	794,290	808,692	826,030
15% undercount series	677,705	693,126	709,946	727,789	746,246	765,151	784,272	802,475	818,471	830,105	841,013	856,262	874,620
Births													
Census-based series	26,217	26,628	27,055	27,485	27,912	28,331	28,739	29,114	29,431	29,664	29,890	30,233	30,678
5% undercount series	27,597	28,029	28,479	28,932	29,381	29,822	30,252	30,646	30,980	31,225	31,463	31,824	32,293
10% undercount series	29,130	29,587	30,061	30,538	31,013	31,479	31,932	32,349	32,701	32,960	33,211	33,592	34,087
15% undercount series	30,844	31,327	31,829	32,335	32,838	33,331	33,811	34,252	34,625	34,899	35,165	35,568	36,092
Deaths													
Census-based series	13,109	12,331	11,888	11,797	11,843	12,078	13,266	15,518	19,542	20,392	16,928	14,629	13,805
5% undercount series	13,799	12,980	12,514	12,418	12,466	12,714	13,964	16,335	20,571	21,465	17,819	15,399	14,532
10% undercount series	14,566	13,701	13,209	13,108	13,159	13,420	14,740	17,242	21,713	22,658	18,809	16,254	15,339
15% undercount series	15,422	14,507	13,986	13,879	13,933	14,209	15,607	18,256	22,991	23,991	19,915	17,211	16,241
Natural increase													
Census-based series	13,108	14,297	15,167	15,688	16,069	16,253	15,473	13,596	9,889	9,272	12,962	15,604	16,873
5% undercount series	13,798	15,049	15,965	16,514	16,915	17,108	16,287	14,311	10,409	9,760	13,644	16,425	17,761
10% undercount series	14,564	15,886	16,852	17,431	17,854	18,059	17,192	15,107	10,988	10,302	14,402	17,338	18,748
15% undercount series	15,422	16,820	17,843	18,456	18,905	19,121	18,204	15,996	11,634	10,908	15,250	18,357	19,851
Crude vital rates													
Birth rate	45.0	44.7	44.3	43.9	43.5	43.0	42.6	42.3	42.0	41.8	41.4	41.1	40.8
Death rate	22.5	20.7	19.5	18.8	18.4	18.3	19.7	22.5	27.9	28.7	23.5	19.9	18.4
Natural increase rate	22.5	24.0	24.8	25.0	25.0	24.7	22.9	19.7	14.1	13.1	18.0	21.2	22.4
Gross reproduction rate	298.6	298.6	298.6	298.6	298.6	298.6	298.6	298.6	298.6	298.6	298.6	298.6	298.6
Expectation of life													
Male	40.58	42.79	44.37	45.15	45.64	45.72	43.99	40.51	34.77	33.80	38.95	43.16	45.13
Female	42.37	44.79	46.45	47.39	47.97	48.09	46.05	42.08	36.03	34.89	40.41	45.01	47.33

MODEL II

Item	1953	1954	1955	1956	1957	1958	1959	1960	1961	1962	1963	1964	1965
Total population													
Census-based series	576,777	588,429	601,141	614,623	628,618	642,949	657,490	671,217	682,349	688,727	694,491	704,153	717,644
5% undercount series	607,134	619,399	632,780	646,972	661,703	676,788	692,095	706,544	718,262	724,976	731,043	741,214	755,415
10% undercount series	640,863	653,810	667,934	682,914	698,464	714,388	730,544	745,797	758,166	765,252	771,657	782,392	797,382
15% undercount series	678,561	692,269	707,225	723,086	739,551	756,411	773,518	789,667	802,764	810,267	817,048	828,415	844,287
Births													
Census-based series	26,217	26,587	26,972	27,357	27,739	28,114	28,481	28,812	29,073	29,229	29,379	29,651	30,058
5% undercount series	27,597	27,986	28,392	28,797	29,199	29,594	29,980	30,328	30,603	30,767	30,925	31,212	31,640
10% undercount series	29,130	29,541	29,969	30,397	30,821	31,238	31,646	32,013	32,303	32,477	32,643	32,946	33,398
15% undercount series	30,844	31,279	31,732	32,185	32,634	33,075	33,507	33,896	34,204	34,387	34,564	34,884	35,362
Deaths													
Census-based series	14,565	13,875	13,490	13,362	13,408	13,573	14,754	17,680	22,695	23,465	19,717	16,160	15,149
5% undercount series	15,332	14,605	14,200	14,065	14,114	14,287	15,531	18,611	23,889	24,700	20,755	17,011	15,946
10% undercount series	16,183	15,417	14,989	14,847	14,898	15,081	16,393	19,644	25,217	26,072	21,908	17,956	16,832
15% undercount series	17,135	16,324	15,871	15,720	15,774	15,968	17,358	20,800	26,700	27,606	23,196	19,012	17,822
Natural increase													
Census-based series	11,652	12,712	13,482	13,995	14,331	14,541	13,727	11,132	6,378	5,764	9,662	13,491	14,909
5% undercount series	12,265	13,381	14,192	14,732	15,085	15,307	14,449	11,717	6,714	6,067	10,170	14,201	15,694
10% undercount series	12,947	14,124	14,980	15,550	15,923	16,157	15,253	12,369	7,086	6,405	10,735	14,990	16,566
15% undercount series	13,709	14,955	15,861	16,465	16,860	17,107	16,149	13,096	7,504	6,781	11,368	15,872	17,540
Crude vital rates													
Birth rate	45.0	44.7	44.4	44.0	43.6	43.2	42.9	42.6	42.4	42.3	42.0	41.7	41.5
Death rate	25.0	23.3	22.2	21.5	21.1	20.9	22.2	26.1	33.1	33.9	28.2	22.7	20.9
Natural increase rate	20.0	21.4	22.2	22.5	22.5	22.4	20.7	16.4	9.3	8.3	13.8	19.0	20.6
Gross reproduction rate	298.3	298.3	298.3	298.3	298.3	298.3	298.3	298.3	298.3	298.3	298.3	298.3	298.3
Expectation of life													
Male	37.94	39.73	41.03	41.83	42.28	42.49	40.91	36.64	30.24	29.36	34.01	39.63	41.82
Female	39.34	41.32	42.69	43.61	44.14	44.41	42.51	37.82	31.17	30.15	35.14	41.20	43.63

MODEL III

Item	1953	1954	1955	1956	1957	1958	1959	1960	1961	1962	1963	1964	1965
Total population													
Census-based series	576,777	588,429	601,175	614,735	628,831	643,315	658,056	672,316	685,083	695,727	706,232	719,109	733,650
5% undercount series	607,134	619,399	632,816	647,089	661,927	677,174	692,690	707,701	721,140	732,344	743,402	756,957	772,263
10% undercount series	640,863	653,810	667,972	683,039	698,701	714,794	731,173	747,018	761,203	773,030	784,702	799,010	815,167
15% undercount series	678,561	692,269	707,265	723,218	739,801	756,841	774,184	790,960	805,980	818,502	830,861	846,011	863,118
Births													
Census-based series	23,304	23,673	24,057	24,442	24,816	25,182	25,539	25,870	26,161	26,402	26,641	26,946	27,316
5% undercount series	24,531	24,919	25,323	25,728	26,122	26,507	26,883	27,232	27,538	27,792	28,043	28,364	28,754
10% undercount series	25,893	26,303	26,730	27,158	27,573	27,980	28,377	28,744	29,068	29,336	29,601	29,940	30,351
15% undercount series	27,416	27,851	28,302	28,755	29,195	29,626	30,046	30,435	30,778	31,061	31,342	31,701	32,136
Deaths													
Census-based series	11,652	10,927	10,497	10,346	10,332	10,441	11,279	13,103	15,517	15,897	13,764	12,405	11,907
5% undercount series	12,265	11,502	11,049	10,891	10,876	10,991	11,873	13,793	16,334	16,734	14,488	13,058	12,534
10% undercount series	12,947	12,141	11,663	11,496	11,480	11,601	12,532	14,559	17,241	17,663	15,293	13,783	13,230
15% undercount series	13,708	12,855	12,349	12,172	12,155	12,284	13,269	15,415	18,255	18,702	16,193	14,594	14,008
Natural increase													
Census-based series	11,652	12,746	13,560	14,096	14,484	14,741	14,260	12,767	10,644	10,505	12,877	14,541	15,409
5% undercount series	12,266	13,417	14,274	14,837	15,246	15,516	15,010	13,439	11,204	11,058	13,555	15,306	16,220
10% undercount series	12,946	14,162	15,067	15,662	16,093	16,379	15,845	14,185	11,827	11,673	14,308	16,157	17,121
15% undercount series	13,708	14,996	15,953	16,583	17,040	17,342	16,777	15,020	12,523	12,359	15,149	17,107	18,128
Crude vital rates													
Birth rate	40.0	39.8	39.6	39.3	39.0	38.7	38.4	38.1	37.9	37.7	37.4	37.1	36.8
Death rate	20.0	18.4	17.3	16.6	16.2	16.0	17.0	19.3	22.5	22.7	19.3	17.1	16.1
Natural increase rate	20.0	21.4	22.3	22.7	22.8	22.7	21.4	18.8	15.4	15.0	18.1	20.0	20.8
Gross reproduction rate	265.4	265.4	265.4	265.4	265.4	265.4	265.4	265.4	265.4	265.4	265.4	265.4	265.4
Expectation of life													
Male	44.0	46.21	47.73	48.65	49.25	49.53	48.16	44.93	40.92	40.53	44.55	47.56	49.03
Female	45.96	48.54	50.29	51.25	51.92	52.25	50.69	47.10	42.74	42.26	46.61	50.06	51.68

MODEL IV

Item	1953	1954	1955	1956	1957	1958	1959	1960	1961	1962	1963	1964	1965
Total population													
Census-based series	577,505	587,700	599,042	611,176	623,807	636,730	649,811	662,370	673,498	682,430	691,129	702,079	714,622
5% undercount series	607,900	618,632	630,570	643,343	656,639	670,242	684,012	697,232	708,945	718,347	727,504	739,030	752,234
10% undercount series	641,672	653,000	665,602	679,084	693,119	707,478	722,012	735,967	748,331	758,256	767,921	780,088	794,024
15% undercount series	679,418	691,412	704,755	719,031	733,891	749,094	764,484	779,259	792,351	802,859	813,093	825,975	840,732
Births													
Census-based series	23,304	23,643	23,995	24,347	24,694	25,032	25,360	25,660	25,918	26,121	26,321	26,585	26,914
5% undercount series	24,531	24,887	25,258	25,628	25,994	26,349	26,695	27,011	27,282	27,496	27,706	27,984	28,331
10% undercount series	25,893	26,270	26,661	27,052	27,438	27,813	28,178	28,511	28,798	29,023	29,246	29,539	29,904
15% undercount series	27,416	27,815	28,229	28,644	29,052	29,449	29,835	30,188	30,492	30,731	30,966	31,276	31,664
Deaths													
Census-based series	13,109	12,301	11,861	11,716	11,771	11,951	12,801	14,532	16,986	17,422	15,371	14,042	13,413
5% undercount series	13,800	12,948	12,485	12,333	12,391	12,580	13,475	15,297	17,880	18,339	16,180	14,781	14,119
10% undercount series	14,566	13,668	13,179	13,018	13,079	13,279	14,223	16,147	18,873	19,358	17,079	15,602	14,903
15% undercount series	15,422	14,472	13,954	13,784	13,848	14,060	15,060	17,096	19,984	20,496	18,084	16,520	15,780
Natural increase													
Census-based series	10,195	11,342	12,134	12,631	12,923	13,081	12,559	11,128	8,932	8,699	10,950	12,543	13,501
5% undercount series	10,731	11,939	12,773	13,295	13,603	13,769	13,220	11,714	9,402	9,157	11,526	13,203	14,212
10% undercount series	11,327	12,602	13,482	14,034	14,359	14,534	13,955	12,364	9,925	9,665	12,167	13,937	15,001
15% undercount series	11,994	13,343	14,275	14,860	15,204	15,389	14,775	13,092	10,508	10,235	12,882	14,756	15,884
Crude vital rates													
Birth rate	40.0	39.8	39.7	39.4	39.2	38.9	38.7	38.4	38.2	38.0	37.8	37.5	37.3
Death rate	22.5	20.7	19.6	19.0	18.7	18.6	19.5	21.8	25.1	25.4	22.1	19.8	18.6
Natural increase rate	17.5	19.1	20.1	20.5	20.5	20.3	19.1	16.7	13.2	12.7	15.7	17.7	18.7
Gross reproduction rate	265.0	265.0	265.0	265.0	265.0	265.0	265.0	265.0	265.0	265.0	265.0	265.0	265.0
Expectation of life													
Male	40.97	43.09	44.56	45.39	45.77	45.87	44.60	41.72	37.98	37.48	40.95	43.69	45.31
Female	42.79	45.12	46.64	47.62	48.09	48.23	46.74	43.54	39.42	38.83	42.61	45.64	47.56

Item	1966	1967	1968	1969	1970	1971	1972	1973	1974	1975	1976
MODEL A (Model III, 1965 Population as Base)											
Total population											
Census-based series	749,059	764,673	780,680	797,058	813,806	830,953	848,498	866,459	884,841	903,639	922,837
5% undercount series	788,483	804,919	821,768	839,008	856,638	874,687	893,156	912,062	931,412	951,199	971,407
10% undercount series	832,288	849,637	867,422	885,620	904,229	923,281	942,776	962,732	983,157	1,004,043	1,025,374
15% undercount series	881,246	899,615	918,447	937,715	957,419	977,592	998,233	1,019,364	1,040,989	1,063,105	1,085,691
Births											
Census-based series	27,682	28,077	28,444	28,805	29,190	29,595	30,017	30,441	30,853	31,236	31,577
5% undercount series	29,139	29,555	29,941	30,321	30,726	31,153	31,597	32,043	32,477	32,880	33,239
10% undercount series	30,758	31,197	31,604	32,006	32,433	32,883	33,352	33,823	34,281	34,707	35,086
15% undercount series	32,567	33,032	33,464	33,888	34,341	34,818	35,314	35,813	36,298	36,748	37,149
Deaths											
Census-based series	12,068	12,070	12,066	12,057	12,043	12,050	12,056	12,059	12,055	12,038	12,021
5% undercount series	12,703	12,705	12,701	12,692	12,677	12,684	12,691	12,694	12,689	12,672	12,654
10% undercount series	13,409	13,411	13,407	13,397	13,381	13,389	13,396	13,399	13,394	13,376	13,357
15% undercount series	14,198	14,200	14,195	14,185	14,168	14,176	14,184	14,187	14,182	14,162	14,142
Natural increase											
Census-based series	15,614	16,007	16,378	16,748	17,147	17,545	17,961	18,382	18,798	19,198	19,556
5% undercount series	16,436	16,850	17,240	17,629	18,049	18,469	18,906	19,349	19,788	20,208	20,585
10% undercount series	17,349	17,786	18,197	18,609	19,052	19,494	19,956	20,424	20,887	21,331	21,729
15% undercount series	18,369	18,832	19,269	19,703	20,173	20,642	21,130	21,626	22,116	22,586	23,007
Crude vital rates											
Birth rate	36.6	36.3	36.1	35.8	35.5	35.2	35.0	34.8	34.5	34.2	33.9
Death rate	15.9	15.6	15.3	15.0	14.6	14.3	14.1	13.8	13.5	13.2	12.9
Natural increase rate	20.6	20.7	20.8	20.8	20.9	20.9	20.9	21.0	21.0	21.0	21.0
Gross reproduction rate	264.8	264.0	262.4	260.3	257.9	255.3	252.3	249.2	245.7	242.0	238.0
Expectation of life											
Male	49.22	49.70	50.19	50.69	51.19	51.66	52.14	52.62	53.10	53.59	54.10
Female	51.84	52.36	52.89	53.42	53.96	54.47	54.98	55.50	56.02	56.56	57.08

MODEL A – Con

Item	1977	1978	1979	1980	1981	1982	1983	1984	1985	1986
Total population										
Census-based series	942,393	962,277	982,437	1,002,771	1,023,201	1,043,620	1,063,901	1,083,850	1,103,195	1,121,572
5% undercount series	991,993	1,012,923	1,034,144	1,055,548	1,077,054	1,098,547	1,119,896	1,140,895	1,161,258	1,180,602
10% undercount series	1,047,103	1,069,197	1,091,597	1,114,190	1,136,890	1,159,578	1,182,112	1,204,278	1,225,772	1,246,191
15% undercount series	1,108,698	1,132,091	1,155,808	1,179,731	1,203,766	1,227,788	1,251,648	1,275,118	1,297,876	1,319,496
Births										
Census-based series	31,866	32,091	32,211	32,225	32,131	31,880	31,423	30,658	29,505	(X)
5% undercount series	33,543	33,780	33,906	33,921	33,822	33,558	33,077	32,272	31,058	(X)
10% undercount series	35,407	35,657	35,790	35,806	35,701	35,422	34,914	34,064	32,782	(X)
15% undercount series	37,489	37,754	37,895	37,912	37,801	37,506	36,968	36,068	34,712	(X)
Deaths										
Census-based series	11,982	11,931	11,877	11,795	11,712	11,599	11,474	11,313	11,128	(X)
5% undercount series	12,613	12,559	12,502	12,416	12,328	12,209	12,078	11,908	11,714	(X)
10% undercount series	13,313	13,257	13,197	13,106	13,013	12,888	12,749	12,570	12,364	(X)
15% undercount series	14,096	14,036	13,973	13,876	13,779	13,646	13,499	13,309	13,092	(X)
Natural increase										
Census-based series	19,884	20,160	20,334	20,430	20,419	20,281	19,949	19,345	18,377	(X)
5% undercount series	20,930	21,221	21,404	21,505	21,494	21,349	20,999	20,364	19,344	(X)
10% undercount series	22,094	22,400	22,593	22,700	22,688	22,534	22,165	21,494	20,419	(X)
15% undercount series	23,393	23,718	23,922	24,036	24,022	23,860	23,469	22,759	21,620	(X)
Crude vital rates										
Birth rate	33.5	33.0	32.5	31.8	31.1	30.3	29.3	28.0	26.5	(X)
Death rate	12.6	12.3	12.0	11.6	11.3	11.0	10.7	10.3	10.0	(X)
Natural increase rate	20.9	20.7	20.5	20.2	19.8	19.2	18.6	17.7	16.5	(X)
Gross reproduction rate	233.8	229.3	224.3	218.7	212.6	205.7	197.7	188.2	176.7	(X)
Expectation of life										
Male	54.61	55.12	55.64	56.17	56.70	57.23	57.77	58.31	58.86	(X)
Female	57.61	58.16	58.70	59.25	59.81	60.37	60.93	61.51	62.09	(X)

(X) Not applicable

MODEL B (Model III, 1965 Population as Base)

Item	1966	1967	1968	1969	1970	1971	1972	1973	1974	1975	1976
Total population											
Census-based series	749,059	764,196	779,283	794,808	810,801	827,288	844,309	861,915	880,133	898,953	917,845
5% undercount series	788,483	804,417	820,298	836,640	853,475	870,829	888,746	907,279	926,456	946,266	966,153
10% undercount series	832,288	849,107	865,870	883,120	900,890	919,209	938,121	957,683	977,926	998,837	1,019,828
15% undercount series	881,246	899,054	916,804	935,068	953,884	973,280	993,305	1,014,018	1,035,451	1,057,592	1,079,818
Births											
Census-based series	27,682	28,123	28,555	29,018	29,510	30,059	30,665	31,286	31,905	32,545	33,179
5% undercount series	29,139	29,603	30,058	30,545	31,063	31,641	32,279	32,933	33,584	34,258	34,925
10% undercount series	30,758	31,248	31,728	32,242	32,789	33,399	34,072	34,762	35,450	36,161	36,866
15% undercount series	32,567	33,086	33,594	34,139	34,718	35,364	36,076	36,807	37,535	38,288	39,034
Deaths											
Census-based series	12,545	13,036	13,030	13,025	13,023	13,038	13,059	13,068	13,085	13,653	14,227
5% undercount series	13,205	13,722	13,716	13,711	13,708	13,724	13,746	13,756	13,774	14,372	14,976
10% undercount	13,939	14,484	14,478	14,472	14,470	14,487	14,510	14,520	14,539	15,170	15,808
15% undercount series	14,759	15,336	15,329	15,324	15,321	15,339	15,364	15,374	15,394	16,062	16,738
Natural increase											
Census-based series	15,137	15,087	15,525	15,993	16,487	17,021	17,606	18,218	18,820	18,892	18,952
5% undercount series	15,934	15,881	16,342	16,834	17,355	17,917	18,533	19,177	19,810	19,886	19,949
10% undercount series	16,819	16,764	17,250	17,770	18,319	18,912	19,562	20,242	20,911	20,991	21,058
15% undercount series	17,808	17,750	18,265	18,815	19,397	20,025	20,712	21,433	22,141	22,226	22,296
Crude vital rates											
Birth rate	36.6	36.4	36.3	36.1	36.0	36.0	35.9	35.9	35.9	35.8	35.8
Death rate	16.6	16.9	16.6	16.2	15.9	15.6	15.3	15.0	14.7	15.0	15.3
Natural increase rate	20.0	19.5	19.7	19.9	20.1	20.4	20.6	20.9	21.2	20.8	20.4
Gross reproduction rate	264.8	264.5	263.7	262.7	261.4	260.0	258.7	257.1	255.3	253.4	251.6
Expectation of life											
Male	48.26	47.78	48.26	48.74	49.22	49.70	50.19	50.69	51.19	50.69	50.19
Female	50.78	50.24	50.78	51.33	51.84	52.36	52.89	53.42	53.96	53.42	52.89

MODEL B – Con

Item	1977	1978	1979	1980	1981	1982	1983	1984	1985	1986
Total population										
Census-based series	936,797	955,765	975,278	995,333	1,015,859	1,036,820	1,058,157	1,079,782	1,101,572	1,123,371
5% undercount series	986,102	1,006,068	1,026,608	1,047,719	1,069,325	1,091,389	1,113,849	1,136,613	1,159,549	1,182,496
10% undercount series	1,040,886	1,061,961	1,083,642	1,105,926	1,128,732	1,152,022	1,175,730	1,199,758	1,223,969	1,248,190
15% undercount series	1,102,114	1,124,429	1,147,386	1,170,980	1,195,128	1,219,788	1,244,891	1,270,332	1,295,967	1,321,613
Births										
Census-based series	33,768	34,298	34,813	35,243	35,664	35,997	36,234	36,327	36,237	(X)
5% undercount series	35,545	36,103	36,645	37,098	37,541	37,892	38,141	38,239	38,144	(X)
10% undercount series	37,520	38,109	38,681	39,159	39,627	39,997	40,260	40,363	40,263	(X)
15% undercount series	39,727	40,351	40,956	41,462	41,958	42,349	42,628	42,738	42,632	(X)
Deaths										
Census-based series	14,800	14,785	14,758	14,717	14,703	14,660	14,609	14,537	14,438	(X)
5% undercount series	15,579	15,563	15,535	15,492	15,477	15,432	15,378	15,302	15,198	(X)
10% undercount series	16,444	16,428	16,398	16,352	16,337	16,289	16,232	16,152	16,042	(X)
15% undercount series	17,412	17,394	17,362	17,314	17,298	17,247	17,187	17,102	16,986	(X)
Natural increase										
Census-based series	18,968	19,513	20,055	20,526	20,961	21,337	21,625	21,790	21,799	(X)
5% undercount series	19,966	20,540	21,110	21,606	22,064	22,460	22,763	22,937	22,946	(X)
10% undercount series	21,076	21,681	22,283	22,807	23,290	23,708	24,028	24,211	24,221	(X)
15% undercount series	22,315	22,957	23,594	24,148	24,660	25,102	25,441	25,636	25,646	(X)
Crude vital rates										
Birth rate	35.7	35.5	35.5	35.0	34.7	34.4	33.9	33.3	32.6	(X)
Death rate	15.6	15.3	15.0	14.6	14.3	14.0	13.7	13.3	13.0	(X)
Natural increase rate	20.0	20.2	20.4	20.4	20.4	20.4	20.2	20.0	19.6	(X)
Gross reproduction rate	249.4	247.1	244.7	241.7	238.8	235.4	231.4	226.6	220.9	(X)
Expectation of life										
Male	49.70	50.19	50.69	51.19	51.66	52.14	52.62	53.10	53.59	(X)
Female	52.36	52.89	53.42	53.96	54.47	54.98	55.50	56.02	56.56	(X)

(X) Not applicable

Item	1966	1967	1968	1969	1970	1971	1972	1973	1974	1975	1976
MODEL C (Model IV, 1965 Population as Base)											
Total population											
Census-based series	728,123	741,015	753,789	766,419	779,493	793,031	807,043	821,589	836,737	852,535	869,037
5% undercount series	766,445	780,016	793,462	806,757	820,519	834,769	849,519	864,830	880,776	897,405	914,776
10% undercount series	809,026	823,350	837,543	851,577	866,103	881,146	896,714	912,877	929,708	947,261	965,597
15% undercount series	856,615	871,782	886,811	901,669	917,051	932,978	949,462	966,575	984,396	1,002,982	1,022,396
Births											
Census-based series	27,245	27,640	28,020	28,414	28,829	29,293	29,833	30,443	31,116	31,840	32,611
5% undercount series	28,679	29,095	29,495	29,909	30,346	30,835	31,403	32,045	32,754	33,516	34,327
10% undercount series	30,272	30,711	31,133	31,571	32,032	32,548	33,148	33,826	34,573	35,378	36,234
15% undercount series	32,053	32,518	32,965	33,428	33,916	34,462	35,098	35,815	36,607	37,459	38,366
Deaths											
Census-based series	14,353	14,866	15,390	15,340	15,291	15,281	15,287	15,295	15,318	15,338	15,671
5% undercount series	15,108	15,648	16,200	16,147	16,096	16,085	16,092	16,100	16,124	16,145	16,496
10% undercount series	15,948	16,518	17,100	17,044	16,990	16,979	16,986	16,994	17,020	17,042	17,412
15% undercount series	16,886	17,489	18,106	18,047	17,989	17,978	17,985	17,994	18,021	18,045	18,436
Natural increase											
Census based series	12,892	13,447	12,630	13,074	13,538	14,012	14,546	15,148	15,798	16,502	16,940
5% undercount series	13,571	13,131	13,295	13,762	14,250	14,750	15,311	15,945	16,630	17,371	17,831
10% undercount series	14,324	14,193	14,033	14,527	15,042	15,569	16,162	16,832	17,553	18,336	18,822
15% undercount series	15,167	15,029	14,859	15,381	15,927	16,484	17,113	17,821	18,586	19,414	19,930
Crude vital rates											
Birth rate	37.1	37.0	36.9	36.8	36.7	36.6	36.6	36.7	36.8	37.0	37.2
Death rate	19.5	19.9	20.2	19.8	19.4	19.1	18.8	18.4	18.1	17.8	17.9
Natural increase rate	17.6	17.1	16.6	16.9	17.2	17.5	17.9	18.3	18.7	19.2	19.3
Gross reproduction rate	264.5	264.2	263.4	262.3	261.0	259.7	258.6	257.8	257.3	257.1	257.0
Expectation of life											
Male	44.05	43.56	43.07	43.56	44.05	44.50	44.97	45.43	45.91	46.38	46.38
Female	46.07	45.52	44.99	45.52	46.07	46.57	47.09	47.61	48.14	48.67	48.67

Item	1977	1978	1979	1980	1981	1982	1983	1984	1985	1986
MODEL C – Cor.										
Total population										
Census-based series	885,977	903,356	920,849	938,112	955,141	972,564	990,383	1,008,206	1,025,663	1,042,685
5% undercount series	932,607	950,901	969,315	987,486	1,005,412	1,023,752	1,042,508	1,061,269	1,079,645	1,097,563
10% undercount series	984,419	1,003,729	1,023,166	1,042,347	1,061,268	1,080,627	1,100,426	1,120,229	1,139,626	1,158,539
15% undercount series	1,042,326	1,062,772	1,083,352	1,103,661	1,123,695	1,144,193	1,165,156	1,186,125	1,206,662	1,226,688
Births										
Census-based series	33,382	34,145	34,896	35,628	36,351	37,075	37,800	38,517	39,219	(X)
5% undercount series	35,139	35,942	36,733	37,503	38,264	39,026	39,789	40,544	41,283	(X)
10% undercount series	37,091	37,939	38,773	39,587	40,390	41,194	42,000	42,797	43,577	(X)
15% undercount series	39,273	40,171	41,054	41,915	42,766	43,618	44,471	45,314	46,140	(X)
Deaths										
Census-based series	16,003	16,652	17,633	18,599	18,928	19,256	19,977	21,060	22,197	(X)
5% undercount series	16,845	17,528	18,561	19,578	19,924	20,269	21,028	22,168	23,365	(X)
10% undercount series	17,781	18,502	19,592	20,666	21,031	21,396	22,197	23,400	24,663	(X)
15% undercount series	18,827	19,591	20,745	21,881	22,268	22,654	23,502	24,776	26,114	(X)
Natural increase										
Census-based series	17,379	17,493	17,263	17,029	17,423	17,819	17,823	17,457	17,022	(X)
5% undercount series	18,294	18,414	18,172	17,925	18,340	18,757	18,761	18,376	17,918	(X)
10% undercount series	19,310	19,437	19,181	18,921	19,359	19,798	19,803	19,397	18,914	(X)
15% undercount series	20,446	20,580	20,309	20,034	20,498	20,964	20,969	20,538	20,026	(X)
Crude vital rates										
Birth rate	37.3	37.4	37.5	37.6	37.7	37.8	37.8	37.9	37.9	(X)
Death rate	17.9	18.3	19.0	19.6	19.6	19.6	20.0	20.7	21.5	(X)
Natural increase rate	19.4	19.2	18.6	18.0	18.1	18.2	17.8	17.2	16.5	(X)
Gross reproduction rate	257.0	257.0	257.0	257.0	257.0	257.0	257.0	257.0	257.0	(X)
Expectation of life										
Male	46.38	45.91	44.97	44.05	44.05	44.05	43.56	42.61	41.65	(X)
Female	48.67	48.14	47.09	46.07	46.07	46.07	45.52	44.49	43.44	(X)

(X)   Not applicable

MODEL D (Model I, 1965 Population as Base)

Item	1966	1967	1968	1969	1970	1971	1972	1973	1974	1975	1976
Total population											
Census-based series	760,300	776,709	793,348	810,253	827,483	844,745	862,068	879,450	896,887	914,356	932,201
5% undercount series	800,316	817,588	835,103	852,898	871,035	889,205	907,440	925,737	944,092	962,480	981,264
10% undercount series	844,778	863,010	881,498	900,281	919,426	938,606	957,853	977,167	996,541	1,015,951	1,035,779
15% undercount series	894,471	913,775	933,351	953,239	973,509	993,818	1,014,198	1,034,647	1,055,161	1,075,713	1,096,707
Births											
Census-based series	31,177	31,723	32,309	32,971	33,676	34,413	35,168	35,930	36,676	37,431	38,217
5% undercount series	32,818	33,393	34,009	34,706	35,448	36,224	37,019	37,821	38,606	39,401	40,228
10% undercount series	34,641	35,248	35,899	36,634	37,418	38,237	39,076	39,922	40,751	41,590	42,463
15% undercount series	36,679	37,321	38,011	38,789	39,619	40,486	41,374	42,271	43,148	44,036	44,961
Deaths											
Census-based series	14,768	15,084	15,404	15,741	16,414	17,090	17,786	18,493	19,207	19,586	19,978
5% undercount series	15,545	15,878	16,215	16,569	17,278	17,989	18,722	19,466	20,218	20,617	21,029
10% undercount series	16,409	16,760	17,116	17,490	18,238	18,989	19,762	20,548	21,341	21,762	22,198
15% undercount series	17,374	17,746	18,122	18,519	19,311	20,106	20,925	21,756	22,596	23,042	23,504
Natural increase											
Census-based series	16,409	16,639	16,905	17,230	17,262	17,323	17,382	17,437	17,469	17,845	18,239
5% undercount series	17,273	17,515	17,794	18,137	18,170	18,235	18,297	18,355	18,388	18,784	19,199
10% undercount series	18,232	18,488	18,783	19,144	19,180	19,248	19,314	19,374	19,410	19,884	20,265
15% undercount series	19,305	19,575	19,889	20,270	20,308	20,380	20,449	20,515	20,552	20,994	21,457
Crude vital rates											
Birth rate	40.6	40.4	40.3	40.3	40.3	40.3	40.4	40.5	40.5	40.5	40.6
Death rate	19.2	19.2	19.2	19.2	19.6	20.0	20.4	20.8	21.2	21.2	21.2
Natural increase rate	21.4	21.2	21.1	21.0	20.6	20.3	20.0	19.6	19.3	19.3	19.4
Gross reproduction rate	298.3	298.0	297.4	296.8	295.9	294.8	293.3	291.5	289.4	287.3	285.5
Expectation of life											
Male	44.05	44.05	44.05	44.05	43.56	43.07	42.59	42.11	41.65	41.65	41.65
Female	46.07	46.07	46.07	46.07	45.52	44.99	44.47	43.95	43.44	43.44	43.44

Item	1977	1978	1979	1980	1981	1982	1983	1984	1985	1986
MODEL D – Con										
Total population										
Census-based series	950,440	969,090	988,156	1,007,660	1,027,125	1,046,493	1,065,666	1,084,589	1,103,194	1,121,848
5% undercount series	1,000,463	1,020,095	1,040,164	1,060,695	1,081,184	1,101,571	1,121,754	1,141,673	1,161,257	1,180,893
10% undercount series	1,056,044	1,076,767	1,097,951	1,119,622	1,141,250	1,162,770	1,184,073	1,205,099	1,225,771	1,246,498
15% undercount series	1,118,165	1,140,106	1,162,536	1,185,482	1,208,382	1,231,168	1,253,725	1,275,987	1,297,875	1,319,821
Births										
Census-based series	39,026	39,856	40,709	41,504	42,239	42,865	43,430	43,924	44,298	(X)
5% undercount series	41,080	41,954	42,852	43,688	44,462	45,121	45,716	46,236	46,629	(X)
10% undercount series	43,362	44,284	45,232	46,116	46,932	47,628	48,256	48,804	49,220	(X)
15% undercount series	45,913	46,889	47,893	48,828	49,693	50,429	51,094	51,675	52,115	(X)
Deaths										
Census-based series	20,376	20,790	21,205	22,039	22,871	23,692	24,507	25,319	25,644	(X)
5% undercount series	21,448	21,884	22,321	23,199	24,075	24,939	25,797	26,652	26,994	(X)
10% undercount series	22,640	23,100	23,561	24,488	25,412	26,324	27,230	28,132	28,493	(X)
15% undercount series	23,972	24,459	24,947	25,928	26,907	27,873	28,832	29,787	30,169	(X)
Natural increase										
Census-based series	18,650	19,066	19,504	19,465	19,368	19,173	18,923	18,605	18,654	(X)
5% undercount series	19,632	20,070	20,531	20,489	20,387	20,182	19,919	19,584	19,635	(X)
10% undercount series	20,722	21,184	21,671	21,628	21,520	21,304	21,026	20,672	20,727	(X)
15% undercount series	21,941	22,430	22,946	22,900	22,786	22,556	22,262	21,886	21,946	(X)
Crude vital rate										
Birth rate	40.7	40.7	40.8	40.8	40.7	40.6	40.4	40.2	39.8	(X)
Death rate	21.2	21.2	21.2	21.7	22.1	22.4	22.8	23.1	23.1	(X)
Natural increase rate	19.4	19.5	19.5	19.1	18.7	18.2	17.6	17.0	16.8	(X)
Gross reproduction rate	284.0	282.8	281.9	280.7	279.2	277.1	274.7	272 .1	268.8	(X)
Expectation of life										
Male	41.65	41.65	41.65	41.15	40.66	40.18	39.70	39.23	39.23	(X)
Female	43.44	43.44	43.44	42.88	42.33	41.79	41.26	40.74	40.74	(X)

(X)   Not applicable

Item	1966	1967	1968	1969	1970	1971	1972	1973	1974	1975	1976
MODEL E (Model I, 1965 Population as Base)											
Total population											
Census-based series	760,300	776,681	793,155	808,106	817,447	816,274	823,865	836,133	850,858	867,915	885,504
5% undercount series	800,316	817,559	834,900	850,638	860,470	859,236	867,226	880,140	895,640	913,595	932,109
10% undercount series	844,778	862,979	881,283	897,896	908,274	906,971	915,406	929,037	945,398	964,350	983,893
15% undercount series	894,471	913,742	933,124	950,713	961,702	960,322	969,253	983,686	1,001,009	1,021,076	1,041,769
Births											
Census-based series	31,145	31,533	31,790	31,776	31,243	31,857	32,793	33,927	35,015	36,065	36,972
5% undercount series	32,784	33,193	33,463	33,448	32,887	33,534	34,519	35,713	36,858	37,963	38,918
10% undercount series	34,606	35,037	35,322	35,307	34,714	35,397	36,437	37,697	38,906	40,072	41,080
15% undercount series	36,641	37,098	37,400	37,384	36,756	37,479	38,580	39,914	41,194	42,429	43,496
Deaths											
Census-based series	14,764	15,059	16,839	22,435	32,416	24,266	20,525	19,202	17,958	18,476	20,796
5% undercount series	15,541	15,852	17,725	23,616	34,122	25,543	21,605	20,213	18,903	19,448	21,891
10% undercount series	16,404	16,732	18,710	24,928	36,018	26,962	22,806	21,336	19,953	20,529	23,107
15% undercount series	17,369	17,716	19,811	26,394	38,136	28,548	24,147	22,591	21,127	21,736	24,466
Natural increase											
Census-based series	16,381	16,474	14,951	9,341	-1,173	7,591	12,268	14,725	17,057	17,589	16,176
5% undercount series	17,243	17,341	15,738	9,832	-1,235	7,991	12,914	15,500	17,955	18,515	17,027
10% undercount series	18,202	18,305	16,612	10,379	-1,304	8,435	13,631	16,361	18,953	19,543	17,973
15% undercount series	19,272	19,382	17,589	10,990	-1,380	8,931	14,433	17,323	20,067	20,693	19,030
Crude vital rates											
Birth rate	40.5	40.2	39.7	39.1	38.2	38.8	39.5	40.2	40.7	41.1	41.4
Death rate	19.2	19.2	21.0	27.6	39.7	29.6	24.7	22.8	20.9	21.1	23.3
Natural increase rate	21.3	21.0	18.7	11.5	-1.4	9.3	14.8	17.5	19.8	20.1	18.1
Gross reproduction rate	298.0	296.3	292.7	286.4	276.2	277.7	279.8	282.2	283.4	283.7	282.8
Expectation of life											
Male	44.05	44.05	41.65	34.39	24.70	31.91	36.88	39.23	41.65	41.65	39.23
Female	46.07	46.07	43.44	35.58	25.19	33.05	38.12	40.74	43.44	43.44	40.74

MODEL E – Con

Item	1977	1978	1979	1980	1981	1982	1983	1984	1985	1986
Total population										
Census-based series	901,680	916,100	925,813	926,095	917,834	921,820	931,889	944,879	960,470	973,983
5% undercount series	949,137	964,316	974,540	974,837	966,141	970,337	980,936	994,609	1,011,021	1,025,245
10% undercount series	1,001,867	1,017,889	1,028,681	1,028,994	1,019,816	1,024,244	1,035,432	1,049,866	1,067,189	1,082,203
15% undercount series	1,060,800	1,077,765	1,089,192	1,089,524	1,079,805	1,084,494	1,096,340	1,111,622	1,129,965	1,145,862
Births										
Census-based series	37,621	37,862	37,449	36,058	36,603	37,464	38,495	39,386	40,156	(X)
5% undercount series	39,601	39,855	39,420	37,956	38,529	39,436	40,521	41,459	42,269	(X)
10% undercount series	41,801	42,069	41,610	40,064	40,670	41,627	42,772	43,762	44,618	(X)
15% undercount series	44,260	44,544	44,058	42,421	43,062	44,075	45,288	46,336	47,242	(X)
Deaths										
Census-based series	23,201	28,149	37,167	44,319	32,617	27,395	25,505	23,795	26,643	(X)
5% undercount series	24,422	29,631	39,123	46,652	34,334	28,837	26,847	25,047	28,045	(X)
10% undercount series	25,779	31,277	41,297	49,243	36,241	30,439	28,339	26,439	29,603	(X)
15% undercount series	27,295	33,116	43,726	52,140	38,373	32,229	30,006	27,994	31,345	(X)
Natural increase										
Census-based series	14,420	9,713	282	-8,261	3,986	10,069	12,990	15,591	13,513	(X)
5% undercount series	15,179	10,224	297	-8,696	4,195	10,599	13,674	16,412	14,224	(X)
10% undercount series	16,022	10,792	313	-9,179	4,429	11,188	14,433	17,323	15,015	(X)
15% undercount series	16,965	11,428	332	-9,719	4,689	11,846	15,282	18,342	15,897	(X)
Crude vital rates										
Birth rate	41.4	41.1	40.4	39.1	39.8	40.4	41.0	41.3	41.5	(X)
Death rate	25.5	30.6	40.1	48.1	35.5	29.6	27.2	25.0	27.5	(X)
Natural increase rate	15.9	10.5	.3	-9.0	4.3	10.9	13.8	16.4	14.0	(X)
Gross reproduction rate	280.4	275.6	267.3	253.8	255.3	257.4	259.8	261.0	261.3	(X)
Expectation of life										
Male	36.88	31.91	24.70	19.73	27.18	31.91	34.39	36.88	34.39	(X)
Female	38.12	33.05	25.19	20.12	27.73	33.05	35.58	38.12	35.58	(X)

(X) Not applicable

Item	1966	1967	1968	1969	1970	1971	1972	1973	1974	1975	1976
MODEL F (Model II, 1965 Population as Base)											
Total population											
Census-based series	732,553	747,109	761,361	775,125	788,128	773,157	713,240	693,358	688,592	696,179	706,171
5% undercount series	771,108	786,430	801,433	815,921	829,608	813,849	750,779	729,850	724,834	732,820	743,338
10% undercount series	813,948	830,121	845,957	861,250	875,698	859,063	792,489	770,398	765,102	773,532	784,634
15% undercount series	861,827	878,952	895,719	911,912	927,209	909,596	839,106	815,713	810,108	819,034	830,789
Births											
Census-based series	30,456	30,745	30,834	30,569	28,107	23,350	24,977	26,871	30,453	32,190	33,501
5% undercount series	32,059	32,363	32,457	32,178	29,586	24,579	26,292	28,285	32,056	33,884	35,264
10% undercount series	33,840	34,161	34,260	33,966	31,230	25,944	27,752	29,857	33,837	35,767	37,223
15% undercount series	35,831	36,171	36,275	35,964	33,067	27,471	29,385	31,613	35,827	37,871	39,413
Deaths											
Census-based series	15,900	16,493	17,070	17,566	43,078	83,267	44,859	31,637	22,866	22,198	21,308
5% undercount series	16,737	17,361	17,968	18,491	45,345	87,649	47,220	33,302	24,069	23,366	22,429
10% undercount series	17,667	18,326	18,967	19,518	47,864	92,519	49,843	35,152	25,407	24,664	23,676
15% undercount series	18,706	19,404	20,082	20,666	50,680	97,961	52,775	37,220	26,901	26,115	25,068
Natural increase											
Census-based series	14,556	14,252	13,764	13,003	-14,971	-59,917	-19,882	-4,766	7,587	9,992	12,193
5% undercount series	15,322	15,002	14,489	13,687	-15,759	-63,070	-20,928	-5,017	7,987	10,518	12,835
10% undercount series	16,173	15,835	15,293	14,448	-16,634	-66,575	-22,091	-5,295	8,430	11,103	13,547
15% undercount series	17,125	16,767	16,193	15,298	-17,613	-70,490	-23,390	-5,607	8,926	11,756	14,345
Crude vital rates											
Birth rate	41.2	40.8	40.1	39.1	36.0	31.4	35.5	38.9	44.0	45.9	47.0
Death rate	21.5	21.9	22.2	22.5	55.2	112.0	63.8	45.8	33.0	31.7	29.9
Natural increase rate	19.7	18.9	17.9	16.6	-19.2	-80.6	-28.3	-6.9	11.0	14.3	17.1
Gross reproduction rate	297.4	295.0	290.2	281.9	253.5	208.8	223.7	238.6	268.4	278.3	283.6
Expectation of life											
Male	41.15	40.66	40.18	39.70	17.77	2.56	9.69	17.62	27.18	29.54	31.91
Female	42.88	42.33	41.79	41.26	17.83	1.26	8.08	17.17	27.73	30.36	33.05

Item	1977	1978	1979	1980	1981	1982	1983	1984	1985	1986
MODEL F – Con										
Total population										
Census-based series	718,364	732,682	748,170	764,954	782,430	800,616	819,493	839,023	859,102	879,181
5% undercount series	756,173	771,244	787,547	805,215	823,610	842,754	862,624	883,182	904,318	925,454
10% undercount series	798,182	814,091	831,300	849,949	869,367	889,573	910,548	932,248	954,558	976,868
15% undercount series	845,134	861,979	880,200	899,946	920,506	941,901	964,109	987,086	1,010,708	1,034,331
Births										
Census-based series	34,655	35,745	36,764	37,757	38,701	39,580	40,364	40,995	41,418	(X)
5% undercount series	36,479	37,626	38,699	39,744	40,738	41,663	42,488	43,153	43,598	(X)
10% undercount series	38,506	39,717	40,849	41,952	43,001	43,978	44,849	45,550	46,020	(X)
15% undercount series	40,771	42,053	43,252	44,420	45,531	46,565	47,487	48,229	48,727	(X)
Deaths										
Census-based series	20,337	20,257	19,980	20,281	20,515	20,703	20,834	20,916	21,339	(X)
5% undercount series	21,407	21,323	21,032	21,348	21,595	21,793	21,931	22,017	22,462	(X)
10% undercount series	22,597	22,508	22,200	22,534	22,794	23,003	23,149	23,240	23,710	(X)
15% undercount series	23,926	23,832	23,506	23,860	24,135	24,356	24,511	24,607	25,105	(X)
Natural increase										
Census-based series	14,318	15,488	16,784	17,476	18,186	18,877	19,530	20,079	20,079	(X)
5% undercount series	15,072	16,303	17,667	18,396	19,143	19,870	20,557	21,136	21,136	(X)
10% undercount series	15,909	17,209	18,649	19,418	20,207	20,975	21,700	22,310	22,310	(X)
15% undercount series	16,845	18,221	19,746	20,560	21,396	22,209	22,976	23,622	23,622	(X)
Crude vital rates										
Birth rate	47.8	48.3	48.6	48.8	48.9	48.9	48.7	48.3	47.7	(X)
Death rate	28.0	27.4	26.4	26.2	25.9	25.6	25.1	24.6	24.6	(X)
Natural increase rate	19.7	20.9	22.2	22.6	23.0	23.3	23.6	23.6	23.1	(X)
Gross reproduction rate	287.2	289.9	292.0	293.8	295.3	296.5	297.4	297.9	298.3	(X)
Expectation of life										
Male	34.39	35.56	36.88	37.34	37.80	38.27	38.75	39.23	39.23	(X)
Female	35.58	36.77	38.12	38.63	39.14	39.66	40.20	40.74	40.74	(X)

(X) Not applicable

Source: John S. Aird, *Estimates and Projections of the Population of Mainland China, 1953–1986* (Washington, D.C.: U.S. Government Printing Office, 1968), pp. 42–49.

19. THE FIRST FOURTEEN NUCLEAR AND TWO SATELLITE TESTS IN CHINA

Nuclear Tests
1. October 16, 1964, Lop Nor, Sinkiang
   Device mounted on a 70-meter steel tower. Uranium-235 was used to produce a yield equivalent to 20,000 tons of TNT.
2. May 14, 1965, Lop Nor, Sinkiang
   The bomb was delivered by an airplane. Uranium-235 was used to produce a yield of 20,000 to 40,000 tons of TNT.
3. May 9, 1966, Lop Nor, Sinkiang
   The bomb was delivered by a bomber. Uranium-235 plus elemental thermonuclear lithium-6 were used to produce a force of 200,000-plus tons of TNT.
4. October 27, 1966, Lop Nor, Sinkiang
   A nuclear warhead (uranium-235) on a medium-range guided missile of the Soviet SS-3 type. Yield: 20,000-plus tons of TNT.
5. December 28, 1966, Lop Nor, Sinkiang
   Tower-mounted. Composition similar to the 3d test. The yield equaled 300,000–500,000 tons of TNT.
6. June 17, 1967, Lop Nor, Sinkiang
   Hydrogen bomb composed of uranium-235, uranium-238, and heavy hydrogen plus lithium. Three megatons of TNT. Air-dropped.
7. December 24, 1967, Lop Nor, Sinkiang
   An air-dropped device believed to be composed of uranium-235, uranium-238 and lithium-6. The yield was in the range of 15,000–25,000 tons of TNT. Test appeared unsuccessful and only fission stage completed.
8. December 27, 1968, Lop Nor, Sinkiang
   Air-dropped hydrogen bomb. The bomb used uranium-235 for the fuse, lithium for the nucleus, and uranium-238 for the crust, producing a force of three megatons of TNT.
9. September 22, 1969
   First underground fission test. Yield: 25,000 tons of TNT.
10. September 29, 1969
    Air-dropped fusion device. Yield: three megatons of TNT.
11. October 14, 1970
    Air-dropped fusion device. Yield: in excess of three megatons of TNT.
12. November 18, 1971, no data on location, presumably Lop Nor, Sinkiang
    Yield: 20 kilotons of TNT.
13. January 7, 1972, no data on location, presumably Lop Nor, Sinkiang
    Yield: 20 kilotons of TNT.
14. March 18, 1972, no data on location, presumably Lop Nor, Sinkiang
    Yield: 100–200 kilotons of TNT.

Satellite Tests
1. April 24, 1970 from Manchuria
   Weight: 173 kilograms.
2. March 3, 1971 from Manchuria
   Weight: 221 kilograms.

Sources: Issues and Studies, 5. No. 5 (Taipei: Institute of International Relations, February, 1969): 1–2; NCNA dispatch, October 4, 1969; and Institute for Strategic Studies, *Strategic Survey, 1970* (London, 1971), p. 34; Hideo Sekino, 'China's Nuclear Armament and its Effect on Pacific Asia,' *Pacific Community*, Vol. 3, No. 4, Tokyo. NCNA Peking, November 19, 1971, and January 9, 1972. For satellite tests, see *1971 Yearbook on Chinese Communism* (Taipei, 1972), p. 11–77, and *Washington Post*, March 4, 1971.

20. EDUCATION ENROLLMENT STATISTICS, 1949–65

Year	Enrollment (in millions)			Estimated Per Cent of Population		
	Primary	Secondary	Higher	Primary	Secondary	Higher
1949–50	24.4	1.27	0.117	4.5	0.23	0.021
1952–53	51.1	3.13	.191	8.9	.54	.033
1957–58	64.3	7.06	.441	10.0	1.09	.668
1958–59	8.64	9.99	.660	13.1	1.52	.100
1959–60	90.0	12.9	.81	13.5	1.93	.121
1960–61	85.0	15.0	.90	12.6	2.22	.133
1961–62	76.0	13.1	.85	11.2	1.93	.125
1962–63	73.0	12.0	.75	10.6	1.75	.100
1963–64	76.0	11.5	.68	10.9	1.65	.098
1964–65	80.0	12.5	.70	11.2	1.75	.098

Source: Jones, 'Emerging Pattern,' in Joint Economic Committee, *Economic Profile*, 1:95. No recent data are available.

21. GRADUATES FROM INSTITUTIONS OF HIGHER LEARNING BY FIELD, 1948–49—1965–66

Year	Total		Engineering		Natural Sciences		Agriculture and Forestry		Medicine		Education		Finance and Economics		Other	
	Number	Per Cent	Number	Per Cent	Number	Per Cent	Number	Per Cent	Number	Per Cent	Number	Per Cent	Number	Per Cent	Number	Per Cent
Total	1,716,000	100	577,840	34	98,387	6	140,149	8	184,868	11	468,417	27	87,140	5	159,199	9
1948–49	21,000	100	4,752	23	1,584	8	1,718	8	1,314	6	1,890	9	3,137	15	6,605	32
1949–50	18,000	100	4,711	26	1,403	8	1,477	8	1,391	8	624	4	3,305	18	5,024	28
1950–51	19,000	100	4,416	23	1,488	8	1,538	8	2,366	12	1,206	6	3,638	19	4,548	23
1951–52	32,000	100	10,213	32	2,215	7	2,361	7	2,636	8	3,077	10	7,263	23	4,235	13
1952–53	48,000	100	14,565	30	1,753	4	2,933	6	2,948	6	9,650	20	10,530	22	5,921	12
1953–54	47,000	100	15,596	33	802	2	3,532	8	4,527	10	10,551	22	6,033	13	5,959	13
1954–55	55,000	100	18,614	34	2,015	4	2,614	5	6,840	12	12,133	22	4,699	8	8,685	15
1955–56	63,000	100	22,047	35	3,978	6	3,541	6	5,403	9	17,243	27	4,460	7	6,328	10
1956–57	56,000	100	17,162	31	3,524	6	3,104	6	6,200	11	15,948	28	3,651	6	6,411	11
1957–58	72,000	100	17,499	24	4,645	6	3,513	5	5,393	8	31,595	44	2,349	3	7,006	10
1958–59	70,000	100	(23,310)	(33)	(4,410)	(6)	6,318	9	9,000	13	(21,000)	(30)	(2,450)	(4)	(3,512)	(5)
1959–60	135,000	100	(44,955)	(33)	(8,505)	(6)	(10,800)	(8)	(14,850)	(11)	(40,500)	(30)	(4,725)	(4)	(10,665)	(8)
1960–61	162,000	100	54,000	33	10,000	6	12,000	7	19,000	12	49,000	30	5,670	4	12,330	8
1961–62	178,000	100	59,000	33	11,000	6	20,000	11	17,000	10	56,000	32	(6,230)	(4)	(8,770)	(5)
1962–63	200,000	100	77,000	38	10,000	5	17,000	8	25,000	12	46,000	23	3,000	2	22,000	16
1963–64	200,000	100	(70,000)	(35)	(11,000)	(6)	(18,000)	(9)	(23,000)	(11)	(56,000)	(28)	(6,000)	(3)	(16,000)	(8)
1964–65	170,000	100	(60,000)	(35)	(10,000)	(6)	(15,000)	(9)	(19,000)	(11)	(48,000)	(28)	(5,000)	(3)	(13,000)	(8)
1965–66	(170,000)	100	(60,000)	(35)	(10,000)	(6)	(15,000)	(9)	(19,000)	(11)	(48,000)	(28)	(5,000)	(3)	(13,000)	(8)

Note: Numbers in parentheses are estimates. Percentage detail may not add to total because of rounding.

Sources: Leo A. Orleans, 'Communist China's Education: Policies, Problems, and Prospects,' in Joint Economic Committee, *Economic Profile*, 2:511. See also Survey Research Corporation, *Directory of Selected Scientific Institutions in Mainland China* (Stanford, Calif.: Published for the National Science Foundation by the Hoover Institution Press, 1970. Orleans lists the following sources for figures: for the first fifteen academic years, C. Y. Cheng, *Scientific and Engineering Manpower in Communist China, 1949–63* (Washington, D.C.: National Science Foundation, 1965), p. 78; for 1963–64, total in *Chung-kuo Ching Nien Pao* (*China Youth Daily*), August 13, 1964, with distribution based on average for three preceding years; for 1965–66, the total was reported in *JMJP*, August 11, 1965, and the distribution figured as for 1963–64; for 1964–65, the total was repeated on the preceding year, assumption that (1) there was no drastic change in figures or distribution at the outset and (2) the students pursued their studies most of the year, although the Cultural Revolution interfered with the orderly completion of studies so that 'most probably the majority of the students received neither a certificate of completion nor a job assignment.'

22. RESEARCH INSTITUTES OF THE ACADEMY OF SCIENCES
(prior to the Cultural Revolution)

1. Institute of Applied Chemistry
2. Institute of Applied Physics
3. Institute of Semiconductors
4. Institute of Atomic Energy
5. Institute of Chemistry
6. Institute of Organic Chemistry
7. Institute of Mathematics
8. Institute of Mechanics
9. Institute of Materia Medica
10. Institute of Computing Technology
11. Institute of Electronics
12. Institute of Physics
13. Tsu-chin-shan Observatory
14. Peking Observatory
15. Shanghai Institute of Mathematics
16. Institute of Chemical Physics
17. Institute of High Polymer
18. Institute of Engineering Mechanics
19. Institute of Acoustics
20. Shanghai Observatory
21. Lanchou Institute of Chemical Physics
22. East China Institute of Computing Technology
23. Institute of Botany
24. Institute of Biochemistry
25. Institute of Biophysics
26. Institute of Experimental Biology
27. Institute of Entomology
28. Institute of Genetics
29. Institute of Hydrobiology
30. Institute of Microbiology
31. Institute of Oceanography
32. Peking Institute of Plant Physiology
33. Institute of Physiology
34. Institute of Plant Physiology
35. Institute of Psychology
36. South China Institute of Botany
37. Wuhan Institute of Microbiology
38. Institute of Zoology
39. Institute of Applied Mycology
40. Institute of Applied Entomology
41. Nanking Institute of Botany
42. Northwest Institute of Biology and Pedology
43. Sinkiang Institute of Water, Soil and Biological Resources
44. The Compilation Committee of the Chinese Flora
45. Amoy Institute of Marine Biology
46. Institute of Forestry and Pedology
47. Institute of Geology
48. Institute of Geophysics and Meteorology
49. Institute of Geology and Paleontology
50. Institute of Pedology
51. Institute of Upper Atmosphere Physics
52. Institute of Geography
53. Institute of Vertebrate Paleontology and Paleoanthropology
54. Institute of Seismology
55. Ch'angch'un Institute of Geology
56. Committee for Publishing National Grand Atlas
57. Institute of Geodesy and Cartography
58. Chungking Laboratory of Soil
59. Institute of Geological Mechanics
60. Lanchou Institute of Geology
61. Institute of Automation and Remote Control
62. Institute of Chemical Metallurgy
63. Institute of Civil Engineering and Architecture
64. Laboratory of Coal

65. Institute of Electrical Engineering
66. Institute of Mechanical Engineering
67. Institute of Metallurgy and Ceramics
68. Institute of Metals
69. Institute of Mining and Metallurgy
70. Institute of Petroleum
71. Institute of Optical and Precision Instruments
72. Institute of Chemistry and Technology of Silicates
73. Institute of Water Conservation
74. Institute of Comprehensive Transportation
75. Institute of Hydrotechnical Research
76. Institute of Metallurgy
77. Institute of Power Engineering
78. Kunming Institute of Precious Metals
79. Institute of Automation
80. Institute of Soil and Water Conservation
81. Institute of Radio Engineering
82. Institute of Coal Chemistry
83. Institute of Petroleum Chemistry
84. Institute of Mechanical and Electrical Engineering
85. Institute of Archaeology
86. Institute of Economics
87. Institute of History
88. Institute of International Relations
89. Institute of Linguistics and Languages
90. Institute of Literature
91. Institute of Philosophy
92. Institute of Minority Languages
93. Institute of Nationalities
94. Institute of Law
95. Institute of Modern History
96. Institute of World Economy

Source: Survey Research Corporation, *Directory of Selected Scientific Institutions in Mainland China* (Stanford, Calif.: Published for the National Science Foundation by Hoover Institution Press, 1970).

23. RESEARCH INSTITUTES OF THE CHINESE ACADEMY OF AGRICULTURAL SCIENCES

(prior to the Cultural Revolution)

1. Institute of Agricultural Economics
2. Institute of Agricultural Mechanization
3. Institute of Agricultural Meteorology
4. Institute of Animal Husbandry
5. Institute of Cotton
6. Institute of Crop Breeding and Cultivation
7. Institute of Agricultural Heredity
8. Institute of Irrigation
9. Institute of Plant Protection
10. Institute of Pomology
11. Institute of Sericulture
12. Institute of Soils and Fertilizers
13. Institute of Tobacco
14. Institute of Agricultural Uses of Atomic Energy
15. Institute of Chinese Veterinary Sciences
16. Institute of Olericulture
17. Institute of Apiculture
18. Institute of Sugar Beets
19. Institute of Tea
20. Institute of Hemp
21. Institute of Potatoes
22. Institute of Marsh Gas
23. Institute of Oil-bearing Vegetables
24. Institute of Oak Silkworm Culture
25. Institute of Peanuts
26. Institute of Poultry
27. Institute of Oranges
28. Institute of Buffaloes
29. Institute of Hogs

Source: Ibid. (same as Section 21, above).

24. RESEARCH INSTITUTES OF THE CHINESE ACADEMY OF MEDICAL SCIENCES

(prior to the Cultural Revolution)

1. Institute of Acupuncture and Moxibustion
2. Institute of Antibiotics
3. Institute of Biologicals
4. Institute of Dermatology and Venereology
5. Institute of Epidemiology and Microbiology
6. Institute of Experimental Medicine
7. Institute of Blood Transfusion and Hematology
8. Institute of Medical Radiology
9. Institute of Neurosurgery
10. Institute of Oncology
11. Institute of Parasitic Diseases
12. Institute of Pediatrics
13. Institute of Pharmacology
14. Institute of Tuberculosis
15. Institute of Hypertension
16. Institute of Traditional Chinese Medicine
17. Institute of Internal Medicine
18. Institute of Surgery
19. Laboratory of Isotopes
20. Institute of Labor Hygiene, Labor Protection, and Occupational Diseases
21. Institute of Medical Biology

Source: Ibid.

25. SCIENTIFIC RESEARCH INSTITUTES AND PERSONNEL IN MEDICAL SCIENCE AND PUBLIC HEALTH, 1958

Number of institutes	101
Personnel,	12,100
including:	
Research and	
technical personnel	2,200

Source: Ten Great Years, p. 203. See also Survey Research Corporation, *Directory of Selected Scientific Institutions in Mainland China* (Stanford, Calif.: Published for the National Science Foundation by Hoover Institution Press, 1970).

26. MEDICAL SCHOOLS, PARTIAL LISTING

1. Anhwei Medical College, Hofei
2. Canton College of Traditional Chinese Medicine, Canton
3. Chungshan Medical College, Canton
4. Chekiang Medical University, Hangchow
5. Ch'engtu College of Traditional Chinese Medicine, Ch'engtu
6. Chinese Medical University, Peking
7. Chungking Medical College, Chungking
8. Dairen Medical College, Dairen
9. Fukien Medical College, Foochow
10. Harbin Medical University, Harbin
11. Honan Medical College, Chengchou
12. Hopei Medical College, Shihchiachuang
13. Hunan Medical College, Ch'angcha
14. Hupei Medical College, Wuhan
15. Inner Mongolia Medical College, Huhehot
16. Kiangsi Medical College, Nanchang
17. Kiangsu Medical College, Nanking
18. Kirin Medical University, Ch'angch'un
19. Kunming Medical College, Kunming
20. Kwangsi Medical College, Kweilin
21. Kweiyang Medical College, Kweiyang
22. Lanchow Medical College, Lanchow
23. Nanking College of Pharmacology, Nanking
24. Nantung Medical College, Nantung
25. Peking College of Traditional Chinese Medicine, Peking
26. Peking Medical College, Peking
27. Shanghai College of Traditional Chinese Medicine, Shanghai
28. Shanghai First Medical College, Shanghai
29. Shanghai Second Medical College, Shanghai
30. Shansi Medical College, Taiyüan
31. Shangtung Medical College, Tsinan
32. Shenyang College of Pharmacology, Shenyang
33. Shenyang Medical College, Shenyang
34. Sian Medical College, Sian
35. Sinkiang Medical College, Urumchi
36. Soochow Medical College, Soochow
37. Szechwan Medical College, Ch'engtu
38. Tientsin Medical University, Tientsin
39. Tsingtao Medical College, Tsingtao
40. Tsitsihar Medical College, Tsitsihar
41. T'ungchi Medical College, Shanghai
42. Wuhan Medical College, Wuhan
43. University of Military Medicine, Shanghai
44. Yenpien Medical College, Yenchi

Source: Survey Research Corporation, *Directory of Selected Scientific Institutions.*

27. HOSPITALS AND MEDICAL CARE, 1949–59, 1962

A. Beds in Hospitals and Sanitoriums

Year	Number of Beds
1949	84,000
1950	106,000
1951	134,000
1952	180,000
1953	215,000
1954	250,000
1955	279,000
1956	328,000
1957	364,000
1958	440,000
1959	570,000
1962	660,000

Sources: 1949–58, *Ten Great Years*, p. 220; 1959 and 1962, *Shin Chugoku Nenkan, 1966 (New China Yearbook)* (Tokyo: Chugoku Kenkyucho, 1967), p. 396.

B. Maternity and Pediatric Hospitals

Year	Maternity Hospitals	Number of Beds	Children's Hospitals	Number of Beds
1949	80	1,762	5	139
1952	98	4,052	6	258
1957	96	6,792	16	2,295
1958	230	7,557	27	3,682

Sources: *Ten Great Years*, p. 221.

28. MEDICAL PERSONNEL, 1949–66

A. Number of Physicians, Nurses, and Midwives

Year	Western-trained Doctors	Doctors' Assistants	Nurses	Midwives
1950	41,000	53,000	38,000	16,000
1952	52,000	67,000	61,000	22,000
1957	74,000	136,000	123,000	36,000
1958	75,000	131,000	138,000	35,000

Source: Ten Great Years, p. 222.

B. Number of Graduates from Institutions of Higher Learning in Medicine

Year	Number
1949	1,314
1950	1,391
1951	2,366
1952	2,636
1953	2,948
1954	4,527
1955	6,840
1956	5,403
1957	6,200
1958	5,393
1959	9,000
1960	(14,850)
1961	19,000
1962	17,000
1963	25,000
1964	(23,000)
1965	(19,000)
1966	(19,000)

Sources: 1949–58, *Ten Great Years*, p. 196; 1959–63, Chun-yuan Cheng, 'Scientific Engineering Manpower in Communist China,' in Joint Economic Committee, *Economic Profile*, 2:531; 1964–66, Orleans, 'Communist China's Education,' p. 511. Figures in parentheses are estimates.

EDITOR AND CONTRIBUTORS

Editor

YUAN-LI WU is Professor of Economics at the University of San Francisco, where he has been a member of the faculty since 1960, and a consultant at the Hoover Institution on War, Revolution, and Peace at Stanford University in California, a post he has also held since 1960. He took a leave of absence from both posts in 1969–70 to serve as Deputy Assistant Secretary of Defense for Policy Planning and National Security Council Affairs in the Nixon administration. He was born in Tientsin, China, in 1920, and did his undergraduate and graduate work at the London School of Economics, receiving his Ph.D. degree in 1946. He has also studied in Berlin. His publications include scores of articles, ten monographs, and nine books, including *The Economy of Communist China: An Introduction* (1965), *The Spatial Economy of Communist China* (1967), and *The Organization and Support of Scientific Research and Development in Mainland China* (1970), which he edited with Robert B. Sheeks.

Contributors

JOHN S. AIRD is Chief of the China Branch of the Foreign Demographic Analysis Division, Bureau of Economic Analysis (formerly of the Bureau of the Census), U.S. Department of Commerce. He received his Ph.D. in sociology from the University of Michigan in 1957. In 1952–53, Dr. Aird served on a UNESCO Social Science Teaching Team at Dacca University in East Pakistan, and he has also taught at several U.S. universities, among them Vanderbilt, where he was Assistant Professor of Sociology in 1956–57.

JOHN A. BERBERET is a physicist with the U.S. Army Nuclear Agency at Fort Bliss, Texas. He received his Ph.D. from the University of Washington in 1952. His study *Science and Technology in Communist China* (1960), which was published when he was a staff member of General Electric-TEMP in Santa Barbara, California, resulted in the first large, unclassified study of China's science and technology. Since that time, Dr. Berberet has published numerous works on Chinese science and technology while continuing his research.

JOHN LOSSING BUCK, an agricultural economist, was Professor of Agricultural Economics at the University of Nanking in China in 1920–34 and 1940–44, and served as U.S. State Department Specialist on the Far East in 1964. He received his Ph.D. from Cornell University in 1933. Among his publications are the pioneering classic, *Land Utilization in China* (1937) and *Food and Agriculture in Communist China* (1966), of which he was co-author with Owen L. Dawson and Yuan-li Wu.

KING C. CHEN is Associate Professor of Political Science at Rutgers University and a Senior Fellow (1972–73) at the Research Institute on Communist Affairs of Columbia University. He is the author of *Vietnam and China: 1938–54* (1969), the editor of and contributor to the forthcoming *The Foreign Policy of China*, and contributor to the forthcoming *The Indochina Crisis*.

S. H. CHEN, before his death in 1971, was Professor of Chinese and Comparative Literature at the University of California at Berkeley, Chairman of the Current Chinese Language Project, and Chairman of the Board of Directors of the Inter-University Program of Chinese Language Studies, administered by Stanford University. His publications include *Biography of Ku K'ai-chih* (1961), as well as other books and numerous articles on Chinese language and literature.

THEODORE H. E. CHEN is Professor of International Education at the University of Southern California. Among his books are *The Chinese Communist Regime: Documents and Commentary* (1967) and the forthcoming *The Maoist Educational Revolution: An Analytical, Philosophical, and Comparative Analysis.*

HUNGDAH CHIU, former Professor of Law at National Chengchi University in the Republic of China, is Research Associate at Harvard Law School. He is the author of *The People's Republic of China and the Law of Treaties* (1972); co-editor, with Shao-chuan Leng, of *Law in Chinese Foreign Policy: Communist China and Selected Problems of International Law* (1972); and editor of the forthcoming *China and the Question of Taiwan: Documents and Analysis.*

GEORGE N. ECKLUND, is Director, Office of Economic Research of the United States Tariff Commission. He received his Ph.D. from the University of Minnesota and has been Associate Professor of Economics at Bethel College in Minnesota and Professorial Lecturer in Economics at American University in Washington, D.C. Dr. Ecklund is the author of several journal articles and a book, *Financing the Chinese Government Budget, Mainland China, 1950–59* (1966).

HAROLD C. HINTON is Professor of Political Science and International Affairs and an Associate of the Institute for Sino-Soviet Studies at The George Washington University. He received his Ph.D. in modern Far Eastern history and politics from Harvard University. Professor Hinton is the author of the forthcoming *An Introduction to Chinese Politics* (1973), *The Bear at the Gate: Chinese Policymaking Under Soviet Pressure* (1971), *China's Turbulent Quest* (1970), and *Communist China in World Politics* (1966).

FRANKLIN W. HOUN was born and educated in China. At present Professor of Political Science at the University of Massachusetts, Professor Houn has also taught Chinese politics and comparative political systems at Michigan State University and the University of Nebraska. He is the author of *A Short History of Chinese Communism* (1967), as well as other books and more than forty articles in both Western and Chinese journals.

CHIAO-MIN HSIEH was born in China and is now Professor of Geography at the University of Pittsburgh. He has taught at several other universities, among them Catholic University and the University of Leeds in England. Among his numerous scholarly works are *China—Ageless Land and Countless People* (1967) and *Taiwan-Ilha Formosa* (1964).

LEONARD A. HUMPHREYS is Assistant Professor of East Asian History at Callison College, University of the Pacific, and Research Associate at the Hoover Institution, Stanford University.

FRED C. HUNG is Professor of Economics at the University of Hawaii. He received his Ph.D. in economics from the University of Washington in 1955. Professor Hung specializes in microeconomics, the economic development of Communist China, and the Hawaiian economy.

ELLIS JOFFE is Senior Lecturer in Chinese Studies and International Relations at the Hebrew University of Jerusalem. He is the author of *Party and Army: Professionalism and Political Control in the Chinese Officer Corps, 1949–1964* (1965). During 1971–72, he was Research Associate at the Center for Chinese Studies of the University of Michigan.

JOYCE K. KALLGREN is Associate Professor of Political Science at the University of California at Davis and Vice-Chairman of the Center for Chinese Studies at the University of California at Berkeley. Professor Kallgren received her Ph.D from

Harvard University. In 1970, she was a recipient of a Social Science Research Council grant for researching the problems of politics and welfare in China. Her research was done in Hong Kong and Taiwan.

LAWRENCE J. LAU is Assistant Professor of Economics at Stanford University. He received his Ph.D in economics in 1969 from the University of California, where he also served as Visiting Assistant Research Economist. He has written numerous articles, many of them focusing on economic aspects of life and government in China.

MICHAEL LINDSAY (Lord Lindsay of Birker) is Professor of Far Eastern Studies at the American University in Washington, D.C. Among his published works are *China and the Cold War* (1955), *Is Peaceful Coexistence Possible?* (1960), and *Educational Problems in Communist China* (1950), as well as many articles. He was with the Chinese Communists in Yenan during World War II, working in radio communications.

WILLIAM T. LIU is Chairman and Professor of the Department of Sociology and Anthropology at the University of Notre Dame, where he has taught since 1963 and where he founded, and served as the first Director of, the Social Science Training and Research Laboratory. He received his Ph.D. in sociology from Florida State University and did postdoctoral work at the University of Chicago. Among his numerous publications are *Chinese Society Under Communism* (1967), *Family and Fertility* (1967), *Catholics/USA: Perspectives for Change* (1970), and *The Emerging Woman: Impact of the Contraceptive Culture* (1970).

JOHN T. MA is the Curator-Librarian of the East Asian Collection of the Hoover Institution at Stanford University. Before coming to Stanford, he was the Associate Librarian of the Missionary Research Library at Columbia University and Chinese Bibliographer at Cornell University. His publications include *East Asian Resources in American Libraries* (1968), *Current Periodicals in the Missionary Research Library* (1961), and *East Asia: A Survey of Holdings at the Hoover Institution on War, Revolution, and Peace* (1971).

FRANZ MICHAEL is Professor of Chinese History and Government and International Affairs at the Institute for Sino-Soviet Studies, George Washington University, and the Chairman of the Inter-university Research Colloquia on Modern China. Until June 30, 1972, he was Director of the Institute. He capped his studies at the Universities of Freiburg, Hamburg, and Berlin from 1925 to 1933, with a Doctor of Jurisprudence degree in 1933. His books include *The Origin of Manchu Rule in China* (1942); *The Far East in the Modern World* (1964), with George E. Taylor; and a three-volume work, *Taiping Rebellion* (1966, 1971).

JAMES T. MYERS is Associate Professor in the Department of Government and International Studies at the University of South Carolina. He received his Ph.D. in political science at The George Washington University in conjunction with that university's Institute for Sino-Soviet Studies, and he has also been a Visiting Scholar at the Free University of Berlin. He has recently completed, with Jürgen Domes, a documentary study of the Cultural Revolution, and he has written numerous articles on Chinese Communist affairs.

K. P. WANG, Supervisory Physical Scientist, Division of Nonmetallic Minerals, U.S. Bureau of Mines, is a specialist in international resources and mineral economics. He previously served as Chief Specialist in International Minerals with the Bureau and as Adjunct Associate Professor in Mineral Economics at Columbia University. He is particularly familiar with Asia and problems of developing countries and has written many articles on China and the Far East.

THOMAS J. WEISS received his Ph.D. in political science from the University of Chicago in 1969. Prior to that, he was a Fulbright-Hayes Fellow in Taiwan and a Public Affairs Fellow of the Hoover Institution at Stanford University. In 1969–71, he was Assistant Professor of Political Science at San Fernando Valley State College and is currently a J.D. candidate at Harvard Law School.

ROBERT M. WORTH was born in Central China and spent most of his life there until the end of World War II, when he moved to the United States. He received his M.D. at the University of California, where he also received his Ph.D. in epidemiology (public health) in 1962. Since 1963, he has been Professor of Public Health at the University of Hawaii. He is the author of numerous articles on medical and public health problems.

CHUN-HSI WU is Research Fellow at the Institute of International Relations in Taipei, Republic of China. His works include *Dollars, Dependants and Dogma: Overseas Chinese Remittances to Communist China* (1967).

RICHARD F. S. YANG was born and raised in China and is a graduate of Yenching University. He received his Ph.D. from the University of Washington in 1955 and taught there for thirteen years. He is now Professor of Chinese Language, Literature, and Culture at the University of Pittsburgh. He has written many articles, and among his books are *Fifty Songs of the Yüan: Poetry of Thirteenth-Century China* (1967) and *Four Plays of the Yüan Drama* (1972).

K. C. YEH is a Senior Economist with The RAND Corporation in Santa Monica, Calif. He received his Ph.D. from Columbia University and is the co-author, with T. C. Liu, of *The Economy of the Chinese Mainland* (1965).

INDEX